Windows 8

the missing manual®

The book that should have been in the box®

Windows 8

the missing manual®

The book that should have been in the box®

David Pogue

O'REILLY®

Beijing | Cambridge | Farnham | Köln | Sebastopol | Tokyo

Windows 8: The Missing Manual
by David Pogue

Printed in the United States of America.

Published by O'Reilly Media, Inc., 1005 Gravenstein Highway North, Sebastopol, CA 95472.

O'Reilly Media books may be purchased for educational, business, or sales promotional use. Online editions are also available for most titles: *safari.oreilly.com.* For more information, contact our corporate/institutional sales department: 800-998-9938 or *corporate@oreilly.com.*

February 2013: First Edition.

ISBN: 978-1-449-31403-3
[LSI] [02/13]

Table of Contents

Chapter 9: Help at the Desktop 321

Chapter 10: Programs & Documents 333

Chapter 11: The Desktop's Starter Programs 375

Part Three: Windows Online

Part Seven: The Windows Network

Part Eight: Appendixes

The Missing Credits

About the Author

David Pogue (author, illustrator) writes a weekly tech column for *The New York Times* and a monthly column for *Scientific American*. He's an Emmy-winning correspondent for *CBS News Sunday Morning*, the host of four *NOVA* miniseries on PBS, and the creator of the Missing Manual series. He's the author or coauthor of over 60 books, including 28 in this series, six in the *For Dummies* line (including *Macs, Magic, Opera,* and *Classical Music*), two novels (one for middle-schoolers), and *The World According to Twitter.* In his other life, David is a former Broadway show conductor, a magician, and a funny public speaker. He lives in Connecticut with his three awesome children.

Links to his columns and funny weekly videos await at *www.davidpogue.com.* He welcomes feedback about his books by email at *david@pogueman.com.*

About the Creative Team

Julie Van Keuren (copy editor, indexer) quit her newspaper job in 2006 to move to Montana and live the freelancing dream. She and her husband, M.H. (who's living the novel-writing dream), have two sons, Dexter and Michael. Email*: little_media@yahoo.com.*

Mike Halsey (technical editor) the author of several Windows books, including *Troubleshoot and Optimize Windows 8 Inside Out*, *Beginning Windows 8,* and the best sellers *Troubleshooting Windows 7 Inside Out* and *Windows 8: Out of the Box*. An English and math teacher by trade, he is also a Microsoft Most Valuable Professional (MVP) awardee (2011, 2012, 2013). He lives in Yorkshire, England with his rescue border collie, Jed. Email: *mike@MVPs.org*. Facebook, Twitter: *HalseyMike.*

Phil Simpson (design and layout) runs his graphic design business from Southbury, Connecticut. His work includes corporate branding, publication design, communications support, and advertising. In his free time, he is a homebrewer, ice cream maker, wannabe woodworker, and is on a few tasting panels. He lives with his wife and three great felines. Email: phil.simpson@pmsgraphics.com.

Acknowledgments

The Missing Manual series is a joint venture between the dream team introduced on these pages and O'Reilly Media. I'm grateful to all of them, and also to a few people who did massive favors for this book. They include Microsoft's Greg Chiemingo, who patiently helped dig up answers to the tweakiest Windows 8 questions; HP and Toshiba for lending me multitouch PCs to test; O'Reilly's Brian Sawyer, who accommodated my nightmarish schedule like a gentleman; and proofreaders Kellee Katagi and Judy Le.

In previous editions of this book, I relied on the talents of several guest authors and editors; some of their prose and expertise lives on in this edition. They include Brian Jepson, Joli Ballew, C.A. Callahan, Preston Gralla, John Pierce, and Adam Ornstein.

Finally, a special nod of thanks to my squadron of meticulous, expert volunteer beta readers who responded to my invitation via Twitter: Shalom Rubdi, Douglas Barry, Robert Stelling, Derek Gibbs, Michael Parente, Adam Sena, Ruben Orozco, Arthur Talansky, Todd E. Murphy, Karl Nicholson, Skip Rynearson, Carter Dudley, John Nicholson, Peter Roehrich, Allen Brandt, Peter Setlak, Niels Siskens, Bonita Smith, Kyle Hartsock, Robindar Nath Batra, James Feighny, Brian N. Bowes, Frank Kachurak, John Greek, Thomas D. Green, Ydder Htnawsaj, Thomas Kerber, Rushir Parikh, Raffi Patatian, Mattia Bellamoli, Eric James, Matt Gibstein, and Ray Richman. They're the superstars of crowdsourcing.

Thanks to David Rogelberg for believing in the idea. Thanks, above all, to Nicki, my muse and my love, and the three Poguelets: Kelly, Tia, and Jeffrey. They make these books—and everything else—possible.

—David Pogue

The Missing Manual Series

Missing Manual books are superbly written guides to computer products that don't come with printed manuals (which is just about all of them). Each book features a handcrafted index; cross-references to specific page numbers (not just "See Chapter 14"); and RepKover, a detached-spine binding that lets the book lie perfectly flat without the assistance of weights or cinder blocks. Recent and upcoming titles include:

For Windows

- *Windows 7: The Missing Manual by* David Pogue
- *Access 2013: The Missing Manual* by Matthew MacDonald
- *Excel 2013: The Missing Manual* by Matthew MacDonald
- *Microsoft Project 2013: The Missing Manual* by Bonnie Biafore
- *Office 2013: The Missing Manual* by Nancy Conner and Matthew MacDonald
- *QuickBooks 2013: The Missing Manual* by Bonnie Biafore
- *Photoshop CS6: The Missing Manual* by Lesa Snider
- *Photoshop Elements 10: The Missing Manual* by Barbara Brundage

For the Mac

- *OS X Mountain Lion: The Missing Manual* by David Pogue
- *AppleScript: The Missing Manual* by Adam Goldstein
- *FileMaker Pro 12: The Missing Manual* by Susan Prosser and Stuart Gripman

- *iMovie '11 & iDVD: The Missing Manual* by David Pogue and Aaron Miller
- *iPhoto '11: The Missing Manual* by David Pogue and Lesa Snider
- *iWork '09: The Missing Manual* by Josh Clark
- *Office 2011: The Missing Manual* by Chris Grover
- *Switching to the Mac: The Missing Manual, Mountain Lion Edition* by David Pogue

Electronics

- *David Pogue's Digital Photography: The Missing Manual* by David Pogue
- *iPhone App Development: The Missing Manual* by Craig Hockenberry
- *iPad: The Missing Manual, Fourth Edition* by J.D. Biersdorfer
- *iPod: The Missing Manual, Tenth Edition* by J.D. Biersdorfer
- *Kindle Fire: The Missing Manual* by Peter Meyers
- *Motorola Xoom: The Missing Manual* by Preston Gralla
- *Netbooks: The Missing Manual* by J.D. Biersdorfer
- *NOOK HD: The Missing Manual* by Preston Gralla
- *Droid X: The Missing Manual* by Preston Gralla
- *Droid X2: The Missing Manual* by Preston Gralla
- *Galaxy S II: The Missing Manual* by Preston Gralla
- *Galaxy Tab: The Missing Manual* by Preston Gralla

Web Technologies

- *Adobe Edge Animate: The Missing Manual*, Third Edition by Chris Grover
- *Creating a Web Site: The Missing Manual*, Third Edition by Matthew MacDonald
- *CSS3: The Missing Manual*, Second Edition, by David Sawyer McFarland
- *Dreamweaver CS6: The Missing Manual* by David Sawyer McFarland
- *Flash CS6: The Missing Manual* by E. A. Vander Veer and Chris Grover
- *Google+: The Missing Manual* by Kevin Purdy
- *HTML5: The Missing Manual* by Matthew MacDonald
- *JavaScript & jQuery: The Missing Manual* by David Sawyer McFarland
- *PHP & MySQL: The Missing Manual* by Brett McLaughlin

Life

- *Personal Investing: The Missing Manual* by Bonnie Biafore
- *Your Brain: The Missing Manual* by Matthew MacDonald
- *Your Body: The Missing Manual* by Matthew MacDonald
- *Your Money: The Missing Manual* by J.D. Roth

Introduction

Wow. Windows 8, huh?

Talk about polarizing. People love this thing; people despise it. People hail Microsoft for boldly acknowledging the era of touchscreen computing; people mock it for taking away the Start menu in the name of trendiness.

Here's one thing most people can probably agree on: Although Windows 8 may not be Microsoft's greatest operating system, it may well be *two* of them.

That's right: When you get right down to it, Windows 8 is two operating systems superimposed. Both are really good. There's the regular desktop, an even more refined version of the popular Windows 7. And then, lying over it, there's the new, colorful world of tiles and modern typography that Microsoft calls—well, Microsoft calls it Windows 8, which doesn't help much. (It desperately needs a name. In this book, I call it "TileWorld.")

Maybe Windows 8 is meant to be a transitional OS. Maybe the next one will be all TileWorld, all touchscreen, all the time.

In the meantime, if you've bought, or have been issued, a Windows 8 machine, you've got a lot to learn. You'll notice immediately that Microsoft has moved the furniture around while you were away. But once you learn where things have wound up, you'll find a lot to like in the redecoration. For example:

- **It's fast.** Windows 8 is very fast, both on the desktop and, especially, in TileWorld. The system requirements for Windows 8 aren't any more demanding than they were for Windows 7.

- **It's graceful.** Windows 8 nags you less than any version ever. You can't believe how many operations have been streamlined and simplified.
- **It's phonelike.** Windows 8 incorporates a lot of features that are standard in smartphones, like the iPhone, Android phones, and Windows Phones. For example, now there's a Lock screen that shows your battery level and the time. There's a Refresh command that resets Windows to its factory-fresh condition without disturbing any of your files. And there's a Reset command that erases it completely (great when you're about to sell your PC to someone).

  And there's an app store that's carefully modeled on the iPhone App Store, for ease in downloading new apps that Microsoft has approved and certified to be virus-free.
- **It's touchscreen friendly.** Microsoft strongly believes that the next generation of computers will have touchscreens—not just tablets, but laptops and desktop computers, too. So Windows 8, especially TileWorld, is filled with touchscreen gestures that work as they do on phones. Tap to click. Pinch or spread two fingers on a photo to zoom in or out. Log in by drawing lines over a photo you've chosen instead of typing a password.
- **It's cloudy.** Your login account can now be stored online—"in the cloud," as the marketers like to say. Why? Because now you can sit down at any Windows 8 computer anywhere, log in, and find all your settings just the way you left them at home: your address book, calendar, desktop wallpaper, Web bookmarks, email accounts, and so on.
- **It's beribboned.** A mishmash of menus and toolbars in desktop windows (now called File Explorer) has been replaced by the Ribbon: a big, fat toolbar atop each window that displays buttons for every possible thing you can do in that window, without hunting.
- **It comes with free virus software.** You read that right. For the first time in Windows history, antivirus software is free and built in.
- **It's had some overhauls.** The Task Manager has been beautifully redesigned. Parental controls have blossomed into a flexible, powerful tool called Family Safety, offering everything from Web protection to daily time limits for youngsters. The Recovery Environment—the screens you use to troubleshoot at startup time—have been beautified, simplified, and reorganized.

Those are the big-picture design changes, but there are dozens of happy surprises here and there—features new to Windows, if not to computing:

- **Storage Spaces** lets you trick Windows into thinking that several hard drives are one big drive, or vice versa, and simultaneously gives you the incredible data safety of a corporate RAID system.
- **File History** lets you rewind any file to a time before it was deleted, damaged, or edited beyond recognition.

- **BitLocker to Go** can put a password on a flash drive—great for corporate data that shouldn't get loose.
- **Windows To Go** (available in the Enterprise version of Windows 8) lets you put an entire PC world—Windows, drivers, programs, documents—on a flash drive. You can plug it into any PC anywhere and find yourself at home—or, rather, at work. And you can use your own laptop without worrying your overlords that you might be corrupting their precious network with outside evilware.
- **New multiple monitor features are a treat.** Now your taskbars and desktop pictures can span multiple monitors. You can have TileWorld on one screen and the desktop on another.
- **Microsoft's Xbox Music service** (no relation to the Xbox game console) has been almost completely ignored in the reviews—but it's great. You can listen to any band, any album, any song, on demand, for free. How's that sound?
- **Narrator**—a weird, sad old feature that would read your error messages to you out loud—has been transformed into a full-blown screen reader for people with impaired vision. It can describe every item on the screen, either in TileWorld or at the desktop. It can describe the layout of a Web page, and it makes little sounds to confirm that you've performed touchscreen gestures correctly.

The Editions of Windows 8—and Windows RT

There are no longer 17,278 different versions of Windows, praise Ballmer. No more Starter, Home, Home Premium, Ultimate, blah blah blah.

Basically, there are only two versions for sale to the public—Windows 8 and Windows 8 Pro—and the differences are minor. The Pro version adds high-end features like these:

- Accepts incoming Remote Desktop connections.
- Can join a corporate network (a Windows Server domain).
- Offers the Encrypting File System (lets you encrypt files at the desktop).
- Includes BitLocker and BitLocker To Go.
- Offers Windows Media Center as a $10 download.

Note: A third version, Enterprise, is available only to corporate buyers.

And then there's Windows RT. Be careful.

Windows RT does not run on computers with Intel processors and does not run traditional Windows software (Photoshop, Quicken, iTunes, and so on). It's designed for low-powered, touchscreen gadgets like tablets—notably Microsoft's own $500 Surface tablet—and maybe a few simple laptops.

Basically, Windows RT is all TileWorld. It runs only TileWorld apps. It still has a desktop underneath, and a few traditional Windows apps like the Calculator and the

Control Panel. (Microsoft also supplies Windows RT versions of Word, Excel, and PowerPoint with its Surface tablet.) But otherwise, Windows RT doesn't run "real" Windows software.

Except where noted, this book covers both Windows 8 and Windows RT.

Note: And what, exactly, does RT stand for? Microsoft says, "Nothing. It's just a brand." But scholars are quick to point out that software companies use a programming tool called Windows Runtime, or WinRT, to write TileWorld apps. Coincidence? You decide.

About This Book

Despite the many improvements in Windows over the years, one feature hasn't improved a bit: Microsoft's documentation. Not only does Windows 8 come with no printed user guide at all, but it actually has very little *electronic* help either! Many TileWorld apps, for example, have no Help command whatsoever.

Even when you do find online help, you'll quickly discover that it's tersely written, offers very little technical depth, and lacks examples. You can't mark your place, underline things, or read it in the bathroom. Some of the help screens are actually on Microsoft's Web site; you can't even see them without an Internet connection. Too bad if you're on a plane somewhere with your laptop.

The purpose of this book, then, is to serve as the manual that should have accompanied Windows. In these pages, you'll find step-by-step instructions for using almost every Windows feature, including those you may not have understood, let alone mastered.

System Requirements for Your Brain

Windows 8: The Missing Manual is designed to accommodate readers at every technical level (except system administrators, who will be happier with a very different sort of book).

The primary discussions are written for advanced-beginner or intermediate PC users. But if you're a first-time Windows user, special sidebar articles called "Up to Speed" provide the introductory information you need to understand the topic at hand. If you're an advanced PC user, on the other hand, keep your eye out for similar shaded boxes called "Power Users' Clinic." They offer more technical tips, tricks, and shortcuts for the veteran PC fan.

About the Outline

This book is divided into seven parts, each containing several chapters:

- Part One, **TileWorld**, is really *book* one. These five chapters offer a complete course in the new, tile-based, touchscreen-focused face of Windows 8. Here's all you need to know about the Start screen, Charms bar, the included TileWorld apps, and other elements of the new world.

  If you have a Windows RT device, these chapters may become your bible.

- Part Two, **The Windows Desktop**, covers the traditional Windows 7–like world that waits for you behind the new Start screen. It's the familiar world of icons, windows, menus, scroll bars, the taskbar, the Recycle Bin, shortcuts, shortcut menus, and so on.

  This part is also dedicated to the proposition that an operating system is a launchpad for *programs*. Chapter 10, for example, describes how to work with applications and documents in Windows—how to open them, switch among them, swap data between them, use them to create and open files, and so on.

  This part also offers an item-by-item discussion of the individual software nuggets that make up this operating system. These include not just the items in your Control Panel, but also the long list of free programs Microsoft threw in: Windows Media Player, WordPad, Speech Recognition, and so on.

- Part Three, **Windows Online**, covers all the special Internet-related features of Windows, including setting up your Internet account, Internet Explorer 10 (for Web browsing), Windows Live Mail (for email), and so on. Chapter 14 covers Windows' dozens of Internet fortification features: the firewall, anti-spyware software, parental controls, and on and on.

- Part Four, **Pictures & Music**, takes you into multimedia land. Here are chapters that cover the Windows Live Photo Gallery picture editing and organizing program, and Windows Media Player (for music playback).

- Part Five, **Hardware & Peripherals**, describes the operating system's relationship with equipment you can attach to your PC—scanners, cameras, disks, printers, and so on. Fonts, printing, and faxing are here, too.

- Part Six, **PC Health**, explores Windows 8's beefed-up backup and troubleshooting tools. It also describes some advanced hard drive formatting tricks and offers tips for making your PC run faster and better.

- Part Seven, **The Windows Network**, is for the millions of households and offices that contain more than one PC. If you work at home or in a small office, these chapters show you how to build your own network; if you work in a corporation where some highly paid professional network geek is on hand to do the troubleshooting, these chapters show you how to exploit Windows' considerable networking prowess. File sharing, accounts and passwords, remote access, and the HomeGroups insta-networking feature are here, too.

At the end of the book, four appendixes provide a guide to installing or upgrading to Windows 8, an introduction to editing the Registry, a master list of Windows keyboard shortcuts, and the "Where'd It Go?" Dictionary, which lists every feature Microsoft moved or deleted on the way to Windows 8.

About→These→Arrows

Throughout this book, and throughout the Missing Manual series, you'll find sentences like this: "Open the Computer→Local Disk (C:)→Windows folder." That's shorthand for a much longer instruction that directs you to open three nested icons in sequence, like this: "Inside the Computer window is a disk icon labeled Local Disk (C:); double-click it to open it. Inside *that* window is yet *another* icon called Windows. Double-click to open it, too."

Similarly, this kind of arrow shorthand helps to simplify the business of choosing commands in menus. See Figure I-1.

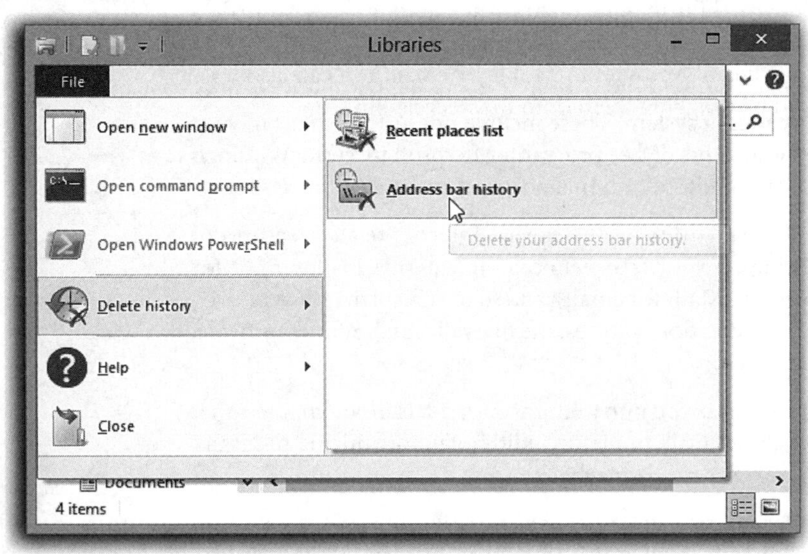

Figure I-1: *When, in this book, you read something like "Choose File→"Delete history"→"Address bar history," that means to open the File menu, and then click the "Delete history" command in its submenu, and then "Address bar history."*

The Very Basics

To get the most out of Windows with the least frustration, it helps to be familiar with the following concepts and terms. If you're new to Windows, be prepared to encounter these words and phrases over and over again—in the built-in Windows Help, in computer magazines, and in this book.

Windows Defined

Windows is an *operating system*, the software that controls your computer. It's designed to serve you in several ways:

- **It's a launching bay.** At its heart, Windows is a home base, a remote-control clicker that lets you call up the various software programs (applications) you use to do work or to kill time. When you get right down to it, applications are the real reason you bought a PC.

  Windows 8 is a well-stocked software pantry unto itself; for example, it comes with such basic programs as a Web browser, a simple word processor, and a calculator.

  If you were stranded on a desert island, the built-in Windows programs could suffice for everyday operations. But if you're like most people, sooner or later, you'll buy and install more software. That's one of the luxuries of using Windows: You can choose from a staggering number of add-on programs. Whether you're a left-handed beekeeper or a German-speaking nun, some company somewhere is selling Windows software designed just for you, its target audience.

- **It's a file cabinet.** Every application on your machine, as well as every document you create, is represented on the screen by an *icon*, a little picture that symbolizes the underlying file or container. You can organize these icons into onscreen file folders. You can make backups (safety copies) by dragging file icons onto a flash drive or a blank CD, or you can send files to people by email. You can also trash icons you no longer need by dragging them onto the Recycle Bin icon.
- **It's your equipment headquarters.** What you can actually see of Windows is only the tip of the iceberg. An enormous chunk of Windows is behind-the-scenes plumbing that controls the various functions of your computer—its modem, screen, keyboard, printer, and so on.

The Right Mouse Button is King

One of the most important features of Windows isn't on the screen—it's in your hand. The standard mouse or trackpad has two mouse buttons. You use the left one to click buttons, to highlight text, and to drag things around on the screen.

When you click the right button, however, a *shortcut menu* appears onscreen, like the one shown in Figure I-2. Get into the habit of *right-clicking* things—icons, folders, disks, text inside a paragraph, buttons on your menu bar, pictures on a Web page, and so on. The commands that appear on the shortcut menu will make you much more productive and lead you to discover handy functions you never knew existed.

Tip: On a touchscreen, you "right-click" something by holding your finger down on it for a second or so. Or, at the Start screen, you can do it by dragging down on a tile a tiny distance.

Figure I-2:
The power of the right-click is everywhere. Whenever you're floundering–whenever you can't figure out what comes next–remember this trick.

(To right-click on a touchscreen, hold your finger down for a moment. Or, at the Start screen, drag down on a tile a short distance.)

This is a big deal: Microsoft's research suggests that nearly 75 percent of Windows users don't use the right mouse button and therefore miss hundreds of timesaving shortcuts.

Tip: Microsoft doesn't discriminate against left-handers…much. You can swap the functions of the right and left mouse buttons easily enough.

Open the Control Panel. (One way: Right-click the lower-left corner of the screen; from the secret menu that appears, click Control Panel. Switch to Classic view. Open the Mouse icon. When the Mouse Properties dialog box opens, click the Buttons tab, and then turn on "Switch primary and secondary buttons." Then click OK. Windows now assumes that you want to use the left mouse button as the one that produces shortcut menus.

Wizards = Interviews

A *wizard* is a series of screens that walk you through the task you're trying to complete. Wizards make configuration and installation tasks easier by breaking them down into smaller, more easily digested steps.

There's More Than One Way to Do Everything

No matter what setting you want to adjust, no matter what program you want to open, Microsoft has provided four or five different ways to do it. For example, here are the various ways to delete a file: Press the Delete key; choose File→Delete; drag the file icon onto the Recycle Bin; or right-click the filename, and then choose Delete from the shortcut menu.

Pessimists grumble that there are too many paths to every destination, making it much more difficult to learn Windows. Optimists point out that this abundance of approaches means that almost everyone will find, and settle on, a satisfying method for each task. Whenever you find a task irksome, remember that you have other options.

(This book generally offers the one or two *shortest* ways to accomplish a task. Life's too short to read all of them.)

UP TO SPEED

"Tap" vs. "Click," "App" vs. "Program"

When you write a book about an operating system that's supposed to be just as good on touchscreen computers as keyboard/mouse ones, what verb do you use for "click"?

If you constantly tell your readers to "click" something, you're ignoring people who are tapping their touchscreens. If you say "tap," you're ignoring mouse people. Neither verb works all the time.

In its help screens online, Microsoft uses the phrase "tap or click." Over and over and over. Unfortunately, if you read "tap or click" 50 times per page of a book, you'd go quietly insane.

In these pages, you're generally directed to "choose," "select," or even "hit" onscreen objects. That, of course, is this book's ingenious solution to the linguistic "tap or click" problem.

There are exceptions. In instructions that are primarily useful for touchscreens, you may read more "tap" instructions; in chapters that document the Windows desktop, which generally requires the mouse, you'll encounter "click" more often.

In any case, now you know the problem. And the solution.

A similar pile of linguistic linguini awaits regarding the terms "app" and "program." Microsoft refers to both TileWorld and desktop software as "apps," which is very confusing.

In this book, "app" is software that runs in TileWorld; "program" generally means "Windows desktop software."

You Can Use the Keyboard for Everything

In earlier versions of Windows, underlined letters appeared in the names of menus and dialog boxes. These underlines were clues for people who found it faster to do something by pressing keys than by using the mouse.

The underlines are hidden in Windows 8, at least in disk and folder windows. (They may still appear in your individual software programs.) If you miss them, you can make them reappear by pressing the Alt key, the Tab key, or an arrow key whenever the menu bar is visible. (When you're operating menus, you can release the Alt key immediately after pressing it.) In this book, in help screens, and in computer magazines, you'll see key combinations indicated like this: Alt+S (or Alt+ whatever the letter key is).

Note: In some Windows programs, in fact, the entire menu bar is gone until you press Alt (or F10).

Once the underlines are visible, you can open a menu by pressing the underlined letter (F for the File menu, for example). Once the menu is open, press the underlined letter key that corresponds to the menu command you want. Or press Esc to close the menu without doing anything. (In Windows, the Esc key always means *cancel* or *stop.*)

If choosing a menu command opens a dialog box, you can trigger its options by pressing Alt along with the underlined letters. (Within dialog boxes, you can't press and release Alt; you have to hold it down while typing the underlined letter.)

In TileWorld, keyboard shortcuts are even more important on computers that don't have touchscreens. Don't miss Appendix D, which lists all of them.

The Start Screen is Fastest

The fastest way to almost anything in Windows 8 is the Search feature in TileWorld.

For example, to open Outlook, you can open the Start screen and type *outlook.* To get to the password-changing screen, you can type *password.* To adjust your network settings, *network.* And so on. *Display. Speakers. Keyboard. BitLocker. Excel. Photo Gallery. Firefox.* Whatever.

Each time, Windows does an uncanny job of figuring out what you want and highlighting it in the results list, usually right at the top. (There's an extra step if you're looking for a setting or a file, as opposed to a program: You have to choose Settings or Files under the search box.)

Here's the thing, though: You don't need the mouse to open the Start screen. You can just tap the ⊞ key.

You also don't need to type the whole thing. If you want the Sticky Notes program, *sti* is usually all you have to type. In other words, without ever lifting your hands from the keyboard, you can hit ⊞, type *sti,* and hit Enter—and you've opened Sticky Notes. Really, really fast.

Now, there is almost always a manual, mouse-clickable way to get at the same function in Windows—in fact, there are usually about six of them. Here, for example, is how you might open Narrator, a program that reads everything on the screen. First, the mouse way:

1. **At the desktop, open the Charms bar (press ⊞+C); click Settings; click Control Panel.**

   The Control Panel opens, teeming with options. If the "View by" pop-up menu doesn't say "Category," then skip to step 3.

2. **Click Ease of Access, then Ease of Access Center.**

   Now another Control Panel screen appears, filled with options having to do with accessibility.

3. **Click Start Narrator.**

   Narrator begins reading what's on the screen.

OK then. Here, by contrast, is how you'd get to exactly the same place using the Start screen method:

1. **Press ⊞ to open the Start screen. Type enough of *narrator* to make Narrator appear in the results list; press Enter.**

   There you go. One step instead of three.

Now, you're forgiven for exclaiming, "What!? Get to things by typing? I thought the whole idea behind the Windows revolution was to eliminate the DOS-age practice of typing commands!"

GEM IN THE ROUGH

Not Your Father's Keyboard

Modern-day Windows machines come with a key bearing the Windows logo (⊞), usually on the left side of the bottom row of the keyboard. No, this isn't just a tiny Microsoft advertising moment; you can press this key to open the Start screen.

On touchscreen gadgets, you may have a ⊞ *button* instead.

On the right, you may find a duplicate ⊞ key, as well as a key whose icon depicts a tiny menu, complete with a microscopic cursor pointing to a command (▤). Press this key to simulate a right-click at the current location of your cursor.

Even better, the ⊞ key offers a number of useful functions when you press it in conjunction with other keys. For a complete list, see Appendix D. But here are a few important ones to get you started:

⊞ opens the Start screen.

⊞+number key opens the corresponding icon on the taskbar, left to right (⊞+1, ⊞+2, and so on).

⊞+D hides or shows all your application windows (ideal for jumping to the desktop for a bit of housekeeping).

⊞+E opens an Explorer window.

⊞+L locks your screen. Everything you were working on is hidden by the Login screen; your password is required to get past it.

⊞+Tab cycles through all open TileWorld apps.

⊞+Z opens the App (options) bar in TileWorld.

⊞+F opens the Search window.

⊞+Q, F, and **W** open the Search pane to search for programs, files, and settings, respectively.

Well, not exactly. Typing has always offered a faster, more efficient way to getting places and doing things—what everyone hated was the *memorizing* of commands to type.

But the Start screen requires no memorization; that's the beauty of it. You can be vague. You can take a guess. And almost every time, the Start screen knows what you want and offers it in the list.

For that reason, this book usually provides the most direct route to a certain program or function: the one that involves the Start screen's search box. There's always a longer, slower, mousier alternative, but hey: This book is plenty fat already, and those rainforests aren't getting any bigger.

About Shift-Clicking

Here's another bit of shorthand you'll find in this book (and others): instructions to *Shift-click* something. That means you should hold down the Shift key and then click before releasing the key. If you understand that much, the meaning of instructions like "Ctrl-click" and "Alt-click" should be clear.

You Could Spend a Lifetime Changing Properties

You can't write an operating system that's all things to all people, but Microsoft has certainly tried. You can change almost every aspect of the way Windows looks and works. You can replace the gray backdrop of the screen (the *wallpaper*) with your favorite photograph, change the typeface used for the names of your icons, or set up a particular program to launch automatically every time you turn on the PC.

When you want to change some *general* behavior of your PC, like how it connects to the Internet, how soon the screen goes black to save power, or how quickly a letter repeats when you hold down a key, you use the Control Panel window (described in Chapter 12).

Many other times, however, you may want to adjust the settings of only one particular element of the machine, such as the hard drive, the Recycle Bin, or a particular application. In those cases, simply right-click the corresponding icon. In the resulting shortcut menu, you'll often find a command called Properties. When you click it, a dialog box appears, containing settings or information about that object.

Tip: As a shortcut to the Properties command, just highlight an icon and then press Alt+Enter.

It's also worth getting to know how to operate *tabbed dialog boxes*. These are windows that contain so many options, Microsoft has had to split them up into separate panels, or *tabs*. To reveal a new set of options, just click a different tab. These tabs are designed to resemble the tabs at the top of file folders.

Tip: You can switch tabs without using the mouse by pressing Ctrl+Tab (to "click" the next tab to the right) or Ctrl+Shift+Tab (for the previous tab).

Every Piece of Hardware Requires Software

When computer geeks talk about their *drivers,* they're not talking about their chauffeurs (unless they're Bill Gates); they're talking about the controlling software required by every hardware component of a PC.

The driver is the translator between your PC's brain and the equipment attached to it: mouse, keyboard, screen, DVD drive, scanner, digital camera, palmtop, and so on. Without the correct driver software, the corresponding piece of equipment doesn't work at all.

When you buy one of these gadgets, you receive a CD containing the driver software. If the included driver software works fine, then you're all set. If your gadget acts up, however, remember that equipment manufacturers regularly release improved (read: less buggy) versions of these software chunks. (You generally find such updates on the manufacturers' Web sites.)

Fortunately, Windows 8 comes with drivers for over 15,000 components, saving you the trouble of scavenging for them on a disk or on the Internet. Most popular gizmos from brand-name companies work automatically when you plug them in—no CD installation required (see Chapter 20).

It's Not Meant to Be Overwhelming

Windows has an absolutely staggering array of features. You can burrow six levels down, dialog box through dialog box, and still not come to the end of it. There are enough programs, commands, and help screens to keep you studying for the rest of your life.

It's crucial to remember that Microsoft's programmers created Windows in modules—the digital-photography team here, the networking team there—with different audiences in mind. The idea, of course, was to make sure that no subset of potential customers would find a feature lacking.

But if *you* don't have a digital camera, a network, or whatever, there's absolutely nothing wrong with ignoring everything you encounter on the screen that isn't relevant to your setup and work routine. Not even Microsoft's CEO uses every single feature of Windows.

About MissingManuals.com

To get the most out of this book, visit *www.missingmanuals.com.* Click the "Missing CD-ROM" link—and then this book's title—to reveal a neat, organized, chapter-by-chapter list of the shareware and freeware mentioned in this book.

The Web site also offers corrections and updates to the book. (To see them, click the book's title, and then click View/Submit Errata.) In fact, please submit such corrections and updates yourself! In an effort to keep the book as up to date and accurate as possible, each time O'Reilly prints more copies of this book, I'll make any confirmed corrections you've suggested. I'll also note such changes on the Web site so that you can mark important corrections into your own copy of the book, if you like.

Part One: TileWorld

1

CHAPTER
1

The Start Screen

Let's start with the elephant in the room: Windows 8 is two operating systems in one. They have separate software programs, control panels, Help systems, Web browsers, application switchers—and separate ways of doing things.

For a single price, here's what you get:

- **Windows desktop,** which is basically Windows 7. It's the familiar world of overlapping windows, the taskbar, and drop-down menus. It's designed for use with a mouse and keyboard. In this environment, you can run any of the four million existing Windows programs (see Figure 1-1).
- **TileWorld,** a new environment designed for touchscreens, like tablets and touchscreen laptops. This environment looks completely different—and works completely differently. There's no taskbar, windows don't overlap, and there are no drop-down menus. For TileWorld, you have to buy and install a completely new kind of app.

Note: Some inexpensive tablets run a version of Windows 8 called *Windows RT,* which is basically TileWorld alone. The Windows desktop is there, but it's just a useless shell; apart from a couple of traditional built-in programs–Notepad and Calculator, for example, and sometimes Microsoft Office–it can't run any other Windows apps.

Now, Microsoft doesn't agree that Windows 8 is really two superimposed OSes. And it certainly doesn't use the term "TileWorld" (see the box on page 19).

But there really are two environments. They look and feel very different. Each has its own techniques for customizing and organizing your stuff. Each requires different techniques.

On a given computer, you'll probably use only *one* environment most of the time. If you have a regular desktop PC or a laptop, you'll spend most of your time at the traditional Windows desktop. If you have a touchscreen tablet, on the other hand, you'll use TileWorld most of the time. And that's totally OK.

Even so, you still have to learn them both. You can't use just one environment *exclusively.* Here and there, the two worlds bleed together.

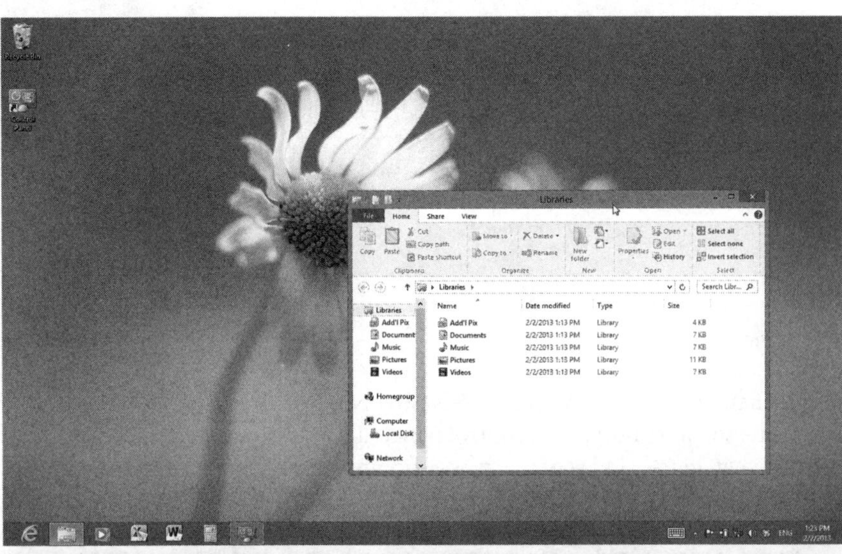

Figure 1-1: *In Windows 8, you'll encounter two different environments. Top: There's Windows Desktop, which looks and works like Windows always has. It runs traditional Windows desktop programs. Bottom: And then there's what this book calls TileWorld, a new environment geared toward touchscreens. It runs a new class of full-screen, colorful, touchscreen-friendly apps.*

The Lock Screen

When you turn on a Windows 8 machine, you know right away that you're not in Kansas anymore. The first thing you see is a new curtain that's been drawn over the computer's world. It's the *Lock screen* (Figure 1-2).

Figure 1-2: *You can control which apps are allowed to add information to the Lock screen in PC Settings. You're not stuck with the Lock screen as Mother Microsoft has installed it. You can change the picture, if you like, or you can eliminate it altogether. Chapter 2 has the details.*

The Lock screen serves the same purpose it does on a smartphone: It gives a quick glance at the time, the date, your WiFi signal strength, the weather, and (on laptops and tablets) your battery charge. As you download and install new apps, they can add informational tidbits to this Lock screen, too.

The point is that sometimes you don't really need to wake the machine up. You just want to know what time it is.

When you do want to go past the Lock screen to log in, there's nothing to it:

- **Touchscreen:** Swipe a finger upward.
- **Mouse:** Click anywhere. Or turn the mouse wheel.
- **Keyboard:** Press any key.

The Lock screen slides up and out of the way, revealing the Accounts screen (Figure 1-3).

The Accounts Screen

As in any modern operating system, you have your own *account* in Windows 8. It's your world of files, settings, and preferences. So the second thing you encounter in Windows 8 is the Accounts screen. Here you see the name and photo for each person who has an account on this machine. Choose yours.

Note: If your machine has only one account, you get to bypass this screen; as soon as you dismiss the Lock screen, you arrive at the Login screen described next.

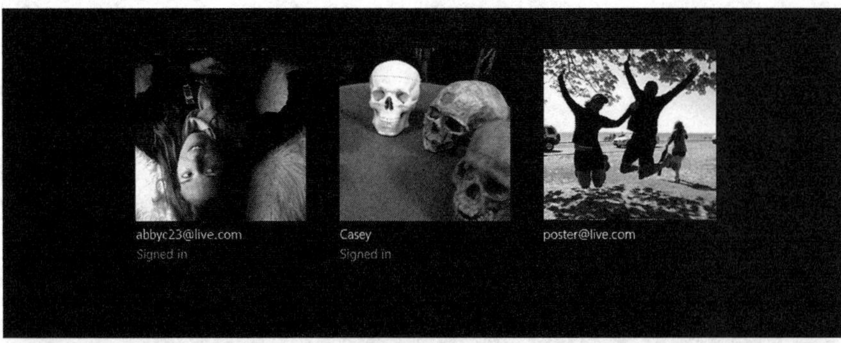

Figure 1-3: *Top: If your machine has more than one account set up, tap or click your icon to sign in.*

Bottom: Typing is so 2009! In Windows 8, you can log into your account using any of several more touchscreen-friendly methods, like drawing three predetermined lines on a photograph. (You don't actually see the lines show up; white lines are shown here so you get the point.)

The Login Screen

Here you provide your account name and password.

But *logging in* no longer has to mean *typing a password.* One of Windows 8's primary goals is to embrace touchscreens, and *typing* is a pain on tablets.

Therefore, you can log in using any of four techniques:

- Draw three lines, taps, or circles on a photo you've selected (Figure 1-3).
- Type in a four-digit number you've memorized.
- Type a traditional password.
- Skip the security altogether. Jump directly to the Start screen when you turn on the machine.

To choose which method you want, see page 52.

In any case, once you've gotten past the security barrier, you finally wind up at the hallmark of Windows 8: the new Start screen.

The Start Screen

This page of colorful tiles is the biggest landmark in Windows 8—and the part that may take the most getting used to (Figure 1-4).

UP TO SPEED

About the Term "TileWorld"

As you can probably guess, "TileWorld" is not Microsoft's name for its new touchscreen environment. The problem is, Microsoft doesn't have *any* good term for it.

At one point, Microsoft was going to call it Metro–but after "discussions with an important European partner" (likely the German store chain Metro), it officially abandoned the Metro term in August 2012.

"Modern" isn't TileWorld's real name, either; Microsoft used that term for awhile, too, but only internally.

The company uses the term "Start screen" to describe the tile-based home screen that replaces the old Start menu, and that's fine. But what about the rest of it–the Charms bar, the gestures, the swiping, the new breed of full-screen apps? Microsoft has no name for it.

So in this book, I'll call it TileWorld.

Now, you can't run traditional Windows programs (Photoshop, Quicken, iTunes, and so on) in TileWorld. TileWorld requires a whole new kind of app, sold exclusively through Microsoft's online store. These apps are full screen, don't have drop-down menus, and are geared toward touchscreen computers, and are generally simpler than traditional apps.

Microsoft doesn't have a good name for these apps, either.

The official name is "Windows Store apps." True, they're available exclusively from Microsoft's online store. Unfortunately, traditional Windows programs (of the Quicken/iTunes variety) are *also* available through the Windows Store. So "Windows Store apps" is not a good name, because *both* kinds of apps are sold at the Windows Store.

So in this book, I'll call these new, touchscreen-oriented, full-screen programs *TileWorld apps*. And I'll call the traditional PC programs *Windows desktop programs*.

Tip: If you miss the old Start menu, it's easy enough to bring it back. Just install the free Classic Menu app. It's available on this book's "Missing CD" page at *www.missingmanuals.com*.

You can think of the Start screen as an exploded view of the old Start menu. It's the launcher for the programs, files, and settings you use most.

***Figure 1-4:** The old Start menu, which has served as the master list of your files and programs since Windows was a toddler, is gone.*

The Start screen is basically the Start menu, spread out.

But it's more than just a launcher. It's also a dashboard. Each tile isn't just a button that *opens* the corresponding program; it's also a little display—a *live tile*, as Microsoft calls it—that can show you real-time information from that program. The Calendar tile shows you your next appointment. Your Mail tile shows the latest incoming subject line. The People tile shows you Twitter and Facebook posts as they pour in.

Tip: Not all Start screen tiles display their own names. Some apps, like the ones for Calendar, People, and Mail, are meant to be visual dashboards only.

To find out such an app's name, point to it with your cursor without clicking. A tinted, rectangular tooltip bar appears, identifying the name.

Here's what you need to know about using the Start screen.

It Displays Both Kinds of Apps

The Start screen is very obviously part of the new TileWorld environment: full screen, new fonts, brightly colored rectangles. But the tiles themselves can represent both kinds of software: Windows desktop programs and the new TileWorld apps.

On Day One, most of the tiles here represent the TileWorld apps that Microsoft provides with Windows 8: Calendar, Mail, Weather, and so on. But you can (and should) install your older programs here, too.

Note: Any new programs you install will gain tiles on the Start screen. But if you've upgraded your PC from an earlier version of Windows, all your old apps appear only in the All Apps screen (page 22)–not as tiles on the Start screen.

Tiles can represent anything that used to be in the Start menu: programs, files, folders, Web sites, and so on. Chapter 2 describes how to edit the Start screen's contents.

It Scrolls Horizontally

As you install more and more programs, the Start screen expands sideways. It can wind up being many screens wide. Here's how you scroll through them:

- **Touchscreen:** Swipe your finger horizontally across the screen—slowly to scroll with precision, quickly to whip through several pages at a time.
- **Mouse:** Turn the scroll wheel on your mouse. (This works on most modern mice.) Or move the mouse until it bumps the right or left edge of the screen to scroll in that direction.

Tip: As soon as you start moving the mouse–or touch the trackpad on a laptop–you also get a horizontal scroll bar at the bottom of the screen. You can drag that, too.

- **Keyboard:** Press the Page Up or Page Down keys to scroll one screenful at a time.

No matter how you wind up scrolling, you'll discover that the pages of the Start screen fly by smoothly and fluidly, as though they have a momentum all their own.

It's a Launcher

Every tile on the Start screen represents something—a program, a person, a Web site, a folder. If it's a Live Tile—one that shows information right on the face of the tile—that's great. You've saved a little time.

But if you want to open the program, file, or folder, tap or click once on its tile.

Tip: If you're keyboard oriented, you can use the arrow keys to highlight the icon you want and then press the Enter key to open it.

The Rest of the Apps

Remember: The Start screen is simply an exploded view of the old Start menu. In other words, it doesn't list *every* program on your computer—only the ones whose icons you want to keep handy.

There's still an All Programs listing, though, where you can see a *complete* list of your apps. To see it, open the App bar (swipe up from the bottom edge of the screen or press ⊞+Z) and tap "All apps." See Figure 1-5.

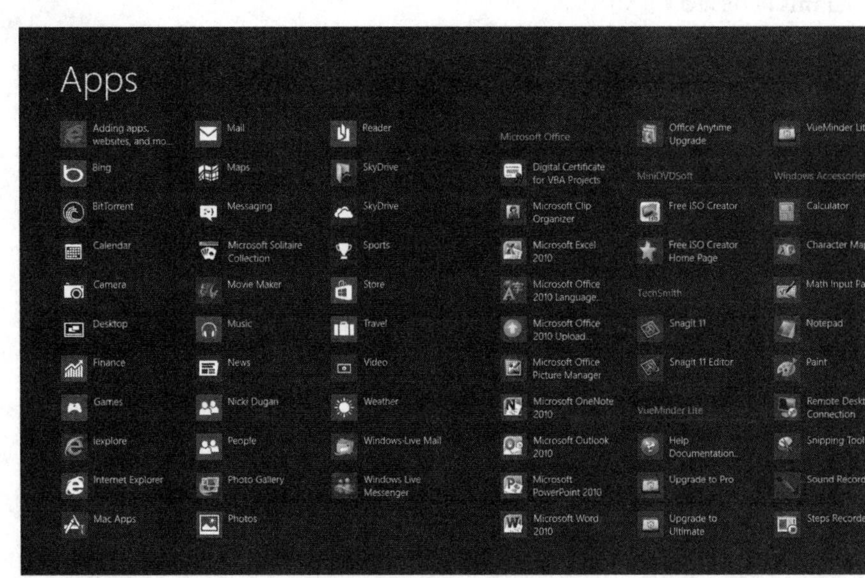

***Figure 1-5:** Here's your master list of every program installed on your computer, both TileWorld apps and Windows desktop apps. They're on a very wide, horizontally scrolling screen, and they're organized by named groups, which correspond to the folders that used to be in the old Start menu.*

Type-Searching

Once the Start screen gets to be many screens wide, the scrolling business can get old. If your machine has a real keyboard, you'll be grateful for the amazing type-selecting shortcut: Just start typing the name of the tile you want. The screen instantly changes to show you nothing but the icons of matching apps and programs, as shown in Figure 1-6.

Chapter 3 covers searching in much more detail.

Returning to the Start Screen

Obviously, the most important things you'll do with your Windows 8 machine involve *leaving* the Start screen. It's a home base, sure, but it's tough to get a lot of work done there.

Once you've done some work, however, you'll probably want to *return* to the Start screen to begin another activity. You can use any of these shortcuts:

- **Touchscreen:** Swipe inward from the right margin of the screen to make the Charms bar appear (page 24). Tap Start.
- **Mouse:** Point to the lower-left corner of the screen. Click the Start-screen miniature that appears.

Tip: If you're already *on* the Start screen, the little lower-left icon represents the program you were most recently using, so that you can hop back and forth.

- **Keyboard:** Press the ⊞ key on the keyboard.

In each case, the Start screen returns.

Tip: On many new computers and tablets (with Windows 8 preinstalled), there may also be a Windows *button*—just below the screen, for example. You can also press it to return to the Start screen.

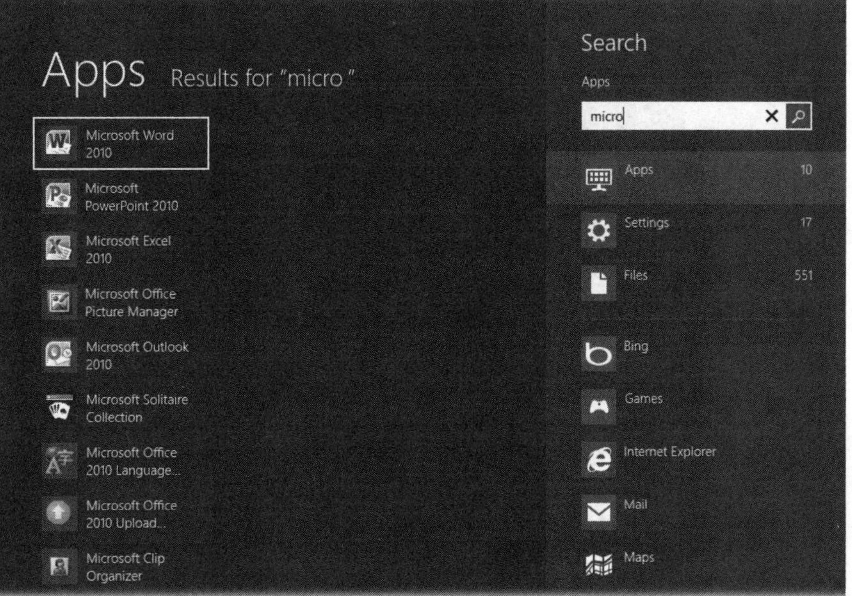

Figure 1-6: *When you begin typing on the Start screen, you automatically enter the search mode. As you type, Windows narrows down the visible icons, showing only matching apps and programs. The first one is always highlighted, so you can just press the Enter key to open it. To back out, press the Esc key a couple of times.*

Corners and Swipes

To be completely blunt, the world of Windows 8 is tailored for touchscreens. You can do everything with a keyboard and a mouse, but Microsoft saved the choicest pleasures for tablets and touchscreens. For example, the Charms bar (right edge) and app switcher (left edge) are positioned where your thumbs are when you're holding a tablet.

The proof is the long list of *gestures* (Figure 1-7) that do things in Windows 8—special finger-on-glass movements that open important panels and do important things.

There are keyboard and mouse equivalents, but finger on glass is almost always quicker and easier.

You'll need to know these techniques whether you have a touchscreen or not, because the panels and options they open are essential to using your computer.

Tip: Every laptop that came with Windows 8 also has a multitouch trackpad. All of the gestures described in this book for touchscreens (pinch, swipe, and so on)—you can also perform on the trackpad itself. (Some older models have multitouch trackpads, too.)

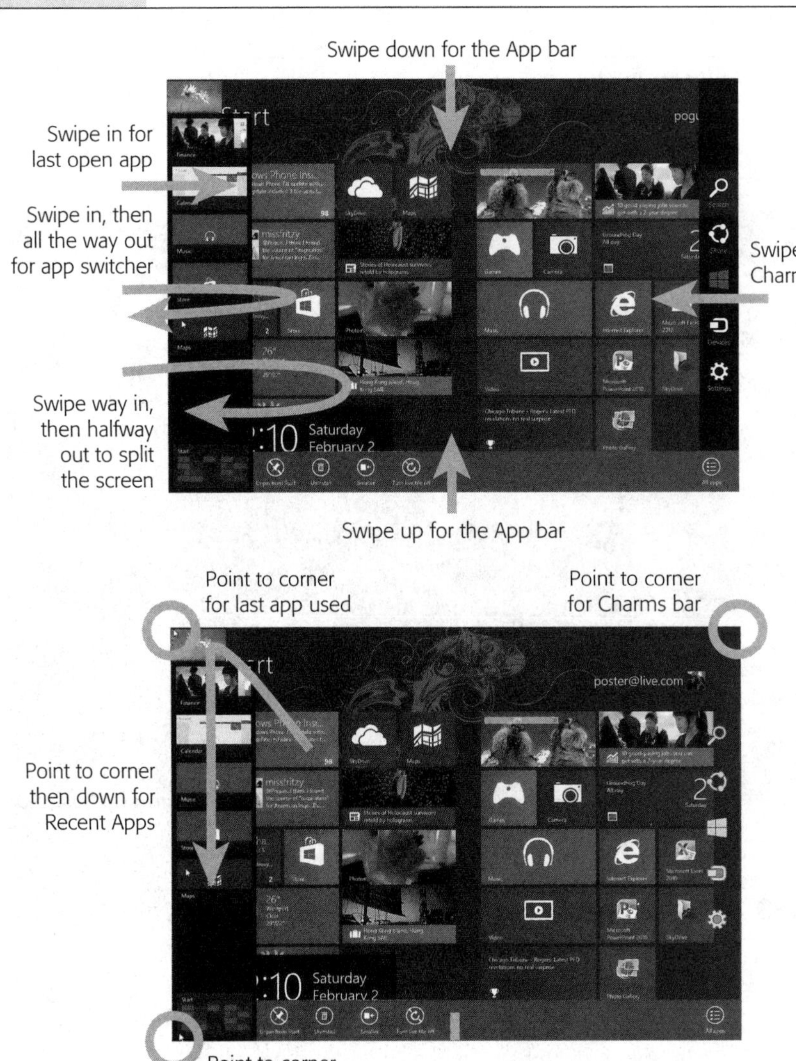

Figure 1-7: *Top: Here's a master diagram, showing all the different ways you can swipe on a touch screen, and all the different panels and options they produce. (Two of them—the app switcher and splitting the screen—are described in Chapter 3.)*

Bottom: And here's a master diagram showing the equivalent gestures if you have a mouse instead of a touchscreen.

The Charms Bar

The Charms bar is new in Windows 8. It's a vertical panel that pops out of the right side of the screen, no matter what you're doing on the computer or what program is open.

Here's how to open the Charms bar:

- **Touchscreen:** Swipe inward from the right edge of the screen.
- **Mouse:** Point to the upper-right corner of the screen.
- **Keyboard:** Press ⊞+C.

In each case, the Charms bar gracefully slides in from the right edge of the screen. As you can see in Figure 1-8, the five icons here provide direct access to some of the most important functions of your computer.

Tip: Whenever the Charms bar opens on the right side of the screen, you simultaneously get a pop-up panel at the lower-*left* side of the screen that shows today's date, the current time, and your battery and WiFi status.

Here are the icons on the Charms bar:

- **Search.** Tap this icon to begin a search of your computer—for anything: programs, documents, settings, email, calendar appointments, and so on. (Figure 1-8, right, shows the panel.) You can read all about searching in Chapter 3.

Figure 1-8: *The Charms bar (left) is named after the jingly silver doodads that dangle from a charm bracelet. In this case, however, they're more than decorative. They give you direct access to some of the most important functions in Windows. For example, the Settings button opens the Settings panel (middle); the Search button opens, of course, the Search panel (right).*

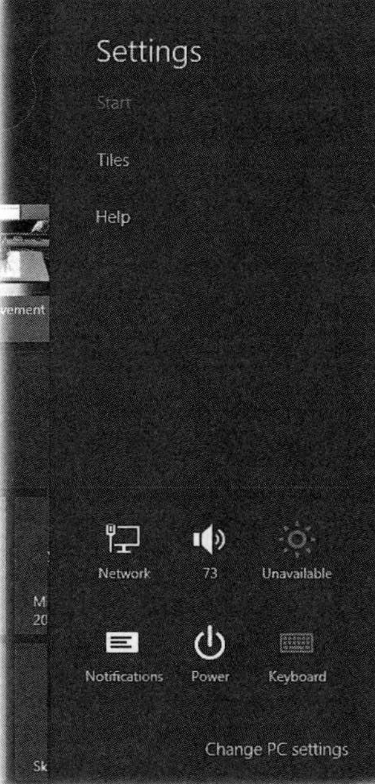

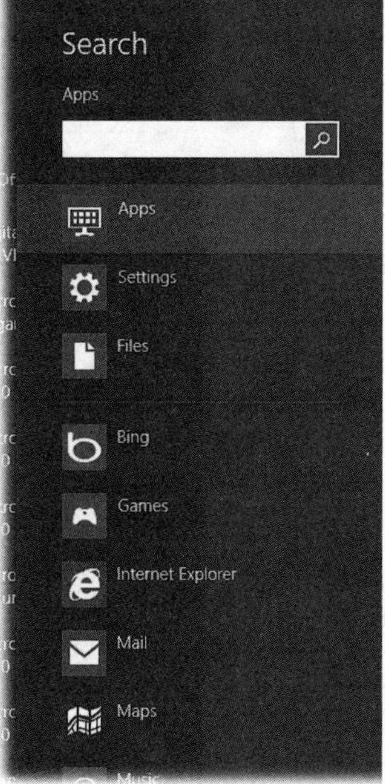

Tip: There are keyboard shortcuts for searching. Press ⊞+F to search for files or ⊞+Q to search for settings. You don't even have to open the Charms bar first.

- **Share.** Tap this icon to send whatever is selected off to your adoring fans—by email or social network, for example.

Tip: Here's another keyboard shortcut: Press ⊞+H to open the Share panel.

The choices you see here vary by program. For example, if you're on a Web page, you might get options like Mail, People (for sending by text message or Twitter), or Post to Facebook. If you're looking at a photo, the options might include Mail or SkyDrive (Microsoft's free online "hard drive"). You can send a location from the Maps app, a news item from the Finance app, or even a contact from the People app.

In each case, you're now offered a new screen where you can tell Windows more about what you want to do. You can address the outgoing email message, or edit the Facebook post, or choose the name of the person you want to receive your shared item, and so on.

You'll read more about the options here in the appropriate sections of this book.

Tip: In PC Settings (page 169), you can turn off individual Share options. For example, if you don't use the SkyDrive, you can turn SkyDrive off here so that the option never appears in the Share panel.

- **Start.** Tap this icon to return to the Start screen.

Tip: If the Start screen is already open, then use this icon to return to whatever app you were using last.

- **Devices.** This icon offers options that pertain to whatever is connected to your computer: TileWorld-compatible printers, projectors, phones, wireless TVs, and so on. For example, this is where you specify how you want a second monitor or external projector to behave—as an extension of your built-in screen, or as a mirror of it.

  And if there aren't any other gadgets connected to your computer, you won't see any options at all here.

Tip: There's a keyboard shortcut for opening the Devices panel: Press ⊞+P.

- **Settings.** Settings, here, means "options for the TileWorld app you're using at the moment." You'll find them on the panel that opens when you tap or click Settings (Figure 1-8, middle).

Note: App settings show up here only in *TileWorld apps*—not in Windows desktop programs. If you open the Settings panel when a Windows desktop program is open, then the top half always lists the same Control Panel shortcuts: Desktop, Control Panel, Personalization, PC Info, and Help.

Below the app settings, you'll find a set of six handy settings icons for your entire computer: network, sound, screen brightness, notifications, power, and keyboard.

As you'll eventually discover, Windows 8 has *three* control panels—different places where you can change settings. (Depending on the kind of computer you have, you might not see them all.) This set of six is only one of those control panels.

Below these, you'll see a link called "Change PC settings" that takes you to a second window full of preferences settings. There's also the traditional Windows Control Panel at the desktop.

Chapter 5 describes all three of the control panels and their settings in exhausting detail.

To hide the Charms bar without tapping any of its buttons, repeat whatever swipe, click, or keystroke you used to make it appear.

Last Open Program

Suppose you've been using BeeKeeper Pro, and now you want to duck back into the last app you used, ProteinFolder Plus.

In the Windows of old, of course, you could press Alt+Tab to jump back and forth between the programs. That still works in Windows 8, but now there are other ways to do the same thing:

- **Touchscreen:** Swipe into the screen from the left edge. With each swipe, you "turn the page" backward to the next older app.
- **Mouse:** Point to the upper-left corner of the screen; when the other program's icon appears, click. (This technique flips back and forth between two apps only.)
- **Keyboard:** Press and release Alt+Tab or ⊞+Tab. (This technique flips back and forth between two apps only.)

Note: The desktop, and all of its own programs, are represented as one app. In other words, if you had three programs open, their windows all appear simultaneously when you flip to the desktop.

See Chapter 3 for more on switching apps.

The App Bar

In the Windows of days gone by, you could click something with the *right* mouse button to open a shortcut menu. That's a brief menu of options, appearing right at your cursor tip, that applies to whatever you just clicked.

At the Start screen, for example, the App menu contains an "All apps" button that displays a list of *all* your programs. (The Start screen shows only a subset of them.) In Internet Explorer, the App menu shows the icons of recently opened pages.

That idea is available in TileWorld, too—but the "shortcut menu" is a horizontal options bar at the bottom of the screen, called the app bar. It contains a few important options for whatever TileWorld program you're using at the moment. In some apps, it pops in from the top of the screen; in others, from the bottom.

Note: The App bar doesn't appear when you're using traditional Windows desktop programs–just for TileWorld apps.

To see the App bar:

- **Touchscreen:** Swipe in from the top *or* bottom edge of the screen.
- **Mouse:** Right-click any blank spot in the window.
- **Keyboard:** Press ⊞+Z. Or press the ▤▾ key, if your keyboard has one, or press Shift+F10.

Tip: At the Start screen, the App bar has a few twists. To see the options for a single tile, swipe down on it with your finger, or right-click it. The resulting buttons apply to that tile: Unpin from Start (gets the tile off the screen), Uninstall, Smaller or Bigger (changes the tile size), and "Turn live tile off" (stops displaying real-time info from online).

Shutting Down

What should you do when you're finished using your computer for the moment?

Millions of people shut their PCs off, but they shouldn't; it's a colossal waste of time. When you shut down, you have to wait for all your programs to close—and then the next morning, you have to reopen everything, reposition your windows, and get everything back the way you had it.

You shouldn't just leave your computer *on* all the time, either. That's a massive waste of electricity, a security risk, and a black mark for the environment.

What you *should* do is put your machine to sleep. Usually, you do that by pressing the physical power button, and that's that. If it's a laptop, just close the lid.

The Sleep/Shut Down/Restart Commands

If you really want to do the sleeping or shutting down thing using the onscreen commands, you'll have to learn their new locations.

For years, Microsoft was ridiculed for a peculiarity of the Windows design: To *shut down* your PC, you had to click a button called *Start.*

Not anymore. The "Shut down" command is now on the *right* side of the screen, in the Charms bar. You can see the official procedure in Figure 1-9.

Tip: If you have a keyboard, you can save yourself some steps. Press ⊞+I to open the Settings panel of the Charms bar; then click Power, and then "Shut down."

As shown in Figure 1-9, shutting down is only one of the options for finishing your work session. Here are your others.

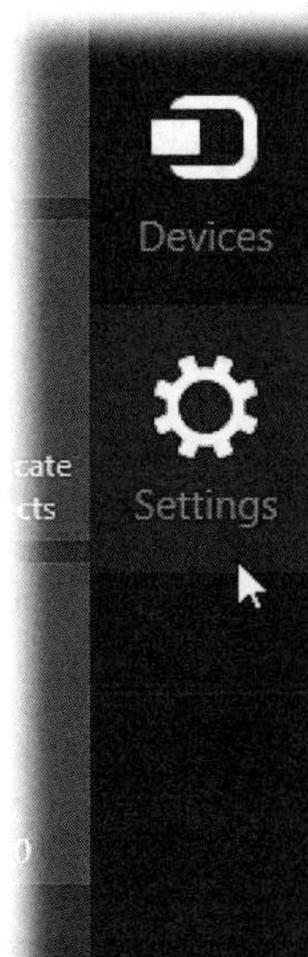

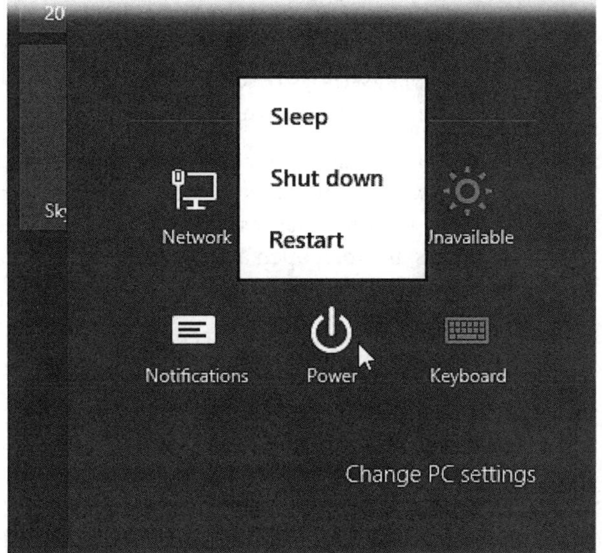

Figure 1-9: *To shut down your computer, open the Charms bar (left). (Swipe inward from the right side, or press ⊞+C.) Click Settings. Right: On the Settings panel, select Power, and then "Shut down."*

Sleep

In the olden days, Windows offered a command called Standby. This special state of PC consciousness reduced the amount of electricity the computer used, putting it in suspended animation until you used the mouse or keyboard to begin working again. Whatever programs or documents you were working on remained in memory.

When using a laptop on battery power, Standby was a real boon. When the flight attendant handed over your microwaved chicken teriyaki, you could take a break without closing all your programs or shutting down the computer.

Unfortunately, there were two big problems with Standby, especially for laptops. First, the PC still drew a trickle of power this way. If you didn't use your laptop for a few days, the battery would silently go dead—and everything you had open and unsaved would be lost forever. Second, drivers or programs sometimes interfered with Standby, so your laptop remained on even though it was closed inside your carrying case. Your plane would land on the opposite coast, you'd pull out the laptop for the big meeting, and you'd discover that (a) the thing was roasting hot, and (b) the battery was dead.

The command is now called Sleep, and it doesn't present those problems anymore. First, drivers and applications are no longer allowed to interrupt the Sleep process. No more Hot Laptop Syndrome.

Second, the instant you put the computer to sleep, Windows quietly transfers a copy of everything in memory into an invisible file on the hard drive. But it still keeps everything alive in memory—the battery provides a tiny trickle of power—in case you return to the laptop (or desktop) and want to dive back into work.

If you do return soon, the next startup is lightning-fast. Everything reappears on the screen faster than you can say, "Redmond, Washington."

If you *don't* return shortly, then Windows eventually cuts power, abandoning what it had memorized in RAM. (You control when this happens using the advanced power plan settings described on page 814.) Now your computer is using no power at all; it's in *hibernate* mode.

Fortunately, Windows still has the hard drive copy of your work environment. So *now* when you tap a key to wake the computer, you may have to wait 30 seconds or so—not as fast as 2 seconds, but certainly better than the 5 minutes it would take to start up, reopen all your programs, reposition your document windows, and so on.

The bottom line: When you're done working for the moment—or for the day—put your computer to sleep instead of shutting it down. You save power, you save time, and you don't risk any data loss.

You can send a laptop to sleep just by closing the lid. On any kind of computer, you can trigger Sleep by clicking Sleep in the Charms bar (Figure 1-9), or by pushing the PC's power button, if you've set it up that way.

POWER USERS' CLINIC

Bringing Back the Hibernate Command

Hibernate mode is a lot like Sleep, except that it *doesn't* offer a period during which the computer will wake up instantly. Hibernate equals the *second* phase of Sleep mode, in which your working world is saved to the hard drive. Waking the computer from Hibernate takes about 30 seconds.

In an effort to make life simpler, Microsoft has hidden the Hibernate command in Windows 8. You won't find it in the pop-up menu shown in Figure 1-9.

You can bring it back, though.

To get there, open the Charms bar (swipe in from the right edge, or press ⊞+C), click or tap Search, click or tap Settings, and type power.

In the search results, click "Choose what the Power buttons do." Now click "Change settings that are currently unavailable" and authenticate yourself, if necessary (Microsoft's way of ensuring that only an administrator can change such important settings).

Finally, scroll down until you see "Shutdown settings." Turn on the "Hibernate: Show in Power menu" checkbox. Click "Save changes."

From now on, the Hibernate option appears in the menu shown in Figure 1-9, just like it did in the good old days.

Restart

This command quits all open programs and then quits and restarts Windows again automatically. The computer doesn't actually turn off. (You might do this to "refresh" your computer when you notice that it's responding sluggishly, for example.)

Shut down

This is what most people would call "really, really off." When you shut down your PC, Windows quits all open programs, offers you the opportunity to save any unsaved documents, exits Windows, and turns off the computer.

In Windows 8, starting up after a full shutdown is a lot faster than before, thanks to something Microsoft calls Hybrid Boot. (It combines element of Hibernation mode with the full shutdown mode, in an effort to save you time the next time you start up.)

Still, there's almost no reason to shut down your PC anymore. Sleep is almost always better all the way around.

The only exceptions have to do with hardware installation. Anytime you have to open up the PC to make a chantge (installing memory, hard drives, or sound or video cards), or to connect something external that doesn't just use a USB or FireWire (1394) port, you should shut the thing down first.

Tip: If you're a keyboardy sort of person, you might prefer this faster route to shut down: Press Ctrl+Alt+Delete to summon the Lock/Switch User screen. Click the ⏻ button in the lower right to shut down.

The Account Menu

See your account name and picture in the upper-right corner of the Start screen (Figure 1-10)?

That's not just helpful information. The picture is also a pop-up menu. And its commands all have to do with switching from one account to another. (In Windows' *accounts* feature, each person who uses this PC gets to see her own desktop picture, email account, files, and so on. See Chapter 24.)

These commands used to be part of the standard Sleep/Restart/Shut Down menu, but they've moved to a new address. Here's what they do.

Tip: Some keystrokes from previous Windows versions are still around. For example, you can still press Ctrl+Alt+Delete to summon the three commands described here: "Lock," "Switch user," and "Sign out"—plus a bonus link for the Task Manager (page 335).

Sign out

When you choose "Sign out," Windows closes all your open programs and documents (giving you an opportunity to save any unsaved documents first). It then presents a new Login screen so that somebody else can log in.

Whatever *you* had running remains open behind the scenes. When you log in again, you'll find all your open programs and documents exactly as you left them.

[Switch user]

What if somebody just wants to log into the computer with her own name and password—to do a quick calendar or email check, for example?

Yes, the "Sign out" command works fine. But the interloper can save a few steps by simply choosing her own account name from the pop-up menu that is your account icon. She'll be asked for her password, of course.

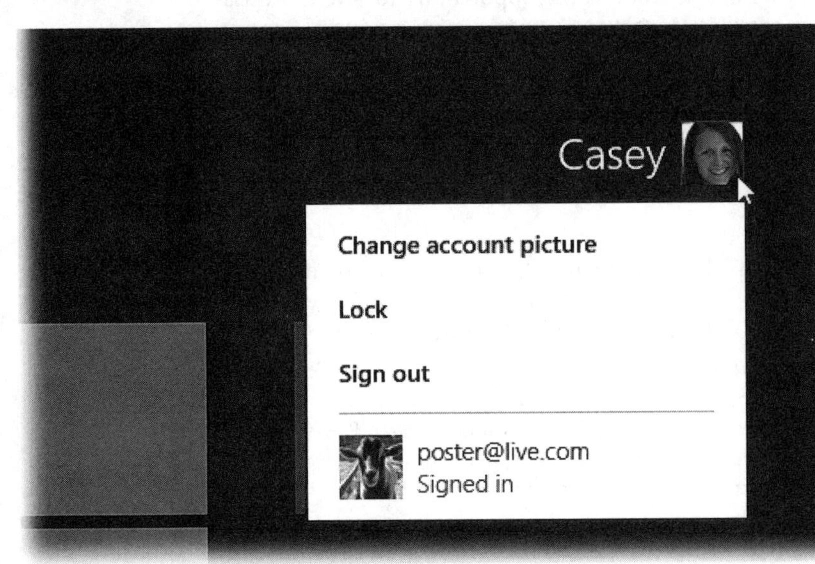

Figure 1-10: *Your account icon isn't just an icon; it's also a pop-up menu. Click it to see the "Sign out" and "Lock" commands, as well as the names of other account holders for fast switching.*

Lock

This command takes you back to the Lock screen described at the beginning of this chapter. In essence, it throws a sheet of inch-thick steel over everything you were doing, hiding your screen from view. This is an ideal way to protect your PC from nosy people who happen to wander by your desk while you're away getting coffee or lunch.

Three Triggers for Sleep/Shut Down–and How to Change Them

You now know how to trigger the "Shut down" command using the Charms bar. But there are even faster ways.

If you have a laptop, just close the lid. If you have a desktop PC, just press its power button (⏻).

In all these cases, though—menu, lid, power button—*you* can decide whether the computer shuts down, goes to sleep, hibernates, or just ignores you.

To find the factory setting that controls what happens when you close the lid or hit the power button, open the Charms bar (swipe in from the right edge, or press ⊞+C), click or tap Search, click or tap Settings, and type *power*.

In the search results, the two relevant options are "Change what closing the lid does" and "Change what the power buttons do."

For each of these options, you can choose "Sleep," "Do nothing," "Hibernate," or "Shut down." And you can set up different behaviors for when the machine is plugged in and when it's running on battery power.

POWER USERS' CLINIC

Shut Down/Restart Buttons on the Start Screen

Here it is again: In general, shutting down your computer is a waste of time. Just Sleep it.

But if you're some oddball who feels better shutting down the computer completely every day, then you'll be relieved to know that you can install a Shut Down button right on the Start screen. In other words, you don't have to burrow into the Charms bar every time you want to shut down. It's a lot of steps, but you have to perform them only once.

Begin at the desktop (click the Desktop tile or press ⊞+D). Right-click a blank spot on the desktop; from the shortcut menu, choose New→Shortcut. In the "Type the location of the item" box, type exactly this:

shutdown.exe -s -t 00

Click Next. In the "Type a name for this shortcut" box, type Shut Down (or Goodnight, or Go Away, or whatever you like). Click Finish.

Now there's a Shut Down shortcut on your desktop. (Optional: Choose a cool icon for it, like the standard ⏻ logo. To do that, right-click the icon; from the shortcut menu, choose Properties. Click Change Icon; click OK; choose a new image from the palette of icons; and then click OK.)

Finally, right-click your desktop shortcut; from the shortcut menu, choose Pin to Start. And presto: The Shut Down command now appears on your Start screen, at the far-right end.

You can also add Restart, Lock, Hibernate, and Sleep buttons to your Start screen, using pretty much the same steps. The only difference is the code you type in the first step:

Restart: shutdown.exe -r -t 00

Lock: rundll32.exe user32.dll,LockWorkStation

Hibernate: rundll32.exe powrProf.dll,SetSuspendState

Sleep: rundll32.exe powrprof.dll,SetSuspendState 0,1,0

For these commands, if you choose to add a custom icon as described above, navigate to Windows/System32/Shell32.dll to find the palette of available images.

CHAPTER

2

Customizing the Lock, Login & Start Screens

As you know from Chapter 1, you pass through three Windows 8 screens before you can actually start getting any work done: the Lock screen, the Login screen, and the Start screen.

Since you'll be spending so much time facing these bastions of modern software design, you'll be glad that you can tweak them to your liking—or, in some cases, eliminate them altogether. Here's the scoop.

Adding or Removing App Tiles

The tiles on the Start screen don't represent *all* of your programs—only the ones to which you want quick access (just like the old Start menu). But there will come a time when you want to add a new program's tile here.

Installing a new app's tile to the Start screen is called *pinning* it. You can pin either TileWorld apps or Windows desktop programs to the Start screen.

And apps are just the beginning. Eventually, you'll discover that you can also pin tiles for Web sites, playlists, photo albums, people from your contacts list, mail accounts or mailboxes, icons from Desktop Windows, and more.

But first things first: pinning apps.

Adding App Tiles to the Start Screen

Windows 8 offers two ways to pin TileWorld apps to the Start screen: from the All Apps list, or from the Search screen.

Pinning from the All Apps list

One way to find the app you want to pin is to use the All Apps screen, as follows:

1. **Open the App bar.**

   Touchscreen: Swipe up from the bottom edge of the screen.

   Mouse: Right-click a blank spot on the Start screen.

   Keyboard: Press ⊞+Z.

   The App bar dutifully appears at the bottom edge of the screen.

2. **Select the "All apps" button at lower right.**

   The master list of every program installed on your computer, both TileWorld apps and Windows desktop programs, is now arrayed before you (Figure 2-1).

Tip: If you have a keyboard, you can press ⊞+Q instead of steps 1 and 2. You go straight to "All apps."

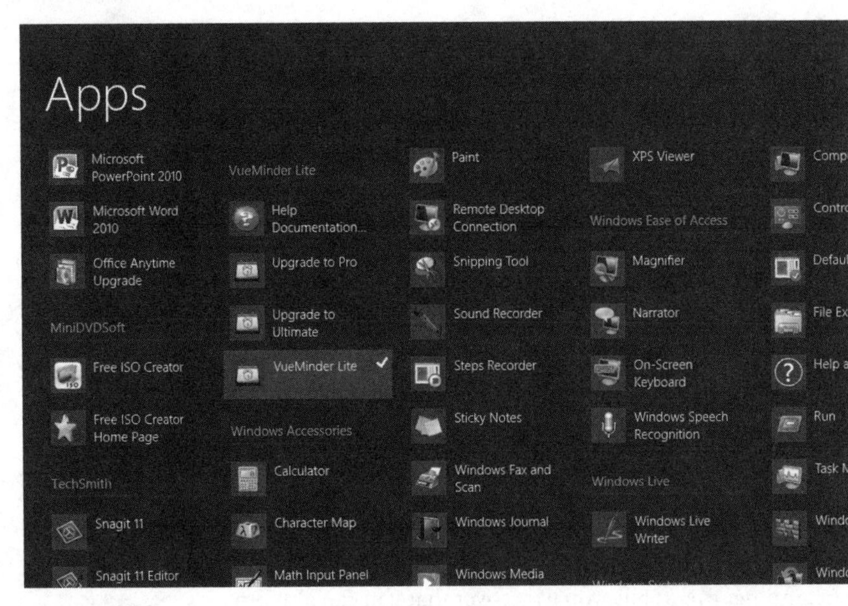

Figure 2-1: *On the "All apps" screen, you see all TileWorld apps and all desktop programs. They're listed the way they would have been in the old Start menu—but instead of folder submenus, you get individually titled groups. You can take this opportunity to pin any of these programs to your Start screen.*

3. **When you find the icon you want to pin to the Start screen, "right-click" it.**

   Touchscreen: Swipe downward from its icon.

   Mouse: Right-click its icon.

   Keyboard: Use the arrow keys to highlight the program's icon, and then press the space bar.

   In each case, the App bar now appears—and it contains a Pin to Start button.

4. **Select Pin to Start.**

   When you select that button, the selected program's icon now appears on the Start screen—at the far right. (You might have to scroll through a few "pages" to see it.) You can always move it into a better position, as described below.

Pinning from Search

If you know the name of the app you want to pin, it may be faster to find it using Search.

- **Touchscreen:** Open the Charms bar (swipe in from the right edge); tap Search. Type the app's name.
- **Keyboard:** From the Start screen, just start typing the app's name.

Once you see the app's name and icon in the search results, proceed as described from step 3 above.

Pinning desktop icons

It may be screamingly obvious that the Start screen belongs to the new TileWorld. But it's going to be your primary launcher for regular Windows desktop icons, too, so you'd better figure out how to pin files, folders, disks, libraries, and programs from the Windows desktop here, too.

1. **From the Start screen, jump to the Windows desktop.**

   Touchscreen: Tap the Desktop tile.

   Mouse: Click the Desktop tile.

   Keyboard: Press ⊞+D.

   You wind up at the traditional Windows desktop.

2. **Right-click the icon you want to pin.**

   It can be anything that would have appeared in the Start menu in days of yore: a folder, a program, a document, a photo, whatever.

UP TO SPEED

Multiple Selections

It's often handy to operate on a whole bunch of apps or tiles simultaneously–to unpin a group of them from the Start screen at once, for example.

As usual, you'll have to learn a different technique depending on whether you have a touchscreen or not.

Touchscreen: Swipe downward on each tile you want to select.

Mouse: Right-click each tile you want.

Keyboard: Use the arrow keys to highlight each icon; press the space bar for each one you want to include.

In each case, a checkmark appears in the upper-right corner of each selected tile.

Now you're ready to unpin the selected tiles en masse.

Tip: It can even be a program whose icon appears in the taskbar.

Here's how you right-click:

Touchscreen: Hold your finger down on its icon.

Mouse: Right-click its icon.

Keyboard: Select the icon; press the ▤ key (or Shift+F10).

In each case, the shortcut menu appears.

3. **In the shortcut menu, choose Pin to Start.**

   It might look like nothing has happened. But in the parallel universe of TileWorld, you have indeed installed this desktop icon's tile on the Start screen. (Once again, it appears at the far right of the last page of the Start screen, so you may have to scroll to find it.)

Unpinning Tiles

Windows software giveth, and Windows software taketh away. You may someday decide that a tile you never use should not be taking up precious real estate on the Start screen. Or some software installer may someday have the gall to put its tile on your Start screen without asking you. Or you may not want to have to look every morning at the junkware that came preinstalled on your Start screen by your PC manufacturer.

Getting rid of a tile is easy as pie:

- **Touchscreen:** Swipe downward on the tile.
- **Mouse:** Right-click the tile.
- **Keyboard:** Use the arrow keys to select the tile, and then press the space bar.

In each case, the App bar now appears at the bottom of the screen. Hit Unpin from Start.

Note: You're not *uninstalling* anything. Whatever you've just unpinned is still on your computer—it just no longer has a tile on the Start screen. If you find yourself seized with remorse, you can always put its tile back *onto* the Start screen as described above.

You can also unpin a bunch of apps all at once; see the box on page 37.

Moving Tiles Around

You can, of course, drag the Start screen's tiles into a new order, putting the *personal* back into *personal computer.*

Most tutorials cheerfully inform you that you can simply drag tiles into new positions. That works fine if you have a mouse.

But if you're using a touchscreen, that instruction leaves out a key fact: If you drag *horizontally*, you'll wind up sliding the Start screen horizontally instead of moving a tile. Instead, follow the trick shown in Figure 2-2.

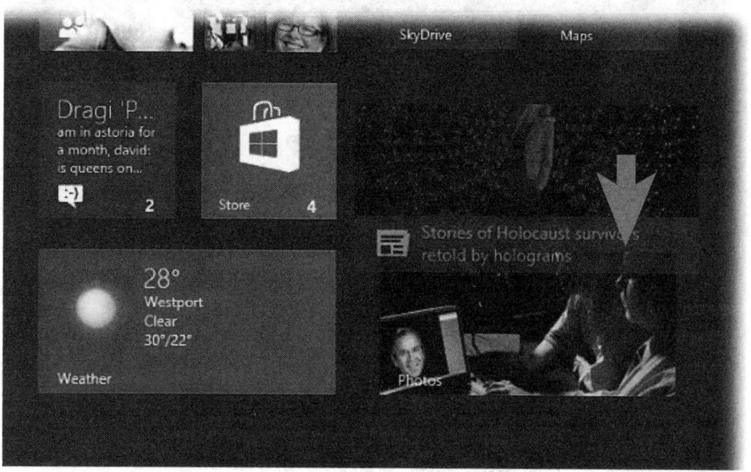

Figure 2-2:
Top: To move a tile, put your finger on a tile.

Bottom: Now make a small vertical move, as though you're unhooking the tile from a picture hook behind it. Once you do that, you're free to drag it anywhere you like; the unhooked tile follows your finger or mouse.

As you drag the unhooked tile, the other tiles scoot out of the way as you find a new place for the unhooked tile.

Tip: Since the Start screen scrolls horizontally—it's as wide as you need it to be—it's good to know that you can even drag a tile to another "page" (another screen) of your Start screen. Just move it up against the edge of the screen and pause briefly; the Start screen scrolls for you automatically.

Grouping Tiles

The Start screen tiles aren't scattered pell-mell; they present an attractive, orderly mosaic. Not only are they mathematically nestled among one another, but they're actually *grouped*. As you can see in Figure 2-3, each cluster of related tiles can bear a *name*, like "Essentials" or "Casey's Faves."

Figure 2-3: *You can make sense of Tile-World by putting your tiles into logically named groups.*

Creating a New Group

To create a new group, choose one tile to be the pioneer. Start moving it as described in the previous paragraphs. But your target is the small blank area *in between* existing groups—or all the way to the *right or left* of existing groups.

When you get there, you'll see a thick vertical bar appear on your screen. That's Windows telling you, "I get the hint. You want to create a new group right here."

Release the tile you're dragging; it's now happily setting up the homestead. Go get some other tiles to drag over into the new group to join it.

Naming and Moving Groups

To change the name that appears over a group of tiles, you'll *zoom out* of the Start screen—a weird and wonderful procedure:

- **Touchscreen:** Put two fingers on the screen (or more), and *pinch inward* against the glass.
- **Mouse:** Move the mouse any amount. Click the tiny – button that appears in the lower-right corner of the screen. (Or turn the scroll wheel down while pressing the Ctrl key.)
- **Keyboard:** Press Ctrl+minus key (–).

Tip: On recent laptops, you can also pinch inward on the trackpad.

You can now see the entire landscape of your Start screen screens—on a single screen (Figure 2-4).

Once you're zoomed out like this, you can operate on your tile groups.

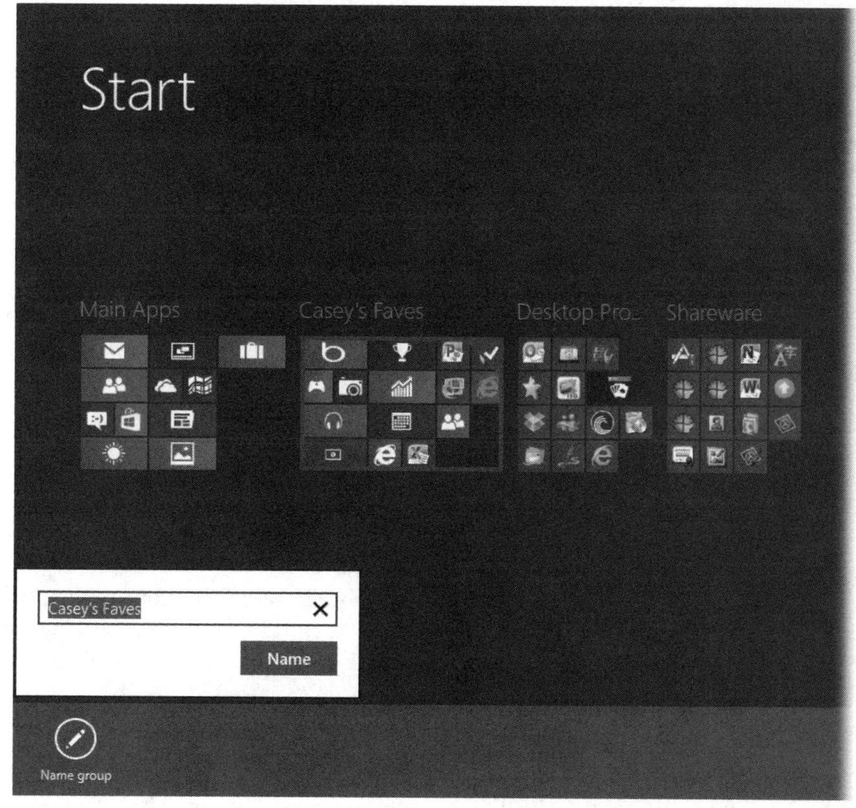

***Figure 2-4:** Pinching with two fingers triggers what Microsoft calls* semantic zoom, *which is a goofy way of saying "the Start screen goes miniature." Now it's easy to name and move groups around.*

Naming a tile group

Zoom out of the Start screen. Then open the App bar for the group you want to rename:

- **Touchscreen:** Make a quick swipe down from the miniaturized group.
- **Mouse:** Right-click the group.
- **Keyboard:** Highlight a group by pressing the arrow keys. Then press the 🗐 key (or Shift+F10).

And lo, a new button appears on the App bar: "Name group." Click that button, type a new name, and hit Name (or press Enter). Your group is now named.

Moving tile groups

While you're zoomed out, you can rearrange your groups, moving entire groups right or left.

You have to use the same technique you use for moving individual tiles: Begin your drag with a slight *up or down* movement; only after you've "unhooked" the group can you slide it horizontally.

The other groups move aside to make room.

Zooming back in

To zoom back in so that you can use the Start screen again, reverse your zooming procedure:

- **Touchscreen:** Tap the glass. (Or spread two fingers.)
- **Mouse:** Click anywhere. Or turn the scroll wheel up while pressing Ctrl.
- **Keyboard:** Press Esc, or press Ctrl+plus sign (+).

More Ways to Tweak the Start Screen

You're going to be seeing a *lot* of the Start screen. You may as well set it up the way you like.

Change the Wallpaper and Color Scheme

Windows wouldn't be Windows if it weren't bristling with options to change the look of your world. In Windows 8, you can change both the background image on the Start screen and the color scheme.

These are related, as it turns out. For example, the Start screen wallpaper pattern actually *changes* to match the color you choose for your Start screen world. You might think that Microsoft gives you only 20 Start screen wallpapers to choose from—but multiply those by the 25 different color schemes, and you'll feel like a regular Sherwin-Williams.

The steps go like this:

1. **Open the Personalize→"Start screen" pane of PC Settings.**

   Touchscreen: Open the Charms bar (swipe in from the right margin). Tap Settings. Tap "Change PC settings." Tap Personalize. Tap "Start screen" at the top.

   Keyboard: At the Start screen, type *start;* select Settings. Confirm that "Start screen" is highlighted in the results, and then press Enter.

   You wind up with something like Figure 2-5.

2. **Tap the various squares below the miniature desktop to try on the different wallpapers.**

   Once you've settled on a background you like, proceed to step 3.

Tip: Microsoft gives you a choice of 20 backgrounds—and no option to choose an image of your own. If you care, check out Stardock's Decor8 ($5). It lets you choose any photo for the Start screen wallpaper—and any color you want for the colors, too! You can download it from this book's "Missing CD" page at *www.missingmanuals.com*.

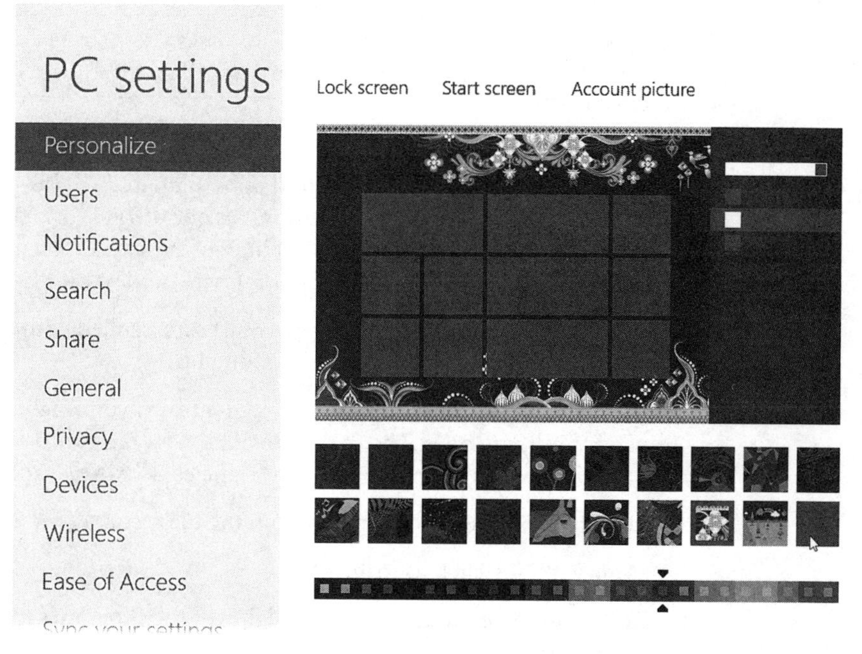

***Figure 2-5:** If you've correctly tapped "Start screen" at the top of the Personalize screen, you get to choose from among these Start screen wallpapers and accent colors. The lower-right one is just a solid dark swatch—no pattern at all.*

3. **Tap the different tiny color squares underneath until you find a color scheme that suits you.**

   As noted above, the color swatch you choose here actually *modifies* the Start screen wallpaper you've chosen.

When everything looks fine, return to the Start screen to see what kind of visual damage you've done.

Resizing Individual Tiles

Tiles come in two sizes: square and rectangle. As part of your Start screen interior decoration binge, you may want to make some of them bigger and some of them smaller. Maybe you want to make the important ones rectangular so you can read more information on them. Maybe you want to make the rarely used ones smaller so that more of them fit into a compact space.

The Larger and Smaller buttons are what you need, and they're hiding on the App bar. So, on the Start screen:

- **Touchscreen:** Swipe downward on the tile whose size you want to change.
- **Mouse:** Right-click the tile.
- **Keyboard:** Use the arrow keys to select the tile, and then press the space bar.

On the App bar, you see a Smaller button (if the tile is rectangular now) or a Larger button (if it's square). Hit that button, and the deed is done.

Note: Some live tiles may continue to show live information when they're shrunken to square size. Some may show less information. Some may not have room to show any at all. You take your chances.

The Silence of the Tiles

The fact that many of your TileWorld apps' tiles are *live tiles*—tiny dashboards that display real-time incoming information—is one of TileWorld's most famous features. There, on the Mail tile, are the subject lines of the last few incoming messages; there, on the Calendar tile, is your next appointment; and so on.

It has to be said, though: Altogether, a Start screen filled with blinky, scrolling icons can look a little like Times Square at midnight.

If you're feeling quite caffeinated enough already, you might not want live tiles so much as, well, *still* ones. The trick to turning off a tile's blinky updating is hiding on the App bar, which appears when you "right-click" the tile. You do it like this:

- **Touchscreen:** Swipe downward from the tile's icon.
- **Mouse:** Right-click its icon.
- **Keyboard:** Use the arrow keys to highlight the program's icon, and then press the space bar.

GEM IN THE ROUGH

Bigger Tiles for All

Windows 8 determines the sizes for your Start screen tiles depending on a bunch of factors, including your screen's size and resolution. Apart from making the square tiles rectangular or vice versa, you don't have much control over the tiles' size.

But you may have *one* degree of control: you can make them all much bigger.

Open the Charms bar; tap Settings; tap "More PC settings." On the PC Settings screen, tap Ease of Access.

See the option called "Make everything on your screen bigger"? If you turn it on, the tiles get even bigger. You can practically use your fist to tap them now.

Truth is, this option is intended for very high-resolution screens (which, because the pixels are tiny, wind up shrinking onscreen objects). If your screen's resolution is less than 1080p high definition (1920 × 1080 pixels), "Make everything on your screen bigger" isn't even available; Microsoft thinks the tiles are already plenty big.

In each case, the App bar now appears—and it contains a "Turn live tile off" button. When you tap it, the tile's current information disappears, and the live updating stops.

Note: That's *if* it was a live tile to begin with. Not all tiles are live–not even all TileWorld apps' tiles are.

To reverse the procedure, "right-click" a dead tile; in this case, the App bar's button says "Turn live tile on" instead.

Administrative Tools

In the old Start menu, there used to be a folder called Administrative Tools. It contained geeky programs like ODBC Data Sources, Component Services, Windows PowerShell, and Resource Monitor.

Well, this folder of nerd catnip is still available, and you can install its apps' tiles right on the Start screen, like this:

1. **Open the Settings pane of the Charms bar.**

   Touchscreen: Swipe inward from the right edge of the screen. Tap Settings.

   Mouse: Move your cursor to the upper-right corner of the screen. Click Settings.

   Keyboard: Press ⊞+I.

2. **Select Tiles.**

   A weird little panel appears, offering a couple of controls.

3. **Set "Show administrative tools" to Yes.**

   Now you can close the panel (tap or click any blank spot on the Start screen).

At the far right of your Start screen, there they are: all the tiles for the Windows administrative application suite.

Notifications

A *notification* is an important status message. You might get one when a text message comes in, a Facebook post goes up, an alarm goes off, a calendar appointment is imminent, or your battery is running low.

In Windows 8, you'll know when some app is trying to get your attention: A message rectangle slides into view at the top right of your screen (Figure 2-6). If you don't take action by clicking or tapping it, the message slides away again after a few seconds.

Tip: On a touchscreen, you can also swipe it away with a finger.

Only TileWorld apps display notifications this way. Desktop programs still use whatever alert mechanisms they always have—pop-up dialog boxes, for example—and you see those only when you're in Desktop world.

Note: Do these "toast" notification bubbles appear on the Lock screen too? That's up to you.

From the Start screen, open the Charms bar. Select Settings, choose "Change PC settings," select Notifications, and turn off "Show app notifications on the lock screen." Those messages no longer appear when the Lock screen is up.

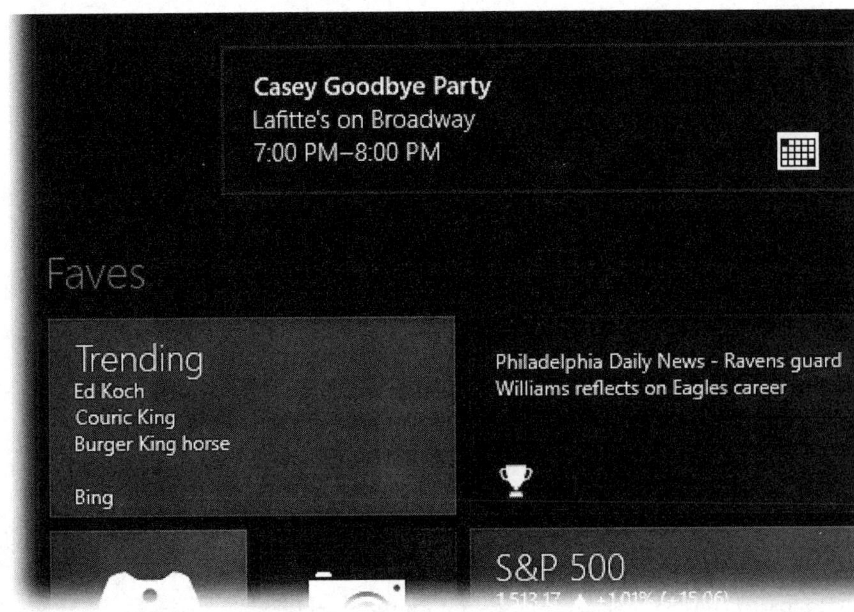

Figure 2-6: *Microsoft's programmers wittily call these alert messages "toast," because they pop up at the right time, just like the delicious breakfast treat. They're intended, of course, to be gentle and inconspicuous alerts that aren't much of a distraction. But if you want to tend to one, click it to open the corresponding app.*

FREQUENTLY ASKED QUESTION

Shutting Up the Bubbles

I'm about to give a presentation on my laptop—I don't need the distraction of those message bubbles in the corner of my screen. Can't they be shut up?

Yes.

Open the Charms bar; tap Settings; tap Notifications. (Keyboard fans: Press ⊞+I, and then click Notifications.)

In the shortcut menu, you're offered three choices: "Hide for 1 hour," "Hide for 3 hours," and "Hide for 8 hours" (that is, the whole workday).

When you're hunkering down for a work session, feel free to shut alerts off. Your messages won't pop up on your screen for the time period you've specified.

You can also turn off these notifications for good. Open PC Settings (page 169); choose Notifications; and turn off "Show app notifications." (Here, too, is where you can turn off "Play notification sounds"—a reference to apps that also ding or chime to get your attention when their notifications appear.)

And by the way: Windows *automatically* shuts up its alert bubbles whenever you're giving a presentation or connected to a projector. Nothing worse than an audience of 500 witnessing the embarrassing subject lines of your incoming email.

Customizing the Notifications

You can (and should) specify *which* apps are allowed to pop onto your screen. There's a special pane in PC Settings just for doing that.

- **Touchscreen:** Swipe in from the right to open the Charms bar. Tap Settings. Tap "Change PC settings." Tap Notifications.
- **Mouse:** Point to the upper-right corner to open the Charms bar. Click Settings. Tap "Change PC settings." Tap Notifications.
- **Keyboard:** At the Start screen, type the beginning of *notifications.* Click Settings. Click Notifications.

Now you see something like Figure 2-7, where there's a master list of every TileWorld app that might want to get your attention: Calendar, Games, Internet Explorer, Mail, Messaging, Store, and so on. Each has an individual On/Off switch, for your toast-stifling pleasure.

Tip: If you use the TileWorld Mail app, you can also stifle the pop-up alerts on an account-by-account basis. Open the Charms panel, tap Settings, tap Accounts, tap the name of the email account you want to change, and scroll down to "Show email notifications for this account."

Figure 2-7: *You have app-by-app control over the "toast" that can pop up to get your attention, right here in Notifications. You can also control how long they remain on the screen, by the way; choose Ease of Access, and then use the "Show notifications for" pop-up menu.*

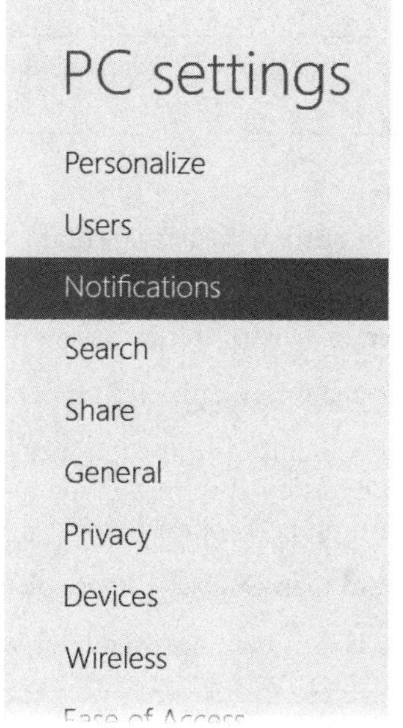

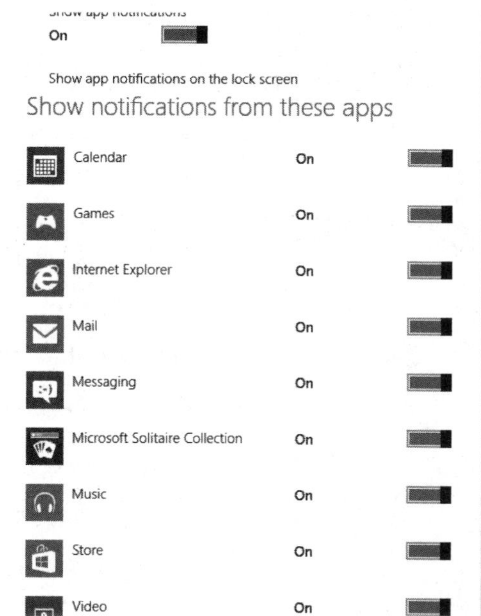

Customizing the Lock Screen

The Lock screen is designed to give you a glimpse of useful information—the time, your battery charge, the current WiFi network signal, the number of new email messages waiting, and so on—without any red tape like having to sign in and type a password.

You can add other programs' information on this choice slice of real estate, too. And you can change the photo that appears as the Lock screen wallpaper. Here's how to proceed.

Lock-Screen Wallpaper

Not everyone has a deep-seated psychological attachment to Seattle, Washington, which is depicted in the standard "wallpaper" for the Lock screen. (Of course, your computer maker—Dell, HP, whatever—might have replaced Seattle with its own wallpaper.) Here's how to choose a photo you prefer:

1. **Open the Charms bar.**

   To open the Charms bar, press ⊞+C, or swipe inward from the right edge of the screen.

2. **Pick Settings.**

   The usual TileWorld Settings panel appears.

Tip: If you have a keyboard, you can combine steps 1 and 2 with a quick press of ⊞+I. You jump directly to the Settings panel.

---

3. **Pick "Change PC settings."**

   Now the PC Settings panel appears at the left side of the screen. Select the Personalize panel, if it's not already selected.

   Microsoft offers you a choice of several starter images for the Lock screen.

4. **If you like one of the suggested images, pick it. If not, tap Browse.**

   You wind up looking at the contents of your computer's Pictures folder. If you've ever accumulated any graphics (saved from the Web, for example, or uploaded from your camera), their thumbnails appear here.

5. **Pick the image you want, and then choose "Choose picture."**

   Presto: Your selected photo is the new, improved Lock screen wallpaper.

Tip: If you have a keyboard, you can press ⊞+L to jump to the Lock screen to examine your handiwork. If not, tap your account picture on the Start screen; from the shortcut menu, tap Lock.

Lock Screen Apps

You're not limited to weather, battery, date, and number of emails; you can introduce other apps' information onto your Lock screen. On the other hand, you don't *have*

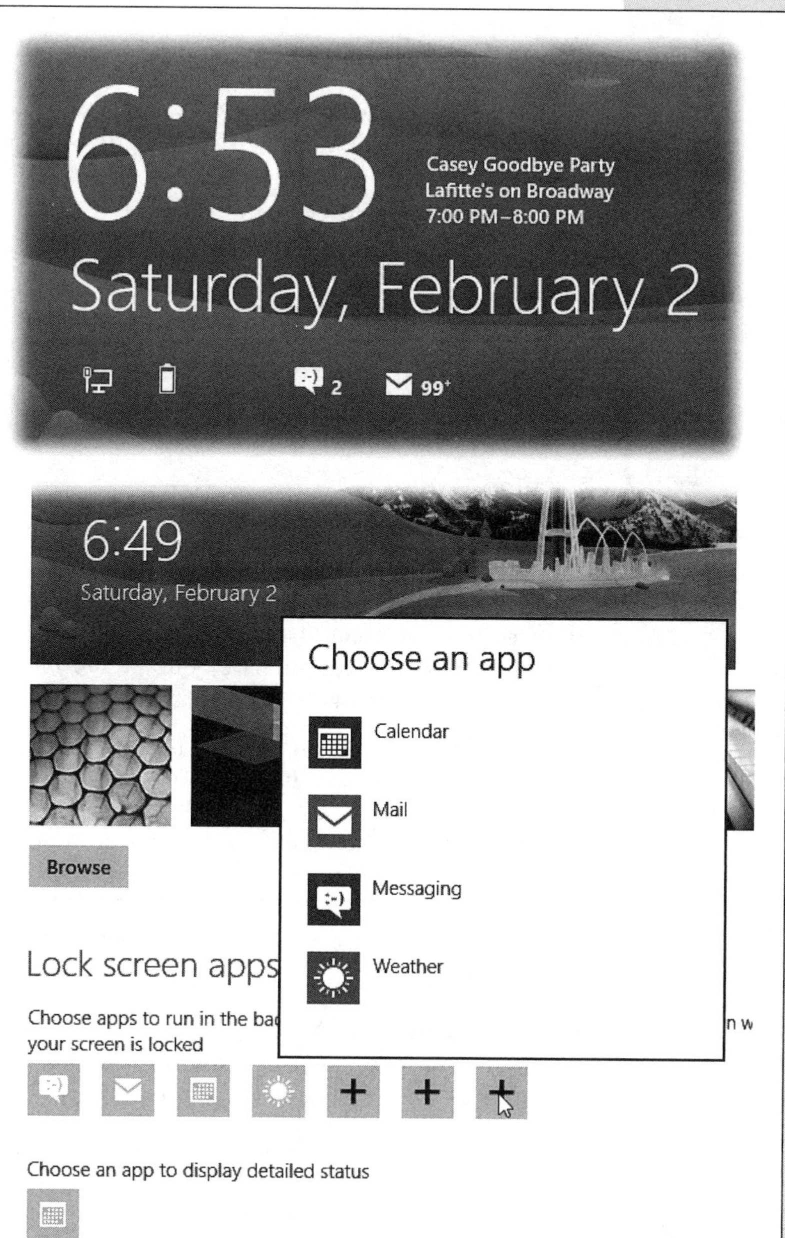

Figure 2-8:
Top: The "detailed status" app gets several lines of text. If you choose Calendar for this job, as shown here, you see a few lines that represent your next appointment. If you choose Weather, you get a quick weather report.

Bottom: What determines how many of the tiny app icons appear on your Lock screen—and which icons they are? You do. In the settings for the Lock screen, you can choose up to seven apps. Their up-to-date info will appear on the Lock screen—as tiny icons. One of them gets special treatment: a multiline textual readout ("detailed status")—in this case, the Calendar.

to look at weather, battery, date, and number of emails, either. The point is, you can add or delete app information from this screen.

To do so, follow steps 1, 2, and 3 above. When you arrive at the Personalize→Lock Screen settings, examine the "Lock screen apps" heading (Figure 2-8).

Here you can see that the Lock screen has room to display info bits from up to seven apps. The icons for Weather, Mail, and Messages are already selected; the slots represented by the + buttons are available for your use. Click one to choose from a list of Lock screen–compatible programs. (Only some apps show up as available, because only some apps can park their data bits on the Lock screen.)

Note: If you choose Weather as one of these seven apps, you will not, in fact, see any weather-related information on your Lock screen except when there's a severe weather alert for your city. If you want to see weather information all the time, choose Weather as the "detailed status" app, as described next.

You can also make an app *stop* appearing on the Lock screen. Follow steps 1, 2, and 3 above. In the row of seven square icons, tap the one you want to squelch, and then tap "Don't show quick status here."

Detailed Status

In Figure 2-8, you can see the peculiar option called, "Choose an app to display detailed status." This one anointed app gets special treatment.

Most Lock screen apps have to convey all their information in the form of a single icon: an envelope to represent Mail, for example (and a small number next to it denoting how many new messages you have). But the app you choose to show *detailed* status gets four lines of text, right next to the big clock on the Lock screen (Figure 2-8, top).

Choosing a new "detailed status" app is quick and easy; just tap the gray-and-white icon that *currently* appears under the "Choose an app" line.

Note: The list of choices includes only apps that have been expressly designed to work with the "detailed status" option. You'll probably find that very few apps show up in this list.

You can also choose *no* app. In the list of apps, tap "Don't show detailed status on the lock screen."

Eliminating the Lock Screen

The Lock screen is handy on a tablet or a laptop. But if you have a desktop PC, you might consider it just another layer of unnecessary red tape.

Fortunately, with a few judicious clicks, you can eliminate the Lock screen (at least if you have the Pro or Enterprise versions of Windows 8). From now on, waking or turning on your computer takes you directly to the password screen. You save a step every time you use your machine.

The steps may sound a tad technical, but you have to go through them only once.

1. **Open the Run dialog box.**

   You can read more about the Run dialog box on page 246. But for now, you open this dialog box by pressing ⊞+R.

   Don't have a keyboard? From the Start screen, type *run*, and then tap the Run icon that appears.

2. **Type *gpedit.msc* and hit OK.**

   The Local Group Policy Editor appears (Figure 2-9).

Note: If it doesn't, you might have to install this app. As you're about to discover, this sort of mucking around is intended for the hopelessly nerdy, but you can handle it.

From the Start screen, type *mmc* and press Enter. In the results, tap *mmc*, and allow the installation.

Now you've opened up the Console app. Choose File→Add/Remove Snap-in. In the following dialog box, select Group Policy Object Editor and then click Add. You should now be able to follow the steps in this tutorial!

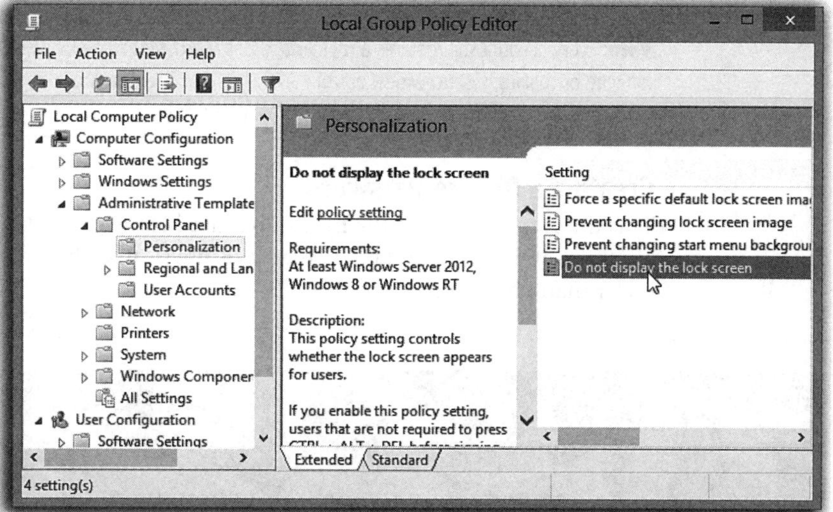

Figure 2-9: *Gpedit is short for the Local Group Policy Editor, a program that lets you mess with all kinds of hidden settings. Click a folder at left to "open" it (expand it to see its contents).*

3. **In the list of folders, expand Administrative Templates→Control Panel→Personalization.**

   In the main window, the "Do not display the lock screen" option is staring you in the face.

4. **Double-click "Do not display the lock screen" and turn on Enabled.**

From now on, whenever you wake up or turn on your computer, you'll go straight to the password screen. The Lock screen is gone forever (or at least until you repeat these steps but turn on "Not configured" in step 4).

Customizing the Login Process

As you now know from Chapter 1, which you've carefully memorized, you can log into your account using any of four methods, of which typing out a password is only one (and a lousy one for touchscreens):

- Draw three lines, dots, or circles on a photo you've selected.
- Type in a four-digit number you've memorized.
- Type a traditional password.
- Skip the security altogether. Jump directly to the Start screen when you turn on the machine.

So how do you specify which method you want? By following these admirably simple steps.

Note: Every account still requires a regular text password; you'll need it when, for example, installing new software or making system-wide Control Panel changes. The drawing-lines thing, the four-digit thing, and the no-password-at-all thing are all *additional* ways to log in.

Creating a Picture Password

This little stunt is one of the most-advertised features of Windows 8. It's perfect for touchscreens, especially tablets that lack physical keyboards, because it's so much easier than typing a password.

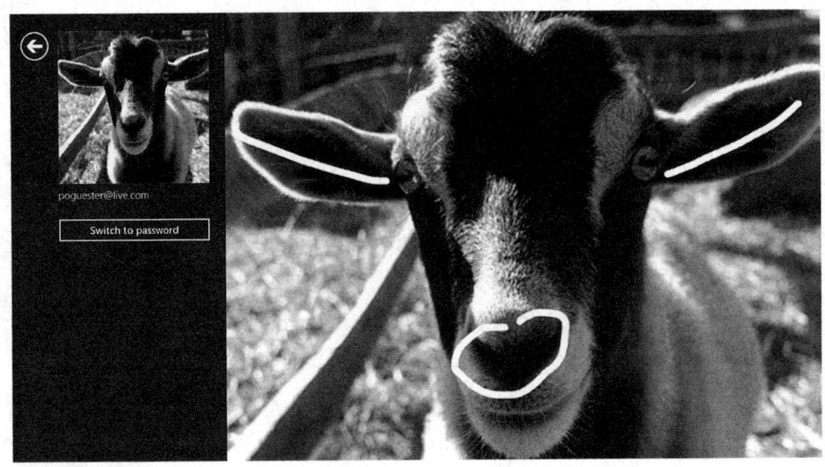

Figure 2-10: *To unlock your account, drag your finger on the photo to recreate your choice of lines, taps, or circles. That's easier than having to type some password. (The lines are shown here in white so you get the idea; they don't appear when you actually draw on your screen. Wouldn't want some bad dude sitting next to you to catch on!)*

The idea is that the password screen will show you a photograph you've chosen. (Before you follow these steps, it's up to you to get a photo into your Pictures folder.) You draw three lines or taps on top of it, as shown in Figure 2-10. The idea is that only you know how and where to draw these lines and taps. That's your security.

Note: Truth is, picture passwords aren't as secure as typed passwords. One reason is that bad guys might be able to learn your photo fingerstrokes by watching you from across the room.

But the even greater security hole is the finger grease you leave behind on your touchscreen. If you drag the same lines over and over, an evildoer can learn your fingerstrokes just by studying the finger-grease marks when the screen is turned off.

You've been warned.

---

1. **Open the Users panel of the PC Settings screen.**

   Keyboard: From the Start screen, type *picture pass*, and then click Settings. In the search results, choose "Create or change picture password."

   Touchscreen: Open the Charms bar (swipe inward from the right margin of the screen), tap Settings, and tap "Change PC settings."

   You wind up on the Users panel of TileWorld's control panel.

2. **Select "Create a picture password." Enter your current typed password to prove that you're not a criminal, and hit OK.**

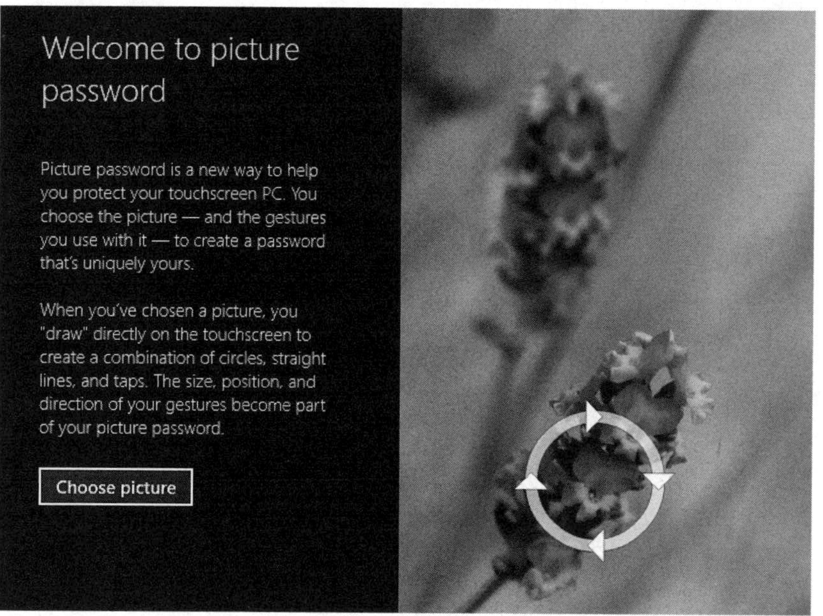

Welcome to picture password
Picture password is a new way to help you protect your touchscreen PC. You choose the picture — and the gestures you use with it — to create a password that's uniquely yours.
When you've chosen a picture, you "draw" directly on the touchscreen to create a combination of circles, straight lines, and taps. The size, position, and direction of your gestures become part of your picture password.
Choose picture

***Figure 2-11:** The rules are simple: Choose a photo from your Pictures folder. Draw three lines on it–circles, curves, or lines. Don't forget them! (Although if you do, the world won't end; you can always use your regular typed password instead.)*

Now you see the screen shown in Figure 2-11, where Windows explains the rules to you.

3. **Hit "Choose picture."**

   You're now shown the contents of your Pictures folder. Choose the one you want to draw on top of, and then hit Open (lower-right corner).

   You now arrive at the "How's this look?" screen, where the photo appears in its full-size majesty. If it's not perfectly suited to your screen dimensions, you can take a moment now to drag it around to fit the screen better. You can also change your mind at this screen ("Choose new picture").

   But if you think it's going to work fine, proceed.

4. **Pick "Use this picture."**

   Now, on the "Set up your gestures" screen, you're supposed to draw on the photo—three taps, lines, or circles in any combination. On a baby photo, for example, you might circle the baby's mouth, tap her nose, and then draw an invisible antenna line right out of her head. Just don't forget what you did.

   You're asked to repeat the three gestures in the same order to make sure you've got it.

   If all went well, Windows says, "Congratulations!" If not—if your two tries weren't similar enough—it prompts you to perform this step again.

5. **Tap Finish.**

Now you're ready to test your picture password. On the Start screen, click your account photo (upper right); from the shortcut menu, choose "Sign out." You arrive back at the Lock screen.

Dismiss it with a swipe up or a keypress (and, if you see the names of more than one account, tap yours). You arrive at the Picture Password screen, with your photo magnificently displayed.

Draw your three lines or taps, as you've set them up (Figure 2-10). If you do a good enough job, Windows logs you into your account.

If you give up, you can always tap "Switch to password" and just type the darned thing.

The Four-Digit Passcode

The four-digit passcode isn't as secure as a full-blown, "f8sh^eir23h*$$%23"-style password, of course. But if the idea is to keep your little brother off your PC, it's plenty.

Note: Here again, you still have to create a regular text password for your account–as a backup method, if nothing else.

---

1. **Open the Users pane of the TileWorld control panel.**

Touchscreen: Open the Charms bar (swipe inward from the right margin of the screen), select Settings, and select "Change PC settings." On the PC Settings screen, choose Users.

Keyboard: From the Start screen, type the first part of *password*, and then click Settings. In the search results, select "Create or change PIN."

In either case, you now wind up on the Users pane of the TileWorld control panel.

2. **Select Create a PIN. Enter your current typed password to prove that you're you, and hit OK.**

   Now you're asked to make up the four-digit PIN (personal identification number). It could be the last four digits of your mom's social security number, the last four digits of your first phone number, or the month and year of your dog's birthday—whatever.

3. **Enter your chosen PIN into both boxes, and then hit Finish.**

Next time you log in, you'll be able to log in with your PIN instead of a password (Figure 2-12). You don't even have to press Enter; after you type the fourth digit, bam— you're signed in.

Note: You'll also be offered a link that says "Sign-in options." When you choose that, you're offered icons that represent all three sign-in options: picture password (if you've set one up), PIN, and regular typed password. So if you can't get in one way, you can try a different method.

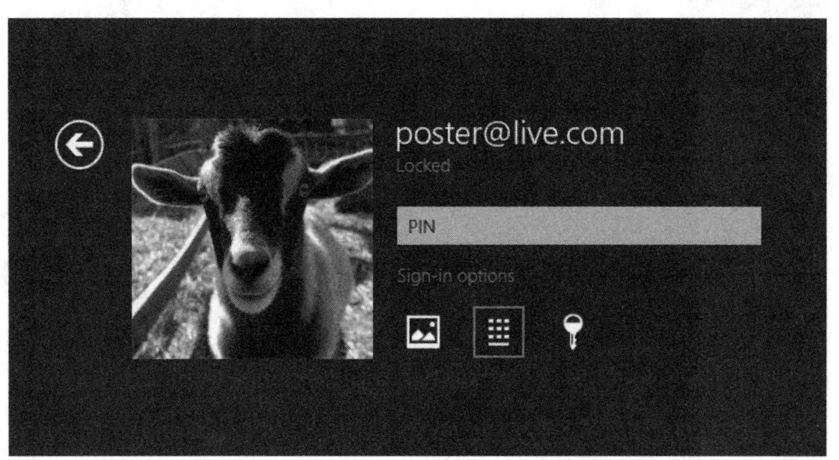

Figure 2-12: *Once you've set up a picture password and/or a PIN password, your login choices become more plentiful. If you click "Sign-in options," you get the three icons shown here. From left, they represent the picture password, the four-digit PIN password, and the traditional typed password.*

Eliminating the Password Requirement

The usual computer book takes this opportunity to stress the importance of a long, complex password—a phrase that isn't in the dictionary, something that's made up of mixed letters and numbers. This is excellent advice if you create sensitive documents and work in a big corporation.

But if you share the computer only with a spouse, or with nobody at all, you may have nothing to hide. You may see the multiple-users feature more as a convenience (keeping your settings and files separate) than a protector of secrecy and security. In these situations, there's no particular urgency to the mission of thwarting the world's hackers with a password.

You may, in other words, prefer to *blow past* the password screen when you turn on or wake up the machine, so you can get right down to work. You may wish you could *turn off* the requirement to log in with a name and password.

Easy enough:

1. **Open the Run dialog box.**

   Details on the Run dialog box are on page 246. But for now:

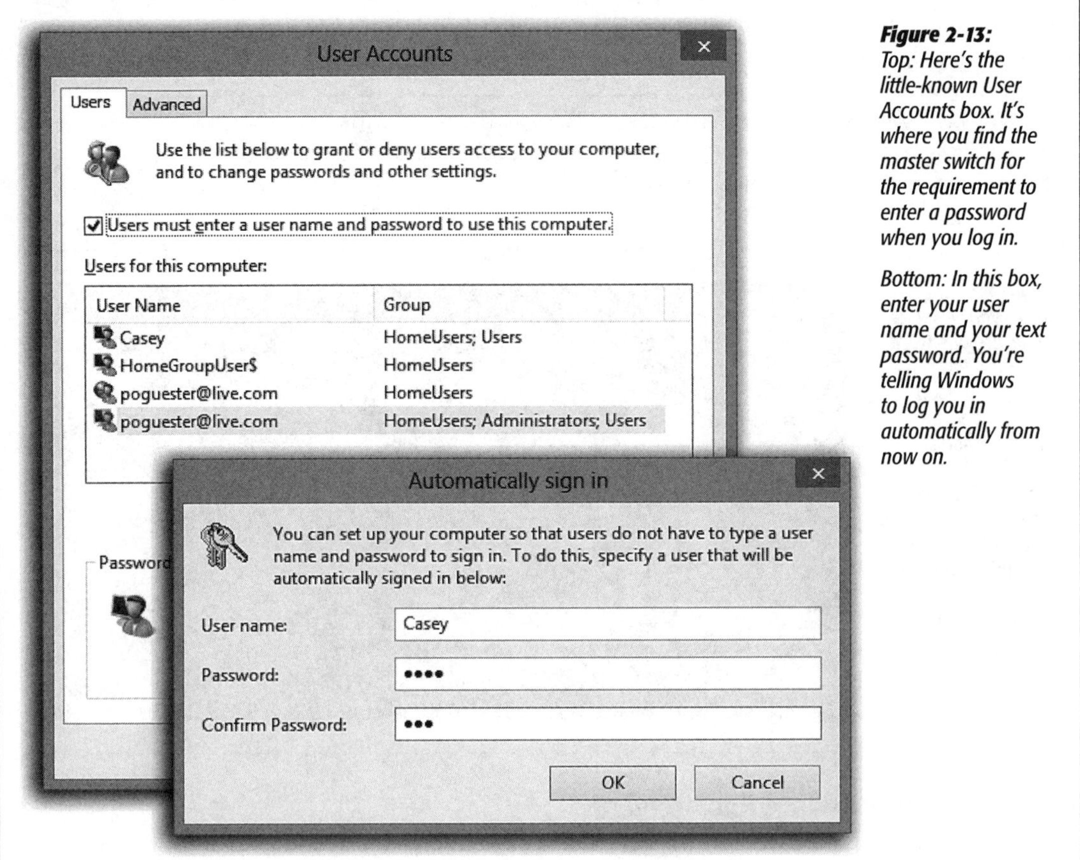

***Figure 2-13:** Top: Here's the little-known User Accounts box. It's where you find the master switch for the requirement to enter a password when you log in.*

Bottom: In this box, enter your user name and your text password. You're telling Windows to log you in automatically from now on.

Keyboard: Press ⊞+R.

Touchscreen: From the Start screen, type *run,* and then tap the Run icon that appears.

2. **In the Run dialog box, type *netplwiz.* Hit OK.**

   You now find yourself in the little-seen User Accounts dialog box (Figure 2-13, top).

3. **Turn off "Users must enter a user name and password to use this computer." Click OK.**

   You've told Windows that you want to sign in automatically. Now you have to tell it *who* gets to sign in automatically (Figure 2-13, bottom).

4. **Enter your account name and password (and the password again), and then hit OK.**

   This is your real text password, not some measly four-digit PIN.

The next time you restart your computer, you'll gasp in amazement as it takes you all the way to the Start screen without bothering to ask for your password.

Note: To restore the password requirement, repeat these steps—but turn *on* "Users must enter a user name and password to use this computer" in step 3.

If you add up the 5 seconds you've just saved times the thousands of times you'll wake or start up your machine, why, you'll wind up with literally *minutes* of free time!

CHAPTER
3

How TileWorld Works

By this point, it may finally be sinking in that Windows 8 is two operating systems in one. And that it runs two different kinds of programs: traditional Windows programs and an all-new class of programs called, for want of a better term, TileWorld apps.

TileWorld apps look and act very different. You'll know right away when you're in one. TileWorld apps:

- **Fill the whole screen, edge to edge.** TileWorld app windows don't overlap, ever.
- **Are fairly simple.** Photoshop, Quicken, Microsoft Access, tax software—complex programs like these will probably never come to TileWorld. TileWorld apps are more like iPad apps.
- **Do not have menus.** There's no menu bar in TileWorld. You can swipe up from the bottom (or down from the top) to see a horizontal bar with a couple of option icons on it, but that's nothing like a real menu bar containing dozens or hundreds of commands.
- **Come from a single source: the Windows Store.** You can't get TileWorld apps from the companies that make them. You can't get them on a disk. You *must* download them, and *only* from the Windows Store. (Tap the Store icon on your Start screen.)
- **Are technically called Windows Store apps.** Microsoft calls them *Windows Store apps* because they come from the Windows Store. Trouble is, Windows desktop programs also come from the Windows Store (although not exclusively), so "Windows Store apps" isn't very descriptive. In this book, Windows Store apps are called TileWorld apps.

- **Do not have viruses.** Since Microsoft is the sole source of TileWorld apps, you don't have to worry about viruses or spyware.
- **Are intended for tablets.** You can run TileWorld apps on a regular mouse-and-keyboard computer—but why?

Because TileWorld apps work so differently from traditional Windows programs, they get their own chapter. You're reading it.

The Windows Store

For years, people installed software onto their computers by buying disks: floppies, CDs, and, later, DVDs. But Microsoft is hoping to pull an Apple here: It wants its *online* software store to be your one-stop software shopping mall.

It's an online catalog of software from huge software companies, tiny one-person software companies, and everything in between. You can read about the apps, check out customer reviews, and, finally, download them directly to your computer.

There are some huge advantages to this system. Since there's no box, DVD, registration card, shipping, or stocking, the software can cost a lot less. Plenty of programs in the Windows Store are actually free, and many paid ones offer a free 7-day trial.

Furthermore, Microsoft controls the transaction on both ends—it knows who you are—so there are no serial numbers to type in. The installation doesn't have to interrupt you with warnings like "Please enter your password to install this software." Once you click Buy, Try, or Install, the software downloads and installs itself automatically, without any interaction from you at all.

There are no disks to store and hunt down later, either. If you ever need to reinstall a program from the Windows Store, or if you ever get a new PC, you just re-download it; the store remembers that you're a legitimate owner. Better yet, you'll be downloading the latest version of that program; you won't have to install all the ".01" patches that have come along since.

Best of all, since Microsoft knows what programs you have, it can let you know when new versions are available. You'll see the word "Updates" in the upper-right corner of the Windows Store, and on the updated app's Start-screen tile; the Store tile on the Start screen shows how many updates await. Tap it to see the apps for which more recent versions are ready. (Tap Install to grab all of them at once.)

Navigating the Store

To use the Windows Store, open the Store tile on your Start screen. As shown in Figure 3-1, the store looks like it's been printed on an endless paper towel roll; it scrolls horizontally for miles.

Each cluster of tiles includes a "Top free" tile (the most-downloaded free apps), "Top Paid," and a "New releases" tile.

At any time, you can jump back to the opening screen by opening the App bar and selecting Home. (To open the App bar, swipe in from the top or bottom of the screen, or right-click.)

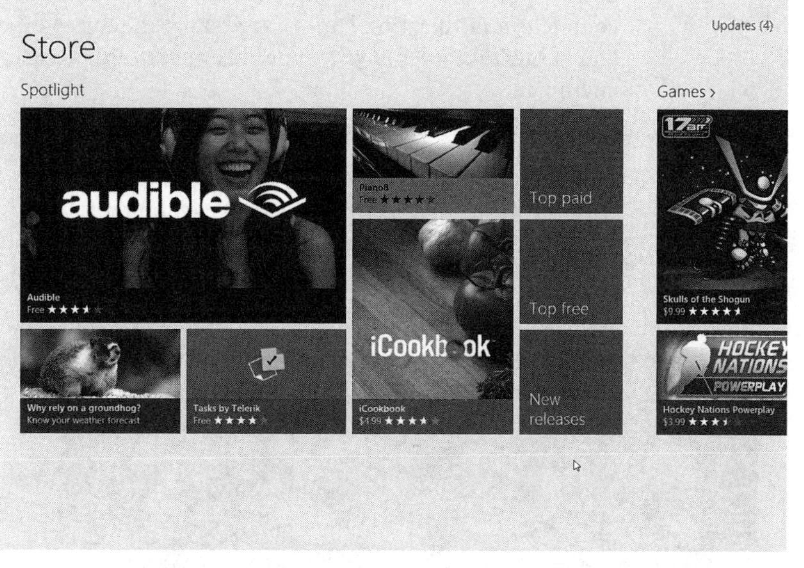

***Figure 3-1:** As you flip through the screens, you can see groupings like Spotlight (apps Microsoft is pushing this week), Games, Social, Entertainment, Music & Video, and so on. Each group is made up of clusters of tiles—hey, just like the Start screen!*

Of course, you can also search for an app by name or by nature. To do that, you don't have to open the Charms bar; at the main screen, just start typing what you're looking for (*piano, stocks, fantasy football,* or whatever).

Tip: You can zoom out of the store so that you can see the big-ticket categories all on a single screen (it's that feature that Microsoft calls *semantic zoom*). You do this zooming the same way you do it in the People app or at the Start screen.

Touchscreen: Put two fingers on the screen (or more), and pinch inward against the glass. *Mouse:* Turn the scroll wheel down while pressing the Ctrl key. *Keyboard:* Press Ctrl+minus key (-) to zoom out, plus key (+) to zoom back in.

In general, the store here works exactly like the app store on a smartphone. Tap a program's icon to open its details page. Here you'll find reviews and ratings from other people, a description, pictures (screenshots) of the program, and much more information to help you make a good buying decision. See Figure 3-2 for more details.

When you find an app that looks good, tap Install (if it's free) or Buy or Try (if it's not). You jump back to the Home screen, where a message lets you know that the download is in progress.

Note: The Windows Store lists desktop apps, too (not just TileWorld apps). But you don't actually buy and download desktop apps from the Windows Store; you get a link to the software company's Web site for that purpose. The only software you can actually download from the Windows Store is TileWorld apps.

You can go right on working while the app downloads. When the download is complete, a notification banner appears at the top-right corner of the screen to let you know. You never have to enter your password, restart, unzip, or manually install anything.

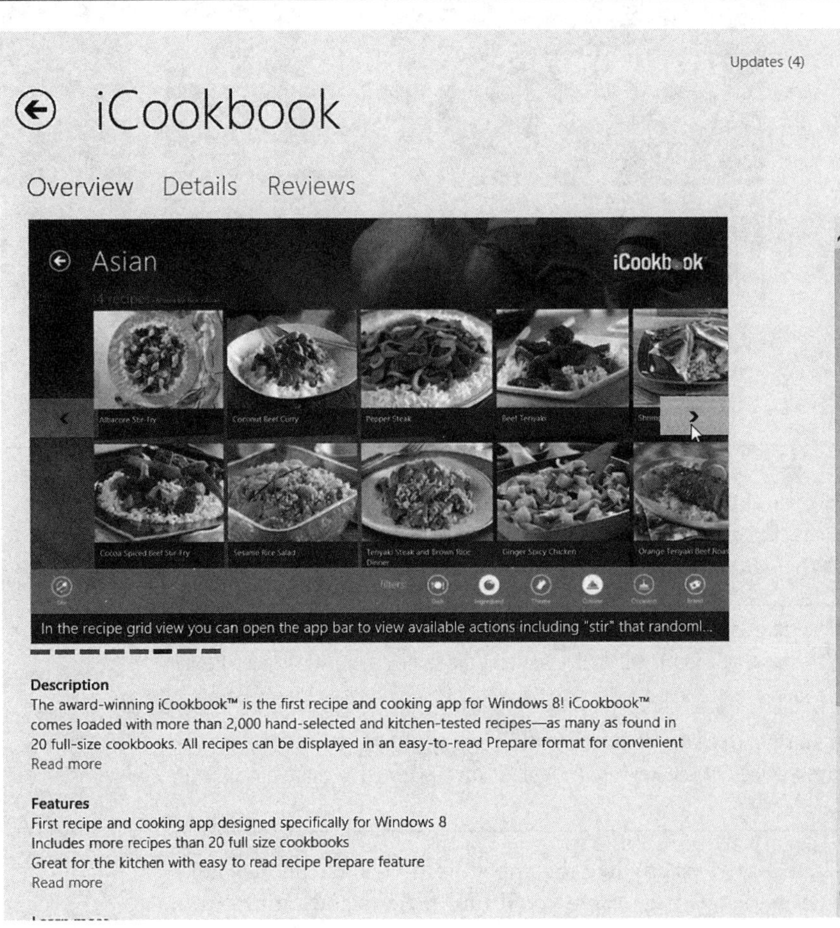

***Figure 3-2:** You won't see all of an app's store page until you realize that you can scroll vertically to see all the text and horizontally to see the other screenshots–on each of the three main pages: Overview, Details, and Reviews (tap these labels at the top of the screen).*

To open the app, you can either tap that notification banner or just hit ⊞ to open your Start screen, where the new app's tile appears to the right of all other tiles and groups.

Tip: Exactly as on phones and tablets, TileWorld apps are frequently updated by their software companies. When you first open the store, you may find the notation "Updates (4)" (or some other number) at the top right, as shown in Figure 3-1. Click for a list of new versions. The App bar opens automatically.

If you don't want one of the updates for some reason, select it to remove the checkmark. (And how do you know what each program's changes are? In the App bar, select Clear. Click an app's tile; now hit "View details" on the App bar.) Finally, click Install (on the App bar) to install all of the checked apps.

Working with TileWorld Apps

To open an app on the Start screen, just tap or click it.

If the app you want isn't visible on the Start screen, and you have a keyboard, you'll love how easy it is to open something: at the Start screen, just begin typing its name. You've instantly entered the search mode; the screen shows you only the names of matching apps as you type.

If the one you want is first in the results, just press Enter to open it. If not, tap or click its tile, or use the arrow keys to highlight a tile and *then* press Enter to open it.

Close a TileWorld App

TileWorld apps don't have Close buttons, so you might wonder what you're supposed to do when you're finished using one.

Answer: Generally, nothing. Leave it open; it doesn't slow your machine down or cost you anything. To use a different app, just return to the Start screen and open it. Or use the app switcher described below.

UP TO SPEED

One App, Five Machines

You can install a certain app on up to five Windows 8 machines, which is handy if you're a multiple-computer family.

So how do you do that?

One easy way is to view the "Your apps" screen. Swipe in from the top or bottom edge of the screen to make the App bar appear. Tap "Your apps." Here's a list of every app you've ever downloaded from the store. The first pop-up menu lists every Windows 8 machine you've ever used (assuming that you've used your Windows ID to sign into each one). You can choose, for example, "Apps installed on Surface" or "Apps installed on HP Envy" to see *only* the apps you installed onto that machine.

You can tap an app and then tap Install (bottom of the screen) to install it on *this* machine. Or tap an app and then tap "View details" to return to that app's store page.

Note, by the way: Paid apps (those you have to pay for) are attached to your Microsoft account. You can install a paid app on up to five machines only if all of them are signed in with the same Microsoft account.

Put another way, if you buy an app and install it on the kitchen PC, other people in the family, logging in with their own Microsoft accounts, won't be able to use it. They have to buy their own darned copies.

But if exiting an app makes you feel better, here's how you do it:

- **Touchscreen:** Swipe *all the way* down the screen, from above the screen to below it. See Figure 3-3.

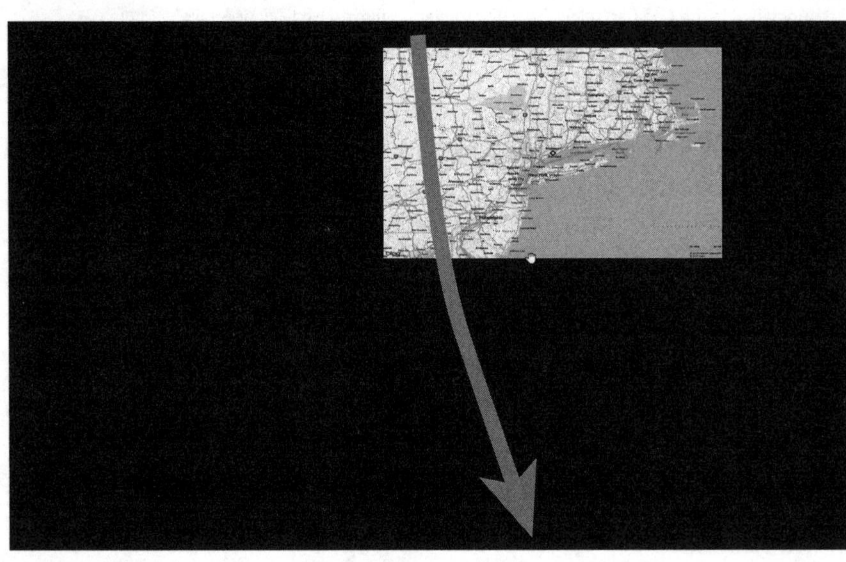

Figure 3-3: *Closing a TileWorld app involves a long, full-height finger-drag down the screen. About halfway down, the app's window abruptly shrinks to half its size and moves along with your fingertip. When you release at the bottom, the app's window disappears.*

- **Mouse:** Point to the top-center edge of the screen so that your cursor becomes a little white hand. Drag all the way down to the bottom of the screen. As the window approaches the bottom of the screen, it shrinks and then vanishes.
- **Keyboard:** Press Alt+F4.

Display Side-by-Side Apps

There are no overlapping windows in TileWorld; the headache of trying to find one window in a haystack is over.

You can, however, display two apps side by side (but only two). In fact, you can display a *TileWorld* app and a *desktop* program side by side, too. That's handy when you want to keep playing some video in one window while you're crunching numbers in another, for example.

Note: Windows doesn't let you split the screen unless its resolution is 1366 × 800 pixels or greater. Microsoft doesn't think anything less would give you enough room for two apps.

- **Touchscreen:** To split the current app's screen with the *most recent* app, see Figure 3-4.

And what if the *most recent* app isn't the one you want as one of the two? You can also split the screen with another running app. To do that, make the app switcher appear (page 69).

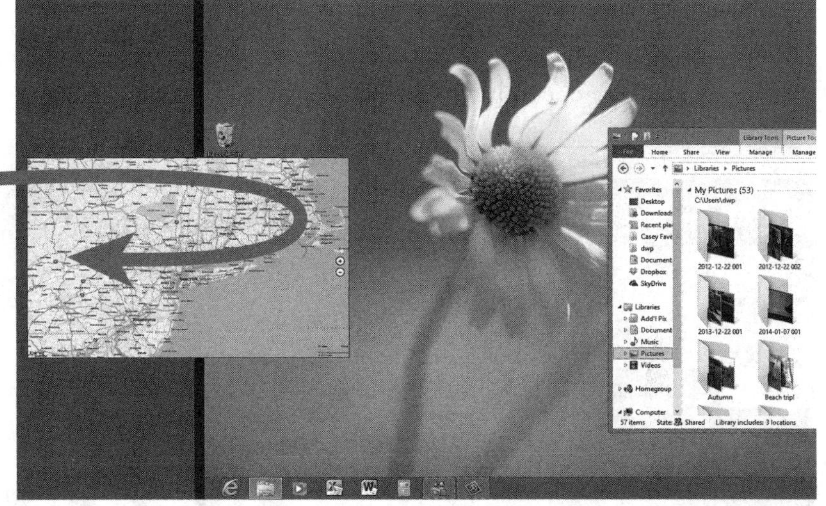

Figure 3-4: *To split the screen, drag your finger slowly in from the left. A miniature of the last app's window follows your finger. To park it to the left of the first one, slide back to the left, stopping about an inch from the left side. To park it to the right of the original app, drag all the way to the right. When the existing app's window shrinks, let go.*

Then drag one of the thumbnails to the right; as described above, pause when your finger is an inch from the edge, so that the current app shrinks. Let go. (Figure 3-4 should make this clear.)

Finally, you can also split the current app's screen with an app you haven't even opened yet. Swipe down from the top edge of the screen, way down, until the current app's window shrinks. Then continue the drag to the right or left so that the current app's window gets parked.

Now you can return to the Start screen and open another app to fill the missing space, or grab a second app's window from the app switcher.

- **Mouse:** Point to the top edge of the open app's screen so that the cursor becomes a little white hand. Drag far down and to the left or right side of the screen until you see the thick vertical divider line appear. Release.
- **Keyboard:** Press ⊞+< or ⊞+>. (That's the comma or the period, but < and > are easier to remember.) The current app's window is now shoved to the left or right side. When you open a second app (from the Start screen or the app switcher), it fills the newly opened space.

Tip: These keyboard shortcuts cycle through three stages. The first press of ⊞+> splits the screen 75 percent/25 percent; the second swaps the proportions so that the leftmost app has 25 percent; the third press restores the original full-screen app.

Once the screen is split, you can drag the vertical divider bar horizontally to adjust the relative space between the two windows. It's not a free choice—you can't split 50/50, for example. One of the apps always occupies about three-fourths of the screen, the other one-fourth.

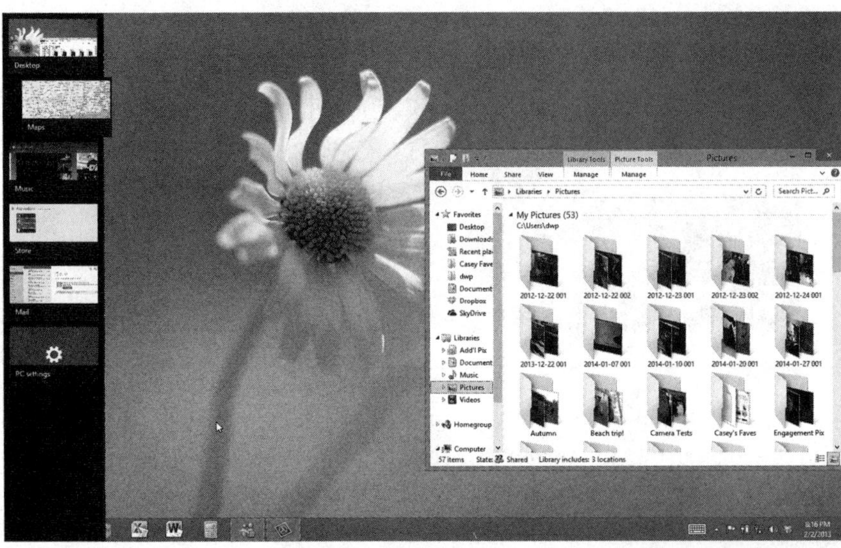

Figure 3-5: *To split the screen with another open app, make the app switcher appear (top). Drag one of the thumbnails toward the center of the screen about an inch, so that the first app scoots out of the way and a divider line appears. At this point, you can adjust the split line by dragging it left or right, thereby redistributing your screen space between the two apps (bottom).*

Note that if one of the apps is, in fact, the Windows desktop, you see thumbnails in the resulting split-screen panel that represent the open programs at the desktop (bottom right).

Tip: If one of the "apps" sharing the screen is the desktop itself, and it's the one you've shrunk to 25 percent of the screen, something weird happens: All the open desktop programs appear as individual icons in that narrow column of screen, as you can see at bottom in Figure 3-5. Tap one to open it full screen. Or, rather, 75 percent screen. (The open TileWorld app crunches down to the remaining 25 percent.)

To turn off the screen-splitting effect, drag the divider bar all the way off one side of the screen or the other. Or press the same keystroke (⊞+< or ⊞+>) twice more.

Uninstalling a TileWorld App

Installing a TileWorld app, as you now know, is infinitely simpler and faster than installing a desktop app. And there's more good news: Getting rid of a TileWorld app is also much easier.

Find the app's icon as though you're about to open it—either by finding it on the Start screen, using the All Apps window, or by searching for it.

Now select the app's tile like this:

- **Touchscreen:** Swipe a small swipe down from the tile.
- **Mouse:** Right-click the tile.
- **Keyboard:** Highlight the tile using the arrow keys, and then press Ctrl+space bar.

Now that Windows knows which tile you want to remove—a checkmark appears in its corner—open the App bar and select Uninstall.

GEM IN THE ROUGH

Multiple Monitors—Two Worlds

If you're lucky enough to have a second monitor connected to your PC, you might say to yourself: "Hey, self! Think how cool this could be! I could have TileWorld on one screen, and a Windows desktop app on the other! Best of both worlds!"

You're absolutely right.

Connect your second monitor to your computer's video output jack, whatever it may be (HDMI cable, VGA cable, whatever).

When everything's powered up, both screens show TileWorld. But that's about to change.

Open the Charms bar. Choose Devices, and then "Second screen." Now you see icons representing the various ways Windows can handle the second screen: "PC screen only" (meaning turn off the second monitor), "Duplicate" (mirror the same image on both screens), "Extend" (use the second monitor as an extension of the main one's area), and "Second screen only" (turn off the main screen).

What you want is Extend. The screens go black for a moment, and then boom: The second monitor now shows the desktop. Using the Desktop tile, you can flip the main screen back and forth between TileWorld (or a TileWorld app) and the desktop.

If you like, you can adjust resolution or swap the screen images using the desktop Control Panel, as described on page 317.

Amazing.

A message warns you that you're about to delete the app *and* all of its data. Hit Uninstall if you're confident you want to nuke all of it right now.

Tip: You're allowed to install a TileWorld app on up to five Windows 8 machines. If you reach that limit, or if you decide to sell or donate an old computer, you can remove it from the list of authorized machines.

To do that, open the Charms bar; hit Settings; hit "Your account." The "Your PCs" list shows all of your computers that Microsoft knows about. Use the Remove button for any computer that you want to remove from your account.

The Two Task Switchers

As mentioned in Chapter 1, there's a quick way to jump back to the last app you had open: Swipe inward from the left border of the screen, or press Alt+Tab.

But what if you have six programs open and you want to jump to the third one?

This, of course, is why the beloved Alt+Tab keystroke was born (Figure 3-6, top).

Alt+Tab still works in Windows 8. It displays the icons of *all* open programs, both TileWorld apps and desktop programs. But now there's a *second* app switcher, a vertical one, that's limited to displaying TileWorld apps.

Note: In the TileWorld task switcher, *all desktop apps* are represented by a single Desktop thumbnail.

The Traditional Task Switcher (Shows All Apps)

To view the traditional app switcher—a horizontal row of icons, depicting both TileWorld apps and traditional Windows programs—proceed like this:

- **Touchscreen:** There's no touchscreen gesture to open the old task switcher. Use the new one (described next) to switch among open TileWorld apps.

  If you want to jump to a Windows desktop program, tap the Desktop tile on the Start screen. (Unless you've moved it, Desktop is the lower-left tile.) You jump back to the traditional Windows desktop, where the icons of all open programs appear on the taskbar (page 227).

- **Mouse:** There's no good mousey way to open this task switcher, either.

- **Keyboard:** If you press Tab while *holding down* the Alt key, a floating palette displays the icons of all running programs, as shown at top in Figure 3-6. Each time you press Tab again (still keeping the Alt key down), you highlight the next icon; when you release the keys, the highlighted program jumps to the front, as though in a high-tech game of duck-duck-goose.

Tip: If you add the Ctrl key, then you don't have to keep the Alt key pressed. The app switcher stays locked onscreen until you click an icon or press Esc to dismiss it.

The New Task Switcher (TileWorld Apps Only)

Here's how to view the new vertical bar that lists the icons of open TileWorld apps (Figure 3-6, bottom):

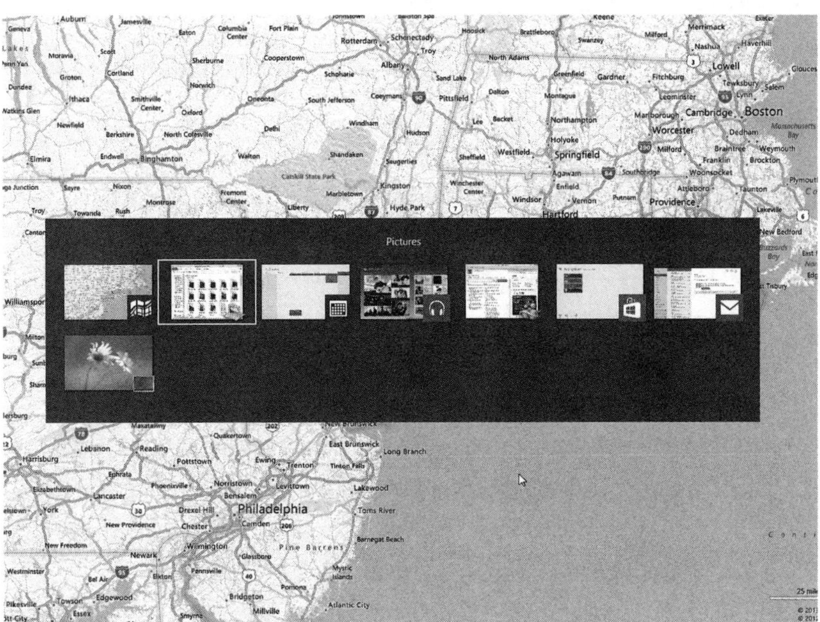

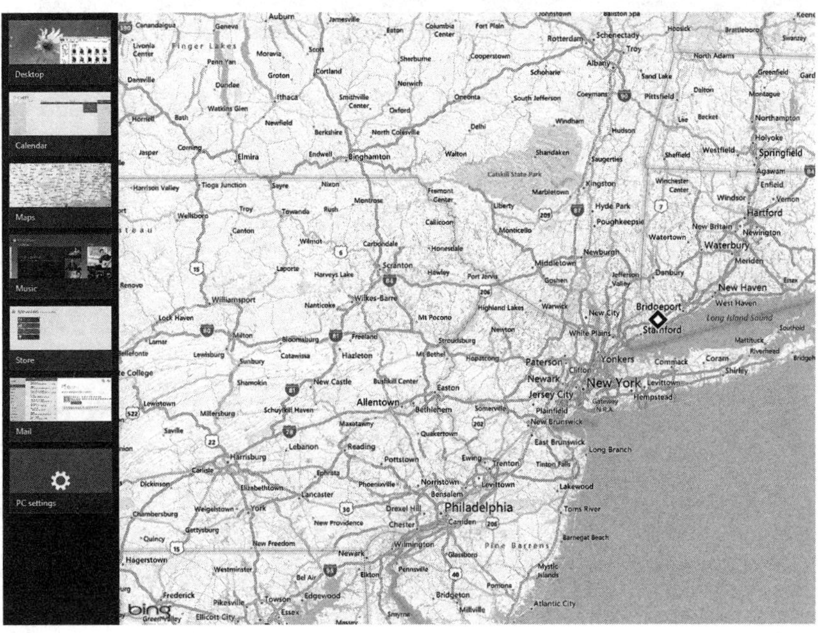

Figure 3-6: *Top: Alt+Tab makes the traditional switcher appear; it lists both desktop and TileWorld apps. Tapping Tab highlights successive icons; add Shift to move backward. (Add the Ctrl key to lock the display, so you don't have to keep Alt down. Tab to the icon you want; then press the space bar or Enter.)*

Bottom: The new switcher displays TileWorld apps only. It appears at the left edge of the screen.

- **Touchscreen:** Swipe into the screen from the left border and then all the way back out again, making a big U-turn with your finger. Now you can tap any thumbnail to jump into the corresponding app.
- **Mouse:** Point to the lower-left corner of the screen so that the icon appears; then move the mouse upward. (Or go from top to bottom instead: Point to the *top*-left corner and then slide downward.) Use the arrow keys or the Tab key to choose the app you want to open, and then press Enter.

  Or, of course, just click its thumbnail.
- **Keyboard:** Press ⊞+Tab, but keep the ⊞ key pressed. Each time you press ⊞, you highlight the next icon; when you release the keys, the highlighted program jumps open.

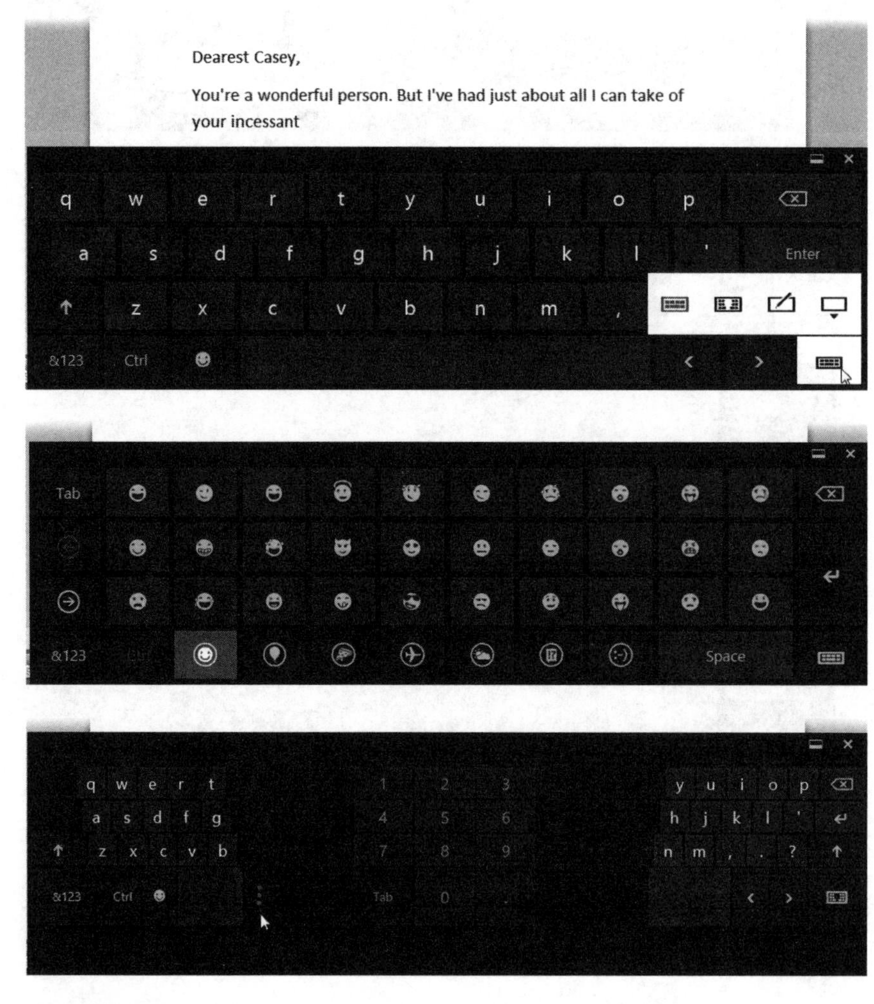

Figure 3-7: *Top: The onscreen keyboard has lots of tricks up its sleeve. When you tap the lower-right key, you get a pop-up menu of different keyboard styles.*

Middle: It can also become a rogue's gallery of emoticons, for those occasions when English just isn't enough.

Bottom: The split keyboard is intended for a tablet—especially one you're holding with fingers beneath, so you can tap with your thumbs. You have a choice of three key sizes; to switch, press the three-vertical-dots button identified by the cursor. It offers you a choice of Small, Medium, or Large, to suit your own thumbs.

The Onscreen Keyboard

If your computer has a physical keyboard, or if your tablet has a removable one, great! But TileWorld was born for touchscreens, and touchscreens generally don't have moving keys. That's why, whenever you tap in a spot where typing is required, the onscreen keyboard pops up (Figure 3-7).

Note: Actually, the onscreen keyboard is available at the Windows desktop, too. Of course, it's primarily useful on touchscreen machines, but you know–whatever floats your boat.

No matter what kind of computer you have, you can force the keyboard to appear–even if you haven't tapped in a typing area. Open the Charms bar, then Settings, then tap Keyboard.

In general, there's not much to know about this keyboard. It works pretty much like any keyboard you've ever used, with a few exceptions:

- **The keys don't move.** Of course not—it's a piece of glass! The keys do everything they can, though, to tell you when they've been struck. They change color and make a little sound.
- **It has a symbol/number layout. Two, actually.** Tap the "&123" key to change all the letter keys into symbol keys: !, @, %, $, &, and so on. Tap the circled ⊕ key to view a second set of them—less common symbols like ©, <, >, and other currency and brackets. And a numeric keypad appears at the right end of the keyboard.

  To return to the regular alphabet keyboard, tap the "&123" key (which is now "lit up" in color) again.

Tip: You don't have to hit the "&123" twice–once to lock, once to unlock. Instead, you can treat it like a Shift key. That is, you can hold it down with one hand and type the symbol you want with the other hand.

- **It has a split, two-thumb version.** If you're holding a tablet, you might prefer the split keyboard shown in Figure 3-7 (bottom). It lets you flail away with both thumbs, with the keys nicely arranged to hug the outer edges of the screen.

  To split the keyboard in this way, tap the keyboard key in the lower-right corner. A tiny palette of keyboard options appears (Figure 3-7, top); tap the second one. Later, you can return to the full keyboard by tapping the *first* icon on this palette.
- **It has a palette of smiley faces.** Tap the smiley-face key (next to the Ctrl key) to change all the letters into a huge array of smiley faces, also called emoticons. These are available wherever you type, but they're most appropriate when you're typing in a chat room or *maybe* an email message. (And even then, plenty of people would argue that they're *never* appropriate.)
- **Its modifier keys are sticky.** If you want to press Shift+D, for example, or Ctrl+N, you don't have to *hold down* the Shift or Ctrl key. Just tap the modifier key (Shift, Ctrl, Alt) and *then* the letter that goes with it.

- **Caps Lock is there.** Just as on a phone, you can lock down the Shift key to type in ALL CAPITALS by *double*-tapping the Shift key. It lights up to show that it's locked down. (Tap it again to unlock it.)
- **Its keys sprout accents.** To produce an accented character (like é, ë, è, ê, and so on), keep your finger pressed on that key for one second. See Figure 3-8.

Tip: Most keys on the symbol keyboard sprout variations, too; for example, the $ key offers an array of alternate currency symbols.

Figure 3-8:
Top: When you hold down a key, a palette of diacritical marks appears; slide onto the one you want. Here's the secret list of keys that sprout these pop-up menus: the five vowels, of course, plus W, T, Y, S, D, G, The, J, ', C, N, comma, period, and ?.

Bottom: When you press the Ctrl key, the letters sprout the keyboard-shortcut commands you'll trigger by tapping them (Cut, Copy, Paste, and so on).

- **The double-space-bar trick is available.** If you press the space bar twice, you get a period, a space, and an automatically capitalized next letter—exactly what you want at the end of a sentence. (It's the same trick that saves you fussing with alternate keyboard layouts on the iPhone, Windows Phone, Android phones, BlackBerry, and so on.)

Note: The on/off switch for this feature is in the Charms bar→Settings→"Change PC settings"→General→"Show text suggestions as I type."

- **There are cursor keys.** See the < and > keys to the right of the space bar? Those don't mean "greater than" and "lesser than." They're cursor keys. They move your cursor left and right through the text.
- **There are typing suggestions.** When you've typed the beginning of a word that Windows can guess—*lu,* for example—a bold word appears in a box just below what you've typed, proposing a suggestion: in this case, *lunch.* If that is indeed the word you wanted, look next to the space bar. The < and > keys have been replaced by a big, colorful Insert key. Tap it to finish the word you'd started using Windows' suggestion. Once you get used to this feature, you can save a lot of time and typos.

Note: The on/off switch for this feature, too, is in the Charms bar→Settings→"Change PC settings"→General→"Show text suggestions as I type."

- **There's a full 101-key PC keyboard layout, too.** The standard Windows 8 keyboard layout was designed to make the letter keys big and easy to type. Microsoft chose to hide a lot of the other stuff you'd find on a real keyboard, including numbers, Tab, Esc, and so on.

Figure 3-9: *If you'd like a full keyboard–number keys above the letter keys, complete set of control keys (Alt, Fn, ⊞, and so on), the works–open the Charms bar. Select Settings, then "Change PC settings," then General. Turn on "Make the standard keyboard layout available.*

But if you'd prefer an onscreen version of the real thing, Windows 8 can accommodate you. Once you follow the steps in Figure 3-9, the standard pop-up menu of keyboard layouts (shown at top in Figure 3-7) offers the full 101-key PC keyboard.

When you're finished typing, tap anywhere outside of the keyboard; it goes away, returning the full screen area to your command.

Handwriting Recognition

The accuracy and convenience of Windows' handwriting recognition have come a very long way—which is great news if you have a tablet. Hey, if tablets can decipher doctors' handwriting, surely you can get your tablet to recognize yours.

Using a pop-up transcription window called the Input panel, you can enter text anywhere you can type: Microsoft Word, your email program, your Web browser, and so on. Windows also comes with a special program called Windows Journal that's a note-taking module designed expressly for tablets.

Handwriting Anywhere

To make Windows recognize your handwriting, open any program where you would otherwise type—a word processor, for example.

Now open the Input panel, which is a floating handwriting window that automatically converts anything you write into typed text (Figure 3-10). To view this panel, start by summoning the regular onscreen keyboard:

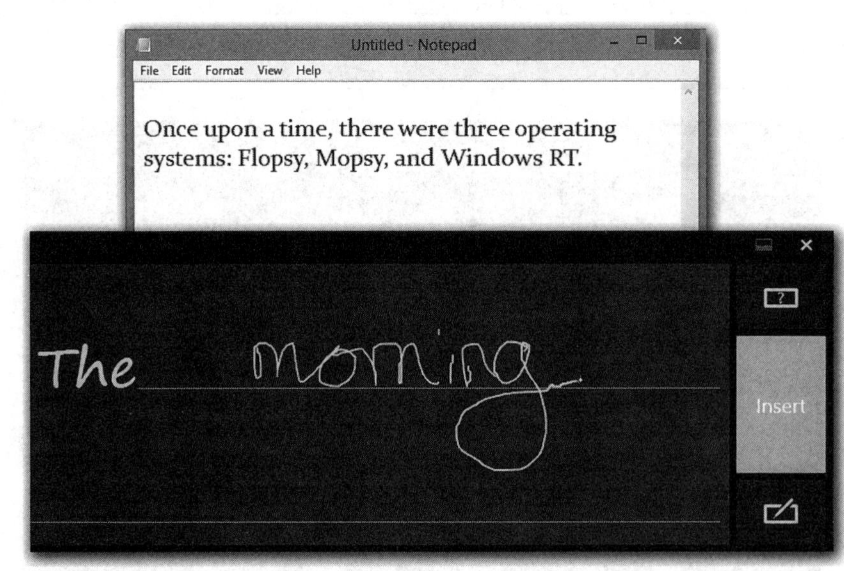

***Figure 3-10:** Write just the way you would on paper—in cursive, printing, or a mixture of both. The main advice here is to be patient. Windows may look like it's transcribing a word before you're finished writing it—but after a moment, it will re-evaluate what you've done and re-transcribe it.*

- **In TileWorld.** Tap to put the insertion point in a text-entry area—an empty word processor document or an email message, for example. The keyboard appears automatically.
- **At the Windows desktop.** Tap the Keyboard icon on the taskbar.

Once the onscreen keyboard appears, tap the keyboard key (lower right); tap the Handwriting icon, third from left. Now the Input panel is ready to use.

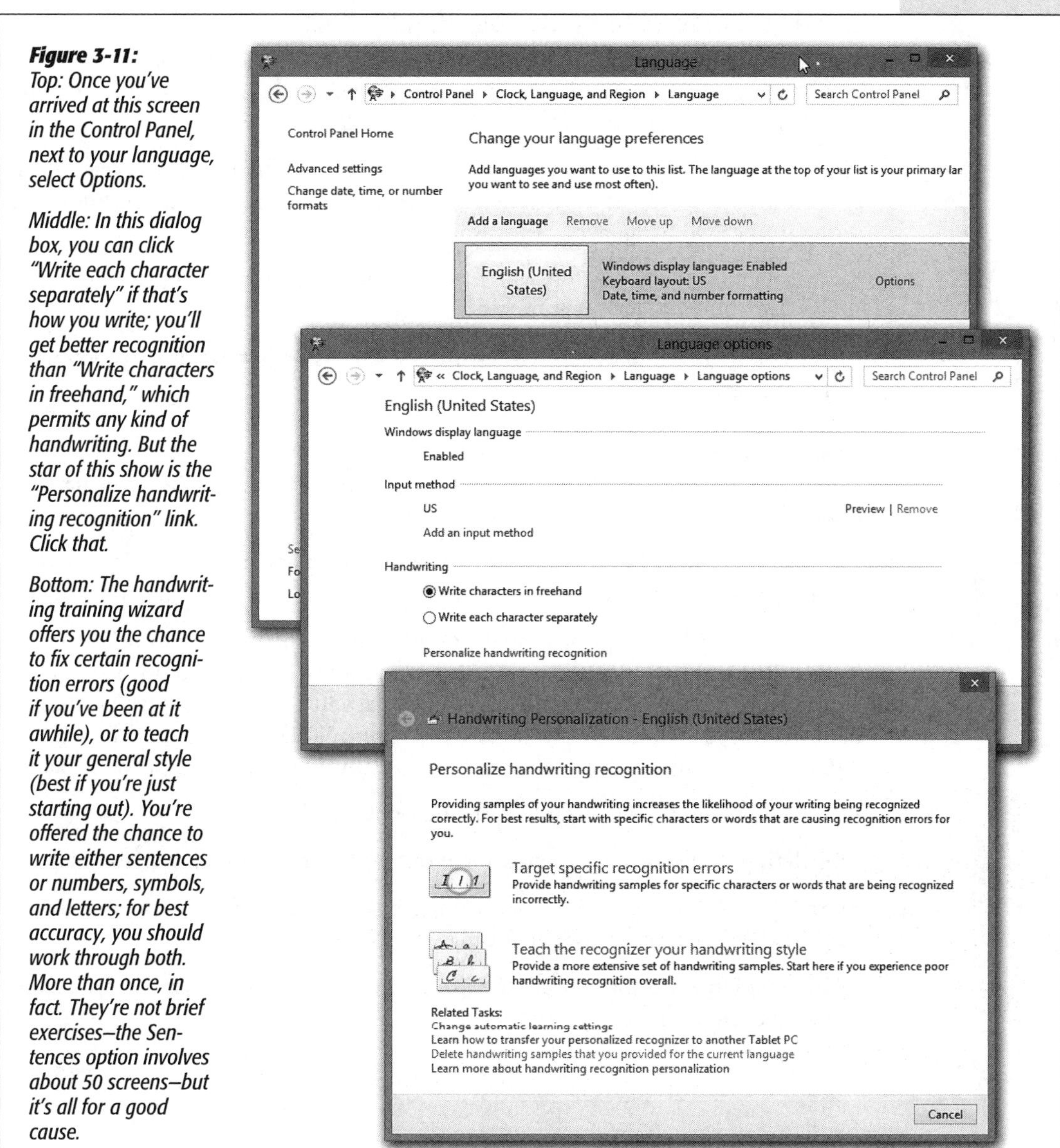

Figure 3-11:
Top: Once you've arrived at this screen in the Control Panel, next to your language, select Options.

Middle: In this dialog box, you can click "Write each character separately" if that's how you write; you'll get better recognition than "Write characters in freehand," which permits any kind of handwriting. But the star of this show is the "Personalize handwriting recognition" link. Click that.

Bottom: The handwriting training wizard offers you the chance to fix certain recognition errors (good if you've been at it awhile), or to teach it your general style (best if you're just starting out). You're offered the chance to write either sentences or numbers, symbols, and letters; for best accuracy, you should work through both. More than once, in fact. They're not brief exercises—the Sentences option involves about 50 screens—but it's all for a good cause.

Just write on either one of the light lines; you're looking at a two-line input panel.

Now then: The "digital ink" doesn't just sit there where you wrote it. A split second after you finish each word, Windows transcribes that word into typed text within the Input panel. Cute how it uses a handwriting-style font to keep you in the mood, eh?

But, finally, when you tap Insert, all of this writing and typing vanishes—and the converted, typed text appears in your document or dialog box.

Training Windows to Know Your Handwriting

Windows 8 does amazingly well at understanding your handwriting right out of the box. But if you plan to use it a lot, you should also *train* it. You provide samples of your handwriting, and Windows studies your style.

Finding the training program is a little tricky, but it can be done if you have a really good computer book. At the Start screen, search for *language.* Select Settings. You'll see an icon called Language in the results pane. Open it.

You're sent back to the desktop, where the Language pane of the Control Panel opens. Proceed as shown in Figure 3-11.

After working through the exercises, you can start using handwriting recognition—with better accuracy.

Fixing mistakes

Windows' handwriting recognition is amazingly accurate. It is not, however, perfect—in part because your handwriting isn't either.

Correcting a mistake is important for two reasons. First, it fixes the error in your document—and second, it *teaches* Windows so that it's less likely to make that mistake again.

To see your correction options, tap the ? button above the Insert button. You get four icons called Correcting, Deleting, Splitting, and Joining. Tap each one to see a little video that illustrates the technique. Basically, what you'll learn is that *tapping* inside the handwriting panel enters correction mode (Figure 3-12). In this mode, the word you tapped expands into individual letter boxes. At this point, you can proceed like this:

- **Correcting.** Replace a letter by drawing right over it.
- **Deleting.** Delete a letter by crossing it out (with a right-to-left horizontal line).
- **Splitting.** Break a word up by drawing a vertical line between two characters. Windows adds a space automatically.
- **Joining.** Draw a smile beneath the space between two words. Windows joins them together into one.

Tap the X (middle top of the Input panel) to exit Correction mode.

Tip: You can also tap the X button (to the right of the suggestions in Correction mode) to make Windows stop proposing the word it's proposing.

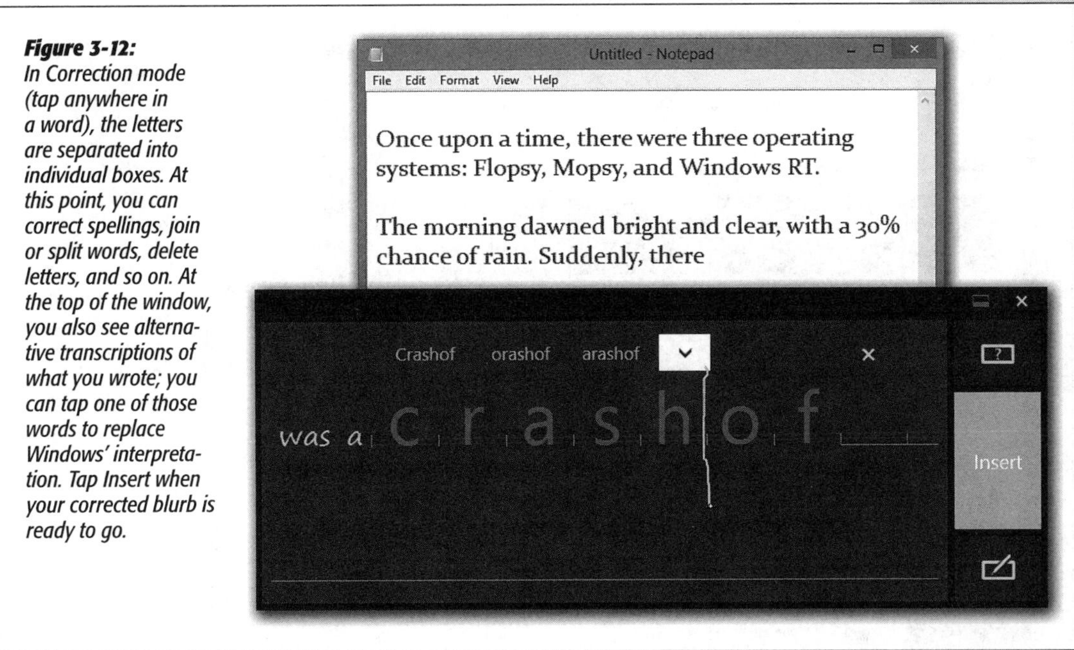

Figure 3-12: *In Correction mode (tap anywhere in a word), the letters are separated into individual boxes. At this point, you can correct spellings, join or split words, delete letters, and so on. At the top of the window, you also see alternative transcriptions of what you wrote; you can tap one of those words to replace Windows' interpretation. Tap Insert when your corrected blurb is ready to go.*

The File Picker

Microsoft's dearest hope for TileWorld is that it will become as ubiquitous, recognizable, and popular as the iPad. And as simple: full screen, no menus, no dialog boxes, no file structure.

What? No file structure? You can't save and name a file, or open an old one?

That's going too far. It may fly on the iPad, but Windows 8 needs to get real work done.

Therefore, here and there in TileWorld apps, you'll run into something called the File Picker (Figure 3-14). In the days of Olde Windows, it was called the Open dialog box. But the idea is the same: It lets you navigate to any folder on your hard drive so that you can hunt for a file or a document that you want to open.

Navigating the File Picker

Now, in the real desktop world, the Save and Open dialog boxes are miniature desktops. They have columns that you can sort or widen, a list of folder links down the left side, a toolbar, and so on.

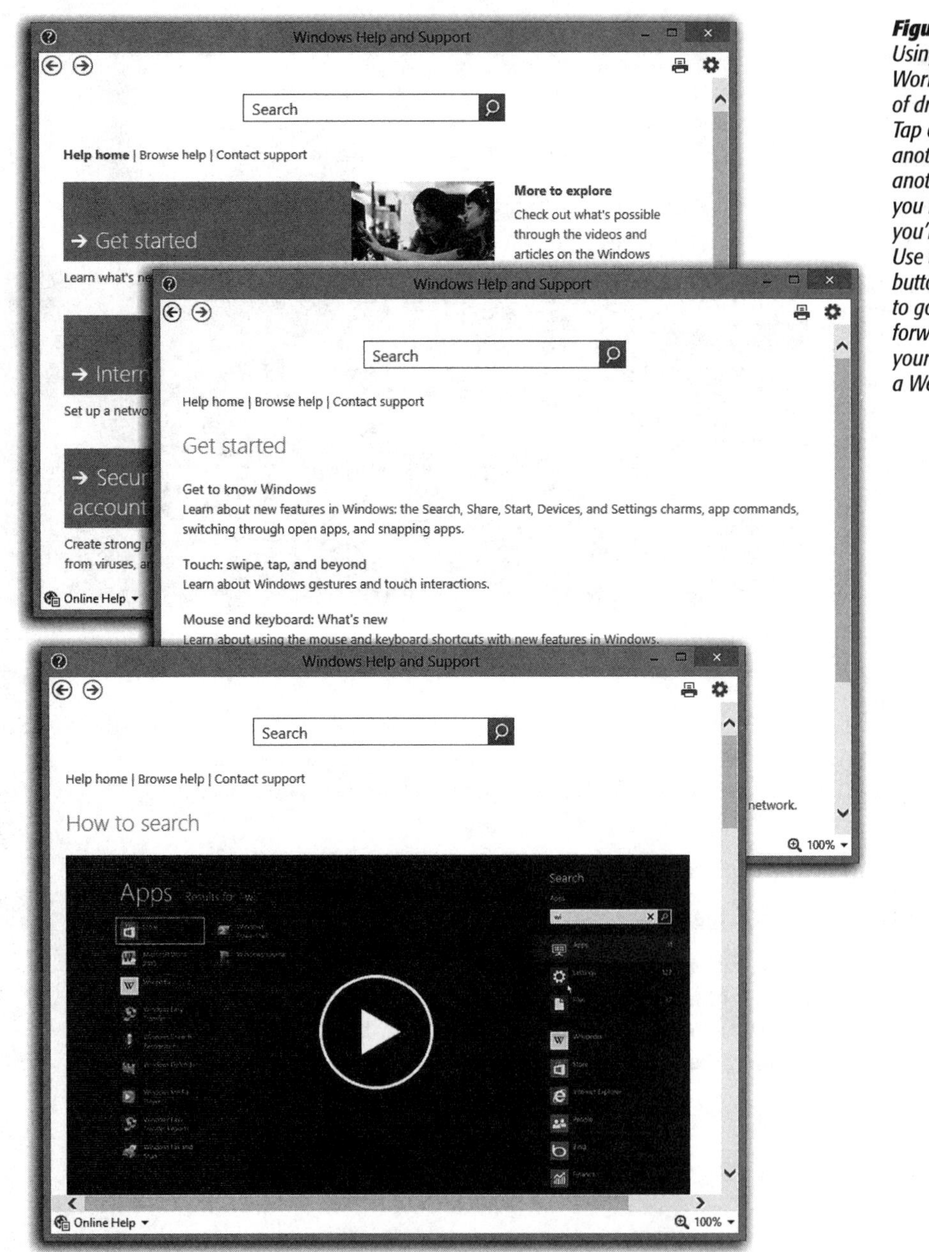

Figure 3-13: *Using Help in Tile-World is a matter of drilling down: Tap one link, then another, and then another, until you find the topic you're looking for. Use the ← and → buttons (top left) to go back and forward through your e, just as in a Web browser.*

The File Picker serves the same purpose—it lets you navigate all the folders of your computer—but it's been incredibly stripped down. If the Open dialog box is a Boeing 767, the File Picker is a kite.

Here are its elements:

- **Files ⌄.** This is actually a pop-up menu. It lists all kinds of frequently used locations on your computer. For example, you can jump directly to the Documents, Pictures, Music, Videos, or Downloads folders, or to the Desktop, your computer's main level, or your network.

  At the bottom of the menu, you see listings for things that aren't folders. For example, if you choose Camera, you activate your computer's built-in camera so that you can take a photo or video right now, on the spot. (You can imagine needing that when you're in the middle of writing an email message, for example. "Dear Casey: You asked about my new haircut. Well…")

  You can also choose Photos, which gives you access to your Photos app—all your pictures, from all your accounts (Facebook, SkyDrive, Flickr, and so on).

  And you can choose SkyDrive for quick access to anything you've stored on your free online "hard drive" (page 169).

Tip: You can operate this menu in all the usual ways: with your finger (if you have a touchscreen), with the mouse, or with the arrow keys (press the space bar to "click" something).

  Once you've chosen a folder, you see its contents, as shown in Figure 3-14. And you see the folder's name at upper right.

- **Go up.** There's no Back button in the File Picker. There is, however, this button. As you'd guess, it takes you up one folder level—in other words, to the folder that contains this one. (For example, if you're currently browsing the contents of the Chicago folder, one click on "Go up" takes you to the Illinois folder; another click opens the United States folder.)

  To go down again—burrowing back *into* folders instead of out of them—you tap or click one of the folders on the screen.

- **Sort by.** This, too, is a pop-up menu. It lets you control how the icons are sorted: chronologically ("by date") or alphabetically ("by name"). If you want to sort them in any other way (by size, tag, rating, and so on), you can always flip back to the desktop.

Choosing Files

All right. So now you've navigated to the proper folder. The time has come at last to do what the File Picker was made for: picking files.

Often, you're allowed to choose only one file (when you're choosing a new desktop wallpaper, for example). In other apps, you can choose several at once (when you're attaching files to an email message, say). Either way, here's how it works.

Previewing a file

The File Picker ordinarily shows you a thumbnail of each file, plus a few details like file size and modification date. But a handy preview box can also show you details like file type, pixel dimensions (for a photo), and folder location (Figure 3-15). To see this box:

- **Touchscreen:** Hold your finger down on the icon momentarily.
- **Mouse:** Point to a tile without clicking.
- **Keyboard:** Press the arrow keys until you've highlighted a tile.

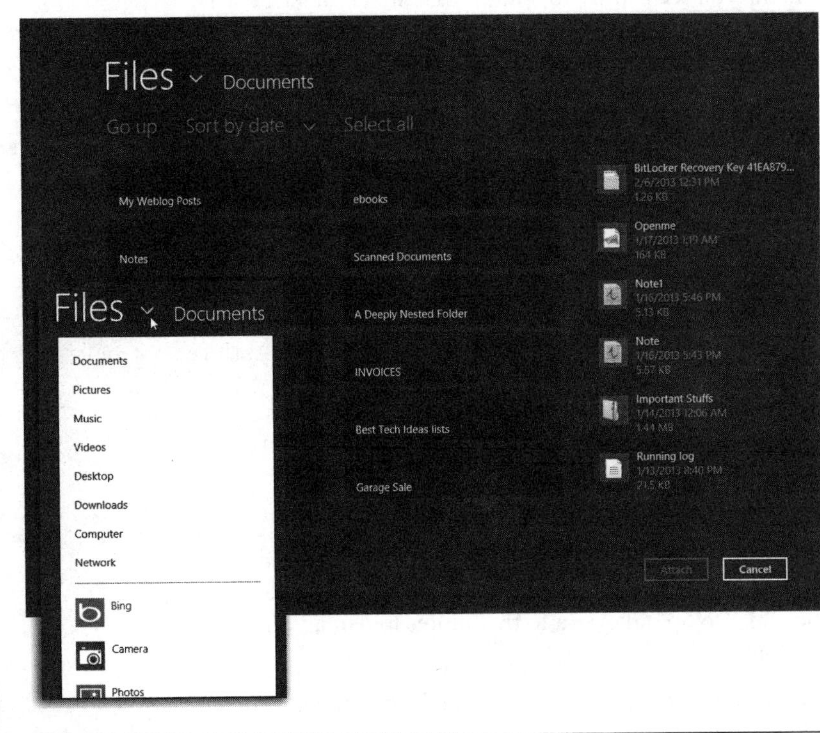

Figure 3-14: *The File Picker appears when, for example, you want to find a file to attach to an outgoing email message. Almost everything you see here is tappable or clickatble.*

Inset: The word "Files" is actually a pop-up menu of folders that Microsoft thinks you might want to visit.

If it turns out you've found the correct file, you should now confirm your choice like this:

- **Touchscreen:** Touch the tile and drag down slightly.
- **Mouse:** Click.
- **Keyboard:** Press the space bar.

When you do that, a checkmark appears in the corner of the file's icon tile.

Note: If you're in a situation where you're allowed to choose multiple files, the File Picker also adds the tiny icon of the newly selected file to the collection of icons at the bottom of the screen.

In some apps, you can go on choosing additional files the same way (when you're choosing files to attach to an email, for example). If you change your mind, you can remove a file from the selection by tapping, clicking, or space-barring again.

When you've checkmarked the right icon(s), use the important-looking button in the lower right to close the File Picker and proceed. That button's wording varies depending on the app you're using—it may say Attach or Choose Picture, for example— but you'll get the idea. It's right next to the Cancel button, which closes the File Picker without choosing any file at all.

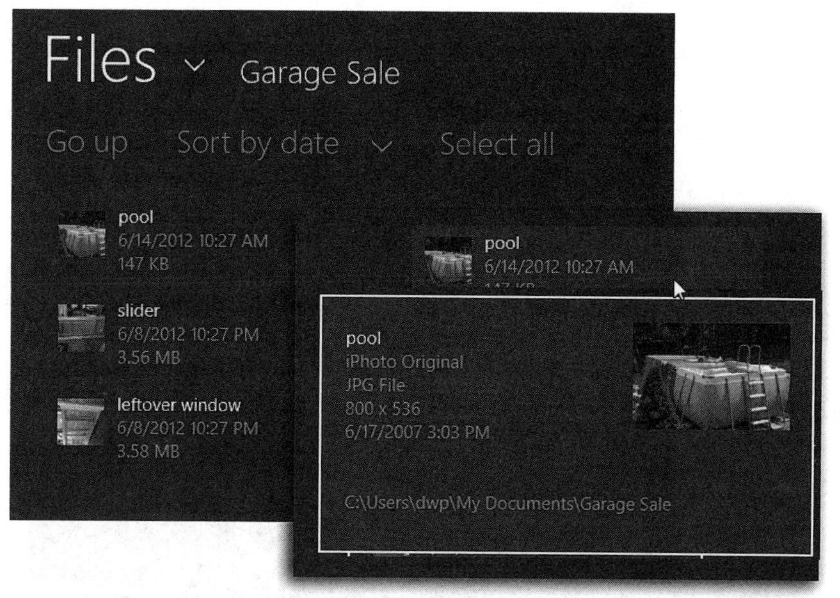

Figure 3-15: *Left: The File Picker shows icons, names, and dates.*

Right: But if you point to an item without clicking, for your convenience, a pop-up box shows the details of that file.

Search

It's one of the best-designed aspects of Windows 8: the new Search. It's always there, hiding in the Charms bar, in every app. It's super fast—it starts showing results even while you're still typing. And it can also search within a single TileWorld app, like Mail or Maps; in TileWorld, you never have to wonder: "Where's the search button in this thing?"

Now, at the desktop, you'll find other search boxes lurking everywhere. The search box at the top of every desktop window searches only that window (including folders within it). Search boxes also appear in the Control Panel window, Internet Explorer, Windows Mail, Windows Media Player, and other spots where it's useful to perform small-time, limited searches.

But the main Search feature, the one that hunts down files, apps, and settings, is the one hiding in the Charms bar. And make no mistake: It may look like it belongs to

TileWorld, but this is the feature you use in both TileWorld and the desktop for general finding purposes. Here's how it works.

Starting the Search

To search for something, open the search box like this:

- **Touchscreen:** Swipe inward from the right edge of your screen to open the Charms bar. Tap Search.
- **Mouse:** Point to the upper- or lower-right corner of the screen to open the Charms bar. Click Search.
- **Keyboard:** Press ⊞+F to open the Charms bar and the search box.

You can immediately begin typing to identify what you want to find (Figure 3-16). For example, if you're trying to find a file called "Pokémon Fantasy League.doc," typing just pok or leag will probably work.

Capitalization doesn't count, and neither do accent marks; typing cafe finds files with the word "café" just fine.

As you type, the familiar Start-screen tiles are replaced by search results (Figure 3-16). This is a live, interactive search; that is, Windows modifies the menu as you type—you don't have to press Enter after entering your search phrase.

Tip: Windows tries to prioritize the results, so that the ones you're most likely looking for appear first. For example, in a music app, you see music files listed first.

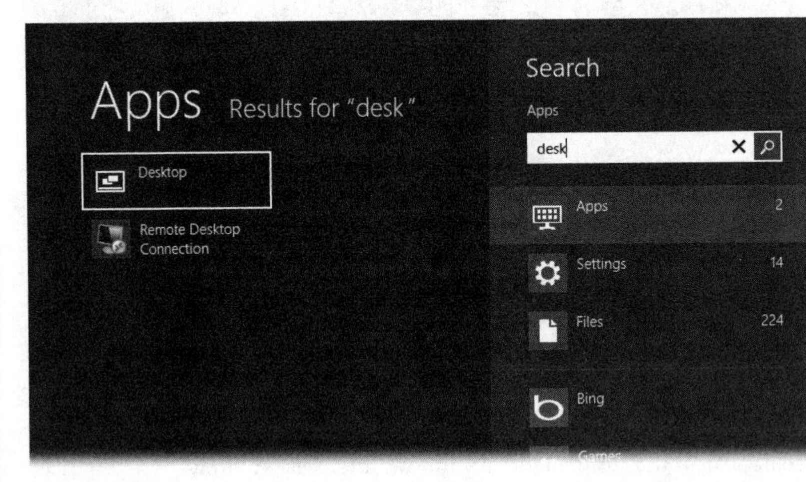

Figure 3-16: *As you type, the left side of the screen fills with matches. You can tap, click, or arrow-key your way to the other searchable categories (Settings, Files, Mail, and so on) to change the focus of your search. The number tells you how many results it's found in that category. In this example, the search found 2 apps or programs, 14 settings panels, and 224 files that match your query.*

If you see what you were looking for, great! Select it to open it (tap it, click it, or arrow-key your way to it and then press the space bar).

If you don't see it, you may have mistyped. You may be searching for something that doesn't exist. And you may be searching for the wrong thing, as described next.

Search for Apps, Settings, and Files

Windows 8 doesn't give you any way to search *everything* on your machine at once. No single search turns up every file, folder, program, email message, address book entry, calendar appointment, and so on. (That's a change from Windows 7.)

Instead, you're supposed to search for things in each category separately.

When you first type into the search box, Windows assumes you're searching for a *program or app.* That's because Search makes a terrific, efficient program launcher. Starting at the Start screen, type *cal* and press Enter, and boom—you've opened Calendar. (In other words, if you have a keyboard, you don't even have to open the Charms bar. *Just start typing* at the Start screen.)

But what if you're not? What if you're searching for a setting or a file? In that case, without having to retype, select Settings or Files in the right-hand column. Windows redoes the search for that item.

Tip: If you have a keyboard, you can perform this switch without taking your hands off the keyboard. Use the down arrow to highlight Settings or Files (or an app's name below that), and then press Enter to "click."

You can also reverse the sequence: You can select Settings or Files *first* and *then* type the search term.

So what do these mean?

- **Settings**. Windows 8 stashes its preference settings in three different places. A few are in the Charms bar when you click Settings. A few more are in "Change PC settings" in that Settings bar. And the full set is in the Control Panel at the Windows desktop. That's a lot of places to look when all you want to do is, say, change your password.

  That's the beauty of a Settings search. You don't have to know where some setting is found, or which of the three places to look. You don't even have to know the *name* of the Control Panel setting.

  Just search for the plain-English *purpose* of the setting you want to change. You can type *wallpaper, WiFi, password, printer, fonts, brightness, volume, keyboard, microphone*—whatever. Search promptly displays all appropriate settings options, written out with convenient verbs (like "Set up a microphone" or "Make everything on your screen bigger").

- **Files.** "Files" means "everything else." This is how you find a picture, a sound, a Word document, a spreadsheet, a PDF file, a music file—anything openable that's not a program or a setting.

Note: There's no way to search for folders using the Search bar. You can do that only at the desktop.

Searching Within Apps

It's one of Windows 8's great design conveniences: the search box within every Tile-World app is in exactly the same place as the *master* search box—in the Charms bar. In other words, when you're in Mail, or People, or Internet Explorer, and you want to search your Inbox, your address book, or a Web page, you open the Charms bar and type your search phrase into the search box. The app knows what you mean: *Search within this app.*

What's unusual about Windows 8, though, is that every app that offers a Search command is listed in the Search panel, even when you're not *in* that app. If you're on the Start screen, you can search Mail. If you're in Calendar, you can search Maps. If you're in Music, you can search Finance. And so on.

All you have to do is open the search box as described above, type what you're looking for, and then select the name of the app you want to search. (Or reverse the steps: Select the app's name and *then* type your search term.) The app opens automatically and performs the search (Figure 3-17).

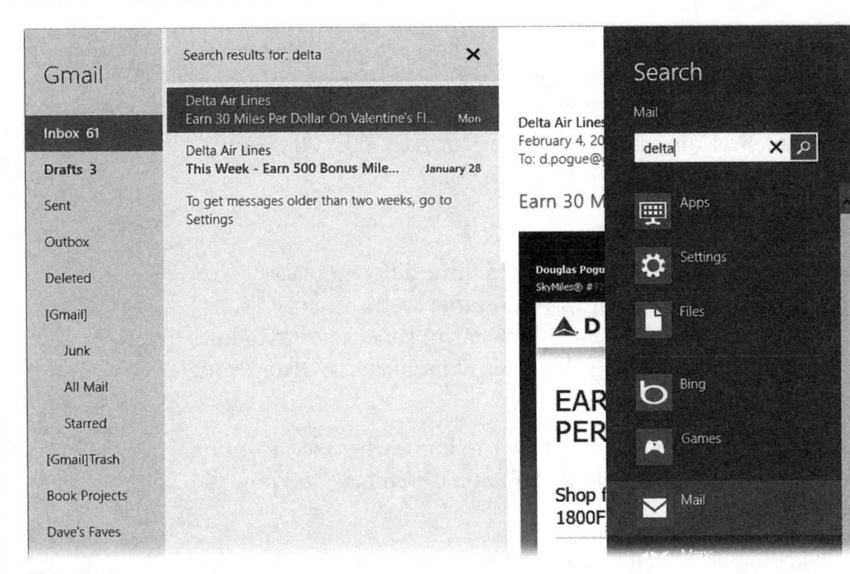

Figure 3-17: *When you type into the search box, you also see the list of TileWorld apps that have their own Search commands. Here's an example: From the Start screen, you can type a search phrase and then hit Mail to seek email messages containing that phrase.*

Text: Selecting, Copying, Pasting

The original copy-and-paste procedure of 1984—putting a graphic into a word processor—has come a long way. Most experienced PC fans have learned to trigger the Cut, Copy, and Paste commands from the keyboard, quickly and without even thinking.

With Mouse and Keyboard

Here's how the copy/paste process works if you have a mouse and a keyboard:

1. **Highlight some material in a document.**

   Drag through some text in a word processor, for example, or highlight graphic, music, movie, database, or spreadsheet information, depending on the program you're using.

2. **Use the Edit→Cut or Edit→Copy command.**

   Or press the keyboard shortcuts Ctrl+X (for Cut—think of the X as a pair of scissors) or Ctrl+C (for Copy). Windows memorizes the highlighted material, socking it away on an invisible storage pad called the Clipboard. If you chose Copy, nothing visible happens. If you chose Cut, the highlighted material disappears from the original document.

3. **Click to indicate where you want the material to reappear.**

   This may entail switching to a different program, a different document, or simply a different place in the same document.

4. **Choose the Edit→Paste command (⌘-V).**

A copy of the material you had originally highlighted now appears at your insertion point—if you're pasting into a program that can accept that kind of information.

POWER USERS' CLINIC

Settings for Search

As you'll quickly discover, the Search command in the Charms bar features a long list of TileWorld apps that can be searched. Mail, Internet Explorer, Maps, People, and so on. The list is probably so long that you'll have to scroll down to see them all.

There are probably apps listed here whose search functions you never actually use. You may as well hide those apps so that they don't take up space on the Search panel.

To do that, open the Charms bar. Select Settings; select "Change PC settings"; select Search in the list of settings at left.

Now, under "Use these apps to search," you see the complete list of searchable apps. Flip the on/off switches to control their presence in your Search panel.

While you're here, by the way, you can also examine two other Search-related on/off switches. "Show the apps I search most often at the top" refers to the order of searchable apps, as they appear in the list on the Search panel. If this option is turned on, then those searchable apps are listed according to how frequently you use their search feature. If it's off, then the searchable apps are listed alphabetically.

Then there's "Let Windows save my searches as future search suggestions." When you click certain apps' names in the Search panel, like Files, Maps, or People, you see, just below the search box, the last three things you searched for within that app. This feature is intended to save you time and typing, on the assumption that you may want to find the same thing again.

But you could also consider it a security risk; how would you feel about your spouse using your computer and discovering that your last three searches were "kidnapping," "ransom," and "tax shelters"?

If that's a worry for you, you can prevent Windows from memorizing your last three searches by turning off "Let Windows save my searches." And you can "Delete history" right now, with a click on the button.

(You won't have much luck pasting, say, a block of spreadsheet numbers into World of Warcraft.)

The most recently cut or copied material remains on your Clipboard even after you paste, making it possible to paste the same blob repeatedly. Such a trick can be useful when, for example, you've designed a business card in your drawing program and want to duplicate it enough times to fill a letter-sized printout. On the other hand, whenever you next copy or cut something, whatever was already on the Clipboard is lost forever.

With Your Finger

If you have a touchscreen, working with text is a little trickier. For one thing, your finger is a lot fatter and less precise than a mouse pointer.

Fortunately, Microsoft has thought this through. You can still make precise copies and pastes using a special onscreen tool called the *gripper.* As shown in Figure 3-18, here's the sequence:

1. **Tap, or hold your finger down at the end of the first word you want to select (Figure 3-18, top).**

   Usually, you'll want to tap the *left* end of the *first* word in the line, paragraph, or blob that you want to cut or copy. (If you want to work backward, you can also tap the *right* end of the *last* word in the selection-to-be.)

   Note: In places where you can't edit the text, like a Web page, you can tap directly on the word to select it.

   You'll notice that a special insertion point appears: a vertical line with a round handle at the bottom. That's the gripper.

2. **Drag the gripper to highlight text.**

   As you move the gripper, everything gets highlighted from the point of your initial tap. In fact, once you start moving it, you get two grippers, one on either end of the selection. You know, in case you change your mind about the starting point.

   All right, then. You've highlighted the text. Now all you have to do is choose Cut or Copy. But remember—TileWorld has no menus. So where are the Cut and Copy commands?

3. **Tap inside the highlighted text.**

   And bingo: A shortcut menu appears, offering the Cut and Copy commands.

   Note: If Windows has underlined the word to show that it's misspelled, the process is a little different: Tapping the word simultaneously highlights the *entire* word and opens the "suggested spelling corrections" shortcut menu.

   If you change your mind, tap anywhere outside the shortcut menu to close it.

4. **Tap the command you want: Cut or Copy, for example.**

   At this point, it's just as though you'd copied text with the mouse.

5. **Tap to indicate where you want the material to reappear.**

   That might mean switching to a different app, or maybe just a different spot in the same one (for example, a search box or email you're writing). In any case, the gripper appears, blinking.

6. **Tap the gripper's round handle (or hold your finger down anywhere) to open the shortcut menu; tap Paste.**

   And voilà: The copied or cut material now appears.

Tip: The usual Windows keyboard shortcuts (Ctrl+C for copy, Ctrl+X for cut, Ctrl+V for Paste) work on touchscreens, too. Of course, that usually means opening the onscreen keyboard, which is a lot less efficient than the tapping method described here. But you know–it's possible.

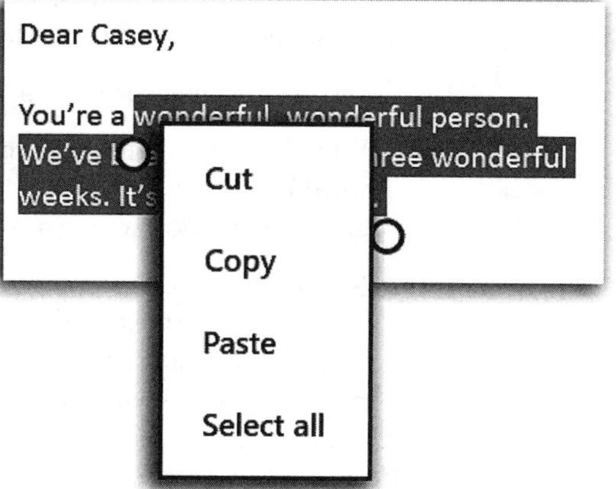

Figure 3-18:
On a touchscreen, copying and pasting text relies on the gripper–the big ball at the bottom of the insertion point.

Top: Tap at one end of the first word you want to select. Drag the gripper to enclose the text you want to select.

Bottom: At that point, you can tap the highlighted text to open the shortcut menu, and then tap Cut or Copy.

Now, tap where you want to paste. Tap the gripper ball; the copied text appears.

The TileWorld Spelling Checker

You might have noticed that as you type, Windows quietly and instantly corrects your obvious typos. Or maybe you *haven't* noticed, which is even more awesome.

In other words, if you type "prolbem," for example, it changes to "problem" the instant you press the space bar at the end of the word. There's no beep, no underline, no error message; the correction just happens.

Tip: You can turn off this feature if you don't find it so helpful–for example, if you're writing a novel starring a character with really bad spelling. In the Charms bar, choose Settings, then "Change PC settings," then General. Then turn off "Autocorrect misspelled words."

You can also teach Windows to stop correcting some word that you know is correct. Right-click a word it just corrected and, from the shortcut menu, choose "Stop correcting [the word]."

That's all well and good if Windows is *sure* of the word you meant to type. But what about a word like "corse"? Did you mean *coarse* or *course?* Windows can't read your mind. (That's supposedly coming in Windows 9.)

In that case, Windows doesn't correct the error—it just flags it by displaying a wavy underline beneath the questionable word. Either you can edit it manually, or you can inspect Windows' proposed corrected spellings, like this:

- **Touchscreen:** Tap the word.
- **Mouse:** Right-click the word.
- **Keyboard:** Press the Menu key (▤).

If one of the proposed corrections is what you intended, select it; Windows replaces your misspelling and forgets that it ever happened.

If you *don't* see the word you intended, then take one of these paths:

- **Select "Add to dictionary."** In other words, you're telling Windows, "This is a real word that I use sometimes. Learn it (add it to your internal spelling dictionary) and don't mark it wrong again."
- **Select Ignore.** You're telling Windows, "I *meant* to type that. Leave it alone. Just this time." (You can achieve the same effect by tapping or clicking outside the shortcut menu, or pressing the Esc key, to close the shortcut menu.) Windows leaves the misspelled word where it is, complete with squiggly underline.

Tip: You can turn off this squiggly-underline feature, too. In the Charms bar, choose Settings, then "Change PC settings," then General. Then turn off "Highlight misspelled words."

Help in TileWorld

Strange as it may sound, TileWorld and the Windows desktop have separate help programs.

To find help in TileWorld, open the Charms bar, tap Settings, and then tap Help. (Help is a kind of setting, isn't it? Sure it is.)

Here's what you need to know about Help:

- You have two options here: Drill down, as shown in Figure 3-13, or search (tap the search box at top). From the search results, you can drill down by tapping topics once again.
- The help you find depends upon the app you're in. In other words, opening Help while you're in Calendar gets you only tips for Calendar.
- In some apps, like People and Mail, Help offers two links to Windows 8 discussion forums, and that's it. In others (like Maps, Weather, and Camera), the Help command doesn't appear at all. That's normal.
- Some help screens contain video tutorials. Tap the ▶ button to play them.

The TileWorld Apps Missing Manual

TileWorld apps are supposed to be extremely easy to use. Many don't have help screens at all (even if they should). You can't get lost, because the app fills your entire screen. You can't get confused, because the apps' functions are very simple—more like iPad apps than Windows desktop programs. You can't get frustrated, because every control is big, broad, and finger-sized, designed from the beginning for touchscreens.

All you need to know boils down to these three tips:

- **Peek into the Charms bar as you learn the app.** You may discover that the Share button offers some cool ways to send whatever you're looking at (map, photo, Web

TROUBLESHOOTING MOMENT

Calibrating the Touch Screen

A touch screen may seem like magic. You're touching glass, and yet somehow the software knows how to react.

But let's face it: It's not really magic. It's actually some incredibly sophisticated layers of sensors, glass, and electronics. And sometimes–rarely–they get misaligned. You might discover one day that when you tap here, the software doesn't register your tap in exactly the right place.

In that case, what the doctor orders is calibration of your screen, which teaches the software to correct its locational abilities.

Open the Charms bar; choose Search. In the search box, type *calibrate*; tap Settings so that "Calibrate the screen for pen or touch input" appears in the search results. Tap it to open the Tablet PC Settings panel.

Tap Setup, and then follow the instructions on the screen.

page...) to other people (by email, Facebook, Twitter...). You may get good use from the Search button, too—it's programmed to search only the app you're *in* first.

You may also discover some useful options under Settings—like Help, in some apps.

- **Don't forget the App bar.** If an app has any controls or commands at all, it's hiding in the App bar that appears when you swipe up from the bottom (or down from the top) of the screen. Or press ⊞+Z. Or right-click a blank spot on the screen, if you have a mouse.
- **Bing apps behave like Web browsers.** Microsoft starts you out with apps called Sports, News, Travel, and Finance. Each is a "Bing app"—something like a Web-based magazine. Swipe horizontally to move through the pages. Tap the ⊕ button at top left to go back to a previous level.

When you're finished with a TileWorld app, there's no need to exit it. Just pop back to the Start screen to open whatever you want to use next.

For a tour of the TileWorld apps that come with Windows 8, see Chapter 4.

CHAPTER

4

TileWorld's Starter Apps

The Windows Store is meant to be the TileWorld Mall of America. That's where you'll find the real gems: thousands of apps that work great on tablets and touchscreens of every ilk. The basics are all there—Netflix, Skype, New York Times, Wikipedia, Evernote, Angry Birds, Fruit Ninja—and the catalog grows all the time.

In the meantime, though, Microsoft starts you out with about 20 TileWorld apps of its own. Here they are: miniature missing manuals for each one. (They're listed here alphabetically, since their specific order on your screen might be different.)

Bing

This "app" is nothing more than a link to Bing.com, Microsoft's version of Google. It's a good starting place when you want to search the Web.

Tip: The background photo changes every day. If you tap or click, small highlighted squares appear. Select one to view a fun fact about that part of the photo.

When you tap or click in the search box, a set of Popular Now buttons appears. And at the bottom of the screen, you'll see a handful of tappable phrases.

All these buttons and links represent what the *rest* of the world is searching for most today: "presidential election," "Bieber marriage," or whatever. That single row of words usually offers a fairly decent indication of what's on the public's mind today—and a quick way for you to catch up on *very* current events.

If you tap the More button (lower right), you wind up at Bing's breaking-news page, filled with tappable headlines.

Anyway, you know the drill: Type a search phrase into the box and then press Enter (or tap the ⌕ button). In the TileWorld version of Bing, you don't get a long list of text results—you get, of course, *tiles* of results (Figure 4-1).

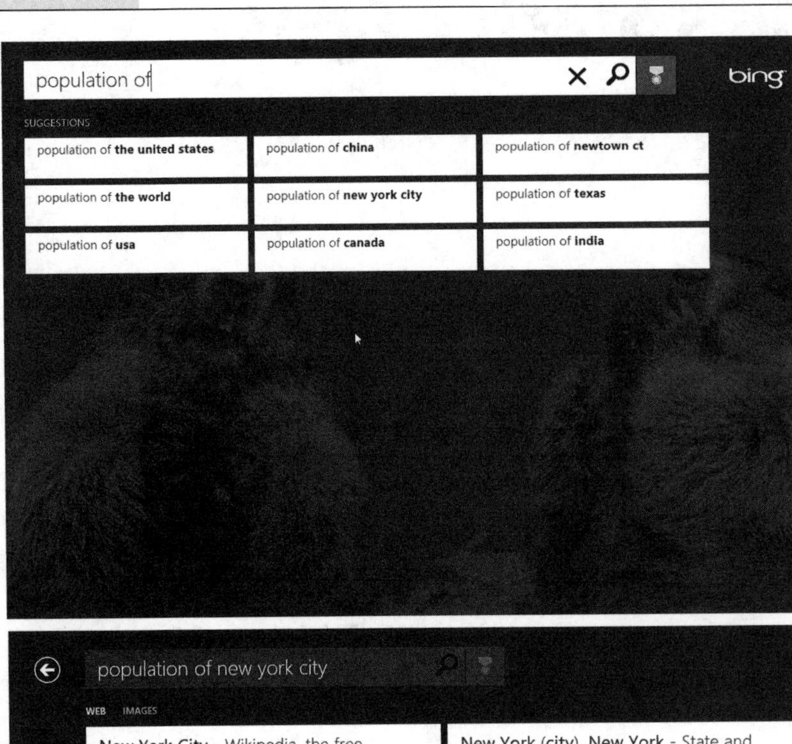

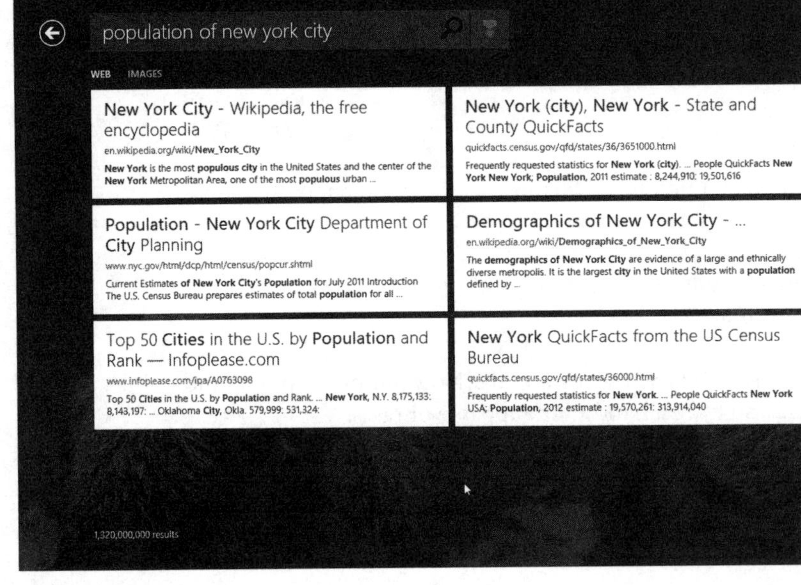

Figure 4-1: *The Bing app is really just a link to Microsoft's search page (top). The results, though, are presented as (what else?) a series of tappable tiles. Scroll horizontally to see more.*

Tip: It's a little bit annoying: You search with one app (Bing), but when you tap a search result, you're sent into a different app (Internet Explorer).

But there's a workaround. Pin the Bing.com (or Google.com) Web site to your Start screen. (Call up Bing.com; open the App bar; tap "Pin this site"; select "Pin to Start.") From now on, use that pinned site instead of the Bing app, and you won't experience the jarring handoff between apps.

Calendar

Calendar is not so different from those "Hunks of the Midwest Police Stations" paper calendars that people leave hanging on the walls for months past their natural life span.

But Calendar offers several advantages over paper calendars. For example:

- **It can automate the process** of entering repeating events, such as weekly staff meetings or gym workouts.
- **Calendar can give you a gentle nudge** (with a sound and a message) when an important appointment is approaching.
- **Calendar can subscribe to online calendars** from Google, Outlook, Hotmail, or even your company's Exchange calendar, so you have all your life's agendas in one place.

Note: There may already be stuff on your calendar the first time you open it–if, elsewhere in Windows, you've already entered account information for an online account. For example, if you've entered your Facebook details, all your friends' birthdays appear in Calendar automatically. You can, of course, turn off one account or another; read on.

That said, you may find that Calendar is among the simplest, most bare-bones calendar programs ever written. At least it won't overwhelm you.

Working with Views

When you open Calendar, you see something like Figure 4-2. On the App bar (page 27), you can switch among these views:

- **Day** looks exactly like a day-at-a-time desk calendar. On the left "page," you get a simple list of appointments for today; on the right, tomorrow. Scroll up and down to see the rest of the day.
- **Week** fills the main display area with seven columns, reflecting the current week.
- **Month** shows the entire month that contains today's date. Double-click a date number to open the Day view for that date.

  If a Month-view square is too small to show everything you've got scheduled that day, you'll see a notation at the top of the square like "5 events." It's letting you know that there may be more events than you can currently see. Switch to Day or Week view to see what they all are.

Tip: If you have a keyboard, you can also hit Ctrl+1, 2, and 3 for Day, Week, and Month views. And while you're at it: Ctrl+N makes a new appointment.

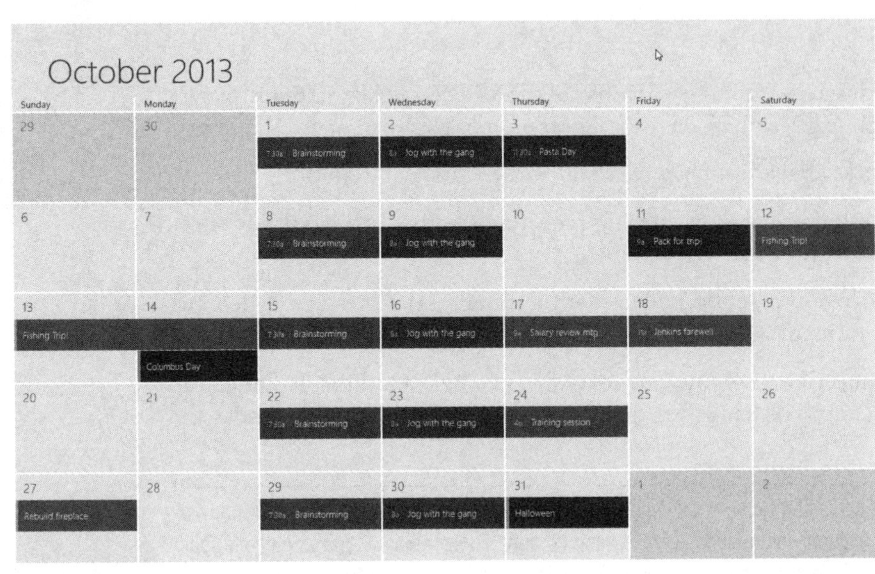

Figure 4-2: *The Windows 8 calendar is very, very simple. In any of the views, just tap or click an appointment to open its information screen (Figure 4-3). If you want to make changes, well, here's your chance.*

Moving among the days, weeks, or months is easy and fun for the whole family:

- **Touchscreen:** Swipe horizontally.
- **Mouse:** Turn the scroll wheel.
- **Keyboard:** The PageUp and PageDown keys jump to the previous or next day, week, or month. (The ← and → keys go to the previous/next day, and the ↑ and ↓ keys go to the previous/next hour.)

You can jump back to today's date in two steps. Open the App bar, and then hit Today. Or, if you have a keyboard, press Ctrl+T.

Making an Appointment

The basic calendar is easy to figure out. After all, with the exception of one unfortunate Gregorian incident, we've been using calendars successfully for centuries.

You can record a new appointment using the Details screen. It opens when any of these things happen:

- **You tap an empty spot** on a day, week, or month square.
- **You open the App bar and select the New button.**

- **You press Ctrl+N.**

In any case, the Details screen now appears (Figure 4-3). Here's where you can specify everything about the new appointment:

- **Account.** At the upper-left corner of the screen, the account name you see here is actually a pop-up menu. Use it to specify which account or category gets this appointment: your Live.com account, Gmail, Exchange, or whatever.
- **Add a title.** That's the large type at the top right—the name of your appointment.

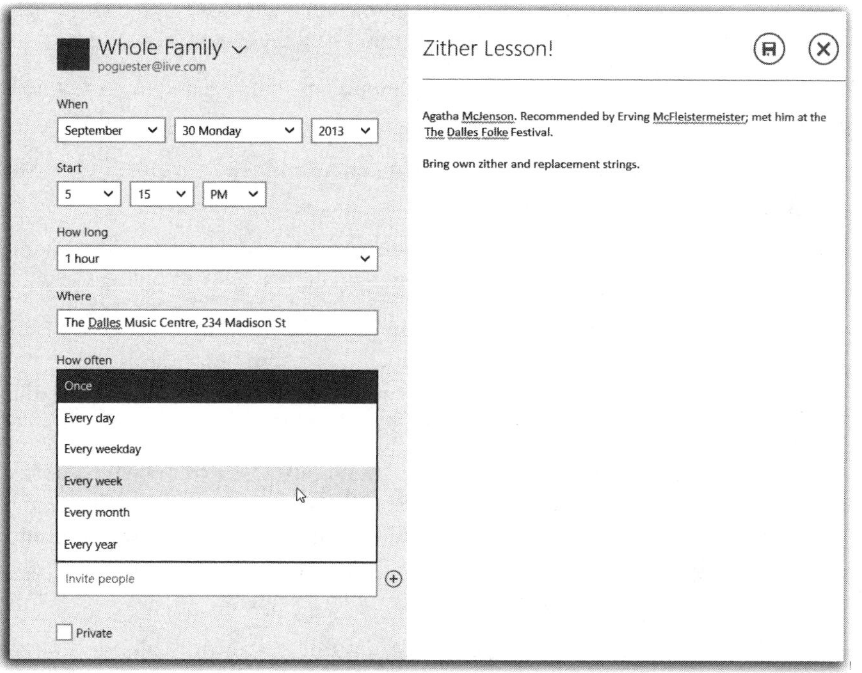

***Figure 4-3:** Here's where you both create a new appointment and edit an old one. The bottom set of controls appears only when you tap "Show more."*

For example, you might type *Fly to Phoenix.*

- **Add a message.** Here's your chance to customize your calendar event. You can type or paste any text you like in the note area—driving directions, contact phone numbers, a call history, or whatever.
- **When.** Separate pop-up boxes offer a choice of month, date/day of week, and year. You can scroll through these lists with your finger, scroll wheel, mouse, or Page Up/Page Down keys.
- **Start.** Here you enter the starting *time* for the appointment.
- **How long.** Your choices are 0 minutes, 30 minutes, 1 hour, 90 minutes, 2 hours, All day, or Custom.

An "All day" event, of course, refers to something that has no specific time of day associated with it: a holiday, a birthday, a book deadline. When you turn on this box, you see the name of the appointment jump to the top of the day/week/month square, in the area reserved for this kind of thing.

You'll probably use the Custom option a lot. It makes a set of "End" controls appear. This is the only way to specify an appointment that (a) has a duration not listed, like "45 minutes" or "3 hours," or (b) lasts more than a day, like a 3-day trip.

- **Where.** This field makes a lot of sense; if you think about it, almost everyone needs to record *where* a meeting is to take place. You might type a reminder for yourself like *My place,* a specific address like *212 East 23,* or some other helpful information, like a contact phone number or a flight number.

- **Calendar.** This pop-up menu lets you specify which online account gets the new appointment.

For each appointment, you can also hit "Show more" to expand the options. Now you can also indicate:

- **How often.** The pop-up menu here contains common options for recurring events: every day, every week, and so on. It starts out saying Once.

  Unfortunately, there's no way to specify any more complicated repeating pattern, like "Tuesdays and Thursdays" or "First Monday of every month." (If you've subscribed to an online calendar like Google, though, oddball repetitions you've set up there work just fine.)

- **Reminder.** This pop-up menu tells Calendar when to notify you when a certain appointment is about to begin. You can specify how much advance notice you want for this particular appointment. If it's a TV show, a reminder 5 minutes before airtime is probably fine. If it's a birthday, you might set up a warning a week in advance, so there's time to buy a present.

- **Status.** This little item communicates to your colleagues when you might be available for meetings. The menu's options are Free, Busy, Out of office, and so on.

  You might think: "Well, *duh*—if I've got something on the calendar, then I'm obviously busy!" But not necessarily. Some Calendar entries might just be placeholders, reminders to self, TV shows you wanted to watch, appointments you'd be willing to change—not things that would necessarily render you unavailable if a better invitation should come along.

- **Who.** If the appointment is a meeting or some other gathering, you can type the participants' names here. If a name is already in your People app, Calendar proposes autocompleting the name for you. Or you can hit the ⊕ button and choose from your People list.

Once you've added a person's name, you can add another, and then another. When you're finished, tap the ⊜ icon at the top-right corner of the screen; your lucky recipients have just been invited by email. Each message comes with an *iCal.ics* attachment: a calendar-program invitation file. In many mail and calendar programs, opening this attachment automatically presents your invitation; the recipients can respond (by choosing the Accept, Maybe, or Decline buttons that appear in *their* calendar programs).

When you're finished setting up the appointment, tap the Save button (®) at the top right (or press Ctrl+S). Your newly scheduled event now shows up on your calendar, complete with the color coding that corresponds to the calendar category you've assigned.

Editing Events

To edit an event, just tap it. You return to the screen shown in Figure 4-3, where you can make any changes you like.

Rescheduling Events

Sometimes things change. In Calendar, alas, you can't drag an appointment block to another time or date. You have to open its Details screen and change its scheduled time or date manually.

Deleting Events

To delete an appointment, just select it to open it. (If you're opening a recurring event, like a weekly meeting, Calendar asks whether you want to operate on only that particular instance of the event or on the whole series from that point forward.)

Then, on the Details screen, tap the Trash icon (⊜), or press Ctrl+D. (If other people have been invited, then Calendar asks if you want to email them to let them know about the change.)

Subscribing to Calendars (Accounts)

In most calendar programs, you can set up different categories, which are often called *calendars.* They can be anything you like. One person might have calendars called Home, Work, and TV Reminders. Another might have Me, Spouse 'n' Me, and Whole Family. A small business could have categories called Deductible Travel, R&D, and R&R.

Alas, the TileWorld Calendar doesn't let you create categories.

It does, however, let you subscribe to online calendars from Hotmail, Google, and Outlook (meaning Microsoft Exchange, Office 365, or Outlook.com). Or, rather, it lets you subscribe to *one* calendar from each account. If your Google Calendar has Home, Work, and Family categories, only one of them will show up in Calendar.

To subscribe to an account, see Figure 4-4.

When you create an appointment, you can use the Calendar pop-up menu to specify *which* account it belongs to, as shown in Figure 4-3.

Tip: You can choose a color for each account. To do that, open the Options panel shown in Figure 4-5.

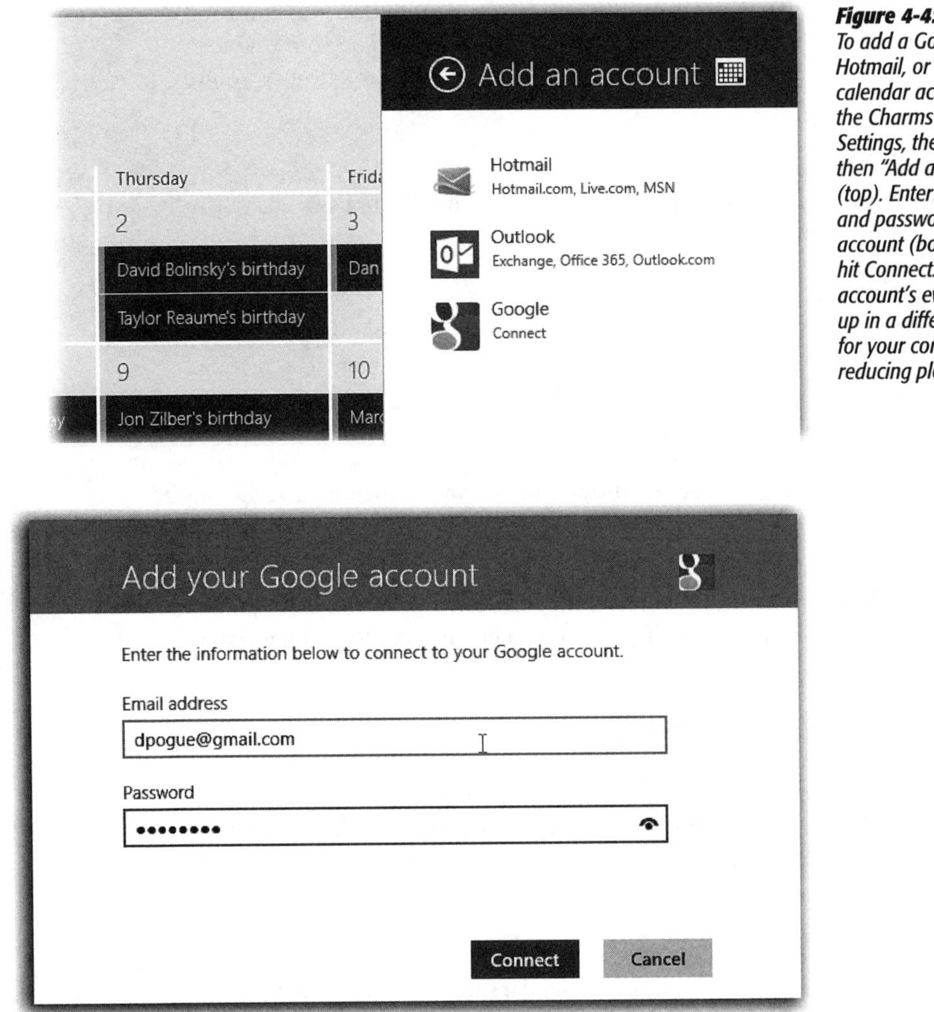

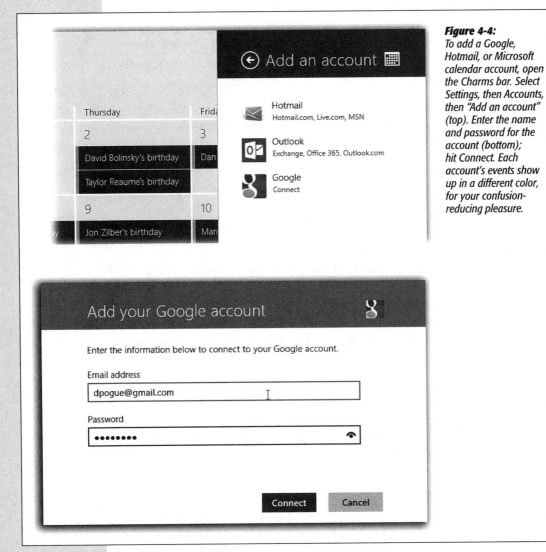

Figure 4-4: *To add a Google, Hotmail, or Microsoft calendar account, open the Charms bar. Select Settings, then Accounts, then "Add an account" (top). Enter the name and password for the account (bottom); hit Connect. Each account's events show up in a different color, for your confusion-reducing pleasure.*

Hiding Accounts

Once you've got a bunch of calendars (accounts) bubbling away in Calendar, each in its own color coding, you may feel a little overwhelmed—or at least crowded, since only a couple of them fit on each calendar square in Month view.

Fortunately, you can hide or show an entire category of appointments at once—a handy trick when you're trying to wade through it all.

To do that, see Figure 4-5. When you're finished tweaking, just tap anywhere on the calendar itself.

Camera

Almost every tablet and laptop these days has a camera—sometimes two (front and back). Even some desktop PCs have Webcams built in. Nobody is going to take profes-

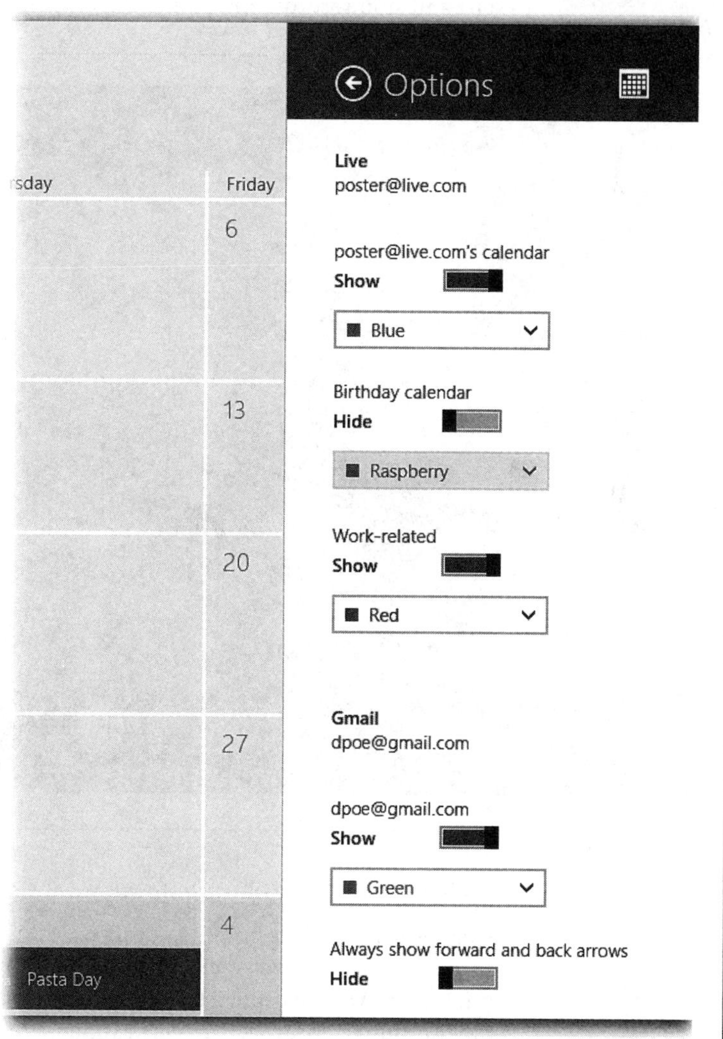

Figure 4-5: *To hide a certain account, open the Charms bar. Tap Settings, then Options. You'll see individual Hide switches for each account. Some, like your Microsoft account, even have sub-switches for things like birthdays and holidays.*

sional portraits with these cameras, but they're just fine for video chats and Facebook snaps. Camera (Figure 4-6) is the app you use for taking pictures and videos.

Note: The first time you open this app, Microsoft's privacy team has your back. "Can Camera use your webcam and microphone?" it asks. It's just making sure that the camera isn't opening on behalf of some nasty piece of spyware.

For many people, the biggest mystery of the Camera app is this: *How do you take a picture?* There's no Take Picture button anywhere.

Sherlock says: *Tap or click the screen.* (If you're in Video mode, tap or click the screen to start and stop recording.)

Figure 4-6: *If you're used to the three-inch screen on the back of a digital camera, discovering that your new preview screen is the entire size of your tablet or laptop comes as quite a shock. In essence, you're seeing the finished photo before you even take it.*

At the bottom of the screen, you see a few icons:

- **Change camera.** This button appears only if your computer has cameras on both the front and the back—a common arrangement on tablets. (Back camera for photography, front camera for video chats, since it's aimed at you.) Each time you tap this button, your view switches to the other camera.

- **Camera options.** This opens a panel containing a few controls, which vary wildly from computer to computer. You may also see different controls in Camera mode and Video mode.

  In camera mode: "Photo resolution" specifies the size and shape of the photo you're about to take, in megapixels (represented here as "MP"). As you're probably aware, higher resolution photos print better but take up more storage space and take more time to send. And remember: The resolution you need for a photo that will be displayed *on a screen* can be far lower than what you'd need to print.

Note: On most tablets, the front camera has a very low resolution, maxing out at maybe 1 megapixel. That's because it's intended for video chats–not for real photos that you intend to print out. The back camera usually has much higher resolution.

  The ratio in parentheses here indicates the *shape* of the photo. "4:3" is roughly square; "16:9" is rectangular and wide, like an HDTV set.

  In video mode: The "Video resolution" control adjusts—you guessed it—the resolution of the video that will be captured. (For reference, 240p is small and cruddy, suitable for attaching to an email; 480p is standard old TV resolution; 720p and higher are high-resolution, rectangular, very sharp videos that take up a lot of storage space.)

  You might also see an on/off option here for video stabilization, on machines that offer it.

  In both modes: "Audio device" lets you switch among your various microphones. Of course, you probably have only one.

  The More link brings up sliders that adjust the video image. Which settings you have depend on your gadget, but Brightness, Contrast, Focus, and Exposure are commonly found here. (For Focus and Exposure, turn off Auto if you'd like to adjust the slider yourself.)

- **Timer.** Yes, kids, your Windows 8 machine has a self-timer. It works in both photo and video modes. It's great for getting a self-portrait or a self-video when you don't want to be right at the machine.

  When you tap this button, it turns white. Now tap the screen to begin the "3…2…1" countdown.

- **Video mode.** When you tap this button, it turns white. Now, when you tap the screen, your camera starts recording video instead of snapping a photo. Tap again to stop recording.

Once you've captured your shot, it lands in a special album called the Camera Roll. (That's to distinguish photos you took with the computer from photos you've rounded up from other sources.) Unfortunately, there's no way to jump to the Camera Roll from within the Camera app. (You'd have to jump back to the Start screen, open Photos, open "Pictures library," and open "Camera roll.")

Fortunately, there's a simpler way to review dr latest shot: just swipe to the right with your finger.

Note: If you don't have a touchscreen, a small left-pointing arrow button appears automatically at the left edge of the screen. Clicking it serves the same purpose as swiping.

Here, as you review your shot, the app offers the two buttons Microsoft thinks you'll need most desperately: Delete and Crop. (If you hit the Crop button, you're offered four corner controls that you can use to enclose the piece of the photo you deem worth keeping. Tap OK to finish the job.)

At any point, you can turn the camera back into a live viewfinder by swiping right to left.

Desktop

This tile takes you to the Windows desktop world, the glorious land of the taskbar, folders, and menus. Tap here (or press ⊞+D) whenever you want to work with disks, folders, and files. And see Chapter 6 whenever you want to know how to *use* the desktop.

Finance

What "Finance" really means is "Financial News." When you open it, you arrive at what looks like a glorious, beautifully designed financial magazine. Swipe horizontally to see stock-market graphs; tiles for the day's winners and losers; article blurbs and headlines; videos; and stats for bonds, rates, currencies, and commodities (Figure 4-7).

Read this chapter's writeup about the News app for a complete understanding of how these apps work. But for now, don't miss the App bar, shown at top in Figure 4-7. (Swipe inward from the top or bottom edge of the screen, right-click any blank spot, or press ⊞+Z.) It offers tiles like these:

- **Today.** Brings you back to the opening collection of news and stats.
- **Watchlist.** Your own portfolio (or just stocks you want to watch). Tap the ⊕ button to specify each company name, or stock symbol, that you want this page to track.
- **Market, Rates.** Huge rows of financial tables representing today's financial-market activity in every conceivable category, or today's interest rates for various mortgages, bank accounts, and credit cards.
- **News, Videos.** A direct link to the financial-news and videos sections of this "magazine."

- **Best of Web.** A display of tiles for Web sites Microsoft thinks you might like—or learn from—on topics like investing, spending, donating, or borrowing.

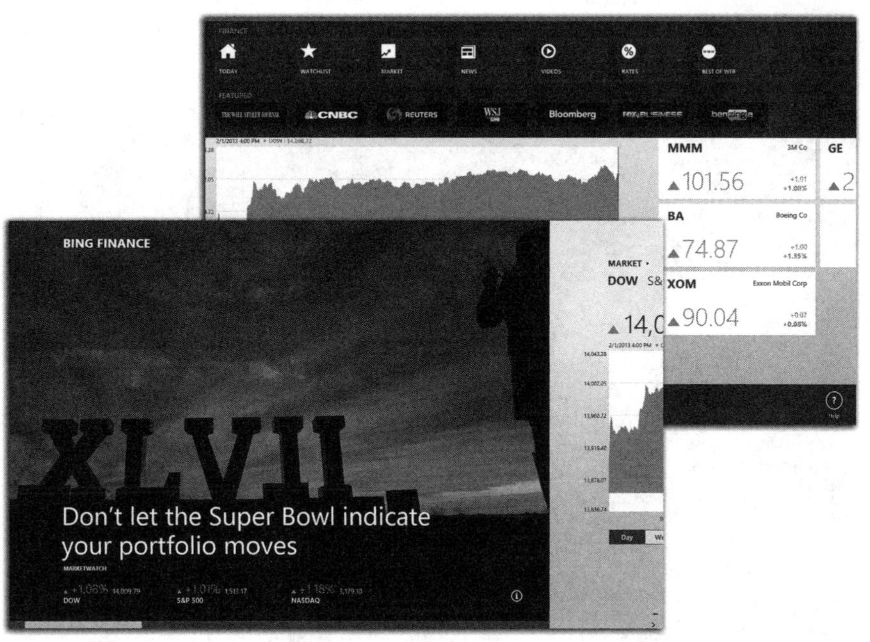

Figure 4-7: *This book would have to be 32 feet wide to show you all the financial goodies that appear in this massively complete, horizontally scrolling financial app. You can tap or click just about anything to drill down for more information.*

A ▾ button next to an App bar tile means, "Click or tap here to open a second row of buttons, providing quicker access to the categories within."

Games

This tile opens the Xbox Games app (Figure 4-8).

Now, try not to get confused. The word "Xbox" here has nothing to do with Microsoft's Xbox game console. Your Windows 8 machine can't play your Xbox games, although that would certainly be nice.

Instead, this app is a store for "Xbox Games on Windows," which is Microsoft code for "TileWorld games." Like all TileWorld apps, these games are available exclusively from the Windows Store—and you're looking at it.

Note: Xbox and Windows 8 games aren't completely separate. Some game companies offer both Xbox and Windows 8 versions–and they sometimes let you sync across machines. Maybe the weapons you've acquired on the console show up in the Windows 8 version of the game, or maybe you can resume your place on the Xbox after pausing on the Windows 8 machine. And your achievements, friends lists, avatars, leaderboards, and in-game rewards may show up on all your different machines, too. It's all up to the game companies.

If you scroll to the left, you'll find your own gamer profile (Gamertag): your name, score, and so on. Links here let you edit your avatar (onscreen cartoon representation), view your game achievements, view incoming friend requests, and so on.

That Achievements screen also shows your game accomplishments from other Microsoft gadgets—Xbox 360, Windows Phone, and so on—as well as Windows 8 games.

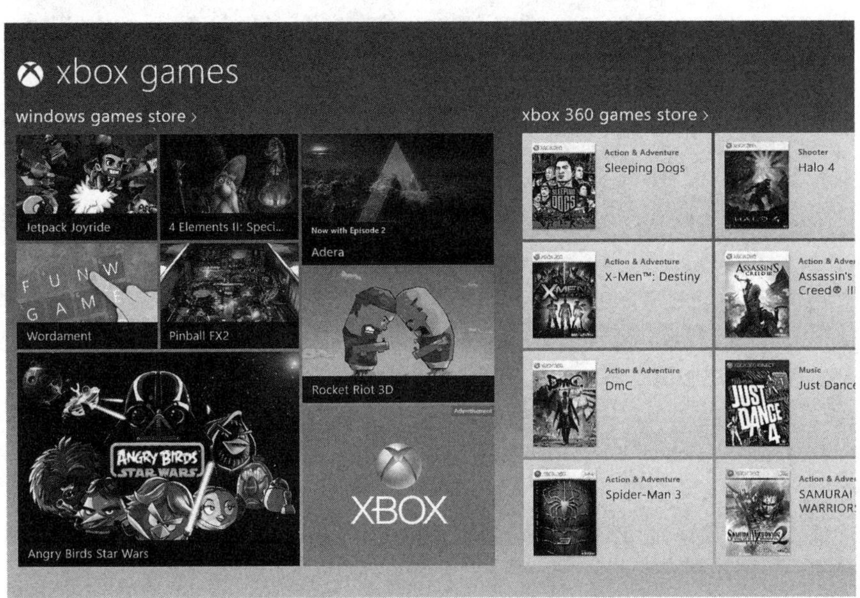

***Figure 4-8:** As you scroll horizontally to the right, you'll find ads for new games; the tiles for games you've recently played (on your computer or Xbox); a link to the Games section of the Windows Store; and a link to the Games section of the Xbox Store.*

All of them appear in one place.

If you choose the art or the Game Details button, you get a full-screen page for a particular game, where you can read (and buy) all about it.

Scroll far enough to the right, and you'll find the Game Activity group of tiles. They represent all the games you've played on all Xbox Games machines. Select a tile to read all about it—and, if it's a TileWorld game, play it.

Internet Explorer

Your copy of Windows 8 actually comes with two versions of Internet Explorer 10. There's the TileWorld version, described here, and the desktop version, described in Chapter 15.

By now, you're probably familiar with the concept of a Web browser. It's the program you use to visit Web sites, of course. The TileWorld version of Microsoft's browser, Internet Explorer (IE for short) has many of the features of a desktop Web browser:

bookmarks, autocomplete (for Web addresses), scrolling shortcuts, cookies, a pop-up ad blocker, password memorization, and so on.

Note: It doesn't work with plug-ins or add-on toolbars, however.

At the outset, though, the TileWorld IE doesn't like to show *anything* except the Web, from edge to edge of your screen; it wants to dedicate as much screen space as possible to the Web's glory. The following pages show you how to make those bells and whistles appear.

Note: You can't designate a Home page (start page) in TileWorld IE. But if you set up a Home page in the desktop version, the TileWorld version will also open to that page.

The Address Bar

Like any Web browser, this one offers several tools for navigating the Web: the address bar, bookmarks, and good old link tapping.

The address bar is the strip at the bottom of the screen where you enter the *URL* (Web address) for a page you want to visit. (URL is short for the even-less-self-explanatory *uniform resource locator.*) See Figure 4-9.

GEM IN THE ROUGH

Xbox SmartGlass

SmartGlass is an app that lets you control your Xbox with your phone or tablet. Impressively enough, this app is available not just for Windows phones, but also for iPhones, iPads, and Android phones and tablets.

It's a touchscreen remote control, which is something every TV ought to have anyway. Using the touchscreen as a trackpad, you can navigate the features at the Xbox Dashboard or the Web, play and pause your Xbox movies, browse Web pages, and so on. (Drag your finger to move the cursor; tap to "click." The B button in the corner of your phone or tablet means Back, just as on a real controller.)

And when you have to enter text—oh, wow. It's a lot faster tapping letters on your touchscreen gadget than having to move the cursor around an onscreen letter grid on your TV.

During music and video playback, the touchscreen offers playback controls. Some movies have been upgraded so that they supply the app with details about what you're watching: cast and crew lists, for example, and scene-selection menus.

In some games, extra information appears on the touchscreen in your hands—a map of the game area, for example. In Halo 4, you can keep your game statistics on the phone or tablet as you play on the TV—if you can figure out how to hold your phone and the Xbox controller simultaneously.

If you have a keyboard, the most efficient way to open the address bar is to press Alt+D, just as in IE versions of old. The address bar appears with the current page's address already typed in—*and highlighted*, meaning that you don't have to delete it before typing. Just begin typing the new address.

Windows tries to save you typing and hunting with three automatic suggestion mechanisms:

Figure 4-9: *Top: When you select the address bar, this scrolling band of tiles appears. It offers one-tap access to sites you've visited often, that you've pinned to your Start screen, or that you've designated as favorites. You can scroll horizontally through them in the usual ways: with your finger (touchscreen), with the mouse, or with the Page Up and Page Down keys.*

Bottom: As you type into the address bar, you see instead a batch of Web sites whose names match what you're typing.

- **Frequent, Pinned, Favorites.** When the address bar is highlighted, but *before* you've started to type, a batch of thumbnail icons appears just above it (Figure 4-9, bottom). These represent three labeled groups of sites: Frequent (sites you visit often), Pinned (sites whose icons you've installed on your Start screen, as described below), and Favorites (bookmarks).
- **Search suggestions.** As you start typing into the address bar, the Frequent/Pinned/Favorites thumbnails get replaced by a batch of even tinier Web-site icons. They represent big-name Web sites that IE thinks you might want to visit, along with

sites you've visited recently. As you continue to type, the suggestions change (Figure 4-9, top).

For example, when you type *n* into the address bar, you see options like *nbcnews.com* and *Netflix.com*. If you continue with a *y*, the choices now include *nypost.com* and *nydailynews.com*. Add a *t*, and you see sites like *nytimes.com*. At any point, of course, you can tap or click one to open it.

- **Autocomplete.** As you type, you see, highlighted in blue, a proposed completion of the Web address you're typing, right there in the address bar. This is the closest thing TileWorld offers to a History list. IE is autocompleting the same sorts of pages: frequently visited ones, pinned ones, and favorites.

If you see the address you're trying to type, then by all means hit Enter (or the ⊕ button) instead of typing out the rest of the URL. The time you save could be your own.

Scrolling

Unless you're reading sites like "A Complete History of Congress's Brilliance and Efficiency," most Web pages are taller than your screen. You'll have to scroll down to read them.

As a result, scrolling is a *constant* activity.

Fortunately, TileWorld gives you about 11,339 different ways to do it.

- **Touchscreen:** Swipe up the screen.
- **Trackpad:** You can use the regular scroll gesture on your laptop—often, that's dragging *two fingers* up or down on the trackpad.

UP TO SPEED

How Scroll Bars Work

These days, swiping with your finger, or tapping the space bar, are the most efficient ways to move down a Web page.

But if you're a mouse addict, you can still operate the vertical scroll bar that appears at the right edge of the window when you move the mouse or touch the trackpad.

In case this whole scrollbar thing is new to you, here's the drill: The scroll bar is a map of your entire document or page. In the middle, there's a sliding

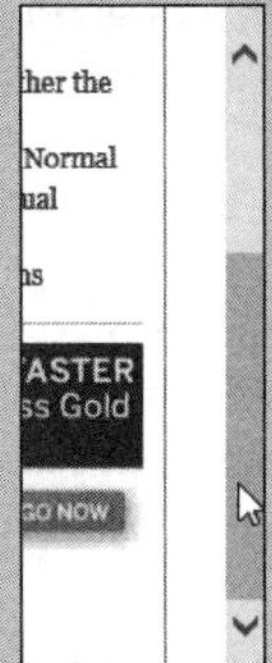

darker rectangle; its height represents how much of the page you're already seeing. For example, if the differently-colored handle is one-third the height or width of the whole screen, then you're already seeing one third of the page.

You can drag the handle manually to move around the page. You can also click or tap in the scroll bar track on either side of the handle to make the window scroll by one screenful.

- **Mouse:** Use the scroll bar that appears as soon as you move the mouse (see the box below). If your mouse has a scroll wheel, it works, too. (Hold Shift while you're rolling the wheel to scroll *horizontally*.)
- **Keyboard:** You can press your ↑ and ↓ keys to scroll one line at a time. Page Up and Page Down scroll in full-screen increments, while Home and End whisk you to the top or bottom of the current Web page.

  But maybe the best way of all is to *tap the space bar* each time you want to see more. Press Shift+space to scroll *up*. (The space bar serves its traditional space-making function only when the insertion point is blinking in a text box or in the address bar.)

Touchscreen Zooming

If you have a touchscreen, you'll get hours of pleasure from the built-in techniques for magnifying a page:

- **Rotate the gadget.** Turn the device 90 degrees in either direction. IE rotates and magnifies the image to fill the wider view.
- **Do the two-finger spread.** Put two fingers on the glass and drag them apart. The Web page stretches before your very eyes, growing larger. Then you can pinch to shrink the page back down again. Great when the type is a little too small. (Most people do several spreads or several pinches in a row to achieve the degree of zoom they want.)

Tip: On most laptops, you can also use this technique right on the trackpad.

- **Magnify with a double-tap.** You can also double-tap a particular spot on a Web page to magnify it by one level; double-tap again to return to the standard size.

Once you've zoomed out to the proper degree, you can then scroll around the page by dragging or flicking with a finger. You don't have to worry about "clicking a link" by accident; if your finger is in motion, IE ignores the tapping action, even if you happen to land on a link.

Tabbed Browsing

Like any other self-respecting browser, TileWorld IE can keep multiple pages open at once, making it easy for you to switch among them. In browsers like the desktop IE, Firefox, Chrome, and Safari, these multiple windows can show up as *tabs*—like filing-folder tabs—at the top of the screen. In TileWorld, the same feature is at work, but the tabs are hidden.

Tip: One handy payoff of this arrangement is that you can start reading one Web page while the others load into their own tabs in the background.

The key to revealing them is to open the App bar. Remember that?

- **Touchscreen:** Swipe inward from the top or bottom edge of the screen.
- **Mouse:** Right-click any blank spot in the window.
- **Keyboard:** Press ⊞+Z.

As you can see in Figure 4-10, in TileWorld, the tabs appear as (what else?) tiles.

- **To open a new tab,** tap the ⊕ button in the upper right. The screen goes blank. The address bar (accompanied by its row of frequents, favorites, and so on) appears at the bottom of the screen so that you can specify *which* Web site you want to visit in the new window.

***Figure 4-10:** This is TileWorld's version of tabbed browsing. The thumbnails at the top of the screen represent all the Web pages you have open at the moment. Tap a tile to jump to that already-open window. Close a tab by tapping its – ⊗ button.*

GEM IN THE ROUGH

inPrivate Browsing

IE's inPrivate browsing feature lets you surf without adding any pages to your History list, searches to your Bing search suggestions, passwords to IE's saved password list, or autofill entries to IE's memory. You might want to turn on inPrivate Browsing before you start visiting Web sites that would, you know, raise interesting questions with your spouse, parents, or boss.

The trick is to tap the ⊙ button and then tap "New inPrivate tab." From this point on, Internet Explorer records nothing while you surf.

When you're ready to browse "publicly" again, close the tab. IE again begins taking note of the pages you visit—but it never remembers the earlier ones.

In other words, what happens inPrivate Browsing stays inPrivate Browsing.

You can open a third window, and a fourth, and so on, and jump among them, using these techniques.

- **To close one tab,** open the App bar. Tap the ⊗ button in the corner of the tile whose tab you want to close. Or, if you have a keyboard, press Ctrl+W.
- **To close all tabs,** tap the ⊖ button; from the shortcut menu, choose "Close tabs."

Tip: You might notice that IE for TileWorld is, ahem, somewhat more stripped down than the "real" IE. Not only is there no real History list, but there's also no way to erase your History if you've been up to no good. Or is there?

There is. Open the Charms bar. Hit Settings, then Internet Options, then (under Delete Browsing History), Delete. You've just erased all the tracks you've left so far in your online travels: your history, saved passwords, temporary files, and cookies.

But that's how you get rid of your tracks after you've left them. Next time, don't leave any tracks to begin with, using inPrivate Browsing (see the box on the previous page).

Stop, Reload

Tap ✖ to interrupt the downloading of a Web page you've just requested (if you've made a mistake, for instance, or if it's taking too long).

Once a page has finished loading, the ✖ button turns into a ↻ (Reload) button. Hit it if a page doesn't look or work quite right. IE re-downloads the Web page and re-interprets its text and graphics.

Back, Forward

Surfing the Web, of course, is a sequence. Often, you start on one page, you tap a link to open a second one, and you tap a link there to move to a third one.

Fortunately, there are Back and Forward buttons and keystrokes in TileWorld IE. ("Back" means "revisit the page I was just on," and "Forward" means "return to the page you were on *before* I went Back.")

- **Touchscreen:** Swipe from the left or right edge of the screen in toward the center (for Back and Forward).

Tip: Begin your swipe within the screen. If your finger starts from off the screen, as you know from Chapter 1, you'll open the Charms bar or the app switcher.

- **Mouse:** Click the ⊖ or ⊕ button.
- **Keyboard:** Press Alt+← or Alt+→.

Flip Ahead

Here's a smart new IE feature that ought to be everywhere.

Often, an article you're reading online is continued on another Web page; you're supposed to select a Next Page button at the bottom of the screen. (And why divide a story up into "pages" in a medium that can scroll forever, like a computer screen? So that the publisher can sell different ads on each page.)

In Windows 8, a new feature called Flip Ahead saves you from having to hunt around for the Next Page button. You just swipe, right to left—or click the ➔ button—and, magically, IE brings the next page onto the screen. It uses crowdsourcing to figure out what link you're likely to want next; that is, it tracks what link was chosen next by the thousands of people who came before you.

So that you won't be taken aback, Microsoft requires that you *turn on* the Flip Ahead feature, as shown in Figure 4-11.

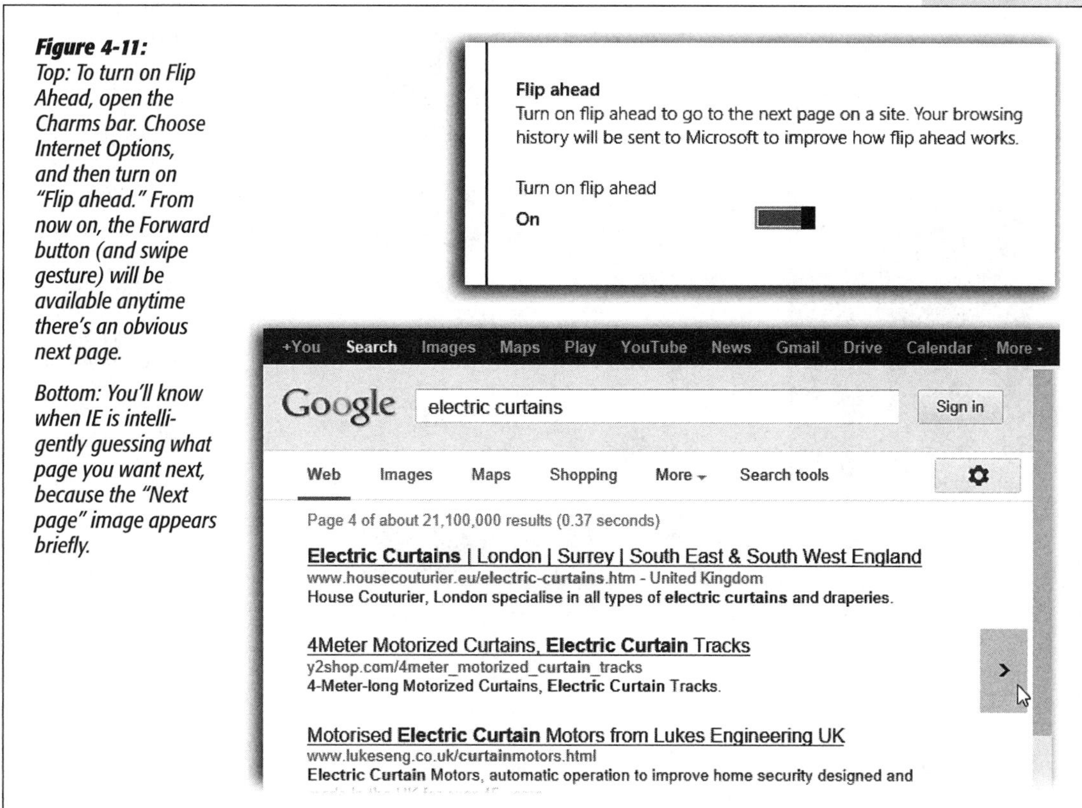

Figure 4-11: *Top: To turn on Flip Ahead, open the Charms bar. Choose Internet Options, and then turn on "Flip ahead." From now on, the Forward button (and swipe gesture) will be available anytime there's an obvious next page.*

Bottom: You'll know when IE is intelligently guessing what page you want next, because the "Next page" image appears briefly.

Now, Flip Ahead isn't always available. (You'll know if you can use it, because the ⊕ button is available even when you haven't backtracked from a page.) It's almost always available when you're reading a multipage article. You can also use it when you've performed a search (using Bing or Google, for example); it takes you to the next page of search results.

It *doesn't* work when IE can't possibly guess where you want to go next—for example, when you pull up the *nytimes.com* home page, filled with hundreds of article headlines.

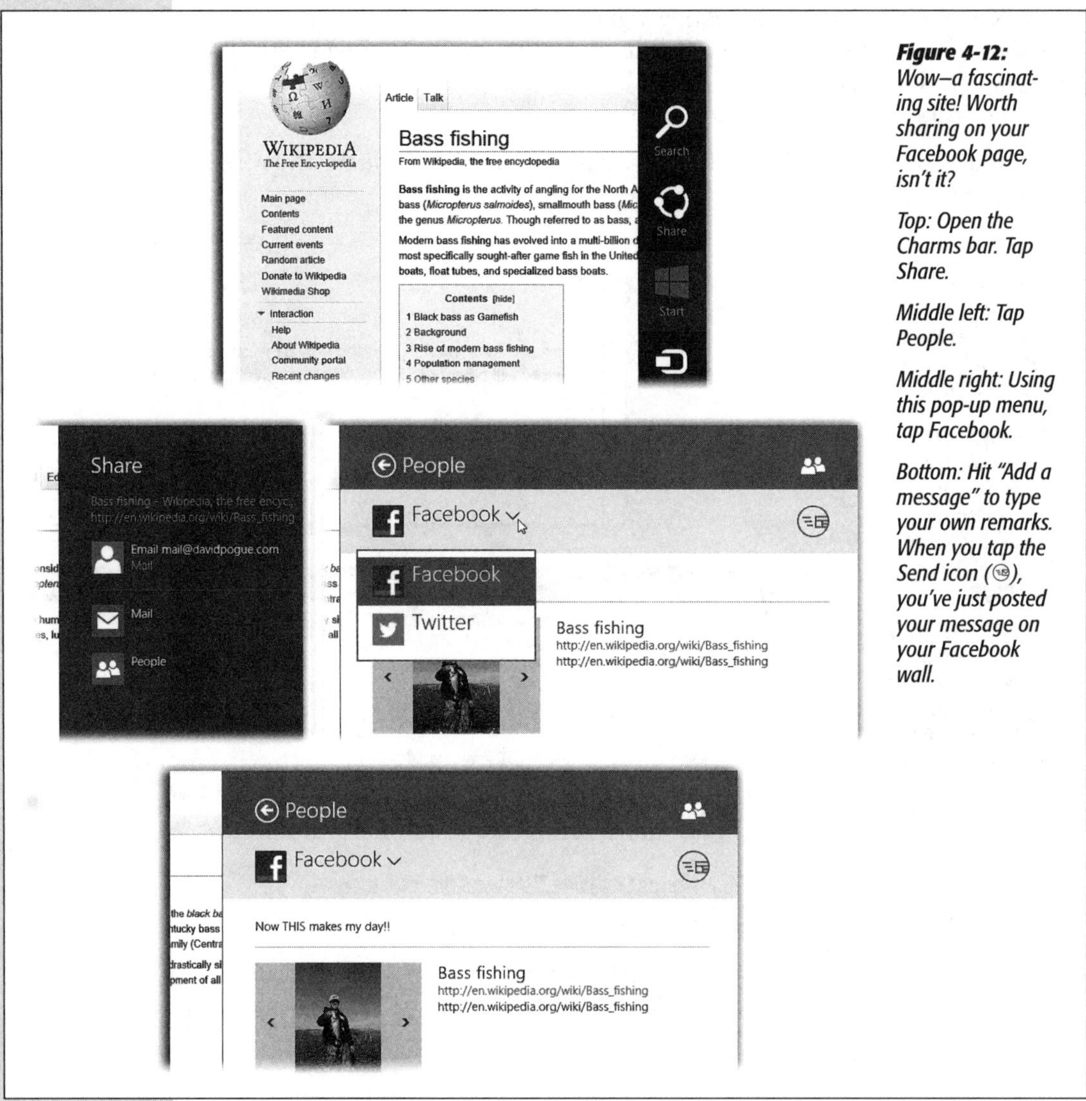

Figure 4-12: *Wow—a fascinating site! Worth sharing on your Facebook page, isn't it?*

Top: Open the Charms bar. Tap Share.

Middle left: Tap People.

Middle right: Using this pop-up menu, tap Facebook.

Bottom: Hit "Add a message" to type your own remarks. When you tap the Send icon (⊜), you've just posted your message on your Facebook wall.

Sharing

When you're on an especially useful page, you can pass it along to other interested parties.

The technique begins, of course, with a visit to the Share button. Open the Charms bar (page 24); select Share.

Now you're offered choices like these:

- **Mail.** Windows prepares for you an outgoing email message containing a link to the page you're sharing, and even a little preview of what's on it. Your job is to address the message, add a little comment ("Hey, Mom—here is written proof that the Great Wall of China is *not* visible from the moon"), and then hit Send.
- **People.** This link offers a new panel that lets you broadcast your discovery on your Facebook wall or Twitter feed; see Figure 4-12.

You may have other options on the Share panel, too, depending on what apps you've installed.

Bookmarks (Favorites)–and Pinning to the Start Page

In TileWorld, there are three ways to identify Web sites you might want to visit again without having to remember and type their URLs. You can create traditional bookmarks (what Microsoft calls favorites); you can create a tile on the Start screen for a certain site; or you can rely on IE's own memory to autocomplete an address you start typing. Here's the drill.

Favorites (Bookmarks)

Here's how you create a favorite.

When you find a Web page you might like to visit again, open the App bar (page 27) and tap the Pin button (⊙). As you can see in Figure 4-13, "Add to favorites" is one of the choices here. Select it.

The next time you highlight the address bar, you'll see a new tile, all the way at the far-right end, that represents the favorite you just designated (Figure 4-12). It bears the name of the site—and, often, an icon of that site's logo.

Here's how you use favorites:

- **Open a favorite page** by tapping or clicking its tile.
- **Open a favorite into a new tab** by choosing "Open in new tab" from its shortcut menu. (To see the shortcut menu, hold your finger down on the tile for a couple of seconds. Or right-click the tile, if you have a mouse.)
- **Delete a favorite** by choosing Remove from its shortcut menu.

- **Lower expectations for favorites.** In TileWorld, you can't rearrange your favorites, rename them, or put them into folders.

Note: The TileWorld and desktop versions of IE use the same favorites. If you add one in TileWorld, it will also show up in the desktop version, and vice versa.

But although you can rearrange, rename, and enfolder favorites in the desktop version, those changes don't show up in TileWorld. Any bookmark you put into a favorites folder in the desktop version shows up in TileWorld as a "loose" icon, nestled among all the others.

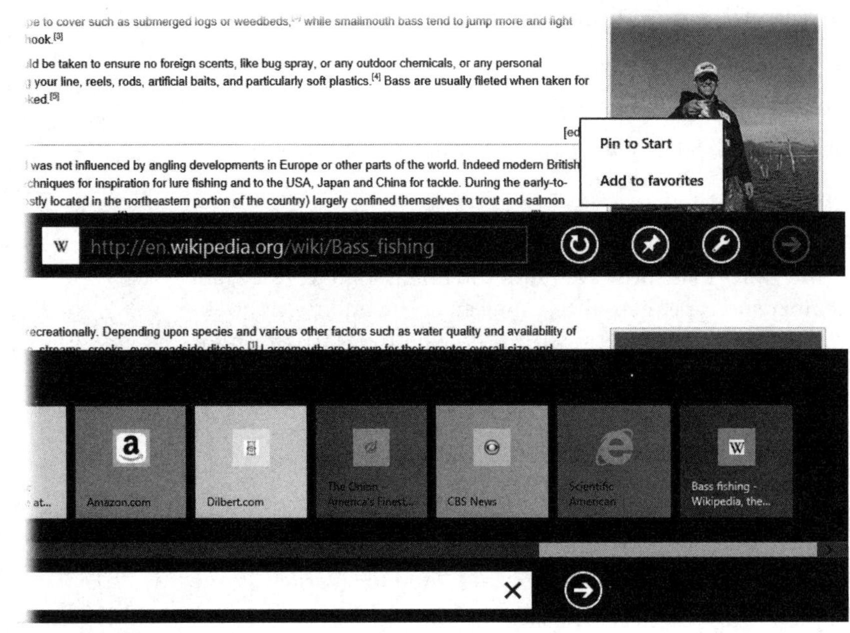

Figure 4-13: *Top: To designate the page you're on as a bookmark, tap "Add to favorites."*

Bottom: Whenever you open the address bar, this row of tiles appears just above it. At the right end, tiles for your favorites appear. (You might have to scroll to the right to find them.)

Pin to Start

If you begin your day with a visit to a few very important sites, you might want to install their tiles on your Start screen. That way, you can jump directly to them without having to open IE first.

Open the page you want to pin. Open the App bar (page 27) and choose Pin (⊘). From the shortcut menu, choose Pin to Start. Rename the tile if you like (Figure 4-14), and then select Pin to Start.

Next time you check out your Start screen, you'll see a tile for your newly pinned Web site. Like all new tiles, it appears at the far-right end of the screen, ready to open with a single tap or click. (See Chapter 2 for details on renaming, moving, and deleting Start screen tiles.)

The History list

Behind the scenes, all Web browsers keep track of the Web sites you've visited in the past week or so, usually organized into subfolders like Earlier Today and Yesterday. It's a great feature when you can't recall the address for a Web site you visited recently—or when you remember it had a long, complicated address.

In TileWorld, there's no History list. There is, however, autocomplete *based* on your history. When you start typing into the address bar, the names and icons of recently visited sites appear just above what you're typing, based on what you've typed so far. They represent your history—it's just that you can't see *when* you visited those sites, and if you don't remember the name of a site, there's no way to view a list of all your recent travels.

Tip: The desktop version of IE still has the traditional History list–so if you're desperate, you can always return to the desktop, open IE, and open its History list. Fortunately, that list keeps track of all sites you've visited in either version of IE.

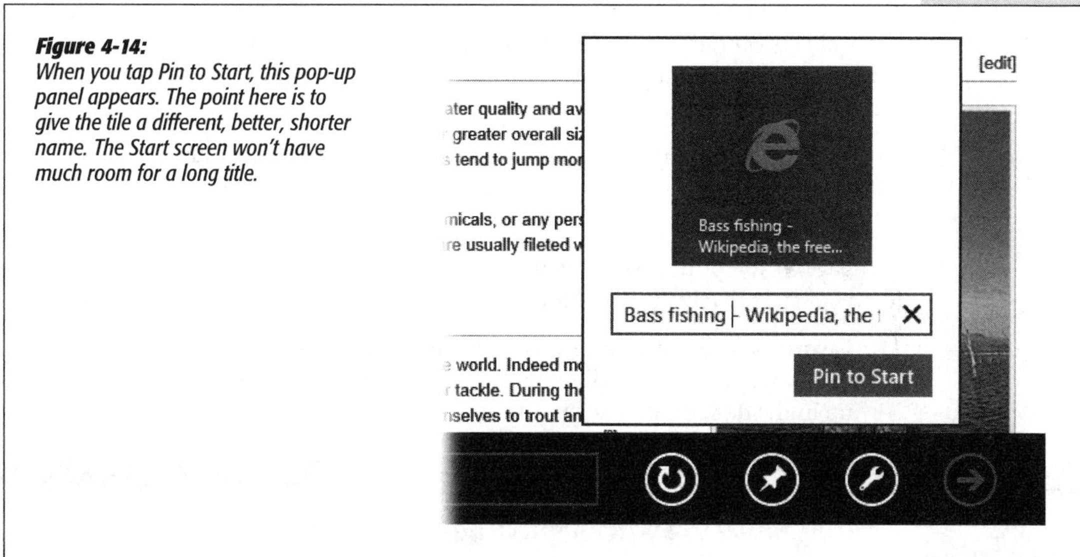

***Figure 4-14:** When you tap Pin to Start, this pop-up panel appears. The point here is to give the tile a different, better, shorter name. The Start screen won't have much room for a long title.*

Saving Graphics

If you find a picture online that you wish you could keep forever, you have two choices. You could stare at it until you've memorized it, or you could save it.

To do that, just touch the image, or hold down the mouse button on it, for about a second. A shortcut menu appears, offering two options: Copy and "Save to picture library."

If you choose Copy, then you nab that graphic and can now paste it into another program. If you choose "Save to picture library," your computer thoughtfully deposits a copy of the image in your Pictures library (page 210).

Searching the Web

The Web is a big place. Heck, there are probably *dozens* of Web sites by now.

So it should come as no surprise that *searching* the Web is an important function of a Web browser. In TileWorld's IE, the search box is exactly where it is in every other app: in the Charms bar.

To search, then, open the Charms bar (page 24) and tap Search.

Tip: If you have a keyboard, pressing ⊞+Q is a faster way to jump directly into the search box.

Type what you're looking for into the search box. Enjoy the suggestions IE proposes to save you typing time. And if you don't see what you're looking for there, then tap the orange ⌕ —or press Enter—to begin the search.

The main part of your screen, on the left, fills with Bing search results.

How the Two IEs are Connected

As you now know, Windows 8 includes two versions of Internet Explorer: the TileWorld version (address bar at the bottom) and the desktop version (address bar at the top). The TileWorld version is greatly simplified, with far fewer features and a design that favors touchscreens.

They're not two *completely* different Web browsers, however. They're connected in some sneaky ways:

- **Home page.** The starting page you set in one browser also becomes your start page in the other, even if you specify a set of home-page *tabs.* (You can set *up* your startup page/pages only at the desktop, however, as described in Chapter 15.)
- **Favorites, frequent sites, history, and typed addresses.** All of this is shared between the browsers, too. If you designate *nytimes.com* as a favorite in TileWorld, it shows up in the desktop IE as a favorite, too.

POWER USERS' CLINIC

Switching to Google

As you'd probably guess, Internet Explorer relies on Microsoft's own search site, Bing.com, instead of the world's most popular one–Google.

In the desktop version of IE, you can switch things up so that it uses Google instead–the Justice Department saw to that. But in TileWorld, the Search box always uses Bing.

If you prefer to search with Google, here are your options:

Download the Google app. Google has written a TileWorld app. Once it's on your Start screen, a Google search is just a click or tap away.

Pin Google to your Start screen. In other words, navigate to Google.com in IE, then pin it to your Start screen as a tile, just as described on page 113.

Tip: In fact, your favorites, frequent sites, history, and typed addresses are synced across all your Windows 8 computers—at least all the ones you sign into using your Microsoft account (page 726). That's pretty handy; sit down at any Windows 8 computer in the world, and boom—your Web bookmarks are there.

- **Choice of search page.** Your choice of search site (Bing, Google, or Yahoo) is also shared between the two Internet Explorer faces. You must make this choice at the desktop, however, as described on page 484.

The two versions of the browser are also *disconnected* in some interesting ways:

- **History list.** The TileWorld version of IE keeps track of Web sites you've visited—for the purpose of autocompleting what you type, for example, and determining what to put into your Frequent Sites list—but you can't see a list of them.
- **RSS feeds.** The desktop version of IE lets you subscribe to *RSS feeds*, which are like news streams published by Web sites that get updated frequently. There's no way to see them in the TileWorld IE.
- **Flash and plug-ins.** In TileWorld, you can't install plug-ins into IE (you still can in the desktop version).

  Unfortunately, that means that most Flash video Web sites don't play in TileWorld. Microsoft permits Flash videos and animations to work only on a specified list of Web sites—big-name ones, usually—whose Flash behavior Microsoft has approved in advance. (Flash still works fine on all sites in the desktop version of IE, although you have to install it yourself at *adobe.com*.)

Mail

TileWorld comes with its own email program—called Mail. In fact, it's the *only* email program that comes with Windows 8.

Mail is fairly stripped down. At least in its first version, it doesn't offer a unified Inbox for multiple accounts, multiple windows, or any way to flag messages for later. If you want something fancier, you'll have to download or buy it yourself. (Of course, then you'll miss out on some of Mail's nice integration with the rest of Windows 8.)

But it's certainly easy to use, it's beautiful, and especially if you have a touchscreen, it offers a fast, fluid way to work.

Before you read another syllable, you need to confront one big piece of what could be bad news: Mail requires an *IMAP account.* It doesn't work with *POP accounts,* which means you may not be able to use Mail at all. Read on.

The POP-Account Problem

There are three kinds of email accounts:

- **Web-based mail.** Some email accounts are designed to be accessed on a Web site, like the free accounts offered by Gmail, Hotmail, or Outlook.com.

- **IMAP accounts** (Internet message access protocol) are the latest type, and they're surging in popularity. IMAP servers keep all your mail online, rather than storing it solely on your computer; as a result, you can access the same mail from any computer (or phone), and you'll always see the same lists of mail. IMAP servers remember which messages you've read and sent, and they even keep track of how you've filed messages into mail folders. (Those free Yahoo email accounts are IMAP accounts, and so are Apple's iCloud accounts and corporate Exchange accounts. Gmail and Outlook.com accounts can be IMAP, too.)

  Windows 8 Mail works fine with IMAP accounts.

Note: Gmail no longer works with Exchange accounts (you'd know if you had one). There is, however, a workaround that involves signing up for a free Outlook.com account. Instructions are here: *http://j.mp/V8hF9s*.)

- **POP accounts** are the oldest, most compatible, and most common type on the Internet. (POP stands for Post Office Protocol, but this won't be on the test.) The big difference: A POP server transfers incoming mail to your computer before you read it. Once it's on your computer, it's no longer on the Internet. (If you try

WORKAROUND WORKSHOP

How to Make Windows 8 Mail Work with POP Accounts

You've probably read by now that Mail can't access POP email accounts. And that is true.

There are, however, some workarounds. You can set up a free Web-based service like Outlook.com or Gmail to fetch your POP account's messages—and then use Windows 8 Mail to fetch it from there. Sounds complicated, maybe, but once it's set up, it's automatic and effortless.

Suppose you decide to use Outlook.com for this purpose. (Outlook.com is Microsoft's new competitor to Gmail. It's a very nice, free, uncluttered, Web-based email system that will eventually replace Hotmail.) Here's how to set things up.

First, sign up for a free account at Outlook.com. From the Settings menu (upper-right corner of the screen), choose "More mail settings."

On the Option screen, under Managing Your Account, choose "Sending/receiving email from other accounts." On the next screen, choose "Add an email account."

Enter your POP account's address and password, and then choose "Advanced settings."

On the next screen, fill in your POP server address, port number, SSL setting, and other settings for your email account. (If you don't know these, ask your email provider, or search for the details using Google. For example, search for Comcast POP email settings.)

Click Next. On the next screen, you're asked where you want mail from your POP account to go (among your Outlook.com folders). Usually, the Inbox is fine. Click Save.

Microsoft sends a confirmation message to your POP account; click the confirmation link. That's it: Now Outlook.com automatically receives incoming mail from your POP account, and you can also send messages from your POP account's address, even while using Outlook.com.

The next step is to add your Outlook.com account to Windows 8 Mail, as described on these pages—and presto! Mail is now sending and receiving mail from a POP account, using Outlook.com as an invisible background helper.

to check your email on your phone, you won't see whatever new messages were downloaded by your computer back at home since you last checked.)

Are you sitting down? Windows 8 Mail doesn't work with POP accounts.

How do you know if yours is a POP account? You'll have to ask the company that provides it to you. Internet providers like Time Warner and Comcast usually provide email addresses as POP accounts.

Now, if you do have a POP account and don't want to ditch it, you have some options. You can use a different email program, of course, although what's nice about Mail is that it's integrated nicely into several Windows features (like notifications).

Some POP accounts can be converted *into* IMAP accounts, the type Windows 8 recognizes; ask your email provider. (There may be a fee.) And most Web-based email systems, like Gmail and Outlook.com, can also supply your mail as an IMAP account.

Finally, you can use a Web-based IMAP account (like Gmail or Outlook.com) as an intermediary that connects your POP account to Windows 8 Mail; see the sidebar box on the facing page for instructions.

Set Up Your Account

All right, then. You've accepted that you can't use Mail with a POP account unless you do some work-arounding. You're ready to set up your IMAP or Exchange account. Here's how to proceed:

1. **Bring up the "Add an account" screen.**

   To get there, see Figure 4-15.

2. **Specify the kind of account you want to add.**

   You're supposed to choose *Hotmail* if you have a Hotmail, Live.com, or MSN email account; *Outlook* if you have an Exchange, Office 365, or Outlook.com account; *Google* if you have a Gmail account; *Yahoo* or *AOL* if you have one of those free accounts; or *Other Account* if you have any other kind of IMAP mail account.

3. **Enter your email address and password.**

   That's generally all Windows needs to set up your account for the big-name email services. (For Other Account, you also have to select "Show more details" and specify your IMAP server address, SSL settings, authentication settings, and ports. This is all information you can get from whatever company provides your email service.)

4. **Hit Connect.**

   If your settings were all correct, you get teleported directly into that account's Inbox, ready to start processing email.

   If you've set up more than one account, their names appear in the lower-left corner of the screen so that you can jump among them. The big number at the right end of each account's name tells you how many new messages are waiting in that account.

If you open the Charms bar and visit Settings→Accounts, you'll see its name appear, a testimony to your technological account-setting-up prowess.

Tip: If you have multiple email accounts, you can switch among them by tapping their buttons at the lower-left corner of the Mail screen. But you can also pin one account's Inbox—or any other mail folder—to your Start screen, for instant access and step-saving. For example, if you have a folder called Stuff to Do, or a folder called Reply to These, you might want them pinned on your Start screen.

To make this happen, tap the folder you want to pin. Then open the App bar (swipe up from the bottom of the screen, or press ⊞+Z), and choose Pin to Start. A pop-up panel offers you the chance to change the folder's name; do that, or not, and then hit Pin to Start. You'll find the pinned folder at the far-right end of your Start screen (you may have to scroll a bit).

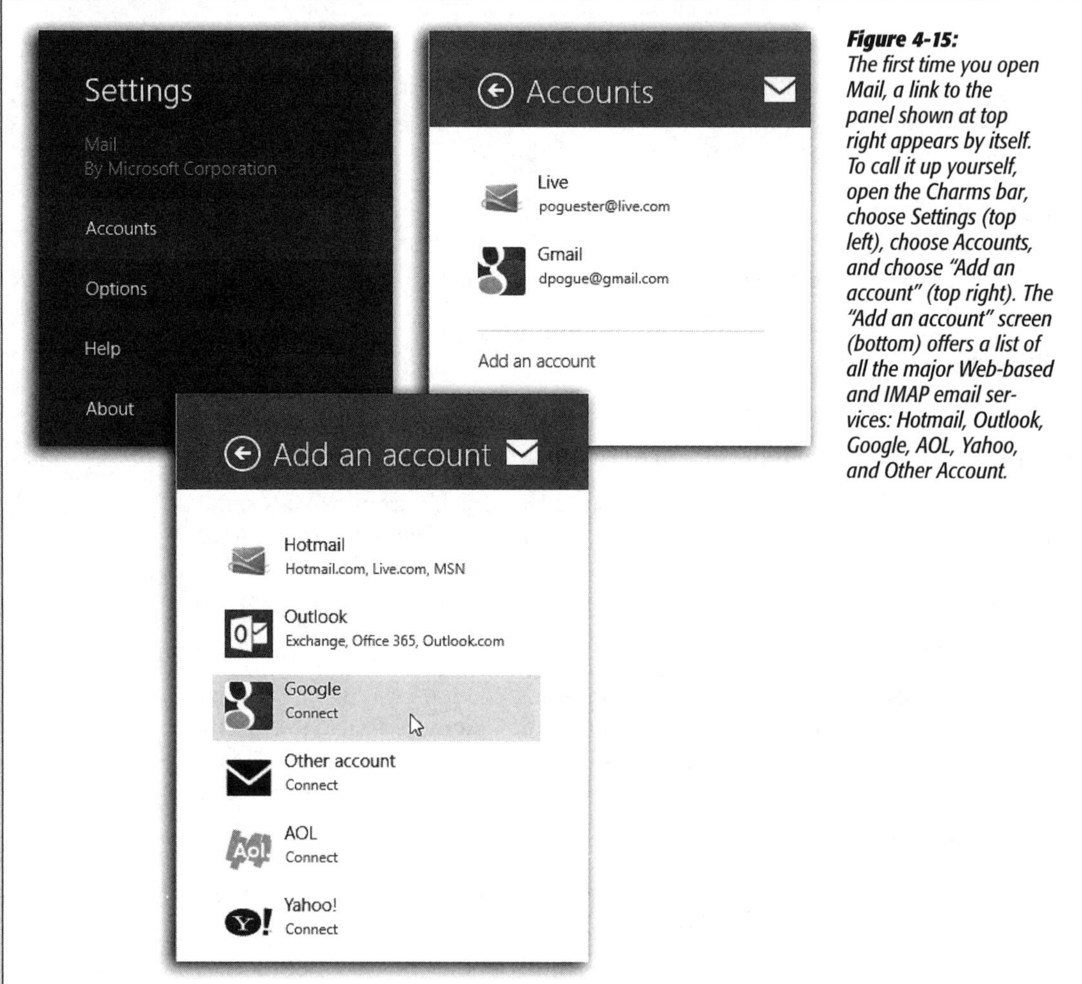

Figure 4-15: *The first time you open Mail, a link to the panel shown at top right appears by itself. To call it up yourself, open the Charms bar, choose Settings (top left), choose Accounts, and choose "Add an account" (top right). The "Add an account" screen (bottom) offers a list of all the major Web-based and IMAP email services: Hotmail, Outlook, Google, AOL, Yahoo, and Other Account.*

Editing or Deleting an Account

Each email account you set up offers some useful options that are worth a visit. To set up an account, follow the steps in Figure 4-16.

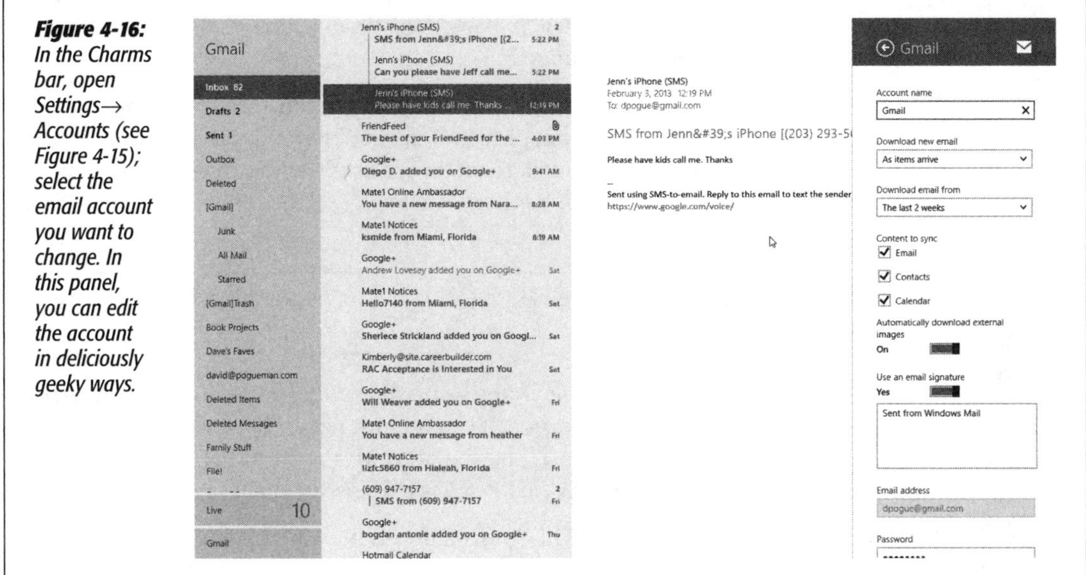

Figure 4-16: *In the Charms bar, open Settings→Accounts (see Figure 4-15); select the email account you want to change. In this panel, you can edit the account in deliciously geeky ways.*

Here are some of the options you find here:

- **Account name.** It doesn't have to say "Yahoo" or "Gmail" or whatever; you can change it to "Chris's Work Mail," "Robin's Mail-O-Rama," or whatever floats your boat.
- **Your name.** Whatever name you type here is what will show up in other people's Inboxes when you write to them.
- **Download new mail.** How often do you want Mail to check for new messages? Usually, "As items arrive" is what you want. Some account types offer only "Every 15 minutes," "Every 30 minutes," and so on.

  (If you choose Manual, Mail never checks unless you tap the Check Mail button.)
- **Content to sync.** Some services, like Google and corporate Exchange servers, offer more than email; those account types also maintain online calendars and address books. Here, turn on the checkboxes of the data types you want your computer to display: Email, Contacts, and/or Calendar.

Note: Of course, Mail displays only email. If you turn on Contacts and Calendar for one of your accounts, your lists of names and appointments show up elsewhere in TileWorld—namely, in the People and Calendar apps.

- **Automatically download external images.** Spammers, the vile undercrust of low-life society, have a famous trick. When they send you email that includes a picture, they don't actually paste the picture into the message. Instead, they include a "bug"—a piece of code that instructs your email program to *fetch* the missing graphic from the Internet. Why? Because that gives the spammer the ability to track who has actually opened the junk mail, making their email addresses much more valuable for reselling to other spammers.

  That's a long explanation for a simple feature: If you turn this option off, then Mail does not fetch "bug" image files at all. You're not flagged as a sucker by the spammers. You'll see empty squares in the email where the images ought to be. The actual pictures don't appear until you manually select the "Download all images in this message" link.

Note: Graphics sent by normal people and legitimate companies are generally pasted right into the email, so they'll still show up just fine.

- **Use an email signature.** A *signature* is a bit of text that gets stamped at the bottom of your outgoing email messages. It can be your name, a postal address, or a pithy quote. Here's where you enter the signature you want to use for outgoing messages from this account. (Also choose Yes for "Use an email signature," of course.)
- **Email address, password.** This information is here in case you want to change it.
- **Show email notifications for this account.** As described on page 46, Windows' *notifications* are pieces of message "toast" that pop quietly into the upper-right corner of the screen to get your attention. Here's where you specify whether or not messages from this account should trigger that kind of notification.
- **Remove account.** Use this button if you decide to get rid of this email account.

Downloading Mail

If your email account offers "As they arrive" mail checking, as described above, then new messages show up on your computer as they arrive, around the clock.

If you have any other kind of account, or if you didn't turn that option on, then Mail checks for new messages automatically on a schedule—every 15, 30, or 60 minutes. It also checks for new messages each time you open the Mail program.

Tip: You can also force Mail to check for new messages and send waiting ones on command. Open the App bar (swipe up from the bottom of the screen), and choose the Sync icon (⊜). Or, if you have a keyboard, press F5.

When new mail arrives, you'll know it at a glance. Mail can notify you with a little alert box (page 46), complete with a little chime, even when you're working in another app. And, of course, the Mail tile on the Start screen updates itself to show you the latest messages (a rotating display of their senders/subjects/first lines). That tile also sprouts a bold number in the corner that tells you how many new messages are waiting.

A Mail Tour

The Mail screen has three columns, as shown in Figure 4-17. At the lower left: the names of your other accounts. (There's no unified Inbox in Mail for the messages from multiple accounts.)

Tip: If you have a keyboard, you can hide or show the folder column by pressing Ctrl+Shift+F, or the Accounts pane by pressing Ctrl+Shift+A. Gets you a little extra reading space.

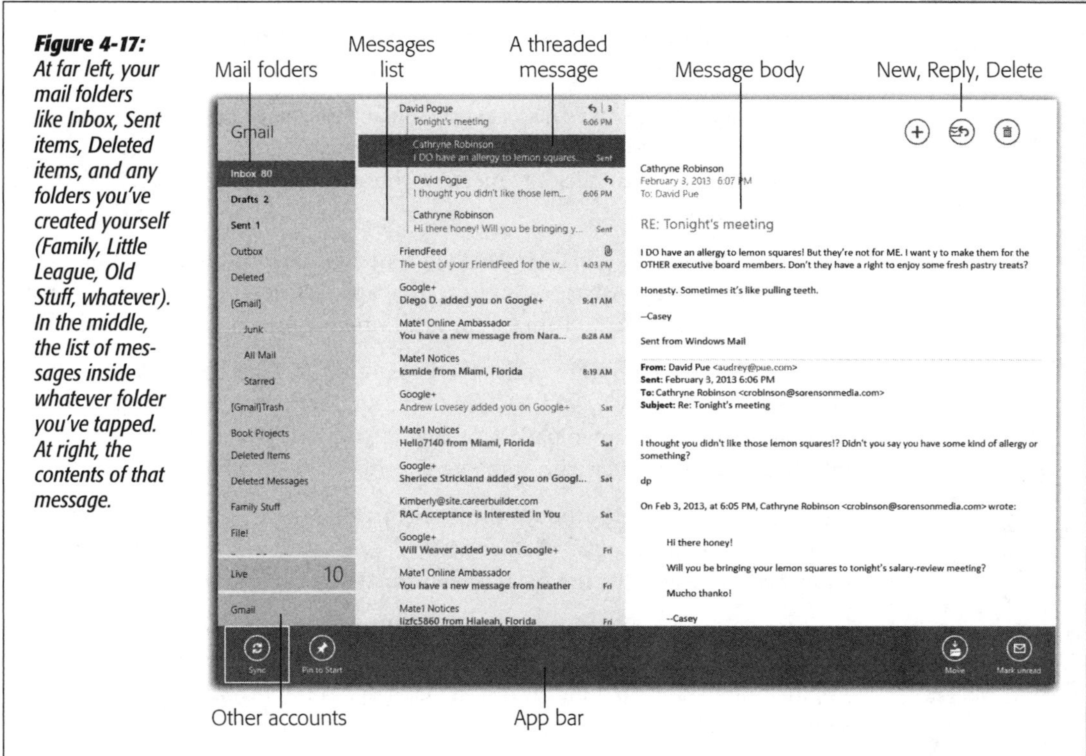

Figure 4-17: *At far left, your mail folders like Inbox, Sent items, Deleted items, and any folders you've created yourself (Family, Little League, Old Stuff, whatever). In the middle, the list of messages inside whatever folder you've tapped. At right, the contents of that message.*

To see all the new messages in the current account, tap Inbox; the new messages appear with bold subject lines.

Tip: Mail now offers message threading, in which back-and-forths on a particular subject appear clumped together in the list. It's a feature you can turn off, if you find it confusing. (In the Charms bar, select Settings, then Options; there's the "Group messages by conversation" on/off switch.

You can flick your finger to scroll the message list, if it's long. Tap a message to read it in all its formatted glory.

Tip: In the Message pane, Mail shows you the name of the sender ("Casey Robin"). To see the email address of whoever sent the message, hold your finger down on the name, or point the mouse to it without clicking. A pop-up bubble shows you the underlying email address.

What to Do with a Message

Once you've read a message, you can respond to it, delete it, file it, and so on. Here's the drill:

- **Read it.** The type size in email messages can be pretty small. Fortunately, you have some great enlargement tricks at your disposal. For example, on a touchscreen, you can spread two fingers to enlarge the entire email message.

- **Next message.** Once you've had a good look at a message and processed it to your satisfaction, you can move on to the next (or previous) message in the list. *Touchscreen or mouse:* Tap or click the message you want in the message list. *Keyboard:* Press the ↑ or ↓ keys.

- **Open an attachment.** You'll know when somebody has attached a file to a message you've received. A paper-clip icon (🔘) appears next to the message's name in the message list, and an icon for the attachment appears at the top of the body.

  If a Download link appears under the icon, select it; Mail clearly hasn't actually downloaded the file yet, and has only indicated its presence. (That's a security feature—you should download files that you know are safe, so you won't wind up infecting your computer with some nasty virus.)

  Once that's done, tapping the attachment icon offers three choices: Open (meaning "open with the usual app"); "Open with" ("open with a different program—I'll choose"), and Save ("let me file this file somewhere on my computer").

- **Reply to it.** To answer a message, select the Reply/Forward icon (↩) at the top of the message. Using the shortcut menu, you can choose Reply. If the message was originally addressed to multiple recipients, "Reply all" sends your reply to everyone simultaneously.

Tip: If you have a keyboard, you can save a couple of steps by pressing Ctrl+R for Reply, or Ctrl+Shift+R for Reply All.

  A new message window opens, already addressed. As a courtesy to your correspondents, Mail places the original message at the bottom of the window. At this point, you can add or delete recipients, edit the subject line or the original message, and so on. When you're finished, tap the Send icon (✉) or press Ctrl+Enter.

- **Forward it.** Instead of replying to the person who sent you a message, you may sometimes want to pass the note on to a third person. To do so, select the Reply/Forward icon (↩) at the top of the message, and this time, choose Forward in the shortcut menu. (Or just press Ctrl+F.) A new message opens, looking a lot like the one that appears when you reply; you're expected to start by filling in the To box.

You may wish to precede the original message with a comment of your own, like, "Frank: I thought you'd be interested in this joke about your mom."

- **Delete it.** Tap the Trash icon (🗑) at the top of the message. (There's no confirmation screen; on the other hand, you can recover the message from the "Deleted items" folder if you change your mind.)
- **File it.** Some mail accounts let you create filing folders to help manage your messages. Once you've opened a message that's worth keeping, you can move it into one of those folders.

  To do that, open the App bar (swipe upward from the bottom edge of the screen, or right-click, or press ⊞+Z). See the Move icon? Tap or click it; Mail dims everything on the screen except the folder list. Choose the one you want.

Tip: The keyboard shortcut for all of that is Ctrl+M. For move, get it?

- **Mark as unread.** In the Inbox, a bold subject line marks any message you haven't yet read. Once you've opened the message, the boldness goes away. By opening the App bar and then choosing Mark as Unread (✉), you make the boldface *reappear*. It's a great way to flag a message for later, to call it to your own attention. The boldface can mean not so much "unread" as "un–dealt with."

  (This button changes to say "Mark as read" if you want to go the *other* way—to flag an unread message, or a bunch of them, as read; see below.)

Tip: Got a keyboard? Press Ctrl+U for "Mark as unread," Ctrl+Q for "Mark as read."

Filing or Deleting Batches of Messages

You can also file or delete a bunch of messages at once. Here's how to select them first, so that all remain highlighted:

- **Touchscreen:** Swipe horizontally across each message in the message list.
- **Mouse:** Right-click each message.

Figure 4-18: *When you've selected multiple messages, the App bar appears automatically. When you've selected all the messages in question, you can delete them all–use the Trash icon (🗑) at the top right–or use the Move or "Mark as read" buttons on the App bar.*

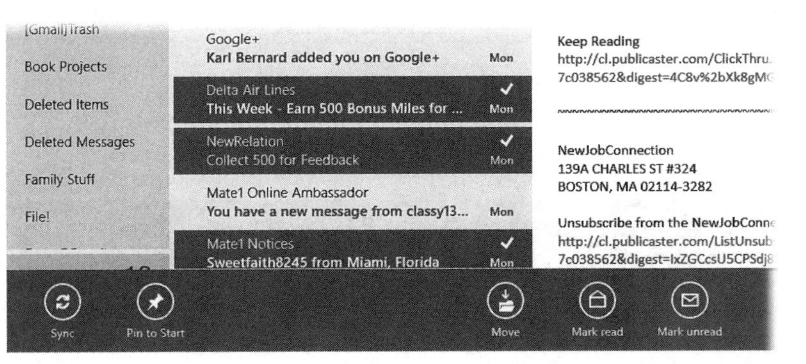

- **Keyboard:** Walk down the list using the arrow keys; press Ctrl+Enter to add the checkmark to the currently highlighted message.

Each message turns dark and sprouts a checkmark to indicate that you've snagged it. You can tap as many messages as you like, scrolling as necessary. See Figure 4-18.

Searching

Praise be—there's a search box in Mail. You get to it the way you get to Search in any app: by opening the Charms bar and choosing Search.

As you type into the search box, Mail hides all but the matching messages in the current mail folder; tap any one of the results to open it. (The title "Search results for:" appears above the message list so you don't freak out and think that all your other messages are gone forever.)

Select any message in the list to read it.

When you're finished, tap the X above the message list. Your full list is restored, and the Search adventure is complete.

Writing Messages

To compose a new piece of outgoing mail, use the + button icon in the top-right corner. A blank new outgoing message appears (see Figure 4-19).

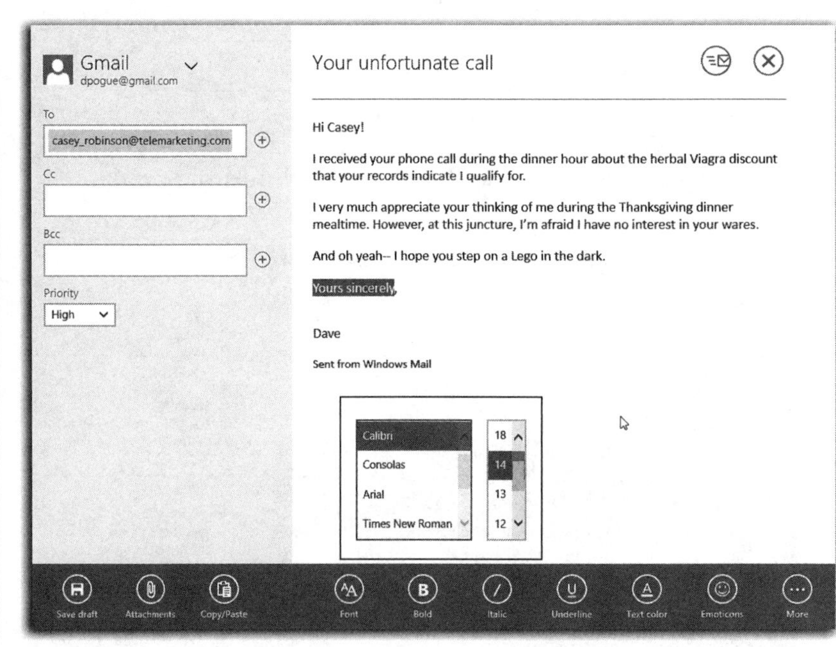

Figure 4-19: *The controls you'd usually expect to find in an email program—like bold, italic, and font controls—are lurking in the App bar. Swipe up, or right-click, or press ⊞+Z, to see it. Here you've just selected the Font button to get this pop-up control.*

Here's how you go about writing a message:

1. **Change the email account you're using, if you like.**

   If you have more than one email account, you can tap the ⌄ next to the account name at the upper-left to open up a list of your accounts. Tap the one you want to use for sending this message.

2. **In the To field, type the recipient's email address—or grab it from Contacts.**

   Often, you won't have to type much more than the first couple of letters of the name or email address. As you type, Mail displays all matching names and addresses so you can choose one from the list instead of typing.

   Alternatively, tap the ⊕ button to open your People app; find the person you want, either by scrolling or by using the Search button in the Charms bar. Then hit the Add button (at the bottom of the People screen).

   You can add as many addressees as you like; just repeat the procedure.

3. **To send a copy to other recipients, enter the address(es) in the "Cc:" or "Bcc:" fields.**

   Cc stands for *carbon copy*. Getting an email message where your name is in the Cc line implies: "I sent you a copy because I thought you'd want to know about this correspondence, but I'm not expecting you to reply."

   If you choose "Show more," the screen expands to reveal a new line beneath the "To:" line: "Bcc:", which stands for *blind* carbon copy (you can see it in Figure 4-19). It's a copy that goes to a third party secretly—the primary addressee never knows who else received it. For example, if you send your coworker a message that says, "Chris, it bothers me that you've been cheating the customers," you could Bcc your supervisor to clue her in without getting into trouble with Chris.

   Each of these lines behaves exactly like the "To:" line. You fill each one up with email addresses in the same way.

Tip: Also hiding in the "Show more" panel: a pop-up menu for Priority. It lets you specify how important your message is, on a three-tiered scale.

The good part about this system is that it lets your recipient see that an email you've sent is, for example, urgent. The bad part is that not every email program displays the priority of email—and even if your recipient's email program *does* display your message's priority, there's no guarantee that it'll make him respond any faster.

---

4. **Type the topic of the message in the "Subject:" field.**

   It's courteous to put some thought into the subject line. (Use "Change in plans for next week," for instance, instead of "Yo.") Leaving it blank only annoys your recipient. On the other hand, don't put the *entire* message into the subject line, either.

5. **Select "Add a message," and then type your message in the message pane.**

   All the usual keyboard tricks apply (Chapter 3). Don't forget that you can use Copy and Paste, within Mail or from other programs. Both text and graphics can appear in your message.

6. **Attach a file, if you like.**

   Open the App bar (swipe up from the bottom edge of the screen, or right-click, or press ⊞+Z). Choose the Attachments icon (Ⓘ) to open the file chooser described on page 77.

   Tap the file you want to send—or several (they all remain selected, with checkmarks)—and then choose Attach. You return to your message in progress, with the files neatly inserted as icons.

7. **Format the text, if you like.**

   You can apply bold, italic, underlining, or colors to Mail text you've typed. You can change the typeface, add smileys, or insert numbered or bulleted lists.

   The trick is to select the text first (page 86). The App bar appears, with icons for Font, Bold, Italic, Underline, Text color, Emoticons, and More (which produces a shortcut menu offering "Bulleted list" and "Numbered list"). Some have an instantaneous effect on your text; the Font and Text color buttons open palettes that let you choose a font or a color.

   (The Emoticons icon changes the entire left side of the screen into a huge gallery of smiley faces, hearts, facial features, heads, and other miniature graphics, ready for insertion into your message.)

8. **To send the message, hit Send (Ⓢ), or press Ctrl+Enter. Or hit Cancel (⊗) to back out of it.**

   If you tap ⊗, Mail wants to know if you want to save the unsent message—maybe because you want to finish it up later. If you tap "Save draft," then the message lands in your Drafts folder. Later, you can open the Drafts folder, tap the aborted message, finish it up, and send it.

   If you choose "Delete draft" instead, the message is either stuffed into the Deleted Items folder—or deleted forever, depending on the account type.

Maps

Windows never had a built-in Maps app before. But now that Windows is a tablet operating system, it's more or less a must-have.

Maps (which is powered by Bing, which is powered by Nokia Maps, which is powered by NAVTEQ) lets you type in any address or point of interest in the United States or many other countries and see it plotted on a map, with turn-by-turn driving directions, just like a $300 windshield GPS unit. It also gives you a live national Yellow Pages business directory and real-time traffic-jam alerts, if you have an Internet connection. You have a choice of a street-map diagram or actual aerial photos, taken by satellite.

Meet Maps

When you open the Maps app, you see—a map.

Note: You also see a question: Maps asks you if it's allowed to use your current location, so that it can show you where you are on the map. The only reason to choose Block is if you think it's creepy that Maps, and by extension Microsoft, knows where you are.

If Maps has an Internet connection and can figure out where you are, it displays a diamond to represent your current location. You can scroll in any direction. You can also zoom in or out, using any of the usual techniques (two-finger pinch or spread; turn the mouse's scroll wheel while pressing Ctrl). You can also double-tap or double-click to zoom into a particular spot.

At any time, you can open the App bar to open a panel of options. You'll be needing the App bar to make Maps perform its best stunts, so make sure you know how to open it:

- **Touchscreen:** Swipe inward from the top or bottom edge of the screen.
- **Mouse:** Right-click any blank spot in the window.
- **Keyboard:** Press ⊞+Z.

So what's on the App bar? These buttons:

- **Show Traffic.** How's this for a cool feature? Free, real-time traffic reporting—the same information you'd have to pay Sirius XM Satellite Radio $10 a month for. Just use the "Show traffic" button (Ⓑ). Now color-coded lines appear on the roadways, showing you the current traffic speed. Green for good traffic flow, yellow for slower traffic, orange for even slower traffic, and red for true traffic jams, for your stressing pleasure.

  If you don't see any colored lines, it's either because traffic is moving fine or because Microsoft doesn't have any information for those roads. Usually, you get traffic info only for highways, and only in metropolitan areas.

- **Map Style.** This icon (◉) opens a shortcut menu with two options: Road view and Aerial view. Road view, of course, is what most maps look like: roads represented as lines. Aerial view, however, superimposes the road lines and place names on top of satellite photos of the real world. Zoom in far enough, and you can find your house.
- **My Location.** The My Location button (◎) on the App bar makes the map scroll and zoom until the "You are here" diamond is dead center on your screen. That's handy if you've scrolled or searched some other part of the world.
- **Directions.** Yes, Maps' best trick is getting you where you need to go. See below.

Searching the Maps

You're not always interested in finding out where you are; often, you want to see where something *else* is.

To search Maps, open the Charms bar and select the Search button. Here's what Maps can find for you:

- **An address.** You can skip the periods (and usually the commas, too). And you can use abbreviations. Typing *710 w end ave nyc* will find 710 West End Avenue, New York, New York. (In this and any of the other examples, you can type a Zip code instead of a city and a state.)
- **An intersection.** Type *57th and lexington, ny ny*. Maps will find the spot where East 57th Street crosses Lexington Avenue in New York City.
- **A city.** Type *chicago il* to see that city. You can zoom in from there.
- **A Zip code or neighborhood.** Type *10024* or *greenwich village nyc.*
- **A point of interest.** Type *washington monument* or *niagara falls.*

When Maps finds a specific address, a black banner identifies the location by name.

Finding Friends and Businesses

You can use Maps as a glorified national Yellow Pages. If you type, for example, *pharmacy 60609,* blue numbered dots show you all the drugstores in that Chicago Zip code. It's a great way to find a gas station, a cash machine, or a hospital in a pinch.

Select a dot to see the name of the corresponding business in the white, vertical "legend" at the left side of the screen.

Tip: You can tap or click either place. That is, you can tap a numbered circle to auto-scroll the info column to the corresponding description, or you can tap a description to auto-scroll the map to the corresponding numbered circle.

For most businesses and points of interest, a **>** button appears within the black banner. You can select the button to view, at the side of the screen, a full dossier about that place (Figure 4-20).

Directions

If you tap Directions (⊛) in the App bar, you get *two* search bars, labeled A and B. That's right: Microsoft is *literally* prepared to get you from Point A to Point B.

Plug in two addresses—the A address may already say "My Location"—and then hit the ➔ button.

Tip: The Swap button (⇅) switches the A and B locations, which is great when you want to find your way home again.

In just a moment, Maps displays an overview of the route you're about to drive. The top of the screen lets you know the distance and the estimated time for that option and identifies the main roads you'll be on.

Now, Maps is not *really* a GPS navigation app of the sort you'd find on a smartphone or a windshield unit. The map doesn't actually know where you are as you drive. It doesn't say anything ("Turn right in 500 feet" or whatever), and it doesn't auto-scroll the map as you drive.

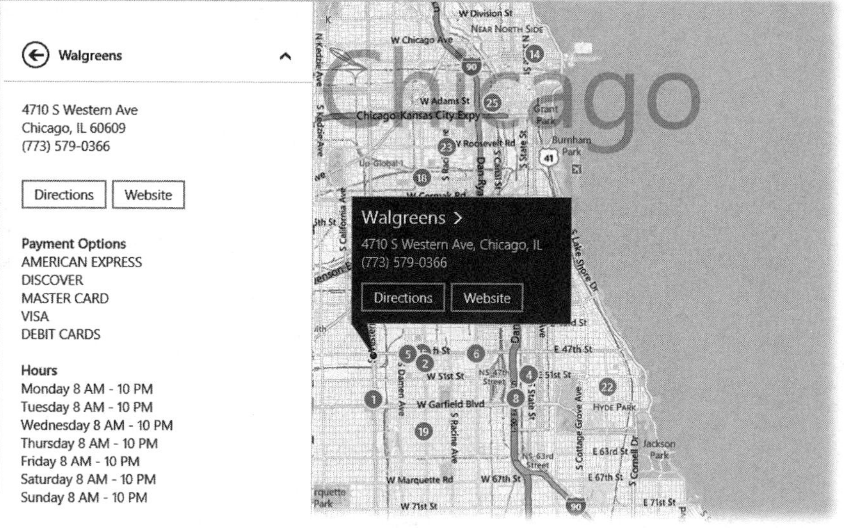

***Figure 4-20:** Top: When you search for something, Maps shows you all the results as blue dots, and as corresponding listings at left.*

Bottom: When you tap the > button on a search result, Maps turns into a full-blown Yellow Pages. It shows you the name, address, phone number, ratings, and other information about the business you've selected. Clearly labeled buttons take you to its Web site—or give you directions from your current location.

Instead, it's more like MapQuest: It shows a written list of turn-by-turn instructions (in the scrolling list at left). And it's more convenient than a paper map; it's at least interactive (see Figure 4-21).

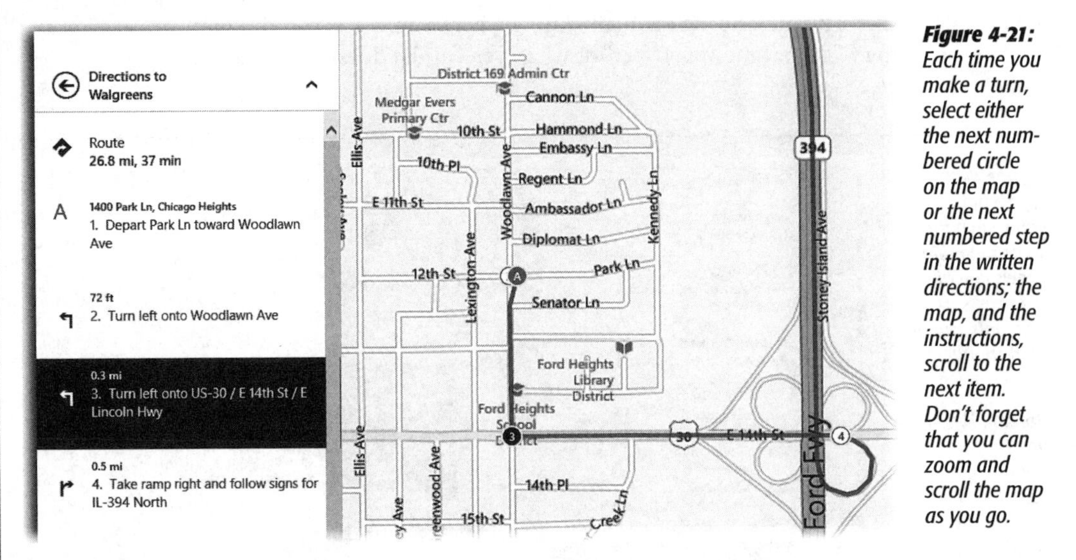

Figure 4-21: *Each time you make a turn, select either the next numbered circle on the map or the next numbered step in the written directions; the map, and the instructions, scroll to the next item. Don't forget that you can zoom and scroll the map as you go.*

Messaging

For your convenience, Windows 8 comes with a built-in chat program. With it, you can send typed messages to anyone on Facebook or Microsoft's own Windows Live Messenger or Skype networks.

Tip: And what if your friends are on some other chat network—like AIM, GChat, ICQ, or Jabber? In that case, it's time to visit the Windows Store and download the IM+ app. It's free, and it works with Facebook and all of those other networks. Use it instead of Messaging.

Messaging doesn't have its own buddy list or address book. Instead, it relies on the People app, Windows 8's master contacts list. In other words, if there's nobody in People, you won't be able to start chatting.

To chat, select the ⊕ button at the top left corner of the window. Now you see the People Picker, which is a miniature version of the People app described later in this chapter. At this point, it shows you everyone in your People list with a Windows Messenger, Skype, or Facebook account (Figure 4-22).

Once you've specified your correspondent, type a message into the text box at bottom. Proceed as shown in Figure 4-23. (If that person isn't online at the moment, he'll get the message the next time he does log in.)

As you can see by the figure, it's possible to keep conversations going with several people simultaneously; just tap the name of the person you want (and for goodness' sake, don't get confused about what you're saying to whom). A colored dot next to somebody's name indicates that a new message is waiting for you there.

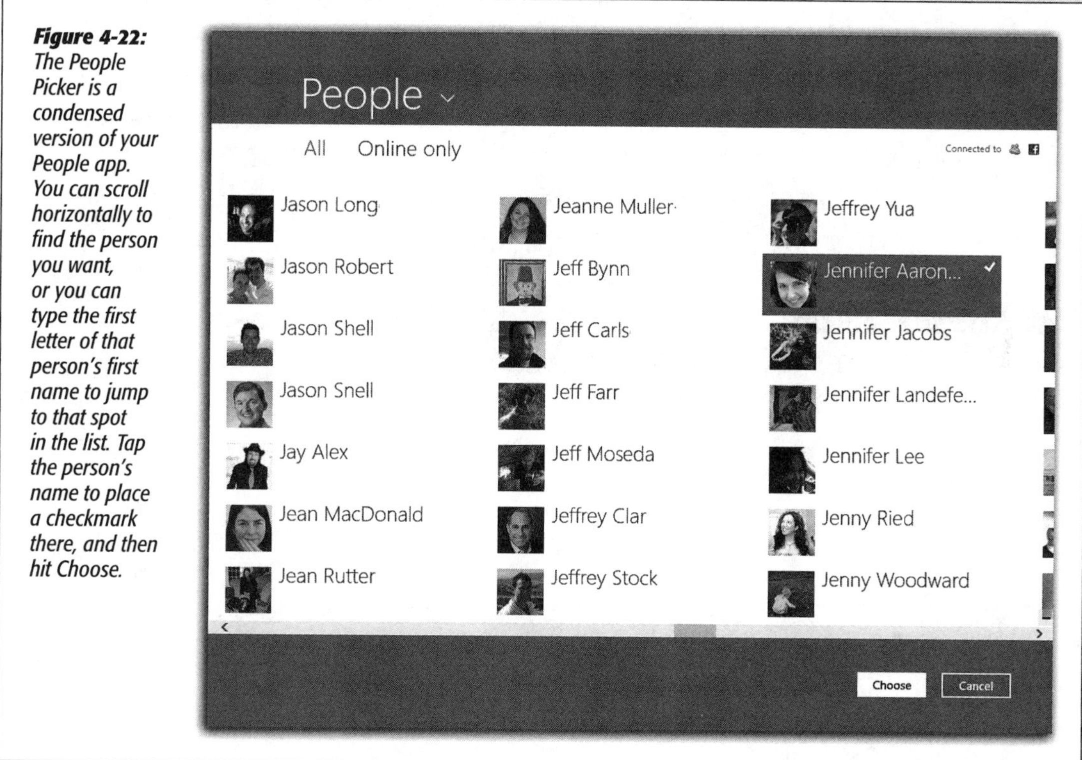

Figure 4-22: *The People Picker is a condensed version of your People app. You can scroll horizontally to find the person you want, or you can type the first letter of that person's first name to jump to that spot in the list. Tap the person's name to place a checkmark there, and then hit Choose.*

In time, the theory goes, that list of names will give you quick access to people you text often. In other words, once you've had a chat with somebody *once*, you won't have to go through the People Picker next time.

The App Bar

Hiding away on the App bar are three useful buttons:

- **Status.** Tap this button to affect whether or not you are reachable. The shortcut menu offers two options: Available and Invisible. Usually, you're Available—people can see that you're online. But for some people, the juicier status option is Invisible. It's like a *Star Trek* cloaking device for your onscreen presence. Great for stalkers!
- **Invite.** Tap this button, and then tap "Add a new friend," to invite one of your Facebook friends to sign up for a Messenger account, so you can start messaging.

- **Delete.** Ordinarily, Windows preserves your witty repartee right there in Messaging. You can return a week later, a year later, and there's the conversation you had today, ready to continue.

  Delete means "Delete the selected chat I've had so far." When you confirm your action by hitting the second Delete button, that transcript, and that person, disappear from the left side of the screen.

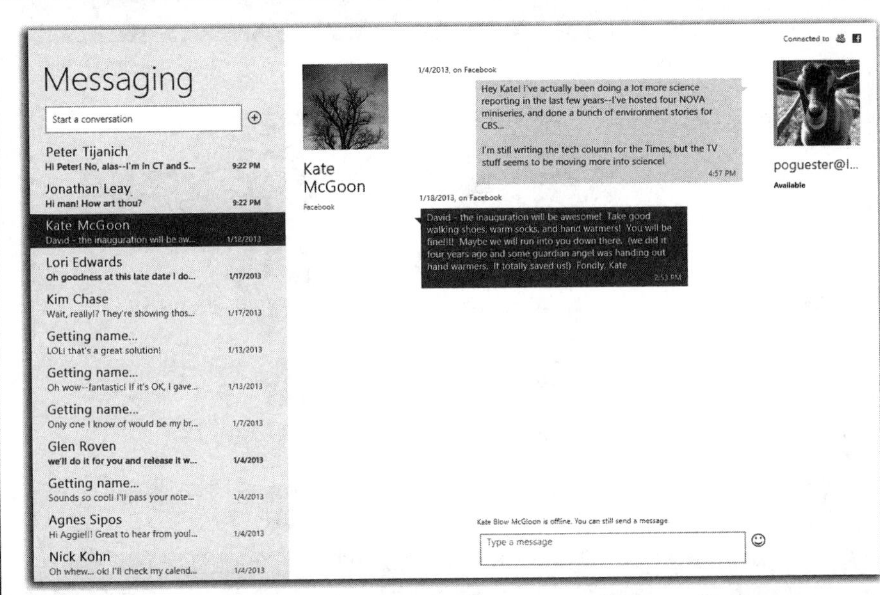

Figure 4-23: *Type your message where it says "Type a message" (duh). Hit the smiley-face icon to produce a palette of smileys, if mere words aren't enough. Press the Enter key to send each message. The conversation grows in the form of a scrolling list of speech bubbles.*

Settings

Hiding in Settings (open the Charms bar), you'll find two useful Messaging morsels:

- **Accounts.** Here's where you can set up your Messenger and Facebook accounts.
- **Options.** There's only one option, actually: "Send/receive messages." It's the master on/off switch for your being online for chats. Turning this switch off is exactly the same as setting your status to Invisible, and turning it on is exactly the same as becoming Available.

Settings also contains a few *not* useful buttons, like a very sparse

option, About, Feedback, Permissions, and "Rate and review."

Tip: Remember the feature that lets you park one app's window side by side with another (page 64)? It's especially useful in Messaging. Chats lend themselves to living in a vertical strip down one-third of the screen while you do work in some other app.

Music

It wouldn't be a computer if it couldn't play your tunes, right?

But this app is much more than a jukebox for songs you already own. It's also the front end for one of Microsoft's best-kept secrets: the Xbox Music service.

Tip: Don't be thrown. When you open the app, you see that its official name is "xbox music," and it lets you work with the Xbox Music service—but it has nothing at all to do with the Xbox game console. "Xbox" is simply the new word for "Microsoft."

Within Microsoft's collection of 30 million songs, Xbox Music combines elements of services like Pandora (it plays endless free music in a style you choose), Spotify (you can listen to any song or any album or any performer, on command, for free), and iTunes (you can buy songs to download). And it's a Windows 8 exclusive; none of your Windows 7 friends can use it.

And it's all free. (If you've signed in with your Microsoft account, that is.)

Note: OK, it's free with occasional interruptions by audio/video ads. Music streaming is free and unlimited for your first six months; after that, you can listen free for 10 hours a month. If you're willing to pay $10 a month (or $100 a year), you can get an Xbox Music Pass, which lets you (a) also listen on a Windows 8 phone and your Xbox 360 (provided you also have a Gold membership), (b) download songs for offline listening, (c) sync your playlists across multiple gadgets, and (d) eliminate the ads.

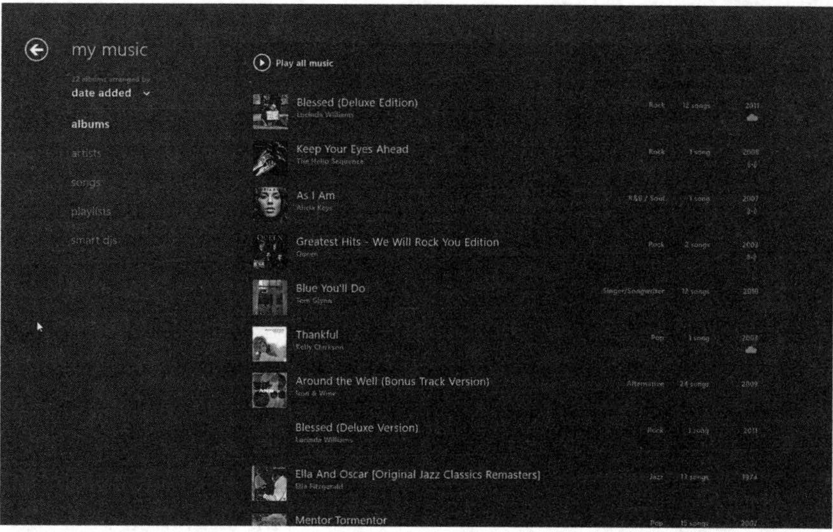

Figure 4-24: *The complete list of your music. You can sort it by tapping the criteria at left—albums, artists, songs, and so on. The ☁ icon marks a song that Microsoft sees you own, and therefore it can offer its own online copy for playback on any gadget; the WiFi icon means you've bookmarked a streaming song that lives only in Microsoft's collection online.*

My Music

Since the Music app is a combination music player/music store, things can get a little confusing. You open it up—and you're looking at a *store*. Not your own music collection.

You can fix that. Scroll to the left, so that the "my music >" tiles appear. Even then, Music shows you the tiles for only a few of your songs, playlists, or albums. You can tap the "my music >" heading to see the *complete* list (Figure 4-24), including playlists and Smart DJs (described below).

(If there's no music on your computer, you'll know right away; the message "It's lonely here" is trying to tell you there are no music files in your Music folder. (If you have none to put there, of course, Microsoft would love for you to go buy some; choose "Find music at the Xbox Music Store.")

The Music app shows *only* songs that are actually in your Music library—no other drives or other folders are eligible (unless, of course, you've added them to your Music *library*).

Tip: You can set things up so that your master list of music (Figure 4-20) appears automatically when you open the Music app, saving you the swipe out of the music store. To do that, open the Charms bar. In Settings, choose Preferences and turn on "Startup view." Now opening the app presents you with a list of your tunes.

Tap a song or album name to open its info screen, which displays the album art, song titles, a "Play album" button, "Explore artist" (bio and photo of the performer), "Play Smart DJ" ("play more songs like this one"), and, if you begin playback, an "Add to now playing" button (Figure 4-25).

UP TO SPEED

The App Bar in the Music App

In most TileWorld apps, the App bar contains useful options. In Music, it contains essential options.

As always, you make it appear by swiping into the screen from the top or bottom, or by right-clicking, or by pressing ⊞+Z.

The bar offers information and cover art for the currently selected song or album, plus Previous, Pause, and Next buttons. The "Playback options" button offers on/off switches for Repeat and Shuffle play, which makes more sense for an album or a playlist than it does for an individual song.

You may also see buttons that let you buy a song or an album, delete one from your "my music" collection, or add one to a playlist. Sometimes there's a Properties button that reveals basic details of the selected song (album, year, length, record company).

But "my music" is only the first stop in Music. Back out of the song list using the ← button at top left; you return to the main Music screen.

If you scroll this full-screen app far enough to the right, you'll discover the rest of the headings.

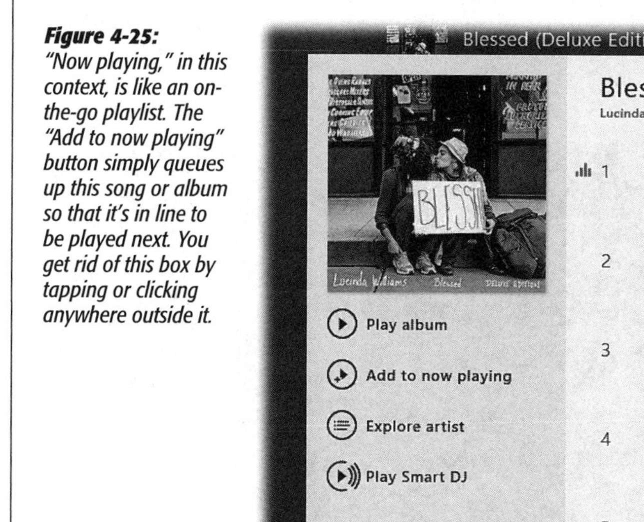

Figure 4-25: *"Now playing," in this context, is like an on-the-go playlist. The "Add to now playing" button simply queues up this song or album so that it's in line to be played next. You get rid of this box by tapping or clicking anywhere outside it.*

Now Playing

If, indeed, you've selected a song or album to play, its album-cover art shows up here (Figure 4-26). Surrounding this major tile, you get options like these:

- **Play an artist.** Microsoft isn't kidding; you can immediately start listening to *any band or singer,* right now, for free. When you choose this tile, you get a pop-up box that lists many popular groups—and offers a search box at the top. Here, you can type in whatever you like: *coldplay, electric light orchestra, london philharmonic,* whatever. When you then hit the ▶ button, boom: You're listening to free streaming music by that performer. You're welcome.

- **New Smart DJ.** This is Microsoft's version of Pandora. When you select this tile, you're asked to enter the name of a band or a singer you like. When you then hit the (▶)) button, Music instantly starts playing songs by that artist *and songs that sound similar.* It's a great way to discover new favorites based on what you know you like, and also a great way to keep the mood going when you find a style you like.

  When you create a Smart DJ, its tile gets added to your "my music" tiles (and to your main "my music" screen shown in Figure 4-24) so that you'll be able to recall it instantly.

If you open the App bar, you get some controls for your Smart DJ. The Pause button does what it says. Hit Previous to hear the same song again. Use the Next button if the Smart DJ plays a song you don't like; it skips to the next song.

- **Play a playlist.** See "Playlists," below.
- **[Performer tiles].** The right side of the "now playing" block offers three tiles for singers Microsoft thinks you might like. Tap one to start listening. And why not? It's all free.

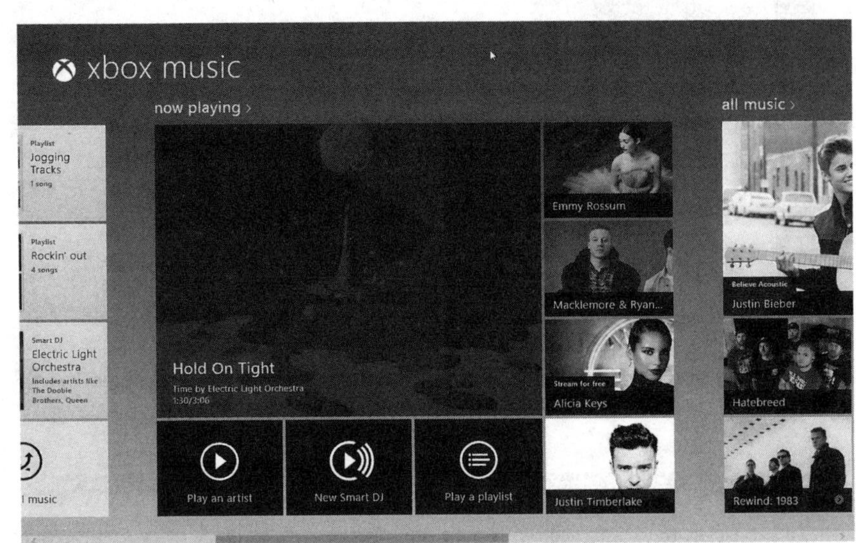

***Figure 4-26:** The "now playing" screen offers album art for the currently playing song, along with buttons that trigger other handy functions–including buttons for three performers Microsoft thinks you'll like.*

All Music, Top Music

Scroll even farther to the right in Music, and you arrive at the "all music" block of tiles. You've scrolled further into Storeland here; these are ads for various bands Microsoft hopes you'll try. The "top music" section, even farther to the right, reveals tiles for what's popular right now.

If you tap the title "all music >" above the tiles, you go down a rabbit hole into Microsoft's huge, huge catalog of music. Using the list of genres in the list at left, you'll find classical music, stand-up comedy recordings, children's albums, movie soundtracks, and more.

Note: As you burrow into Microsoft's music store, you'll eventually notice that not all songs, albums, and bands have given Xbox Music the same permissions. Sometimes, you'll be able to see a song but not play it. Other times, you can play a song but not add it to a playlist. You take your chances, and you're grateful for what it gives you.

Search

Don't forget that the old standby, the Search command, is hiding in the Charms bar, ready to pluck some musical needle out of Microsoft's enormous haystack. (Press ⊞+Q if you have a keyboard.)

Type in the name of a song, an album, or a musician. Just beneath the search box, the app offers some common suggestions to save you typing. When you hit Enter or tap the ⌕ icon, the main screen shows the search results. You can choose "artists," "albums," "songs," or "all results" to filter out the findings.

It's all available to play right now, on demand, for free.

Tip: You can't shrink Music down to a tiny miniplayer, as you can most Windows music apps. But you can split the screen so that it huddles in a vertical strip while you do other work; see page 64.

The Artist Screen

Sometimes it's handy that Microsoft is a billion-dollar corporate giant; it can tackle large-scale projects like the Artist screen.

You can see it in Figure 4-27. It's a full-screen display—actually, it's even *wider* than a full screen (you have to scroll)—of information about a singer or band. You get a photo slideshow, a biography, and a list of albums. Just about everything is tappable.

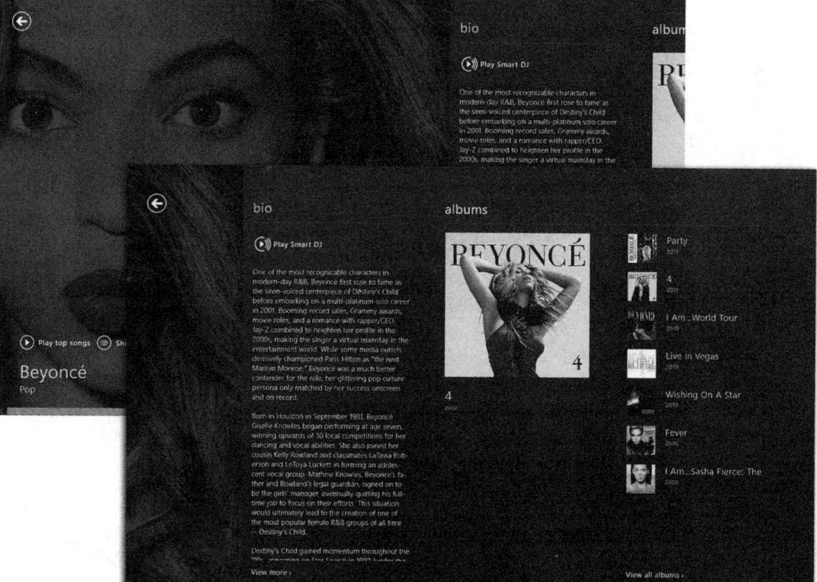

Figure 4-27: *The Artist screen scrolls horizontally to reveal more information about this performer and related albums. The Play Smart DJ instantly starts playing songs by this artist, and songs that sound similar. "Play top songs" and "Show song list" do just what they say. It's a complete database/jukebox, yours free.*

To get to the Artist screen, select an album cover anywhere it appears, and then choose "Explore artist."

The Artist screen also appears when you tap the words "now playing >" above the tiles.

Playlists

A playlist is a group of songs you've placed together, in a sequence that makes sense to you. One might consist of party tunes; another might hold romantic dinnertime music; a third might be drum-heavy workout cuts.

Tip: If all you want to do is create a lineup of songs you want to hear right now, in a queue (list), you don't have to muck with playlists. The Music app always maintains a temporary lineup of upcoming songs, called "now playing." You can add a song to it wherever you see the "Add to now playing" button.

One easy place to find it: on the App bar (swipe up from the bottom of the screen, or press ⊞+Z). Or add a song to "my music" first. That is, you'll see a button called "Add to my music"; after you tap it, the same button changes to say "Add to now playing."

To see the "now playing" list, choose the "now playing >" heading, and then select "Show song list" in the lower-left corner. You can't make changes to it, but you can skip through it using the buttons on the App bar.

Creating playlists

To create a new playlist, start by selecting (clicking or tapping) an album *or* a song; you can add either one to a playlist.

Now open the App bar. Tap "Add to playlist." If this is the first time you've ever fooled around with playlists, a shortcut menu appears, offering only one command: "Create new playlist." Choose it, type a name for the playlist ("Rockout Toonz," "Makeout Music," whatever), and hit Save.

The next time you open the App bar, you'll see that the "Add to playlist" button has been joined by another button, labeled "Rockout Toonz" (or whatever you called

GEM IN THE ROUGH

Universal Playback Controls

You can start music playing and then dive into other apps or programs; the music continues to play. You know—background music for your work session.

But what if you have to take a phone call or speak sternly to a child? Do you have to muddle all the way back to the Music app to pause playback?

Don't be silly. Just tap one of your keyboard's volume keys. Up pops this handy audio palette, containing Previous Song, Next Song, Pause, and volume controls. The album cover appears here, too—a very nice touch.

your latest list). Now you can breeze through your music collection, or Microsoft's online version, and add more songs and albums to that new playlist just by tapping that new button in the App bar.

To create a *second* playlist, repeat these steps. But this time, when you hit "Add to playlist" in the App bar, you see the "Create new playlist" command *and* the names of all your existing playlists (Figure 4-28). In other words, that one button lets you add songs or albums to any playlist you've created so far.

Editing, rearranging, and deleting playlists

The App bar may offer quick access to playlist creation buttons, but the real playlist hub is hiding in the "my music" area. If you tap the "my music >" heading, you'll see the "playlists" heading (Figure 4-28, top). It reveals a list of all your playlists.

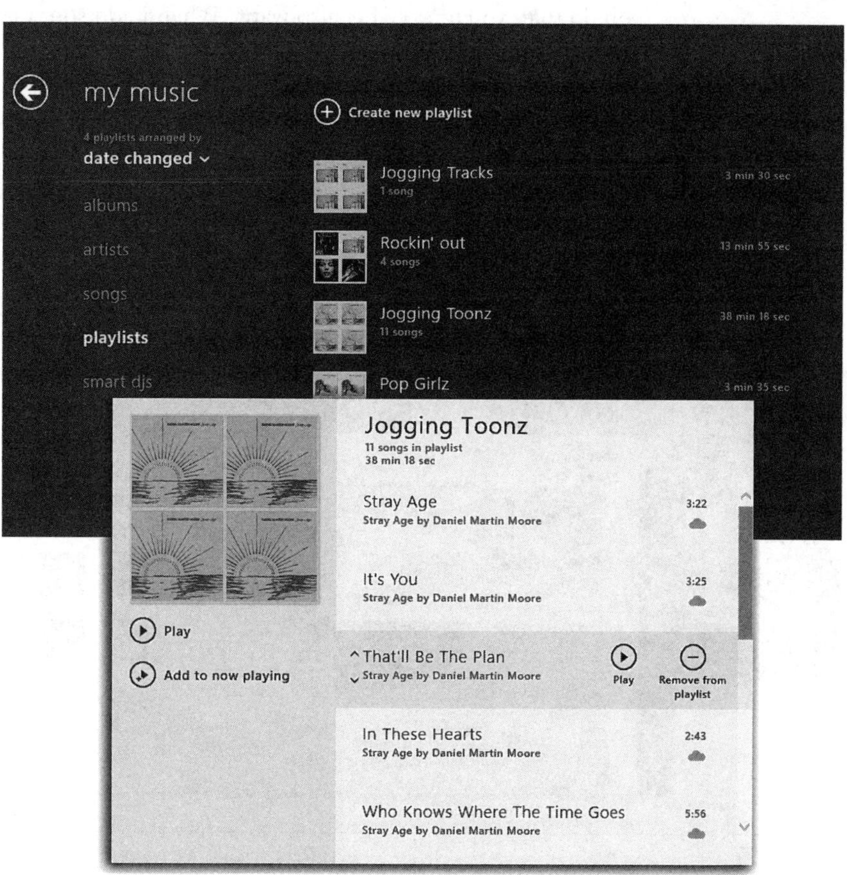

Figure 4-28: *Top: This is Grand Central Playlist. Tap a playlist's name to see what songs are inside and how much time they'll take to play (bottom). Tap a song's name to reveal the "Play" and "Remove from playlist" buttons. You can also tap the little ^ and ⌄ buttons to slide the selected song up or down within the playlist.*

To delete a selected playlist, open the App bar and use the Delete button. The Rename button is hiding in there, too.

Settings

In the Charms bar, the Settings icon opens a panel of useful options:

- **Account.** Here's where you can sign up for a paid Xbox Music account or change the settings for it (and your regular Xbox account, if you have one). The buttons here let you redeem free-music codes, change your credit-card information, add or remove new Windows phones/tablets/computers on your account, and so on.
- **Preferences.** These on/off switches control a few miscellaneous Music options. "When the app opens, show my music" means that you'll see your "my music" view when you open Music, instead of the music store. "Ask me to sign in" is good protection if young music lovers might buy music without your awareness.

  "Xbox Music Cloud" stores your own, purchased music files online so that you can listen to them from any Windows device with an Xbox Music connection. If you do that, you'll probably also want "When I add songs to my music on other devices, download them here too"; it ensures that buying a song or an album on one Windows device sends it to the Music app on all of them.

  Finally, there's no good reason to turn off "Automatically retrieve and update album art and metadata." This handy feature is responsible for the art and information that appears for each song, album, or musician in your collection.

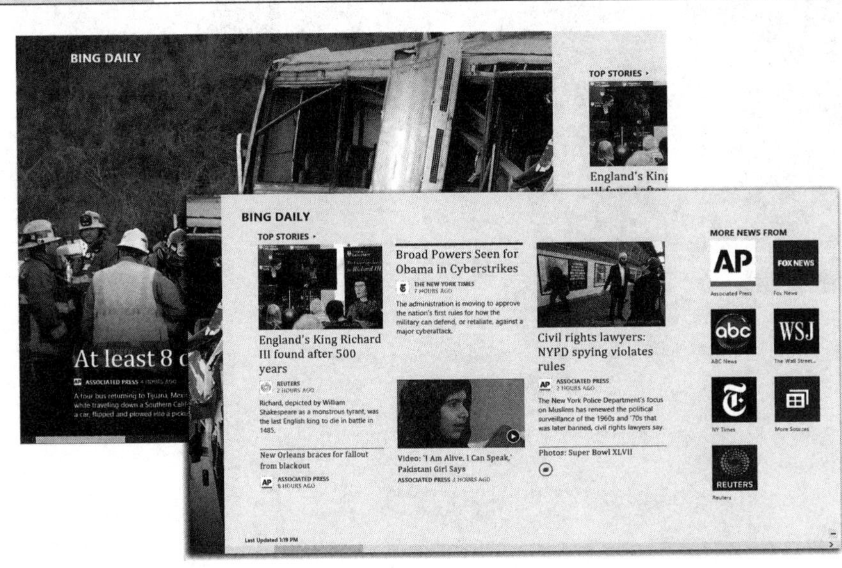

***Figure 4-29:** Microsoft doesn't actually write these articles; it just grabs them from other news sources, like* The New York Times, *Reuters, and The Associated Press. Tap or click any story to read it; tap the Back arrow (⊖) to return to the opening "table of contents" spread.*

Tip: Like many of Microsoft's TileWorld apps, Music is intended to be bare bones and simple. It offers the basic functions and no more; for example, it doesn't let you rip your audio CDs to your computer, edit song information, or create "smart playlists."

If you'd prefer something a little fuller fledged, don't forget that Windows Media Player is waiting for you back at the Windows desktop. Or you could download a nicer, more complete free program like MusicBee. It's available from this book's "Missing CD" page at *www.missingmanuals.com*. (Both of these two alternatives are for the full Windows, not Windows RT, alas.)

News

The News app (technically called Bing News) is one of several free, daily, full-screen magazines that come preinstalled in TileWorld. (Sports, Finance, and Travel are the others.)

This is a *fantastic* feature. At its core, Bing is simply grabbing articles from over 300 different big-name news Web sites: *The New York Times, The Wall Street Journal, The New Yorker,* CNN, Huffington Post, and so on.

But it reformats everything into one uniform, attractive, screen-friendly layout (Figure 4-29). No hard-to-read color schemes or ugly fonts. No blinking ads, banners, or obnoxious animations. If the 300 publications presented here pique your interest at all, the News app is, for sure, the way to read them.

They all work essentially alike. You open the app (Internet connection required). You see a huge cover photo. Tap or click it to read the associated article.

Or scroll *horizontally* to see headlines and teaser blurbs for other articles.

As it turns out, News is more like a newspaper than you might think. It actually has *sections,* like a real newspaper.

If you swipe down from the top (or right-click, or press ⊞+Z), a bunch of tile buttons appear (Figure 4-30).

- **Bing Daily.** Select this button to return to the opening spread.

  See the ▾ button hugging the Bing Daily tile? It opens a second row of tiles, bearing the names of the "sections" of your "magazine": U.S., World, Technology, Politics, Business, Entertainment, and Sports. Each button takes you directly to a similar spread of photos, headlines, and blurbs just for that section.

- **My News.** It turns out that your Bing magazine is *customizable.* You can ask it to bring you stories about your favorite actor, your favorite toothpaste, or even *you.*

  When you select My News, you see a new spread, showing only articles on subjects you've asked for. At the outset, of course, there's nothing here at all except some Microsoft news, put there to give you the idea.

But if you use the "Add a section" button, you get to type in any topic you like. *Justin Bieber. Electric cars. Seedless watermelon.* Whatever you might like your customized newspaper to show you.

The instant you then hit the Add button, a new section of news blurbs appears automatically, shoving Microsoft (or whatever other topics you've got in there) off to the right. You can add as many new topics as you like.

Tip: To remove a topic you've added, open the App bar. Use the Remove button to summon a screen of sections. Tap the tile of the one you want to zap out of existence.

Once you've added some topics of your own, you'll notice that the My News tile has a ▾ button. It opens a new row of tile buttons, representing the various topics you've set up for yourself. Use them to jump directly to one of your own pet topic pages.

- **Sources.** This tile (Figure 4-30, bottom) reveals a huge screenful of logos—one for every publication Windows 8 uses as fodder for its magazine. *The New Yorker,* Fox News, *The New York Times,* CNN, BBC News, *The Atlantic,* NPR, *Forbes, The Economist,* CNET, *Wired, Entertainment Weekly,* and on and on.

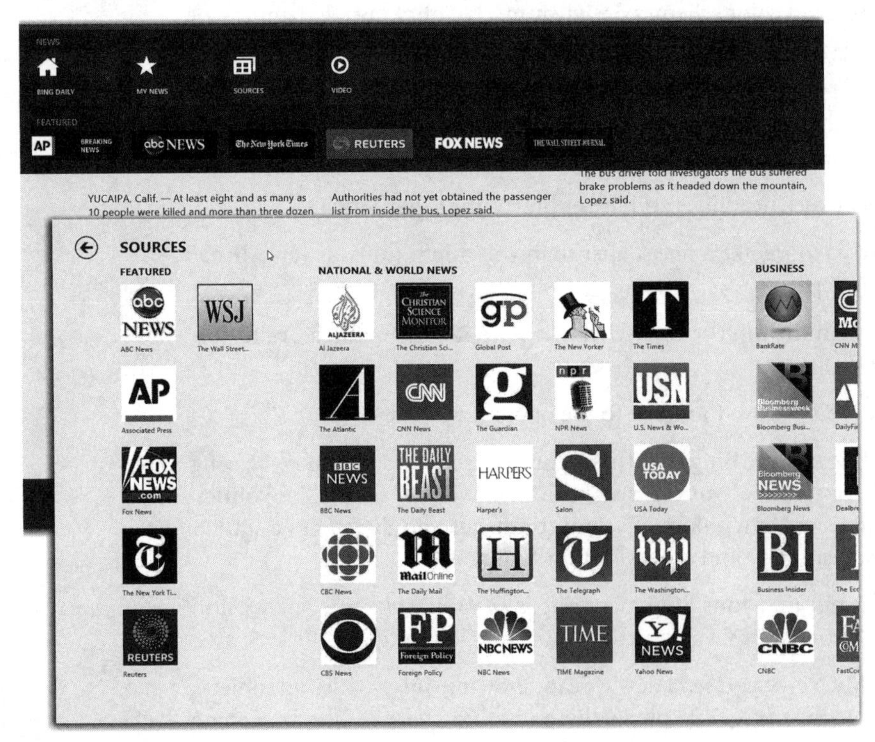

Figure 4-30: *In the News app, (top) the App bar appears at both the top and bottom of the screen. At top, you get four primary tiles that let you slice and dice Bing's 300 news sources in different ways. If you select Sources, you get to choose which online news sources you want as your news suppliers (bottom).*

The idea here is twofold: First, to marvel at the enormous range of material Microsoft culls every day. Second, to allow you to choose any of these icons to jump directly to a Bing-style layout of its current articles.

- **Video.** This tile gives you direct access to *videos* from Bing's multitude of sources. That's something a typical printed magazine doesn't usually offer.

On a tablet, wow—News is one of the best things to come along since hyperlinks.

People

The People app is Windows 8's address book. It's a centralized database of everybody in your social circles: their email and mailing addresses, Twitter and Facebook handles, phone numbers, and so on (Figure 4-31).

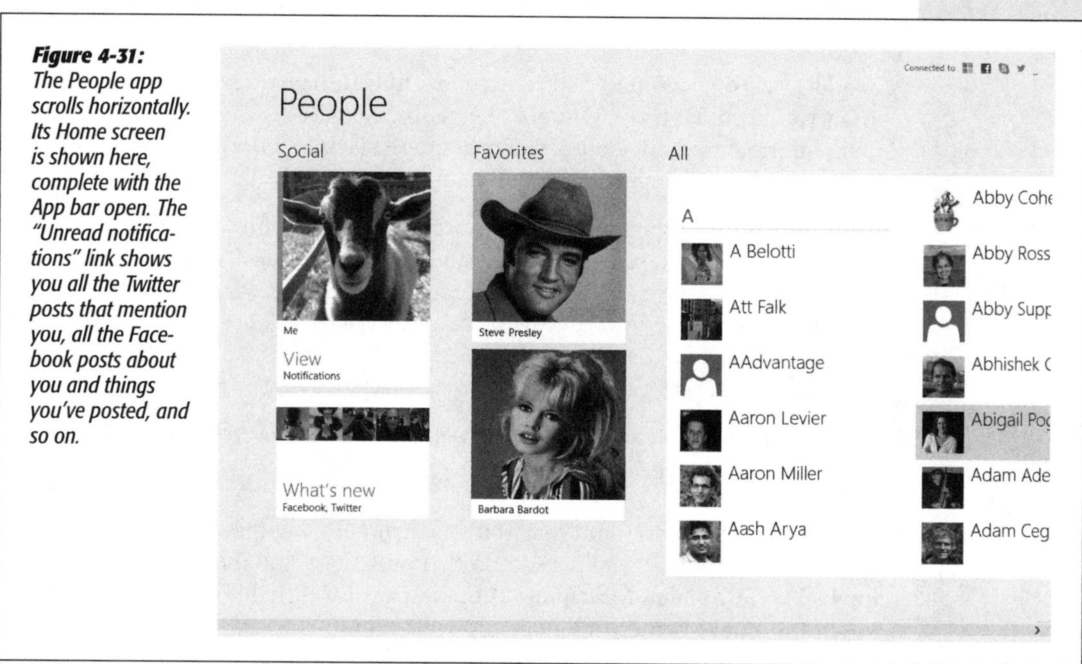

***Figure 4-31:** The People app scrolls horizontally. Its Home screen is shown here, complete with the App bar open. The "Unread notifications" link shows you all the Twitter posts that mention you, all the Facebook posts about you and things you've posted, and so on.*

But it's more than that. It's also where you can see what your friends are *saying* on Twitter and Facebook.

Tip: This app has many screens that go many layers deep. Most of the time, you can find your way back by tapping the ⊖ at the top left of the screen. But there's also a Home button hiding at the left side of the App bar. Whenever you're feeling navigationally woozy, swipe up from the bottom of the screen (or press ⊞+Z) and then hit Home. You wind up back on the screen shown in Figure 4-31.

Adding Addresses

If you've signed up for a Microsoft ID and told it all about your Facebook, Twitter, or LinkedIn account, then the People app probably has people listed in it the very first time you open it. If not, it's probably empty when you first open it.

You can add your contacts' information either one person at a time, or en masse, by slurping in everybody you know from an online service like Gmail, Facebook, Twitter, or LinkedIn.

Importing from Gmail, Facebook, or another Internet service

The People app can synchronize its contacts with online Rolodexes that may be very important to you: your Gmail (Google) contacts, Facebook contacts, Skype contacts, LinkedIn, Twitter, and various Microsoft email accounts.

To add an account, open the Charms bar and choose Settings, then Accounts. There, staring you in the face, are names of the accounts you've set up already.

To add a new one, use the "Add an account" link at the bottom. Tap the kind of account you want: Hotmail, Outlook, LinkedIn, Google, or whatever. Enter your account information, and boom—you're done. The People app is now synced with your online accounts. Change information in one place and it's also changed in the other.

You can repeat the process to add more accounts; in fact, you can even have *multiple* accounts for certain types (like Google and Microsoft email accounts).

Note: You can unsubscribe from one of your online accounts just as easily. In the Charms bar, hit Settings, then Accounts, then the account you want to dump, then "Remove account." You're not actually deleting any names or addresses from Facebook, Twitter, or whatever–just preventing them from showing up in People.

(Deleting your Microsoft account is different. If you do that, you really are deleting all your contacts–and your calendar, and your messages, and your mail.)

It's important to understand that you're actually linking those Internet services *to your Microsoft account*. You have to do that only once, and then all your TileWorld apps—Mail, Calendar, Messaging, People—can use their information. You've just woven Facebook, Twitter, or Gmail into your Windows world.

The big payoff comes when you sign into another Windows 8 machine (or a Windows 8 phone). To your delight and amazement, you'll see that your address book is already filled in with all your contacts and accounts. Your Favorites list is even pre-filled with the favorites you've set up on other Microsoft products. Progress!

Creating address cards manually

Each entry in People is like a paper Rolodex card, with predefined spaces to hold all the standard contact information.

To add a new person:

- **Touchscreen:** Swipe up from the bottom of the screen to reveal the App bar. Tap "New contact."
- **Mouse:** Right-click the screen to open the App bar; click "New contact."
- **Keyboard:** Press Ctrl+N.

In each case, the "New contact" screen (Figure 4-32).

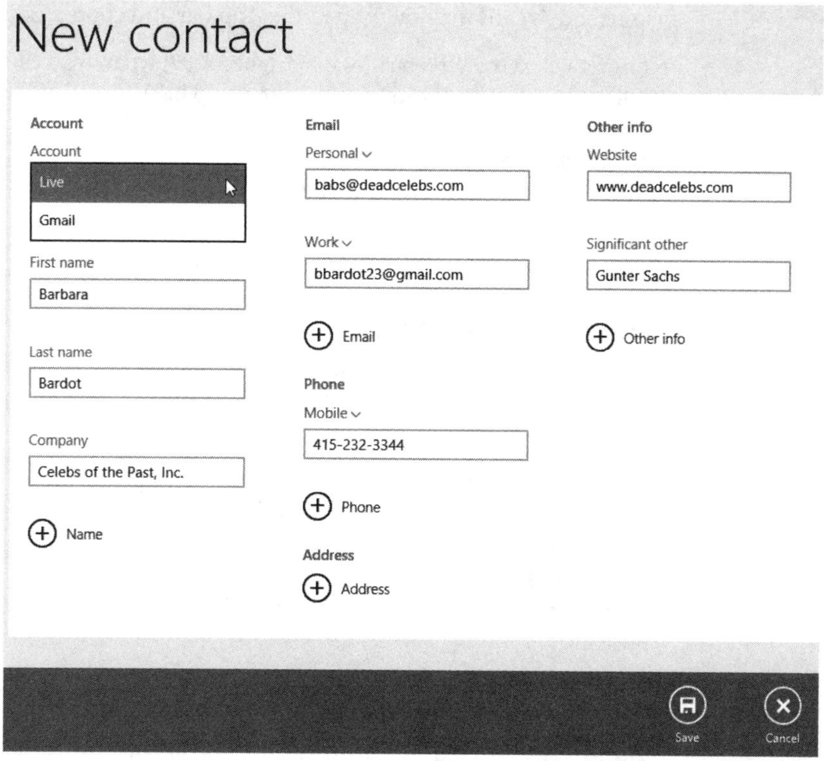

Figure 4-32: *It shouldn't take you very long to figure out how to fill in this form: You tap in a box and type. Fill in this person's name, email address, phone number, and so on, pressing the Tab key to move from field to field. To change the label for a number ("mobile," "home," "work," and so on), tap the ⌄ button next to the current label.*

The first box, Account, lets you specify what online email address book you want this name stored in: your Gmail account, Outlook account, or whatever. (This assumes you've actually set *up* some email accounts.)

Tip: If you have an Android phone, choose Gmail; Windows will thoughtfully add this person to your phone's built-in address book automatically via your Google account.

Now, the trouble with people these days is that they often have more than one phone number, more than one email address, and more than one mailing address. Fortunately, all of these boxes are infinitely expanding. Choose the ⊕ button to add another blank box of the same type: another phone-number field, for example.

Tip: You can also add fields for "Job title," "Significant other," "Website," or "Notes." They're hiding in the "Other info" button. Select its ⊕ button to see those choices.

Once you've added the complete dossier for this person, open the App bar and hit Save (or just press Ctrl+S). Both take you back to the main People screen.

Editing an address

People move, people quit, people switch cellphone carriers. To make changes to somebody's card manually, open the App bar and choose Edit.

You return to the screen shown in Figure 4-32, where you can add, remove, and edit fields. Use the Save button (also on the App bar) when you're finished.

Adding pictures

One nice thing about snagging info cards from Facebook, Twitter, or LinkedIn is that they come with headshots already.

Unfortunately, you can't add a photo to a People entry photo manually.

Favorites and Start Screen Tiles

If you're like most of us, you care more about some people than others. You might have 10,000 people in your master database of contacts, but you might not be interested in seeing what *all* of them had for lunch.

Fortunately, People lets you promote certain people to VIP status, where you can find them, or follow them, apart from the crowd.

Designating favorites

Open the card of your special friend. Open the App bar and choose Favorite (or press Ctrl+F).

From now on, you'll see this person's picture at the top of the list on the People home page. That way you have quick access to the links for emailing, calling, or messaging.

(To Un-favorite someone, open her card, open the App bar, and tap Favorite again so that the button is no longer white.)

Pinning someone to Start

You can also turn a person in People into a Start screen tile, where his latest Facebook and Twitter updates will stare you in the face all day. You should reserve this treatment for the *really* important handful of people in your life. Figure 4-33 has the instructions. (If you have a keyboard, Ctrl+Shift+1 does the trick.)

Next time you visit the Start screen, you'll see that person's photo, way off to the right side, where new tiles always appear. The tile alternates between showing the photo, this person's latest Facebook post, and this person's latest tweet.

Tap the tile to jump to the corresponding person's page in People, for quick calling, emailing, or messaging.

(To un-pin someone, open the card, open the App bar, and tap Unpin from Start.)

Figure 4-33:
Start by opening the lucky individual's screen. Open the App bar. Choose Pin to Start. Edit the name, if you want–Windows proposes the actual name, but you can substitute "Mom" or "Honeybunch" or whatever–and then hit Pin to Start.

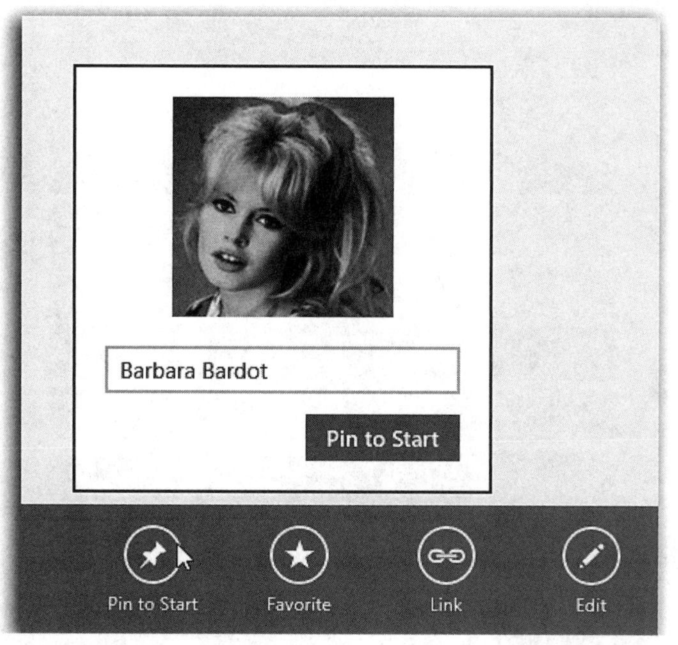

Finding Someone

There are three ways to find someone in your digital Rolodex:

- **Scroll horizontally.** Microsoft has decided to present your contacts alphabetically—not a bad notion—and the whole thing scrolls left to right. (Keyboard: PageUp and PageDown keys scroll; Home and End jump to the beginning or end of the list.)
- **Search.** As usual, the Search button is hiding in the Charms bar. But you don't have to expend precious calories opening the Charms bar; this search works just the way it does on the Start screen. When you're on the main People screen, *just type.* The search box in the Charms bar opens automatically.

  Once you've typed part of a person's first or last name, press Enter (or hit the ⌕ icon), and boom—the results screen appears.

- **Use the alphabetical index.** You can *zoom out* of People, reducing your whole social circle to nothing but a screen full of alphabet blocks, the better to jump to a particular part of the alphabet. Figure 4-34 has details.

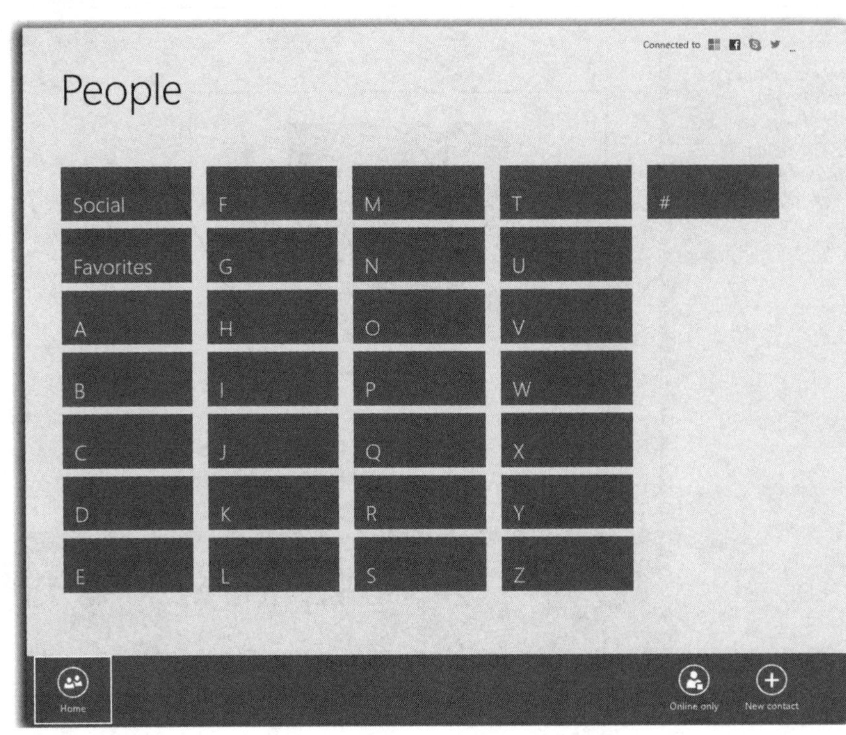

Figure 4-34: *To get from the regular People screen to the alphabetical index, zoom out from the screen. Pinch with two fingers (or more), or turn your mouse's scroll wheel down while pressing the Ctrl key, or press Ctrl+minus key (-). This is the feature Microsoft calls "semantic zoom," but it really means you can now hop directly to any part of the alphabet with a tap or a click.*

Once you're viewing the index, tap or click a letter to jump into that part of the alphabet.

GEM IN THE ROUGH

Who's Online Right Now?

As you peruse your archipelago of people, you might discover a vertical colored bar flanking the photos of certain people. These are the ones who are online right now—on Facebook at this moment, for example. That's a helpful flag; it shows you who might be available for a question or a chat.

But who wants to scroll through hundreds of thumbnails on a quest for people who have no life? Windows 8 can round them up for you!

Open the App bar (shown in Figure 4-34). Choose "Online only" to hide everyone in your People app except those who are online right now. (Hit the same button again to restore your full complement of friends.)

The Person Screen

Once you've found the tile for the person you seek, tap or click to open up the Details screen shown in Figure 4-35. Here's an amazing dossier on this friend, relative, or associate. If you scroll the screen horizontally, you'll find the following screens full of information.

Figure 4-35: *The Person screen offers contact information, followed immediately by this person's latest Twitter and Facebook news. After that comes photos this person has posted to Facebook or Twitter, sorted by which camera or app took them.*

Contact

Here are buttons for every conceivable way to reach this person. The exact buttons depend on what information you have for him, but these are some of the possibilities:

- **Send email.** Use the pop-up menu to specify which email address you want to use. Then hit "Send email"; the Mail app opens a new, outgoing message, pre-addressed to the person you chose. Add a subject line and a message, and send away.
- **Send message.** It means "Send a message via Facebook."
- **Call mobile.** (Use the pop-up menu to choose a Home number, Work number, or another number.) Of course, your computer is not a phone any more than your toaster is a VCR. But it *can* call phone numbers—using Skype, the famous texting/calling/videochatting app that Microsoft bought a few years ago.

  It's not free; you have to buy "Skype credit." (You'll get the chance when you try to make the call.) Once you connect via Skype, your computer's mike and speakers will simulate a phone. You can use the pop-up menu to choose a different phone number—Home or Work, for example.

- **Map address.** The Maps app opens and pinpoints this person's address on a map. (If you've specified more than one address, then use the pop-up menu to choose the one you mean.)
- **View profile.** "Profile," in this case, refers to your person's details screen. It's an ever-expanding, horizontally scrolling presentation of every scrap of contact information you have for that person.

What's new

If you scroll rightward, past the Contact block, you may find a "What's new" block of tiles. ("What's new" is also a tile on your home screen.) It shows this person's latest Facebook and Twitter posts, complete with the usual buttons at the bottom—Like, Retweet, Comment, Reply, and so on.

GEM IN THE ROUGH

Linking Contacts

As you know, the People app can sync up with different accounts. It might list three sets of names and numbers: one from Facebook, one from Twitter, and one from your corporate Exchange server at work. In the old days, therefore, certain names might have shown up in the list two or three times–not an optimal situation.

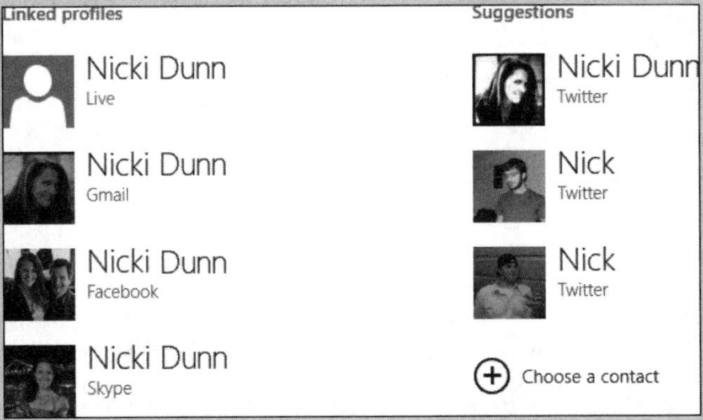

Linked profiles | Suggestions

Nicki Dunn – Live | Nicki Dunn – Twitter
Nicki Dunn – Gmail | Nick – Twitter
Nicki Dunn – Facebook | Nick – Twitter
Nicki Dunn – Skype | Choose a contact

Now, as a favor to you, Windows displays each person's name only once. If you tap that name, you open the unified information screen for that person. It includes all the details from all the underlying accounts for that person.

You can, however, link or unlink a unified "card." (Unlinking means splitting it back into its original component "cards.") You might do that if, for example, People has linked two cards incorrectly. (It can happen. There is, after all, more than one person on earth named John Smith.)

To unlink, open the unified card. Open the App bar (swipe up from the bottom edge, right-click a blank spot, or press ⊞+Z).

Select the Link button. (A tiny digit appears on this button, indicating how many cards have been consolidated.) The "Links for [this person's name]" screen appears. Linked cards are represented (under the heading "Links for [this person]") by thumbnails.

Select the thumbnail of the card you want to unlink. Presto: Its thumbnail pops over to the Suggestions column, no longer associated with this person.

You can use this same procedure to link to cards manually. Open a person's card, open the App bar, and then choose Link. Now, if the Suggestions column correctly guesses the additional card you want to link, choose it. If not, use the "Choose a contact" option to go find the right one; hit Add.

The "View all" button expands that notion, filling the whole screen with a horizontally scrolling display of recent posts. You can tell by the little icon beneath each post which service it comes from (like Twitter, Facebook, or LinkedIn).

In other words, you can see all of each person's online activities, from all their accounts, all in one place.

Tip: On this screen, you can also hide all the posts from one service or another. Open the App bar; the Filter button offers a list–Facebook, Twitter, All–that lets you control which posts you're seeing.

To return to the main contact page, use the ⊖ button at top left.

Photos

Finally, off to the right again, there may be a third block of tiles: photos this person has posted online. They're rounded up from Facebook and Twitter.

Each tile represents an app (like Instagram or Hipstamatic), a program (like iPhone or Picasa), or a source (like the Facebook Timeline) for a group of photos. Tap or click one of these tiles to see the photos within.

When you see an especially compelling photo, select it. It fills the screen—all except for a panel at the right side where you can type a comment about it ("Great pic!!!" is typical) or express your approval with a click or a tap on the Like button.

You can work your way back to the person's main card screen using the ⊖ button, or you can back all the way out to People's "front door" using the Home button on the App bar.

Hiding an Account (Filtering)

You can hide all the people from a certain account—Facebook or Twitter, for example—so that they're not cluttering up your People app. That's handy if you use People mainly for looking up email addresses or phone numbers and don't really care about their social-network posts right now.

Just open the Charms bar, hit Settings, and then choose Options. Boom: There they are, checkboxes for Facebook, Gmail, Twitter, Skype, Outlook, and whatever other accounts you've set up. Turn off the checkboxes for the accounts whose contacts you want to hide. (You can always bring them back by turning their checkboxes on again.)

Sharing a Contact

There's a lot of work involved in entering someone's contact information. It would be thoughtful, therefore, if you could spare the next guy all that effort—by sending a fully formed electronic business card to him. It can be yours or that of anyone in your People list.

To do that, open the contact's card. Open the Charms bar; choose Share; choose Mail, OneNote, or whatever sharing method you prefer. (In theory, as you install new programs, your list of options here may grow.)

If you chose Mail, you're asked to address the outgoing email message; do so and then choose Send. You've just fired off an email containing the chosen contact info. The recipient, assuming he has a half-decent smartphone or address-book program on the receiving end, can install that person's information with a single tap on the attachment.

Posting

You can also post to your social networks—Facebook, Twitter, whatever—right from the People app. See Figure 4-36 for the step-by-step.

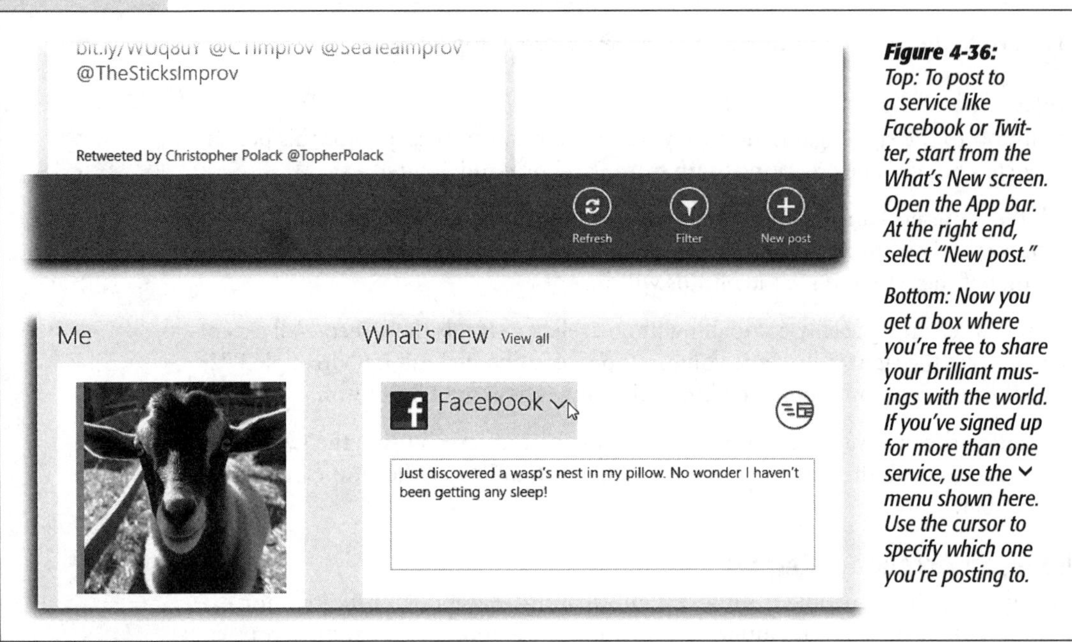

Figure 4-36: *Top: To post to a service like Facebook or Twitter, start from the What's New screen. Open the App bar. At the right end, select "New post."*

Bottom: Now you get a box where you're free to share your brilliant musings with the world. If you've signed up for more than one service, use the ˅ menu shown here. Use the cursor to specify which one you're posting to.

Photos

The old Photo Viewer of Windows 7 fame is gone. In its place: the TileWorld app called Photos. Its job is to grab photo albums from everywhere fine photos are stored—your own Pictures folder, other PCs on your network, Facebook, Flickr, your SkyDrive, and so on—and display them all in one place. Especially if you have a touchscreen, you'll find Photos a graceful, fluid, lovely way to browse your shots.

Your Pictures Folder

Back at the desktop, behind the scenes of TileWorld, you have a Pictures folder. Any photos in this folder show up in the Photos app automatically.

Maybe there are pictures here already—perhaps because you upgraded a Windows 7 machine to Windows 8. If not, maybe now is the time to move your pictures into Pictures.

The Photos app can't show you pictures that lie in any other folder on your PC. It's the Pictures folder or nothing.

Tip: Well, actually, there's one exception. If you keep pictures in another folder and don't want to move them, you can add that folder to the Pictures library, as described on page 210.

Setting Up Online Accounts

Before you can have much fun with Photos, you have to provide your account information for Facebook, Flickr, and/or SkyDrive. To do that one service at a time, select the appropriate tile at the bottom of the Photos screen: SkyDrive, Facebook, Flickr, or whatever.

You're asked for your *Microsoft* ID, which is itself supposed to be linked to your Facebook and other online accounts.

Note: If you haven't yet told Windows 8 to store your account info for these services, now is a good time. Opportunities to link those accounts to your Microsoft account are everywhere: in Messages, Mail, and People, for example. In any of these apps, open the Charms bar, choose Settings, and choose Accounts. There you'll find the "Add an account" link.

Then, after a few heart-pounding moments, the magic begins: Photos fills up with photos it's snagged from the Web (Figure 4-37).

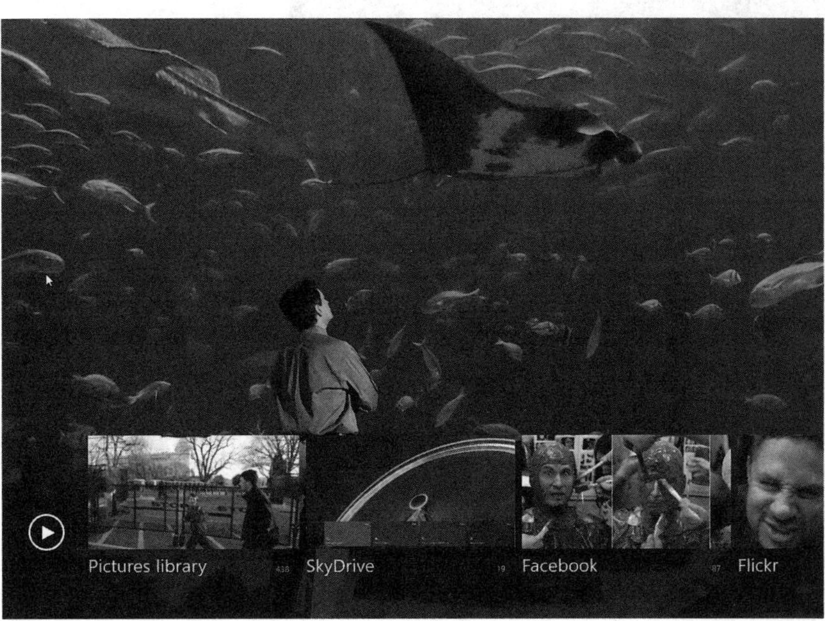

***Figure 4-37:** In the Photos app, the various sources of photos are represented as big tiles; scroll horizontally to see them all. Meanwhile, the thumbnails of photos within each source occasionally perform micro-slideshows, just to tease you.*

Tip: Once you've linked an account to your Microsoft account, its photos show up in Photos automatically—which you may not want. For example, you might enjoy having Facebook hooked up to the People app, but you may feel that seeing your Facebook account's pictures in Photos isn't really necessary.

Fortunately, you're not condemned to looking at all of them. At any time, you can hide the photos from one account or another. Open the Charms bar; tap Settings; tap Options; tap "Show photos and videos from"; and then turn off the checkboxes of the sources you'd rather hide.

Slurping in Photos from a Camera

Not all photos originate online, thank heaven. Photos is also proud to display pictures you've taken yourself. It can import photos from a camera or memory card, too.

If you open the App bar (page 27), you'll find the Import button. It's available at the Photos home screen or on any screen full of tiles or thumbnails—not when you've opened an individual photo.

The Import button brings in pictures from your camera, a USB flash drive, or some other drive. See Figure 4-38.

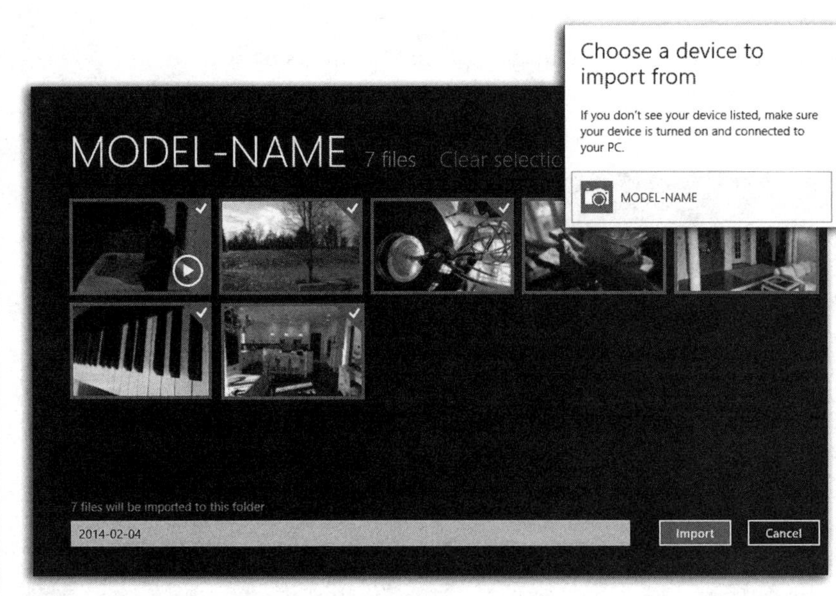

Figure 4-38: *Inset: When you select Import, you're first asked to choose the device you want to import from.*

Bottom: You see the photos and videos on it. All the new ones are selected and ready to import, but you can select or deselect them as you see fit. (Swipe down from a thumbnail if you have a touch-screen; right-click if you don't.) Name the folder for the new arrivals; then hit Import.

When it's all over, Windows offers you an "Open folder" button so you can see the newly imported goodies in the Photos app.

Playing with Photos

The rules of Photos are simple:

- By tapping or clicking, select a source, then an album within it, and then a photo within *it*. When you've drilled down as far as you can go, the picture fills most of the screen.
- To move through the photos, swipe horizontally (touchscreen), click the ‹ and › buttons at the edges of the screen (mouse), or press the ← and → keys (keyboard).
- The ▶ button in the lower-left corner starts a slideshow of all photos in this batch.

Tip: You can interrupt the slideshow by tapping (if you have a touchscreen) or by pressing the Esc key (if you don't).

- Search for a photo by name (choose Search on the Charms bar).
- Send a photo to somebody by email or text message (tap Share on the Charms bar; see page 26).

Note: That's all Photos can do: show photos. You can't do even the most minimalist editing—can't even rotate or crop a photo. For those purposes, consider downloading a free, far more powerful program, like Picasa. (It's a Windows desktop program, so Picasa isn't an option on a Windows RT tablet.)

POWER USERS' CLINIC

Photos from Other PCs

In general, Photos is automatic. The "Pictures library" tile shows the photos in your Pictures folder right now. The SkyDrive, Facebook, and Flickr tiles show what's online in your accounts.

But there's one more available source of photos that's not so automatic—although it's super handy: other Windows 8 computers. Yes, you, seated at your Windows 8 machine, can peruse the photos sitting in the Pictures folders of other PCs. Not just on your network, but across the Internet. From your hotel room in Honolulu, you can examine the photos on your desktop PC in Detroit.

The common link is your SkyDrive, Microsoft's free online "hard drive."

To get started, install the SkyDrive desktop app on the PC in Detroit. (You can download it from *https://apps.live.com/skydrive*). Make sure you've signed into the same Microsoft account on both machines.

Now, on your own Windows 8 machine, run through the SkyDrive setup utility as usual. Turn on "Make files on this PC available to me on other devices."

That's all there is to it. If your computer is online, then after a few minutes, your Detroit PC's photos show up, represented by a new Photos tile on your Honolulu Windows 8 machine.

(As a bonus, you now have a SkyDrive folder on each PC. It's like the free Dropbox software, if you've ever used that: Any files you put into the SkyDrive folder are instantly available and synced among all your PCs—even Macs—and SkyDrive.com, for access anywhere you go. Whenever you add, change, or delete files on one machine, all the others get updated.)

What's great is that the SkyDrive is just acting as a conduit for your photos—it's not actually storing them. So these photos don't count against your 7 GB SkyDrive storage limit.

Zooming In, Zooming Out

When you've opened an individual photo, you can enlarge or shrink it in the usual ways:

- **Touchscreen:** Spread two fingers apart on the glass; pinch to zoom back out.
- **Mouse:** Click the + and – buttons at the right edge of the horizontal scroll bar to zoom in or out. Or turn the scroll wheel while pressing the Ctrl key.
- **Keyboard:** Press Ctrl and the + or – keys.

When zooming gets complicated is *after* you've restored a photo to its original fit-the-screen size. If you continue to zoom out, you backtrack into the album or other batch from which the photo came. If you zoom out *more,* you shrink the album's thumbnails. You wind up with a mosaic view of your album that you can't get to any other way, the better with which to survey your collection.

Viewing by Date

In theory, photographs are a record of your life—so *when* they were taken is a rather important tidbit. The Photos app offers a secret way to view your photos in chronological chunks; see Figure 4-39.

Slapping a Photo onto the Lock Screen, Photos Tile, or Photos Screen

Also hiding on the App bar: the Set As button. Its shortcut menu lets you slap the current photo onto any of these billboards:

- **Lock screen.** That's a reference to the big photo that appears when you first wake up a Windows 8 machine, the one that bears the current time. Here's one easy way to change it to a photo of your own.
- **App tile.** Usually, the image that represents Photos on the Start screen changes every few seconds. It rotates through different pictures. But using this command, you can stamp the selected photo onto that tile for all time. (The tile no longer rotates through photos.)

GEM IN THE ROUGH

Playing Photos on Your TV

Your tablet is one thing. But if you want to show your pictures to more than a couple of people, your big-screen TV is the way to go. Fortunately, the Photos app is nicely hooked up to the Devices icon that's been staring you in the face ever since you first opened the Charms bar.

For example, if you have an Xbox 360, it's easy to select a slideshow or video in the Photos app, open the Charms bar, tap Devices, and tap the Xbox's name to send the slideshow to your TV. (This works only if you're signed into Windows 8 and the Xbox with the same Microsoft account.)

Presto: Instant on-TV slideshow!

- **App background.** You may have noticed the handsome Ferris-wheel-at-night photo that fills the Photos screen the first time you open it. And you may also have grown tired of it.

  You can replace this image, too, with one of your own. That's the purpose of this shortcut menu command.

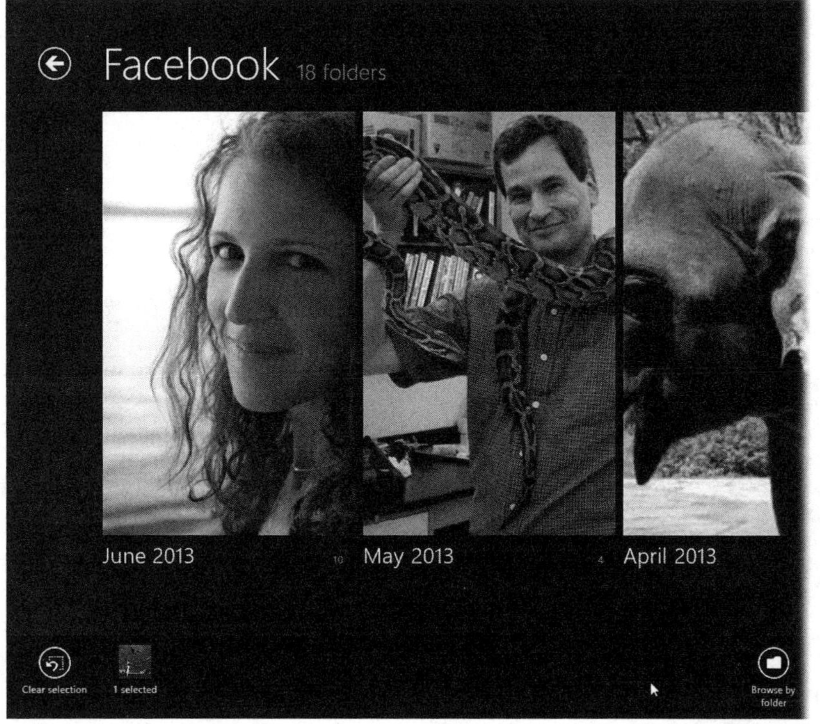

Figure 4-39: *Once you've opened a source tile (for example, Facebook or "Pictures library"), open the App bar and choose "Browse by date." Suddenly these vertical tiles appear, representing months' worth of photos, newest first.*

Selecting and Sharing Photos

Photos wouldn't be much fun if your screen were the only place you could see them. Fortunately, the Photos app is happy to zap them away to your adoring fans electronically.

Selecting photos

The first step is telling Photos which pictures you want to send. To do that, drill down until you're looking at the thumbnails of some batch. Then, for each photo you want to include, do this:

- **Touchscreen:** Flick downward on the thumbnail.
- **Mouse:** Right-click the thumbnail.

- **Keyboard:** Use the arrow keys to highlight a thumbnail, and then press the ⊞ key.

Tip: You can remove a thumbnail from the current selection by using the same technique a second time.

In each case, the thumbnail sprouts a colored outline, and a checkmark appears in its top-right corner. You can repeat the procedure for another photo, and another, until all the ones you want are checkmarked.

Note: You can't select photos from two different sources at once–your Pictures folder and a Facebook album, for example. In fact, if you try to select photos from one source while some others are still selected in another, Windows complains and asks that you de-select the earlier group.

To do that, you don't have to revisit the earlier thumbnails. Instead, just open the App bar and use the "Clear selection" button. Now no photos are selected in any album.

Sharing selected photos

Once you've chosen the photos you want to share, open the Charms bar (page 24). Hit Share.

The options here vary, but a couple of them are sure things:

- **Mail.** That's right—you can send photos by email, directly from Photos. If you choose Mail, a new panel appears, showing an outgoing message; the photos are attached. Address it, type a subject line and maybe a message, and then hit the ⊜ button to send it.
- **SkyDrive.** Your free online SkyDrive disk is a handy intermediary for photos that shuttle between computers (see the box on page 157). So it's no surprise that Microsoft made it easy to send photos from Photos to your online SkyDrive—if nothing else, it's a great way to back them up.

  You're asked to enter your Microsoft ID and password (or to sign up for a Microsoft account, if you don't have one). Then you see a list of the folders on your SkyDrive; choose the one you want to receive the new photos. (The one called Pictures is usually a good bet.) When you're finished, choose Upload.

Printing Pictures

You can, of course, print out photos so that you can hang them handsomely on the wall or hand them proudly to admirers.

Start by opening the Pictures tile in Photos. (You can't print pictures from online accounts or ones that live on other computers—only ones that are actually on your computer.)

Open the first photo you want to print so that it's filling your screen. Open the Charms bar (page 24); choose Devices; choose your printer.

Photos shows you a preview of the printout-to-be. On this screen, you can specify how many copies you want and how you want the photo printed—upright (portrait orientation) or sideways (landscape). The "More settings" button reveals additional options specific to your printer, like paper type and print quality.

When everything looks good, hit the Print button.

SkyDrive

The SkyDrive is one of Microsoft's great unsung offerings. It's a free, 7-gigabyte online hard drive on the Internet, accessible from any computer. How is it handy? Let us count the ways:

- It's a trustworthy "disk" for backing up important files.
- It's a central online location for files you want to access from any machine that can get online.
- It's a perfect pit stop for files you want to shuttle from one computer to another.
- It's an intermediary for sharing big files with other people far away.
- It's integrated into the latest versions of Microsoft Office (for Mac and Windows). That is, you can save a document directly onto your SkyDrive from Word, Excel, or PowerPoint—or open a SkyDrive document directly from within those programs.
- It's also integrated into Microsoft's email services like Hotmail and Outlook.com. For example, if someone sends you a Microsoft Office attachment, you can open and edit it right online and save it to your SkyDrive.

You can pull the SkyDrive onto almost any gadget's screen, wherever you go, saving you the trouble of carrying around a physical disk to transport files. Microsoft offers free SkyDrive apps for Windows; Xbox; Mac OS X; iPhone/iPad; Windows Phone; and Android phones. These apps let you see and organize what's on your SkyDrive and even synchronize files across all your machines.

The SkyDrive is part of your free Microsoft account (page 726).

The purpose of this app is to show you what's on your SkyDrive and give you the chance to organize, download, add, or delete files on it.

Navigating the SkyDrive

Like almost everything else in TileWorld, the contents of your SkyDrive are represented by big rectangular tiles (Figure 4-40). In the first block, each one represents a folder. Microsoft starts you off with folders like Public (everyone in the world can see the contents) and Documents, but you can create your own folders, too, as described below.

Tip: You can use the ⌄ button next to the folder's name, at the top of the screen, to jump to a different folder.

The App Bar

If you didn't know about the App bar, you'd never make new folders, delete any files, or add anything new to your SkyDrive. Fortunately, you *do* know about it (swipe up from the bottom of the screen, or right-click, or press ⊞+Z). Here are the options that appear:

- **Refresh.** Remember, various computers all over the world can access your SkyDrive simultaneously. The Refresh button is here for those occasions when you're collaborating with someone at another location and want to be sure you're seeing the latest versions of the files. It means "update the list."
- **New folder.** Creates a new folder (after you name it and hit the "Create folder" button).
- **Upload.** How do you put new files into your SkyDrive from TileWorld? Clearly, you can't drag and drop from the desktop; there *is* no desktop in TileWorld.

  Answer: Use this button. You're shown the File Picker (page 77) so that you can choose a file to copy to your SkyDrive.
- **Details.** Most of the time, the SkyDrive app prefers to display your files as tiles. But there's something to be said for a traditional list view, where you can see your files' or folders' sizes, modification dates, and (for folders) number of items inside. The Details button produces just such a view.

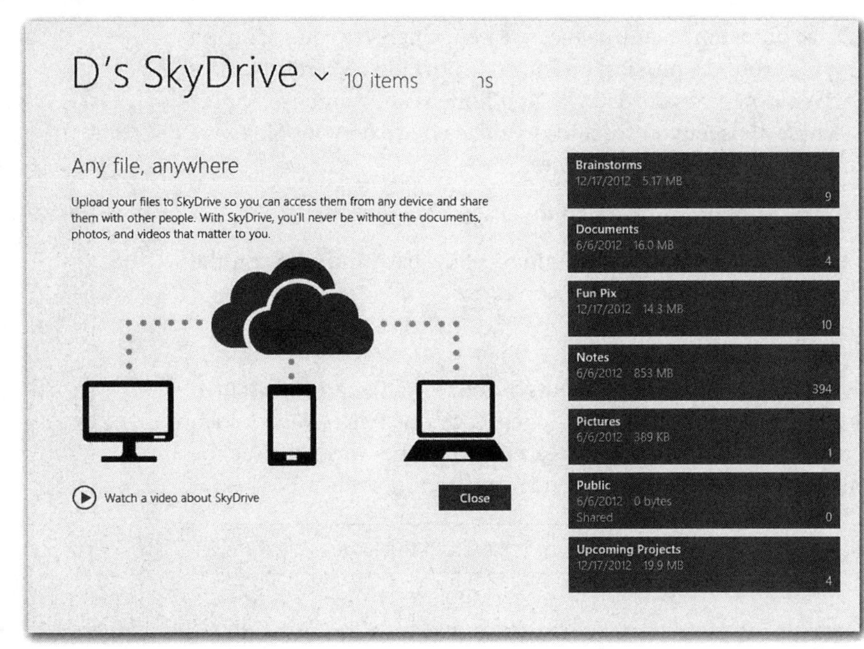

Figure 4-40: *Tap or click to open a folder and see what's inside. If it's a Microsoft Office document, a picture, a text file, or some other common file type, you can open it with one more tap or click. Use the ⊖ button to return to the previous folder.*

In Details view, the same button changes to say "Thumbnails" so that you can return to Tiles view if you get all detailed out.

- **Select all, Clear selection.** In the SkyDrive, you can't share, delete, or download files until you first select them. You do that in the usual TileWorld way.

  Touchscreen: Swipe down from an icon to make a checkmark appear in its corner. *Mouse*: Right-click. *Keyboard*: Use the arrow keys to highlight a tile, and then press the ▤ key.

  Of course, if you want to select everything in the current folder, the "Select all" button is just the ticket. And "Clear selection" *de*selects everything.

- **Delete.** This button appears only when you've selected some tiles or icons. After you confirm your intention, Windows removes the selected files or folders from the SkyDrive.

- **Download.** This button copies the selected files or folders to the machine you're using right now.

- **Open with.** When a single document icon is selected, you can use this button to specify which Windows program or app you want to open it (Figure 4-41).

Figure 4-41:
You'll use this option primarily with generic file types like JPEG pictures, text files, and MP3 music files–documents for which you might own multiple "parent" programs. Here you see some photos in Details view.

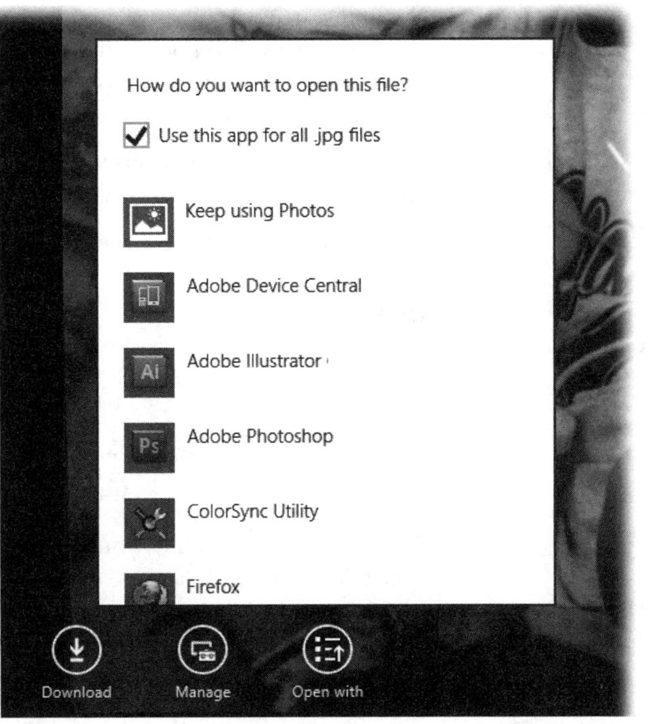

Sharing a File

As always in TileWorld, the Share button is a powerful tool that's only one tap or click away—in the Charms bar (page 24). In other words, you can fire off a link to some SkyDrive file by email, or you can slap a post on Facebook or a tweet on Twitter, incorporating a link to one of your SkyDrive files.

Note: The gotcha: The SkyDrive app can send only one file at a time. The Share button isn't available if you've selected two or more.

Select the file's tile or thumbnail, as described above. Open the Charms bar, hit Share, and then choose your weapon:

- **Mail.** You're asked to address an outgoing message, add a subject line, and select the Send (⊜) button. Once your colleagues receive your email, they have but to select the link in the message to visit your folder and download the file immediately. They can do it even if they don't have Windows Live accounts and even if they're on a Mac or whatever.

Tip: This is a fantastic way to send really huge files to people—files that are much too big to send as email attachments.

- **Facebook or Twitter.** You might not immediately understand that the People button here means "Facebook or Twitter," but there you have it. Once you've selected People, a panel opens with a pop-up menu at the top, which lets you choose either Facebook or Twitter.

  The "Add a message" area lets you type your Facebook post or tweet; hit the Send icon (⊜) to blast a link to your attachment to that social network.

As always, other apps, in time, may add additional icons to the Share panel.

Sports

Here's another online magazine, composed of attractively laid out articles that Microsoft swipes from 300 big-name online news sources.

The app works exactly like the News app (page 143), with a few exceptions:

- It's all about sports.
- If you scroll horizontally, you'll find pages and pages of scores, statistics, and schedules, along with news.
- Open the App bar. See the various league buttons (NFL, NBA, MLB, Golf, and so on)? There are lots of them. You may actually have to *scroll* the App bar—that's something you probably haven't seen before—to view them all. Each league button offers a ▾ button that opens a second row of "section" heads: Top Stories, Videos, Preview Articles, Recap Articles, Standings, Player Stats, and Team Stats, for example (Figure 4-42).

- The App bar contains a Favorite Teams tile. It lets you create a new "section" that displays news of *only* the teams you like. (Hit the ⊕ button to add one.) You can start typing the team name, like *dolphins*, or the city, like *miami;* the app displays a list of matches that narrows down as you type.

  You'll find a similar Favorite Teams block off to the scrollable right of any sports "section," like NFL, NBA, or whatever.

***Figure 4-42:** The Sports app is your interactive, real-time sports rag. Many of the App-bar buttons show you current standings or scores for your chosen team or sport.*

Store

This is it: the Windows Store, source of all TileWorld apps and many regular Windows desktop apps. You can read all about it in Chapter 3.

Travel

Here's yet another Bing magazine family member. Like News, Finance, and Sports, it's an attractive, horizontally scrolling "magazine."

As you'd guess, the theme of Bing Travel is getting away. As you scroll to the right, the various blocks include Featured Destinations (profiles of various vacation spots), Panoramas (cool 360-degree photos that let you "turn your head" inside the scene), and Magazine Articles (drawn from various travel Web sites).

As usual, the most interesting stuff is hiding in the App bar:

- **Destinations.** It's vacation porn: page after page of photo tiles, each depicting a glamorous tourist destination. Select one for details.
- **Flights, Hotels.** Yep, Microsoft's mighty Expedia travel Web site is built right in. Search and book flights and hotel rooms, right from inside the app.
- **Best of Web.** An excellent motley assortment of travel-related Web sites and tools. The various blocks of tiles feature sites dedicated to Road Trips, Food and Wine, Sustainable Travel, Family Travel, and Frequent Travel. Select any tile to open that site in Internet Explorer.

  Don't miss the Tools section, which includes links to currency converters, time/distance/cost calculators, language translators, and, perhaps most important of all, TheBathroomDiaries.com, a global directory of public restrooms.

Video

This "app" is a lot like the Music app described earlier. It serves two purposes:

- **It's a gateway to Microsoft's TV and movie stores.** Scroll off to the right, and you see tiles representing the latest rentable or buyable movies and TV episodes (Figure 4-43, top).
- **It's a player for your own videos.** The Video app opens up to Microsoft's store. But if you scroll to the *left,* you find tiles that represent your own video collec-

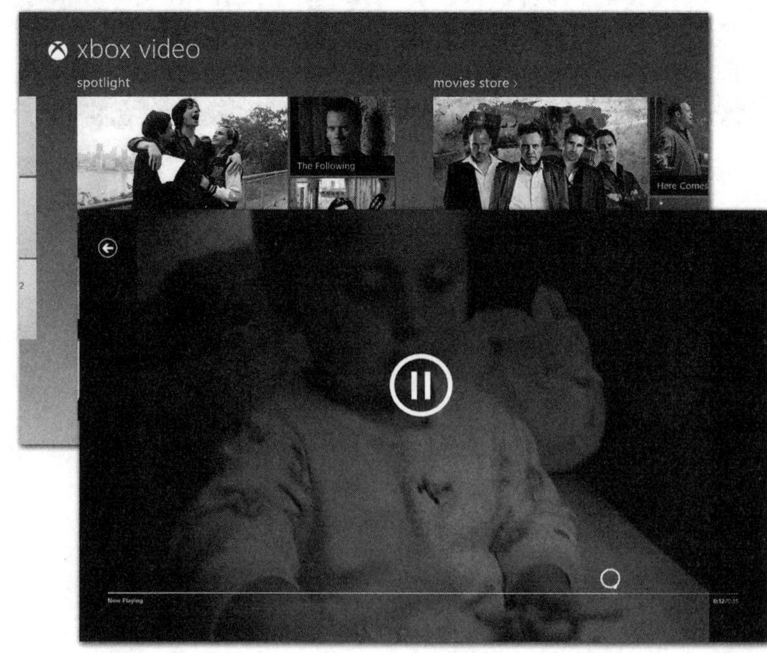

Figure 4-43: *Exactly as in the Xbox Music app, the Xbox Video app is basically a billboard for stuff Microsoft thinks you might want to buy; the Search command is, as always, waiting in the Charms bar if you want to find some particular movie or show to watch. When you choose one of your videos, it opens full screen and begins to play. The only controls are the huge Play/Pause button and the scrollbar; both fade away after a couple of seconds. Move the mouse to bring them back. You can also use the space bar to start or stop playback.*

tion—whatever files you've added to the Videos library folder at the desktop (page 210). See Figure 4-43 (bottom).

Weather

This app opens into a lovely, colorful weather report. Right off the bat, you see the current weather (as though the full-screen background photo didn't give it away). There's the five-day forecast. In a panel on the right, you see the hour-by-hour forecast for today, so you can see exactly what time your softball game will get rained out.

Most people probably never bother drilling past this screen, but there's much more to do here. For example, you can choose the right arrow (➔) to check out the *next* five days' forecast. Or you can choose the expand-o-triangle (▽) to open up a new row of details—wind speed, visibility, humidity, barometer, and the predicted highs and lows. You pilots know who you are.

But the most surprising part of the Weather app is the more complete weather station that lurks beyond this opening screen. If you scroll to the right, you'll discover additional blocks like these:

- **Hourly forecast.** The Hourly column that appears on the main screen is actually only the left end of a wider Hourly display.
- **Maps** are cool visual representations of current meteorological data for the whole country: radar, regional temperature, precipitation, cloud cover, severe weather alerts, and so on.
- **Historical weather.** This handy graph shows you a snapshot of your current location's weather history. The big graph shows temperature, rainfall, and snowfall (depending on which of the three round icons you select beneath it). The little table at the right gives you stats like the average high and low for today's date, the record high and low for today's date, and monthly averages for rainfall, snowy days, and rainy days.
- **Advertisement.** There's also an ad at the far right. Thank goodness you have to go out of your way to find it.

There is, by the way, a table of contents for these different data blocks (Figure 4-44). You might never even find it if you didn't zoom out:

- **Touchscreen:** Pinch two fingers on the screen or trackpad.
- **Mouse:** Move the mouse so that the horizontal scrollbar appears. Hit the tiny – button at lower right.
- **Keyboard:** Press Ctrl+minus key (hyphen).

In each case, the Weather app "shrinks" down into five stacked rectangular bars, representing the main weather screen (Bing Weather), the Hourly Forecast, Maps,

Historical Weather, and Advertisement. Each takes you directly to the corresponding block of tiles without your having to scroll.

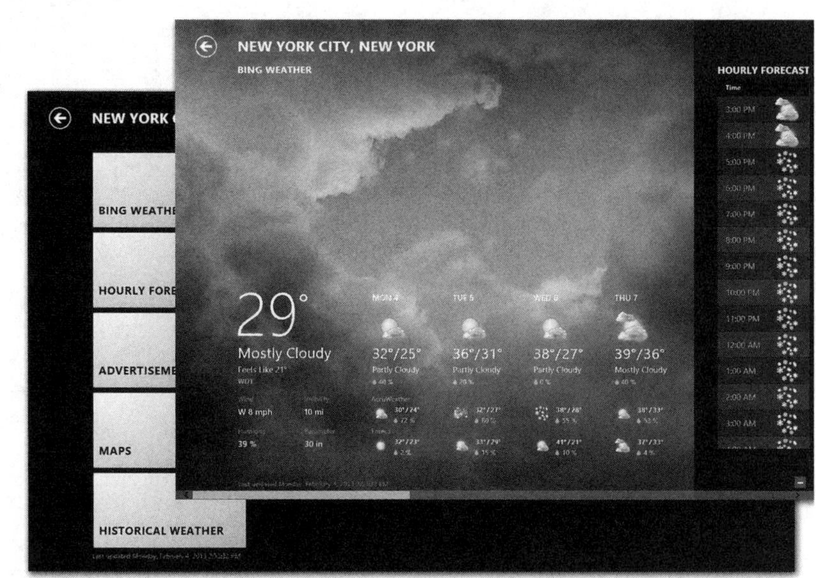

Figure 4-44:
Top: The pages of the Weather app scroll horizontally, just like many of the other built-in TileWorld apps.

Bottom: If you pinch to zoom out (what Microsoft calls "semantic zoom"), you get the table of contents shown here.

CHAPTER
5

TileWorld Settings

TileWorld, where rectangles rule, has its own way of doing things. No overlapping windows, no menus, every app runs full screen—and, of course, everything runs best on a touchscreen. TileWorld has its own version of Internet Explorer, its own technique for right-clicking—and its own special Control Panel, filled with settings that control only the TileWorld world.

The traditional Control Panel still exists at the desktop, and still gets its own chapter in this book (see Chapter 12). Here, though, is a complete rundown of the settings you can change just in TileWorld.

The Six Charms-Panel Settings

When you open the Charms bar (page 24) and then choose Settings, the bottom half of the Settings panel offers icons for the six settings Microsoft thinks you'll want to adjust most often (Figure 5-1). They are:

- **Network.** You use this icon to connect to a network—a WiFi hotspot, for example, that gets you onto the Internet. Details are in Chapter 13.
- **Volume.** Here's your speaker-volume control. When you select it, a volume slider appears; tap, click, or drag anywhere in the vertical "track" to make the volume louder or softer. The number tells you where you are, on a scale of Mute to 100.
- **Brightness.** This icon works just like the volume slider—except it adjusts your screen brightness.

Tip: If you have a tablet or some kind of freaky hybrid Frankenstein laptop, a little surprise lies in store at the top of the Brightness slider; see Figure 5-1.

Figure 5-1:
If you open the Charms bar and select Settings, you get to see these six icons. They give you direct access to the four settings Microsoft thinks you'll need most often, plus two functions that really have nothing to do with settings (Power and Keyboard).

If you tap the Screen icon, you may see a tiny screen-rotation icon above the brightness slider. It appears on any machine whose screen image rotates when you turn it–usually a tablet.

It's the Rotation Lock icon. You can tap it to stop the image from rotating when you turn the screen. (A tiny padlock appears when rotation is locked.)

You might find that useful when, for example, you want to read an ebook in bed–lying on your side.

- **Notifications.** This icon opens a pop-up menu with three options: "Hide for 1 hour," "Hide for 3 hours," and "Hide for 8 hours." It's referring to the notifications—pop-up messages that let you know about incoming mail, messages, updates, and so on. You might want them to stop appearing for an hour while you give a presentation, for example.
- **Power.** This icon isn't really a setting at all, of course. But its shortcut menu offers the Sleep, Shut down, and Restart commands, as described on page 30.
- **Keyboard.** This one's not a setting, either. It hides or shows the onscreen keyboard described on page 71.

Those six are pretty useful—and also pretty self-explanatory.

The rest of the TileWorld settings (Figure 5-2), however, don't appear until you select "Change PC settings" at the bottom of the Settings pane. They're described next.

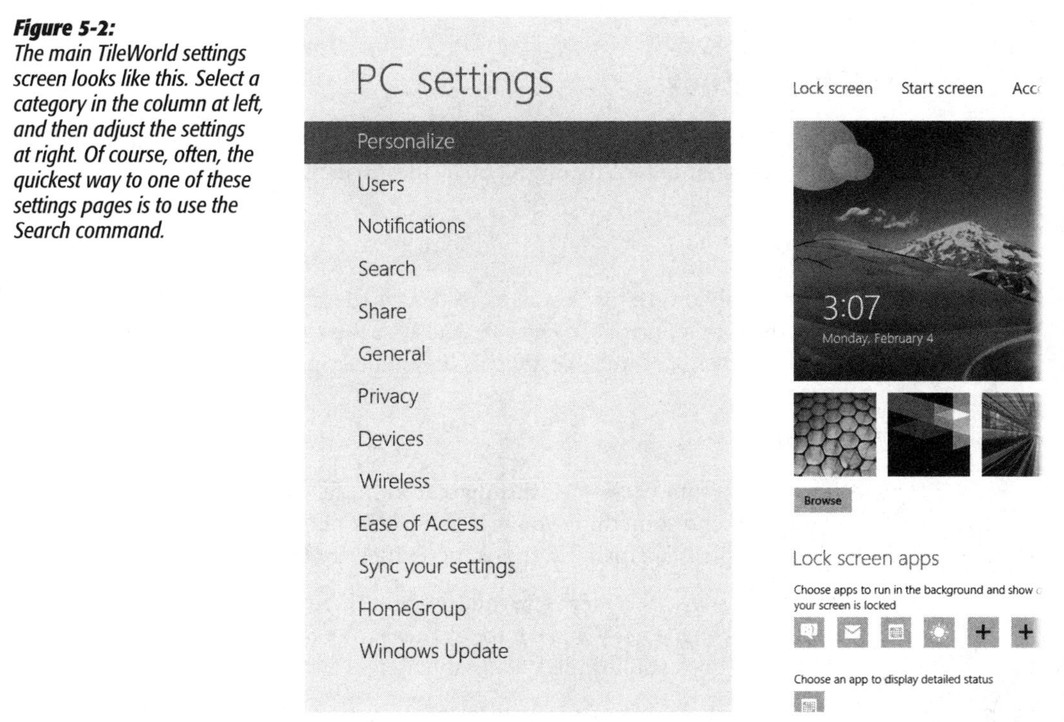

Figure 5-2: *The main TileWorld settings screen looks like this. Select a category in the column at left, and then adjust the settings at right. Of course, often, the quickest way to one of these settings pages is to use the Search command.*

Personalize

There are actually three panes to this panel, which you open using the three tabs across the top:

- **Lock screen.** Here's where you choose a photo as your Lock screen backdrop and control which apps are allowed to run in the background so they can display information on the Lock screen itself. See page 48 for details.
- **Start screen.** Choose a graphic to use as the background for your Start screen, and then choose a color scheme from the row of colored squares below.
- **Account picture.** What image do you want to represent you on the Login screen, and at the upper-right corner of the Start screen? That's the question you're asked here. Use the Browse button to choose an existing picture of yourself from your Pictures folder, or use the Camera button to take a picture of yourself right now, using the built-in Camera app.

Users

On this panel, you can set up additional *accounts* for logging into Windows—usually one for each person who uses this machine—or make changes to your own. Details are in Chapter 24.

Notifications

These switches govern which apps are allowed to bug you with onscreen TileWorld alert boxes—reminders, incoming mail, and so on. Details are in Chapter 2.

Search

These controls govern the Search panel described on page 25. You can read about the "Search history" controls on page 85. The "Use these apps to search" controls hide or show the names of searchable apps, as they appear in the Charms bar's Search panel.

Share

As you know from Chapter 1, the Share icon in the Charms bar is handy whenever you want to send something you're looking at (a photo or a Web page, for example) to other people (via email, Facebook, or Twitter, for example).

When you first install Windows 8, you have only three ways to share material: via Mail, via People (which gives you a choice of Facebook or Twitter), or via your SkyDrive. In time, new apps you install can add themselves to this list.

Which is all a long way of saying that the Share controls govern *which* of those apps (Mail, People, SkyDrive, other apps) are allowed to show up as ways to share stuff. Anything you turn off here won't appear in the Share panel.

Then there's "Show apps I use most often at the top of the app list," which means just what it says (if this is off, then the apps are listed alphabetically). And there's "Show a list of how I share most often," which adds a short list of your most frequently chosen sharing methods—which particular email accounts, for example—at the top of the Share panel. (The "Items in list" control lets you specify how long that list of shortcuts is, and there's a "Clear list" button in case you worry about other people in your family snooping to see how you've been sharing recently.)

General

"General," in this case, means "miscellaneous." Here's what you find here (Figure 5-3):

- **Time.** Here's where you can set your computer's clock, time zone, and daylight saving settings.

- **App switching.** Microsoft has given you the option to *turn off* the convenient swipe gestures for opening the TileWorld app switcher (page 68) and jumping back to the last open app. The inclusion of the "Clear history" button suggests that all of this is intended to protect your privacy—that fellow officemates who wander by while you're up getting coffee might be able to see what apps you've been using recently (gasp!).

Figure 5-3:
This panel of the PC Settings world scrolls vertically. Don't miss any of your exciting options!

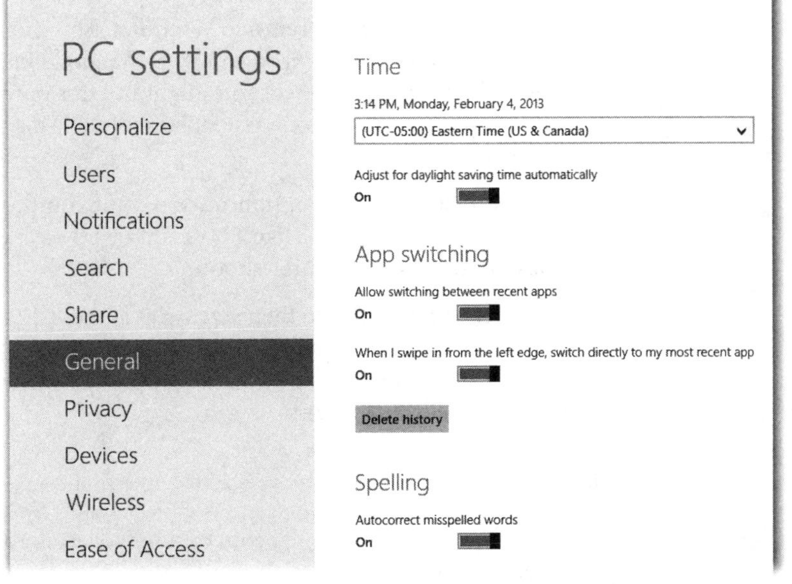

- **Touch keyboard.** These options appear only on touchscreen computers. Most are pretty self-explanatory; you can probably figure out what "Capitalize the first letter of each sentence" means.

  "Show suggestions as I type" is the on/off switch for the word autocomplete suggestions that appear next to your insertion-point cursor as you type. "Make the standard keyboard layout available" is described on page 73.

- **Spelling.** These are the on/off switches for the autocorrect and auto-misspelling underlines described on page 88.

- **Language.** The "Language preferences" link takes you directly to the desktop world, where the Language Preferences panel of the Control Panel opens. Here you can install new languages and keyboard layouts, as described on page 427.

- **Available storage.** How much room is left on your computer? (In the olden days, you might have said "on your hard drive"—but of course, tablets and some laptops don't have actual spinning hard drives anymore. Now it's flash memory (solid-state drives, or SSDs). But the idea is the same.)

Tip: If you're wondering what's eating up all your "disk space," click "View app sizes." It opens a tidy list of all your apps–and shows you exactly how much space they're taking up.

- **Refresh your PC without affecting your files.** The option to *refresh* your PC is new in Windows 8. In essence, it resets your computer. Your files and settings are untouched, but basic computer settings are reset to their factory states, and apps that didn't come from the Windows App Store are deleted. Chapter 21 has more on the refreshing process.
- **Remove everything and reinstall Windows.** This more dramatic troubleshooting technique erases *everything* except what Windows installed on Day One. All your files and settings are deleted. You might use this option on the day you're selling your computer to someone else, for example. This option, too, is described in Chapter 21.
- **Advanced startup.** This option restarts your computer so that you can boot up from some external drive, like a DVD or a USB flash drive, or change startup settings in the course of troubleshooting.

  The screen blinks off, and then you arrive at the "Choose an option" screen, where you can restart into Windows 8, troubleshoot (refresh or reset the PC, or use the advanced troubleshooting and configuration tools described in Chapter 21), or just turn the computer off.

Privacy

This panel offers three miscellaneous options governing apps that want to access your personal information:

- **Let apps use my location.** Clearly, this item is generally intended for tablets and laptops—computers that get moved around. It refers to apps that function best if they know where you are: a movie-listing app, for example, that can show you what's playing at local theaters.

  Of course, letting such apps know where you are also means that your location might also get transmitted to the software companies that wrote those apps. If you turn this option off, then apps can't use your location information (or collect it).
- **Let apps use my name and account picture.** Some app might want to grab your Windows account photo to use as your headshot for other services (Facebook or Twitter, for example). But only if you give permission here.
- **Help improve Windows by sending URLs for the web content that apps use.** If you turn on this switch, then whenever one of your apps fetches data from the Web, Microsoft finds out about it. (That includes Web sites you visit in Internet Explorer or another browser.) Microsoft, of course, would say that it needs this information to make sure that Windows is correctly handling the sort of Web information that apps typically request.

Devices

This is the master screen that lists every external device your computer knows about: printer, scanner, mouse, keyboard, USB camera, and so on.

This is also where you add new devices (that is, introduce them to Windows) and delete old ones. See Chapter 20 for details.

The "Download over metered connection" option is relevant only if you have a laptop or tablet with a built-in cellular modem that lets it get online anywhere you can get a cellphone signal. Sometimes, Windows needs to grab drivers or apps for new hardware gadgets you've installed. Keeping this option turned off ensures that that process will wait until you're in a WiFi hotspot, to avoid running up your bill.

Wireless

These are the on/off switches for your machine's wireless antennas: WiFi, Bluetooth, and cellular (3G or 4G, for example).

Here, too, is the Airplane Mode switch. As you're probably aware, you're not allowed to make cellphone calls on U.S. airplanes. According to legend (if not science), a cellphone's radio can interfere with a plane's navigational equipment.

But come on. Are you supposed to deprive yourself of all the music, videos, movies, and email that you could be using in flight, just because wireless gadgets are forbidden?

Nope. Just turn on Airplane Mode (so that this switch says On). Now a airplane icon appears wherever your WiFi signal-strength bars would appear, including on your desktop taskbar. (You can tap it to turn Airplane Mode off again.)

Now it's safe (and permitted) to use your machine in flight—at least after takeoff, when you hear the announcement about "approved electronics"—because the cellular and WiFi features are turned off completely. You can't make calls or get online, but you can do anything else in the computer's bag of nonwireless tricks.

Note: You can't turn WiFi on when Airplane Mode is on, too. If your flight has WiFi, don't use Airplane Mode.

Ease of Access

Windows offers all kinds of tools to make computing easier if you have trouble seeing or hearing. Most of them are in the *real* Control Panel, which is described in Chapter 12.

But a small sampling of them appear here, in TileWorld:

- **High contrast.** When you turn this switch on, you reverse the screen's colors black for white, like a film negative. It creates a higher-contrast effect that some people find is easier on the eyes. (The other colors reverse, too—red for green, and so on.)

- **Make everything on your screen bigger.** When you turn this option on, everything in TileWorld—text and graphics—gets larger. Bigger Start screen tiles, bigger Charms bar icons, and so on.

  And now, the fine print: If this option is dimmed out on your machine, and there's a line underneath that says "Your display doesn't support this setting," it must mean that your screen's resolution is lower than 1920 × 1080 pixels. You can't make things bigger. Microsoft thinks things are already big enough.

  Note, too, that can't control how much things get bigger. These controls don't affect the desktop, which has its own size controls in the Control Panel. And you may discover that some layouts, like Web pages, look a little funny.

- **Pressing Windows + Volume Up.** It would be handy if you could turn on some of Windows' ease-of-access features with one quick button press, without having to burrow all the way into the desktop Control Panel. And indeed you can, thanks to this handy control.

  Use the pop-up menu to specify *which* feature you want to turn on when you hold down the ⊞ key and press your machine's Volume Up key or button: the Magnifier (a window that enlarges everything you point to), the Narrator (reads aloud everything the cursor touches), or the On-Screen Keyboard. Yes, that's right: You can make the onscreen keyboard appear by pressing physical buttons.

  (For more on the Magnifier and the Narrator, see pages 381 and 384.)

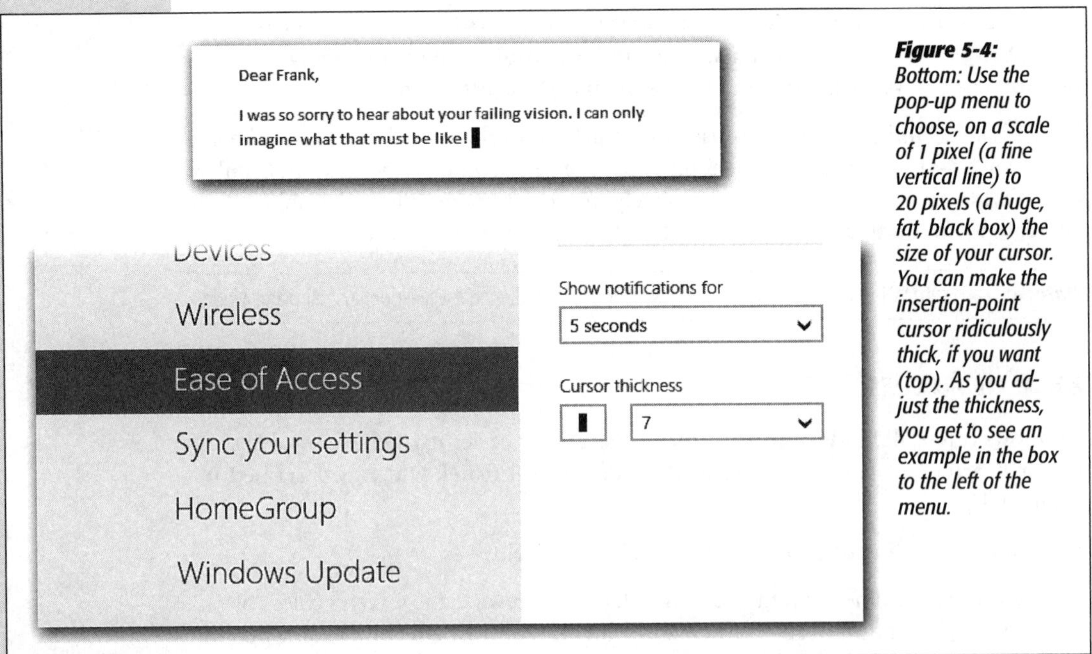

Figure 5-4: *Bottom: Use the pop-up menu to choose, on a scale of 1 pixel (a fine vertical line) to 20 pixels (a huge, fat, black box) the size of your cursor. You can make the insertion-point cursor ridiculously thick, if you want (top). As you adjust the thickness, you get to see an example in the box to the left of the menu.*

- **Show notifications for.** Remember the Notification bubbles described in Chapter 2? Usually they pop up to remind you of something, or to let you know that some new message has arrived, and then they disappear. But using this pop-up menu, you can control how long they stick around before vanishing—from 5 seconds to 5 minutes (a good setting if you're *really* slow on the draw).
- **Cursor thickness.** How thick do you want the text cursor to be? (Not the arrow pointer—the vertical bar that blinks where the next typing will appear.) See Figure 5-4.

Sync Your Settings

If you log into your computer using an online Microsoft account, as described in Chapter 24, you get a delicious perk: Your settings, passwords, browser favorites, and other preferences magically appear on any Windows 8 machine you use. (Or at least any machine you sign into with that Microsoft name and password.) They're all synchronized over an Internet connection.

This panel gives you individual on/off switches for the data you want to synchronize in this way. For details, see Chapter 24.

Homegroup

A Homegroup is a quick, easy way to set up networking among several Windows machines in the same house or office. Without having to know anything about security or system administration, you can easily share documents, music, pictures, videos, printers, and other peripherals with other computers on the same Homegroup.

Here's where you create a Homegroup, join an existing one, and specify which folders you want to share (Documents, Music, Pictures, and so on). For complete details, see Chapter 27.

Windows Update

Windows is software and can therefore be updated, debugged, and improved. (Software is handy that way.) Windows Update is Microsoft's system for sending you patches and fixes over the Internet.

If you choose "Turn on recommended settings," then Windows 8 will periodically query the mother ship to see if there are any new patches for you to install. You can also force a check right now, using the "Check for updates now" button. See page 671 for more on Windows Update.

2

Part Two: The Windows Desktop

CHAPTER
6

File Explorer, Folders & the Taskbar

Let's be honest: TileWorld, the subject of this book's first five chapters, is ideally suited for touchscreens. The mouse and keyboard are afterthoughts. But another environment is sitting there behind TileWorld's attractive rectangles: the traditional Windows desktop. The taskbar, folders, menus, Explorer windows—it's all there, patiently waiting.

Someday, Microsoft hopes, nobody will need the desktop. Someday, all computers will have touchscreens, and everybody will live in TileWorld all the time.

For now, though, a lot of administrative work still requires the desktop. Organizing files and folders. Working with disks. Connecting to networks. And above all, *running programs*; the 4 million Windows programs that existed before Windows 8 still run—but only at the desktop.

The rest of this book, therefore, describes the desktop world.

The Windows Desktop

It's easy enough to *get* to the desktop. On the Start screen, tap or click the Desktop tile. (Unless you've moved it, it's the lower-left tile.) Or press ⊞+D. Either way, TileWorld instantly vanishes—and the desktop appears.

Tip: Move the Desktop tile to the *top* left position on the Start screen. Now, no matter what you're doing, you can jump to the Desktop with a quick press of the ⊞ key (to open the Start screen) and then Enter (to open the first item).

When it first appears, the desktop's wallpaper (background photo) is probably something installed by your PC's manufacturer. By all means choose one of the much more attractive Windows desktop pictures, as described in Chapter 8.

All the traditional Windows landmarks are here at the desktop—the taskbar, the Recycle Bin—except one: the Start menu. You're supposed to use the Start screen to open programs and files now.

To get to the Start screen from the desktop:

- **Touchscreen:** Press the ⊞ button.
- **Mouse:** Point to the lower-left corner of the screen; click the Start-screen tile that pops up.
- **Keyboard:** Press the ⊞ key.

Restoring the Start Menu

If you're feeling instantly lost without the old Start menu, you're not alone. Thousands of PC fans would argue that the Start menu offers a more compact, concise, customizable listing of programs and files.

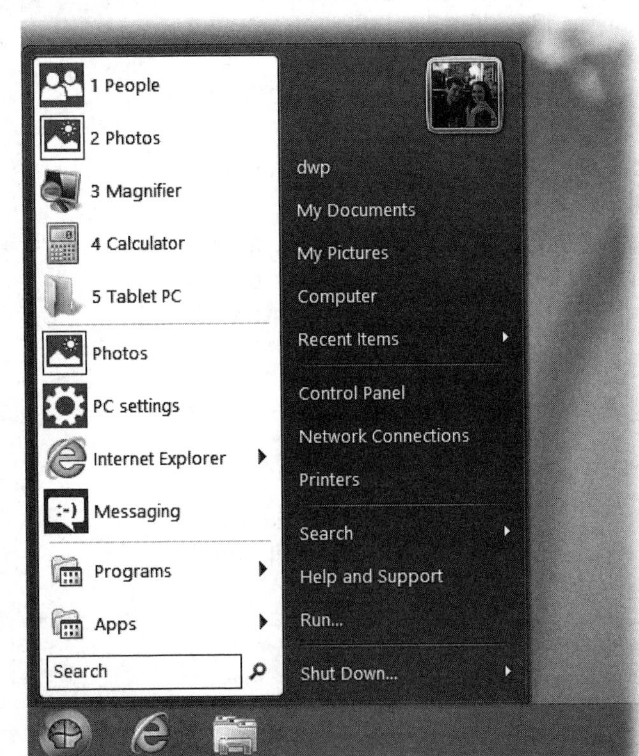

Figure 6-1:
Classic Shell is a free, open-source program (that is, a program written corroboratively by volunteers all over the Internet). It restores the traditional Start menu to the Windows 8 desktop–in your choice of Windows XP, Windows Vista, or Windows 7 styles.

You can drag icons into the lower-left part of the menu to install them there. If you right-click the Start-menu icon (lower left), you access Classic Shell's settings. Among other advantages, they offer an option called Skip Metro Screen. It lets your machine start up directly to the desktop, bypassing TileWorld altogether. You can even disable Windows 8's "hot corners," so that the Charms bar and other new elements don't pop up accidentally.

Microsoft scoffs at that idea. It points out that *every* time there's a new version of Windows, there's an instant spike in popularity of shareware programs that make it work like the *previous* version of Windows. Eventually, the public stops panicking and learns to trust the new design.

Still, even if you want the old Start menu back during your transitional learning time, that's easy to do. All kinds of free or cheap programs are available to restore the Start menu to its rightful place at the desktop, bearing names, like StartIsBack, Classic Shell, Start8, Power8, Pokki, and StartW8 (see Figure 6-1).

The best of them, including Classic Shell and Start8, also offer the option to start up your PC directly to the desktop, bypassing TileWorld altogether. In other words, you can, using one of these programs, live almost entirely at the desktop; you can almost pretend TileWorld doesn't even exist.

Desktop Windows: File Explorer

Windows got its name from the rectangles on the screen—the windows—where all your computer activity takes place. You look at a Web page in a window, type into a window, read email in a window, and look at lists of files in a window. But as you create more files, stash them in more folders, and open more programs, it's easy to wind up paralyzed before a screen awash with cluttered, overlapping rectangles.

Fortunately, Windows has always offered icons, buttons, and other inventions to help you keep these windows under control—and Windows 8 positively crawls with them.

The primary tool at the desktop is now called File Explorer (formerly Windows Explorer), which just means "a window that contains files and folders." But there's more to it than meets the eye, as you'll find out shortly.

Universal Window Controls

A lot has changed in windows since the Windows of a few years ago. If you're feeling disoriented, firmly grasp a nearby stationary object and read the following breakdown.

Here are the controls that appear on almost every window, whether in an application or in File Explorer (see Figure 6-2):

- **Control menu.** This tiny icon sat in the upper-left corner of every Explorer window in Windows XP. It was invisible (but still functional) in Windows 7. And now it's back.

  In any case, the Control menu contains commands for sizing, moving, and closing the window. One example is the Move command. It turns your cursor into a four-headed arrow; at this point, you can move the window by dragging *any* part of it, even the middle. Why bother, since you can always just drag the top edge of a window to move it? Because sometimes, windows get dragged *past* the top of your screen. You can hit Alt+space to open the Control menu, type *M* to trigger the Move command, and then move the window by pressing the arrow keys (or by dragging *any* visible portion). When the window is where you want it, hit Enter to "let go," or the Esc key to return the window to its original position.

Tip: You can double-click the Control menu spot to close a window.

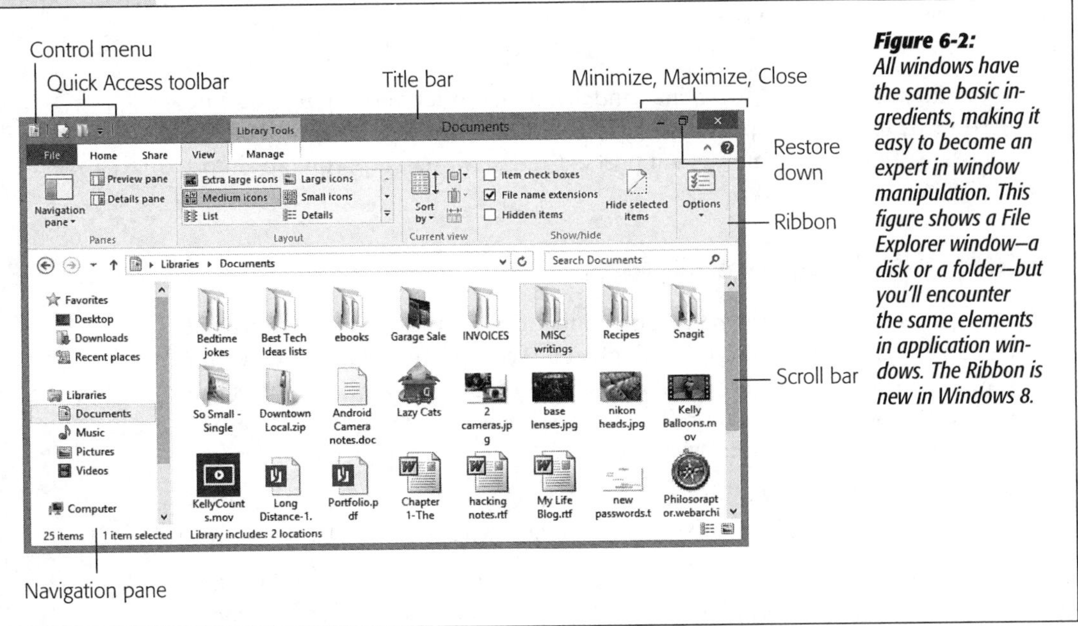

***Figure 6-2:** All windows have the same basic ingredients, making it easy to become an expert in window manipulation. This figure shows a File Explorer window—a disk or a folder—but you'll encounter the same elements in application windows. The Ribbon is new in Windows 8.*

- **Quick Access toolbar.** New in Windows 8: You can dress up the left end of the title bar with tiny icons for functions you use a lot—like Undo, Properties, New Folder, and Rename. And how do you choose which of these commands show up? By turning them on and off in the Customize Quick Access Toolbar menu (⏷), which is always the last icon *in* the Quick Access toolbar.

Tip: As you can see in the ⏷ menu, the Quick Access toolbar doesn't have to appear in the title bar (although that is the position that conserves screen space the best). You can also make it appear as a thin horizontal strip below the Ribbon, where it's not so cluttered. Just choose—what else?—"Show below the ribbon."

- **Title bar.** This big, fat top strip is a giant handle you can use to drag a window around. It also bears the name of the window or folder you're examining.

Tip: The title bar offers two great shortcuts for maximizing a window, making it expand to fill your entire screen exactly as though you had clicked the Maximize button described below. Shortcut 1: Double-click the title bar. (Double-click it again to restore the window to its original size.) Shortcut 2: Drag the title bar up against the top of your monitor.

- **Ribbon.** That massive, tall toolbar at the top of a File Explorer window is the Ribbon. It's a dense collection of controls for the window you're looking at. You can hide it, eliminate it, or learn to value it, as described in the next section of this chapter.
- **Navigation pane.** Some form of this folder tree, a collapsible table of contents for your entire computer, has been part of Windows for years. It's described on page 205.
- **Window edges.** You can reshape a window by dragging any edge—even the very top. Position your cursor over any border until it turns into a double-headed arrow. Then drag inward or outward to make the window smaller or bigger. (To resize a full-screen window, click the Restore Down ⧉ button first.)

Tip: You can resize a window in two dimensions at once by dragging one of its corners. Sometimes a dotted triangle appears at the lower-right corner, sometimes not; in either case, all *four* corners work the same way.

- **Minimize, Maximize, Restore Down.** These three window-control buttons, at the top of every Windows window, cycle a window among its three modes—minimized, maximized, and restored, as described on the following pages.
- **Close button.** Click the ⊠ button to close the window. *Keyboard shortcut:* Press Alt+F4.

Tip: Isn't it cool how the Minimize, Maximize, and Close buttons "darken up" when your cursor passes over them?

Actually, that's not just a gimmick; it's a cue that lets you know when the button is clickable. You might not otherwise realize, for example, that you can close, minimize, or maximize a *background* window without first bringing it forward. But when the background window's Close box "glows dark," you know.

- **Scroll bar.** A scroll bar appears on the right side or bottom of the window if the window isn't large enough to show all its contents.

Sizing, Moving, and Closing Windows

A Windows window can cycle among three altered states.

Maximized

A maximized window is one that fills the screen, edge to edge, so you can't see anything behind it. It gets that way when you do one of these things:

- Click its Maximize button (▭).
- Double-click the title bar.
- Drag the window up against the top of the screen.
- Press ⊞+↑. That's an awesome shortcut.

Maximizing the window is an ideal arrangement when you're surfing the Web or working on a document for hours at a stretch, since the largest possible window means the least possible scrolling.

Once you've maximized a window, you can restore it to its usual, free-floating state in any of these ways:

- Drag the window away from the top edge of the screen.
- Double-click the title bar.
- Click the Restore Down button (🗗). (It's how the Maximize button appears when the window is *already* maximized.)
- Press ⊞+↓.

Tip: If the window *isn't* maximized, this keystroke minimizes it instead.

- Press Alt+space, then R.

Minimized

When you click a window's *Minimize* button (–), the window gets out of your way. It shrinks down into the form of a button on your taskbar at the bottom of the screen. Minimizing a window is a great tactic when you want to see what's behind it. *Keyboard shortcut:* ⊞+↓.

You can bring the window back, of course (it'd kind of be a bummer otherwise). Point to the taskbar button that represents that window's *program.* For example, if you minimized an Explorer (desktop) window, point to the Explorer icon.

On the taskbar, the program's button sprouts handy thumbnail miniatures of the minimized windows when you point to it without clicking. Click a window's thumbnail to restore it to full size. (You can read more about this trick later in this chapter.)

Restored

A *restored* window is neither maximized nor minimized; it's a loose cannon, floating around on your screen as an independent rectangle. Because its edges aren't attached to the walls of your monitor, you can make it any size you like by dragging its borders.

Moving a Window

Moving a window is easy—just drag the big, fat top edge.

Closing a Window

Microsoft wants to make absolutely sure you're never without some method of closing a window. It offers at least nine ways to do it:

- Click the Close button (the ✕ in the upper-right corner).

Tip: If you've managed to open more than one window, Shift-click that button to close *all* of them.

- Press Alt+F4. (This one's worth memorizing. You'll use it everywhere in Windows.)
- Double-click the window's upper-left corner.
- Right-click the window's taskbar button, and then choose Close from the shortcut menu.
- Point to a taskbar button without clicking; thumbnail images of its windows appear. Point to a thumbnail; a ☒ button appears in its upper-right corner. Click it.
- Right-click the window's title bar (top edge), and choose Close from the shortcut menu.
- In an Explorer window, choose File→Close. That works in most other programs, too.
- Quit the program you're using, log off, or shut down the PC.

Be careful. In many programs, including Internet Explorer, closing the window also quits the program entirely.

Tip: If you see *two* ☒ buttons in the upper-right corner of your screen, then you're probably using a program like Microsoft Excel. It's what Microsoft calls an MDI, or *multiple document interface* program. It gives you a window within a window. The outer window represents the application itself; the inner one represents the particular *document* you're working on.

If you want to close one document before working on another, be careful to click the *inner* Close button. If you click the outer one, you'll exit the entire program.

Layering Windows

When you have multiple windows open on your screen, only one window is *active*, which affects how it works:

- It's in the foreground, *in front* of all other windows.
- It's the window that "hears" your keystrokes and mouse clicks.
- Its Close button is red. (Background windows' Close buttons are transparent or window-colored, at least until you point to them.)

As you would assume, clicking a background window brings it to the front.

Tip: And pressing Alt+Esc sends an active window to the *back.* Bet you didn't know that one!

And what if it's so far back that you can't even see it? That's where Windows's window-management tools come in; read on.

Tip: For quick access to the desktop, you can press ⊞+D. Pressing that keystroke again brings all the windows back to the screen exactly as they were.

There's a secret button that does the same thing when clicked or tapped, too. It's the Show Desktop button–a tiny, skinny rectangle that occupies the *farthest-right sliver* of the taskbar. (It was there in Windows 7 , too, but you could see it. Now you just have to know it's there.)

Window Tricks

Windows 8 carries on the window-stunt tradition of Windows 7: special shortcuts expressly designed for managing windows. Most of them involve some clever *mouse gestures*—special dragging techniques. Thanks to those mouse movements and the slick animations you get in response, goofing around with your windows may become the new Solitaire.

Here's the rundown:

- **Maximize a window** by dragging its title bar against the top edge of your monitor.
- **Restore a maximized window** by dragging its title bar *down* from the top of the screen.
- **Make a full-height, half-width window** by dragging it against one side of your screen.

Tip: Actually, it's faster to use the keyboard shortcuts: ⊞+← to snap the window against the left side, or ⊞+→ to snap it against the right. To move the window back again, either hit the same keystroke a few more times (it cycles left, right, and original spot, over and over), or use the ⊞ key with the opposite arrow key.

And if you have more than one monitor, add the Shift key to move the frontmost window to the next monitor, left or right.

NOSTALGIA CORNER

Turn Off All the Snapping and Shaking

It's cool how Windows now makes a window snap against the top or side of your screen. Right? That is, it's better than before, right?

It's perfectly OK to answer, "I don't think so. It's driving me crazy. I don't want my operating system manipulating my windows on its own."

In that case, you can turn off the snapping and shaking features. Open the Start screen. Type enough of the word *shaking* until you see "Turn off automatic window arrangement." Click it.

You've just opened the "Make the mouse easier to use" control panel. At the bottom, turn on "Prevent windows from being automatically arranged when moved to the edge of the screen," and then click OK.

From now on, windows move only when and where you move them. (Shaking a window's title bar doesn't hide other windows now, either.)

And why would you bother? Well, a full-height, half-width window is ideal for reading an article, for example. You wouldn't want your eyes to keep scanning the text all the way across the football field of your screen, and you wouldn't want to spend a lot of fussy energy trying to make the window tall enough to read without scrolling a lot. This gesture sets things up for you with one quick drag.

But this half-screen-width trick is even more useful when you apply it to *two* windows, as shown in Figure 6-3. Now it's simple to compare two windows' contents, or to move or copy stuff between them.

Figure 6-3: *Parking two windows side by side is a convenient preparation for copying information between them or comparing their contents—and it's super-easy. Just drag the first window against the right or left side of your screen; then drag the second window against the opposite side (shown here in progress on the right). Each one gracefully snaps to the full height of your monitor, but only half its width.*

- **Make a window the full height of the screen.** This trick never got much love from Microsoft's marketing team, probably because it's a little harder to describe. But it can be very useful.

  It's not the same as the previous trick; this one doesn't affect the *width* of the window. It does, however, make the window exactly as tall as your screen, sort of like *half*-maximizing it; see Figure 6-4.

Tip: There's a keyboard shortcut for this feature: Shift+⊞+↑ to create the full-height effect, and (of course) Shift+⊞+↓ to restore the window's original height.

To restore the window to its original dimensions, drag its top or bottom edge away from the edge of your screen.

Note: These new window-morphing tricks make a good complement to the traditional "Cascade windows," "Show windows stacked," and "Show windows side by side" commands that appear when you right-click an empty spot on the taskbar.

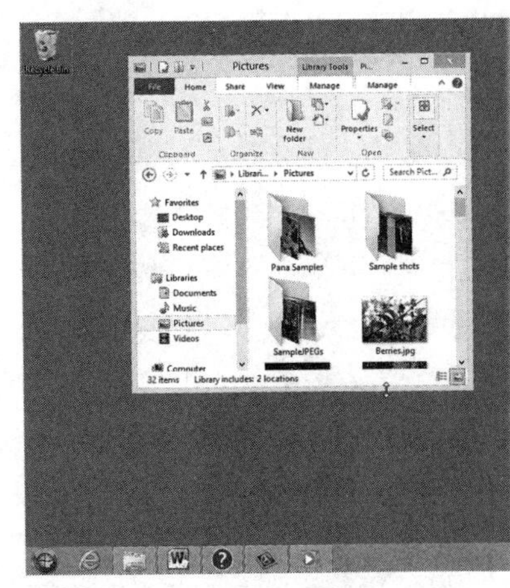

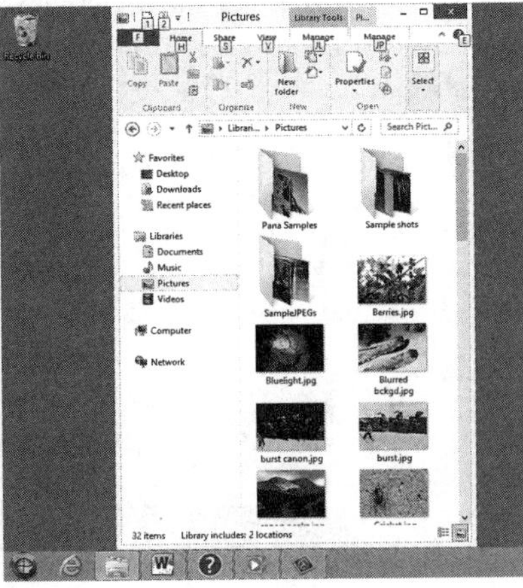

Figure 6-4: *The before-and-after effect of the full-screen-height feature. To make this work, grab the bottom edge of your window (left) and drag it down to the bottom edge of your screen. The window snaps only vertically, but maintains its width and horizontal position (right).*

- **Hide all other windows.** If you've become fond of minimizing windows—and why not?—then you'll love this one. If you give your window's title bar a rapid back-and-forth *shake*, you minimize all *other* windows. The one you shook stays right where it was (Figure 6-5).

Tip: This shaking business makes a very snazzy YouTube demo video, but it's not actually the easiest way to isolate one window. If the window you want to focus on is already the frontmost window, then you can just press ⊞+Home key to achieve the same effect. Press that combo a second time to restore all the minimized windows.

Handily enough, you can bring all the hidden windows back again, just by giving the hero window another title-bar shake.

Note: Dialog boxes (for example, boxes with OK and Cancel buttons) aren't affected by this shaking thing–only full-blown windows.

The Show Desktop Button

The horizontal strip of square tiles at the bottom of the desktop is one of Windows' most famous landmarks: the taskbar. If you asked most people, "What's on the far right of the taskbar?" they'd probably say, "the system tray" or "the notification area" (that little row of status icons for battery, WiFi strength, and so on).

But they'd be wrong. What's actually at the far right of the taskbar is the Show Desktop button.

In Windows 7, it was a bizarre little reflective-looking stick of Trident. In Windows 8, it's still there, but with absolutely no visual clue that it exists.

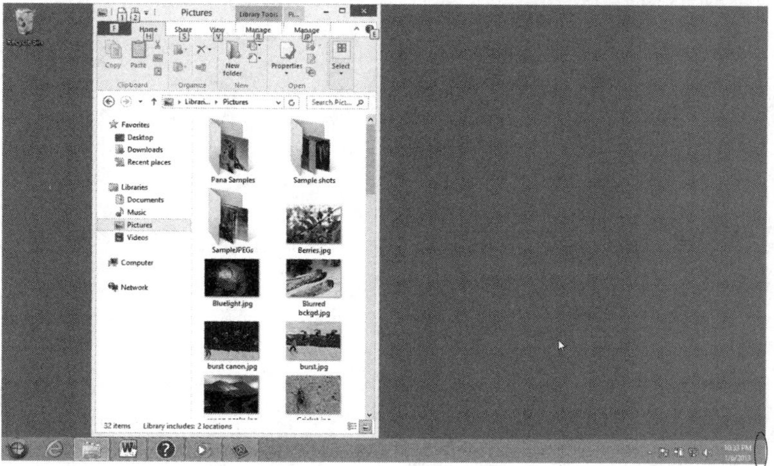

Figure 6-5: *Top: OK, this is the state of your screen. You want to have a look at your desktop—but oy, what a cluttered mess!*

Bottom: So you give this window's title bar a little shake—at least a couple of horizontal or vertical back-and-forths—and boom! All other windows are minimized to the taskbar, so you can see what you're doing. Give the title bar a second shake to bring the hidden windows back again.

The tiny circle at lower right indicates the position of the invisible Show Desktop button. It's a tiny slice at the far-right end of the taskbar.

Click that spot to make all windows and dialog boxes disappear *completely*, so you can do some work on your desktop. They're not minimized—they don't shrink down into the taskbar—they're just gone. Click the Show Desktop button a second time to bring them back from invisible-land.

Tip: There's a less flashy but more efficient keyboard trick that achieves the same effect. Next time you want to minimize all windows, revealing your entire desktop, press ⊞+M (which you can think of as M for "Minimize all"). Add the Shift key (Shift+⊞+M) to bring them all back.

The Ribbon

In previous versions of Windows, there were all kinds of crazy ways to shape, sort, group, slice, and dice the contents of an Explorer window. In Windows 8, somebody at Microsoft got fed up and decided to stuff them all into one convenient place: the new Ribbon.

The Ribbon is a glorified toolbar. (Word, PowerPoint, Excel, and other Microsoft programs have Ribbons, too.) In File Explorer, it comes with several tabs full of buttons. They can differ from window to window; for example, in a window full of pictures, you get buttons that are especially useful for managing picture files (Figure 6-6).

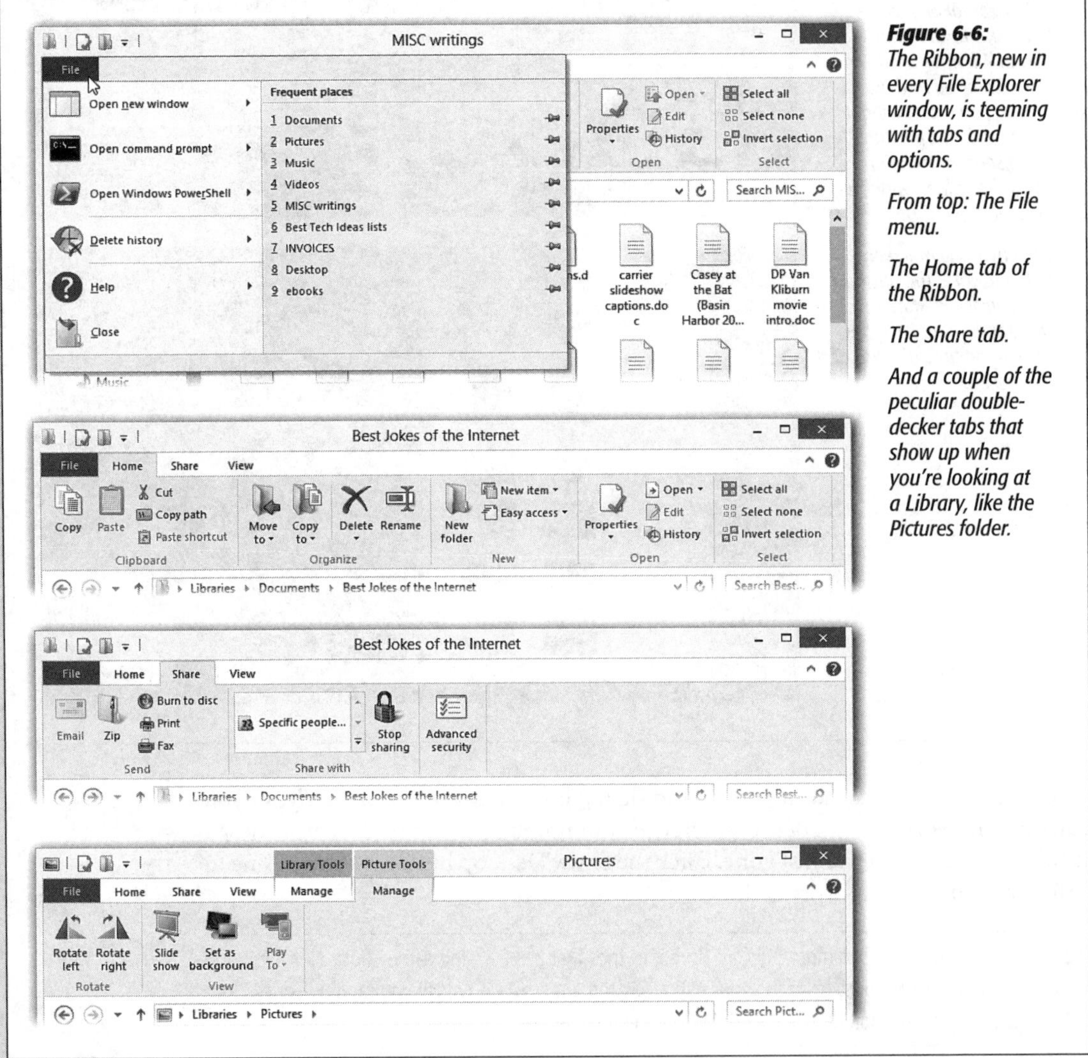

Figure 6-6: *The Ribbon, new in every File Explorer window, is teeming with tabs and options.*

From top: The File menu.

The Home tab of the Ribbon.

The Share tab.

And a couple of the peculiar double-decker tabs that show up when you're looking at a Library, like the Pictures folder.

You can collapse the Ribbon to get it out of your way; it is, after all, pretty tall. You do that by clicking the ⌄ button at the window's upper-right corner, or by pressing Ctrl+F1. (Later, you can bring it back by clicking the ^ button, or by pressing Ctrl+F1 again. But that might not be necessary; even when the Ribbon is collapsed, its tab names—File, Home, Share, View, and so on—are still visible for quick clicking.)

Tip: The Ribbon also goes away in full-screen mode, in which your Explorer window fills the entire screen. (Press F11 to start or stop full-screen mode.)

You can also get rid of it permanently, using the free Ribbon Disabler program. You can download it from this book's "Missing CD" page at *www.missingmanuals.com.*

But before you go whole-hog into a Ribbon-cutting ceremony, consider what the Ribbon has to offer.

File Tab

Ha, fooled you! The word File here looks like all the other tabs, but it's actually a weird kind of menu (Figure 6-6, top). The idea, as always, is to cram every possible command you might want into one central place, so you don't have to hunt. Here's a rundown:

NOSTALGIA CORNER

Bringing Back Aero Peek

In Windows 7, that invisible Show Desktop button (the tiny sliver at the right end of the taskbar) housed a gimmicky but cool additional feature. Instead of just clicking it to hide all windows, you could also point to it *without* clicking—and you'd trigger something called Aero Peek.

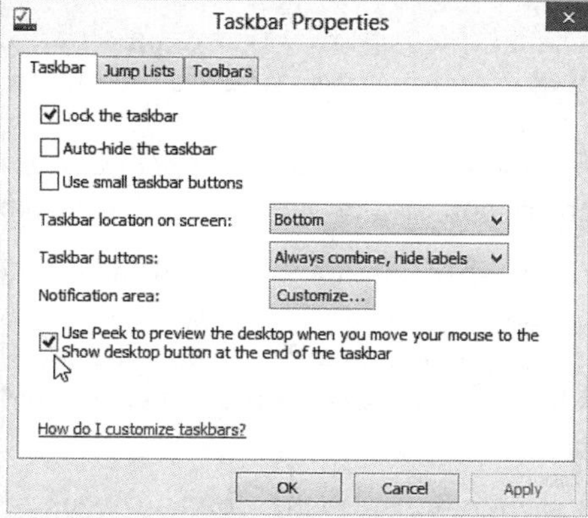

That's when all the windows stay where they are on your screen—but they become transparent. Only their outlines indicate where they used to be.

That feature no longer works. After all, pointing to the lower-right corner of the screen has a new meaning in Windows 8: It makes the Charms bar appear. Microsoft reasoned that it might confuse people if that action made the Charms bar appear *and* made the windows go all hollow-like.

But you can bring Aero Peek back from the dead, if you like. Right-click the taskbar; from the shortcut menu, choose Properties. In the Properties dialog box, on the Taskbar tab, turn on "Use Peek to preview the desktop when you move your mouse to the Show Desktop button at the end of the taskbar." Click OK.

Now when you point to the lower-right corner of the screen, you summon the Charms bar *and* make all windows disappear (except for their outlines). Eat your heart out, Cheshire Cat.

- **Open new window.** It's a submenu, actually. It offers two sub-commands: "Open new window" (opens a new Explorer window) and "Open new window in new process." (A *process* is a computer's train of thought. Hard-core PC geeks sometimes like to open a new window, or a second copy of the same one, in a new computer process in case the first one crashes. Not, admittedly, something you'll do every day.)
- **Open command prompt.** The command prompt is a *command line*, a text-based method of performing a task. You type a command, click OK, and something happens as a result. Power users can type long sequences of commands and symbols at the command prompt.

  Working at the command line is becoming a lost art in the world of Windows, because most people prefer to issue commands by choosing from menus using the mouse. However, some old-timers still love the command prompt, and even mouse-lovers encounter situations when a typed command is the only way to do something.

  You have a choice of two variations: "Open command prompt" and "Open command prompt as administrator," which gives you greater powers over your PC domain, once you enter an administrator password to prove your worth. Either way, the white-text-on-black command prompt window opens, ready for your typed input.
- **Open Windows PowerShell.** PowerShell is a command console and scripting language. If you're a programmer, PowerShell lets you write your own simple programs, called *cmdlets* ("commandlets") that can perform all kinds of automated drudgery for you: Copy or move folders, manipulate files, open or quit programs, and so on.

  You harness all this power by typing up *scripts* in PowerShell's command-line interface (which means no mouse, no menus, no windows—all text, like in the DOS days). In short, PowerShell is not for the layperson. If you're an ambitious layperson, however, a Google search for *PowerShell tutorial* unveils all kinds of Web sites that teach you, step by step, how to harness this very advanced tool.
- **Delete History.** Two commands wait in the submenu here; both are designed to erase your navigational tracks, for privacy purposes. "Recent places list" erases the list of recent folders that Windows maintains in the File menu, as described above. "Address bar history" erases the list of computer folders you've visited in the address bar.
- **Help.** The Help command in the submenu opens the onscreen help for the Windows desktop world, as described on page 89. The About Windows command just opens a dialog box that identifies which version of Windows 8 you have.
- **Close.** Closes the Explorer window.
- **Frequent places.** Here, for your convenience, is a listing of important folders in your account (Documents, Pictures, Music, Videos), plus folders you've accessed recently. The idea is to save you some burrowing.

Tip: If you have a keyboard, you can save time by hitting the indicated number. In Figure 6-6, for example, you could hit the number 3 to open the Music folder.

As you can tell by the underlines, in fact, *all* of the File menu commands offer keyboard shortcuts. See how it says "Open new window"? That means you can type the N key to open a new window, rather than using the mouse or a finger.

Home Tab

This tab of the Ribbon is, more or less, an exploded view of the shortcut menu that would appear if you right-clicked a desktop icon. But Microsoft research shows that a huge number of Windows users don't even *know* about the shortcut menus—so by putting these commands in the Ribbon, the company hopes to make these useful commands more "discoverable."

- **Copy, Paste, Cut.** These commands let you copy, cut, and paste icons from one window to another.
- **Copy path.** This command copies the icon's navigational *path* to the Clipboard, ready for pasting somewhere. (See page 808.)
- **Paste Shortcut.** If you've copied an icon to the Clipboard, then this command pastes a shortcut icon of it—another handy way to make a shortcut (page 282).
- **Move To, Copy To.** These handy buttons/menus make it quick and easy to move or copy selected icons to another place on your computer. The pop-up menu lists frequently and recently opened folders; you can also hit "Choose location" to specify a folder that's not listed here. Either way, the beauty is that you can move or copy icons without having to open and position the destination window.

POWER USERS' CLINIC

Power Keys for the Ribbon

The Ribbon is supposed to enhance your efficiency by putting every conceivable command in one place, with nothing hidden. But how efficient is a tool that requires mousing?

Fortunately, the Ribbon is fully keyboard-operable. It even has a built-in cheat sheet.

To see it, press the Alt key, which is the universal Windows shortcut for "show me the keyboard shortcuts." You see the little boxed letter-key shortcuts for each of the tabs, as shown here. (Those keystrokes work, however, even if you haven't first summoned the cheat sheet.)

Sometimes, you'll actually see *two*-letter codes. In a Pictures library, for example, the Picture Tool tab of the Ribbon offers RLL and RR as the keyboard shortcuts for "Rotate Left" and "Rotate Right."

But the idea is the same: to save you time and mousing.

- **Delete.** The pop-up menu offers two commands: "Recycle" (moves the selected icon to the Recycle Bin) and "Permanently delete" (deletes the file forever without its usual stop in the Recycle Bin). The third item, "Show recycle confirmation," isn't a command—it's an on/off switch for the "Are you sure?" message that usually appears when you put something into the Recycle Bin.
- **Rename.** Opens the selected icon's name-editing box.
- **New Folder.** Makes a new, empty folder in the current window, ready for you to name and fill up with icons.
- **New item.** Here's a catch-all pop-up menu that lists new things you might want to create in the open window: a new folder, a shortcut (page 282), a contact (that is, a new person page in the People app), a Microsoft Word document, a Journal document, a text document, a compressed (zipped) folder, and so on. You may see different items here, since different programs can modify this menu to make your life more convenient.
- **Easy access.** Here's an even more miscellaneous pop-up menu of useful commands; all of them apply to icons you've selected in the window. There's "Pin to Start," which adds a tile for the highlighted icon to the Start screen, as described in Chapter 1. "Include in library" adds the selected icon to one of your libraries (page 208). "Add to favorites" adds the selected icon to the navigation pane at the left side of every Explorer window.

  To understand "Map as drive," read page 808.

  The remaining commands—"Always available offline," "Sync," and "Work offline," pertain to the offline files feature described on page 815.
- **Properties.** This button/menu offers two options: "Properties" opens the selected icon's Properties dialog box, where you can read a wealth of detail about its size, type, and so on. "Remove properties" strips all of that stuff off of a file, usually because you're about to send it to somebody and don't want them to know about its revision history, modification dates, and so on.

Tip: You can just click the icon to open the Properties dialog box. That is, you don't actually have to choose from the submenu.

- **Open.** Do you really need a button that opens the selected icon? Yes, if it's the type of file that *more than one program can open.* For example, suppose you have a picture file. Do you want to open it in Photoshop or in Picasa? This pop-up menu changes to reflect the programs that are capable of opening the selected icon.
- **Edit** opens the highlighted icon in the first program Windows finds that can edit that file type.
- **History.** This button opens a window that tracks the file's editing history. It's an essential part of the new Windows 8 *File History* feature described on page 696; it lets you rewind a certain document to an earlier version.

- **Select all, Select none.** As you'd guess, these commands highlight all the icons in the window, or none of them.
- **Invert selection.** This command swaps what you've selected. In other words, if you've highlighted files A and B (but not C and D), then this command highlights files C and D, and deselects A and B.

Share Tab

This tab offers a full line of controls for sharing the icons in the window—via email, fax, printer, or other people on your network.

- **Email.** Click to open a new outgoing email message, with the selected file(s) attached, ready to address and send.
- **Zip.** Compresses the selected file(s) into one more compact, self-contained zip file. Great for sending a batch of related files to somebody in a way that contains all the necessary pieces.
- **Burn to disc.** Prompts you to insert a blank CD or DVD; Windows will burn a copy of the selected files onto that disc.
- **Print.** Opens the document and, depending on what kind of file it is, prepares it for printing.
- **Fax.** Sends the selected file to your fax modem, if you have one.
- **Specific people.** Makes the selected file(s) available for accessing over the network by people you specify. (Chapter 27 has details.) When you click here, a window opens up with a list of people on the network, so you can choose the lucky collaborators.
- **Stop sharing.** Turns off network sharing, so that once again, you're the only person who can see the selected files.
- **Advanced security.** This control, too, affects file sharing on the network. It gives you much finer control over who's allowed to do what to the selected file: See it? Open it? Change it? Chapter 27 contains more on these file permissions.

View Tab

This tab controls the look, arrangement, and layout of the icons in the window: list view, icon view, sorted alphabetically, sorted chronologically, and so on. Page 215 has a complete rundown of these options.

Library Tools/Manage Tab

In a few places, you get a bonus tab—with a weird double-stacked title. These tabs appear only when you've opened the window of a library—a special class of folder that can display the contents of other folders, wherever they may actually sit on your machine, without having to move them. You can read more about libraries on page 208.

Music Tools/Play Tab

When you've opened your Music library (either the one Windows gives you, or one you've made yourself), the window bears a new double-decker tab called Music Tools/ Play. These are your options:

- **Play.** Opens your music-playback program (the TileWorld app called Music) and begins playing the highlighted music.
- **Play all.** Opens the Music app and begins playing everything in the window.
- **Play To.** This pop-up menu lets you direct audio or video playback to another device—usually an Xbox connected to your TV, but there are other Play To–compatible receivers. If you do, in fact, own one of these gadgets, and you've configured it right, you'll see it listed in this pop-up menu. Choose its name to redirect sound. (If you don't have any other compatible playback gadgets, this button is dimmed.)
- **Add to playlist.** Adds the highlighted music file to a new, untitled playlist in Windows Media Player (Chapter 18). The idea is that you can root around here, in an Explorer window, adding files to a playlist without having to open Media Player first.

Picture Tools/Manage Tab

Opening the Pictures library folder offers a special double-decker tab, too, stocked with commands for controlling pictures. They include these:

- **Rotate left, Rotate right.** Turns the selected photos 90 degrees. Handy if they're coming up turned sideways because of the way you held the camera.
- **Slide show.** Starts an immediate full-screen slideshow. Click the mouse or tap to go to the next picture; press the arrow keys to go faster forward or backward; press the Esc key to stop the show.
- **Set as background.** Instantly applies the selected photo to your desktop, as its new wallpaper!
- **Play To.** Here, again, is the Play To command. If you have an Xbox or another playback gadget attached to your TV, then you can send a photo or slideshow from your Windows 8 machine to the big screen with this one click. See page 607 for more on Play To.

Tabucopia

Incredibly, that's not all the tabs. You'll see other tabs appear when you open certain window types. There's a Ribbon tab just for the Recycle Bin. There's a Disk Tools tab (when you open a disk window), a Shortcut Tools tab (for a shortcut), Application Tools (for a program), and so on. Part of the fun is encountering new tabs you've never seen before.

Explorer Window Controls

When you're working at the desktop—that is, opening Explorer folder windows—you'll find a few additional controls dotting the edges. They're quite a bit different from the controls of Windows XP and its predecessors.

Address Bar

In a Web browser, the address bar is where you type the addresses of the Web sites you want to visit. In an Explorer window, the address bar is more of a "bread-crumbs bar" (a shout-out to Hansel and Gretel fans). That is, it now shows the path you've taken—folders you burrowed through—to arrive where you are now (Figure 6-7).

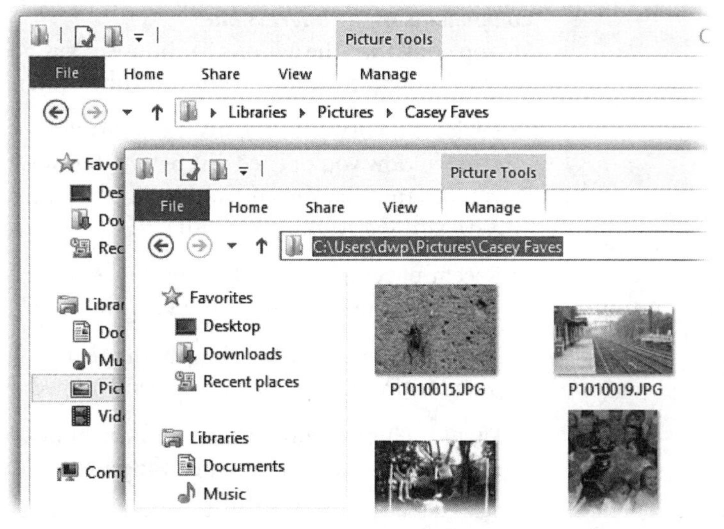

Figure 6-7: *Top: The notation in the address bar, Libraries ▸ Pictures ▸ Casey Faves, indicates that you, Casey, opened your Personal folder (page 263), then opened the Pictures library inside, and finally opened the Casey Faves folder inside that.*

Bottom: If you press Alt+D, then the address bar restores the slash notation of Windows versions gone by so that you can type in a different address.

There are three especially cool things about this address bar:

- **It's much easier to read.** Those ▸ little ▸ triangles are clearer separators of folder names than the older\slash\notation. And instead of drive letters like C:, you see the drive *names.*

Tip: If the succession of nested folders' names is too long to fit the window, then a tiny « icon appears at the left end of the address. Click it to reveal a pop-up menu showing, from last to first, the other folders you've had to burrow through to get here.

(Below the divider line, you see, for your convenience, the names of all the folders on your desktop.)

- **It's clickable.** You can click any breadcrumb to open the corresponding folder. For example, if you're viewing the Casey ▸ Pictures ▸ Halloween folder, you can click the *word* Pictures to backtrack to the Pictures folder.

- **You can still edit it.** The address bar of old was still a powerful tool, because you could type in a folder address directly (using the slash notation).

  Actually, you still can. You can "open" the address bar for editing in any of four different ways: (1) Press Alt+D. (2) Click the tiny icon to the left of the address. (3) Click any blank spot. (4) Right-click anywhere in the address; from the shortcut menu, choose Edit Address.

  In each case, the address bar changes to reveal the old-style slash notation, ready for editing (Figure 6-7, bottom).

Tip: After you've had a good look, press Esc to restore the ▸ notation.

Components of the address bar

On top of all that, the address bar houses a few additional doodads that make it easy for you to jump around on your hard drive (Figure 6-8):

- **Back** (⊖), **Forward** (⊕). Just as in a Web browser, the Back button opens whatever window you opened just before this one. Once you've used the Back button, you can then use the Forward button to return to the window where you started. *Keyboard shortcuts:* Alt+←, Alt+→.
- **Recent pages list.** Click the ▾ to the left of the address bar to see a list of folders you've had open recently; it's like a multilevel Back button.
- **Recent folders list.** Click the ⌄ at the *right* end of the address bar to see a pop-up menu listing addresses you've recently typed.
- **Up** (↑). This delightful new button, right next to the address bar, makes its debut in Windows 8. It means "Open the parent folder of this one."

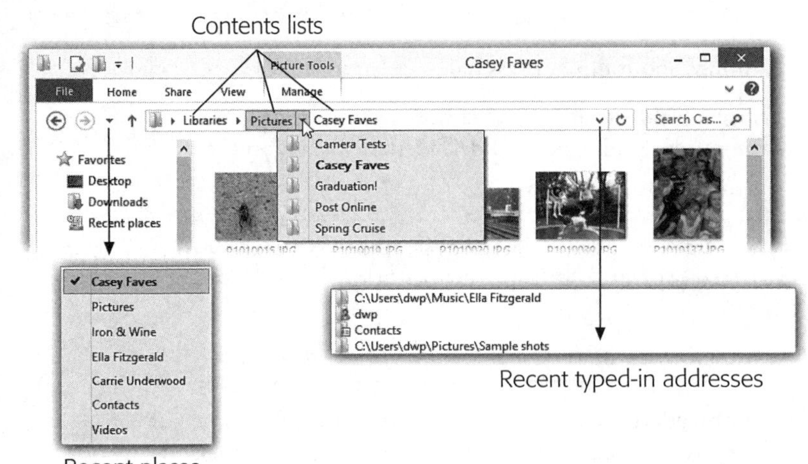

Figure 6-8: *The address bar is crawling with useful controls and clickable gizmos. It may take you awhile to appreciate the difference between the little ▾ to the left of the address bar and the ⌄ to its right, though. The left-side one shows a list of folders you've had open recently; the right-side one shows addresses you've explicitly typed (and not passed through by clicking).*

For example, if you've drilled down into the USA→Texas→Houston folder, you could hit Alt+↑ to pop "upward" to the Texas folder, again for the USA folder, and so on. If you hit Alt+↑ enough times, you wind up at your desktop.

(There's always been an Alt+↑ keystroke for this purpose, but a dedicated button is more novice-friendly.)

- **Contents list.** This one takes some explaining, but for efficiency nuts, it's a gift from the gods.

  It turns out that the little ▸ next to each breadcrumb (folder name) is actually a pop-up menu. Click it to see what's *in* the folder name to its left.

  How is this useful? Suppose you're viewing the contents of the USA ▸ Florida ▸ Miami folder, but you decide that the file you're looking for is actually in the USA ▸ California folder. Do you have to click the Back button, retracing your steps to the USA folder, only to then walk back down a different branch of the folder tree? No, you don't. You just click the ▸ that's next to the USA folder's name and choose California from the list.

POWER USERS' CLINIC

The Master Explorer-Window Keyboard-Shortcut List

If you arrive home one day to discover that your mouse has been stolen, or if you simply like using the keyboard, you'll enjoy the shortcuts that work in File Explorer:

F6 or **Tab** cycles the "focus" (highlighting) among the different parts of the window: Favorite Links, address bar, main window, search box, and so on.

F4 highlights the address bar and pops open the list of previous addresses. (Press Alt+D to highlight the address bar without opening the pop-up menu.)

Alt+← opens the previously viewed window, as though you'd clicked the Back button in a browser. Once you've used Alt+←, you can press Alt+→ key to move *forward* through your recently open windows.

Backspace does the same thing as Alt+←. It, too, walks you backward through the most recent windows you've had open. That's a change from Windows XP, when Backspace meant "up," as in, "Take me to the parent folder" (see Alt+↑, below).

Alt+↑ opens the parent window of whatever you're looking at now—just like the new button next to the address bar.

Alt+double-clicking an icon opens the Properties window for that icon. (It shows the same sort of information you'd find in the Details pane.) Or, if the icon is already highlighted, press Alt+Enter.

F11 enters or exits full-screen mode, in which the current window fills the entire screen. Even the taskbar and Ribbon are hidden. This effect is more useful in a Web browser than at the desktop, but you never know; sometimes you want to see everything in a folder.

Shift+Ctrl+N makes a new empty folder.

Shift+Ctrl+E adjusts the navigation pane so that it reveals the folder path of whatever window is open right now, expanding the indented folder icons as necessary.

Press the Ctrl key while turning the mouse's scroll wheel to magnify or shrink the icons in your window. You can also press the letter keys to highlight a folder or file that begins with that letter, or the ↑ and ↓ keys to "walk" up and down a list of icons.

- **Refresh (↻).** If you suspect that the window contents aren't up to date (for example, that maybe somebody has just dropped something new into it from across the network), click this button, or press F5, to make Windows update the display.
- **Search box.** Type a search phrase into this box to find what you're looking for *within this window.*

What to type into the address bar

When you click the tiny folder icon at the left end of the address bar (or press Alt+D), the triangle ▸ notation changes to the slash\notation, meaning that you can edit the address. At this point, the address bar is like the little opening in the glass divider that lets you speak to your New York cab driver; you tell it where you want to go. Here's what you can type there (press Enter afterward):

- **A Web address.** You can leave off the *http://* portion. Just type the body of the Web address, such as *www.sony.com,* into this strip. When you press Enter (or click the → button, called the Go button), Internet Explorer opens to the Web page you specified.

Tip: If you press Ctrl+Enter instead of just Enter, you can surround whatever you've just typed into the address bar with *http://www.* and *.com.* See Chapter 15 for even more address shortcuts along these lines.

- **A search phrase.** If you type some text into this strip that isn't obviously a Web address, Windows assumes you're telling it, "Go online and search for this phrase." From here, it works exactly as though you'd typed into the Address/Search bar of Internet Explorer.
- **A folder name.** You can also type one of several important folder names into this strip, such as *Computer, Documents, Music,* and so on. When you press Enter, that particular folder window opens.

Tip: This window has AutoComplete. That is, if you type *pi* and then press Tab, the address bar will complete the word *Pictures* for you. (If it guesses wrong, press Tab again.)

- **A program or path name.** In this regard, the address bar works just like the Run command (page 246).

In each case, as soon as you begin to type, a pop-up list of recently visited Web sites, files, or folders appears below the address bar. Windows is trying to save you some typing. If you see what you're looking for, click it with the mouse, or press the ↓ key to highlight the one you want, and then press Enter.

Note: Remember the colored strip that appeared just below the address bar in Windows 7? It was called the task toolbar. It's gone in Windows 8; the Ribbon incorporates all of its functions and more.

Optional Window Panes

Most File Explorer windows have some basic informational stuff across the top: the address bar and the Ribbon, at the very least.

But that's just the beginning. As shown in Figure 6-9, you can add a new panel to the right side of any Explorer window. It can take one of two forms: a Preview (of the selected icon) or a panel of Details. Turning one of these panels on may make your window feel a bit claustrophobic, but at least you'll know absolutely everything there is to know about your files and folders.

The on/off switch for this panel is on the View tab of the Ribbon, as shown in Figure 6-9.

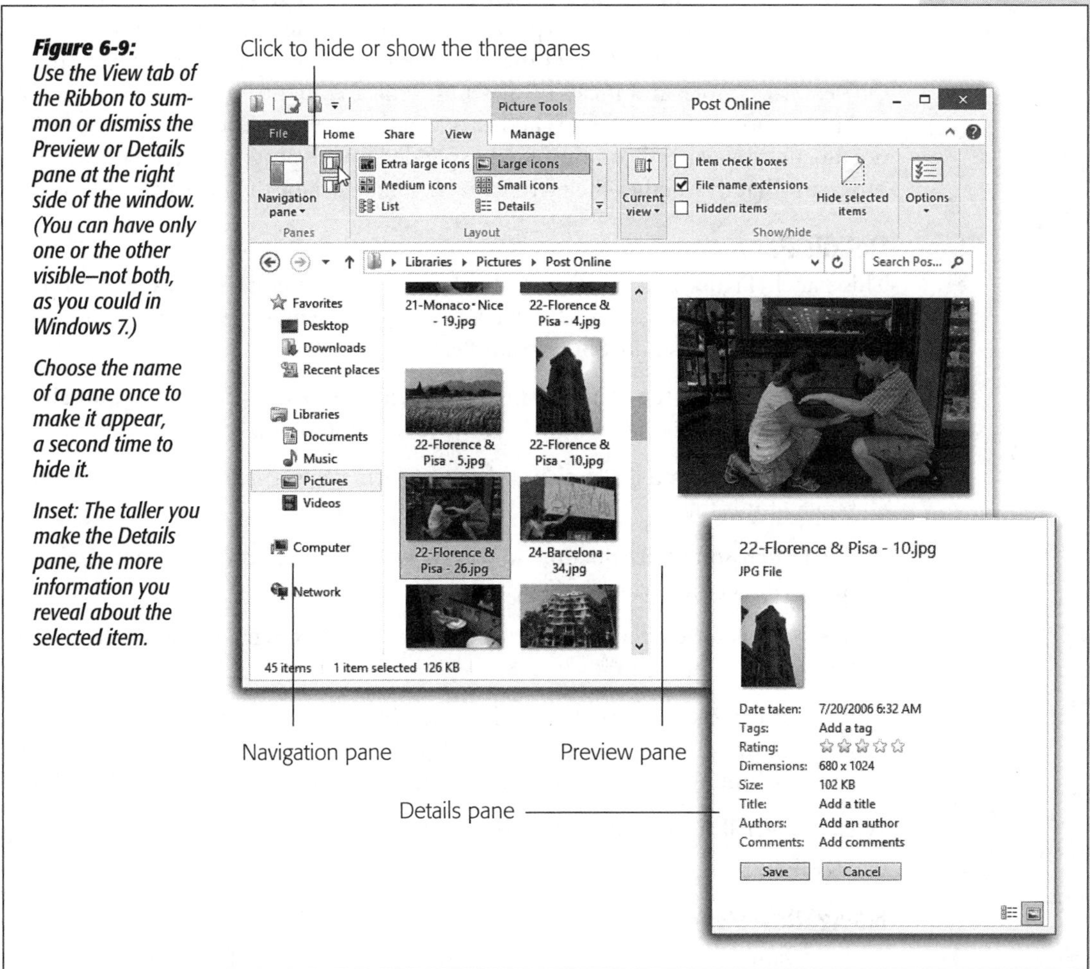

Figure 6-9: *Use the View tab of the Ribbon to summon or dismiss the Preview or Details pane at the right side of the window. (You can have only one or the other visible–not both, as you could in Windows 7.)*

Choose the name of a pane once to make it appear, a second time to hide it.

Inset: The taller you make the Details pane, the more information you reveal about the selected item.

Tip: You can adjust the size of any pane by dragging the dividing line that separates it from the main window. (You know you've got the right spot when your cursor turns into a double-headed arrow.)

Preview Pane

The Preview pane appears either when you click the Preview pane button (shown by the cursor in Figure 6-9) or when you press Alt+P.

It can be handy when you're examining common file types like pictures, text files, RTF files, and Office documents. As you click each icon, you see a magnified thumbnail version of what's actually *in* that document. (Alas, the Preview pane can no longer play back music and movie files, right in place.)

Now, the Preview pane isn't omniscient; right out of the box, Windows can't display the contents of oddball document types like, say, sheet-music documents or 3-D modeling files. But as you install new programs, the Preview pane can get smarter. Install Office, for example, and it can display Office files' contents; install Adobe Acrobat, and it can show you PDF files. Whether or not the Preview pane recognizes a certain document type depends on the effort expended by the programmers who wrote its program (that is, whether they wrote *preview handlers* for their document types).

Details Pane

This panel (Figure 6-9, inset) can also be extremely useful. It reveals all kinds of information about whatever icon you've clicked in the main part of the window: its size, date, type, and so on. Some examples:

- For a music file, the Details pane reveals the song's duration, band and album names, genre, the star rating you've provided, and so on.
- For a disk icon, you get statistics about its formatting scheme, capacity, and how much of it is full.
- For a Microsoft Office document, you see when it was created and modified, how many pages it has, who wrote it, and so on.
- If *nothing* is selected, you get information about the open window itself: namely, how many items are in it.
- If you select several icons at once, this pane shows you the sum of their file sizes—a great feature when you're burning a CD, for example, and don't want to exceed the 650 MB limit. You also see the *range* of dates when they were created and modified.

What's especially intriguing is that you can *edit* many of these details, just by clicking and typing.

Navigation Pane

The navigation pane is the helpful folder map at the left side of an Explorer window. It's come a long way, baby, since the folder hierarchy of Windows XP, and even since the navigation pane of Windows Vista. Today, it's something like a master map of your computer, with a special focus on the places and things you might want to visit most often.

Favorite Links list

At the top of the navigation pane, there's a collapsible list of Favorites. These aren't Web-browser bookmarks, even though Microsoft uses the same term for those. Instead, these are *places* to which you want quick access. Mostly, that means folders or disks, but saved searches and libraries are eligible, too (both are described later in this chapter).

Tip: You can hide the Favorites list completely, if you like. On the Ribbon's View tab, click Options. On the General tab of the resulting dialog box, turn off "Show favorites."

Since this pane will be waiting in every Explorer window you open, taking the time to install your favorite folders here can save you a lot of repetitive folder-burrowing. One click on a folder name opens the corresponding window. For example, click the Pictures icon to view the contents of your Pictures folder in the main part of the window (Figure 6-10).

Figure 6-10: *Top: The quickest way to install a folder into Favorites is just to drag it there, as shown here.*

Bottom: But there's another way, too, that's not so invisible. On the Home tab of the Ribbon, the "Easy access" pop-up menu offers an "Add to favorites" command. You can choose that (or type the letter A) to add the selected icon(s) to the Favorites list in one fell swoop.

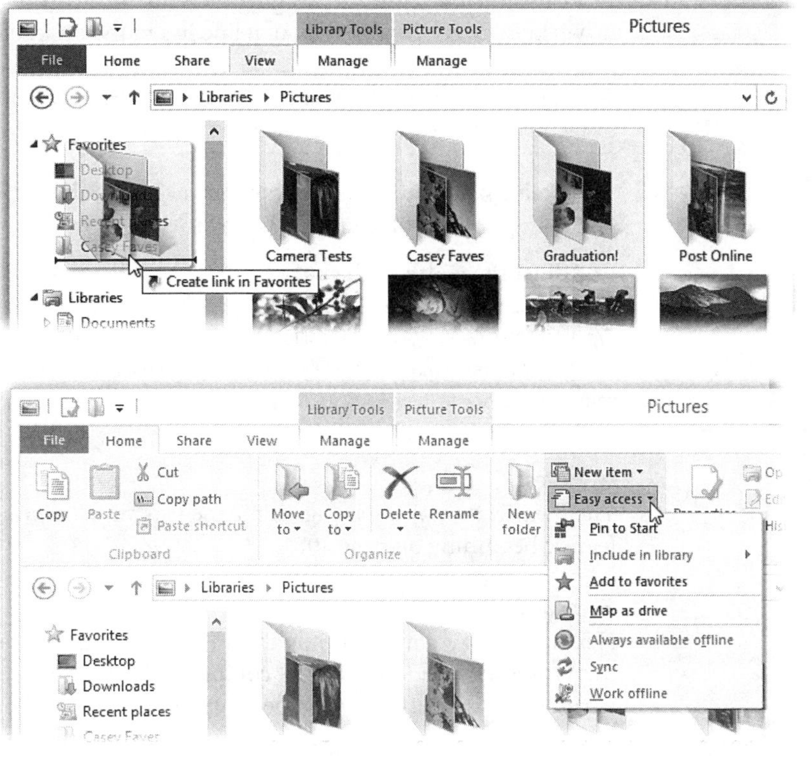

Out of the box, this list offers icons for your desktop, your Downloads folder (which is actually inside your Personal folder), plus a Recent Places link that reveals all the folders and Control Panel items you've opened recently.

Tip: If you click the word "Favorites" itself, you open the Favorites window, where the shortcuts for all your Favorites are stored. Now you have a quick way to add, delete, or rename the items in your favorite links all at once.

The beauty of this parking lot for containers is that it's so easy to set up with *your* favorite places. For example:

- **Remove** an icon by dragging it out of the window entirely and onto the Recycle Bin icon; it vanishes from the list. Or right-click it and, from the shortcut menu, choose Remove. (You haven't actually removed anything from your *PC;* you've just unhitched its alias from the navigation pane.)

Tip: If you delete one of the starter icons (Desktop, Downloads, Recent Places) and later wish you had it back, no big deal. Right-click the word "Favorites"; from the shortcut menu, choose "Restore favorite links."

- **Rearrange** the icons by dragging them up or down in the list. Release the mouse when the thick black horizontal line lies in the desired new location.

Tip: You can also sort this list alphabetically. Right-click the word "Favorites"; from the shortcut menu, choose "Sort by name."

- **Install a new folder, disk, library, or saved search** by dragging its icon off of your desktop (or out of a window) into any spot in the list.
- **Adjust the width** of the pane by dragging the vertical divider bar right or left.

Tip: If you drag carefully, you can position the divider bar *just* to the right of the disk and folder icons, thereby hiding their names almost completely. Some people find it a tidier look; you can always identify the folder names by pointing to them without clicking.

Libraries

The next section of the navigation pane lists your *libraries.* You can read about this feature beginning on page 208.

Homegroup

Next in the nav pane, you might find the Homegroup heading. Here's a list of all the Windows 7 and Windows 8 computers in your house that you've joined into a harmonious unit using the Homegroup networking feature described in Chapter 27.

Computer

The next heading is Computer. When you expand this heading, you see a list of all your drives (including the main C: drive), each of which is also expandable (Figure 6-11). In essence, this view can show you every folder on the machine at once. It lets you burrow very deeply into your hard drive's nest of folders without ever losing your bearings.

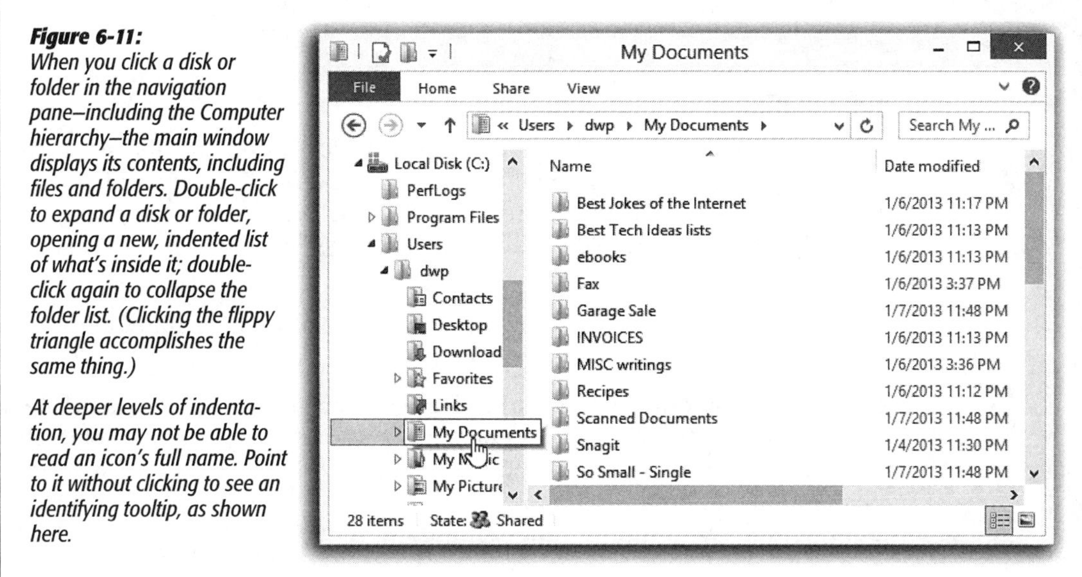

Figure 6-11: *When you click a disk or folder in the navigation pane–including the Computer hierarchy–the main window displays its contents, including files and folders. Double-click to expand a disk or folder, opening a new, indented list of what's inside it; double-click again to collapse the folder list. (Clicking the flippy triangle accomplishes the same thing.)*

At deeper levels of indentation, you may not be able to read an icon's full name. Point to it without clicking to see an identifying tooltip, as shown here.

Network

Finally, the Network heading shows your entire network. Not just Windows 7 and 8 PCs that have been connected as a homegroup, but the *entire* network—Macs, PCs running older Windows versions, Linux boxes, whatever.

Flippy triangles

As you can see, the navigation list displays *only* disks and folders, never individual files. To see those, look at the main window, which displays the contents (folders *and* files) of whatever disk or folder you click.

To expand a folder or disk that appears in the nav pane, double-click its name, or click the tiny ▸ next to its name. You've just turned the nav list into an outline; the contents of the folder appear in an indented list, as shown in Figure 6-11. Double-click again, or click the flippy triangle again, to collapse the folder listing.

Tip: Windows can, if you like, expand the folder list automatically as you navigate your folders. Open the Music folder with your mouse, for example, and the Music folder's flippy triangle is automatically opened, giving you a visual representation of where you are. Sound useful? Turn it on like this: On the Ribbon's View tab, click Options. On the General tab of the resulting dialog box, turn on "Automatically expand to current folder."

By selectively expanding folders like this, you can, in effect, peer inside two or more folders simultaneously, all within the single navigation list. You can move files around by dragging them onto the tiny folder icons, too.

Tip: Ordinarily, the nav pane shows only folders that Microsoft thinks you'd be interested in–folders that contain your stuff, for example. But if you like, it can display more Windowsy folders like the Control Panel and Recycle Bin, too. On the Ribbon's View tab, click Options. On the General tab of the resulting dialog box, turn on "Show all folders."

Libraries

Libraries, which debuted in Windows 7, are like folders, with one difference: They can display the contents of *other* folders from all over your PC—and even from other PCs on your network. In other words, a library doesn't really contain anything at all. It simply monitors *other* folders and provides a single "place" to work with all their contents.

Windows starts you out with four libraries: Documents, Music, Pictures, and Videos. (You can make libraries of your own, too.)

Sure, XP and Vista came with *folders* bearing those names, but libraries are much more powerful. The Pictures library, for example, seems to contain all your photos—but in real life, they may be scattered all over your hard drive, on external drives, or on other PCs in the house.

So what's the point? Well, consider the advantages over regular folders:

- **Everything's in one spot.** When it comes time to put together a year-end photo album, for example, you might be very grateful to find your pictures, your spouse's

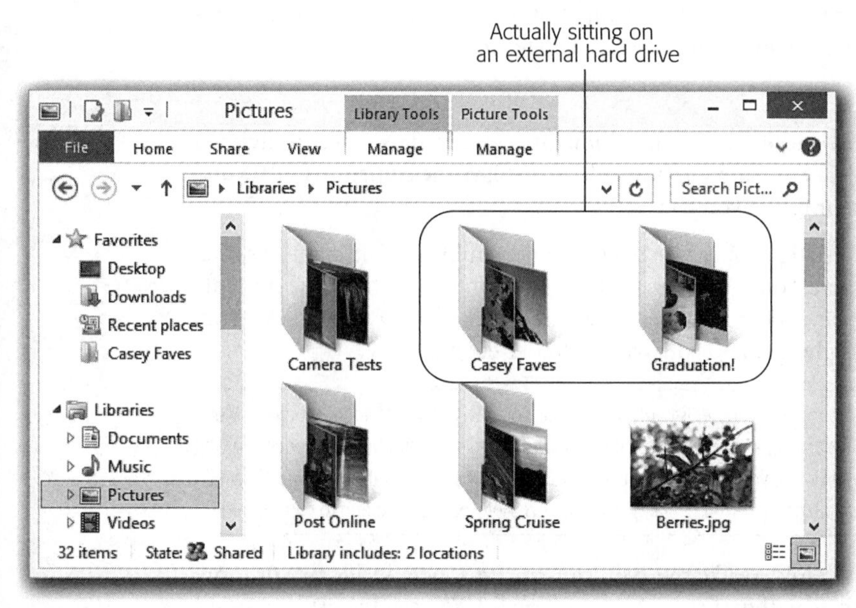

Figure 6-12: *The Pictures library window seems to contain a bunch of photo folders, all in one place. As a bonus, you can access all this from the Save and Open dialog boxes within your programs, too. But don't be fooled; In real life, these folders are scattered all over your system.*

pictures from the upstairs PC, and the pictures from your kids' laptop all in one central place, ready for choosing. Figure 6-12 shows the idea.

- **Happy laptop reunions.** When you come home with your laptop and connect to the network, you're instantly reunited with all those music, pictures, and video files you store on other drives.
- **Easy backup or transfer.** You can back up or transfer all the files corresponding to a certain project or time period in one fell swoop, even though the originals are in a bunch of different places or reside on different collaborators' computers.
- **Manipulate en masse.** You can *work* with the contents of a library—slicing, dicing, searching, organizing, filtering—just as you would a folder's contents. But because you're actually working with folders from all over your computer and even your network, you can be far more efficient.

Working with Library Contents

To use a library, click its name in your navigation pane. (Try Pictures, for example.)

A few clues tell you that you're not in a regular folder. First, there's the appearance of a special Library Tools tab on the Ribbon. The status bar at the bottom of the window, furthermore, says something like "Includes: 2 locations," letting you know that you're actually looking at the consolidated contents of two folders.

Tip: Remember, the icons in a library aren't really there; they're just a mirage. They're stunt doubles for files that actually sit in other folders on your hard drive.

Fortunately, when you're getting a bit confused as to what's really where, there's a way to jump to a file or folder's actual location. Right-click its icon in the library; from the shortcut menu, choose "Open file location" (or "Open folder location"). You jump right to the real thing, sitting in its actual File Explorer window.

POWER USERS' CLINIC

Hiding and Showing Libraries

Microsoft thinks libraries are very important. After all, libraries get one of the coveted spots in the navigation pane at the left side of every single Explorer window.

You, however, may not consider all of them equally important. You might not use your PC for music at all. You might not have any videos.

Or maybe you love libraries, but you don't want all of them listed in the nav pane, either for privacy reasons or clutter reasons.

In each of these cases, it's nice to know you can hide a library so that its name doesn't appear in the nav pane. Just right-click the library's name; from the shortcut menu, choose "Don't show in navigation pane." Poof! It's gone (just the listing, not the library itself).

You can, fortunately, bring the library listing back. It's still sitting in your Personal→Libraries folder. To see it, click the word "Libraries" in any window's navigation pane. Right-click the library's icon; from the shortcut menu, choose "Show in navigation pane." Foop! It's back in the list. (Or, if you've really made a mess, right-click the word "Libraries" in the nav pane; from the shortcut menu, choose "Restore default libraries.")

Adding a Folder to an Existing Library

A library is nothing without a bunch of folders to feed into it. You can add a folder to a library (like Pictures or Music) in any of four ways, depending on where you're starting.

- **You can see the folder's icon.** If the folder is on the desktop or in a window, right-click it. From the shortcut menu, choose "Include in library"; the submenu lists all your existing libraries so you can choose the one you want. Figure 6-13 shows the idea.

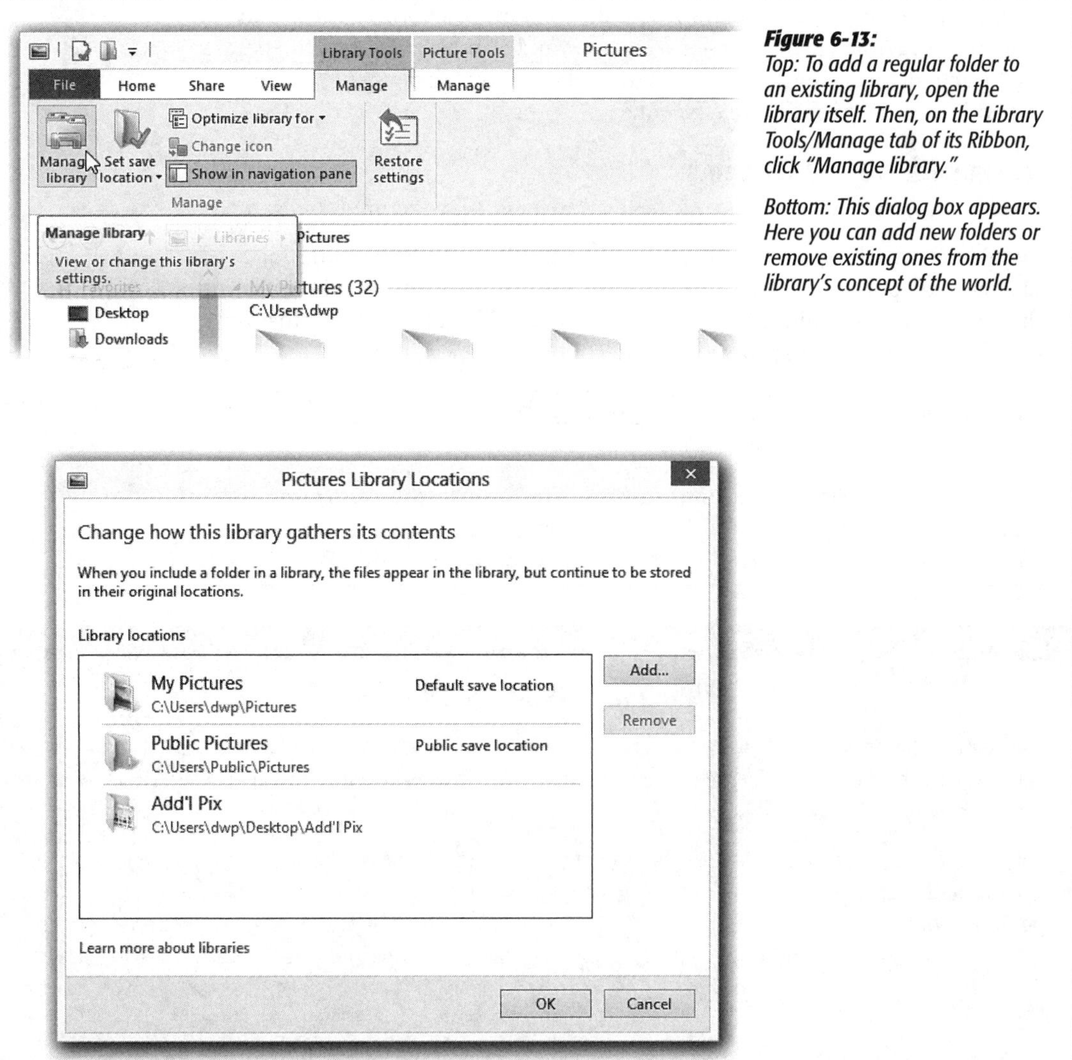

Figure 6-13:
Top: To add a regular folder to an existing library, open the library itself. Then, on the Library Tools/Manage tab of its Ribbon, click "Manage library."

Bottom: This dialog box appears. Here you can add new folders or remove existing ones from the library's concept of the world.

- **You can see the folder's icon (alternate).** Use the right mouse button to drag the folder onto a library's name in the navigation pane. Release the mouse button when it's on the library name. From the shortcut menu, choose "Include in library."
- **You've opened the library window.** If you're already *in* the library, you can add a folder to it using the dialog box shown in Figure 6-13. Click Add, and then find and double-click the folder you want. You see it added to the "Library locations" list in the dialog box. Click OK.

The fine print

All the techniques above also work for folders on external drives, USB flash drives, and shared folders on your network. There is, however, some important fine print:

- You can't add a folder that's on a CD or a DVD.
- You *can* add a folder that's on a USB flash drive, as long as that flash drive's icon shows up in the navigation pane when it's inserted, under the Computer/Hard Drives heading. (A few oddball models appear under Devices With Removable Storage; they're not allowed.) Furthermore, the folder won't be available in the library when the flash drive isn't inserted (duh).
- You can't add a networked folder to a library *unless* it's been *indexed for searching* on the PC that contains it; see page 253 for details on that process. (If it's a Windows 7 machine that's part of a homegroup [page 788], then you're all set; it's been indexed.)

  As an alternative, you can turn on the "available offline" feature for that networked folder, as described on page 815. The good news is that the folder can now be part of your library even when the other PC on the network is turned off. The bad news is that you've basically copied that folder to your own PC, which eats up a lot of disk space and sort of defeats the purpose of adding a networked folder to your library.

FREQUENTLY ASKED QUESTION

Your Preferred "Save Into" Folder

So let me get this straight: A library is just a fiction. It contains links to a bunch of folders. So when I'm in, say, Microsoft Word, and I save a new document "into the library," which real folder am I saving it into?

That's up to you.

In an Explorer window, click the library in question. Where it says "Includes:" at the top of the window, click "locations." In the Library Locations dialog box (shown in Figure 6-13), right-click the folder you want to be the standard location for new files you save into this library. From the shortcut menu, choose "Set as default save location," and then click OK.

Removing a Folder from a Library

Getting rid of a folder is pretty straightforward, really. You can use any of these techniques:

- **If the library window is open:** Use the "Manage library" button shown at top in Figure 6-13. Click the folder's name and then click Remove.
- **If the library's name is visible in the navigation pane:** Expand the library to show the folder you want to remove. Right-click the folder's name. From the shortcut menu, choose "Remove location from library."

Remember: You're not deleting anything important. A library only *pretends* to contain other folders; the real ones are actually sitting in other places on your PC or network, even after the library is gone.

Creating a New Library

The starter libraries (Pictures, Music, Documents, and Videos) are awfully useful right out of the box. Truth is, they're as far as most people probably go with the libraries feature.

But you may have good reasons to create new ones. Maybe you want to create a library for each client—and fill it with the corresponding project folders, some of which have been archived away on external drives. Maybe you want to round up folders full of fonts, clip art, and text, in readiness for submitting a graphics project to a print shop.

In any case, here are the different ways to go about it:

- **From the navigation pane.** Right-click the word "Library" in any window's navigation pane, or any blank spot inside a library folder. From the shortcut menu, choose New→Library.

  A new, empty library appears, both in the Libraries window and in the list of libraries in the nav pane. It's up to you to add folders to it, as described earlier.

- **From a folder.** Right-click any folder. From the shortcut menu, choose "Include in library"→"Create new library." *Bing!* A new library appears in the Libraries list, named after the folder you clicked. As a handy bonus, this library already contains its first folder: the one you clicked, of course.

Tip: Once you've created a library, you can specify which canned library style it resembles most: General Items, Pictures, Music, Documents, or Videos. (Why does it matter? Because the library style determines which commands are available in the Ribbon. Pictures offers a tab that offers slideshow and rotation tools; Music offers choices like "Play" and "Add to playlist.")

Anyway, to make this choice, open the library. In the Ribbon, on the Library Tools/Manage tab, use the "Optimize library for" pop-up menu. Click the type you want.

Tags, Metadata, and Properties

See all that information in the Details pane—Date, Size, Title, and so on? It's known by geeks as *metadata* (Greek for "data about data").

Different kinds of files provide different sorts of details. For a document, for example, you might see Authors, Comments, Title, Categories, Status, and so on. For an MP3 music file, you get Artists, Albums, Genre, Year, and so on. For a photo, you get Date Taken, Title, Author, and so on.

Oddly (and usefully) enough, you can actually edit some of this stuff (Figure 6-14).

Figure 6-14: *Click the information you want to change; if a text-editing box appears, you've hit pay dirt. Type away, and then press Enter (or click the Save button at the bottom of the dialog box). To input a list (of tags or authors, for example), type a semicolon (;) after each one.*

Some of the metadata is off limits. For example, you can't edit the Date Created or Date Modified info. (Sorry, defense attorneys of the world.) But you *can* edit the star ratings for music or pictures. Click the third star to give a song a 3, for example.

Most usefully of all, you can edit the Tags box for almost *any* kind of icon. A tag is just a keyword. It can be anything you want: McDuffy Proposal, Old Junk, Back Me Up—anything. Later, you'll be able to round up everything on your computer with a certain tag, all in a single window, even though they physically reside in different folders.

You'll encounter tags in plenty of other places in Windows—and in this book, especially when it comes to searching for photos and music.

Note: Weirdly, you can't add tags or ratings to BMP, PNG, AVI, or MPG files.

Many of the boxes here offer autocompletion, meaning that Windows proposes finishing a name or a text tidbit for you if it recognizes what you've started to type.

Tip: You can tag a bunch of icons at once. Just highlight them all and then change the corresponding detail in the Details pane *once*. This is a great trick for applying a tag or star rating to a mass of files quickly.

Click Save when you're finished.

Properties

The Details pane shows some of the most important details about a file, but if you really want to see the entire metadata dossier for an icon, open its Properties dialog box using one of these tactics:

- **Select it.** From the Home tab of the Ribbon, click Properties.
- **Right-click it.** From the shortcut menu, choose Properties.
- **Alt+double-click it.**
- **If the icon is already highlighted,** press Alt+Enter.

In each case, the Properties dialog box appears. It's a lot like the one in previous versions of Windows, in that it displays the file's name, location, size, and so on. But in Windows 8, it also bears a scrolling Details tab that's sometimes teeming with metadata details (Figure 6-15).

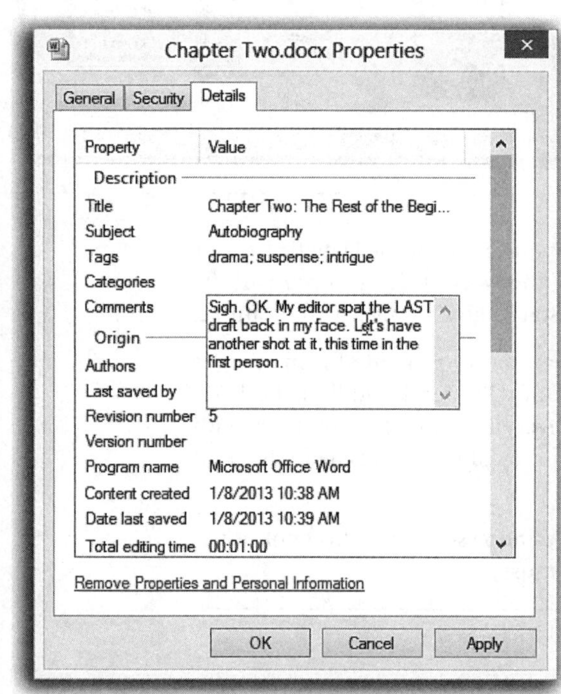

Figure 6-15:
If Windows knows anything about an icon, it's in here. Scroll, scroll, and scroll some more to find the tidbit you want to see—or to edit. As with the Details pane, many of these text morsels are editable.

Icon and List Views

Windows' windows look just fine straight from the factory; the edges are straight, and the text is perfectly legible. Still, if you're going to stare at this screen for half of your waking hours, you may as well investigate some of the ways these windows can be enhanced.

For starters, you can view the files and folders in an Explorer window in either of two ways: as icons (of any size) or as a list (in several formats). Figure 6-16 shows some of your options.

Every window remembers its view settings independently. You might prefer to look over your Documents folder in List view (because it's crammed with files and folders), but you may prefer to view the Pictures library in Icon view, where the icons look like miniatures of the actual photos.

To switch a window from one view to another, you have eight options, all of which involve the View tab of the Ribbon, as shown in Figure 6-16:

Tip: You can point to the icons in the View tab without clicking. The files in the window change as you hover, so you can preview the effect before committing to it.

So what *are* these various views? And when should you use which? Here you go:

- **Extra large icons, Large icons, Medium icons, Small icons.** In an icon view, every file, folder, and disk is represented by a small picture—an *icon*. This humble image, a visual representation of electronic bits, is the cornerstone of the entire Windows religion. (Maybe that's why it's called an icon.)

GEM IN THE ROUGH

How to Shed Your Metadata's Skin

At the bottom of the Details pane (of the Properties dialog box) is a peculiarly worded link: "Remove Properties and Personal Information."

This is a privacy feature. What it means is "Clean away all the metadata I've added myself, like author names, tag keywords, and other insights into my own work routine."

Microsoft's thinking here is that you might not want other people who encounter this document (as an email attachment, for example) to have such a sweeping insight into the minutiae of your own work routine.

When you click this link, the Remove Properties dialog box appears, offering you a scrolling list of checkboxes: Title, Rating, Tags, Comments, and lots and lots of others.

You can proceed in either of two ways. If you turn on "Create a copy with all possible properties removed," then *all* the metadata that's possible to erase (everything but things like file type, name, and so on) will be stripped away. When you click OK, Windows instantly creates a duplicate of the file (with the word "Copy" tacked onto its name), ready for distribution to the masses in its clean form. The original is left untouched.

If you choose "Remove the following properties from this file" instead, you can specify exactly *which* file details you want erased from the original. (Turn on the appropriate checkboxes.)

Interestingly, in Windows 8, folder icons appear turned 90 degrees. Now, in real life, setting filing folders onto a desk that way would be idiotic; everything inside would tumble out. But in Windows-land, the icons within a folder remain exactly where they are. Better yet, at larger icon sizes, they peek out just enough so that you can see them. In the Music folder, for example, a singer's folder shows the first album cover within; a folder full of PowerPoint presentations shows the first slide or two; and so on.

Small icons put the files' names to the right of the icons; the other views put the name *beneath* the icon. You might want one of the large settings for things like photos and the small settings when you want to see more files without scrolling.

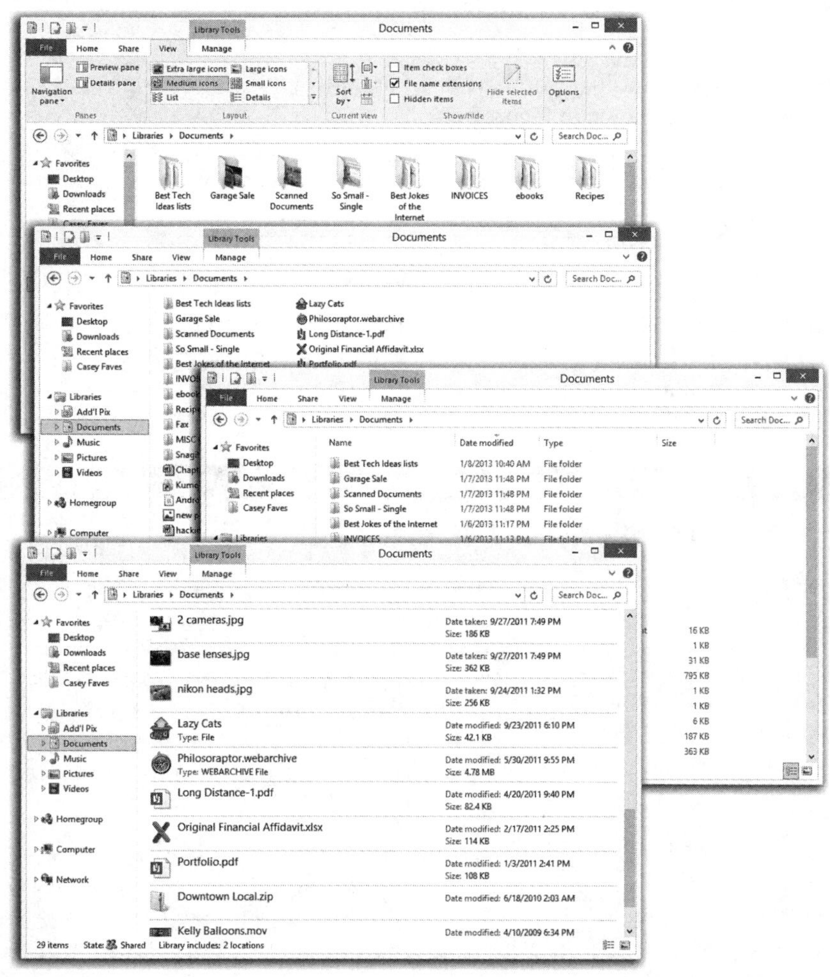

Figure 6-16: *Here's a survey of window views in Windows 8's desktop world. From top: Medium Icons, List view, Details view, and Content view. List and Details views are great for windows with lots of files. Extra Large Icons (not shown) is great if you're 30 feet away.*

Tip: If you have a touchscreen, you can use the two-finger spreading gesture to enlarge icons, or the pinching gesture to shrink them, right on the glass. If you have a mouse, you can enlarge or shrink all the icons in a window by turning your mouse's scroll wheel while you press the Ctrl key. This trick even works on desktop icons.

- **List view.** This one packs, by far, the most files into the space of a window; each file has a tiny icon to its left, and the list of files wraps around into as many columns as necessary to maximize the window's available space.

POWER USERS' CLINIC

Secrets of the Details View Columns

In windows that contain a lot of icons, Details view is a powerful weapon in the battle against chaos. Better yet, *you* get to decide how wide the columns should be, which of them should appear, and in what order. Here are the details on Details:

Add or remove columns. When you choose "Add columns" in the Ribbon's View tab, or right-click any column heading (like Name or Size), you see a shortcut menu with checkmarks next to the visible columns: Name, Date Modified, Size, and so on. Choose a column's name to make it appear or disappear.

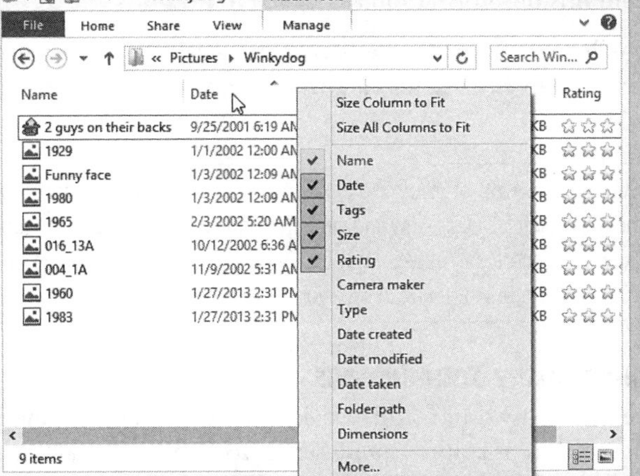

But don't think that you're stuck with that handful of common columns. If you click "Choose columns" or "More" in the shortcut menu, you open the Choose Details dialog box, which lists *300 more* column types, most of which are useful only in certain circumstances: Album Artist (for music files), Copyright, Date Taken, Exposure Time (for photos), Nickname (for people), Video Compression (for movies), and on and on. To make one of these columns appear, turn on its checkbox and then click OK; by the time you're done, your Explorer window can look like a veritable spreadsheet of information.

Rearrange the columns. You can rearrange your Details columns just by dragging their gray column headers horizontally. (You can even drag the Name column out of first position.)

Change column widths. If some text in a column is too long to fit, Windows displays an ellipsis (...) after the first few letters of each word. In that case, here's a trick: Carefully position your cursor at the right edge of the column's header (Name, Size, or whatever—even to the right of the ▾ button). When the cursor sprouts horizontal arrows, double-click the divider line to make the column adjust *itself,* fitting automatically to accommodate the longest item in the column.

If you'd rather adjust the column width manually, just drag the divider line horizontally. Doing so makes the column to the *left* of your cursor wider or narrower.

Or use the "Size all columns to fit" command. It's in the shortcut menu and also on the Ribbon's View tab, and it makes all columns exactly as wide as necessary.

- **Details view.** This is the same as List view, except that it presents only a single column of files. It's a table, really; additional columns reveal the size, icon type, modification date, rating, and other information.

  Microsoft thinks you'll really dig Details view. It's so important that it even has a keystroke (Ctrl+Shift+6) and a dedicated "Switch to Details view" icon at the lower-right corner of every window .

  Furthermore, whenever you're in Details view, you get two bonus icons on the Ribbon's View tab: "Add columns" and "Size all columns to fit." They're described in the box on the previous page.

- **Tiles view.** Your icons appear at standard size, with name and file details just to the *right*.

- **Content view.** This view attempts to cram as many details about each file as will fit in your window. Yes, that's right: It's a table that shows not just a file's icon and name, but also its metadata (Properties) and, in the case of text and Word files, even the first couple of lines of text *inside* it. (If you're not seeing all the file details you think you should, then make the window bigger. Windows adds and subtracts columns of information as needed to fit.)

  You'll get to know Content view very well indeed once you start using the Search feature, which uses this view to display your results when you search in an Explorer window.

Tip: At the lower right of every Explorer window, you see repeats of the two styles Microsoft thinks you'll find the most useful: Details view and large thumbnails. (As their pop-out tooltip balloons indicate, they even have keyboard shortcuts: Ctrl+Shift+6 for Details, Ctrl+Shift+2 for large thumbnails.) By duplicating these controls here, Windows is trying to save you the effort of opening the Ribbon if it doesn't happen to be open.

Immortalizing Your Tweaks

Once you've twiddled and tweaked an Explorer window into a perfectly efficient configuration of columns and views, you needn't go through the same exercises for each folder. Windows can immortalize your changes as the standard setting for *all* your windows.

On the Ribbon's View tab, click Options. Click the View tab. Click Apply to Folders, and confirm your decision by clicking Yes.

At this point, all your disk and folder windows open up with the same view, sorting method, and so on. You're still free to override those standard settings on a window-by-window basis, however. (And if you change your mind again and want to make all your maverick folder windows snap back to the standard settings, repeat the process, but click Reset Folders instead.)

Sorting, Grouping, and Filtering

It's a computer—it had darned well better be able to sort your files alphabetically, chronologically, or in any other way. But that's only one way to impose order on your teeming icons. Grouping, filtering, and searching can be handy, too.

Sorting Files

Sorting the files in a window alphabetically or chronologically is nice, but it's *so* 2005. In Windows 8, you can sort up, down, and sideways.

The trick is to click the "Sort by" pop-up icon, which is on the View tab of the Ribbon. As you can see, it lists every conceivable sorting criterion: Name, Date modified, Type, Size, and on and on. And if those 10 ways to sort aren't enough, you can choose "Choose columns" from this menu to add even more options to it: Attachments, Copyright, Data rate, and so on.

Sorting in Details view

In Details view, you get another way to sort. See the column headings, like Name, Size, and Type? They aren't just signposts; they're also buttons. Click Name for alphabetical order, "Date modified" for chronological order, Size to view largest files at the top, and so on (Figure 6-17).

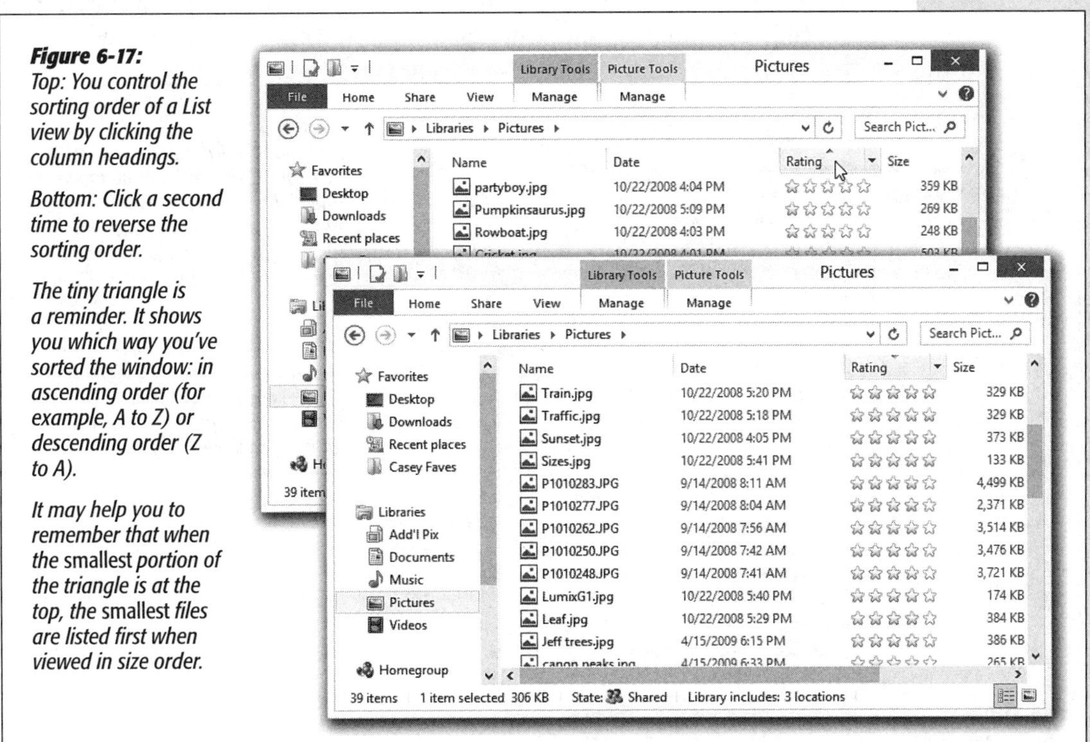

Figure 6-17: *Top: You control the sorting order of a List view by clicking the column headings.*

Bottom: Click a second time to reverse the sorting order.

The tiny triangle is a reminder. It shows you which way you've sorted the window: in ascending order (for example, A to Z) or descending order (Z to A).

It may help you to remember that when the smallest portion of the triangle is at the top, the smallest files are listed first when viewed in size order.

To reverse the sorting order, click the column heading a second time. The tiny triangle turns upside-down.

Note: Within each window, Windows groups *folders* separately from *files*. They get sorted, too, but within their own little folder ghetto.

Sorting using the shortcut menu

You can sort your icons in any window view without using the Ribbon, like this: Right-click a blank spot in the window. From the shortcut menu, choose "Sort by" and choose the criterion you want (Name, Date, Type…) from the submenu.

There's no handy triangle to tell you *which way* you've just sorted things; is it oldest to newest or newest to oldest? To make *that* decision, you have to right-click the window a second time; this time, from the "Sort by" submenu, choose either Ascending or Descending.

Grouping

Grouping means "adding headings within the window and clustering the icons beneath the headings." The effect is shown in Figure 6-18, and so is the procedure. Try it out; grouping can be a great way to wrangle some order from a seething mass of icons.

Don't forget that you can flip the sorting order of your groups. Reopen that shortcut menu and the "Group by" submenu, and specify Ascending or Descending.

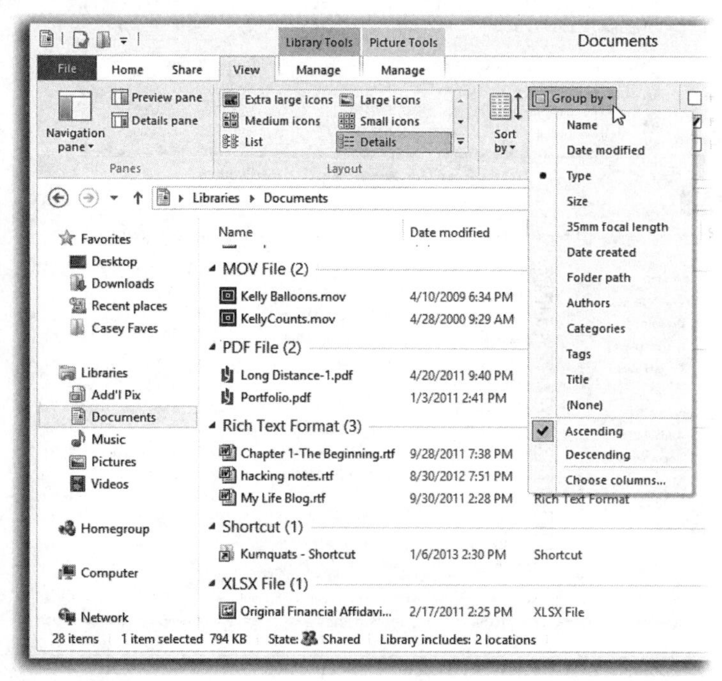

Figure 6-18:
To group the icons in a window, use the "Group by" pop-up menu in the Ribbon, on the View tab. (If the window isn't especially wide, then you might see only the icon for the menu, not the actual words "Group by.")

You can also find the "Group by" menu by right-clicking a blank spot in the window. Use the shortcut menu that results; that way, you don't need the Ribbon.

Filtering

Filtering, a feature available only in Details view, means hiding. When you turn on filtering, a bunch of the icons in a window *disappear*, which can make filtering a sore subject for novices.

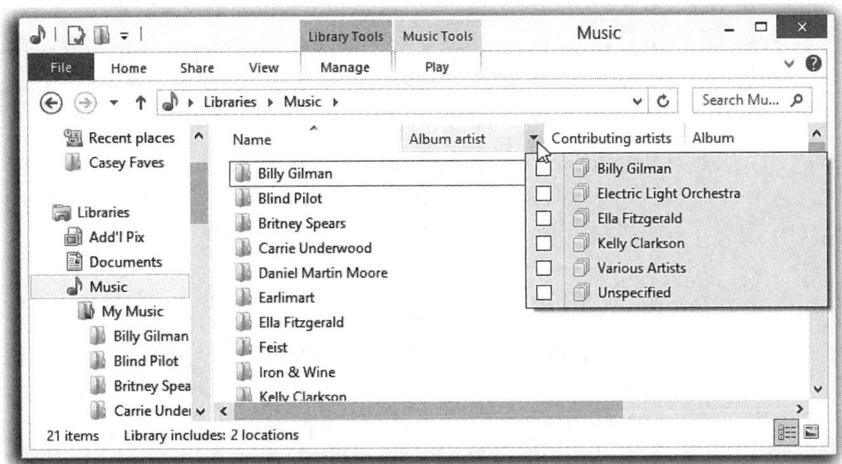

Figure 6-19: *You can turn on more than one checkbox. To see music by Ella Fitzgerald or Kelly Clarkson, turn on both checkboxes. In fact, you can turn on checkboxes from more than one heading—music by Kelly Clarkson, rated four stars or higher, for example.*

POWER USERS' CLINIC

The Little Filtering Calendar

Some of the column-heading pop-up menus in Details view—"Date modified," "Date created," "Date taken," and so on—display a little calendar, right there in the menu. You're supposed to use it to specify a date or a date range. You use it, for example, if you want to see only the photos taken last August, or the Word documents created last week. Here's how the little calendar works:

To change the month, click the ◂ or ▸ buttons to go one month at a time. Or click the month name to see a list of all 12 months; click the one you want.

To change the year, click the ◂ or ▸ buttons. Or, to jump further back or forward, double-click the month's name. You're offered a list of all 10 years in this decade. Click a third time (on the decade heading) to see a list of *decades*. At this point, drill down to the year you want by clicking. (The calendar goes from the years 1601 to 9999, which should pretty much cover your digital photo collection.)

To see only the photos taken on a certain date, click the appropriate date on the month-view calendar.

To add photos taken on other dates, click additional squares. You can also drag horizontally, vertically, or diagonally to select blocks of consecutive dates.

If you "back out" until you're viewing the names of months, years, or decades, then you can click or drag to choose, for example, only the photos taken in June or July 2012.

The checkboxes below the calendar offer one-click access to photos taken earlier this week, earlier this year, and before the beginning of this year ("a long time ago").

Tip: In case you one day think you've lost a bunch of important files, look for the checkmark next to a column heading. That's your clue that filtering is turned on, and Windows is deliberately hiding something from you.

On the positive side, filtering means screening out stuff you don't care about. When you're looking for a document you know you worked on last week, you can tell Windows to show you *only* the documents edited last week.

You turn on filtering by opening the pop-up menu next to the column heading you want. For instance, if you want to see only your five-star photos in the Pictures folder, open the Rating pop-up menu.

Sometimes, you'll see a whole long list of checkboxes in one of these pop-up menus (Figure 6-19). For example, if you want to see only the songs in your Music folder by The Beatles, turn on the checkmark for The Beatles.

Note: Filtering, by the way, can be turned on *with* sorting or grouping.

Once you've filtered a window in Details view, you can switch to a different view; you'll still see (and not see) the same set of icons. The address bar reminds you that you've turned on filtering; it might say, for example, "Research notes→LongTimeAgo→DOC file," meaning "ancient Word files."

To stop filtering, open the heading pop-up menu again and turn off the Filter checkbox.

Searching in an Explorer Window

You might suppose that the search mechanism that's now part of TileWorld is the only way to search the desktop world, but you'd be wrong; there's a search box in the upper-right corner of every Explorer window. It's described in the next chapter.

The "Folder Options" Options

In the battle between flexibility and simplicity, Microsoft comes down on the side of flexibility almost every time. Anywhere it can provide you with more options, it will.

Explorer windows are a case in point, as the following pages of sometimes preposterously tweaky options make clear. The good news: If Explorer windows already work fine for you the way they are, you can ignore all of this.

But if you'd like to visit the famed Folder Options dialog box, here's the new Windows 8 way to do it: On the View tab of the Ribbon, click the Options button. You see the dialog box shown in Figure 6-20.

Here you see an array of options that affect *all* the folder windows on your PC. When assessing the impact of these controls, *earth-shattering* isn't the adjective that springs to mind. Still, you may find one or two of them useful.

General Tab

On the General tab, you find these intriguing options:

- **Browse folders.** When you double-click a folder, Windows can react in one of two ways. It can either *open a second window*, overlapping the first; now moving or copying an icon from one into the other is a piece of cake. Or it can *replace the original window with a new one.* This only-one-window-at-all-times behavior keeps your desktop from becoming crowded with windows. If you need to return to the previous window, the Back button takes you there. Of course, you'll have a harder time dragging icons from one window to another using this method.

  Whatever you decide, you tell Windows using these buttons. Click either "Open each folder in the same window" or "Open each folder in its own window," as you like.

- **Click items as follows.** This option lets you single-click icons to open them instead of double-clicking—a feature that might make life easier if you have a touchscreen. See page 223.

- **Navigation pane.** Here are three handy options that let you customize the navigation pane at the left side of every Explorer window; they're described on pages 205–208.

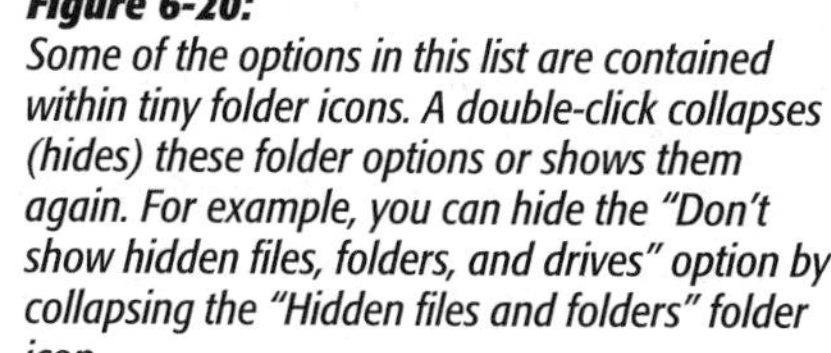

Figure 6-20:
Some of the options in this list are contained within tiny folder icons. A double-click collapses (hides) these folder options or shows them again. For example, you can hide the "Don't show hidden files, folders, and drives" option by collapsing the "Hidden files and folders" folder icon.

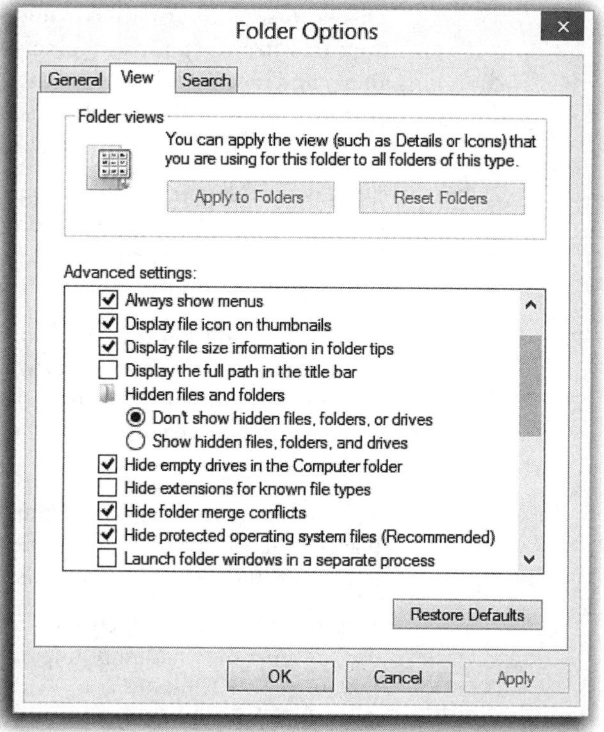

View Tab

Here are the functions of the various checkboxes:

- **Always show icons, never thumbnails.** Windows takes great pride in displaying your document icons *as* documents. That is, each icon appears as a miniature of the document itself—a feature that's especially useful in folders full of photos.

  On a slowish PC, this feature can make your processor gasp for breath. If you notice that the icons are taking forever to appear, consider turning this checkbox on.

- **Always show menus.** This checkbox forces the traditional Windows menu bar (File, Edit, View, and so on) to appear in every Explorer window, without your having to tap the Alt key.

- **Display file icon on thumbnails.** Ordinarily, you can identify documents (think Word, Excel, PowerPoint) because their icons display the corresponding logo (a big W for Word, and so on). But in Windows' icon views (medium and larger), you see the *actual document* on the icon—an image of the document's first page. So does that mean you can no longer tell at a glance what *kind* of document it is?

  Don't be silly. This option superimposes, on each thumbnail icon, a tiny "badge," a sub-icon, that identifies what kind of file it is. (It works on only some kinds of documents, however.)

- **Display file size information in folder tips.** A *folder tip* is a rectangular balloon that appears when you point to a folder—a little yellow box that tells you what's in that folder and how big it is on the disk. (It appears only if you've turned on the "Show pop-up description" checkbox described below.) You turn off *this* checkbox if you want to see only the description, but not the size. Talk about tweaky!

- **Display the full path in the title bar.** When this option is on, Windows reveals the exact location of the current window in the title bar of the window—for example, *C:\Users\Chris\Documents.* See page 202 for more on folder paths. Seeing the path can be useful when you're not sure which disk a folder is on, for example.

- **Hidden files and folders.** Microsoft grew weary of answering tech-support calls from clueless or mischievous customers who had moved or deleted critical system files, rendering their PCs crippled or useless. The company concluded that the simplest preventive measure would be to make them invisible (the files, not the customers).

  This checkbox is responsible. Your personal and Windows folders, among other places, house several invisible folders and files that the average person isn't meant to fool around with. Big Brother is watching you, but he means well.

  By selecting "Show hidden files, folders, and drives," you, the confident power user in times of troubleshooting or customization, can make the hidden files and folders appear (they show up with dimmed icons, as though to reinforce their delicate nature). But you'll have the smoothest possible computing career if you leave these options untouched.

Note: Actually, there's a much quicker way to turn hidden files on and off. The Ribbon's View tab has a "Hidden files" button dedicated just to this purpose.

- **Hide empty drives in the Computer folder.** For years, the Computer window has displayed icons for your removable-disk drives (floppy, CD, DVD, memory-card slots, whatever) even if nothing was in them. Now, though, that's changed. Now you see icons only when you insert a *disk* into these drives. (It works like the Mac, if that's any help.)

- **Hide extensions for known file types.** Windows normally hides the *filename extension* on standard files and documents (.doc, .jpg, and so on), in an effort to make Windows seem less technical and intimidating. Your files wind up named "Groceries" and "Frank" instead of "Groceries.doc" and "Frank.jpg."

  There are some excellent reasons, though, why you should turn *off* this option. See page 357 for more on this topic.

Note: There's a dedicated on/off switch for showing filename extensions right on the Ribbon's View tab ("File name extensions"). It's a lot easier to reach than the Folder Options dialog box.

- **Hide folder merge conflicts.** When you drag a file into a window that contains an identically named file, Windows warns you; it doesn't want you to replace one file with another accidentally.

  When you drag a *folder* into a window that contains an identically named *folder*, however, whether or not Windows warns you is up to you. If you turn this box on, you get no warning—just an insta-replace.

- **Hide protected operating system files.** This option is similar to "Show hidden files, folders, and drives"—except that it refers to even more important files, system files that may not be invisible but are nonetheless so important that moving or deleting them might turn your PC into a $2,000 paperweight. Turning this off, in fact, produces a warning message that's meant to frighten away everybody but power geeks.

- **Launch folder windows in a separate process.** This geekily worded setting opens each folder into a different chunk of memory (RAM). In certain rare situations, this largely obsolete arrangement is more stable—but it slows down your machine slightly and unnecessarily uses memory.

- **Restore previous folder windows at logon.** Every time you log off the computer, Windows forgets which windows were open. That's a distinct bummer, especially if you tend to work out of your Documents window, which you must therefore manually reopen every time you fire up the old PC.

  If you turn on this useful checkbox, then Windows will automatically greet you with whichever windows were open when you last logged off.

- **Show drive letters.** Turn off this checkbox to hide the drive letters that identify each of your disk drives in the Computer window (in the navigation pane, click

Computer). In other words, "Local Disk (C:)" becomes "Local Disk"—an option that might make newcomers feel less intimidated.

- **Show encrypted or compressed NTFS files in color.** This option won't make much sense until you've read pages 708 and 712, which explain how Windows can encode and compact your files for better security and disk space use. Turning on this checkbox turns the names of affected icons green and blue, respectively, so you can spot them at a glance. On the other hand, encrypted or compressed files and folders operate quite normally, immediately converting back to human form when double-clicked; hence, knowing which ones have been affected isn't particularly valuable. Turn off this box to make them look just like any other files and folders.
- **Show pop-up description for folder and desktop icons.** If you point to an icon, a taskbar button, a found item in Search, or whatever (without clicking), you get a *tooltip*—a floating, colored label that identifies what you're pointing to. If you find tooltips distracting, then turn off this checkbox.
- **Show preview handlers in preview pane.** This is the on/off switch for one of Windows' best features: seeing a preview of a selected document icon in the Preview pane. Turn it off only if your PC is grinding to a halt under the strain of all this graphics-intensive goodness.
- **Show status bar.** This option, new in Windows 8, refers to the horizontal strip that you can summon at the bottom of every Explorer window. It shows you, in tiny type, how many items are in the window. When you select some of them, it tells you how many you've highlighted and how much disk space they take up—a great way to anticipate whether or not they'll fit on some flash drive or CD.
- **Use check boxes to select items.** Now here's a weird one: This option makes a *checkbox* appear on every icon you point to with your mouse, for ease in selection. Page 272 explains all.

Tip: There's a duplicate, easier way to access this option: Turn on "Item check boxes" on the Ribbon's View tab.

- **Use Sharing Wizard (Recommended).** Sharing files with other computers is one of the great perks of having a network. As Chapter 27 makes clear, this feature makes it much easier to understand what you're doing. For example, it lets you specify that only certain people are allowed to access your files, and it lets you decide how much access they have. (For example, can they change them or just see them?)
- **When typing into list view.** When you've got an Explorer window open, teeming with a list of files, what do you want to happen when you start typing?

  In the olden days, that'd be an easy one: "Highlight an icon, of course!" That is, if you type *piz,* you highlight the file called "Pizza with Casey.jpg." And indeed, that's what the factory setting means: "Select the typed item within the view."

  But Windows 8 has a search box in every Explorer window. If you turn on "Automatically type into the Search Box," then each letter you type arrives in that box, performing a real-time, letter-by-letter search of all the icons in the window. Your savings: one mouse click.

Taskbar 2.0

For years, the *taskbar*—the strip of colorful icons at the bottom of your screen—has been one of the most prominent and important elements of the Windows interface (Figure 6-21). Today, you can call it Taskbar, Extreme Makeover Edition; starting in Windows 7, it began doing a lot of things it had never done before.

Figure 6-21: *The taskbar offers buttons for every program you're running–and every program you've pinned there for easy access later.*

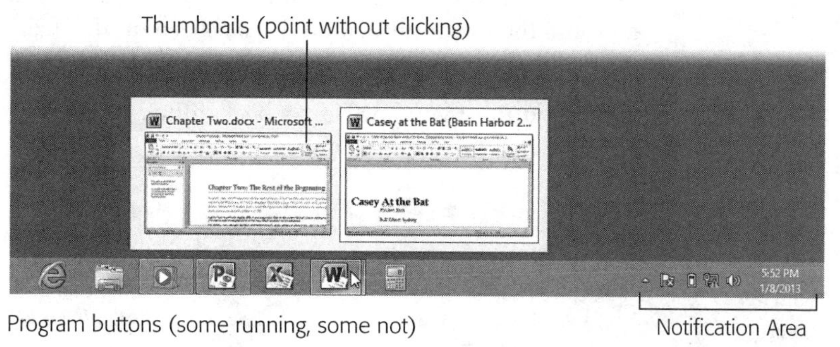

Here's an introduction to its functions, old and new:

- **The Start menu is gone now.** As you know from the beginning of this chapter, the Start *screen* now replaces the old Start *menu* (although it's easy enough to bring back the Start menu).
- **The taskbar lists your open programs and windows.** The icons on the taskbar make it easy to switch from one open program to another—from your Web browser to your email programs, for example—or even to specific windows *within* those programs.
- **The taskbar lets you open your favorite programs.** You read that right. The taskbar is now a *launcher,* just like the Dock in the Mac's OS X or the QuickLaunch toolbar in old Windows versions. It's a mini-Start menu.
- **The system tray (notification area) is at the right end.** These tiny icons show you the status of your network connection, battery life, and so on.
- **The Show Desktop button hides at the far-right end.** You can read more about this invisible button on page 188.

You've already read about the Start screen; the following pages cover the taskbar's other functions.

Tip: You can operate the taskbar entirely from the keyboard. Press ⊞+T to highlight the first button on it, as indicated by a subtle glow. Then you can "walk" across its buttons by pressing the left/right arrow keys, or by pressing ⊞+T (add the Shift key to "walk" in the opposite direction). Once a button is highlighted, you can tap the space bar to "click" it, press Shift+F10 to "right-click" it, or press the Menu key on your keyboard to open the icon's jump list. Who needs a mouse anymore?

Taskbar as App Switcher

Every open window is represented by a button—an actual miniature of the window itself—that sprouts from its program's taskbar icon. These buttons make it easy to switch among open programs and windows. Just click one to bring its associated window into the foreground, even if it has been minimized.

Once you know what to look for, you can distinguish an open program from a closed one, a frontmost window from a background one, and so on (see Figure 6-22).

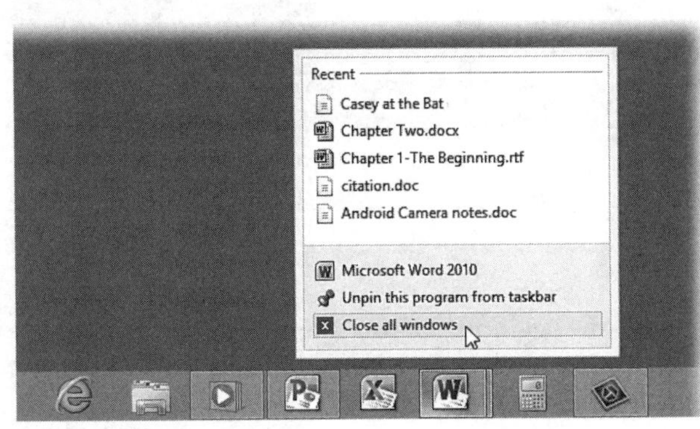

Figure 6-22: *An icon without a border is a program you haven't opened yet (the first and second ones here, for example). A brightened background indicates the active (frontmost) program. Right-clicking one of these buttons lets you perform tasks on all the windows together, such as closing them all at once.*

Handy Window Miniatures

If you point to a program's button without clicking, it sprouts thumbnail images of *the windows themselves.* Figure 6-23 shows the effect. It's a lot more informative than just reading the windows' *names,* as in days of yore (your previous Windows versions, that is). The thumbnails are especially good at helping you spot a particular Web page, photo, or PDF document.

Tip: There's a tiny Close button (☒) in each thumbnail, too, which makes it easy to close a window without having to bring it forward first. (Or click the thumbnail itself with your mouse's scroll wheel, or use your middle mouse button, if you have one.) Each thumbnail also has a hidden shortcut menu. Right-click to see your options!

Full-Size Peeking

Those window miniatures are all fine, but the taskbar can also show you *full-screen* previews of your windows.

To see them, point to one of the *thumbnails* without clicking. As you can see in Figure 6-23, Windows now displays that window at full size, right on the screen, even if it was minimized, buried, or hidden. Keep moving your cursor across the thumbnails (if there are more than one); each time the pointer lands on a thumbnail, the full-size window preview changes to show what's in it.

When you find the window you want, click on the thumbnail you're already pointing to. The window pops open so you can work in it.

***Figure 6-23:** Pointing to a taskbar button produces "live" thumbnail previews of the windows themselves, which can be a huge help. Click a thumbnail to open its window.*

Then, as long as you're pointing around, try pointing to one of the thumbnails. You see a full-size preview of the corresponding window (in this case, a Web window). Click the thumbnail to make that window active.

Button Groups

In the old days, opening a lot of windows might produce a relatively useless display of truncated buttons. Not only were the buttons too narrow to read the names of the windows, but the buttons appeared in chronological order, not software-program order.

As you may have noticed, though, Windows now automatically consolidates open windows into a single program button. (There's even a subtle visual sign that a program has multiple windows open: Its taskbar icon appears to be "stacked," like the first icon in Figure 6-23.) All the Word documents are accessible from the Word icon, all the Excel documents sprout from the Excel icon, and so on.

Point to a taskbar button to see the thumbnails of the corresponding windows, complete with their names; click to jump directly to the one you want.

Despite all the newfangled techniques, some of the following time-honored basics still apply:

- If a program has only *one window* open, you can hide or show it by clicking the program's taskbar button—a great feature that a lot of PC fans miss. (To hide a *background* window, click its taskbar button *twice:* once to bring the window forward, then a pause, then again to hide it.)
- To minimize, maximize, restore, or close a window, even if you can't see it on the screen, point to its program's button on the taskbar. When the window thumbnails pop up, right-click the one you want, and choose from the shortcut menu.
- Windows can make all open windows visible at once, either by *cascading* them, *stacking* them, or displaying them in side-by-side vertical slices. (All three options are shown in Figure 6-24.) To create this effect, right-click a blank spot on the taskbar and choose Cascade Windows from the shortcut menu.

Figure 6-24: *Top: Cascading windows are neatly arranged so you can see the title bar for each window. Click any title bar to bring that window to the foreground as the active window.*

Bottom: You may prefer to see your windows displayed stacked (left) or side by side (right).

- To hide all open windows in one fell swoop, press ⊞+D. Or right-click a blank spot on the taskbar and choose "Show the desktop" from the shortcut menu. Or point to (or click) the Show Desktop rectangle at the far-right end of the taskbar.

To bring the windows back, repeat that step.

Tip: When the taskbar is crowded with buttons, it may not be easy to find a blank spot to click. Usually there's a little gap near the right end; you can make it easier to find some blank space by *enlarging* the taskbar, as described on page 240.

The Taskbar as App Launcher

Each time you open a program, its icon appears on the taskbar. That's the way it's always been. And when you exit that program, its icon disappears from the taskbar.

These days, however, there's a twist: You can *pin* a program's icon to the taskbar so that it's always there, even when it's not open. One quick click opens the app. The idea, of course, is to put frequently used programs front and center, always on the screen, so you don't have to flip back to the Start screen to find them.

To pin a program to the taskbar in this way, use one of these two tricks:

- **Drag a program's icon** directly to any spot on the taskbar, as shown in Figure 6-25. You can drag them from any Explorer window or from the desktop.

Figure 6-25: *To install a program on your taskbar, drag its icon to any spot; the other icons scoot aside to make room.*

(Here a program is being dragged from the Program Files folder, the behind-the-scenes source of all desktop programs.)

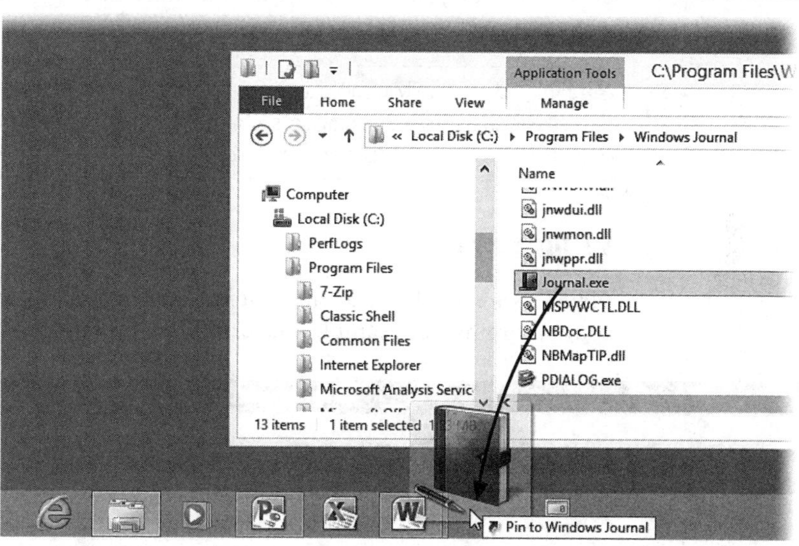

- **Right-click a program's icon (or its shortcut icon)**, wherever it happens to be. From the shortcut menu, choose Pin to Taskbar. The icon appears instantly at the right end of the taskbar. This technique requires less mousing, of course, but it also deprives you of the chance to specify *where* the new icon goes.

- **Right-click an open program's taskbar icon,** wherever it happens to be. From the shortcut menu, choose Pin to Taskbar. In other words, the program's icon might be on the taskbar *now*, because it's running—but you've just told it to stay there even after you exit it.

Once an icon is on the taskbar, you can open it with a single click. By all means, stick your favorites there; over the years, you'll save yourself thousands of unnecessary Start-screen trips.

Tip: If you Shift-click a taskbar icon, you open another window for that program–for example, a new Web-browser window, a new Microsoft Word document, and so on. (Clicking with your mouse's scroll wheel, or middle mouse button, does the same thing.) Add the Ctrl key to open the program as an administrator.

And if you Shift-right-click a taskbar icon, you see the same menu of window-management commands (Cascade, Restore, and so on) that you get when you right-click a blank spot on the taskbar.

If you change your mind about a program icon you've parked on the taskbar, it's easy to move an icon to a new place—just drag it with your mouse.

You can also remove one altogether. Right-click the program's icon—in the taskbar or anywhere on your PC—and, from the shortcut menu, choose "Unpin this program from taskbar."

Note: The taskbar is really intended to display the icons of programs. If you try to drag a file or a folder, you'll succeed only in adding it to a program's jump list, as described next. If you want quick, one-click taskbar access to files, folders, and disks, you can have it–by using the Links toolbar (page 243).

Jump Lists

Jump lists are handy submenus that list frequently or recently opened files in each of your programs. For example, the jump list for Internet Explorer shows the Web sites

GEM IN THE ROUGH

Secret Keystrokes of the Taskbar Icons

There's secret keyboard shortcuts lurking in them thar taskbar icons.

It turns out that the first 10 icons, left to right, have built-in keystrokes that "click" them: the ⊞ key plus the numbers 1, 2, 3, and so on (up to 0, which means 10).

If you use this keystroke to "click" the icon of a program that's not running, it opens up as though you'd clicked it. If you "click" a program that has only one window open, that window pops to the front. If you "click" a program with more than one window open, the icon sprouts thumbnail previews of all of them, and the first window pops to the front.

Remember that you can drag icons around on the taskbar, in effect reassigning those 1-through-0 keystrokes.

you visit most often; the jump list for Windows Media Player shows songs you've played a lot lately.

All of this is designed to save you time, mousing, and folder-burrowing. You can *re*open a file just by clicking its name—to resume work on something you had open recently, for example.

Often, jump lists also include shortcut-menu-ish commands, like New Message (for an email program), Play/Pause (for a jukebox program), or Close All Windows (for just about any program). As Microsoft puts it, it's like having a separate Start menu for *every single program.*

To see a jump list, right-click a program's icon on the taskbar (Figure 6-26).

Figure 6-26:
Tip: Instead of right-clicking the taskbar icon, you can drag upward from the icon with your mouse or trackpad finger. This gesture was intended for use on touchscreen computers, where right-clicking is awfully hard to do with your pointer finger. But it works equally well on any PC.

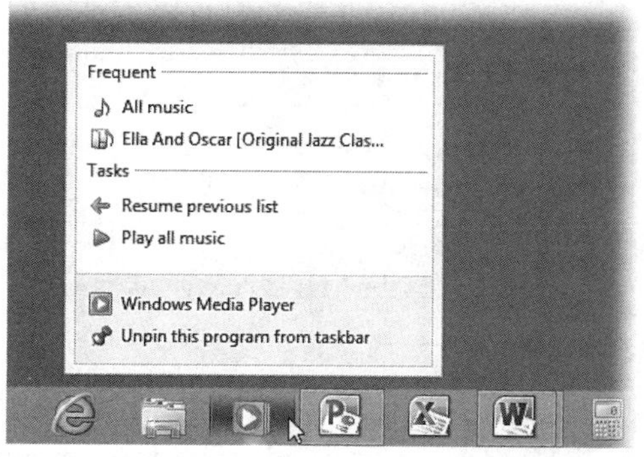

Pinning

In general, jump lists maintain themselves. Windows decides which files you've opened or played most recently or most frequently and builds the jump lists accordingly. New document listings appear, older ones vanish, all without your help.

But you can also install files *manually* into a program's jump list—in Windows-ese, you can *pin* a document to a program's jump list so it's not susceptible to replacement by other items.

For example, you might pin the chapters of a book you're working on to your Word jump list. To the File Explorer jump list, you might pin the *folder and disk* locations you access often.

You can pin a file or folder to a jump list in any of three ways:

- **Drag an icon directly onto a blank spot on the taskbar.** You can drag a document (or its file shortcut) from the desktop or an Explorer window. (You can drag it onto its "parent" program's icon if you really want to, but the taskbar itself is a bigger target.)

As shown in Figure 6-27, a tooltip appears: Pin to Adobe Photoshop (or whatever the parent program is). Release the mouse. You've just pinned the document to its program's taskbar jump list.

Note: If the document's parent program didn't already appear on the taskbar, it does now. In other words, if you drag a Beekeeper Pro document onto the taskbar, Windows is forced to install the Beekeeper Pro program icon onto the taskbar in the process. Otherwise, how would you open the jump list?

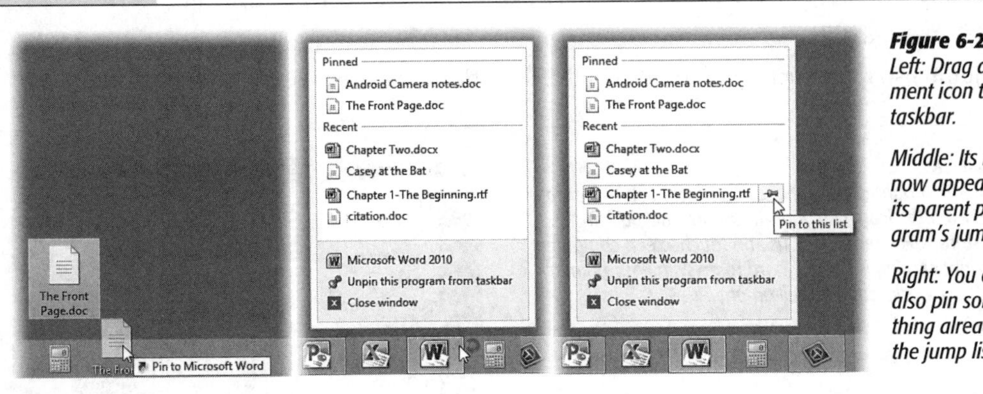

Figure 6-27: *Left: Drag a document icon to the taskbar.*

Middle: Its name now appears in its parent program's jump list.

Right: You can also pin something already in the jump list.

- **In an existing jump list, click the pushpin icon** (Figure 6-27, right). If the document already appears in a jump list, you can move it up into the Pinned list at the top of the jump list this way. Now it won't be dislodged over time by other files you open.

Tip: If you drag a *folder* (or a shortcut of one) onto the taskbar, it gets pinned in the File Explorer icon's jump list.

- **If the file appears in *another* program's jump list, drag it onto the new program's taskbar icon.** For example, maybe you opened a document in WordPad (it's in WordPad's jump list), but you want to move it to Microsoft Word's jump list.

  To do that, drag the document's name out of WordPad's list and then drop it onto Word's taskbar icon. It now appears pinned in *both* programs' jump lists.

Removing things from your taskbar jump lists is just as easy. Open a program's jump list, point to anything in the Pinned list, and click the "Unpin from this list" pushpin.

Note: Once it's unpinned, the file's name may jump down into the Recent section of the jump list, which is usually fine. If it's not fine, you can erase it from there, too; right-click its name and, from the shortcut menu, choose "Remove from this list." (Of course, you're not actually deleting the file.)

You can also erase your jump lists completely—for privacy, for example. For details, and for other caveats about jump lists, see the following pages.

Deleting One Item

For privacy, for security, or out of utter embarrassment, you may not want some file or Web site's name to show up in a jump list. Just right-click and, from the shortcut menu, choose "Remove from this list."

Jump List Caveats

Jump lists are great and all, but you should be aware of a few things:

- They don't know when you've deleted a document or moved it to another folder or disk; they continue to list the file even after it's gone. In that event, clicking the document's listing produces only an error message. You're offered the chance to delete the listing (referred to as "this shortcut" in the error message) so you don't confuse yourself again the next time.
- Some people consider jump lists a privacy risk, since they reveal everything you've been up to recently to whatever spouse or buddy happens to wander by. (You know who you are.) In that case, you can turn off jump lists, or just the incriminating items, as described next.

Tip: Of course, even if you turn off jump lists, there's another easy way to open a document you've recently worked on—from within the program you used to create it. Many programs maintain a list of recent documents in the File menu.

Jump List Settings

There are all kinds of ways to whip jump lists into submission. To see them, right-click a blank spot on the taskbar. From the shortcut menu, choose Properties. Click the Jump Lists tab. Now you can perform tasks like these:

- **Turn off jump lists.** If the whole idea of Windows (or your boss) tracking what you've been working on upsets you, you can turn this feature off entirely. To do that, turn off "Store recently opened programs" and "Store and display recently opened items in Jump Lists" and then click OK.
- **Clear a jump list completely.** At other times, you may want to wipe out *all* your jump lists—and all your tracks. To do that, turn off the checkbox that says "Store and display recently opened items in Jump Lists" (that's the master on/off switch for jump lists). Click Apply; you've just erased all the jump lists.

  If you didn't intend to turn off jump lists for good, though, turn the "Store and display" checkbox back on again before clicking OK. Your jump lists are now ready to start memorizing *new* items.
- **Change the number of documents in the list.** Ordinarily, jump lists track the 10 most recent (or most frequently used) items, but you can goose that number up or down. To do that, adjust the "Number of recent items to display in Jump Lists" item at the top of the dialog box, and then click OK.

Tip: Jump-list items are draggable. For example, suppose you're composing an email message, and you want to attach your latest book outline. If it's in a jump list, you can drag the document's icon directly from the jump list into your email message to attach it. Cool.

The Notification Area (System Tray)

The notification area gives you quick access to little status indicators and pop-up menus that control various functions of your PC (Figure 6-28).

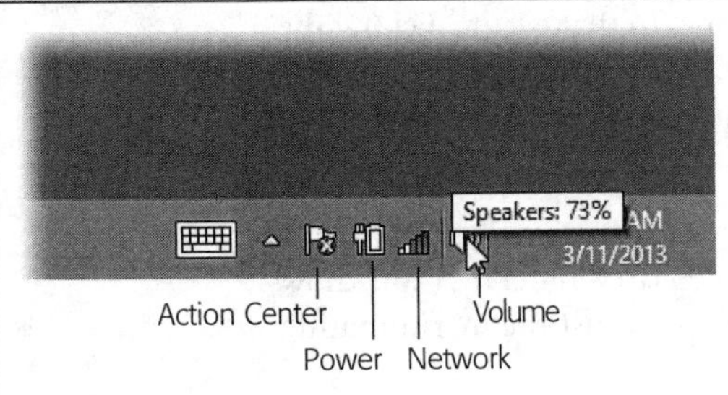

Figure 6-28:
You can point to a status icon's name without clicking (to see its name) or click one to see its pop-up menu of options.

This area has been a sore spot with PC fans for years. Many a software installer inserts its own little icon into this area: fax software, virus software, palmtop synchronization software, and so on. So the tray eventually filled with junky, confusing little icons that had no value to you—but made it harder to find the icons you *did* want to track.

Now, all that is history. Out of the box, only a handful of Windows icons appear here. Each one offers three displays: one when you *point without clicking,* one when you *click the icon,* and a third when you *right-click* the icon. Here's what you start with:

- **Action Center** (⚐). This humble, tiny icon is the front end for the Action Center: a single, consolidated command center for all the little nags that Windows used to bury you with.

  Nowadays, Windows may still whimper because your backup is out of date, because there are Windows updates to install, or whatever. But this icon will sprout a balloon just once, for a few seconds, and then leave you alone after that.

Note: When all is well, the Action Center icon looks like a tiny flag (⚐); when you've ignored some of its warnings, a circled X appears on the flag (⚐).

  If you actually care what Windows is griping about, you have several options. Point to the icon without clicking to see how many important messages are waiting. Click to see the most important messages (or click a link to take care of them). Right-click for links to the Action Center itself (Chapter 21), a troubleshooting wizard, or Windows Update (page 671).

- **Power (, portables only).** Point to the tiny battery icon without clicking to view the time-remaining (and percentage-remaining) readout for your laptop battery. Click for a choice of power plan (page 425)—and for a detailed battery juice–remaining readout, in minutes and in percentage of capacity. Right-click for access to the Power Options control panel and the Windows Mobility Center (see Chapter 28).
- **Network (or).** Point to see the name of your current network and whether or not it's connected to the Internet. Click for a list of available networks; the wireless (WiFi) ones in the list come with icons for signal strength and "locked" (password-protected) status. You can switch networks by clicking one's name. Right-click for a shortcut menu that offers direct access to a troubleshooting screen and to the Network and Sharing Center.
- **Volume ().** Point to see a tooltip that says, for example, "Speakers: 67%" (of full volume). Click for a volume slider that controls your PC's speakers. Right-click for a shortcut menu that offers direct access to various Control Panel screens, like Sounds, Recording Devices, and so on.
- **Clock.** Shows the current date and time. Point to see today's full date, with day of the week ("Thursday, January 16, 2014"). Click for a pop-up clock and mini-calendar, which you can use to check, for example, what day of the week March 9, 2016, falls on. (Right-clicking the Clock doesn't offer anything special—just the same shortcut menu that appears when you right-click a blank spot on the taskbar. The subtle difference: Choosing Properties from this one opens the Properties dialog box for the system-tray icons instead of the taskbar.)

Tip: You can drag system-tray icons around to rearrange them—not just these starter icons, but any that you install, as described below. A vertical insertion-point line appears to show you where the icon will go when you release the mouse.

Revealing the hidden status icons

So if these are the only authorized status icons, then what happened to all the other junky ones deposited there by your software programs?

They're hidden until you summon them. Click the tiny ▲ at the left end of the system tray to see them, safely corralled in a pop-up palette (Figure 6-30).

Reinstating the hidden icons

OK, so now you know where the additional, non-Microsoft status icons are hidden. Thank you, Windows, for sparing us from Creeping Iconitus.

But what if you *want* one of those inferior icons to appear in the system tray? What if you *don't* want Windows to hide them away in the popup window (Figure 6-30)?

No big whoop. Just drag them *out* of the "hidden" corral and back onto the taskbar.

Or you can do it the long way, by opening the notification area control panel and bringing them back (see Figure 6-29).

Here you see a list of all those secondary, usually hidden status icons. For each one, you can use the pop-up menu to choose from the following:

- **Show icon and notifications.** This icon will always appear in the system tray, unhidden at last.

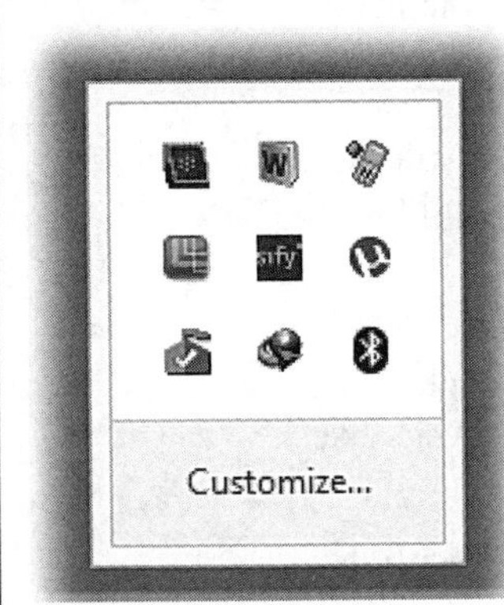

Figure 6-29:
Left: Nowadays, your taskbar isn't overrun by useless software-company icons. They're all hidden in this pop-up corral.

Right: You can drag them around within this bubble to rearrange them, or drag them into or out of the bubble to hide or un-hide specific icons.

- **Hide icon and notifications.** The icon is hidden. If the icon wants to get your attention by popping up a message, too bad; Windows stifles all notifications.
- **Only show notifications.** This icon is hidden, but if it needs your attention, Windows will still show you its notification pop-ups.

Hiding icons you rarely use is a noble ambition. Most of the time, you truly won't miss them, and their absence will make the icons you *do* use stand out all the more.

It's worth noting, by the way, that you have these options even for the basic Windows icons described above: Volume, Network, Power, and so on. If you don't want the date and time eating up taskbar space, then, by golly, you can hide them.

Tip: Actually, the Clock item doesn't appear in the dialog box shown in Figure 6-31. If you want to hide the date and time, click "Turn system icons on or off" at the bottom of that box. You arrive in another dialog box, this one dedicated exclusively to on/off switches for the basic Windows icons: Power, Action Center, Network, Volume–and, yes, Clock.

Revealing all system-tray icons

One last thought: If your intention in visiting the Notification Area Icons box (Figure 6-30) is to turn on *all* system-tray icons—maybe to recreate the halcyon days of Windows XP—you can save yourself some time. Just turn on "Always show all icons and notifications on the taskbar." (It's at the bottom of the dialog box.)

Now all the icons appear in the system tray, the Behaviors pop-up menus are dimmed to show you've overridden them, and the little ▲ button at the left end of the system tray goes away. That's a lot faster than adjusting the Behaviors pop-up menu individually for each icon.

Tip: You have complete keyboard control over the system tray. Press ⊞+B to highlight the first icon–the little ▲ button. Then press the arrow keys to "walk through" the other icons. Press the space bar to "click" whatever icon is highlighted, opening its menu. (Press the Menu key to "right-click" the icon.)

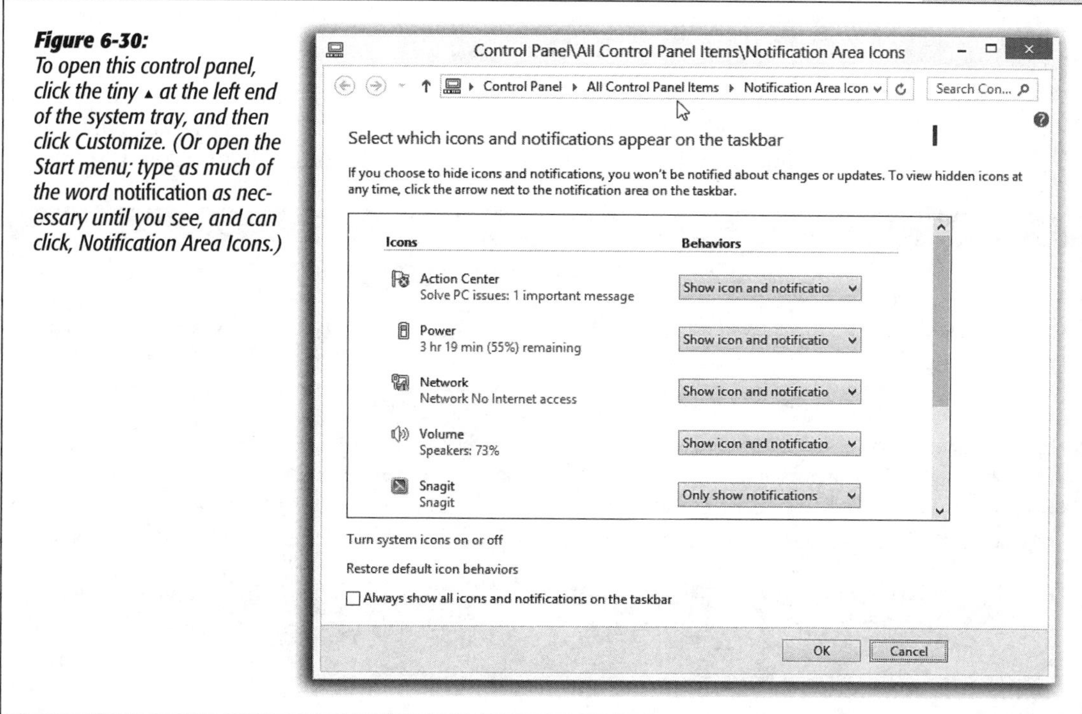

Figure 6-30:
To open this control panel, click the tiny ▲ at the left end of the system tray, and then click Customize. (Or open the Start menu; type as much of the word notification *as necessary until you see, and can click, Notification Area Icons.)*

Three Ways to Get the Taskbar Out of Your Hair

The bottom of the screen isn't necessarily the ideal location for the taskbar. Virtually all screens are wider than they are tall, so the taskbar eats into your limited vertical screen space. You have three ways out: Hide the taskbar, shrink it, or rotate it 90 degrees.

Auto-Hiding the Taskbar

To turn on the taskbar's auto-hiding feature, start by right-clicking a blank spot on the taskbar, and then choose Properties from the shortcut menu. The dialog box that appears offers a checkbox called "Auto-hide the taskbar." This feature makes the taskbar disappear whenever you're not using it—a clever way to devote your entire screen to application windows and yet have the taskbar at your cursor tip when needed.

When this feature is turned on, the taskbar disappears whenever you click elsewhere, or whenever your cursor moves away from it. Only a thin line at the edge of the screen indicates that you have a taskbar at all. As soon as your pointer moves close to that line, the taskbar joyfully springs back into view.

Changing the Taskbar's Size

Even with the button-grouping feature, the taskbar can still accumulate a lot of buttons and icons. As a result, you may want to enlarge the taskbar to see what's what:

- **The draggy way.** First, ensure that the toolbar isn't *locked* (which means you can't move or resize it). Right-click a blank spot on the taskbar; from the shortcut menu, uncheck "Lock the taskbar," if necessary.

  Now position your pointer on the upper edge of the taskbar (or, if you've moved the taskbar, whichever edge is closest to the center of the screen). When the pointer turns into a double-headed arrow, drag to make the taskbar thicker or thinner.

NOSTALGIA CORNER

Bringing Back the Old Taskbar

The taskbar's tendency to consolidate the names of document windows into a single program button saves space, for sure.

Even so, it's not inconceivable that you might prefer the old system, in which there's one taskbar button for every single window. For example, the new consolidated-window scheme means you can't bring a certain application to the front just by clicking its taskbar button. (You must actually choose one particular window from among its thumbnails, which is a lot more effort.)

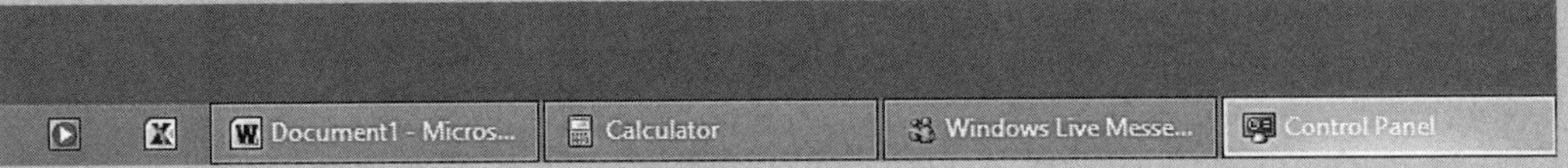

To make Windows display the taskbar the old way, right-click an empty area of the taskbar and choose Properties from the shortcut menu. From the "Taskbar buttons" pop-up menu, choose either "Never combine" or "Combine when taskbar is full" (meaning "only as necessary"). Click Apply; you now have the wider, text-labeled taskbar buttons from the pre-Win7 days, as shown here.

While you're rooting around in here, consider also turning on "Use small taskbar buttons." That step replaces the inch-tall, unlabeled, Mac-style taskbar icons with smaller, half-height ones. Click OK.

The only weirdness now: Icons representing programs that aren't open—icons you've pinned to the taskbar for quick access—appear only as icons, without labels, and the effect is somewhat disturbing. You can get rid of them, if you want; just right-click each and choose "Unpin this program from taskbar."

Now you have a taskbar that looks almost exactly like the Windows XP taskbar—except that it still has a rectangular, plain, modern look. Without add-on shareware, that's as far back into the past as you're allowed to rewind Windows; the Classic theme, if you even remember it, is gone from Windows 8.

Note: If you're resizing a taskbar that's on the top or bottom of the screen, it automatically changes its size in full taskbar-height increments. You can't fine-tune the height; you can only double or triple it, for example.

If it's on the left or right edge of your screen, however, you can resize the taskbar freely. If you're not careful, you can make it look really weird.

- **The dialog-box way.** In the Properties dialog box for the taskbar (right-click it; choose Properties from the shortcut menu), an option called "Use small taskbar buttons" appears. It cuts those inch-tall taskbar icons down to half size, for a more pre-Win7 look.

Moving the Taskbar to the Sides of the Screen

Yet another approach to getting the taskbar out of your way is to rotate it so that it sits vertically against a side of your screen. You can rotate it in either of two ways:

- **The draggy way.** First, ensure that the toolbar isn't *locked*, as described above. (Right-click a blank spot; from the shortcut menu, uncheck "Lock the taskbar.")

  Now you can drag the taskbar to any edge of the screen, using any blank spot in the central section as a handle. (You can even drag it to the *top* of your screen, if you're a true rebel.) Release the mouse when the taskbar leaps to the edge you've indicated with the cursor.

Tip: No matter which edge of the screen holds your taskbar, your programs are generally smart enough to adjust their own windows as necessary. In other words, your Word document will shift sideways so that it doesn't overlap the taskbar you've dragged to the side of the screen.

- **The dialog-box way.** Right-click a blank spot on the taskbar; from the shortcut menu, choose Properties. Use the "Taskbar location on screen" pop-up menu to choose Left, Right, Top, or Bottom. (You can do this even if the taskbar is locked.)

You'll probably find that the right side of your screen works better than the left. Most programs put their document windows against the left edge of the screen, where the taskbar and its labels might get in the way.

Note: When you position your taskbar vertically, what was once the right side of the taskbar becomes the bottom. In other words, the clock appears at the bottom of the vertical taskbar. So as you read references to the taskbar in this book, mentally substitute the phrase "bottom part of the taskbar" when you read references to the "right side of the taskbar."

Taskbar Toolbars

You'd be forgiven if you've never even heard of taskbar *toolbars*; this is one obscure feature.

These toolbars are separate horizontal sections on the taskbar that offer special-function features. You can even build your own toolbars—for example, one stocked with documents related to a single project. (Somewhere, there's a self-help group for people who spend entirely too much time fiddling with this kind of thing.)

To make a toolbar appear or disappear, right-click a blank spot on the taskbar and choose from the Toolbars submenu that appears (Figure 6-31). The ones with checkmarks are the ones you're seeing now; you can click to turn them on and off.

Tip: You can't adjust the toolbars' widths until you unlock the taskbar (right-click a blank spot and turn off "Lock the taskbar"). Now each toolbar is separated from the main taskbar by a dotted "grip strip." Drag this strip to make the toolbar wider or narrower.

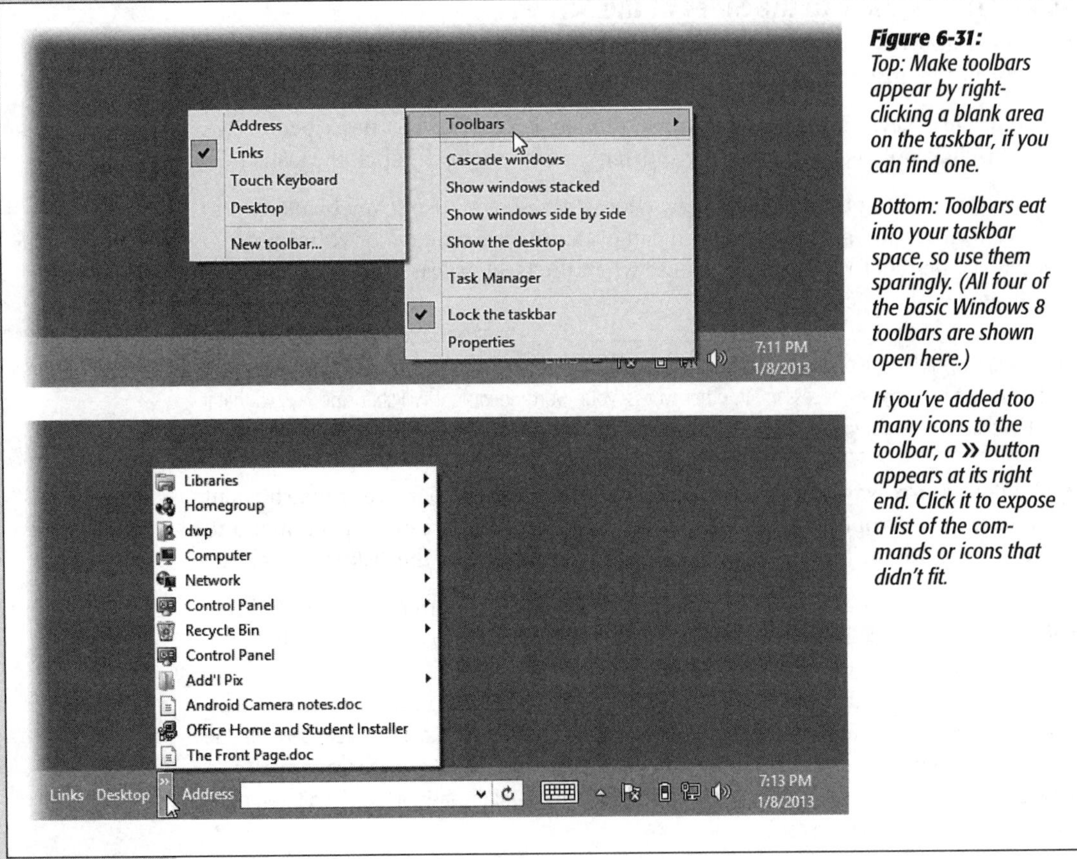

Figure 6-31: *Top: Make toolbars appear by right-clicking a blank area on the taskbar, if you can find one.*

Bottom: Toolbars eat into your taskbar space, so use them sparingly. (All four of the basic Windows 8 toolbars are shown open here.)

If you've added too many icons to the toolbar, a » button appears at its right end. Click it to expose a list of the commands or icons that didn't fit.

Here's a rundown of the ready-made taskbar toolbars at your disposal.

Address Toolbar

This toolbar offers a duplicate copy of the address bar that appears in every Explorer window, complete with a Recent Addresses pop-up menu—except that it's always available, even if no Explorer window happens to be open.

Links Toolbar

From its name alone, you might assume that the purpose of this toolbar is to provide links to your favorite Web sites. And sure enough, that's one thing it's good for.

But in fact, you can drag *any icon at all* onto this toolbar—files, folders, disks, programs, or whatever—to turn them into one-click buttons.

In other words, the Links toolbar duplicates the "park favorite icons" function of the Start screen, taskbar, and Quick Launch toolbar. But in some ways, it's better. It can display *any* kind of icon (unlike the taskbar). It's always visible (unlike the Start screen). And it shows the icons' names.

Note: The Links toolbar is a mirror of the Favorites toolbar in Internet Explorer (Tools→Toolbars→Favorites), just in case you were baffled. Edit one, you edit the other.

Here are a few possibilities of things to stash here, just to get your juices flowing:

- Install icons of the three or four programs you use the most (or a few documents you work on every day).
- Install the Recycle Bin's icon, so you don't have to mouse all the way over to… wherever you keep the real Recycle Bin.
- Install icons for shared folders on the network. This arrangement saves several steps when you want to connect to them.
- Install icons of Web sites you visit often so you can jump directly to them when you sit down in front of your PC each morning. (In Internet Explorer, you can drag the tiny icon at the left end of the address bar directly onto the Links toolbar to install a Web page there.)

You can drag these links around on the toolbar to put them into a different order, or remove a link by dragging it away—directly into the Recycle Bin, if you like. (They're only shortcuts; you're not actually deleting anything important.) To rename something here—a good idea, since horizontal space in this location is so precious—right-click it and choose Rename from the shortcut menu.

Tip: Dragging a Web link from the Links toolbar to the desktop or an Explorer window creates an *Internet shortcut file*. When double-clicked, this special document connects to the Internet and opens the specified Web page.

Touch Keyboard

This "toolbar" is actually the onscreen typing keyboard, the one you'll need if you have a touchscreen tablet that doesn't have a keyboard. In other words, you can make the onscreen keyboard appear and disappear by clicking this button. Chapter 3 has the details.

Desktop Toolbar

The Desktop toolbar (Figure 6-31, bottom) offers quick access to whichever icons are sitting on your desktop—the Recycle Bin, for example, and whatever else you've put there. As a convenience, it also lists a few frequently used places that *aren't* on the desktop, including your Personal folder, libraries, Homegroup, Network, Control Panel, and so on.

When it first appears, the Desktop toolbar takes the form of a >> button at the right end of the taskbar. You can widen the Desktop toolbar if you like, making its buttons appear horizontally on the taskbar. But if you leave it compressed, then many of its icons sprout pop-up *submenus* that give you direct access to their *contents.* That's a useful way to get at your stuff when your screen is filled with windows.

NOSTALGIA CORNER

Bringing Back the Quick Launch Toolbar

The whole point of the old Quick Launch toolbar was to display the icons of programs you used a lot–exactly like the new Windows 7/8 taskbar itself. So Microsoft took the Quick Launch toolbar out behind the barn and shot it.

Besides, if "a toolbar filled with icons of my choosing, ready for one-click opening" is the idea behind the Quick Launch toolbar, then why not use the Links toolbar or the "build your own" toolbar described on these pages?

Well, all right. If you really feel it's that important to have the Quick Launch toolbar–the actual, original one–you can bring it back.

Start by creating a folder that contains the icons for everything you want displayed on the toolbar.

Now right-click a blank spot on the taskbar. From the shortcut menu, choose Toolbars→New Toolbar. In the resulting dialog box, type this (AutoComplete is there to help you save typing)...

%appdata%\Microsoft\Internet Explorer\Quick Launch

...and then click Select Folder.

And presto: The Quick Launch toolbar now appears on your taskbar. It works exactly like the Links toolbar, in that you can drag anything onto it for easy access: folder, file, disk, shortcut, program, anything with an icon.

It still doesn't look much like the old Quick Launch toolbar, though. But you can fix that.

First, unlock the taskbar. (Right-click it; from the shortcut menu, choose "Lock the taskbar," if necessary, so that the checkmark disappears.)

Now right-click the Quick Launch toolbar itself; turn off Show Title and Show Text. Drag the dotted "grip strip" handle at the toolbar's left edge all the way to the left so that it's right next to the Start menu, where the old Quick Launch toolbar used to be. Drag the right-side "grip strip" to adjust the width. Relock the taskbar, if you like.

From now on, you can install any file, folder, or disk onto this toolbar just by dragging it there. It shows up, tiny but legible, ready for opening with one click.

If you change your mind, you can get rid of the Quick Launch toolbar. Right-click the taskbar; from the shortcut menu, choose Toolbars→"Quick Launch toolbar," so that the checkmark disappears.

Redesigning Your Toolbars

To change the look of a toolbar, first unlock it. (Right-click it; from the shortcut menu, choose "Lock the taskbar," if necessary, so that the checkmark disappears. Later, repeat this procedure to lock the taskbar again.)

Next, right-click any blank spot on the toolbar. The resulting shortcut menu offers these choices, which appear *above* the usual taskbar shortcut menu choices:

- **View** lets you change the size of the icons on the toolbar.
- **Open Folder** works only with the Quick Launch and Links toolbars.

  It turns out that the icons on these toolbars reflect the contents of corresponding *folders* on your PC. To see one, right-click a blank spot on the toolbar itself; from the shortcut menu, choose Open Folder.

  Why is that useful? Because it means you can add, rename, or delete icons en masse, by working in the folder instead of on the toolbar itself. Of course, you can also delete or rename any icon on these toolbars by right-clicking it and choosing Delete or Rename from the shortcut menu. But a window isn't nearly as claustrophobic as the toolbar itself.
- **Show Text** identifies each toolbar icon with a text label.
- **Show Title** makes the toolbar's name (such as "Quick Launch" or "Desktop") appear on the toolbar.
- **Close Toolbar** makes the toolbar disappear.

Tip: How much horizontal taskbar space a toolbar consumes is up to you. Drag the border at the left edge of a toolbar to make it wider or narrower. That's a good point to remember if, in fact, you can't *find* a blank spot to right-click on. (Sub-tip: In a pinch, you can right-click the clock.) Don't forget that you have to unlock the toolbar before you can change its size (right-click, and then choose "Lock the taskbar" so the checkmark disappears).

Build Your Own Toolbars

The Quick Launch and Links toolbars are such a delight that you may find that having only one isn't enough. You may wish to create several *different* Links toolbars, each stocked with the icons for a different project or person. One could contain icons for all the chapters of a book you're writing; another could list only your games.

Fortunately, it's easy to create as many different custom toolbars as you like, each of which behaves exactly like the Links toolbar.

Windows creates toolbars from *folders,* so before creating a toolbar of your own, you must create a folder and fill it with the stuff you want to toolbar-ize.

Next, right-click a blank spot on the taskbar. From the shortcut menu, choose Toolbars→New Toolbar to open the New Toolbar dialog box, as shown in Figure 6-32. Find and click the folder you want, and then click Select Folder.

Now there's a brand-new toolbar on your taskbar, whose buttons list the contents of the folder you selected. Feel free to tailor it as described—by changing its icon sizes, hiding or showing the icon labels, or installing new icons onto it by dragging them from other Explorer windows.

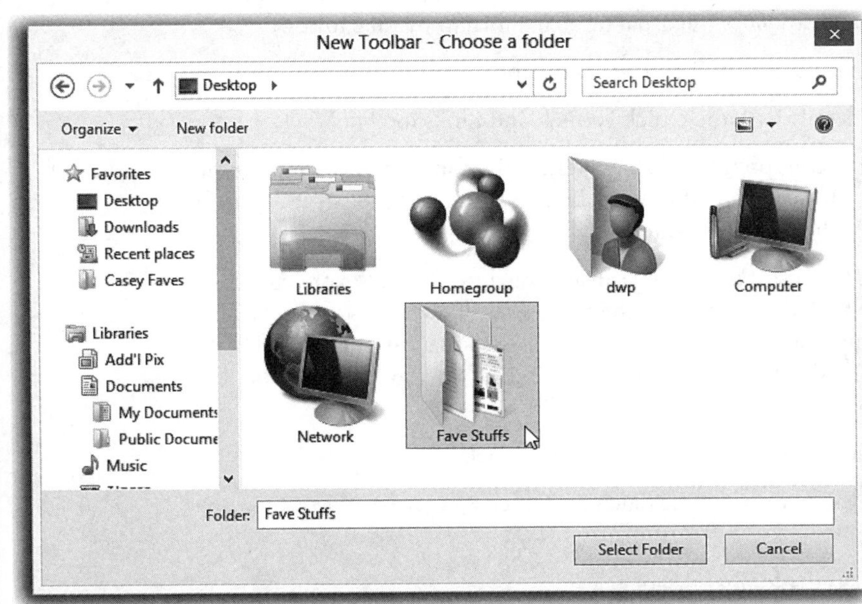

Figure 6-32: *To create a new toolbar, begin by making a folder. Stock it with the icons you want to access from the taskbar. Amaze your friends!*

The Run Command

The Start screen doesn't ordinarily include the Run command. But power users and über-geeks may well want to put it back into the Start screen, following the instructions in Chapter 2.

Or don't bother. Whenever you want the Run command, you can just press ⊞+R, or type *run* at the Start screen, or right-click the lower-left corner of the screen and choose Run from the secret Utilities menu.

The Run command gets you to a *command line*, as shown in Figure 6-33. A command line is a text-based method of performing a task. You type a command, click OK, and something happens as a result.

Note: The command line in the Run dialog box is primarily for *opening* things. Windows also comes with a program called Command Prompt that offers a far more complete environment—not just for opening things, but also for controlling and manipulating them. Power users can type long sequences of commands and symbols in Command Prompt.

If you're a PC veteran, your head probably teems with neat Run commands you've picked up over the years. If you're new to this idea, however, the following are a few of the useful and timesaving functions you can perform with the Run dialog box.

Open a Program

For example, you can use the Run command as a program launcher. Just type any program's *program filename* in the Open text box and then press Enter. For both pros and novices, it's frequently faster to launch a program this way than to click the Start→All Programs menu with the mouse.

Unfortunately, the program filename isn't the same as its plain-English name; it's a cryptic, abbreviated version. For example, if you want to open Microsoft Word, you must type *winword*. That's the actual name of the Word program icon as it sits in your Computer→Local Disk (C:)→Program Files→Microsoft Office→Office folder. Here are some other common program filenames:

Program's real name	Program's familiar name
iexplore	Internet Explorer
explorer	File Explorer
write	WordPad
msworks	Microsoft Works
msimn	Mail
wmplayer	Windows Media Player
control	Classic Control Panel
regedit	Registry Editor
cleanmgr	Disk Cleanup
defrag	Disk Defragmenter
calc	Calculator

To discover the real filename of a certain program, open Computer→Local Disk (C:) →Program Files. Inspect the folders there; with the window in Details view, you'll be able to spot the icons whose type is "application."

Note: True, the search box at Start screen offers another way to find and open any program without taking your hands off the keyboard. But the Run method is more precise and may require less effort because you're not typing the *entire* program name.

In fact, keyboard lovers, get this: You can perform this entire application-launching stunt without using the mouse at all. Just follow these steps in rapid succession:

1. **Press ⊞+R.**

   That's the keyboard shortcut for the Run command, whose dialog box now opens.

2. **Type the program file's name in the Open box.**

   If you've typed the name before, just type a couple of letters; Windows fills in the rest of the name automatically.

3. Press Enter.

   Windows opens the requested program instantly. Keystrokes: 4; Mouse: 0.

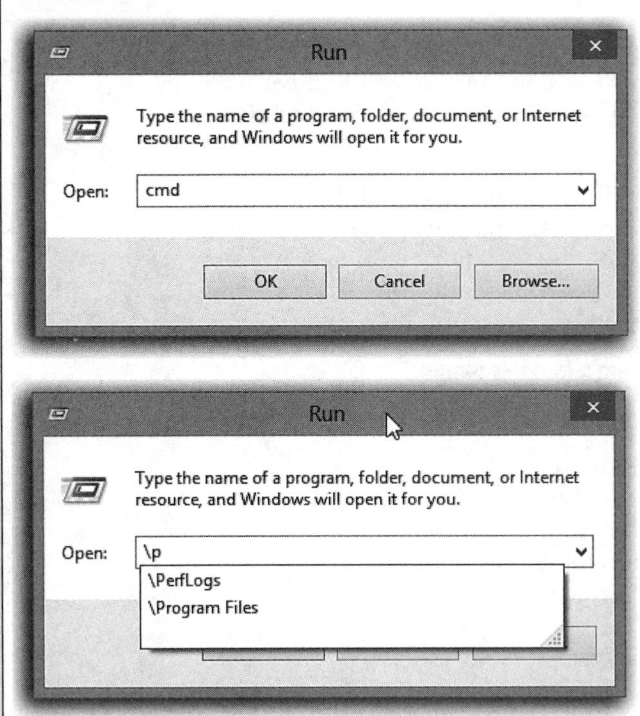

Figure 6-33: *Top: The last Run command you entered appears automatically in the Open text box. You can use the drop-down list to see a list of commands you've previously entered.*

Bottom: The Run command knows the names of all your folders and also remembers the last few commands you typed here. As you go, you're shown the best match for the characters you're typing. When the name of the folder you're trying to open appears in the list, click it to prevent having to type the rest of the entry.

Open Any Program or Document

Using the Run dialog box is handy for opening favorite applications, because it requires so few keystrokes. But you can also use the Run dialog box to open *any* file on the computer.s

The trick here is to type in the entire *path* of the program or document you want. (See page 202 if you're new to the idea of file paths.) For example, to open the family budget spreadsheet that's in Harold's Documents folder, you might type *C:\Users\Harold\Documents\familybudget.xls.*

Of course, you probably wouldn't *actually* have to type all that, since the AutoComplete pop-up menu offers to complete each folder name as you start to type it.

Tip: Typing the path this way is also useful for opening applications that don't appear on the Start screen. (If a program doesn't appear there, you must type its entire *pathname*—or click Browse to hunt for its icon yourself.)

For example, some advanced Windows utilities (including the *Registry Editor,* an advanced diagnostic program) are accessible only through the command line. You also need to use the Run command to open some older command-line programs that don't come with a listing in the All Programs menu.

Open a Drive Window

When you click Computer at the desktop, you see that Windows assigns a letter of the alphabet to each disk drive attached to your machine—the hard drive, the DVD drive, the floppy drive, and so on. The floppy drive is A:, the hard drive is usually C:, and so on. (There hasn't been a B: drive since the demise of the two-floppy computer.)

By typing a drive letter followed by a colon (for example, *C:*) into the Run box and pressing Enter, you make a window pop open, showing what's on that drive.

Open a Folder Window

You can also use the Run dialog box to open the window for any folder on your machine. To do so, type a backslash followed by the name of a folder (Figure 6-33, bottom). You might type, for example, the first few letters of *\Program Files* to see your complete software collection.

Note: The Run command assumes you're opening a folder on drive C:. If you want to open a folder on a different drive, add the drive letter and a colon before the name of the folder (for example, *D:\data)*.

If you're on a network, you can even open a folder that's sitting on another computer on the network. To do so, type *two* backslashes, the computer's name, and then the shared folder's name. For instance, to access a shared folder called Budgets on a computer named Admin, enter *\\admin\budgets.* (See Chapter 27 for more on sharing folders over the network.)

It might make you feel extra proficient to know that you've just used the *Universal Naming Convention,* or UNC, for the shared folder. The UNC is simply the two-backslash, computer name\folder name format (for example: *\\ComputerName\foldername)*.

Tip: In any of these cases, if you don't remember the precise name of a file or folder you want to open in the Run dialog box, then click the Browse button to display the Browse dialog box, as shown in Figure 6-33, bottom.

Connect to a Web Page

You can jump directly to a specific Web page by typing its Web address (URL)—such as *http://www.bigcompany.com*—into the Run dialog box and then pressing Enter. You don't even have to open your Web browser first.

Once again, you may not have to type very much; the drop-down list in the Run dialog box lists every URL you've previously entered. Simply click one (or press the ↓ key to highlight the one you want, and then press Enter) to go to that site.

The Secret Utilities Menu

As you may be starting to appreciate, Microsoft didn't make many changes to the Windows 8 desktop. Sure, the Start menu is gone and the Ribbon was added, but almost everything else is mostly the same as Windows 7.

The secret Utilities menu

There is one new feature, however—a feature Microsoft has scarcely said anything about. It's for power users. It's a secret menu full of advanced commands—a little thank-you note to veterans who've put in the years to master Windows. It's the little-known Utiliies menu. You can make it appear in any of these ways:

- **Mouse:** Point to the lower-left corner of the screen, so that the Start-screen thumbnail appears. Right-click it.
- **Keyboard:** Press ⊞+X.

There, in all its majesty, is the X menu, seething with shortcuts to toys for the technically inclined (Figure 6-34).

All of these items are described elsewhere in this book, but a few are especially useful to have at your mousetip—System (a window that provides every possible detail about your machine), Control Panel, Task Manager, and Search, for example. (Having the option to choose Search here saves you a trip into TileWorld and its Charms menu.)

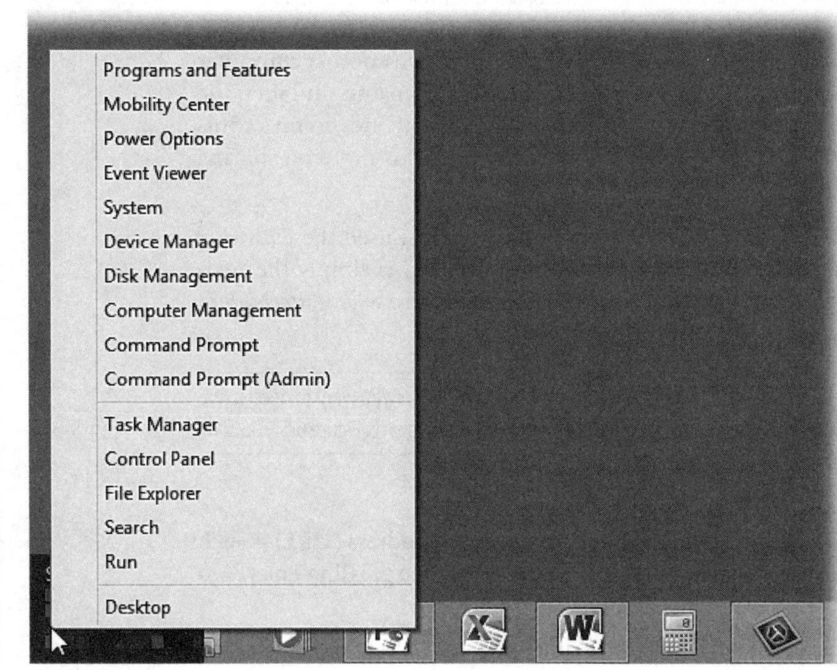

Figure 6-34: *The secret Utilities menu is intended for the power-using elite—people who know exactly what to do with the Device Manager and the Computer Management console.*

But almost anyone can get pleasure from the shortcuts to everyday options like Search, Task Manager, and Control Panel—and will be grateful to have them still there in a pseudo-Start menu that doesn't require a hike to TileWorld.

CHAPTER

7

Searching & Organizing Your Files

Every disk, folder, file, application, printer, and networked computer is represented on your screen by an icon. To avoid spraying your screen with thousands of overlapping icons seething like snakes in a pit, Windows organizes icons into folders, puts those folders into *other* folders, and so on. This folder-in-a-folder-in-a-folder scheme works beautifully at reducing screen clutter, but it means that you've got some hunting to do whenever you want to open a particular icon.

Helping you find, navigate, and manage your files, folders, and disks with less stress and greater speed is one of the primary design goals of Windows—and of this chapter. The following pages cover the desktop version of Search, plus icon-management life skills like selecting them, renaming them, moving them, copying them, making shortcuts of them, assigning them to keystrokes, deleting them, and burning them to CD or DVD.

Tip: To create a new folder to hold your icons, right-click where you want the folder to appear (on the desktop or in any desktop window except Computer), and choose New→Folder from the shortcut menu. The new folder appears with its temporary "New Folder" name highlighted. Type a new name for the folder and then press Enter.

Desktop Search

Every computer offers a way to find files. You already know about the principal method in Windows 8: the search box in the Charms bar, back in TileWorld.

It's important to note, though, that you can also search for files at the desktop. The Start menu may be gone, but the search box at the upper-right corner of every File Explorer window lives on.

This, too, is a piece of the Search empire. But there's a big difference: The search box in the Charms bar searches *your entire computer.* The search box in an Explorer window searches *only that window* (and folders within it).

And what if you prefer the search mechanism at the desktop to the TileWorld version? True, Explorer's search box looks only in one window—but there's nothing to stop you from defining "that window" as your entire account folder, or even your entire computer. Just click your Personal folder, or the Computer icon in the Navigation pane, before you search.

The window changes to show search results (in Content view) *as* you type into the search box (see Figure 7-1).

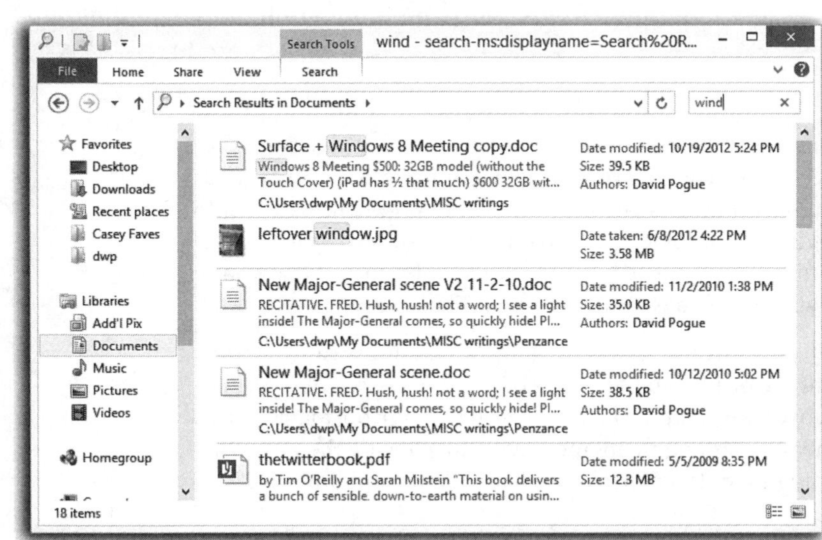

Figure 7-1: *You won't always see your search term highlighted in the results list like this. That's because Windows is also searching inside the files. The matching result may be a word inside the text of a document, or even in the invisible tags associated with a file.*

You don't have to type an entire word. Typing *kumq* will find documents containing the word "kumquat." However, it's worth noting that Windows recognizes only the

UP TO SPEED

Directories vs. Folders

Before Windows took over the universe, folders were called directories, and the folders inside them were called subdirectories. Keep that in mind the next time you're reading an old user guide, magazine article, or computer book.

beginnings of words. Typing *umquat* won't find a document containing—or even named—"Kumquat."

Press the ↑ or ↓ keys to walk through the results list one item at a time.

Once the results appear in the main window, you can change the window view if that's helpful, or sort, filter, and group them, just as you would in any other Explorer window.

Tip: The filtering feature of Windows 7, which let you screen the search results by file type and other criteria, is gone in Windows 8.

Results-Listing Tips

It should be no surprise that a feature as important as Search comes loaded with options, tips, and tricks. Here it is—the official, unexpurgated Search Tip-O-Rama:

- The standard Content window view, preferred by the search results, offers lots of detail about the found files. But if you switch into any other view, you can learn more about a search result by pointing to it without clicking. The pop-up tooltip balloon shows you the details. For a file, you see size, date, and other info; for a program or control panel, you see a description.
- You can jump to the actual icon of a search result, sitting there in its actual window, instead of opening it. To do that, right-click its name and, from the shortcut menu, choose "Open file location." The Esc key (top-left corner of your keyboard) is a quick "back out of this" keystroke. Tap it to close the results menu.
- To clear the search box—to try a different search, for example—click the little ⌧ at the right end of the search box.
- Among a million other things, Windows tracks the *tags* (keywords) you've applied to your pictures. As a result, you can find, open, or insert any photo at any time, no matter what program you're using. This is a fantastic way to insert a photo into an outgoing email message, a presentation, or a Web page you're designing. (In a page-layout program, for example, use the Insert command, and then use the search box that appears at the top of the Open dialog box.)

The Search Index

You might think that typing something into the search box triggers a search. But to be technically correct, Windows has already *done* its searching. In the first 15 to 30 minutes after you install Windows—or in the minutes after you attach a new hard drive—it invisibly collects information about everything on your hard drive. Like a kid cramming for an exam, it reads, takes notes on, and memorizes the contents of all your files.

And not just the names of your files. That would be *so* 2004!

No, Windows actually looks *inside* the files. It can read and search the contents of text files, email, Windows Contacts, Windows Calendar, RTF and PDF documents, and documents from Microsoft Office (Word, Excel, and PowerPoint).

In fact, Windows searches over 300 bits of text associated with your files—a staggering collection of tidbits, including the names of the layers in a Photoshop document, the tempo of an MP3 file, the shutter speed of a digital-camera photo, a movie's copyright holder, a document's page size, and on and on. (Technically, this sort of secondary information is called *metadata*. It's usually invisible, although a lot of it shows up in the Details pane described on page 203.)

Windows stores all this information in an invisible, multimegabyte file called, creatively enough, the *index*. (If your primary hard drive is creaking full, you can specify that you want the index stored on some other drive; see page 258.) This index serves both the TileWorld and the desktop versions of Search.

Once it's indexed your hard drive in this way, Windows can produce search results in seconds. It doesn't have to search your entire hard drive—only that single card-catalog index file.

After the initial indexing process, Windows continues to monitor what's on your hard drive, indexing new and changed files in the background, in the microseconds between your keystrokes and clicks.

Where Windows Looks

Windows doesn't actually scrounge through *every* file on your computer. Searching inside Windows' own operating-system files and all your programs, for example, would be pointless to anyone but programmers. All that useless data would slow down searches and bulk up the invisible index file.

What Windows *does* index is everything in your Personal folder: email, pictures, music, videos, program names, entries in your People and Calendar apps, Office documents, and so on. It also searches all your *libraries* (page 208), even if they contain folders from other computers on your network.

Similarly, it searches *offline files* that belong to you, even though they're stored somewhere else on the network. Finally, it indexes everything on the Start screen.

Note: Windows indexes all the drives connected to your PC, but not other hard drives on the network. You can, if you wish, add other folders to the list of indexed locations manually (page 255).

Windows does index the Personal folders of everyone else with an account on your machine (Chapter 24), but you're not allowed to search them. So if you were hoping to search your spouse's email for phrases like "Meet you at midnight," forget it.

If you try to search anything Windows *hasn't* incorporated into its index—in a Windows system folder, for example, or a hard drive elsewhere on the network—a message appears. It lets you know that because you're working beyond the index's wisdom, the search is going to be slow, and the search will include filenames only—not file *contents* or metadata.

Furthermore, this kind of outside-the-index searching doesn't find things *as* you type. This time, you have to press Enter after typing the name (or partial name) of what you want to find.

Adding New Places to the Index

On the other hand, suppose there's some folder on another disk (or elsewhere on the network) that you really do want to be able to search the *good* way—contents and all, nice and fast. You can do that by adding it to your PC's search index.

And you can do *that* in a couple of ways:

Figure 7-2:
In the Indexing Options box, you can add or remove disks, partitions, or folders, thereby editing the list of searchable items.

Start by opening Indexing Options (left), and then click Modify. Now expand the flippy triangles, if necessary, to see the list of folders on your hard drive. Turn a folder's checkbox on (to have Windows index it) or off (to remove it from the index, and therefore from searches). In this example, you've just told Windows to stop indexing your Downloads folder. Click OK.

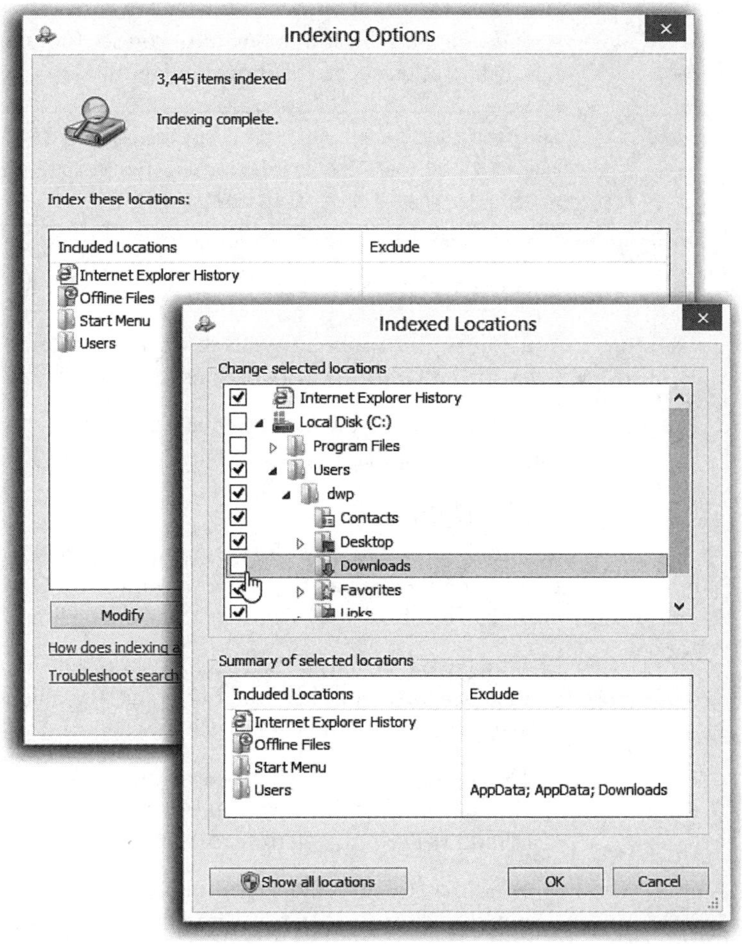

- **Add it to a library.** Drag any folder into one of your libraries (page 208). After a couple of minutes of indexing, that folder is now ready for insta-searching, contents and all, just as though it were born on your own PC.

- **Add it to the Indexing Options dialog box.** Windows maintains a master list of everything in its search index. That's handy, because it means you can easily *add* folders to the index—folders from an external hard drive, for example—for speedy searches.

  You can *remove* folders from the index, too, maybe because you have privacy concerns (for example, you don't want your coworkers searching your stuff while you're away from your desk). Or maybe you just want to create more focused searches, removing a lot of old, extraneous junk from Windows' database.

  Either way, the steps are simple. Open the Indexing Options control panel; the quickest way is to open the Charms bar, click Search, click Settings, and start typing *indexing* into the search box until you see Indexing Options in the search results. Click it, and proceed as shown in Figure 7-2.

Tip: If you're trying to get some work done while Windows is in the middle of building the index, and the indexing is giving your PC all the speed of a slug in winter, you can click the Pause button. Windows will cool its jets for 15 minutes before it starts indexing again.

Customizing Search

You've just read about how Search works fresh out of the box. But you can tailor its behavior, either for security reasons or to customize it to the kinds of work you do.

Unfortunately for you, Microsoft has stashed the various controls that govern searching into three different places. Here they are, one area at a time.

Folder Options

The first source is in the Folder Options→Search dialog box. To open it, find the View tab on the Ribbon in any Explorer window; click Options. In the resulting dialog box, click the Search tab. You wind up at the dialog box shown in Figure 7-3.

- **Find partial matches.** Turn this off if you want Windows to find only whole-word matches, meaning that you'll no longer be able to type *waff* to find *Mom's Best Waffle Recipes of the Eighties.doc.*

- **Don't use the Index when searching in file folders for system files.** If you turn this item on, Windows won't use its internal Dewey Decimal System for searching Windows itself. It will, instead, perform the names-only, slower type of search.

  So who on earth would want this turned on? You, if you're a programmer or system administrator and you're worried that the indexed version of the system files might be out of date. (That happens, since system files change often, and the index may take some time to catch up.)

- **Include system directories.** When you're searching a disk that hasn't been indexed, do you want Windows to look inside the folders that contain Windows itself (as opposed to just the documents people have created)? If yes, then turn this on.

Figure 7-3:
Search actually works beautifully right out of the box. For the benefit of the world's tweakers, however, this dialog box awaits, filled with technical adjustments to the way Search works.

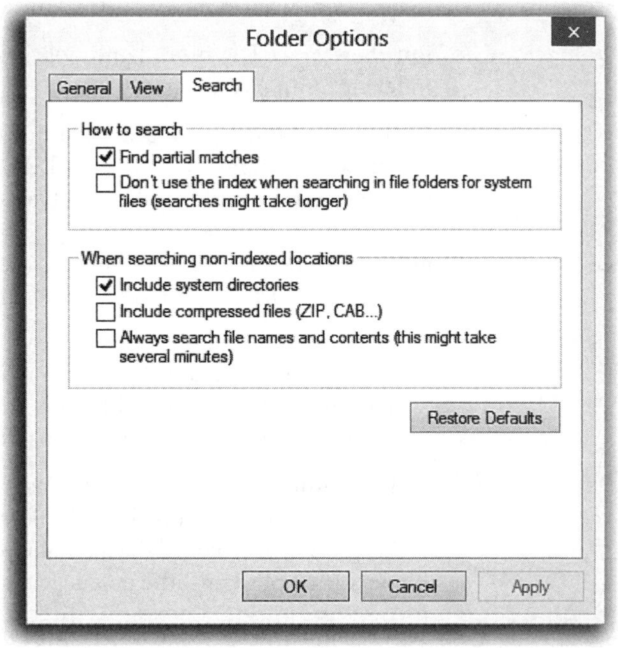

- **Include compressed files (.ZIP, .CAB…).** When you're searching a disk that hasn't been indexed, do you want Windows to search for files inside compressed archives, like .zip and .cab files? If yes, then turn on this checkbox. (Windows doesn't ordinarily search archives, even on an indexed hard drive.)

- **Always search file names and contents.** As the previous pages make clear, the Windows search mechanism relies on an *index*—an invisible database that tracks the location, contents, and metadata of every file. If you attach a new hard drive, or attempt to search another computer on the network that hasn't been indexed, Windows ordinarily just searches its files' *names*. After all, it has no index to search for that drive.

  If Windows did attempt to index those other drives, you'd sometimes have to wait awhile, at least the first time, because index-building isn't instantaneous. That's why the factory setting here is Off.

  But if you really want Windows to search the text inside the other drives' files, even without an index—which can be painfully slow—turn this checkbox on instead.

Indexing Options

The dialog box shown in Figure 7-2 is the master control over the search *index*, the massive, invisible, constantly updated database file that tracks your PC's files and what's in them. As described earlier, you can use this dialog box to add or remove folders from what Windows is tracking.

But there are a few more handy options here, too, lurking behind the Advanced Indexing Options button.

To find this third area of search options, start in the Indexing Options dialog box (Control Panel) and click Advanced. Authenticate if necessary. Now you're ready to perform these powerful additional tweaks.

Index Settings Tab

On the first tab, here's the kind of fun you can have:

- **Index encrypted files.** Windows can *encrypt* files and folders with a quick click, making them unreadable to anyone who receives one by email, say, and doesn't have the password. This checkbox lets Windows index these files (the ones that *you've* encrypted, of course; this isn't a back door to files you can't otherwise access).
- **Treat similar words with diacritics as different words.** The word "ole," as might appear cutely in a phrase like "the ole swimming pool," is quite a bit different from "olé," as in, "You missed the matador, you big fat bull!" The difference is a *diacritical mark* (øne öf mâny littlé lañguage märks).

  Ordinarily, Windows ignores diacritical marks; it treats "ole" and "olé" as the same word in searches. That's designed to make it easier for the average person who can't remember how to type a certain marking, or even which direction it goes. But if you turn on this box, then Windows will observe these markings and treat marked and unmarked words differently.
- **Troubleshooting.** If the Search command ever seems to be acting wacky—for example, it's not finding a document you *know* is on your computer—Microsoft is there to help you.

  Your first step should be to click "Troubleshoot search and indexing." (It appears both here, on the Advanced panel, and on the main Indexing Options panel.) The resulting step-by-step sequence may fix things.

  If it doesn't, click Rebuild. Now Windows *wipes out* the index it's been working with, completely deleting it—and then begins to rebuild it. You're shown a list of the disks and folders Windows has been instructed to index; the message at the top of the dialog box lets you know its progress. With luck, this process will wipe out any funkiness you've been experiencing.
- **Move the index.** Ordinarily, Windows stores its invisible index file on your main hard drive. But you might have good reason for wanting to move it. Maybe your

main drive is getting full. Or maybe you've bought a second, faster hard drive; if you store your index there, searching will be even faster.

In the Advanced Options dialog box, click "Select new." Navigate to the disk or folder where you want the index to go, and then click OK. (The actual transfer of the file takes place the next time you start up Windows.)

File Types Tab

Windows ordinarily searches for just about every kind of *useful* file: audio files, program files, text and graphics files, and so on. It doesn't bother peering inside things like Windows operating system files and applications, because what's inside them is programming code with little relevance to most people's work. Omitting these files from the index keeps the index smaller and the searches fast.

But what if you routinely traffic in very rare Venezuelan Beekeeping Interchange Format (VBIF) documents—a file type your copy of Windows has never met before? You won't be able to search for their contents unless you specifically teach Windows about them.

In the Advanced Options dialog box, click the File Types tab. Type the filename extension (such as VBIF) into the text box at the lower left. Click Add and then OK. From now on, Windows will index this new file type.

On the other hand, if you find that Windows uses up valuable search-results menu space listing, say, Web bookmarks—stuff you don't need to find very often—you can tell it not to bother. Now the results list won't fill up with files you don't care about.

Turn the checkboxes on or off to make Windows start or stop indexing them.

Using the "How should this file be indexed" options at the bottom of the box, you can also make Windows stop searching these files' contents—the text within them—for better speed and a smaller index.

GEM IN THE ROUGH

Beyond Your Own Stuff

Ordinarily, Windows searches only what's in *your* account—your Personal folder. From the Start screen, you can't search what's inside somebody else's stuff.

Yet you *can* search someone else's account—just not from the Start screen and not without permission.

Start by opening the Computer→Users folder. Inside, you'll find folders for all other account holders. Open the one you want to search, and then search using the search box at the top of the Explorer window.

You won't be given access, though, without first supplying an administrator's password. (You don't necessarily have to know it; you could just call an administrator over to type it in personally.) After all, the whole point of having different accounts is to ensure privacy for each person—and only the administrator, or *an* administrator, has full rein to stomp through anyone's stuff.

Saved Searches

Once you've performed an Explorer-window search, you may notice a little button on the Ribbon's Search Tools/Search tab called "Save search."

This button generates a *saved search*. Whenever you click it, you get an instantaneous update of the search you originally set up. (Behind the scenes, it's a special document with the filename extension *.search-ms*.)

To create a saved search, open an Explorer window and perform a search. By all means, use the *search filters* described earlier for more exactitude.

Now, as you survey the search results, click "Save search" (Figure 7-4, top). You're asked to name and save your search. Windows proposes stashing it in your Saved Searches folder (which is in your Personal folder), but you can expand the Save As box and choose any location you like—including the desktop.

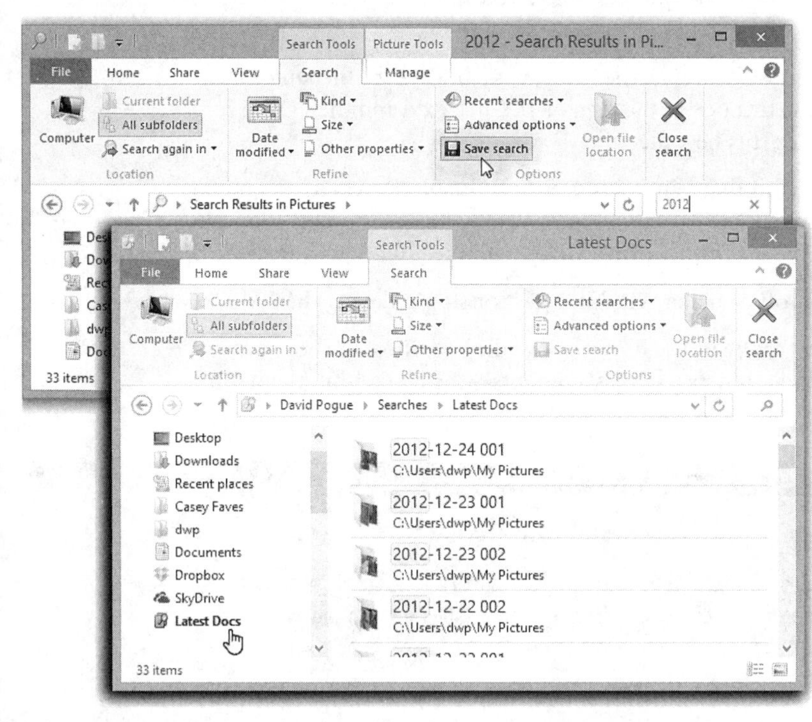

Figure 7-4: *Windows can preserve your search as a saved search that does its duties instantly every time you click it.*

Top: First, do the search using the usual controls. Click "Save search," shown here.

Save the search folder wherever you like; give it a good name.

Bottom: Your saved search is ready to use! Its icon (here called Latest Docs) appears in the Favorite Links list at the left side of every window.

Either way, you also wind up with an icon for your saved search. Unless you changed the location manually, it shows up as an icon in the Favorites section of the Navigation pane in every Explorer window.

Here's a common example: Suppose that every week you want to round up all the documents authored by either you or your business partner that pertain to the Higgins proposal and burn them onto a CD. A search folder can do the rounding-up part with a single click.

So you open your Documents library (or even your Personal folder) and set up a search. In the search box, you type *tags: Higgins authors: casey OR authors: robin*. That text turns blue, meaning that Windows understands what you're looking for: anything with the Higgins tag that was written by Casey or Robin (or whatever your names are).

(Of course, you've been painstakingly tagging your documents with author names and tags, in readiness for this glorious moment.)

You click "Save search." You name the search something like "Our Higgins Files" and save it.

From now on, whenever you click the "Our Higgins Files" icon in your Navigation pane, it opens to reveal all the files you've worked on that were tagged with "Higgins" and written by you or your partner. The great part is that these items' real locations may be all over the map, scattered in folders throughout your PC. But through the magic of the saved search, they appear as though they're all in one neat window.

Unfortunately, there's no easy way to edit a search folder. If you decide your original search criteria need a little fine-tuning, then the simplest procedure is to set up a new search—correctly this time—and save it with the same name as the first one; accept Windows's offer to replace the old one with the new.

Tip: Speaking of memorized searches: You might have noticed that the Search box in every Explorer window maintains a running list of all the searches you've performed so far. They appear in a drop-down menu when you click in the Search box.

If that list contains, ahem, some searches of a personal nature, or maybe just some annoying typos, you might wish you could delete individual items from this list. You can. Press ↑ or ↓ to highlight the one you want (or, rather, don't want), and then press Delete.

The Folders of Windows 8

The top-level, all-encompassing, mother-ship window of your PC is the Computer window. From within this window, you have access to every disk, folder, and file on your computer. Its slogan might well be, "If it's not in here, it's not on your PC."

To see it, open an Explorer window and click Computer in the Navigation pane.

You wind up face to face with the icons of every storage gizmo connected to your PC: hard drives, CD and DVD drives, USB flash drives, digital cameras, and so on (Figure 7-4).

Tip: Ordinarily, every drive has an icon in here, even if no disk or memory card is in it. That can be annoying if your laptop has, for example, four memory-card slots, each for a different kind of card, labeled D:, E:, F:, and G:, and your Computer window is getting a little hard to navigate.

Fortunately, Windows can hide your drive icons when they're empty, just as on the Mac. To turn that on or off, open Folder Options (click Options on the Ribbon's View tab). Click the View tab. Click "Hide empty drives in the Computer folder," and then click OK.

If you leave this option on, then your removable-disk/card drives appear only when something's in them–a CD, a DVD, or a memory card, for example.

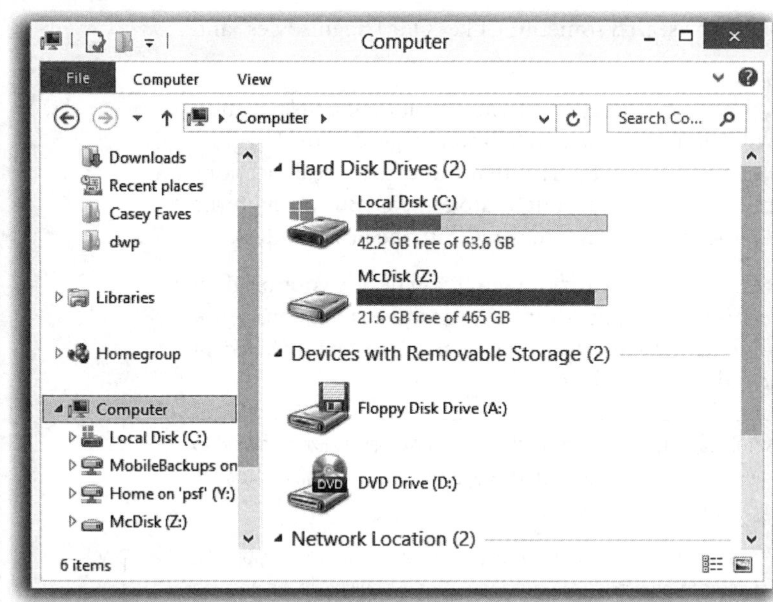

Figure 7-4: *The Computer window is the starting point for any and all folder-digging. It shows the "top-level" folders: the disk drives of your PC. If you double-click the icon of a removable-disk drive (such as your CD or DVD drive), you receive only a "Please insert a disk" message, unless there's actually a disk in the drive.*

Most people, most of the time, are most concerned with the Local Disk (C:), which represents the internal hard drive preinstalled in your computer. (You're welcome to rename this icon, by the way, just as you would any icon.)

Tip: The drive lettering, such as C: for your main hard drive, is an ancient convention that doesn't offer much relevance these days. (Back at the dawn of computing, the A: and B: drives were floppy drives, which is why you don't see those letters anymore.)

Since Windows now displays icons and plain-English names for your drives, you might consider the drive-letter display to be a bit old-fashioned and cluttery. Fortunately, you can hide the drive letter (page 225).

What's in the Local Disk (C:) Window

If you double-click the Local Disk (C:) icon in Computer—that is, your primary hard drive—you'll find, at least, these standard folders.

PerfLogs

Windows Reliability and Performance Monitor is one of Windows' hidden maintenance apps that knowledgeable tech gurus can use to measure your PC's health and speed. This folder is where it dumps its *logs,* or reports.

Program Files

This folder contains all your desktop programs—Word, Excel, Internet Explorer, games, and so on.

Of course, a Windows program isn't a single, self-contained icon. Instead, it's usually a *folder,* housing both the program and its phalanx of support files and folders. The actual application icon itself generally can't even run if it's separated from its support group.

Program Files (x86)

If you've installed a 64-bit version of Windows, this folder is where Windows puts all your older 32-bit programs.

Users

Windows' *accounts* feature is ideal for situations where different family members, students, or workers use the same machine at different times. Each account holder will turn on the machine to find her own separate, secure set of files, folders, desktop pictures, Web bookmarks, font collections, and preference settings. (Much more about this feature in Chapter 24.)

In any case, now you should see the importance of the Users folder. Inside is one folder —one *Personal folder*—for each person who has an account on this PC. In general, standard account holders (page 728) aren't allowed to open anybody else's folder.

Note: Inside the Documents library, you'll see Public Documents; in the Music library, you'll see Public Music; and so on. These are nothing more than pointers to the master Public folder that you can also see here, in the Users folder. (Anything you put into a Public folder is available for inspection by anyone else with an account on your PC, or even other people on your network.)

Windows

Here's a folder that Microsoft hopes you'll just ignore. This most hallowed folder contains the thousands of little files that make Windows, well, Windows. Most of these folders and files have cryptic names that appeal to cryptic people.

In general, the healthiest PC is one whose Windows folder has been left alone.

Your Personal Folder

Everything that makes your Windows experience your own sits inside the Local Disk (C:)→Users→[your name] folder. This is your *Personal folder*, where Windows stores your preferences, documents, email, pictures, music, Web favorites, cookies (described below), and so on.

Tip: Actually, it would make a lot of sense for you to install your Personal folder's icon in the Favorites list at the left side of every Explorer window. Drag its icon directly into the Favorites list.

Inside your Personal folder, you'll find folders like these:

- **Contacts.** An address-book program called Windows Contacts came with Windows Vista, but Microsoft gave it the ol' pink slip for Windows 7. All that's left today is this folder, where it used to stash the information about your social circle. (Some other companies' address-book programs can use this folder, too.)

- **Desktop.** When you drag an icon out of a folder or disk window and onto your desktop, it may *appear* to show up on the desktop. But that's just an optical illusion—a visual convenience. In truth, nothing in Windows is ever really on the desktop; it's just in this Desktop *folder,* and mirrored on the desktop.

  Everyone who shares your machine, upon logging in, sees his own stuff sitting out on the desktop. Now you know how Windows does it; there's a separate Desktop folder in every person's Personal folder.

  You can entertain yourself for hours trying to prove this. If you drag something out of your Desktop folder, it also disappears from the actual desktop. And vice versa.

Note: A link to this folder appears in the Navigation pane of every Explorer window.

- **Downloads.** When you download anything from the Web, Internet Explorer suggests storing it on your computer in this Downloads folder. The idea is to save you the frustration of downloading stuff and then not being able to find it later.

Tip: The Downloads folder appears in your Favorite Links list, too, so you can find your downloaded goodies with a single click.

- **Favorites.** This folder stores shortcuts of the files, folders, and other items you've designated as *favorites* (that is, Web bookmarks). This can be handy if you want to delete a bunch of your favorites all at once, rename them, or whatever.

- **Links.** This folder's icons correspond exactly to the easy-access links in the Favorite Links list at the left side of your Explorer windows. Knowing this little tidbit can be handy if you want to delete these links, rename them, or add to them. (Yes, you can perform these duties directly in the Favorite Links lists, but only one link at a time.)

- **My Documents.** Microsoft suggests that you keep your actual work files in this folder. Sure enough, whenever you save a new document (when you're working in Word or Photoshop Elements, for example), the Save As box proposes storing the new file in this folder.

Tip: You can move the My Documents folder, if you like. For example, you can move it to a *removable* drive, like a pocket hard drive or a USB flash drive, so that you can take it back and forth to work with you and always have your latest files at hand.

To do so, open your My Documents folder. Right-click a blank spot in the window; from the shortcut menu, choose Properties. Click the Location tab, click Move, navigate to the new location, and click Select Folder.

What's cool is that the Documents *link* in every Explorer window's Navigation pane still opens your My Documents folder. What's more, your programs still propose storing new documents there—even though it's not where Microsoft originally put it.

- **My Music, My Pictures, My Videos.** You guessed it: These are Microsoft's proposed homes for your multimedia files. These are where song files from ripped CDs, photos from digital cameras, and videos from camcorders go.
- **Saved Games.** When you save a computer game that's already in progress, it should propose storing it here, so you can find it again later. (Needless to say, it may take some time before all the world's games are updated to know about this folder.)
- **Searches.** Back in the Windows 7 days, when you could *save* searches for reuse later, this folder stored shortcuts for them. Today, this folder lives on solely for the sake of backward compatibility in case you upgraded to Windows 8 from Windows 7.

Note: Your Personal folder also stores a few hidden items reserved for use by Windows itself. One of them is AppData, a very important folder that stores all kinds of support files for your programs (it was called Application Data in Windows XP). For example, it stores word-processor dictionaries, Web cookies, your Media Center recordings, Internet Explorer security certificates, and so on. In general, there's not much reason for you to poke around in them, but in this book, here and there, you'll find tips and tricks that refer you to AppData.

Life with Icons

File Explorer has only one purpose in life: to help you manage the *icons* of your files, folders, and disks. You could spend your entire workday just mastering the techniques of naming, copying, moving, and deleting these icons—and plenty of people do.

Here's the crash course.

Renaming Your Icons

To rename a file, folder, printer, or disk icon, you need to open up its "renaming rectangle." You can do so with any of the following methods:

- Highlight the icon and then press the F2 key.
- Highlight the icon. On the Home tab of the Ribbon, click Rename.
- Click carefully, just once, on a previously highlighted icon's name.
- Right-click the icon and choose Rename from the shortcut menu.

Tip: You can even rename your hard drive so you don't go your entire career with a drive named "Local Disk." Just rename its icon (in the Computer window) as you would any other.

In any case, once the renaming rectangle has appeared, type the new name you want and then press Enter. Use all the standard text-editing tricks: Press Backspace to fix a typo, press the ← and → keys to position the insertion point, and so on. When you're finished editing the name, press Enter to make it stick. (If another icon in the folder has the same name, Windows beeps and makes you choose another name.)

Tip: If you highlight a bunch of icons at once and then open the renaming rectangle for any *one* of them, you wind up renaming *all* of them. For example, if you've highlighted three folders called Cats, Dogs, and Fish, then renaming one of them to *Animals* changes the original set of names to Animals (1), Animals (2), and Animals (3).

If that's not what you want, press Ctrl+Z (that's the keystroke for Undo) to restore all the original names.

A folder or filename can technically be up to 260 characters long. In practice, though, you won't be able to produce filenames that long; that's because that maximum must also include the *file extension* (the three-letter suffix that identifies the file type) and even the file's *folder path* (like C:\Users\Casey\My Pictures).

Note, too, that because they're reserved for behind-the-scenes use, Windows doesn't let you use any of these symbols in a Windows filename: \ / : * ? " < > |

You can give more than one file or folder the same name, as long as they're not in the same folder.

Note: Windows comes factory-set not to show you filename extensions. That's why you sometimes might *think* you see two different files called, say, "Quarterly Sales, " both in the same folder.

The explanation is that one filename may end with *.doc* (a Word document), and the other may end with *.xls* (an Excel document). But because these suffixes are hidden, the files look like they have exactly the same name. To un-hide filename extensions, turn on the "File name extensions" checkbox. It's on the View tab of the Ribbon.

Icon Properties

Properties are a big deal in Windows. Properties are preference settings that you can change independently for every icon on your machine.

To view the properties for an icon, choose from these techniques:

- Right-click the icon; choose Properties from the shortcut menu.
- Highlight the icon in an Explorer window; click the Properties button. (It's the wee tiny icon at the upper-left corner of the window, in the Quick Access toolbar. Looks like a tiny page with a checkmark.)
- Highlight the icon. On the Ribbon, on the Home tab, click Properties.

- While pressing Alt, double-click the icon.
- Highlight the icon; press Alt+Enter.

Tip: You can also see some basic info about any icon (type, size, and so on) by pointing to it without clicking. A little info balloon pops up, saving you the trouble of opening the Properties box or even the Details pane.

These settings aren't the same for every kind of icon, however. Here's what you can expect when opening the Properties dialog boxes of various icons (Figure 7-5):

Computer (System Properties)

There are about 500 different ways to open the Properties dialog box for your Computer icon. For example, you can click Computer in the navigation bar of any window and then click "System properties" on the Ribbon's Computer tab. Or right-click the Computer icon (in the nav bar again); from the shortcut menu, choose Properties.

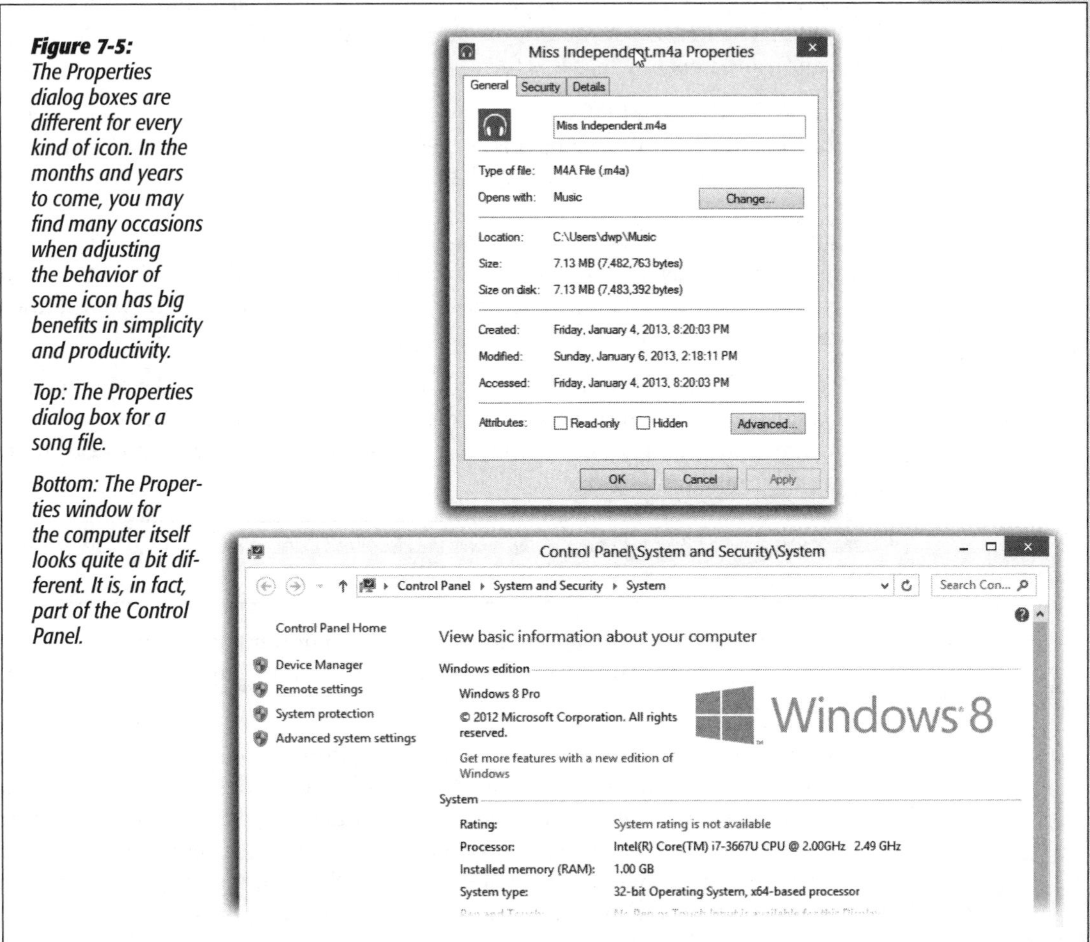

Figure 7-5: *The Properties dialog boxes are different for every kind of icon. In the months and years to come, you may find many occasions when adjusting the behavior of some icon has big benefits in simplicity and productivity.*

Top: The Properties dialog box for a song file.

Bottom: The Properties window for the computer itself looks quite a bit different. It is, in fact, part of the Control Panel.

The System Properties window is packed with useful information about your machine: what kind of processor is inside, how much memory (RAM) it has, whether or not it has a touchscreen, and what version of Windows you've got.

The panel at the left side of the window (shown in Figure 7-5) includes some useful links—"Device Manager," "Remote settings," "System protection," and "Advanced system settings"—all of which are described in the appropriate chapters of this book.

Note, however, that most of them work by opening the *old* System Properties Control Panel, also shown in Figure 7-5. Its tabs give a terse, but more complete, look at the tech specs and features of your PC. These, too, are described in the relevant parts of this book—all except "Computer Name." Here, you can type a plain-English name for your computer ("Casey's Laptop," for example). That's how it will appear to other people on the network, if you have one.

Disks

In a disk's Properties dialog box, you can see all kinds of information about the disk itself, like its name (which you can change right there in the box), its capacity (which you can't), and how much of it is full.

This dialog box's various tabs are also gateways to a host of maintenance and backup features, including Disk Cleanup, Error-checking, Defrag, Backup, and Quotas; all of these are described in Chapters 21 and 23.

Data files

The properties for a plain old document depend on what kind of document it is. You always see a General tab, but other tabs may also appear (especially for Microsoft Office files).

- **General.** This screen offers all the obvious information about the document—location, size, modification date, and so on. The *read-only* checkbox locks the document. In the read-only state, you can open the document and read it, but you can't make any changes to it.

Note: If you make a *folder* read-only, it affects only the files already inside. If you add additional files later, they remain editable.

Hidden turns the icon invisible. It's a great way to prevent something from being deleted, but because the icon becomes invisible, you may find it a bit difficult to open *yourself.*

The Advanced button offers a few additional options. "File is ready for archiving" means "Back me up." This message is intended for the old Backup and Restore program described in Chapter 22, and it indicates that this document has been changed since the last time it was backed up (or that it's never been backed up). "Allow this file to have contents indexed in addition to file properties" lets you indicate that this file should, or should not, be part of the Search index described earlier in this chapter.

"Compress contents to save disk space" is described later in this chapter. Finally, "Encrypt contents to secure data" is described on page 712.

- **Security** has to do with the technical NTFS permissions of a file or folder, technical on/off switches that govern who can do what to the contents. You see this tab only if the hard drive is formatted with NTFS.
- **Custom.** The Properties window of certain older Office documents includes this tab, where you can look up a document's word count, author, revision number, and many other statistics. But you should by no means feel limited to these 21 properties.

  Using the Custom tab, you can create properties of your own—Working Title, Panic Level, Privacy Quotient, or whatever you like. Just specify a property type using the Type pop-up menu (Text, Date, Number, Yes/No); type the property name into the Name text box (or choose one of the canned options in its pop-up menu); and then click Add.

  You can then fill in the Value text box for the individual file in question (so that its Panic Level is Red Alert, for example).

Note: This is an older form of tagging files—a lot like the tags feature described on page 213—*except* that you can't use Windows Search to find them. Especially technical people can, however, perform query-language searches for these values.

- The **Details** tab reveals the sorts of details—tags, categories, authors, and so on—that *are* searchable by Windows' search command. You can edit these little tidbits right in the dialog box.

  This box also tells you how many words, lines, and paragraphs are in a particular Word document. For a graphics document, the Summary tab indicates the graphic's dimensions, resolution, and color settings.
- The **Previous Versions** tab appears only if you've gone to the extraordinary trouble of resurrecting Windows 7's Previous Versions feature, which lets you revert a document or a folder to an earlier version. See page 696.

Folders

The Properties dialog box for a folder offers five (or six) tabs:

- **General, Security.** Here you find the same sorts of checkboxes and options as you do for data files, described above.
- **Sharing** makes the folder susceptible to invasion by other people—either in person, when they log into this PC, or from across your office network (see Chapter 29).
- **Location.** This tab appears only for folders you've included in a library (page 208). It identifies where the folder *really* sits.
- **Customize.** The first pop-up menu here lets you apply a *folder template* to any folder: General Items, Documents, Pictures, Music, or Videos. A template is noth-

ing more than a canned layout with a predesigned set of Ribbon tabs, icon sizes, column headings, and so on.

You may already have noticed that your Pictures library displays a nice big thumbnail icon for each of your photos, and that your Music library presents a tidy Details-view list of all your songs, with Ribbon buttons like "Play all," "Play To," and "Add to playlist." Here's your chance to apply those same expertly designed templates to folders of your own making.

This dialog box also lets you change the *icon* for a folder, as described in the next section.

Program files

There's not much here that you can change yourself, but you certainly get a lot to look at. For starters, there are the General and Details tabs described above.

But you may also find an important Compatibility tab, which may one day come to save your bacon. It lets you trick a pre–Windows 8 program into running on Microsoft's latest.

Changing Your Icons' Icons

You can change the actual, inch-tall illustrations that Windows uses to represent the little icons replete in your electronic world. You can't, however, use a single method to do so; Microsoft has divided up the controls between two different locations.

Standard Windows icons

First, you can change the icon for some of the important Windows desktop icons: the Recycle Bin, Documents, and so on. To do so, right-click a blank spot on the desktop. From the shortcut menu, choose Personalize.

In the resulting window, click "Change desktop icons" in the task pane at the left side. You'll see a collection of those important Windows icons. Click one, and then click Change Icon to choose a replacement from a collection Microsoft provides. (You haven't *lived* until you've made your Recycle Bin look like a giant blue thumbtack!)

Folder or shortcut icons

Ordinarily, when your Explorer window is in Tiles, Content, or a fairly big Icon view, each folder's icon resembles what's in it. You actually see a tiny photo, music album, or Word document peeking out of the open-folder icon.

This means, however, that the icon may actually *change* over time, as you put different things into it. If you'd rather freeze a folder's icon so it doesn't keep changing, you can choose an image that will appear to peek out from inside that folder.

Note: The following steps also let you change what a particular shortcut icon looks like. Unfortunately, Windows offers no way to change an actual document's icon.

Actually, you have two ways to change a folder's icon. Both begin the same way: Right-click the folder or shortcut whose icon you want to change. From the shortcut menu, choose Properties, and then click the Customize tab. Now you have a choice (Figure 7-6):

- **Change what image is peeking out of the file-folder icon.** Click Choose File. Windows now lets you hunt for icons on your hard drive. These can be picture files, icons downloaded from the Internet, icons embedded inside program files and .dll files, or icons you've made yourself using a freeware or shareware icon-making program. Find the graphic, click it, click Open, and then click OK.

  It may take a couple of minutes for Windows to update the folder image, but eventually, you see your hand-selected image "falling out" of the file-folder icon.

Figure 7-6:
Left: The original folder icon.

Middle: You've replaced the image that seems to be falling out of it.

Right: You've completely replaced the folder icon.

- **Completely replace the file-folder image.** Click Change Icon. Windows offers up a palette of canned graphics; click the one you want, and then click OK. Instantly, the original folder bears the new image.

Selecting Icons

Before you can delete, rename, move, copy, or otherwise tamper with any icon, you have to be able to *select* it somehow. By highlighting it, you're essentially telling Windows what you want to operate on.

Use the Mouse

To select one icon, just click it once. To select *multiple* icons at once—in preparation for moving, copying, renaming, or deleting them en masse, for example—use one of these techniques:

- **Select all.** Highlight all the icons in a window by using the "Select all" button on the Ribbon's Home tab. (Or press Ctrl+A, its keyboard equivalent.)

- **Highlight several consecutive icons.** Start with your cursor above and to one side of the icons, and then drag diagonally. As you drag, you create a temporary shaded blue rectangle. Any icon that falls within this rectangle darkens to indicate that it's been selected.

Alternatively, click the first icon you want to highlight, and then Shift-click the last file. All the files in between are automatically selected, along with the two icons you clicked. (These techniques work in any folder view: Details, Icon, Content, or whatever.)

Tip: If you include a particular icon in your diagonally dragged group by mistake, Ctrl-click it to remove it from the selected cluster.

- **Highlight nonconsecutive icons.** Suppose you want to highlight only the first, third, and seventh icons in the list. Start by clicking icon No. 1; then Ctrl-click each of the others. (If you Ctrl-click a selected icon *again*, you *de*select it. A good time to use this trick is when you highlight an icon by accident.)

Tip: The Ctrl key trick is especially handy if you want to select *almost* all the icons in a window. Press Ctrl+A to select everything in the folder, then Ctrl-click any unwanted subfolders to deselect them.

Use the Keyboard

You can also highlight one icon, plucking it out of a sea of pretenders, by typing the first few letters of its name. Type *nak,* for example, to select an icon called "Naked Chef Broadcast Schedule."

Checkbox Selection

It's great that you can select icons by holding down a key and clicking—if you can remember *which* key must be pressed.

Turns out novices were befuddled by the requirement to Ctrl-click icons when they wanted to choose more than one. So Microsoft created a checkbox mode. In this

FREQUENTLY ASKED QUESTION

Why "My" is Back

OK, I remember that Windows XP and earlier versions had "My" in front of all the folder names. You know: My Pictures, My Music, My Documents. I always thought it looked a little goofy, like, you know, it was My First Operating System.

Then the "My" disappeared in Windows Vista, which I thought was great.

But now "My" is back on those folder names in Windows 8! What gives?

In testing, Microsoft found that potential Windows users were getting confused. They couldn't tell the difference between the Documents *library* and each individual's Documents *folder*. (Review page 208 for the difference.)

Now, it's true that your My Documents folder is one of the folders that makes up the Documents library, but it's still really easy to get confused.

So Microsoft put "My" back on those folder names so you can tell them apart from the libraries that have similar names.

If the "My" on the names of your folders (in your Personal folder) bugs you, though, no biggie. You can rename those folders just as you would any other folder. Take off the "My," if you're so inclined. No harm done.

mode, any icon you point to temporarily sprouts a little checkbox that you can click to select it (Figure 7-7).

To turn this feature on, open any Explorer window, and then turn on "Item check boxes," which is on the View tab of the Ribbon (visible in Figure 7-7).

Figure 7-7: *Each time you point to an icon, a clickable checkbox appears. Once you turn it on, the checkbox remains visible, making it easy to select several icons at once. What's cool about the checkboxes feature is that it doesn't preclude your using the old click-to-select method; if you click an icon's name, you deselect all checkboxes except that one.*

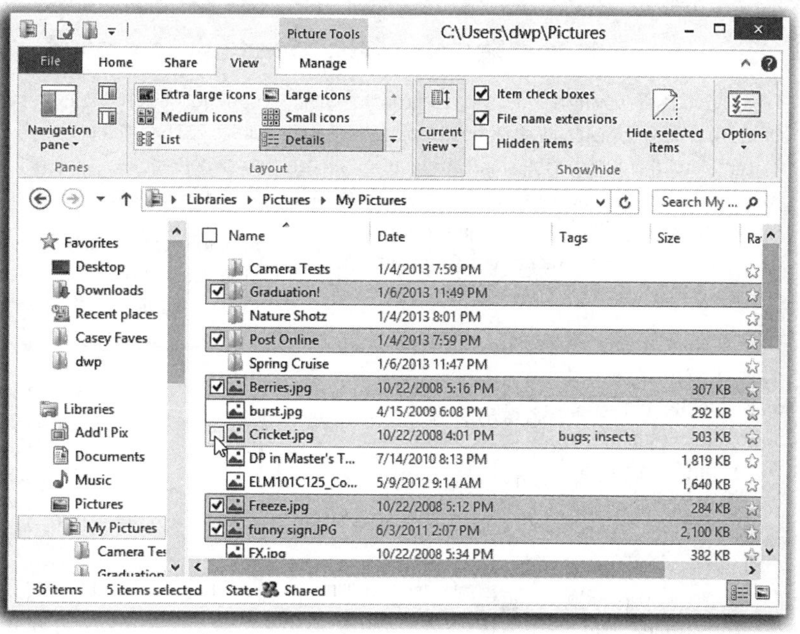

Now, anytime you point to an icon, an on/off checkbox appears. No secret keystrokes are necessary now for selecting icons; it's painfully obvious how you're supposed to choose only a few icons out of a gaggle.

Eliminating Double-Clicks

In some ways, a File Explorer window is just like Internet Explorer, the Web browser. It has a Back button, an address bar, and so on.

If you enjoy this PC-as-browser effect, you can actually take it one step further. You can set up your PC so that *one* click, not two, opens an icon. It's a strange effect that some people adore, that some find especially useful on touchscreens—and others turn off as fast as their little fingers will let them.

In any File Explorer window, on the View tab of the Ribbon, click Options.

The Folder Options control panel opens. Turn on "Single-click to open an item (point to select)." Then indicate *when* you want your icon's names turned into underlined links by selecting "Underline icon titles consistent with my browser" (that is, *all* icons' names appear as links) or "Underline icon titles only when I point at them." Click OK. The deed is done.

Now, if a single click opens an icon, you're entitled to wonder how you're supposed to *select* an icon (which you'd normally do with a single click). Take your pick:

POWER USERS' CLINIC

Secrets of the "Send to" Command

If you find yourself copying or moving certain icons to certain folders or disks with regularity, it's time to exploit the "Send to" command that lurks in the shortcut menu for almost every icon. Unlike the "Move to" and "Copy to" commands on the Ribbon, the "Send to" commands can send files to *services* (like your DVD burner or email program), not just folders.

This command offers a quick way to copy and move highlighted icons to popular destinations. For example, you can teleport a copy of a highlighted file directly to your CD burner by choosing "Send to"→DVD-RW Drive, or to the desktop background by choosing "Send to"→Desktop (create shortcut).

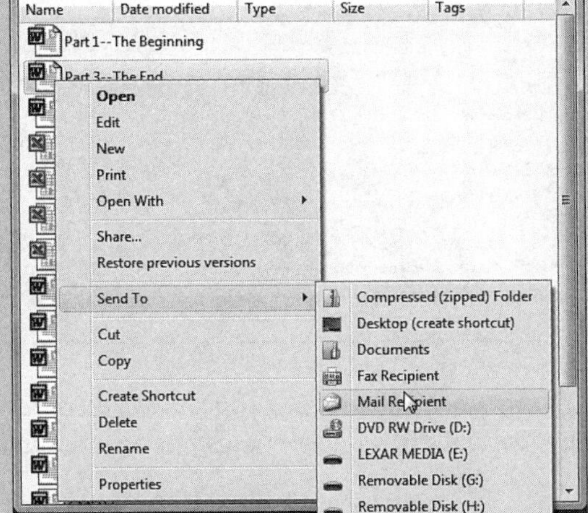

Then there's the "Send to"→Mail Recipient, which bundles the highlighted icon as an email attachment that's ready to send. You can also zip up a folder (see the end of this chapter) by choosing "Send to"→"Compressed (zipped) Folder."

If you start getting into "Send to"—and you should—check this out. If you press Shift while you right-click, you get a much longer list of "Send to" options, including all the essential folders (Downloads, Desktop, Favorites, Links, Searches, and so on). Cool.

But if the folder you want isn't there, it's easy enough to make the "Send to" command accommodate your *own* favorite or frequently used folders. Lurking in your Personal folder (page 263) is a folder called SendTo. Any shortcut icon you place here shows up instantly in the "Send to" menus within your desktop folders and shortcut menus.

Alas, this folder is among those Microsoft considers inappropriate for inspection by novices. As a result, the SendTo folder is *hidden*.

You can still get to it, though. In the address bar of any Explorer window, type *shell:sendto*, and then press Enter. (That's a quick way of getting to the C:\Users\[your name]\AppData\Roaming\Microsoft\Windows\SendTo folder.)

Most people create shortcuts here for folders and disks (such as your favorite backup disk). When you highlight an icon and then choose "Send to"→Backup Disk, for example, Windows copies the icon to that disk. (Or, if you simultaneously press Shift, you *move* the icon to the other disk or folder.) You can even add shortcuts of *applications* (program files) to the SendTo folder. By adding WinZip to this "Send to" menu, for example, you can drop-kick a highlighted icon onto the WinZip icon (for decompressing) just by choosing "Send to"→WinZip. Or add a Web server to this menu, so you can upload a file with a quick right-click. You can even create shortcuts for your printer or fax modem so you can print or fax a document just by highlighting its icon and choosing File→"Send to"→ [printer or fax modem's name].

- Point to it for about a half-second without clicking. (To make multiple selections, press the Ctrl key as you point to additional icons. And to *drag* an icon, just ignore all this pointing stuff—simply drag as usual.)
- Turn on the checkbox mode described above.

Copying and Moving Folders and Files

Windows offers two techniques for moving files and folders from one place to another: dragging them and using the Copy and Paste commands. In both cases, you'll be delighted to find out how much more communicative Windows is during the copy process (Figure 7-9).

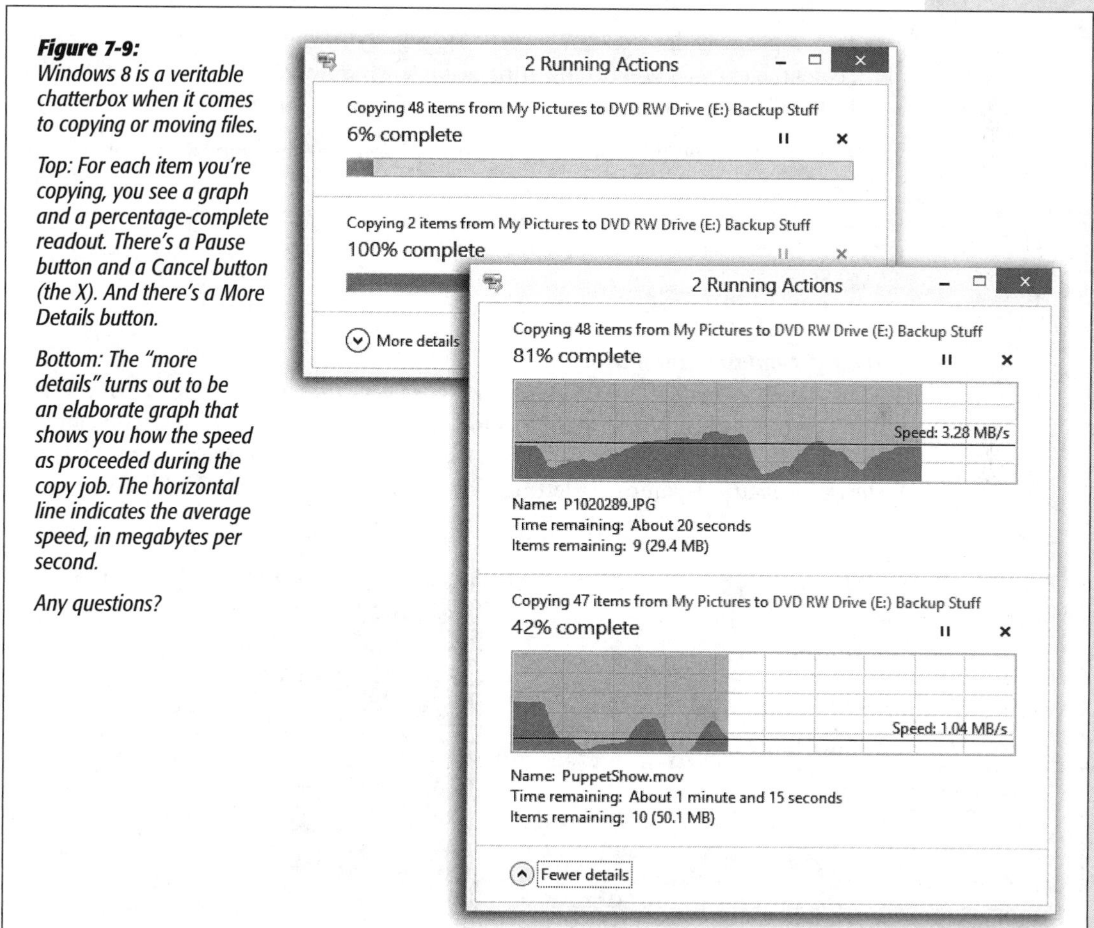

Figure 7-9: *Windows 8 is a veritable chatterbox when it comes to copying or moving files.*

Top: For each item you're copying, you see a graph and a percentage-complete readout. There's a Pause button and a Cancel button (the X). And there's a More Details button.

Bottom: The "more details" turns out to be an elaborate graph that shows you how the speed as proceeded during the copy job. The horizontal line indicates the average speed, in megabytes per second.

Any questions?

Whichever method you choose, you start by showing Windows which icons you want to copy or move—by highlighting them, as described on the previous pages. Then proceed as follows.

Copying by Dragging Icons

You can drag icons from one folder to another, from one drive to another, from a drive to a folder on another drive, and so on. (When you've selected several icons, drag any *one* of them, and the others will go along for the ride.)

Here's what happens when you drag icons in the usual way, using the left mouse button:

- Dragging to another folder on the same disk *moves* the folder or file.
- Dragging from one disk to another *copies* the folder or file.
- Holding down the Ctrl key while dragging to another folder on the same disk *copies* the icon. (If you do so within a single window, Windows creates a duplicate of the file called "[Filename] - Copy.")
- Pressing Shift while dragging from one disk to another *moves* the folder or file (without leaving a copy behind).

Tip: You can move or copy icons by dragging them either into an open window or directly onto a disk or folder *icon*.

The right-mouse-button trick

Think you'll remember all those possibilities every time you drag an icon? Probably not. Fortunately, you never have to. One of the most important tricks you can learn is to use the *right* mouse button as you drag. When you release the button, the menu shown in Figure 7-8 appears, letting you either copy or move the selected icons.

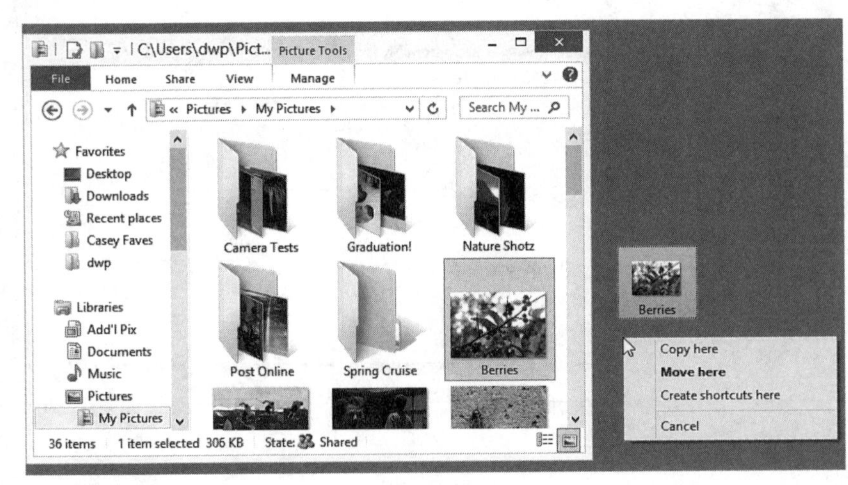

Figure 7-8: *Thanks to this shortcut menu, right-dragging icons is much easier and safer than left-dragging when you want to move or copy something. If you're dragging more than one item, a tiny numeric "badge" on the cursor reminds you how many things you're about to move or copy.*

Tip: Press the Esc key to cancel a dragging operation at any time.

Dragging icons into the Navigation pane

You may find it easier to copy or move icons using the Navigation pane, since the two-pane display format makes it easier to see where your files are and where they're going.

Just expand the triangles of the Navigation pane until you can see the destination folder.

Tip: If you accidentally click a folder in the Navigation pane, its contents will pop up in the right pane, covering up the icon you wanted to copy. Click the Back button to get back to where you once belonged.

Then find the icon you want to move in the right pane, and drag it to the appropriate folder in the left pane (Figure 7-9), or vice versa. Windows copies the icon.

Tip: This situation is also a good time to use the window Snap feature. Drag the icon's home window against the right side of your screen; drag the destination window against the left side. Now they're perfectly set up for drag-copying between them.

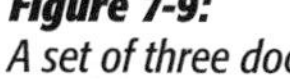

Figure 7-9: *A set of three documents is being dragged to the folder named A Deeply Nested Folder (in the My Documents folder). As the cursor passes each folder in the left pane, the folder's name darkens. Release the mouse when it's pointing to the correct folder or disk.*

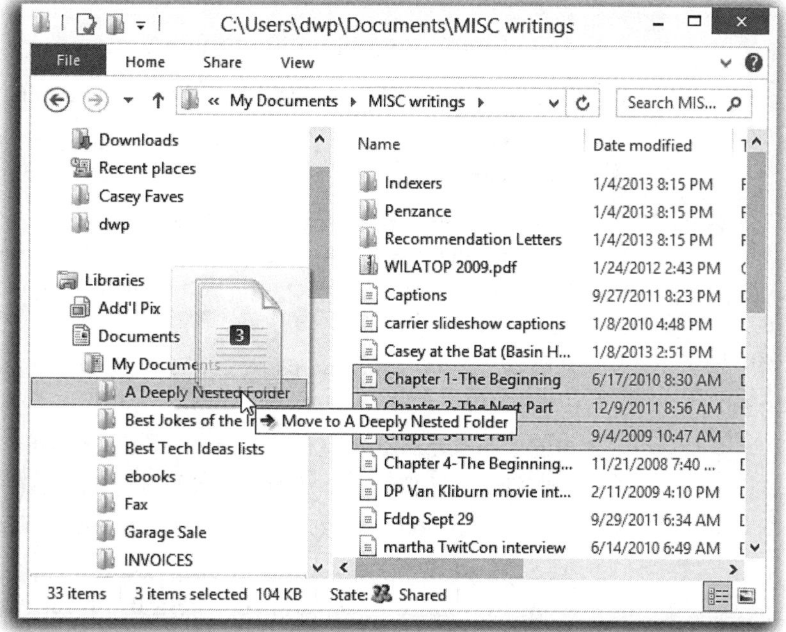

Copying or Moving Files with the Ribbon

Dragging icons to copy or move them feels good because it's so direct; you actually see your arrow cursor pushing the icons into the new location.

But you also pay a price for this satisfying illusion. That is, you may have to spend a moment or two fiddling with your windows, or clicking in the Explorer folder hierarchy, so you have a clear "line of drag" between the icon to be moved and the destination folder.

In Windows 8, moving or copying icons can be a one-step operation, thanks to the "Move to" and "Copy to" buttons on the Ribbon's Home tab. The pop-up menu for each one lists frequently and recently used folders. (If the destination folder isn't listed, choose "Choose location" and navigate to it yourself.)

In other words, you just highlight the icons you want to move; hit "Move to" or "Copy to" and then choose the destination folder. The deed is done, without ever having to leave the folder window where you began.

Copying with Copy and Paste

You can also use the pre–Windows 8 method to move icons from one window into another: the Cut, Copy, and Paste commands. The routine goes like this:

1. **Highlight the icon or icons you want to move.**

   Use any of the tricks described on page 271.

2. **Right-click one of the icons. From the shortcut menu, choose Cut or Copy.**

   You may want to learn the keyboard shortcuts for these commands: Ctrl+C for Copy, Ctrl+X for Cut. Or use the Cut and Copy buttons on the Ribbon's Home tab.

   The Cut command makes the highlighted icons appear dimmed; you've stashed them on the invisible Windows Clipboard. (They don't actually disappear from their original nesting place until you paste them somewhere else—or hit the Esc key to cancel the operation.)

   The Copy command also places copies of the files on the Clipboard, but it doesn't disturb the originals.

3. **Right-click the window, folder icon, or disk icon where you want to put the icons. Choose Paste from the shortcut menu.**

   Once again, you may prefer to use the appropriate Ribbon button, Paste.

   Either way, you've successfully transferred the icons. If you pasted into an open window, you see the icons appear there. If you pasted onto a closed folder or disk icon, you need to open the icon's window to see the results. And if you pasted right back into the same window, you get a duplicate of the file called "[Filename] - Copy."

The Recycle Bin

The Recycle Bin is your desktop trash basket. This is where files and folders go when they've outlived their usefulness. Basically, the Recycle Bin is a waiting room for data oblivion, in that your files stay there until you *empty* it—or until you rescue the files by dragging them out again.

While you can certainly drag files or folders onto the Recycle Bin icon, it's usually faster to highlight them and then perform one of the following options:

- Press the Delete key.
- Click the Delete button on the Ribbon's Home tab.
- Choose File→Delete.
- Right-click a highlighted icon and choose Delete from the shortcut menu.

Windows asks if you're sure you want to send the item to the Recycle Bin; in Windows 8, it provides a good chunk of information about the file in the warning window, for your safety. (You don't lose much by clicking Yes, since it's easy enough to change your mind, as noted below.) Now the Recycle Bin icon looks like it's brimming over with paper.

You can put unwanted files and folders into the Recycle Bin from any folder window or even from inside the Open File dialog box of many applications.

Note: All these methods put icons from your *hard drive* into the Recycle Bin. But deleting an icon from a removable drive (flash drives, for example), from other computers on the network, or from a .zip file, does *not* involve the Recycle Bin. Those files go straight to heaven, giving you no opportunity to retrieve them. (Deleting anything with the Command Prompt commands *del* or *erase* bypasses the Recycle Bin, too.)

Making the Recycle Bin Less Naggy

When you get right down to it, you really have to *work* to get rid of a file in Windows. First you have to put the thing in the Recycle Bin. Then you have to confirm that, yes, you're sure. Then you have to *empty* the Recycle Bin. Then you have to confirm that, yes, you're sure about *that.*

Fortunately, those are just the factory settings. There are all kinds of ways to eliminate some of these quadruplicate confirmations. For example:

- **Squelch the "Are you sure?" message.** On the Ribbon's Home tab, click the ▾ beneath the Delete button. From the shortcut menu, turn off "Show recycle confirmation." Or, in the Recycle Bin's Properties dialog box (Figure 7-10), turn off "Display delete confirmation dialog." Now you'll never get that message when you put something into the Recycle Bin.
- **Bypass the Recycle Bin just this time.** Again, use the ▾ beneath the Delete button on the Ribbon's Home tab. From the shortcut menu choose "Permanently delete"; you've just deleted the file permanently, skipping its layover in the Recycle Bin.

Note: Pressing Shift while you delete a file (and then clicking Yes in the confirmation box, or hitting Enter), also deletes the file instantly. The Shift-key trick works for every method of deleting a file: pressing the Delete key, choosing Delete from the shortcut menu, and so on.

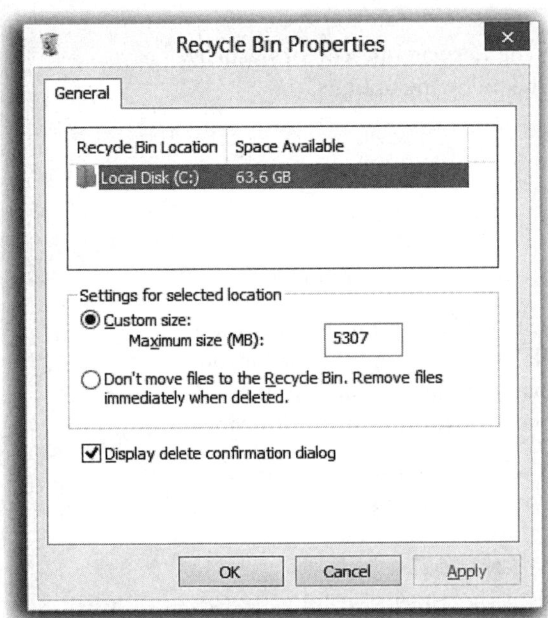

Figure 7-10:
Use the Recycle Bin Properties dialog box to govern the way the Recycle Bin works, or even if it works at all. If you have multiple hard drives, the dialog box offers a tab for each of them so you can configure a separate and independent Recycle Bin on each drive.

- **Bypass the Recycle Bin for good.** If you, a person of steely nerve and perfect judgment, never delete a file in error, then your files can *always* bypass the Recycle Bin. No confirmations, no second chances. You'll reclaim disk space instantly when you press the Delete key to vaporize a highlighted file or folder.

  To set this up, right-click the Recycle Bin. From the shortcut menu, choose Properties. Select "Don't move files to the Recycle Bin. Remove files immediately when deleted" (Figure 7-10).

  And voilà! Your safety net is gone (especially if you *also* turn off the "Display delete confirmation dialog" checkbox—then you're *really* living dangerously.)

Note: That really is living dangerously. The Shift-key trick might be a better safety/convenience compromise.

Restoring Deleted Files and Folders

If you change your mind about sending something to the software graveyard, simply open the Recycle Bin by double-clicking. A window like the one in Figure 7-11 opens.

To restore a selected file or folder—or a bunch of them—click the "Restore this item" link on the task toolbar. Or right-click any one of the selected icons and choose Restore from the shortcut menu.

Figure 7-11: *When you double-click the Recycle Bin (top), its window (bottom) displays information about each folder and file it holds. It's a regular Explorer window, so you can inspect a selected item in the Details view, if you like.*

Restored means returned to the folder from whence it came—wherever it was on your hard drive when deleted. If you restore an icon whose original folder has been deleted in the meantime, Windows even recreates that folder to hold the restored file(s). (If nothing is selected, the toolbar button says "Restore all items," but be careful: If there are weeks' worth of icons in there, and Windows puts them all back where they came from, recreating original folders as it goes, you might wind up with a real mess.)

Tip: You don't have to put icons back into their original folders. By *dragging* them out of the Recycle Bin window, you can put them back into any folder you like.

Emptying the Recycle Bin

While there's an advantage to the Recycle Bin (you get to undo your mistakes), there's also a downside: The files in the Recycle Bin occupy as much disk space as they did when they were stored in folders. Deleting files doesn't gain you additional disk space until you *empty* the Recycle Bin.

That's why most people, sooner or later, follow up an icon's journey to the Recycle Bin with one of these cleanup operations:

- Right-click the Recycle Bin icon, or a blank spot in the Recycle Bin window, and choose Empty Recycle Bin from the shortcut menu.
- In the Recycle Bin window, click Empty Recycle Bin on the Ribbon's Recycle Bin Tools/Manage tab.
- In the Recycle Bin window, highlight only the icons you want to eliminate, and then press the Delete key. (Use this method when you want to nuke only *some* of the Recycle Bin's contents.)
- Wait. When the Recycle Bin accumulates so much stuff that it occupies a significant percentage of your hard drive space, Windows empties it automatically, as described in the next section.

The first three of these procedures produce an "Are you sure?" message.

Auto-emptying the Recycle Bin

The Recycle Bin has two advantages over the physical trash can behind your house: First, it never smells. Second, when it's full, it can empty itself automatically.

To configure this self-emptying feature, you specify a certain fullness limit. When the Recycle Bin contents reach that level, Windows begins deleting files (permanently) as new files arrive in the Recycle Bin. Files that arrived in the Recycle Bin first are deleted first.

Unless you tell it otherwise, Windows reserves 10 percent of your drive to hold Recycle Bin contents.

To change that percentage, open the Recycle Bin; on the Ribbon, click "Recycle bin properties." Now you can edit the "Maximum size" number, in megabytes (Figure 7-10). Keeping the percentage low means you're less likely to run out of the disk space you need to install software and create documents. On the other hand, raising the percentage means you have more opportunity to restore files you decide to retrieve.

Note: Every disk has its own Recycle Bin, which holds files and folders you've deleted from that disk. As you can see in the Recycle Bin Properties dialog box, you can give each drive its own trash limit and change the deletion options shown in Figure 7-10 for each drive independently. Just click the drive's name before changing the settings.

Shortcut Icons

A *shortcut* is a link to a file, folder, disk, or program (see Figure 7-12). You might think of it as a duplicate of the thing's icon—but not a duplicate of the thing itself. (A shortcut occupies almost no disk space.) When you double-click the shortcut icon, the original folder, disk, program, or document opens. You can also set up a keystroke for a shortcut icon so you can open any program or document just by pressing a certain key combination.

Shortcuts provide quick access to the items you use most often. And because you can make as many shortcuts of a file as you want, and put them anywhere on your PC, you can, in effect, keep an important program or document in more than one folder. Just create a shortcut to leave on the desktop in plain sight, or drag its icon onto the Links toolbar. In fact, every link in the top part of your Navigation pane is a shortcut.

Tip: Don't confuse the term *shortcut*, which refers to one of these duplicate-icon pointers, with *shortcut menu*, the context-sensitive menu that appears when you right-click almost anything in Windows. The shortcut *menu* has nothing to do with the shortcut icons feature; maybe that's why it's sometimes called the *context* menu.

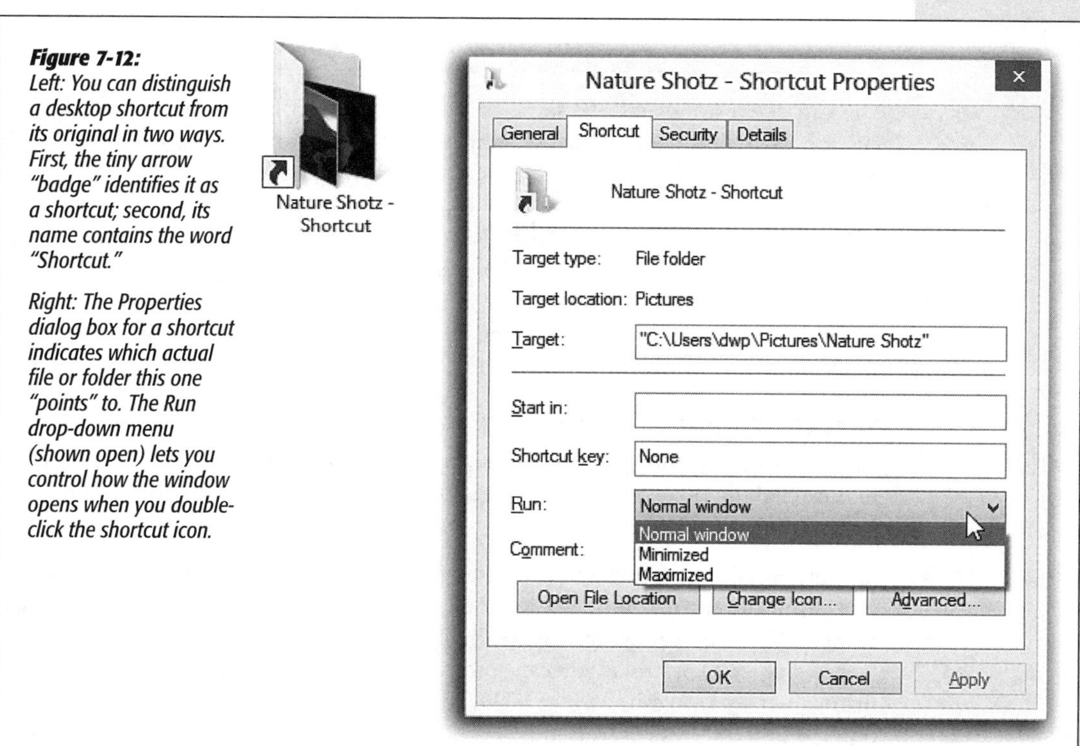

Figure 7-12: *Left: You can distinguish a desktop shortcut from its original in two ways. First, the tiny arrow "badge" identifies it as a shortcut; second, its name contains the word "Shortcut."*

Right: The Properties dialog box for a shortcut indicates which actual file or folder this one "points" to. The Run drop-down menu (shown open) lets you control how the window opens when you double-click the shortcut icon.

Among other things, shortcuts are great for getting to Web sites and folders elsewhere on your network, because you're spared having to type out their addresses or burrowing through network windows.

Creating and Deleting Shortcuts

To create a shortcut, use any of these tricks:

- Right-click an icon. From the shortcut menu, choose "Create shortcut."

- Right-drag an icon from its current location to the desktop. When you release the mouse button, choose "Create shortcuts here" from the menu that appears.

Tip: If you're not in the mood to use a shortcut menu, just left-drag an icon while pressing Alt. A shortcut appears instantly. (And if your Alt key is missing or broken—hey, it could happen—drag while pressing Ctrl+Shift instead.)

- Copy an icon, as described earlier in this chapter. Open the destination window; then, on the Ribbon's Home tab, click "Paste shortcut."
- Drag the tiny icon at the left end of the address bar onto the desktop or into a window.

Tip: This also works with Web sites. If your browser has pulled up a site you want to keep handy, drag that little address-bar icon onto your desktop. Double-clicking it later will open the same Web page.

You can delete a shortcut the same as any icon, as described in the Recycle Bin discussion earlier in this chapter. (Of course, deleting a shortcut *doesn't* delete the file it points to.)

Unveiling a Shortcut's True Identity

To locate the original icon from which a shortcut was made, right-click the shortcut icon and choose Properties from the shortcut menu. As shown in Figure 7-12, the resulting box shows you where to find the "real" icon. It also offers you a quick way to jump to it, in the form of the Open File Location button.

Shortcut Keyboard Triggers

Sure, shortcuts let you put favored icons everywhere you want to be. But they still require clicking to open, which means taking your hands off the keyboard—and that, in the grand scheme of things, means slowing down.

Lurking within the Shortcut Properties dialog box is another feature with intriguing ramifications: the Shortcut Key box. By clicking here and then pressing a key combination, you can assign a personalized keystroke for the shortcut. Thereafter, by pressing that keystroke, you can summon the corresponding file, program, folder, printer, networked computer, or disk window to your screen, no matter what you're doing on the PC. It's *really* useful.

Three rules apply when choosing keystrokes to open your favorite icons:

- The keystrokes work only on shortcuts stored *on your desktop.* If you stash the icon in any other folder, the keystroke stops working.
- Your keystroke can't incorporate the space bar or the Enter, Backspace, Delete, Esc, Print Screen, or Tab keys.
- Your combination *must* include Ctrl+Alt, Ctrl+Shift, or Alt+Shift, and another key.

Windows enforces this rule rigidly. For example, if you type a single letter key into the box (such as *E*), Windows automatically adds the Ctrl and Alt keys to your combination (Ctrl+Alt+E). This is the operating system's attempt to prevent you from inadvertently duplicating one of the built-in Windows keyboard shortcuts and thoroughly confusing both you and your computer.

Tip: If you've ever wondered what it's like to be a programmer, try this. In the Shortcut Properties dialog box (Figure 7-12), use the Run drop-down menu at the bottom of the dialog box to choose "Normal window," "Minimized," or "Maximized." By clicking OK, you've just told Windows what kind of window you want to appear when opening this particular shortcut.

Controlling Windows in this way isn't exactly the same as programming Microsoft Excel, but you are, in your own small way, telling Windows what to do.

If you like the idea of keyboard shortcuts for your files and programs, but you're not so hot on Windows' restrictions, consider installing a free *macro program* that lets you make *any* keystroke open *anything anywhere.* The best-known one is AutoHotKey, which is available from this book's "Missing CD" page at *www.missingmanuals.com,* but there are plenty of similar (and simpler) ones. (Check them out at, for example, *www.shareware.com.)*

Compressing Files and Folders

Windows is especially effective at compressing files and folders to reduce the space they occupy on your hard drive—which is ironic, considering the fact that hard drives these days have enough capacity to stretch to Steve Ballmer's house and back three times.

Even so, compressing files and folders can occasionally be useful, especially when hard drive space is running short, or when you want to email files to someone without dooming them to an all-night waiting session. Maybe that's why Microsoft has endowed Windows with two different schemes for compressing files and folders: *NTFS compression* and *zipped folders.*

NTFS Compression

Windows 8, since you asked, requires a hard drive that's formatted using a software scheme called *NTFS*. It's a much more modern formatting scheme than its predecessor, something called FAT32—and among its virtues is, you guessed it, NTFS *compression*.

This compression scheme is especially likable because it's completely invisible. Windows automatically compresses and decompresses your files, almost instantaneously. At some point, you may even forget you've turned it on. Consider:

- Whenever you open a compressed file, Windows quickly and invisibly expands it to its original form so you can edit it. When you close the file again, Windows instantly recompresses it.

- If you send compressed files (via disk or email, for example) to a PC whose hard drive doesn't use NTFS formatting, Windows once again decompresses them, quickly and invisibly.
- Any file you copy into a compressed folder or disk is compressed automatically. (If you only *move* it into such a folder from elsewhere on the disk, however, it stays compressed or uncompressed—whichever it was originally.)

There's only one downside to all this: You don't save a *lot* of disk space using NTFS compression (at least not when compared with Zip compression, described in the next section). Even so, if your hard drive is anywhere near full, it might be worth turning on NTFS compression. The space you save could be your own.

Compressing files, folders, or disks

To turn on NTFS compression, right-click the icon for the file, folder, or disk whose contents you want to shrink; from the shortcut menu, choose Properties. Proceed as shown in Figure 7-13.

Tip: To compress an entire hard drive, the steps in Figure 7-13 are even simpler. Just right-click the drive's icon (in your Computer window); choose Properties; and turn on "Compress this drive to save disk space." Click OK.

Figure 7-13: *In the Properties dialog box for any file or folder, click Advanced. Turn on "Compress contents to save disk space," and then click OK. For a folder, Windows offers to compress all the files and folders inside this one, too.*

Many Windows veterans wind up turning on compression for the entire hard drive, even though it takes Windows several hours to do the job. (If you plan to go see a movie while Windows is working, though, wait until the appearance of the first message box letting you know about some "open file" that can't be compressed; then click Ignore All. A few files will remain uncompressed when you get back from the

Cineplex, but at least you won't have had to stay home, manually clicking to dismiss every "open file" complaint box.)

When Windows is finished compressing files, their names appear in a different color, a reminder that Windows is doing its part to maximize your disk space.

Note: If the files don't change color, somebody—maybe you—must have turned off the "Show encrypted or compressed NTFS files in color" option (see page 226).

Zipped Folders

NTFS compression is ideal for freeing up disk space while you're working at your PC. But as soon as you email your files to somebody else or burn them to a CD, the transferred copies bloat right back up to their original sizes.

Fortunately, there's another way to compress files: Zip them. If you've ever used Windows before, you've probably encountered Zip files. Each one is a tiny little suitcase, an *archive*, whose contents have been tightly compressed to keep files together, to save space, and to transfer them online faster (see Figure 7-14). Use this method when you want to email something to someone, or when you want to pack up a completed project and remove it from your hard drive to free up space.

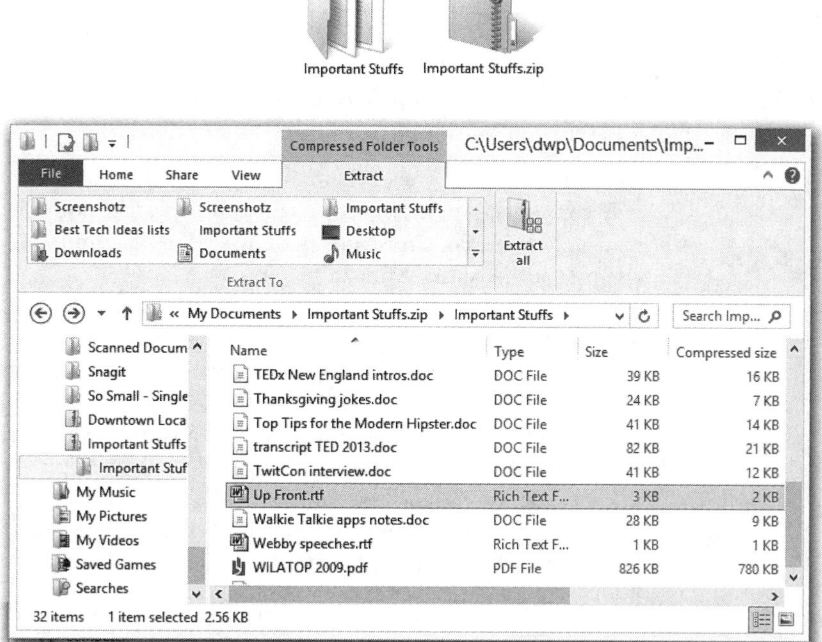

Figure 7-14: *Top: A Zip archive looks just like an ordinary folder—except for the tiny little zipper.*

Bottom: Double-click one to open its window and see what's inside. The Size, Compressed Size, and Ratio columns tell you how much space you've saved. (JPEG and GIF graphics usually don't become much smaller than they were before zipping, since they're already compressed formats. But word processing files, program files, and other file types reveal quite a bit of shrinkage.)

Creating zipped folders

You can create a Zip archive in either of two ways:

- Right-click any blank spot on the desktop or an open window. From the shortcut menu, choose New→"Compressed (zipped) Folder." (Or, from the Ribbon's Home tab, choose "New item"→"Compressed (zipped) Folder.") Type a name for your newly created, empty archive, and then press Enter.

  Now, each time you drag a file or folder onto the archive's icon (or into its open window), Windows automatically stuffs a *copy* of it inside.

  Of course, you haven't exactly saved any disk space, since now you have two copies (one zipped, one untouched). If you'd rather *move* a file or folder into the archive—in the process deleting the full-size version and saving disk space—then *right*-drag the file or folder icon onto the archive icon. Now from the shortcut menu, choose Move Here.

- To turn an *existing* file or folder into a Zip archive, right-click its icon. (To zip up a handful of icons, select them first, and then right-click any one of them.) Now, from the shortcut menu, choose "Send to"→"Compressed (zipped) Folder." You've just created a new archive folder *and* copied the files or folders into it.

Tip: At this point, you can right-click the zipped folder's icon and choose "Send to"→Mail Recipient. Windows automatically whips open your email program, creates an outgoing message ready for you to address, and attaches the zipped file to it. It's now set for transport.

Working with zipped folders

In many respects, a zipped folder behaves just like any ordinary folder. Double-click it to see what's inside.

If you double-click one of the *files* you find inside, however, Windows opens a *read-only* copy of it—that is, a copy you can view, but not edit. To make changes to a read-only copy, you must use the File→Save As command and save it somewhere else on your hard drive first.

Note: Be sure to navigate to the desktop or Documents folder, for example, before you save your edited document. Otherwise, Windows will save it into an invisible temporary folder, where you may never see it again.

To decompress only some of the icons in a zipped folder, just drag them out of the archive window; they instantly spring back to their original sizes. Or, to decompress the entire archive, right-click its icon and choose Extract All from the shortcut menu (or, if its window is already open, click "Extract all files" on the Ribbon's Compressed Folder Tools/Extract tab). A dialog box asks you to specify where you want the resulting files to wind up.

Tip: Windows no longer lets you password-protect a zipped folder, as you could in Windows XP. But the Web is teeming with zip-file utilities, many of them free, that do let you assign a password. You might try, for example, SecureZIP Express. It's available from this book's "Missing CD" page at *www.missingmanuals.com*.

Burning CDs and DVDs from the Desktop

Burning a CD or DVD is great for backing stuff up, transferring stuff to another computer, mailing to somebody, or archiving older files to free up hard drive space. These days, you can buy blank CDs and DVDs very inexpensively in bulk via the Web or a discount store.

If your computer has a drive at all, it can burn *both* CDs and DVDs. Many Windows 8 machines, however, are designed to be small and light—tablets and ultralight laptops, for example—and don't have disc drives at all. In that case, you can always buy an external USB burner; they're dirt cheap.

Before you dig in, however, here's a brief chalk talk about CD data formats.

A Tale of Two Formats

Turns out Windows can burn blank CDs and DVDs using your choice of *two* formats:

- **Mastered (ISO).** This is what most of the world is used to. It's what everybody burned before Windows Vista came along. The primary virtue of discs burned this way is compatibility; they play in just about any computer, including Macs, PCs, and CD or DVD players that play MP3 CDs and digital video.

  To make one, insert the blank disc and then drag files and folders into its window. The PC duplicates the items, parking them in an invisible, temporary holding area until you're ready to burn. You burn all the files and folders at once.

  Trouble is, you're therefore *doubling* the space requirement of the files you intended to burn. If you're burning a DVD to get older files off your hard drive because you're running low on space, you could wind up in a Catch-22: You can't free up drive space without burning a DVD—but you don't have enough drive space to burn a DVD!

Tip: To be fair, you *can* change the location of the temporary holding folder–if you have another hard drive. In your Computer window, right-click your burner's icon; from the shortcut menu, choose Properties. Click the Recording tab; from the drive menu, choose the hard drive you prefer, authenticating when you're asked.

- **Live File System (UDF).** This newer, more modern format—Windows 8's factory setting—is light-years more convenient. It lets you use a blank CD or DVD exactly as though it's a USB flash drive. You can drag files and folders onto it, move icons around on it, rename them, and so on. There's no momentous Moment of Burn; files are copied to the CD in real time, whenever you put them there. You can leave a disc in your drive, dragging stuff onto it throughout the week as it's convenient—without ever having to click a Burn button.

  What's more, you can the eject the CD, store it, or share it—and then, later, put it back into your PC and *burn more stuff onto it.* That's right—you can burn a single CD as many times as you like. And we're talking regular, cheapie CD-R discs, not CD-RW (rewritable).

What Windows creates, in other words, is a *multisession* disc.

Of course, the downside is that discs you burn this way play back only on relatively recent Macs and PCs. And you can record *more* stuff onto them only on a PC running Windows XP or later.

UP TO SPEED

All About AutoPlay

When you insert a CD, what should Windows do with it?

Start playing the music files on it? Open up a slideshow of the pictures on it? Just open an Explorer window to show you the files on it?

What about a DVD? What about the memory card from your camera? What kind of automatic action should Windows take when you insert one of those?

It's all up to you, thanks to the AutoPlay feature. For each kind of disc or card, AutoPlay lets you specify what you want Windows to do. It saves your having to indicate your preference each time you plug in a certain kind of storage. (AutoPlay doesn't handle flash drives and hard drives, however–basically, it's for discs, memory cards, cameras, camcorders, and phones.)

As you can see in the inset figure, Windows generally asks you to make such a choice each time you connect a storage gadget. But the master control center for AutoPlay is in the Control Panel. To get there, press the W key (to open the Start screen). Type *autoplay* and then click Settings, so that AutoPlay appears in the search results. Open it.

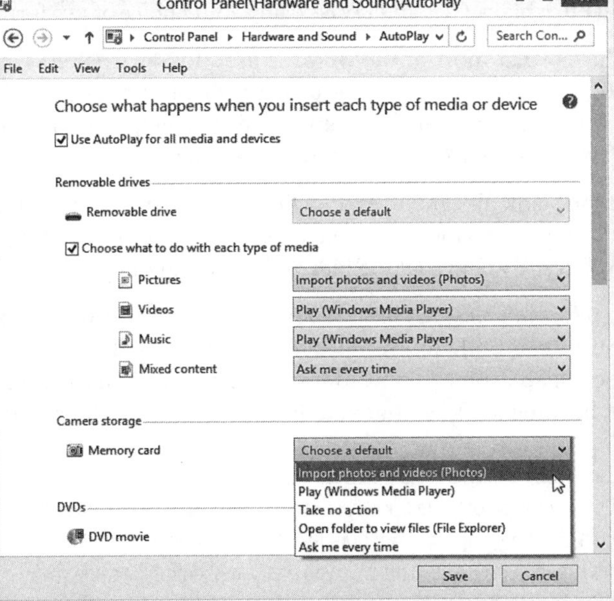

Here you can see that each kind of disk (CD, DVD, removable drive like a flash drive or a memory card) has a pop-up menu of logical "what to do when I'm inserted" choices. For a music CD, for example, your options are Play (Windows Media Player will open and start playing the songs), "Take no action" (nothing happens at all), "Open folder to view files" (a File Explorer window will open so you can inspect the MP3 files), or "Ask me every time" (these choices will appear each time you insert a music CD).

If your tablet offers Microsoft's Tap and Do feature, you'll find an option for handling incoming Tap and Send files here, too.

This Control Panel also lets you turn off AutoPlay completely; turn off "Use AutoPlay for all media and devices." Now when you insert a disk or card, nothing happens. Or turn it off just for one kind of media, using the corresponding checkboxes. Click Save.

Tip: Even if you've turned off AutoPlay, you can still force it to kick in just this once: Hold down the Shift key as you insert or connect the disc, card, or gadget.

Tip: If it helps you to remember which format is which, here's a mnemonic for you: The last letter of the format name (ISO, UDF) lets you know whether this is the *Older* format or the *Future* one.

Burning, Step by Step

Now that, with luck, you understand the difference between the Mastered (ISO) and Live File System (UDF) formats, you're ready to proceed.

1. **Insert a blank disc into your PC.**

   Windows starts asking how you want to handle blank discs (see Figure 7-15, top left).

2. **In the Navigation pane of an Explorer window, click the name of your DVD burner.**

   The Burn a Disc dialog box appears (Figure 7-15, top right).

3. **Type a name for the disc.**

   But don't click Next yet. This crucial moment is your only chance to change the disc's format.

   If you're OK with burning in the delicious, newfangled UDF format described above, leave "Like a USB flash drive" selected; skip to step 4.

POWER USERS' CLINIC

Closing the Session

Every time you eject a Live File System disc, Windows *closes the session,* which means sort of shrink-wrapping the disc so it can be used on other computers. (Even computers that can't understand Live File System, like Macs or pre-XP PCs, can play these discs. They just can't record more stuff onto them.)

But each time Windows does that, you lose another 20 megabytes of disc space and 2 minutes of your time.

If you, the power user, would like session closing to be a decision left up to you, you can make Windows *stop* automatically closing sessions. Right-click the burner's icon in your Computer window; from the shortcut menu, choose Properties. In the dialog box, click the Recording tab and then the Global Settings button.

Here, you can turn off "Single session-only discs are ejected," which makes Windows stop auto-closing discs that can be burned only once (DVD-R, DVD+R, DVD-RAM, DVD+R DL, DVD-R DL, and BD-RE).

Or turn off "Multi session-capable discs are ejected," which refers to discs that you can record onto many times (CD-RW, DVD+RW, DVD-RW, and BD-R discs).

From now on, Windows won't close your session—or use up 20 megabytes—unless *you* right-click your burner's icon in the Computer window or nav bar and choose "Close session." This way, you can maximize the space and speed of CDs and DVDs that you keep on your desk and *don't* distribute to other people.

Tip: If you try the CD or DVD in somebody else's machine and it doesn't work—and you realize that you forgot to close the session—all is not lost. You can always return the disc to your machine and close the session there.

And now, help yourself to some aspirin.

If you want this disc to be usable by a CD or DVD player, or somebody using a version of Windows before Windows XP, though, you want to take this moment to click "With a CD/DVD player."

Once that's done, you can go on to step 4.

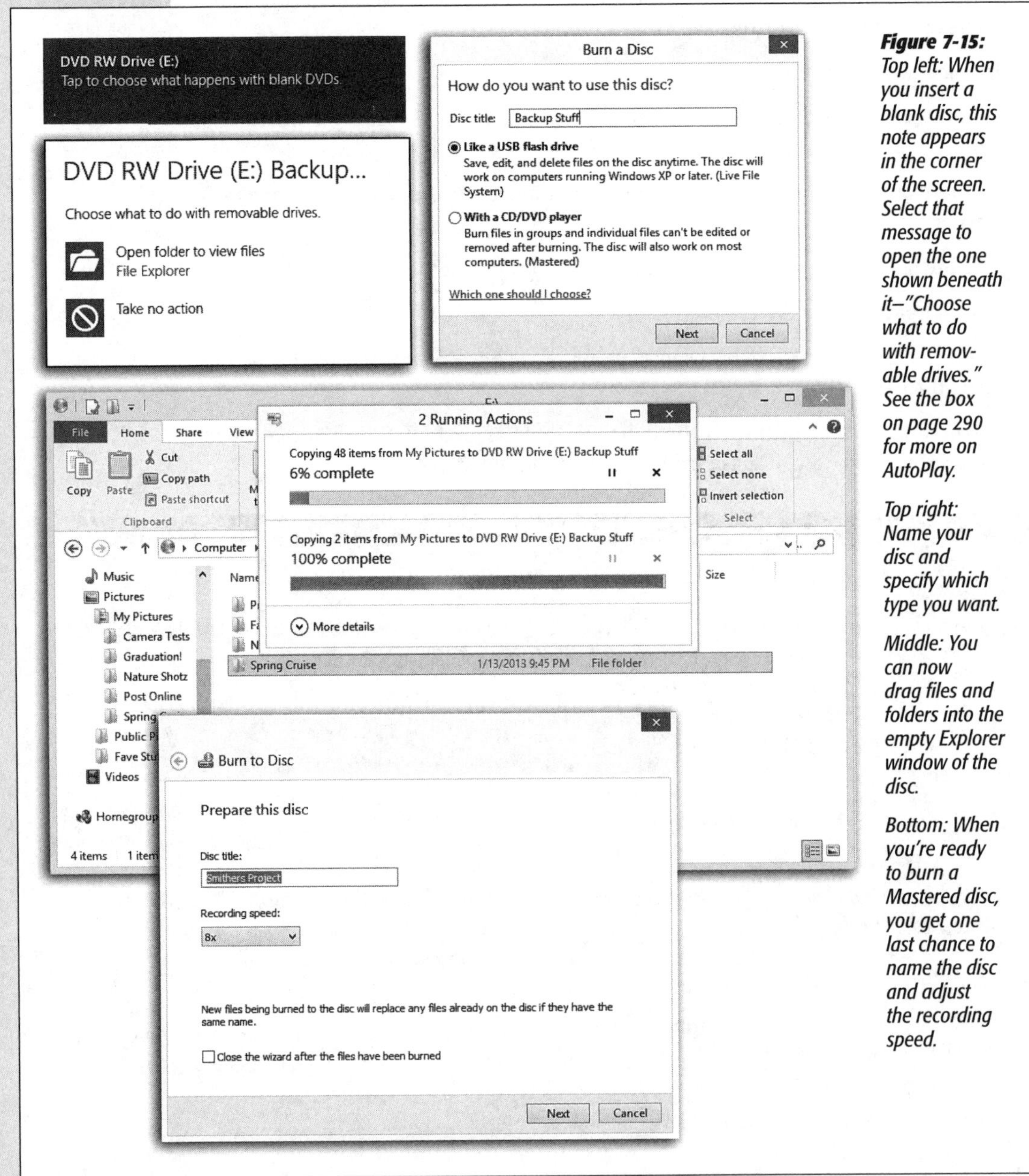

Figure 7-15: *Top left: When you insert a blank disc, this note appears in the corner of the screen. Select that message to open the one shown beneath it—"Choose what to do with removable drives." See the box on page 290 for more on AutoPlay.*

Top right: Name your disc and specify which type you want.

Middle: You can now drag files and folders into the empty Explorer window of the disc.

Bottom: When you're ready to burn a Mastered disc, you get one last chance to name the disc and adjust the recording speed.

4. **Click Next.**

   Your PC takes a moment—a long one—to format the blank disc.

   When it's finished, you're left facing the disc's empty Explorer window. The words "Drag files to this folder to add them to the disc" hint at what you're supposed to do next.

5. **Begin putting files and folders into the disc's window.**

   You can use any combination of these three methods:

   First, you can scurry about your hard drive, locating the files and folders you want on the CD. Drag their icons into the open CD/DVD window, or onto the disc burner's icon in the Computer window (Figure 7-15, middle).

   Second, you can highlight the files and folders you want burned onto the CD. From the Home tab on the Ribbon, click Copy. Click in the CD or DVD's window, and then click Paste (in the Ribbon) to copy the material there.

   Finally, you can explore your hard drive. Whenever you find a file or folder you'd like backed up, right-click it. From the shortcut menu, choose "Send to"→DVD/CD-RW Drive (or whatever your burner's name is).

   To finish the job, see "The final steps," below, for the kind of disc you're burning.

Tip: The Details pane at the bottom of the CD/DVD window gives you a running tally of the disc space you've filled up so far. (It may say, for example, "223.2 MB of 702.8 used on disc.") At last you have an effortless way to exploit a blank disc's capacity with precision.

The final steps: Mastered (ISO) format

When you put files and folders into the disc's window, Windows actually *copies* them into a temporary, invisible holding-tank folder. (If you must know, this folder is in your Personal folder→Local Settings→AppData→Local→Microsoft→Windows→Burn→Temporary Burn Folder.)

In other words, you need plenty of disk space before you begin burning a CD—at least double the size of the CD files themselves.

Tip: Remember that a standard CD can hold only about 650 MB of files. To ensure that your files and folders will fit, periodically highlight all the icons in the Computer→CD window (choose Organize→Select All). Then inspect the Details pane to confirm that the size is within the legal limit.

What you see in the disc's window, meanwhile, is nothing but shortcuts (denoted by the downward arrows on their icons). The little down arrows mean, "This icon hasn't been burned to the disc yet. I'm just waiting my turn."

At last, when everything looks ready to go, click "Finish burning." (This button appears on the Drive Tools/Manage tab of the Ribbon.) Or right-click the burner's icon, or any blank spot in its window, and, from the shortcut menu, choose "Burn to disc."

The Burn to Disc dialog box appears (Figure 7-15, bottom). The PC's laser proceeds to record the CD or DVD, which can take some time. Feel free to switch into another program and continue working.

When the burning is over, the disc pops out and you have a freshly minted CD or DVD, whose files and folders you can open on any PC or even Macintosh.

At this point, Windows asks: "Do you want to burn another disc using these same files?" This is your chance to insert another blank disc and make a copy of what you just did—without having to wait for all that copying business a second time. Click the Yes checkbox if so; click Finish if not.

The final steps: Live File System (UDF) format

If you've been dragging files and folders into the window of a Live File System-formatted disc, there are no more steps. You can eject the disc and put it to use.

To eject the disc, click Eject on the Drive Tools/Manage tab of the Ribbon. (You can also right-click your burner's icon; from the shortcut menu, choose Eject.) Windows takes a moment to "close the session" and then ejects the disc.

You can play this disc on Macs or PCs running Windows XP and later.

Better yet, you can put this disc back into any XP-or-later PC and pick up right where you left off, adding and erasing files as though it's a big flash drive.

Final Notes

Here are a few final notes on burning CDs and DVDs at the desktop:

- To erase an RW type disc (rewritable, like CD-RW or DVD-RW), click your drive's icon (in the nav bar or Computer window); on the Drive Tools/Manage tab of the Ribbon, click Format. (Or right-click the burner's icon; from the shortcut menu, choose Format.) Change the file-system format if you like, and then turn on Quick Format. Finally, click Start to erase the disc.

Tip: Of course, you don't have to erase the disc completely. You can always select and delete individual icons from it using the Delete key.

- If you do a lot of disc burning, a full-fledged burning program like Nero adds myriad additional options. Only with a commercial CD-burning program can you burn MP3 music CDs, create *mixed-mode* CDs (containing both music and files), create Video CDs (low-quality video discs that play on DVD players), and so on.

ISO Disk Images

Programs you download from the Web (not the Windows Store) often arrive in a specially encoded, compressed form—a *disk image* file, also known as an ISO image (Figure 7-16).

Disk images are extremely handy; they behave exactly like discs, in that they can include a whole bunch of related files, folders, and pieces, all distributed online in just the way the software company intended. And here's the good news: In Windows 8, you can work with ISO images just as though they're discs, too. (In the old days, you had to buy a program like Virtual CloneDrive to get this feature.)

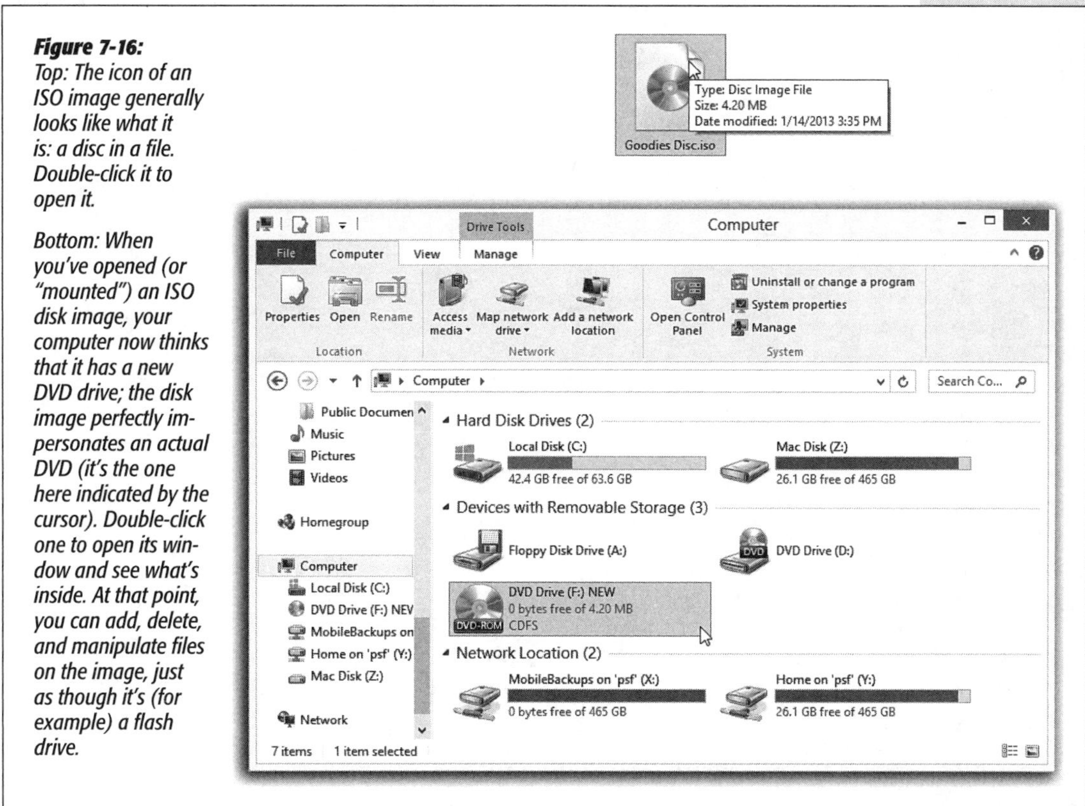

Figure 7-16: *Top: The icon of an ISO image generally looks like what it is: a disc in a file. Double-click it to open it.*

Bottom: When you've opened (or "mounted") an ISO disk image, your computer now thinks that it has a new DVD drive; the disk image perfectly impersonates an actual DVD (it's the one here indicated by the cursor). Double-click one to open its window and see what's inside. At that point, you can add, delete, and manipulate files on the image, just as though it's (for example) a flash drive.

Just double-click the downloaded ISO icon. (You can also right-click it; from the shortcut menu, choose Mount. Or click its icon and use the Mount button on the Ribbon's Disk Tools/Manage tab.)

After a moment, it magically turns into a disk icon in your Nav pane or Computer window, which you can work with just as though it were a real disk. Windows even assigns it a drive letter, like D: or L:; you've got yourself a virtual disc. The software you downloaded is inside.

In theory, you could also create an ISO image from a DVD or Blu-ray disc, so you'll have "the disc" with you when you travel (even if your machine doesn't have a disc drive). Games, for example, run faster from a disk image than from an actual disc. The Web is full of free programs that let you turn folders or groups of files into ISO images.

Tip: If an ISO image doesn't mount (open) when you double-click it, check your file associations. It's possible that you've associated .iso file types to open with a different program, like WinZip or Nero. That program is therefore intercepting your attempt to open the ISO image.

When you're finished working with the disk image, you can eject it exactly as you would a CD or DVD—using the Eject button on the Drive Tools tab of the Ribbon, for example.

CHAPTER
8

Redesigning Your Desktop World

As you now realize, TileWorld doesn't look anything like the Windows the world thought it knew. The bright colors, the lack of window buttons, the crisp rectangles everywhere—that's all new, and especially great on touchscreens.

But the desktop world is still there, and it's every bit as tweakable as previous versions of Windows. You can change the picture on your desktop, or tell Windows to change it *for* you periodically. You can bump up the text size for better reading by over-40 eyeballs.

As Microsoft might say, "Where do you want to redesign today?"

Note: Customizing the Start screen is described in Chapter 2; customizing the taskbar is covered in Chapter 6.

Turning Off the New Look

The Windows 8 desktop doesn't look much different from the Windows 7 desktop. (There's no Start menu, there's a Ribbon in Explorer windows, and window edges are no longer transparent—but that's about it for changes.)

But if you're used to anything earlier, things look a lot different. You may love the changes; you may miss the less flashy, more utilitarian look of Windows Vista or XP. If you're in that category, don't worry; Windows comes with a whole trainload of Off switches.

Turning Off Window Snapping and Shaking

If you drag a window close to the top edge of your screen, the window expands to fill the *whole* screen. If you drag it close to a side of your screen, the window expands to fill *half* the screen. If all this auto-snapping makes you crazy, turn it off as described on page 188.

Turning Off the Inch-Tall Taskbar

The Windows 8 taskbar shows giant, inch-tall icons—with no text labels. And you no longer get one button for each open window; Windows consolidates open windows within each program to save taskbar space.

You can make the taskbar look like it did in Vista or even Windows XP, if you like. Details are on page 240.

Turn Off All Those Glitzy Animations

Then there are all those other things Windows does to show off: Windows seem to zoom open or closed; the Close, Minimize, and Maximize buttons glow when you point to them; menu commands and tooltips fade open and closed; and so on.

It turns out that there's a master list of these effects, filled with individual on/off switches for Win8's various animations, pop-up previews, simulated mouse and window shadows, and so on.

To see it, open the Start screen. Type *effects* and click Settings. "Adjust the appearance and performance of windows" appears in the search results. Click it.

Now you're in the Performance Options dialog box (see Figure 8-1). Now, these aren't exactly the kind of special effects they make at Industrial Light & Magic for use in *Star Wars* movies. In fact, they're so subtle, they're practically invisible. But the more of them you turn off, the faster the desktop will seem to work. (You can turn all of them off with one click—select "Adjust for best performance." Some examples:

- **Enable Peek.** Yes, you can turn off the Peek feature, which lets you (a) point to a taskbar thumbnail to see its full-size window pop to the fore and (b) point to the Show Desktop button (right end of the taskbar) to make all windows transparent.

- **Smooth edges of screen fonts.** If you look very closely at the characters on your screen, they look a bit ragged on the curves. But when this option is turned on, Windows softens the curves, making the text look more professional (or slightly blurrier, depending on your point of view).

- **Show shadows under windows/mouse pointer.** Take a look: In Windows 8, open windows actually seem to cast faint, light gray drop shadows, as though floating an eighth of an inch above the surface behind them. It's a cool, but utterly superfluous, special effect.

- **Show window contents while dragging.** If this option is off, then when you drag a window, only a faint outline of its border is visible; you don't see all the items *in* the window coming along for the ride. As soon as you stop dragging, the contents reappear. If this option is on, however, then as you drag a window across your screen, you see all its contents, too—a feature that can slow the dragging process on really slow machines.

Bring Back the Start Menu

No, silly, you're not stuck with the Start screen as your sole method of opening programs and files. See page 182.

Figure 8-1:
Select "Adjust for best performance" to turn everything off, leaving you with, more or less, Windows XP. Alternatively, turn off only the animations you can live without.

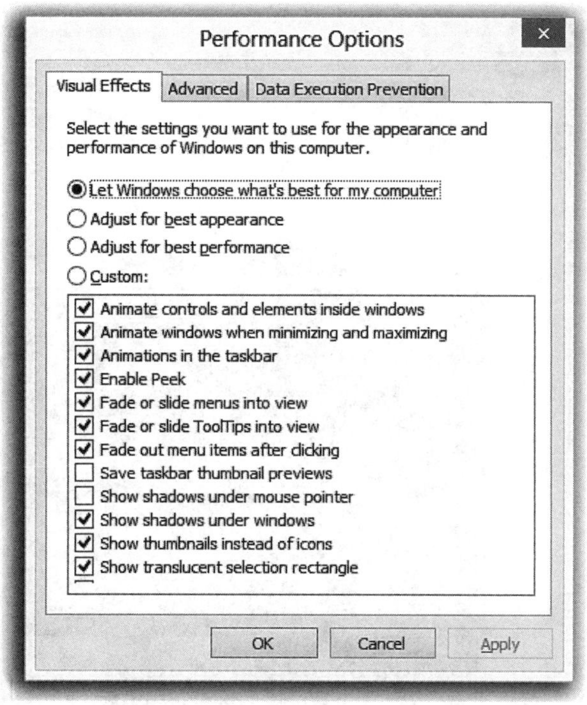

A Gallery of Themes

As you can see in Figure 8-2, Windows includes a number of predesigned design themes that affect the look of your desktop and windows.

Each design theme controls these elements of Windows:

- Your wallpaper (desktop picture).
- Your screen saver.
- The design of icons like Computer, Network, Control Panel, and Recycle Bin.
- The color scheme for your window edges, plus any tweaks you make in the Color and Appearance dialog box (font size, window border width, and so on).
- The size and shape of your arrow cursor.
- The sounds your PC uses as error and alert beeps.

It's fun to customize your PC (especially because it's your opportunity to replace, at last, that huge Dell or HP logo that came as your preinstalled wallpaper). This is also yet another way to shut off some of Windows' predefined cosmetics.

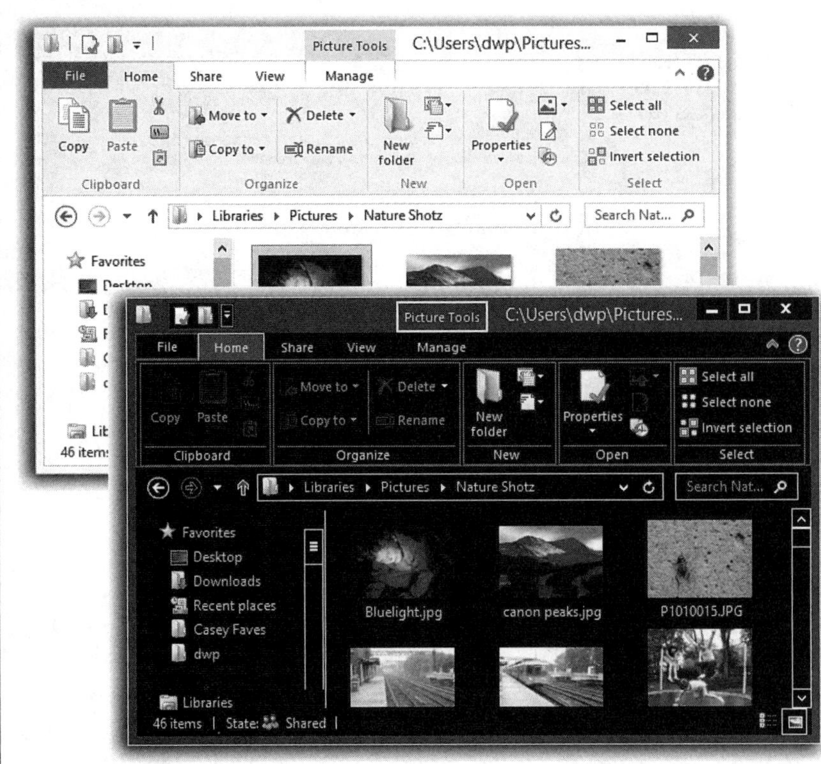

Figure 8-2: *Top: Most people's Windows desktop windows look like this. But your computer may look different, especially if you've turned on one of the other styles–like a high-contrast theme (bottom).*

To see your theme choices, right-click a blank spot on the desktop. From the shortcut menu, choose Personalize.

The Personalization control panel opens, revealing a window full of factory-installed icons for different visual themes (Figure 8-3). Clicking one applies its look to your desktop world instantaneously, making it simple to try on different themes.

Note: Don't miss the "Get more themes online" link; it takes you to a download-more-themes Web site.

Basic and High-Contrast Themes

The control panel offers three categories of themes: My Themes (ones you've modified yourself), Windows Default Themes (Microsoft's canned starter designs), and High Contrast themes. These are designed to help out people with limited vision, who require greater differences in color between window elements. High-contrast themes more closely resemble the squared-off windows and dialog boxes of Windows 2000.

The real fun, however, awaits when you choose one of the canned themes and then *modify* it. Four of the modification tactics are represented by buttons at the bottom of the window (Desktop Background, Window Color, Sounds, and Screen Saver); two more are represented by links at the left side of the window (Desktop Icons and Mouse Pointers). The following pages cover each of these elements in turn.

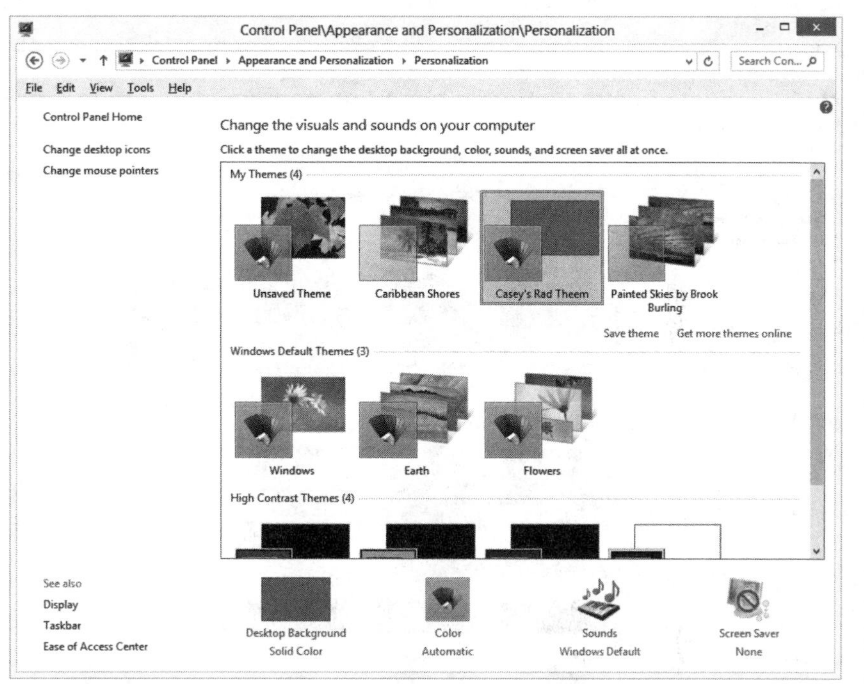

***Figure 8-3:** A theme is more than a color scheme. It also incorporates a desktop background, a standard screen saver, and even a coordinated set of alert sounds. The four icons across the bottom show you the current desktop, color, sound, and screen saver settings for whatever theme you click.*

Desktop Background (Wallpaper)

Windows comes with a host of desktop pictures, patterns, and colors for your viewing pleasure. You want widescreen images for your new flat-panel monitor? You got 'em. Want something gritty, artsy, in black and white? They're there, too. And you can use any picture you'd like as your background as well.

To change yours, right-click the desktop; choose Personalize; and, at the bottom of the box, click Desktop Background.

Now you're looking at the box shown in Figure 8-4. It starts you off examining the Microsoft-supplied photos that come with Windows. Use the "Picture locations" pop-up menu to choose a category:

- **Windows Desktop Backgrounds** includes gorgeous nature photos.
- **Pictures Library** displays all your *own* photos—at least those in your Pictures library. It's more fun to use one of your *own* pictures on the desktop. That might

be an adorable baby photo of your niece, or it might be Sofia Vergara with half her clothes off; the choice is yours.

Feel free to click Browse to forage through other photo folders on your PC, if you have them.

- **Top Rated Photos** displays the photos in your collection to which you've given the highest star ratings.

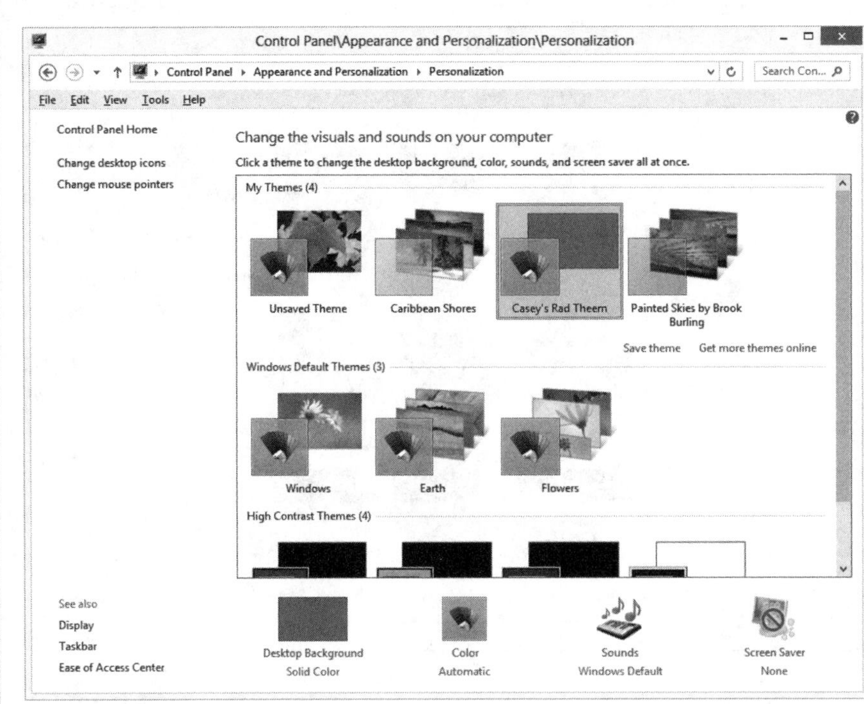

***Figure 8-4:** Desktop backgrounds have come a long way since Windows 3.1. The desktop backgrounds include outdoors scenes, illustrations, and more. There are lots to choose from, so feel free to look around.*

- **Solid Colors** is a palette of simple, solid colors for your desktop background. It's not a bad idea, actually; it's a little easier to find your icons if they're not lost among the rocks and trees of a nature photo.
- **Desktop Background** appears if you've downloaded additional themes. These are the included wallpaper options.
- **Computer** shows any pictures you've added yourself to the Computer→Web→Wallpaper folder.

If you see something you like, you can click it to slap it across the entire background of your desktop.

Or you can use the feature that *changes* your desktop picture periodically, so you don't get bored.

Auto-Picture Changing

The novelty of any desktop picture is likely to fade after several months of all-day viewing. Fortunately, you can choose *multiple* desktop pictures from the gallery; see Figure 8-5.

Now, from the "Change picture every:" pop-up menu, specify when you want your background picture to change: every day, every hour, every 5 minutes, or whatever. (If you're *really* having trouble staying awake at your PC, you can choose every 10 seconds.)

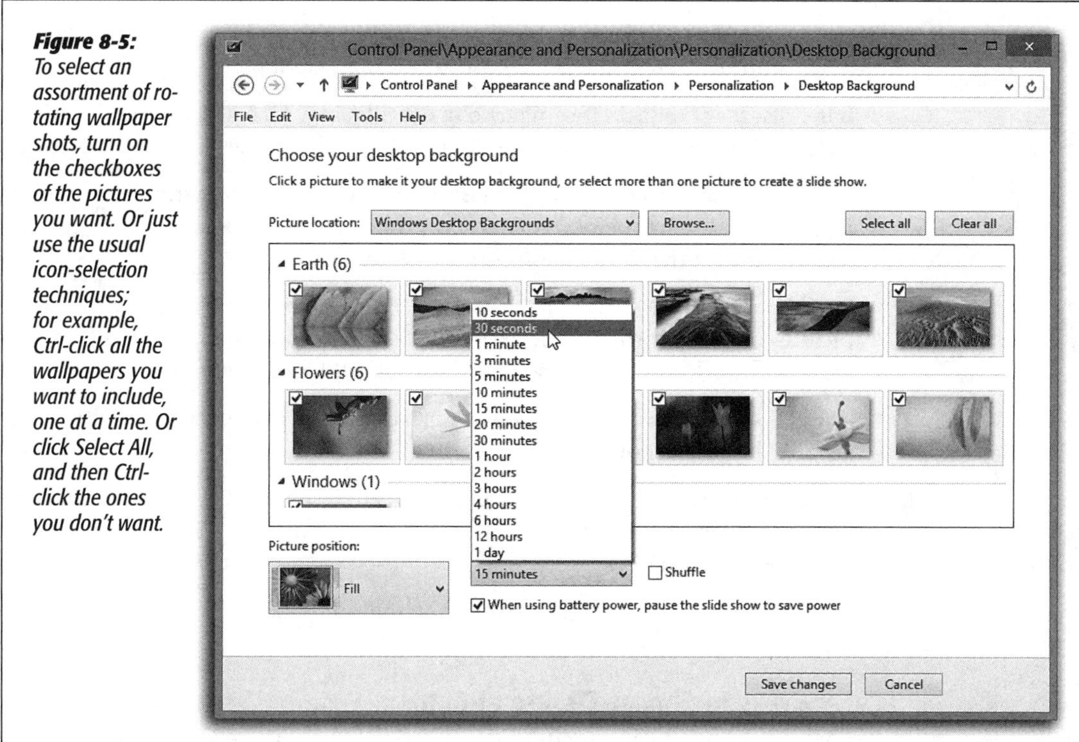

Figure 8-5: *To select an assortment of rotating wallpaper shots, turn on the checkboxes of the pictures you want. Or just use the usual icon-selection techniques; for example, Ctrl-click all the wallpapers you want to include, one at a time. Or click Select All, and then Ctrl-click the ones you don't want.*

Finally, turn on "Shuffle," if you like. If you leave it off, your desktop pictures change in the sequence shown in the gallery.

Now, at the intervals you specified, your desktop picture changes automatically, smoothly cross-fading between the pictures in your chosen source folder like a slideshow. You may never want to open another window, because you'd hate to block your view of the show.

Note: If you have a tablet or laptop, by all means turn on "When using battery power, pause the slide show to save power." Changing wallpapers is nice and all, but not if it means showing up for your talk with a dead laptop.

Making the Pictures Fit

No matter which source you use to choose a photo, you have one more issue to deal with. Unless you've gone to the trouble of editing your chosen photo so that it matches the precise dimensions of your screen (1280 × 800 or whatever), it probably isn't exactly the same size as your screen.

Fortunately, Windows offers a number of solutions to this problem. Using the "Picture position" pop-up menu, you can choose any of these options:

- **Fill.** Enlarges or reduces the image so that it fills every inch of the desktop without distortion. Parts may get chopped off, but this option never distorts the picture.
- **Fit.** Your entire photo appears, as large possible without distortion *or* cropping. If the photo doesn't precisely match the proportions of your screen, you get "letterbox bars" on the sides or at top and bottom.
- **Stretch.** Makes your picture fit the screen exactly, come hell or high water. Larger pictures may be squished vertically or horizontally as necessary, and small pictures are drastically blown up *and* squished, usually with grisly results.
- **Tile.** This option makes your picture repeat over and over until the multiple images fill the entire monitor.
- **Center.** Centers the photo neatly on the screen. If the picture is smaller than the screen, it leaves a swath of empty border all the way around. If it's larger, the outer edges get chopped off.
- **Span.** If you have more than one monitor, this option lets you slap a single photo across multiple screens.

Other Ways to Choose Desktop Photos

Really, the Desktop Backgrounds screen described above is the wallpaper headquarters. But there are "Set as desktop background" commands hiding everywhere in Windows, making it simple to turn everyday images into wallpaper. You'll find that command, for example, when you right-click a graphics icon in an Explorer window or a graphic on a Web page.

Color

This button opens the box shown in Figure 8-6; it lets you specify a color for the taskbar background and window borders.

Note: In Windows Vista and Windows 7, there was a button here called "Advanced appearance settings." It opened a dialog box that let you change every single aspect of the selected visual theme independently—scroll-bar thickness, tooltip text size, icon fonts, and so on. Alas, that box, and those options, are no longer available in Windows 8.

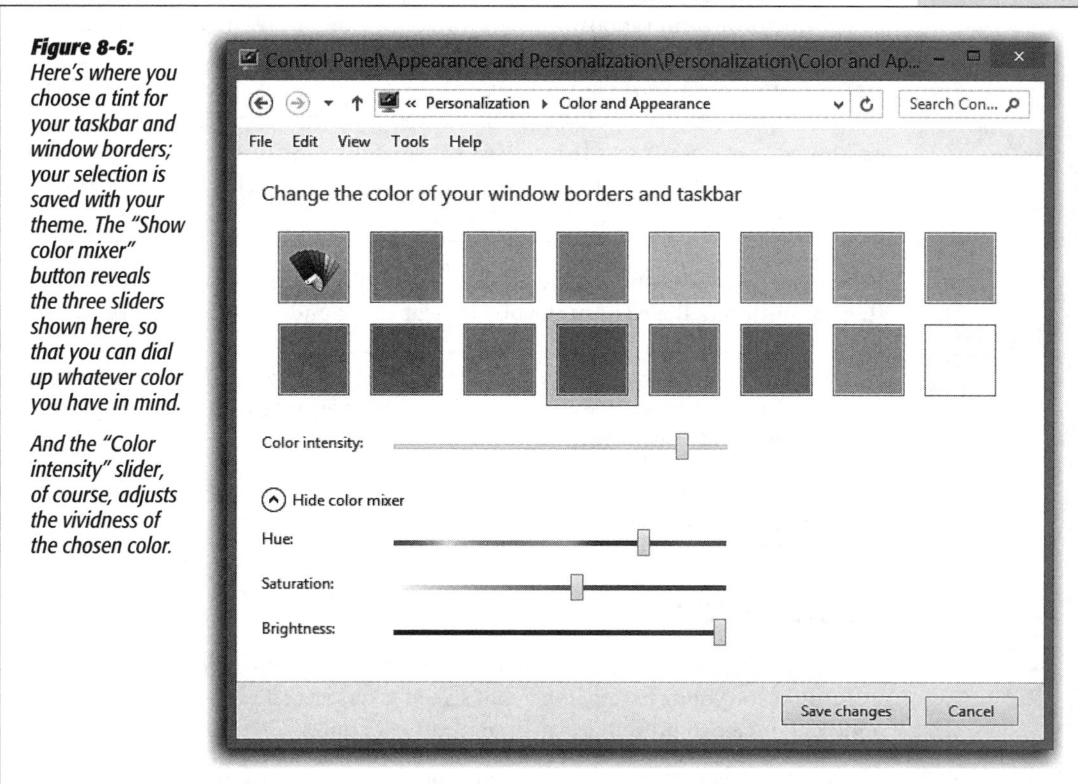

***Figure 8-6:** Here's where you choose a tint for your taskbar and window borders; your selection is saved with your theme. The "Show color mixer" button reveals the three sliders shown here, so that you can dial up whatever color you have in mind.*

And the "Color intensity" slider, of course, adjusts the vividness of the chosen color.

Sounds

Windows plays beeps and bloops to celebrate various occasions: closing a program, yanking out a USB drive, logging in or out, getting a new fax, and so on. You can turn these sounds on or off, or choose new sounds for these events.

Sounds, too, are part of a theme. To edit the suite of sounds that goes with your currently selected theme, click Sounds at the bottom of the Personalization dialog box (Figure 8-3).

See the list of Program Events? A speaker icon represents the occasions when a sound will play. Double-click a sound (or click the Test button) to see what it sounds like.

Or, if you click the name of some computer event (say, Low Battery Alert), you can make these adjustments:

- Remove a sound from the event by choosing (None) from the Sounds drop-down list.
- Change an assigned sound, or add a sound to an event that doesn't have one, by clicking Browse and choosing a new sound file from the list in the Open dialog box.

Tip: When you click the Browse button, Windows opens the Local Disk (C:)→Windows→Media folder, which contains the *.wav* files that provide sounds. If you drag *.wav* files into this Media folder, they become available for use as Windows sound effects. Many people download *.wav* files from the Internet and stash them in the Media folder to make their computing experience quirkier, more fun, and richer in *Austin Powers* sound snippets.

When you select a sound, its filename appears in the Sounds drop-down list. Click the Test button to the right of the box to hear the sound.

Tip: Each set of sounds is called a sound *scheme*. Sometimes the sound effects in a scheme are even sonically related. (Perhaps the collection is totally hip-hop, classical, or performed on a kazoo.) To switch schemes, use the Sound Scheme pop-up menu.

You can also define a new scheme of your own. Start by assigning individual sounds to events, and then click the Save As button to save your collection under a name that you create.

Screen Savers

The term "screen saver" is sort of bogus; today's flat-panel screens *can't* develop "burn-in." (You're too young to remember, but screen savers were designed to bounce around a moving image to prevent burn-in on those old, bulky, CRT screens.)

No, screen savers are mostly about entertainment—and, especially in the business world, security. You can wander away from your desk without fear of snoopers.

The idea is simple: A few minutes after you leave your computer, whatever work you were doing is hidden behind the screen saver; passers-by can't see what's on the screen. To exit the screen saver, move the mouse, click a mouse button, or press a key.

Choosing a Screen Saver

To choose a screen saver, click Screen Saver at the bottom of the Personalization dialog box (Figure 8-3). The Screen Saver Settings dialog box appears.

Now use the "Screen saver" drop-down list. A miniature preview appears in the preview monitor on the dialog box (see Figure 8-7).

To see a *full-screen* preview, click the Preview button. The screen saver display fills your screen and remains there until you move your mouse, click a mouse button, or press a key.

The Wait box determines how long the screen saver waits before kicking in, after the last time you move the mouse or type. Click the Settings button to play with the chosen screen saver module's look and behavior. For example, you may be able to change its colors, texture, or animation style.

Figure 8-7:
"On resume, display logon screen" is a handy security measure. It means you'll have to input your password to get back into your PC once the screen saver has come on–a good barrier against nosy coworkers who saunter up to your PC while you're out getting coffee.

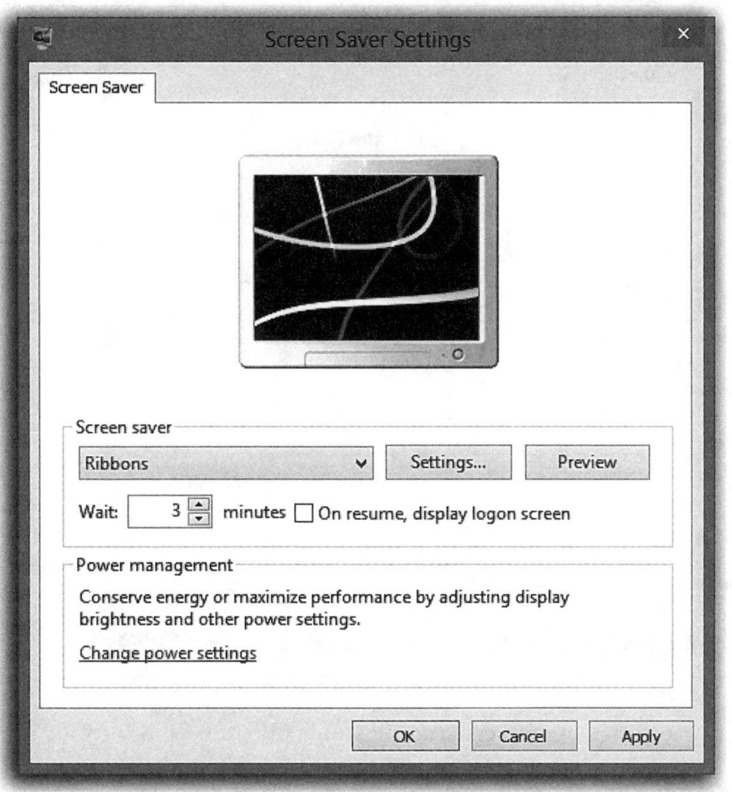

At the bottom of this tab, click "Change power settings" to open the Power Options window described on page 425.

Tip: If you keep graphics files in your Pictures folder, try selecting the Photos screen saver. Then click the Settings button and choose the pictures you want to see. When the screen saver kicks in, Windows puts on a spectacular slideshow of your photos, bringing each to the screen with a special effect (flying in from the side, fading in, and so on).

Desktop Icons

Thanks to the "Change desktop icons" link at the left side of the Personalization screen, you can specify which standard icons sit on your desktop for easy access, and what they look like.

To choose your icons, just turn on the checkboxes for the ones you want (see Figure 8-8).

Figure 8-8: *Microsoft has been cleaning up the Windows desktop in recent years, and that includes sweeping away some useful icons, like Computer, Control Panel, Network, and your Personal folder. But you can put them back, just by turning on these checkboxes.*

You can also substitute different *icons* for your icons. Click, for example, the Computer icon, and then click Change Icon. Up pops a collection of pre-drawn icons in a horizontally scrolling selection box. If you see a picture you like better, double-click it.

Click OK if you like the change, Cancel if not.

Mouse Makeover

If your fondness for the standard Windows arrow cursor begins to wane, you can assert your individuality by choosing a different pointer shape. For starters, you might want to choose a *bigger* arrow cursor—a great solution on today's tinier-pixel, shrunken-cursor monitors.

Begin by clicking "Change mouse pointers" at the left side of the Personalization dialog box shown in Figure 8-3. In a flash, you arrive at the dialog box shown in Figure 8-9.

At this point, you can proceed in any of three ways:

- **Scheme.** There's more to Windows cursors than just the arrow pointer. At various times, you may also see the spinning circular cursor (which means, "Wait; I'm thinking," or "Wait; I've crashed"), the I-beam cursor (which appears when you're editing text), the little pointing-finger hand that appears when you point to a Web link, and so on.

  All these cursors come prepackaged into design-coordinated sets called *schemes.*

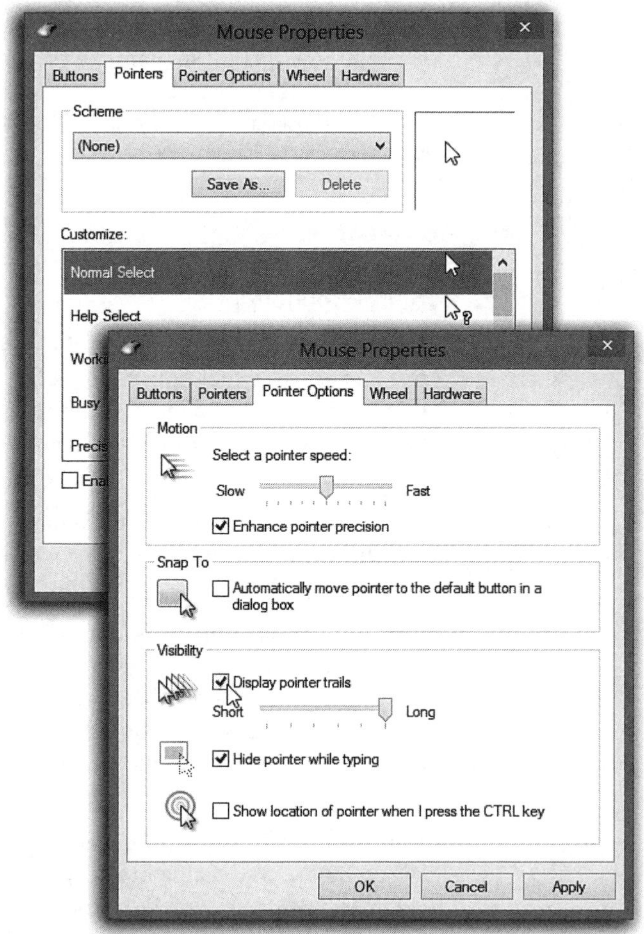

Figure 8-9:
Top: The Pointers dialog box, where you can choose a bigger cursor (or a differently shaped one).

Bottom: The Pointer Options tab. Ever lose your mouse pointer while working on a laptop with a dim screen? Maybe pointer trails could help. Or have you ever worked on a desktop computer with a mouse pointer that seems to take forever to move across the desktop? Try increasing the pointer speed.

To look over the cursor shapes in a different scheme, use the Scheme drop-down list; the corresponding pointer collection appears in the Customize list box. The ones whose names include "large" or "extra large" offer jumbo, magnified cursors ideal for very large screens or failing eyesight. When you find one that seems like an improvement over the factory-setting set, click OK.

- **Select individual pointers.** You don't have to change to a completely different scheme; you can also replace just one cursor. To do so, click the pointer you want to change, and then click the Browse button. You're shown the vast array of cursor-replacement icons (which are in the Local Disk (C:)→Windows→Cursors folder). Click one to see what it looks like; double-click to select it.

- **Create your own pointer scheme.** Once you've replaced a cursor shape, you've also changed the scheme to which it belongs. At this point, either click OK to activate your change and get back to work, or save the new, improved scheme under its own name, so you can switch back to the original when nostalgia calls. To do so, click the Save As button, name the scheme, and then click OK.

Tip: The "Enable pointer shadow" checkbox at the bottom of this tab is pretty neat. It casts a shadow on whatever's beneath the cursor, as though it's skimming just above the surface of your screen.

Pointer Options

Clicking the Pointer Options tab offers a few more random cursor-related functions (Figure 8-9, bottom):

- **Pointer speed.** It comes as a surprise to many people that the cursor doesn't move five inches when the mouse moves five inches on the desk. Instead, you can set things up so that moving the mouse one *millimeter* moves the pointer one full *inch*—or vice versa—using the "Pointer speed" slider.

  It may come as an even greater surprise that the cursor doesn't generally move *proportionally* to the mouse's movement, regardless of your "Pointer speed" setting. Instead, the cursor moves farther when you move the mouse faster. How *much* farther depends on how you set the "Select a pointer speed" slider.

  The Fast setting is nice if you have an enormous monitor, since it prevents you from needing an equally large mouse pad to get from one corner to another. The Slow setting, on the other hand, can be frustrating, since it forces you to constantly pick up and put down the mouse as you scoot across the screen. (You can also turn off the disproportionate-movement feature completely by turning off "Enhance pointer precision.")

- **Snap To.** A hefty percentage of the times when you reach for the mouse, it's to click a button in a dialog box. If you, like millions of people before you, usually click the *default* (outlined) button—such as OK, Next, or Yes—then the Snap To feature can save you the effort of positioning the cursor before clicking.

  When you turn on Snap To, every time a dialog box appears, your mouse pointer jumps automatically to the default button so that all you need to do is click. (And to click a different button, like Cancel, you have to move the mouse only slightly to reach it.)

- **Display pointer trails.** The options available for enhancing pointer visibility (or invisibility) are mildly useful under certain circumstances, but mostly they're just for show.

If you turn on "Display pointer trails," for example, you get ghost images that trail behind the cursor like a bunch of little ducklings following their mother. In general, this stuttering-cursor effect is irritating. On rare occasions, however, you may find that it helps locate the cursor—for example, if you're making a presentation on a low-contrast LCD projector.

- **Hide pointer while typing** is useful if you find that the cursor sometimes gets in the way of the words on your screen. As soon as you use the keyboard, the pointer disappears; just move the mouse to make the pointer reappear.
- **Show location of pointer when I press the CTRL key.** If you've managed to lose the cursor on an LCD projector or a laptop with an inferior screen, this feature helps you gain your bearings. After turning on this checkbox, Windows displays an animated concentric ring each time you press the Ctrl key to pinpoint the cursor's location.

Tip: You can also fatten up the insertion point–the cursor that appears when you're editing text. See page 177.

Preserving Your Tweaks for Posterity

The previous pages describe six ways to modify one of Windows' canned themes. You can change the desktop picture, the window color schemes, the sound scheme, the screen saver, the desktop icons, and the mouse-pointer shapes. The basic concept is simple: You choose one of Microsoft's canned themes as a starting point and then adjust these six aspects of it as suits your mood.

When that's all over, though, you return to the Personalization box, where all the modifications you've made are represented at the top of the screen—as an icon called Unsaved Theme (Figure 8-10).

Well, you wouldn't want all that effort to go to waste, would you? So click "Save theme," type a name for your new, improved theme, and click Save.

From now on, the theme you've created (well, OK, *modified)* shows up in a new row of the Personalization dialog box called My Themes. From now on, you can recall the emotional tenor of your edited look with a single click on that icon.

If you make *further* changes to that theme (or any other theme), another Unsaved Theme icon appears, once again ready for you to save and name. You can keep going forever, adding to your gallery of experimentation.

You can also delete a less-inspired theme (right-click its icon; from the shortcut menu, choose Delete Theme). On the other hand, when you strike creative gold, you can package up your theme and share it with other computers—your own, or other people's online. To do that, right-click the theme's icon; from the shortcut menu, choose "Save theme for sharing." Windows asks you to name and save the new .themepak file, which you can distribute to the masses. (Just double-clicking a .themepak file installs it in the Personalization dialog box.)

Note: If your theme uses sounds and graphics that aren't on other people's PCs, they won't see those elements when they install your theme.

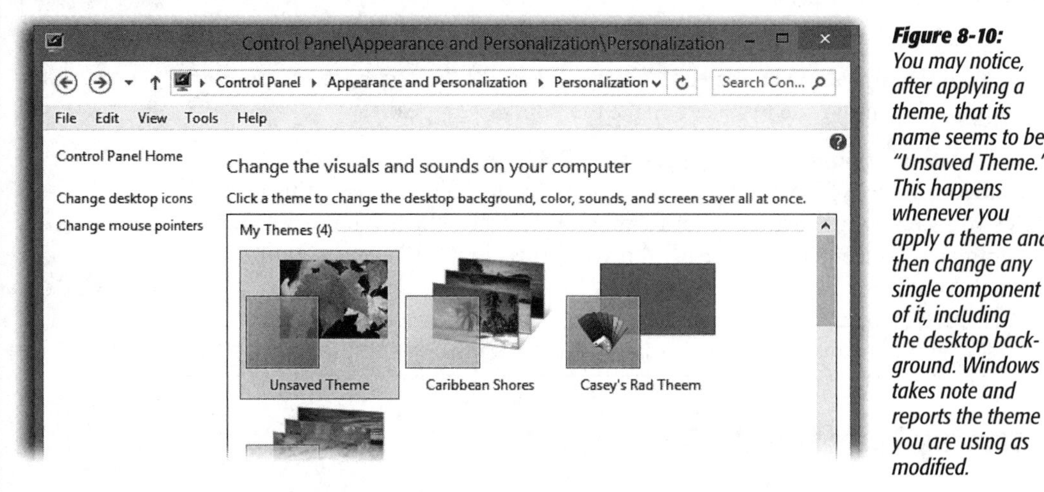

Figure 8-10: *You may notice, after applying a theme, that its name seems to be "Unsaved Theme." This happens whenever you apply a theme and then change any single component of it, including the desktop background. Windows takes note and reports the theme you are using as modified.*

Monitor Settings

You wouldn't get much work done without a screen on your computer. It follows, then, that you can get *more* work done if you tinker with your screen's settings to make it more appropriate to your tastes and workload.

Four Ways to Enlarge the Screen

There are two reasons why Windows offers a quick-and-easy way to magnify *everything* on the screen.

First, people tend to get older—even you. Come middle age, your eyes may have trouble reading smaller type.

Second, the resolution of computer screens gets higher every year. That is, more and more dots are packed into the same-sized screens, and therefore those dots are getting smaller, and therefore the *type and graphics* are getting smaller.

Microsoft finally decided enough was enough. That's why there's a one-click way to enlarge all type and graphics, with crisp, easier-to-see results.

There are also various older schemes for accomplishing similar tasks. Here's a rundown of all of them.

Change the resolution

Your screen can make its picture larger or smaller to accommodate different kinds of work. You perform this magnification or reduction by switching among different *resolutions* (measurements of the number of dots that compose the screen).

When you use a low-resolution setting, such as 800 × 600, the dots of your screen image get larger, enlarging (zooming in on) the picture—but showing a smaller slice of the page. Use this setting when playing a small movie on the Web, for example, so that it fills more of the screen.

At higher resolutions, such as 1280 × 1024, the dots get smaller, making your windows and icons smaller but showing more overall area. Use this kind of setting when working on two-page spreads in your page-layout program, for example.

Unfortunately, adjusting the resolution isn't a perfect solution if you're having trouble reading tiny type. On a flat-panel screen—that is, the *only* kind sold today—only one resolution setting looks really great: the maximum one. That's what geeks call the *native* resolution of that screen.

POWER USERS' CLINIC

Some Clear Talk About ClearType

ClearType is Microsoft's word for a sneaky technology that makes type look sharper on your screen than it really is.

Imagine a lowercase *s* at a very small point size. It looks great on this page, because this book was printed at 1,200 dots per inch. But your monitor's resolution is far lower–maybe 96 dots per inch–so text doesn't look nearly as good. If you were to really get up close, you'd see that the curves on the letters are actually a little jagged.

Each dot on an LCD screen is actually composed of three subpixels (mini-dots): red, green, and blue. What ClearType does is simulate smaller pixels in the nooks and crannies of letters by turning on only some of those subpixels. In the curve of that tiny *s*, for example, maybe only the blue subpixel is turned on, which to your eye looks like a slightly darker area, a fraction of a pixel; as a result, the type looks finer than it really is.

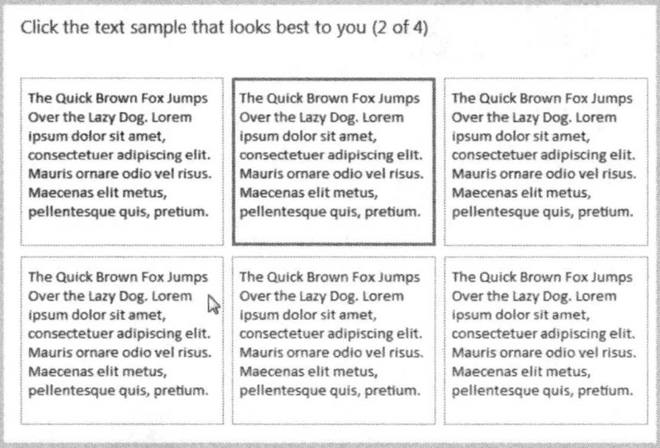

ClearType's behavior is adjustable. To see the options, open the Start screen. Type *cleartype;* click Settings; when you see "Adjust ClearType text" in the results list; click it.

On the first screen, you have an on/off checkbox for ClearType. It's there just for the sake of completeness, because text on an LCD screen really does look worse without it.

If you click Next, Windows walks you through a series of "Which type sample looks better to you?" screens, where all you have to do is click the "Quick Brown Fox Jumps Over the Lazy Dog" example that you find easiest to read. Behind the scenes, of course, you're adjusting ClearType's technical parameters without even having to know what they are. When it's all over, you'll have the best-looking small type possible.

That's because on flat-panel screens, every pixel is a fixed size. At lower resolutions, the PC does what it can to blur together adjacent pixels, but the effect is fuzzy and unsatisfying. (On the old, bulky CRT monitors, the electron gun could actually make the pixels larger or smaller, so you didn't have this problem.)

If you still want to adjust your screen's resolution, here's how you do it. Right-click the desktop. From the shortcut menu, choose "Screen resolution." In the dialog box (Figure 8-11), use the Resolution pop-up menu.

Tip: Depending on your monitor, you may see a weird Orientation pop-up menu here. Believe it or not, this control lets you flip your screen image upside-down or left/right, forming a mirror image.

These options make hilarious practical jokes, of course, but they were actually designed to accommodate newfangled PC designs where, for example, the screen half of a laptop flips over, A-frame style, so people across the table from you can see it.

In any case, once you choose an orientation and click Apply or OK, a dialog box lets you either keep or discard the setting. Which is lucky, because if the image is upside-down on a regular PC, it's really hard to get any work done.

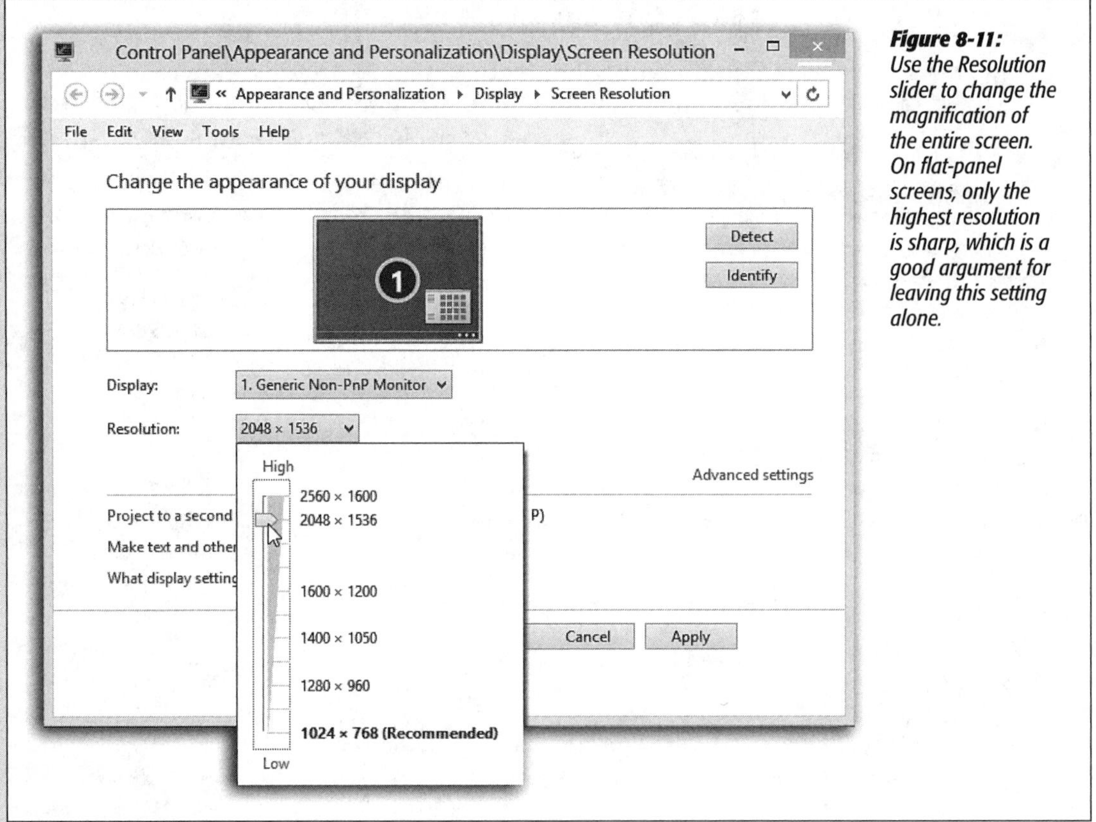

Figure 8-11: *Use the Resolution slider to change the magnification of the entire screen. On flat-panel screens, only the highest resolution is sharp, which is a good argument for leaving this setting alone.*

Enlarge just the type and graphics

This feature is one of Microsoft's most inspired, most useful—and least publicized. It turns out that you can enlarge the type and graphics on the screen *without* changing the screen's resolution. So type gets bigger without getting blurrier, and everything else stays sharp, too.

To make this adjustment, right-click the desktop; from the shortcut menu, choose Resolution. In the resulting dialog box, click "Make text and other items larger or smaller."

Now you arrive at a new dialog box; proceed as directed in Figure 8-12.

Tip: The box in Figure 8-12 offers only two fixed degrees of magnification: 125% and 150%. You can actually dial up any amount you like, though. Click "Custom sizing options" to produce the dialog box shown at bottom in Figure 8-12.

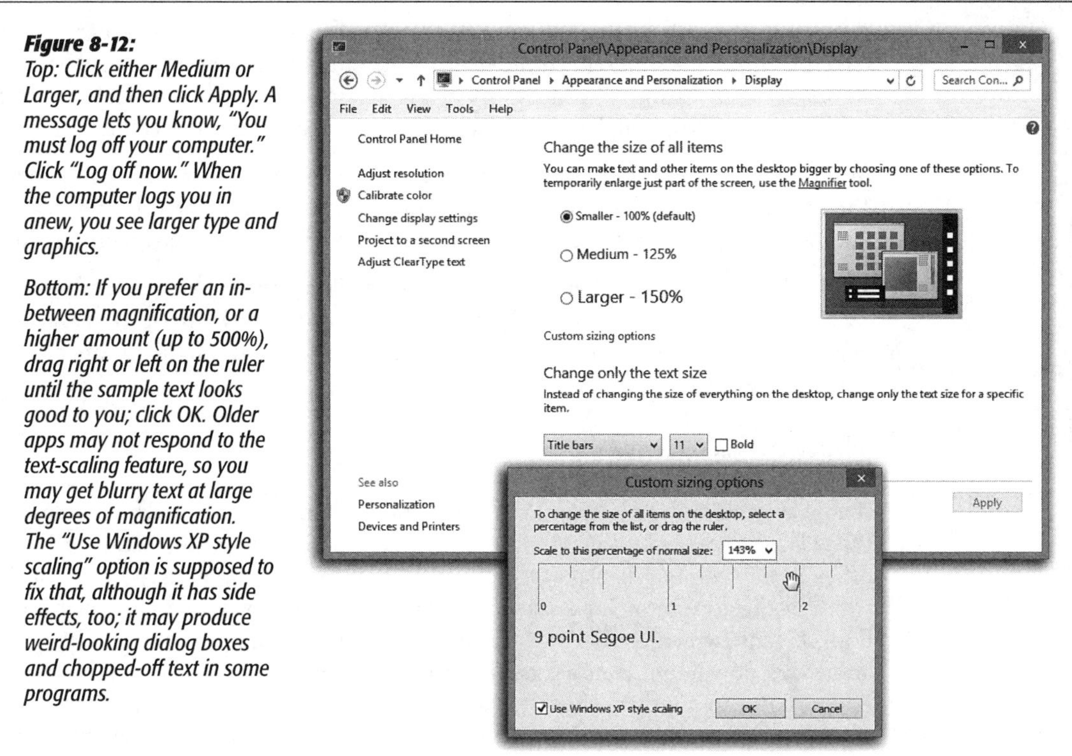

Figure 8-12: *Top: Click either Medium or Larger, and then click Apply. A message lets you know, "You must log off your computer." Click "Log off now." When the computer logs you in anew, you see larger type and graphics.*

Bottom: If you prefer an in-between magnification, or a higher amount (up to 500%), drag right or left on the ruler until the sample text looks good to you; click OK. Older apps may not respond to the text-scaling feature, so you may get blurry text at large degrees of magnification. The "Use Windows XP style scaling" option is supposed to fix that, although it has side effects, too; it may produce weird-looking dialog boxes and chopped-off text in some programs.

Enlarge specific window elements

In Windows 7, you could open an Advanced Appearance Options dialog box that let you change every single aspect of the selected visual theme independently. That box is gone now, but the heart of it lives on—in the "Change only the text size" pop-up menu at the bottom of the dialog box shown in Figure 8-12.

Proceed with your interior-decoration crusade by choosing from the drop-down list: Title bars, Menus, Message boxes, Palette titles, Icons, or Tooltips. Then use the font-size pop-up menu to its right to suit your artistic urges and eyeglasses prescription.

You can even make some of these elements appear in boldface, if you so desire (turn on Bold).

When you've exhausted your options—or just become exhausted—click Apply. You can now explore the world of your new, larger-type icon and window elements.

The Magnifier

If your "type is too small" problem is only occasional, you can call up Windows' Magnifier. It's like a software magnifying glass that fills the top portion of your screen; as you move your pointer around the real-size area beneath, the enlarged image scrolls around, too. Details are on page 381.

Colors

Today's video cards offer different *color depth* settings, each of which permits the screen to display a different number of colors simultaneously. You usually have a choice between settings like Medium (16-bit), which was called High Color in early versions of Windows; High (24-bit), once known as True Color; and Highest (32-bit).

In the early days of computing, higher color settings required a sacrifice in speed. Today, however, there's very little downside to leaving your screen at its highest setting. Photos, in particular, look best when you set your monitor to higher-quality settings.

To check your settings, right-click the desktop. From the shortcut menu, choose "Screen resolution." In the dialog box, click "Advanced settings" to open the Properties dialog box for your monitor. Click the Monitor tab, and use the Colors pop-up menu to choose your color depth.

Multiple Monitors

If your computer has a jack for an external monitor (most do these days—including the video-output jacks on laptops and even tablets), or if your new tablet or laptop offers WiDi (wireless display) technology, then you can hook up a second monitor (or even third monitor) or a projector. You can either display the same picture on both screens (which is what you'd want if your laptop were projecting slides for an audience), or you can create a gigantic virtual desktop, moving icons or toolbars from one monitor to another. The latter setup also lets you keep an eye on Web activity on one monitor while you edit data on another. It's a *glorious* arrangement, even if it does make the occasional family member think you've gone off the deep end with your PC obsession.

Now, as you know, Windows 8 is really two operating systems in one. You actually wind up with two different multiple-monitor centers: one in TileWorld, one at the desktop.

Quick and Simple: The Charms Bar

The quick, easy way to introduce a second screen is to open the Devices pane of the Charms bar and then hit "Second screen" (see Figure 8-13). The resulting options let you mirror the same image on both screens ("Duplicate"), use the second monitor as an extension of the first ("Extend"—perfect for displaying TileWorld on one screen and the desktop on another), or to light up only one screen or the other.

Figure 8-13:
If you just want a quick, easy way to hook up a second monitor or a projector, open the Charms bar (page 24). Hit the Devices button, then hit "Second screen."

If you have a keyboard, you can save a lot of those steps by simply pressing ⊞+P (for "projector"–get it?).

Either way, you wind up at this panel, where you can specify exactly what appears on which screen.

This panel is an extremely thoughtful touch for laptop luggers, because it avoids the staggeringly confusing keyboard-based system you previously had to use. That's where you'd press, for example, F8 three times to cycle among the three modes: image on laptop only (projector dark), image on projector only (laptop screen dark), or image on both at once. Windows 8's method is much easier.

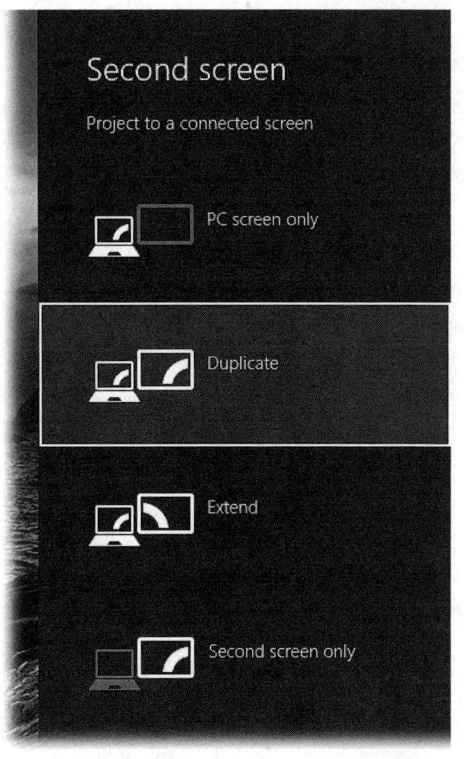

That's all fine for quick jobs, like boardroom PowerPoint setups. But if you have a second monitor at home, you might want more control; you might want to specify which monitor is on the left and which is on the right, for example, or to indicate the screen resolution for each monitor separately. Fortunately, the old desktop Control Panel is still around.

Flexibility and Options: The Screen Resolution Panel

For the beating heart of Windows' multiple-monitor controls, right-click the desktop. From the shortcut menu, choose "Screen resolution."

In the resulting dialog box (Figure 8-14), you see icons for both screens (or even more, if you have them, you lucky thing). It's like a map. Click the screen whose settings (like resolution) you want to change. If Windows seems to be displaying these miniatures out of sequence—if your external monitor is really to the *left* of your main screen, and Windows is showing it to the right—you can actually drag their thumbnails around until they match reality. (Click Identify if you get confused; that makes an enormous digit fill each real screen, which helps you match it to the digits on the miniatures.)

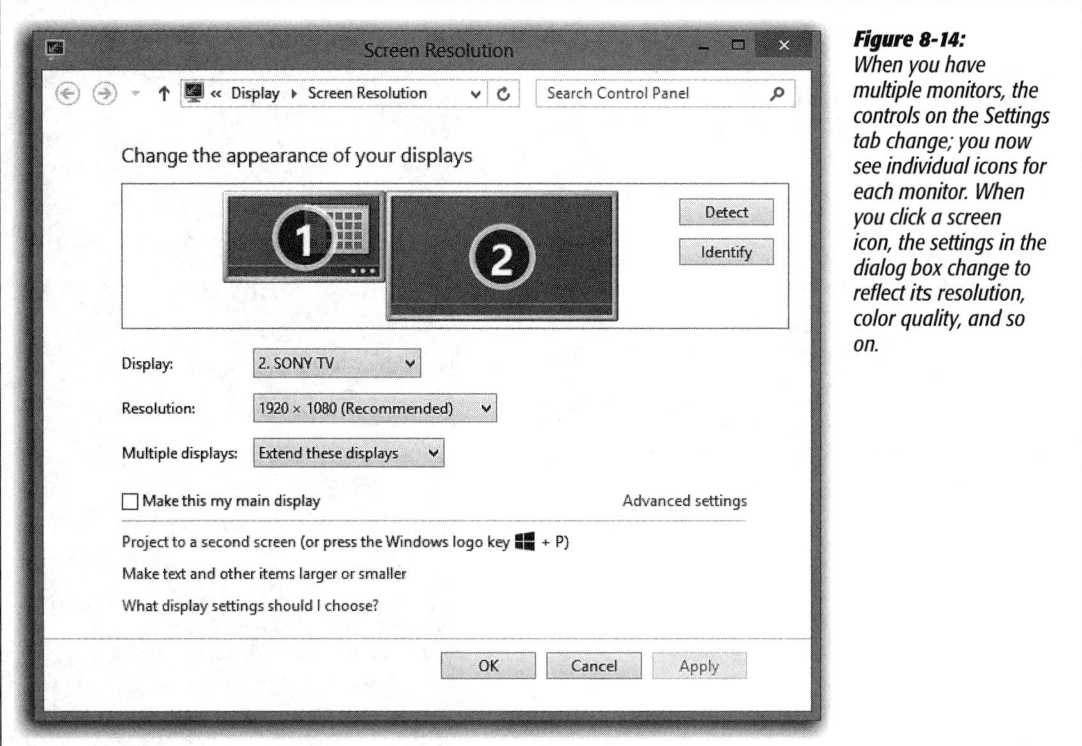

Figure 8-14: *When you have multiple monitors, the controls on the Settings tab change; you now see individual icons for each monitor. When you click a screen icon, the settings in the dialog box change to reflect its resolution, color quality, and so on.*

To bring about that extended-desktop scenario, use the "Multiple displays" pop-up menu. It offers commands like "Duplicate these displays" and "Extend these displays."

Advanced Settings

If you click the Advanced button on the Settings tab, you're offered a collection of technical settings for your particular monitor model. Depending on your video driver, there may be tab controls here that adjust the *refresh rate* to eliminate flicker, install an updated adapter or monitor driver, and so on. In general, you rarely need to adjust these controls—except on the advice of a consultant or help-line technician.

Life with Eight Corners

Once you've hooked up a second monitor and told Windows what to show there, the fun has only just begun. Let the tips flow:

- The corners of both monitors are "live" for Windows 8 purposes. In other words, you can push the mouse into the upper- or lower-right corner of *any* monitor to make the Charms bar appear. You can push it into the lower-left corner of *any* monitor to make the Start-screen button appear. You can summon the thumbnail of the last-used app by pushing it into the upper-left corner of *any* monitor. (You'll discover that Windows fattens up the corner targets as your mouse approaches, so you don't have to hit the corner exactly. They're now 6 pixels square instead of 1.)

  Put another way, you can open the Start screen, Charms bar, or Recent Apps thumbnail column on any screen at any time.

Note: When you press the ⊞ key, the Start screen appears on whichever screen it was on most recently.

- You can zap a TileWorld app's window from one monitor to the other by pressing ⊞+Page Up or ⊞+PageDown.
- Similarly, you can toss a desktop program's window from one screen to the other by pressing ⊞+← or ⊞+→.
- You can drag a TileWorld app from screen to screen with the mouse, even if it's a split-screen, "snapped" app. (Use the top edge of the app's screen as a handle.)
- The desktop, and regular Windows apps, can appear on multiple screens at once—but TileWorld, and the Start screen, can never appear on more than one screen.
- As you now know, you can open the Start screen on any screen; when you click there, that becomes the new TileWorld screen.
- The System tray (notification area) never appears on any monitor except the main one.
- You can't pin different items onto each screen's taskbar.
- You can give each screen its own desktop wallpaper, exactly as you'd hope. But the method for doing it is a little counterintuitive.

  Right-click the desktop background on any monitor; from the shortcut menu, choose Personalize. In the Personalization window, click "Desktop background." You arrive at the control panel shown in Figure 8-5.

  Find the thumbnail that represents the wallpaper you want for the first monitor; right-click the thumbnail; from the shortcut menu, choose "Set for monitor 1." Right-click another thumbnail; from the shortcut menu, choose "Set for monitor 2." Lather, rinse, repeat.

Tip: See the "Picture position" pop-up menu? When you have multiple monitors, it sprouts a new option called Span. When you choose it, you can make one single desktop picture stretch across your multiple screens.

Taskbar Complications

If you have multiple monitors, a question arises: where is the taskbar supposed to be? If it's on Monitor #1, then your mouse has an awfully long way to travel if it's starting out on Monitor #3.

Fortunately, you can make the taskbar appear on *all screens simultaneously*, which can make life a lot easier. To do that, open the Charms bar, select Search, type *taskbar*, and select Settings. In the search results, open Taskbar. You arrive at the Taskbar Properties dialog box; proceed as shown in Figure 8-15.

That illustration also explains how to adjust which buttons appear on the taskbar of each monitor; you have extremely fine-grained control.

You might also discover a new pop-up menu at the bottom of that dialog box, called "Buttons on other taskbars." It's a duplicate of the "Taskbar buttons" pop-up menu described on page 229, except that, of course, it affects the taskbars on other monitors, not the main one.

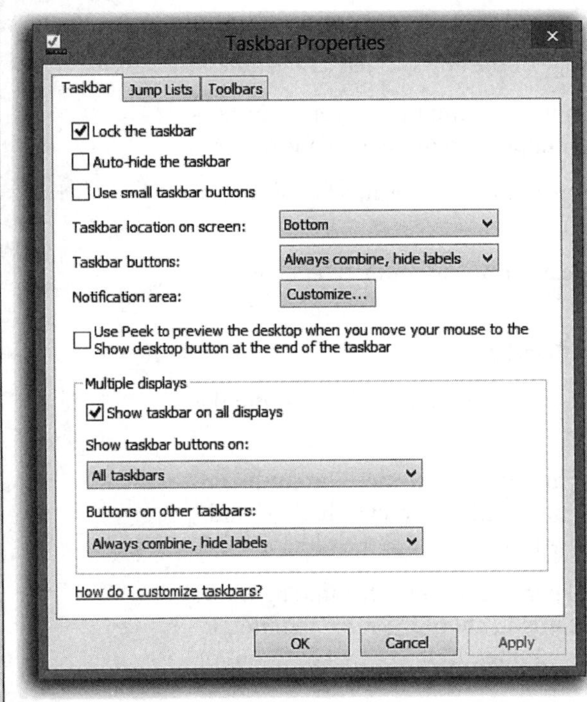

Figure 8-15:
Here's how to make the taskbar appear on all monitors simultaneously: turn on "Show taskbar on all displays." That's new in Windows 8, and very welcome.

The "Show taskbar buttons on" pop-up menu is tweaky—it's intended for power users. If you choose "All taskbars," then the same taskbar appears on every screen.

If you choose "taskbar where the window is open," then each screen's taskbar bears the icons of only the windows that are on that monitor. If Internet Explorer and Word are on Monitor #2, then only those two icons appear on Monitor #2's taskbar.

And if you choose "Main taskbar and taskbar where window is open," then the main monitor shows the full taskbar, containing buttons for all windows on all monitors. The other monitors' taskbars have buttons only for the windows actually on them.

CHAPTER
9

Help at the Desktop

In Windows 8, you get two Help systems for the price of one—TileWorld and the desktop each have their own online Help mechanisms. The TileWorld Help can be sparse or, in some apps, nonexistent. But the full desktop Help system has little videos, links to Web articles, and even links that do certain jobs for you. It may take all weekend, but eventually you should find written information about this or that Windows feature or problem.

This chapter covers not only the Help system, but also some of the ways Windows can help you get help from a more experienced person via your network or the Internet.

Navigating the Help System

To open the Help system, choose File→Help in any Explorer window, or press ⊞+F1. The Help and Support window appears, as shown in Figure 9-1. From here, you can home in on the help screen you want using one of two methods: using the Search box or clicking your way from the Help home page.

Search the Help Pages

By typing a phrase into the Search Help box at the top of the main page and then pressing Enter (or clicking the tiny magnifying glass button), you instruct Windows to rifle through its thousands of help pages—and many more that reside online—to search for the phrase you typed.

Here are a few pointers:

- When you enter multiple words, Windows assumes you're looking for help screens that contain *all* those words. For example, if you search for *video settings*, then help screens that contain both the words "video" and "settings" (although not necessarily next to each other) appear.

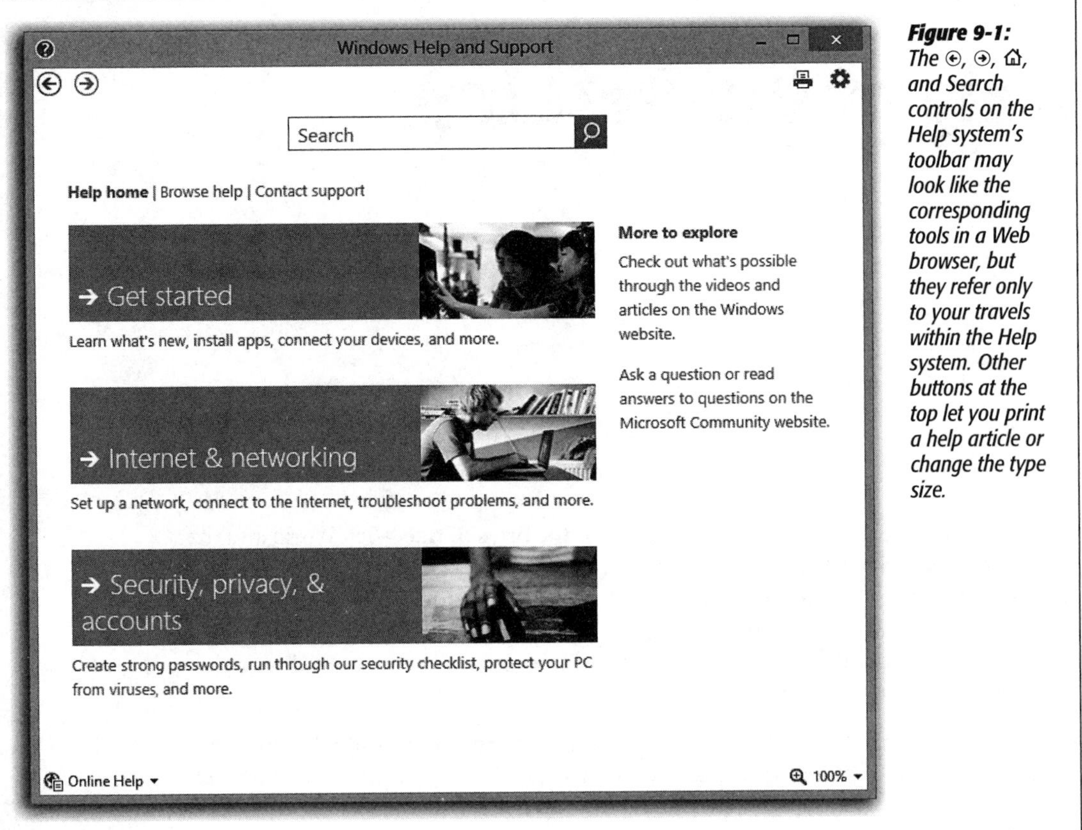

Figure 9-1: *The ⊖, ⊕, ⌂, and Search controls on the Help system's toolbar may look like the corresponding tools in a Web browser, but they refer only to your travels within the Help system. Other buttons at the top let you print a help article or change the type size.*

- To search for an exact phrase, put quotes around it ("video settings").
- Once you've clicked your way to an article that looks promising, you can search within that page, too—but only from the keyboard. Press Ctrl+F to open the Find box.

Tip: The Help pages included with your PC actually aren't very complete; most of the good stuff is online. If you know what's good for you, you'll click the ✲ icon at upper right and, in the dialog box, make sure "Get online Help" is turned on.

Drilling Down

If you're not using the same terminology as Microsoft, you won't find your help topic by using the search box. Sometimes, you may have better luck unearthing a certain help article by drilling down through the Table of Contents.

The main Help screen offers three points of entry: "Get started," "Internet & networking," and "Security, privacy, & accounts." But if you click "Browse help" at the top of the window, you're offered a more comprehensive table of contents for the entire Help system.

Each one lists subtopics. Keep clicking until you arrive at an actual help article (Figure 9-2).

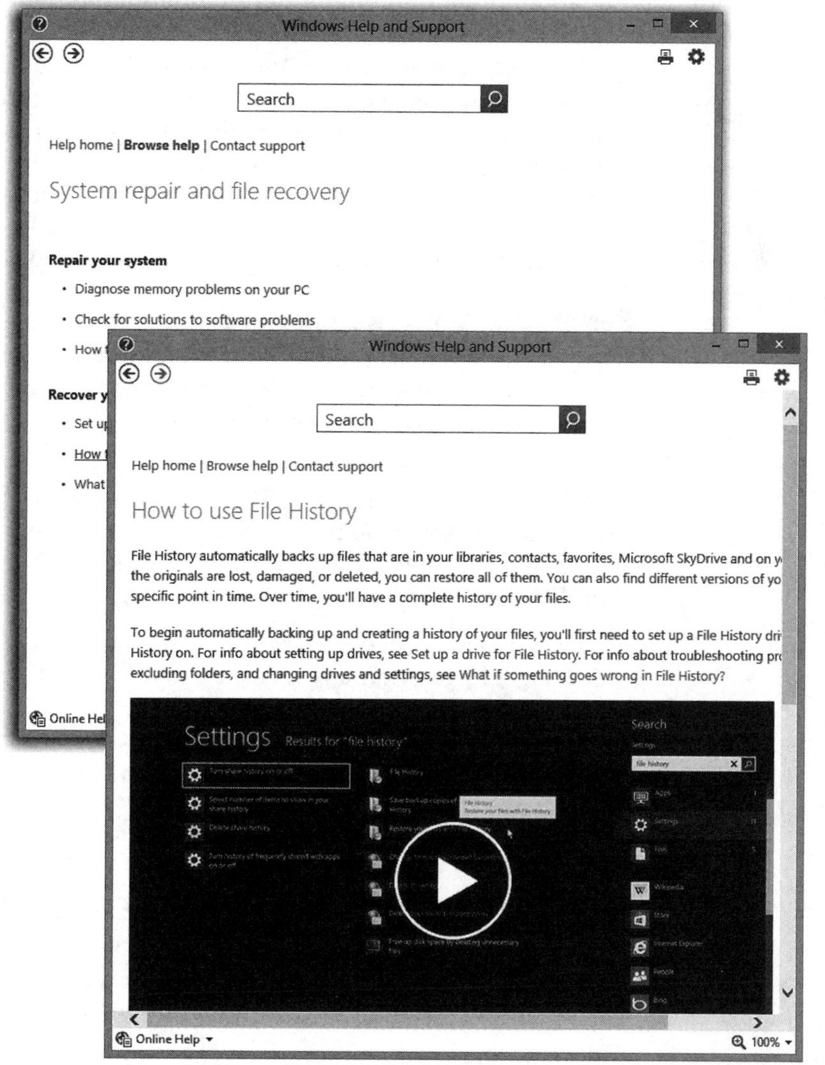

Figure 9-2: *Keep clicking on each more finely grained subtable of subcontents until you find the help topic you want. Sometimes you'll be offered a "Tap or click to open..." instruction, which takes you directly to the relevant program or settings screen.*

When you get really lucky, you actually get a video tutorial.

Remote Assistance

You may think you know what stress is: deadlines, breakups, downsizing. But nothing approaches the frustration of an expert trying to help a PC beginner over the phone—for both parties.

The expert is flying blind, using Windows terminology that the beginner doesn't know. Meanwhile, the beginner doesn't know what to look for and describe on the phone. Every little step takes 20 times longer than it would if the expert were simply seated in front of the machine. Both parties are likely to age 10 years in an hour.

Fortunately, that era is at an end. Windows' Remote Assistance feature lets somebody having computer trouble extend an invitation to an expert, via the Internet. The expert can actually see the screen of the flaky computer and can even take control of it by remotely operating the mouse and keyboard. The guru can make even the most technical tweaks—running utility software, installing new programs, adjusting hardware drivers, even editing the Registry (Appendix B)—by long-distance remote control. Remote Assistance really *is* the next best thing to being there.

Remote Assistance: Rest Assured

Of course, these days, most people react to the notion of Remote Assistance with stark terror. What's to stop some troubled teenager from tapping into your PC in the middle of the night, rummaging through your files, and reading your innermost thoughts?

Plenty. First of all, you, the help-seeker, must begin the process by sending a specific electronic invitation to the expert. The invitation has a time limit: If the helper doesn't respond within, say, an hour, then the electronic door to your PC slams shut again. Second, the remote-control person can only *see* what's on your screen. She can't actually manipulate your computer unless you grant another specific permission.

Finally, you must be present *at your machine* to make this work. The instant you see something fishy going on, a quick tap on your Esc key disconnects the interloper.

Tip: If you still can't stand the idea that there's a tiny wormhole into your PC from the Internet, open the Start screen. Type *remote;* on the Search panel, select Settings. In the results list, select "Allow remote access to your computer." In the resulting dialog box, turn off "Allow Remote Assistance connections to this computer." Click OK. Now you've effectively removed the use of the Remote Assistance feature from Windows.

Starting Up Remote Assistance: If You're Both on Windows 7 or 8

A great feature in Windows drastically shortens the number of steps necessary to set up a Remote Assistance session. It's called, self-explanatorily enough, Easy Connect. But it works only if both of you are using Windows 7 or 8.

If the novice or the expert is using an older version of Windows, then skip to the next section.

Instructions for the novice

OK, let's say you're the one who needs help. And you're running Windows 8. And you know somebody else with Windows 7 or 8 who might be able to help you by remote control. Here's what you do:

1. **Open Windows Remote Assistance.**

   There are a bunch of ways to do that, but the quickest is to search for it. On the Start screen, type *assist*; below the search box, select Settings. Select "Invite someone to connect to your PC and help you, or offer to help someone else" in the results list.

   You now arrive at a "Do you want to ask for or offer help?" screen.

2. **Click "Invite someone you trust to help you."**

   If you now see an error message ("This computer is not set up to send invitations"), then click Repair. Usually, the problem is that the Windows Firewall is blocking the outgoing signal—and usually, clicking Repair fixes it after a moment.

   At this point, what you see depends on whether you've used Easy Connect before. If so, you see a list of people who've helped you in the past; you can resend an invitation to your usual savior just by clicking that person's name.

   If you're inviting someone new, on the other hand, you get the box shown in Figure 9-3, offering three ways to send the invitation to your friendly neighborhood guru.

3. **Click Use Easy Connect.**

   Now Windows shows you a 12-character password (Figure 9-3, bottom).

POWER USERS' CLINIC

Invitation Expiration Dates

If you're the one who wants help, then you'll be sending out an invitation to invade your machine. For security's sake, it has an expiration date. If your guru doesn't cash in on the opportunity within 6 hours, the ticket expires, and you'll have to reissue the invitation another time.

It's worth pointing out that you can adjust that expiration period. From the Start screen, type *remote*; select Settings below the search box; select "Allow remote access to your computer" in the results list. In the System Properties dialog box, click Advanced (the button, not the tab). Here you find two key security options:

Allow this computer to be controlled remotely. This is the master switch for permitting your guru to operate your PC from afar, not just see what's onscreen.

Invitations. Here's where you specify how quickly an invitation to a guru expires. It may give you an extra level of comfort knowing that after, say, 3 hours of waiting for your guru to come home and get your invitation, the window of opportunity will close. On the other hand, if you change it to, say, 99 days, and you're not especially worried that somebody might try to hack into your system (you do have to be present and approve the connection, of course), then you'll save yourself some time and effort the next time you need help. Click OK twice to close the dialog boxes.

4. **Provide the password to your expert friend.**

   You can send it by email, read it to her over the phone, type it to her in a chat program, send a text message, whatever.

   If your expert friend does indeed have a clue, then in a moment, you see a message from that person asking permission to see your screen ("Would you like to allow Casey to connect to your computer?"). Close whatever windows on the screen might be displaying incriminating information, and then—

5. **Click Yes.**

   And voilà: Your guru friend can now see what you're doing—and what you're doing wrong.

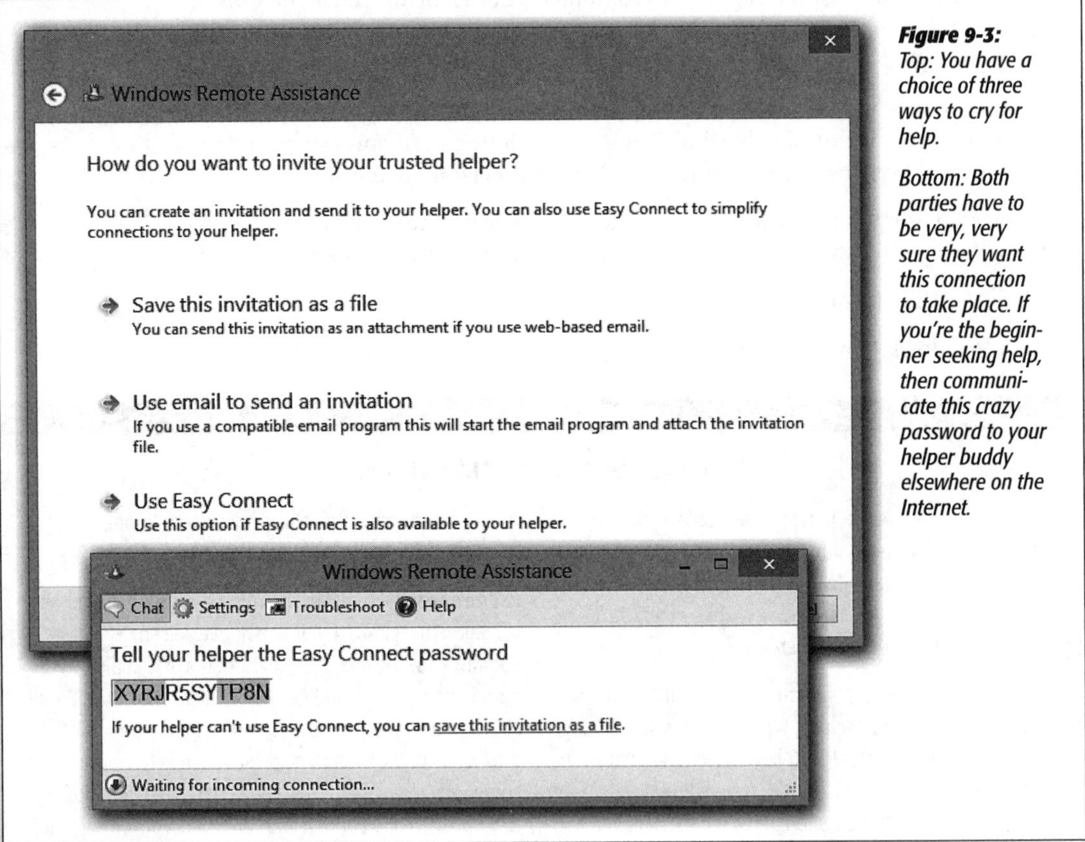

Figure 9-3: *Top: You have a choice of three ways to cry for help.*

Bottom: Both parties have to be very, very sure they want this connection to take place. If you're the beginner seeking help, then communicate this crazy password to your helper buddy elsewhere on the Internet.

Instructions for the expert

If you and your clueless friend are both using Windows 7 or 8 and you receive an invitation to help out—in the form of the 12-character Easy Connect password described above—here's what to do with it:

1. **Open Windows Remote Assistance.**

   The quickest way is to type *assist* at the Start screen; below the search box, select Settings. Select "Invite someone to connect to your PC and help you, or offer to help someone else" in the results list.

2. **Click "Help someone who has invited you."**

   Now you're shown a list of people you've helped out before (if any). If you see your desperate friend's name, click it. Otherwise…

3. **Click "Help someone new." In the next window, click Use Easy Connect.**

   Now Windows asks you for that 12-character password.

4. **Type in the 12-character password.**

   Capitals don't matter. Press Enter when you're finished.

   If your inviter approves the connection, then after a moment, the session begins, as described below.

Starting Up Remote Assistance: If You're Not Both on Windows 7/8

If the helper and the helpee aren't both using Windows 7/8, you can still use Remote Assistance; there are just more steps.

In fact, anybody with Windows XP, Vista, or Server (2003 or later) can help anyone else with one of those operating systems.

The steps, however, are different depending on whether you're the flailer or the helper. In the following steps, suppose you're running Windows 7/8. (It's a pretty good assumption; you are reading a book about Windows 8, aren't you?)

Tip: If you and your guru are both fans of Windows Live Messenger, Microsoft's chat program, then you have at your disposal a more direct way of starting a Remote Assistance session. When you see that your guru is online in Messenger, choose Actions→Start Request Remote Assistance.

If the guru accepts, and you accept the acceptance, then a Remote Assistance session begins, without your having to go through all the email rigmarole described below.

Instructions for the novice

If you're the novice, and you have Windows 8, and you need help, here's how to request it from your more experienced friend:

1. **Open the Windows Remote Assistance program.**

   See the previous Step 1 for details.

2. **Click "Invite someone you trust to help you."**

   The phrase "you trust" is Microsoft's little way of reminding you that whomever you invite will be able to see anything you've got open on the screen. (Those who would rather keep that private know who they are.)

Note: If you now see an error message ("This computer is not set up to send invitations"), then click Repair. As noted above, Windows will fix your Windows Firewall so that you can connect; then read on.

   In any case, the "How do you want to invite your trusted helper?" screen appears.

Tip: If you click "Save this invitation as a file" at this point, then Windows invites you to save a *ticket file*–a standalone invitation file–to your hard drive. You have to do that if you have a Web-based email account like Gmail, Hotmail, or Yahoo Mail. (Make up a password first–see step 5, below, for an explanation–and then attach the file you've saved in this step when sending a message to your guru.)

Saving the file is also handy because you can save some steps by resending it to your guru the next time you're feeling lost.

---

3. **Click "Use email to send an invitation."**

   This assumes, of course, that you have a working email program on your PC. If not, set up your account as described in Chapter 16. Or get on the phone and ask your guru to drive over to your place to help you in person.

   If you do have working email, then your email program now opens, and Windows composes an invitation message *for* you. "Hi," it begins. "I need help with my computer. Would you please use Windows Remote Assistance to connect to my computer so you can help me?" (You're welcome to edit this message, of course—perhaps to something that does a little less damage to your ego.)

   Now Windows displays a password like the one shown in Figure 9-3. It's designed to ensure that your guru, and only your guru, can access your machine.

4. **Type your guru's email address into the To box, and then send the message.**

   Windows sends an electronic invitation to your good Samaritan.

5. **Let your guru know the password.**

   Of course, you need to find some way of *telling* that person the password—maybe calling on the phone, sending a text message, or sending a separate email. The password isn't automatically included in the invitation mail.

Now there's nothing to do but sit back, quietly freaking out, and wait for your guru to get the message and connect to your PC. (See the next section.)

If your buddy accepts the invitation to help you, Windows asks if you're absolutely, positively sure you want someone else to see your screen. If you click Yes, the assistance session begins.

If you get a note that your expert friend wants to take control of your PC, and that's cool with you, click OK.

Now watch in amazement and awe as your cursor begins flying around the screen, text types itself, and windows open and close by themselves.

As noted earlier, if the expert's explorations of your system begin to unnerve you, feel free to slam the door by clicking the "Stop sharing" button on the screen—or just by pressing the Esc key. Your friend can still see your screen but can no longer control it. (To close the connection completely so that your screen isn't even visible anymore, click the Disconnect button.)

Instructions for the expert

When the novice sends you an email invitation, it arrives in your email program with an attachment—a tiny file called Invitation.msrcincident. This is your actual invitation, a Remote Assistance *ticket*.

When you open it, you're asked to supply the password that your helpless newbie created in step 5 above. Once that's done, the online help session can begin.

Tip: And by the way, if the novice, a trusting individual, sends you a Remote Assistance ticket that doesn't expire for a very long time (99 days, for example), keep it around on your desktop or pinned to your Start screen. From now on, both of you can skip all the invitation-and-response rigmarole. Now, whenever he needs your help, he can just call you up or email you. And all you have to do is double-click your ticket and wait for the OK from the other side.

Once You're Connected

Once you, the expert, and your little novice friend have completed all the inviting and permission-granting, you observe a strange sight: the other person's screen in a special Remote Assistance window (Figure 9-4). To communicate with your troubled comrade, chat on the phone, if you like, or click the Chat button to type back and forth.

Tip: If the victim's screen isn't exactly the same size as yours, click the "Actual size" button. With each click on that button, you cycle your display between two modes.

In the first one, the other person's screen is represented at full size, although you may have to scroll around to see all of it. With another click, Windows compresses (or enlarges) the other person's screen image to fit inside your Remote Assistance window, even though the result can be distorted and ugly.

When you want to take control of the distant machine, click "Request control" on the toolbar at the top of your screen. Of course, all you've actually done is just ask *permission* to take control.

If it's granted, then you can use your mouse, keyboard, and troubleshooting skills to do whatever work you need to do. You can type messages back and forth (click Chat on the toolbar) or even send files back and forth (click Send Files on the toolbar).

You can do anything to the distant PC that the novice would be able to do—and you can't do anything the novice isn't allowed to do. (For example, if the novice doesn't have an administrative account, you won't be able to do administratory things like installing apps or creating accounts.)

When your job is done, click the window's Close button—or wait for your grateful patient to click Cancel on the toolbar.

> ***Tip:*** Once you've taken control of the other person's screen, your first instinct might be to close the gargantuan Remote Assistance window that's filling most of the screen. Don't. If that window closes, the connection closes, too. What you really want is to *minimize* it, so it's out of your way but not closed.

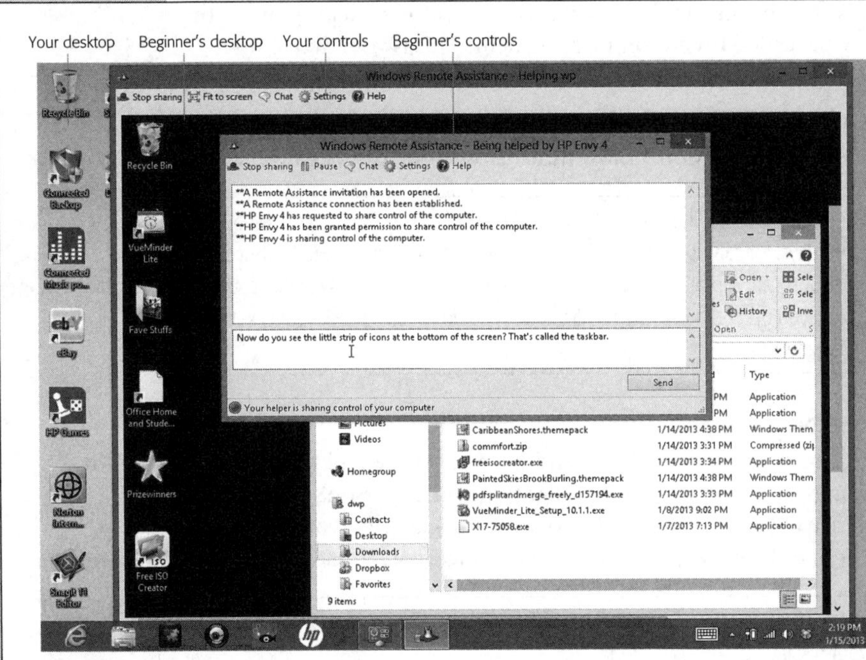

Figure 9-4: *This is what you see, wise master, as you watch the flailing beginner from across the Internet. You are now ready to tell him what he's doing wrong.*

If you're the person being helped, by the way, your toolbar has some useful options, too. "Stop sharing" is your emergency Off button if you think the remote guru is getting into places you consider private. You can also click Pause, which freezes the image the other person is seeing so you can do something personal without fear of being watched.

Getting Help from Microsoft

If you run into trouble with installation—or with any Windows feature—the world of Microsoft is filled with sources of technical help. For example, you can follow any of these avenues, all of which have direct links from the "Contact support" page of the Help system (click "Contact support" at the top of the Help window):

- **Support articles and videos.** This is the mother lode: the master Web site for help and instructions on running Windows. You can search it, use its links to other pages, read articles, study FAQs (frequently asked questions), or burrow into special-topic articles.

  Of course, a lot of these online articles are built right into the regular Help system described at the beginning of this chapter. You generally don't have to go online to search a second time.

- **Windows 8 Forums.** This link takes you to a discussion site about Windows issues. You can post questions to the multitudes all over the Internet and return later to read the answers.

- **Windows Website.** Here's the basic Windows 8 promotional Web site, with a few very basic getting-started pages.

- **Microsoft Community Website.** This link takes you to exactly the same forums as the "Windows 8 Forums" link described above.

Microsoft Customer Support

If you bought Windows separately (that is, it didn't come on your computer), then you have a few additional options.

Most of them begin here: *http://support.microsoft.com/get-support.*

At this site, you can search the online help articles, ask a question in the forums, or get chatroom-style help from an actual, living human being.

Getting help over the phone is a little bit harder. If Windows came preinstalled on your machine, you're supposed to call the computer company with your Windows questions. You *can* call Microsoft, but it'll cost you $100 per problem.

But if you promise that you bought Windows 8 directly from Microsoft, you can call Microsoft for free during business hours. In the United States, that's 800-MICROSOFT. The company is especially interested in helping you get Windows installed. In fact, you can call as often as you like on this subject.

After that, you get a 90-day warranty. During that time, you can call Microsoft as many times as you like. After that, it's $100 per "issue." (They say "per issue" to make it clear that if it takes several phone calls to solve a particular problem, it's still just one charge.) This service is available 24 hours a day; the U.S. number is (800) 936-5700.

Tip: If you're not in the United States, direct your help calls to the local Microsoft office in your country. You can find a list of these subsidiaries at *http://support.microsoft.com.*

CHAPTER 10

Programs & Documents

When you get right down to it, an operating system is nothing more than a home base from which to launch applications (programs). And you, as a Windows person, are particularly fortunate, since more programs are available for Windows than for any other operating system on earth.

But when you launch a program, you're no longer necessarily in the world Microsoft designed for you. Programs from other software companies work a bit differently, and there's a lot to learn about how Windows handles programs that were born before it was.

This chapter covers everything you need to know about installing, removing, launching, and managing programs; using programs to generate documents; and understanding how documents, programs, and Windows communicate with one another.

Opening Desktop Programs

Windows lets you launch (open) programs in many different ways:

- Choose a program's name from the Start screen.
- Choose a program's name from the "All apps" list. (On the Start screen, right-click, or swipe up from the bottom of the screen, to reveal the app bar; select "All apps.")
- Click a program's icon on the taskbar.
- Double-click an application's program-file icon in the Computer→Local Disk (C:)→Program Files→application folder, or highlight the application's icon and then press Enter.

- Press a key combination you've assigned to be the program's shortcut.
- Press ⊞+R, type the program file's name in the Open text box, and then press Enter.
- Let Windows launch the program for you, either at startup (page 685) or at a time you've specified (see Task Scheduler, page 662).
- Open a document using any of the above techniques; its "parent" program opens automatically. For example, if you used Microsoft Word to write a file called "Last Will and Testament.doc," then double-clicking the document's icon launches Word and automatically opens that file.

What happens next depends on the program you're using (and whether or not you opened a document). Most programs present you with a new, blank, untitled document. Some, like FileMaker and Microsoft PowerPoint, welcome you instead with a question: Do you want to open an existing document or create a new one? And a few oddball programs don't open any window at all when launched. The appearance of tool palettes is the only evidence that you've even opened a program.

Exiting Desktop Programs

When you exit, or quit, an application, the memory it was using is returned to the Windows pot for use by other programs.

If you use a particular program several times a day, like a word processor or calendar, you'll save time in the long run by keeping it open all day long. (You can always minimize its window when you're not using it.)

But if you're done using a program for the day, exit it, especially if it's a memory-hungry one like, say, Photoshop. Do so using one of these techniques:

- Choose File→Exit.
- Click the program window's Close box, or double-click its Control-menu spot (at the upper-left corner of the window).
- Right-click the program's taskbar button; from the shortcut menu, choose Close or Close Group.
- Point to the program's taskbar button; when the thumbnail preview pops up, click the little ☒ button in its upper-right corner. (If the program had only one window open, the program exits.)
- Press Alt+F4 to close the window you're in. (If it's a program that disappears entirely when its last document window closes, you're home.)
- Press Alt+F, then X.

After offering you a chance to save any changes you've made to your document, the program's windows, menus, and toolbars disappear, and you "fall down a layer" into the window that was behind it.

When Programs Die: The Task Manager

Windows 8 may be a revolution in stability (at least if you're used to, say, Windows Me), but that doesn't mean that *programs* never crash or freeze. They crash, all right—it's just that you rarely have to restart the computer as a result.

When something goes horribly wrong with a program, your primary interest is usually exiting it. But when a program locks up (the cursor moves, but menus and tool palettes don't respond) or when a dialog box tells you a program has "failed to respond," exiting may not be so easy. After all, how do you choose File→Exit if the File menu doesn't open?

As in past versions of Windows, the solution is to open up the Task Manager dialog box.

Tip: Actually, there may be a quicker solution. Try right-clicking the frozen program's taskbar button; from the shortcut menu, choose Close. This trick doesn't always work–but when it does, it's much faster than using the Task Manager.

UP TO SPEED

Sending an Error Report to Microsoft

Whenever Windows detects that a program has exited, shall we say, *eccentrically*–for example, it froze and you had to terminate it–your PC quietly sends a report back to Microsoft, the mother ship, via the Internet. It provides the company with the technical details about whatever was going on at the moment of the freeze, crash, or premature termination.

The information includes the name and version number of the program, the date and time, and other details. Microsoft swears that it doesn't collect any information about *you*.

Microsoft says it has two interests in getting this information. First, it collates the data into gigantic electronic databases, which it then analyzes using special software tools. The idea, of course, is to find trends that emerge from studying hundreds of thousands of such reports. "Oh, my goodness, it looks like people who own both Speak-it Pro 5 and Beekeeper Plus who right-click a document that's currently being printed experience a system lockup," an engineer might announce one day. By analyzing the system glitches of its customers en masse, the company hopes to pinpoint problems and devise software patches with much greater efficiency than before.

Second, Microsoft's computers may also react to the information on the spot and send you a dialog box that lets you know about an available fix.

Windows XP did this report-sending, too, but it asked you *each time* a program crashed. In Windows Vista, the report-sending feature was either turned *on* all the time or *off* all the time. In Windows 7 and 8, these automatic connections are once again up to you.

To adjust the settings, open the Start screen. Type *problems* and select Settings under the search box. In the search results, click "Choose how to report problems." There, before you, are the controls for the auto-reporting. You can opt to have Windows check for solutions, check for solutions and report to Microsoft what happened, ask for permission before each sending, or never check for solutions.

This dialog box offers various other privacy controls. For example, you can "Select programs to exclude from reporting." (This one's for you, owners of Music Piracy Plus 4.0.)

For details on Windows's automatic error-reporting system, see page 335.

Here are three ways to do it:

- Invoke the new "three-fingered salute," Ctrl+Shift+Esc.
- Right-click the taskbar and, from the shortcut menu, choose Task Manager.
- Right-click the lower-left corner of the screen; from the secret Utilities menu, choose Task Manager.

In any case, now you see a list of every open program. You should now also realize that the Windows 8 Task Manager has had a serious overhaul; in its freshly opened state, it doesn't let you do anything but (a) double-click a program's name to switch to it, or (b) click a program's name and then hit "End task" to close it.

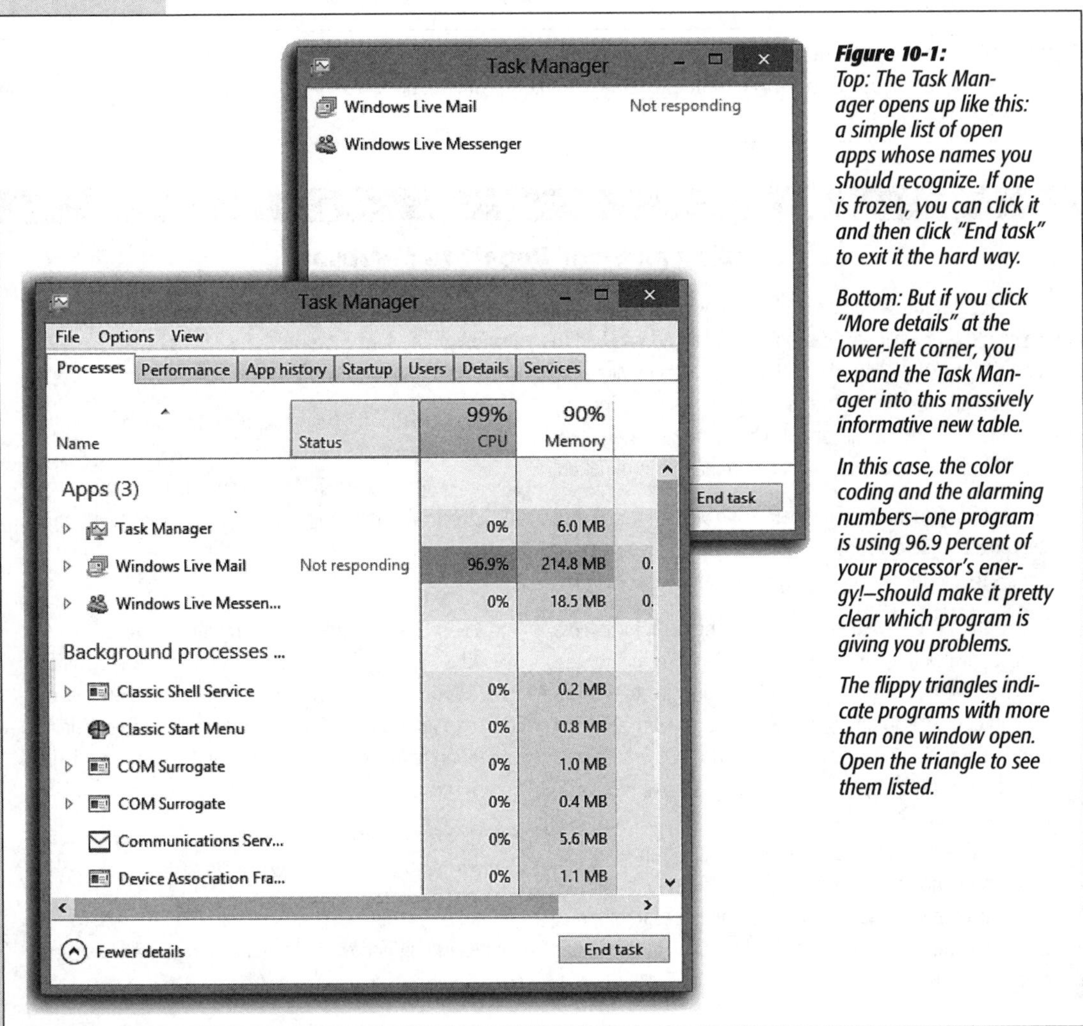

Figure 10-1: *Top: The Task Manager opens up like this: a simple list of open apps whose names you should recognize. If one is frozen, you can click it and then click "End task" to exit it the hard way.*

Bottom: But if you click "More details" at the lower-left corner, you expand the Task Manager into this massively informative new table.

In this case, the color coding and the alarming numbers–one program is using 96.9 percent of your processor's energy!–should make it pretty clear which program is giving you problems.

The flippy triangles indicate programs with more than one window open. Open the triangle to see them listed.

But if you click "More details," then wow, are your nerd genes in for a treat. The Task Manager blossoms into a full-blown spreadsheet of details about all the programs you're running at the moment—including invisible, background programs ("processes") you might not even have known were there. Figure 10-1 shows the Task Manager in both its tiny and expanded states.

The Status column should make clear what you already know: that one of your programs—labeled "Not responding"—is ignoring you.

Tip: Now, "not responding" could just mean "in the middle of crunching away." If the nonresponsive program is some huge mega-hog and you just chose some command that's going to take awhile, give it a chance to finish before you conclude that it's locked up.

Shutting down the troublesome program is fairly easy; just click its name and then click the "End task" button.

Note: In the old Task Manager, you sometimes got yet another dialog box at this point, telling you, "This program is not responding." You had to click the End Now button to put it away for good.

That no longer happens. "End task" kills a program completely and instantly–and no longer gives you the chance to save unsaved changes.

If you click "More details," you expand the Task Manager into its newly beefed-up state, shown at bottom in Figure 10-1. Clearly, this mode is intended for power geeks only; if you're among them, then hours of fun await you. Read on.

Note: TileWorld apps are listed here, too, but Microsoft says they never slow down your PC and never need task-managing. When a TileWorld app is in the background, it goes totally silent, uses no resources, and eventually exits automatically if you don't use it for awhile.

Heat Map

Microsoft noticed that people often sorted the Task Manager by CPU (how much of your processor's attention is dedicated to each program) or memory (how much memory each program is using). When your computer slows down, it's often because one out-of-control program is hogging the system—and that's how you can figure out which one.

The new Task Manager's "heat map" effect saves you the trouble. The "heat map" uses darker shades of color to flag the programs that are using the most computer resources—not just CPU cycles or memory, but also network bandwidth and disk space. In other words, you can now spot the resource hogs without having to sort the columns or even understanding the numbers (for example, Microsoft Word in Figure 10-1).

Similarly, when one resource is being gobbled up disproportionately, Task Manager darkens that column title (CPU, Memory, Disk, Network) to get your attention. If your computer has been slowing down, check that column first.

Tip: The new Task Manager tries to use plain-English names for the programs and processes it displays–a welcome change from the old days of cryptic programmery names. But you'll still see unfamiliar items listed here. Fortunately, you can right-click anything in the list and, from the shortcut menu, choose "Search online." You'll go directly to a page of Bing or Google search results to read about the mystery item.

The Other Tabs

The Task Manager offers seven tabs now. They're crammed with information that's either useful or useless, depending on just how technical a person you are. Here's a crash course:

- **Processes.** This is the tab that most people visit most often. It lists all programs and processes (background operations) that are running right now.

Tip: Click a column heading to sort the table by that criterion. Right-click a column heading to get a choice of additional columns that you can add–including PID, the process ID (a favorite of geekheads).

- **Performance.** Cool graphs—one each for CPU (processor time), Memory, Disk, and Network. Shows how much you've got, how much is in use, and what the trend is.
- **App history.** A table that shows how much data each of your programs and apps has used for the current user account. This table could tell you all kinds of things about, for example, what your kid's been doing on the family PC. (The Metered column means "cellular connections." Since an app that uses a lot of data over cellular connections costs you money, this is a critical tool in keeping your bills under control.)
- **Startup.** Shows you exactly which items are starting up automatically when you turn on the computer. (This is information that used to require a trip to the user-unfriendly MSCONFIG program.) Some you may not even know about.

  If your computer seems to be taking an unusually long time to start up, here's the first place you should check; Task Manager even shows you the impact of each item on your startup process.

  You can turn one off by right-clicking it; from the shortcut menu, choose Disable. You can also read about something unfamiliar by choosing "Search online" from the shortcut menu.
- **Users.** If you've set up multiple user accounts on this machine, this little table shows which are logged in right now, and how much of the computer's resources they're using.
- **Details.** Stand back. This massive, nearly infinitely expandable table looks like a space shuttle cockpit. It's a far more detailed version of the Processes tab; for example, it uses the true process names instead of the plain-English ones. You start out with seven columns, but you can add many more; right-click any column header, and from the shortcut menu, choose "Select columns."

- **Services.** This table lists all of Windows' behind-the-scenes "services"—background features that run all the time. (For example, the indexing of your hard drive, to keep your Search feature up to date, is a service. So are background printing, the computer's clock if you've told it to set itself, and Windows Messenger, which stays alert in case someone tries to instant-message you.)

Tip: On any of these tabs, you can drag columns horizontally to move them around.

Saving Documents

In Calculator, Solitaire, and most TileWorld apps, you don't actually create any documents; when you close the window, no trace of your work remains.

Most desktop programs, however, are designed to create *documents*—files you can reopen for further editing, send to other people, back up on another disk, and so on.

That's why these programs offer File→Save and File→Open commands, which let you preserve the work you've done, saving it onto the hard drive as a new file icon so you can return to it later.

Figure 10-2: *The Save box may appear in either of two forms: the full-blown, File Explorerish view shown at top, or the collapsed form shown at bottom.*

Use the Hide Folders button to collapse the big version, or the Browse Folders button to expand the collapsed version.

Type a name, choose a folder location, and specify the format for the file you're saving.

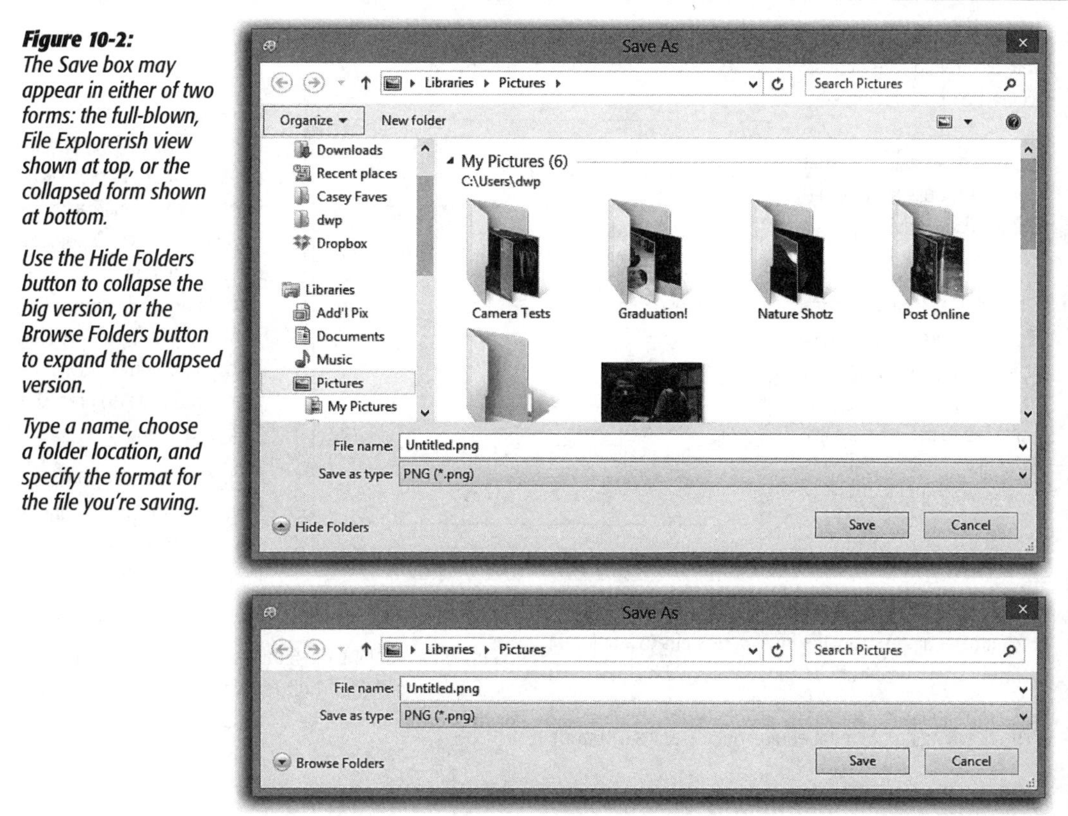

The Save Dialog Box

When you choose File→Save for the first time, you're asked where you want the new document stored on your hard drive (Figure 10-2). These days, this Save As dialog box is a *full Explorer window,* complete with taskbar, Navigation pane, search box, a choice of views (Icon/List/Details), and an Organize menu. All the skills you've picked up working at the desktop come into play here; you can even delete a file or folder right from within the Save or Open box. (The Delete command is in the Organize menu.)

To give it a try, open any Windows program that has a Save or Export command—WordPad, for example. (Not all programs from other software companies have updated their Save dialog boxes yet.) Type a couple of words and then choose File→Save. The Save As dialog box appears (Figure 10-2).

Saving into Your Documents Folder

The first time you use the File→Save command to save a file, Windows suggests putting your newly created document in your Documents library.

UP TO SPEED

Dialog Box Basics

To the delight of the powerful Computer Keyboard Lobby, you can manipulate almost every element of a Windows dialog box by pressing keys on the keyboard. If you're among those who feel that using the mouse to do something takes longer, you're in luck.

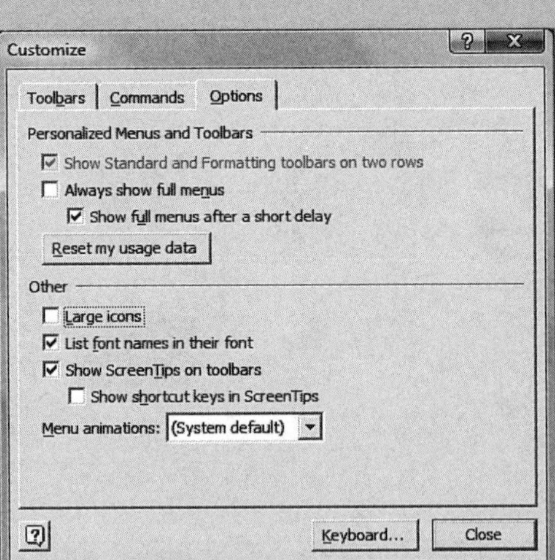

The rules for navigating a dialog box are simple: Press Tab to jump from one set of options to another, or Shift+Tab to move backward. If the dialog box has multiple *tabs,* like the one shown here, press Ctrl+Tab to "click" the next tab, or Ctrl+*Shift*+Tab to "click" the previous one.

Each time you press Tab, the PC's *focus* shifts to a different control or set of controls. Windows reveals which element has the focus by using text highlighting (if it's a text box or drop-down menu), or a dotted-line outline (if it's a button). In the illustration shown here, the "Large icons" checkbox has the focus.

Once you've highlighted a button or checkbox, simply press the space bar to "click" it. If you've opened a drop-down list or a set of mutually exclusive *option buttons* (or *radio buttons*) then press the ↑ or ↓ keys. (Once you've highlighted a drop-down list's name, you can also press the F4 key to open it.)

Each dialog box also contains larger, rectangular buttons at the bottom (OK and Cancel, for example).

Efficiency fans should remember that tapping the Enter key is always the equivalent of clicking the *default* button–the one with the darkened or thickened outline (the Close button in the illustration here). And pressing Esc almost always means Cancel (or "Close this box").

For many people, this is an excellent suggestion. First, it means your file won't accidentally fall into some deeply nested folder where you'll never see it again. Instead, it will be waiting in the Documents library, which is very difficult to lose.

Second, it's very easy to make a backup copy of your important documents if they're all in one folder. There's a third advantage, too: The Documents folder is also what Windows displays whenever you use a program's File→*Open* command. In other words, the Documents library saves you time both when *creating* a new file and when *retrieving* it.

Tip: If the Documents library becomes cluttered, feel free to make subfolders inside it to hold your various projects. You could even create a different default folder in Documents for each program.

Saving into Other Folders

Still, the now-familiar Navigation pane, address bar, and search box also appear in the Save dialog box. (The Nav pane appears only in the Save box's expanded form; see Figure 10-2.) You always have direct access to other places where you might want to save a newly created file.

All the usual keyboard shortcuts apply: Alt+↑, for example, to open the folder that *contains* the current one. There's even a "New folder" button on the toolbar, so you can generate a new, empty folder in the current list of files and folders. Windows asks you to name it.

In fact, if on some project you often find yourself having to navigate to some deeply buried folder, press ⊞+D to duck back to the desktop, open any Explorer window, and drag the folder to your Favorites list. From now on, you'll have quick access to it from the Save dialog box.

GEM IN THE ROUGH

Why You See Document Names in the Save Dialog Box

In the Save dialog box, Windows displays a list of both folders *and documents* (documents that match the kind you're about to save, that is).

It's easy to understand why *folders* appear here: so you can double-click one if you want to save your document inside it. But why do *documents* appear here? After all, you can't very well save a document into another document.

Documents are listed here so you can perform one fairly obscure stunt: If you click a document's name, Windows copies its name into the "File name" text box at the bottom of the window. That's a useful shortcut if you want to *replace* an existing document with the new one you're saving. By saving a new file with the same name as the existing one, you force Windows to overwrite it (after asking your permission, of course).

This trick also reduces the amount of typing needed to save a document to which you've assigned a different version number. For example, if you click the "Thesis Draft 3.1" document in the list, Windows copies that name into the "File name" text box; doing so keeps it separate from earlier drafts. To save your new document as "Thesis Draft 3.2," you need to change only one character (change the 1 to 2) before clicking the Save button.

Tip: Many programs let you specify a different folder as the proposed location for saved (and reopened) files. In Microsoft Word, for example, you can change the default folders for the documents you create, where your clip art is stored, and so on.

Navigating the List by Keyboard

When the Save As dialog box first appears, the "File name" text box is automatically selected so you can type a name for the newly created document.

But a Windows dialog box is elaborately rigged for keyboard control. In addition to the standard Tab/space bar controls, a few special keys work only within the list of files and folders. Start by pressing Shift+Tab (to shift Windows' attention from the "File name" text box to the list of files and folders) and then do the following:

- Press various letter keys to highlight the corresponding file and folder icons. To highlight the Program Files folder, for example, you could type *PR*. (If you type too slowly, your keystrokes are interpreted as separate initiatives—highlighting first the People folder and then the Rodents folder, for example.)
- Press the Page Up or Page Down keys to scroll the list up or down. Press Home or End to highlight the top or bottom item in the list.
- Press the ↑ or ↓ keys to highlight successive icons in the list.
- When a folder (or file) is highlighted, you can open it by pressing the Enter key (or double-clicking its icon, or clicking the Open button).

The File Format Drop-Down Menu

The Save As dialog box in many programs offers a menu of file formats (usually referred to as file *types*) below or next to the "File name" text box. Use this drop-down menu when preparing a document for use by somebody whose computer doesn't have the same software.

For example, if you've typed something in Microsoft Word, you can use this menu to generate a Web page document or a Rich Text Format document that you can open with almost any standard word processor or page-layout program.

Closing Documents

You close a document window just as you'd close any window: by clicking the close box (marked by ☒) in the upper-right corner of the window, by double-clicking the top-left corner, by clicking the ☒ in its taskbar icon's preview thumbnail, or by pressing Alt+F4. If you've done any work to the document since the last time you saved it, Windows offers a "Save changes?" dialog box as a reminder.

Sometimes closing the window also exits the application, and sometimes the application remains running, even with no document windows open. And in a few *really* bizarre cases, it's possible to exit an application (like Windows Mail) while a document window (an email message) remains open on the screen, lingering and abandoned!

The Open Dialog Box

To reopen a document you've already saved and named, you can pursue any of these avenues:

- Open your Documents library (or whichever folder contains the saved file). Double-click the file's icon.
- If you've opened the document recently, choose its name from the taskbar's jump list.
- If you're already in the program that created the document, choose File→Open. (Or check the bottom of the File menu, where many programs add a list of recently opened files.)
- Type the document's path and name into the Run dialog (⊞+R) or the address bar. (You can also browse for it.)

The Open dialog box looks almost identical to the Save As dialog box. Once again, you start out by perusing the contents of your Documents folder; once again, the dialog box otherwise behaves exactly like an Explorer window. For example, you can press Backspace to back *out* of a folder you've opened.

When you've finally located the file you want to open, double-click it or highlight it (from the keyboard, if you like), and then press Enter.

Most people don't encounter the Open dialog box nearly as often as the Save As dialog box. That's because Windows offers many more convenient ways to *open* a file (double-clicking its icon, choosing its name from the Start→Documents command, and so on), but only a single way to *save* a new file.

Moving Data Between Documents

You can't paste a picture into your Web browser, and you can't paste MIDI music into your word processor. But you can put graphics into your word processor, paste movies into your database, insert text into Photoshop, and combine a surprising variety of seemingly dissimilar kinds of data. And you can transfer text from Web pages, email messages, and word processing documents to other email and word processing files; in fact, that's one of the most frequently performed tasks in all of computing.

Cut, Copy, and Paste

Most experienced PC users have learned to quickly trigger the Cut, Copy, and Paste commands from the keyboard—without even thinking.

Bear in mind that you can cut and copy highlighted material in any of three ways. First, you can use the Cut and Copy commands in the Edit menu; second, you can press Ctrl+X (for Cut) or Ctrl+C (for Copy); and third, you can right-click the highlighted material and, from the shortcut menu, choose Cut or Copy (Figure 10-3).

When you do so, Windows memorizes the highlighted material, stashing it on an invisible Clipboard. If you choose Copy, nothing visible happens; if you choose Cut, the highlighted material disappears from the original document.

Pasting copied or cut material, once again, is something you can do either from a menu (choose Edit→Paste), from the shortcut menu (right-click and choose Paste), or from the keyboard (press Ctrl+V).

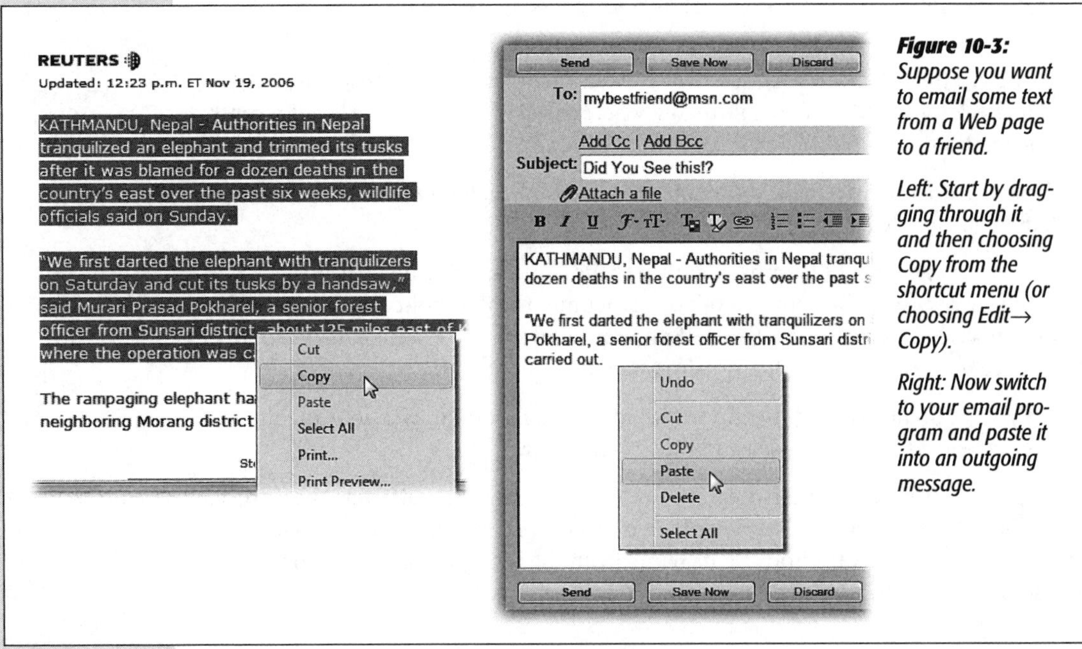

***Figure 10-3:** Suppose you want to email some text from a Web page to a friend.*

Left: Start by dragging through it and then choosing Copy from the shortcut menu (or choosing Edit→Copy).

Right: Now switch to your email program and paste it into an outgoing message.

The most recently cut or copied material remains on your Clipboard even after you paste, making it possible to paste the same blob repeatedly. Such a trick can be useful when, for example, you've designed a business card in your drawing program and want to duplicate it enough times to fill a letter-sized printout. On the other hand, whenever you next copy or cut something, whatever was previously on the Clipboard is lost forever.

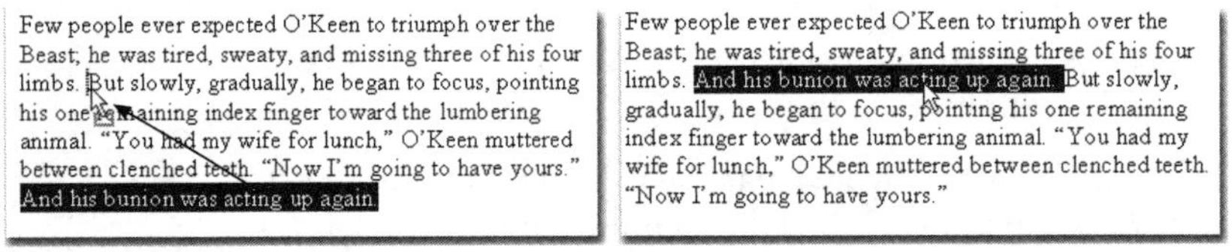

Few people ever expected O'Keen to triumph over the Beast; he was tired, sweaty, and missing three of his four limbs. But slowly, gradually, he began to focus, pointing his one remaining index finger toward the lumbering animal. "You had my wife for lunch," O'Keen muttered between clenched teeth. "Now I'm going to have yours." And his bunion was acting up again.

Few people ever expected O'Keen to triumph over the Beast; he was tired, sweaty, and missing three of his four limbs. And his bunion was acting up again. But slowly, gradually, he began to focus, pointing his one remaining index finger toward the lumbering animal. "You had my wife for lunch," O'Keen muttered between clenched teeth. "Now I'm going to have yours."

***Figure 10-4:** You can drag highlighted text (left) to another place in the document–or to a different window or program (right).*

Drag-and-Drop

As useful and popular as it is, the Copy/Paste routine doesn't win any awards for speed; after all, it requires four steps. In many cases, you can replace it with the far more direct (and enjoyable) drag-and-drop method. Figure 10-4 illustrates how it works.

Tip: To drag highlighted material offscreen, drag the cursor until it approaches the top or bottom edge of the window. The document scrolls automatically; as you approach the destination, jerk the mouse away from the edge of the window to stop the scrolling.

Several of the built-in Windows programs work with the drag-and-drop technique, including WordPad and Mail. Most popular commercial programs offer the drag-and-drop feature, too, including email programs and word processors, Microsoft Office programs, and so on.

Note: Scrap files–bits of text or graphics that you can drag to the desktop for reuse later–no longer exist in Windows.

As illustrated in Figure 10-4, drag-and-drop is ideal for transferring material between windows or between programs. It's especially useful when you've already copied something valuable to your Clipboard, since drag-and-drop doesn't involve (and doesn't erase) the Clipboard.

FREQUENTLY ASKED QUESTION

When Formatting Is Lost

How come pasted text doesn't always look the same as what I copied?

When you copy text from Internet Explorer, for example, and then paste it into another program, such as Word, you may be alarmed to note that the formatting of that text (bold, italic, font size, font color, and so on) doesn't reappear intact. In fact, the pasted material may not even inherit the current font settings in the word processor. There could be several reasons for this problem.

First, not every program *offers* text formatting–Notepad among them. And the Copy command in some programs (such as Web browsers) doesn't pick up the formatting along with the text. So when you copy something from Internet Explorer and paste it into Word or WordPad, you may get plain, unformatted text. (There is some good news along these lines, however. Word maintains formatting pasted from the latest Internet Explorer.)

Finally, a note on *text wrapping*. Thanks to limitations built into the architecture of the Internet, email messages aren't like word processor documents. The text doesn't flow continuously from one line of a paragraph to the next, reflowing as you adjust the window size. Instead, email programs insert a press of the Enter key at the end of each line *within* a paragraph.

Most of the time, you don't even notice that your messages consist of dozens of one-line "paragraphs." When you see them in the email program, you can't tell the difference. But if you paste an email message into a word processor, the difference becomes painfully apparent–especially if you then attempt to adjust the margins.

To fix the page, delete the invisible carriage return at the end of each line. (Veteran PC users sometimes use the word processor's search-and-replace function for this purpose.) Or, if you just need a quick look, reduce the point size (or widen the margin) until the text no longer breaks oddly.

Its most popular use, however, is rearranging the text in a single document. In, say, Word or WordPad, you can rearrange entire sections, paragraphs, sentences, or even individual letters, just by dragging them—a terrific editing technique.

Tip: Using drag-and-drop to move highlighted text within a document also deletes the text from its original location. By pressing Ctrl as you drag, however, you make a *copy* of the highlighted text.

Export/Import

When it comes to transferring large chunks of information from one program to another—especially address books, spreadsheet cells, and database records—none of the data-transfer methods described so far in this chapter does the trick. For such purposes, use the Export and Import commands found in the File menu of almost every database, spreadsheet, email, and address-book program.

These Export/Import commands aren't part of Windows, so the manuals or help screens of the applications in question should be your source for instructions. For now, however, the power and convenience of this feature are worth noting. Because of these commands, your four years' worth of collected names and addresses in, say, an old address-book program can find its way into a newer program, such as Mozilla Thunderbird, in a matter of minutes.

Speech Recognition

For years, there's been quite a gulf between the promise of computer speech recognition (as seen on *Star Trek*) and the reality (as seen just about everywhere else). You say "oxymoron"; it types "ax a moron." (Which is often just what you feel like doing, frankly.)

Microsoft has had a speech-recognition department for years. But until recently, it never got the funding and corporate backing it needed to do a really bang-up job.

The speech recognition in today's Windows, however, is another story. It can't match the accuracy of its chief rival, Dragon NaturallySpeaking, but you might be amazed to discover how elegant its design is now, and how useful it can be to anyone who can't, or doesn't like to, type.

In short, Speech Recognition lets you not only *control* your PC by voice—open programs, click buttons, click Web links, and so on—but also *dictate text* a heck of a lot faster than you can type.

To make this all work, you need a PC with a microphone. The Windows Speech Recognition program can handle just about any kind of mike, even the one built into your laptop's case. But a regular old headset mike—"anything that costs over $20 or so," says Microsoft—will give you the best accuracy.

Take the Tutorial

The easiest way to fire up Speech Recognition for the first time is to open the Start screen. Type *speech*. In the search results, click "Windows Speech Recognition."

The first time you open Speech Recognition, you arrive at a very slick, very impressive full-screen tutorial/introduction, featuring a 20-something model in, judging by the gauzy whiteness, what appears to be heaven.

Click your way through the screens. Along the way, you're asked to do the following:

- **Specify what kind of microphone you have.** Headset, desktop, array, or built-in?
- **Read a sample sentence,** about how much Peter loves speech recognition, so your PC can gauge the microphone's volume.
- **Give permission to Windows to study your documents and email collection.** Needless to say, there's no human rooting through your stuff, and none of what Speech Recognition finds is reported back to Microsoft. But granting this permission is a great way to improve your ultimate accuracy, since the kinds of vocabulary and turns of phrase you actually use in your day-to-day work will be built right into Speech Recognition's understanding of your voice.
- **Print the reference card.** This card is critical when you're first learning how to operate Windows by voice. Truth is, however, you don't really need to print it. The same information appears in this chapter, and you can always call the reference card up on the screen by saying into your microphone, "What can I say?"
- **Practice.** The tutorial is excellent; it'll take you about half an hour to complete. It teaches you how to dictate and how to operate buttons, menus, windows, programs, and so on.

  But there's another, better reason to try the tutorial: At the outset, Windows is just *simulating* its responses to what you say. But behind the scenes, it's actually studying your real utterances, learning about your voice, and shaping your voice profile. This, in other words, is the "voice training" session you ordinarily have to perform with commercial dictation programs.

Now you're ready to roll. Operating Windows by voice entails knowing three sets of commands:

- Controlling Speech Recognition itself.
- Controlling Windows and its programs.
- Dictating.

The following sections cover these techniques one at a time.

Controlling Windows Speech Recognition

Slip on your headset, open Windows Speech Recognition, and have a gander at these all-important spoken commands:

- **"Start listening"/"Stop listening."** These commands tell your PC to start and stop listening to you. That's important, because you don't want it to interpret everything you say as a command. It would not be so great if it tried to act when you said to your roommate, "Hey, Chris, close the window."

So say, "Start listening" to turn on your mike—you see the microphone button on the Speech palette (Figure 10-5) darken. Say "Stop listening" when you have to take a phone call.

Tip: Once you've opened the Speech Recognition program, you can hit a keystroke to turn listening on and off instead. That key combo is Ctrl+⊞. Get it? "Control Windows"?

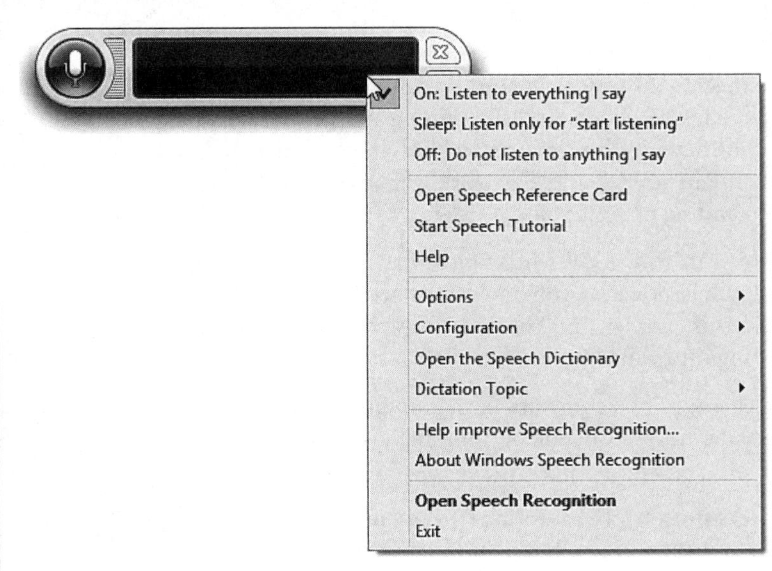

Figure 10-5:
The Speech palette is how Windows holds up its end of the conversation. If it doesn't understand something you said, for example, its text says, "What was that?" The Speech shortcut menu opens when you say "Show Speech Options." It's as though you right-clicked the little palette.

- **"What can I say?"** This one's incredibly important. If you can't figure out how to make Windows do something, look it up by saying this. You get the Speech Recognition page of the Windows Help system, complete with a collapsible list of the things you can say.
- **"Show Speech Options."** This command opens the shortcut menu for the Speech palette, as shown in Figure 10-5. From this menu, you can leap into further training, open the "What can I say?" card, go to the Speech Recognition Web site, and so on.
- **"Hide Speech Recognition"/"Show Speech Recognition"** hides or shows the Speech palette itself when screen real estate is at a premium.

Controlling Windows and Its Programs

The beauty of controlling Windows by voice is that you don't have to remember what to say; you just say whatever you would click with the mouse.

For example, to open the little Calculator program using the mouse, you'd open the Charms bar, click to go to the Start screen, right-click to open the App bar to get to All Programs, and finally click Calculator. To do the same thing using speech recognition, you just *say*, "Start Calculator."

Here's the cheat sheet for manipulating programs. In this list, any word in *italics* is meant as an example (and other examples that work just as well are in parentheses):

- "Start *Calculator* (Word, Excel, Internet Explorer…)." Opens the program you named, without your having to touch the mouse. Super convenient.
- "Switch to *Word* (Excel, Internet Explorer…)." Switches to the program you named.
- "*File. Open.*" You operate menus by saying whatever you would have clicked with the mouse. For example, say "Edit" to open the Edit menu, then "Select All" to choose that command, and so on.
- "*Print* (Cancel, Desktop…)." You can also click any button (or any tab name in a dialog box) by saying its name.
- "*Contact us* (Archives, Home page…)." You can click any link on a Web page just by saying its name.
- "Double-click *Recycle Bin*." You can tell Windows to "double-click" or "right-click" anything you see.

GEM IN THE ROUGH

Mousegrid

The voice commands described in this section are all well and good when it comes to clicking onscreen objects. But what about *dragging* them?

When you say the word "Mousegrid," Speech Recognition superimposes an enormous 3 × 3 grid on your screen, its squares numbered 1 through 9.

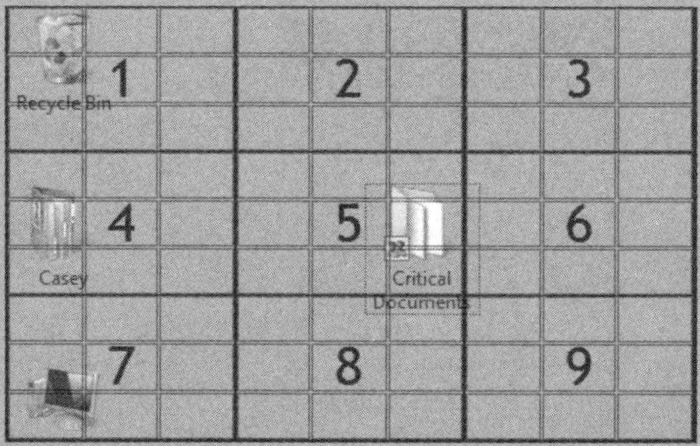

Say "Five" and a new, much smaller 3 × 3 grid, also numbered, appears in the space previously occupied by the 5 square. You can keep shrinking the grid in this way until you've pinpointed a precise spot on the screen.

Dragging something—say, an icon across the desktop—is a two-step process.

First, use Mousegrid to home in on the exact spot on the screen where the icon lies; on your last homing-in, say, "Four mark." (In this example, the icon you want lies within the 4 square. "Mark" means "This is what I'm going to want to drag.")

When you say "mark," the Mousegrid springs back to the full-screen size; now you're supposed to home in on the *destination* point for your drag. Repeat the grid-shrinking exercise—but in the last step say, "Seven click." Watch in amazement as Windows magically grabs the icon at the "mark" position and drags it to the "click" position.

You can use Mousegrid as a last resort for *any* kind of click or drag when the other techniques (like saying button or menu names, or saying, "Show numbers") don't quite cut it.

- "Go to *Subject* (Address, Body…)." In an email message, Web browser, or dialog box, "Go to" puts the insertion point into the text box you name. "Address," for example, means the address bar.
- "*Close* that." Closes the frontmost window. Also "Minimize that," "Maximize that," "Restore that."
- "Scroll *up* (down, left, right)." Scrolls the window. You can say "up," "down," "left," or "right," and you can also append any number from one to 20 to indicate how many lines: "Scroll down 10."
- "Press *F* (Shift+F, capital B, down arrow, X three times…)." Makes Windows press the key you named.

Tip: You don't have to say "press" before certain critical keys: Delete, Home, End, Space, Tab, Enter, Backspace. Just say the key's name: "Tab."

Show numbers

It's great to know you can click any button or tab by saying its name. But what if you don't *know* its name? What if it's some cryptic little icon on a toolbar? You can't exactly say, "Click the little thing that looks like a guy putting his head between two rollers."

For this purpose, Microsoft has created a clever command called "Show numbers." When you say that, the program overlays *every clickable thing* with superimposed colorful numbers; see Figure 10-6.

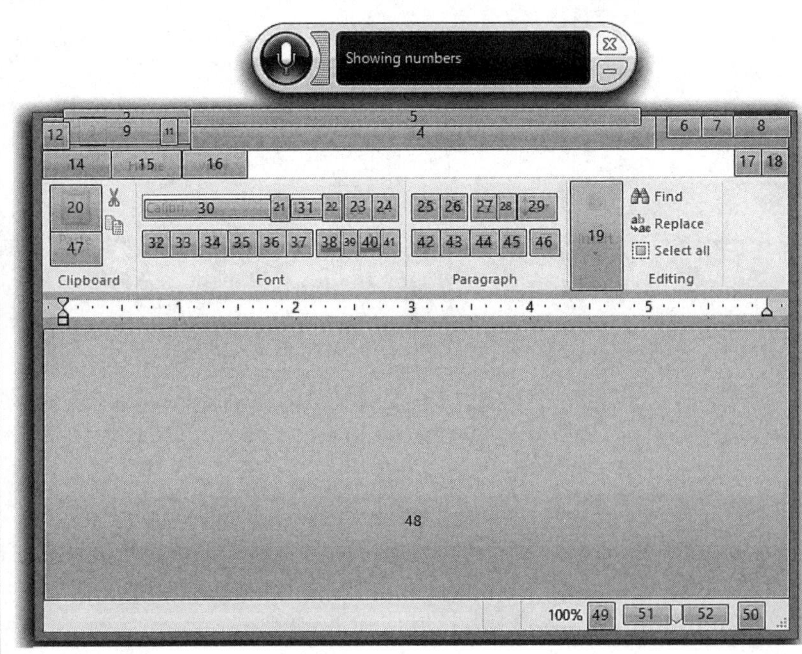

Figure 10-6: *When you say a number, that number turns green and changes into an OK logo—your clue that you must now say "OK" to confirm the selection. (You can run these utterances together without pausing—for example, "Three OK.") Not all programs respond to the "Show numbers" command, alas.*

The numbers appear automatically if there's more than one button of the same name on the screen, too—several Settings buttons in a dialog box, for example. Say, "One OK."

Tip: This trick also works great on Web pages. Say "Show numbers" to see a number label superimposed on every clickable element of the page.

Controlling Dictation

The real Holy Grail for speech recognition, of course, is *dictation*—you speak, and Windows transcribes your words, typing them into any document. (This feature is especially important on tablet PCs that don't have keyboards.)

Windows' dictation accuracy isn't as good as, say, Dragon NaturallySpeaking's. But it's a close second, it's free, and it's a lot of fun.

Figure 10-7: *You make your corrections in the Alternates panel. It shows a numbered list of other possible interpretations of what you said. To choose one of these alternates, say its number and then OK (no pause needed)—for example, "Two OK."*

It's also very easy. You just talk—at regular speed, into any program where you can type. The only real difference is that you have to *say* the punctuation. You know: "Dear Mom (comma, new line), How are things going (question mark)? Can't believe I'll be home for Thanksgiving in only 24 more weeks (exclamation mark)!"

Correcting errors

Sooner or later—probably sooner—Speech Recognition is going to misunderstand you and type out the wrong thing. It's very important that you correct such glitches—for two reasons. First, you don't want your boss/family/colleagues to think you're incoherent. Second, each time you make a correction, Windows *learns*. It won't make that mistake again. Over time, over hundreds of corrections, Speech Recognition gets more and more accurate.

Suppose, then, that you said, "I enjoyed the ceremony," and Speech Recognition typed out, "I enjoyed this era money." Here's how you'd proceed:

1. **Say, "Correct *this era money.*"**

   Instantly, the Alternates panel pops up (Figure 10-7).

2. **If the correct transcription is among the choices in the list, say its number and then "OK."**

   As noted in Figure 10-7, you don't have to pause before "OK."

Figure 10-8:
Just spell out the word you really wanted: "F-I-S-H," for example. For greater clarity, you can also use the "pilot's alphabet": Alpha, Bravo, Charlie, Delta, and so on–or even "A as in alligator" (any word you like). If it mishears a letter you've spoken, say the number over it ("three") and then repronounce the letter. Say "OK" once you've gotten the word right.

3. **If the correct transcription *doesn't* appear in the list, then speak the correct text again.**

   In this example, you'd say, "the ceremony." Almost always, the version you wanted now appears in the list. Say its number and then "OK."

4. **If the correct transcription *still* doesn't appear in the list, say "Spell it."**

   You arrive at the Spelling panel; see Figure 10-8.

When you finally exit the Alternates panel, Speech Recognition replaces the corrected text *and* learns from its mistake.

More commands

Here are the other things you can say when you're dictating text. The first few are extremely important to learn.

- "Select *next* (previous) *two* (10, 14, 20...) *words* (sentences, paragraphs)." Highlights whatever you just specified—for example, "Select previous five sentences."

  At this point, you're ready to copy, change the font or style, say "Cap that" to capitalize the first words—or just redictate to replace what you wrote.

Tip: If the phrase you want to highlight is long, you can say, "Select *My country* through *land of liberty."* Windows highlights all the text from the first phrase through and including the second one.

- "Correct *ax a moron.*" Highlights the transcribed phrase and opens the Alternates panel, as described above. (You can say a whole phrase or just one word.)
- "Undo." Undoes the last action.
- "Scratch that." Deletes the last thing you dictated. ("Delete that" works, too.)
- "Delete *your stupid parents.*" Instantly deletes the text you identified.

GEM IN THE ROUGH

Text to Speech

The big-ticket item, for sure, is that speech-to-text feature. But Windows can also convert typed text *back* to speech, using a set of voices of its very own.

To hear them, open the Start screen. Type *speech* and select Settings under the search box. In the search results, click "Change text to speech settings." Click Preview Voice to hear the astonishing realism of Microsoft David, the primary voice of Windows (no relation). You can even control his speaking rate using the "Voice speed" slider.

So when can you hear Microsoft David do his stuff? Primarily in Narrator (page 384). If you master the Narrator keyboard shortcuts, David can read back *whatever you want,* like stuff you've written or articles you find on the Web. Why not let him read the morning news to you while you're getting breakfast ready each day?

Tip: If you use commands like "Delete," "Select," "Capitalize," or "Add hyphens to" on a word that occurs more than once in the open window, Speech Recognition doesn't try to guess. It puts colorful numbered squares on every occurrence of that word. Say, "One OK" (or whatever the number is) to tell it *which* occurrence you meant.

- "Go to *little.*" Puts the insertion point right before the word "little."
- "Go after *lamb.*" Puts the insertion point right after the word "lamb."
- "Go to the *start* (end) of the *sentence* (paragraph, document)." Puts the insertion point where you said.
- "Caps." Capitalizes the first letter of the next word you dictate (no pause is necessary). Saying "All caps" puts the next word ENTIRELY in caps.

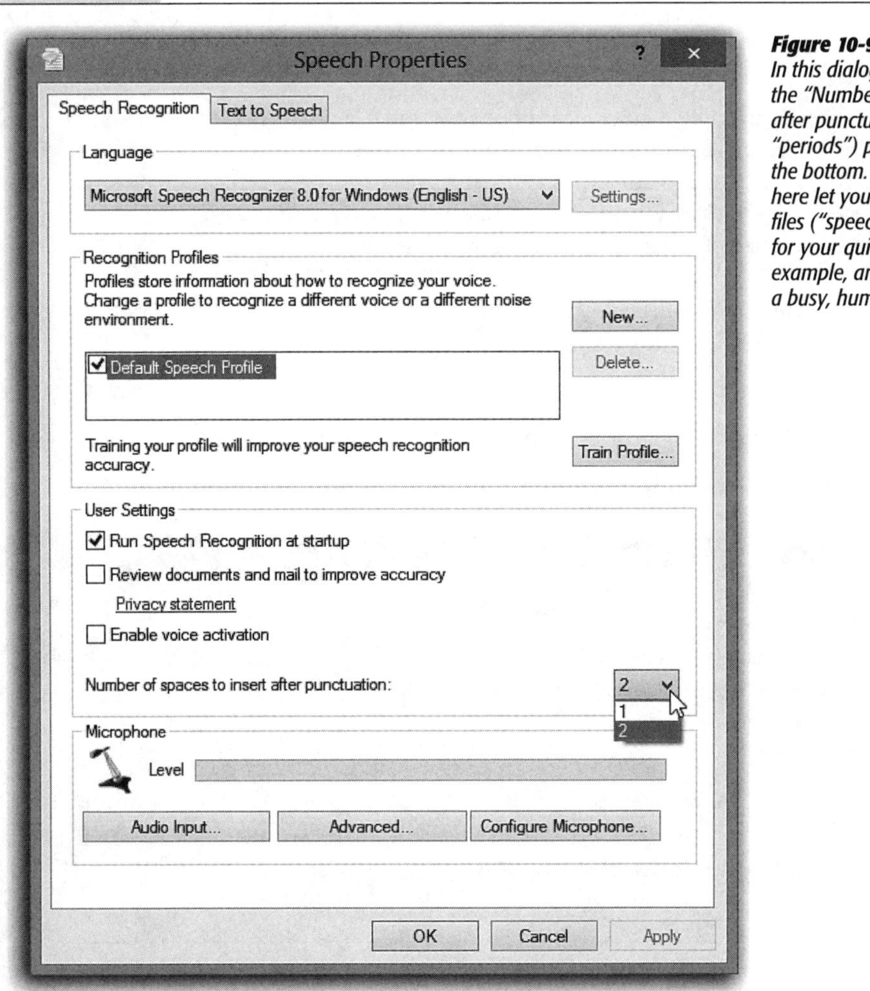

Figure 10-9: *In this dialog box, you can find the "Number of spaces to insert after punctuation" (meaning "periods") pop-up menu near the bottom. The other controls here let you create new voice files ("speech profiles")–one for your quiet home office, for example, and another for use in a busy, humming office.*

- "*Ready* no space *Boost*." Types "ReadyBoost"—no space.
- "He typed the word literal *comma*." The command "literal" tells Speech Recognition to type out the word that follows it ("comma"), rather than transcribing it as a symbol.
- "Add hyphen to *3D*." Puts a hyphen in the word ("3-D").
- "Start typing I, P, C, O, N, F, I, G; stop typing." When you say "Start typing" (and then pause), you enter Typing mode. Now you can spell out anything, letter by letter, in any program on earth. It's a handy way to dictate into programs that don't take dictation well, like PowerPoint and Excel.

Speech recognition tips

There are zillions of secrets, tips, and tricks lurking in speech recognition—but here are a few of the most useful:

- You can teach Speech Recognition new words—unusual last names, oddball terminology—by adding them directly to its dictionary. Say "Show speech options" to open the shortcut menu, and then click (or say), "Open the Speech Dictionary." You're offered the chance to add words, change existing words, or stop certain words from being transcribed.
- When you want to spell out a word, say, "Spell it," and then launch right into the spelling: "F, R, E, A, K, A, Z, O, I, D." You don't have to pause between letters or commands.
- In the Spelling window, say the digit over the wrong letter, and then say, "A," or "Alpha," or "A as in alligator" (or any word that starts with that letter).
- Beginning any utterance with "How do I" opens up Windows Help; the next part of your sentence goes into the search box.
- "Computer" forces the interpretation of your next utterance as a command; "Insert" forces it to be transcribed.
- Out of the box, Speech Recognition puts two spaces after every period—a very 1980s thing to do. Nowadays, that kind of gap looks a little amateurish. Fortunately, you can tell Speech Recognition to use only one space.

  Making this change requires you to visit the little-known Advanced Speech Options dialog box. Open the Start screen. Start typing *speech* until you see "Speech Recognition" in the results list; click it. In the task pane at left, click "Advanced speech options" (Figure 10-9).

Filename Extensions and File Associations

Every operating system needs a mechanism to associate documents with the applications that created them. When you double-click a Microsoft Word document icon, for example, Word launches and opens the document.

In Windows, every document comes complete with a normally invisible *filename extension* (or just *file extension)*—a period followed by a suffix that's usually three letters long.

Here are some common examples:

When you double-click this icon...	**...this program opens it.**
Fishing trip.docx	Microsoft Word
Quarterly results.xlsx	Microsoft Excel
Home page.htm	Internet Explorer
Agenda.wpd	Corel WordPerfect
A home movie.avi	Windows Media Player
Animation.dir	Macromedia Director

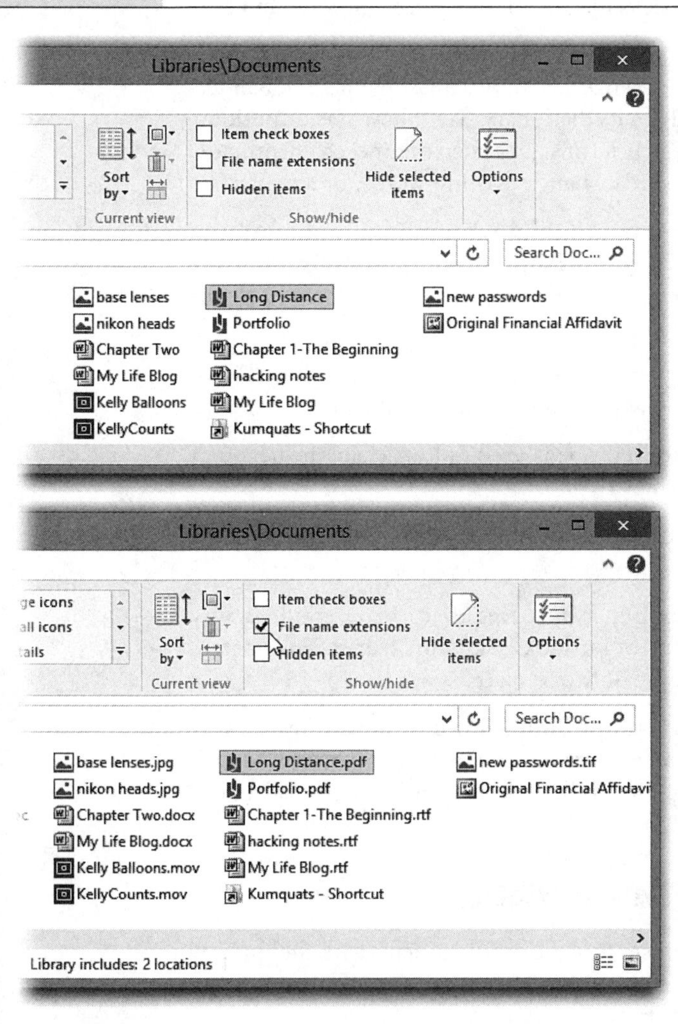

Figure 10-10:
As a rule, Windows shows filename extensions only on files whose extensions it doesn't recognize. The JPEG graphics and Word files at top, for example, don't show their suffixes.

Bottom: You can ask Windows to display all extensions, all the time. Just use the "File name extensions" checkbox on the Ribbon's View tab, indicated by the cursor.

Tip: For an exhaustive list of every file extension on the planet, visit *www.whatis.com*; click the link for "Every file extension in the world."

Behind the scenes, Windows maintains a massive table that lists every extension and the program that "owns" it. More on this in a moment.

Displaying Filename Extensions

It's possible to live a long and happy life without knowing much about these extensions. Because file extensions don't feel very user-friendly, Microsoft designed Windows to *hide* the suffixes on most icons (Figure 10-10). If you're new to Windows, you may never have even seen them.

Some people appreciate the way Windows hides the extensions, because the screen becomes less cluttered and less technical-looking. Others make a good argument for the Windows 3.1 days, when every icon appeared with its suffix.

For example, in a single Explorer window, suppose one day you discover that three icons all seem to have exactly the same name: PieThrower. Only by making filename extensions appear would you discover the answer to the mystery: that one of them is called PieThrower.ini, another is an Internet-based software updater called PieThrower.upd, and the third is the actual PieThrower program, PieThrower.exe.

If you'd rather have Windows reveal the file suffixes on *all* icons, then open an Explorer window. On the Ribbon's View tab, turn on "File name extensions," as shown in Figure 10-10. Now the filename extensions for all icons appear.

Figure 10-11: *Left: If you're pretty sure your PC has a program that can open this mystery file, then give it a little help–click "More options."*

Right: Use this list to select a program for opening the mystery file.

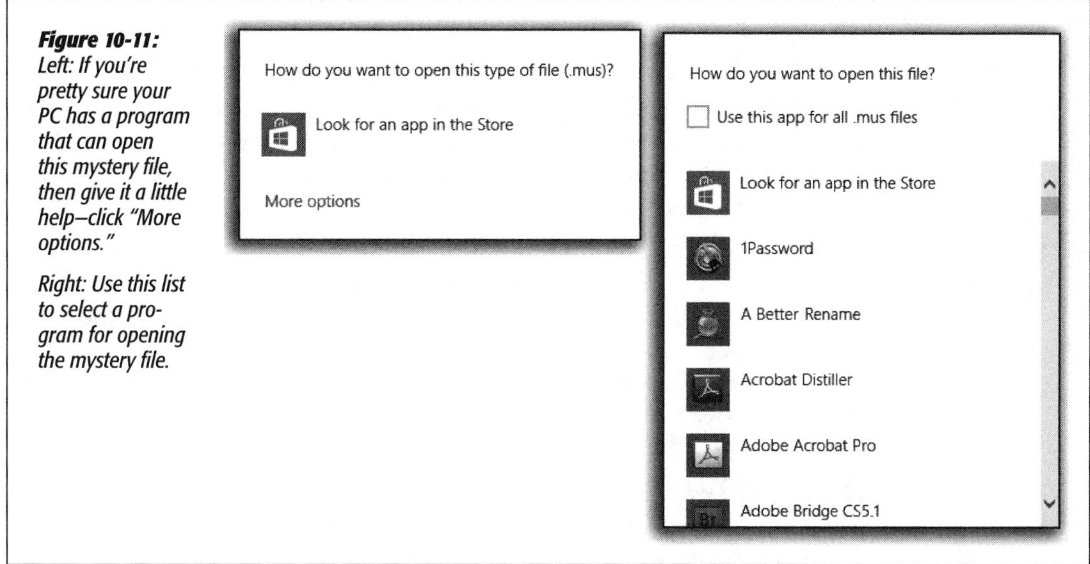

Hooking Up an Unknown File Type

Every now and then, you might try to open a mystery icon—one whose extension is missing, or whose extension Windows doesn't recognize. Maybe you've been sent some weirdo document created by a beekeeper or a banjo transcriber using a program you don't have, or maybe you're opening a document belonging to an old DOS program that doesn't know about the Windows file-association feature. What will happen when you double-click that file?

Windows *asks* you.

Windows offers you two options, shown in the dialog box Figure 10-11. First, it encourages you to go online to the Windows Store in hopes of finding a TileWorld app that can open this file type. Good luck with that.

Usually, you'll want to click "More options." As shown in Figure 10-11 at right, you now see a list of all programs and TileWorld apps that are capable of opening this document. Click the name of the program you want, and then turn on "Use this app for all [mystery filename extension] files," if you like.

Hooking Up a File Extension to a Different Program

Windows comes with several programs that can open text files with the extension *.txt*—Notepad and WordPad, for example. There are also plenty of programs that can open picture files with the extension *.jpg*. So how does Windows decide *which* program to open when you double-click a .txt or .jpg file?

Easy—it refers to its internal database of preferred *default programs* for various file types. But at any time, you can reassign a particular file type (file extension) to a different application. If you've just bought Photoshop, for example, you might want it to open up your JPEG files, rather than the TileWorld app called Photos.

This sort of surgery has always confused beginners. Yet it was important for Microsoft to provide an easy way of reprogramming documents' mother programs; almost everyone ran into programs like RealPlayer that, once installed, "stole" every file association they could. The masses needed a simple way to switch documents back to their preferred programs.

Whether or not the *three* file-association mechanisms described next are actually superior to the *one* old one from Windows versions of old—well, you be the judge.

Tip: The File Types tab of the Folder Options dialog box, once the headquarters of document-to-program relationships, no longer exists in Windows 8.

Method 1: Start with the document

Often, you'll discover a misaligned file-type association the hard way. You double-click a document and the wrong program opens it.

For that reason, Microsoft has added a new way of reprogramming a document—one that starts right in Explorer, with the document itself.

Right-click the icon of the file that needs a new parent program. From the shortcut menu, choose Open With.

If you're just trying to open this document into the new program *this once*, you may be able to choose the new program's name from the Open With submenu (Figure 10-12). Windows doesn't always offer this submenu, however.

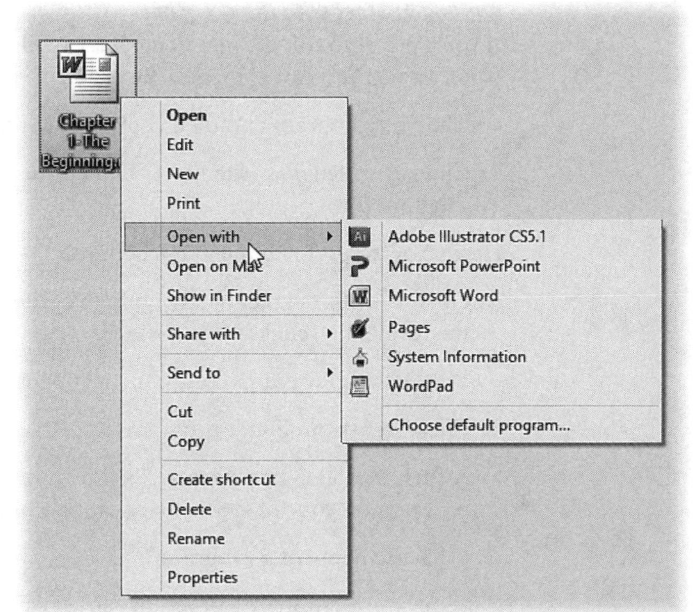

Figure 10-12:
Top: To reassign a document to a new parent program, use its Open With shortcut menu. If you're lucky, you get a submenu of available programs that can open the document.

Bottom: Windows is prepared to show you a list of every program that can open the mystery file. Scroll through the list of installed programs to select the one you want. By turning on the checkbox at the bottom of the dialog box, you create a file association that will handle similar files (those with the same file extension) in the future.

If you choose "Choose default program" from the submenu, or if there's no submenu at all, then the new Open With list appears, as shown in Figure 10-12. It's supposed to list every program on your machine that's capable of opening the document.

And now, a critical decision: Are you trying to make *this document only* open in a different program? Or *all documents of this type?*

If it's just this one, then click the program you want and stop reading. If it's *all* files of this type (all JPEGs, all MP3s, all DOC files…), then also turn on "Use this app for all [filename extension] files" before you click the program name.

You should now be able to double-click the original document—and smile as it opens in the program you requested.

Note: If the program isn't listed, you can go find it yourself. Scroll to the very bottom of the list of proposed apps. If you see "More options," click that. Now scroll to the very bottom again until you see the last item: "Look for another app on this PC." Now you're shown a standard Open File dialog box so that you can peruse the entire contents of your Programs folder on a quest for just the right software.

By the way, it's sometimes useful to associate a particular document type with a program that *didn't* create it. For example, you might prefer that double-clicking a text file created with WordPad should really open into Microsoft Word.

Method 2: Start with the program

If you'd prefer to edit the master database of file associations directly, a special control panel awaits. You can approach the problem from either direction:

- Choose a program and then choose which file types you want it to take over; or
- Choose a filename extension (like .aif or .ico) and then choose a new default program for it.

Here's how to perform the first technique:

1. **Open the Start screen. Start typing *default* until you see "Default Programs" in the results list; click it.**

   The Default Programs control panel opens.

2. **Click "Set your default programs."**

   A curious dialog box appears, as shown in Figure 10-13 at top. It's a list of every program on your machine that's capable of opening multiple file types.

3. **Click the name of a program.**

   For example, suppose a program named FakePlayer 3.0 has performed the dreaded Windows Power Grab, claiming a particular file type for itself without asking you. In fact, suppose it has elected itself King of *All* Audio Files. But you want Windows Media Player to play everything *except* FakePlayer (.fkpl) files.

   In this step, then, you'd click Windows Media Player.

   If you want Media Player to become the default player for *every* kind of music and video file, you'd click "Set this program as default." But if you want it to open only *some* kinds of files, proceed like this:

4. **Click "Choose defaults for this program."**

Now yet another dialog box opens (Figure 10-13, bottom). It lists every file type the selected program knows about.

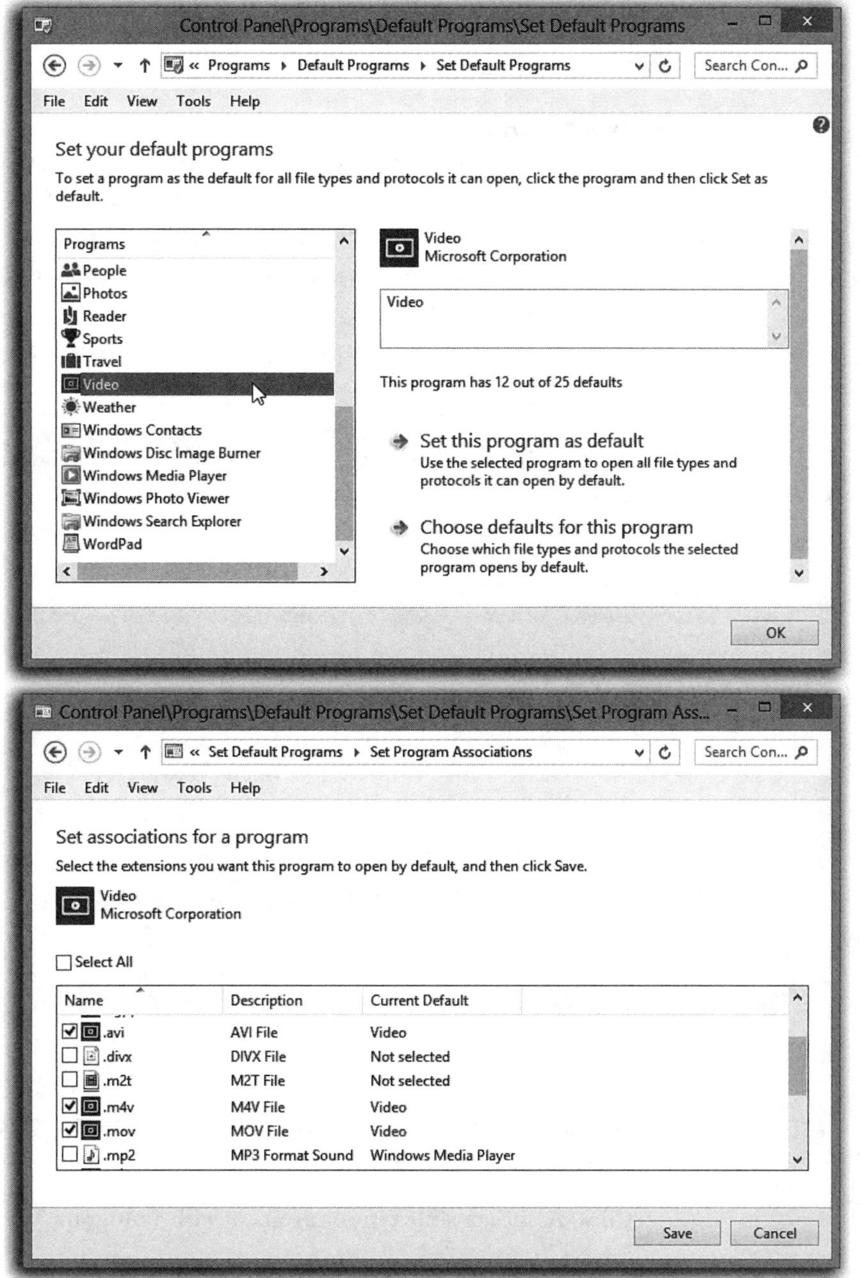

Figure 10-13: *Top: Each software program you install must register the file types it uses. The link between the file type and the program is called an association. This dialog box displays each program on your PC that's capable of opening documents.*

Bottom: If you click "Choose defaults for this program," you get this box, where you can manually inform Windows of which file types the selected program is allowed to open. In this example, the box tells you which types of files will open in the Video TileWorld app when double-clicked.

5. **Turn on the checkboxes of the file types for which you want this program to be the default opener.**

   Of course, this step requires a certain amount of knowledge that comes from experience—how the heck would the average person know what, say, a .wvx file is?—but it's here for the power user's benefit.

6. **Click Save, and then OK.**

Method 3: Start with the file type

Finally, you can approach the file-association problem a third way: by working through a massive alphabetical list of filename extensions (.aca, .acf, .acs, .aif, and so on) and hooking each one up to a program of your choice.

1. **Open the Start screen. Start typing *default* until you see "Default Programs" in the results list; click it.**

   The Default Programs control panel opens (Figure 10-14, top).

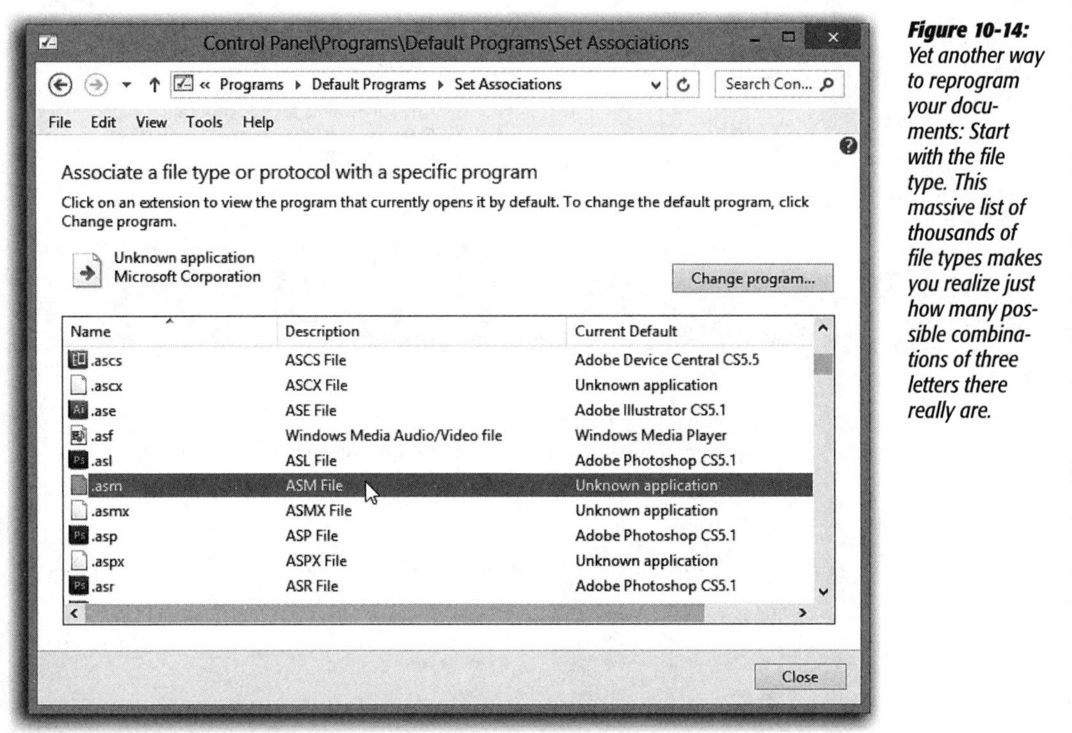

***Figure 10-14:** Yet another way to reprogram your documents: Start with the file type. This massive list of thousands of file types makes you realize just how many possible combinations of three letters there really are.*

2. **Click "Associate a file type or protocol with a program."**

   After a moment, a massive filename extensions list opens.

3. **Select the filename extension you want, and then click "Change program."**

   Now the Open With dialog box appears (the same one shown in Figure 10-12).

FREQUENTLY ASKED QUESTION

Program Access and Defaults

OK, I've just barely understood your description of the control panel where I can hook up documents to programs or programs to documents. So what, exactly, is this other *link in that panel, called "Set program access and computer defaults?"*

Well, it's kind of a long story.

In its 2002 agreement with the U.S. Department of Justice, Microsoft agreed to give other companies a fighting chance at competing with programs like Internet Explorer, Outlook Express, and Windows Media Player.

If you open the Default Programs applet and click "Set program access and computer defaults," you get the dialog box shown here. After you authenticate yourself, you're offered three or four options:

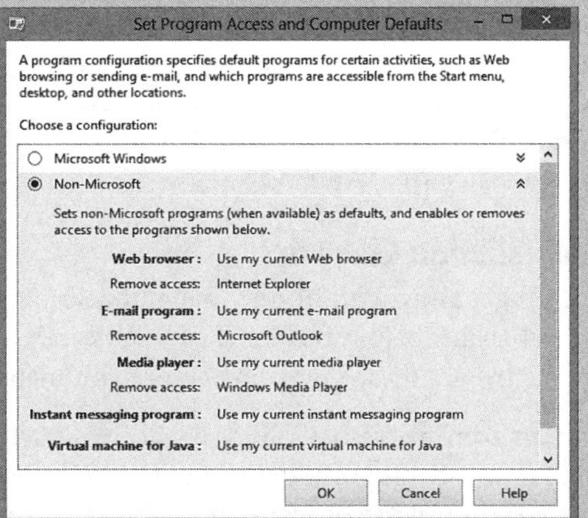

Microsoft Windows means, "Use all of Microsoft's utility programs, as always." You're saying you prefer Microsoft's Web browser (Internet Explorer), music/video player (Windows Media Player), and instant messaging program (Windows Messenger).

Selecting this option doesn't *prevent* you from using other browsers, email programs, and so on—you can still find them listed on the Start screen's All Programs list. But this option does put the Internet Explorer and Windows Media Player icons, for example, into prime positions on the Start screen for quick and easy access.

Non-Microsoft means, "Use *anything* but Microsoft's programs! Instead, use Netscape Navigator, Eudora, RealPlayer, Sun's Java, or whatever—just nothing from Microsoft."

You should install your preferred alternate programs *before* selecting this option. Otherwise, the only programs this feature "sees" are Microsoft programs, which would make selecting this option a tad pointless.

As with the "Microsoft" option, choosing this option places your preferred programs' icons prominently on your Start screen. But this option also *removes access* to the corresponding Microsoft programs. If you choose a non-Microsoft program as your browser, for example, Internet Explorer disappears completely from your PC.

Microsoft's programs aren't really gone—they're just hidden. They pop right back when you choose the "Microsoft Windows" option, or when you choose Custom and then click the associated "Enable access to this program" checkbox. Just remember to click OK to apply your changes.

Computer Manufacturer means, "Use whatever programs are recommended by Dell" (or whoever made the PC and signed deals with AOL, Real, and so on). This option doesn't appear on all PCs.

Custom lets you choose each kind of program independently, whether from Microsoft or not. For example, you can choose Firefox, Internet Explorer, or any other Web browser as your default browser. (They'll all be listed here when you click the double-arrow button to expand the dialog box.)

During your selection process, note the "Enable access to this program" checkbox. It really means, "List this baby at the top of the Start screen, and also put its icon on the desktop, and wherever else important programs are listed."

4. **Click the name of the new default program.**

   Once again, if you don't see it listed here, you can click Browse to find it yourself.

5. **Click OK and then Close.**

Installing Desktop Software

Most people don't buy their computers from Microsoft. Most computers come from companies like Dell, HP, Acer, and Lenovo; they install Windows on each computer before customers take delivery.

Many PC companies sweeten the pot by preinstalling other programs, such as Quicken, Microsoft Works, Microsoft Office, more games, educational software, and so on. The great thing about preloaded programs is that they don't need installing. Just double-click their desktop icons, or choose their names from the Start screen, and you're off and working.

Sooner or later, though, you'll probably want to exploit the massive library of Windows software and add to your collection. Today, almost all new desktop software comes to your PC from one of two sources: a disc (CD or DVD) or the Internet. (The following discussion doesn't apply to TileWorld apps, which are simpler to find and install.)

An installer program generally transfers the software files to the correct places on your hard drive. The installer also adds the new program's name to the Start screen, tells Windows about the kinds of files (file extensions) it can open, and makes certain changes to your *Registry* (Appendix B).

The Preinstallation Checklist

You can often get away with blindly installing some new desktop program without heeding the checklist below. But for the healthiest PC and the least time on hold with tech support, answer these questions before you install anything:

- **Are you an administrator?** Windows derives part of its security and stability by handling new software installations with suspicion. For example, you can't install most programs unless you have an *administrator account* (page 728).

FREQUENTLY ASKED QUESTION

Microsoft InstallShield?

I'm a bit confused. I bought a program from Infinity Workware. But when I run its installer, the welcome screen says InstallShield. Who actually made my software?

Most of the time, the installer program isn't part of the software you bought or downloaded, and doesn't even come from the same company. Most software companies pay a license to installer-software companies. That's why, when you're trying to install a new program called, say, JailhouseDoctor, the first screen you see says InstallShield. (InstallShield is the most popular installation software.)

- **Does it run in Windows 8?** If the software or its Web site specifically says it's compatible with 8, great. Install away. Otherwise, consult the Microsoft Web site, which includes a list—not a complete one, but a long one—of Win8-compatible programs.

Tip: See "Running Pre-Windows 8 Programs" later in this chapter for compatibility tips.

- **Is the coast clear?** Exit all your open programs. You should also turn off your virus-scanning software, which may take the arrival of your new software the wrong way.
- **Am I prepared to backtrack?** If you're at all concerned about the health and safety of the software you're about to install, remember that the System Restore feature (page 691) takes an automatic snapshot of your system just before any software installation. If the new program turns out to be a bit hostile, you can rewind your system to its former, happier working condition.

Installing Software from a Disc

Some commercial software comes on CD or DVD. On each one is a program called Setup.exe, which, on most installation discs, runs automatically when you insert the disc into the machine. You're witnessing the *AutoPlay* feature at work.

If AutoPlay is working, then a few seconds after you insert the disc, the "wait" cursor appears. A few seconds later, the welcome screen for your new software appears, and you may be asked to answer a few onscreen questions (for example, to specify the folder into which you want the new program installed). Along the way, the program may ask you to type in a serial number, which is usually on a sticker on the disc envelope or the registration card.

When the installation is over—and sometimes after restarting the PC—the Start screen now displays an icon, at the far right, for the new program. It's now ready for action.

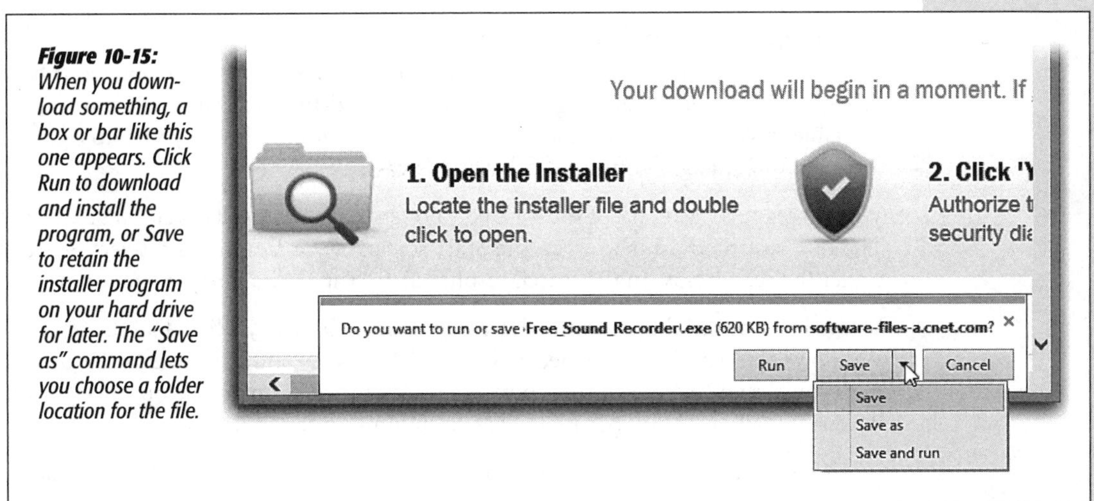

Figure 10-15: *When you download something, a box or bar like this one appears. Click Run to download and install the program, or Save to retain the installer program on your hard drive for later. The "Save as" command lets you choose a folder location for the file.*

Installing Downloaded Software

When you download a new program from the Internet (see Figure 10-15), you have a couple of decisions to make:

- **Are you darned sure?** Internet downloads are the most common sources of PC virus infections. If you're downloading from a brand-name site like Shareware.com or Versiontracker.com (or a software company's site, like Microsoft.com), you're generally safe. But if the site is unfamiliar, be very, very afraid.
- **Run or Save?** You can find thousands of Windows programs (demos, free programs, and shareware) at Web sites like *www.download.com, www.tucows.com,* or *www.versiontracker.com.*

  When you actually click a program's Download button, though, you're asked if you want to Run its installer or Save it (Figure 10-15). Most of the time, Run is fine; that means your PC will download the installer program to your hard drive, open the installer, install the software you wanted, and then completely disappear. There's no cleanup to worry about.

  If you click Save instead, your browser will download the installer program to your hard drive—and that's it. Your job is to find that installer program, double-click it, install the program—and then delete the installer program later, if you have no further use for it.

Tip: Ordinarily, Windows puts the downloaded installer into your Downloads folder. But if you prefer to stash it somewhere else–on the desktop, for example , where it will be easier to find–choose "Save as" from the Save pop-up menu, as shown in Figure 10-15. (That's a feature of Internet Explorer 10, although other Web browsers offer similar features.) After the download is complete, quit or hide your browser. Unzip the file, if necessary, and then run the downloaded installer.

Installing Windows Components

The Windows installer may have dumped over a gigabyte of software onto your hard drive, but it was only warming up. Plenty of second-tier programs and features are available to Windows—stuff that Microsoft didn't want to burden you with right off the bat, but copied to your hard drive just in case.

Want to see the master list of software components you have and haven't yet installed? The quickest method is to open the Start screen. Type *features* and select Settings under the search box. In the search results, click "Turn Windows features on or off."

You've just opened the Windows Features Wizard—basically a list of all the optional Windows software chunks. Checkmarks appear next to some of them; these are the ones you already have. The checkboxes that aren't turned on are the options you still haven't installed. As you peruse the list, keep in mind the following:

- To learn what something is, point to it without clicking. A description appears in a tooltip balloon.

- Turn on the checkboxes for software bits you want to install. Turn off the checkboxes of elements you already have but would like Windows to hide.

Note: Turning off an optional feature *doesn't* remove it from your hard drive. Turning off a feature simply hides it and doesn't return any disk space to you. You can make a feature magically reappear just by turning the checkbox back on, without having to download or install anything.

- Some of these checkboxes' titles are just catchalls for bigger groups of independent software chunks (see Figure 10-16).

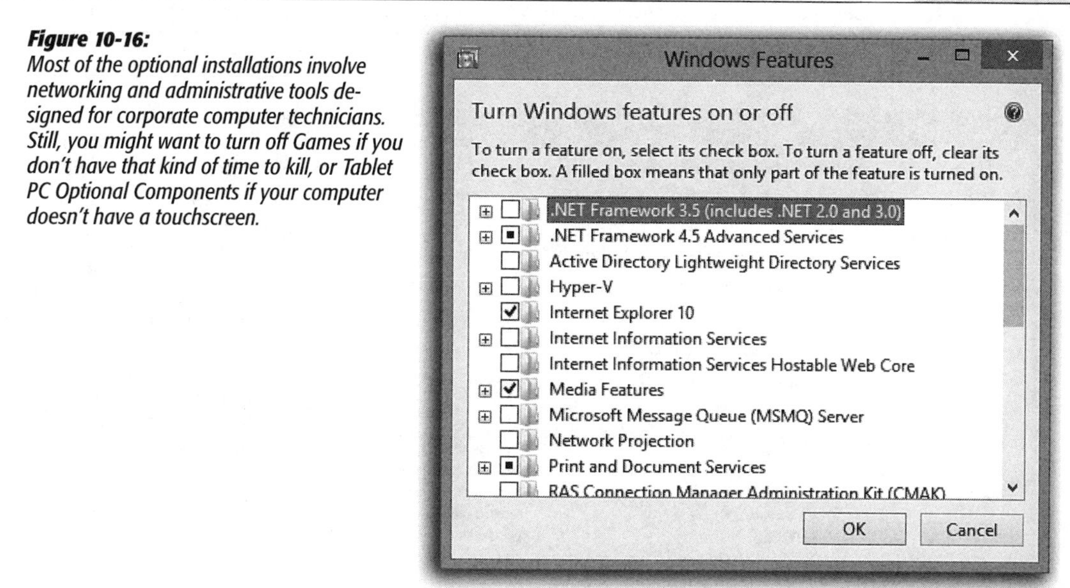

Figure 10-16: *Most of the optional installations involve networking and administrative tools designed for corporate computer technicians. Still, you might want to turn off Games if you don't have that kind of time to kill, or Tablet PC Optional Components if your computer doesn't have a touchscreen.*

Uninstalling Software

When you've had enough of a certain program and want to reclaim the disk space it occupies, don't just delete its folder. The typical application installer tosses its software components like birdseed all over your hard drive; therefore, only some of the program is actually in the program's folder.

Instead, ditch software you no longer need using the Programs and Features program. (Open the Start screen. Type *programs* and select Settings under the search box. In the search results, click Programs and Features.)

Now your master list of installed programs (and driver updates) appears, as shown in Figure 10-17. Click the one you no longer want, and then click Uninstall on the toolbar.

Tip: If your computer is a member of a workgroup and you're using Fast User Switching (see page 751), then don't delete a program until you've verified that it isn't running in somebody else's account behind the scenes.

Even after you uninstall a program, the folder that contained it may still exist, especially if it contains configuration files, add-ons, or documents you created while the program was still alive. If you're sure you won't need those documents, it's safe to remove the folder (discussed later in this section), along with the files inside it.

Note: In Windows XP, the list in this dialog box was cluttered up with dozens upon dozens of "Windows Hotfixes"—the little security patches Microsoft sends out weekly or monthly via the Internet just to make your life interesting.

Nowadays, they get a list of their own. Click "View installed updates" (one of the links in the task pane at the left side). That's useful to remember if you suspect one day that a certain patch has broken something on your PC.

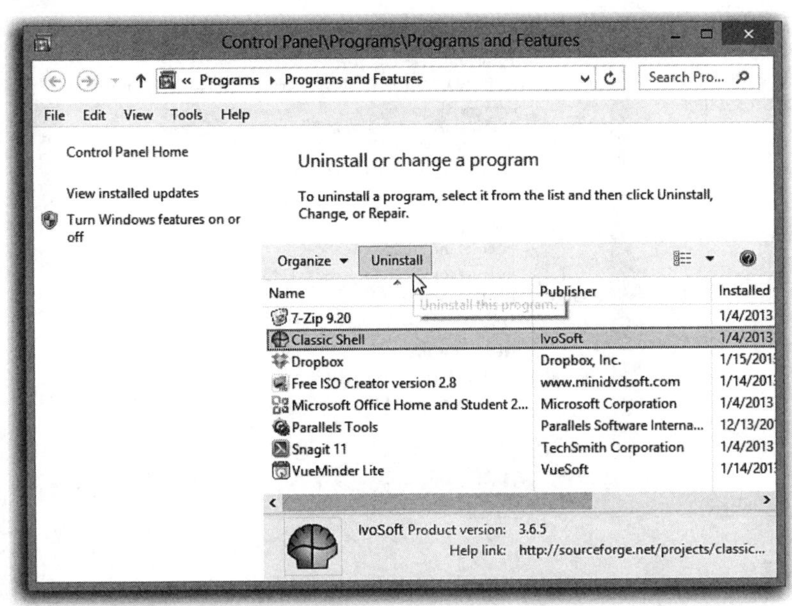

Figure 10-17: *To vaporize a program, click its name to reveal the toolbar, as shown here, and then click Uninstall. Here's a tip—right-click the column headings to add or remove columns. If you choose More, you see some really useful columns, like Last Used On (shows you the last date you ran this program) and Used (how often you've run it).*

FREQUENTLY ASKED QUESTION

This File Is in Use

Hey, I tried to uninstall a program using Programs and Features, like you said. But during the process, I got this scary message saying that one of the deleted program's files is also needed by other programs. It asked me if I was sure I wanted to delete it! Heck, I wouldn't have the faintest idea. What should I do?

Don't delete the file. Leaving it behind does no harm, but deleting it might render one of your other applications nonfunctional.

When Uninstalling Goes Wrong

That's the *theory* of uninstalling Windows programs, of course. In practice, you'll probably find that the Programs and Features program should more accurately be called the "Add or I'll-Make-My-Best-Effort-to-Remove-Programs-But-No-Guarantees" program. A disappointing percentage of the time, one error message or another pops up, declaring that the uninstallation can't proceed because Windows can't find this or that component.

Most of the time, it's not the fault of Windows. Programs and Features is simply a list of links. When you highlight an entry and click Uninstall, Windows just fires up the program's own uninstaller program. When the uninstaller doesn't work, thanks to some bug or glitch, the fun begins.

The truth is, the world won't end if you just leave the crippled program on board your PC. You can join millions of other PC fans who slog along, hard drives corroded with bits of software they can't seem to remove. Apart from the waste of space and the uneasy feeling that your PC is getting clogged arteries, there's no harm done.

But if you'd rather wipe the slate clean, start by visiting the Web site of the company that made your program. Dig into its support section to see if the company has provided a fix or any removal instructions. (Some companies discover bugs in their uninstaller utilities just like they might in any other part of their programs, and then release patches—or even special removal tools—that let their customers remove their software.)

If that step doesn't lead anywhere, you can get serious by eliminating the stubborn bits by hand. Because the process is manual and technical—and because, heaven willing, you won't need it often—it's been offloaded to a free bonus article called "Removing Stubborn Programs." You can find it on this book's "Missing CD" page at *www.missingmanuals.com.*

Program Compatibility Modes

"You can't make an omelet without breaking a few eggs." If that's not Microsoft's motto, it should be. Each successive version of Windows may be better than the previous one, but each inevitably winds up "breaking" hundreds of programs, utilities, and drivers that used to run fine.

Microsoft is well aware of this problem and has pulled every trick in the book to address it. Here, for example, is the chain of second chances you'll experience:

Warning When You Upgrade to Windows 8

In theory, you'll know about incompatible programs well in advance. You'll have run the Windows 8 Upgrade Advisor program (page 838) before you even installed Windows 8, for example, and learned which programs will give you trouble. Even if you skip that step, the Windows installer is supposed to quarantine all incompatible programs.

Warning Right When You Install an Older App

If you try to install an old, incompatible program later, the Program Compatibility Assistant may appear to bring you the bad news.

This app works by consulting a database of programs that Microsoft has determined to have problems with Windows 8. It might tell you a newer version is available for downloading.

Or it might announce that the installation didn't go smoothly. In that case, you can click "Reinstall using recommended settings," which makes Windows run the installer again using different compatibility settings. (For example, it might use one of the compatibility modes described below.)

Compatibility Mode

In principle, programs that were written for recent versions of Windows should run fine in Windows 8. Unfortunately, some of them contain software code that deliberately sniffs around to find out what Windows version you have. These programs (or even their installer programs) may say, "Windows *what?*"—and refuse to open.

Fortunately, Windows 8's Compatibility mode has some sneaky tricks that can fool them into running. You can use it to make "let me run!" changes to a stubborn app either the non-techie way (you just answer questions in a screen-by-screen interview

FREQUENTLY ASKED QUESTION

Really Ancient Apps

Will Windows 8 run my really old, really important app?

You'll never really know until you try. And this chapter outlines all the tools available to help you make the old app run. But here are some specifics on what you can expect.

16-bit programs are so old, they were written when Windows 3.1 roamed the earth and the first George Bush was president. (Programs written for Windows 95 and later are known as *32-bit* programs; Windows 8 can even run *64-bit* programs.) But amazingly enough, the 32-bit versions of Windows 8 (though not the 64-bit versions) can run most of these programs. They do so in a kind of software simulator—a DOS-and-Windows 3.1 PC impersonation called a *virtual machine*.

As a result, these programs don't run very fast, don't understand the long filenames of modern-day Windows, and may crash whenever they try to "speak" directly to certain components of your hardware. (The simulator stands in their way, in the name of keeping Windows stable.) Furthermore, if just one of your 16-bit programs crashes, *all* of them crash, because they all live in the same memory bubble.

Even so, it's impressive that they run at all, 10 years later.

DOS programs are 16-bit programs, too, and therefore they run just fine in 32-bit versions of Windows, even though DOS no longer lurks beneath the operating system.

To open the black, empty DOS window that's familiar to PC veterans, press ⊞+R, type *command.com*, and press Enter.

For the best possible compatibility with DOS programs—and to run DOS programs in a 64-bit copy of Windows—try out DOSBox (*www.dosbox.com/*), which emulates a classic 16-bit computer, complete with DOS compatibility. It's great for those old DOS games that haven't run correctly on Windows since the days of Windows 95.

Programs written for Windows 95, 2000, and XP usually run OK in the Compatibility mode described on these pages.

format, and let Windows make the changes behind the scenes) or the expert way (changing compatibility settings manually).

Compatibility mode: the wizardy way

To let Windows fix your compatibility headache, open the Start screen. Type *compatibility* and select Settings under the search box. In the search results, click "Run programs made for previous versions of Windows."

Tip: Here's another way to get to the wizard: Right-click a program's icon (in the Program Files folder, for example), or its shortcut's icon; from the shortcut menu, choose "Troubleshoot compatibility."

The Program Compatibility program opens. It's a wizard—a series of dialog boxes that interview you. On the way, you're asked to click the name of the program you're having trouble with. On the following screen, you have a choice of automatic or manual modes:

- **Try recommended settings** means, "Let Windows try to figure out how to make my stubborn program run. I don't really care what it has to tinker with under the hood."
- **Troubleshoot program** means, "Let me adjust the compatibility settings myself."

  You'll be asked to choose from options like, "The program worked in earlier versions of Windows," "The program opens but doesn't display correctly," and so on. Work through the question screens the best you can. When it's all over, you get a "Start the program" button that lets you see if the program finally runs without problems.

  Whether things are fixed or not, after you've checked out the app, return to the troubleshooting wizard and click Next. You'll be able to (a) save the fixed settings for the future, (b) start a new round of troubleshooting, or (c) send a report to Microsoft that you never did solve the problem.

Compatibility mode: the manual way

If you know what you're doing, you can save some time and cut to the chase by invoking Compatibility mode yourself. To do that, right-click a program's icon (or its shortcut's icon). From the shortcut menu, choose Properties; click the Compatibility tab.

Now the dialog box shown in Figure 10-18 appears. The options here are precisely the same choices Windows makes for you automatically when you use the wizard described above—it's just that now you can adjust them yourself. Here's what you get:

- **Compatibility mode.** This is the part that tricks the program into believing you're still running Windows 95, Windows XP, or whatever.
- **Reduced color mode.** Makes the program switch your screen to certain limited-colors settings required by older games.
- **Run in 640 × 480 screen resolution.** Runs the app in a small window—the size monitors used to be in the olden days. You might try this option if the app doesn't look right when it runs.

- **Disable display scaling on high DPI settings.** If you've bumped up the type size for your screen, but your fonts are looking really weird in an older app, turn on this checkbox.
- **Run this program as an administrator** lets you run the program as though you have an administrator account (page 728; it's not available if you are *actually* logged in as an administrator).

  This mode is designed to accommodate poorly written programs that, in the XP days, had to be run in administrative mode, back when everyone ran their PCs that way and didn't realize how many virus doors that left open. The downside of turning on this option is that you'll have to authenticate yourself every time you run the program.

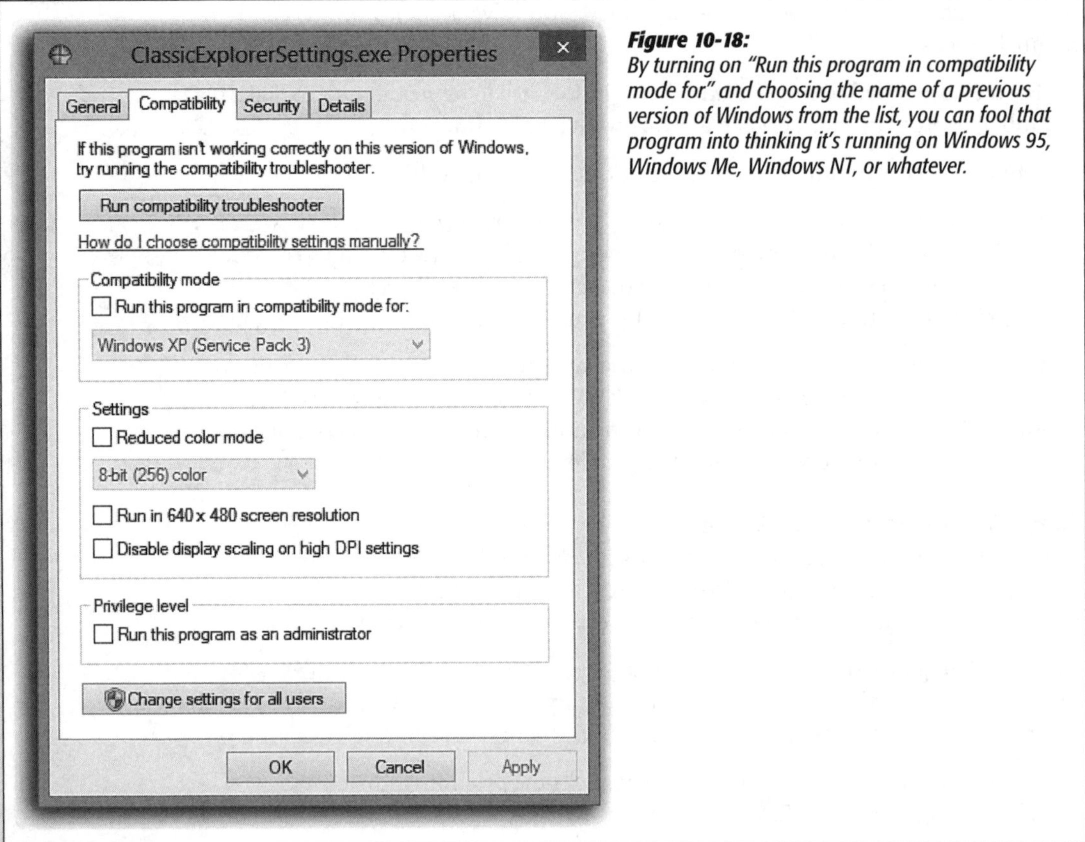

Figure 10-18:
By turning on "Run this program in compatibility mode for" and choosing the name of a previous version of Windows from the list, you can fool that program into thinking it's running on Windows 95, Windows Me, Windows NT, or whatever.

- **Change settings for all users.** If more than one person has an account on this PC, this applies the changes you've just made to everyone's accounts.

Finally, two footnotes:

- You're much better off securing an updated version of the program, if it's available. Check the program's Web site to see if a Win8-compatible update is available.
- Don't try this "fake out the app" trick with utilities like virus checkers, backup programs, CD-burning software, and hard drive utilities. Installing older versions of these with Windows 8 is asking for disaster.

Note: In Windows 7, there was Windows XP Mode: an actual Windows XP simulator that could run all those legacy and specialty programs. Alas, it's gone in Windows 8. You can find some iffy hacks online to restore it—let Google be your friend—but for all real-world purposes, Windows XP Mode is gone and buried.

UP TO SPEED

A Little Bit About 64 Bits

Windows 8 is available in both 32-bit and 64-bit versions. (Both come in the same package if you buy Windows 8 Pro on disc.)

Right. 64-what?

If you want your eyes to glaze over, you can read the details on 64-bit computing on Wikipedia. But the normal-person's version goes like this:

For decades, the roadways for memory and information that passed through PCs were 32 "lanes" wide—they could manage 32 chunks of data at once. It seemed like plenty at the time. But as programs and even documents grew enormous, and computers came with the capacity to have more and more memory installed, engineers began to dream of 64-lane circuitry.

To reach 64-bit nirvana, however, you need a 64-bit computer running the 64-bit version of Windows.

Sometimes, you don't have a choice. For example, if your PC comes with at least 4 gigabytes of memory, it has 64-bit Windows, like it or not. And if you buy a netbook, it probably comes with the 32-bit version.

Otherwise, though, you probably have a choice. Which version should you go for?

In the short term, the most visible effect of having a 64-bit computer is that you can install a lot more memory. A top-of-the-line 32-bit PC, for example, is limited to 4 GB of RAM—and only about 3 GB is actually available to your programs. That once seemed like a lot, but it's suffocatingly small if you're a modern video editor, game designer, or number-crunchy engineer.

On a 64-bit PC with 64-bit Windows, though, you can install just a tad bit more memory: 192 GB.

Eventually, there may be other benefits to a 64-bit PC. Programs can be rewritten to run faster. Security can be better, too. For now, though, there are some downsides to going 64-bit.

For example, much of the world's software has yet to be rewritten as 64-bit apps. The older, 32-bit programs mostly run fine on a 64-bit machine. But some won't run at all, and 32-bit drivers for your older hardware (sound card, graphics card, printer, and so on) may give you particular headaches.

(That's why, for example, 64-bit Windows 8 actually runs the 32-bit version of Internet Explorer—because the world's Internet Explorer plug-ins are mostly 32-bit, and they wouldn't work with the 64-bit version of Internet Explorer.)

You can't run 16-bit programs at all in 64-bit Windows, either (at least not without an add-on program like DOSBox).

If you have taken the 64-bit plunge, you generally don't have to know whether your apps are running in 32- or 64-bit mode; every kind of program runs in the right mode automatically. If you ever want to see how many of your apps are actually 32-bitters, though, press Ctrl+Shift+Esc to open the Task Manager; then click the Processes tab. The 32-bit programs you have open are indicated by "*32" after their names.

CHAPTER
11

The Desktop's Starter Programs

Even after a fresh installation of Windows 8, your computer teems with a rich array of preinstalled programs—as an infomercial might put it, they're your *free bonus gifts*. This chapter offers a tour of these programs. (A few of them merit chapters of their own in this book.)

For your reference pleasure, they're described here alphabetically. They may appear on the All Programs screen in various groups, under various headings (Figure 11-1). But in this chapter, they're all alphabetical, for your sanity's sake.

Windows Essentials

Before the software tour begins, however, a word about Windows Essentials.

If you can believe it, Windows 8 doesn't come with a desktop email program. It doesn't come with a chat program, video-editing app, or basic photo-management software, either (only the Photos viewing app in TileWorld).

It's not because Microsoft doesn't have the talent; it's because of the lawyers. Microsoft grew sick and tired of defending itself in antitrust lawsuits ("If you include all the software anybody would ever need, you're stifling your competition!"). So nowadays, Microsoft leaves out all those controversial programs.

But even if they've been left out, they're not actually gone. These programs are one click away, a one-shot free download from the Web, in a package called Windows Essentials (formerly known as Microsoft Lawsuit Bait).

Most of them, anyway. The Windows Essentials suite includes these apps:

- **Windows Live Mail.** Yes, it's the classic free Microsoft email program. Once, long ago, it went by the name Outlook Express.
- **Photo Gallery.** This is Microsoft's "digital shoebox" program for managing, organizing, and touching up all your photos.
- **Messenger.** It's the chat program that uses Microsoft's chat network, rival to AIM and Yahoo IM. (Microsoft is replacing it with Skype, which it bought.)
- **Movie Maker.** Simple video-editing program. (DVD Maker, alas, has gone to the great Circuit City in the sky. Steve Ballmer giveth, and Steve Ballmer taketh away.)
- **SkyDrive.** Turns your free online SkyDrive into a virtual hard drive for everyday file stashing.
- **Toolbar.** A toolbar for your Web browser that taps into Microsoft's mail, chat, and other services.
- **Windows Live Writer.** A tool for composing blog posts.

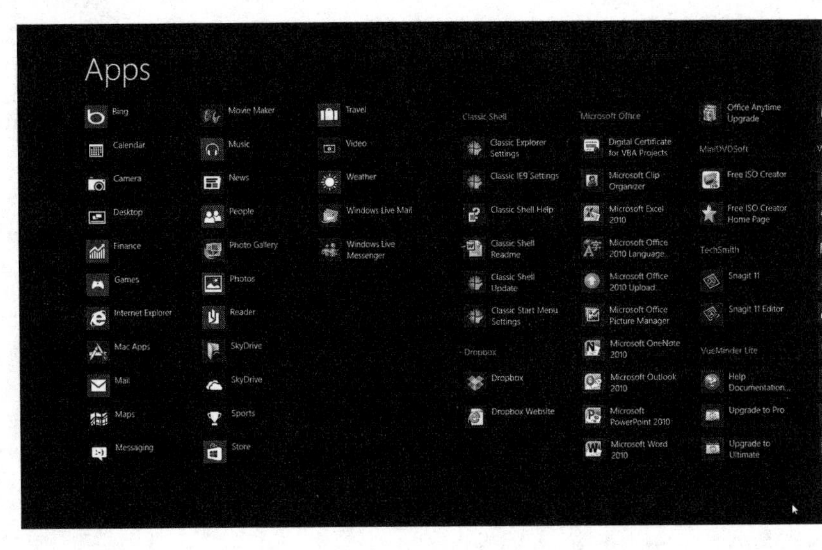

Figure 11-1:
From the Start screen, open the App bar and choose "All apps" to see the master list of every app and program. At the left: TileWorld apps. To the right, in groups: desktop apps.

With two weird exceptions: Windows Essentials, which are desktop apps, appear among the TileWorld apps. And the desktop Internet Explorer doesn't appear at all.

The following pages assume that you have, in fact, downloaded the Windows Essentials. You can download it from this link: *http://j.mp/V3jvo8*. (That's a shorter-to-type substitute for the real address: *http://windows.microsoft.com/en-US/windows-live/essentials-home.*)

Calculator

At first glance, this calculator looks like nothing more than a 2-D version of every pocket calculator you've ever seen (Figure 11-2). You can operate it either by clicking the buttons with your mouse or by pressing the corresponding keys on your keyboard.

Tip: Choosing View→Digit Grouping instructs Calculator to display numbers with commas (123,456,789) or whatever separator your country uses, making large numbers (123456789) a lot easier to read.

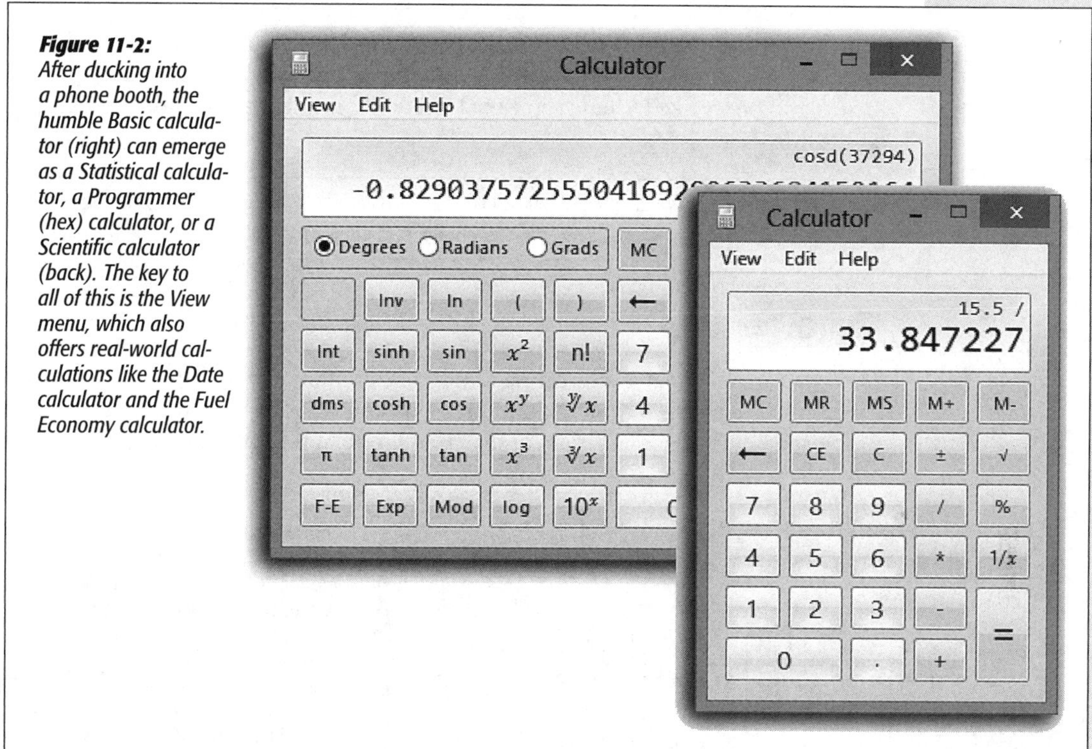

***Figure 11-2:** After ducking into a phone booth, the humble Basic calculator (right) can emerge as a Statistical calculator, a Programmer (hex) calculator, or a Scientific calculator (back). The key to all of this is the View menu, which also offers real-world calculations like the Date calculator and the Fuel Economy calculator.*

Most of the buttons look just like the ones on the plastic calculator that's probably in your desk drawer at this very moment, but several require special explanation. The slash means "divided by" in computerese; the asterisk (*) is the multiplication symbol. To use the % button, type in one number, click the * button, type a second number, and then click this button to calculate what percentage the first number is of the second.

Then there's the ratio button (1/x). It makes the currently displayed number appear as the denominator of a fraction. That is, it turns 4 into ¼, which it expresses as 0.25.

The Calculator harbors some advanced calculatory goodies in the View menu. For example, choose View→Scientific to turn this humble five-function calculator into a full-fledged scientific number-cruncher, as shown in Figure 11-2.

Similarly, Programmer mode is a full-blown hexadecimal calculator. (And if you have no idea what a hexadecimal calculator is, then you must not, yourself, be a Programmer.)

Statistics mode offers functions like Sum, Average, and Standard Deviation. Enter each number in the batch you want to analyze, clicking Add after each one; they line up in the top half of the window. Then click the button you want. (Those little symbols mean average, average of the square, sum, sum of the square, standard deviation, and standard deviation of population.)

At the bottom of the View menu, you get a few really useful real-world options like Unit Conversion, Date Calculation, and Worksheets (Mortgage, Vehicle lease, and Fuel economy). Each makes a new panel pop out, filled with easy-to-understand pop-up menus and boxes like Distance and Fuel Used. Fill in the blanks, and let Calculator do the thinking for you.

Tip: In Standard and Scientific modes, you can choose View→History to see a paper trail of the numbers you've typed. You can then make a correction by double-clicking one of those numbers and retyping.

Character Map

Your computer is capable of creating hundreds of different typographical symbols—the currency symbols for the yen and British pound, diacritical markings for French and Spanish, various scientific symbols, trademark and copyright signs, and so on.

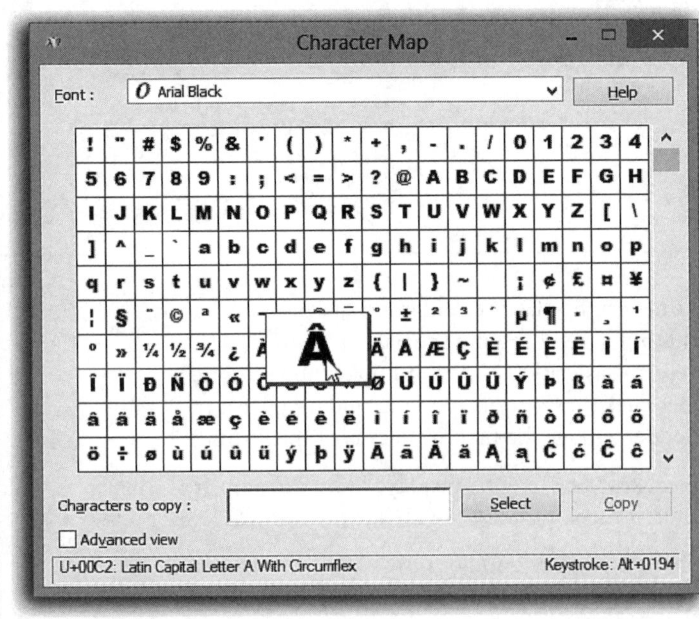

Figure 11-3: *Double-click a character to transfer it to the "Characters to copy" box, as shown here. (Double-click several in a row if you want to capture a sequence of symbols.) You may have to scroll down quite a bit in some of today's modern Unicode fonts, which contain hundreds of characters. Click Copy, and then Close. When you've returned to your document, use the Paste command to insert the symbols.*

Obviously, these symbols don't appear on your keyboard; to provide enough keys, your keyboard would have to be the width of Wyoming. You *can* type the symbols, but they're hidden behind the keys you do see.

The treasure map that reveals their locations is the Character Map. When first opening this program, use the Font pop-up menu to specify the font you want to use (because every font contains a different set of symbols). Now you see every single symbol in the font. As you click on each symbol, a magnified version of it appears to help you distinguish them. See Figure 11-3 for details on transferring a particular symbol to your document.

Tip: Some email programs can't handle the fancy kinds of symbols revealed by the Character Map. That explains why your copyright symbols, for example, can turn into a gibberish character on the receiving end.

Command Prompt

The Command Prompt opens a *command line interface:* a black, empty screen with the time-honored *C:>* prompt where you can type out instructions to the computer. This is a world without icons, menus, or dialog boxes; even the mouse is almost useless.

Surely you can appreciate the irony. The whole breakthrough of Windows was that it *eliminated* the DOS command-line interface that was still the ruling party on the computers of the day. Most nongeeks sighed with relief, delighted that they'd never have to memorize commands again. Yet here's Windows 8, Microsoft's supposedly ultramodern operating system, complete with a command line! What's going on?

Actually, the command line never went away. At universities and corporations worldwide, professional computer nerds kept right on pounding away at the little *C:>* prompts, appreciating the efficiency and power such direct computer control afforded them.

You never *have* to use the command line. In fact, Microsoft has swept it far under the rug, obviously expecting that most people will use the beautiful icons and menus of the regular desktop.

FREQUENTLY ASKED QUESTION

Clipboard Viewer

Hey, what happened to the Clipboard Viewer? It used to be in the System Tools group of my Start→Programs→Accessories menu, and now it's gone.

Yes, Clipboard Viewer was a cool little program for seeing the material you'd most recently copied.

It's gone. You can't even use the Run command to issue the *Clipbrd.exe* command anymore.

Fortunately, the shareware world is ready to step into the breach. Take a look, for example, at AccelClip (available, among other places, from this book's "Missing CD" page at *www.missingmanuals.com*).

Tip: You can also open the Command Prompt directly from the Start menu. Just type *command* into the search box, and then press Enter.

If you have a little time and curiosity, however, the Command Prompt opens up a world of possibilities. It lets you access corners of Windows that you can't get to from the regular desktop. (Commands for exploring network diagnostics are especially plentiful—*ping, netstat,* and so on.) It lets you perform certain tasks with much greater speed and efficiency than you'd get by clicking buttons and dragging icons. And it gives you a fascinating glimpse into the minds and moods of people who live and breathe computers.

Here are a few examples:

Command	Purpose	Example
control	Opens a Control Panel applet	*control date/time*
ping	Checks to see if a server is responding	*ping nytimes.com*
ipconfig	Reveals your PC's IP address and other network info	*ipconfig*
mkdir	Make directory (that is, create a folder)	*mkdir \Reports*
copy	Copy files from one folder to another	*copy c:\Reports*.* \Backup*

You can also type the true, secret name of any program to open it, quickly and efficiently, without having to mouse around through the Start menu. For example, you can type *winword* to open Word, or *charmap* to open Character Map.

To learn a few of the hundreds of commands at your disposal, consult the Internet, which is filled with excellent lists and explanations. To find them, visit a search page like *www.google.com* and search for *Windows command line reference.* You'll find numerous ready-to-study Web sites that tell you what to type at the Command Prompt. (Here's an example from Microsoft: *http://bit.ly/bx0xo4.)*

Tip: You can open a Command Prompt for any folder just by Shift+right-clicking a folder. From the shortcut menu, choose Open Command Window Here.

Computer

Opening this "program" does nothing more than open your Computer window— the same one you'd see when you click Computer in the Navigation pane of any Explorer window. It's not really a program at all, just a convenience.

Control Panel

Opens the Control Panel, which gets its very own chapter (Chapter 12).

Default Programs

This item is a link to the Default Programs control panel. It's described in Chapter 12.

File Explorer

Is File Explorer really a program? Yes, it probably is. In any case, this is nothing more than a link to the basic desktop file-organizing window described in Chapter 6.

Help and Support

Here's yet another way to open the desktop Help system described in Chapter 9.

Magnifier

Magnifier puts a floating magnifying-glass icon on your screen (Figure 11-4, top left). When you click it, you get the Magnifier toolbar (top right).

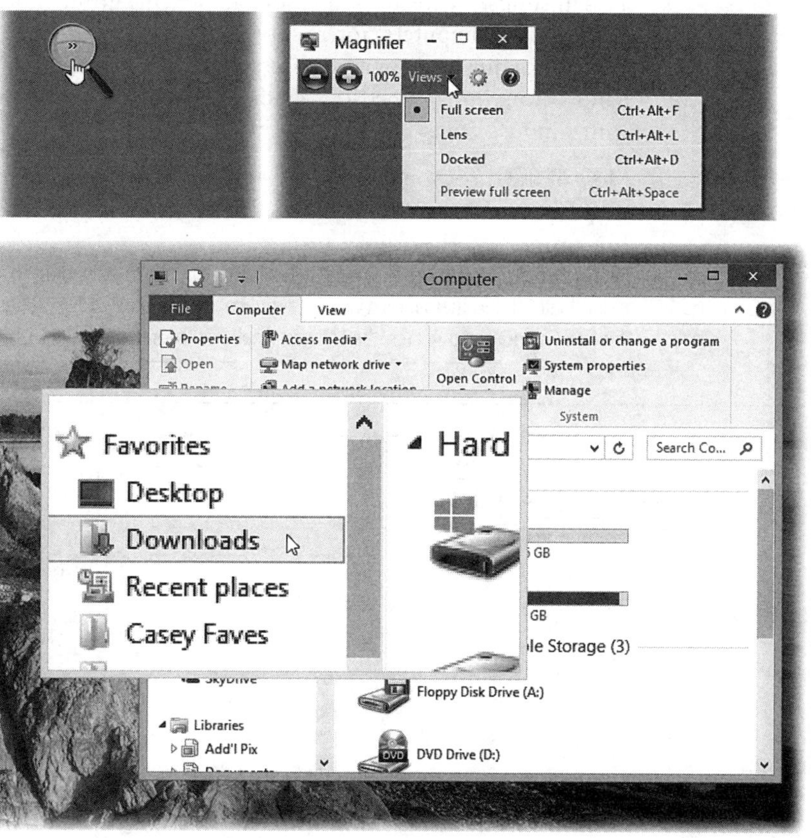

Figure 11-4: *Magnifier enlarges whatever part of the screen your cursor is touching. In Lens or Docked modes, note that you can adjust the size of the magnified area by dragging its edge. In Docked mode, you can also tear the pane away from the edge of the screen so it becomes a floating window; just drag anywhere inside it.*

Magnifier creates various magnification effects—great when your eyes are tired or old, or when you're trying to study something whose font is just too dang small.

Using the View menu, you can choose "Full screen" (the entire screen image grows when you click the + button), "Lens" (you get a floating magnification inset that follows your cursor, as shown at bottom in Figure 11-4), or "Docked" (the top strip of the screen is one giant magnification inset; the rest of the screen is normal size).

In each case, the magnified area scrolls as you move your cursor, tab through a dialog box, or type, enlarging whatever part of the screen contains the action. Using the Magnifier Settings dialog box (click the ✿ in the toolbar), you can specify how the magnification area should follow your cursor.

Tip: Whenever Magnifier is turned on, you can zoom in or out with Ctrl+plus or Ctrl+minus.

Math Input Panel

This unsung little freebie is intended for an elite group indeed: mathematicians with touchscreen computers. You're supposed to write out math equations in the writing area using your finger or a touchscreen stylus and marvel as Windows translates your handwriting into a typed-out mathematical expression. (You *can* use this program with a mouse; it just might feel a little odd.)

Most of the time, you'll want to use MIP when you're writing in a word processor—preparing a math test for students, writing a white paper, whatever.

Note: This program can insert its finished math expressions only into programs that recognize something called MathML (Mathematical Markup Language). Microsoft Word, Excel, and PowerPoint do, and so does the free OpenOffice.org. (Yes, the software itself has the same name as its Web site.)

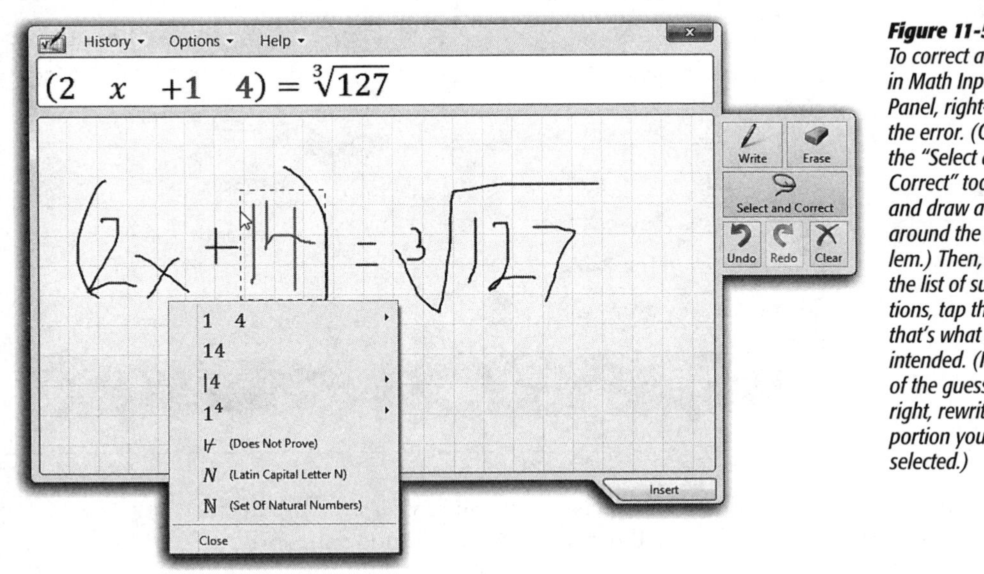

Figure 11-5: *To correct an error in Math Input Panel, right-click the error. (Or use the "Select and Correct" tool, and draw a circle around the problem.) Then, from the list of suggestions, tap the one that's what you intended. (If none of the guesses are right, rewrite the portion you've selected.)*

If you have a touchscreen computer and you're working in the Windows Journal program, you can also use MIP to analyze your previously *handwritten* math expressions and make them properly typeset. (Use the selection tool to highlight your handwriting, and then drag the expression *into* the MIP window.)

To use MIP on any other computer, write out the mathematical expression, as neatly as you can, in the writing area. In the Preview area (see Figure 11-5), you see Windows' stab at recognizing your handwriting.

If it's all correct, tap Insert to drop the equation into your word processor.

If something needs correcting, you can show MIP what it got wrong in one of several ways:

- **Right-click the mistake.** Or, if the mistaken transcription is more than one symbol, circle the error while pressing the right mouse button.
- **Tap the mistake while pressing your stylus's button.** (Or, again, circle the mistake while pressing the pen's button.)
- **Click the Select and Cancel button.** Now tap the erroneous symbol, or circle the larger part that's wrong.

Tip: It's better to correct errors after you've written out the whole thing.

Immediately, a pop-up menu of alternative transcriptions appears. Proceed as shown in Figure 11-5.

If the expression is now complete, tap Insert. If you have more to write, just keep on going. (If you got into symbol-correction mode by tapping Select and Cancel, then you have to tap Write before you continue.)

FREQUENTLY ASKED QUESTION

Where Did All the Games Go?

Hey, what happened to all the Windows games?

It's true: From the misty dawn of Microsoft time, Windows has always come with at least one game. At least Solitaire.

But no more. Windows 8 does not include a single game. Microsoft wants its corporate customers, the ones who buy 500 copies of Windows at a time, to know that Windows means business.

But Microsoft isn't completely out of the free-games business; with a couple of clicks, you can download a set of free new TileWorld card games that include Solitaire and FreeCell (two of the missing games), plus Klondike, Spider Solitaire, TriPeaks, and Pyramid.

To get them: From the Start screen, type *freecell*; in the Search panel, select Store (you may have to scroll down). You're taken online to the Windows Store, where the results of your search appear. The one you want is "Microsoft Solitaire Collection." Download away.

You'll soon discover that Windows is as good at helping you waste time as it ever was.

Tip: You can tap any entry in the History menu to re-input an expression you've entered before. When you're working on, for example, a proof, or a drill with many similar problems, that can save you a lot of time.

Narrator

Narrator began life as a little program that could read aloud certain items on the screen, like dialog boxes and error messages. But in Windows 8, it's had a huge upgrade. Now it can read anything that's on the screen. If you're blind, you may find that Narrator comes very close to serving as a basic screen reader. It can describe every item on the screen, either in TileWorld or the desktop; it can describe the layout of a Web page; and it can make sounds to confirm that you've performed a touchscreen gesture correctly.

Even if you're not blind, Narrator is still handy; it can read your email back to you, or read Web articles as you're getting dressed in the morning.

When you open Narrator, you wind up at its Settings dialog box (Figure 11-6)—and the voice of Microsoft David starts talking, reading everything on the screen.

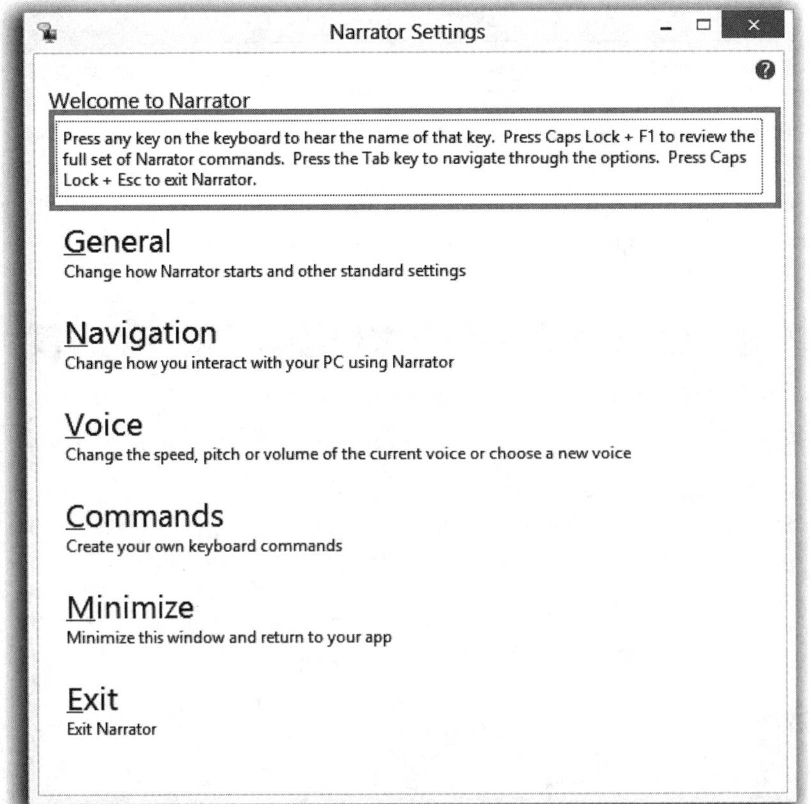

Figure 11-6: *Narrator's entire visual presence is nothing more than this Settings dialog box–and a colored rectangular frame that moves around the screen as you touch it (or arrow-key it). Whatever the frame encloses, Narrator speaks. That way, you can figure out where you are on the screen even if you can't see it.*

As you'll soon discover, mastering Narrator takes a lot of time and patience; it's something like a complete operating system in itself. But here are the basics.

Touchscreen Basics

Narrator is especially important on touchscreen computers; if you're blind, how else are you supposed to navigate the screen?

Drag your finger around the touchscreen; Narrator speaks everything you touch, so that you can get a feel for the layout of things. You can also tap to hear a single item identified; you don't have to worry about opening something accidentally.

Of course, if touching something makes it say its name, then how are you supposed to open it? Simple: Add another tap. That is, you *double-tap* when a single tap usually works (or press-and-hold) and *triple-tap* when you'd ordinarily double-tap.

To see the master cheat sheet of touch gestures in Narrator (and hear it read to you), tap *three times with four fingers* against the screen. You'll learn essential tips like these:

To do this	Use this touch command
Stop Narrator from reading	Tap once with two fingers
Read current window	Swipe up with three fingers
Click	Double-tap
Double-click	Triple-tap
Start dragging	Tap with three fingers
Show/hide Narrator window	Tap with four fingers
Move to previous/next item	Flick left/right with one finger
Scroll	Swipe any direction with two fingers
Tab forward and backward	Swipe left/right with three fingers

As you can see from that little table, flicking left or right makes Narrator read the previous or next item. But when you're on a Web page or in an email message, what's an "item"? Is it a word? A paragraph? A headline?

Answer: That's up to you. The new up/down flick changes the increment of the right/left flick. In other words, each time you flick downward with one finger, you'll hear the voice say these things, in sequence:

- **"Heading view."** Each right/left swipe of your finger speaks and highlights the next headline on the page. Great for exploring a newspaper's front page. When you find a headline that sound interesting, swipe down with three fingers to make Narrator start reading the entire article.
- **"Item view."** Each right/left swipe of your finger speaks and highlights the next *item* on the page, whether that's a graphic, headline, ad, or table.
- **"Paragraph view."** Each right/left swipe of your finger speaks and highlights the next *paragraph*. Great for skimming an article.
- **"Line view."** Each right/left swipe of your finger speaks and highlights the next line of text.

- "**Word view.**" Each right/left swipe of your finger speaks and highlights the next word.
- "**Character view.**" Each right/left swipe of your finger speaks and highlights the next character. Very useful if you're trying to figure out how a word is spelled.
- "**Table view.**" Each right/left swipe of your finger speaks and highlights the next table on the page.
- "**Link view.**" Each right/left swipe of your finger speaks and highlights the next clickable link on the page.

Tip: If you have a keyboard, pressing Ctrl plus the four arrow keys performs the same functions as swiping up, down, left, or right.

It's also worth noting that each kind of gesture—scroll, swipe, tap, and so on—plays a different sound effect. That kind of immediate feedback helps you figure out what you're actually doing in Windows 8.

Keyboard Basics

When Narrator is running, the Caps Lock key becomes specially dedicated to it. Press Caps Lock+V, for example, to make Narrator repeat whatever it just said. Caps Lock+plus or minus makes the voice speed up or slow down. Press Caps Lock+Esc to exit Narrator.

Here are a few of the most useful commands:

To do this	Use this keystroke
"Click" the selected object	Space bar or Enter
Move around on the screen	Tab and arrow keys
Stop reading	Ctrl
Read item	Caps Lock+D
Read whole document	Caps Lock+H
Repeat that	Caps Lock+V
Read window	Caps Lock+W
Adjust voice volume	Caps Lock+Page Up or Page Down
Adjust reading speed	Caps Lock+plus (+) or minus (-)
Move to previous/next item	Caps Lock+← or →
Turn Caps Lock on or off	Press Caps Lock twice quickly
Exit Narrator	Caps Lock+Esc

Tip: On the Commands tab of the Narrator Settings dialog box (Figure 11-6), you can change any of these keystrokes to anything you like.

Settings

You could spend the rest of your life fiddling with Narrator's settings to make it work exactly the way you like. But here are some important examples. (To open the Settings panel, open Narrator itself.)

General tab

- **Lock the Narrator key so you don't have to press them for each command.** What Microsoft means is, "Change all those keyboard shortcuts so I don't need the Caps Lock key to trigger them."
- **Enable visual highlighting of narrator cursor.** This is a reference to the colored rectangle that identifies whatever Narrator thinks has "the focus" (whatever it's speaking at the moment). You can hide that box, if you like, by turning this off.
- **Read hints for common items.** Turning this off makes Narrator stop giving you the handy hints like, "Double-tap to activate."
- **Enable visual highlighting of narrator cursor.** This is a reference to the colored rectangle that identifies whatever Narrator thinks has "the focus" (whatever it's speaking at the moment). You can hide that box, if you like, by turning this off.

Voice tab

Here's where you get to adjust the speed, volume, and pitch of Narrator's speaking voice—or even choose a different voice. You get a choice of three: David, a red-blooded American male (of course); Hazel, a British woman; and Zira, an American woman.

Commands tab

Change Narrator's keyboard shortcuts to whatever floats your boat. Select one of the 72 commands in the list, and then hit "Change command keyboard shortcut."

Notepad

Notepad is a bargain-basement *text editor,* which means it lets you open, create, and edit files that contain plain, unformatted text, like the ReadMe.txt files that often accompany new programs. You can also use Notepad to write short notes or to edit text that you intend to paste into your email program after editing it.

Notepad Basics

Notepad opens automatically when you double-click text files (those with the file extension *.txt*). You can also find Notepad by typing *notep* at the Start screen.

You'll quickly discover that Notepad is the world's most frill-free application. Its list of limitations is almost longer than its list of features.

For example, the Notepad window has no toolbar and can work with only one file at a time.

Above all, Notepad is a *text* processor, not a *word* processor. That means you can't use any formatting at all—no bold, italic, centered text, and so on. That's not necessarily bad news, however. The beauty of text files is that any word processor on any kind of computer—Windows, Mac, Unix, whatever—can open plain text files like the ones Notepad creates.

About Word Wrap

In the old days, Notepad didn't automatically wrap lines of text to make everything fit in its window. As a result, chunks of text often went on forever in a single line or got chopped off by the right side of the window, which could produce disastrous results when you were trying to follow, say, a soufflé recipe.

Now, lines of text wrap automatically, exactly as they do in a word processor. But you're still seeing nothing more than the effects of the Format→Word Wrap command—an option you can turn off, if you like, by choosing the command again. (You can tell when Word Wrap is on by the presence of a checkmark next to the command in the Format menu.)

Onscreen Keyboard

In the new world of touchscreen tablets, not everyone has a physical keyboard. Windows 8 offers this onscreen version, which is described on page 71.

Paint

You can use Paint to "paint" simple artwork or to edit graphics files from other sources. You might say Paint is something like Adobe Photoshop (well, in the same way you might say the local Cub Scout newsletter is something like *The New York Times*). Common tasks for this program include making quick sketches, fixing dust specks on scanned photos, and entertaining kids for hours on end.

GEM IN THE ROUGH

Notepad Log Files

As stripped-down as it is, Notepad has one surprising feature not available in any other text processor or word processor: automated log files. Every time you open a certain file, Notepad can automatically insert the current date and time at the bottom of the file, creating a tidy record of when you last worked on it–a nifty way to keep any type of a log, like a record of expenditures or a secret diary.

To set this up, create a new Notepad document (choose File→New). Then type the phrase *.LOG* at the top of the new document. (Capitalize "LOG," and put nothing, not even a space, before the period.)

Now save the document (File→Save) wherever you like, and give it a name. (Notepad adds the extension *.txt* automatically.)

When you next open the file, Notepad types out the date and time automatically and puts your cursor on the next line. Now you're ready to type the day's entry.

To make your log file easier to read, press the Enter key to insert a blank line after each entry before saving the file.

When you first open Paint, you get a small, empty painting window. Go like this:

1. **From the File menu, choose Properties to specify the dimensions of the graphic you want to create. Click OK.**

   Later in your life, you can revisit that command to adjust your graphic's dimensions.

2. **Click a tool on the Home tab, like the Pencil.**

   If you need help identifying one of these tools, point to it without clicking. A tooltip identifies the icon by name, and a help message appears at the bottom of the window.

3. **Click a "paint" color from the palette.**

   You may also want to change the "brush" by clicking the Brushes palette, like the spray-paint splatter shown in Figure 11-7.

Figure 11-7: *The Paint tools include shapes, pens for special uses (straight lines and curves), and coloring tools (including an airbrush). The Select tools don't draw anything. Instead, they select portions of the image for cutting, copying, or dragging to a new location.*

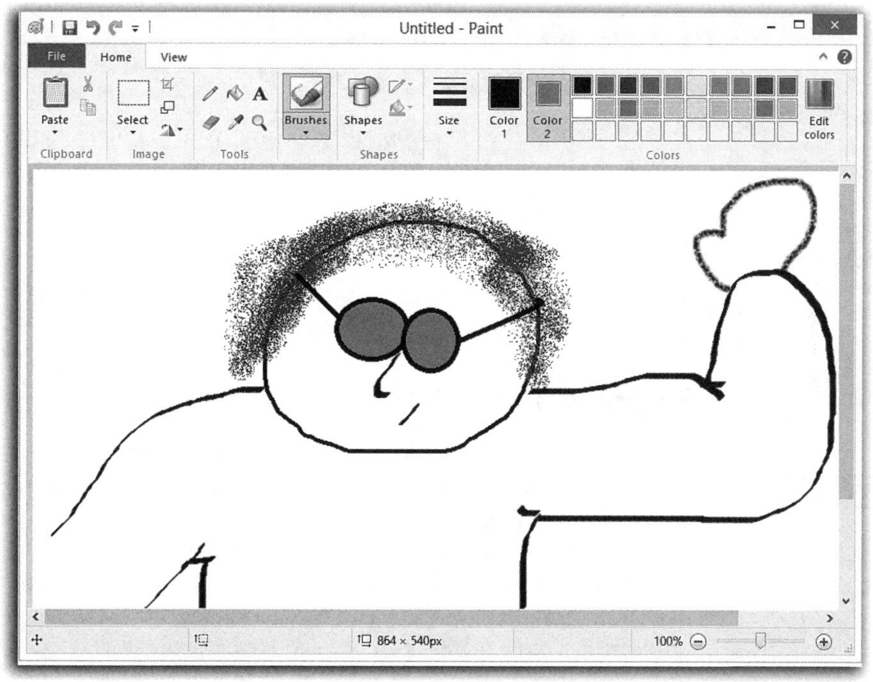

4. **If you've selected one of the enclosed-shape tools, use the Fill pop-up menu to specify a texture (Watercolor, Crayon, or whatever); click Color 2, and then a color swatch, to specify the color for the inside of that shape.**

Some tools produce enclosed shapes, like squares and circles. You can specify one color for the border, and a second color for the fill color inside.

5. **Finally, drag your cursor in the image area (see Figure 11-7).**

   As you work, don't forget that you can click the Undo button (the counterclockwise arrow at the very top edge of the window), "taking back" the last painting maneuvers you made.

   For fine detail work, click the View tab, and then click Zoom In. You've just enlarged it so every dot is easily visible.

Paint can open and create several different file formats, including BMP, JPEG, and GIF—every file format you need to save graphics for use on a Web site.

Tip: Paint also offers a nifty way to create wallpaper. After you create or edit a graphic, open the File menu. Choose "Set as desktop background"; from the submenu, choose Fill, Tile, or Center to transfer your masterpiece to your desktop.

Remote Desktop Connection

Remote Desktop Connection lets you sit at your home PC and operate your office PC by remote control. Details are in Chapter 28.

Run

When you want to open something with just a few keystrokes, the little Run command-line window is there for you. See page 246 for details.

Snipping Tool

Snipping Tool (Figure 11-8) takes pictures of your PC's screen, for use when you're writing up instructions, illustrating a computer book, or collecting proof of some secret screen you found buried in a game. You can take pictures of the entire screen or capture only the contents of a rectangular selection. When you're finished, Snipping Tool displays your snapshot in a new window, which you can print, close without saving, edit, or save (as a JPEG, GIF, PNG, or embedded HTML file), ready for emailing or inserting into a manuscript or page-layout program.

Now, as experienced PC enthusiasts already know, Windows has *always* had shortcuts for capturing screenshots: Press the Print Screen (or PrtScn) key to print a picture of the whole screen; add the Alt key to copy it to your Clipboard; or press WW+Print Screen to save the screenshot as a file into a Screenshots folder in your Pictures library.

So why use Snipping Tool instead? Because it's infinitely more powerful and flexible. Here's how it works:

1. **Open Snipping Tool.**

The screen goes foggy and light, and the Snipping Tool palette appears.

2. **From the New shortcut menu, specify what area of the screen you want to capture.**

   These are your choices:

   Free-form Snip means you can drag your cursor in any crazy, jagged, freehand, nonrectangular shape. Snipping Tool outlines it with a red border.

Tip: You can change the border color in the Options dialog box. It appears when you click Options on the main Snipping palette, or when you choose Tools→Options in the editing window.

   Rectangular Snip lets you drag diagonally across the frozen screen image, thus capturing a square or rectangular area. Unfortunately, you can't adjust the rectangle if your aim was a little off; the instant you release the mouse button, the program captures the image in the rectangle.

   A **Window Snip** neatly captures an entire window, automatically cropping out the entire background. And *which* window does it capture? That's up to you. As you point to each window, a red border appears around it to illustrate what Snipping

Figure 11-8: *Top: The Snipping Tool program begins life as a tiny floating toolbar. Tell it what part of the screen you want to capture.*

Bottom: After you capture a snip, the editing window appears, with your screen grab right in the middle of it. The Pen, Highlighter, and Eraser tools are there to help you annotate, draw attention to, or erase parts of your illustration. (The Eraser works only on pen and highlighter strokes–not the snip itself.)

Tool *thinks* you intend to capture. When the correct one is highlighted, click the mouse to capture.

Tip: A "window," in this context, doesn't have to be a window. It can also be the taskbar, a Sidebar gadget, a dialog box, and so on.

And a **Full-screen Snip,** of course, captures the entire screen.

3. **Specify what you want to capture, if necessary.**

   That is, drag across the screen for a Free-form or Rectangular snip, or click the window (object) you want for a Window Snip. (Skip this step if you chose Full-screen Snip. In that case, Snipping Tool pretty much knows what to do.) Now the editing window appears (Figure 11-8).

What you do with your finished graphic is up to you. For example:

- **Paste it.** The edited image may be in the window in front of you, but the original, unedited image is *also* on your invisible Windows Clipboard. Close the editing window without saving changes, pop into your graphics, word processing, or email program, and paste (Ctrl+V) what you've copied. Often, that's exactly what you want to do.

Tip: On the other hand, the Snipping Tool's tendency to copy everything to the Clipboard can be *bad* if there was already something *on* the Clipboard you wanted to keep. (The Clipboard can hold only one thing at a time.) If that syndrome is driving you nuts, you can turn off the copy-to-Clipboard feature in Options.

- **Send it.** The little envelope button on the editing-window toolbar automatically prepares an outgoing email message with your graphic already pasted in (or, if your email program is set to send plain, unformatted text messages only, as an attachment).

POWER USERS' CLINIC

May I Please See a Menu?

Snipping Tool, as you've already seen, is a heck of a lot better than the old PrtScn keystroke. But at first glance, you might assume that it still can't take a picture of a menu or a shortcut menu. After all, the instant you try to drag to highlight the menu, the menu closes!

Actually, you can capture menus—if you know the secret.

Open Snipping Tool, and then *minimize* it, which hides its window but keeps it running.

Now open the menu you want to capture, using the mouse or keyboard. Once the menu is open, press Ctrl+PrtScn. That's all it takes; Snipping Tool is smart enough to know that you intend to capture just the menu.

That's workable, but still a bit complicated. That's why, if you're *actually* going to write a computer book or manual, you probably want a proper screen-capture program like Snagit (*www.techsmith.com*). It offers far more flexibility than any of Windows' own screenshot features. For example, you have a greater choice of file formats and capture options, you can dress up the results with arrows or captions, and (with its companion program, Camtasia Studio) you can even capture *movies* of screen activity.

- **Save it.** If your intention is to save the capture as a file, click the Save (floppy-disk) icon, or choose File→Save, or press Ctrl+S. When the Save As dialog box appears, type a name for your graphic, choose a file format for it (from the "Save as type" pop-up menu), specify a folder location, and then click Save.

Tip: If you capture the screen of a Web page and save it in HTML format, Snipping Tool helpfully prints the original URL (Web address) at the bottom of the image, so you'll know where it came from. You can turn off this "subtitling" feature in the Options dialog box of Snipping Tool.

Sound Recorder

Windows comes with a generous assortment of sound files you can use as error beeps. But no error beep is as delightful as one you've made yourself—of your 2-year-old saying, "Nope!" for example, or your own voice saying, "Dang it!"

Using Sound Recorder (Figure 11-9) requires a sound card, speakers, and a microphone. If your PC is appropriately equipped, you can use this little program to record various snippets of your life, which can serve a number of purposes, including becoming error beeps.

Figure 11-9:
Sound Recorder has been lobotomized since the Windows XP version, but it does the job.

Recording a New Sound

Here's how to do it:

1. **Open Sound Recorder.**

   For example, on the Start screen, start typing *sound* until Sound Recorder pops up in the results list. Select it. The window shown in Figure 11-9 appears.

2. **Click Start Recording. Make the sound, and then click Stop Recording as soon as possible thereafter.**

   If you see the green animated bar dance in the Sound Recorder window, great; that's your VU (sound level) meter. It tells you that the PC is hearing you. If you don't see this graphic, however, then the sound isn't getting through. Most likely, the problem is that your PC control panel isn't set to record the appropriate sound source. Visit the Control Panel and open the Sound panel to investigate.

   As soon as you click Stop Recording, the Save As box appears.

3. **Type a name for your sound file in the "File name" text box, choose a folder for it, and then click the Save button.**

You've just created a .wma file, a standard kind of Windows sound file.

What to Do with Sounds

When you double-click a .wma file, the file opens in Windows Media Player and plays back immediately. (Press Esc to halt playback.) Sound files are ideal for emailing to other people, posting on Web sites, transferring over the network, and so on. Many a Bart Simpson sound bite proliferates via the Internet in exactly this way.

Steps Recorder

This weird little program is designed to record exactly where you're clicking or tapping, and to capture a screen picture each time you do so. Why? So that you can document some problem you're having. You can send the resulting recording to someone who wants to see exactly what steps you were taking when you run into trouble.

Of course, this is a similar scenario to the times when you might use Windows Remote Assistance, where the wise guru can *watch* you perform the steps that are frustrating you. But because Steps Recorder lets you type a little message each time you click the mouse, it's a better, more permanent way to record some problem you're having.

When you're ready to record the steps, click Start Record. Now do whatever it is, on your computer, that produces the problem: Click here, use that menu, drag that slider, whatever. As you go, you can do the following:

- **Pause the recording.** Click Pause Record. (Click Resume Record to continue.)
- **Type an annotation for a particular step.** ("Here's where I double-clicked.") Click Add Comment, highlight the part of the screen that you want to comment on, type your note into the box, and then click OK.

Note: Anything you type outside that comment box doesn't get recorded; that's a security precaution.

When you're finished, click Stop Record.

The Recorded Steps window, new in Windows 8, appears. It shows you each screenshot that Steps Recorder captioned, complete with its time stamp and text description ("User left-click on 'File Explorer' button," for example). This is your chance to make sure you're not about to send away personal information (or naughty photos) that might have been on the screen while you recorded.

If everything looks good, click either Save (creates a compressed archive—a .zip file—that you can later open to look at the report again in your Web browser) or Email (to send to an expert).

Sticky Notes

Sticky Notes creates virtual Post-it notes that you can stick anywhere on your screen—a triumphant software answer to the thousands of people who stick notes on the edges of their actual monitors.

You can type quick notes and to-do items, paste in Web addresses or phone numbers you need to remember, or store any other little scraps and snippets of text you come across (Figure 11-10).

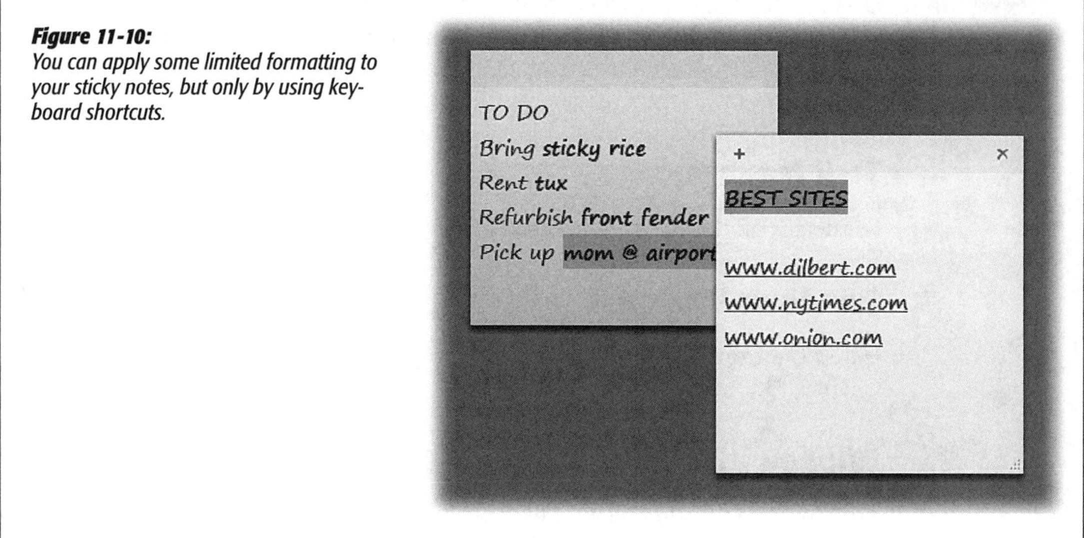

Figure 11-10:
You can apply some limited formatting to your sticky notes, but only by using keyboard shortcuts.

Creating Notes

To create a new note, click the **+** button in the upper-left corner of the starter note, or press Ctrl+N. Then fill the note by typing or pasting.

Note the resize handle on the lower-right corner of each note. Drag it to make notes larger or smaller onscreen.

Formatting Notes

You can format the text of a note—a *little* bit. There are no menus, of course, so you have to use keyboard shortcuts:

- **Bold, Italic, Underline.** Press Ctrl+B, Ctrl+I, or Ctrl+U.
- **Strikethrough style.** Press Ctrl+T.
- **Create a bulleted list.** Press Ctrl+Shift+L.

Tip: Press Ctrl+Shift+L a second time to produce a numbered list.

- **Change the type size.** Press Ctrl+Shift+> (larger font) or Ctrl+Shift+< (smaller).

You can also change the "paper" color for a note to any of five other pastel colors. To do that, right-click the note and then choose from the shortcut menu.

Deleting Notes

To get rid of a note, click the little ✕ in the upper-right corner. (You may have to point to it to see it.) When the program asks if you're sure, click Yes.

On the other hand, you can *exit* Sticky Notes without worrying that you'll lose what you've already typed. Right-click the Sticky Notes icon on the taskbar, for example, and choose "Close window" from the shortcut menu. The program disappears, but all your notes will be there the next time you open it.

Task Manager

For details on this newly redesigned program-killing tool, see page 335.

Windows Defender

Here's the front panel for Windows 8's built-in antivirus software. Details are in Chapter 13.

Windows Easy Transfer

This program transfers all your files and settings from an old PC to a new one—over a cable, over a network, or on a disk. Details are on page 847.

Windows Easy Transfer Reports

It's not crystal clear why this program gets its own icon on your All Programs screen, when important things like Internet Explorer for the desktop don't. But in any case, once you've used Windows Easy Transfer, open this program to read about what that program moved where on your new computer.

Windows Fax and Scan

See Chapter 19 for full details on sending and receiving faxes from your PC—and on scanning documents using a scanner.

Windows Journal

Windows Journal is for taking notes (Figure 11-11). But unlike Notepad or WordPad, Journal is specially designed for touchscreens. You can take your notes in handwriting, and later ask the program to convert it into typed text. Try *that* on an iPad!

Journal opens up to a blank note page; File→New Note opens another one.

Tip: The standard new note looks like a sheet of lined notebook paper. But if you choose File→New Note from Template, you get to choose from a bunch of different looks for your new note: graph paper, Sudoku-ish paper, even musical staff paper.

You can create your own design templates, too. Use the File→Page Setup command to specify the paper size, paper color, line pattern, background picture, and other elements of your page. Then choose File→Save As, and choose the template format as you name your new sheet of "stationery."

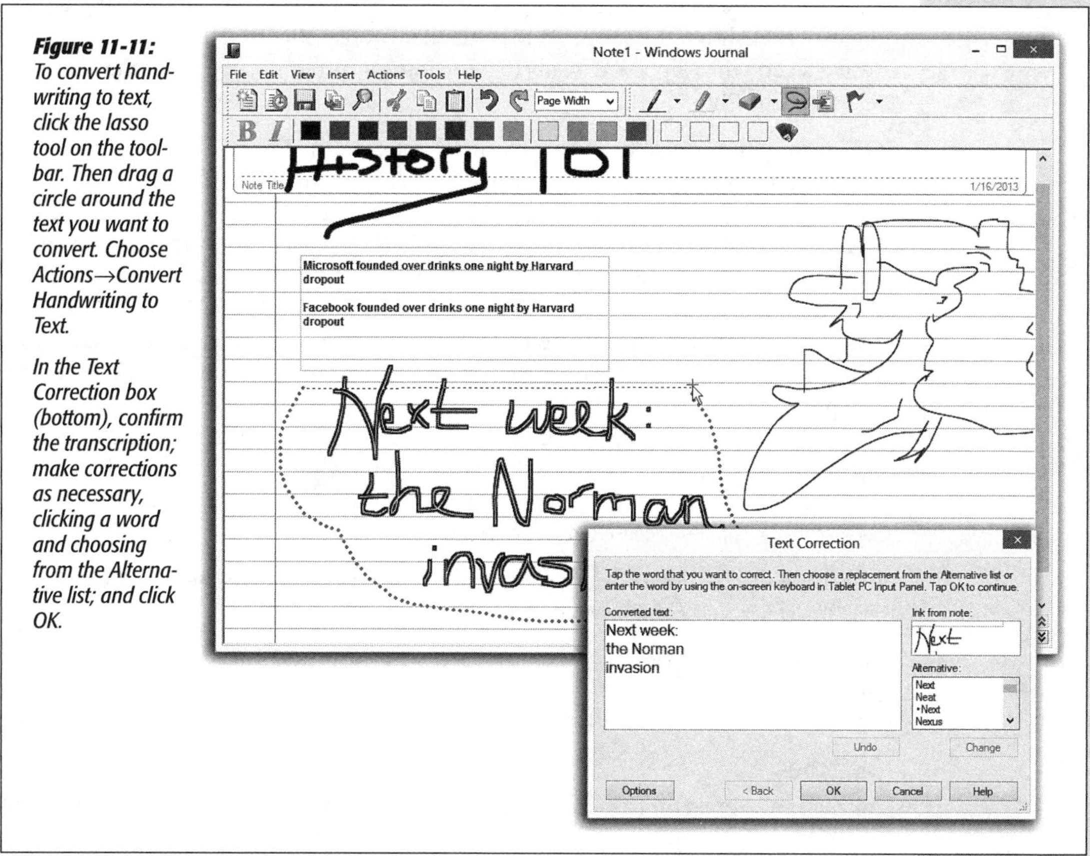

Figure 11-11: *To convert handwriting to text, click the lasso tool on the toolbar. Then drag a circle around the text you want to convert. Choose Actions→Convert Handwriting to Text.*

In the Text Correction box (bottom), confirm the transcription; make corrections as necessary, clicking a word and choosing from the Alternative list; and click OK.

Handwriting

All you have to do is start writing, using your finger or, for less frustration, a stylus. The toolbar offers a pop-up menu of pen thicknesses; for a choice of colors, choose View→Toolbars→Format.

Tip: You can change your pen thickness or color even after your writing is on the page—something that's very difficult to do with real pen marks. Select the writing using the lasso tool, and then choose Edit→Format Ink. Make your changes in the resulting dialog box.

An eraser tool is available on the toolbar if you mess up. There's also a highlighter pen that lets you draw over the most important parts of your notes for emphasis.

Even when your notes are still in handwritten-scrawl form, Journal can still search for text. Depending on how messy your writing is, this trick can seem like something of a miracle. Just choose File→Search and type the text you're trying to find. Journal highlights the matching handwritten phrase, wherever it appears in your notes.

Later, when the lecture or meeting is over, you can convert the handwriting to text; Figure 11-11 shows the steps. They conclude with an offer to either (a) put the converted text on the Clipboard, ready to paste into any program, or (b) put the converted text into a text box on the page.

Of course, you can also type into a Journal note; use the Insert→Text Box command to plop a rectangle onto the page, which you can fill with typing.

Tip: To move the text box, click the Selection lasso tool. Point to the text box's border; when the pointer becomes a four-headed arrow, you can drag to move the text box.

You can also import an existing text document into Journal, and then mark it up with your pen or finger (hello, proofreaders!). Use the File→Import command for this purpose.

Tip: When you first open Journal, you're asked if you want to install the Journal Note Writer driver. Say yes. It adds, to the Print menus of other programs, a new "printer" that sends any document to Journal. (If you declined that opportunity, choose Tools→Repair Journal Note Writer.)

For example, suppose you're in Word. You can choose File→Print, and then choose Journal Note Writer as your "printer." Click Print; name and save the resulting file.

Now you can switch to Journal, use File→Open, and open that file, which has now turned into a Journal document.

Sketches

Journal is also great for freehand drawing, of course. Sure beats the back of an envelope.

The program can even help clean up your work. If you draw a rough approximation of a line, square, or circle, you can select it with the Selection lasso and then use the Action→Change Shape To command. The submenu options (Line, Square, Circle/Ellipse) turn your scratched shape into a perfectly, computer-drawn version.

Exporting

When your masterpiece is ready for the viewing public, you can:

- Use the File→Export command to save it as a TIFF graphics file (great for sketches).
- Select some writing with the Selection lasso, and then choose Action→Convert to email. Journal converts the writing to typed text as described above, and then puts it into a new outgoing email message.

Windows Live Mail

If you downloaded the Essentials software, as described at the beginning of this chapter, then you have a much more complete email program than the TileWorld app included with Windows 8. See Chapter 16 for a full writeup.

Windows Live Messenger

Somewhere between email and the telephone lies a unique communication tool called *instant messaging*. Messenger, of course, is Microsoft's very own instant messenger program; it's part of the Essentials suite described at the start of this chapter.

Messenger does four things very well:

- **Instant messaging.** If you don't know what instant messaging is, there's a teenager near you who does.

  It's like live email. You type messages in a chat window, and your friends type replies back to you in real time. Instant messaging combines the privacy of email and the immediacy of the phone.

- **Free long distance.** If your PC has a microphone, and your buddy's does, too, the two of you can also chat *out loud,* using the Internet as a free long-distance phone.
- **Free videoconferencing.** If you and your buddies all have broadband Internet connections and cameras, you can have *video* chats, no matter where you happen to be in the world. This arrangement is a jaw-dropping visual stunt that can bring distant collaborators face to face without plane tickets—and it costs about $99,900 less than professional videoconferencing gear.
- **File transfers.** Got an album of high-quality photos or a giant presentation file that's too big to send by email? Forget about using some online file-transfer service or networked server; you can drag that monster file directly to your buddy's PC, through Messenger, for a direct machine-to-machine transfer.

This would be the perfect place to read about Messenger, if it weren't for one inconvenient detail: Microsoft bought Skype for $8.5 billion—and is using it to replace its own Messenger program.

In short, Microsoft courteously requests that you download Skype instead. Once you sign in with your Microsoft ID, guess what? All your old Messenger buddies appear automatically. You'll hardly know you're using a different program.

Windows Live Writer

If WordPad is a basic word processor, and Notepad is a basic text processor, then Writer is a basic *blog* processor. It's a simple program for composing blogs (Web logs—frequently updated Web pages full of text and photos) and, more important, posting them online. If you don't already have a blog, Writer makes it easy to create one that's hosted by Microsoft for free.

When you first open Writer, you're asked to set up your new blog. After the welcome screen, you have to specify *where* on the Web you want your blog to live.

- **If you already have a blog account,** either on Microsoft's SharePoint or one of its rivals (Blogger, WordPress, TypePad, or some other site), click the appropriate button. When you click Next, you're asked for the blog's Web address and your account name and password.
- **If you don't already have a blog account,** click "Create a new blog." You're instructed to visit *wordpress.com* and create a blog account there manually. (That process involves answering a lot of questions and replying to a confirmation email.)

  When that's all over, return to the first page of the Writer setup screen—and this time, choose the WordPress button. Because now, after all, you have a WordPress account. When you're asked if you want to download the WordPress template, click Yes.

***Figure 11-12:** Writer is Microsoft's blog-writing tool. It lets you compose fully formatted and illustrated blog posts (text, graphics, links, tables) and post them online with just a couple of clicks.*

Note: There's no reason you can't maintain multiple blog accounts. Just choose Tools→Accounts at any time, and click Add to add on a new account.

Then, after a moment, you name your new blog ("Cat Diaries" or whatever)—and then you're ready to begin writing!

The process goes like this:

- **Make up a title for your post.** Each new post (mini-article) on your blog needs a title. Type it into the "Enter a post title" headline box.
- **Write.** Go ahead and type or paste into the big empty, white box. You can use the formatting tools on the toolbar (see Figure 11-12) to dress up the formatting. (Don't miss the "HTML styles" pop-up menu, which offers different canned styles for headings.)
- **Add pictures, links, tables, or videos.** On the Insert tab, you'll find buttons that let you link to another Web page ("Hyperlink"), drop in a photo ("Picture"), or insert a table ("Table"). The other buttons here even let you insert a video or a map.

Tip: When you click a photo you've inserted, a new Picture Tools/Format tab appears on the Ribbon. It offers all kinds of options: You can make your text wrap around the photo, add a drop shadow border, change the size of the photo, crop it, rotate it, or adjust its contrast. The "Picture effects" pop-up menu even lets you apply cheesy special effects, like Black and White, Sharpen, Emboss, and so on.

When it's all over, and everything looks good, and you've checked your spelling (click Spelling at the right end of the Home tab), and you've clicked Preview to see what the thing will look like on the Web, you can publish your little writeup for your fans worldwide to enjoy. Just click Publish on the Home tab of the Ribbon.

After a moment, your Web browser opens, with your fresh, hot, piping blog post in all its glory. Now all you have to do is send the address of your blog to your friends and loved ones so your fan base can start to grow.

Windows Media Player

This massive music and video player is described in Chapter 18.

Note: What happened to Windows Meeting Space, which would ordinarily appear here in the alphabetical list? It's gone. Microsoft has eliminated it. The requirements were too steep, the setup was too confusing, and pretty much nobody used it. Then again, Microsoft SharedView offers pretty much the same features in a free, simpler form: *http://connect.microsoft.com/site94*.

Windows PowerShell

PowerShell is a command console and scripting language. If you're a programmer, PowerShell lets you write your own simple programs, called *cmdlets* ("commandlets") that can perform all kinds of automated drudgery for you: Copy or move folders, manipulate files, open or quit programs, and so on.

You harness all this power by typing up *scripts* in PowerShell's command-line interface (which means no mouse, no menus, no windows—all text, like in the DOS days). In short, PowerShell is not for the layperson. If you're an *ambitious* layperson, however, a Google search for *PowerShell tutorial* unveils all kinds of Web sites that teach you, step-by-step, how to harness this very advanced tool.

Windows Speech Recognition

Windows offers a surprisingly useful (and accurate) speech-recognition feature. You can read all about it on page 346.

WordPad

WordPad is a basic word processor (see Figure 11-13). Among other blessings, WordPad has a toolbar ribbon for quick access to formatting commands, and it can open and create Microsoft Word files. Yes, you can get away with not buying Microsoft Office, and none of your email business partners will ever know the difference.

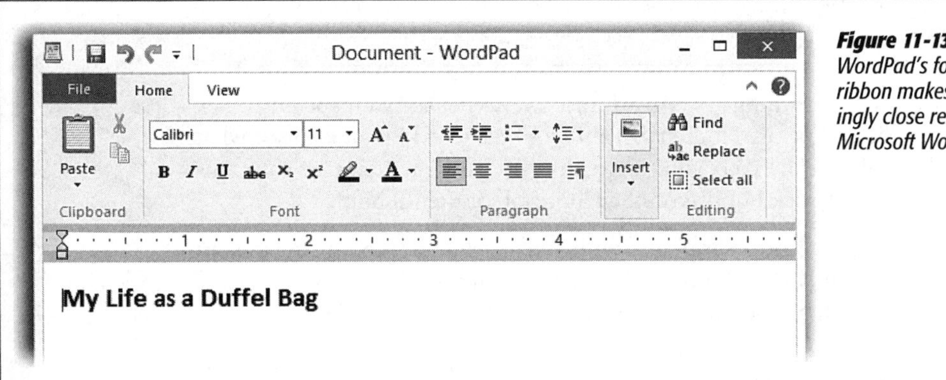

Figure 11-13: *WordPad's formatting ribbon makes it a surprisingly close relative to Microsoft Word.*

And it's not just Word files. WordPad also can open and create plain text files, Rich Text Format (RTF) documents, and OpenOffice.org files.

Using WordPad

When WordPad first opens, you see an empty sheet of electronic typing paper. Just above the ruler, the Ribbon offers menus and buttons that affect the formatting of your text. As in any word processor, you can apply these formats (like bold, italic, or color) to two kinds of text:

- **Text you've highlighted by dragging the mouse across it.**

- **Text you're *about* to type.** In other words, if you click the *I* button, the next characters you type will be italicized. Click the *I* button a second time to turn off the italics.

The Font formatting buttons let you change the look of selected text: font, size, color, subscript, and so on. The Paragraph formatting buttons affect entire paragraphs, as shown in Figure 11-4.

Figure 11-14:
These buttons make paragraphs flush left, centered, flush right, or bulleted as a list. You can drag through several paragraphs before clicking these buttons, or you can click these buttons to affect just the paragraph where your insertion point already is. The little L's on the ruler indicate tab stops that have been clicked into place; each press of the Tab key makes the insertion point jump to the next one.

WordPad doesn't offer big-gun features like spell checking, style sheets, or tables. But it does offer a surprisingly long list of core word-processing features. For example:

- **Find, Replace.** Using the Find button (right end of the Home tab on the Ribbon), you can locate a particular word or phrase instantly, even in a long document. The Replace command takes it a step further, replacing that found phrase with another one (a great way to change the name of your main character throughout your entire novel, for example).

- **Indents and Tab stops.** As shown in Figure 11-14, you click on the ruler to place tab stops there. Each time you press the Tab key, your insertion point cursor jumps in line with the next tab stop.

- **Bulleted lists.** You're reading a bulleted list right now. To apply bullets to a bunch of paragraphs, click the Bullets button (☰). If you click the ▾ next to it, you can create a numbered or lettered list instead.
- **Insert object.** This button lets you create or slap in a picture, graph, chart, sound, movie, spreadsheet, or other kind of data. (The "Paint drawing" button opens up a temporary Paint window so that you can whip up a quick sketch that then gets dropped into your WordPad document.)

Tip: If you click "Date and time," you get a dialog box full of date and time formats (12/18/2013; 12-Dec-2013; Wednesday, December 18, 2013, and so on). Double-click one to insert that date into your document at the insertion point.

- **Drag-and-drop editing.** Instead of using the three-step Copy and Paste routine for moving words and phrases around in your document, you can simply drag highlighted text from place to place on the screen.

XPS Viewer

This little app is dedicated to letting you read XPS files that people send you. (Hint: Nobody will.)

UP TO SPEED

Text-Selection Fundamentals

Before doing almost anything to text in a word processor, like making it bold, changing its typeface, or moving it to a new spot in your document, you have to *highlight* the text you want to affect. For millions of people, this entails dragging the cursor extremely carefully, perfectly horizontally, across the desired text. And if they want to capture an entire paragraph or section, they click at the beginning, drag diagonally, and release the mouse button when they reach the end of the passage.

That's all an enormous waste of time. Selecting text is the cornerstone of every editing operation in a word processor, so there are faster and more precise ways of going about it.

For example, double-clicking a word highlights it, instantly and neatly. In fact, by keeping the mouse button pressed on the second click, you can now drag horizontally to highlight text in crisp one-word chunks–a great way to highlight text faster and more precisely. These tricks work anywhere you can type.

In most programs, including Microsoft's, additional shortcuts await. For example, *triple*-clicking anywhere within a paragraph highlights the entire paragraph. (Once again, if you *keep* the button pressed at the end of this maneuver, you can then drag to highlight your document in one-paragraph increments.)

In many programs, including Word and WordPad, you can highlight exactly one sentence by clicking within it while pressing Ctrl.

Finally, here's a universal trick that lets you highlight a large blob of text, even one that's too big to fit on the current screen. Start by clicking to position the insertion point cursor at the very beginning of the text you want to capture. Now scroll, if necessary, so the ending point of the passage is visible. Shift+click there. Windows instantly highlights everything between your click and your Shift+click.

You know how Microsoft always comes up with its own version of anything popular? iPod, iPad, Web browser, whatever?

Its latest software target is the PDF document, the brainchild of Adobe.

A PDF document, of course, is a file that opens up on any kind of computer—Mac, Windows, Unix, anything—looking exactly the way it did when it was created, complete with fonts, graphics, and other layout niceties. The recipient can't generally make changes to it, but can search it, copy text from it, print it, and so on. It's made life a lot easier for millions of people because it's easy, free, and automatic.

And now Microsoft wants a piece o' dat. Its Microsoft XPS document format is pretty much the same idea as PDF, only it's Microsoft's instead of Adobe's.

To turn any Windows document into an XPS document, choose File→Print. In the Print dialog box, choose Microsoft XPS Document Writer as the "printer," and then click Print. You're asked to name it and save it.

The result, when double-clicked, opens up in the Reader app in TileWorld.

But a message lets you know that it can also open into this program, XPS Viewer—a bare-bones program that does nothing but open XPS files. Either program offers the usual PDF-type options: find a phrase, jump to a page, zoom in or out, switch to double-page view, print, save a copy, and so on. XPS Viewer also has commands for unlocking password-protected XPS documents.

Truth is, Microsoft has a long battle ahead if it hopes to make the XPS format as commonplace as PDF.

But then again, long battles have never fazed it before.

CHAPTER
12

The Control Panel

Like the control panel in the cockpit of an airplane, the Control Panel is an extremely important feature of Windows 8. It's teeming with miniature applications (or *applets*) that govern every conceivable setting for every conceivable component of your computer. Some are so important that you may use them (or their corresponding notification-area icons) every day. Others are so obscure that you'll wonder what on earth inspired Microsoft to create them.

Now, the Control Panel isn't the only source of settings in Windows 8. Some of the most frequently used controls are right there in the Charms bar (hit Settings). Another set, mostly pertaining to TileWorld, await when you tap "Change PC settings" on said Charms panel.

This chapter, however, covers the real deal, The Big One, the main event: the traditional desktop Control Panel.

Note: Here and there, within the Control Panel, you'll spot a little Windows security-shield icon. It tells you that you're about to make an important, major change to the operating system, something that will affect everyone who uses this PC—fiddling with its network settings, for example, or changing its clock. To prove your worthiness (and to prove that you're not an evil virus attempting to make a nasty change), you'll be asked to *authenticate* yourself; see page 743 for details.

Many Roads to Control Panel

There are two ways to change a setting in the Control Panel. There's the traditional way, which begins with opening the Control Panel and drilling down from there. And there's the Search way. That's when you jump directly to the setting you want, using the Start screen's Search mechanism.

Opening the Control Panel Itself

You can reach the main Control Panel window in a number of ways. Here are the three fastest:

- **Fast.** From the Start screen, type *control*. (That, of course, opens the Search panel and conducts a search.) Control Panel is the first result; press Enter (or select it) to open it.
- **Faster.** Open the Charms panel; click Settings; click Control Panel. (Weirdly enough, that Control Panel link appears only when you're at the desktop—not in TileWorld.)
- **Fastest.** Press ⊞+X, or right-click the lower-left corner of the desktop, to open the X menu in that corner; click Control Panel.

Tip: Wouldn't it be great if the Control Panel's icon were right on the Start screen, so you could open it with one click, just like any other program? Yes, it would. See the box on the facing page.

In each case, the Control Panel window opens (Figure 12-1). The "View by" pop-up menu (upper right) shows that there are a few ways to view the complete collection of control panels: by category or as a list of small or large icons.

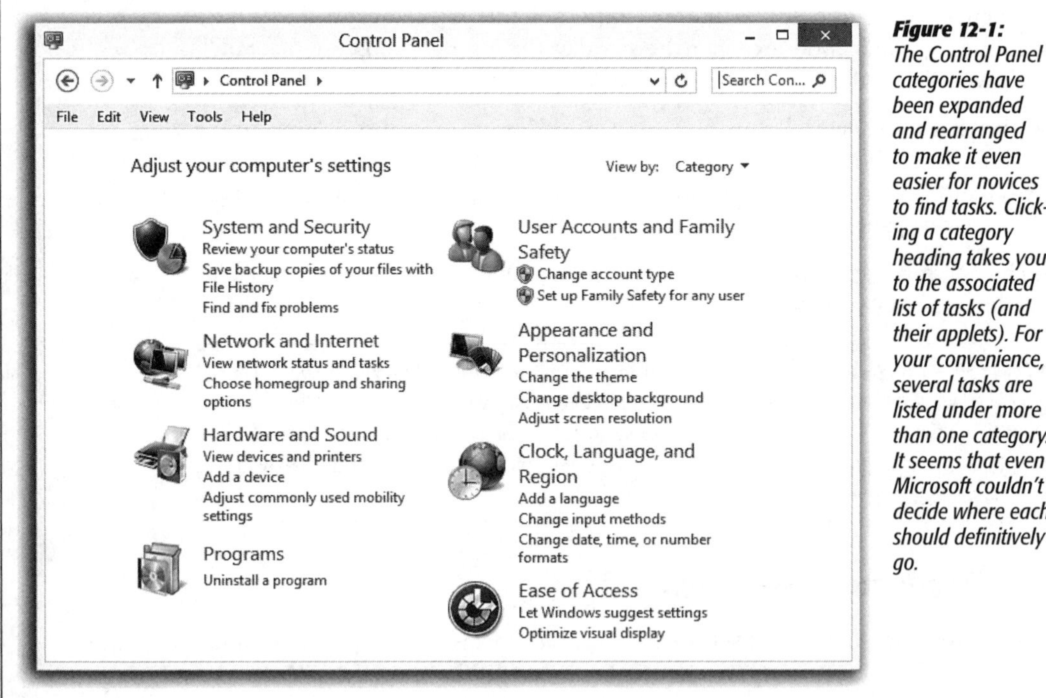

Figure 12-1: *The Control Panel categories have been expanded and rearranged to make it even easier for novices to find tasks. Clicking a category heading takes you to the associated list of tasks (and their applets). For your convenience, several tasks are listed under more than one category. It seems that even Microsoft couldn't decide where each should definitively go.*

Category View

Here's a rundown of the Control Panel home categories:

- **System and Security.** In this category are system and administrative tasks like backing up and restoring (including the new File History feature), and setting your power and security options (firewall, encryption, and so on).
- **Network and Internet.** This category contains settings related to networking, Internet options, offline files, and Sync Center (to manage synchronizing data between computers and network folders).
- **Hardware and Sound.** Here you find everything for managing gadgets connected to your computer: printer settings, projector settings, laptop adjustments, and so on.

POWER USERS' CLINIC

Control Panel on the Start Screen

Want to know the most convenient place of all for the Control Panel icon? On the Start screen, of course. Why on earth isn't the Control Panel there in the first place?

You can put it there. It requires patience, but you only have to do it once. And it's really not bad.

Phase 1: Make a shortcut of the Control Panel.

To do that, right-click the desktop; from the shortcut menu, choose New→Shortcut.

In the resulting dialog box, carefully type this geeky blob of code into the Location box. It looks complex, but it's just careful typing.

```
%windir%\explorer.exe shell:::{26EE0668-A00A-44D7-9371-BEB064C98683}
```

(Yes, type the hyphen after 9371.)

Click Next. Type *Control Panel* and then click Finish. Presto! There's a Control Panel icon on your desktop now.

Unfortunately, its icon looks like an Explorer folder.

Phase 2: Change the icon to look like the Control Panel.

Right-click the Control Panel shortcut you just made. From the shortcut menu, choose Properties.

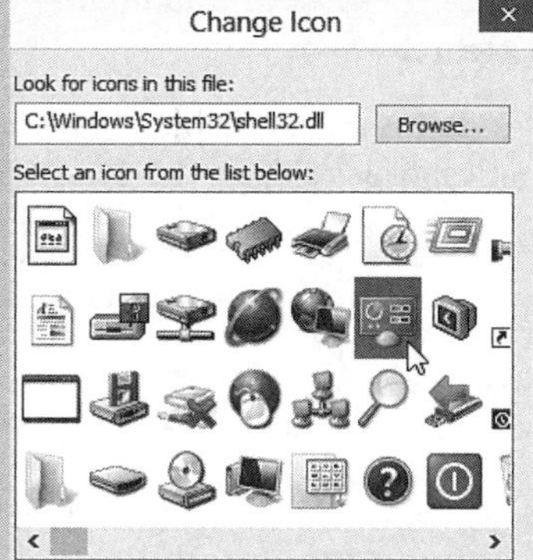

In the Properties dialog box, on the Shortcut tab, click Change Icon. Then click Browse. Navigate to the C:→Windows→System32 folder, and find the icon called Shell32.dll. Open it.

Now you get to see another array of icon possibilities; double-click the one that looks like the Control Panel. Click OK, and then OK again. Your shortcut now looks like the Control Panel.

Phase 3: Add the shortcut to the Start screen.

Right-click the Control Panel shortcut icon. From the shortcut menu, choose Pin to Start.

Congratulations! You've just added the Control Panel to the Start screen. It's way off to the right, of course, but you can drag it anywhere you like. From now on, you're in control of the Control Panel.

- **Programs.** You'll probably use this one a lot. Here's how you uninstall programs, choose which program is your preferred one (for Web browsing or opening graphics, for example), turn Windows features on and off, and manage your desktop gadgets.
- **User Accounts and Family Safety.** This category contains the settings you need to manage the accounts on the computer, including the limited accounts that parents can create for their children.
- **Appearance and Personalization.** Here's a big category indeed. It covers all things cosmetic, from how the desktop looks (plus taskbar, Sidebar, and personalization settings) to folder options, fonts, and ease-of-access settings.
- **Clock, Language, and Region.** These time, language, and clock settings all have one thing in common: They differ according to where in the world you are.
- **Ease of Access.** This revamped category is one-stop shopping for every feature Microsoft has dreamed up to assist the disabled. It's also the rabbit hole into Speech Recognition Options.

Classic View

The category concept sounds OK in principle, but it'll drive veterans nuts. You don't want to guess what category Fax wound up in—you just want to open the Print and Fax control panel, right now.

Fortunately, Classic view is still available. That's where the Control Panel displays all 50 icons in alphabetical order (Figure 12-2).

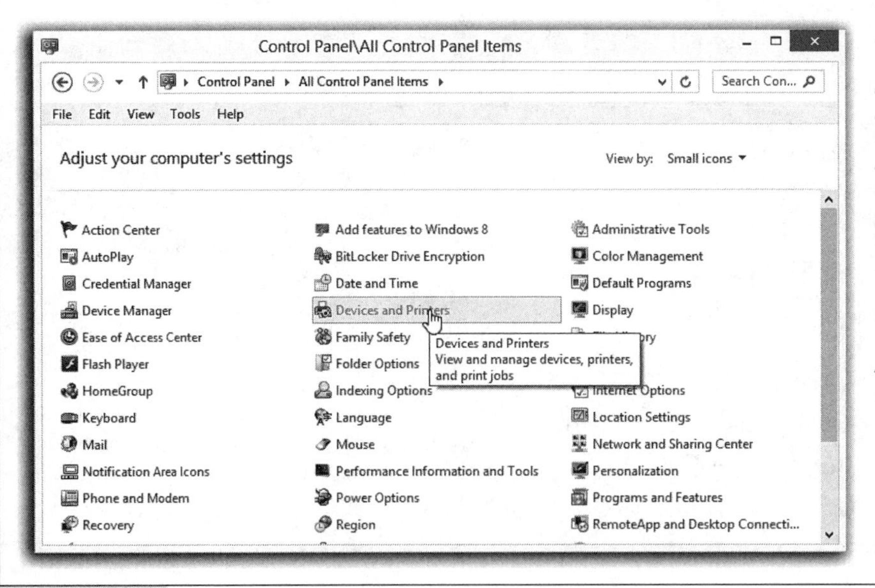

Figure 12-2: *Classic view might be overwhelming for novices, because the task icons give little indications about what settings they actually contain. Here's a hint: Remember that you can just move your mouse over a task and pause there. A tooltip pops up, giving you an idea of what's inside.*

Use the "View by" pop-up menu in the upper right, and choose either "Small icons" or "Large icons." Then double-click the icon of the applet you'd like to use.

Control Panel via Search

Ever try to configure a setting in the Control Panel but forget which applet it's in? Happens all the time. It's perfectly possible to waste some time, clicking likely categories, opening and closing a few applet icons, backing out, and trying again.

Use the search box in the Charms bar instead. It's uncannily good at taking you to the control panel you really want.

Quick: Where do you go to set up your monitor's color settings? Would it be under the System and Security category? Hardware and Sound? Appearance and Personalization?

Don't worry about it. Press the ⊞ key or button to open the Start screen; type *color*; select Settings. Now you see Color Management in the results list; tap or click to open it. (On other quests, you might type *fonts, sound, battery, accounts, date, CDs, speech,* or whatever.)

Yes, you've had to type, just like in the ancient DOS days—but you saved a lot of time, steps, and fumbling. (There's a similar search box right in the Control Panel window itself.)

Tip: There are other shortcuts to the Control Panel, too, that don't require typing. If you don't mind a cluttered desktop, make a shortcut for the applets you access most. To do that, open the Control Panel. Right-click the icon you want; from the shortcut menu, choose "Create shortcut." It automatically places it on the desktop for you.

The Control Panel, Applet by Applet

Icon view is the perfect structure for a chapter that describes each Control Panel applet, since it's organized in alphabetical order. The rest of this chapter assumes that you're

FREQUENTLY ASKED QUESTION

What Happened to AutoRun?

What the heck? I've inserted a flash drive that I know contains a software installer, but it doesn't run automatically like it did in Windows Vista. What's going on?

Microsoft made a big change back in Windows 7: It turned off the ability for software installers to autorun from USB gadgets like flash drives.

Why? Because the bad guys were using the AutoRun feature as an evil back door for installing viruses and other nasties on your PC. You'd insert a flash drive, and bing!—something would auto-install without your awareness.

Nowadays, if you really want to run an installer from a flash drive, open the Computer window, open the drive's icon, and run the installer manually by double-clicking it.

looking at the Control Panel in one of the two Icon views. (You may see additional applets, depending on the features of your particular computer.)

Action Center

Here's the Action Center: a single, consolidated window listing every security- and maintenance-related concern that Windows has at the moment. Be grateful: These all used to be separate balloons harassing you from the right end of the taskbar. For details, see Chapter 21.

Add Features to Windows 8

This is the humble successor to what used to be called Anytime Upgrade. It lets you upgrade to a fancier version of Windows 8 by paying the price difference.

For example, if you have the standard version of Windows 8, you can upgrade to Windows 8 Pro without disturbing any of your files or programs. And if you already have Pro, you can pay $10 to download Windows Media Center.

Administrative Tools

This icon is actually a folder containing a suite of technical administrative utilities. Many of these tools, intended for serious technowizards only, are explained in Chapters 21 and 23.

AutoPlay

What do you want to happen when you insert a CD? Do you want to see a window of what's on it? Do you want the music on it to start playing? Do you want to auto-run whatever software installer is on it? Do you want whatever photos it contains to get copied to your Pictures library?

The answer, of course, is "Depends on what kind of CD it is," and also "That should be up to me." That's the purpose of the AutoPlay feature. It differentiates among different kinds of audio CDs and DVDs, video CDs and DVDs, programs (like software and games), pictures, video and audio files, and blank CDs and DVDs. Page 290 tells all.

BitLocker Drive Encryption

BitLocker encrypts the data on your drives to keep them from being accessed by the bad guys who might steal your laptop. For details, see Chapter 23.

Color Management

Microsoft created this applet in conjunction with Canon in an effort to make colors more consistent from screen to printer. Details are on page 627.

Credential Manager

Credential Manager (formerly Windows Vault) is designed to memorize your name/password combinations, of the sort that you use to log into things. The panel offers two tabs: Web Credentials (stores your Web-site passwords) and Windows Credentials (passwords for shared network drives and corporate-intranet Web sites).

When you click the ⌄ next to an item's name, you see details about the stored item; a Remove button; and a Show button, which (if you correctly enter your Windows login password to prove your worth) reveals the actual stored password for that item.

At the top of the window, "Back up Credentials" and "Restore Credentials" offer you the chance to back up your entire array of memorized passwords.

You don't need to bother, though, if you log in with a Microsoft account [page 726]; in that case, your passwords are backed up automatically online—and any time you log into another Windows 8 computer, your passwords are already stored and ready to use.

Date and Time

Your PC's concept of what time it is can be very important. Every file you create or save is stamped with this time, and every email you send or receive is marked with it. When you drag a document into a folder that contains a different draft of the same

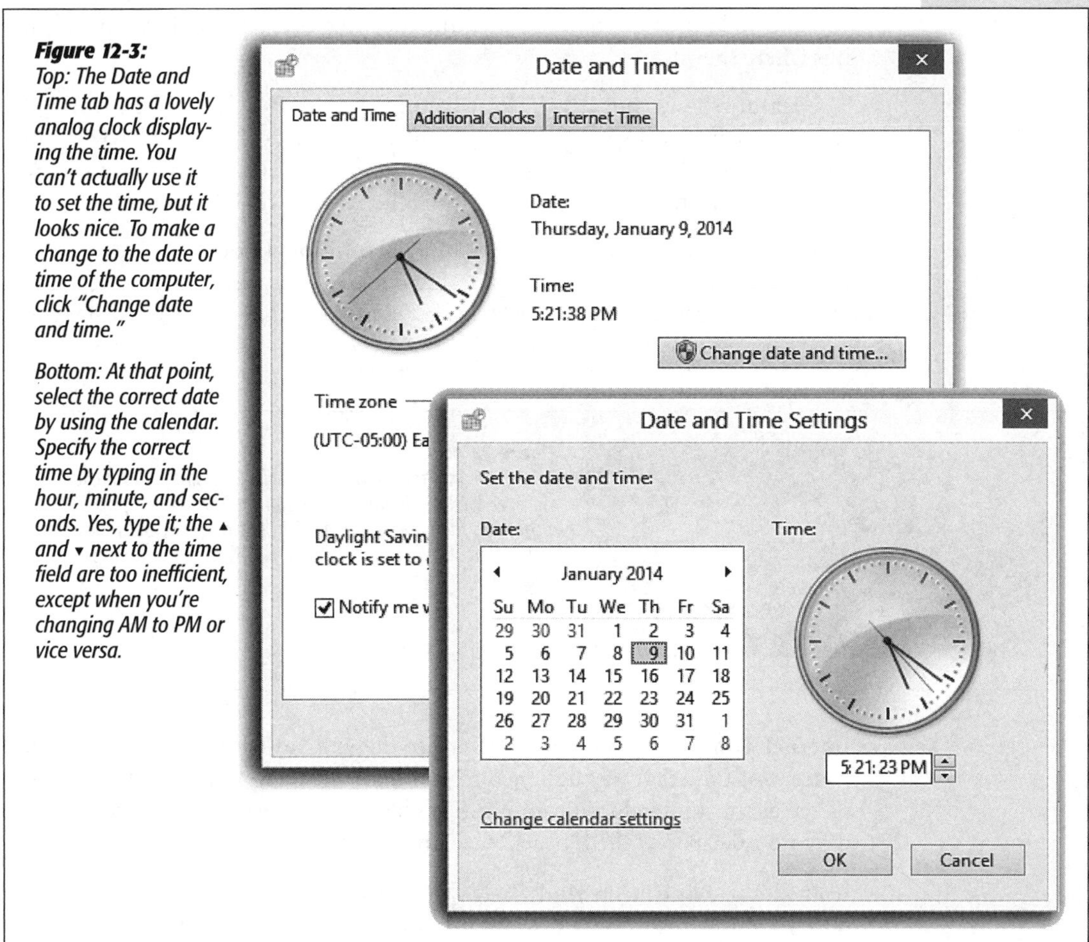

Figure 12-3: *Top: The Date and Time tab has a lovely analog clock displaying the time. You can't actually use it to set the time, but it looks nice. To make a change to the date or time of the computer, click "Change date and time."*

Bottom: At that point, select the correct date by using the calendar. Specify the correct time by typing in the hour, minute, and seconds. Yes, type it; the ▲ and ▼ next to the time field are too inefficient, except when you're changing AM to PM or vice versa.

thing, Windows warns that you're about to replace an older version with a newer one (or vice versa)—but only if your clock is set correctly.

This program offers three tabs:

- **Date and Time.** Here's where you can change the time, date, and time zone for the computer (Figure 12-3)—if, that is, you'd rather not have the computer set its own clock (read on).

Tip: In the "Time zone" section of the Date and Time tab, you can find exactly when Windows thinks daylight saving time is going to start (or end, depending on what time of year it is). In addition, there's an option to remind you a week before the time change occurs, so you don't wind up unexpectedly sleep-deprived on the day of your big TV appearance.

- **Additional Clocks.** If you work overseas, or if you have friends, relatives, or clients in different time zones, you'll like this one; it's the only thing that stands between you and waking them up at three in the morning because you forgot what time it is where they live.

  This feature shows you, at a glance, what time it is in other parts of the world. You can give them any display name you want, like "Paris" or "Mother-in-Law time." Note that the additional clocks' times are based on the PC's own local time. So if the computer's main clock is wrong, the other clocks will be wrong, too.

  Figure 12-4 shows how to check one of your additional clocks.

Tip: If you *click* the time on the taskbar instead of just pointing to it (Figure 12-4), you get three large, beautiful *analog* clocks in a pop-up window.

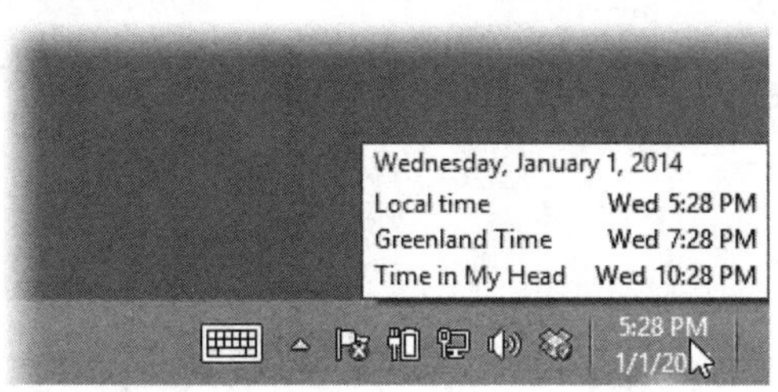

Figure 12-4:
To see the time for the additional clocks, point without clicking over the time in the notification area. You get a pop-up displaying the time on the additional clock (or clocks) that you configured.

- **Internet Time.** This option has nothing to do with Swatch Internet Time, a 1998 concept of time that was designed to eliminate the complications of time zones. (Then again, it introduced complications of its own, like dividing up the 24-hour day into 1,000 parts called "beats," each one being 1 minute and 26.4 seconds long.)

  Instead, this tab teaches your PC to set its own clock by consulting one of the highly accurate scientific clocks on the Internet. To turn the feature on or off, or to specify which atomic Internet clock you want to use as the master clock, click

Change Settings. (No need to worry about daylight saving time, either; the time servers take that into account).

Note: Your PC resets its clock once a week–*if* it's connected to the Internet at the time. If not, it gives up until the following week. If you have a dial-up modem, in other words, you might consider connecting to the Internet every now and then and using the "Update now" button to compensate for all the times your PC unsuccessfully tried to set its own clock.

Default Programs

In an age when Microsoft is often accused of leveraging Windows to take over other realms of software, like Web browsing and graphics, the company created this command center. It's where you choose your preferred Web browser, music-playing program, email program, and so on—which may or may not be the ones provided by Microsoft.

You're offered four links:

- **Set your default programs.** Here's where you teach Windows that you want your own programs to replace the Microsoft versions. For instance, you can say that, when you double-click a music file, you want to open iTunes and not Windows Media Player. For details, see page 415.
- **Associate a file type or protocol.** This window lets you specify exactly what kind of file you want to have opened by what program. (That's essentially what happens in the background when you set a default program.) File associations are covered in more depth on page 355.
- **Change AutoPlay Settings.** This option opens the AutoPlay applet described on page 290.
- **Set program access and computer defaults.** Here you can not only manage what programs are used by default, like browsing with Internet Explorer or getting email with Windows Mail, but also disable certain programs so they can't be used at all. It's organized in rather combative schemes: You can choose to prefer Microsoft products (disabling access to the non-Microsoft interlopers), non-Microsoft products (pro–third party, anti-Microsoft), or create a custom scheme, in which you can specifically choose a mix of both. See page 363 for more information.

Device Manager

The Device Manager console shows you where all your hardware money was spent. Here you or your tech-support person can troubleshoot a flaky device, disable and enable devices, and manage device drivers. If you're comfortable handling these more advanced tasks, then Chapter 20 is for you.

Devices and Printers

Double-click to open the Devices and Printers window, where everything you've attached to your PC—Webcam, printer, scanner, mouse, whatever—appears with its own picture and details screen. Chapter 20 has the details.

Display

This one opens the "Make it easier to read what's on your screen" window. The task pane on the left side offers links to other screen-related controls, like "Adjust resolution," "Change display settings," and so on.

Ease of Access Center

The Ease of Access Center is designed to make computing easier for people with disabilities, although some of the options here can benefit anyone. See page 175 for details.

Family Safety

This applet lets you, the wise parent, control what your inexperienced or out-of-control loved one (usually a child, but sometimes a spouse) can and cannot do on (or with) the computer. For more information, see page 475.

File History

Here's the on/off switch for File History, Windows 8's new automated file-backup feature. Specify which kinds of files you want included and, when disaster strikes, bring your files back from the dead. Details in Chapter 21.

Folder Options

This box appears when you click Options on the Ribbon's View tab in an Explorer window. Its three tabs (General, View, Search) are described beginning on page 224.

Fonts

This icon is a shortcut to a folder; it's not an applet. It opens into a window that reveals all the typefaces installed on your machine, as described in Chapter 19.

Homegroup

The Homegroup icon opens the "Change homegroup settings" screen, where you can change the password or perform other administrative tasks related to your Homegroup (home file-sharing network). Homegroups are described in Chapter 27.

Indexing Options

The Start menu's search box is so magnificently fast because it doesn't actually root through all your files. Instead, it roots through an *index* of your files, an invisible, compact database file that Windows maintains in the background.

This dialog box lets you manage indexing functions and change what gets indexed, and it lets you know how many items have been indexed. To learn more about the particulars of indexing and how to use it, see Chapter 7.

Internet Options

A better name for this program would have been "Web Browser Options," since all its settings apply to Web browsing—and, specifically, to Internet Explorer. As a matter of fact, this is the same dialog box that opens from the Tools→Internet Options menu command within Internet Explorer. Its tabs break down like this:

- **General, Security, Privacy, and Content.** These tabs control your home page, cache files, search-field defaults, and History list. They also let you define certain Web pages as off-limits for your kids, and manage RSS feeds, as well as block pop-up windows. Details on these options are in Chapter 14.
- **Connections.** Controls when your PC modem dials, and lets you set up VPN (virtual private networking) connections.
- **Programs.** Use this tab to manage browser add-ons, decide whether or not Internet Explorer should warn you whenever it is not the default browser (for your protection, of course), or choose the default programs that open when you click a link to email someone, to open a media file, or to view the HTML source of a Web page (View→Source).
- **Advanced.** On this tab, you find dozens of checkboxes, most of which are useful only in rare circumstances and affect your Web experience only in minor ways. For example, "Enable personalized favorites menu" shortens your list of bookmarks over time, as Internet Explorer hides the names of Web sites you haven't visited in a while. (A click on the arrow at the bottom of the Favorites menu makes them reappear.)

  Similarly, turning off the "Show Go button in Address bar" checkbox hides the Go button at the right of the address bar. After you've typed a Web address (URL), you must press Enter to open the corresponding Web page instead of clicking the Go button on the screen. And so on.

Keyboard

You're probably too young to remember the antique known as a *typewriter.* On some electric versions of this machine, you could hold down the letter X key to type a series of XXXXXXX's—ideal for crossing something out in a contract, for example.

On a PC, *every* key behaves this way. Hold down any key long enough, and it starts spitting out repetitions, making it easy to type, "No WAAAAAY!" or "You go, grrrrrl!" for example. (The same rule applies when you hold down the arrow keys to scroll through a text document, hold down the = key to build a separator line between paragraphs, hold down Backspace to eliminate a word, and so on.) The Speed tab of this dialog box (Figure 12-5) governs the settings:

- **Repeat delay.** This slider determines how long you must hold down the key before it starts repeating (to prevent triggering repetitions accidentally).
- **Repeat rate.** The second slider governs how fast each key spits out letters once the spitting has begun.

  After making these adjustments, click the "Click here and hold down a key" test box to try out the new settings.
- **Cursor blink rate.** The "Cursor blink rate" slider actually has nothing to do with the *cursor,* the little arrow that you move around with the mouse. Instead, it governs the blinking rate of the *insertion point,* the blinking marker that indicates where typing will begin when you're word processing, for example. A blink rate that's too slow makes it more difficult to find your insertion point in a window filled with data. A blink rate that's too rapid can be distracting.

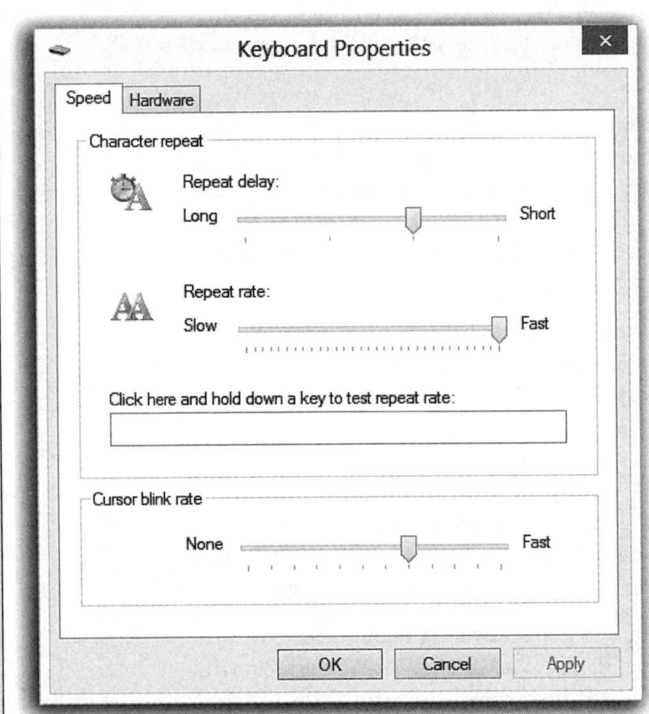

Figure 12-5:
How fast do you want your keys to repeat? This dialog box also offers a Hardware tab, but you won't go there very often. You'll use it exclusively when you're trying to troubleshoot your keyboard or its driver.

Language

Here you can install multiple input language kits on your computer and switch among them when the mood strikes. The key term here is *default input language*; the language for the operating system doesn't change. If you installed Windows in English, you still see the menus and dialog boxes in English.

But when you switch the input language, your keyboard can type the characters necessary for the selected language.

The "Add a language" button lets you install additional language packs to your computer (Figure 12-6, top); the Options button lets you download them from Microsoft's Web site (Figure 12-6, bottom).

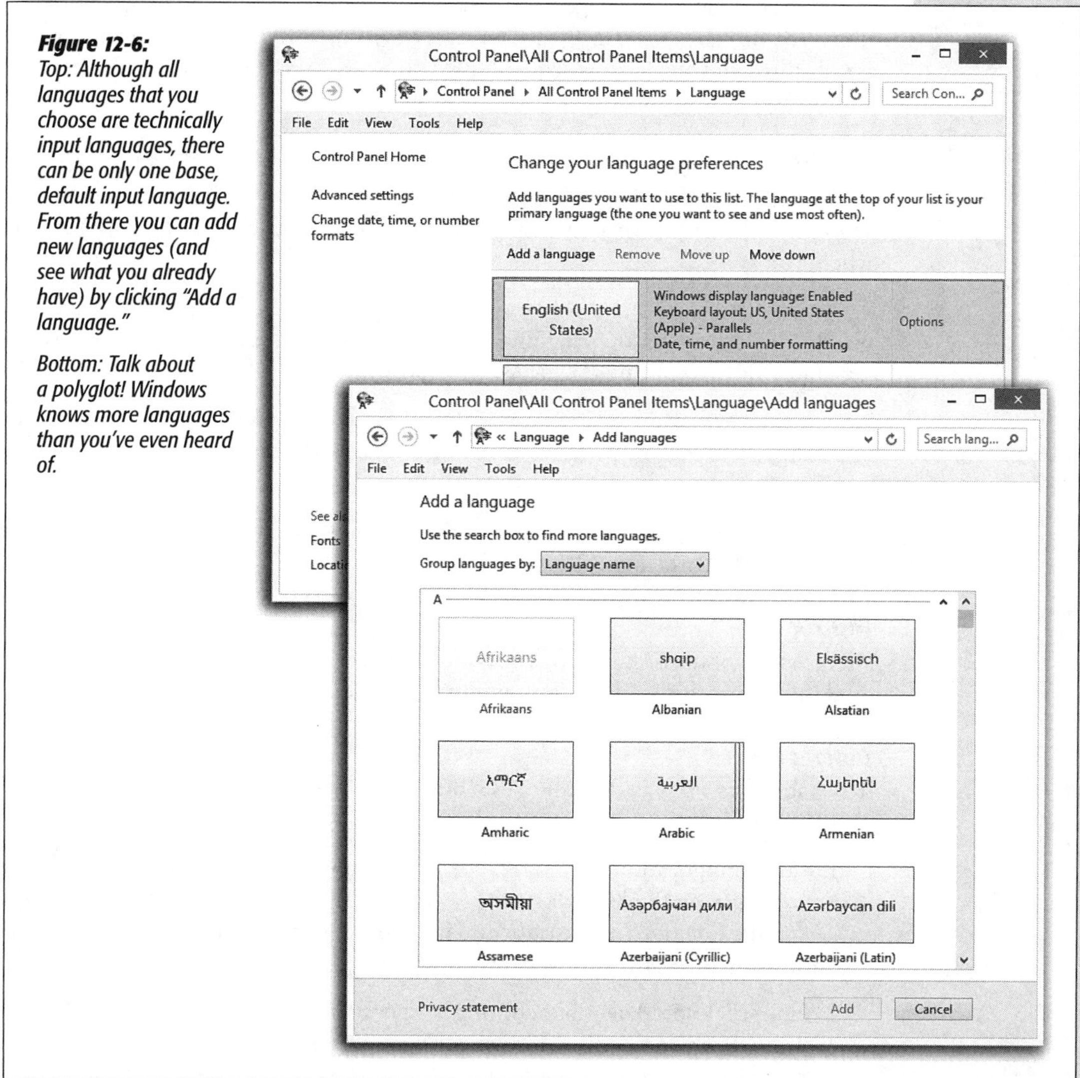

Figure 12-6: *Top: Although all languages that you choose are technically input languages, there can be only one base, default input language. From there you can add new languages (and see what you already have) by clicking "Add a language."*

Bottom: Talk about a polyglot! Windows knows more languages than you've even heard of.

If you click "Advanced settings," you can specify how you switch languages as you work. For example, you can turn on the Language bar, which either floats on the desktop or sits nestled in your system tray. It's a toolbar that lets you switch input languages on the fly.

Click Options to see the possible settings. For example, you can make the Language bar transparent, display text labels, and even add additional Language bar icons in the taskbar.

If you click "Change language bar hot keys," you can set up a keyboard combination to use to switch between layouts. The factory setting is the left Alt key+Shift, which scrolls through your layouts sequentially with each press, but you can also assign a combination to each specific layout.

Location Settings

These days, tablets and some laptops can tell where they are. They might have GPS sensors, for example, or they might use WiFi hotspot triangulation to figure out where you are.

This, of course, is a hot-button issue for privacy advocates. This panel is the master on/off switch for desktop programs' ability to use your location. (A movie-listings program, for example, might suggest theaters near you.)

Even if you've turned on "Turn on the Windows Location platform" here, however, you still have to turn on "Use my location" in *each individual program* that wants to use this information.

(There's a separate Location Settings switch in TileWorld's "PC settings" panel, too; it governs TileWorld apps.)

Mouse

All the icons, buttons, and menus in Windows make the mouse a very important tool. And the Mouse dialog box is its configuration headquarters (Figure 12-7).

Buttons tab

This tab offers three useful controls: "Button configuration," "Double-click speed," and "ClickLock."

- **Button configuration.** This checkbox is for people who are left-handed and keep their mouse on the left side of the keyboard. Turning on this checkbox lets you switch the functions of the right and left mouse buttons so that your index finger naturally rests on the primary button (the one that selects and drags).
- **Double-click speed.** Double-clicking isn't a very natural maneuver. If you double-click too slowly, the icon you're trying to open remains stubbornly closed. Or worse, if you accidentally double-click an icon's name instead of its picture, Windows sees your double-click as two single-clicks, which tells it that you're trying to rename the icon.

  The difference in time between a double-click and two single-clicks is usually well under a second. That's an extremely narrow window, so let Windows know what you consider to be a double-click by adjusting this slider. The left end of the slider bar represents 0.9 seconds, and the right end represents 0.1 seconds. If you need more time between clicks, move the slider to the left; if your reflexes are highly tuned (or you drink a lot of coffee), try moving the slider to the right.

Each time you adjust the slider, remember to test your adjustment by double-clicking the little folder to the right of the Speed slider. If the folder opens, you've successfully double-clicked. If not, adjust the slider again.

Figure 12-7:
If you're a southpaw, you've probably realized that the advantages of being left-handed when you play tennis or baseball were lost on the folks who designed the computer mouse. It's no surprise, then, that most mice are shaped poorly for lefties—but at least you can correct the way the buttons work.

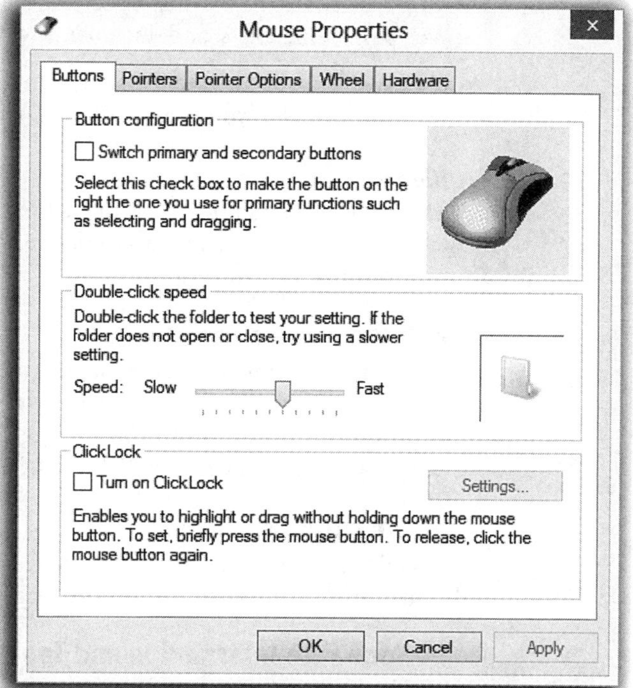

- **ClickLock.** ClickLock is for people blessed with large monitors or laptop trackpads who, when dragging icons onscreen, get tired of keeping the mouse button pressed continually. Instead, you can make Windows "hold down" the button automatically, avoiding years of unpleasant finger cramps and messy litigation.

  When ClickLock is turned on, you can drag objects on the screen like this: First, point to the item you want to drag, such as an icon. Press the left mouse or trackpad button for the ClickLock interval. (You can specify this interval by clicking the Settings button in this dialog box.)

  When you release the mouse button, it acts as though it's still pressed. Now you can drag the icon across the screen by moving the mouse (or stroking the trackpad) without holding any button down.

  To release the button, hold it down again for your specified time interval.

Pointers tab

See page 308 for details on changing the shape of your cursor.

Pointers Options tab

See page 308 for a rundown of these cursor-related functions.

Wheel tab

The scroll wheel on the top of your mouse may be the greatest mouse enhancement since they got rid of the dust-collecting ball on the bottom. It lets you zoom through Web pages, email lists, and documents with a twitch of your index finger.

Use these controls to specify just how *much* each wheel notch scrolls. (You may not see this tab at all if your mouse doesn't have a wheel.)

Hardware tab

The Mouse program provides this tab exclusively for its Properties buttons, which take you to the Device Manager's device properties dialog box. Useful if you have to troubleshoot a bad driver.

Network and Sharing Center

This network command center offers, among other things, a handy map that shows exactly how your PC is connected to the Internet. It also contains a tidy list of all networking-related features (file sharing, printer sharing, and so on), complete with on/off switches. See Chapter 27 for details.

Notification Area Icons

Double-click to open up a screen where you can hide or show specific icons in your system tray (at the right end of your taskbar), as described in Chapter 2.

Performance Information and Tools

Windows 8 needs a fast computer. Just how fast is yours? This control panel breaks it down for you, even going so far as to give your PC a grade for speed.

In addition, this window has convenient links to tabs of several other applets (like Power Options, Indexing Service, and System Performance), as well as access to the old Disk Cleanup utility. For power users, there's even a kickin' Advanced Tools window stocked with speed-related goodies, logs, and reports. For details, see Chapters 21 and 23.

Personalization

Have you ever admired the family photo or space shuttle picture plastered across a coworker's PC desktop? Wished your cursor was bigger? Been annoyed that you have to log in again every time your screen saver kicks in?

All these are aspects of the Personalization applet. It's such a big topic, it gets its own chapter: Chapter 8.

POWER USERS' CLINIC

The Story of God Mode

It started on a blog called jkOnTheRun: the crazy rumor that Microsoft had created a secret Control Panel view called God Mode, and that only power users could access it.

Crazy thing is, it's true. "God Mode" is a simple folder that brings all aspects of Windows control—Control Panel functions, interface customization, accessibility options—to a single location.

To create this all-powerful Control Panel folder, start by creating an empty folder anywhere. Give it this name:

GodMode.{ED7BA470-8E54-465E-825C-99712043E01C}

One typo, and you're toast. But if you type it correctly, the folder transforms into a strange little icon called GodMode. Open it, and you get the super-cool Control Panel view shown here, with major headings and minor ones in a tidy alphabetical list—and even a Search GodMode box. Convenient! Slick! Secret!

Or not.

As it turned out, the bloggers had gotten just about everything about God Mode wrong. It isn't unique to Windows 7/8, it isn't unique to the Control Panel, and it isn't actually called God Mode. The bloggers made up "God Mode"; in fact, you can type any folder name you want before the first period. Call it Master Control Panel, or All Tasks, or whatever.

Finally, this Control Panel thing isn't secret; it's a documented shortcut for programmers. Actually, "God Mode" is only one of a dozen summary folders you can create. You can also create folders that offer lists of what's in the Action Center, the Devices and Printers window, and so on.

Here are a few of the folders you can create. In each case, you can type anything you want before the period, as long as the hexadecimal code that follows is correct:

AutoPlay.{9C60DE1E-E5FC-40f4-A487-460851A8D915}

DateandTime.{E2E7934B-DCE5-43C4-9576-7FE4F75E7480}

FolderOptions.{6DFD7C5C-2451-11d3-A299-00C04F8EF6AF}

Fonts.{93412589-74D4-4E4E-AD0E-E0CB621440FD}

Homegroup.{67CA7650-96E6-4FDD-BB43-A8E774F73A57}

InternetOptions.{A3DD4F92-658A-410F-84FD-6FBBBEF2FFFE}

NetworkandSharingCenter.{8E908FC9-BECC-40f6-915B-F4CA0E70D03D}

PowerOptions.{025A5937-A6BE-4686-A844-36FE4BEC8B6D}

Sound.{F2DDFC82-8F12-4CDD-B7DC-D4FE1425AA4D}

SpeechRecognition.{58E3C745-D971-4081-9034-86E34B30836A}

Troubleshooting.{C58C4893-3BE0-4B45-ABB5-A63E4B8C8651}

Mobility Center.{5ea4f148-308c-46d7-98a9-49041b1dd468}

There are many more, as a quick Google search will tell you. Not all of them work in Windows 8 (sometimes the folder you're renaming with the magic name simply doesn't change its icon and adopt its new personality). And of course, there's not a whole lot of point in going to this trouble; if you really want direct access to a certain Control Panel applet, you can simply drag it to your desktop right from the Control Panel window!

But even if it's not that secret, not that special, and not that new, it's still cool.

Phone and Modem

You'll probably need to access these settings only once: the first time you set up your PC or laptop to dial out. Details in Chapter 13.

Power Options

The Power Options program (Figure 12-8) manages the power consumption of your computer. That's a big deal when you're running off a tablet or laptop battery, of

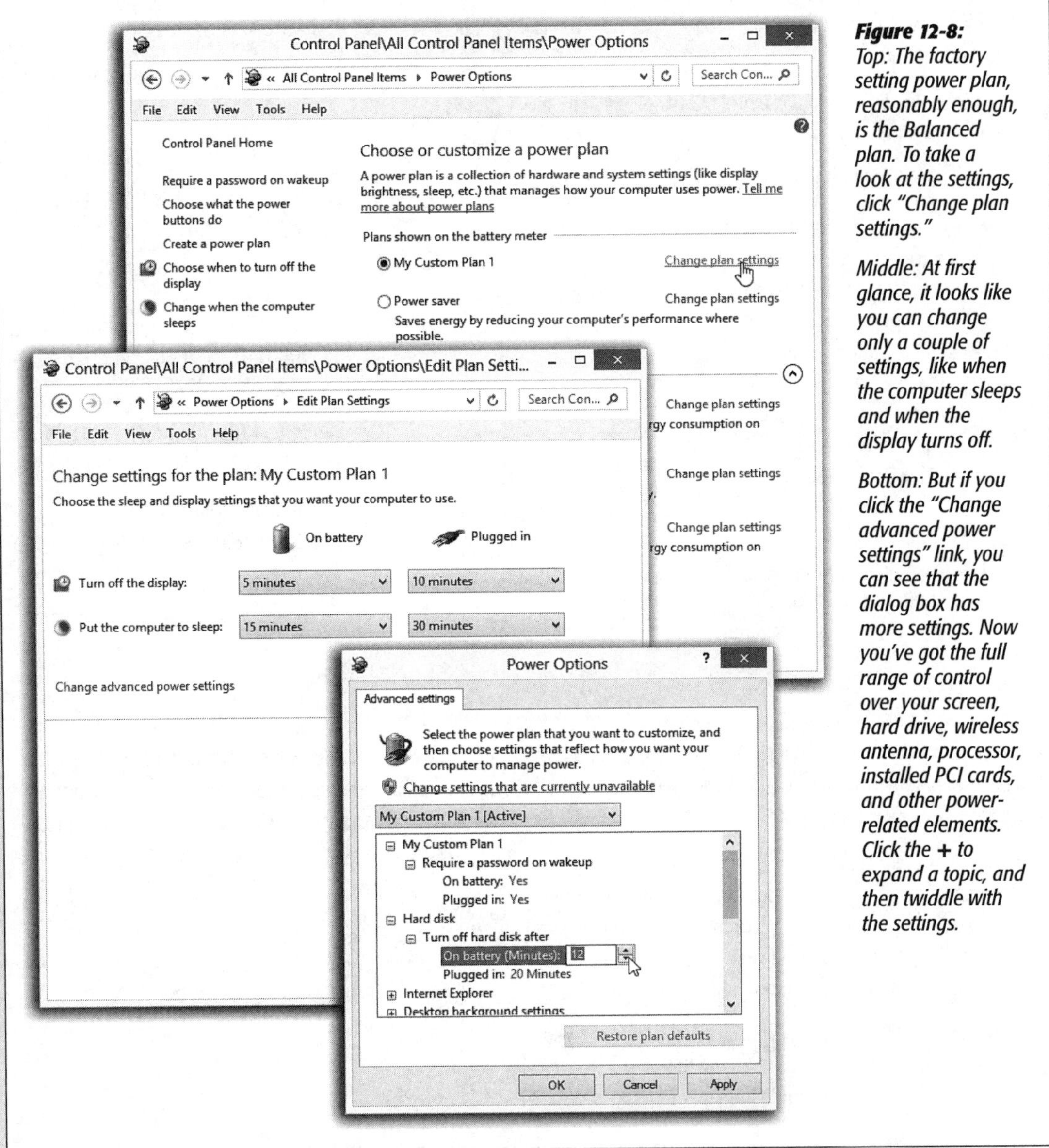

Figure 12-8: *Top: The factory setting power plan, reasonably enough, is the Balanced plan. To take a look at the settings, click "Change plan settings."*

Middle: At first glance, it looks like you can change only a couple of settings, like when the computer sleeps and when the display turns off.

Bottom: But if you click the "Change advanced power settings" link, you can see that the dialog box has more settings. Now you've got the full range of control over your screen, hard drive, wireless antenna, processor, installed PCI cards, and other power-related elements. Click the + to expand a topic, and then twiddle with the settings.

course, but it's also important if you'd like to save money (and the environment) by cutting down on the juice consumed by your *desktop* PC.

The options you see depend on your PC's particular features. Figure 12-8 displays the Power Options for a typical computer.

A *power plan* dictates things like how soon the computer goes to sleep, how bright the screen is, what speed the processor cranks at, and so on. This panel presents you right up front with three premade power plans:

- **Balanced,** which is meant to strike a balance between energy savings and performance. When you're working hard, you get all the speed your PC can deliver; when you're thinking or resting, the processor slows down to save juice.
- **Power saver** slows down your computer, but saves power—a handy one for laptop luggers who aren't doing anything more strenuous than word processing.
- **High performance** (click "Show additional plans" to see it) sucks power like a black hole but grants you the computer's highest speed possible.

Tip: You don't have to open the Control Panel to change among these canned plans. On a laptop, for example, you can just click the battery icon in your notification area and choose from the pop-up menu.

Creating your own plan

But adding to Microsoft's three starter plans can be useful, not only because you gain more control, but also because you get to see exactly what a plan is made of. You create a new plan by modifying one of Microsoft's three starter plans.

Start by clicking "Create a power plan" (left side of the window). On the next screen, click the plan you want to modify, type a name for your plan (say, PowerPoint Mode), and then click Next.

The "Change settings" dialog box now appears. Yeah, yeah, you can use the pop-up menus to specify how soon your PC sleeps and turns off its monitor; if you're using a laptop, you can even specify *different* timings depending on whether you're running on battery power or plugged into the wall. Boring!

The real fun begins when you click "Change advanced power settings" (Figure 12-8, bottom). Lots of these subsettings are technical and tweaky, but a few are amazingly useful (click the **+** button next to each one to see your options):

- **Require a password on wakeup.** Nice security feature if you're worried about other people in your home or office seeing what you were working on before your machine went to sleep to save power.
- **Hard disk.** Making it stop spinning after a few minutes of inactivity saves a lot of juice. The downside: The PC takes longer to report in for work when you return to it and wake it up.

- **Wireless Adapter Settings.** If you're not using your computer, you can tell it to throttle back on its WiFi wireless networking signals to save juice.
- **Sleep.** How soon should the machine enter low-power sleep state after you've left it idle? And should it sleep or hibernate?
- **Power buttons and lid.** What should happen when you close the lid of your laptop or press its Power or Sleep button (if it has one)?
- **PCI Express.** If you've got any adapter cards installed, and they're modern and Windows 7/8–aware, then they, too, can save you power by sleeping when not in use.
- **Processor power management.** When you're running on battery power, just how much are you willing to let your processor slow down to save juice?
- **Display.** These controls govern how fast your monitor turns off to save power.
- **Multimedia settings.** These controls have little to do with electricity and everything to do with not ruining your big PowerPoint pitch. They let you specify that the computer should not sleep if you're in the middle of playing a song, a movie, or a PowerPoint deck.
- **Battery.** "Critical battery action" dictates what the laptop should do when the battery's all out: hibernate, sleep, or shut down. The other settings here let you govern when Windows' two low-battery warnings appear (that is, at what percentage-remaining levels).

Some of these options also appear in the task pane at the left side of the Power Options control panel, for your convenience. They affect whatever plan is currently selected.

In any case, click OK to close the "Advanced settings" box. Click "Save changes" to immortalize your newly created power plan. From now on, you can choose its name from the Battery icon on the system tray (if you have a laptop), or switch to it right in the control panel (if you have a desktop).

Tip: To delete a plan you've created, open the Power Options control panel; click "Change plan settings," and then click "Delete this plan."

Programs and Features

Programs and Features is about managing the software you have installed, managing updates, and buying software online. It replaces the old Add/Remove Programs program. ("Add" was dropped from the name because it was unnecessary; all programs these days come with their own installer. When was the last time you installed a program through Add/Remove Programs?)

This window is useful for fixing (which might simply mean reinstalling), changing, or uninstalling existing programs, and it's the only place you can go to turn on (or off) Windows features like Fax and Scan, Telnet Client, and more.

Recovery

The Recovery icon is nothing more than a trio of links: "Create a recovery drive" lets you turn a flash drive into an emergency startup disk. Open System Restore and Configure System Restore are both part of the System Restore feature that rewinds your computer to an earlier, better-behaved state (page 691). There's also a link here to the new PC Refresh feature (page 675).

Region

Windows can accommodate any conceivable arrangement of date, currency, and number formats (Figure 12-9); comes with fonts for dozens of Asian languages; lets you remap your keyboard to type non-English symbols of every ilk; and so on.

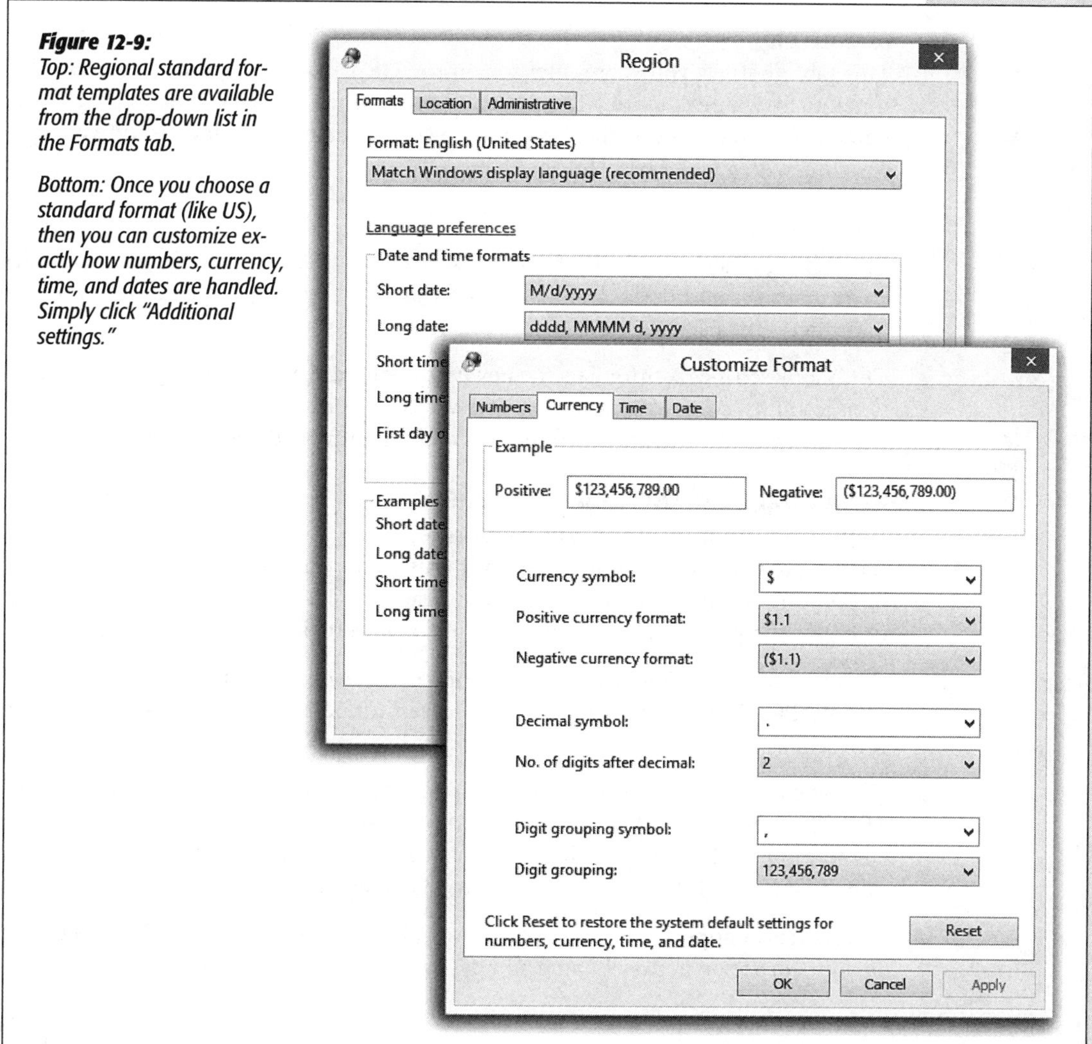

Figure 12-9:
Top: Regional standard format templates are available from the drop-down list in the Formats tab.

Bottom: Once you choose a standard format (like US), then you can customize exactly how numbers, currency, time, and dates are handled. Simply click "Additional settings."

Formats tab

If you think that 7/4 means July 4 and that 1.000 is the number of heads you have, then skip this section.

But in some countries, 7/4 means April 7, and 1.000 means one thousand. If your PC isn't showing numbers, times, currency symbols, or dates in a familiar way, choose your country from the "Current format" pop-up menu. (Or, if you're a little weird, use the "Customize this format" button to rearrange the sequence of date elements; see Figure 12-9.)

Tip: The Customize Format box (Figure 12-9) is where you can specify whether you prefer a 12-hour clock ("3:05 PM") or a military or European-style, 24-hour clock ("1505").

Location tab

This tab identifies your computer's location. (If it has GPS, you don't have to tell it manually where you are.) The point is so that when you go online to check local news and weather, you get the *right* local news and weather—a handy feature if you're traveling with a tablet or a laptop.

Administrative

The "Change system locale" button on this tab lets you specify which language handles error messages and the occasional dialog box. (Just changing your input language may not do the trick.)

The "Copy settings" button lets the newly configured language settings apply to new user accounts, so anyone who gets a new account on this computer will have your language, format, and keyboard settings conveniently available to them.

RemoteApp and Desktop Connections

With Windows 8, Microsoft continues its service to the world's corporate IT nerds. As in the past, these corporate system administrators can "publish" certain programs, or even entire computers, at the company headquarters—and you, using your laptop or home computer, can use them as though you were there.

But in Windows 8, these "published" resources behave even more like programs right on your PC. They're listed on your Start screen, for heaven's sake, and you can search for them as you'd search for any app.

The whole cycle begins when your company's network nerd provides you with the URL (Internet address) of the published program. Once you've got that, open the RemoteApp and Desktop Connections control panel, and then click "Set up a new connection with RemoteApp and Desktop Connections."

A wizard now appears; its screens guide you through pasting in that URL and typing in your corporate network name and password.

When it's all over, you see a confirmation screen, and your new "connection" is listed in the control panel.

Sound

This box contains four tabs that control every aspect of your microphone and speakers: Playback, Recording, Sounds, and Communications. See Figure 12-10.

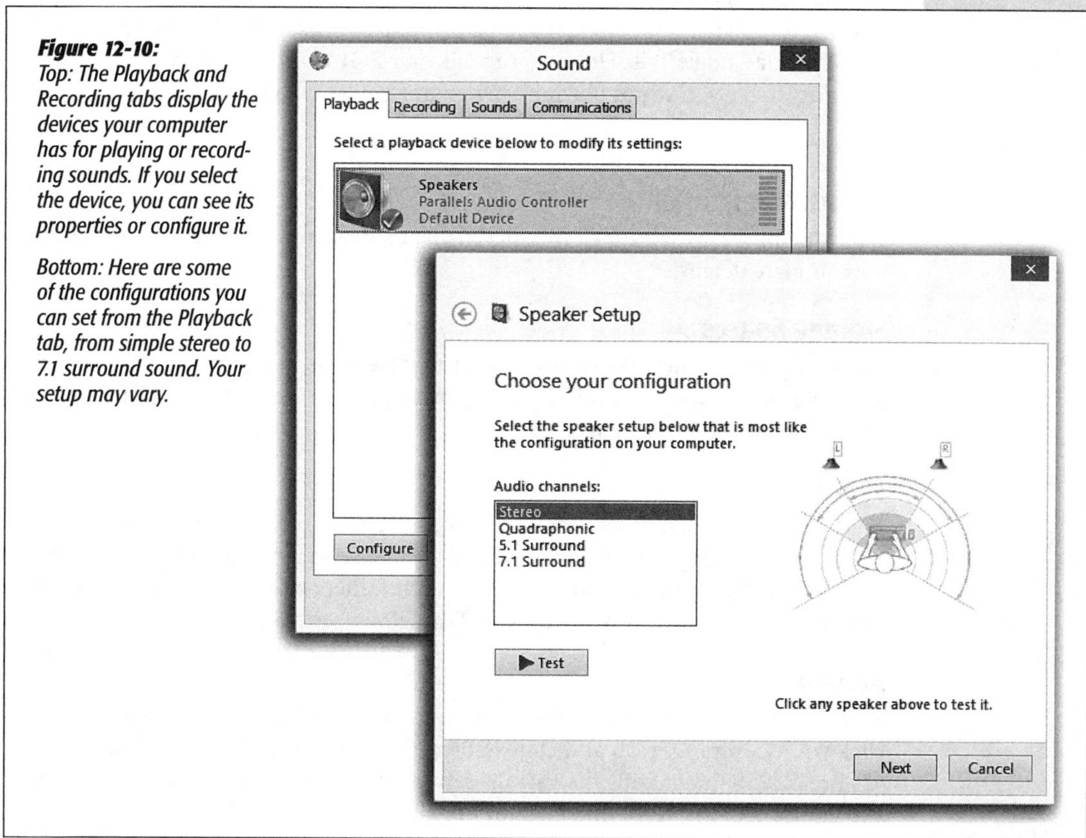

Figure 12-10: *Top: The Playback and Recording tabs display the devices your computer has for playing or recording sounds. If you select the device, you can see its properties or configure it.*

Bottom: Here are some of the configurations you can set from the Playback tab, from simple stereo to 7.1 surround sound. Your setup may vary.

Playback and Recording tabs

These tabs simply contain the icons for each attached sound device. To change a device's settings, select it, and then click Configure.

If you're configuring an output ("playback") device like a speaker or a headset, then you get a quick wizard that lets you set the speaker configuration (stereo or quadraphonic, for example). If you're configuring a microphone ("recording"), then you're taken to the Speech Recognition page, where you can set up your microphone.

Sounds tab

Windows comes with a tidy suite of little sound effects—beeps, musical ripples, and chords—that play when you turn on the PC, trigger an error message, empty the Recycle Bin, and so on. This tab lets you specify which sound effect plays for which situation; see page 305 for details.

Communications tab

This tab is designed for people who make phone calls using the PC, using a program like Skype or Google Talk. Here you can tell your PC to mute or soften other sounds—meaning music you've got playing—whenever you're on a PC call.

Nice touch.

Speech Recognition

This little program sets up all the speech-related features of Windows. See page 346 for complete details.

Storage Spaces

Storage Spaces is a new Windows 8 feature that lets you use two or more hard drives as a super-safe, super-redundant backup system. Even if one dies, your files are still protected. Details are on page 703.

Sync Center

The Sync Center used to be where you managed connected devices (like smartphones or palmtops) and synchronized them with your calendar and address book. In Windows 8, it's strictly for syncing your files with folders elsewhere on your corporate network, so you'll always be up to date. For details, see page 819.

System

This advanced control panel window is the same one that appears when you right-click your Computer icon and choose Properties from the shortcut menu (or press ⊞+Break key). It contains the various settings that identify every shred of circuitry and equipment inside, or attached to, your PC.

When you open the System icon in Control Panel, you're taken to the System window (Figure 12-11). Here you can find out:

- What edition of Windows is installed on your computer. As you know, Windows 8 comes in several editions. Not all editions are made equal; if you're flailing to find some feature that you could have sworn you were supposed to have, it's good to check here. You might find out that the feature you want is available only on higher-priced versions.
- Your PC's performance rating—a statistic for establishing your superiority over lesser PC owners.
- The model name and speed of your PC's processor (such as Intel Core i7, 2.0 GHz).

- How much memory your PC has. That's a very helpful number to know, particularly if you need to improve your computer's speed.
- Your computer's name, domain, or workgroup, which can be modified with the "Change settings" button. Remember, your computer name and description are primarily useful on a network, since that's how other people will identify your computer. Unless you tell it otherwise, Windows names your computer after your login name, something like Casey Robbins-PC.
- Whether or not your operating system is activated. For more on Activation, check Appendix A.
- What the Product ID key is for your system. Every legal copy of Windows has a Product ID key—a long serial number that's required to activate Microsoft software. For more information about Product ID keys, see Appendix A.

Tip: In the Windows Activation section, you can do something unprecedented (and this is a really good thing): You can change your Product ID simply by clicking "Change product key" in the System window without having to reinstall your operating system. That's progress.

***Figure 12-11:** The System window is a one-stop shop for all things computer-related. From your hardware (and what Windows thinks of it) to your product ID key, System's got you covered.*

At the left side of the window, you'll find a few links:

- **Device Manager.** This very powerful console lists every component of your PC: CD-ROM, Modem, Mouse, and so on. Double-clicking a component's name (or clicking the **+** symbol) discloses the brand and model of that component. For more on the Device Manager, see Chapter 20.

- **Remote settings.** To read about Remote Assistance—the feature that lets a technical help person connect to your PC (via the Internet) to help you troubleshoot—turn to page 324.
- **System Protection.** This link takes you to the System Protection tab in the System dialog box. Here you can keep track of the automatic system restores (snapshot backups of a system) or even create a new restore point. And if your computer has begun to act like it's possessed, you can go here to restore it to a previous restore point's state. Check out Chapter 21 for more details.
- **Advanced system settings.** Clicking this link opens the Advanced tab of the System Properties dialog box. This tab is nothing more than a nesting place for four buttons that open other dialog boxes—some of which aren't "advanced" in the least.

  The first Settings button opens the **Performance Options** dialog box, described on page 669. The second Settings button opens the **User Profiles** box, which is covered in Chapter 24. The third Settings button opens a **Startup and Recovery** window. It contains advanced options related to *dual-booting* (Appendix A) and what happens when the system crashes.

  Finally, the **Environment Variables** button opens a dialog box that will get technically minded people excited. It identifies, for example, the path to your Windows folder and the number of processors your PC has. If you're not in the computer-administration business, avoid making changes here.

Taskbar

This program controls every conceivable behavior of the taskbar. You can read all about these options—the same ones that appear when you right-click the taskbar or the Start button and choose Properties from the shortcut menu—in Chapter 6.

Troubleshooting

Here's a list of Windows' troubleshooters—step-by-step interview screens that walk you through fixing various problems. [Insert your own joke here about Windows' need for an entire program dedicated to troubleshooting.]

Anyway, you can find links here for running older programs under Windows 8, getting online, figuring out why your speakers aren't working, sleuthing out why your PC is getting so slow, and so on.

User Accounts

This control panel is the master switch and control center for the user-accounts feature described in Chapter 23. If you're the only one who uses your PC, you can (and should) ignore it.

Windows 7 File Recovery

If you've used the backup feature described in Chapter 21, and something goes wrong, this is where you go to recover files from the backup. (Why is it called "Windows 7" when this is Windows 8? Because Microsoft doesn't want you using this backup feature anymore. You have better tools, like File History. But this is here in case you upgraded a machine to Windows 8 after having used Windows 7 to make a backup.)

Windows Defender

Windows Defender is Microsoft's free anti-spyware/antivirus program, built into Windows. For an extensive look at what it can do for you, see Chapter 14.

Windows Firewall

In this age of digital technology, when most people's computers are connected at all times to the Internet (and therefore always vulnerable to the Internet), it's a good and reasonable idea to have a firewall protecting your computer from possible attacks and exploitation. To learn more about Windows Firewall, see Chapter 14.

Windows Mobility Center

Here's a one-stop shopping center for the most important laptop features: battery, wireless networking, external projector connection, and so on. You can read all about it in at the beginning of the Road Warrior's Handbook (Chapter 28).

Windows Update

Because Windows is a constant work in progress, Microsoft frequently releases updates, fixes, patches, and drivers, in hopes of constantly (or at least one Tuesday a month) improving your computer's speed and security. Windows Update is the tool used to acquire, install, and track those useful fixes. For a more in-depth look at Windows Update, see Chapter 21.

3

Part Three: Windows Online

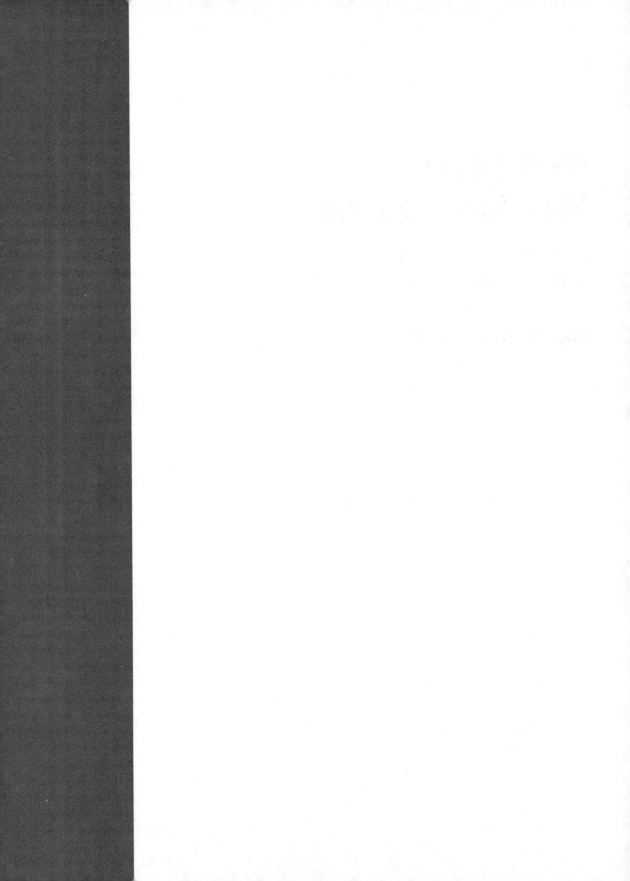

CHAPTER 13

Hooking Up to the Internet

Plenty of people buy a PC to crunch numbers, scan photos, or cultivate their kids' hand-eye coordination. But for millions of people, Reason One for using a PC is to get on the Internet. Few computer features have the potential to change your life as profoundly as the Web and email.

There are all kinds of ways to get your PC onto the Internet these days:

- **WiFi.** Wireless hotspots, known as WiFi, are glorious conveniences, especially if you have a laptop. Without stirring from your hotel bed, you're online at high speed. Sometimes for free.
- **Cable modems, DSL.** Over half of the U.S. Internet population connects over higher-speed wires, using broadband connections that are always on: cable modems, DSL, or corporate networks. (These, of course, are often what's at the other end of an Internet hotspot.)
- **Cellular modems.** A few well-heeled individuals enjoy the go-anywhere bliss of USB cellular modems, which get them online just about anywhere they can make a phone call. These modems are offered by Verizon, Sprint, AT&T, and so on, and usually cost $60 a month.
- **Tethering.** Tethering is letting your cellphone act as a glorified Internet antenna for your PC, whether connected by a cable or a Bluetooth wireless link. The phone company charges you maybe $20 a month extra for this convenience.

- **Dial-up modems.** It's true: Plenty of people still connect to the Internet using a modem that dials out over ordinary phone lines. They get cheap service but slow connections, and their numbers are shrinking.

This chapter explains how to set up each one of these. (For the basics of setting up your own network, see Chapter 25.)

Tip: If you upgraded to Windows 8 from an earlier version of Windows, then you can already get online, as the installer is thoughtful enough to preserve your old Internet settings. (So is Windows Easy Transfer, described in Appendix A.) That's the best news you'll hear all day.

Connecting to a WiFi Network

Almost every computer today has a built-in WiFi antenna, officially known as 802.11 (WiFi) wireless networking technology. WiFi can communicate with a wireless base station up to 300 feet away, much like a cordless phone. Doing so lets you surf the Web from your laptop in a hotel room, for example, or share files with someone across the building from you.

Chapter 25 has much more information about *setting up* a WiFi network. The real fun begins, however, when it comes time to *join* one.

Sometimes you just want to join a friend's WiFi network. Sometimes you've got time to kill in an airport, and it's worth a $7 splurge for half an hour. And sometimes, at some street corners in big cities, WiFi signals bleeding out of apartment buildings might give you a choice of several free hotspots to join.

If you're in a new place, and Windows discovers, on its own, that you're in a WiFi hotspot, then the icon sprouts an asterisk. And where is the icon? It's in two places:

- On the taskbar (Figure 13-1, top left).
- On the Settings pane of the Charms bar. (In other words, open the Charms bar and select Settings.)

Figure 13-1 shows you how to proceed. Along the way, you'll be offered the "Connect automatically" checkbox; if you turn it on, you'll spare yourself all this clicking the next time your PC is in range. It'll just hop on that network by itself.

Some hotspots (most these days, actually) are protected by a password. It serves two purposes: First, it keeps everyday schlumps from hopping onto that network, and it also encrypts the connection so that hackers armed with sniffing software can't intercept the data you're sending and receiving.

Tip: Some modern WiFi routers offer a feature called WPS (Wi-Fi Protected Setup). If you press the special WPS button at this point, it will transmit the password automatically to your PC, saving you the trouble of filling in the password yourself. (This technology is great because it transmits a huge, complicated password that nobody would ever be able to guess. But it's not so great because if any other WiFi gadget–one that doesn't have the WPS feature–tries to get online, you'll have to type in that endless password manually.)

One more note: The first time you connect to a new network—the first time you use a wireless hotspot, the first time you connect to a dial-up ISP, the first time you plug into an office network—you're asked the question at lower right in Figure 13-1.

The choice you make here tells Windows how much *security* to apply to the network you've just joined.

Figure 13-1:
Top left: Hey, look! On the taskbar, and on the Settings pane of the Charms bar, my icon is has an asterisk–there's WiFi here!*

(Tip: If you point to the taskbar icon without clicking, you see your current network's name and signal strength. And if you right-click the icon, you get links to a troubleshooting app and the Network and Sharing Center.)

OK, so there are available networks. Suppose I select that icon?

Top right: This panel pops up, identifying all the available WiFi networks.

Suppose I select one of them?

Lower left: You're offered a Connect button. If you don't want to have to go through all this the next time you're in this hotspot, turn on "Connect automatically."

Lower right: If a password is required, type it now.

Lower lower right: "No, don't turn on sharing" tells Windows that this is a public hotspot (café, for example). "Yes, turn on sharing" means you're at home or work. This is all to keep evil WiFi -sniffing geeks out of your files.

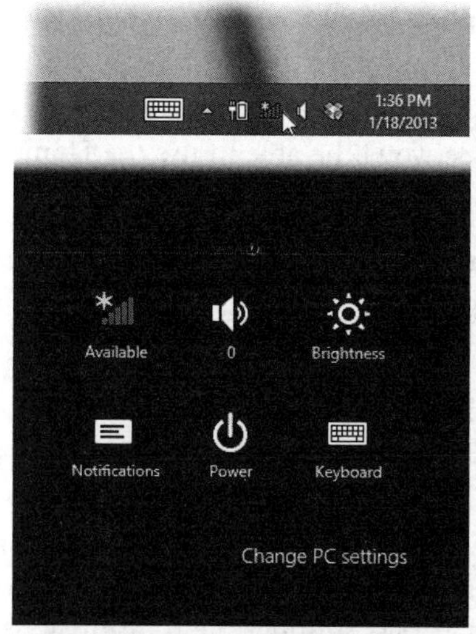

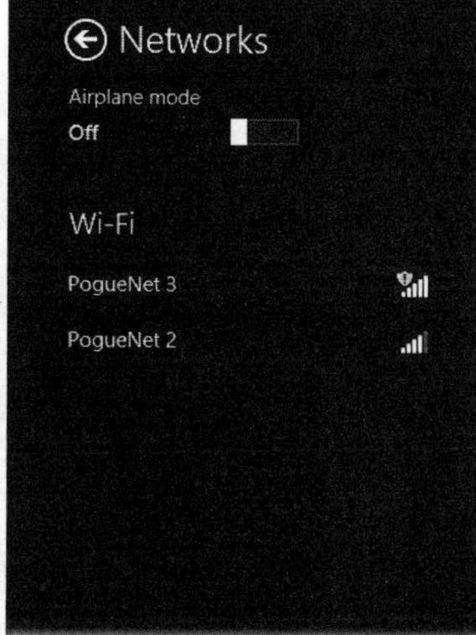

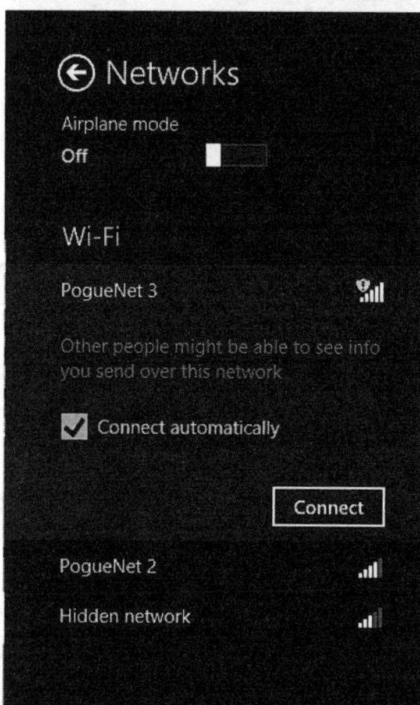

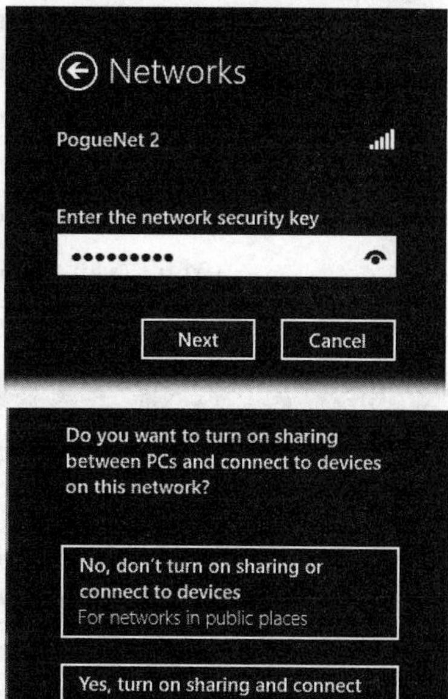

If you choose "No, don't turn on sharing or connect to devices," for example, Windows makes your computer invisible to other computers nearby. (Technically, it turns off the feature called *network discovery*.) That's not ideal for file sharing, printer sharing, and so on—but it means hackers have a harder time "sniffing" the airwaves to detect your presence. This is what you'd want for public hotspots, like coffee shops.

If you make this choice, you may be visited quite a bit by the "Unblock?" messages from the Windows firewall. That's just Windows being insecure, asking for permission every time any program (like a chat program) tries to get through the firewall.

If you choose "Yes, turn on sharing and connect to devices," on the other hand, you'll find it much easier to share files, printers, and other goodies on your own home network. For example, you'll be able to use the Homegroups feature described in Chapter 27. This is the right choice for a home or office network.

When You Can't Get On

That should be all that's necessary to get you onto a WiFi hotspot. You should now be able to surf the Web or check your email.

Before you get too excited, though, some lowering of expectations is in order. There are a bunch of reasons why your icon might indicate that you're in a hotspot, but you can't actually get online:

- **It's locked.** If there's no little icon next to the hotspot's signal strength in the pop-up list of networks, then the hotspot has been password-protected. That's partly to prevent hackers from "sniffing" the transmissions and intercepting messages, and partly to keep random passersby like you off the network.
- **The signal isn't strong enough.** Sometimes the WiFi signal is strong enough to make the hotspot's name show up, but not strong enough for an actual connection.
- **You're not on the list.** Sometimes, for security, hotspots are rigged to permit only specific computers to join, and yours isn't one of them.
- **You haven't logged in yet.** Commercial hotspots (the ones you have to pay for) don't connect you to the Internet until you've supplied your payment details on

TROUBLESHOOTIING MOMENT

Wrong Network Type–Oops

Oh dear. When I connected to my home WiFi network, I clicked "No, don't turn on sharing" by accident. Now I can't see any of my shared files, music, printers, and so on. What to do?

You should change the setting to "Yes, turn on sharing."

To do that, open the Charms bar. Select Settings. Select the WiFi icon, so you see the name of the network in question.

Now right-click the network's name (or hold your finger down on it for a couple of seconds). From the shortcut menu, choose "Turn sharing on or off." (Bet you didn't know these items had shortcut menus, did you?)

Now you're right back at the options shown at lower right in Figure 13-1, so you can correct your miscategorized network type.

a special Web page that appears automatically when you open your browser, as described below.

- **The router's on, but the Internet's not connected.** Sometimes wireless routers are broadcasting, but their Internet connection is down. It'd be like a cordless phone that has a good connection back to the base station in the kitchen—but the phone cord isn't plugged into the base station.

Tip: If you point to the icon on the taskbar without clicking, you'll know. It will say either "Internet access" (good) or "No Internet access" (bad).

Commercial Hotspots

Choosing the name of the hotspot you want to join is generally all you have to do—if it's a home WiFi network.

Unfortunately, joining a commercial hotspot—one that requires a credit card number (in a hotel room or an airport, for example)—requires more than just connecting to it. You also have to sign into it before you can send so much as a single email message.

To do that, open your browser. You see the "Enter payment information" screen either immediately or as soon as you try to open a Web page of your choice. (Even at free hotspots, you might have to click OK on a welcome page to initiate the connection.)

Supply your credit card information or (if you have a membership to this WiFi chain, like Boingo or T-Mobile) your name and password. Click Submit or Proceed, try not to contemplate how this $8 per hour is pure profit for somebody, and enjoy your surfing.

Memorized Hotspots

If you turned on "Connect automatically," then whenever your laptop enters this hotspot, it will connect to the network automatically. You don't have to do any clicking at all.

POWER USERS' CLINIC

PPPoE and DSL

If you have DSL service, you may be directed to create a PPPoE service.

It stands for PPP over Ethernet, meaning that although your DSL "modem" is connected to your Ethernet port, you still have to make and break your Internet connections manually, as though you had a dial-up modem.

To set this up, open the Network and Sharing Center (page 773). Click "Set up a new connection or network." In the next box, click "Connect to the Internet."

In the next box–which is known as the "Connect to the Internet" wizard–click "Broadband (PPPoE)." Fill in the PPPoE box as directed by your ISP (usually just your account name and password). From here on in, you start and end your Internet connections exactly as though you had a dial-up modem–for example, by clicking the icon on your taskbar tray, and then clicking the network name.

Behind the scenes, Windows is capable of piling up quite a list of these hotspots, representing a bread-crumb trail of the hotspots you've used at every hotel, airport, coffee shop, and buddy's house.

In Windows 7, there was a "Manage wireless networks" link that let you look over the list and delete the ones you didn't need. That's gone in Windows 8.

But you can still tell Windows to force-forget a network it can see. Open the Charms bar; select Settings, then the WiFi icon. Then right-click the name of the network you want Windows to forget (or hold your finger down on it). From the shortcut menu, choose "Forget this network."

But what about the much longer list of hotspots you've told Windows to memorize, including those you're not actually *in* right now? For that purpose, you need a free software tool like WiFi Profile Manager 8. You can download it from this book's "Missing CD" page at *www.missingmanuals.com*.

Wired Connections

The beauty of Ethernet connections is that they're superfast and supersecure. No bad guys sitting across the coffee shop, armed with shareware "sniffing" software, can intercept your email and chat messages, as they theoretically can when you're on wireless.

And 99 percent of the time, connecting to an Ethernet network is as simple as connecting the cable to the computer. That's it. You're online, quickly and securely, and you never have to worry about connecting or disconnecting.

Automatic Configuration

Most broadband wired connections require no setup whatsoever. Take a new PC out of the box, plug the Ethernet cable into your cable modem, and you can begin surfing the Web instantly.

That's because most cable modems, DSL boxes, and wireless base stations use DHCP. It stands for dynamic host configuration protocol, but what it means is: "We'll fill in your Network Control Panel automatically." (Including techie specs like IP address and DNS Server addresses.)

Manual Configuration

If, for some reason, you're not able to surf the Web or check email the first time you try, it's remotely possible that your broadband modem or your office network doesn't offer DHCP. In that case, you may have to fiddle with the network settings manually.

See "Connection Management" on page 445 for details.

Tethering and Cellular Modems

WiFi hotspots are fast and usually cheap—but they're *spots*. Beyond 150 feet away, you're offline.

No wonder laptop luggers across America are getting into cellular Internet services. Your tablet or laptop can get onto the cellular data network in any of four ways:

- **Tethering.** If you have a smartphone, like an iPhone, Android, or Windows phone, you can use it as a glorified WiFi hotspot. You have to pay, for example, $20 a month extra to your cellphone company. And tethering eats up battery power like crazy. But for quick Internet checks wherever you are, there's nothing as convenient.
- **MiFi.** The MiFi is a pocket-sized, thick-credit-card-looking thing that grabs the cellular signal and converts it into a WiFi signal for your Windows machine. Here again, you pay a monthly fee. But the nice part is that up to five people can use the WiFi hotspot simultaneously, and this arrangement doesn't slurp down your phone's battery power.
- **USB sticks.** All the big cellphone companies offer ExpressCards or USB sticks that let your laptop get online at high speed anywhere in major cities.
- **Built-in cellular.** Plenty of laptops and tablets even have cellular circuitry built right inside, so you have nothing to insert or eject.

Imagine: No hunting for coffee shops. With cellular Internet service, you can check your email while zooming down the road in a taxi. (Outside the metropolitan areas, you can still get online wirelessly, though much more slowly.)

And if your phone, MiFi, USB stick, or cellular computer has 4G LTE-type cellular, wow—you'll get speeds approaching a cable modem.

To make the connection, turn on the cellular gadget (phone, MiFi, whatever). After about 20 seconds, the name of your private WiFi hotspot shows up in the list as shown in Figure 13-1.

Dial-Up Connections

High-speed Internet is where it's at, baby! But there are plenty of reasons why you may be among the 10 percent of the Internet-using population who connect via dial-up

FREQUENTLY ASKED QUESTION

Laptop's Lament: Away from the Cable Modem

When I'm home, I connect my laptop to my cable modem. But when I'm on the road, of course, I have to use my dial-up ISP. Is there any way to automate the switching between these two connection methods?

If there weren't, do you think your question would have even appeared in this chapter?

The feature you're looking for is in the Internet Options control panel. (Quickest way to open it: Open the Start menu; start typing *Internet options* until you see Internet Options in the results list; press Enter to open it.

Click the Connections tab, and then turn on "Dial whenever a network connection is not present."

From now on, your laptop will use its dial-up modem only when it realizes that it isn't connected to your cable modem.

modem, slow though it is. Dial-up is a heck of a lot less expensive than broadband. And its availability is incredible—you can find a phone jack in almost any room in the civilized world, in places where the closest Ethernet or WiFi network is miles away.

To get online by dial-up, you need a PC with a modem—maybe an external USB model—and a dial-up *account*. You sign up with a company called an Internet service provider (or *ISP*, as insiders and magazines inevitably call them).

National ISPs like EarthLink and AT&T have local telephone numbers in every U.S. state and in many other countries. If you don't travel much, you may not need such broad coverage. Instead, you may be able to save money by signing up for a local or regional ISP. In fact, you can find ISPs that are absolutely free (if you're willing to look at ads), or that cost as little as $4 per month (if you promise not to call for tech support). Google can be your friend here.

Even if you have a cable modem or DSL, you can generally add dial-up access to the same account for another few bucks a month. You'll be happy to have that feature if you travel a lot (unless your cable modem comes with a *really* long cord).

In any case, dialing the Internet is a local call for most people.

Microsoft expects that you've contacted an ISP on your own. It assumes that you're equipped with either (a) a setup CD from that company or (b) a user name, password, and dial-up phone number from that ISP, which is pretty much all you really need to get online.

Your only remaining task is to plug that information into Windows. (And, of course, to plug your computer into the phone jack on the wall.)

POWER USERS' CLINIC

Secret Hotspots

It's entirely possible for you to be standing right in the middle of a juicy, strong WiFi hotspot–and not even know it. Its name doesn't show up in the list.

It turns out that the owner can choose whether or not the hotspot should broadcast its name. Sometimes, he might want to keep the hotspot secret–to restrict its use to employees at a coffee shop, for example, so that the common customer riffraff can't slow it down. In these cases, you'd have to know (a) that the hotspot exists, and (b) what its name is.

Sometimes, you see "Unidentified network" right there in the list of available networks (shown in Figure 13-1, top right). If so, great–select it, enter the name and password, and off you go.

If not, open the Network and Sharing Center (page 773). Select "Set up a new connection or network." On the next screen, choose "Manually connect to a wireless network," and then hit Next.

Now enter the network's exact name and password. You'll probably want to turn on "Start this connection automatically," too, if you think you might encounter the hotspot again later.

When you click Next, you'll get a notification that you've successfully connected (if, in fact, you have).

To do that, open the Network and Sharing Center (page 773). In the main window, click "Set up a new connection or network." Double-click "Set up a dial-up connection," and follow the instructions on the screen.

Connection Management

No matter what crazy combination of Internet connections you've accumulated on your computer, Windows represents each one as a *connection icon.* You can view them, rename them, change their settings, or just admire them by opening the window shown at top in Figure 13-2.

To get there, open the Network Connections window. Here's the quickest way to go about it: Open the Start screen. Type *view net* and then select Settings. You see "View network connections" in the results; select it.

These icons are handy because their Properties boxes are crammed with useful information. A dial-up connection icon stores your name, password, phone number, and so on; a broadband or wireless icon stores various technical Internet connection details.

In these and other situations, you need a way to make manual changes to your connections. Here, for example, is how you might change the Internet settings for a cable modem, DSL, or wireless connection:

1. **Double-click a connection icon.**

   You get the dialog box shown in Figure 13-2, lower left.

2. **Click Properties.**

   Authenticate yourself, if necessary.

3. **Double-click the listing that says Internet Protocol Version 4.**

   An even more intimidating dialog box now appears (Figure 13-2, lower right).

UP TO SPEED

IP Addresses and You

Every computer connected to the Internet, even temporarily, has its own exclusive *IP address* (IP stands for Internet Protocol). When you set up your own Internet account, as described on these pages, you're asked to type in this string of numbers. As you'll see, an IP address always consists of four numbers separated by periods.

Some PCs with high-speed Internet connections (cable modem, DSL) have a permanent, unchanging address called a *static* or *fixed* IP address. Other computers get assigned a new address each time they connect (a *dynamic* IP address). That's always the case, for example, when you connect via a dial-up modem. (If you can't figure out whether your machine has a static or fixed address, ask your Internet service provider.)

If nothing else, dynamic addresses are more convenient in some ways, since you don't have to type numbers into the Internet Protocol (TCP/IP) Properties dialog box shown in Figure 13-2.

4. **Edit the connection details.**

   Most of the time, Internet companies instruct you to turn on "Obtain an IP address automatically" and "Obtain DNS server address automatically." You're lucky; you've been saved from typing in all the other numbers in this dialog box. Otherwise, turn on "Use the following IP address" and type in the appropriate numbers. Do the same with "Use the following DNS server addresses."

5. **Click OK.**

   Windows doesn't make you restart the PC for your new settings to take effect.

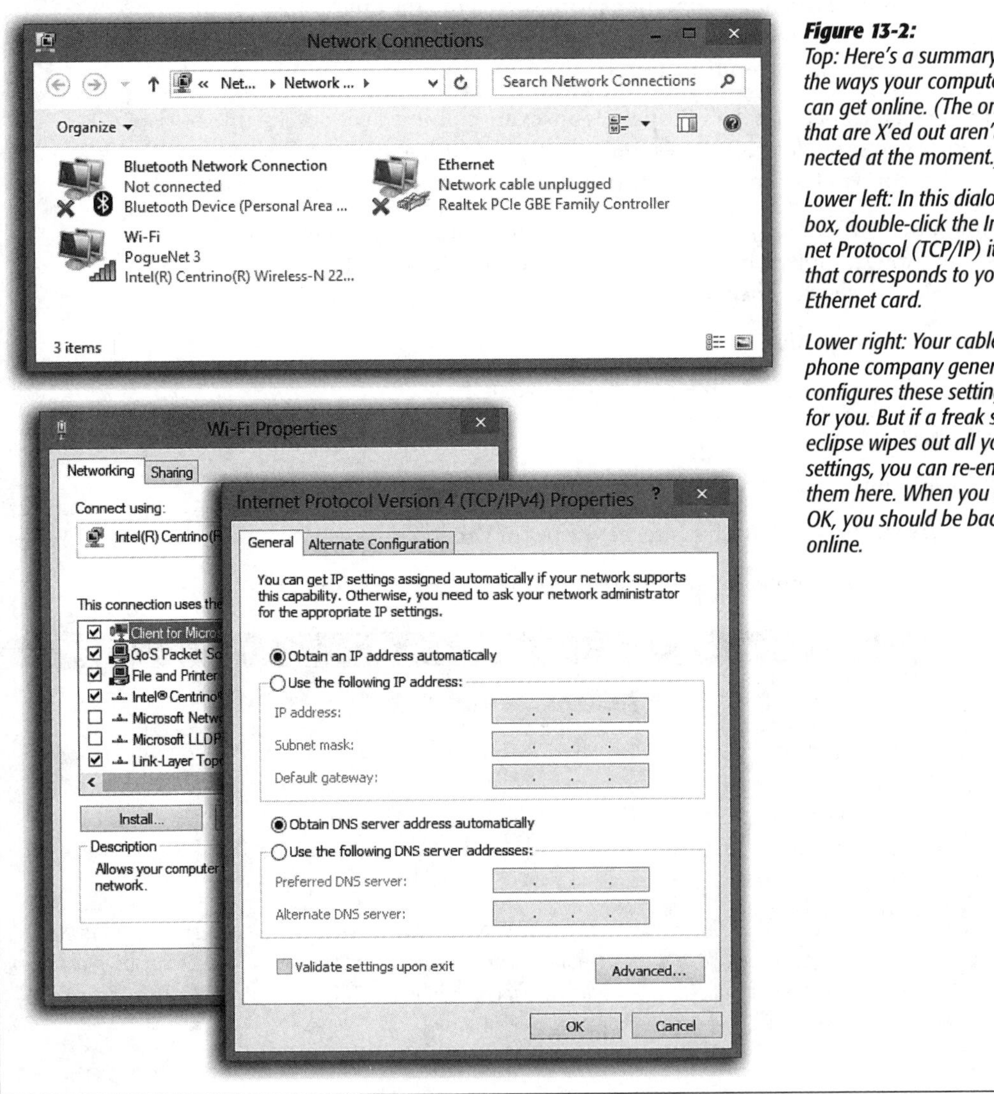

Figure 13-2:
Top: Here's a summary of the ways your computer can get online. (The ones that are X'ed out aren't connected at the moment.)

Lower left: In this dialog box, double-click the Internet Protocol (TCP/IP) item that corresponds to your Ethernet card.

Lower right: Your cable or phone company generally configures these settings for you. But if a freak solar eclipse wipes out all your settings, you can re-enter them here. When you click OK, you should be back online.

CHAPTER 14

Security & Privacy

If it weren't for that darned Internet, personal computing would be a lot of fun. After all, it's the Internet that lets all those socially stunted hackers enter our machines, unleashing their viruses, setting up remote hacking tools, feeding us spyware, trying to trick us out of our credit-card numbers, and otherwise making our lives an endless troubleshooting session. It sure would be nice if they'd cultivate some other hobbies.

In the meantime, these lowlifes are doing astronomical damage to businesses and individuals around the world—along the lines of $100 billion a year (the cost to fight viruses, spyware, and spam).

In the days of Windows XP, these sorts of Internet attacks were far more common. Microsoft left open a number of back doors that were intended for convenience (for example, to let system administrators communicate with your PC from across the network) but wound up being exploited by hackers.

Microsoft wrote Windows Vista, and later Windows 7 and Windows 8, for a lot of reasons: to give Windows a cosmetic makeover, to give it up-to-date music and video features, to overhaul its networking plumbing—and, of course, to make money. But Job Number One was making Windows more secure. Evil strangers will still make every attempt to make your life miserable, but one thing is for sure: They'll have a much, much harder time of it.

Note: Most of Windows' self-protection features have to do with Internet threats–because, in fact, virtually all the infectious unpleasantness that can befall a PC these days comes from the Internet. A PC that never goes online probably won't get infected.

So why is Internet Explorer (IE) the most popular hacking target? First, it's by far the most popular browser on the planet. Second, Internet Explorer includes hooks directly into Windows itself, so a hacker can wreak havoc on Windows by using Internet Explorer as a back door.

Lots of Windows' security improvements are invisible to you. They're deep in the plumbing, with no buttons or controls to show you. If you're scoring at home, they include the following features:

- **Application isolation.** A program can't take over important tasks performed by Windows itself.
- **Service hardening.** Windows *services* are programs that run in the background: the print spooler that comes with Windows, virus checkers from other companies, and so on. Service hardening prevents rogue services (or services that have been surreptitiously modified by nasties from the Internet) from making changes to parts of the system they're not supposed to touch; for example, they can't change important system files or the Registry (Appendix B).
- **Protected Mode.** Protected Mode shields the operating system from actions taken by Internet Explorer or its add-ons. So even if a nasty piece of software breaks through all of Internet Explorer's security features, it can't do harm to your PC, because Protected Mode locks IE inside a safe box. What happens in Internet Explorer stays in Internet Explorer.
- **Address Space Layout Randomization.** When a program is running, it keeps a lot of information in system memory. Because many viruses and worms depend on their author's knowledge of *how* vulnerable programs keep that information organized, ASLR scrambles that information—though not so much that the programs can't run—to make it harder for them to break into your system.
- **Network Access Protection.** On a corporate domain network, this feature prevents you from connecting to an insufficiently protected PC on the network—one lacking virus protection, for example.
- **PatchGuard.** This prevents non-Microsoft software from touching the beating heart of Windows.
- **Code Integrity.** Software is checked before it runs to make sure it hasn't been modified somehow.

The rest of this chapter describes features that *aren't* invisible and automatic—the ones you can control.

Note: And does it work? Do all these tools and patches actually reduce the number of virus and spyware outbreaks?

Apparently yes. The years of annual front-page headlines about national virus outbreaks–called things like Melissa (1999), Blaster (2003), and Sasser (2004)–seem to be over. There will always be clever new attacks–but they'll be much less frequent and much harder to write.

Note, however, that built-in security tools can't do the whole job of keeping your PC safe; you play a role, too. So keep in mind these basic tips before you or your family go online:

- **Don't trust a pretty face.** It doesn't take much expertise to build a snazzy-looking Web site. Just because a Web site looks trustworthy doesn't mean you can trust it. If you're visiting a little-known Web site, be careful what you do there.
- **Don't download from sites you don't know.** The Web is full of free software offers. But that free software may, in fact, be spyware or other *malware*. (Malware is a general term for viruses, spyware, and other Bad Software.) So be very careful when downloading anything online.
- **Don't click pop-up ads.** Pop-up ads are more than mere annoyances; some of them, when clicked, download spyware to your PC. As you'll see later in this chapter, Internet Explorer includes a pop-up blocker, but it doesn't block all pop-ups. So to be safe, don't click.

With all that said, you're ready to find out how to keep yourself safe when you go online.

Windows Defender

It's historic. It's amazing. After all these decades, Microsoft has finally built free antivirus software right into Windows. Thanks to Defender, you have no more excuse not to protect your PC. The X on the system-tray nag flag (🏴), complaining that your PC is unprotected, will go away.

Important: Most new PCs come with aggressive, in-your-face trial versions of commercial antivirus programs like Norton and McAfee–programs that require an annual fee forever. Those companies may not like it, but *you don't need them.* Windows Defender does a perfectly good job, and you already have it.

But to pacify the Nortons and McAfees of the world, Microsoft agreed to let PC companies ship new PCs with *Defender turned off.* So if you want Defender to defend you, you should (a) uninstall the Norton or McAfee trial version so it'll quit bugging you, and then promptly (b) turn Defender *on*. To do that, open Windows Defender as described below; you'll see the big, red "Turn on" button staring you in the face on the Home tab.

The antivirus portion of this program used to be called Microsoft Security Essentials, and you had to download it separately. (Security Essentials no longer works in Windows 8, but of course you don't need it now.) There was something called Windows Defender in Windows 7, but it protected you only from spyware, not from viruses. In Windows 8, Defender protects you from *both* threats—both kinds of malware.

Windows Defender

Malware is software you don't know you have: viruses and spyware. You usually get it in one of two ways. First, a Web site may try to trick you into downloading it. You see what looks like an innocent button in what's actually a phony Windows dialog box, or maybe you get an empty dialog box—and clicking the Close button actually triggers the installation.

Second, you may get spyware or viruses by downloading a program you *do* want—"cracked" software (commercial programs whose copy protection has been removed) is a classic example—without realizing that a secret program is piggybacking on the download.

Once installed, the malware may make changes to important system files, install ads on your desktop (even when you're not online) or send information about your surfing habits to a Web site that blitzes your PC with pop-up ads related in some way to your online behavior.

Spyware can do thinks like hijacking your home page or search page so that every time you open your browser, you wind up at a Web page that incapacitates your PC with

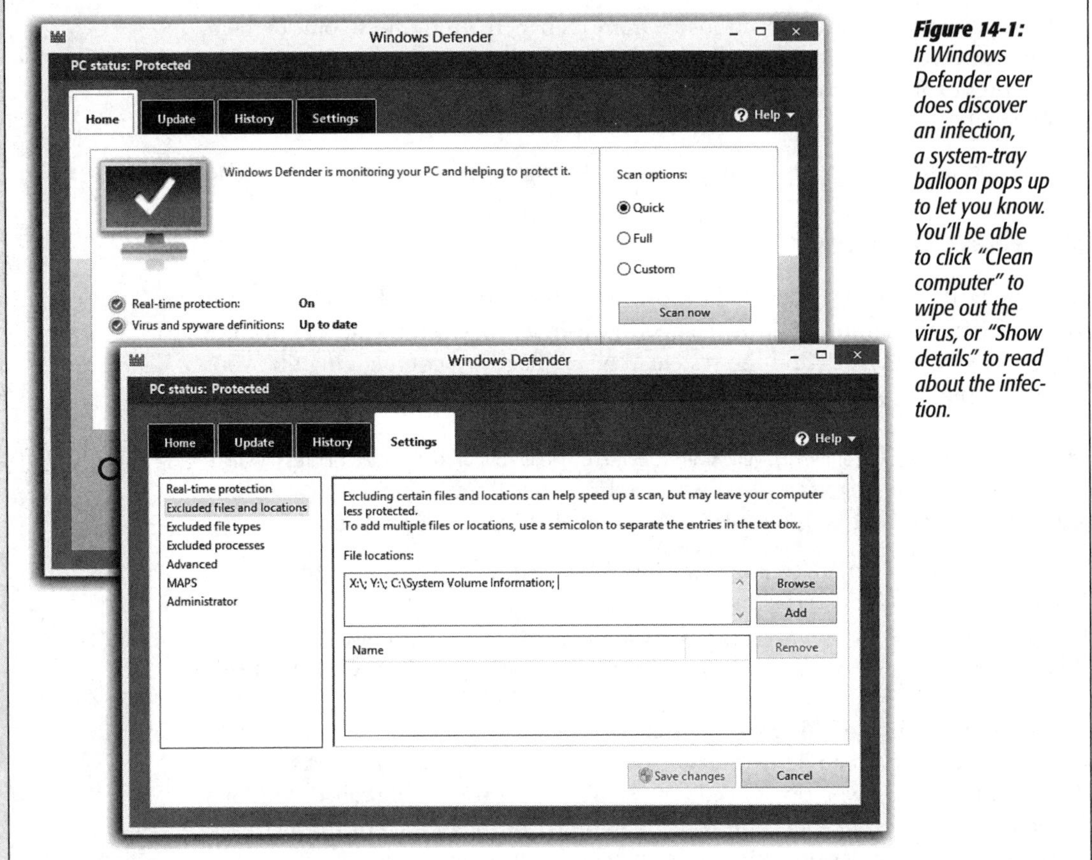

Figure 14-1: *If Windows Defender ever does discover an infection, a system-tray balloon pops up to let you know. You'll be able to click "Clean computer" to wipe out the virus, or "Show details" to read about the infection.*

a blizzard of pop-ups. *Keylogger* spyware can record all your keystrokes, passwords and all, and send them to a snooper.

Like any good antivirus program, Defender (Figure 14-1) has two functions: real-time scanning and on-demand scanning.

Real-Time Protection

Defender watches over your PC constantly, as a barrier against new infections of viruses and spyware. Each day, the program auto-downloads new *definitions files*—behind-the-scenes updates to its virus database, which keep it up to date with the latest new viruses that Microsoft has spotted in the wild.

Note: The Update tab shows you what definitions database you've got and offers a big fat Update button to download the latest one right now.

If it recognizes a virus or piece of a spyware on your PC, Defender generally zaps it automatically. Occasionally, it asks if you want to allow the questionable software to keep working, or instead remove it.

On-Demand Scanning

Defender also has a scanning function that's designed to clean out infections you already have (a feature that, thank heaven, you'll rarely need).

Ordinarily, the program scans your PC continuously. But if you're feeling a little antsy, you can also trigger a scan manually.

To do that, on the Home tab, specify what you want it to check out for you:

- **Quick.** Scans the most vulnerable parts of your system software, in an effort to save time.
- **Full.** A full scan of everything on your hard drive. As you'd guess, this can take a long time.

UP TO SPEED

Is It Spyware or Adware?

Spyware has a less-malignant cousin called *adware*, and the line between the two types is exceedingly thin.

Adware is free software that displays ads (the free version of Eudora, for example). In order to target those ads to your interests, it may transmit reports on your surfing habits to its authors. (Windows Defender doesn't protect against adware.)

So what's the difference between adware and spyware? If it performs malicious actions, like incapacitating your PC with pop-ups, it's spyware for sure.

Proponents of adware say, "Hey—we've gotta put bread on our tables, too! Those ads are how you pay for your free software. Our software doesn't identify you personally when it reports on your surfing habits, so it's not really spyware."

But other people insist that any software that reports on your activities is spyware, no matter what.

- **Custom.** This feature lets you scan one particular disk, folder, or file—something you just got as an email attachment, for example. When you click Custom and then "Scan now," you're shown a checkbox hierarchy of your entire computer. Expand the disks and folders until you can turn on the exact items you want scanned; then click OK to start the scan.

Tip: Similarly, you can exclude certain disks, folders, kinds of files, or open programs from the usual automated scanning–to shut Defender up, for example, when it keeps complaining about a certain item that you know is pristine. On the Settings tab, click "Excluded files and locations," "Excluded file types," or "Excluded processes" (meaning programs) to specify what you want omitted. Once you've set things up, click "Save changes" (and authenticate if necessary).

When Defender Strikes

When Defender finds spyware, it puts the offending software into a quarantined area where it can't do any more harm. On the History tab, you can see the quarantined software, delete it, or restore it (take it out of quarantine). In general, restoring spyware and viruses is a foolhardy move.

Here's what you see on the History tab:

- **Quarantined items.** Click this button and then "View details." You see each program Defender has taken action on, the alert level, and the date. You can use "Remove all" if you don't recognize any of it, or you can select just one, or a few, and then click Remove or Restore. (Restore means "It's fine. Put it back and let me run it.")
- **Allowed items.** If Defender announces that it's found a potential piece of malware, but you allow it to run anyway, it's considered an allowed item. From now on, Defender ignores it, meaning that you trust that program completely. Allowed programs' names appear when you click this button and then click "View details."

  If you highlight a program's name and then click Remove From List, it's *gone* from the Allowed list, and therefore Defender monitors it once again.

Now, Defender is certainly not the only antivirus program on the planet; it's not even the best one.

Several rival antivirus programs are free for personal use, like Avast (*www.avast.com*). These do have their downsides—some nag you to buy the Pro versions, for example, and there's nobody to call for tech support.

In any case, the bottom line is this: If your PC doesn't have antivirus software working for you right now, then getting some should be at the top of your to-do list.

Note: Get antivirus software written especially for Windows 8. Antivirus software from the old days won't work.

Action Center

One of the biggest annoyances in Windows of old was the nagginess. Windows was constantly bugging you, sending up balloons, popping up "Attention!" boxes, demanding your name and password at every turn. It's great that Microsoft tightened up security, but come on; it was like living with a needy 5-year-old.

Today, Windows harangues you much less. In fact, 10 categories of not-that-urgent, security-related nags don't interrupt your work at all; instead, they quietly collect themselves into a central message station called the Action Center. You can poke in there from time to time to have a look.

The only indication you have that Windows is still on the job, in fact, is Action Center's front man: the tiny flag icon on your taskbar tray. When there's an X on it like this: flag-with-X icon,

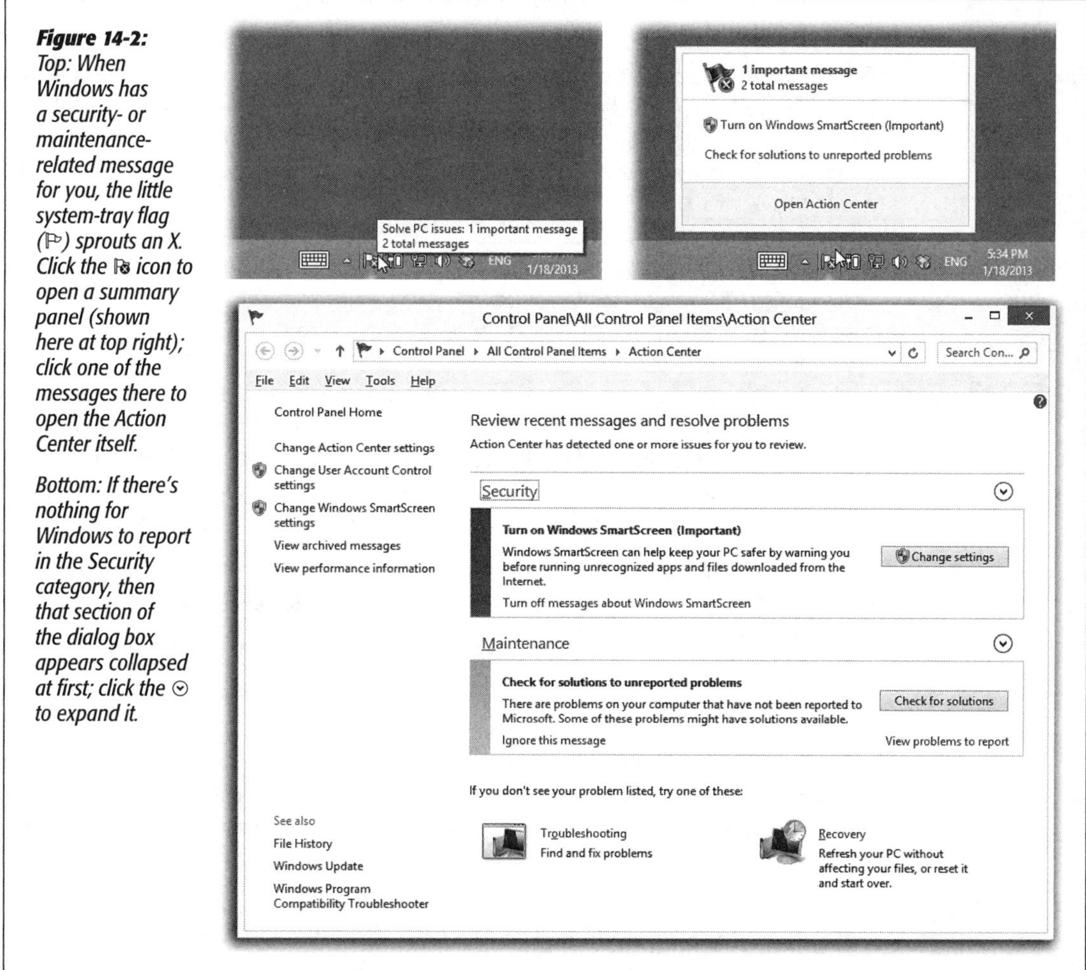

Figure 14-2: *Top: When Windows has a security- or maintenance-related message for you, the little system-tray flag (flag icon) sprouts an X. Click the flag-with-X icon to open a summary panel (shown here at top right); click one of the messages there to open the Action Center itself.*

Bottom: If there's nothing for Windows to report in the Security category, then that section of the dialog box appears collapsed at first; click the ⊙ to expand it.

Windows has something to say to you (Figure 14-2, top). If Windows considers the problem to be urgent, then a message balloon sprouts from the flag, too.

Tip: If you point to the flag icon without clicking, then a status balloon appears to let you know how many messages Windows has saved up for you.

If you click the ⚑, you get a pop-up summary of the problem (and others that Windows has noticed). Sometimes there's a link you can click to solve the problem right in the summary bubble. Other times, you may want to just click Open Action Center in the shortcut menu; the Action Center appears, as shown in Figure 14-2, bottom. (If you ever see a message balloon appearing from the ⚑ icon, you can also open the Action Center by clicking the balloon itself.)

Here's where Windows collects all messages related to antivirus software, antispyware software, Windows Update settings, Internet security settings, your firewall software, and your backup settings.

If the Security heading is collapsed and you see no messages, then Windows thinks that all is well. Expand the ⊙ button next to the Security heading, if you like, to see the full panoply of security settings. Here you see the state of firewall security, automatic updating, malware protection, and other security settings. "On" or "OK" means you're protected.

Tip: Each message comes with a "Turn off" link. Click it if you no longer want to be bothered by messages on this subject. Or click "Change Action Center settings"; you're shown a complete list of the kinds of situations Action Center monitors–and you can turn off a bunch of them at once.

A color-coded bar indicates the urgency of the messages here: red for dire (for example, you don't have an antivirus program), yellow for not-so-urgent messages (for example, you don't have Windows Update set to auto-download patches). Each message comes with a button that proposes an action Windows thinks you should take: turning on your antivirus program, setting up an automatic backup system, and so on.

Conveniently enough, both Microsoft and non-Microsoft security programs can patch into Action Center; if you use Norton Antivirus, for example, you see its messages here, too.

Windows Firewall

If you have a broadband, always-on connection, you're connected to the Internet 24 hours a day. It's theoretically possible for some cretin to use automated hacking software to flood you with files or to take control of your machine. Fortunately, the Windows *Firewall* feature puts up a barrier to such mischief.

The firewall acts as a gatekeeper between you and the Internet. It examines all Internet traffic and lets through only communications that it knows are safe; all other traffic is turned away at the door.

How It Works

Every kind of electronic message sent to or from your PC—instant messaging, music sharing, file sharing, and so on—conducts its business on a specific communications channel, or *port*. Ports are numbered tunnels for certain kinds of Internet traffic.

The problem with Windows before Vista came along was that Microsoft left all your ports *open* for your convenience—and, as it turns out, for the bad guys'. Starting with Vista, all the ports arrive on your PC *closed*.

The firewall blocks or permits signals based on a predefined set of rules. They dictate, for example, which programs are permitted to use your network connection, or which ports can be used for communications.

You don't need to do anything to turn on the Windows Firewall. When you turn on Windows, it's already at work. But the Windows Firewall *can* be turned off.

To do that, or to fiddle with any of its settings, there are plenty of ways to find it. It's an icon in the Control Panel, for example. Or you can find it from the Start screen; type *firewall*. Select Settings. Select Windows Firewall in the results list.

As you can see in Figure 14-3, the Firewall screen is pretty simple.

Tip: It's perfectly OK to use the Windows Firewall and another company's firewall software–a first for Windows. If you're a supergeek, you can assign each to handle different technical firewall functions.

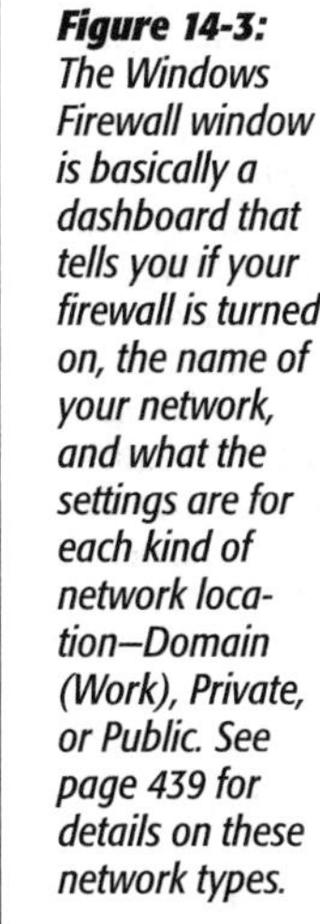

Figure 14-3: *The Windows Firewall window is basically a dashboard that tells you if your firewall is turned on, the name of your network, and what the settings are for each kind of network location–Domain (Work), Private, or Public. See page 439 for details on these network types.*

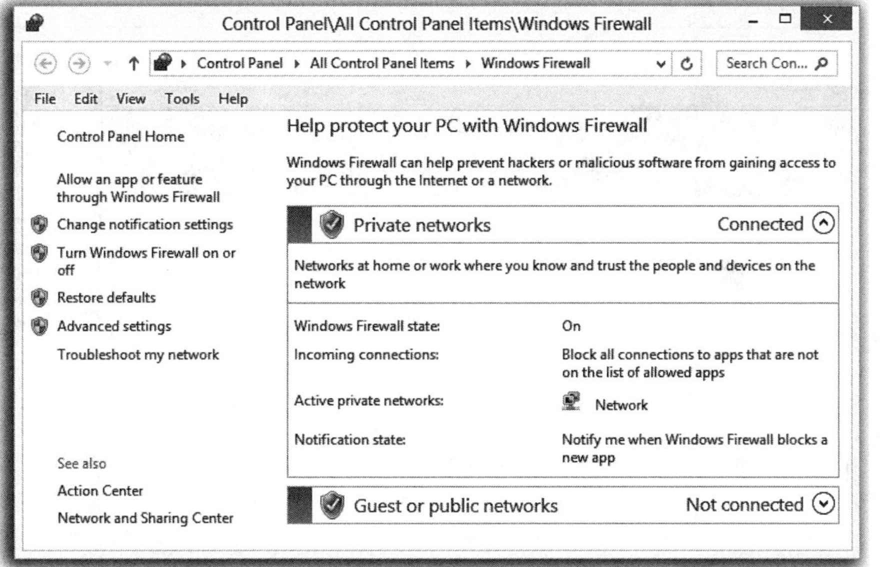

Firewall Settings

To see the ways you can adjust the Windows Firewall, click "Turn Windows Firewall on or off" in the left-side task panel. (Authenticate yourself if necessary.)

The resulting screen lets you tweak the settings for each location (Public, Private, Domain) independently. You have these options:

- **Block all incoming connections, including those in the list of allowed apps.** When you're feeling especially creeped out by the threat of hackerishness—like when you're at the coffee shop of your local computer-science grad school—turn on this box. Now your computer is pretty much completely shut off from the Internet except for Web browsing, email, and instant messaging.
- **Notify me when Windows Firewall blocks a new app.** Windows will pop up a message that lets you know when a new program has attempted to get online, on the off chance that it's some evil app. Most of the time, of course, it's some perfectly innocent program that you happen to be using for the first time; just click Allow in the box and go on with your life.

Note: If you really are on a domain (Chapter 25), then you may not be allowed to make any changes to the firewall settings, because that's something the network nerds like to be in charge of.

- **Turn off Windows Firewall.** Yes, you can turn the firewall off entirely. There's very little reason to do that, though, even if you decide to install another company's firewall; its installer turns off the Windows Firewall if necessary.

Figure 14-4: *From time to time, your life with Windows will be interrupted by this message. It's your firewall speaking. It's telling you that a program is trying to get online, as though you didn't know. Most of the time, you can just hit Unblock and get on with your life.*

You also might be tempted to turn off the firewall because you have a *router* that distributes your Internet signal through the house—and most routers have *hardware* firewalls built right in, protecting your entire network.

Still, there's no harm in having *both* a hardware and a software firewall in place. In fact, having the Windows Firewall turned on protects you from viruses you catch from other people on your own network (even though you're both "behind" the router's firewall). And if you have a laptop, this way you won't have to remember to turn the firewall on when you leave your home network.

Punching Through the Firewall

The firewall isn't always your friend. It can occasionally block a perfectly harmless program from communicating with the outside world—a chat program or a game that you can play across the Internet, for example.

Fortunately, whenever that happens, Windows lets you know with a message like the one shown in Figure 14-4. Most of the time, you know exactly what program it's talking about, because it's a program you just opened *yourself*—a program you installed that might legitimately need Internet access. In other words, it's not some

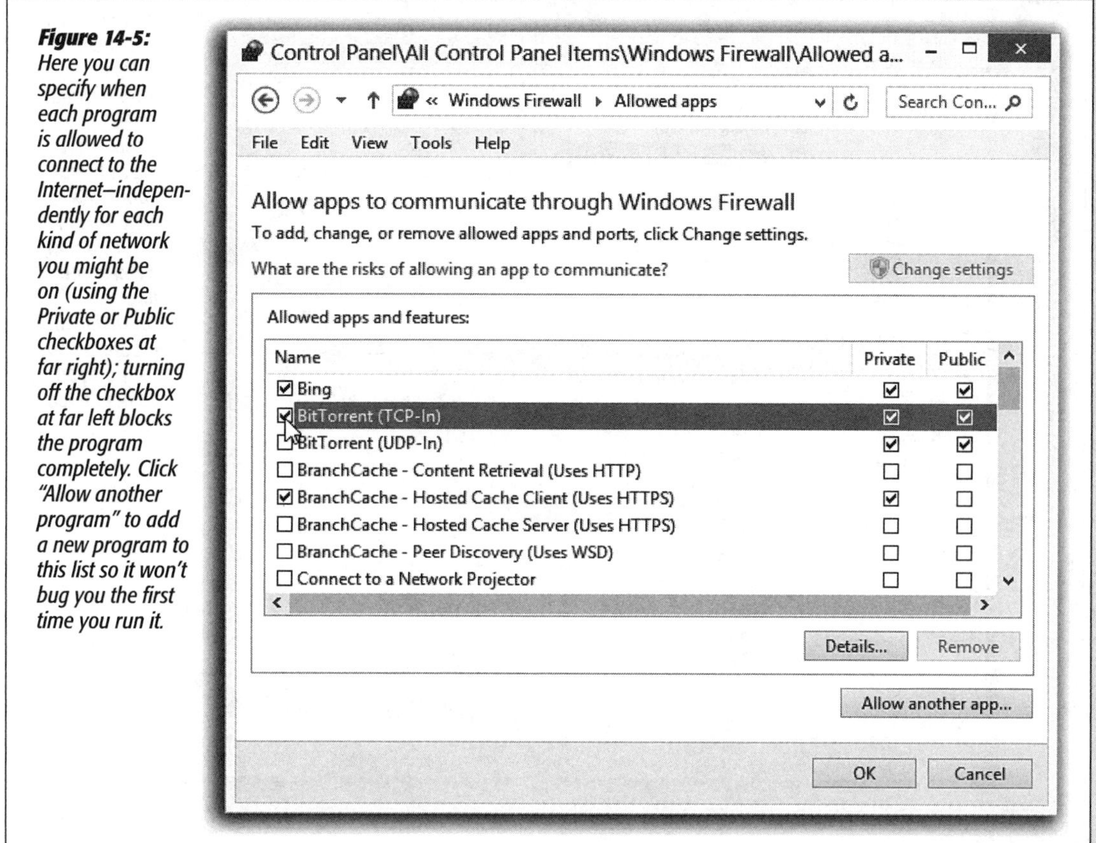

Figure 14-5: *Here you can specify when each program is allowed to connect to the Internet–independently for each kind of network you might be on (using the Private or Public checkboxes at far right); turning off the checkbox at far left blocks the program completely. Click "Allow another program" to add a new program to this list so it won't bug you the first time you run it.*

rogue spyware on your machine trying to talk to the mother ship. Click "Allow access" and get on with your life.

Alternatively, you can set up permissions for your apps in advance. At the left side of the firewall screen shown in Figure 14-3, click "Allow a program or feature through Windows Firewall." Proceed as shown in Figure 14-5.

Advanced Firewall

The Windows Firewall screen gives you a good deal of control over how the Windows Firewall works. But it doesn't offer nearly the amount of tweakiness that high-end geeks demand, like control over individual ports, IP addresses, programs, and so on. It also offers no way to create a log (a text-file record) of all attempts to contact your PC from the network or the Internet, which can be handy when you suspect that some nasty hacker has been visiting you in the middle of the night.

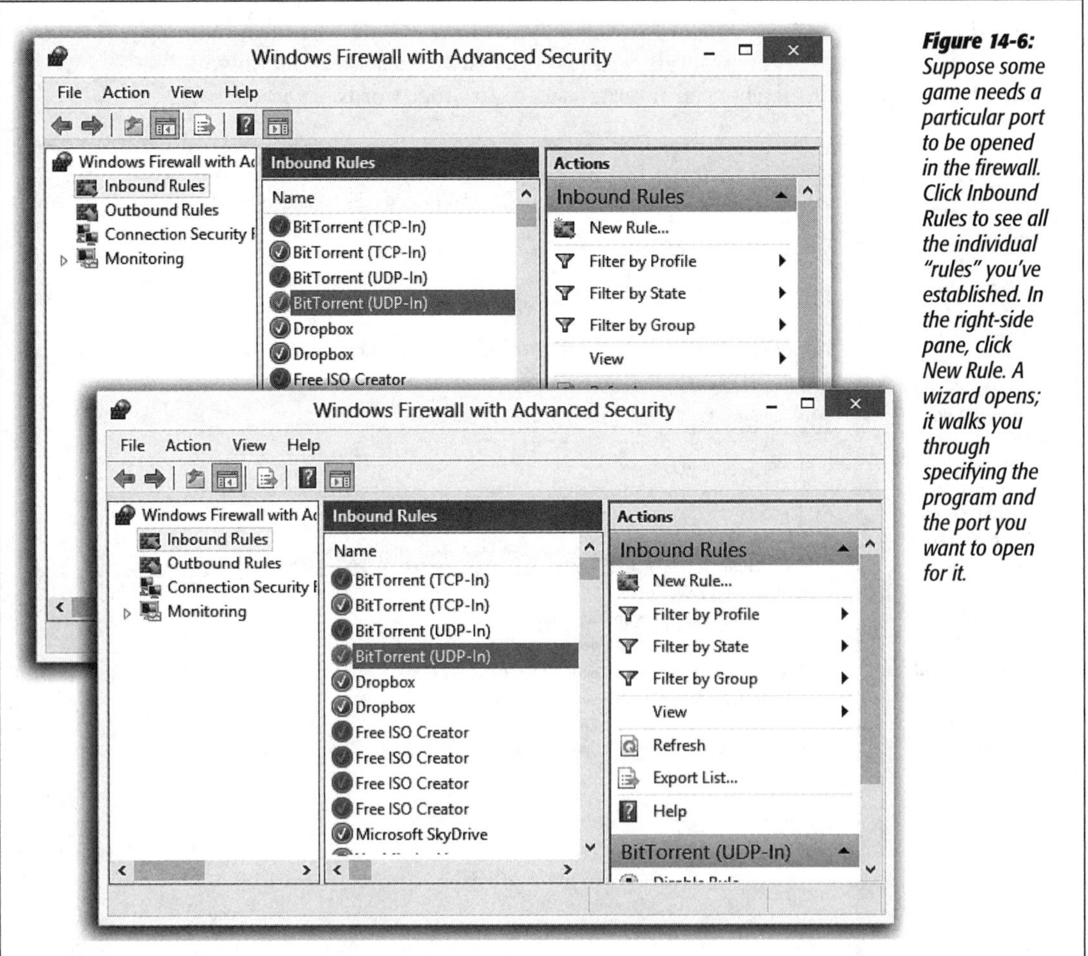

Figure 14-6: *Suppose some game needs a particular port to be opened in the firewall. Click Inbound Rules to see all the individual "rules" you've established. In the right-side pane, click New Rule. A wizard opens; it walks you through specifying the program and the port you want to open for it.*

There is, however, an even more powerful firewall control panel. In an effort to avoid terrifying novices, Microsoft has hidden it, but it's easy enough to open. It's called the Windows Firewall with Advanced Security.

Get there by clicking "Advanced settings" at the left side of the Windows Firewall window. Authenticate if necessary. Figure 14-6 shows you the very basics. But if you're really that much of an Advanced Security sort of person, you can find Microsoft's how-to guide for this console at *http://bit.ly/hxR0i.*

Windows SmartScreen

SmartScreen, in Windows 7, was an anti-phishing technology built into Internet Explorer. It's still working for you in Windows 8. If you try to visit a Web site that Microsoft knows is suspicious, it blocks your path with a huge warning banner.

In that situation, close the page, click "Go to my home page instead," or go to another site. (If you're just researching phishing sites, and you know full well what trouble you're getting yourself into, and you really want to proceed, then click "More information" and then "Disregard and continue"; you'll go through to the phony site.)

If Internet Explorer isn't quite sure about a certain site's phishiness, but it has a funny feeling in its bones, a yellow button appears next to the address bar saying "Suspicious Website." Unless you absolutely know the site is legitimate, it's a good idea to head somewhere else.

In Windows 8, SmartScreen has grown a lot more powerful. Now SmartScreen also warns you when you try to open a downloaded *program* that might be fishy, even if you downloaded it in a browser other than Internet Explorer. One day, when you least expect it, you'll get a pop-up warning.

SmartScreen works by comparing the file's original Web site address against a massive list of Web sites and file downloads that have been reported to Microsoft as unsafe. If it blocks the program you're trying to open, just click "More info" and then (if you're sure it's OK) "Run anyway."

UP TO SPEED

Is It Spyware or Adware?

What's phishing? That's when you're sent what appears to be legitimate email from a bank, eBay, PayPal, or some other financial Web site. The message tells you the site needs to confirm your account information, or warns that your account has been hacked, and needs you to help keep it safe.

If you, responsible citizen that you are, click the provided link to clear up the supposed problem, you wind up on what looks like the bank/eBay/PayPal Web site. But it's a fake, carefully designed to look like the real thing; it's run by a scammer. If you type in your password and login information, as requested, then the next thing you know, you're getting credit-card bills for $10,000 charges at high-rolling Las Vegas hotels–the scammer has collected your login information. The fake sites look so much like the real ones that it can be extremely difficult to tell them apart.

Phine-Tuning the Philter

There's not much to controlling SmartScreen; basically, you can turn it on or off. (And by golly, you should check right now; on many PCs, it comes from the factory turned off.)

In fact, you control the two parts of SmartScreen—Web blocking and app blocking—separately.

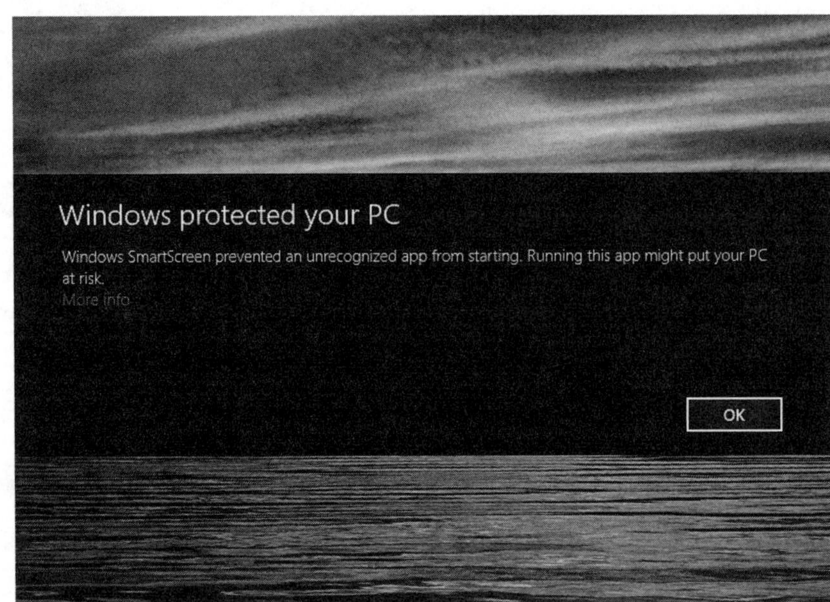

Figure 14-7: *This screen means that SmartScreen has checked your downloaded program against a list of known evil apps and determined that it's suspicious.*

This program isn't necessarily bad; it could just be something Microsoft doesn't recognize.

If you're sure it's OK, click "More info"; on the next screen, click "Run anyway." The app opens as scheduled.

FREQUENTLY ASKED QUESTION

Sherlock Explorer

How does Internet Explorer know what's a phishing site and what's not?

IE uses three bits of information to figure out whether a site is legitimate or a phishing site.

Its first line of defense is a Microsoft-compiled, frequently updated database of known phishing sites that, believe it or not, sits right on your own hard drive. Whenever you head to a Web site, Internet Explorer consults that database. If the Web site appears in the list, you get the warning. (The database is compiled from several phish-tracking companies, including Cyota, Internet Identity, and MarkMonitor, as well as from direct user feedback.)

Second, Internet Explorer uses *heuristics,* a sort of low-level artificial intelligence. It compares characteristics of the site you're visiting against common phishing-site characteristics. The heuristics tool helps IE recognize phishing sites that haven't yet made it into the database of known sites.

Finally, Internet Explorer quietly sends addresses of some of the sites you visit to Microsoft, which checks it against a frequently updated list of reported phishing sites (not the database on your PC).

SmartScreen Web Settings

In Internet Explorer, press the Alt key to make the menu bar appear. Choose Tools→SmartScreen Filter→Turn off SmartScreen Filter. In the confirmation box, click "Turn off SmartScreen filter" and then click OK.

SmartScreen App Settings

To change the settings, open the Start screen. Type *smartscreen* and select Settings under the search box. In the search results, click "Windows SmartScreen."

Here you see the on/off switch for Windows SmartScreen. If it says "Turn on Windows SmartScreen (Recommended)" with a big red bar, then click "Change settings" (authenticate if necessary). If SmartScreen is already on, then click "Change SmartScreen settings" on the pane at left.

Either way, you have three options here:

- **Get administrator approval before running an unrecognized app from the Internet.** In other words, you'll have to enter an administrator's password (page 728) before you can bypass the warning and open the fishy app.
- **Warn before running an unrecognized app, but don't require administrator approval.** Even your minions, those with standard accounts, can bypass the warning.
- **Don't do anything (turn off Windows SmartScreen).** You're flying without a net now, pal.

  And why would you ever want to turn this feature off? Because maybe you're a privacy nut. SmartScreen works by sending the Web address of each page you visit, and the details of each program you download, back to Microsoft, where it's compared against the list of evil sites and apps. It's all transmitted in encrypted form, and none of it, according to Microsoft, is stored anywhere. And no information associated with the site is sent, like search terms you've used, information you've entered into forms, or cookies.

  Still. If that transmitting business creeps you out, you can turn the whole thing off.

Privacy and Cookies

Cookies are something like Web-page preference files. Certain Web sites—particularly commercial ones like Amazon.com—deposit them on your hard drive like little bookmarks so they'll remember you the next time you visit. On Amazon, in fact, a greeting says "Hello, Casey" (or whatever your name is), thanks to the cookie it uses to recognize you.

Most cookies are perfectly innocuous—and, in fact, are extremely helpful. They can let your PC log into a site automatically or let you customize what the site looks like and how you use it.

But fear is on the march, and the media fan the flames with tales of sinister cookies that track your movement on the Web. Some Web sites rely on cookies to record which pages you visit on a site, how long you spend on a site, what kind of information you like to find out, and so on.

If you're worried about invasions of privacy—and you're willing to trade away some of the conveniences of cookies—Internet Explorer is ready to protect you.

The Terminology of Cookies

Before you begin your cookie-fortification strategy, you'll have to bone up on a little terminology. Here are a few explanations to get you started:

- A **first-party cookie** is created by the site you're currently visiting. These kinds of cookies generally aren't privacy invaders; they're the Amazon type described above, designed to log you in or to remember how you've customized, for example, the Google home page.

POWER USERS' CLINIC

Data Execution Prevention

Data Execution Prevention (DEP), one of Windows' advanced security features, isn't well known, but it protects you against a variety of threats. It monitors important Windows services (background programs) and programs to make sure that no virus has hijacked them to your PC from within its own system memory. If DEP finds out that an attack is under way, it automatically closes the offending service or program.

DEP comes set to protect only Windows itself–not other programs. You can, though, ask DEP to monitor *every* program on your system, or just programs that you specify. The upside is better protection; the downside is that DEP could conflict with those programs, causing them to run erratically or not at all. In such cases, though, you can always turn off DEP protection for the affected programs.

(Note: If DEP suddenly starts interfering with important Windows files and features, a recently installed program could be at fault. Try uninstalling it, or inquire if the publisher has a DEP-friendly version; that may solve the problem.)

To turn on DEP for some or all programs: Open the Start screen. Type *advanced system* and select Settings under the search box. In the search results, click "View advanced system settings." In the Performance section, click Settings, and then click the Data Execution Prevention tab, shown at left. Select "Turn on DEP for all programs and services except those I select," and then click OK.

Should you find that DEP interferes with a program, click Add, and then follow the directions for selecting it.

Incidentally, at the bottom of the Data Execution Prevention screen, you can see whether or not your PC offers DEP *circuitry*, which reduces its speed impact. If not, Windows runs a software-based version of DEP.

- **Third-party cookies** are deposited on your hard drive by a site other than the one you're currently visiting—often by an advertiser. Needless to say, this kind of cookie is more objectionable. It can track your browsing habits and create profiles about your interests and behaviors.
- A **compact privacy statement** is a Web site's publicly posted privacy policy that describes how its cookies are used. Here you'll find out why cookies are used, for example, and how long they stay on your PC. (Some cookies are automatically deleted when you leave a Web site, and others stay valid until a specified date.)
- **Explicit consent** means you've granted permission for a Web site to gather information about your online activity; that is, you've "opted in."
- **Implicit consent** means you haven't OK'd that info gathering, but the site assumes that it's OK with you because you're there on the site. If a Web site uses the implicit-consent policy, it's saying, "Hey, you're fair game, because you haven't opted out."

Cookie Options

In Internet Explorer, choose Tools→Internet Options→Privacy to get to the Privacy tab shown in Figure 14-8. (To make the Tools menu appear, press the Alt key.)

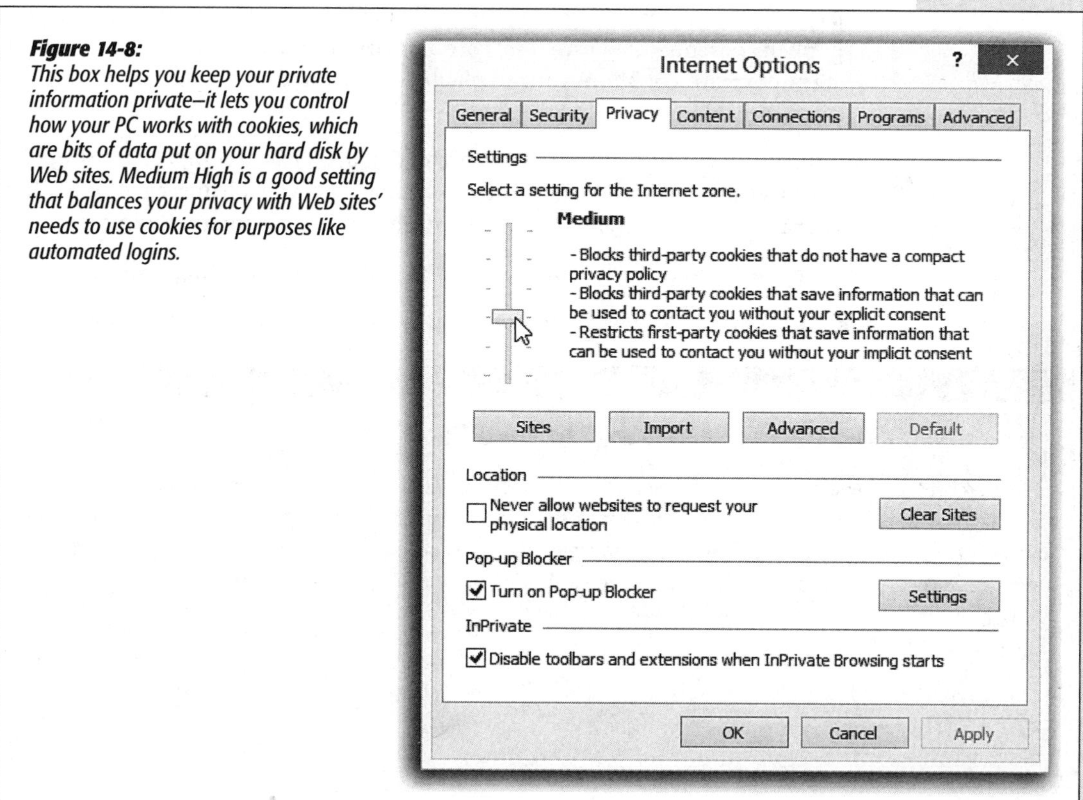

Figure 14-8:
This box helps you keep your private information private–it lets you control how your PC works with cookies, which are bits of data put on your hard disk by Web sites. Medium High is a good setting that balances your privacy with Web sites' needs to use cookies for purposes like automated logins.

Tip: You can also accept or reject cookies on a site-by-site basis. To do that, click the Sites button on the Privacy tab (Figure 14-8). The Per Site Privacy Actions dialog box appears. Type the name of the site in question, and then click either Block or Allow.

The slider on the left side lets you pick your compromise on the convenience/privacy scale, ranging from Accept All Cookies to Block All Cookies. Here are a few examples (and good luck with the terminology):

- **Block All Cookies.** No cookies, no exceptions. Web sites can't read existing cookies, either.
- **High.** No cookies from any Web site that doesn't have a compact privacy policy. No cookies from sites that use personally identifiable information without your consent.
- **Medium High.** Blocks third-party cookies from sites that don't have a compact privacy policy or that use personally identifiable information without your explicit consent. Blocks first-party cookies that use personally identifiable information without your implicit consent.
- **Medium (Default).** Blocks third-party cookies from sites that don't have a compact privacy policy or that use personally identifiable information without your implicit consent. Accepts first-party cookies from sites that use personally identifiable information without your implicit consent, but deletes them when you close Internet Explorer.
- **Low.** Blocks third-party cookies from sites that don't have a compact privacy policy. Accepts third-party cookies that use personally identifiable information without your implicit consent, but deletes them when you close Internet Explorer.
- **Accept All Cookies.** All cookies OK. Web sites can read existing cookies.

Choose the setting you want, and then click OK. You're ready to start browsing.

POWER USERS' CLINIC

Backing Up Your Cookies

This is probably deeper cookie information than you really wanted to know, but here it is: You may want to consider *backing up* your cookies. You could do that, for example, and transfer your cookies to another PC, for your auto-login convenience. Or you could back up the cookies just in case yours get somehow deleted.

To export or back up your cookies, open Internet Explorer. Press the Alt key to make the menus appear. Then choose File→Import and Export. The Import/Export Wizard appears. Choose Export Cookies and follow the directions. A single text file containing all your cookies is created in your Documents folder (or a folder you specify).

To import cookies to another computer (or to the same one after a disaster), launch the Import/Export Wizard, choose Import Cookies, and then browse to the folder where you stashed the backup file.

Note: Some sites don't function well (or at all) if you choose to reject all cookies. So if you choose High Privacy, and you run into trouble browsing your favorite sites, then return here and change the setting to Medium High. (The factory setting is Medium.)

If you're ever curious whether a Web site you've visited in your current browser session has placed any cookies on your hard disk, press the Alt key to make Internet Explorer's menu bar appear. Choose View→Webpage Privacy Policy. You'll see a list of the sites you've visited and whether any have placed cookies on your PC.

History: Erasing Your Tracks

You'd be shocked to see the kinds of information Internet Explorer stores about you. Behind the scenes, it logs every Web site you ever visit. It stashes your cookies, of course, plus passwords and information you type into Web forms (your name and address, for example). Your hard drive also keeps cache files—graphics and text files that make up the Web pages themselves, stored on your hard drive to speed up their reappearance if you visit those sites again.

Now, some people find it unnerving that Internet Explorer maintains a complete list of every Web site they've seen recently, in plain view of any family member or coworker who wanders by. Fortunately, you can delete any or all of these tracks easily enough.

- To delete just one particularly incriminating History listing, right-click it in the History list. (Click the ☆ at the upper-right corner of the window; click History; click the day in question.) From the shortcut menu, choose Delete.

  You can also delete any other organizer icon in the History list: one of the little Web-site folders, or even one of the calendar folders like Three Weeks Ago.

- To erase the entire History menu, choose Tools→Delete Browsing History, turn on History, and then click Delete.

POWER USERS' CLINIC

Examine Individual Cookies

Want to see the actual cookies themselves as they sit on your hard drive–the individual cookie files?

They're in your Personal folder→AppData→Roaming→Microsoft→Windows→Cookies folder. (You won't be able to see it until you visit Folder Options–page 256. Click "Show hidden files, folders, and drives," and turn off "Hide protected operating system files." Remember to switch these back to the factory settings when you're finished with this little experiment.)

Each cookie is named something like *casey@abcnews.com[1].txt*. The name of the Web site or ad network usually appears after the @, but not always–sometimes you just see a number.

To inspect a cookie, open the file as you would any other text file (in Notepad or WordPad, for example). Usually, there's nothing but a list of numbers and letters inside, but you might occasionally find useful information like your user name and the password for the Web site.

If you don't want the cookie on your hard disk, simply delete it as you would any other text file.

- The same dialog box (Figure 14-9) offers individual buttons for deleting the other kinds of tracks—the passwords, cache files, and so on.

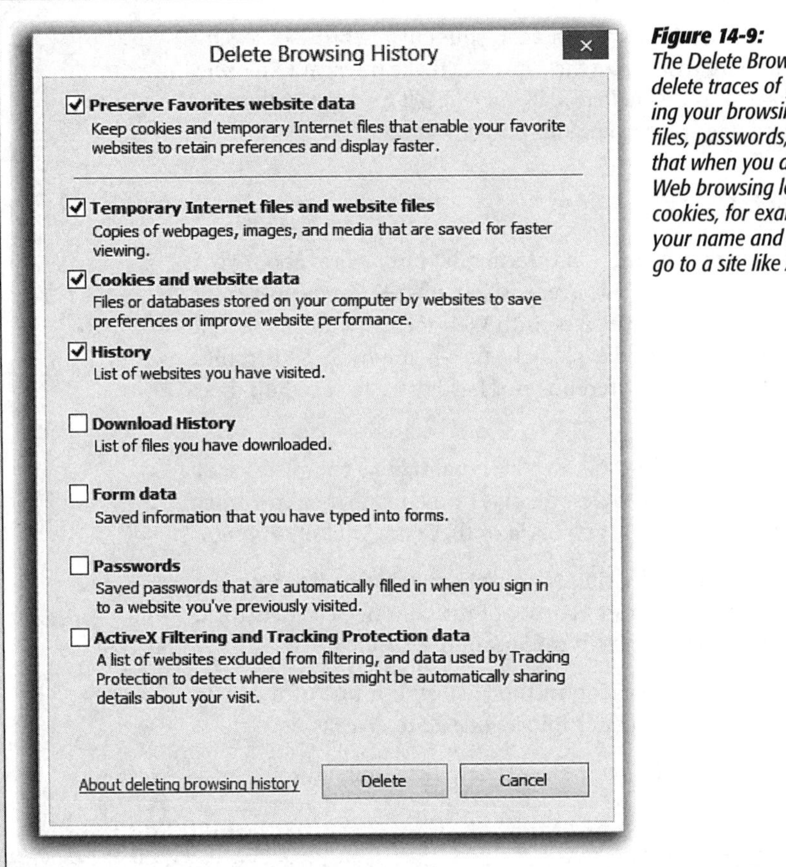

Figure 14-9:
The Delete Browsing History dialog box lets you delete traces of your Internet activities, including your browsing history, cookies, temporary files, passwords, and forms data. Keep in mind that when you delete some of this, it may make Web browsing less convenient. Delete your cookies, for example, and you'll have to enter your name and password again every time you go to a site like Amazon.

This is good information to know; after all, you might be nominated to the Supreme Court someday.

The Pop-Up Blocker

The ad banners at the top of every Web page are annoying enough—but nowadays, they're just the beginning. The world's smarmiest advertisers have begun inundating us with *pop-up* and *pop-under* ads: nasty little windows that appear in front of the browser window or, worse, behind it, waiting to jump out the moment you close your browser. They're often deceptive, masquerading as error messages or dialog boxes… and they'll do absolutely anything to get you to click inside them (Figure 14-10).

Pop-ups are more than just annoying; they're also potentially dangerous. They're a favorite trick that hackers use to deposit spyware on your PC. Clicking a pop-up can begin the silent downloading process. That's true even if the pop-up seems to serve a legitimate purpose—asking you to participate in a survey, for example.

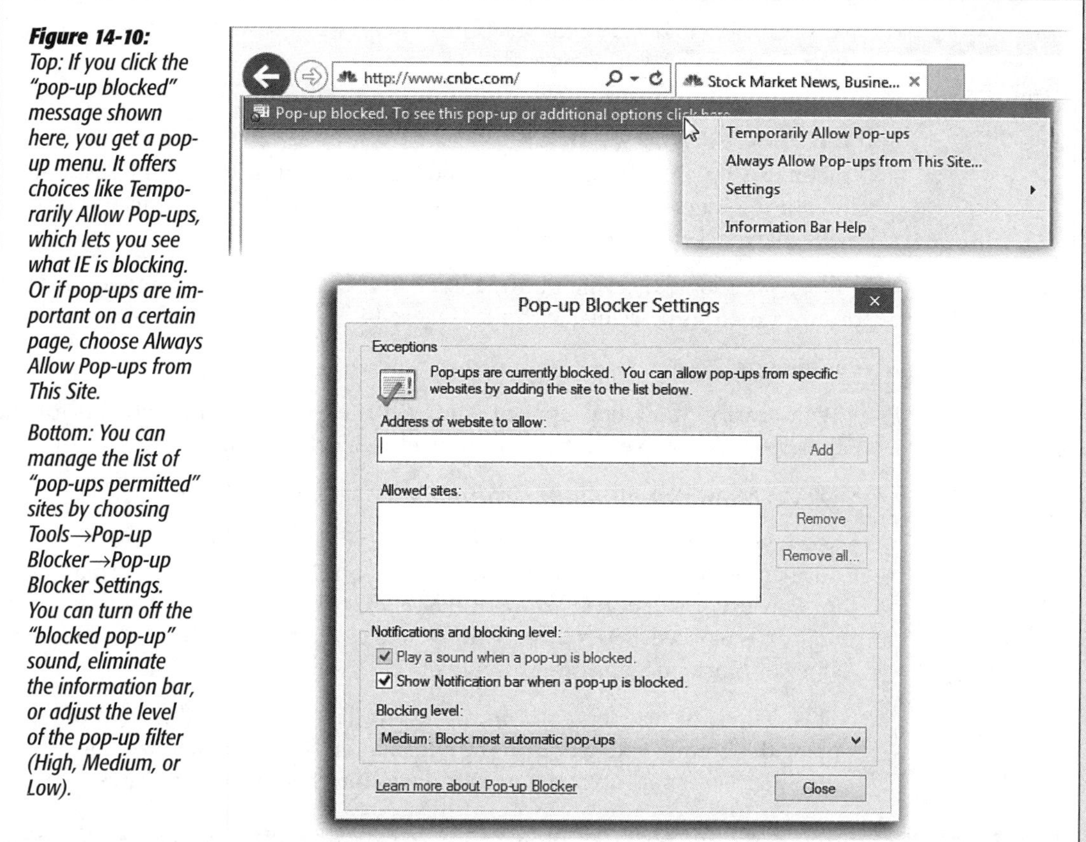

Figure 14-10: *Top: If you click the "pop-up blocked" message shown here, you get a pop-up menu. It offers choices like Temporarily Allow Pop-ups, which lets you see what IE is blocking. Or if pop-ups are important on a certain page, choose Always Allow Pop-ups from This Site.*

Bottom: You can manage the list of "pop-ups permitted" sites by choosing Tools→Pop-up Blocker→Pop-up Blocker Settings. You can turn off the "blocked pop-up" sound, eliminate the information bar, or adjust the level of the pop-up filter (High, Medium, or Low).

Internet Explorer, fortunately, has a pop-up *blocker*. It comes automatically turned on; you don't have to do anything. You'll be browsing along, and then one day you'll see the "Pop-up blocked" message in the yellow information bar (Figure 14-10, top).

Tip: At the outset, IE does more than just show the info bar message. It also opens a little dialog box—yes, a pop-up—to brag that it's blocked a pop-up. For best results, click "Don't show this message again," and then click OK. (The "Pop-up blocked" message still shows on the information bar, so you'll always know when a pop-up is sent into the ether.)

Note that IE blocks only pop-ups that are spawned *automatically,* not those that appear when you click something (like a seating diagram on a concert-tickets site). And it doesn't block pop-ups from your local network, or from Web sites you've designated as Trusted (choose Tools→Internet Options→Security, click "Trusted sites," and then click Sites).

Tip: As you can read in Figure 14-10, there *is* a High setting that blocks *all* pop-ups, even the ones that appear when you click a link. Even then, you still have a way to see the occasional important pop-up: Hold down the Ctrl key as your Web page is loading.

Overriding the Pop-up Block

Sometimes, though, you *want* to see the pop-up. Some sites, for example, use pop-up windows as a way to deliver information—showing you a seating chart when you're buying plane tickets, for example.

In those situations, click the information bar. A box appears that lets you manage pop-ups from this particular Web site (Figure 14-10, top).

Your options:

- **Temporarily Allow Pop-ups** lets this Web site's pop-ups through just for this browsing session. Next time, pop-ups will be blocked again.
- **Always Allow Pop-ups from This Site** does what it says.
- **Settings** lets you configure the pop-up blocker. From the menu that appears, select Turn Off Pop-up Blocker to turn the blocker off. Turn off Show Information Bar for Pop-ups if you don't even want the yellow information bar to appear when a pop-up is blocked. Select More Settings, and a screen appears that lets you always allow or block pop-ups from specific sites.

  This dialog box also lets you control how you're notified in the event of a pop-up: with a sound, with a note in the information bar, or neither. You can also use the Filter Level pop-up menu to tone down Internet Explorer's aggressiveness in

FREQUENTLY ASKED QUESTION

The Wisdom of Internet Explorer

How does the pop-up blocker know a good pop-up from a bad one, anyway?

Internet Explorer generally tries to distinguish between pop-ups it considers necessary for a site to run and those it considers annoying or dangerous.

Although it doesn't always succeed, there is some logic behind its thinking.

At the factory setting, some pop-ups get through. For example, it allows pop-ups that contain "active content"–for example, important features, brought to you by ActiveX controls and browser add-ons, that are integral to the proper functioning of a Web site: seating charts, flight-details screens, and so on.

The blocker doesn't block pop-ups from sites in your Local Intranet or Trusted Sites zones, either (page 470).

Finally, if you already have a spyware infection, pop-ups may appear constantly; the pop-up blocker isn't designed to block spyware pop-ups.

blocking pop-ups. The High level, for example, blocks *all* pop-ups, even the ones Internet Explorer determines to be necessary for the site to run properly.

Tip: If you've installed some other company's pop-up blocker, you can turn off IE's version by choosing Tools→Pop-up Blocker→Turn Off Pop-up Blocker.

InPrivate Browsing

If, ahem, not everything you do on the Web is something you want your spouse/parents/boss/teacher to know about, then Microsoft has heard you.

Of course, you can erase individual History entries, as described earlier. But those aren't the only tracks you leave as you browse the Web. Your hard drive collects cookies and temporary files; Internet Explorer collects passwords and other stuff you type into boxes; the address bar memorizes addresses you type, so you'll have AutoFill working for you later; and so on.

But in Internet Explorer 10, a feature called InPrivate browsing lets you surf wherever you like within a single browser window. Then, when you close that window, all that stuff is wiped out. No History items, no cookies, no saved password list, no AutoFill entries, and so on. In other words, what happens in InPrivate browsing stays in InPrivate browsing.

POWER USERS' CLINIC

Add-On Manager

Internet Explorer is more than just a browser. In fact, it's practically a kind of mini-operating system that lets lots of little add-on programs run inside it. The most common category of these plug-ins is called ActiveX controls. They grant all kinds of superpowers to Internet Explorer; for example, the Flash add-on makes possible animations and movies on YouTube and many other sites.

But ActiveX controls and other add-ons can cause problems. Install too many, and your browser can get sluggish. Sometimes add-ons conflict, resulting in an Internet Explorer crash. And some—this is the really nasty part—may actually be malicious code, designed to gum up your browser or your PC.

You'll know when some page needs an ActiveX control to proceed. You'll see a yellow warning bar just under the address bar, letting you know you have to click to proceed. (If you're pretty sure this is a reliable Web site that really needs to install this add-on feature, click the information bar; from the shortcut menu, choose Allow Blocked Content.) Gone are the days when evildoers could invade your PC by downloading these things without your knowledge.

To help you get a handle on your plug-in situation, choose Tools→Manage Add-ons. You get a list of all your add-ons and ActiveX controls. They're listed in several different categories, like those currently loaded into Internet Explorer and ActiveX controls you've downloaded.

Highlight one to read details about it, and to summon the Disable, Enable, and (in some categories) Remove buttons.

(Hint: Before clicking any of these buttons, do a Google search on the name or the file name. You'll find out soon enough if the plug-in is trustworthy. Be especially wary of add-ons in the Browser Helper Objects [BHOs] category. These can be useful, but also very dangerous.)

- To start InPrivate browsing, press the Alt key to make the menu bar appear. Then choose Tools→InPrivate Browsing, or press Shift+Ctrl+P. A new window opens (Figure 14-11). Nothing you do in this window—or in the tabs within it—will leave tracks.

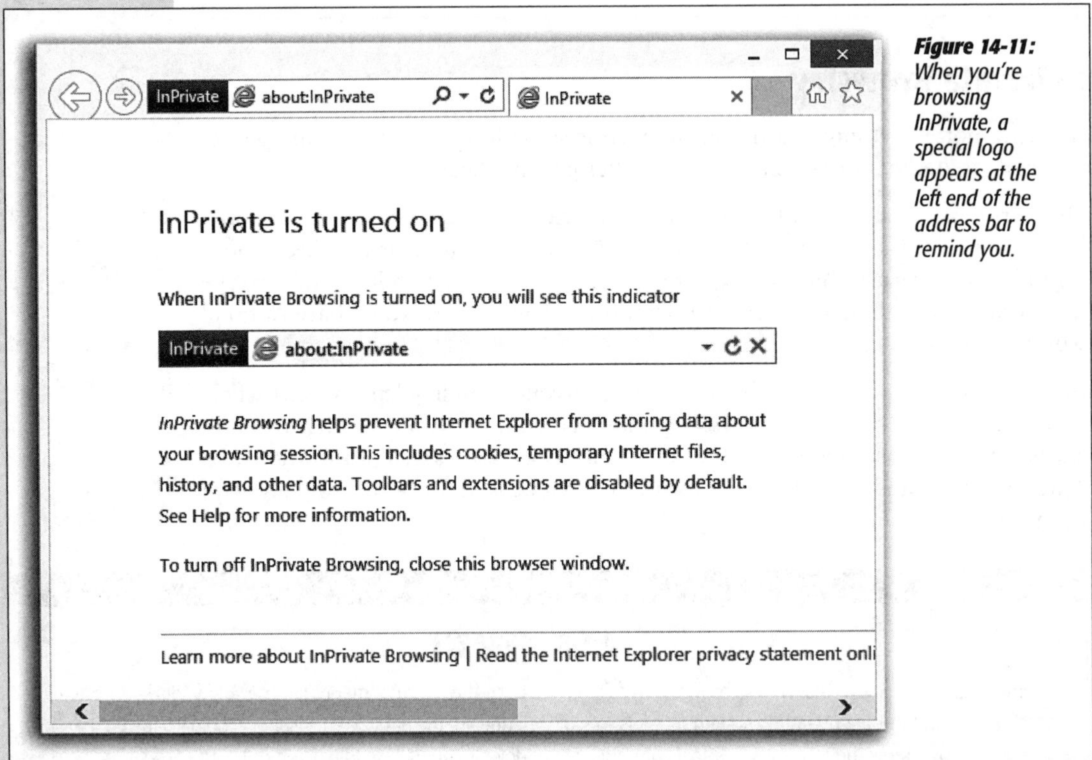

Figure 14-11: *When you're browsing InPrivate, a special logo appears at the left end of the address bar to remind you.*

- To stop InPrivate browsing, just close the window. Open a new Internet Explorer window to continue browsing "publicly."

Note: Casual snoopers will never know you've been looking over the racy photos on the Midwestern Shirtless Accountants Web site. But you're not completely untraceable. Nobody using your PC can see where you've been, but your network administrator, or a nearby hacker, could watch you from across the network.

Internet Security Zones

In the real world, you usually have a pretty good sense of where the bad parts of town are, and how to avoid them after dark. On the Web, it's not so easy. The most elegant-looking Web page may be a setup, a trick by sleazy hackers to install viruses on your PC.

Security zones is an older Internet Explorer feature designed to limit the number of paths the bad guys have into your PC. It's fairly confusing, which is why almost nobody uses it.

Under this scheme, if you have tons of time, you can place individual Web sites into different classifications (zones) according to how much you trust them. Internet Explorer refuses to download potential bad stuff (like those ActiveX plug-ins) from sites in the seedier zones. Your PC, sanitized for your protection.

For example, internal company Web sites, right there on the corporate network, are pretty unlikely to be booby-trapped with spyware and viruses (unless you have a really twisted network administrator). Such internal sites are automatically part of the low-security Local Intranet zone. If you maintain a Web site at home, it's in that zone, too.

The rest of the Internet starts out in the very big Internet zone (medium security). As you browse, though, you can manually place them into zones called Trusted Sites (medium security) or Restricted Sites (high security).

To see your options, choose Tools→Internet Options→Security from within Internet Explorer (Figure 14-12).

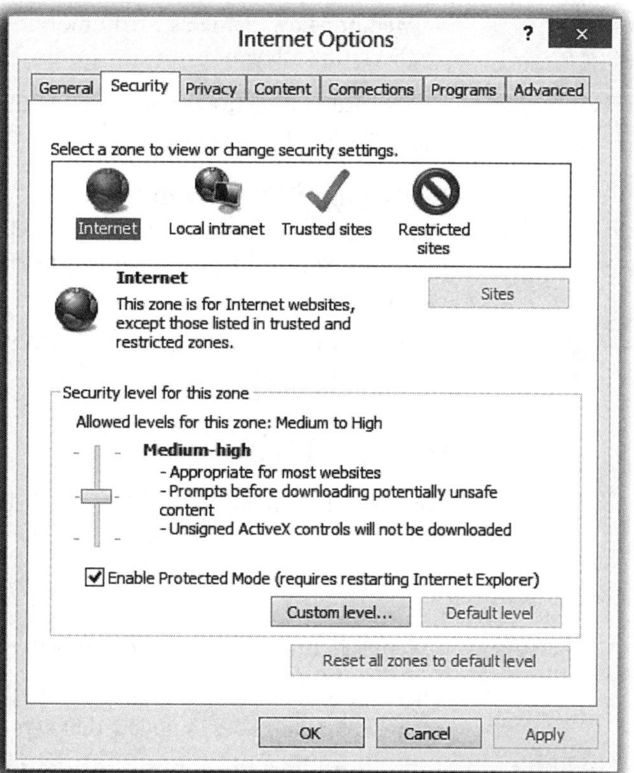

Figure 14-12: *The Internet Options Security tab lets you control Internet Explorer's security settings for browsing the Web. You can customize the settings for each zone by moving the slider up for more security, or down for less security.*

Security Levels

And what, exactly, is meant by "Medium security" or "High security"? These settings control what can and can't be done when you're visiting such a site. For example, they govern whether or not you're allowed to download files, and whether or not Internet Explorer runs embedded Web-page programs like Java applets or ActiveX controls. (Java applets are little programs that offer interactivity on Web sites, like games and interactive weather maps.)

Here's the cheat sheet:

- **High** security blocks all kinds of features that could conceivably be avenues for bad guys to infect your browser: ActiveX controls, Java and Java applets, and downloads.
- **Medium** security means that whenever a Web site triggers an ActiveX control to run, you're asked for permission. Unsigned ActiveX controls—those whose origins aren't clear to Internet Explorer—don't get run at all. Downloads and Java applets are OK.
- **Medium-Low.** Same as Medium, but some ActiveX programs run without first checking with you.
- **Low.** Runs all ActiveX controls and other little Web programs. Rarely asks you for permission for things.

Classifying Sites by Hand

To place a certain Web site into the Trusted or Restricted zone, choose Tools→Internet Options→Security. Click either Trusted Sites or Restricted Sites, and then click the Sites button.

In the resulting dialog box, the current Web site's address appears automatically. Click Add, and then Close.

Do Not Track

You know how there's a "Do not call" list? If you register your phone number with this list, telemarketers are legally forbidden to call you.

Now there's a "Do not track" list, too. If you turn this feature on in your browser—like Internet Explorer 10—then Web advertisers are supposed to not track your Web activities in order to market to you better.

There's a difference, though. Advertisers' respect for your Do Not Track setting is entirely *optional*. There's no law that says they *have* to obey it.

Originally, the advertisers (in the form of the Digital Advertising Alliance trade group) promised the U.S. government that they'd all respect the Do Not Track setting—as long as this feature came turned *off* on all new computers.

But Do Not Track comes *turn* on in Internet Explorer 10, to the great unhappiness of the advertising industry. In retaliation, the ad industry has vowed to ignore the Do Not Track feature altogether. As a result, it's essentially a useless feature.

If you care, you can find the Do Not Track setting like this: Press the Alt key to make the Tools menu appear. Choose Tools→Internet Options. In the resulting dialog box, click the Advanced tab. Scroll down to the Security heading, and tun turn on "Always send Do Not Track header." Restart the computer.

Hotspot Security

One of the greatest computing conveniences of the new millennium is the almighty public wireless hotspot, where you and your WiFi-enabled laptop can connect to the Internet at high speed, often for free. There are thousands of them at cafés, hotels, airports, and other public locations (see *www.jiwire.com* for a national directory).

But unless you're careful, you'll get more than a skinny latte from your local café if you connect to its hotspot—you may get eavesdropped on as well. It's possible for someone sitting nearby, using free shareware programs, to "sniff" the transmissions from your laptop. He can intercept email messages you send, names and passwords, and even the images from the Web pages you're visiting.

Now, you don't have to sell your laptop and move to the Amish country over this. There are a few simple steps that will go a long way toward keeping yourself safe:

- **Tell Windows you're on a public network.** When you first connect to a wireless network, Windows asks whether it's a public or a private one (see the figure on page 439). Choosing Public gives you extra protection. Technically speaking, Windows turns off *network discovery,* the feature that makes your PC announce its presence to others on the network. (Unfortunately, lurking hackers using special scanning software can still find you if they're determined.)

- **Turn off file sharing.** You certainly don't want any of your over-caffeinated neighbors to get access to your files. Open the Start screen. Start typing *sharing* until you see "Manage advanced sharing settings" in the results list; click it. In the resulting window, turn of all the Sharing options.

- **Watch for the padlock.** You generally don't have to worry about online stores and banks. Whenever you see the little padlock icon in your Web browser (or whenever the URL in the address bar begins with "https" instead of "http"), you're visiting a secure Web site. Your transmissions are encrypted in both directions and can't be snooped.

- **Look over your shoulder.** Hacking isn't always high-tech stuff; it can be as simple as "shoulder surfing," in which someone looks over your shoulder to see the password you're typing. Make sure no one can look at what you're typing.

- **Don't leave your laptop alone.** Coffee has a way of moving through your system fast, but if you have to leave for the restroom, don't leave your laptop unattended.

Pack it up into its case and take it with you, or bring along a lock that you can use to lock it to a table.

- **Use a virtual private network (VPN).** If somebody intercepts your "Hi, Mom" email, it may not be the end of the world. If you're doing serious corporate work, though, and you want maximum safety, you can pay for wireless virtual private network (VPN) software that encrypts all the data you're sending and receiving. Nobody will be able to grab it out of the air using snooping software at a hotspot.

  For example, HotSpotVPN (*www.hotspotvpn.com*) costs $3.88 per day or $8.88 per month. You get a password, user name, and the Internet address of a VPN server.

  Open the Network and Sharing Center (quickest link to it: the Network icon on your system tray). Click "Set up a new connection or network." Select "Connect to workplace," and then follow the prompts for creating a new VPN connection with the information provided to you by HotSpotVPN.

Protect Your Home Wireless Network

Public wireless hotspots aren't the only ones that present a theoretical security risk; your wireless network at home harbors hacker potential, too. It's theoretically possible (barely) for so-called war drivers (people who drive around with laptops, looking for unprotected home WiFi networks) to piggyback onto home networks to download child pornography or to send out spam.

This one's easy to nip in the bud:

- **Turn on wireless encryption.** When you first set up your WiFi router (your base station or access point), you're offered the chance to create a password for your network. Take the chance. (Modern wireless routers offer two different types of password-protected encryption, called WEP and WPA. If it's available, choose the more modern, more secure one, which is WPA.)

  You then have to enter the password when you first connect to that hotspot from each wireless PC on your network.

Note: You won't have to type this password every time you want to get onto your own network! Windows offers to memorize it for you.

- **Ban unwanted PCs.** Many routers include a feature that lets you limit network access to specific computers. Any PC that's not on the list won't be allowed in. The feature is called MAC address filtering, although it has nothing to do with Macintosh computers. (It stands for media access control address, is a serial number that uniquely identifies a piece of networking hardware.)

  Not all routers can do this, and how you do it varies from router to router, so check the documentation. In a typical Linksys router, for example, you log into the router's administrator's screen using your Web browser and then select Wireless→Wireless

Network Access. On the screen full of empty boxes, type the MAC address of the PC that you want to be allowed to get onto the network.

Tip: To find out the MAC address of a PC, press ⊞+R to open the Run dialog box. Type *cmd* and press Enter. Type *ipconfig/all*, and press Enter. In the resulting info screen, look for the Physical Address entry. That's the MAC address.

Type all the MAC addresses into the boxes on the Linksys router, click Save Settings, and you're all done.

- **Place your router properly.** Placing your WiFi router centrally in the house minimizes the "leaking" of the signal into the surrounding neighborhood.

Family Safety (Parental Controls)

Many parents reasonably worry about the volatile mixture of kids+computers. They worry about kids spending too much time in front of the PC, rotting their brains instead of going outside to play stickball in the street like we did when we were their age, getting fresh air and sunshine. They worry that kids are playing disgusting, violent video games. They worry that kids are using programs they really shouldn't be using, corrupting themselves with apps like Skype or Quicken. (That's a joke.)

Above all, parents worry that their kids might encounter upsetting material on the Internet: violence, pornography, hate speech, illegal drug sites, and so on.

A special Windows feature gives you a fighting chance at keeping this stuff off your PC: Family Safety, formerly called Parental Controls. It's easy to use and fairly complete (it's been beefed up since Windows 7).

Specifically, Family Safety has four features to protect your youngsters:

- Block inappropriate Web sites from their impressionable eyes.
- Set daily time limits on their computer use.
- Monitor which programs your kids are using, and limit games and TileWorld apps they buy from the Windows Store.
- Send you activity reports so you know what they're up to.

Turn on Family Safety

Before you can set up parental controls, some housekeeping is required. You, the parent, are presumably in charge of the computer and should therefore have an Administrator account (page 728). And it must be password-protected; if it's not, then the kid whose innocence you're trying to preserve can just log in as you and turn Parental Controls off.

Your children, on the other hand, must have Standard accounts. You can create one account that all your kids share, or you can set up a different account for each kid; that way, you can set up different safety restrictions for each person.

Family Safety (Parental Controls)

When you create a kid's Standard account, as described in Chapter 23, you'll see how incredibly simple it is to turn on Family Safety: Just click the box that says, "Is this a child's account? Turn on Family Safety to get reports of their PC use."

Without doing a single thing more, you've enabled the weekly monitoring feature. Each week, you'll get emailed a report for each of your kids that summarizes the following:

- Which Web sites they've visited most often this week.
- What words they've searched for online.
- How much time they spent on the computer each day.

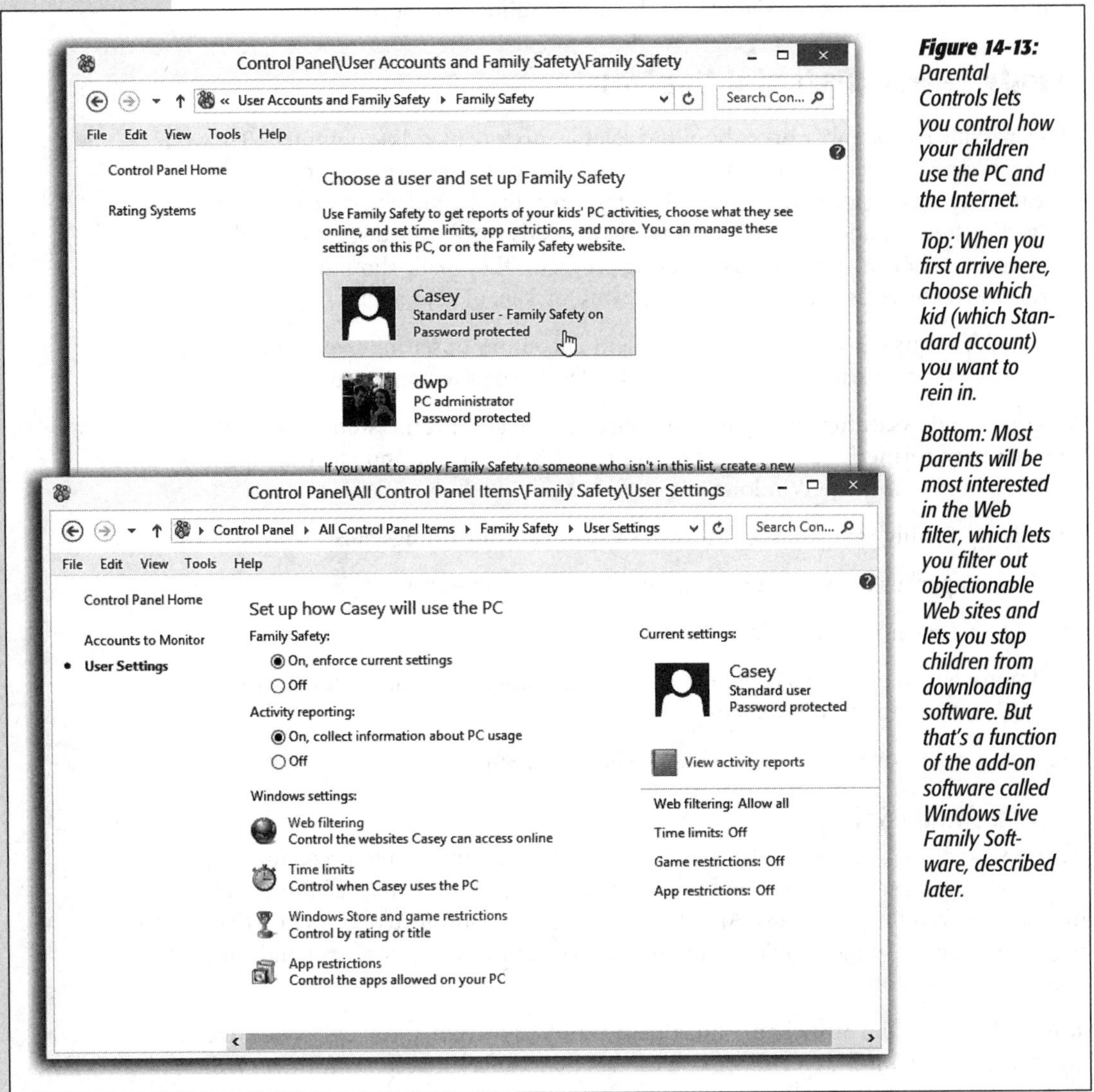

Figure 14-13: *Parental Controls lets you control how your children use the PC and the Internet.*

Top: When you first arrive here, choose which kid (which Standard account) you want to rein in.

Bottom: Most parents will be most interested in the Web filter, which lets you filter out objectionable Web sites and lets you stop children from downloading software. But that's a function of the add-on software called Windows Live Family Software, described later.

- Which programs and games they've used most this week.
- What apps they've downloaded from the Windows Store.

On/Off Switches

Once your kid turns 18, or finally seems to be developing a little maturity, for crying out loud, you can turn off either the weekly reports or the Family Safety feature as a whole.

To do that, sign in using your Administrator account. You can open the Family Safety panel in either of these ways:

- **Open the Start screen.** Type *family* and select Settings under the search box. In the search results, choose "Set up Family Safety."
- **Open the Control Panel** (for example, by right-clicking the lower-left corner of the screen and then choosing Control Panel from the secret Utilities menu). In the User Accounts and Family Safety category, click "Set up Family Safety for any user."

Authenticate yourself if necessary (page 743). The dialog box shown at top in Figure 14-13 appears, listing all the user *accounts* on the PC (Chapter 23). Click the kid's account that you want to adjust.

Here you'll find the master On/Off switch for the entire Family Safety feature (for this account holder); it's shown at bottom in Figure 14-13. You can also turn off just the weekly reports by clicking the "Activity reporting" Off button.

Turning on Restrictions

If the prospect of being monitored by those weekly emails to you isn't all your kids need to steer them straight, you can also turn on some restrictions.

One of the key advantages of the accounts system is that you can set up separate "worlds" for each person in your family—and now comes the payoff. Click your kid's account to open up its parental controls screen (Figure 14-13, bottom).

If "On, enforce current settings" is selected (Figure 14-13, bottom), you can now set up these limits for your offspring's PC use in Family Safety's big four categories. Here they are, blow by blow.

Web Filtering

Web filtering prevents your youngsters from opening inappropriate Web sites—dirty pictures, hate speech, and so on. You can either trust Microsoft's ever-evolving "blacklist" of known naughty sites, or you can add individual Web addresses to the blocked list.

To set it up, click Web Filtering on the account holder's setup page (Figure 14-13, bottom). Turn on "Casey [or whatever the kid's name is] can only use the websites I allow."

Click "Set web filtering level." Now you have five levels of blocking options. Each builds on the previous:

- **Allow list only.** Your little ragamuffin can't open any Web sites except the ones that appear on the list when you click "Click here to change Allow List."
- **Designed for children.** The only sites available are the ones on the Allow List and those designed expressly for kids.
- **General interest.** Includes the sites described above, plus general-interest, non-pornographic regular sites.
- **Online communication.** Includes all of the above, plus social networking, chat, and email Web sites.
- Warn and adult. All Web sites are available—but a message pops up to warn the kid (or invite him, depending on your point of view) before he tries to open a porn site.

This page also offers a "Block file downloads" checkbox. You know who you are.

Time Limits

This feature lets you control when your little tyke can use the computer—a much more automated method than constant "Why don't you go out and play?" nagging.

In Windows 8, you have two ways to limit this account holder's brain-rotting time: by total number of hours each day, or by specific times of the day (no computer on school nights, for example):

- **Time Limits.** Click "Set time allowance" to view the dialog box shown at top in Figure 14-14. When you click "Casey can only use the PC for the amount of time I allow," a set of pop-up menus appears. You can use them to specify a time allotment for each weekday (Mon-Fri) or each weekend day (Sat-Sun). Or, by opening the ^, you can assign different time limits for each individual day of the week (Figure 14-14).
- **Curfew.** If you click "Set curfew" instead, then you get the box shown at bottom in Figure 14-14. Drag your mouse through the grid for the hours when computer use is *forbidden*. You might want to block use during normal sleeping hours, for example.

Windows Store and Game Restrictions

This option prevents your youngsters from playing games altogether or lets you specify which kinds of games they can play.

For example, if you click "Casey can only use games and Windows Store apps I allow," you see that you have two ways to limit games:

- **Set games and Windows Store ratings.** Click this link to permit only games in a certain age bracket: Early Childhood, say, or Adults Only.

  (Caution: Not all game programs on your PC identify themselves as games. Some appear just as regular old programs. Of course, you can always block them using the "specific programs" options described next.)

Note: To make this feature work, Windows consults a tiny GDF (game definition file) that software companies can put into their games. Game companies usually use ratings bestowed by a ratings board like the Entertainment Software Ratings Board (ESRB).

If a publisher uses information from a different ratings board, or doesn't have a rating file (GDF) at all, then Windows consults Microsoft's own 2,000-game database. And if even *that* source draws a blank, Windows considers the game unrated. That's why this screen offers a "Block games with no rating" option; it's designed just for such situations.

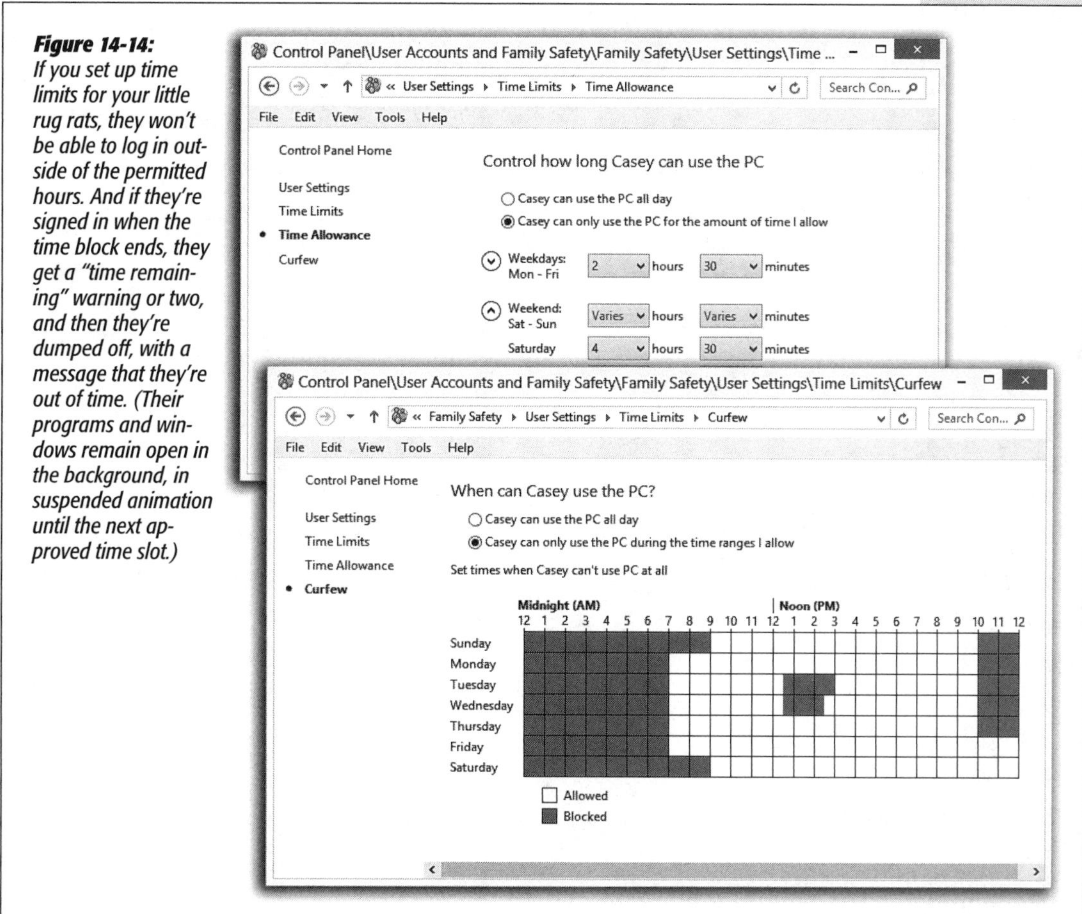

***Figure 14-14:** If you set up time limits for your little rug rats, they won't be able to log in outside of the permitted hours. And if they're signed in when the time block ends, they get a "time remaining" warning or two, and then they're dumped off, with a message that they're out of time. (Their programs and windows remain open in the background, in suspended animation until the next approved time slot.)*

- **Allow or block specific games** lets you declare individual programs on your PC to be off limits. Windows presents you with a list of every game on your PC; for each one, you can choose "Always block," "Always allow," or "User rating setting" (meaning, "fall back to the game ratings system described above").

  If your lovable young ruffian does attempt to run an off-limits program, a box appears that says, "Family Safety has blocked this program." If he clicks "Ask an administrator for permission," the UAC box appears (page 743) so he can call you or some other older, wiser account holder over to the PC. You can type in a name and administrator password to "unlock" the program—just for this time.

CHAPTER
15

Internet Explorer 10

Internet Explorer is the most famous Web browser on earth, thanks in part to several years of Justice Department scrutiny. It also has more syllables than any other Web browser, which is probably why most people just call it IE.

As you know, there are two Internet Explorers in Windows 8—the TileWorld version and the desktop version. Actually, although they have separate faces, they share some internal organs.

You can read about the TileWorld version on page 105. This chapter covers the desktop version, which is far more complete. (For one thing, it can run plug-ins, and it can show you Flash sites.)

All these goodies and more are described in this chapter. Chapter 14, meanwhile, covers Internet Explorer's security and privacy features.

Note: OK, you may have to read this slowly:

When you first get Windows 8, the TileWorld version of Internet Explorer is your *default* browser. It's the one that opens when you click a link in some email, or do a search for *Internet Explorer*, or click its tile on the Start screen (which bears a big "e" logo, with the name *Internet Explorer* beneath).

But if you install a different program, like Chrome or Firefox, as your default browser, then the Start screen tile changes. The "e" logo is small, and the name *Internet Explorer* appears *above* it. This is the *desktop* version of Internet Explorer, and it's the one that opens when you click the tile or do a search for "Internet Explorer."

IE10 Desktop: The Grand Tour

There's only one easy way to open the desktop Internet Explorer: Click its icon on the desktop taskbar. It comes preinstalled there.

Now, you might reasonably object: "What's the big deal? I can always get to it the way I get to any other program: with a quick search at the Start screen."

But you'd be wrong. Desktop IE is, for some reason, completely invisible to the Search command and does not appear as a tile on the Start screen. The only version you can find by searching, and the only version on the Start screen, is the TileWorld version.

Tip: Actually, you *can* pin desktop IE to the Start screen. Open a Windows Explorer window at the desktop. Open your Computer→Program Files→Internet Explorer window. Right-click the icon called *iexplore.exe*; from the shortcut menu, choose Pin to Start.

And there you go. Your desktop IE, called "iexplore," appears as a tile at the right end of the Start screen. Now you can select it or even search for it (although you have to use its Windows name, iexplore).

There's one other sneaky way to open desktop IE, one that may actually be quicker sometimes. Just type a Web address—a *URL* (Uniform Resource Locator)—into any Explorer window's address bar, and then hit Enter. Desktop IE opens automatically and pulls up that page. (A Web page URL usually begins with the prefix *http://*, but you can leave that part off when typing into the address bar.)

Figure 15-1: *The Internet Explorer window offers tools and features that let you navigate the Web almost effortlessly; these various toolbars and status indicators are described in this chapter. Chief among them: the newly unified address/search bar, which displays the address (URL) of the Web page you're currently seeing and also serves as the search box when you want to find something on the Web.*

As you can see in Figure 15-1, the Internet Explorer window is filled with tools designed to facilitate a smooth trip around the World Wide Web.

A Note About the Menu Bar

You'd never know it by looking, but Internet Explorer has a menu bar. A really important one. But to help maximize window space, Microsoft generally hides it. Whenever you need it, press the Alt key. There it is: File, Edit, View, Favorites, Tools, and Help.

In this chapter, you'll frequently be directed to choose a menu command. Now you know that in every case, you'll have to tap the Alt key to see the menu bar as a first step.

Tip: Either that, or you can tell IE to display the menu bar *all the time*. To do that, right-click the top strip of the window; from the shortcut menu, choose "Menu bar." Now it will never leave you.

Links and Underlines

A link (or hyperlink) is a bit of text, or a little graphic, that's been programmed to serve as a button. When you click a link, you're transported from one Web page to another. One may be the home page of General Motors; another might have baby pictures posted by a parent in Omaha. About a billion pages await your visit.

Tip: Text links aren't always blue and underlined. In fact, modern Web designers sometimes make it very difficult to tell which text is clickable and which is just text. When in doubt, move your cursor over some text. If the arrow changes to a pointing-finger cursor, you've found yourself a link.

Actually, you can choose to hide *all* underlines, a trick that makes Web pages look cleaner and more attractive. Underlines appear only when you point to a link (and wait a moment). If that arrangement appeals to you, open Internet Explorer. Choose Tools→Internet Options, click the Advanced tab, scroll down to "Underline links," select the Hover option, and then click OK.

The Address/Search Bar

Often, of course, you'll want to begin browsing by typing in a Web address; that's the purpose of the address/search bar identified in Figure 15-1. In IE10, though, a single, unified box serves as both the address bar and the search bar. If you type a Web address there, like *amazon.com,* pressing Enter takes you to that Web site; if you type anything else, like *cashmere sweaters* or just *amazon,* pressing Enter gives you the Bing search results for that phrase.

In general, it's handy to have a combined address bar/search bar (many other browsers work this way, too).

Searching the Web

Press Alt+D to deposit your insertion point inside the new unified toolbar. As you type something you're looking for—*phony baloney,* say—a pop-up menu of autocomplete suggestions appears beneath your typing, as shown in Figure 15-2. When you finish typing and press Enter (or when you click one of those suggestions), IE takes you directly to the Bing results page.

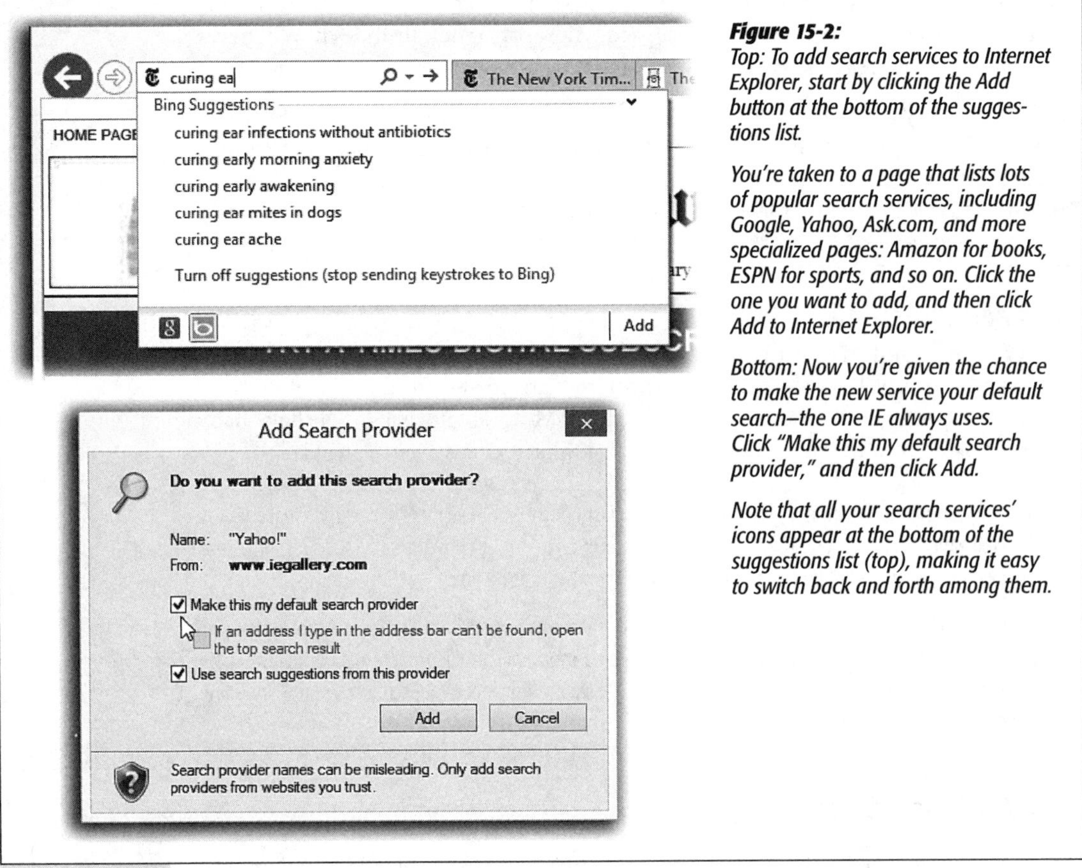

Figure 15-2:
Top: To add search services to Internet Explorer, start by clicking the Add button at the bottom of the suggestions list.

You're taken to a page that lists lots of popular search services, including Google, Yahoo, Ask.com, and more specialized pages: Amazon for books, ESPN for sports, and so on. Click the one you want to add, and then click Add to Internet Explorer.

Bottom: Now you're given the chance to make the new service your default search–the one IE always uses. Click "Make this my default search provider," and then click Add.

Note that all your search services' icons appear at the bottom of the suggestions list (top), making it easy to switch back and forth among them.

Now, in order to supply those suggestions, IE has to send what you've typed to Microsoft's computers. If that notion bugs you, the privacy fan, just click "Turn off suggestions (stop sending keystrokes to Bing") at the bottom of the pop-up menu.

Adding Google

You're not obligated to use Microsoft's Bing search service. There is, after all, another very good search engine out there called Google. You might have heard of it.

Fortunately, you can make IE use Google instead of (or in addition to) Bing, like this:

1. **Start typing something into the address/search bar.**

   The autocomplete suggestions appear, as shown in Figure 15-2.

2. **Click the Add button at its lower right.**

   You wind up at a huge gallery of online search services.

3. **Click the Google Search icon.**

   A new page appears, giving details about Google search.

4. **Click Add to Internet Explorer.**

   Now a dialog box appears (Figure 15-2, bottom). It offers two checkboxes: "Make this my default search provider" and "Use search suggestions from this provider."

5. **Turn on the checkboxes you prefer, and then click Add.**

From now on, much to Microsoft's dismay, you'll be using Google instead of Bing for searching. As an added convenience, the logos of *all* search services—Bing, Google, and whatever others you add using this technique—appear at the bottom of the suggestions menu (shown at top in Figure 15-2). You can click them to switch back and forth between results and suggestions.

Entering an Address

Because typing out Internet addresses is so central to the Internet experience and such a typo-prone hassle, the address bar is rich with features that minimize keystrokes. For example:

- You don't have to click in the address bar before typing; just press Alt+D.
- You don't have to type out the whole Internet address. You can omit the *http://www* and *.com* portions; if you press Ctrl+Enter after typing the name, Internet Explorer fills in those standard address bits for you.

GEM IN THE ROUGH

Let AutoFill Do the Typing

Internet Explorer can remember the user names and passwords you type into those "Please sign in" Web sites.

You can't miss this feature; each time you type a password into a Web page, this box appears at the bottom of the screen.

Do you want Internet Explorer to remember the password for nytimes.com? Yes No ×

It's a great time- and brain-saver, even though it doesn't work on all Web sites. (Of course, use it with caution if you share an account on your PC with other people.)

When you want IE to "forget" your passwords—for security reasons, for example—choose Tools→Internet Options. Click the Content tab. In the AutoComplete section, click Settings, and then click "Delete AutoComplete history."

You get the box shown on page 466, where you can delete all kinds of stuff Internet Explorer memorizes: cookies, forms (your name, address, and so on), your History list, user names and passwords, and so on. Turn on the checkboxes you want (or, rather, don't want), and then click Delete.

To visit Amazon.com, for example, you can press Alt+D to highlight the address bar, type *amazon,* and then press Ctrl+Enter.

- Even without the Ctrl+Enter trick, you can still omit the *http://* from any Web address. (Most of the time, you can omit the *www.,* too.) To jump to today's Dilbert cartoon, type *dilbert.com* and then press Enter.
- When you begin to type into the address/search bar, the AutoComplete feature compares what you're typing against a list of Web sites you've recently visited. IE displays a drop-down list of Web addresses that seem to match what you're typing (Figure 15-2). To save typing, just click the correct complete address with your mouse, or use the ↓ key to reach the desired listing and then press Enter. The complete address you selected then pops into the address bar.

  (To make AutoComplete *forget* the Web sites you've visited recently—so that nobody will see what you've been up to—delete your History list, as described on page 465.)
- If the *first item* in the list of suggestions is the site you want, you don't have to click it, and you don't have to do any more typing. Just press Shift+Enter to open that site.
- Press F4 (or click the ▾ inside the right end of the address/search bar) to view a list of URLs you've visited recently—your History list, in other words—as well as sites you've bookmarked (which Microsoft calls Favorites). Once again, you can click the one you want—or press the ↓ or ↑ keys to highlight one, and the Enter key to select it.

Topside doodads

Around the address/search bar, you'll find several important buttons. Some of them lack text labels, but all offer tooltip labels:

- **Back button (⊖), Forward button (⊖).** Click the ⊖ button to revisit the page you were just on. (*Keyboard shortcut:* Backspace or Alt+←.)

Tip: Pressing Shift as you turn your mouse's scroll wheel up or down also navigates forward and back. Cool.

  Once you've clicked Back, you can then click the ⊖ button (or press Shift+Backspace or Alt+→) to return to the page you were on *before* you clicked the Back button. Click and hold on either button for a list of all the Web pages you've visited during this online session (that is, within this browser window, as opposed to your long-term History list).

- **Refresh button.** Click the ↻ at the right end of the address bar if a page doesn't look or work quite right, or if you want to see the updated version of a Web page that changes constantly (such as a stock ticker). This button forces Internet Explorer to redownload the Web page and reinterpret its text and graphics.
- **Stop (✖) button.** Click this button, at the far right end of the address/search bar, to interrupt the downloading of a Web page you've just requested (by mistake, for example). (*Keyboard shortcut:* Esc.)

Window Controls

These last items wrap up your grand tour of Internet Explorer's window gizmos:

- **Scroll bars.** Use the scroll bar, or the scroll wheel on your mouse, to move up and down the page—or to save mousing, press the space bar each time you want to see more. Press Shift+space bar to scroll *up*. (The space bar has its traditional, space-making function only when the insertion point is blinking in a text box or the address/search bar.)

  You can also press your ↑ and ↓ keys to scroll. Page Up and Page Down scroll in full-screen increments, while Home and End whisk you to the top or bottom of the current Web page.

- **⌂ button.** Click to bring up the Web page you've designated as your home page—your starter page.

  And which page is that? Whichever one you designate. Open a good startup page (Google, NYTimes.com, Dilbert.com, whatever). Then right-click this icon; from the shortcut menu, choose "Add or change home page."

  You're asked if you want this one page to be your startup page, or if you want to add it to your home-page tabs. In other words, you can have several sites open up *simultaneously* when you click Home, on separate *tabs* (see below)—and IE is asking if you want this page added as one of those tabs. Make your choice and click Yes.

- **Status bar.** The status bar at the bottom of the window tells you what Internet Explorer is doing (such as "Opening page..." or "Done"). When you point to a link without clicking, the status bar also tells you which URL will open if you click it.

  And when you're opening a new page, a graph appears here, showing that your PC is still downloading (receiving) the information and graphics on the Web page. In other words, you're not seeing everything yet.

  So how come you can't see your status bar? Because it starts out hidden. You have to summon it by choosing View→Toolbars→Status Bar (press Alt to make the status bar appear).

Tabbed Browsing

Beloved by hard-core surfers the world over, *tabbed browsing* is a way to keep a bunch of Web pages open simultaneously—in a single, neat window, without cluttering up your taskbar with a million buttons.

Figure 15-3 illustrates.

Tip: When you open new tabs by clicking links on a Web page, the tabs are color-coded to match the color of the originating page, so you can tell where they came from (shown in Figure 15-3). The newly sprouted tab appears right next to its source tab.

Shortcut-O-Rama

Tabbed browsing unlocks a whole raft of Internet Explorer shortcuts and tricks, which are just the sort of thing power surfers gulp down like Gatorade:

- **To open a new, empty tab** in front of all others, press Ctrl+T (for *tab*), or click the New Tab stub identified in Figure 15-3. From the empty tab that appears, you can navigate to any site you want.

***Figure 15-3:** When you Ctrl-click a link, or type an address and press Alt+Enter, you open a new tab, not a new window as you ordinarily would. You can now pop from one open page to another by clicking the tabs above the window, or close one by clicking its* ✖ *button (or pressing Ctrl+W).*

- **To open a link into a new tab,** Ctrl-click it. Or click it with your mouse wheel.

  Or, if you're especially slow, right-click it and, from the shortcut menu, choose Open in New Tab.

Note: Ctrl-clicking a link opens that page in a tab *behind* the one you're reading. That's a fantastic trick when you're reading a Web page and see a reference you want to set aside for reading next, but you don't want to interrupt whatever you're reading now.

But if you want the new tab to appear in *front, then* add the Shift key.

- **To close a tab,** click the ✖ on it, press Ctrl+W, or click the tab with your mouse wheel or middle mouse button, if you have one. (If you press Alt+F4, you close all tabs. If you press Ctrl+Alt+F4, you close all tabs *except* the one that's in front.)

Tip: If you close a tab, or a group of tabs, by accident, you can call them back from the dead. Click the New Tab button (see Figure 15-3). The resulting New Tab page displays the addresses of tabs you've recently closed; click the one you want.

If you've exited Internet Explorer in the meantime, you lose your chance to recover those closed tabs. But speaking of which: If that happens, you can always choose Tools→Reopen Last Browsing Session, a command that brings back all the pages you had open when you quit the program.

- **Switch from one tab to the next** by pressing Ctrl+Tab. Add the Shift key to move backward through them.
- **Jump to a specific tab** by pressing its number along with the Ctrl key. For example, Ctrl+3 brings the third tab forward.
- **Save a tab configuration.** If there's a certain set of Web sites you like to visit daily, open them all into tabs. Click the Favorites (☆) button, and then, from the "Add to favorites" pop-up menu, choose "Add current tabs to favorites." Type a name for the group, and then click Add.

  Later, you can recreate your current setup—with all of them in a tabbed window—by selecting the resulting listing in the Favorites menu (on the Favorites tab) and then clicking the blue ➔ button beside its name. The beauty of this arrangement is that you can start reading the first Web page while all the others load into their own tabs in the background.
- **Close all?** When you close Internet Explorer, a dialog box appears asking if you really want to close *all* the tabs, or just the frontmost one. If you grow weary of answering that question, turn on "Always close all tabs" before making your selection.

Tab Settings

People get *really* obsessive over tabs for some reason. They want tabs to behave *just* the way they expect, or it's back to Firefox they go.

No worries—IE lets you customize tabs' behavior to within an inch of their lives. Start by choosing Tools→Internet Options→General; in the Tabs section of the dialog box, click Tabs. Here's the most useful of what you'll find:

- **Enable Tabbed Browsing.** This is the on/off switch for the whole tab feature.
- **Warn me when closing multiple tabs.** If tabs are open when you close Internet Explorer, a confirmation box appears: "Do you want to close all tabs?" It's semi-annoying but semi-useful, because you may not realize that you're about to close all your tabs.
- **Always switch to new tabs when they are created.** Makes every new tab appear in front of the others, even if you Ctrl-click a link rather than Ctrl+Shift-click it. (Even if you leave this option off, though, Ctrl+Shift-clicking a link still opens the tab in front.)
- **Show previews for individual tabs in the taskbar.** Ordinarily, pointing to the Internet Explorer icon on the taskbar produces the handy pop-up thumbnails for

each tab you have open. Turn this option off if you want only a thumbnail for each window. (You won't see the effect until the next time you turn on your computer.)

- **Enable Quick Tabs.** This is the on/off switch for the feature shown in Figure 15-4. (Switching this setting, too, requires a restart.)
- **Enable Tab Groups.** When you're on one tab, and you open a new tab from it (for example, by right-clicking a link and choosing "Open link in new tab"), IE color-codes the two tabs so you can tell that they sprouted from the same source. It also puts them together on the row of tabs. This feature is called tab grouping, and you can turn it off by clicking this box (and then restarting).
- **Open only the first home page when Internet Explorer starts.** Got a tab group set as your home page? Turn on this box if you want only the first tab to open when IE starts, rather than the whole tab group.
- **When a new tab is opened, open:** When you click the New Tab tab (Figure 15-3), a special, mostly blank New Tab page opens. It contains icons for sites you visit often, plus links like "Reopen last session" and "InPrivate Browsing." This pop-up menu lets you choose to have your home page appear instead, or even a completely blank page.
- **When a pop-up is encountered.** When a "good" pop-up window opens, should it open in a new window or in a new tab? Or should Internet Explorer try to figure out which would be most helpful? (If the Web programmer has specified a specific size for the pop-up, it appears in a window; otherwise, in a tab.)
- **Open links from other programs in:** If you click a link in an email message, should the resulting Web page open in a new window or in a new tab? Or should it replace whatever is currently in the frontmost window or tab? Only you can decide.

Actually, there's one more useful tabbed-browsing setting that's *not* here—for some reason, Microsoft stuck it on the Tools→Internet Options→Advanced tab. It's "Use most recent order when switching tabs with Ctrl+Tab."

Ordinarily, pressing Ctrl+Tab moves you through your tabs from left to right; adding Shift moves you backward.

But if you turn this option on, then Ctrl+Tab jumps through the tabs you've visited in *reverse chronological order.* It's just the way Alt+Tab works when you're switching between Windows programs. This arrangement makes it very easy to compare two Web pages, because pressing Ctrl+Tab bounces you back and forth between them.

Note: This option also affects what happens when you hit Ctrl+W repeatedly to *close* tabs. They close in reverse chronological order.

Quick Tabs (Thumbnails)

Once you've got a bunch of tabs open, you may face a horizontal screen-space crunch. How much, exactly, of the text "Welcome to Bass World—The Internet's Global Resource for Bass Fisherfolk" can you see on a half-inch tab?

Not much. But how, then, are you supposed to tell your tabs apart?

By using another feature called Quick Tabs. Figure 15-4 shows all.

Note, however, that Quick Tabs aren't available until you *turn on* this feature, as described on the previous page.

Tip: You can *close* a tab directly from the Quick Tabs screen, too—just click the ✖ button in the upper-right corner of the thumbnail.

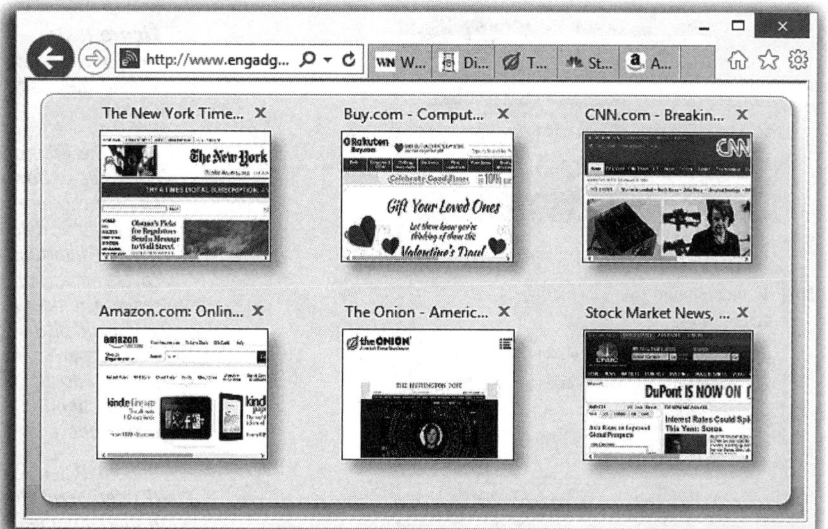

***Figure 15-4:** Quick Tabs shows you thumbnails of all the Web pages you've opened into tabs, making it simple to tell them apart. One click on a thumbnail returns it to full size, in front of the others. All you have to learn is the Quick Tabs keystroke, which is Ctrl+Q. (Repeat the trigger to exit the Quick Tabs view without changing anything.)*

Favorites (Bookmarks)

When you find a Web page you might like to visit again, press Ctrl+D. That's the keyboard shortcut for the Add to Favorites command. (The long way is to click the ☆ button to make the Favorites pane appear, and then click the "Add to favorites" button, identified in Figure 15-5—but who's got the time?) Type a shorter or more memorable name, if you like, and then click Add.

Tip: Actually, here's a trick that may save you even more time. You can drag a Web site's icon (the tiny one just to the left of its address in the address/search bar) directly onto Internet Explorer's taskbar icon. (This works with any browser, actually—Firefox or whatever.) When you release the mouse, that site's name appears at the top of the icon's jump list, in the pinned area. Next time you want to visit that site, just click the Internet Explorer icon (even if it's not running) and click the site's name in the jump list.

The page's name appears instantly in the Favorites Center, which is the panel indicated by the yellow star (Figure 15-5). The next time you want to visit that page, open this menu—or press Alt+C—and click the Web site's name in the list. (Your Favorites also appear in a tidy list that appears when you click the ▾ at the right end of the address/search bar.)

Tip: You can send your list of Favorites to or from other browsers or other PCs, which can save you a lot of time.

To do that, open the Add to Favorites menu (Figure 15-5); choose "Import and export." The Import/Export wizard appears to guide you through the process. Consider saving them onto, for example, a flash drive, for ease in transporting to another location or computer.

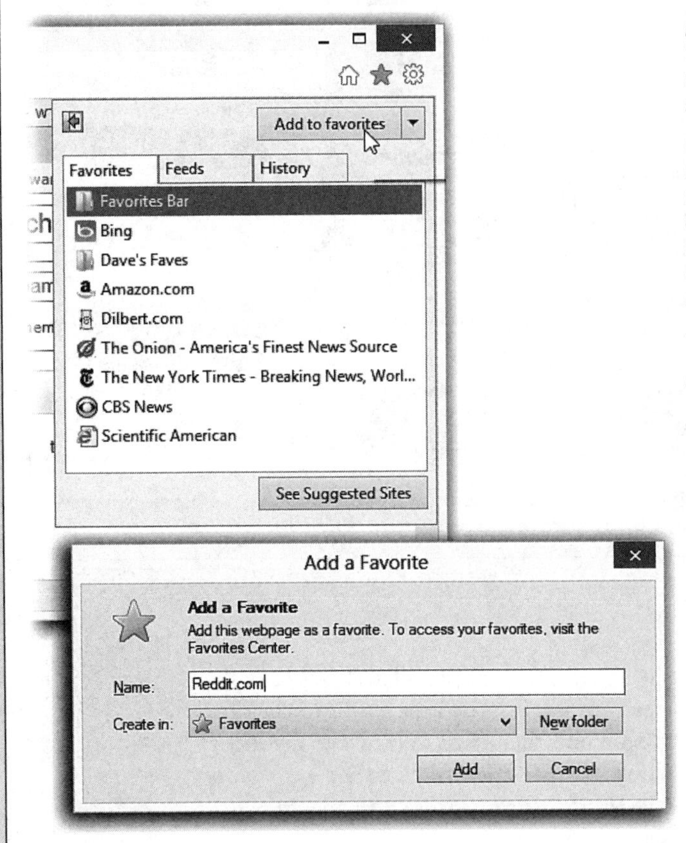

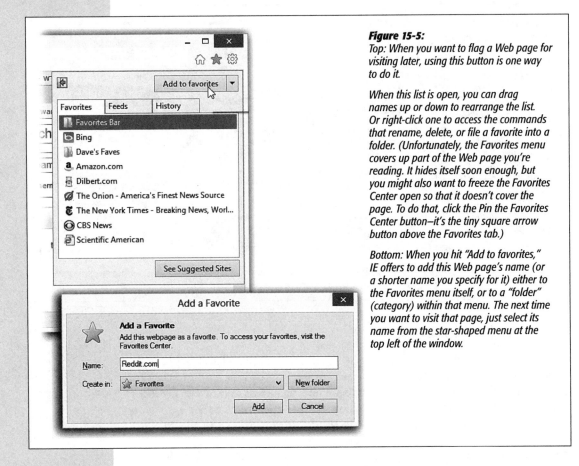

Figure 15-5:
Top: When you want to flag a Web page for visiting later, using this button is one way to do it.

When this list is open, you can drag names up or down to rearrange the list. Or right-click one to access the commands that rename, delete, or file a favorite into a folder. (Unfortunately, the Favorites menu covers up part of the Web page you're reading. It hides itself soon enough, but you might also want to freeze the Favorites Center open so that it doesn't cover the page. To do that, click the Pin the Favorites Center button–it's the tiny square arrow button above the Favorites tab.)

Bottom: When you hit "Add to favorites," IE offers to add this Web page's name (or a shorter name you specify for it) either to the Favorites menu itself, or to a "folder" (category) within that menu. The next time you want to visit that page, just select its name from the star-shaped menu at the top left of the window.

You can rearrange the commands in your Favorites menu easily enough. Open the Favorites Center (Figure 15-5, top), and then drag the bookmarks up and down in the list.

Or, for more elaborate organizing tasks—creating and deleting folders, renaming sites, and so on—open the "Add to favorites" pop-up menu and, from the shortcut menu, choose "Organize favorites." You get a little dialog box that makes all those tasks easy.

The Favorites Toolbar

The Favorites pane is one way to maintain a list of Web sites you visit frequently. But opening a Web page in that pane requires *two mouse clicks*—an exorbitant expenditure of energy. The Favorites toolbar, on the other hand, lets you summon a few, very select, *very* favorite Web pages with only *one* click.

You make the toolbar appear by choosing Tools→Toolbars→Favorites Bar. Figure 15-6 illustrates how to add buttons to, and remove them from, this toolbar. Once they're there, you can rearrange these buttons simply by dragging them horizontally. (Whatever you stash here also turns up on the Links bar at the desktop, weirdly enough.)

Tip: As shown in Figure 15-6, you can drag a link from a Web page onto your Favorites toolbar. But you can also drag it directly to the desktop, where it turns into a special Internet shortcut icon. To launch your browser and visit the associated Web page, just double-click this icon whenever you like.

Better yet, stash a few of these icons on your Start screen for even easier access. (Moreover, if you open your Computer→(C:) drive→Users→[Your Name]→Favorites folder, you see these shortcut icons for *all* your favorite links. Feel free to drag them to the desktop, the Links bar, or wherever you like.)

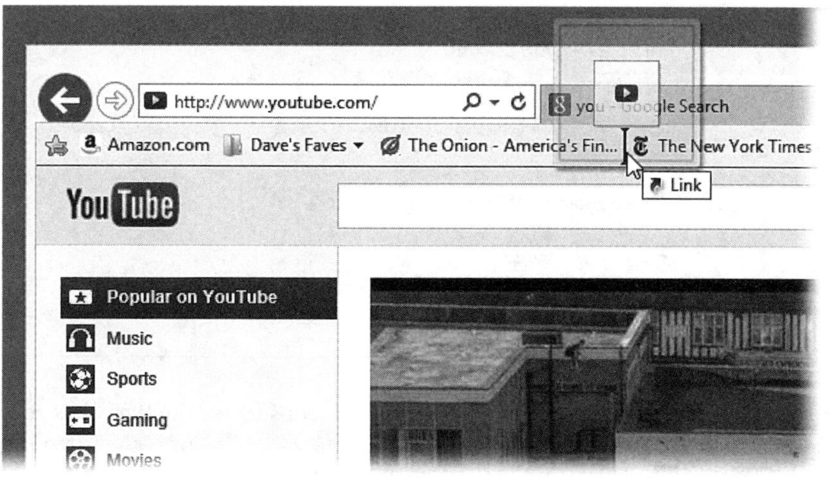

Figure 15-6: *Drag the tiny page icon to the Links bar. Right-click a link to choose Rename (to pick a shorter name that fits better).*

History List

This *history* is a list of the Web sites you've visited. It's the heart of three IE features: AutoComplete, described at the beginning of this chapter; the drop-down list at the right side of the address/search bar; and the History list itself.

That's the pane that appears when you click the Favorites (★) button and then click History—or just press Ctrl+H. Figure 15-7 presents the world's shortest History class.

History List

The History pane lists the Web sites you've visited in the past week or so, neatly organized into subfolders like "Today" and "Last Week." These are great features if you can't recall the URL for a Web site you remember having visited recently.

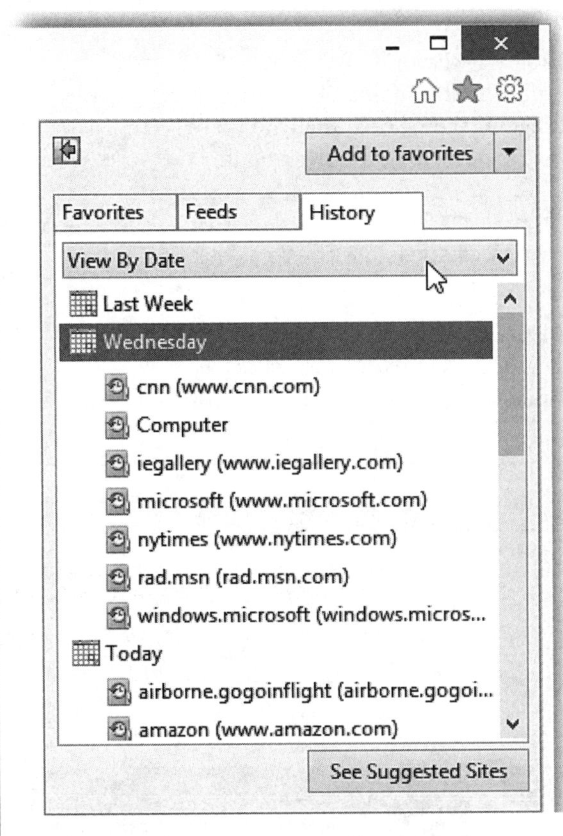

Figure 15-7: *You can expand or contract the day folders with a click.*

The pop-up menu indicated here by the cursor lets you sort the list by Web site, date, frequency of visits—or you can see only the sites you've visited today, in order. The same little pop-up menu offers a command called Search History so that you can search for text in the History list—not the actual text on those pages, but text within the page addresses and descriptions.

Click one of the time-period icons to see the Web sites you visited during that era. Click the name of a Web site to view a list of each visited page *within* that site—and click an actual URL to reopen that Web page in the main window.

You can configure the number of days for which you want your Web visits tracked. To do so, choose Tools→Internet Options→General; where it says "Browsing history," click Settings. At the bottom of the dialog box, you see the "Days to keep pages in history" control.

Tip: The more days IE tracks, the easier it is for you to refer to those addresses quickly. On the other hand, the more days it tracks, the longer the list becomes, which may make it harder to use the list efficiently.

Oh, and if you set "Days to keep pages in history" to 0, Internet Explorer doesn't track your movements at all. (You know who you are.)

For details on *erasing* your History list for security purposes, see page 465.

RSS: The Missing Manual

In the beginning, the Internet was an informational Garden of Eden. There were no banner ads, pop-ups, flashy animations, or spam messages. People thought the Internet was just the greatest.

Those days, unfortunately, are long gone. Web browsing now entails a constant battle against intrusive advertising and annoying animations. And with the proliferation of Web sites and blogs, just reading your favorite sites can become a full-time job.

Enter RSS, a technology that lets you subscribe to *feeds*—summary blurbs provided by thousands of sources around the world, from Reuters to Microsoft to your nerdy next-door neighbor. News and blog sites usually publish RSS feeds, but RSS can also bring you podcasts (recorded audio broadcasts), photos, and even videos.

You used to need a special RSS *reader* program to tune into them—but no longer. Internet Explorer can "subscribe" to updates from such feeds so you can read any new articles or postings at your leisure.

The result? You spare yourself the tedium of checking for updates manually, plus you get to read short summaries of new articles without ads and blinking animations.

WORKAROUND WORKSHOP

Compatibility View

For years, Internet Explorer didn't respect the programming conventions of the Web. Web-page designers would carefully follow the rules to create, say, a picture with a 3-point blue box around it–but in Internet Explorer, it would look wrong. Microsoft just said: "We're the 800-pound gorilla. We do things our own way."

So Web designers had to use all sorts of programming hacks and kludges, writing the HTML code for their sites so that they'd look right in Internet Explorer. (Many went to the effort of designing a different site just for the "all other browsers" category. Which version you'd see when you visited that page depended on what browser you had.)

But with millions of people choosing other free Web browsers, Microsoft realized that it couldn't remain cocky forever. So it cleaned up its act; today's version of Internet Explorer strictly sticks to modern Web standards.

The irony, of course, is that now all those millions of pages written for the *old* IE look funny in the new IE!

Now Microsoft gets to know what it feels like to be one of the other browsers, the ones that have always worked properly.

In any case, if you find a Web page that looks odd, or the text spills out of its box, or the buttons don't line up, or whatever, you can use Compatibility View. You can turn it on in either of two ways:

- Click the Compatibility View button (☒). It appears on the address/search bar automatically whenever you're on a page that hasn't been updated for IE8 or later.
- Choose Tools→Compatibility View.

In this mode, IE10 impersonates IE6, believe it or not, displaying the page the way the creator intended. IE will remember to use this view for this Web site until (a) you turn Compatibility View off, or (b) the site is rewritten for IE10.

And if you want to read a full article, you can click its link in the RSS feed to jump straight to the main Web site.

Note: RSS stands for either Rich Site Summary or Really Simple Syndication. Each abbreviation explains one aspect of RSS—either its summarizing talent or its simplicity. (Web feeds and XML feeds are the same thing.)

Figure 15-8: *Top: When the Feeds button on the command bar changes color, you've got yourself a live one: a Web site that publishes a feed. Click the Feeds button.*

Middle: Now you see what the feed looks like. You can use the Displaying box like a search filter—type a topic to see only matching items. Or use the sorting and filtering commands in the same box.

Bottom: If you like the looks of this feed, click the Favorites button (★) and then click "Subscribe to this feed," as shown here.

You're asked to name this feed; then your personalized clipping service is always ready to read. It's hiding in the Favorites button (★) on the Feeds tab.

Viewing an RSS Feed

So how do you sign up for these free, automatic RSS "broadcasts"? Open the command bar. It's one of the toolbars available when you right-click the top edge of the window.

On that command bar, you find a bunch of little icons—including the Feeds button ( ). Watch that icon as you're surfing the Web. When the turns orange, IE is telling you, "This site has an RSS feed available."

(Sometimes, in fact, the site has *multiple* feeds available—for example, in different formats—in which case you can choose among them using the ▾ menu next to the icon.)

Tip: To find more RSS feeds, visit a site like *www.syndic8.com*.

By the way, Internet Explorer isn't the only RSS reader. If you catch the RSS bug, you might want to try out a more powerful RSS reader. Visit *www.downloads.com,* for example, and search for *RSS readers,* or try a Web-based one like *www.reader.google.com.*

To see what the fuss is all about, click that button. Internet Explorer switches into RSS-viewing mode, as shown in Figure 15-9, middle.

At this point, you have three choices:

- **Massage the feed.** Once you're looking at the feed, you can sort the headline items by date, title, and author, or use the search box to find text among all the articles.

GEM IN THE ROUGH

Web Slices

A Web slice is a Microsoft invention with a lot in common with an RSS feed: It's information from other Web sites, automatically updated and placed in front of you for easy reviewing.

But a Web slice is a pop-up panel that sprouts from a button on your Favorites toolbar. That is, you don't lose your place on the Web; you stay on whatever page you were on and just pop up a Web slice panel for a quick look at the weather, the latest headlines, current stock prices, your Hotmail inbox, or whatever.

Supposedly, when a Web site offers a Web slice, the Slices icon ( ) appears and lights up green. (This icon appears on the command bar, which you have to open manually as described above.) Click the Slices icon, or press Alt+J, to see a list of the RSS feeds and Web slices available on that page. Click the one you want to subscribe to.

From now on, you can click that button on the toolbar to see the latest information. If the slice's name appears in bold, that means it's been updated since the last time you looked.

Not every Web page offers a Web slice–in fact, hardly any do. A Web page's programmer has to create a Web slice. And since Internet Explorer is the only Web browser that can exploit them, Web slices have been very slow to catch on. In fact, they're practically dead.

- **Subscribe.** Click the Favorites button (★) and then the Feeds tab; then click "Subscribe to this feed." Name and save the feed into a folder, if you like. From now on, you'll be able to see whether the RSS feed has had any new articles posted—without actually having to visit the site.

Note: Once you've subscribed to a feed, Internet Explorer checks the originating Web site once a day for updates.

You can make it check a bit more obsessively, if you like (as often as every 15 minutes), or cool its jets (once a week). To adjust the schedule, choose Tools→Internet Options→Content; click Settings at the bottom of the dialog box. Use the "Every:" pop-up menu to specify the frequency.

While you're here, turn on "Play a sound" if you want a little sonic heads-up, too, when IE finds that a Web page you've just opened has an available RSS feed.

- **Close the RSS feed.** Click any of the feed's headlines to jump to its corresponding full-blown Web page.

Tips for Better Surfing

Internet Explorer is filled with shortcuts and tricks for better speed and more pleasant surfing. For example:

Full-Screen Browsing

The Web is supposed to be a *visual* experience; losing a bunch of your monitor's real estate to toolbars and other window dressing isn't necessarily a good thing.

But if you press F11 (or choose View→Full Screen from the Classic menus), all is forgiven. The browser window explodes to the very borders of your monitor, hiding the Explorer bar, toolbars, and all. The Web page you're viewing fills your screen, edge to edge—a glorious, liberating experience.

You can return to the usual crowded, toolbar-mad arrangement by pressing F11 again—but you'll be tempted never to do so.

Picking a Home Page

The first Web site you encounter when IE connects to the Internet is a Microsoft Web site—or one of Dell's, or EarthLink's; the point is, *you* didn't choose it. This site is your factory-set *home page.*

Unless you actually work for Microsoft, Dell, or EarthLink, you'll probably find Web browsing more fun if you specify your *own* favorite Web page as your startup page.

The easiest way to go about it is to follow the instructions shown in Figure 15-9.

Google makes a nice home page; so does a news site. But here are a couple of possibilities that might not have occurred to you:

- **A blank page.** If you can't decide on a home page, or if your mood changes from day to day, set up a blank—empty—home page. This setup makes IE load very quickly when you first launch it. Once this window opens, *then* you can tell the browser where you want to go today.

  To set this up, choose Tools→Internet Options→General. In the "To create home page tabs" box at the top, type *about:blank*. (Not kidding; that's how you do it.) Click OK.

- **Multiple home page tabs.** This is a cool one. You can designate a *bunch* of tabs to open all at once each time you fire up Internet Explorer. It's a great way to avoid wasting time by calling up one site after another, because they'll all be loading in the background as you read the first one.

Note: See "Tab settings" on page 489; a few settings there pertain exclusively to home page tab groups.

The quickest way to set up a Home tab set: Open all the Web sites into their own tabs, just the way you'll want IE to do automatically in the future. Then, from the Home shortcut menu shown in Figure 15-11, choose "Add or change home page."

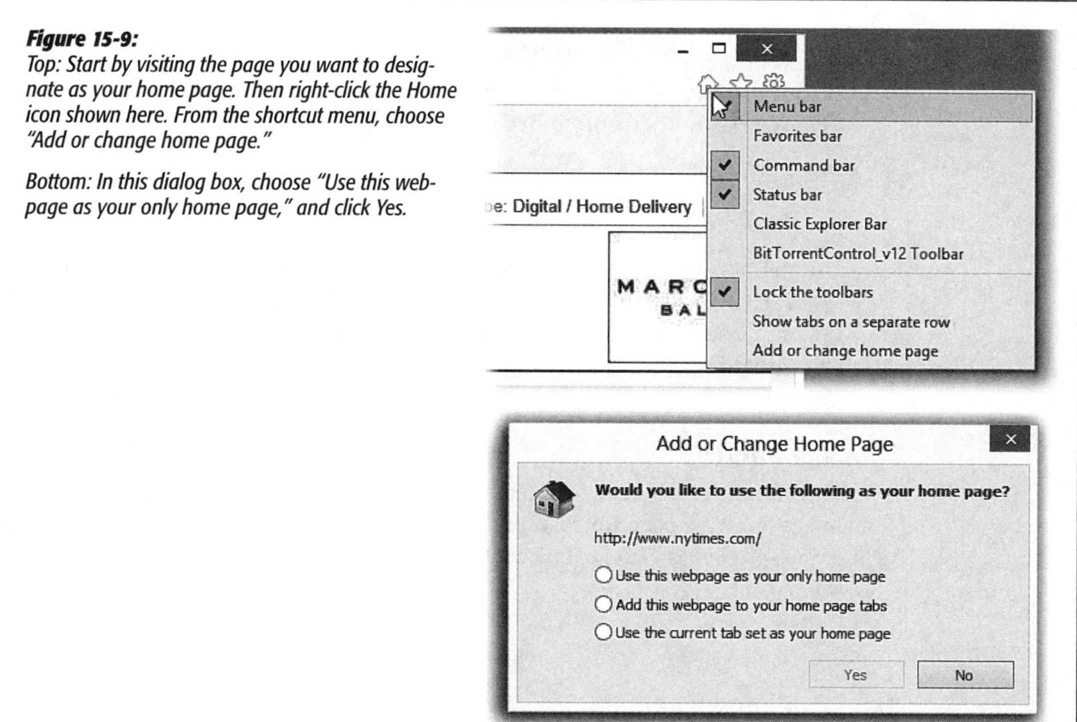

Figure 15-9:
Top: Start by visiting the page you want to designate as your home page. Then right-click the Home icon shown here. From the shortcut menu, choose "Add or change home page."

Bottom: In this dialog box, choose "Use this webpage as your only home page," and click Yes.

Next, in the dialog box (Figure 15-9, bottom), select "Use the current tab set as your home page," and click Yes.

Thereafter, you can always add additional tabs to this starter set by choosing "Add this webpage to your home page tabs," the middle option shown in Figure 15-9.

Note: Although it's a little more effort, you can also edit your home page (or home page tab sets) manually in a dialog box, rather than opening them up first.

Choose Tools→Internet Options→General. In the "Home page" text box, type each address, complete with *http://* and so on. If you want to create a home page tab set, type each address on its own line. (Leave the box empty for a blank home page.) Click OK, OK?

Bigger Text, Smaller Text

When your eyes are tired, you might like to make the text bigger. When you visit a site designed for Macintosh computers (whose text tends to look too large on PC screens), you might want a smaller size. You can adjust the point size of a Web page's text using the View→Text Size command.

Zooming In and Out

So much for magnifying the *text;* what about the whole Web page?

There are plenty of ways to zoom in or out of the whole affair:

- If you have a touchscreen, pinch or spread two fingers against the glass.
- If you have a scroll-wheel mouse, press the Ctrl key as you turn the mouse's wheel. (This works in Microsoft Office programs, too.)
- Press Ctrl+plus or Ctrl+minus on your keyboard.
- Use the ✿→Zoom submenu.
- Use the pop-up menu in the right corner of the status bar, if you've made that visible (it probably says "100%" at the moment). Just clicking the digits repeatedly cycles the page among 100, 125, and 150 percent of actual size. Alternatively, you can use its ▾ menu to choose a degree of zoom from 50 to 400 percent—or choose Custom to type anything in between.

Online Photos

Internet Explorer is loaded with features for handling graphics online. Right-clicking an image on a Web page, for example, produces a shortcut menu that offers commands like "Save picture as," "E-mail picture," "Print picture," and "Set as background" (that is, wallpaper).

By the way, when you see a picture you'd like to keep, right-click it and choose "Save picture as" from the shortcut menu. After you name the picture and then click the Save button, the result is a new graphics file on your hard drive containing the picture you saved. (You can also choose Set as Background, which makes the picture part of your desktop image itself.)

Saving Pages

You can make Internet Explorer *store* a certain Web page on your hard drive so that you can peruse it later—on your laptop during your commute, for example.

The short way is to choose ⚙→Page→Save As.

For greatest simplicity, choose "Web Archive, single file (*.mht)" from the "Save as type" drop-down list. (The other options here save the Web page as multiple files on your hard drive—a handy feature if you intend to edit them, but less convenient if you just want to read them later.) Name the file and click the Save button. You've just preserved the Web page as a file on your hard drive, which you can open later by double-clicking it.

Sending Pages

Internet Explorer provides two ways of telling a friend about the page you're looking at. You might find that useful when you come across a particularly interesting news story, op-ed piece, or burrito recipe.

Hiding in the Page menu are commands that let you email the page to someone, or only the link to it.

Accelerators

Accelerators are time-saving commands that process selected Web text in useful ways. Highlight an address: An accelerator can show you where it is on a map. Highlight a sentence or a paragraph in another language: An accelerator can translate it into your language. Highlight a term you want to look up online: An accelerator feeds it directly to Google or Bing. And so on.

Better yet, accelerators are a kind of plug-in; you can add new ones as other people write them.

Note: The first time you open Internet Explorer, you're asked if you want a starter set of accelerators installed. If you decline them at that time, you can always install them (or a different set) later, as described below.

How to use an accelerator

When you see some text that you want to map, define, translate, or otherwise process with one of your accelerators, highlight it. When you point to the highlighted text, the Accelerator icon (⧉) appears at the corner of the selection. Click it to see the menu of accelerators (Figure 15-10).

As you can see in the figure, some accelerators reveal their goodies when you just point to their names. That's handy, since you don't lose your place on the Web. Other times, you have to click the accelerator's name, which takes you to a different Web page containing the desired info.

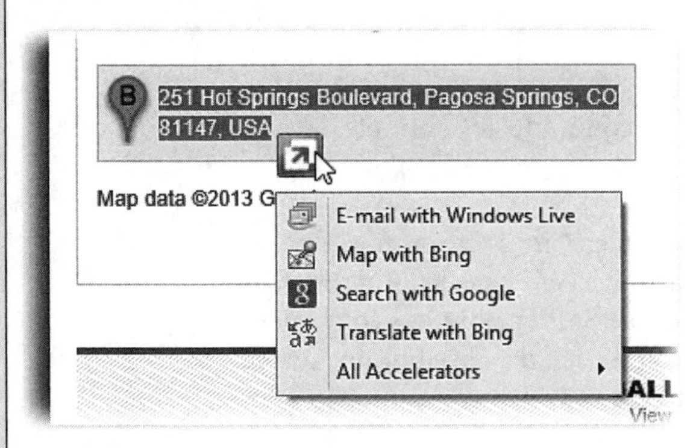

Figure 15-10:
Click the Accelerator icon to see this menu. You can point to one without clicking to view a preview of the results (like a map); sometimes, as with a dictionary definition, that's all you need to do. Other times, click the accelerator's name to trigger its magic.

Here's what the starter accelerators do:

- **Email with Windows Live.** Again, this option appears if you've installed the Essentials. The accelerator sends the highlighted text into a new, outgoing email message. Great for little "I told you so" notes! ("According to this article, I was right about the Steelers' starting lineup in 1973!")
- **Map with Bing.** If you've highlighted a street address, this opens up the Bing maps site and shows you the address on a map.
- **Search with Bing/Search with Google.** Copies the selected text into the Bing or Google search box—and actually performs the search for you.
- **Translate with Bing.** Sends the highlighted text to the Bing translation Web site. Use the pop-up menus there to specify what languages you want the text translated from and to. (Keep in mind that it's a computer, not a person; there may be some goofy words and phrases in the automated translation.)

Turning off accelerators

If you find your shortcut menu of accelerators cluttered by commands you never use, you can turn them off. Choose Tools→"Manage Add-ons," click Accelerators (in the "Add-on Types" column); click the one you're tired of, and then click either Disable or Remove. (You can also find the Manage Accelerators command in the shortcut menu that appears when you click the actual Accelerator icon ◪.)

Adding more accelerators

The starter accelerators are only the beginning; you can install a world of additional ones.

Choose Tools→"Manage Add-ons," click Accelerators (in the "Add-on Types" column), and then click Find More Accelerators (bottom of the screen).

On the site that appears, you find additional accelerators that send the selected text to Google Maps, Yahoo Maps, LinkedIn, Hotmail, Bing Shopping, Digg, eBay, Facebook search, a dictionary, and on and on. Click Add to Internet Explorer for each one you want to try out.

Tip: A lot of these features duplicate one another. There's Yahoo Maps, Bing Maps, Google Maps, and so on. That's why, when you add a new accelerator in an existing category, the confirmation box offers a "Make this my default provider for the Accelerator Category" option. Turn it on to make that your main Maps option, for example.

If you have several accelerators in a single category, you can always get to the nondefault ones by choosing All Accelerators from the Accelerator (⧅) shortcut menu.

Later, you can always change the default option for each category in the Manage Accelerators box described previously.

Happy accelerating!

Printing Pages

The decade of chopped-off printouts is over. In IE10, when you press Ctrl+P or choose Print (the little printer icon), *all* the page's text is auto-shrunk to fit within the page.

Tip: You can print only *part* of a page, too. Drag through the portion you want, press Ctrl+P, click Selection, and then click Print.

Better yet, if you choose Print Preview from the little printer icon (it's on the command bar), you get a handsome preview of the end result. The icons in the Print Preview window include buttons like these:

- **Portrait, Landscape (Alt+O, Alt+L)** controls the page orientation: upright or sideways.
- **Turn headers and footers on or off (Alt+E)** hides or shows the header (the text at the top of the printout, which usually identifies the name of the Web site you're printing and the number of pages) and the footer (the URL of the Web page and the date).
- **View Full Width (Alt+W)** blows up the preview to fill your screen, even if it means you have to scroll down to see the whole page. (This option has no effect on the printout itself.)
- **View Full Page (Alt+1)** restores the original view, where the entire print preview is shrunk down to fit your screen.
- **The 1 Page View pop-up menu** governs how many pages fit in the preview window at a time.

- **The Change Print Size pop-up menu** affects the size of the image on the printed pages. Shrink to Fit adjusts the printout so it won't be chopped off, but you can manually magnify or reduce the printed image by choosing the other percentage options in this menu.

Tip: Lots of Web sites have their own "Print this Page" buttons. When they're available, use them instead of Internet Explorer's own Print command. The Web site's Print feature not only makes sure the printout won't be chopped off, but it also eliminates ads, includes the entire article (even if it's split across multiple Web pages), and so on.

Turn Off Animations

If blinking ads make it tough to concentrate as you read a Web-based article, choose Tools→Internet Options→Advanced tab, and then scroll down to the Multimedia heading. Turn off "Play animations in web pages" to stifle most animated ads. Alas, it doesn't stop *all* animations; the jerks of the ad-design world have grown too clever for this option.

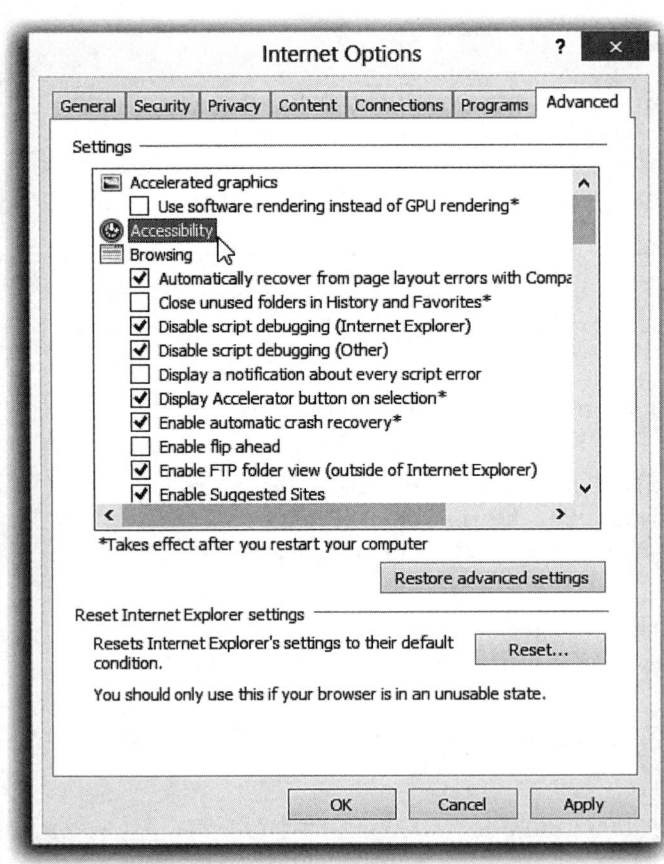

Figure 15-11: *Choosing Tools→Internet Options opens this dialog box, the identical twin of the Internet Options program in the Control Panel. Double-click one of the headings (like "Accessibility") to collapse all of its checkboxes. Your sanity is the winner here.*

Take a moment, too, to look over the other annoying Web page elements that you can turn off, including sounds.

Internet Options

Internet Explorer's Options dialog box offers roughly 68,000 tabs, buttons, and nested dialog boxes. Most of the useful options have been described in this chapter, with their appropriate topics (like Tabbed Browsing). Still, by spending a few minutes adjusting Internet Explorer's settings, you can make it more fun (or less annoying) to use.

To open this cornucopia of options, choose Tools→Internet Options (Figure 15-11).

The Keyboard Shortcut Master List

Before you set off into the Internet Explorer sunset, it's worth admitting that surfing the Web is one of the things most people do *most* with their PCs. And as long as you're going to spend so much time in this single program, it's worth mastering its keyboard shortcuts. Once you've learned a few, you save yourself time and fumbling.

Here it is, then: the complete master list of every Internet Explorer keyboard shortcut known to Microsoft. Clip and save.

Viewing	
Full Screen mode (on/off)	F11
Cycle through links on a page	Tab
Search the text on a page	Ctrl+F
Open the current page in a new window	Ctrl+N
Print this page	Ctrl+P
Select all items on the page	Ctrl+A
Zoom in/out by 10 percent	Ctrl+plus, Ctrl+minus
Zoom to 100%	Ctrl+0
Override pop-up blocker	Ctrl+Alt
Shut up this page's background sounds	Esc
Bars and menus	
Highlight the address/search bar	Alt+D
Open URL in the address bar in a new tab	Alt+Enter
View previously typed addresses	F4
Highlight the information bar	Alt+N
Open Home menu	Alt+M
Open Feeds menu	Alt+J
Open Print menu	Alt+R
Open Page menu	Alt+P
Open Tools menu	Alt+O
Open Help menu	Alt+L
Open Favorites menu	Alt+C, Ctrl+I
Open Favorites in pinned mode (won't auto-close)	Ctrl+Shift+I
Organize Favorites dialog box	Ctrl+B
Open Feeds list	Ctrl+J

Open Feeds in pinned mode	Ctrl+Shift+J
Open History	Ctrl+H
Open History in pinned mode	Ctrl+Shift+H
Add *http://www.* and *.com* to the text in address bar	Ctrl+Enter
Add *http://www.* and *.net* or *.org* to the text in address bar	Ctrl+Shift+Enter

Tip: To set up this last trick, open Tools→Internet Options→General tab→Langauges. In the Suffix box, enter whatever suffix you want IE to insert when you press Ctrl+Shift+Enter: *.org, .net, .edu, .jp,* or whatever you like.

Navigation

Scroll down a screenful	space bar (or Page Down)
Scroll up a screenful	Shift+space bar (or Page Up)
Go to home page	Alt+Home
Go back a page	Alt+←
Go forward a page	Alt+→
Refresh page	F5
Super refresh (ignore any cached elements)	Ctrl+F5
Stop downloading this page	Esc
Open link in a new window	Shift-click
Add current page to Favorites	Ctrl+D
"Right-click" any highlighted item	Shift+F10

Search bar

Highlight the search bar	Ctrl+E
Open list of search services	Ctrl+↓
Open search results in new tab	Alt+Enter

Tabbed browsing

Open link in new background tab	Ctrl-click*
Open link in new foreground tab	Ctrl+Shift-click (left or middle button)
Close tab (closes window if only one tab is open)	Ctrl+W, Ctrl+F4*
Quick Tab view	Ctrl+Q
Open new empty tab	Ctrl+T
View list of open tabs	Ctrl+Shift+Q
Switch to next tab	Ctrl+Tab
Switch to previous tab	Ctrl+Shift+Tab
Switch to tab #1, #2, etc.	Ctrl+1, Ctrl+2, etc.
Switch to last tab	Ctrl+9

* or scroll wheel–click, or middle button–click

CHAPTER
16

Windows Live Mail

Email is a fast, cheap, convenient communication medium; these days, it's almost embarrassing to admit you don't have an email address. To spare you that humiliation, Microsoft offers you Windows Live Mail. It's a renamed, revamped version of the program that, through the years, has been called Windows Mail, Windows Live Desktop Mail, and Outlook Express. It lets you receive and send email, subscribe to RSS feeds (Web-site update blurbs), and read *newsgroups* (Internet bulletin boards).

Now, Mail doesn't exactly come *with* Windows 8; the lawyers saw to that. But it is part of the free, easy-to-download Windows Essentials suite (page 375), so you have very little excuse for not having a decent email program. Download it now.

(Of course, Windows 8 does come with a Mail app—it's part of the starter set of TileWorld apps, and it's described in Chapter 4. But that's a quite basic mail app with very few options and features. Use the program described in *this* chapter if you want something a little fuller featured.)

Setting Up Windows Live Mail

To start up Mail for the first time, you can use either of the two standard Windows methods: Either click its icon on the Start screen, or go to the Start screen and type *mail;* click Windows Live Mail in the results list.

You might see a Microsoft Services Agreement screen filled with legalese (the most significant part of which is that Microsoft can send you updated versions of the software). Click Accept.

Now you're offered the "Add your email accounts" screen.

Now, if you had a Microsoft email account or program already, Windows Live Mail imports *everything* automatically: mail, address book, calendar, account settings. You're ready to start doing email.

If not, it's fairly easy to enter your email settings information for the first time. All you have to do is type your email name and password into the box (Figure 16-1). If Mail recognizes the suffix (for example, *@gmail.com)*, then it does the heavy lifting for you.

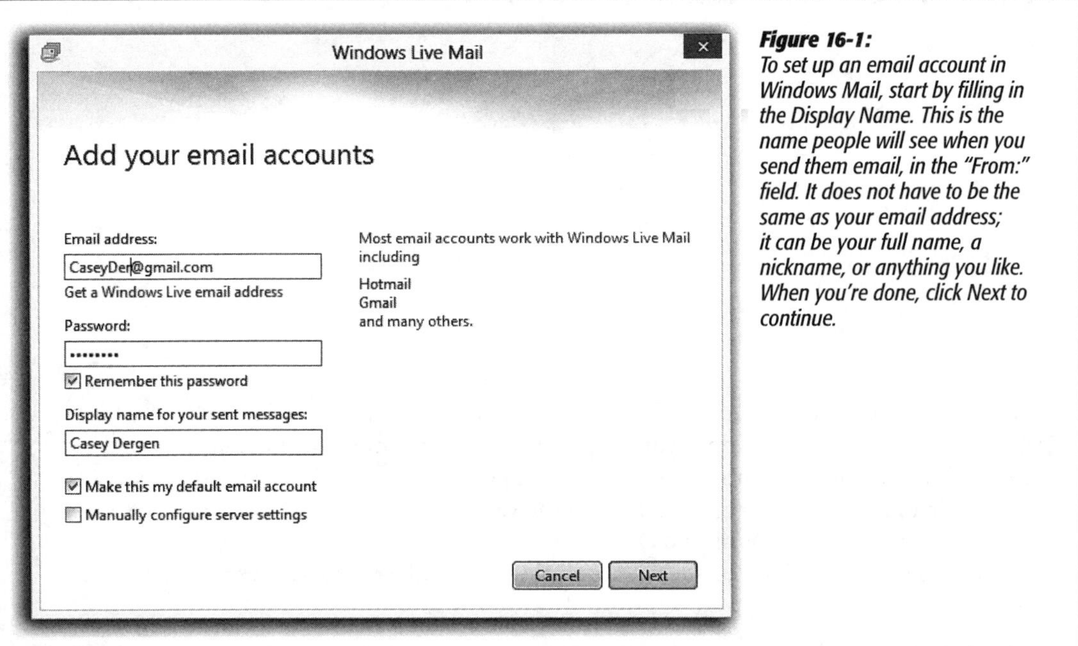

Figure 16-1: *To set up an email account in Windows Mail, start by filling in the Display Name. This is the name people will see when you send them email, in the "From:" field. It does not have to be the same as your email address; it can be your full name, a nickname, or anything you like. When you're done, click Next to continue.*

Mail auto-recognizes the necessary server settings for all the common email services—Outlook.com, Hotmail, Gmail, Yahoo, Comcast, and so on, so your name and password are all you need to set those up.

If you use a service provider that Mail *doesn't* recognize when you type in your name and password—you weirdo!—then you have to set up your mail account the long way. Mail prompts you along, and you confront a dialog box where you're supposed to type in various settings to specify your email account. Some of the information may require a call to your Internet service provider (ISP).

Note: If you used the Easy Transfer Wizard (page 847) to bring over your files and settings from an older PC, then Windows Mail is probably already set up quite nicely. If that's the case, skip to the next section.

Click Next to step through the wizard's interview process, during which you'll provide the following information:

- **Incoming mail server details.** Enter the information your ISP provided about its mail servers: the type of server (POP3, IMAP, or HTTP), the name of the incoming mail server, and the name of the outgoing mail server. Most of the time, the incoming server's name is connected to the name of your ISP. It might be *pop.gmail.com*, for example, or *mail.comcast.net.*

  The outgoing mail server (the *SMTP server*) usually looks something like *smtp.gmail.com* or *smtp.comcast.net.*

Note: For a crash course in the difference between IMAP and POP accounts, see page 118.

- **Security settings.** All that stuff about "This server requires a secure connection" and "Requires authentication"? You'll never guess it. Contact your ISP (or its Web pages, which almost always include these details).

When you click Next, if all is well, you get a congratulations message (click Finish), and then you return to the main Mail screen, where your folder list and then the messages come flooding in (Figure 16-2).

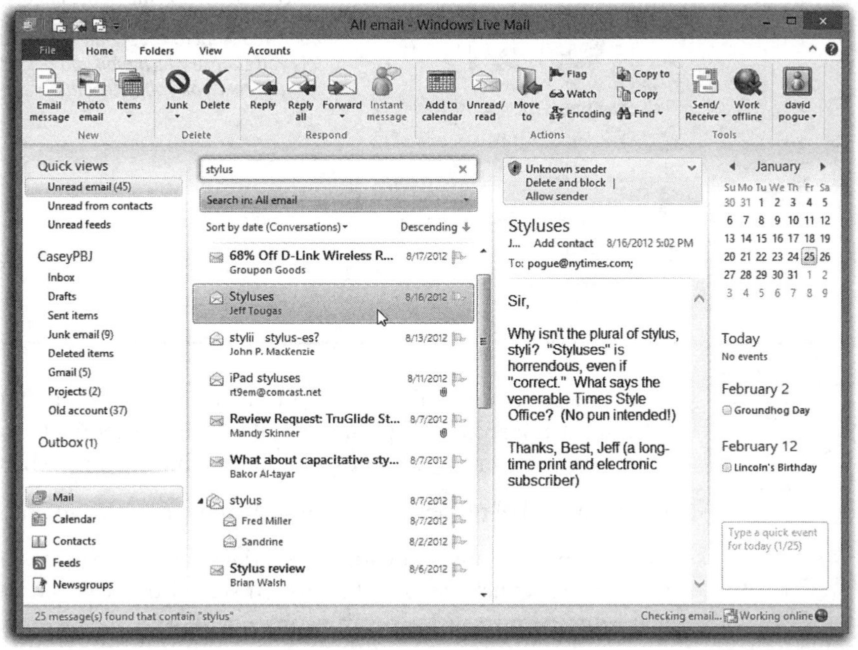

Figure 16-2: *Windows Live Mail has four major columns: mail folders, messages in the current folder, contents of the current message, and the calendar pane. On top: the Ribbon, filled with every conceivable control.*

To sort the message list, click a column heading: From, Subject, and so on. You can rearrange or adjust the widths of the columns, too.

After a moment, you see that Mail has created a listing for your email account in the list at the left side, complete with subfolders like Inbox, Drafts, and Sent Items.

To add another email account, click the Accounts tab of the Ribbon and then click Email. The wizard you worked through previously reappears. You've just met a great feature of Mail: It can manage a bunch of different email accounts all in one place.

Tip: If you want to import a stash of mail from an older email program, like Outlook Express, then choose File→Import Messages.

Checking Email

Whenever you want to receive and send new mail, you use the Send/Receive button shown in Figure 16-3. To tell you the truth, just learning to press Ctrl+5 or F5 is a lot simpler.

Note: In all the instructions having to do with email, this chapter assumes that you've clicked Mail in the list of modules at the lower-left corner of the Mail window. Not Calendar, not Contacts: Mail. (Pressing Shift+Ctrl+J also selects the Mail module.)

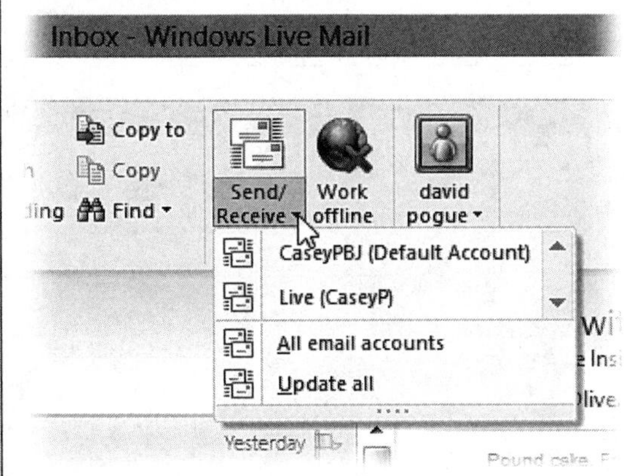

Figure 16-3: *Most of the time, you'll want to simply click the Send/ Receive icon. It's on the Home tab of the Ribbon.*

But if you want to check only one account, the ▾ beside it lets you choose which mail you'd like to get, if you don't want to check all your accounts.

You can also set up Mail to check your email accounts automatically according to a schedule. Choose File→Options→Mail. On the General tab, you see the "Check for new messages every __ minutes" checkbox, which you can change to your liking.

In any case, Mail retrieves new messages and sends any outgoing messages.

In the second column on your screen, the names of new messages show up in bold type; in the "Quick views" list at the left side of the window, parentheses show how many unread messages are waiting in each folder.

Tip: Mail groups your inbox into conversations or threads, meaning that related back-and-forths on a certain subject, with a certain person, appear as a single item marked by a flippy triangle (▸). Click that triangle to expand the listing, showing all the individual messages within that flurry of communication.

To turn off this feature, use the Off command that sprouts from the Conversations button (on the View tab of the Ribbon).

Mail Folders in Windows Live Mail

At the left side of the screen, Mail organizes your email into *folders*. To see what's in a folder, click it once:

- **Inbox** holds mail you've received.
- **Outbox** holds mail you've written but haven't sent yet.
- **Sent Items** holds copies of messages you've sent.
- **Deleted Items** holds mail you've deleted. (There's a separate Deleted folder for each account.) It works a lot like the Recycle Bin, in that messages placed there don't actually disappear. Instead, they remain in the Deleted Items folder, awaiting rescue if you opt to retrieve them. To empty this folder, right-click it and then choose "Empty 'Deleted Items' Folder" from the shortcut menu.

POWER USERS' CLINIC

The Mighty Morphing Interface

You don't have to be content with the factory-installed design of the Mail screen; you can control which panes are visible, how big they are, and which columns show up in List views.

To change the size of a pane, drag its border to make it larger or smaller, as shown here.

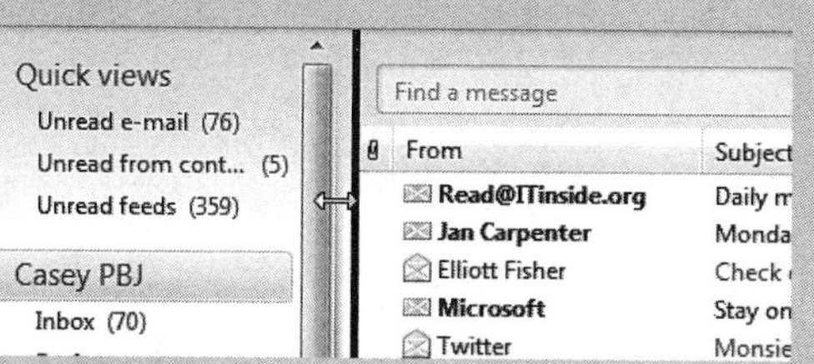

There's also a vast array of layout options on the View tab of the Ribbon. For example, using the "Reading pane" pop-up menu, you can control where the message body pane appears: under the message list, or to its right—a great arrangement if your screen has the width.

Using the "Message list" pop-up menu on the Ribbon, you can show one-line or two-line previews.

Another batch of buttons hides or shows various interface elements, like the "Calendar pane" button, the "Status bar" button, the "Compact view" button (collapses the folder list down to simple, skinny icons, leaving more room for messages and lists), and the "Compact shortcuts" button (collapses the list of modules at lower left—Mail, Calendar, Contacts, and so on—down to simple icons to save space).

The "Storage folders" button controls the appearance of folders that hold messages on your PC, as opposed to the Web-based folders from a Gmail, Yahoo, or Hotmail account.

Tip: To make the folder empty itself every time you exit Mail, choose File→Options→Mail, click the Advanced tab, and then click the Maintenance button. In the Maintenance dialog box, turn on "Empty messages from the 'Deleted Items' folder on exit."

- **Drafts** holds messages you've started but haven't finished—and don't want to send just yet.
- **Junk E-Mail** holds messages deemed as junk (spam) by Mail's Junk E-Mail Protection. (More about that later.)

You can also add to this list, creating folders for your own organizational pleasure—Family Mail, Work Mail, or whatever. See page 522.

Composing and Sending Messages

To send a message, click "Email message" on the Home tab of the Ribbon (or press Ctrl+N). The New Message form opens (Figure 16-4).

Tip: You can also start writing a message by clicking Contacts (lower left). In the Contacts window, click the person's name, and then click E-Mail on the Ribbon. A blank, outgoing piece of mail appears, already addressed to the person whose name you clicked.

Come to think of it, it's faster to hit Ctrl+N.

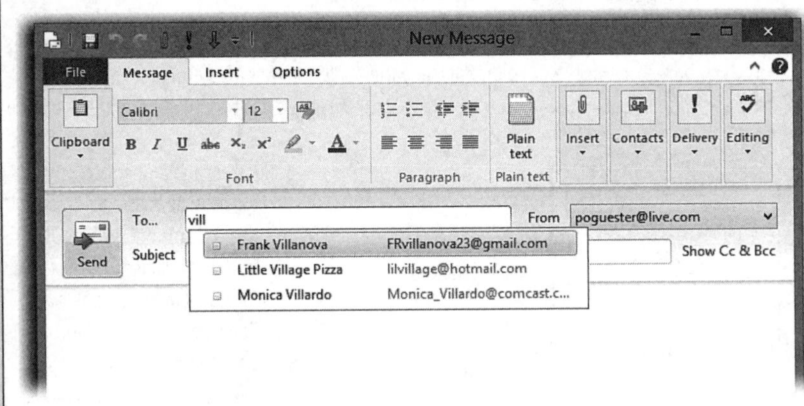

***Figure 16-4:** In the New Message window, type the name of your message's recipients, separated by commas or semicolons, in the "To:" field. If Mail doesn't automatically complete the name for you (by consulting your address book and recent recipients list)–or even present multiple-choice matches–click Check Names on the Ribbon.*

Composing the message requires several steps:

1. **Type the email address of the recipient into the "To:" field.**

   If you want to send a message to more than one person, then separate their email addresses using commas or semicolons, like this: *bob@earthlink.net; billg@microsoft.com; tim@apple.com.*

As you begin typing the person's plain-English name, the program attempts to guess who you mean (if it's somebody in your Contacts list)—and fills in the email address automatically to save you typing, as shown in Figure 16-4.

If it guesses the correct name, great; press Tab to move on to the next text box. If it guesses wrong, just keep typing. The program quickly retracts its suggestion and watches what you type next.

Tip: You can also click the actual word "To:" to open your Contacts list; double-click a name to address your message.

As usual in Windows dialog boxes, you can jump from blank to blank in this window (from the "To:" field to the "Subject:" field, for example) by pressing the Tab key.

Note: If you have more than one email account, use the "From:" pop-up menu to specify which you want to use for sending this message.

---

2. **To send a copy of the message to other recipients, enter the additional email address(es) in the "Cc:" field.**

   Cc stands for *carbon copy.* There's very little difference between putting all your addressees on the "To:" line (separated by commas or semicolons) and putting them on the "Cc:" line. The only difference is that using the "Cc:" line implies, "I sent you a copy because I thought you'd want to know about this correspondence, but I'm not expecting you to reply."

   To make the "Cc:" (and "Bcc:"; see box below) lines appear, click "Show Cc & Bcc," a link that appears to the right of the "Subject:" line.

   Press Tab when you're finished.

UP TO SPEED

Blind Carbon Copies

A *Bcc:* or *blind carbon copy* is a secret copy. This feature lets you send a copy of a message to somebody secretly, without any of the other recipients knowing. The names in the "To:" and "Cc:" fields appear at the top of the message for all recipients to see, but nobody can see the names you typed into the "Bcc:" box. To view this box, click "Show Cc & Bcc" in the New Message window.

You can use the "Bcc:" field to quietly signal a third party that a message has been sent. For example, if you send your coworker a message that says, "Chris, it bothers me that you've been cheating the customers," you could Bcc your boss or supervisor to clue her in without getting into trouble with Chris.

The Bcc box is useful in other ways, too. Many people send email messages (containing jokes, for example) to a long list of recipients. You, the recipient, must scroll through a very long list of names the sender placed in the "To:" or "Cc:" field.

But if the sender uses the "Bcc:" field to hold all the recipients' email addresses, then you, the recipient, won't see any names but your own at the top of the email. (Unfortunately, spammers–the miserable cretins who send you junk mail–have also learned this trick.)

3. **Type the topic of the message in the "Subject:" field.**

   It's courteous to put some thought into the subject line. (For example, use "Change in plans for next week" instead of "Hi.")

   Press the Tab key to move your cursor into the message area.

4. **Format the message, if you like.**

   When it comes to formatting a message's body text, you have two choices: *plain text* or *HTML* (Hypertext Markup Language).

   Plain text means you can't format your text with bold type, color, specified font sizes, and so on. HTML, on the other hand, is the language used to create Web pages, and it lets you use formatting commands (such as font sizes, colors, and bold or italic text). It also lets you paste in pictures.

   But there's a catch: HTML mail is much larger, and therefore slower to download, than plain-text messages. Certain Internetters remain fairly hostile toward heavily formatted email. Plain text tends to feel more professional, never irritates anybody—and you're guaranteed that the recipient will see exactly what was sent.

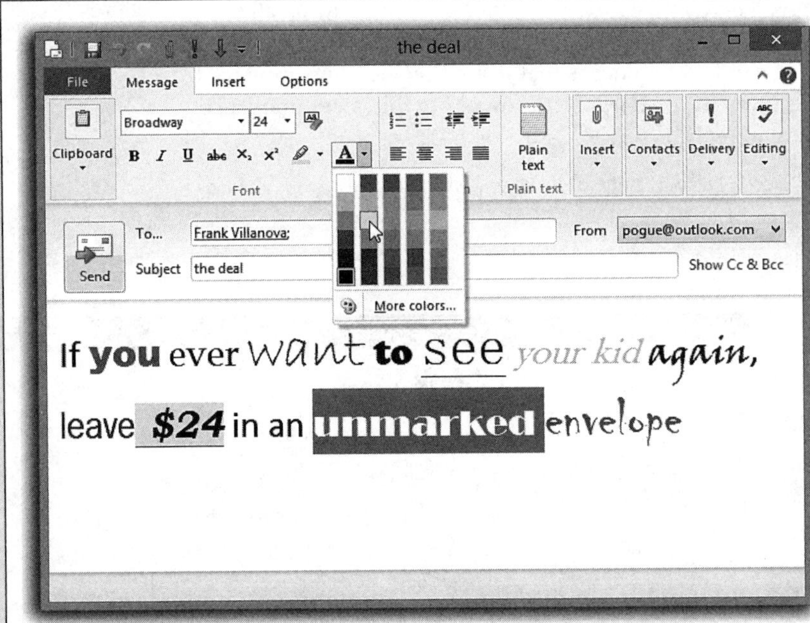

***Figure 16-5:** When you're composing an email using the HTML format, the New Message window gives you options for choosing fonts; formatting options like bold, italic, and underline; and colors (from a handy color palette).*

To specify which format Windows Live Mail *proposes* for all new messages (plain text or HTML), choose File→Options→Mail→Send tab. Next, in the section labeled Mail Sending Format, choose either the HTML or Plain Text button, and then click OK.

No matter which setting you specify there, however, you can always switch a *particular* message you're writing to the opposite format. Just click the button on the Ribbon's Message bar; it says either Rich Text (HTML) or Plain Text, whichever your message currently is *not*.

Whenever you're creating a formatted HTML message, you can use the Message ribbon's various buttons for formatting, font, size, color, paragraph indentation, line spacing, and other word processor–like formatting controls (Figure 16-5).

Just remember: Less is more. If you go hog wild formatting your email, the message may be difficult to read, especially if you also apply stationery (a background).

5. **Enter the message in the message box (the bottom half of the message window).**

   You can use all the standard editing techniques, including Cut, Copy, and Paste, to rearrange the text as you write it.

Tip: You should also spell check your outgoing mail. Just click Spelling on the Ribbon's Message tab, or press F7.

6. **Add a signature, if you wish.**

   Signatures are bits of text that get stamped at the bottom of outgoing email messages. They typically contain a name, a mailing address, or a *Star Trek* quote.

   To create a signature, choose File→Options→Mail→Signatures tab; click the New button. The easiest way to compose your signature is to type it into the Edit Signatures text box at the bottom of the window. (If you poke around long enough in this box, you'll realize that you can actually create multiple signatures—and even assign each one to a different outgoing email account.)

   Once you've created a signature (or several), you can tack it onto your outgoing mail for all messages (by turning on "Add signatures to all outgoing messages" at the top of this box) or on a message-by-message basis (press Shift+Ctrl+S, or choose Signature from the Ribbon's Insert tab).

7. **Click the Send button.**

   Alternatively, press Alt+S or Ctrl+Enter. Your PC connects to the Internet and sends the message.

If you're working offline, you might prefer Mail to place each message you write in the Outbox folder, saving them up until you click the Sync button on the toolbar; see "Send Tab" on page 532.

You can also schedule a piece of mail so that it auto-sends at a specified time. That's a handy way to post an article, for example, only after the news blackout period has expired. To do that, click the Ribbon's Options tab, click "Send later," and dial up the correct time and date.

Inserting Links, Lines, or Smileys

You can dress up any HTML-formatted message with links to the Web, with emoticons (smiley-face symbols), or with horizontal lines to separate chunks of your message. Use the corresponding buttons on the Message tab of the Ribbon.

Attaching Files or Photos

Sending little text messages is fine, but it's not much help when you want to send somebody a photograph, a sound recording, a Word or Excel document, and so on. Fortunately, attaching such files to email messages is one of the world's most popular email features. To attach a file to a message, use either of two methods:

- **The long way.** Click the "Attach file" or "Photo album" button on the Message tab of the Ribbon. When the Open dialog box appears, locate the file and select it. (In the resulting navigation window, you can Ctrl-click multiple files to attach them all at once.)

  Now the name of the attached file appears in the message, in the Attach text box. When you send the message, the file tags along.

- **The short way.** If you can see the icon of the file you want to attach—in its folder window behind the Mail window, on the desktop, or wherever—then attach it by *dragging* its icon directly into the message window. That's a handy technique when you're attaching many different files.

Tip: To remove a file from an outgoing message before sending it, just click it and then press the Delete key.

UP TO SPEED

Selecting Messages

In order to process a group of messages simultaneously–to delete, move, or forward them, for example–you must first master the art of multiple message selection.

To select two or more messages that appear consecutively in your message list, click the first message, and then Shift-click the last. Known as a *contiguous selection*, this trick selects the two messages you clicked and every message between them.

To select two or more messages that *aren't* adjacent in the list (that is, skipping a few messages between selected ones), Ctrl-click the messages you want. Only the messages you click get selected–no filling in of messages in between this time.

After using either technique, you can also *deselect* messages you've managed to highlight–just Ctrl-click them again.

Photos are even easier to send. You can paste one, or drag-and-drop it from the desktop, right into an outgoing message (provided it's an HTML-formatted one). You can even edit the pictures before you send them, using the surprisingly complete Picture Tools/Format tab on the Ribbon.

Tip: You can also send an entire *album* of high-resolution photos. Use the Ribbon's Insert tab; choose "Photo album"; select the photos, or a folder of them. Behind the scenes, the photos actually reside on your SkyDrive; your recipient just has to click a link to download them all.

Reading Email

Just seeing a list of the *names* of new messages in Mail is like getting wrapped presents—the best part's yet to come. There are two ways to read a message: using the Reading pane, and opening the message into its own window.

When you click a message's name in the List pane, the body of the message appears in the Reading pane below or to the right. Don't forget that you can adjust the relative sizes of the List and Preview panes by dragging the border between them up or down.

To open a message into a window of its own, double-click its name in the List pane. An open message has its own Ribbon, along with Previous and Next buttons.

Once you've read a message, you can view the next one in the list either by pressing Ctrl+→ (next message), by pressing Ctrl+U (next *unread* message), or by clicking its name in the List pane. (If you haven't opened a message into its own window, you can also press the ↑ or ↓ keys to move from one message to the next.)

Tip: To mark a message you've read as an *unread* message, so that its name remains bolded, right-click its name in the List pane and then choose "Mark as unread" from the shortcut menu.

Here's another timesaver: To hide all the messages you've already read, click the Ribbon's View tab. From the "Filter messages" pop-up menu, choose "Hide read messages." Now only unread messages are visible in the selected folder. To bring the hidden messages back, choose "Show all messages" from the same icon.

When Pictures are Part of the Message

Mail comes set up to block images, because these images sometimes serve as "bugs" that silently report back to the sender when you open the message. At that point, the spammers know that they've found a working email address—and a sucker who opens email from strangers. Now you're on their hit list, and the spam flood *really* begins.

You'll know if pictures were meant to appear in the body of a message; see the strip that appears at the top in Figure 16-6.

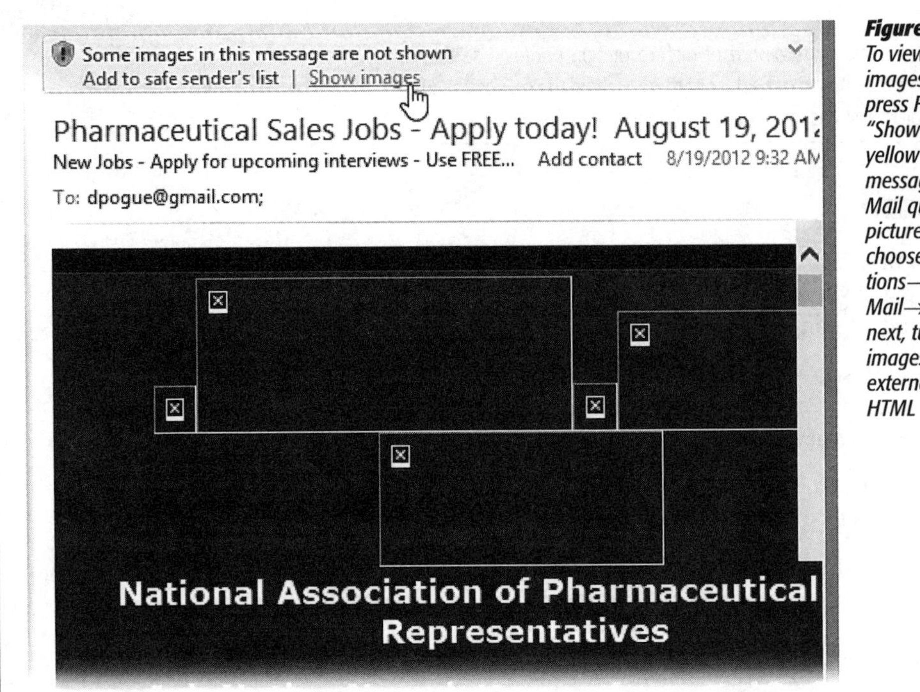

Figure 16-6: *To view blocked images in a message, press F9, or click "Show images" in the yellow strip above the message. Or, to make Mail quit blocking pictures altogether, choose File→Options→Mail→Security; next, turn off "Block images and other external content in HTML messages."*

Quick Views, Custom Views (Filters)

You already know that there are about 65,000 different ways to customize the way Mail looks. Don't look now—it's about to get worse (or better, depending on your taste).

With a couple of clicks, you can command Mail to show you only unread mail. Or only high-priority mail. Or only mail from your boss. All other messages are temporarily hidden.

This feature is called Views, and it comes in a couple of different flavors.

Quick Views

Mail comes with a few useful views already set up. They're called Quick Views, and you can see them at the top of the folder list (Figure 16-7): "Unread mail," "Unread mail from contacts," and so on. Click one to filter your inbox so that it shows only messages that meet those criteria.

Tip: If you never use this feature, you can hide the Quick Views so their names don't take up room in your folder list. On the Ribbon's View tab, turn off Quick Views.

Not all the available Quick Views appear in the folder list, though. To see the other options awaiting you, click "Quick views" (on the Ribbon's View tab), and proceed as described in Figure 16-7.

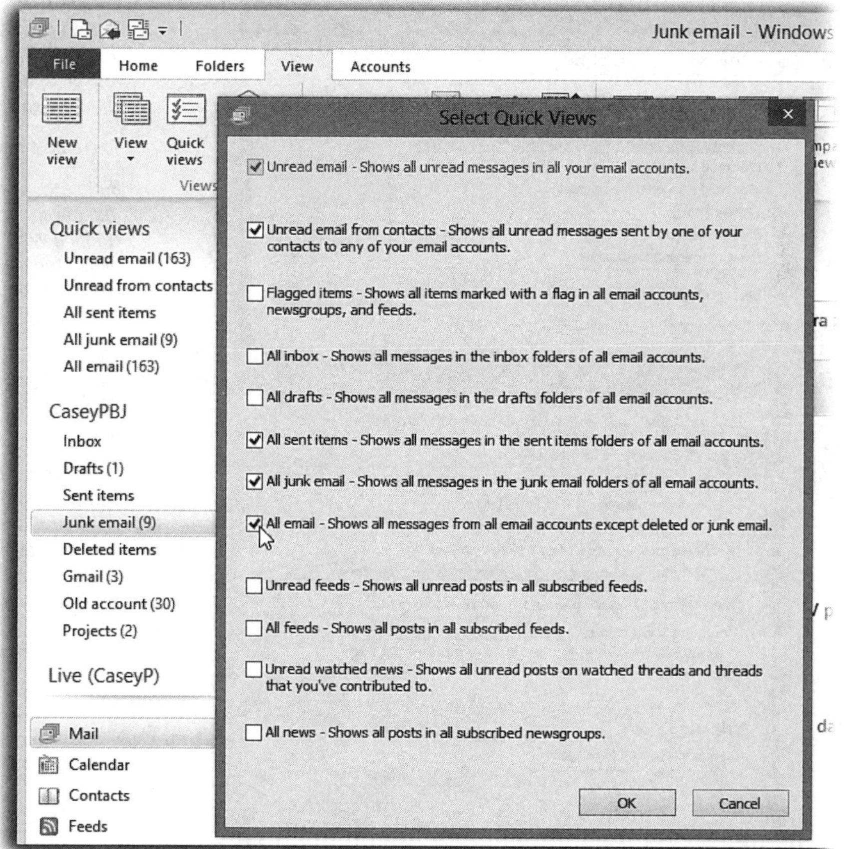

Figure 16-7: *Mail comes with a long list of Quick Views—memorized "hide messages that don't meet these criteria" views. For each checkbox that you turn on here, another entry appears in the "Quick views" list at the top of the folder list, visible at top left here.*

Custom Views

Turns out you can set up even more sophisticated views of your mail lists—self-updating folders that show you all your mail from your boss, for example, or every message with "mortgage" in its subject line. They're folders whose contents are based around criteria you specify.

To create a view, click "New view" on the Ribbon's View tab. A list of all your custom views appears. Proceed as shown in Figure 16-8.

There's no quick way to apply one of your custom views once you've created it; it doesn't appear in the folder list like Quick Views do, for example. Whenever you want to summon a view you've created, click "New view" (on the View tab of the Ribbon); when the box shown in Figure 16-8 at top appears, click the view you want. Click Apply View, and then (when you're asked) specify whether you want your filter to affect only the currently selected folder or all folders.

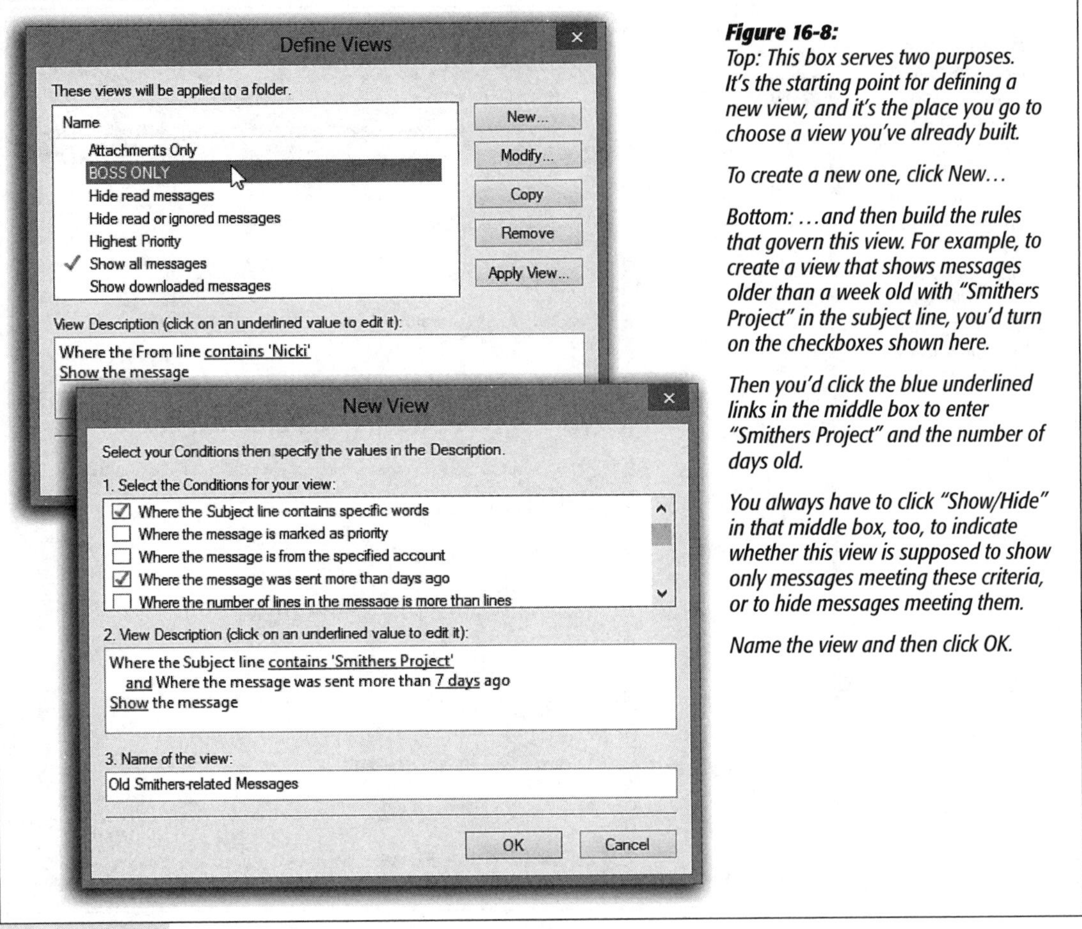

Figure 16-8:
Top: This box serves two purposes. It's the starting point for defining a new view, and it's the place you go to choose a view you've already built.

To create a new one, click New…

Bottom: …and then build the rules that govern this view. For example, to create a view that shows messages older than a week old with "Smithers Project" in the subject line, you'd turn on the checkboxes shown here.

Then you'd click the blue underlined links in the middle box to enter "Smithers Project" and the number of days old.

You always have to click "Show/Hide" in that middle box, too, to indicate whether this view is supposed to show only messages meeting these criteria, or to hide messages meeting them.

Name the view and then click OK.

How to Process a Message

Once you've read a message and savored the feeling of awe brought on by the miracle of instantaneous electronic communication, you can handle the message in any of several ways.

Deleting Messages

Sometimes it's junk mail, sometimes you're just done with it; either way, it's a snap to delete a message. Click the Delete button on the Ribbon's Home tab, press the Delete key, or hit Ctrl+D. (You can also delete a batch of selected messages simultaneously.)

Tip: Above any message from somebody who's not in your Contacts, in the yellow bar, there's a "Delete and block" link. What a great way to slam the door in some idiot's face! You'll never hear from this person again.

The messages don't actually disappear. Instead, they move to the Deleted Items folder for that email account. If you like, click this folder to view a list of the messages you've deleted. You can even rescue some simply by dragging them into another folder (even right back into the inbox).

Mail doesn't truly vaporize messages in the Deleted Items folder until you "empty the trash." You can empty it in any of several ways:

- **Right-click the Deleted Items folder.** Choose "Empty 'Deleted Items' folder" from the shortcut menu.
- **Click the X button** to the right of the Deleted Items folder's name.
- **Click a message, or a folder, within the Deleted Items folder list, and then click the Delete button on the Ribbon's Home tab (or press the Delete key).** You're asked to confirm its permanent deletion.
- **Set up Mail to delete messages automatically** when you quit the program. To do so, choose File→Options→Mail→Advanced. Click the Maintenance button, and then turn on "Empty messages from the 'Deleted Items' folder on exit." Click OK.

Replying to Messages

To reply to a message, click the Reply button on the Ribbon's Home tab, or press Ctrl+R. Mail creates a new, outgoing email message, preaddressed to the sender's return address. (If the message was sent to you *and* a few other people, and you'd like to reply to all of them at once, click "Reply all" instead.)

UP TO SPEED

About Mailing Lists

During your email experiments, you're likely to come across something called a mailing list—a discussion group conducted via email. By searching Yahoo.com or other Web directories, you can find mailing lists covering just about every conceivable topic.

You can send a message to all members of such a group by sending a message to a single address—the list's address. The list is actually maintained on a special mail server. Everything sent to the list gets sent to the server, which forwards the message to all the individual list members.

That's why you have to be careful if you're actually trying to reply to *one person* in the discussion group; if you reply to the list and not to a specific person, you'll send your reply to every address on the list—sometimes with disastrous consequences.

To save additional time, Mail pastes the entire original message at the bottom of your reply (either indented, if it's HTML mail, or marked with the > brackets that serve as Internet quoting marks); that's to help your correspondent figure out what you're talking about.

Note: To turn off this feature, choose File→Options→Mail, click the Send tab, and then turn off "Include message in reply."

Mail even tacks "*Re:*" (meaning "regarding") onto the front of the subject line.

Your insertion point appears at the top of the message box. Now, just begin typing your reply. You can also add recipients, remove recipients, edit the subject line or the message, and so on.

Tip: Use the Enter key to create blank lines within the bracketed original message in order to place your own text within it. Using this method, you can splice your own comments into the paragraphs of the original message, replying point by point. The brackets preceding each line of the original message help your correspondent keep straight what's yours and what's hers. Also, if you're using HTML formatting for the message, you can format what you've written in bold, italics, underline, or even in another color for easier reading.

Forwarding Messages

Instead of replying to the person who sent you a message, you may sometimes want to *forward* the message—pass it on—to a third person.

To do so, click Forward on the Ribbon's Home tab, or press Ctrl+F. A new message opens, looking a lot like the one that appears when you reply. Once again, before forwarding the message, you have the option of editing the subject or the message. (For example, you may wish to precede the original message with a comment of your own, along the lines of, "Frank: I thought you'd be interested in this joke about Congress.")

All that remains is for you to specify who receives the forwarded message. Just address it as you would any outgoing piece of mail.

Printing Messages

Sometimes there's no substitute for a printout of an email message—an area where Mail shines. Choose File→Print, or press Ctrl+P. The standard Windows Print dialog box pops up so you can specify how many copies you want, what range of pages, and so on. Make your selections, and then click Print.

Filing Messages

Mail lets you create new folders in the Folders list; by dragging messages from your inbox onto one of these folder icons, you can file away your messages into appropriate cubbies. You might create one folder for important messages, another for order confirmations from shopping on the Web, still another for friends and family, and so on. In fact, you can even create folders *inside* these folders, a feature beloved by the hopelessly organized.

To create a new folder, see Figure 16-9.

Tip: To rename an existing folder, right-click it and choose Rename from the shortcut menu.

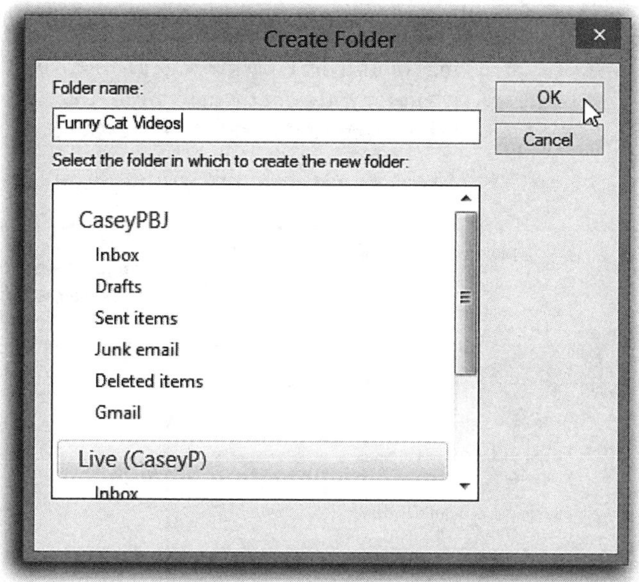

Figure 16-9: *To create a new folder, click "New folder" on the Ribbon's Folders tab. Or press Shift+Ctrl+D.*

No matter which way you choose, this window appears. Name the folder and then, by clicking, indicate which folder you want this one to appear in.

To move a message (or several at once) into a folder, proceed like this:

- **Drag it out of the List pane and onto the folder icon.** You can use any part of a message's "row" in the list as a handle. You can also drag messages en masse into a folder after selecting them.
- **Select a message (or several).** On the Ribbon's Home tab (or Folder tab), click "Move to folder." In a dialog box, the folder list appears; select the one you want, and then press Enter or click OK.
- **Right-click a message (or one of several you've highlighted).** From the shortcut menu, choose "Move to folder." In a dialog box, the folder list appears; select the one you want, and then press Enter or click OK.

Tip: When you click a ▸ triangle in the Folder list, you see all folders contained within that folder, exactly like in File Explorer. You can drag folders inside other folders, nesting them to create a nice hierarchical folder structure. (To drag a nested folder back into the list of "main" folders, just drag it to the Storage Folders icon.)

You can also drag messages between folders; just drag one from the message list onto the desired folder at the left side of the screen.

This can be a useful trick when you apply it to a message in your outbox. If you decide to postpone sending it, drag it into any other folder. Mail won't send it until you drag it *back* into the outbox.

Flagging Messages

Sometimes, you'll receive an email message that prompts you to some sort of action, but you may not have the time or the fortitude to face the task at the moment. ("Hi there…it's me, your accountant. Would you mind rounding up your expenses for 1996 through 2004 and sending me a list by email?")

That's why Mail lets you *flag* a message, positioning a small, red flag in the corresponding column next to a message's name. These little flags are visual indicators that mean whatever you want them to mean. You can bring all flagged messages to the top of the list by choosing "Sort by"→Flag (the pop-up menu above the message list).

To flag a message in this way, see Figure 16-10.

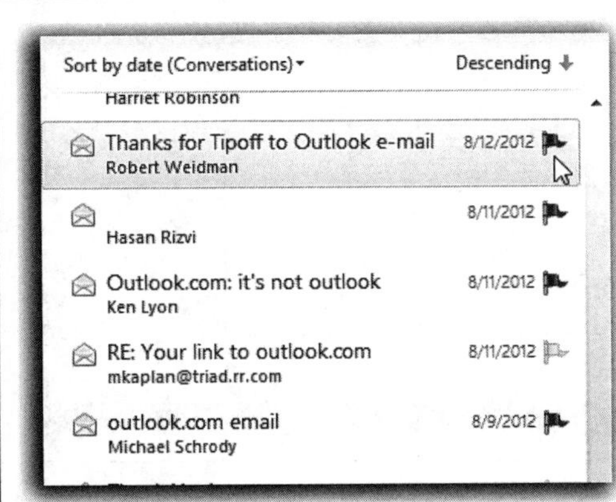

Figure 16-10: *To flag a message, click in the Flag column. Or, if you want to flag a whole batch of selected messages, select them and then click Flag on the Ribbon's Home tab.*

Opening Attachments

Just as you can attach files to a message, people can send files to you. You know when a message has an attachment because a paper-clip icon appears next to its name in the inbox.

To free an attached file from its message, releasing it to the wilds of your hard drive, use one of the following methods:

- **Right-click the attachment's name (in the message),** select "Save as" from the shortcut menu, and then specify a folder for the saved file (Figure 16-11).
- Double-click the attachment's name. After you click Open to confirm the risk (it's *always* risky to open an email attachment), it opens right up in Word, Excel, or whatever.

- Drag the attachment's icon out of the message window and onto any visible portion of your desktop.

Figure 16-11:
One way to rescue an attachment from an email message is to right-click its name and choose "Save as." You can also drag an attachment's icon onto your desktop. Either way, you take the file out of the Mail world and into your standard Windows world, where you can file it, trash it, open it, or manipulate it as you would any file.

Message Rules

Once you know how to create folders, the next step in managing your email is to set up *message rules*. These are filters that can file, answer, or delete an incoming message *automatically* based on its subject, address, or size.

Message rules require you to think like the distant relative of a programmer, but the mental effort can reward you many times over. In fact, message rules can turn Mail into a surprisingly smart and efficient secretary.

Tip: Sadly, Mail's rules work only on POP email accounts, not the increasingly common IMAP accounts.

Setting up message rules

Now that you're thoroughly intrigued about the magic of message rules, here's how to set one up:

1. **On the Ribbon's Folders tab, click "Message rules."**

   If you've never created a message rule, you see what's shown in Figure 16-12. If you *have* created message rules before, you see the Message Rules window first (Figure 16-13), in which case you should click New to open the New Mail Rule window shown in Figure 16-12.

2. **Use the top options to specify how Mail should select messages to process.**

   For example, if you'd like Mail to watch out for messages from a particular person, you would choose, "Where the From line contains people."

To flag messages containing "*loan*," "*$$$$*," "*XXX*," "*!!!!*," and so on (favorites of spammers), choose, "Where the Subject line contains specific words."

If you turn on more than one checkbox, you can set up another condition for your message rule. For example, you can set up the first criterion to find messages *from* your uncle, and a second that watches for subject lines that contain "joke." If you click the Options button, you get to specify whether the message has to contain *all* the words you've specified, or *any* of them.

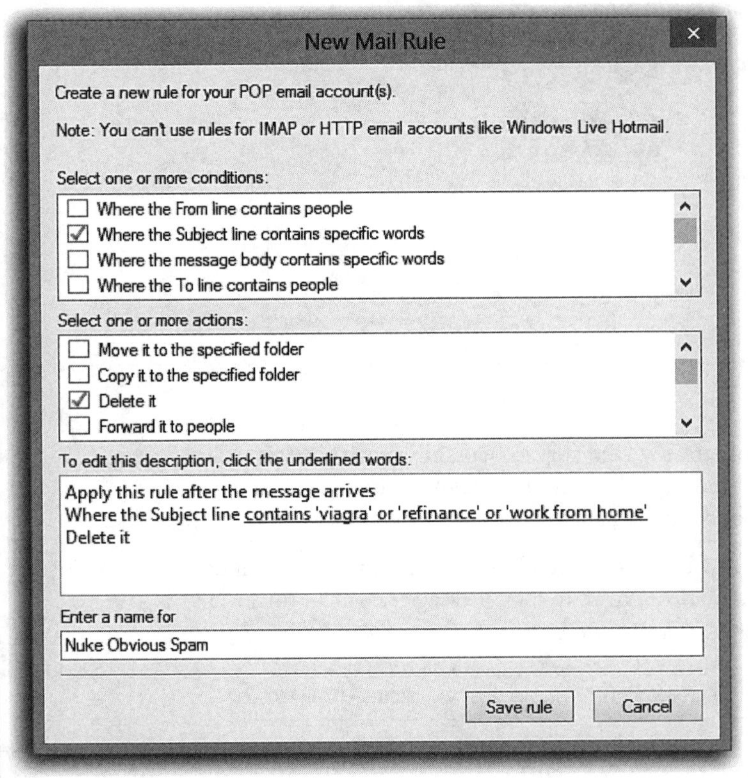

Figure 16-12: *Building a message rule entails specifying which messages you want Mail to look for–and what to do with them. By adding the underlined words, as shown here, you specify what criteria you're looking for. Here, any email with the words "Rolex," "Refinance," or "Viagra" in the subject line is automatically deleted.*

3. **Using the second set of checkboxes, specify what you want to happen to messages that match the criteria.**

   If, in step 2, you told your rule to watch for messages from your uncle containing the word "joke" somewhere in the message body, here's where you can tell Mail to delete or move the message into, say, a Spam folder.

   With a little imagination, you'll see how these checkboxes can perform absolutely amazing functions with your incoming email. Windows Live Mail can delete, move, or print messages; forward or redirect them to somebody; automatically reply to certain messages; and even avoid downloading files bigger than a certain number of kilobytes (ideal for laptop lovers on slow hotel room connections).

4. **Specify *which* words or people you want the message rule to watch out for.**

   In the bottom of the dialog box, you can click any of the underlined phrases to specify which people, which specific words, which file sizes you want Mail to watch out for—a person's name, or "*Viagra*," in the previous examples.

   If you click "contains people," for example, a dialog box appears that lets you open your Contacts list to select certain individuals whose messages you want handled by this rule. If you click "contains specific words," you can type in the words you want a certain rule to watch out for. And so on.

5. **In the very bottom text box, name your mail rule. Click OK.**

   Now the Message Rules dialog box appears (Figure 16-13).

Tip: Windows Live Mail applies rules as they appear–from top to bottom–in the Message Rules window. If a rule doesn't seem to be working properly, it may be that an earlier rule is intercepting and processing the message before the "broken" rule even sees it. To fix this, try moving the rule up or down in the list by selecting it and then clicking the Move Up or Move Down buttons.

Figure 16-13:
Once a rule is created, it lands in the Message Rules list. Here you can manage the rules you've created, choose a sequence for them (those at the top get applied first), and apply them to existing messages (by clicking "Apply now").

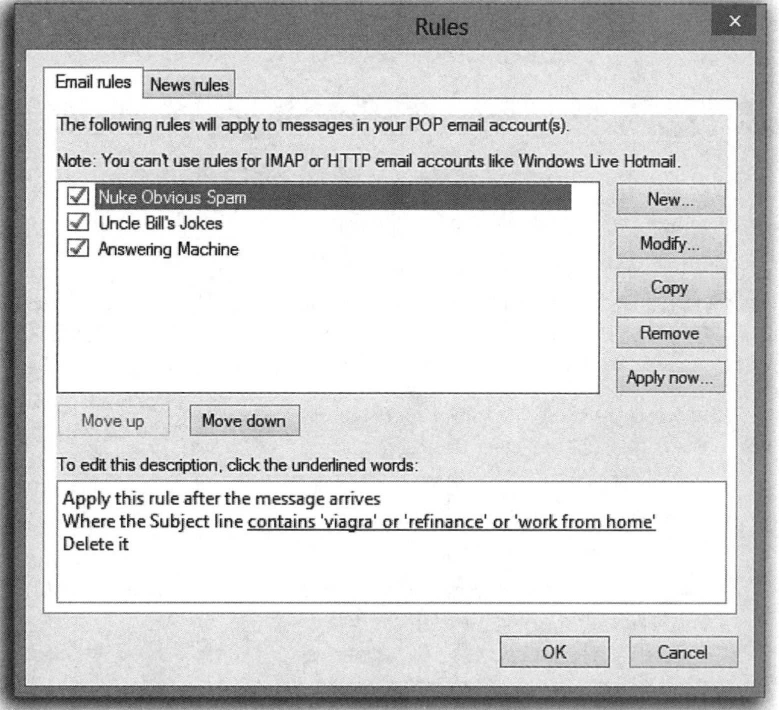

Two sneaky message-rules tricks

You can use message rules for many different purposes. But here are two of the best:

- **File mail from specific people.** For instance, if you have a few friends who constantly forward their idea of funny messages, create a rule that sends any email from them to a specific folder automatically. At the end of the day, look through the folder just to make sure you haven't missed anything and, if you have time, read the "most excellent funny emails in the whole wide world."
- **The email answering machine.** If you're going on vacation, turn on "For all messages" in step 2, and then "Reply with message" in step 3. In other words, you can turn Windows Live Mail into an email answering machine that automatically sends a canned "I'm away until the 15th" message to everyone who writes you.

Tip: Unsubscribe from, or turn off, any email mailing lists before you turn on "For all messages." Otherwise, you'll incur the wrath of the other list members by littering their email discussion groups with copies of your autoreply message.

Junk Email

Mail's Junk filter automatically channels what it believes to be spam into the "Junk E-mail" folder in the folder list.

FREQUENTLY ASKED QUESTION

Canning Spam

Help! I'm awash in junk email! How do I get out of this mess?

Spam is a much-hated form of advertising that involves sending unsolicited emails to thousands of people. While there's no instant cure for spam, you can take certain steps to protect yourself from it.

1. Above all, never post your main e-mail address online, ever. Use a different, dedicated email account for online shopping, Web site and software registration, and newsgroup posting.

   Spammers have automated software robots that scour every Web page, automatically recording email addresses they find. These are the primary sources of spam, so at least you're now restricting the junk mail to one secondary mail account.

2. Even then, when filling out forms or registering products online, look for checkboxes requesting permission for the company to send you email or to share your email address with its "partners." Just say no.
3. When posting messages in a newsgroup, insert the letters NOSPAM, SPAMISBAD, or something similar somewhere into your email address. Anyone replying to you via email must manually remove it from your email address, which, though a hassle, keeps your email address away from the spammer's robots. (They're getting smarter every day, though; a trickier insert may be required, along the lines of REMOVETOEMAIL or SPAMMERSARESCUM.)
4. Create *message rules* to filter out messages containing typical advertising words such as *casino, Rolex, herbal,* and so forth. (Instructions are on page 525.)
5. Buy an antispam program like SpamAssassin.

Tip: You may not have a "Junk E-mail" folder for Web-based email accounts like Gmail and Yahoo. Those online mail services usually have their own spam filters.

The Junk filter's factory setting is Low, meaning that only the most obvious spam gets sent to the "Junk E-mail" folder. You'll probably still get a ton of spam, but at least almost no legitimate mail will get mistakenly classified as spam.

You can configure the level of security you want in the Junk E-Mail Options window, shown in Figure 16-14.

Junk E-Mail Safety Options

Junk E-Mail Safety Options offers six tabs. The Options tab is shown in Figure 16-14. These are the other tabs:

- **Safe Senders.** Messages from any contacts, email addresses, or domain names that you add to this list are never treated as junk email. (A domain name is what comes after the @ sign in an email address, as in *bob@herbalviagra.com*.) Click Add to begin.

Tip: The two checkboxes below the list are also useful in preventing "false positives." The first, "Also trust e-mail from my Contacts," means that anyone in your own address book is not a spammer. The second, "Automatically add people I e-mail to the Safe Senders list," means that if you send mail *to* somebody, it's someone you don't consider a spammer.

Figure 16-14:
To visit this dialog box, choose File→Options→"Safety options." Choose No Automatic Filtering, Low, High, or Safe List Only. You can also opt to permanently delete suspected spam instead of moving it to the Junk E-Mail folder. No matter what setting you choose, though, always go through the Junk E-Mail folder every few days to make sure you haven't missed any important messages that were flagged as spam incorrectly.

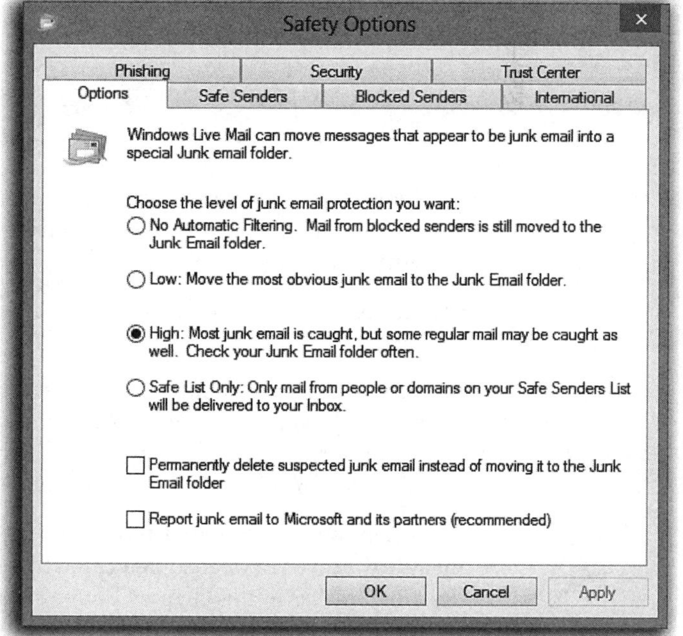

- **Blocked Senders.** This one's the flip side of Safe Senders: It's a list of contacts, email addresses, and domain names that you always want flagged as spam.
- **International.** You can also block email in foreign languages or messages that originate overseas. (A huge percentage of spam originates overseas, since U.S. antispam laws have no jurisdiction there.) See Figure 16-15.

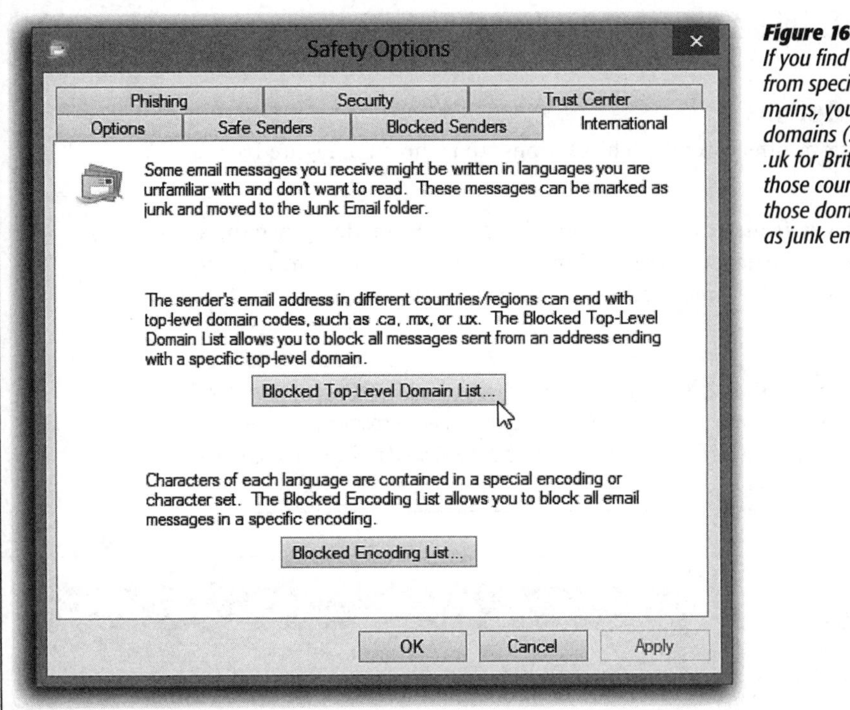

Figure 16-15: *If you find you're getting email from specific countries or domains, you can select the top-level domains (.ca for Canadian mail, .uk for British mail, and so on) for those countries. All email from those domains now gets treated as junk email.*

- **Phishing.** *Phishing* email is designed to look like it came from your bank, eBay, or PayPal—but it's a trick to get you to surrender your account information so the bad guys can steal your identity.

  Mail keeps phishing email out of your inbox unless you turn off this feature on this tab.
- **Security.** This tab contains options for sending secure mail, using digital IDs and encryption. If you're using Mail in a business that requires secure email, the system administrator will provide instructions. Otherwise, you'll find that most of these settings have no effect.

  The exceptions are the antivirus and antispam features, like "Do not allow attachments to be saved or opened that could potentially be a virus" and "Block images," described earlier in this chapter. For best results, leave these settings as they are.

Tip: One of these options is very useful in the modern age: "Warn me when other applications try to send mail as me." That's a thinly veiled reference to viruses that, behind the scenes, send out hundreds of infected emails to everybody in your Contacts list, with you identified as the sender. This option ensures that if some software—not you—tries to send messages, you'll know about it.

When the Junk Filter Goes Wrong

Windows Live Mail doesn't always get it right. It labels some good messages as junk and some spam messages as OK.

Over time, though, it's supposed to get better—*if* you patiently help it along. Every time you see a good piece of email in the "Junk E-mail" folder, click it, and then click "Not junk" on the Ribbon's Home tab.

Better yet, use that icon's ▾ menu to choose one of these two options:

- **Add sender to safe senders list.** No future mail from this person will be misfiled.
- **Add sender's domain to safe senders list.** No future mail from this person's entire company or ISP will be marked as spam.

On the other hand, you can reverse all this logic if you find a piece of spam in your inbox. That is, click it and then click the Junk button on the toolbar.

You can also use the "Add sender to blocked senders list" (or "Add sender's domain") commands in that same shortcut menu; unfortunately, spammers rarely use the same address or domain twice, so it's probably faster just to hit the Delete key.

The World of Mail Settings

Mail has enough features and configuration options to fill a very thick book. You can see them for yourself by choosing File→Options→Mail. Here's a brief overview of some of the most useful options (Figure 16-16).

General Tab

Most of the controls here govern what Mail does when you first open the program. Take note of the options to connect automatically; you can opt to have Mail check for messages every few minutes and then use the drop-down list to say how, and whether, to connect at that time if you're not already online.

Read Tab

Use these options to establish how the program handles messages in the inbox. One of these options marks a message as having been read—changing its typeface from bold to nonbold—if you leave it highlighted in the list for 1 second or more, even without opening it. That's one option you may want to consider turning off. (This tab is also where you choose the font you want to use for the messages you're reading, which is an important consideration.)

Receipts Tab

You can add a *return receipt* to messages you send. When the recipient reads your message, a notification message (receipt) is emailed back to you under two conditions: *if* the recipient agrees to send a return receipt to you, and *if* the recipient's email program offers a similar feature. (Mail, Outlook, and Eudora all do.)

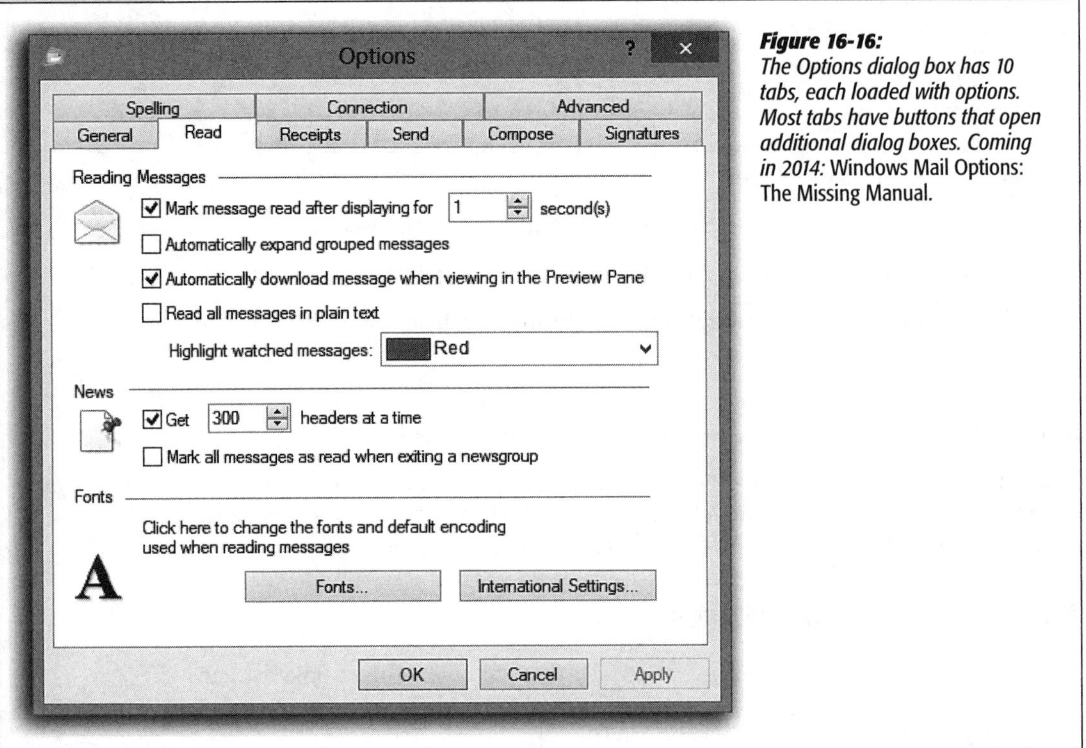

Figure 16-16: *The Options dialog box has 10 tabs, each loaded with options. Most tabs have buttons that open additional dialog boxes. Coming in 2014:* Windows Mail Options: The Missing Manual.

Send Tab

The options here govern outgoing messages. One option to consider turning *off* here is the factory-set option "Send messages immediately." That's because as soon as you click the Send button, Mail sends your message, even if you haven't had time to fully consider the consequences of the rant inside it—aimed at an ex, a boss, or a coworker—which could land you in hot water.

Tip: It's also a good choice if you're on a dial-up connection. All this dialing—and *waiting* for the dialing—drives some people crazy, especially in households with only one phone line.

If you turn this option off, then clicking the Send button simply places a newly written message into the outbox. As you reply to messages and compose new ones, the outbox collects them. They're not sent until you click the Sync button, or press Ctrl+M. Only at that point does Mail send your email.

Tip: To see the messages waiting in your outbox, click the Outbox icon at the left side of the screen. At this point, you can click a message's name (in the upper-right pane of the screen) to view the message itself in the *lower*-right pane, exactly as with messages in your inbox.

Don't bother to try *editing* an outgoing message in this way, however; Mail won't let you do so. Only by double-clicking a message's name (in the upper-right pane), thus opening it into a separate window, can you make changes to a piece of outgoing mail.

The Send tab also includes features for configuring replies. For example, you can disable the function that includes the original message in the reply.

Finally, the "Automatically put people I reply to in my address book after the third reply" option can be a real timesaver. It means that if somebody seems to have become a regular in your life, his email address is automatically saved in your Contacts list. The next time you want to write him a note, you won't need to look up the address—just type the first few letters of it in the "To:" box.

Tip: The option here called "Upload larger images to the Web when sending a photo e-mail" works if you have signed into your Microsoft account, as described on page 726. It means you don't have to worry about photo file sizes; your big-mama files will be "hosted" on the Windows Live site (for 30 days). Your recipient gets a smaller version of the photos, which she can click to see or download the bigger ones.

Compose Tab

Here's where you specify the font you want to use when writing emails and newsgroup messages.

This is also the control center for *stationery (*custom-designed templates, complete with fonts, colors, backgrounds, borders, and other formatting elements that you can use for all outgoing email).

To choose a stationery style for all outgoing messages, turn on the Mail checkbox, and then click the Select button. You're offered a folder full of Microsoft stationery templates; click one to see its preview. You can also click the Create New button, which launches a wizard that walks you through the process of creating your own background design.

Tip: You don't have to use one particular stationery style for all outgoing messages. When composing a message, use the Stationery pop-up menu to view the list of stationery templates. In other words, you can choose stationery on a message-by-message basis.

Signatures Tab

Use this tab to design a *signature* for your messages (page 122). By clicking the New button and entering more signature material in the text box, you can create several *different* signatures: one for business messages, one for your buddies, and so on.

Spelling Tab

The Spelling tab offers configuration options for the Mail spell-checking feature. You can even force the spell checker to correct errors in the *original* message when you send a reply, although your correspondent may not appreciate it.

Tip: Mail's spelling checker is so smart, it's supposed to be able to recognize the language of the message and to use the appropriate spelling dictionary automatically.

Connection Tab

Here you can tell Mail to hang up automatically after sending and receiving messages (and reconnect the next time you want to perform the same tasks). This, of course, is for the six people left who still use a dial-up modem.

Advanced Tab

This tab is your housekeeping and settings center for Mail. You can configure what you want Mail to do with your contacts' vCards (virtual business cards), whether you want to compose your replies at the bottom of emails instead of at the top, and whether you want to mark message threads in newsgroups as "watched."

Don't miss the Maintenance button. It lets you clear out old deleted messages, clean up downloads, purge newsgroup messages, and so on.

The Contacts List

If you've read Chapter 4, then you know about the People app in TileWorld. It's your master address book, and it eliminates the need to enter complete email addresses whenever you want to send a message.

But here's a little-known fact: If you've downloaded Windows Live Mail, you can work with your contacts at the desktop, too. Click the Contacts button (lower left of the window), or press Ctrl+Shift+B; then, to begin adding names and email addresses, click Contact on the Ribbon.

Tip: Windows Live Mail offers a convenient timesaving feature: "Add sender to contacts" (right-click a message in the list). Whenever you choose it, Mail automatically stores the email address of the person whose message you clicked.

Mail uses this list to autocomplete email addresses that you start to type. Using the Ribbon buttons, you can have all kinds of other fun: you can edit your contacts (except the ones inherited from Facebook and other online sources); change the way they're displayed; import or export addresses; incorporate corporate directories; create categories; and more.

Mail's Calendar

Windows 8 comes with a calendar app—but it's a TileWorld app, and it's so bare-bones, it makes a skeleton look overdressed.

If you need anything more powerful, you're in luck; there's a calendar built into Windows Live Mail. Sometimes, its integration with Mail makes sense (like when potential appointments come to you via email), and sometimes not so much (like when you have to fire up Mail just to see what you're doing on Thursday night).

You can keep the calendar open, in miniature form, in a pane of its own as you work on email; if you don't see it already, click Calendar on the Ribbon's View tab.

But to do any more substantial work, you'll want to fill the screen with the calendar. To do that, click the Calendar button in the lower-left corner of the screen, or press Shift+Ctrl+X. You'll soon discover that this calendar offers some nice perks. For example:

Figure 16-17: *Top: Week view. The miniature navigation calendar provides an overview of adjacent months. You can jump to a different week or day by clicking the triangle buttons and then clicking within the numbers. If the event is recurring, it bears an icon that looks like two curly arrows chasing each other.*

Bottom: Month view. Pretty lame—you don't see what time any appointment is for—but it's something. You can make more room by hiding the navigation pane.

- Your Mail calendar is synced with your Windows Live online calendar. Make a change on the Web calendar and you'll find it changed on your PC, and vice versa.

Tip: Truth be told, the online calendar has even more features than this one. For example, the Windows Live one has a to-do list, which the Mail calendar lacks.

- You can "subscribe" to calendars on the Internet, like the ones published by your family members/classmates/baseball team members/downtrodden employees. For example, you can subscribe to your spouse's Google Calendar, thereby finding out if you've been committed to after-dinner drinks on the night the big game is on TV.

Working with Views

When you open Mail's calendar, you see something like Figure 16-17. By clicking the buttons on the Ribbon (or pressing Ctrl+Alt+1, +2, or +3), you can switch among any of these views:

- **Day** shows the appointments for a single day in the main calendar area, broken down by time slot.

Tip: Calendar provides a quick way to get to the current day's date: Click Today on the Ribbon.

- **Week** fills the main display area with seven columns, reflecting the current week.
- **Month** shows the entire current month. Double-click a date square or a date number to create a new appointment.

Tip: Your mouse's scroll wheel can be a great advantage in this calendar. For example, when entering a date, turning the wheel lets you jump forward or backward in time. It also lets you change the time zone as you're setting it.

Making an Appointment

You can quickly record an appointment using any of several techniques:

- In any view, double-click a time slot on the calendar.
- In any view, right-click a date or a time slot, and then choose either "New event" or "New all day event" from the shortcut menu.
- In any view, click the ▾ next to a calendar (category)'s name; choose either "New event" or "New all day event" from the shortcut menu.
- Click Event on the Ribbon.
- Press Ctrl+Shift+E (for *event*).

Tip: In Day or Week view, drag vertically through the time slots for the appointment you're trying to create (10 a.m. down to 12:30 p.m., for example) before taking one of the steps above. That way, you've already specified the start and end times, saving yourself a lot of tedious typing.

In each case, the New Event dialog box appears (Figure 16-18), where you type the details for your new appointment. For example, you can tab your way to the following information areas:

- **Subject.** That's the name of your appointment. For example, you might type, *Fly to Phoenix.*
- **Location.** You can record a location, a flight number, a phone number—anything that you'll find helpful later.
- **Start, End.** Most appointments have the same Start and End dates, thank heaven (although we've all been in meetings that don't seem that way). But you can click the little calendar buttons to change the dates.

Tip: If you specify a different ending date, you get a *banner* across the relevant dates in the Month view.

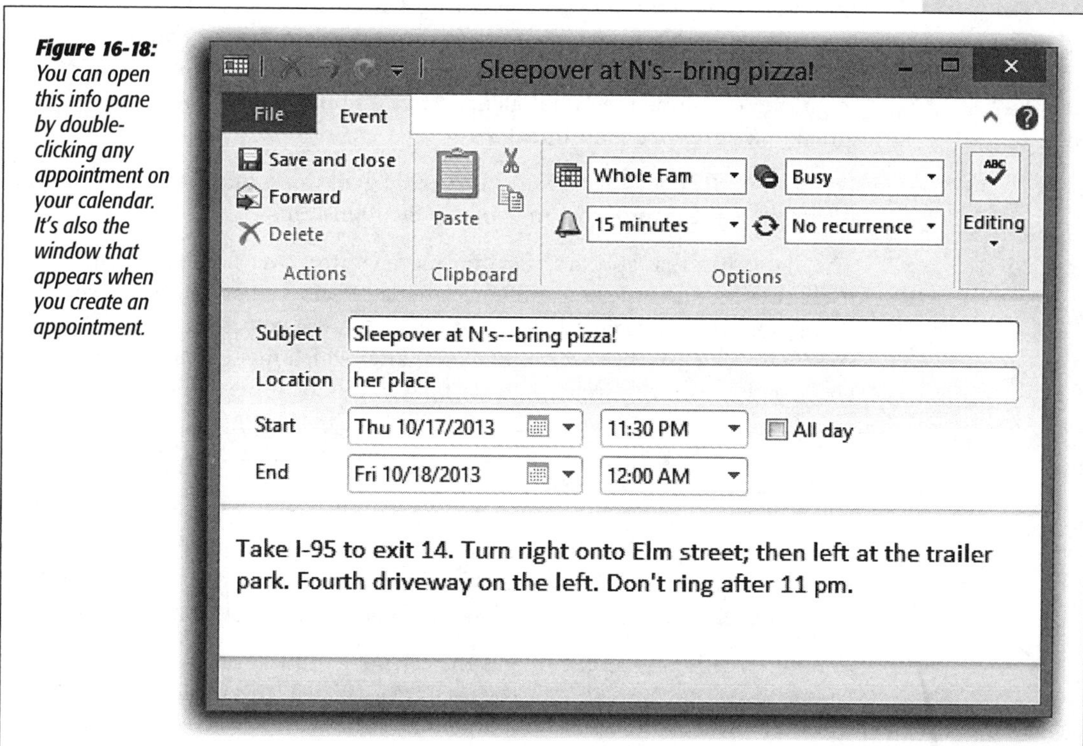

***Figure 16-18:** You can open this info pane by double-clicking any appointment on your calendar. It's also the window that appears when you create an appointment.*

Then set the start and end time for this appointment, either by using the pop-up menu or by editing the text (like "9:30 a.m.") with your mouse and keyboard.

- **All day.** An "all-day" event, of course, is something with no specific time of day associated with it, like a birthday or a trip. All-day appointments appear at the top of the daily- or weekly-view screens, in the area reserved for this kind of thing.

- **My Calendar.** A *calendar*, in Microsoft's confusing terminology, is a subset—a category—into which you can place various appointments. You can create one for yourself, another for whole-family events, another for book-club appointments, and so on. Later, you'll be able to hide and show these categories at will, adding or removing them from the calendar with a single click. For details, read on.

Tip: Use this same pop-up menu to *change* an appointment's category. If you filed something in Company Memos that should have been in Sweet Nothings for Honey-Poo, open the event's dialog box and reassign it. Quick.

- **No recurrence.** The pop-up menu here contains common options for repeating events: "Daily," "Weekly," and so on. It starts out saying "No recurrence."

  The somewhat goofy part is that if you choose any of those convenient commands in the pop-up menu, the calendar assumes that you want to repeat this event every day/week/month/year *forever.* You don't get any way to specify an end date. You'll be stuck seeing this event repeating on your calendar until the end of time. That may be a good choice for recording your anniversary, especially if your spouse might be consulting the same calendar. But it's not a feature for people who are afraid of long-term commitments.

  If you want the freedom to *stop* your weekly gym workouts or monthly car payments, choose Custom from the pop-up menu instead.

  The dialog box that appears offers far more control over how this event repeats itself. You can make the repeating stop after a certain number of times, which is a useful option for car and mortgage payments. And if you choose "After," you can specify the date (or the number of times) after which the repetitions come to an end; use this option to indicate the last day of school, for example.

Tip: This dialog box also lets you specify days of the week. For example, you can schedule your morning runs for Monday, Thursday, and Saturday.

- **Busy.** This pop-up menu lets you block off time during which you're unavailable (or tentatively available). The point here is for coworkers who might be looking over your calendar online to know when you're *not* available for meetings.

- **Reminder.** This pop-up menu tells the calendar you want to be notified when a certain appointment is about to begin. Unfortunately, this feature isn't built into the Mail calendar—it's actually a function of the Windows Live Web service.

  If you're cool with that, then the news is good: Windows Live can remind you of an event by email, as a notice in the Windows Live Messenger chat program, or even with a text message to your cellphone.

Note: To set up these reminders, click Reminders on the Ribbon. Your Web browser opens to the Windows Live page where you change your mail, chat, and cellphone options for getting reminders.

Use the pop-up menu to specify how much advance notice you want. If it's a TV show you like to watch, you might set up a reminder only 5 minutes before airtime. If it's a birthday, you might set up a 2-day warning to give yourself enough time to buy a present, and so on.

- **Notes.** Here's your chance to customize your calendar event. In the big, empty part of the window, you can type, paste, or drag any text you like in the notes area—driving directions, contact phone numbers, a call history, or whatever.

When you're finished entering all the details, click "Save & close" (or press Ctrl+S). Your newly scheduled event now shows up on the calendar, complete with the color coding that corresponds to the calendar category you've assigned.

What to Do with an Appointment

Once you've entrusted your agenda to Calendar, you can start putting it to work. Here are a few of the possibilities.

Editing events

To edit a calendar event's name or details, double-click it. You don't have to bother with this if all you want to do is *reschedule* an event, however, as described next.

Lengthening or shortening events

If a scheduled meeting becomes shorter or your lunch hour becomes a lunch hour-and-a-half (in your dreams), changing the length of a selected calendar event is as easy as dragging the top or bottom border of its block in Day or Week view (see Figure 16-19).

Figure 16-19: *You can resize any calendar event just by dragging its border. As your cursor touches the bottom edge of a calendar event, it turns into a double-headed arrow. You can now drag the event's edge to make it take up more or less time on your calendar.*

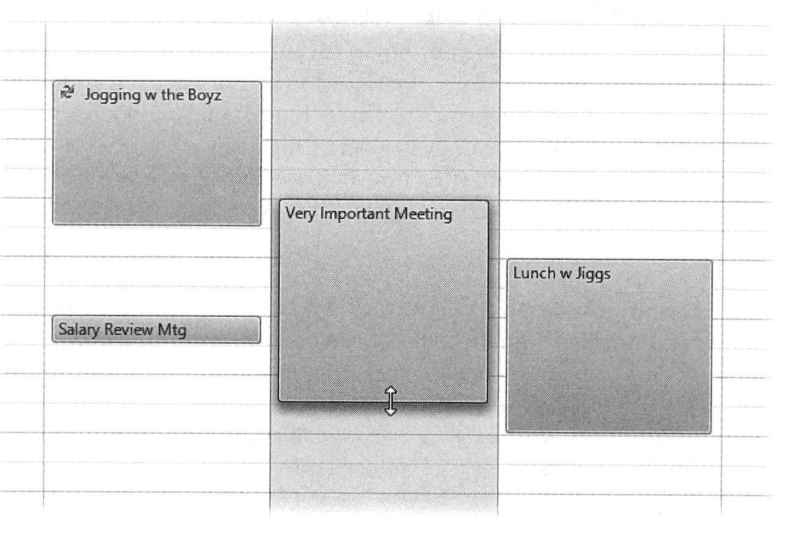

Tip: In Week view, if you've grabbed the top or bottom edge of an appointment's block so that the cursor changes, you can drag *horizontally* to make an appointment cross the midnight line and extend into a second day.

Rescheduling events

If an event in your life gets rescheduled, you can move an appointment just by dragging the rectangle that represents it. In Day or Week view, drag the event vertically in its column to change its time on the same day; in Week or Month view, you can drag it to another date.

If something is postponed for, say, a month or two, it's more of a hassle; you can't drag an appointment beyond its month window. You have no choice but to open the Event dialog box and edit the starting and ending dates or times—or just cut and paste the event to a different date.

Printing events

To commit your calendar to paper, choose File→Print, or press Ctrl+P. The resulting Print dialog box lets you specify a range of dates and which view you want (Week, Month, or whatever).

Deleting events

To delete an appointment, just click its box and then press the Delete key. If you delete a recurring event (like a weekly meeting), the calendar asks whether you want to delete only that particular instance of the event or the entire series.

The "Calendar" Category Concept

Everyone in your house (or office) can have a different set of appointments on the same calendar, color-coded so you all can tell your schedules apart. The red appointments might be yours; the blue ones, your spouse's; the green ones might be your kid's. You can overlay all of them simultaneously to look for conflicts (or mutually available meeting times), if you like. It's a great feature, one that the TileWorld Calendar app doesn't offer.

Each such set of appointments is called, confusingly enough, a *calendar* (Figure 16-20).

To create a calendar, click Calendar on the Ribbon, or press Shift+Ctrl+D. Type a name that defines the category in your mind, and choose the color you want for its appointments.

Tip: Whenever you're about to create an appointment, click a calendar name *first*. That way, the appointment will already belong to the correct calendar.

To change the name or color-coding of an existing category, click the ▾ next to its name; from the shortcut menu, choose Properties to reopen the dialog box.

You assign an appointment to one of these categories using the pop-up menu on its Details pane. After that, you can hide or show an entire category of appointments at once just by turning on or off the appropriate checkbox in the list of calendars.

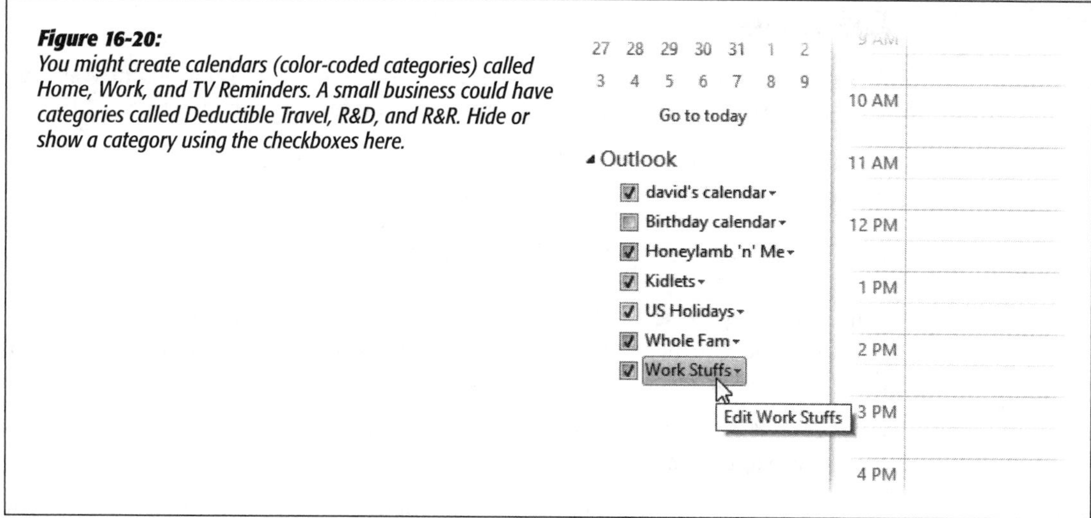

Figure 16-20:
You might create calendars (color-coded categories) called Home, Work, and TV Reminders. A small business could have categories called Deductible Travel, R&D, and R&R. Hide or show a category using the checkboxes here.

Syncing Calendars with Windows Live

If you've signed into your Windows Live account, a great feature awaits: Your Mail calendar and your Windows Live calendar on the Web are automatically brought up to date with each other. In other words, you can check your schedule from any PC in the world over the Internet.

You don't have to do anything to make this happen; it's automatic.

Publishing Calendars

One of Windows Live Calendar's best features is its ability to post your calendar on the Web so that other people—or you, using a different computer—can subscribe to it, which adds *your* appointments to *their* calendars. For example, you might use this feature to post the meeting schedule for a club you manage, or to share the agenda for a series of upcoming financial meetings that all your coworkers will need to consult.

Note: This isn't the same thing as the Windows Live syncing described above. Publishing a calendar lets you control which appointments people see, which people see them, and what permission they have to make changes to it.

And you're not the only one who can publish a calendar. The Web is full of such schedules published by *other* people, ready for adding to your *own* calendar: team schedules, company meetings, national holidays, and so on.

Unfortunately, the calendar in *Mail* can't do any of this publishing; only the Web-based copy of it at the Windows Live Web site can. Fortunately, your Mail calendar is a mirror of what's online, so the difference may not be so huge.

RSS Feeds

RSS feeds are like free headline services, reporting what's new on different Web sites (news, sports, tech, whatever). There's a great description of them on page 495.

Microsoft must think a lot of RSS feeds, because it's given you at least two different programs that can read them: Internet Explorer and Windows Live Mail.

Tip: If you subscribe to feeds in Internet Explorer, they show up in Mail, and vice versa.

Start by clicking the Feeds button (lower left of the Mail window), or by pressing Shift+Ctrl+K. The main window starts out empty; you're expected to know the URL (Web address) of a feed you want to read.

If you're an RSS fan, then you're an executive-summary kind of person—and so here's the executive summary:

- **To add a new feed**, click Feed on the Ribbon; in the resulting box, paste or type in the URL (the Web address) of that feed. Click OK. That feed's name appears in the list at left.

  Keep expanding the flippy triangles until you see the list of individual headlines in the center column, where email messages would normally appear. Click one to read, in the Reading pane, the summary that it represents.

  You can work with feeds exactly the way you work with email: forward them, file them in folders, print them, and so on.

- **To change the frequency of a feed (and how many headlines to keep)**, right-click its name; from the shortcut menu, choose "Manage feeds." In the Manage Your

UP TO SPEED

Newsgroups Explained

Newsgroups (often called *Usenet*) started out as a way for people to conduct discussions via a bulletin board–like system, in which a message is posted for all to see and reply to. These public discussions are divided into categories called newsgroups, which cover the gamut from photographic techniques to naval aviation.

These days, Usenet has a certain seedy reputation as a place to exchange pornography, pirated software, and MP3 files with doubtful copyright pedigrees. Even so, there are tens of thousands of interesting, informative discussions going on, and newsgroups are great places to get help with troubleshooting, to exchange recipes, or just to see what's on the minds of your fellow Usenet fans.

Feeds dialog box, expand the flippy triangles until you can see the feed in question. Click its name, and then click Edit Feed.

- **To remove a feed,** right-click its name and choose Delete from the shortcut menu (and confirm the deletion).

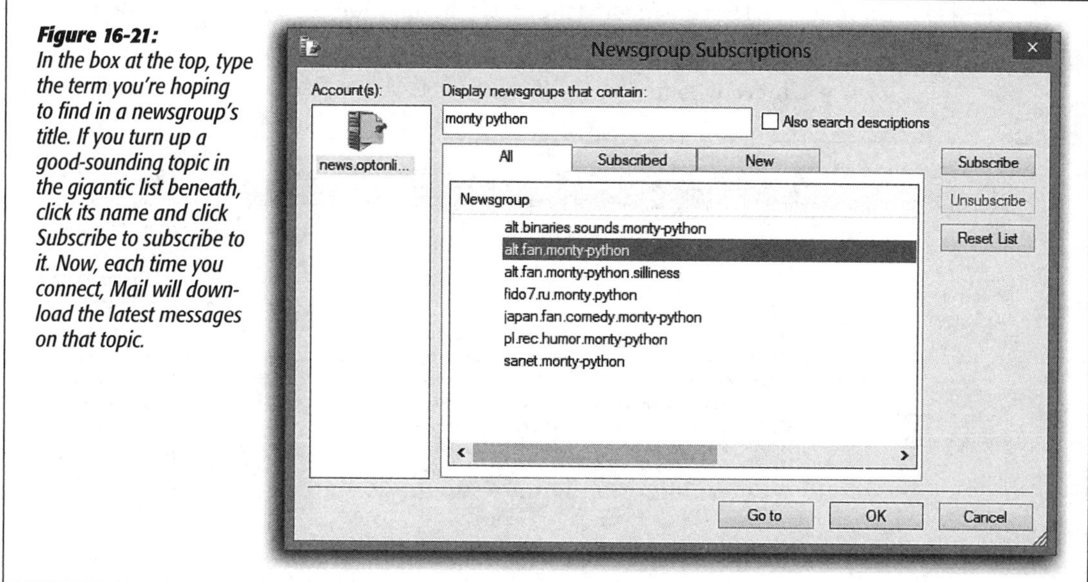

Figure 16-21: *In the box at the top, type the term you're hoping to find in a newsgroup's title. If you turn up a good-sounding topic in the gigantic list beneath, click its name and click Subscribe to subscribe to it. Now, each time you connect, Mail will download the latest messages on that topic.*

Newsgroups

Newsgroups have nothing to do with news; in fact, they're Internet bulletin boards. There are hundreds of thousands of them on every conceivable topic: pop culture, computers, politics, and every other special (and *very* special) interest; in fact, there are thousands just about Windows. You can use Mail to read and reply to these messages almost exactly as though they were email messages.

Subscribing to a Newsgroup

Subscribing to your first newsgroup can be quite an experience, simply because there are just so many newsgroups to choose from.

To get started with newsgroups, click the Newsgroups button (lower left of the Mail window), or press Shift+Ctrl+L.

On the Accounts tab of the Ribbon, click Newsgroup. A wizard walks you through adding your name (as you'll be represented in these discussions); your email address (*do not use your main one* unless you want an ocean of spam!); and your news server address.

Right: Your *what?*

A news server is a central computer that lists and manages the thousands of newsgroups. Your Internet service provider has one. You can find it out by Googling it (*comcast newsgroup server*, for example). Or you can type in a free one like *www.eternal-september.org*. (You have to go to that Web site and sign up for a free account first.)

When you're finished with the wizard, Mail downloads a list of newsgroups available on your server. Wait patiently; the list can be quite long—tens of thousands of entries. Fortunately, it's a one-time deal.

Now you're ready to find yourself some good online discussions; see Figure 16-21.

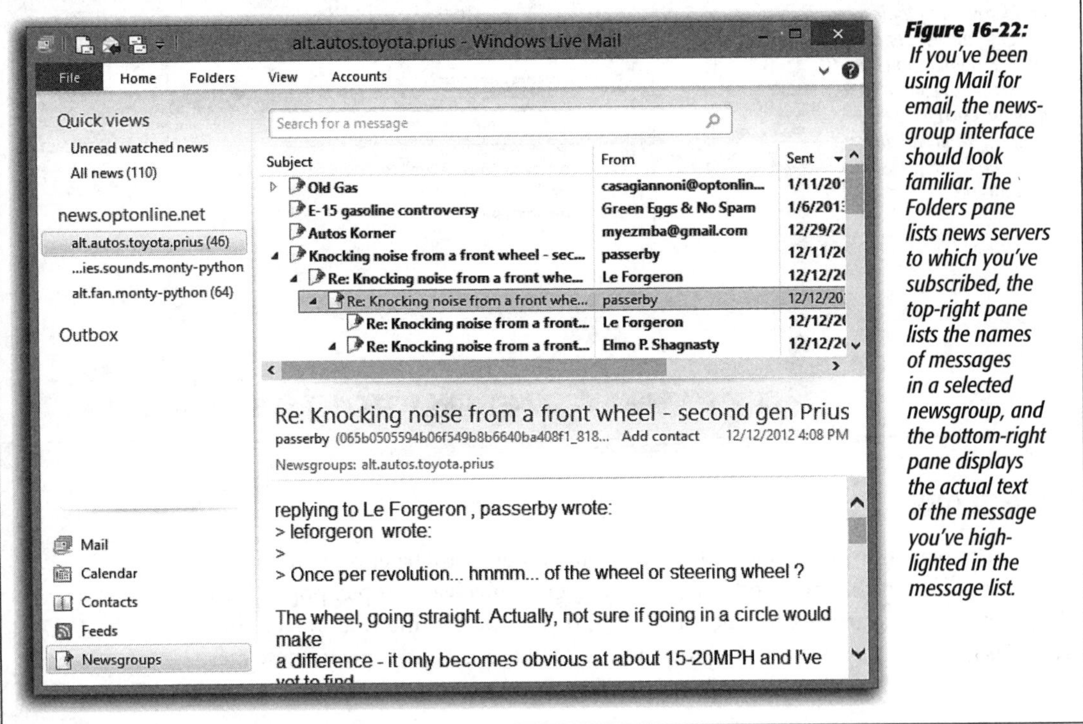

Figure 16-22: *If you've been using Mail for email, the newsgroup interface should look familiar. The Folders pane lists news servers to which you've subscribed, the top-right pane lists the names of messages in a selected newsgroup, and the bottom-right pane displays the actual text of the message you've highlighted in the message list.*

Reading Messages

Once you've subscribed to a newsgroup, Mail downloads all the message summaries in the discussions to which you've subscribed. (There may be just a few messages, or several hundred; they may go back only a few days or a couple of weeks, depending on the amount of "traffic" in each discussion and the storage space on the news server.)

To read the messages in a newsgroup, either click an entry in the list of messages to display it in the Preview window (Figure 16-22), or double-click an entry to open the list of messages in a new window.

Tip: You can set up message rules for newsgroups to screen out messages from certain people, messages with certain phrases in their subject lines, and so on. It works exactly like the message rules for email, as described earlier in this chapter. Just click "Message rules" on the Ribbon's Folders tab.

In fact, *many* email features also work in newsgroups, exactly as described in this chapter: replying, custom views, searching, filing in folders, and so on.

Replying, Composing, and Forwarding Messages

Working with newsgroup messages is very similar to working with email messages, except that you must be conscious of whether you're replying to the individual sender of a message or to the entire group. Otherwise, you can reply to messages, forward them, or compose them exactly as described earlier in this chapter. You can include file attachments, too, by using the Attach toolbar button, for example.

Tip: Aside from posting ads and HTML-formatted messages, the best way to irritate everyone on a newsgroup is to ask a question that has already been answered recently on the newsgroup. Before asking a question, spend 5 minutes reading the recent newsgroup messages to see whether someone has already answered your question. Also consider visiting the Groups tab at *www.google.com,* a Web site that lets you search all newsgroups for particular topics.

4

Part Four: Pictures & Music

CHAPTER 17

Windows Photo Gallery

Your digital camera is brimming with photos. You've snapped the perfect graduation portrait, captured that jaw-dropping sunset over the Pacific, or compiled an unforgettable photo essay of your 2-year-old attempting to eat a bowl of spaghetti. It's time to use your PC to gather, organize, and tweak all these photos so you can share them with the rest of the world.

Microsoft has addressed photo organizing/editing with a vengeance. You have, of course, a very simple photo program waiting for you in TileWorld — the Photos app. But all it does is display photos. It doesn't offer any tools for editing them, cropping them, rating them, or organizing them. It can't play or handle video clips.

That's where Windows Live Photo Gallery comes in. It's a beautiful, full-blown digital camera companion for Windows at the desktop, and it's the subject of this chapter.

It's not built into Windows. You have to download it as part of the Windows Live Essentials software suite described on page 375. But once you have it, you'll realize that it's an important part of Windows.

Tip: Then again, you may prefer Google's Picasa—a free photo-editing program that you could argue is faster, easier, and more powerful. And it connects to a beautiful online photo gallery. Just sayin'.

Photo Gallery: The Application

Photo Gallery approaches digital photo management as a four-step process: importing the photos to your Pictures folder; organizing, tagging, and rating them; editing them; and sharing them (via prints, onscreen slideshows, DVD slideshows, email, your screen saver, and so on).

The first time you open Windows Live Photo Gallery, you're subjected to a battery of interview questions:

- **Sign in with your Windows Live name and password.** (Why? So Photo Gallery will be able to post your photos online when you're ready for that.)
- **Do you want Photo Gallery to open when you double-click common photo types (like JPEG, PNG, and TIFF)?** Probably. Otherwise, they'll continue to open in Windows Photo Viewer, which does nothing but *show* photos—it doesn't let you organize or edit them.
- **Some photos can't be displayed.** If you have any video clips that are in a format Photo Gallery doesn't understand—specifically, Apple's QuickTime format—then this dialog box appears to let you know. Click Download to go get the necessary adapter software that lets Photo Gallery recognize those file types.

Once you do that, you finally arrive at the program's main window, the basic elements of which are shown in Figure 17-1.

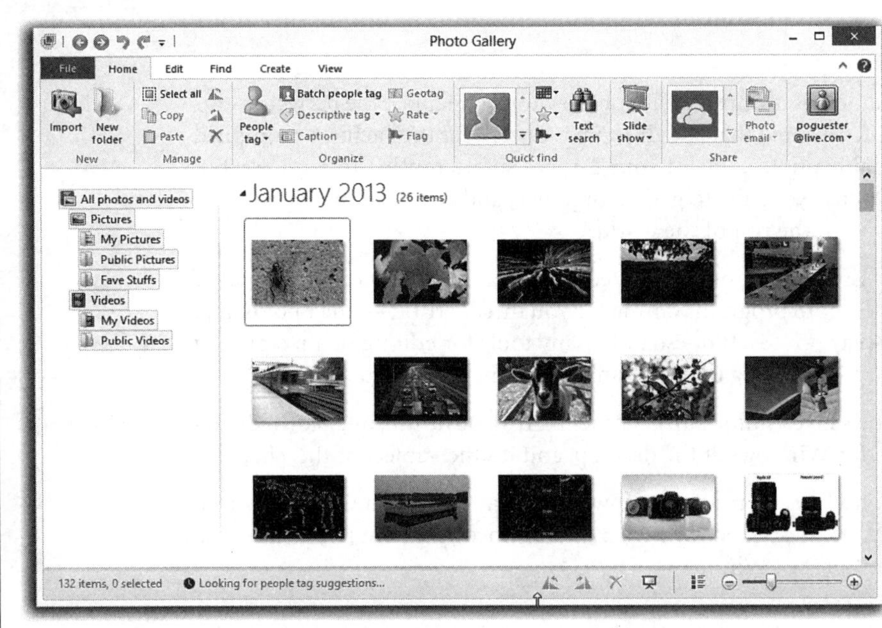

Figure 17-1: *Here's what Photo Gallery looks like once you've added a few photos. The viewing area is where thumbnails of your photos appear. The Ribbon shows all the stuff you can do with them. To adjust their size, drag the lower-right slider. All the thumbnails expand or contract simultaneously.*

Getting Pictures into Photo Gallery

The very first time you open it, Photo Gallery displays all the digital photos it can find in your Pictures and Videos folders.

This is important: You're looking at the *actual files* on your hard drive. If you delete a picture or a movie from Photo Gallery, you've just deleted it from your PC. (Well, OK, you've actually moved it to your Recycle Bin. But still, that's a step closer to oblivion.)

If you store your photos in other folders, you can make Photo Gallery aware of those, too. You can go about this task in either of two ways:

- **The menu way.** Choose File→"Include folder"; navigate to and select the additional folder, and then click OK.
- **The draggy way.** Find the folder on your desktop or in any Explorer folder. Drag the folder directly onto the heading "All photos and videos" in the left-side list, or directly into Photo Gallery's window (see Figure 17-2). Windows not only makes the contents appear in Photo Gallery, but also copies them to your Pictures folder for safekeeping.

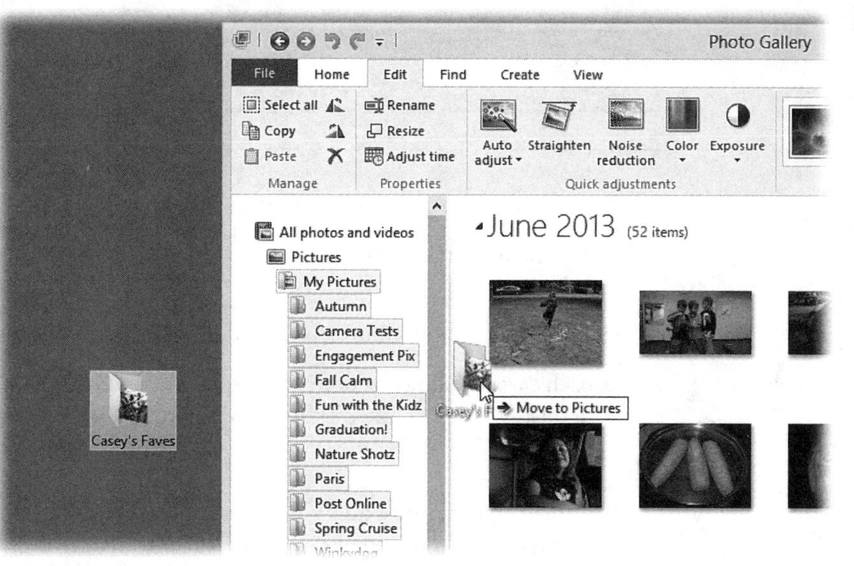

Figure 17-2: *You can add a "watched folder" to Photo Gallery by dragging it off the desktop (or any from folder window) right onto a Pictures heading or into the main window, as shown here. The cursor changes to let you know that Photo Gallery understands your intention.*

Photos from a Digital Camera

In Windows Live Photo Gallery, Microsoft has done a lot of work to make the camera-importing process smoother and smarter. Here's how it goes:

1. **Open Windows Live Photo Gallery.**

   For example, open the Start screen. Type *gallery* until you see the program's name; click it.

2. **Connect your camera to the PC. Turn the camera on.**

   Now, if this is the first time you've ever connected a camera, you may be shown the standard AutoPlay dialog box—otherwise known as the "What am I supposed to do with this thing?" box; see Figure 17-3.

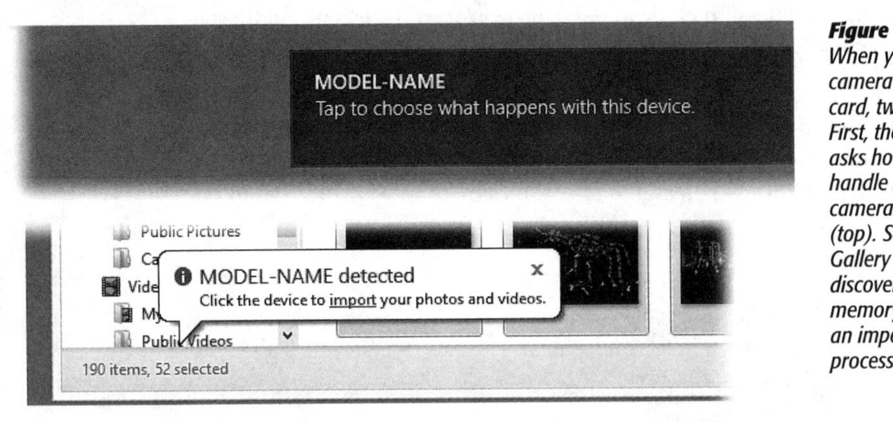

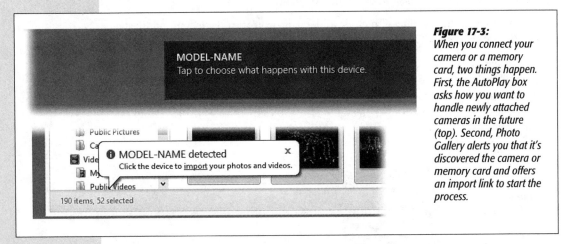

Figure 17-3: *When you connect your camera or a memory card, two things happen. First, the AutoPlay box asks how you want to handle newly attached cameras in the future (top). Second, Photo Gallery alerts you that it's discovered the camera or memory card and offers an import link to start the process.*

   You can read about AutoPlay on page 290; for now, just ignore the box.

3. **Begin the importing process.**

   You have three options: Click the "import" link shown at bottom in Figure 17-3, click Import on the Ribbon, or choose File→"Import photos and videos."

   In each case, a dialog box appears, displaying the camera's memory card as though it's a disk. Make sure the disk is highlighted (Figure 17-4, top).

4. **Click Import.**

   Now the Import Photos and Videos dialog box appears (Figure 17-4, middle). Here the steps branch. If you'd like to review the photos and import only certain batches (by date), go on to step 5a. If you'd rather just import them all now, without all the examining and grouping, skip to step 5b.

5a. **Click "Review, organize and group items to import," and then click Next.**

   Now you see the impressive dialog box shown in Figure 17-4 (bottom).

   In the old days, Photo Gallery just imported everything on your camera in one gigantic clump—even if it included photos from several different events, shot weeks apart. Now it automatically analyzes the time stamps in the incoming photos and puts them into individually named groups according to when you took them. Click "View all 20 items" (or whatever the number is) to see thumbnail previews of the photos in each batch, so you know what you're talking about.

Your job here, then, is to click "Enter a name" and type a name for each event whose photos you're about to import. It could be *Disney Trip, Casey's Birthday,* or *Baby Meets Lasagna,* for example—anything that helps you organize and find your pictures later.

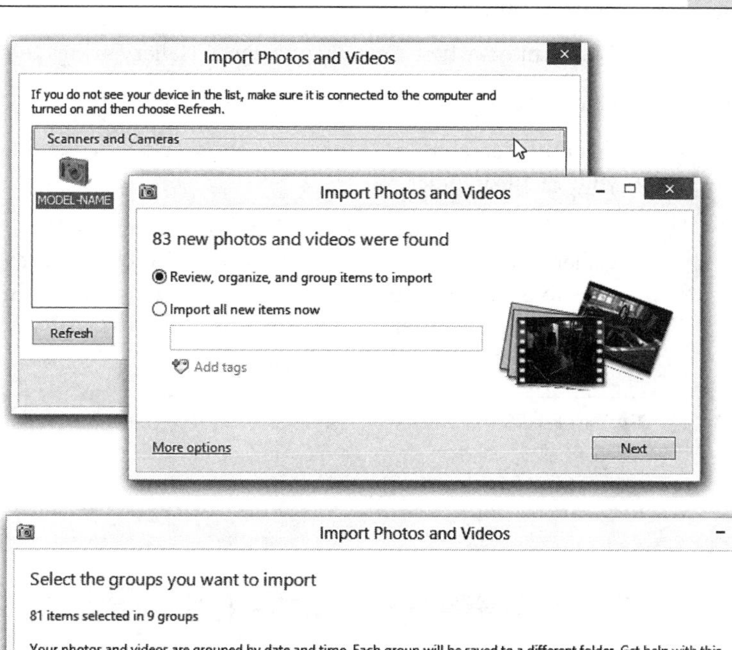

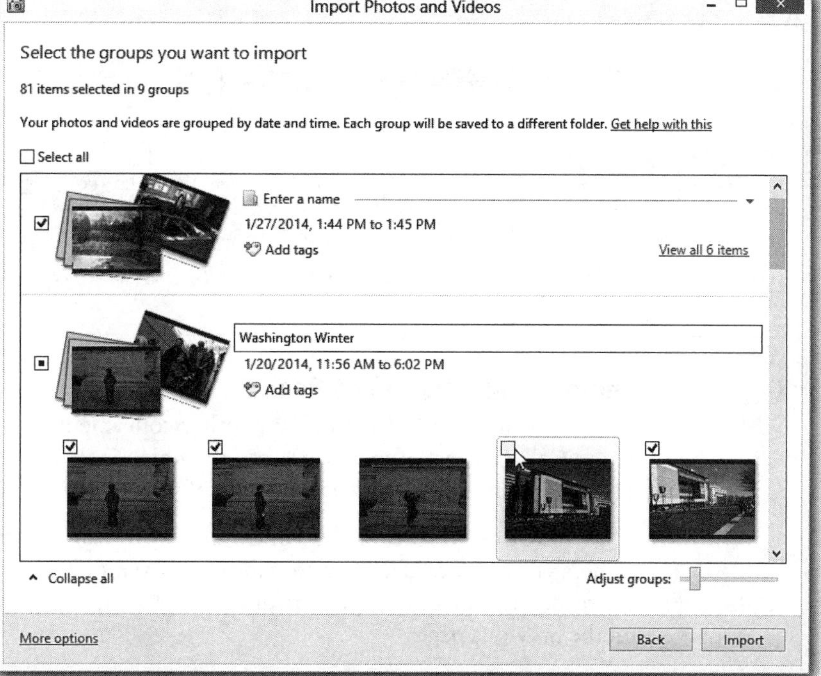

Figure 17-4: *Top: Do you want to examine the various clumps of photos before importing them? Or do you want to just slurp them all in at once and organize them later?*

Bottom: In this box, you can break up the camera's contents into batches by date. You can also apply tags (keywords) to each batch. Above all, you can turn each group's checkbox on or off, thereby importing only certain ones.

Out of the box, Photo Gallery starts a new group after every 30 minutes of no picture-taking. But the "Adjust groups" slider can make that interval greater—a couple of hours, a whole day, even a whole month—which results in fewer separate groups. You can even drag the slider all the way to the right for "All items in one group," if you like.

5a. Click "Import all new items now." Enter a description, like "Fall Fun."

Photo Gallery also invites you to type in *tags* to each of the incoming photos, separated by semicolons. More on tags later in this chapter; for now, it's enough to know that you can use them to specify who was on the trip, the circumstances of the shoot, and so on.

Click Import when you're ready. Photo Gallery brings the photos onto your PC.

6. **Click Import.**

Windows sets about sucking in the photos from the camera and placing them into your Pictures folder.

Not all loose and squirming—that'd be a mess. Instead, it neatly creates a Photo Gallery folder bearing the name or description you provided in step 5. (If you were to open the Pictures folder in File Explorer, you'd discover that there's a new folder *there*, too, bearing the same name. Photo Gallery is just a mirror of what's in your Pictures folder.) See Figure 17-5.

Tip: You can fiddle with Windows' folder- and photo-naming conventions by choosing File→Options→Import in Photo Gallery. For example, you can opt to have the subfolder named after the date the pictures were *taken* instead of the date they were *imported*.

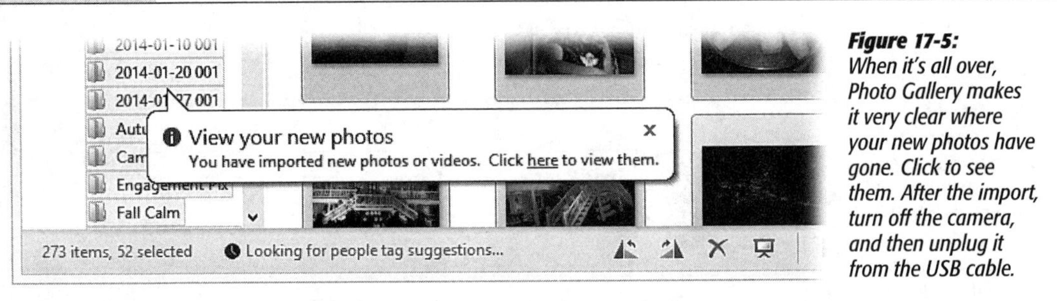

***Figure 17-5:** When it's all over, Photo Gallery makes it very clear where your new photos have gone. Click to see them. After the import, turn off the camera, and then unplug it from the USB cable.*

Photos from a USB Card Reader

A USB *memory card reader* offers another convenient way to transfer photos into Photo Gallery. Most of these card readers, which look like tiny disk drives, are under $15; some can read more than one kind of memory card.

If you have a reader, then instead of connecting the camera to the PC, you can slip the camera's memory card directly into the reader. Windows, or Photo Gallery, recognizes the reader as though it's a camera and offers to import the photos, just as described on the previous pages.

This method eliminates the battery drain involved in pumping the photos straight off the camera. Furthermore, it's less hassle to pull a memory card out of your camera and slip it into your card reader (which you can leave always plugged in) than it is to constantly plug and unplug camera cables.

The File Format Factor

Photo Gallery recognizes the most common photo file formats: JPEG, TIFF, PNG, BMP, and WPD, for example. (It doesn't recognize GIF files or Photoshop files.)

Movies

Photo Gallery can also import and organize camera videos, *if* the movies are in a format that Movie Maker can understand, like .mov, .wmv, .asf, .mpeg, or .avi format.

To play one of these movies once they're in Photo Gallery, see Figure 17-6.

Figure 17-6: *The first frame of each video clip shows up as though it's a photo in your library. Your only clues that it's a movie and not a photo are the film sprocket holes along the sides and the tooltip that identifies the movie's running time. If you double-click one, it opens up and begins to play immediately.*

GEM IN THE ROUGH

Auto Card Erase

Ordinarily, each time your camera's card is full, you'll want to dump all the selected pictures onto your PC.

The question is: After you've finished dumping them, do you want the memory card erased, so that it's empty and ready to reuse?

Or would you prefer to leave the photos on the card, either to erase yourself or to add more photos to them?

If it's safety you're worried about, don't bother. There's zero risk that you'll lose pictures if lightning strikes in mid-import; Photo Gallery doesn't delete your pictures until *after* it has successfully copied them all to the Pictures folder. Even so, Windows doesn't delete imported photos unless you tell it to.

To do that, in Photo Gallery, choose File→Options. Click the Import tab. There you see the "Delete files from this device after importing" checkbox.

RAW files

Finally, Photo Gallery can work with RAW files. And what's a RAW file? Most digital cameras work like this: When you squeeze the shutter button, the camera studies the data picked up by its sensors. The circuitry then makes decisions about sharpening level, contrast, saturation, white balance, and so on—and then saves the processed image as a compressed JPEG file on your memory card.

For millions of people, the result is just fine, even terrific. But all that in-camera processing drives professionals nuts. They'd much rather preserve every last shred of original picture information, no matter how huge the resulting file—and then process the file *by hand* once it's been safely transferred to the PC, using a program like Photoshop.

That's the idea behind the RAW file format, an option in many pricier digital cameras. (RAW stands for nothing in particular.) A RAW image isn't processed at all; it's a complete record of all the data passed along by the camera's sensors. As a result, each RAW photo takes up much more space on your memory card.

But once RAW files open up on the PC, image-manipulation nerds can perform astounding acts of editing to them. They can actually change the lighting of the scene—retroactively! And they don't lose a speck of image quality along the way.

Most people use a program like Photoshop or Photoshop Elements to do this kind of editing. But humble little Photo Gallery can at least open and organize them—usually. Its success at this depends on *which* kind of RAW files you've added to your Pictures folder. Each camera company (Canon, Nikon, and so on) has created a different flavor of RAW files—their filename suffixes are things like .cr2, .crw, .dng, .nef, .orf, .rw2, .pef, .arw, .sr2, and .srf—and it's up to Microsoft to keep Photo Gallery updated. If there are RAW files in your Pictures folder but they're not showing up in Photo Gallery, well, now you know the reason.

UP TO SPEED

Scanning Photos

Microsoft has outsourced the task of scanning to two different programs. When you want to scan documents, you're supposed to use Windows Fax and Scan. When you want to scan photos, though, stay right where you are–in Photo Gallery.

When a scanner is turned on and connected to the PC, choose File→"Import from a camera or scanner," clicking the scanner's name in the next dialog box and then clicking Import. The New Scan dialog box appears. From the Profile list, choose Photo. You can also specify a color format, file format, resolution, and so on.

Click Preview to see what lies ahead. If it all looks good, click Scan.

As usual, Photo Gallery offers to tag the picture; click Import. After a moment, the freshly scanned photo pops up in the Photo Gallery viewer, ready for you to fix and organize it.

Behind the scenes, Photo Gallery dumps the scanned file into the Pictures folder. (You can override this setting by choosing File→Options→Import tab within Photo Gallery. Click "Settings for," choose Cameras, click Browse, and then find the folder you prefer.)

Note: You can open a RAW file for editing in Photo Gallery, but you're never making changes to the original file. Photo Gallery automatically creates a *copy* of the photo–in JPEG format–and lets you edit *that*.

The Post-Dump Slideshow

If you're like most people, the first thing you want to do after dumping the photos from your camera into your PC is to see them at full size, filling your screen. That's the beauty of Photo Gallery's slideshow feature.

To begin the slideshow, specify which pictures you want to see. For example:

- To see the pictures you most recently imported, click the folder Photo Gallery just created.
- If "All photos and videos" (your whole library) is selected, then click one of the photo-batch headings in the main window—for example C:\Users\Public\Pictures\Ski Trip.

Now click the Slideshow button at the bottom of the window (), or just hit F12 or Alt+S. Photo Gallery fades out of view, and a big, brilliant, full-screen slideshow of the new photos—and even self-playing videos—begins (Figure 17-7).

Figure 17-7: *As the slideshow progresses, you can pause the show or change the transition effects, courtesy of these controls.*

What's really useful are the controls shown in Figure 17-7. You make them appear by wiggling your mouse once the show begins.

Click Back to Photo Gallery, or press the Esc key, to end the slideshow.

Note: Photo Gallery can't play music with your slides. (Bummer.) Microsoft cheerfully suggests that if you want music, you can first pop into another program (like Windows Media Player) to start playback, then return to Photo Gallery to start the slides.

Or, if you're really serious and you're willing to put in some effort, click "Create movie." Photo Gallery hands off the project to Movie Maker, where you can add music (and even upload the result to YouTube).

Slideshow themes

If you wiggle the mouse during a slideshow to make the control bar appear, you see an odd little button called "Change theme" at the left side.

A theme is a canned special-effect set for a slideshow: panning, zooming, and cross-fading in various different ways. For example, "Pan and Zoom" makes the pictures smoothly crossfade, panning and zooming as they go, as in a Ken Burns documentary on PBS. "Black and white" and "Sepia" take out all the color.

Sharing a slideshow

The "Share slide show" link lets you post your magnificent slideshow online, on any of the usual movie or photo-sharing Web sites: Facebook, YouTube, Vimeo, or Flickr. You can also drop it directly onto your SkyDrive.

If you choose a Web site's name, you're asked to log in with your name and password for that service. In most cases, you have to enter a title, a description, and a category. When it's all over, Photo Gallery turns your slideshow into a movie file, showing your adoring fans exactly the same fading, panning, zooming slideshow you saw on your screen.

The Digital Shoebox

If you've imported your photos into Photo Gallery, you now see a neatly arranged grid of thumbnails in the main photo-viewing area. This is, presumably, your entire photo collection, including every last picture you've ever imported—the digital equivalent of that old shoebox you've had stuffed in the closet for the past 10 years.

Your journey out of chaos has begun. From here, you can sort your photos, give them titles, group them into smaller subcollections (called albums), and tag them with keywords so you can find them quickly.

The Bigger Picture

If you point to a photo thumbnail without clicking, Photo Gallery is kind enough to display, at your cursor tip, a larger version of it. Think of it as a digital version of the magnifying loupe that art experts use to inspect gemstones and paintings.

Tip: If this feature gets on your nerves, choose File→Options, and then turn off "Show photo and video previews in tooltips."

You can also make *all* the thumbnails in Photo Gallery grow or shrink using the Size slider—the horizontal slider at the lower-right corner of the window. Drag the slider all the way left, and you get micro-thumbnails so small that you can fit 200 or more of them in the window. If you drag it all the way to the right, you end up with such large thumbnails that only a few fit the screen at a time.

For the biggest view of all, though, double-click a thumbnail. It opens all the way, filling the window. At this point, you can edit the picture, too, as described below.

The Navigation Tree

Even before you start naming your photos, assigning them keywords, or organizing them into albums, Photo Gallery imposes an order of its own on your digital shoebox.

The key to understanding it is the *navigation tree* at the left side of the Photo Gallery window. This list grows as you import more pictures and organize them.

The first icon in the navigation tree, "All photos and videos," is a very reassuring little icon, because no matter how confused you may get in working with subsets of photos later in your Photo Gallery life, clicking this icon returns you to your entire picture collection. It makes *all* your photos and videos appear in the viewing area.

Click a folder in the list to see only those photos.

Tip: You can Ctrl-click several folders in the list at once. For example, if you want to see both Family photos *and* Vacation photos, click Family, and then Ctrl-click Vacation.

Click the My Pictures or My Videos subhead to filter out the thumbnails so that *only* photos or *only* videos are visible.

Tip: You can drag thumbnails onto folders in the Folder list to sort them into different locations. (Yes, you can actually move them around the hard drive this way.)

Working with Your Photos

Browsing, selecting, and opening photos is straightforward. Here's everything you need to know:

- Use the vertical scroll bar, or your mouse's scroll wheel, to navigate through your thumbnails.
- To create the most expansive photo-viewing area possible, you can hide or show two space-eating panels: the Ribbon and the "Tag and caption pane" at the right side of the window.

  To collapse the Ribbon, click the ^ button at its upper right. To hide or show the tag and caption pane, click "Tag and caption pane" on the Ribbon's View tab.

Category Groupings

Each time you import a new set of photos into Photo Gallery, it appears with its own heading. Each batch is like one film roll you've had developed. Photo Gallery starts out sorting your photo library chronologically, meaning that the most recently imported photos appear at the top of the window.

Tip: If you'd prefer that the most recent items appear at the *bottom* of the Photo Gallery window instead of the top, click "Reverse sort" on the Ribbon's View tab.

You can exploit these mini-categories within Photo Gallery in several ways:

- For speed in scrolling through a big photo collection, you can *collapse* these groupings so only their names are visible. To do that, just click the tiny ▸ button at the left end of each horizontal line.
- The "categories" don't have to be chronological. You can also ask Photo Gallery to cluster your photos into other logical groups: by rating (all the five-starrers together), by date taken, by person (who's in the photo), and so on. Just click the desired button at the left end of the Ribbon's View tab.

Selecting Photos

To highlight a single picture in preparation for printing, opening, duplicating, or deleting, click its thumbnail once with the mouse.

That much may seem obvious. But first-time PC users may not know how to manipulate *more* than one icon at a time—an essential survival skill.

To highlight multiple photos, use one of these techniques:

- **To select all the photos.** Select all the pictures in the set you're viewing by pressing Ctrl+A (the equivalent of the Select All command on the Ribbon's Edit tab).
- **To select several photos by dragging.** You can drag diagonally to highlight a group of nearby photos. You don't even have to enclose the thumbnails completely; your cursor can touch any part of any icon to highlight it. In fact, if you keep dragging past the edge of the window, the window scrolls automatically.
- **To select consecutive photos.** Click the first thumbnail you want to highlight, and then Shift-click the last one. All the files in between are automatically selected, along with the two photos you clicked. This trick mirrors the way Shift-clicking works in a word processor, the Finder, and many other kinds of programs.
- **To select nonconsecutive photos.** If you want to highlight only, for example, the first, third, and seventh photos in a window, start by clicking the photo icon of the first one. Then Ctrl-click each of the other two. Each thumbnail darkens to indicate that you've selected it. (You can also click the checkbox in the upper-left corner of each photo as you point to it.)

  If you're highlighting a long string of photos and then click one by mistake, you don't have to start over. Instead, just Ctrl-click it again, and the highlighting disappears. (If you do want to start over from the beginning, however, just deselect all selected photos by clicking any empty part of the window.)

The Ctrl-key trick is especially handy if you want to select *almost* all the photos in a window. Press Ctrl+A to select everything in the folder, and then Ctrl-click any unwanted photos to deselect them. You'll save a lot of time and clicking.

Tip: You can also combine the Ctrl-clicking business with the Shift-clicking trick. For instance, you could click the first photo, then Shift-click the 10th, to highlight the first 10. Next, you could Ctrl-click photos 2, 5, and 9 to *remove* them from the selection.

Once you've highlighted multiple photos, you can manipulate them all at once. For example, you can drag them en masse out of the window and onto your desktop—a quick way to export them.

In addition, when multiple photos are selected, the commands in the shortcut menu (which you can access by right-clicking any *one* of the icons)—like Rotate, Copy, Delete, Rename, or Properties—apply to all the photos simultaneously.

Deleting Photos

As every photographer knows—make that every *good* photographer—not every photo is a keeper. You can relegate items to the Recycle Bin by selecting one or more thumbnails and then performing one of the following:

- Right-click a photo, and then choose Delete from the shortcut menu.
- Click the red, slashy X button at the bottom of the window, or the Delete button on the Ribbon's Home tab.
- Press Ctrl+D, or press the Delete key on your keyboard.

Note: That's the forward-delete key, not the regular delete (Backspace) key. In Photo Gallery, the Backspace key means "go back to the previous view," just as in a Web browser.

GEM IN THE ROUGH

Syncing Photo Collections Between Two PCs

How's this for an unsung feature? Photo Gallery can keep your photo collection synchronized between two computers. If you return from a trip, your laptop bristling with new shots, they'll be automatically copied into your big desktop PC.

To set this up, sign into Windows Live on both PCs (click "Sign in" in the upper-right corner of Photo Gallery, if necessary). On the laptop, sign out again (click "Sign out," top right), and then sign right back in again. You're asked if you want your gallery synced with the other PC. Click Sync.

The rest is automatic. (Note: This feature is brought to you by your SkyDrive.)

If you suddenly decide you don't really want to get rid of any of these trashed photos, it's easy to resurrect them. Switch to the desktop, open the Recycle Bin, and then drag the thumbnails out of the window and back into your Pictures folder.

(Of course, if you haven't deleted the imported pictures from your camera, you can still recover the original files and reimport them even after you empty the Recycle Bin.)

Duplicating a Photo

It's often useful to have two copies of a picture. For example, a photo whose dimensions are appropriate for a slideshow or a desktop picture (that is, a 4:3 proportion) isn't proportioned correctly for ordering prints (4 × 6, 8 × 10, or whatever). To use the same photo for both purposes, you really need to crop two copies independently.

To make a copy of a photo, you can copy and paste it right back where it is. That's easy, thanks to the Copy and Paste icons on the Ribbon's Home tab.

The Info Pane

Behind the scenes, Photo Gallery stores a wealth of information about each individual photo in your collection. To take a peek, highlight a thumbnail; if you don't already see the details pane at the right side of the window (Figure 17-8), then click the "Tag and caption pane" button on the Ribbon's View tab.

How does Photo Gallery know so much about how your photos were taken? Most digital cameras embed a wealth of image, camera, lens, and exposure information in the photo files they create, using a standard data format called *XMP* (Extensible Metadata Platform) or *EXIF* (Exchangeable Image Format). With that in mind, Photo Gallery automatically scans photos for XMP or EXIF data as it imports them (see Figure 17-8).

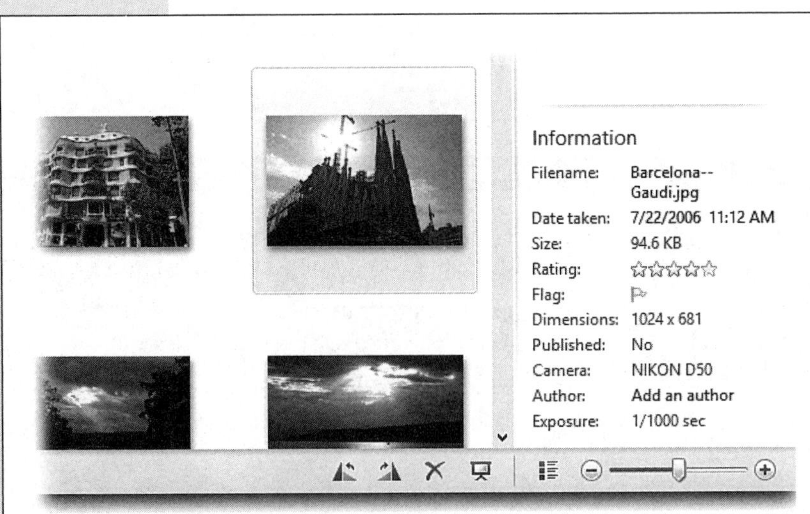

Figure 17-8: *The Information pane reveals a picture's name, rating, creation time and date, dimensions (in pixels), file size, camera settings, and any comments you've typed into the Captions area. It isn't just a place to look at the details of your pictures, though. You can also edit a lot of it. You can even change the date a photo was taken–a good tip to remember if you're a defense attorney.*

Note: Some cameras do a better job than others at embedding EXIF data in photo files. Photo Gallery can extract this information only if it's been properly stored by the camera when the digital photo was created. Of course, most of this information is missing if your photos didn't come from a digital camera (if they were scanned in, for example).

Titles

You can rename a photo easily enough. Just click its existing name in the Info panel, and then retype it.

Tip: Most people find this feature especially valuable when it comes to individual photographs. When you import them from your digital camera, the pictures bear useless gibberish names like CRS000321.JPG, CRS000322.JPG, and so on. If you highlight a *bunch* of photos and then change the title, you're renaming *all* of them at once. Photo Gallery even numbers them.

You can also *batch rename* a bunch of photos—so that they're called Spaghetti On Baby's Head 1, Spaghetti On Baby's Head 2, and so on. Just select the batch and then click the Rename button on the Ribbon's Edit tab.

While you can make a photo's title as long as you want, it's smart to keep it short (about 10 characters or so). This way, you can see all or most of the title in the Title field (or under the thumbnails).

Tip: Once you've gone to the trouble of naming your photos, you can make these names appear right beneath the thumbnails for convenient reference. On the Ribbon's View tab, click "File name."

Conveniently enough, the same tab has buttons for *other* things you can display beneath each photo: "File size," "Date taken," "Image size," "Date modified," and so on. Each of these infobits can appear in place of the file name.

Dates

Weirdly enough, you can even edit the dates the pictures were taken—a handy fix if, for example, the camera's clock wasn't set right. Just click the date or time, and then either retype the date digits or click the ▾ button to open a clickable calendar.

FREQUENTLY ASKED QUESTION

Your Own Personal Sorting Order

I want to put my photos in my own order. I'm making a slideshow, and I want to dictate the sequence. How do I do that?

You can't.

At least not without a lot of effort–namely, by manually renaming the photos so that their names are 000 Beach, 001 Sunset, and so on.

To rename a photo, click it once. See the Info pane at the right side of the window? (If not, click Info in the toolbar.) Click the photo's name to open its photo-editing box.

If you want to *drag* photos into a new order–say, for the purposes of a slideshow movie–you have to do it in Movie Maker.

Ratings, flags
Read on!

People, Tags, Geotags, Captions, Ratings, and Flags

It's awfully hard for software to search for a photo by what it *shows*. Scientists are working on this problem, but at the moment, only a human can quickly spot a photo that shows "Uncle Frank looking humiliated on his porch."

Photo Gallery helps to solve this problem with five powerful text bits that you can associate with each photo—and search for them:

- **People tags.** The program can instantly locate all photos of a certain person—either because you've hand-labeled those photos, or because you've used its face-recognition feature to label those photos automatically.
- **Descriptive tags** are descriptive keywords—like *Family*, *Vacation*, or *Kids*—that you can use to label and categorize your photos and videos.
- **Geotags.** Some cameras (and most phones) can automatically stamp each photo not just with the time and date you took it, but also with *where* you took it. The geographic coordinates are embedded right into the file itself.
- **Captions.** Sometimes you need more than a one- or two-word title to describe a picture. Fortunately, Photo Gallery lets you add much longer captions to your photos.
- **Ratings** are, of course, star ratings from 0 to 5, meaning that you can categorize your pictures by how great they are.

The beauty of people tags, geotags, captions, descriptive tags, and ratings is that they're searchable. Want to comb through all the photos in your library to find every closeup taken of your children during summer vacation? Instead of browsing through dozens of folders, just click the tags *Kids*, *Vacation*, *Closeup*, and *Summer* in the navigation tree. You'll have the results in seconds.

Or want to gather only the cream of the crop into a slideshow or DVD? Let Photo Gallery produce a display of only your five-star photos.

Here's a walkthrough of these five data features.

People Tags

Photo Gallery may not be able to tell what's in a photo, but it's taken one giant step toward that ambitious software goal: It can automatically identify whose *face* is in a photo. Once it knows who's in which photos, it's easy to round up all photos of, say, Grandpappy. And when you post photos to Facebook, those "who is this?" tags go along for the ride; they're alive even when they're on your Facebook page.

Tagging one person at a time

You have to help Photo Gallery out first, though, by holding a few training sessions, like this:

1. **On the Ribbon's Home tab, click "People tag."**

   A new panel appears at the right side of the screen, called "People tags." It's a list of everybody in your Contacts app (Figure 17-9, top) (This feature doesn't work unless you've signed into your Microsoft account—and linked your Facebook account to it.)

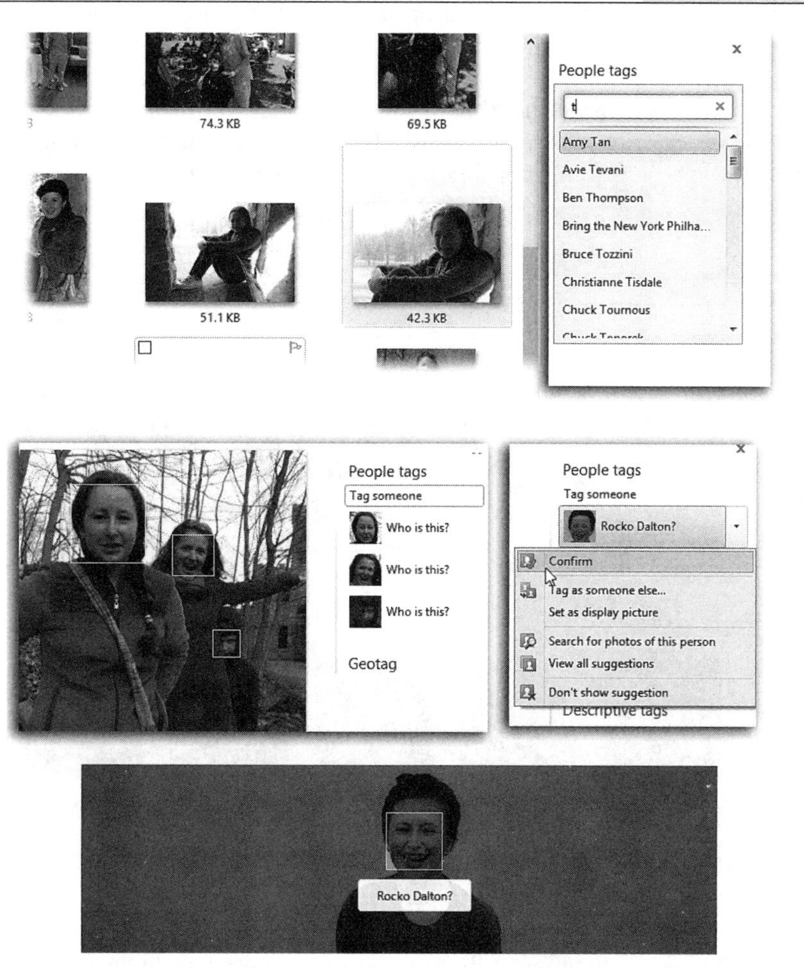

Figure 17-9: *Work through your photos, either thumbnails (top) or opened pictures (bottom), identifying who's in them. Photo Gallery has no trouble picking out faces in your pictures; it just needs you to tell it whose faces they are.*

Once you've done a few, the program seems to get the hang of it. It starts to guess who's in the shot (middle); all you have to do is confirm the guess.

2. **Click a photo's thumbnail. Click where it says "Who is this?" in the "People tags" pane, and tell Photo Gallery who it is.**

   As you type, the program narrows down your master Contacts list. If the person's name isn't already in the list, type the correct name and then click "Add new person."

3. **Press Enter to confirm the name. Click the next thumbnail. Repeat the process.**

   Once you've identified a certain person in a few photos, Photo Gallery starts to catch on. It starts guessing that person's name (Figure 17-9, middle). Whenever it makes a guess, you can click the guess and, from the shortcut menu, choose Confirm.

   You can also tag people in photos you've opened up to full size by double-clicking their thumbnails (Figure 17-9, bottom).

Batch tagging

Once you've tagged a few people, you can blow through your entire photo collection, confirming many people's faces at once.

Click "Batch people tag" on the Ribbon's Home tab, and then proceed as shown in Figure 17-10.

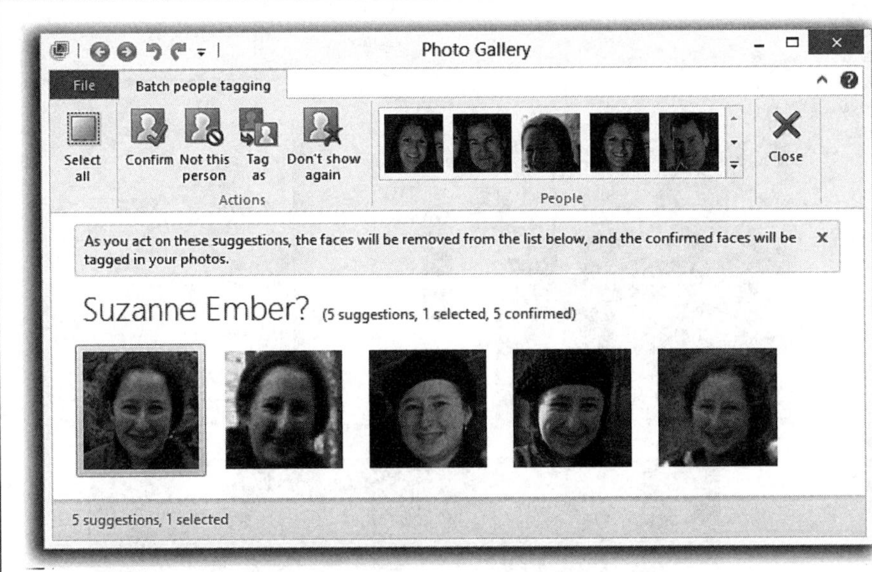

Figure 17-10: *Click the first face in the rogue's gallery at top; Photo Gallery displays closeups of everyone in your photo collection that seems to be that person. Select each thumbnail (or Select All) and click Confirm. Click the next headshot at top; lather, rinse, repeat.*

In essence, Photo Gallery is rounding up all the faces it can find that seem to match, and allowing you to confirm all of them at once. (Well, about 11 at a time.)

If you see a face that Photo Gallery can't put a name to, click it and then click "Tag as."

As you go, you can always re-tag someone, remove a tag, or combine two tags into a single new name, using the commands in the menu shown in Figure 17-9, middle.

Using people tags

The fun begins once you've tagged your photos so that Photo Gallery knows who's in them. Does your kid need a really good shot of Grandpa for a school project? One click later, you're looking at your entire Grandpa collection.

On the Home tab of the Ribbon, just click the face of the person you want to find. (If you're not seeing all known faces, then use the tiny vertical scroll arrows.) Or just point without clicking to scan your various people collections.

A similar set of "click me" headshots awaits on the Find tab of the Ribbon. It's handy both because it shows more headshots without scrolling, and also because it has "and" and "or" buttons. That's handy when, for example, you want to find a photo that contains Grandpa and Grandma together. Click Grandpa's face, then the "and" button, and then Grandma's face. Photo Gallery shows you only photos of the couple.

Descriptive Tags

As you work with your photos (and read this chapter), you'll soon discover the convenience of adding *tags* (keywords) to them, like Family, Trips, or Baby Pix.

A tag is a keyword you can attach to a photo so it's easier to search for it later. You can create as many tag labels as you want to create a meaningful, customized list.

To build your list, you can operate in either of two ways:

- **In the "Tags and captions" pane.** On the Ribbon's Home tab, click "Descriptive tags." Your cursor pops into the "Descriptive tags" box in the "Tags and captions" pane, so that you can type a tag. As you type, Photo Gallery proposes previous tags spelled the same way to save you typing.
- **In the Manage Tags window.** On the Ribbon's Home tab, click the ▾; from the shortcut menu, choose "Manage tags." You get a Manage Tags window, where you can rapidly enter a bunch of tag names.

It may take some time to develop a really good master set of keywords. The idea is to assign labels that are general enough to apply across your entire photo collection, but specific enough to be meaningful when conducting searches.

Applying tags

Photo Gallery offers two methods of applying tags to your pictures:

- **Method 1: Drag the picture.** One way to apply tags to photos is, paradoxically, to apply the *photos* to the *tags*. That is, drag relevant photos directly onto the tags in the navigation tree, as shown in Figure 17-11.

Tip: You can apply as many tags to an individual photo as you like. A picture of your cousin Rachel at a hot dog–eating contest in London might bear all of these keywords: Rachel, Relatives, Travel, Food, Humor, and Medical Crises. Later, you'll be able to find that photo no matter which of these categories you're hunting for.

This method is best when you want to apply a whole bunch of pictures to one or two keywords. It's pretty tedious, however, when you want to apply a lot of different keywords to a single photo. That's why Microsoft has given you a second method, described next.

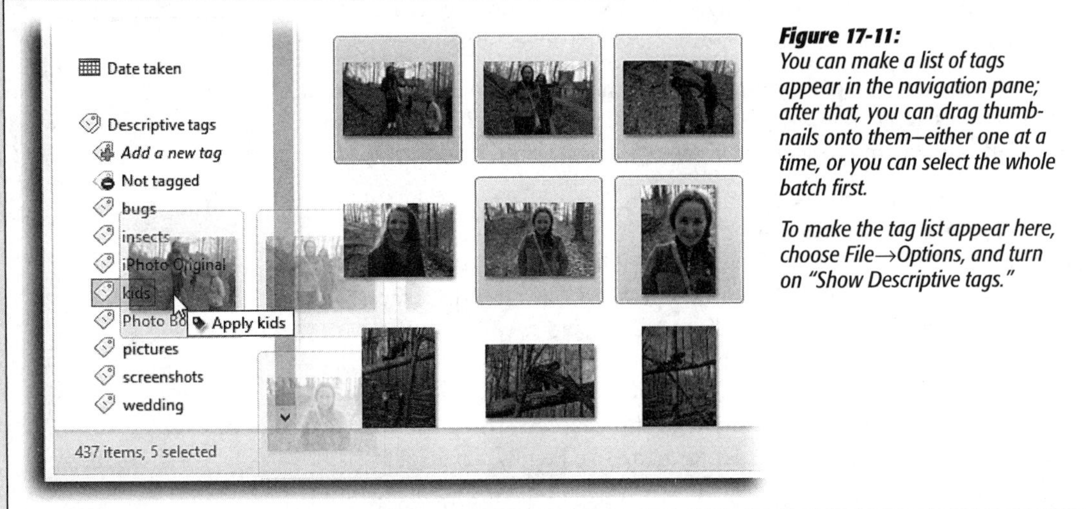

Figure 17-11: *You can make a list of tags appear in the navigation pane; after that, you can drag thumbnails onto them–either one at a time, or you can select the whole batch first.*

To make the tag list appear here, choose File→Options, and turn on "Show Descriptive tags."

- **Method 2: Use the tag and captions pane.** Highlight a thumbnail. On the tag and captions pane, you find a simple list of all the tags you've applied to this photo. Add a tag by clicking "Add descriptive tags" and then typing a tag name (or as much as necessary for Photo Gallery to AutoComplete it).

  The beauty of this system is that you can *keep the little info pane open* on the screen as you move through your photo collection. Each time you click a photo—or, in fact, select a group of them—the tags list updates itself to reflect the tags of whatever is now selected.

Editing or removing tags

To *remove* tag assignments from a certain picture, right-click the name of the tag. From the shortcut menu, choose "Remove tag."

To edit a tag: On the Ribbon's Home tab, click the ▾; from the shortcut menu, choose "Manage tags." You get a Manage Tags window, where you can edit a tag name by clicking it and then retyping.

Note: Be careful about renaming tags after you've started using them; the results can be messy. If you've already applied the keyword *Fishing* to a batch of photos but later decide to replace it with *Romantic* in your keyword list, then all the fishing photos automatically inherit the keyword Romantic. Depending on you and your interests, this may not be what you intended.

Using tags

The big payoff for your diligence arrives when you need to get your hands on a specific set of photos, because Photo Gallery lets you *isolate* them with one quick click.

To round up all the photos with, say, the Kids tag, click the Find tab of the Ribbon. From the Tags pop-up menu, choose the tag you want. (You can also point to the tag names in this menu without clicking for real-time previews of the matching photos.) Photo Gallery immediately rounds up all photos labeled with that tag, displays them in the photo-viewing area, and hides all others.

Note: Windows can't embed metadata (and therefore tags or star ratings) to BMP, PNG, GIF, or MPEG files. Actually, you can apply such identifying information to those file types *in Photo Gallery,* but it won't show up in Explorer windows or anywhere else in Windows (like the Photo Viewer program).

You also won't be able to apply Windows-wide metadata to files that are locked, in use by another program, or corrupted.

More tips:

- To find photos that match multiple keywords, just open the Tags pop-up menu (on the Find tab of the Ribbon) and click additional tag labels. For example, if you click Travel and click Holidays, Photo Gallery reveals all the pictures that have *both* of those keywords.

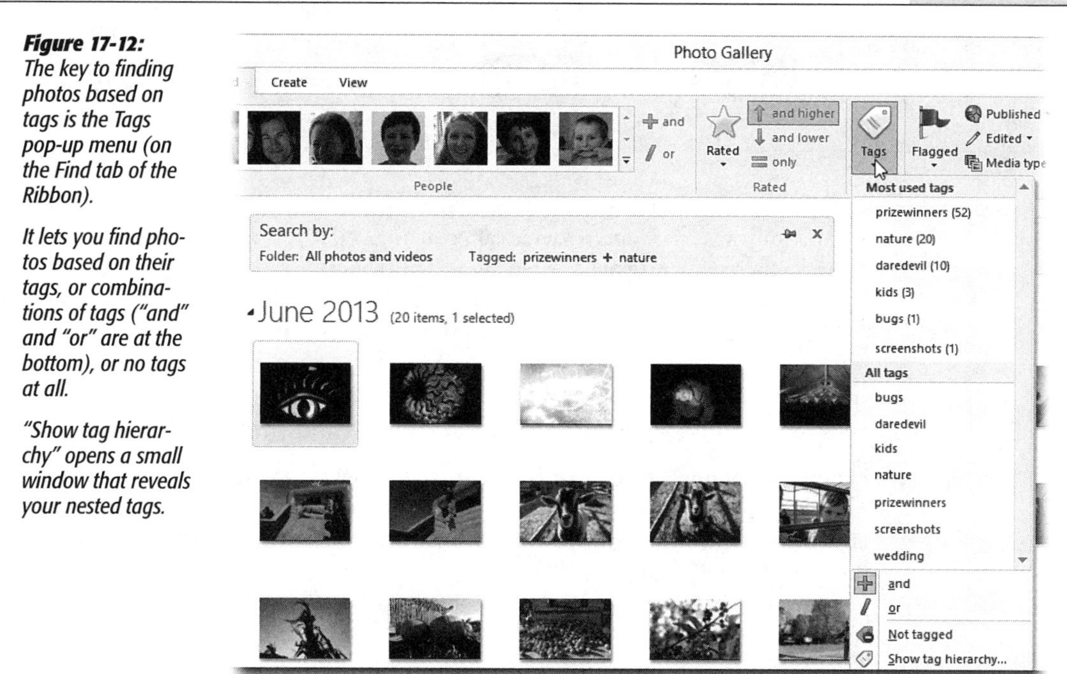

Figure 17-12: *The key to finding photos based on tags is the Tags pop-up menu (on the Find tab of the Ribbon).*

It lets you find photos based on their tags, or combinations of tags ("and" and "or" are at the bottom), or no tags at all.

"Show tag hierarchy" opens a small window that reveals your nested tags.

- You can even perform an "or" keyword roundup—that is, to find pictures that have *either* Travel *or* Holidays tags. To do that, choose "or" from the Tags pop-up menu.
- As you find photos based on tags, the information bar above the thumbnails summarizes what you've done so far, as shown in Figure 17-13. Click the **×** at the right end to conclude your finding mission and restore the full view of all thumbnails.

Figure 17-13: *As you refine your search using the various pop-up menus and icons on the Find tab, the "Search by" bar reveals the search criteria you've built so far.*

If you make a mistake, you can point to a criterion to reveal its **×** *(Remove) button. Or click the main* **×** *button (top right of the "Search by" bar) to cancel the search.*

- If you've added the tag list to the navigation tree as described in Figure 17-11,you can drag tags up or down to rearrange them. And if you drag a tag *on top of* another one, it becomes a *subtag* (nested tag). That is, you could have a tag called Trips, and then subtags called Vermont, Florida, and Ohio. As the tag list grows, remember that you can collapse any branch of the tree by clicking its flippy triangle.

Geotags

Your camera invisibly stamps the time on every photo—why not the place?

Most smartphones, some cameras, and some memory cards do exactly that. They have GPS circuitry that embeds location coordinates on every shot you take. In Photo Gallery, you can search or sort your photos by where they were shot, or even look at their origins on a map.

The geotagging information is visible on the tag and caption pane, right along with all the other information about a selected photo. (If the pane isn't open, click Geotag on the Ribbon's Home tab. Or "Tag and caption pane" on the View tab, for that matter.)

Most cameras, of course, don't have GPS features; fortunately, you can also add location data manually. Select a photo (or a bunch); under the Geotag heading in the tag and caption pane, click "Add geotag." Start typing a place name (city, state, country) until Photo Gallery autocompletes it for you.

Tip: This feature requires an Internet connection. Microsoft's Bing servers supply the place info.

After you've assigned some geotags, you can harness their power like this:

- **Sort by location.** On the Ribbon's View tab, in the box at far left, click Geotag. All your thumbnails are now sorted by location, with place-name headings to match.
- **Search by location.** On the Ribbon's Find tab, click "Text search." Now you can find photos by typing a place name.
- **See on a map.** If you right-click the geotag itself (in the tag and caption pane), you can choose "Map it" from the shortcut menu. You're taken into your Web browser, where the correct slice of Bing Maps appears. A numbered circle identifies the exact spot where the photo was taken. (Other programs, like Picasa, and Web sites like Flickr, can also show you geotags on a map.)

Tip: Usually, the tag and caption pane identifies only the city name. But if it has more specific details, like a street address, you can point to the geotag without clicking to see a tooltip containing the full address.

Captions

Tags are fine, but a word or two is not very descriptive. Fortunately, you can also add true captions to your photos. The best thing about adding them is that they're searchable. After you've entered all this free-form data, you can use it to quickly locate a photo using the "Text search" button on the Ribbon's Find tab, as described below.

To add a caption, click the Caption button (on the Ribbon's Home tab). The corresponding box appears in the "Tag and caption" pane; type away.

Even if you don't write full-blown captions for your pictures, you can use the Captions box to store little details, such as the names, places, dates, and events associated with your photos.

Ratings

Photo Gallery offers another way to slice and dice your photo collection: by how great they are! You can assign each picture a rating, from one to five stars, and then use the ratings to sort your library or round up only, for example, the cream of the crop for a book or a slideshow.

Here are a couple of ways to rate your digital masterpieces. In each case, begin by highlighting a thumbnail (or several). Then:

- From the Ribbon's Home tab, use the Rate ▾ pop-up menu to choose 0, 1, 2, 3, 4, or 5 stars.
- Highlight a thumbnail (or several); press the number keys on your keyboard, from 0 through 5.
- Click the corresponding star in the "Tag and caption" pane.

Once you've rated your photos, you can make that effort pay off in any number of ways:

- **Sort by ratings.** At the left end of the Ribbon's View tab, there's a set of icons that control how the photos are sorted. Click Ratings.

  Usually, the best photos appear at the top, and the worst ones (0 stars) at the bottom. Click "Reverse sort" to put the unrated photos and the duds at the top.
- **View ratings.** On the Ribbon's View tab, click the big Rating icon. The program displays a small row of stars beneath every thumbnail, showing you all the ratings at once.
- **Find by ratings.** You can round up all the five-star photos in the current folder. On the Ribbon's Find tab, use the Ratings pop-up menu to choose a number of stars (from 0 to 5). Then click either "and higher," "and lower," or "only." So to find photos rated three stars or better, you'd choose three stars and click "and higher"; to find only your five-starrers, you'd choose five stars and click "only."

  Click the **×** button (at the top of the "Search by" bar above the thumbnails) to un-hide all the photos.

Flags

Just in case it's not enough to annotate your photos by name, tag, caption, rating, and geotag, Photo Gallery also offers a simple Flag button. A photo can be either flagged or not.

So what does the flag mean? Anything you want it to mean, but usually for temporary organizational tasks.

For example, you might want to cull only the most appropriate images from a photo album for use in a slideshow. As you browse through the images, flag each shot you want. Later you can round up all the images you flagged so you can drag them all into a new album en masse.

To flag a photo, select its thumbnail and click Flag on the Ribbon's Home tab. (You can flag a bunch of them at once, too.) The Flag button darkens whenever this thumbnail is selected. (Unflag the photo by clicking the same button again.)

Tip: Ordinarily, you don't see any flag mark on the *photo itself*—unless you click the Flags button on the Ribbon's View tab.

Now suppose you've worked through all your photos for some purpose, carefully flagging them as you go. Here's the payoff: rounding them up so that you can delete them all, hide them all, incorporate them into a slideshow, export them as a batch, and so on.

On the Ribbon's Find tab, click the Flags button. (You can also find all unflagged photos. Use that button's ▾ button; choose "Unflagged photos" from the pop-up menu.)

Now Photo Gallery shows you all flagged photos in your entire library.

Searching for Photos

Once you've put in all the time required to flag, caption, rate, and people-tag your pictures, you're finally ready to enjoy the fruits of your labors. You can round up certain photos with ridiculous amounts of specificity (Figure 17-13).

On the Ribbon, click the Find tab. Build your search like this:

- Pinpoint the date of the desired photos using the Date, Months, and Years pop-up menus. You can click, say, the 2012 icon to see just the ones you took during that year.

Note: Photo Gallery shows *only* the months and dates in which you actually took pictures; that's why 2013, for example, may show only April, July, and October.

- Pinpoint who's in the photos by clicking the thumbnail headshots.
- Pinpoint the photos' ratings using the Ratings pop-up menu.
- Pinpoint the descriptive tags using the Tags pop-up menu.
- Pinpoint the photos you've flagged using the Flagged pop-up menu.
- Use the Published, Edited, and "Media type" pop-up menus to further characterize the pix you're looking for.
- Using the "Text search" icon, find photos according to the text associated with them: their names, captions, geotags, or folder locations (that is, their folder *paths*).

  As you type, you filter the thumbnails down to just the pictures that match what you've typed so far. You don't have to finish a word, press Enter, or use wildcard characters (*).

  You can type two words (or parts of words) to find pictures that match both. To find all photos of Zelda in Brazil, typing *zel br* will probably do the trick.

  Only beginnings of words count. Typing *llweg* won't find pictures of Renee Zellweger, but *zell* will.

Here's the crazy thing: You can combine all of these search techniques. For example, you can click the Casey tag, and then choose the five-star rating, to find only the very best pictures of Casey. You could then even choose "2013" from the Years icon to further restrict the photos you're seeing.

But why stop there? Then choose Video from the "Media type" pop-up menu, and now you're seeing only the five-star *videos* of Casey in 2013.

Editing Your Shots

Straight from the camera, digital snapshots often need a little bit of help. A photo may be too dark or too light. The colors may be too bluish or too yellowish. The focus may be a little blurry, the camera may have been tilted slightly, or the composition may be somewhat off.

Fortunately, Photo Gallery lets you fine-tune digital images in ways that, in the world of traditional photography, would have required a fully equipped darkroom, several bottles of smelly chemicals, and an X-Acto knife.

In Photo Gallery, you can't paint in additional elements, mask out unwanted backgrounds, or apply 50 different special-effects filters, as you can with editing programs like Photoshop and Photoshop Elements. Nonetheless, Photo Gallery handles basic photo fix-up tasks, many of which work with a single click.

All Photo Gallery editing controls are hanging out on the Ribbon's Edit tab, which appears automatically when you double-click a photo thumbnail to open it.

You exit Edit mode by clicking "Close file" (top right of the window) or by tapping the Esc key.

Ways to Zoom

Before you get deeply immersed in the editing process, it's well worth knowing how to zoom and scroll around, since chances are you'll be doing quite a bit of it.

- **Maximize.** One way to zoom is to change the size of the window itself. Maximize Photo Gallery to enlarge the image.
- **The Size pop-up menu.** Use the Size slider (lower right) to zoom in or out.

Note: The icon beside the size slider means "Fit the photo in the window once again, no matter how much zooming I did." Pressing Ctrl+0 does the same thing.

- **The keyboard.** Press Ctrl+plus and Ctrl+minus to zoom in or out.
- **The mouse wheel.** If your mouse has a scroll wheel on the top, you can zoom in or out by turning that wheel, which is surely the most efficient way of all.

When you're zoomed in, the cursor changes to a friendly little white glove—your clue that you can now scroll the photo in any direction just by dragging. That's more direct than fussing with two independent scroll bars.

Ten Levels of Undo

As long as you remain in Edit mode, you can back out of your latest 10 changes by pressing Ctrl+Z. To change your mind about the *last* change you made, just click the Undo button at the *bottom* of the Fix pane.

But once you leave Edit mode—by returning to the gallery—you lose the ability to undo your individual edits. At this point, the only way to restore your photo to its original state is to click "Revert to original," which removes *all* the edits you've made to the photo since importing it.

Rotate

If your digital camera has a built-in orientation sensor, Photo Gallery attempts to figure out which orientation the photos are supposed to be (horizontal or vertical) at the time you import them.

If it missed a few, however, you can use any of these methods to turn them right-side up:

- Click one of the tiny blue Rotate buttons at the bottom of the main Photo Gallery window. They work either on thumbnails or an open photo.
- Click one of the similar Rotate buttons on the Edit tab of the Ribbon.
- Right-click a thumbnail; from the shortcut menu, choose one of the Rotate commands.

Tip: After importing a batch of photos, you can save a lot of time and mousing if you first select *all* the thumbnails that need rotating (by Ctrl-clicking each, for example). Then use one of the rotation commands above to fix all the selected photos in one fell swoop.

Auto Adjust

The "Auto adjust" button on the Ribbon provides a simple way to improve the appearance of less-than-perfect digital photos. One click applies four fixes at once: straightens out a crooked photo, reduces "noise" (digital grain in low-light pictures), balances and boosts colors, and fixes the exposure (brightness/darkness overall).

You may find that Auto Adjust only minimally improves some photos but dramatically affects others.

Tip: To control which of these four changes the button makes, choose Settings from the button's ▾ menu.

Cropping

You'd be surprised at how many photographs can benefit from selective cropping. You can eliminate parts of a photo you just don't want, improve a photo's composition (filling the frame with your subject often has greater impact), or fit a photo to specific proportions (an important step if you're going to turn your photos into standard-size prints).

Here are the steps for cropping a photo you've double-clicked to open:

1. **On the Ribbon's Edit tab, click Crop.**

   The Crop controls appear.

2. **Constrain the rectangle proportions, if you like (Figure 17-14).**

   In the ▾ menu of the Crop button, you're offered some useful options. The **Proportion** submenu controls the behavior of the cropping tool. When the menu is set to Custom, you can draw a cropping rectangle of any size and proportion, in essence going freehand.

Figure 17-14: *When you crop a picture, you draw a rectangle in any direction using the crosshairs pointer to define the part of the photo you want to keep. (To deselect this area—when you want to start over, for example—click anywhere in the dimmed area.) Once you've drawn the rectangle and clicked Crop, the excess falls to the digital cutting room floor, thus enlarging your subject.*

POWER USERS' CLINIC

Editing Dates, Names, and Resolutions

The instructions in this section help you edit how your photos look. But the Edit tab of the Ribbon also offers three buttons that let you edit some behind-the-scenes photo data that may be just as useful.

The **Rename** button lets you turn a batch of selected thumbnails into a numbered sequence: "Spring Break (1)," "Spring Break (2)," and so on.

The **Resize** button lets you scale down a photo, making it smaller so that it takes up less disk space. You're offered a choice of standard sizes, plus a Custom box.

Finally, there's **Adjust time**. Feel like changing history? This command—actually, the resulting dialog box—lets you change the time stamp on a photo. (If you've selected multiple photos, their time stamps get changed relative to the first one.)

That's a handy feature that lets you fix things up when your camera's clock wasn't set correctly—or when you're a defense attorney trying to twist evidence.

When you choose one of the other options in the pop-up menu, however, Photo Gallery constrains the rectangle you draw to preset proportions. It prevents you from coloring outside the lines, so to speak.

Most digital cameras produce photos whose proportions are 4:3 (width to height). This size is ideal for onscreen slideshows and DVDs, because most PC screens and TVs use 4:3 dimensions, too—but it doesn't divide evenly into standard print photograph sizes.

That's why the Proportion pop-up menu offers canned choices like 4 × 6, 5 × 7, and so on. Limiting your cropping to one of these preset sizes guarantees that your cropped photos will fit perfectly into Kodak (or Shutterfly) prints. If you don't constrain your cropping this way, Kodak—not you—will decide how to crop them to fit.

As soon as you make a selection from this pop-up menu, Photo Gallery draws a preliminary cropping rectangle—of the proper dimensions—on the screen, turning everything outside it slightly dim.

In general, this rectangle always appears in landscape (horizontal) orientation. To make it vertical, click "Rotate frame" from the Crop button's menu.

Often, you'll want to give the cropping job the benefit of your years of training and artistic sensibility by *redrawing* the cropping area.

3. **Drag the tiny white control handles to reshape the cropping rectangle.**

   Drag inside the rectangle to move it relative to the photo itself.

4. **When the cropping rectangle is just the way you want, click the Crop button on the Ribbon (or press Enter).**

   Photo Gallery throws away all the pixels outside the rectangle. Of course, the Undo and Revert commands are always there if you change your mind.

Note: Remember that cropping always shrinks your photos. Remove too many pixels, and your photo may end up too small (that is, with a resolution too low to print or display properly).

Red Eye

You snap a near-perfect family portrait: The focus is sharp, the composition is balanced, everyone's smiling. And then you notice it: Uncle Mitch, standing dead center in the picture, looks like a vampire. His eyes are glowing red, as though illuminated by the evil within.

Red eye is light reflected back from your subject's eyes. The bright light of your flash passes through the pupil of each eye, illuminating and bouncing off of the blood-red retinal tissue at the back of the eye. Red-eye problems worsen when you shoot pictures in a dim room, because your subjects' pupils are dilated wider, allowing even more light from the flash to shine on the retina.

The best course of action is to avoid red eye to begin with—by using an external (not built-in) flash, for example. But if it's too late for that, and people's eyes are already glowing demonically, there's always Photo Gallery's Red Eye tool. It lets you alleviate red-eye problems by digitally removing the offending red pixels.

To fix red eye, zoom in and scroll so that you have a closeup view of the eye with the red-eye problem. Click "Red eye," and then drag a box around each affected eye.

Photo Gallery neutralizes the red pixels, painting them solid black. Of course, this means that everybody winds up looking like they have black eyes instead of red ones—but at least they look a little less like the walking undead.

Retouch

Sometimes an otherwise perfect portrait is spoiled by the tiniest of imperfections—a stray hair or an unsightly blemish, for example. Professional photographers, whether working digitally or in a traditional darkroom, routinely remove such minor imperfections from their final prints—a process known as *retouching*, for clients known as *self-conscious*. (Kidding!)

The Retouch tool lets you do the same thing with your own digital photos. You can paint away scratches, spots, hairs, or any other small flaws in your photos with a few quick strokes.

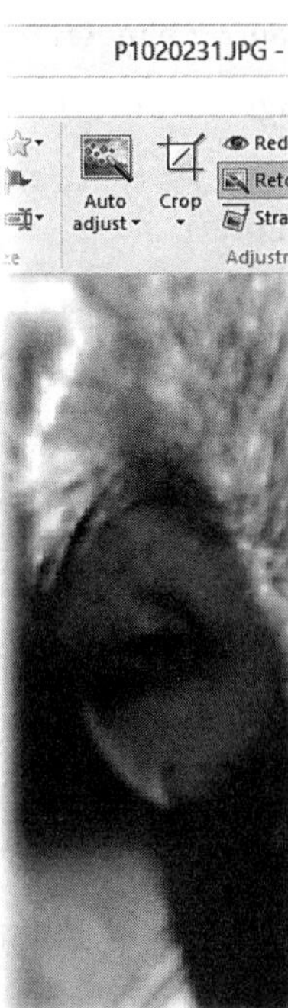

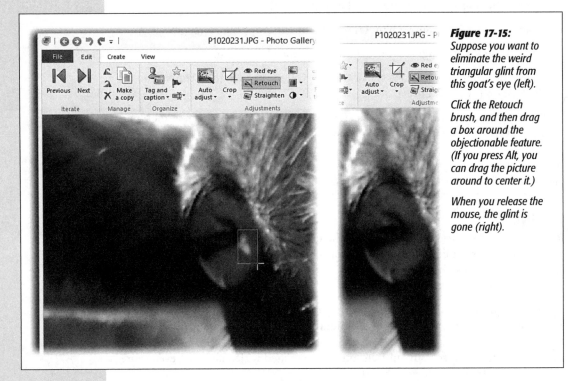

***Figure 17-15:** Suppose you want to eliminate the weird triangular glint from this goat's eye (left).*

Click the Retouch brush, and then drag a box around the objectionable feature. (If you press Alt, you can drag the picture around to center it.)

When you release the mouse, the glint is gone (right).

The operative word here is *small*. The Retouch brush can't completely erase somebody's mustache. It's intended for tiny touch-ups that don't involve repainting whole sections of a photo. (For that kind of photo overhaul, you need a pixel-editing program like Photoshop Elements.)

The Retouch brush works its magic by blending the colors in the tiny area that you're fixing. You can see the effect in Figure 17-15.

Once you've clicked Retouch on the Ribbon, find the imperfection and drag a box around it. If you don't get it right—Retouch can produce some hideous results— you can use the Undo command (Ctrl+Z) to rewind.

Note: On high-resolution photos, it can take a moment or two for Photo Gallery to catch up with you.

Straighten

Off-axis, tilted photos are a fact of photography, and especially of scanning; Photo Gallery makes fixing them incredibly easy. One click on the Straighten button (on the Edit tab of the Ribbon) automatically straightens out most images. The software looks for obvious horizontal or vertical lines in your composition and tilts things so that they're straight.

If you think about it, you can't rotate a rectangular photo without introducing skinny empty triangles at the corners of its "frame." Fortunately, Photo Gallery sneakily eliminates that problem by very slightly magnifying the photo as you straighten it (and thereby slightly losing resolution). Now you're losing skinny triangles at the corners, but at least you don't see empty triangular gaps when the straightening is over.

In other words, the straightening tool isn't a free lunch.

Noise Reduction

In photographic terms, *noise* means graininess—colored speckles. Noise is a common problem in digital photography, especially in low-light shots. Some cameras, for example, claim to have "anti-blur" features that turn out to be nothing more than goosed-up ISO (light-sensitivity) settings in low light. But over ISO 800 or so, the resulting digital noise can be truly hideous.

If a photo looks noisy (grainy), you can lessen the effect with a click on this button (on the Ribbon's Edit tab). It doesn't work wonders. But by subtly smoothing neighboring pixels, it sometimes does a reasonable job of removing noise from low-light photos.

Automatic Color and Exposure Adjustments

Plenty of photos need no help at all. They look fantastic right out of the camera. And plenty of others are ready for prime time after only a single click on the "Auto adjust" button, as described earlier.

If you click Color on the Ribbon, though, you auto-fix only the color tint and saturation. If you click Exposure, you auto-fix just the overall brightness.

Tip: Both of these buttons also have pop-up menus that offer nine other adjustment preset icons. You can point to them without clicking to get a real-time preview of how they'll affect your photo.

Manual Adjustments

The "Fine tune" button opens a panel (Figure 17-16) where you can make *gradations* of the kinds of changes that the Straighten, Noise Reduction, Color, and Exposure buttons make. For example, if a photo looks too dark and murky, you can bring details out of the shadows without blowing out the highlights. If the snow in a skiing shot looks too bluish, you can de-blue it. If the colors don't pop quite enough in the prize-winning-soccer-goal shot, you can boost their saturation levels.

In short, there are fixes the Adjust panels can make that no one-click magic button can touch.

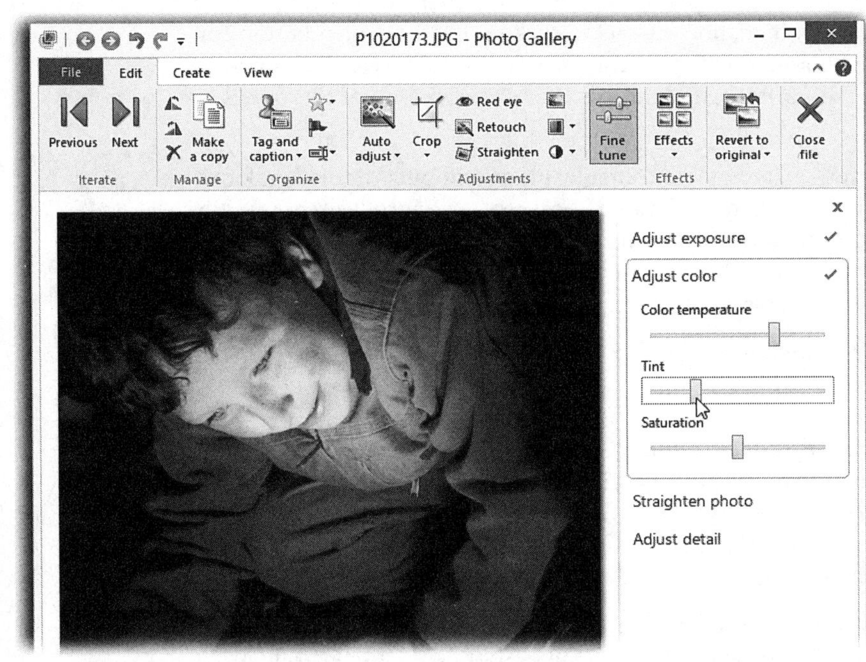

***Figure 17-16:** You can drag the handle of a slider, of course, but that doesn't give you much accuracy. Sometimes you may prefer to click directly on the slider, which makes the handle jump to the spot. The checkmark means "You've fooled with this parameter."*

Exposure

Click "Adjust exposure" to see the five controls available to tweak the photo's brights and darks.

- When you move the **Brightness** slider, you're making the *entire* image lighter or darker. In other words, if the picture's contrast is already exactly as you want it, but the whole picture could use darkening or lightening, Brightness should be your tool of choice.

- The **Contrast** slider, on the other hand, affects the difference between the darkest and lightest tones in your picture. If you increase the contrast, you create darker blacks and brighter whites. If you decrease the contrast (too much), you create flat or muddy tones.
- The **Shadows** slider attempts to recover lost detail in the darkest parts of the photo, and the **Highlights** slider attempts to recover detail from white, blown-out parts. Both of them work surprisingly well—in moderation. (Too much makes the photo look weird.)
- You can also drag the little handles on the *histogram* to more professionally adjust the brights and darks, as described in the box below.

Color balance

One of the most common failings of digital cameras (and scanners) is that they don't capture color very accurately. Digital photos sometimes have a slightly bluish or greenish tinge. Or maybe you just want to take color adjustment into your own hands, not only to get the colors right, but also to create a specific mood for an image—icy blue for a freezing day, for example.

The "Adjust color" panel offers three sliders that wield power over this sort of thing:

- **Color Temperature.** This slider adjusts the photo along the blue-orange spectrum. Move the slider to the left to make the image "cooler," or slightly bluish—a good way to improve overly yellowish scenes shot in incandescent lighting. Move the slider to the right to warm up the tones, or make them more orange—a particu-

POWER USERS' CLINIC

The Histogram

The histogram, the little graph in the Exposure panel, is a self-updating visual representation of the dark and light tones that make up your photograph, and it's a tool that's beloved by photographers.

If the mountains of your graph seem to cover all the territory from left to right, that means you have a roughly even distribution of dark and light tones in your picture, so you're probably in good shape. But if the mountains seem clumped up at either the left side or the right side of the graph, your photo is probably either muddy/too dark or overexposed/too bright. (Your eye could probably have told you that, too.) Anyway, you might want to make an adjustment.

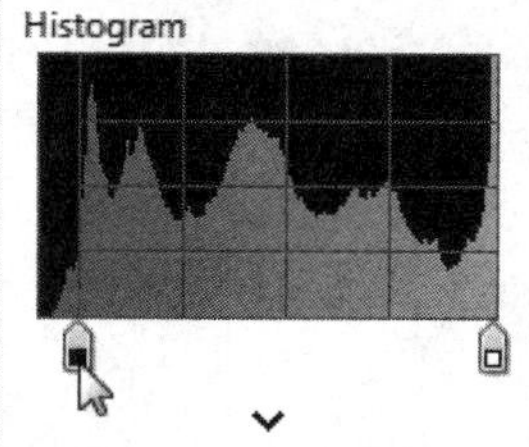

To fix this situation, drag the right or left pointer on the slider inward, toward the base of the "mountain." If you move the right indicator inward, the whites become brighter, but the dark areas stay pretty much the same; if you drag the left indicator inward, the dark tones change, but the highlights remain steady.

In general, avoid moving these endpoint handles inward beyond the outer edges of the mountains. Doing so adds contrast, but it also throws away whatever data is outside the handles, which generally makes for a lower-quality printout.

larly handy technique for breathing life back into subjects that have been bleached white with a flash.

- **Tint.** Nudge the slider to the right to add a greenish tint, left to add red. Adjusting this slider is helpful for correcting skin tones and compensating for difficult lighting situations, like pictures you took under fluorescent lighting.
- **Saturation.** When you increase the saturation of a photo's colors, you make them more vivid; you make them "pop" more. You can also improve photos that have harsh, garish colors by dialing *down* the saturation, so that the colors end up looking a little less intense than they appeared in the original snapshot. That's a useful trick in photos whose *composition* is so strong that the colors are almost distracting.

Tip: Drag the Saturation slider all the way to the left for an instant black-and-white rendition of your shot.

Straighten photo, Adjust detail

These last two sections of the Fine Tune panel duplicate buttons on the Edit tab of the Ribbon—but give you more control over the degree of correction, thanks to the sliders.

Reverting to the Original

Photo Gallery includes built-in protection against overzealous editing—a feature that can save you much grief. If you end up cropping a photo too much, or cranking up the brightness of a picture until it seems washed out, or accidentally turning someone's lips black with the Red-Eye tool, then you can undo all your edits at once with the "Revert to original" command. That strips away *every change you've ever made* since the picture arrived from the camera. It leaves you with your original, unedited photo.

The secret of the "Revert to original" command: Whenever you use any editing tools, Photo Gallery—without prompting and without informing you—instantly makes a duplicate of your original file. With an original version safely tucked away, Photo Gallery lets you go wild on the copy. Consequently, you can remain secure in the

FREQUENTLY ASKED QUESTION

Originals Folder Auto-Cleanup

Let me get this straight: Every time I edit a photo, even slightly, I wind up with a duplicate copy of it in some hidden folder on my hard drive? Seems like that's a recipe for a lot of wasted disk space.

True enough: The auto-backup feature means you wind up with *two* copies of every photo you ever edit, the edited one visible in Photo Gallery, and the original stashed on your hard drive. If left unchecked, all those originals could eat up a distressingly large chunk of your hard drive.

For that reason, Photo Gallery can auto-delete the secret originals after a certain amount of time has passed. If it's been a year since you touched a photo, after all, you're probably happy with the changes you made to it, and you may not need the space-eating safety net anymore.

To turn on this feature, choose File→Options within Photo Gallery. In the Options dialog box, under the Original Images heading, you can specify how long Windows should keep those unedited originals on hand.

knowledge that, in a pinch, Photo Gallery can always restore an image to the state it was in when you first imported it.

Note: Windows keeps your unedited original photos in your Personal→AppData→Local→Microsoft→Windows→Original Images folder. (It's OK to open this folder to inspect its contents and even open photos inside, but don't delete, move, or rename any of them; you'll wind up completely confusing Photo Gallery.)

To restore a selected photo to its original, click "Revert to original" on the Ribbon. Photo Gallery asks you to confirm the change; if you click OK, it swaps in the original version of the photo. You're back where you started.

Tip: Clearly, Photo Gallery has all the basics covered. But if you want more editing control–for example, if you want to edit only *part* of an image, or if you want to add text or something–you'll have to rely on another program.

Fortunately, Photo Gallery plays well with others. Once you've opened a photo, you can use the "More tools"→"Open with" submenu, on the Ribbon's Create tab, to send it off to any other graphics program–say, Photoshop Elements–for additional tweaking.

But even if you make changes in that other program, you're still protected by the warmth and security of the Revert command.

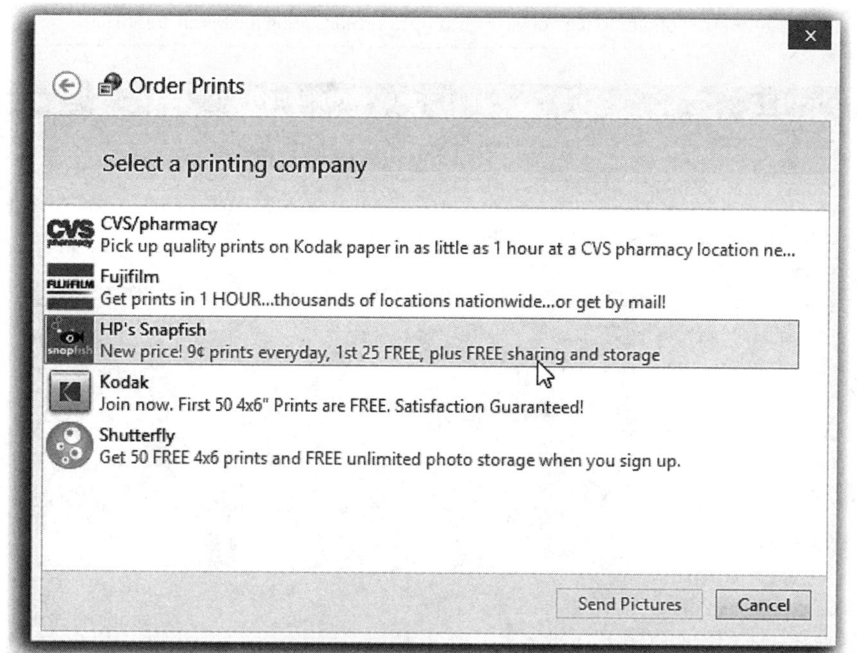

Figure 17-17: *Thanks to deals that Microsoft has cut with online photo print shops, you can order prints directly from within Photo Gallery. After you select the size and quantity of the pictures you want, one click is all it takes to transmit your photos and bill your credit card. The rates range from 19 cents for a single 4 × 6 print to about $4 for an 8 × 10. You get photos printed on high-quality glossy paper in the mail.*

Finding Your Audience

The last stop on your digital photos' cycle of greatness is, of course, a showing for other people. Photo Gallery offers several ways to make that happen.

Make Prints

If you highlight some photo thumbnails and then choose File→Print, the submenu offers you two choices:

- **Print.** Here you can specify what printer, paper, and quality options you want in order to print your own pictures at home—on an inkjet printer, for example.
- **Order Prints.** Even if you don't have a high-quality color printer, traditional prints of your digital photos are only a few clicks away—if you're willing to spend a little money, that is. Figure 17-17 has the details.

  The best part is that you get to print only the photos you actually want, rather than developing a roll of 36 only to find that just two of them are any good.

Tip: If you plan to order prints, first crop your photos to the proper proportions (4 × 6, for example), using the Crop tool described earlier in this chapter. Most digital cameras produce photos whose shape doesn't quite match standard photo-paper dimensions. If you send photos to Shutterfly uncropped, you're leaving it up to Shutterfly to decide which parts of your pictures to lop off to make them fit. (More than one PC fan has opened the envelope to find loved ones missing the tops of their skulls.) You can always restore the photos to their original uncropped versions using the Revert command.

GEM IN THE ROUGH

The Automatic Panorama

If you're one of those clever shutterbugs who tries to capture really wide-angle scenes by taking multiple side-by-side photos, Photo Gallery is here to help you. Its automatic panorama-stitching feature can combine those side-by-side shots into one superwide megavista.

To make this work, select all the side-by-side shots in Photo Gallery. On the Create tab of the Ribbon, click Panorama.

After the program crunches away for a while, it proposes a name for the resulting shot ("Flower stitch," for example); fix the name, if you like, and then click Stitch.

Now the panorama opens up at full size. Sometimes you see that the edges don't quite align, or that the exposure was slightly different from shot to shot.

Click Edit on the Ribbon and use the cropping tool to shave away the jagged edges. (There's not much you can do about the mismatched lighting–except to remember that the next time you take panorama shots, it's best to turn off your camera's automatic mode. Choose one exposure and stick with it for all the side-by-side shots.)

Panorama

See the box on the facing page.

Photo Fuse

Of course it's happened to you: In a group shot, you look good in one take, and your buddy looks good in a different one. Photo Fuse is a feature that can actually combine the faces from different shots into a single, unified shot where everybody looks his best.

See Figure 17-18 for details.

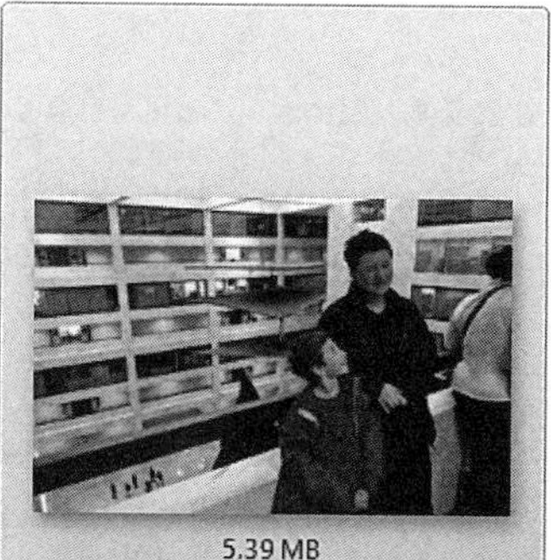

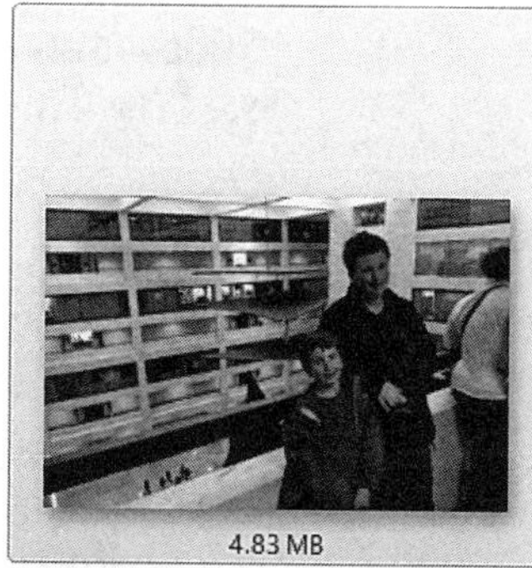

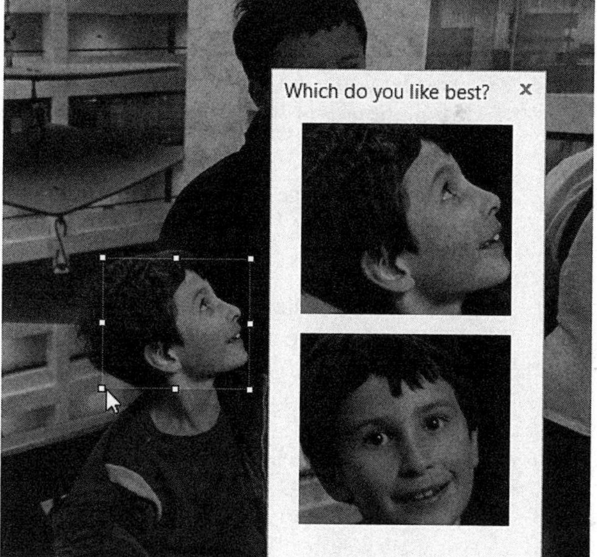

Figure 17-18:
To use Photo Fuse, start by selecting the thumbnails of the group photos that need merging (top).

They must be images taken of the same people in the same poses with the same lighting at the same angle. It's software, not Gandalf.

On the Create tab of the Ribbon, click Photo Fuse.

Now click to place a rectangle on the piece of the photo that looks better in one shot than another—the kid's face, for example. Drag its handles to change its size and shape.

The software shows you the contents of that exact rectangle in every selected photo (bottom). Click the version that looks best—the one where the kid's not *looking away from the camera or* not *blinking.*

Repeat as necessary. When you click Save, Photo Gallery creates a new photo that seamlessly combines the preferred head from each photo into a single perfect one. (Usually.)

Auto Collage

School projects and Valentine's Day gifts will never be the same. This feature lets you select a bunch of photos, click one button, and wind up with a beautiful, full-poster collage. No gaps, nothing important covered up, softly faded edges.

Just select the photos you want to include (seven or more, please). On the Ribbon's Edit tab, click the Auto Collage button—or, from its ▾ menu, choose the page size and orientation you prefer. In a few seconds, Photo Gallery asks you to save the finished collage file to your hard drive. Name it and click Save.

Now you get to see the finished collage. Lovely!

Slideshows

See "The Post-Dump Slideshow" at the beginning of this chapter.

Email

You can, if you like to live dangerously, select some photos and then, on the Ribbon's Create tab, open the "Photo email" icon's ▾ menu and choose "Send photos as attachments."

Unfortunately, *full-size photos are usually too big to email.* They're huge files, and the original camera shots won't even fit on a modern PC monitor—they're much bigger, in terms of pixels—without shrinking. Your recipient's email system might even bounce the message back to you because it exceeds the maximum attachment size.

So when you choose "Send photos as attachments," Photo Gallery asks how much smaller you want the photo attachments to be. In each case, it throws away size and resolution in order to squish the attachments down in size.

Fortunately, you have an ingenious alternative: Photo Gallery can send a handsome preview message that contains links to the actual, full-resolution photo files that actually reside on your SkyDrive. This feature works *if* you have a Microsoft account and *if* Windows Live Mail (Chapter 16) is your email program.

Once you've selected the photo(s) you want to email, click "Photo email" on the Ribbon's Create tab. Photo Gallery hands off the photos to your email program. It prepares an outgoing message with the photos already attached, in preview form; see Figure 17-19.

The beautiful part is that the thumbnails in the message are linked to the full-size originals as they sit on your SkyDrive. Your recipient doesn't have to worry about attachment sizes—and doesn't need a Microsoft account or even Windows. She can just click either "View slideshow" or "Download all."

Address the message, add a note if you like, and click Send.

Blog Post

This button, on the Ribbon, is a quick way to hand off some photos to Windows Live Writer, the blogging software described in Chapter 11. You get a new blog post with the photos already placed, ready to title, write up, and post.

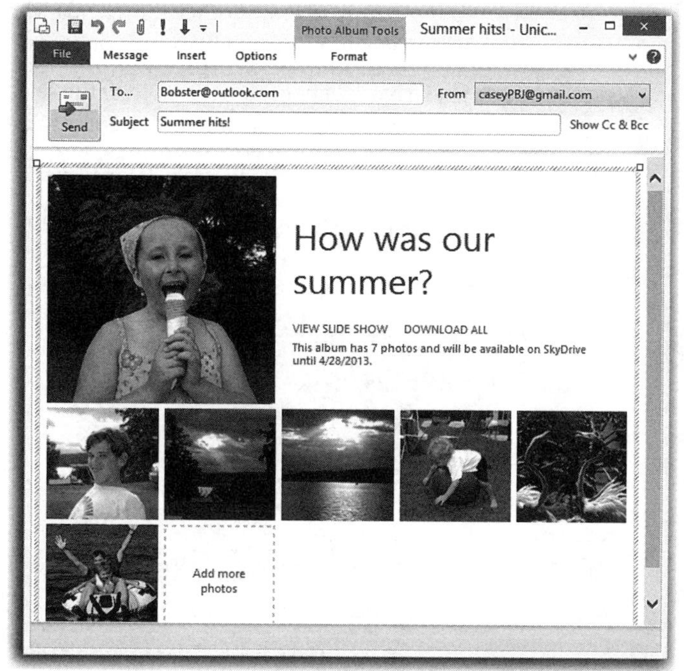

Figure 17-19: *When Photoshop Gallery opens your email program, you're shown a nearly completed outgoing message. You should edit the title to something more descriptive than "Enter album name here."*

You can also write your own message above the photos area, or add more photos by clicking "Add more photos."

Your recipients will be able to see a slideshow of these photos or to download the originals–as long as they do so within the three-month deadline.

Movie

If you highlight some photo thumbnails and then choose Movie, Photo Gallery automatically hands them off to Windows Movie Maker and lays them out in the timeline as a slideshow, all ready to go.

All you have left to do is rearrange them, add music and credits, and save as a digital movie file for publishing online or distributing to your hip friends. (Check out the free PDF appendix "Windows Movie Maker" from this book's "Missing CD" at *www.missingmanuals.com.*)

If a Movie Maker slideshow project is already open, then this button adds the photos to it.

Publish to Facebook, YouTube…

This set of icons stands ready to "publish" a selected batch of photos to the online service of your choice. The icons represent these services:

- **Groups** refers to address-book groups. (You can set one up here, if you haven't built any already.) You can define one group for your immediate family, another for your coworkers, another for friends who like to get your photos. Once you've set up a group, you can blast new photos to them with one click on this icon.
- **SkyDrive.** Click this button to copy the selected pictures to your virtual Microsoft hard drive. You're asked to put them into an album, either an existing one or one

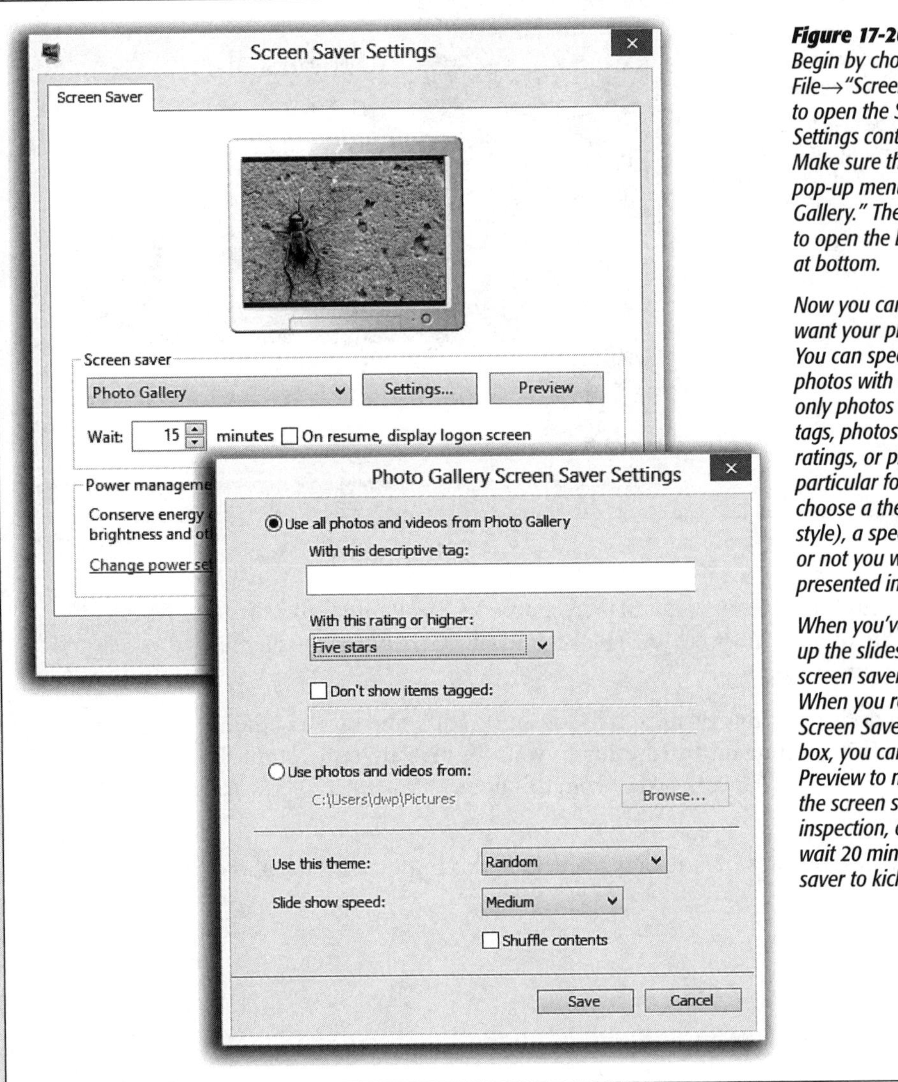

Figure 17-20: *Begin by choosing File→"Screen saver settings" to open the Screen Saver Settings control panel (top). Make sure the "Screen saver" pop-up menu says "Photo Gallery." Then click Settings to open the box shown here at bottom.*

Now you can choose how you want your photos selected. You can specify only the photos with certain tags, only photos without certain tags, photos with certain star ratings, or photos from a particular folder. You can also choose a theme (animation style), a speed, and whether or not you want the photos presented in a random order.

When you've finished setting up the slideshow—that is, screen saver—click Save. When you return to the Screen Saver Settings dialog box, you can either click Preview to manually trigger the screen saver for your inspection, or click OK and wait 20 minutes for the screen saver to kick in by itself.

you create on the spot. You can also choose whether to post the originals or, to save SkyDrive space, smaller versions.

- **Facebook, YouTube, Flickr, Vimeo.** If you choose one of these free sharing sites, you're asked to log in with your name and password for that service. In most cases, you have to enter a title, description, and category, and you can specify whether your photos are visible to the public, or only to you.

  When it's all over, Photo Gallery posts the selected photos. (For the movie sites YouTube and Vimeo, you wind up with an animated slideshow.)

Burn to a Disc

Photo Gallery offers a great way to back up or archive your pictures and movies. Select some photo thumbnails and then choose File→Burn a CD. Insert a blank CD when you're asked. Photo Gallery copies the full-quality originals you've selected to that disc.

Build a Photo Screen Saver

This feature is really nice. You can turn any arbitrary batch of photos into your PC's very own screen saver. After half an hour (or whatever) of inactivity, the screen darkens, thunder rolls, and *your* friends and family begin to appear, gracefully panning and zooming and crossfading, as your coworkers spill their coffee in admiration and amazement.

The hard part is specifying *which* pictures you want to be part of the show; you can't just highlight a bunch of them in Photo Gallery and say, "Use these." Instead, you have to isolate your screen saver–bound shots, either by giving them a certain tag, applying a certain rating, or confining them to a certain folder. See Figure 17-20 for details.

CHAPTER
18

Windows Media Player

In the beginning, Windows Media Player was the headquarters for music and video on your PC. It was the Grand Central Terminal for things like music CDs (you could play 'em, copy songs off 'em, and burn 'em); MP3 files and other digital songs (you could sort 'em, buy 'em online, and file 'em into playlists); pocket music players of the non-iPod variety (fill 'em up, manage their playlists); Internet radio stations; DVD movies (watch 'em); and so on.

Media Player still does all that, and more. But it's no longer clear that this is the program you'll use for these activities. Gradually, the Media Player audience is splintering.

POWER USERS' CLINIC

Missing In Action: Music Store and DVD Playback

In Windows 7, Media Player offered two handy features that are now gone. First, it offered a window into online music stores, where you could stream or buy songs. That's over now; Microsoft figures that the Music app (in TileWorld) offers more than enough streaming and buying options, thanks to the XBox Music service.

The other missing feature takes more effort to replace: Windows Media Player can no longer play DVDs. You can no longer insert a Hollywood movie and play it on your PC—at least not without downloading some add-on software.

Solution 1: Buy the Windows Media Center add-on. It costs $10, and requires Windows 8 Pro. (See the last page of this chapter.) It can now play both DVDs and Blu-Ray discs.

Solution 2: Download a free DVD-playback program like VLC. It's a super-feature-packed program for playing DVDs and Internet videos, it doesn't cost $10, and it doesn't require Windows 8 Pro. You can download it from this book's "Missing CD" page at *www.missingmanuals.com.*

Nowadays, a certain percentage of people are using alternative programs like Apple's iTunes software or other non-Microsoft candidates.

Still, *most* of the Windows world continues to use Windows Media Player as their music-file database. The current version has some excellent features, including a cleaner design, free streaming through your house—or even over the Internet—to other computers, and playback of more kinds of audio and video files (the new types include H.264, AAC, Xvid, and DivX). It's worth getting to know.

Note: In its insatiable quest to dominate the world of digital music and video, Microsoft keeps updating Windows Media Player, usually redesigning it beyond recognition with each update. For example, this chapter describes Media Player version 12, included with Windows 8 out of the gate. But sure as shootin', version 13 will be coming your way within a year or so. (Windows' automatic-update feature will let you know when version 13 is fully baked and ready to download.)

The Lay of the Land

The first time you open Windows Media Player, you confront the usual Microsoft interrogation about your privacy tolerance. If it's pretty much OK with you for Microsoft to do what it wants with (anonymous) details of your Media Player habits, click Recommended and get on with your life.

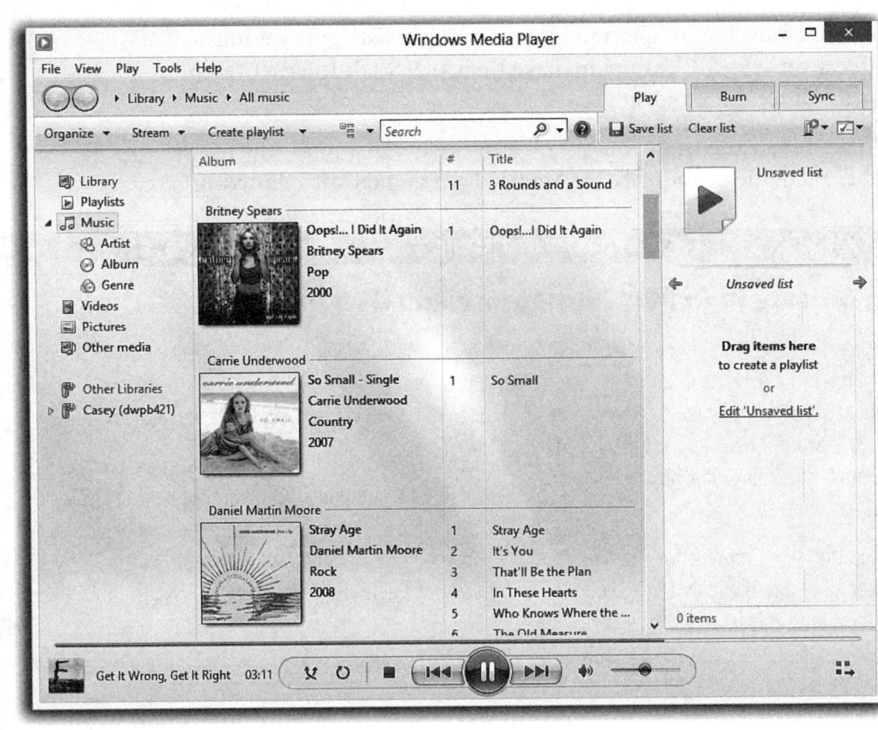

Figure 18-1: *When you click a label at left, the main portion of the window changes to show you your music collection, using the actual album-cover artwork as icons. It's very visual, but not especially stingy with screen space. Fortunately, you also have a more compact List view available–choose Details from the View Options pop-up menu (☷) next to the search box.*

In any case, eventually, you wind up at the main Media Player screen (Figure 18-1).

Down the left side of the window is a navigation tree—a list of the music, videos, pictures, recorded TV shows, and playlists in your collection. The flippy triangles next to the major headings make it easy to collapse sections of the list. Under the Library headings, you can click Artist, Album, Genre, or whatever, to see your entire music library sorted by that criterion (Figure 18-1).

Media Player's top edge, as you may have noticed, offers three horizontal strips:

- **The menu bar.** As in so many Windows programs, this one has a very useful menu bar, but Microsoft has hidden it in hopes of making Media Player seem less complicated. Fine, but you *need* the menu bar. Make it appear by pressing Alt+M. The rest of this chapter assumes that you've done so, as shown in Figure 18-1.
- **Address bar.** This "bread crumbs trail" of Media Player places shows what you've clicked to get where you are: for example, Library▸Music▸Genre▸Classical. You can click any of these words to backtrack.
- **Toolbar.** Here are the one- or two-word commands you'll use most often.

The largest portion of the window is filled by the Details pane—basically, your list of music, videos, or photos. The wider you make the window, the more information you can see here.

Tip: The pop-up menu next to the search box lets you change how the album covers, videos, and photos are displayed: in a list, as icons only, or as icons with details.

When you're in any kind of List view, don't forget that you can right-click the column headings to get the "Choose columns" command. It lets you change what kinds of detail columns appear here. You can get rid of Length and Rating, if you like, and replace those columns with Mood and Conductor. (If you're weird, that is.)

At the right side, you may see the Play, Burn, and Sync tabs; more on these in a moment. Down at the bottom, there's a standard set of playback controls.

UP TO SPEED

Custom Express

The first time you open Media Player, a welcome message appears. It offers you two choices:

Express Settings. This option is "Recommended" because it makes Media Player the main music and video player for your PC, sends Microsoft anonymous details about what you buy and listen to, and downloads track lists and other details from the Internet when you insert a CD or DVD.

Custom Settings. If you'd rather be a little less free with your private information, or If you'd like Media Player not to do quite such a big land grab of your multimedia playback rights, then choose this option. You're walked through three settings screens where you can tone down Media Player's ambitions: Turn off its transmission or recording of your activities, opt out of the link to the Media Guide online music store, or specify which file types Media Player considers itself the "owner" of (that will open in Media Player when double-clicked).

Importing Music Files

When you first open Media Player, it automatically searches the usual folders on your hard drive—Music, Pictures, Videos, Recorded TV—for files that it can play. It leaves the files where they are, but in the navigation pane, it *lists* everything it finds.

Actually, it's *monitoring* those folders. If any new music files (or video or pictures) arrive in those folders, they're automatically listed in Media Player.

But what if there's some music in a *different* folder? Fortunately, you can add that new folder to Media Player's awareness.

Choose Organize→"Manage libraries"→Music. Proceed as shown in Figure 18-2.

Note: Any song, video, or photo that you ever play in Media Player gets automatically added to its Library—*if* it's on your hard drive or the Internet. If it's on another PC on the network, or on a removable disk like a CD, Media Player doesn't bother adding it, because it probably won't be there the next time you want it.

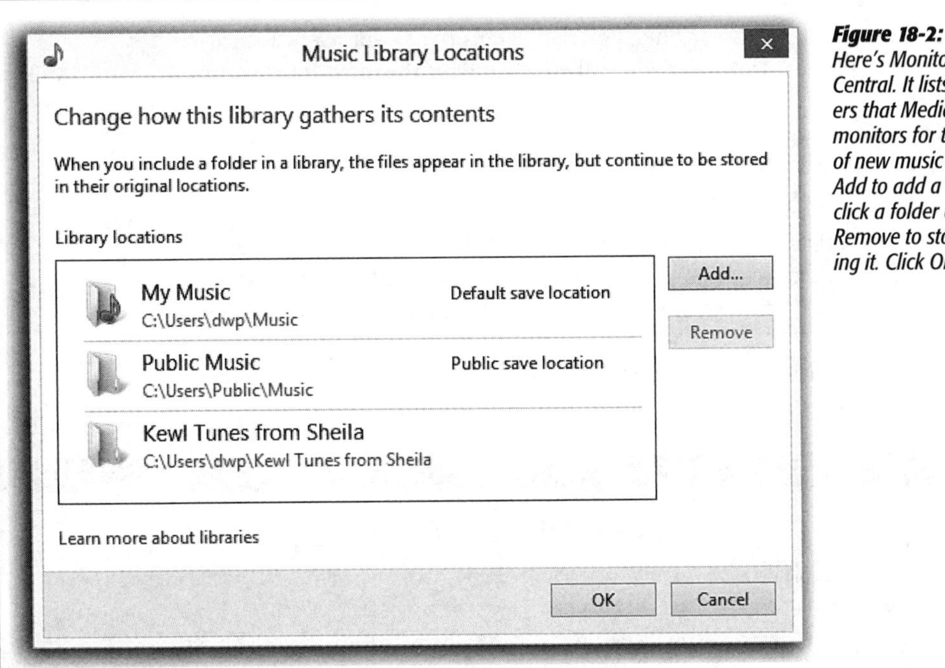

Figure 18-2: *Here's Monitored Folder Central. It lists the folders that Media Player monitors for the arrival of new music files. Click Add to add a new folder; click a folder and click Remove to stop monitoring it. Click OK.*

You can also drag sound or video files directly from your desktop or folder windows into the Media Player window.

Music Playback

You can sort your collection by performer, album, year released, or whatever, just by clicking the corresponding icons in the navigation tree. Whenever you want to play back some music, just click your way to the song or album you want—there's no need to hunt around in your shoeboxes for the original CD the songs came from.

But that's just the beginning of Media Player's organizational tools; see Figure 18-3.

Figure 18-3: *On the Library tab, the navigation tree (left) lists your playlists. Under the Music heading, you see various ways to sort your collection. The button that starts out looking like this (next to the search box) changes the layout in the central window: List view, Icon view, and so on. Don't miss the search box at the top, which searches all text related to your songs and videos as you type, hiding entries that don't match.*

You can pick something to listen to in a couple of different ways:

- Under Music in the navigation pane, click Artist, Album, or Genre. Double-click an album cover to see what songs are on that album. Double-click a song to start playing it.
- Use the Search command to find a song, composer, album, or band.

When you've found something worth listening to, double-click to start playback. You can use the space bar to start and stop playback.

Tip: If you point to a song without clicking, a little Preview bubble pops up. Click the ▶ button to hear a 15-second snippet of it; click the ⏭ button to skip ahead.

How is this feature any better than just clicking the song and hitting the space bar? Microsoft only knows.

Fun with Media Player

When your everyday work leaves you uninspired, here are a few of the experiments you can conduct on the Media Player screen design:

- **Shrink the window to Now Playing size.** If the Media Player window is taking up too much screen space, making it harder for you to work on that crucial business plan as you listen to Adele, no problem: You can shrink it down to a three-inch square, a little panel called the Now Playing window (Figure 18-4). You can park this window off to the side of your screen as you do other work. It shows the current album cover, and when you point at it, playback controls appear.

  To fire up the Now Playing screen, press Ctrl+3, or choose View→Now Playing, or click the icon in the lower-right corner of the window.

  Press Ctrl+1 to return the Media Player window to its full-sized glory.

UP TO SPEED

Redesigning the Navigation Pane

The navigation pane starts out looking a little baffling. Under the Music heading, it looks like you can sort by only Artist, Album, or Genre—why not rating or composer?

And what's the deal with the Pictures category? You've already got two photo-playback programs (Photos in TileWorld and Photo Gallery)—why would you use Media Player to play photos?

And why is there a Recorded TV folder here, even on the vast majority of PCs that cannot, in fact, record TV?

Fortunately, it's easy enough to hide the items you'll never use and add the ones you will.

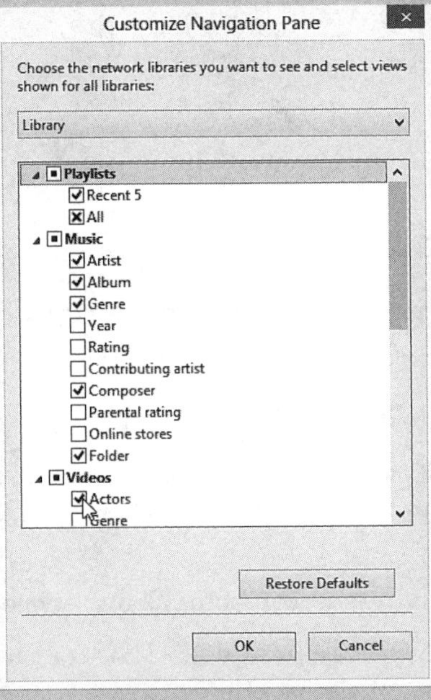

The key is to choose Organize→"Customize navigation pane." For Music, you're offered a long list of additional music-sorting categories, like Year, Rating, Composer, Folder, and so on. Turn on the checkboxes you want.

Meanwhile, the other nav-pane headings have checkboxes here, too. Go ahead and turn off Recorded TV (you may have to click the checkbox twice to make it empty) or Pictures, if you like. If you don't plan to buy any music online, then turn off Show Music Services below the list, too.

Finally, click OK. You've finally made Media Player your player.

Tip: Of course, you can also just minimize Media Player, as you would any window. In fact, when you do that, Media Player's icon on the taskbar sprouts a jump list. In other words, you can right-click it to see a pop-up menu of handy commands, like "Resume previous list" and "Play all music." It also lists your most frequently played tunes.

- **Switch visualizations.** A *visualization* is a sort of laser light show, a screen saver that pulses in time to the music. It's available only in the Now Playing mode described above (Figure 18-4, right).

Figure 18-4: *Left: When the Now Playing window is on your screen, you get to see the album art and, when the mouse is in the window, a very tiny set of playback controls.*

Right: Visualizations R Us.

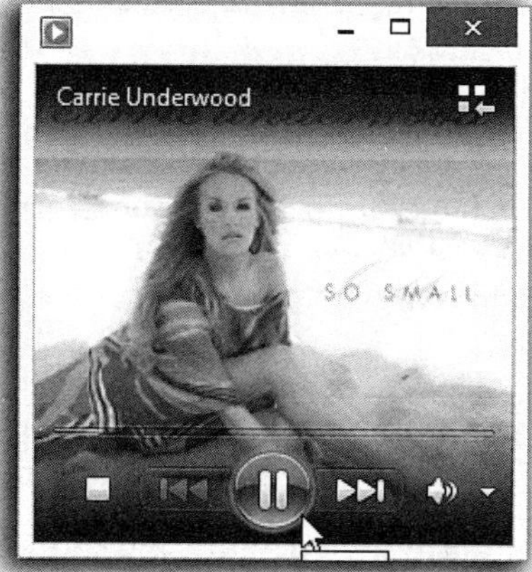

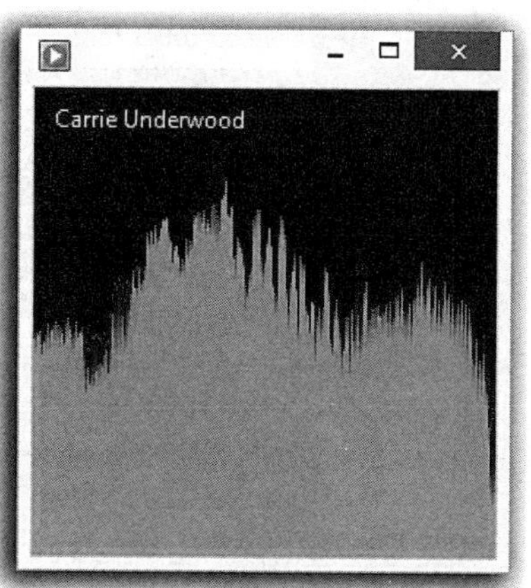

  To see it, right-click the Now Playing window. From the shortcut menu, choose Visualizations; from the submenu (and sub-submenus), choose a visualization style. Ctrl-click the window (to see the next style) or Shift+Ctrl-click (for the previous one).

  And if you tire of the displays built into Windows, download more of them by choosing Visualizations→"Download visualizations" from the same shortcut menu.

- **Expand the window.** On the other hand, if your PC is briefly serving as a glorified stereo system at a cocktail party, double-click the visualization display itself (or press Alt+Enter). The screen-saver effect now fills the entire screen, hiding all text, buttons, and controls. If you have an available laptop and a coffee table to put it on, you've got yourself a great atmospheric effect. (When the party's over, just double-click again, or press Alt+Enter again, to make the standard controls reappear.)

- **Fool around with the sound.** Don't miss the graphic equalizer, a little row of sliders that lets you adjust the bass, treble, and other frequencies to suit your particular speakers and your particular ears. In the Now Playing window, right-click an empty spot. From the shortcut menu, choose Enhancements→Graphic Equalizer.

  The same submenu offers a number of other audio effects, including Quiet Mode (smooths out the highs and the lows so that sudden blasts don't wake up the kids) and something called SRS WOW, which simulates a 3-D sound experience through nothing more than stereo speakers or headphones.

- **Fool around with the speed.** If you're in a hurry to get through an album, or just think the tempo's too slow, right-click an empty spot in the Now Playing window. From the shortcut menu, choose Enhancements→"Play speed settings." You're offered a new window containing a playback-speed slider for your music—a weird and wonderful feature.

- **Change the skin.** In hopes of riding the world's craze for MP3 files, Microsoft has helped itself to one of the old Winamp program's most interesting features: *skins.* A skin is a design scheme that completely changes the look of Windows Media Player, as shown in Figure 18-5.

  To choose a new skin, choose View→Skin Chooser. Then click each of the available skins, listed down the left side, to see a preview of its appearance. When you click the Apply Skin button (at the top-left corner of the window), your player takes on the look of the skin you chose *and* shrinks down into the compact Skin mode, as described in the previous tip.

Playing Music CDs

For its next trick, Media Player can simulate a $25 CD player. To fire it up, just insert an audio CD into your computer's CD or DVD drive.

If you insert a CD when you're at the desktop, and it's the first time you've ever taken this dramatic action, you get the AutoPlay interview shown in Figure 18-6. It asks how you want Windows to handle inserted CDs. Do you want it to *play* them? Or *rip* them (start copying their songs to your hard drive)? And if you said "play," do you want to use Media Player or Media *Center*, if you have it?

For now, click "Play audio CD using Windows Media Player."

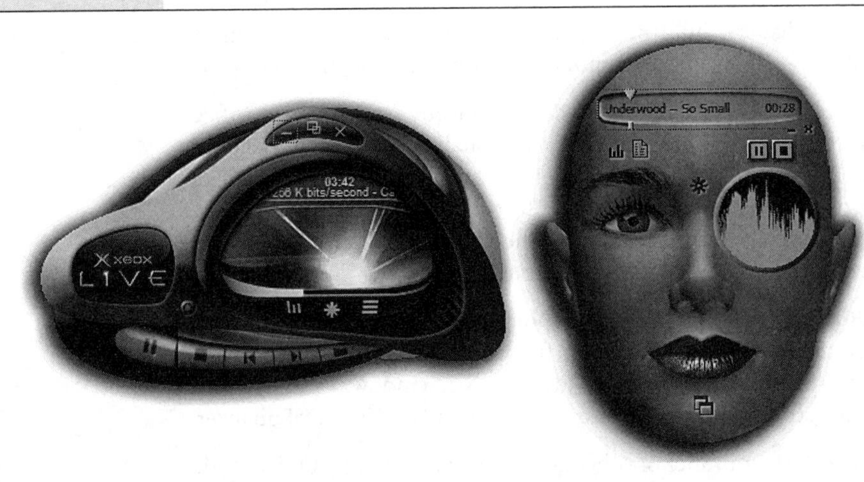

Figure 18-5: *To change the skin, choose View→Skin Chooser from the menu. A directory of skins appears; it's empty at the outset. Click More Skins; Windows sends you online to Microsoft's grisly-sounding Skin Gallery.*

If you're in Media Player, on the other hand, the CD's contents show up right away.

Either way, you can start playing the CD just as though the files were on your PC, using the playback controls at the bottom of the window. All of the usual tricks—Now Playing, visualizations, and so on—are available for the CD playback.

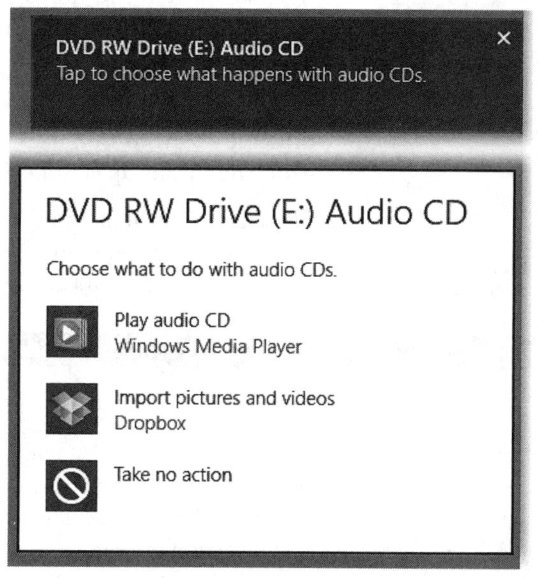

Figure 18-6:
Top: Windows may ask what you want it to do with a music CD. Tap or click this message to open the one shown here at bottom.

Bottom: If you accept the "Play audio CD" option by clicking OK or pressing Enter, Media Player opens automatically and begins to play the songs on your CD.

Ripping CDs to Your Hard Drive

You can copy an album, or selected tracks, to your hard drive in the form of standalone music files that play when double-clicked. The process is called *ripping,* much to the consternation of sleepless record executives who think that's short for *ripping off.*

Having CD songs on your hard drive is handy, though:

- You can listen to your songs without having to hunt for the CDs they came from.
- You can listen to music even if you're using the CD-ROM drive for something else (like a CD-based game).
- You can build your own *playlists* (sets of favorite songs) consisting of tracks from different albums.
- You can compress the file in the process, so that each song takes up much less disk space.
- You can transfer the songs to a portable player or burn them onto a homemade CD.

If you're sold on the idea, open the "Rip settings" pop-up menu on your toolbar. Inspect your settings. For example:

- **Format.** Microsoft has designed Windows Media Player to generate files in the company's own format, called Windows Media Audio (.wma) format. But many people prefer, and even require, MP3 files. For example, certain CD players and portable music players (including the iPod) can play back MP3 files—but won't know what to do with WMA files.

  If you'd prefer the more universally compatible MP3 files, choose "Rip settings"→Format→MP3 (Figure 18-7).

- **Audio quality.** The "Audio quality" submenu controls the tradeoff, in the resulting sound files, between audio quality and file size. At 128 kbps, for example, a 3-minute MP3 file might consume about 2.8 megabytes. At 192 kbps, the same file sounds better, but it eats up about 4.2 MB. And at a full 320 kbps, the file's roughly 7 MB.

  These are important considerations if you're ripping for an MP3 player. For instance, a 20-gigabyte music player can hold 142 hours of music you've ripped at 320 kbps, or 357 hours at 128 kbps.

GEM IN THE ROUGH

Filling in Track Names

Weird though it may seem, precious few audio CDs come programmed to know their own names (and song titles). (Remember, CDs were invented before the MP3/iTunes era; nobody expected them to be played on computers.)

Every day, millions of people insert music CDs into their computers and see the songs listed as nothing more than "Track 1," "Track 2," and so on–and the album itself goes by the catchy name "Unknown Album."

Fix #1. If your PC is online when you insert a certain music CD, you'll bypass that entire situation. Windows takes a quick glance at your CD, sends a query to *www.allmusic.com* (a massive database on the Web containing information on over 15 million songs), and downloads the track list and a picture of the album cover for your particular disc.

Fix #2. If *allmusic.com* draws a blank, as it often does for classical recordings, no big deal. Media Player makes it easy to search the Web for this information at a later time. In the main Media Player window (Ctrl+1), click Album in the nav pane. Right-click an album cover, and then, from the shortcut menu, choose "Find album info." (Alternatively, you can highlight the names of the *tracks* with missing information; right-click one and then choose "Find album info.")

Fix #3. You can type in the names of your songs manually. Begin on the Library tab. Select the tracks you want to edit. (By Shift-clicking or Ctrl-clicking, you can add information to multiple tracks simultaneously–for example, if they all came from the same album.)

Now click carefully in the *specific column* you want to edit–Artist, Album, or whatever. A little text box opens so that you can type in the track information manually.

Fix #4. This is pretty cool: In the navigation tree, click the criterion that's missing, like Artist or Album. Now you can *drag* an incorrectly labeled track or album *onto* one with the correct labeling–and marvel as Media Player copies the correct info onto the dragged item.

(If an album is missing its cover art, you can paste in a graphic you've copied from, for example, the Web. Just right-click it and, from the shortcut menu, choose "Paste album art.")

No matter how the track names and album art get onto your PC, Windows saves this information in your music library. Therefore, the next time you insert this CD, the Media Player will recognize it and display the track names and album information automatically.

For MP3 files, most people find the 192 kbps setting to produce great-sounding, relatively compact files. For WMA, 128 kbps might be a good starting point. Needless to say, let your ears (and the capacity of your portable music player) be your guide.

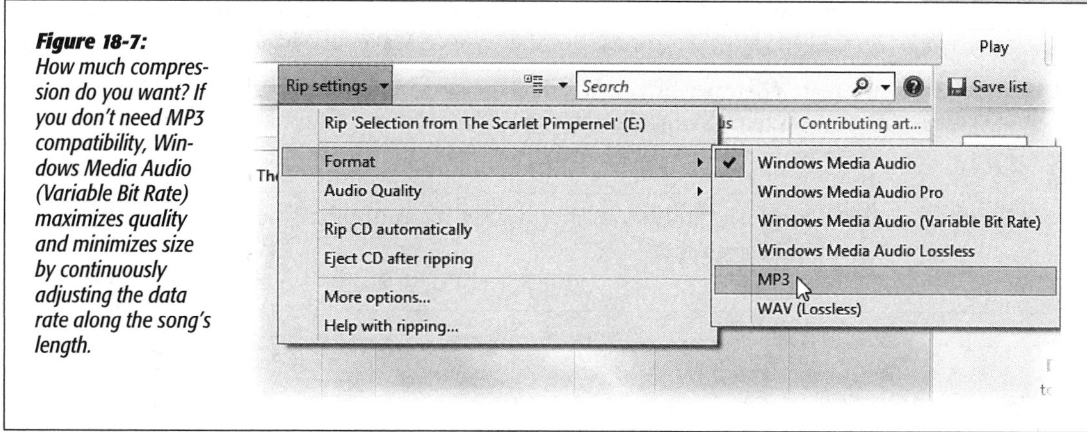

Figure 18-7: *How much compression do you want? If you don't need MP3 compatibility, Windows Media Audio (Variable Bit Rate) maximizes quality and minimizes size by continuously adjusting the data rate along the song's length.*

- **Storage location.** Windows likes to copy your song files into your Personal→Music folder. If you'd prefer it to stash them somewhere else, choose "Rip settings"→"More options."

Tip: If you have a stack of CDs to rip, don't miss the two commands in the "Rip settings" menu: "Rip CD Automatically" and "Eject CD after ripping." Together, they turn your PC into an automated ripping machine, leaving nothing for you to do but feed it CDs and watch TV.

Here's how you rip:

1. **Insert the music CD.**

   The list of songs on the CD appears.

2. **Turn on the checkboxes of the tracks you want to copy.**

   You've waited all your life for this: At last, you have the power to eliminate any annoying songs and keep only the good ones.

3. **On the toolbar, click Rip CD.**

   Windows begins to copy the songs onto your hard drive. The Rip CD button changes to "Stop rip," which you can click to interrupt the process.

When it's all over, the CD's songs are now part of your library, nestled among whatever other files you had there.

Playlists

Microsoft recognizes that you may not want to listen to *all* your songs every time you need some tunes. That's why Media Player lets you create *playlists*—folders in the navigation list that contain only certain songs. In effect, you can devise your own albums, mixing and matching songs from different albums for different purposes: one called "Downer Tunes," another called "Makeout Music," and so on.

To create a new playlist, make sure the Play tab is selected (right side). That pane starts out empty. (If it's not, click "Clear list" at the top.) It says, "Drag items here to create a playlist." Well, hey—it's worth a try. See Figure 18-8.

Tip: You can also right-click any album or song and, from the shortcut menu, choose "Add to"; the submenu lists all your existing playlists.

Figure 18-8: *To create a playlist, just start dragging tracks or whole albums to the Playlist pane. Switch views, or use the search box, as necessary to find the tracks you want. Drag songs up and down in the Playlist pane to reorder them. Click where it now says "Untitled Playlist" to give your playlist a name. Use the upper-right pop-up menu to scramble or sort the playlist.*

Once you've created a playlist, click "Save list" at the top of the pane. Thrill to the appearance of a new icon in the Playlists category of the navigation tree.

Note: To create another playlist right away, close the first one by clicking the red ✕ beside its name.

Whenever you want to delete a selected song, playlist, or almost anything else, press the Delete key. Media Player generally asks if you want it deleted only from the library, or if you really want it gone from your computer.

Burning Your Own CDs

The beauty of a CD burner is that it frees you from the stifling restrictions put on your musical tastes by the record companies. You can create your own "best of" CDs that play in any CD player—and that contain only your favorite songs in your favorite order. The procedure goes like this:

1. **Click the Burn tab. Insert a blank CD.**

   If you've inserted a rewriteable disc like a CD-RW, and you've burned it before, right-click its icon in the navigation tree. Then, from the shortcut menu, choose "Erase disc" before you proceed.

GEM IN THE ROUGH

Auto Playlists

Auto playlists constantly rebuild themselves according to criteria you specify. You might tell one playlist to assemble 45 minutes' worth of songs you've rated higher than four stars but rarely listen to, and another to list your most-often-played songs from the '80s.

To make an auto playlist, choose "Create playlist"→"Create auto playlist" (on the toolbar). The dialog box shown here appears. The controls are designed to set up a search of your music database. Click "Click here to add criteria," click the first criterion (like Artist), and then click each underlined phrase ("is"/"is not") to build a sentence. For example, "Artist" "Is" "Beatles."

The last set of controls in this dialog box let you limit the playlist's total size, playback time, or song quantity.

When you click OK, your auto playlist is ready to show off; it appears in the navigation tree like any other playlist. The difference, of course, is that it updates itself as you work with your music collection. This playlist gets updated as your collection changes, as you change your ratings, as your play count changes, and so on.

(To edit an auto playlist, right-click it; from the shortcut menu, choose Edit.)

2. **Specify which songs you want to burn by dragging them into the Burn List (where it says "Drag items here").**

You can add music to your CD-to-be in just about any kind of chunk: individual songs, whole albums, playlists, random audio files on your hard drive, and so on. You drag them into the Burn list, just as you'd drag them into a playlist like the one shown in Figure 18-8.

To add a whole playlist to the Burn List, drag its name right across the screen from the navigation tree. To add a file that's not already in Media Player, drag it out of its Explorer window directly into the Burn List. Drag tracks up or down in the Burn list to change their sequence.

As you go, keep an eye on the time tally above your list of tracks. It lets you know how much you've put on your CD, measured in minutes:seconds. If you go over the limit (about an hour), Media Player will have to burn additional CDs. ("Next disc" markers will let you know where the breaks will come.)

Tip: Media Player adds 2 seconds of silence between each song, which might explain why you may not be able to fit that one last song onto the disc even though it seems like it should fit. It also applies volume leveling, which is great when you're mixing songs from various albums that would otherwise be at different volume levels. (You control both the gaps and the volume leveling by opening the Burn menu and choosing "More burn options.")

3. **Click "Start burn" above the list of songs.**

It takes awhile to burn a CD. To wind up with the fewest "coasters" (mis-burned CDs that you have to throw away), allow your PC's full attention to focus on the task. Don't play music, for example.

POWER USERS' CLINIC

CD and DVD Format Fun

Most of the time, you'll probably want to burn a regular audio CD, of the type that plays in the world's 687 quintillion CD players. But you can also use the Burn tab to make a *data* CD or DVD—a disc designed to play in *computers.* That's a good way, for example, to make a backup of your tunes.

Actually, most recent CD players can also play *MP3 CDs,* which are basically data CDs filled with MP3 files. That's a great feature, because a single MP3 CD can hold 100 songs or more. (A few can even play *WMA CDs,* meaning CDs containing files in Microsoft's own audio format.)

You specify what kind of disc you intend to burn by choosing its name from the "Burn options" menu (upper-right).

If you're ever in doubt about how you burned a certain CD (audio or data?), here's a trick: Insert it into your PC, open its window, and examine its contents. If you see files with the suffix .cda, you've got yourself an audio CD; if it's full of other kinds of files, like .mp3, .wma, or even .jpg and .doc, it's a data CD.

Copying to a Portable Player or Windows Phone

If you have a pocket gizmo that's capable of playing music (like a SanDisk Sansa) or a Windows Phone, then the process for loading your favorite material onto it is very similar to burning your own CD. The only difference in the procedure is that you do your work on the Sync tab instead of the Burn tab.

If you attach a player or phone with a capacity greater than 4 gigabytes, Media Player automatically copies your entire collection onto it, if possible. If it's smaller, or if your whole library won't fit, Media Player switches into manual-sync mode, in which you handpick what gets copied.

Automatic sync

Connect the player or phone. Media Player announces that it will perform an automatic sync. Click Finish. Smile. Wait.

From now on, just connecting the player to Media Player brings it up to date with whatever songs you've added or deleted on your PC. As your library grows, shrinks, or gets edited, you can sleep soundly, knowing that your gadget's contents will be updated automatically the next time you hook it up to your PC's USB port.

Manual sync

Connect the player or phone. Read the dialog box. Click Finish.

In Media Player, click the Sync tab. Drag songs, videos, playlists, or albums into the List pane, exactly as you would when preparing to burn a CD. Click "Start sync."

Tip: If you'd like to surrender to the serendipity of Shuffle mode, you can let Media Player choose the songs you get. From the Sync options (▾) menu, choose the name of your player or phone; from the submenu, choose "Shuffle list." Each time you sync, you get a different random selection from your collection.

Sharing Music on the Network

When Microsoft called it "Windows Media Player," it wasn't kidding. This app can play music and video up, down, and sideways—and even across the network.

In a couple of ways, actually. For example:

- **Listen to other people's music.** If all the PCs in your house are part of the same network, you can sit at *your* PC and see what music and videos are on everyone *else's* PCs, right from within Media Player. Oh, yeah—see them and *play* them.
- **Send your music to another computer.** Using the new Play To command, you can use your PC as a glorified remote control that operates playback on a *different* PC, sending your music to it from across the network.

Note: And not just a different PC. This feature can also send music to a new generation of gear bearing the DLNA (Digital Living Network Alliance) logo–TV sets, video recorders, and so on. That's the theory, anyway.

- **Listen to your home music collection from across the Internet.** Yes, that's right: From any PC in the world, you can listen to the music that's on your PC back home—no charge.

Here are the step-by-steps.

Note: Amazingly, the record companies seem to be OK with all this music sharing. Microsoft has designed these features cleverly enough that it's always you (or your family) listening to your own collection. So the record companies, at least in principle, have nothing to worry about.

Browse One Another's Collections–Homegroup Method

If you've joined your home's Windows computers together into a *homegroup* (Chapter 27), then you'll have a particularly effortless job of sharing one another's Media Player collections. You'll have to do—absolutely nothing.

As shown in Figure 18-9, your other computers' Media Player collections show up automatically at the bottom of the navigation pane. Each shared *account* on each *PC* shows up here. Just click the flippy triangle to expand the name of an account or a PC.

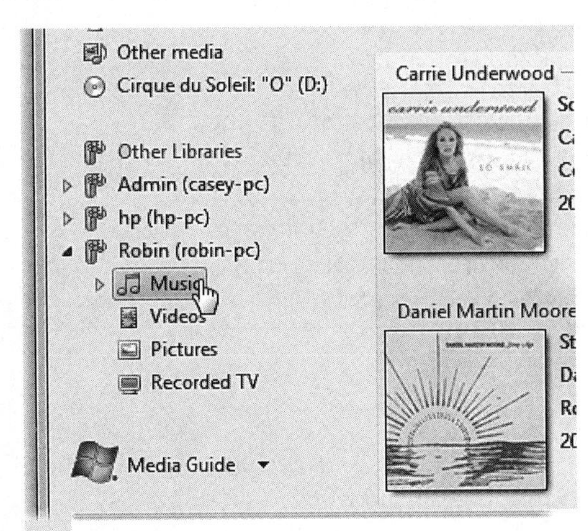

Figure 18-9: *As you sit here at the Casey PC, you can see two other computers on the network–"hp" and Robin–and one other account on your own PC–"Admin." Within, you see a duplicate of your own Media Player categories: Music, Videos, and so on. You can organize and play them exactly as though they're on your own PC.*

Now, it's *possible* that you're on a homegroup and didn't turn on the "Stream my media" at the time you set it up, as suggested in Chapter 27. No problem.

If you're sitting at PC #1, and PC #2 isn't showing up in your copy of Media Player, walk over to PC #2 and choose Stream→"Turn on home media streaming." (If you don't see that command, then it's already turned on.)

Now everything should work as described here.

Browse One Another's Collections—Manual Method

The homegroup method is great, because there aren't really any steps at all. But not every PC can be part of a homegroup, because not every PC on earth (or even in your home) is running Windows 7 or 8. And you can't be in a homegroup without Windows 7 or 8.

Fortunately, you're not out of luck. Even if there's no homegroup, even if some of the PCs aren't running Windows 7/8, you can still share one another's music.

The only difference is that each person must explicitly *turn on* sharing for his own PC.

To do that on your computer, in Media Player, choose Stream→"Turn on media sharing"; in the dialog box, click "Turn on media sharing." (You may be asked to authenticate [page 743].) Now everybody else can see and play your Media Player collection.

It's up to you to persuade *them* to turn on that feature on *their* machines (if you're not seeing them already in your copy of Media Player).

Play To

This feature is one of the most interesting Windows tricks. In this scenario, you *send* music or video from your PC to another PC in the house.

Note: As noted above, you can also send your Media Player playback to any TV, stereo, or other gadget that bears the DLNA logo—and that you can figure out how to use.

Why? Because you probably keep *most* of your music on a single computer, and it can't be everywhere. Suppose you're planning to have a dinner party, but your music collection is on the PC in the attic office. Thanks to the Play To feature, you can line up enough background music for the whole evening, up there in the attic, and send it down to the laptop with the nice speakers in the kitchen. You won't have to keep

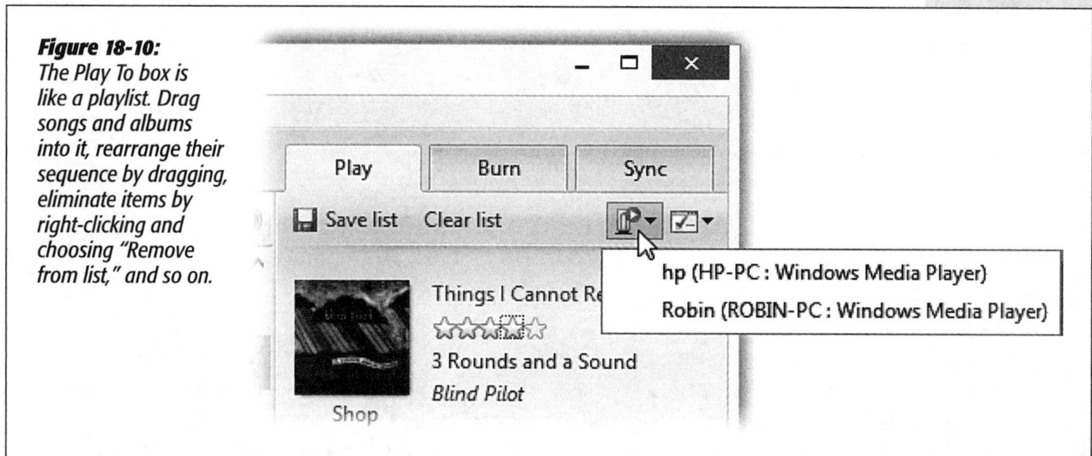

Figure 18-10: *The Play To box is like a playlist. Drag songs and albums into it, rearrange their sequence by dragging, eliminate items by right-clicking and choosing "Remove from list," and so on.*

running back upstairs to choose more music. You can stay downstairs and enjoy the whole party, uninterrupted.

There's one step of setup on the PC that will be *receiving* the playback (in this example, the laptop in the kitchen). Open Media Player. Choose Stream→"Allow remote control of my Player." In the resulting confirmation box, click—you guessed it—"Allow remote control on this network."

Note: This option doesn't work on networks you've designated as Public; see page 439.

Leave Media Player running (you can minimize it if you like).

FREQUENTLY ASKED QUESTION

Shutting Out Others From Your Music

I'm especially annoyed with my sister right now. I don't think she deserves the privilege of listening to my music. Can I block just her PC from listening to my stuff over the network?

But of course.

In Media Player, choose Stream→"More streaming options." (This option appears only after you've turned on streaming.) You see, in a scrolling list, the individual PCs on your network–and you can use the pop-up menu to its right to choose Blocked.

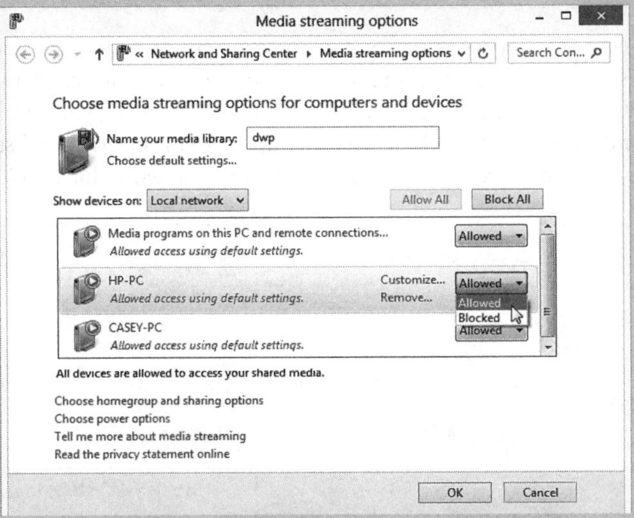

Now she can't get to your music–until she apologizes for her behavior and you change this setting back to Allowed.

If you want to stop everyone from listening to your stuff–we've all had days when we've felt like that–there's a much easier step you can take. Just choose Stream→"Automatically allow devices to play my media" so that the checkmark disappears. That's the master on/off switch for letting other people play with your stuff.

Finally, it's worth noting that you can also limit what other people are allowed to see of your collection. For example, you might want only the best stuff to be available (the highest star ratings) so your network doesn't bog down because your library is so huge. Or you might want to limit what's shared to music or movies with certain parental ratings, so you don't corrupt your kids' minds with filth.

To do that, choose Stream→"More streaming options." In the dialog box that appears, you can click either "Choose default settings" (meaning that you're going to limit what everyone shares) or "Customize" (next to the first computer in the list), to limit what you're sharing.

In the resulting dialog box, turn off "Use default settings," if necessary. Now you see the controls that let you limit what's shared to, for example, "3 stars or higher." Or, in the "Choose parental ratings" box, turn off the checkboxes of "Rated R" or whatever you don't want your impressionable young minds to see. Click OK.

Now go to the attic PC. In Media Player, on the Play tab, click the Play To icon (). Its pop-up menu lists all the PCs in your house that have been prepared for remote controlling, including the kitchen laptop. Choose its name.

If all has gone well, the Play To window appears. It's a waiting list of music that will play in sequence. Fill it up with albums, songs, and playlists, as shown in Figure 18-10.

When you click the big ▶ button in the Play To window, the music, amazingly enough, begins to play on the kitchen laptop. Go downstairs and have some fun.

Play over the Internet

For its final stunt, Media Player lets you listen to your home music collection from *anywhere in the world*—across the Internet.

How does it know it's you, and not some teenage software pirate who just wants free music? Because you have to sign in with your Microsoft account at both ends.

To set this up, open Media Player on your home computer. Choose Stream→"Allow Internet access to home media." Proceed as shown in Figure 18-11.

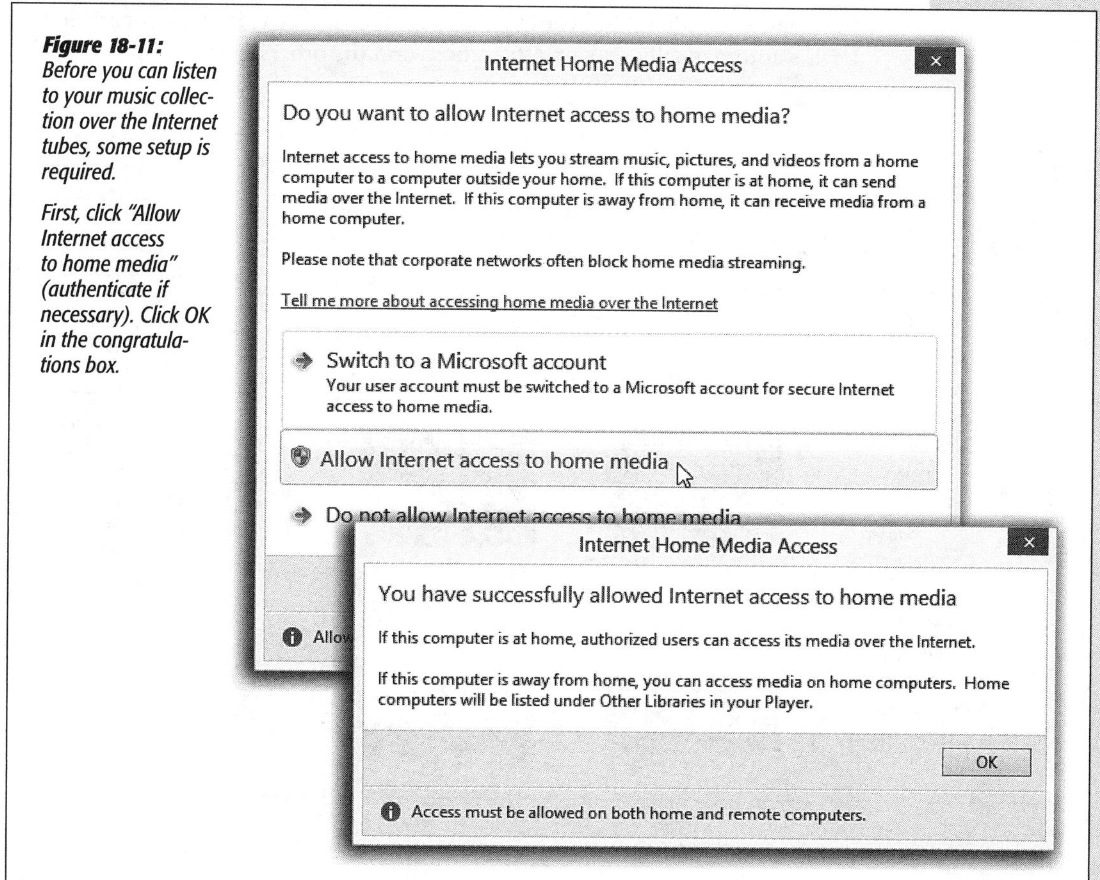

Internet Home Media Access
Do you want to allow Internet access to home media?
Internet access to home media lets you stream music, pictures, and videos from a home computer to a computer outside your home. If this computer is at home, it can send media over the Internet. If this computer is away from home, it can receive media from a home computer.
Please note that corporate networks often block home media streaming.
Tell me more about accessing home media over the Internet
Switch to a Microsoft account
Your user account must be switched to a Microsoft account for secure Internet access to home media.
Allow Internet access to home media
Do not allow Internet access to home media
Internet Home Media Access
You have successfully allowed Internet access to home media
If this computer is at home, authorized users can access its media over the Internet.
If this computer is away from home, you can access media on home computers. Home computers will be listed under Other Libraries in your Player.
OK
Access must be allowed on both home and remote computers.

Figure 18-11: *Before you can listen to your music collection over the Internet tubes, some setup is required.*

First, click "Allow Internet access to home media" (authenticate if necessary). Click OK in the congratulations box.

Now, on any other PC that's online and has Media Player 12 or later, repeat the steps shown in Figure 18-11. And presto: In the Other Libraries category of your navigation pane, your home music library shows up! It's ready to examine and play, across the Internet. If that ain't magic, what is?

Pictures and Videos

Microsoft may like to think that music, photos, and videos are all equally important in Media Player; photos, recorded TV shows, and videos all get equal billing with music.

But that's just silly. Media Player is really all about music, and everyone knows it. If you want to play your photos and videos, Windows Photo Gallery is infinitely better suited to the task; for example, you can't edit photos or apply tags within Media Player.

Nevertheless, here's the rundown.

Start by clicking Pictures or Videos in the navigation tree. The screen changes to something that closely resembles Photo Gallery (Figure 18-12). Here's what you can do in Pictures or Videos mode:

- **See a photo or video at full size** by double-clicking it. The video plays, or a slideshow begins automatically, showing that photo and the others in its group.

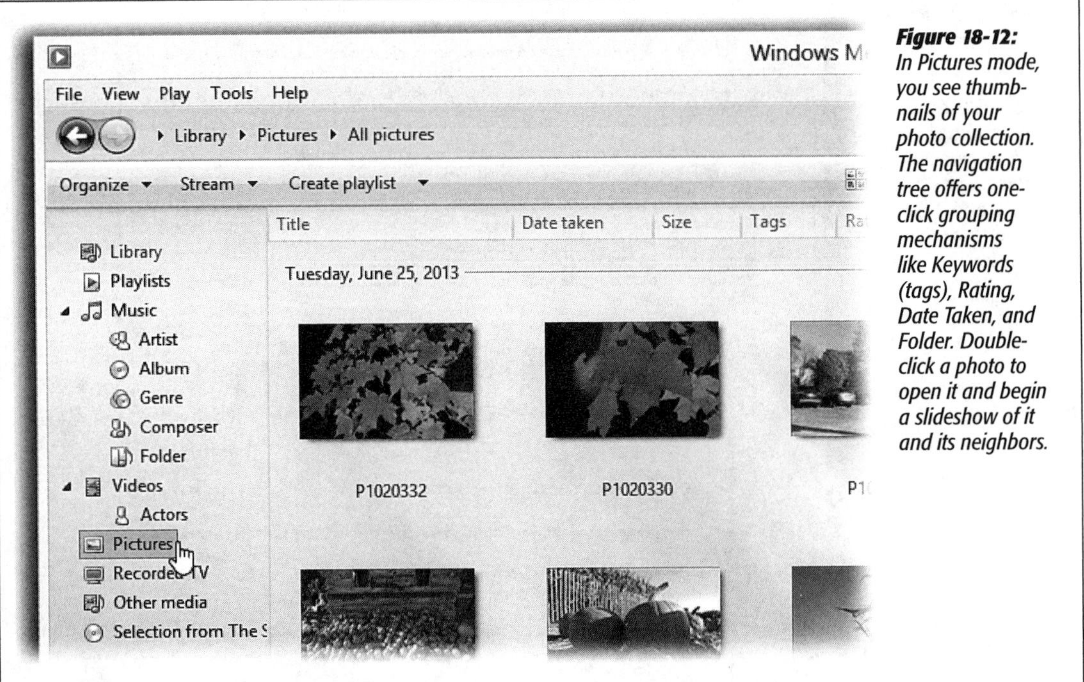

Figure 18-12: *In Pictures mode, you see thumbnails of your photo collection. The navigation tree offers one-click grouping mechanisms like Keywords (tags), Rating, Date Taken, and Folder. Double-click a photo to open it and begin a slideshow of it and its neighbors.*

- **Rate a photo or video** by right-clicking it and, from the shortcut menu, choosing Rate→4 Stars (or whatever).

Tip: In Tiles view, it's easier to rate pictures and videos, because a row of stars appears next to each thumbnail. You just click the third star (for example). Use the View Options pop-up menu next to the search box to choose Tiles view.

- **Create a playlist** by dragging thumbnails into the List pane at right (on the Library tab). In the context of photos or videos, a playlist basically means a slideshow or a sequence of self-playing videos. Click the big ▶ button at the bottom of the screen to see it.
- **Delete a photo or video** by clicking its thumbnail and then pressing the Delete key. Media Player asks if you want it removed only from the library, or from your computer altogether.

POWER USERS' CLINIC

Windows Media Center

Most of the time, you sit about three feet away from the computer screen.

But the modern PC is a digital hub for your photos, music, and videos; the concept of Microsoft's Windows Media Center program, therefore, is to transform playback of these goodies into a 10-foot-away experience. You can play them on your TV while you're sitting on the couch, or you can play them on your PC from across the room. Media Center uses jumbo fonts, buttons, and controls, so you can see them, and lets you operate them with a wireless mouse and keyboard, or a special Media Center remote control.

Better still, Media Center can turn your PC into a full-blown digital video recorder, like a TiVo. If your PC has a TV tuner card, you can watch TV, pause it, rewind and then fast-forward it, record it, and even burn the result to a DVD.

This program was included with certain versions of Windows Vista and Windows 7, but it's no longer included with any version of Windows 8. You can still download it, though—for a fee. It's $10, and available only if you have Windows 8 Pro.

To get it, go to the Start screen and type "add features"; click Settings, and choose "Add features to Windows 8" in the search results. You're taken online and offered the chance to pay the 10 bucks for Windows Media Center.

5

Part Five: Hardware & Peripherals

CHAPTER
19

Printing, Fonts & Faxing

Technologists got pretty excited about "the paperless office" in the 1980s, but the PC explosion had exactly the opposite effect. Thanks to the proliferation of inexpensive, high-quality PC printers, the world generates far more printouts than ever. Fortunately, there's not much to printing from Windows 8.

Installing a Printer

A printer is a peripheral device—something outside the PC—and as such, it won't work without a piece of *driver software* explaining the new hardware to Windows. In general, getting this driver installed is a simple process. It's described in more detail in Chapter 20.

The good news, though, is that Windows 8 comes with the drivers for thousands of printers, all different brands, ready to be installed. Read on.

USB Printers

If the technology gods are smiling, then here's the entire set of instructions for installing a typical inkjet USB printer:

1. **Connect the printer to the computer.**

   That's it. Turn on the printer— you're ready to print. No driver operations, no setup.

If you have a really old printer, its drivers might not be compatible with Windows 8. Check the manufacturer's Web site, such as *www.epson.com* or *www.hp.com,* or a central driver repository like *www.windrivers.com,* to see if there's anything newer.

Network Printers

If you work in an office where people on the network share a single printer (usually a laser printer), the printer usually isn't connected directly to your computer. Instead, it's elsewhere on the network; your PC's Ethernet cable or wireless antenna connects you to it indirectly.

In general, there's very little involved in ensuring that your PC "sees" this printer, either. Its icon simply shows up in your Print dialog box.

Ancient Printers

Although USB printers are the world's most popular type today, there was, believe it or not, a time before USB. In those days, most home printers fell into categories described by the ports they connected to: parallel, serial, and infrared, for example.

Sometimes you get lucky, and these printers work just like modern USB printers: You connect the printer, turn on your PC, and delight in the "Found new hardware" message that appears on your taskbar. You're ready to print.

But if Windows doesn't recognize the printer model you've hooked up, it can't install its drivers automatically. In that case, you'll have to call upon the mighty powers of the wizard shown in Figure 19-1.

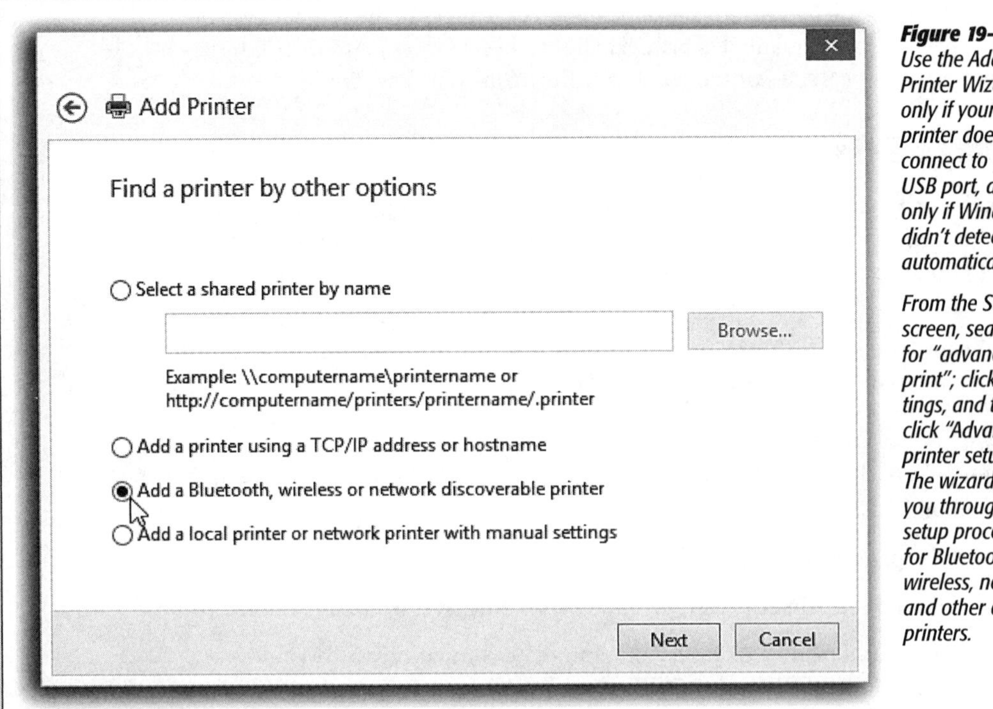

Figure 19-1: *Use the Add Printer Wizard only if your printer doesn't connect to your USB port, and only if Windows didn't detect it automatically.*

From the Start screen, search for "advanced print"; click Settings, and then click "Advanced printer setup." The wizard walks you through the setup procedure for Bluetooth, wireless, network, and other oddball printers.

The Devices and Printers Window

If your driver-installation efforts are ultimately successful, you're rewarded by the appearance of an icon that represents your printer.

This icon appears in the *Devices and Printers* window—an important window that you'll be reading a lot about in this chapter. You can open the window in several ways:

- Open the Start screen. Type *printers* and select Settings under the search box. In the search results, click Devices and Printers.
- At the desktop, open the Control Panel. (For example, right-click the lower-left corner of the screen to open the secret Utilities menu.) If the Control Panel is in Category view, click "View devices and printers" (under Hardware and Sound).

  If you view your Control Panel in the Small Icons or Large Icons view, then click the Devices and Printers icon.

In any case, the Devices and Printers window contains big, good-looking icons representing every gadget plugged into your PC—including the printers you've installed (Figure 19-2).

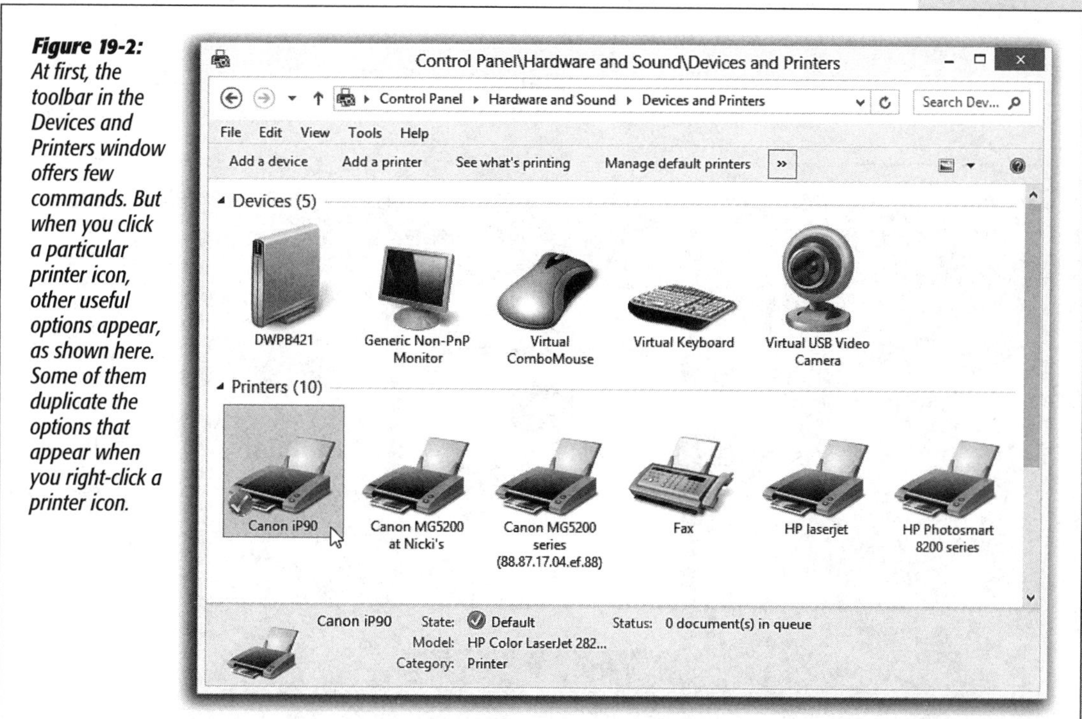

Figure 19-2: *At first, the toolbar in the Devices and Printers window offers few commands. But when you click a particular printer icon, other useful options appear, as shown here. Some of them duplicate the options that appear when you right-click a printer icon.*

If you have a printer from a big-name company, double-clicking its icon here might open the Device Stage: a mini–Web page full of details and useful links like what's printing now, ink levels, and so on. Other devices and printers may open a more generic preference pane or management program. (Device Stage was a much-hyped new feature in Windows 7, but very few manufacturers bothered creating the required details pages. If your gadget has a photorealistic, accurate icon, it probably has a Device Stage page.)

No matter which approach you take, printer icons come in handy in several different situations, as the rest of this chapter clarifies.

Note: When you're finished with a printer–when you sell it, for example–you can eliminate its icon from your Devices and Printers window. Right-click its icon; from the shortcut menu, choose "Remove device."

Printing

Once you've connected a printer or three, printing is little more than a one-click operation.

Printing from TileWorld Apps

After you've created a document you want to see on paper, start the printout. The steps differ depending on which world you're in:

If you're using a TileWorld app, then Open the Charms bar; select Devices to see the list of printers (Figure 19-3, left). Tap the one you want, and then savor the spartan

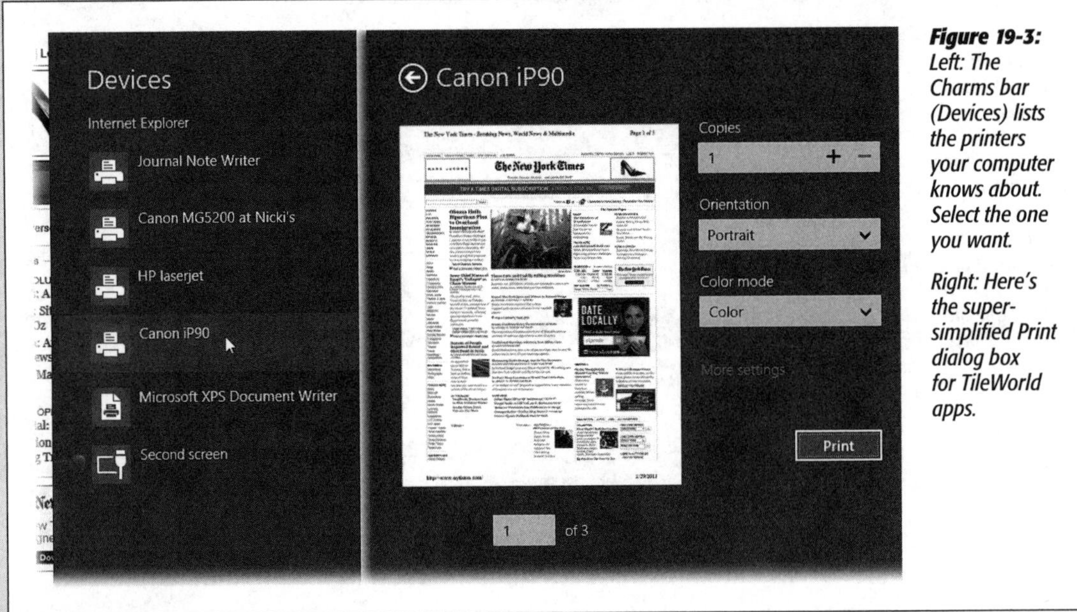

Figure 19-3: *Left: The Charms bar (Devices) lists the printers your computer knows about. Select the one you want.*

Right: Here's the super-simplified Print dialog box for TileWorld apps.

simplicity of the TileWorld Print dialog box (Figure 19-3, right).

Whereas the traditional Windows Print dialog box looks like a space shuttle cockpit, there's nothing to set up in TileWorld except the number of copies you want, the page orientation, and the color mode (for color printers).

If the printout is longer than one page, you can also use the number box below the page preview to have a glance at a different page of the preview.

Printing from Desktop Programs

In a desktop program, choose File→Print, click the Print button on the toolbar, or press Ctrl+P. The Print dialog box appears, as shown at top in Figure 19-4.

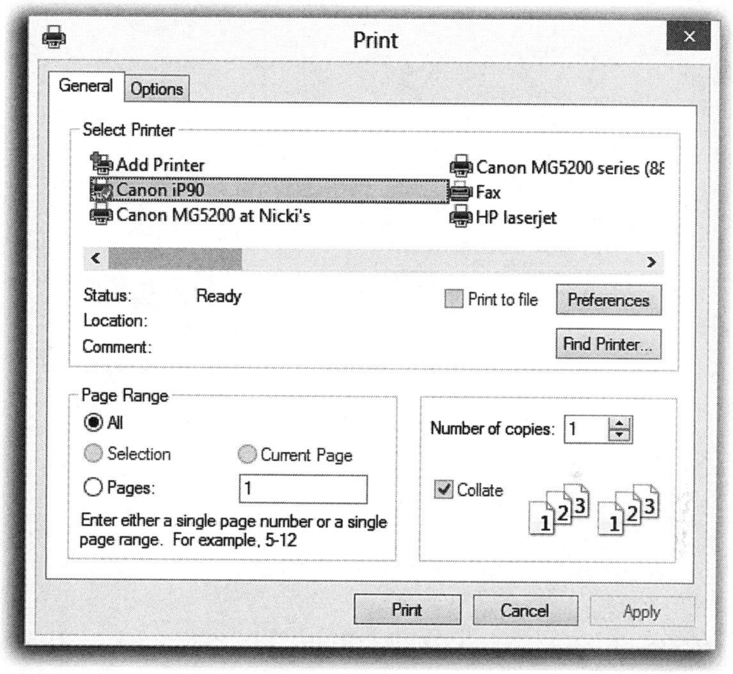

Figure 19-4: *The options in the Print dialog box are different for each printer model and each program, so your Print dialog box may look slightly different. Most of the time, the factory settings shown here are what you want (one copy, print all pages). Just click OK or Print (or press Enter) to close this dialog box and send the document to the printer.*

This dialog box, too, changes depending on the program you're using—the Print dialog box in Microsoft Word looks a lot more intimidating than the WordPad version—and the printer model. But you'll usually find the basics here:

- **Select Printer.** If your PC is connected to several printers, choose the one you want from this list of printers.
- **Preferences/Properties.** Clicking this button opens a version of the printer's Properties dialog box, as shown in Figure 19-5.
- **Page range** controls which pages of the document you want to print. If you want to print only some of the pages, click the Pages option and type in the page numbers you want (with a hyphen, like *3-6* to print pages 3 through 6).

Tip: You can also type in individual page numbers with commas, like *2, 4, 9,* to print only those three pages—or even add hyphens to the mix, like this: *1-3, 5-6, 13-18.*

Click Current Page to print only the page where you've placed the blinking insertion point. Click Selection to print only the text you selected (highlighted) before opening the Print dialog box. (If this option button is dimmed, it's because you didn't highlight any text—or because you're using a program that doesn't offer this feature.)

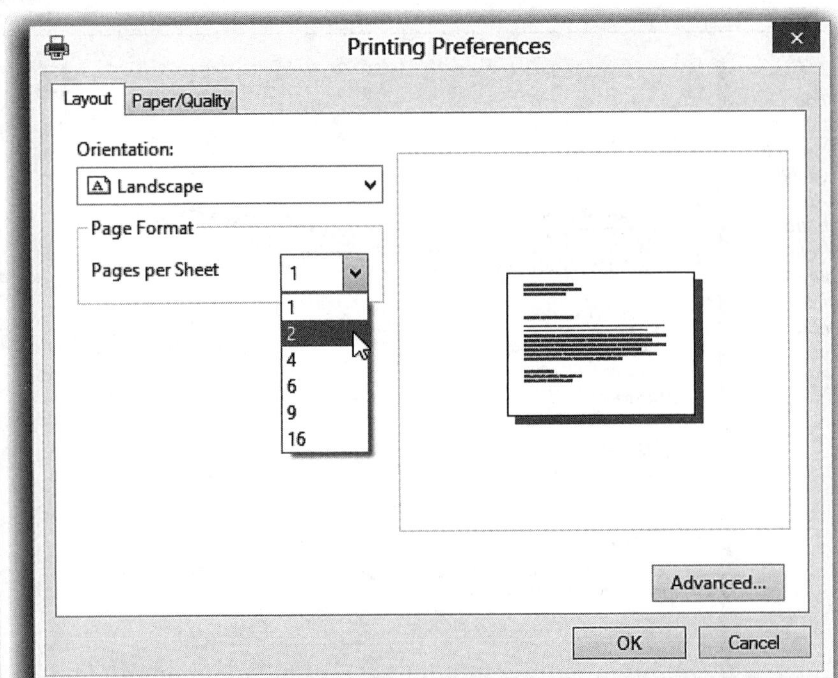

Figure 19-5: *When you open Properties from the Print dialog box, you can specify the paper size you're using, whether you want to print sideways on the page (landscape orientation), what kind of photo paper you're using, and so on. Here you're making changes only for a particular printout; you're not changing any settings for the printer itself. (The specific features of this dialog box depend on the program you're using.)*

- **Number of copies.** To print out several copies of the same thing, use this box to specify the exact number. You get several copies of page 1, then several copies of page 2, and so on, in sequence—*unless* you also turn on the Collate checkbox, which produces complete sets of pages, in order.
- **Print.** The Print drop-down list that might appear in the lower-left section of the dialog box offers three options: "All pages in range," "Odd pages," and "Even pages."

  Use the Odd and Even pages options when you have to print on both sides of the paper but your printer has no special feature for this purpose. You'll have to print all the odd pages, turn the stack of printouts over, and run the pages through the printer again to print even pages.

- **Application-specific options.** The particular program you're using may add a few extra options of its own to an Options tab in this dialog box. For example, Internet Explorer offers an Options tab (Figure 19-6).

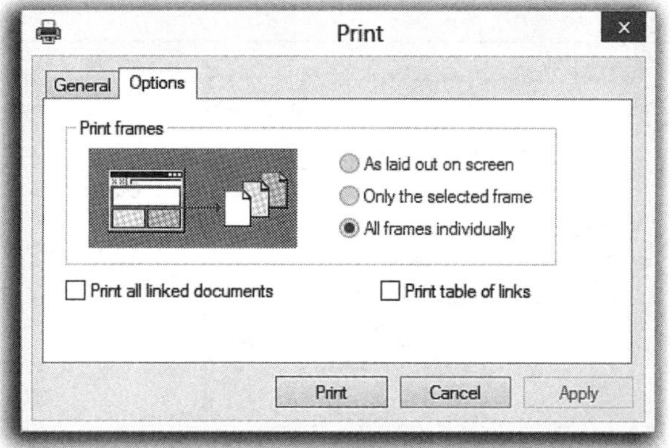

Figure 19-6:
Say you're printing something from Internet Explorer. The Web page about to be printed uses frames (individual, independent, rectangular sections). The Print dialog box in Internet Explorer recognizes frames and lets you specify exactly which frame or frames you want to print. If the page contains links to other Web pages (and these days, what Web page doesn't?), you can print those Web pages, too, or just print a table of the links (a list of the URLs).

When you've finished making changes to the print job, click OK or Print, or press Enter. Thanks to the miracle of *background printing* (also called spooling), you don't have to wait for the document to emerge from the printer before returning to work on your PC. In fact, you can even exit the application while the printout is still under way, generally speaking. (Just don't put your machine to sleep until it's finished printing.)

Tip: During printing, the tiny icon of a printer appears in your notification area. Pointing to it without clicking produces a pop-up tooltip that reveals the background printing activity.

Printing from the Desktop

You don't necessarily have to print a document while it's open in front of you. You can, if you wish, print it directly from the desktop or from an Explorer window in a couple of ways:

- Right-click the document icon, and then choose Print from the shortcut menu. Windows opens the program that created it—Word or Excel, for example. The document is then printed automatically to the default printer.
- If you've opened the printer's own print queue window (Figure 19-7) by right-clicking the Printers icon in your Devices and Printers window and choosing "See what's printing," then you can drag any document icon directly into the list of waiting printouts. Its name joins the others on the list.

These methods bypass the Print dialog box and therefore give you no way to specify which pages you want to print, or how many copies. You just get one copy of the entire document.

Controlling Printouts

Between the moment you click OK in the Print dialog box and the arrival of the first page in the printer's tray, there's a delay. Usually, it's brief, but when you're printing a complex document with lots of graphics, the delay can be considerable.

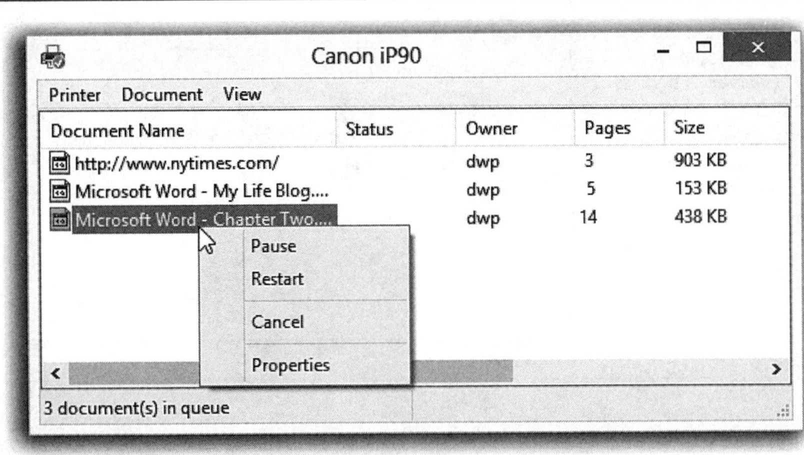

Figure 19-7: *By right-clicking documents in this list, you can pause or cancel any document in the queue–or all of them at once.*

Fortunately, the waiting doesn't necessarily make you less productive, since you can return to work on your PC, or even quit the application and go watch TV. An invisible program called the *print spooler* supervises this background printing process. The spooler collects the document that's being sent to the printer, along with all the codes the printer expects to receive, and then sends this information, little by little, to the printer.

Note: The spooler program creates huge temporary printer files, so a hard drive that's nearly full can wreak havoc with background printing.

To see the list of documents waiting to be printed—the ones that have been stored by the spooler—open the Devices and Printers window, right-click your printer's icon, and then choose "See what's printing" to open its window.

Tip: While the printer is printing, a printer icon appears in the notification area. As a shortcut to opening the printer's window, just double-click that icon.

The printer's window lists the documents currently printing and waiting; this list is called the *print queue* (or just the *queue*), as shown in Figure 19-7. (Documents in the list print in top-to-bottom order.)

You can manipulate documents in a print queue in any of the following ways during printing:

- **Put one on hold.** To pause a document (put it on hold), right-click its name, and then choose Pause from the shortcut menu. When you're ready to let the paused document continue to print, right-click its listing and choose Resume (Figure 19-7).
- **Put them all on hold.** To pause the printer, choose Printer→Pause Printing from the window's menu bar. You might do this when, for example, you need to change the paper in the printer's tray. (Choose Printer→Pause Printing again when you want the printing to pick up from where it left off.)
- **Add another one.** As noted earlier, you can drag any document icon directly *from its disk or folder window* into the printer queue. Its name joins the list of printouts-in-waiting.
- **Cancel one.** To cancel a printout, click its name and then press the Delete key. If you click Yes in the confirmation box, the document disappears from the queue; it'll never print out. (Or right-click it and choose Cancel from the shortcut menu.)
- **Cancel all of them.** To cancel the printing of all the documents in the queue, choose Printer→Cancel All Documents.

Note: A page or so may still print after you've paused or canceled a printout. Your printer has its own memory (the *buffer*), which stores the printout as it's sent from your PC. If you pause or cancel printing, you're only stopping the spooler from sending *more* data to the printer.

- **Rearrange them.** To rearrange the printing order, start by right-clicking the name of one of the printouts-in-waiting; from the shortcut menu, choose Properties. On the General tab, drag the Priority slider left or right. Documents with higher priorities print first.

Fancy Printer Tricks

The masses of Windows users generally slog through life choosing File→Print, clicking OK, and then drumming their fingers as they wait for the paper to slide out of the printer. But your printer can do more than that—much more. Here are just a few of the stunts that await the savvy PC fan.

Sharing a Printer

If you have more than one PC connected to a network, as described in Chapter 24, they all can use the same printer. In the old days, this convenience was restricted to expensive network printers like laser printers. But in Windows 8, you can share even the cheapest little inkjet connected to the USB port of one computer.

To begin, sit down at the computer to which the printer is attached. Open the Devices and Printers window (Figure 19-2). Right-click the printer's icon; from the shortcut menu, choose "Printer properties." Continue as described in Figure 19-8.

Once you've *shared* the printer, its icon shows up in the Devices and Printers windows of all other computers on the same networking Homegroup (Chapter 25). It's listed in their Print dialog boxes, their Printer windows, and so on.

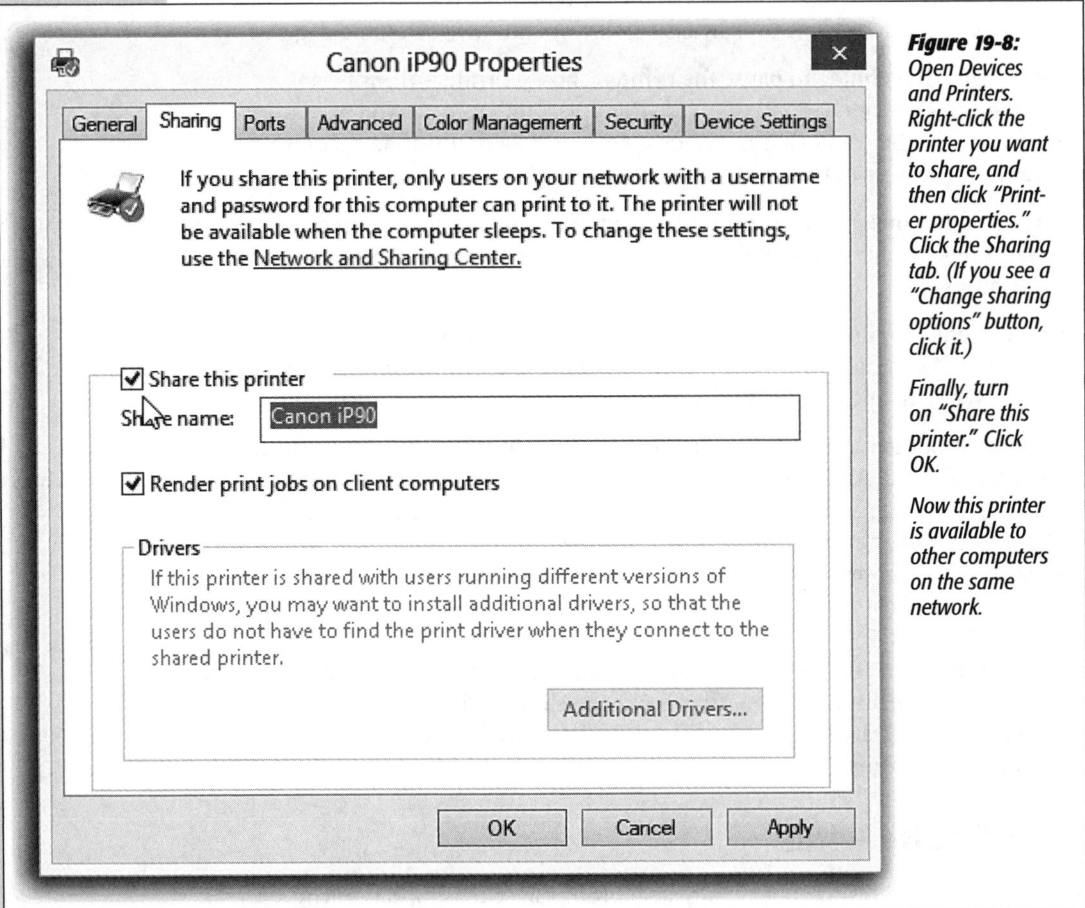

Figure 19-8: *Open Devices and Printers. Right-click the printer you want to share, and then click "Printer properties." Click the Sharing tab. (If you see a "Change sharing options" button, click it.)*

Finally, turn on "Share this printer." Click OK.

Now this printer is available to other computers on the same network.

Limiting Hours of Access

If it's just you, your Dell, and a color inkjet, then you're entitled to feel baffled by this feature, which lets you declare your printer off-limits during certain hours of the day. But if you're the manager of some office whose expensive color laser printer makes printouts that cost a dollar apiece, you may welcome a feature that prevents employees from hanging around after hours in order to print out 500 copies of their headshots.

To specify such an access schedule for a certain printer, follow the instructions in Figure 19-9.

Add a Separator Page

If your PC is on a network whose other members bombard a single laser printer with printouts, you might find *separator pages* useful—the printer version of fax cover sheets. A separator page is generated before each printout, identifying the document and its owner.

This option, too, is accessible from the Advanced tab of the printer's Properties dialog box (Figure 19-9). Click the Separator Page button at the bottom of the dialog box. In the Separator Page dialog box, click the Browse button to choose a *.sep* (separator page) file.

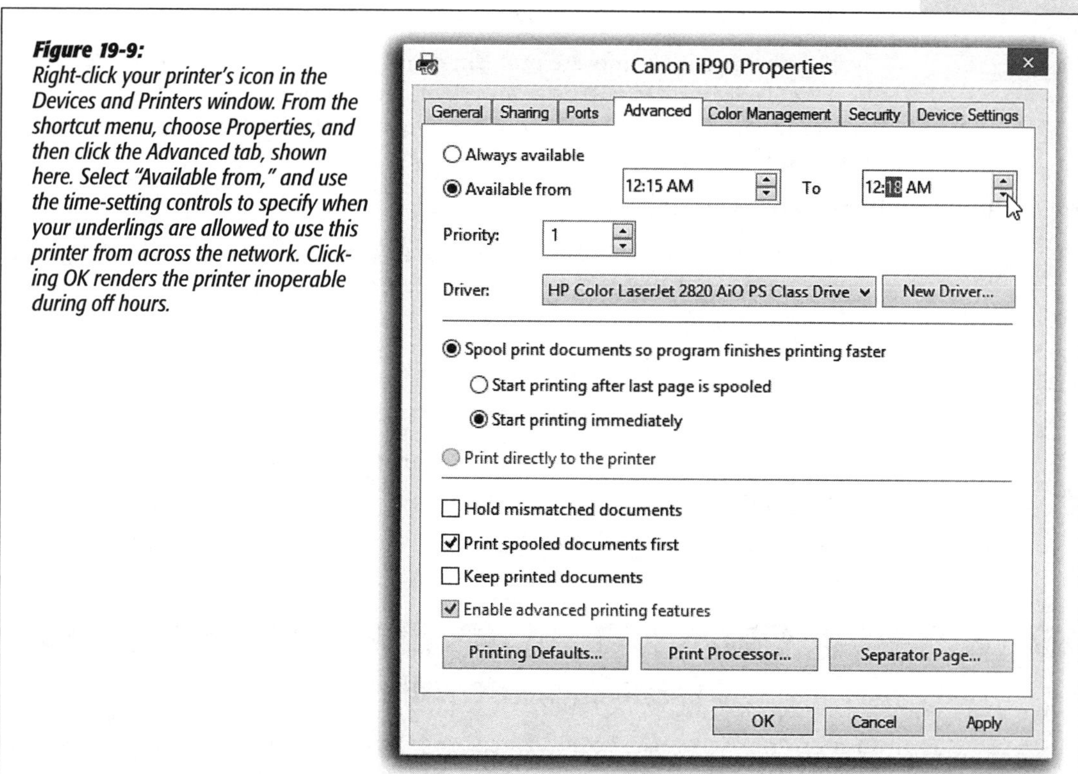

Figure 19-9:
Right-click your printer's icon in the Devices and Printers window. From the shortcut menu, choose Properties, and then click the Advanced tab, shown here. Select "Available from," and use the time-setting controls to specify when your underlings are allowed to use this printer from across the network. Clicking OK renders the printer inoperable during off hours.

If you scroll to the very bottom of the resulting list of geeky Windows folder names, you'll find four of them:

- **Sysprint.sep** is the one you probably want. Not only does this page include the name, date, time, and so on, but it also automatically switches the laser printer to PostScript mode—if it's not already in that mode, and if it's a PostScript printer.
- **Pcl.sep** is the same idea, except that it switches the laser printer to PCL mode—commonly found on HP printers—before printing. (PostScript and PCL are the two most common languages understood by office laser printers.)

- **Pscript.sep** switches the printer to PostScript mode but doesn't print out a separator page.
- **Sysprtj.sep** prints a separator page, switches the printer to PostScript mode, and sets Japanese fonts, if they're available on your printer.

Printer Troubleshooting

If you're having a problem printing, the first diagnosis you must make is whether the problem is related to *software* or *hardware*. A software problem may mean the driver files have become damaged. A hardware problem means there's something wrong with the printer, the port, the cable, the toner, the ink, or whatever.

If you're guessing it's a software problem—fairly likely—reinstall the printer driver. Open the Devices and Printers window, right-click the printer's icon, and then choose Remove Device from the shortcut menu. Then reinstall the printer as described at the beginning of this chapter.

If the problem seems to be hardware-related, try these steps in sequence:

- Check the lights or the LED panel readout on the printer. If you see anything other than the normal "Ready" indicator, then check the printer's manual to diagnose the problem.
- Turn the printer off and on to clear any memory problems.
- Check the printer's manual to learn how to print a test page.
- Check the cable to make sure both ends are firmly and securely plugged into the correct ports.
- Test the cable. Use another cable, or take your cable to another computer/printer combination.

UP TO SPEED

Location-Aware Printing

Speaking of shared printers, if you're working on a laptop, you can let Windows handle the printing chores that arise when you move from one network to another. Windows uses a feature called location-aware printing to do this.

When you're at home, for example, and printing to your family's Homegroup printer, Windows uses that as your default printer. When you head back to the office the next day and log onto your company's network, Windows knows which printer you used the last time you printed at the office and switches to that printer as the default.

To associate a printer with a particular network, open your Devices and Printers window. Click the printer's icon. On the toolbar, click "Manage default printers."

In the resulting dialog box, you can tell Windows to use the same printer as your default all the time (if that's your preference) or to change default printers network to network. Use the Select Network and Select Printer lists to assign the printers you want to use.

If none of these steps leads to an accurate diagnosis, you may have a problem with the port, which is more complicated. Or even worse, the problem may originate from your PC's motherboard (main circuit board), or the printer's. In that case, your computer (or printer) needs professional attention.

Fonts

Some extremely sophisticated programming has gone into the typefaces that are listed in the Fonts dialog boxes of your word processor and other programs. They

POWER USERS' CLINIC

Color Management

As you may have discovered through painful experience, computers aren't great with color. That's because each device you use to create and print digital images "sees" color a little bit differently, which explains why the deep amber captured by your scanner may be rendered as brownish on your monitor but come out as a bit orangey on your Epson inkjet printer. Since every gadget defines and renders color in its own way, colors are often inconsistent as a print job moves from design to proof to press.

The Windows *color management system* (CMS) attempts to sort out this mess, serving as a translator among all the different pieces of hardware in your workflow. For this to work, each device (scanner, monitor, printer, copier, and so on) must be calibrated with a unique *CMS profile*—a file that tells your PC exactly how your particular monitor (or scanner, or printer, or digital camera) defines colors. Armed with the knowledge contained within the profiles, the CMS software can make on-the-fly color corrections, compensating for the quirks of the various devices.

Most of the people who lose sleep over color fidelity do commercial color scanning and printing, where "off" colors are a big deal—after all, a customer might return a product if the actual product color doesn't match the photo on a Web site. Furthermore, not every gadget comes with a CMS profile, and not every gadget can even accommodate one. (If yours does, you'll see a tab called Color Management in the Properties dialog box for your printer.)

If you're interested in this topic, open the Color Management tab for your printer. (Opening the Color Management applet in the Control Panel gets you to the same place, shown here.) The Automatic setting usually means that Windows came with its own profile for your printer, which it has automatically assigned. If you click Manual, you can override this decision and apply a new color profile (that you downloaded from the printer company's Web site, for example).

Remember to follow the same procedure for the other pieces of your color chain—monitors, scanners, and so on. Look for the Color Management tab or dialog box, accessible from their respective Properties dialog boxes.

use *OpenType* and *TrueType* technology, meaning that no matter what point size you select for these fonts, they look smooth and professional—both on the screen and when you print.

Managing Your Fonts

Windows comes with several dozen great-looking fonts: Arial, Book Antiqua, Garamond, Times New Roman, and so on. But the world is filled with additional fonts. You may find them on Web sites or in the catalogs of commercial typeface companies. Sometimes you'll find new fonts on your system after installing a new program, courtesy of its installer.

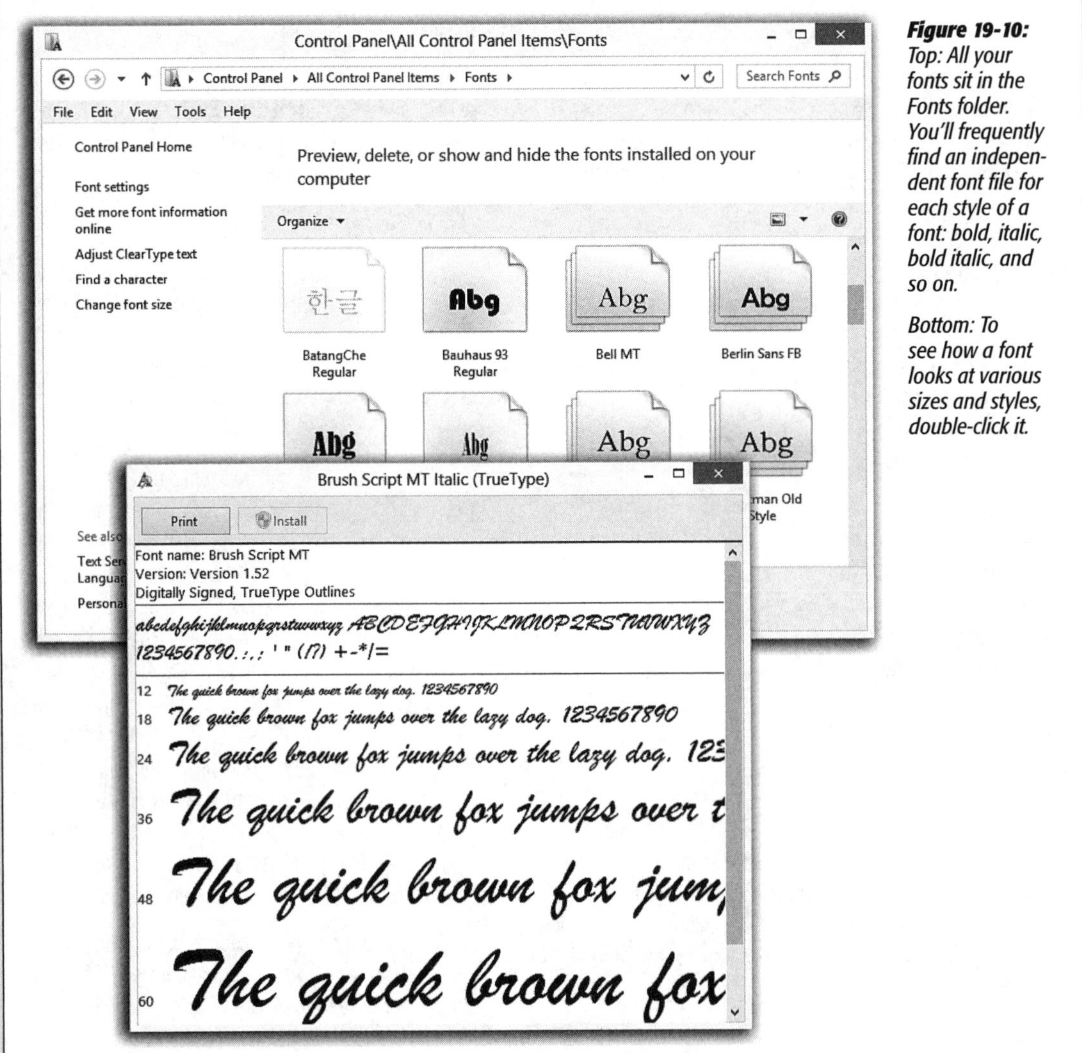

Figure 19-10: *Top: All your fonts sit in the Fonts folder. You'll frequently find an independent font file for each style of a font: bold, italic, bold italic, and so on.*

Bottom: To see how a font looks at various sizes and styles, double-click it.

To review the files that represent your typefaces, open the Fonts icon in the Control Panel. (Switch to Large Icons or Small Icons view to see the Fonts icon.) As Figure 19-10 illustrates, it's easy and enlightening to explore this folder.

Tip: The Fonts icon in your Control Panel window is only a shortcut to the *real* folder, which is in your Local Disk (C:)→Windows→Fonts folder.

To remove a font from your system, right-click it and then choose Delete from the shortcut menu, or highlight it and then click Delete on the toolbar. To install a new font, first download the font (from the Internet, for example) and then drag its file icon into this window (or right-click the font and then click Install). You can also choose to show or hide specific fonts in your programs. The Fonts window in Control Panel includes a column that shows the status of a font. Select a font, and then click Show or Hide to make this font available in the programs you use.

Whatever you do, you see the changes immediately reflected in your programs' Font dialog boxes; you don't even have to quit and reopen them.

Faxing

In the increasingly rare event that your PC has a built-in fax modem, and your PC is connected to a phone line, it can serve as a true-blue fax machine. This feature works like a charm, saves money on paper and fax cartridges, and may even spare you the expense of buying a physical fax machine.

Sending a fax is even easier on a PC than on a real fax machine; you just use the regular Print command (Ctrl+P), exactly as though you were making a printout of the onscreen document. When faxes come *in,* you can opt to have them printed automatically, or you can simply read them on the screen. You even get a dedicated program, Windows Fax and Scan, for the purpose of managing faxes

Tip: The similarity with printing doesn't stop there. The Devices and Printers folder even contains a Fax icon that works just like a printer icon.

Sending a Fax from Any Program

Now, the one big limitation of PC-based faxing is that you can transmit only documents that are, in fact, *on the computer.* That pretty much rules out faxing notes scribbled on a legal pad, clippings from *People* magazine, and so on (unless you scan them first).

If you're still undaunted, the procedure for sending a fax is very easy:

1. **Open up whatever document you want to fax. Choose File→Print.**

   The Print dialog box appears.

2. **Click the Fax icon (or choose Fax from the Select Printer list, as shown in Figure 19-11), and then click OK or Print.**

   The very first time you try faxing, you encounter the Fax Setup Wizard. It first asks you to connect to a fax modem. Choose that option, and then type a name for your fax modem.

   Next it wants you to specify what happens when someone sends a fax to *you* (that is, when the phone line your PC is connected to "rings"). Click "Answer automatically" if you want Windows to answer incoming calls after five rings, assuming that if you haven't picked up by that time, the incoming call is probably a fax.

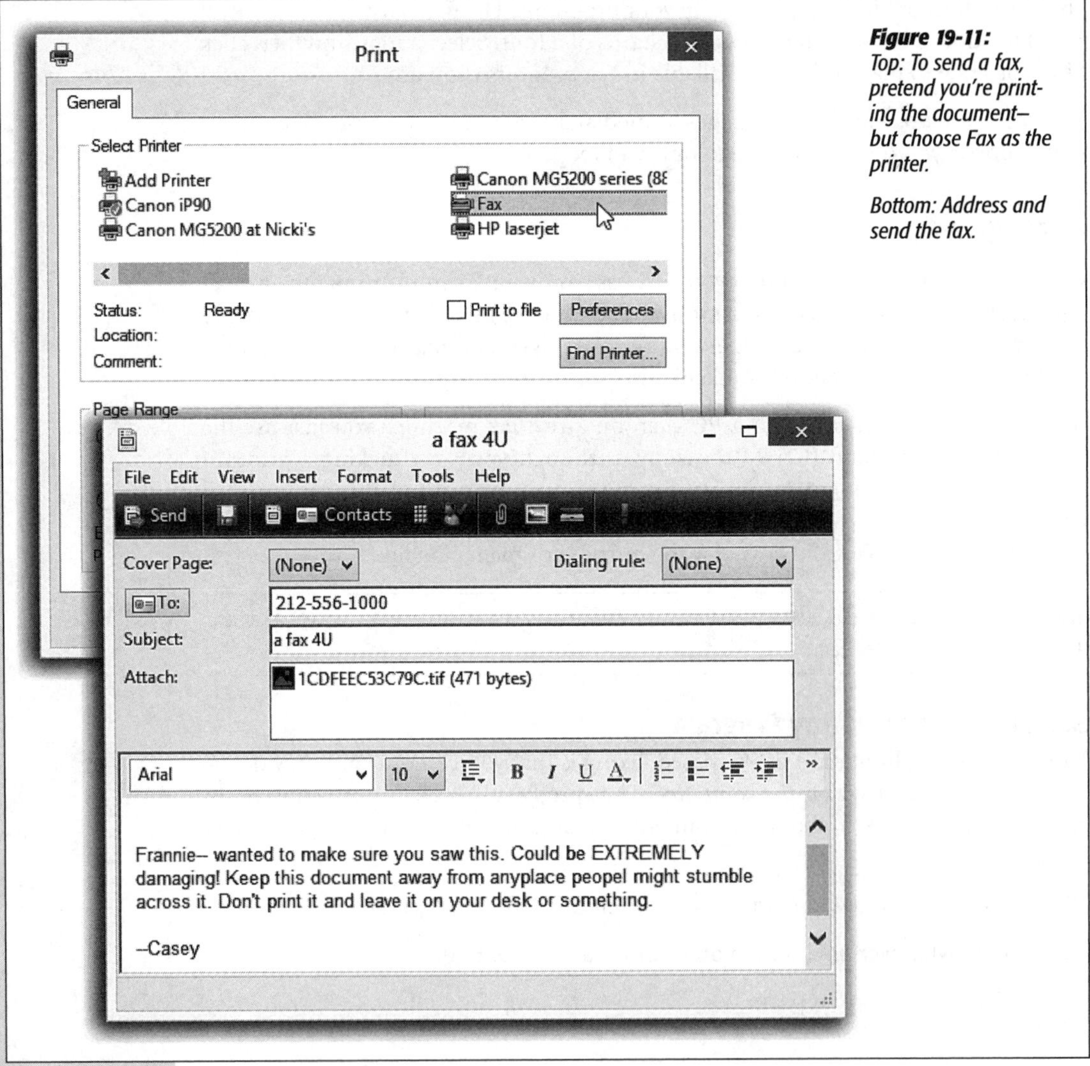

Figure 19-11:
Top: To send a fax, pretend you're printing the document—but choose Fax as the printer.

Bottom: Address and send the fax.

If you choose "Notify me," then each incoming call triggers an onscreen message, asking you whether you want the PC to answer as a fax machine. And if you choose "I'll choose later," you can postpone the decision and get on with sending your first fax.

Note: At this point, the Windows Firewall, rather stupidly, may interrupt to ask if it's OK for Windows Fax and Scan to run. Click Unblock.

Finally, you arrive at a New Fax window (like a New Message window) (Figure 19-11, bottom).

3. **Type the recipient's fax number into the "To:" box.**

   Or click the tiny envelope next to "To:" to open up the Select Recipients list (where you can find people listed as your Windows Contacts and others). Double-click the name of the fax-equipped buddy you want.

4. **If you want a cover page, choose a cover-page design from the Cover Page drop-down menu.**

   A new text box opens up, where you can type a little note, which also appears on the cover page.

Note: You can ignore the main message box at the bottom of the window for now. It's intended for creating faxes from thin air, as described below, rather than faxes that began life as documents on your PC.

   At this point, type a subject for your fax. You may also want to choose View→Preview (or click the tiny Preview icon on the toolbar) to give it a final inspection before it goes forth over the wires. When you're finished looking it over, your fax is ready to send.

5. **Click Send in the toolbar.**

   Your modem dials, and the fax goes on its merry way. A status dialog box appears (although its progress bar doesn't actually indicate how much time remains). You can go do other work on the PC; when the fax goes through, a cheerful message appears in your notification area.

Your recipient is in for a real treat. Faxes you send straight from your PC's brain emerge at the receiving fax machine looking twice as crisp and clean as faxes sent from a standalone fax machine. After all, you never scanned them through a typical fax machine's crude scanner on your end.

Faxing Using Windows Fax and Scan

If you just have a few quick words to fax to somebody, you can use Fax and Scan by itself, without first opening a document on your PC. Open the Fax and Scan program by searching for it at the Start screen.

Click New Fax in the toolbar, fill in the fax number, and choose a cover page as described in the preceding steps. This time, however, you can use the broad message area at the bottom of the window to type the body of your text.

Tip: Cover pages automatically include your name, fax number, and so on. And how does it know all this? Because, in Fax and Scan, you chose Tools→Sender Information and filled it out.

Receiving Faxes

There are several reasons why you may *not* want your PC to receive faxes. Maybe you already have a standalone fax machine that you use for receiving them. Maybe your house has only one phone line, whose number you don't want to give out to people who might blast your ear with fax tones.

But receiving faxes on the PC has a number of advantages, too. You don't pay a cent for paper or ink cartridges, for example, and you have a handy, organized software program that helps you track every fax you've ever received.

Note: The discussion here applies to normal people who send faxes using a computer's built-in fax modem. If you work in a corporation where the network geeks have installed a *fax server,* life is even easier. Incoming faxes automatically arrive in the inbox of the Fax and Scan program.

POWER USERS' CLINIC

Cover-Page Art Class

You don't have to be content with the handful of fax cover pages that Microsoft provides. The Fax and Scan program comes with its own little cover-page design studio. To get started, choose Tools→Cover Pages.

At this point, you could click the New button to call up a pure, empty, virginal cover page. But by far the easiest way to get going is to open one of the existing cover pages, make changes to it, and then save it under a different name.

To do so, click the Copy button now in front of you, and then open one of the four cover-page templates that Windows presents. Windows puts it into what's now a one-item list. Select the item and click Rename to give it a new name, if you like, and then click Open to begin work on your redesign.

The design program works like any standard drawing program. In order to type text that won't change—a confidentiality notice, for example—click the Text tool on the toolbar (which looks like this: **ab|**), and then click the page. Use the commands in the Insert menu to plop placeholder text boxes onto the page—special rectangles that, on the actual cover sheet, will be filled by your name, fax number, the number of pages, and so on. You can transfer your own company logo onto the page just by pasting it there (Edit→Paste).

Every item you place on the page—a text block, a graphic, and so on—is a separate object that you can move around independently using the arrow tool. In fact, you can even move a selected object in front of, or behind, other objects, using the commands in the Layout menu.

When you're finished with your masterpiece, choose File→Save. It gets saved into your Documents→Fax→Personal CoverPages folder (meaning that only you have access to it—not other people who share the PC and log in with their own accounts).

Exactly what happens when a fax comes in is up to you. Start by opening Windows Fax and Scan; then choose Tools→Fax Settings, and proceed as shown in Figure 19-12.

You have two options for receiving faxes:

- **Manually answer.** This option is an almost-perfect solution if your PC and telephone share the same phone line—that is, if you use the line mostly for talking,

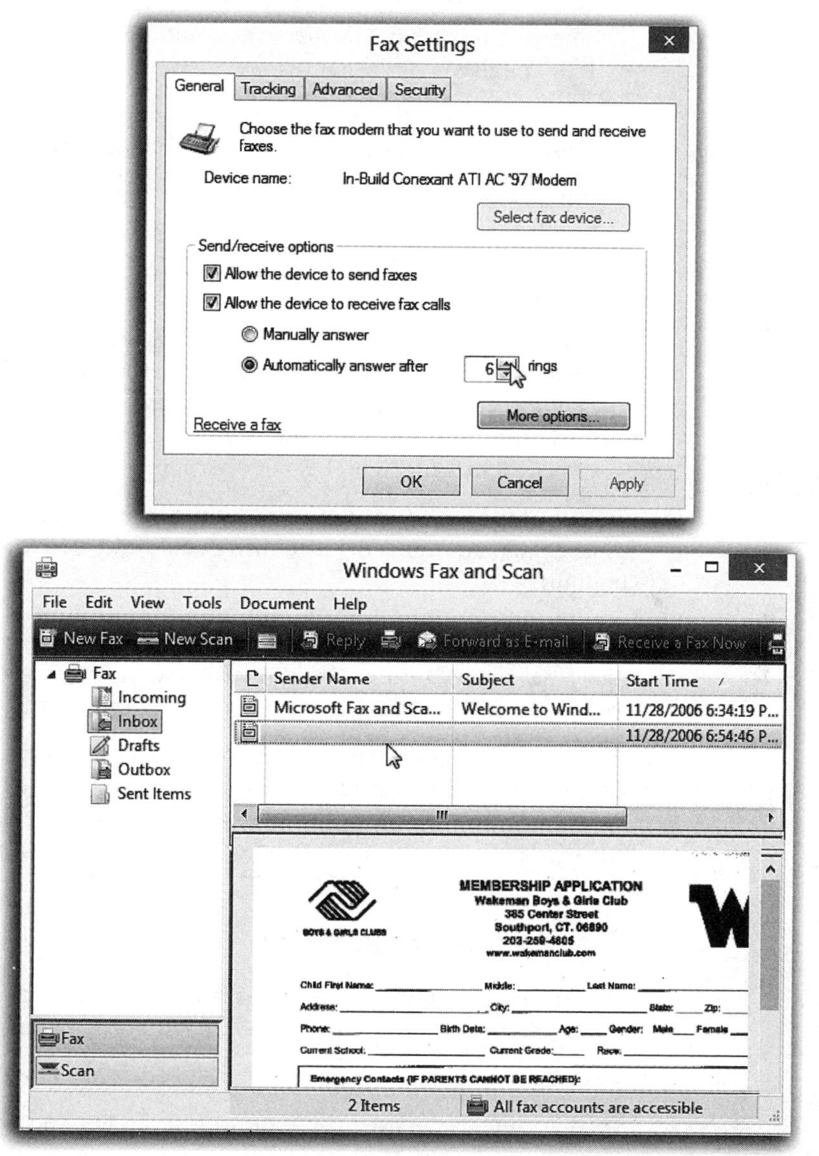

Figure 19-12: *Top: Click the General tab and then turn on "Allow device to receive fax calls." If you choose "Automatically answer," you can also specify how many rings you want to go by before the PC answers; you don't want it answering regular incoming voice calls before you've had a chance to pick up.*

Bottom: Windows Fax and Scan takes over and begins to download the fax. The incoming fax winds up in your inbox, just as though it's a particularly old-fashioned email message.

but occasionally receive a fax. From now on, every time the phone rings, a balloon in your notification area announces: "Incoming call from [the phone number]. Click here to answer this call as a fax call." (See Figure 19-12.)

When you do so, your PC answers the phone and begins to receive the fax. To see it, open Fax and Scan.

- **Automatically answer after.** Use this option if your PC has a phone line all to itself. In this case, incoming faxes produce a telephone-ringing sound, but there's otherwise no activity on your screen until the fax has been safely received. Once again, received faxes secret themselves away in your Fax and Scan program.

While you're setting things up in the Fax Settings dialog box, don't miss the "More options" button. It's the gateway to two useful features:

- **Print a copy to.** If you like, Windows can print out each incoming fax, using the printer you specify here. Of course, doing so defeats the environmental and cost advantages of viewing your faxes onscreen, but at least you've got something you can hold in your hand.
- **Save a copy to.** Ordinarily, incoming faxes are transferred to your Fax and Scan program. If you turn on this option, however, you can direct Windows to place a *duplicate* copy of each one—stored as a graphics file—in a folder of your choice. (Either way, it's handy to know that these are standard TIFF graphics files that you can email to somebody else—or even edit.)

To look at the faxes you've received, open Fax and Scan. Click the inbox to see a list of faxes that have come in—and then double-click one to open it up (Figure 19-12, bottom).

Tip: Another great way to capitalize on the power of your PC for fax purposes is to sign up for J2 or eFax (*www.j2.com* and *www.efax.com*). These services issue you your own personal fax number. And here's the twist–all faxes sent to that number arrive at your PC as email attachments.

The brilliance of the system, of course, is that you don't need another phone line for this, and you can get these faxes anywhere in the world, even on the road. And here's the best part: As of this writing, both of these services are absolutely free. (You might consider reserving a separate email address just for your J2 or eFax account, however, since waves of junk mail are part of the "free" bargain.)

Scanning Documents

Faxing isn't the only technology that turns paper into digital bits. Scanning is the other—and that, too, is a talent of Windows Fax and Scan.

First, install your scanner (and its driver) as described in Chapter 20.

Load it up with the page you want to scan. In Fax and Scan, click New Scan. The New Scan dialog box appears. Click Preview to trigger a quick, temporary scan so that you can see how the document will look after the scan (Figure 19-13). If it all looks good, click Scan.

Once the document has magically turned into a graphic in your Scan list, you can do all kinds of neat things with it: Forward it as a fax or an email attachment (click Forward as Fax or Forward as E-mail on the toolbar); export it as a JPEG, GIF, BMP, TIFF, or PNG document (click "Save as" on the toolbar); print it; or delete it.

Figure 19-13: *In this box, you have the chance to specify what sort of thing you want to scan—picture? document?—and specify its resolution and color settings.*

Choose 300 to 600 dots per inch resolution (dpi) for professional scans; for everyday scanning, 150 to 200 dpi is plenty. The more dots, the bigger the resulting file.

FREQUENTLY ASKED QUESTION

Scanning Text—and then Editing It

I scanned an article from a magazine. How do I copy a couple of paragraphs from it into my word processor?

When you scan an article or a page of a book, you're not capturing text; you're just taking a *picture* of text. You can no more copy and paste a paragraph out of the resulting graphics file than you can copy text out of a photograph. Your PC sees everything on the scanned page as one gigantic graphic.

If you want to edit text you've scanned, then you need *optical character recognition (OCR)* software, which comes free with certain scanners. This kind of software analyzes the patterns of dots in a scanned graphics file and does a fairly good job of turning it into a word processor document that contains the original text. When businesses decide to convert old paper documents into computer files (insurance policies, research papers, and so on), OCR software is what they use.

CHAPTER 20

Hardware & Drivers

If your Windows 8 machine is a tablet, good for you. You probably won't have to spend much time mucking around with peripherals and their drivers. But if you have a regular PC, adding new gear is part of the fun. Hard drives, flash drives, cameras, phones, printers, scanners, network cards, video cards, keyboards, monitors, game controllers, and other accessories all make life worth living. When you introduce a new piece of equipment to the PC, you must hook it up and install its *driver,* the software that lets a new gadget talk to the rest of the PC.

UP TO SPEED

The Master Compatibility List

Windows 8 is another leap ahead in the evolution of the operating system. Discovering that a piece of your existing equipment is now flaky or nonfunctional is par for the course.

If you'd like to eliminate every glitch and every shred of troubleshooting inconvenience, limit your add-on gear to products that pass the test—the one administered by the Windows 7 Upgrade Assistant. That's a little program you can download from this Web site:

http://windows.microsoft.com/en-US/windows-8/upgrade-to-windows-8

Even if your computer uses Windows Vista—which means it's probably fine for Windows 8—running the Upgrade Assistant is a good idea. You should know how many of your peripherals won't work *before* you install Windows 8. (The Upgrade Assistant takes the place of the old Hardware Compatibility List [HCL], an online list of every gadget and program on earth that had been shown to work with Windows XP.)

Plug in all your external gadgets—scanners, printers, hard drives, and so on—and then run the Assistant program you've downloaded.

The driver issue was once a chronic, nagging worry for the average Windows fan, however. Drivers conflicted; drivers went missing; drivers went bad; drivers went out of date.

Fortunately, Microsoft has made further strides in addressing the driver problem. Windows 8 comes with thousands upon thousands of drivers for common products already built in, and Microsoft deposits dozens more on your hard drive, behind the scenes, with every Windows Update. Chances are good that you'll live a long and happy life without ever having to lose a Saturday manually configuring new gizmos, as your forefathers did.

Most of the time, you plug in some new USB gadget, and bam—it's ready to use. You don't have to install anything, walk through any wizards, or sacrifice any small animals.

This chapter counsels you on what to do when the built-in, autorecognized drivers don't do the trick.

Note: Chapter 19 contains additional hardware-installation details specific to printers.

External Gadgets

Over the years, various engineering organizations have devised an almost silly number of different connectors for printers, scanners, and other *peripherals* (Figure 20-1 shows a typical assortment). The back panel—or front, or even side panel—of your PC may include any of these connector varieties.

USB Jacks

Man, you gotta love USBs (Universal Serial Bus). The more of these jacks your PC has, the better.

The USB jack itself is a compact, thin, rectangular connector that's easy to plug and unplug. It often provides power to the gadget, saving you one more cord and one

UP TO SPEED

Of Hubs and Power

If your PC doesn't have enough built-in USB jacks to handle all your USB devices, you can also attach a USB *hub* (with, for example, four or eight additional USB ports), in order to attach multiple USB devices simultaneously.

Whether the jacks are built in or on a hub, though, you have to be aware of whether or not they're *powered* or *unpowered* jacks.

Unpowered ones just transmit communication signals with the USB gadget. These kinds of USB gadgets work fine with unpowered jacks: mice, keyboards, flash drives, and anything with its own power cord (like printers).

Powered USB jacks also supply current to whatever's plugged in. You need that for scanners, Webcams, hard drives, and other gadgets that don't have their own power cords but transmit lots of data.

The bottom line? If a gadget isn't working, it may be because it requires a powered jack and you've given it an unpowered one.

more bit of clutter. And it's hot-pluggable, so you don't have to turn off the gadget (or the PC) before connecting or disconnecting it.

Tip: Be careful, though, not to yank a USB flash drive or hard drive out of the PC when it might be in the middle of copying files.

USB accommodates a huge variety of gadgets: USB hard drives, scanners, mice, phones, keyboards, printers, palmtop cradles, digital cameras, camcorders, and so on.

Most modern PCs come with at least two USB ports, often on both the front and back panels.

Note: Today's USB gadgets and PCs offer *USB 3.0* jacks—a faster, enhanced form of USB. You can still plug the older, slower USB 1.1 and 2 gadgets into USB 3.0 jacks, and vice versa—but you'll get the older, slower speed.

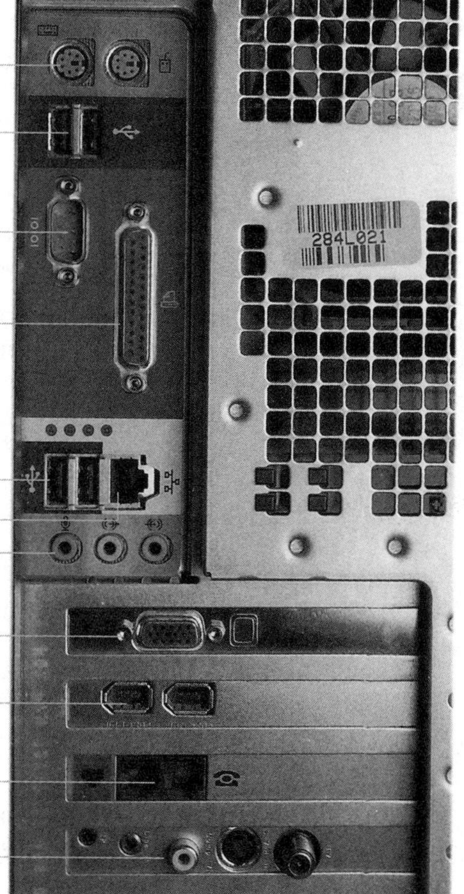

Figure 20-1:
The back panel of a PC. Not every computer has every kind of jack—some of the ones shown here are rapidly disappearing, and occasionally a new type crops up.

A few not shown on this older PC: Thunderbolt (for monitors and certain hard drives); HDMI (to connect a hi-def television); and DisplayPort (to connect monitors and projectors).

Other Jacks

At one time, the backs of PCs were pockmarked with all manner of crazy jacks: serial ports, PS/2 ports, SCSI ports, parallel ports, keyboard ports. Today, all these connectors are rapidly disappearing, thanks to the all-powerful superiority of the USB jack.

Here's what else you may find on the modern PC, though:

- **FireWire port.** The faster FireWire 800 has a rectangular jack; the original, FireWire 400 jack is a rectangle-with-one-V-shaped-end. (Various companies may also call it IEEE 1394 or i.Link.) It's a hot-pluggable, extremely high-speed connector that's ideal for digital camcorders (for video editing) and external hard drives.
- **Thunderbolt port.** This fairly rare jack connects to fairly rare Thunderbolt-compatible hard drives and monitors. Superfast.
- **Bluetooth adapters.** Bluetooth is a fascinating short-range wireless technology. Don't think of it as a networking scheme—it's intended for the elimination of *cable clutter.* A Bluetooth-equipped PC can print to a Bluetooth printer, or "talk" to a Bluetooth headset, or sync with a Bluetooth phone, from up to 30 feet away.
- **PC card or ExpressCard slot.** These slots are found primarily on older laptops. They accommodate miniature expansion cards, which look like metal Visa cards. Each card adds a useful feature to your laptop: additional USB jacks, a cellular high-speed modem, external eSATA adapters (for plugging in hard drives), and so on.

  ExpressCard is a newer, narrower type of card. (Actually, there are *two* ExpressCard types—one narrow, and one *really* narrow.) Just make sure, before you buy any card, that it fits the kind of slot your laptop has.
- **Video (VGA), DVI, or DisplayPort.** These are all ways to connect a second monitor or a projector. The older but widely compatible VGA is a narrow female connector with 15 holes along three rows. The DVI (digital visual interface) jack has 24 pins and is designed for modern LCD screens. And DisplayPort, which is intended to replace VGA and DVI (but retain compatibility via adapters), looks like a USB jack with one diagonally clipped corner.
- **HDMI.** Handy! This kind of jack sends high-def video and audio to an HDTV set.
- **SD card reader.** Pop the SD memory card out of your camera and straight into this slot to import the photos. Sweet.

Connecting New Gadgets

In books, magazines, and online chatter about Windows, you'll frequently hear people talk about *installing* a new component. In many cases, they aren't talking about physically hooking it up to the PC—they're talking about installing its driver software.

But remember the insanely complete collection of drivers that come with Windows 8, especially for USB gadgets. When you plug the thing into the PC for the first time,

Windows 8 autodetects its presence, digs into its trunk for the driver, and installs it automatically. A flurry of balloons in the notification area may or may not appear (Figure 20-2).

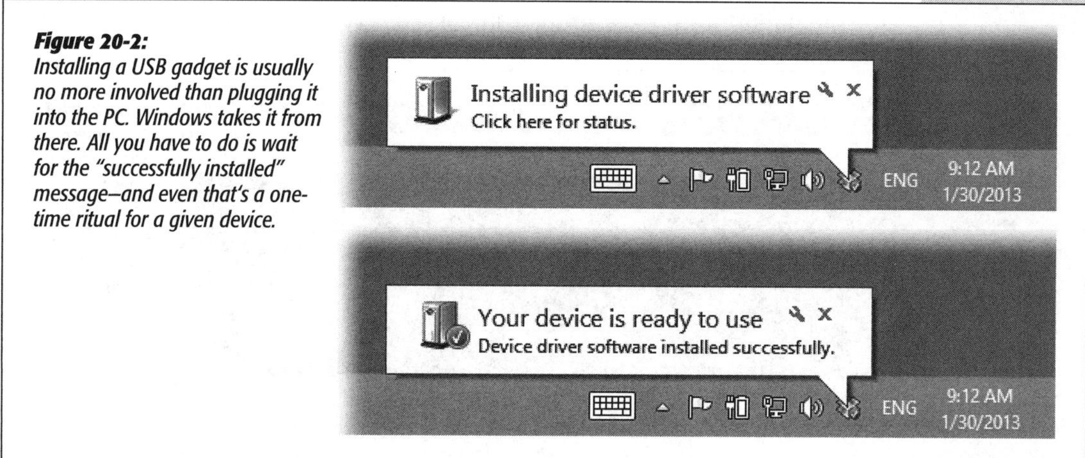

Figure 20-2: *Installing a USB gadget is usually no more involved than plugging it into the PC. Windows takes it from there. All you have to do is wait for the "successfully installed" message—and even that's a one-time ritual for a given device.*

If Windows can't find the driver, a dialog box appears, suggesting that you insert whatever software-installation disc came with the gadget.

And now, the fine print:

- Usually the process shown in Figure 20-2 is all it takes—that is, you start by plugging the device in. Sometimes, though, you're supposed to install the driver before connecting the gizmo. (Check the manual.)
- Usually, the device should be turned on before you plug it in. Again, though, check the manual, because some devices are supposed to be switched on during the installation.

In either case, your gear is now completely installed—both its hardware and its software—and ready to use.

Device Stage

The *Device Stage*, a feature introduced in Windows 7, is supposed to demystify the sometimes baffling world of external gadgets. Its mission: to depict, in visual form, Windows' understanding of whatever gadgets you've connected to it.

Microsoft refers to Device Stage as a "home page" for the most popular kinds of gadgets: cellphones, music players, cameras, printers, scanners, multifunction printers, mice, and keyboards. They can be connected to your PC by a USB cable or even a wireless Bluetooth or WiFi connection. To open a gadget's Device Stage window, you double-click its icon in the Devices and Printers window.

For each gadget, the Device Stage window (Figure 20-3) is supposed to display highly specific information and links. For a camera, you might see a handsome photo of the camera model you've plugged in, the number of photos on it to be downloaded, how much space remains on the card, and the current battery level—and you're offered links to import the photos, read the manual, buy accessories, and so on.

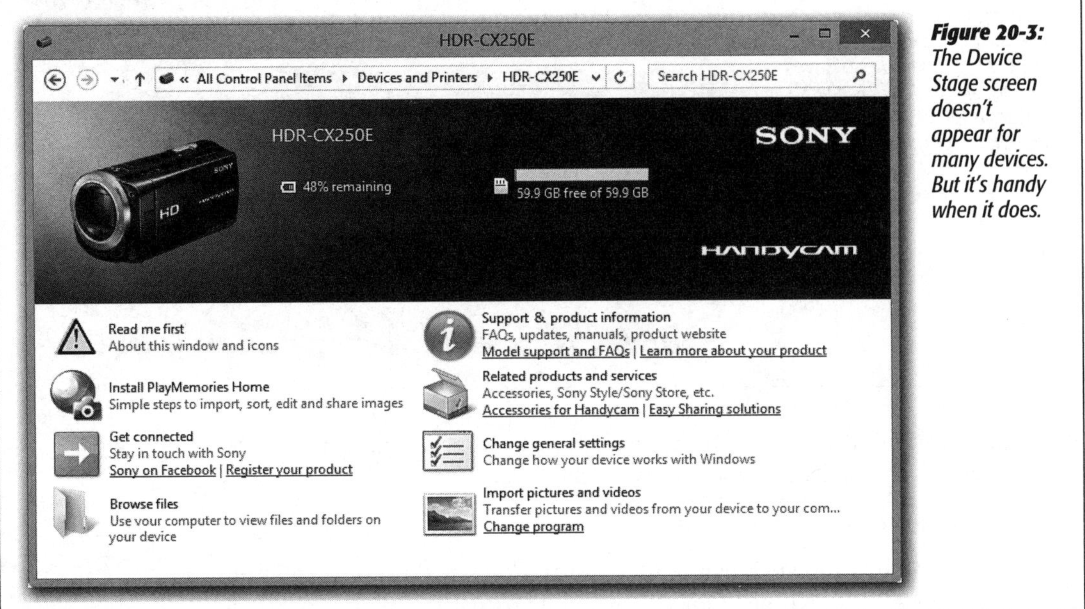

Figure 20-3: *The Device Stage screen doesn't appear for many devices. But it's handy when it does.*

For a printer, you might see ink-level details, options to buy paper and ink online, and so on; for a cellphone, you see options to edit or buy ringtones, sync with your Windows address book and calendar, and so on. For any kind of gadget, you probably get a link to the manufacturer's Web site, too.

Microsoft doesn't create these little model-specific pages; the gadget manufacturers are supposed to do it and submit them to Microsoft. When you attach the device to your PC, you see its own custom Device Stage page.

Now, the bad news: Very few gadgets *do* have Device Stage information built in. Most gadgets—including the several trillion pre-Windows 7 models—produce either no Device Stage at all, or, sometimes a generic one. This "baseline" page may offer the basic tasks—import pictures from a camera, for example—but doesn't offer the photo and functions of your exact model.

Note: When the hardware makers get around to it, they'll update their Device Stage screens, or add them to gizmos that are currently showing you only the generic basic pages. You'll know when an updated Device Stage is available, because the top of the window will sprout a little banner inviting you to download it.

Installing Cards in Expansion Slots

Modems and adapter cards for video, TV, sound, network cabling, disk drives, and tape drives generally take the form of circuit boards, or *cards*, that you install inside your PC's case. These slots are connected to your PC's *bus*, an electrical conduit that connects all the components of the machine to the brains of the outfit: the processor and memory.

The two common (and incompatible) kinds of slots are called *PCI* and *PCI Express (PCIe)*. The PCI slot (Peripheral Component Interconnect) has been around since the dawn of the PC in the early 1990s. PCI Express is newer and offers much better speed, but is typically used only for graphics cards. Most computers in use today have both kinds of slots.

Note: There's a third type of slot in some computers, called AGP (Accelerated Graphics Port). This slot is almost always occupied by a graphics card. PCIe is the most popular slot type for graphics cards, but you may encounter AGP in older PCs.

Knowing the characteristics of the different bus types isn't especially important. What *is* important is knowing what type of slots your computer has free, so you can purchase the correct type of expansion card. To do this, you'll have to open your PC's case to see which type of slots are empty:

- PCIe slots come in different lengths, depending on their speed (from x1, the slowest, to x16, the fastest and most common). The have metal pins or teeth in the center and a small crossbar partway down the slot. There's also a slot on one end that the card uses to lock into place.
- The plastic wall around a PCI slot is usually white or off-white, and shorter than an ISA slot. A PCI slot has a metal center and a crossbar about three-quarters of the way along its length.

Installing a card usually involves removing a narrow plate (the *slot cover*) from the back panel of your PC, which allows the card's connector to peek through to the outside world. After unplugging the PC and touching something metal to discharge static, unwrap the card, and then carefully push it into its slot until it's fully seated.

Note: Depending on the type of card, you may have to insert one end first, and then press the other end down with considerable force to get it into the slot. A friendly suggestion, however: Don't press so hard that you flex and crack the motherboard.

Troubleshooting Newly Installed Gear

If, when you connect a new component, Windows doesn't display a "successfully installed" message like the one at the bottom of Figure 20-2, it probably can't "see" your new device.

- If you've installed an internal card, make sure that it's seated in the slot firmly (after shutting down your computer, of course).
- If you attached something external, make sure that it's turned on, has power (if it came with a power cord), and is correctly connected to the PC.

In either case, before panicking, try restarting the PC. If you still have no luck, try the Add Hardware wizard described in the box below. (And if even *that* doesn't work, call the manufacturer.)

If your new gadget didn't come with a disc (or maybe just a disc with drivers, but no installer), then hooking it up may produce a "Found New Hardware" balloon in the notification area, but no message about happy success. In that case, click the balloon to make the Add Hardware wizard appear.

If you have the drivers on a CD from the manufacturer, select the first option, "Locate and install driver software." Now Windows asks for the driver CD. Windows either finds the compatible driver and installs it automatically, or it offers you a choice. If

WORKAROUND WORKSHOP

The Add Hardware Wizard

Microsoft really, really hopes you'll never need the Add Hardware wizard. This little program is a holdover from Windows past, designed for very old, pre-Plug-and-Play gadgets (what Microsoft calls "legacy hardware") that Windows doesn't autorecognize when you plug them in.

Begin by connecting the new gear; turn off the computer first, if necessary. Turn the machine on again, and then open the Add Hardware wizard program, which takes a few steps. Right-click the lower-left corner of your screen; from the X menu, choose Device Manager. Then, in the Device Manager window, right-click your PC at the top of the list and choose "Add legacy hardware" from the shortcut menu.

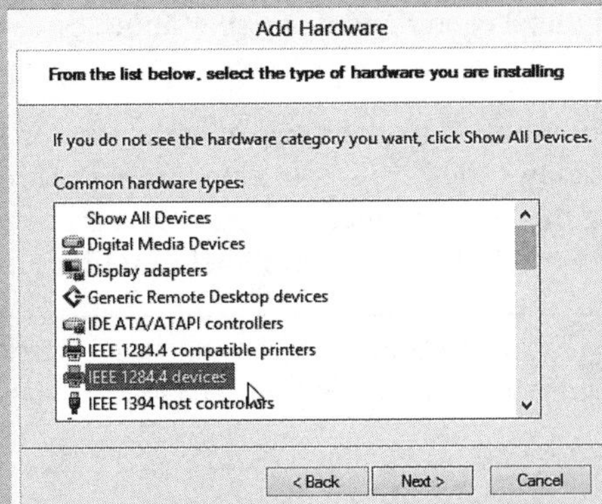

The wizard makes another attempt to detect the new equipment and install its driver. If a happy little "Found new hardware" balloon appears in your notification area, all is well; the wizard's work is done. If not, you're walked through the process of specifying exactly *what* kind of gadget seems to have gone missing, choosing its manufacturer, inserting its driver disc, and so on.

If you choose "Install the hardware that I manually select from a list" and click Next (or if the previous option fails), the wizard displays a list of device types, as shown here. From that list, find and select the type of hardware you want to install—"Imaging devices" for a digital camera or a scanner, for example, "PCMCIA adapters" for a PC card, and so on. (Click Show All Devices if you can't figure out which category to choose.)

Click Next to forge on through the wizard pages. You may be asked to select a port or configure other settings. When you click the Finish button on the last screen, Windows transfers the drivers to your hard drive. As a final step, you may be asked to restart the PC.

you do not, in fact, have the CD, click "I don't have the disc." You're offered two final, fatalistic options: "Check for a solution" (Windows dials the mother ship on the off chance that a driver has miraculously cropped up since its last update) or "Browse my computer," designed for people who have downloaded a driver from the Web on their own.

Driver Signing

Every now and then, when you try to install the software for one new gadget or another, you see a warning box that says, "Windows can't verify the publisher of this driver software."

It's not really as scary as it sounds. It's just telling you that Microsoft has not tested this driver for Windows 8 compatibility and programming solidity. (Technically speaking, Microsoft has not put its digital signature on that driver; it's an *unsigned driver.*)

Note: In very rare circumstances, you may also see messages that say, "This driver software has been altered" or "Windows cannot install this driver software." In those cases, go directly to the hardware maker's Web site to download the official driver software; Windows is trying to warn you that hackers may have gotten their hands on the driver version you're trying to install.

In theory, you're supposed to drop everything and contact the manufacturer or its Web site to find out if a Windows 8–certified driver is now available.

In practice, just because a driver isn't signed doesn't mean it's no good; it may be that the manufacturer simply didn't pony up the testing fee required by Microsoft's Windows Hardware Quality Labs. After all, sometimes checking with the manufacturer isn't even possible—for example, it may have gone to that great dot-com in the sky.

So most people just plow ahead. If the installation winds up making your system slower or less stable, you can always uninstall the driver, or rewind your entire operating system to its condition before you installed the questionable driver. (Use System Restore, described on page 691, for that purpose. Windows automatically takes a snapshot of your working system just before you install any unsigned driver.)

The Device Manager

The Device Manager is an extremely powerful tool that lets you troubleshoot and update drivers for gear you've already installed. It's a master list of every component that makes up your PC: floppy drive, CD-ROM drive, keyboard, modem, and so on (Figure 20-4). It's also a status screen that lets you know which drivers are working properly and which ones need some attention.

The quickest way to open the Device Manager is to right-click the lower-left corner of the screen, which makes the secret Utilities menu appear; from the shortcut menu, choose Device Manager. (You can also use the Start screen. Type *device manager* and select Settings under the search box. In the search results, click "Device Manager" in the results list.)

Authenticate yourself if necessary. You then arrive at the screen shown in Figure 20-4.

The Curse of the Yellow ! Badge

A yellow circled exclamation point next to the name indicates a problem with the device's driver. It could mean that either you or Windows installed the *wrong* driver, or that the device is fighting for resources being used by another component. It could also mean that a driver can't find the equipment it's supposed to control. That's what happens to your Webcam driver, for example, if you've detached the Webcam.

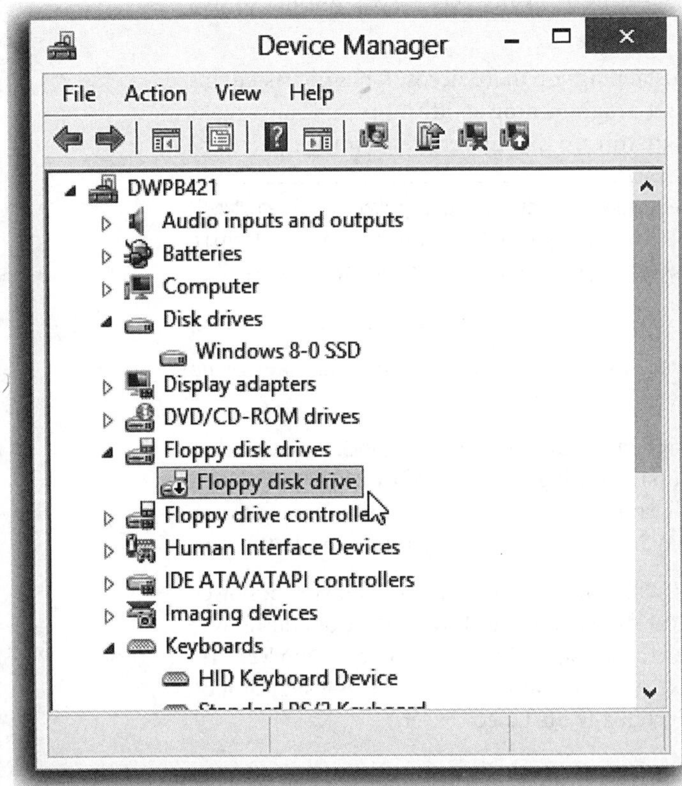

Figure 20-4:
The Device Manager lists types of equipment; to see the actual model(s) in each category, you must expand each sublist by clicking the flippy triangle.

A device that's having problems is easy to spot, thanks to the black down-arrows and yellow exclamation points.

You can see a disabled driver (↓ logo) on the "Floppy disk drive" entry in this illustration.

FREQUENTLY ASKED QUESTION

Driver vs. Driver

Which is better: the drivers that come with Windows, or the drivers I've downloaded from the manufacturer's Web site?

In many cases, they're the same thing. The drivers included with Windows usually did come from the hardware's manufacturer, which gave them to Microsoft. However, you should still use the drivers that came from your gadget's manufacturer whenever possible, especially if you got them from the manufacturer's Web site. They're likely to be newer versions than the ones that came with Windows.

The yellow badge may also be the result of a serious incompatibility between the component and your computer, or the component and Windows. In that case, a call to the manufacturer's help line is almost certainly in your future.

Tip: To find out which company actually created a certain driver, double-click the component's name in the Device Manager. In the resulting Properties dialog box, click the General tab, where you see the name of the company, and the Driver tab to see the date the driver was created, the version of the driver, and so on.

Duplicate devices

If the Device Manager displays icons for duplicate devices (for example, two modems), remove *both* of them. (To remove a device, click Uninstall in the dialog box shown in Figure 20-5.) If you remove only one, Windows will find it again the next time the PC starts up, and you'll have duplicate devices again.

If Windows asks if you want to restart your computer after you remove the first icon, click No, and then delete the second one. Windows won't ask again after you remove the second incarnation; you have to restart your computer manually.

Figure 20-5: *To get here, double-click a component listed in your Device Manager and then click the Driver tab. Here, you find four buttons and a lot of information. The Driver Provider information, for example, lets you know who's responsible for your current driver—Microsoft or the maker of the component.*

Click the Driver Details button to find out where on your hard drive the actual driver file is. Or click Update Driver to install a newer version, the Roll Back Driver button to reinstate the earlier version, the Disable button to hide this component from Windows until you change your mind, or the Uninstall button to remove the driver from your system entirely—a drastic decision.

(If the buttons here are dimmed, click the General tab, click "Change settings," and then authenticate.)

When the PC starts up again, Windows finds the hardware device and installs it (only once this time). Open the Device Manager and make sure there's only one of everything. If not, contact the manufacturer's help line.

Resolving resource conflicts

If the yellow-! problem isn't caused by a duplicate component, then double-click the component's name. Here you find an explanation of the problem.

Turning Components Off

The Driver tab shown in Figure 20-5 contains another useful tool: the Disable button. It makes your PC treat the component in question as though it's not even there.

You can use this function to test device conflicts. For example, if a yellow exclamation point indicates that there's a resource conflict, then you can disable one of the two gadgets, which may clear up a problem with its competitor.

When you disable a component, a circled ↓ appears next to the component's listing in the Device Manager. To undo your action, click the device's name and click the Enable button in the toolbar (formerly the Disable button).

Updating Drivers

If you get your hands on a new, more powerful (or more reliable) driver for a device, you can use the Device Manager to install it. (Newer isn't *always* better, however; in the world of Windows, the rule "If it ain't broke, don't fix it" contains a grain of truth the size of Texas.)

Open the dialog box shown in Figure 20-5, and then click the Update Driver button. The Update Device Driver wizard walks you through the process.

Along the way, the wizard offers to search for a better driver, or to display a list of drivers in a certain folder so you can make your own selection. In either case, you may have to restart the PC to put the newly installed driver into service.

Roll Back Driver

Suppose that you, the increasingly proficient PC user, have indeed downloaded a new driver for some component—your scanner, say—and successfully installed it using the instructions in the previous paragraphs. Life is sweet—until you discover that your scanner no longer scans in color.

In this situation, you'd probably give quite a bit for the chance to return to the previous driver, which, though older, seemed to work better. That's the beauty of the Roll Back Driver function. To find it, open the dialog box shown in Figure 20-5 and click Roll Back Driver.

Windows 8, forgiving as always, instantly undoes the installation of the newer driver and reinstates the previous driver.

6

Part Six: PC Health

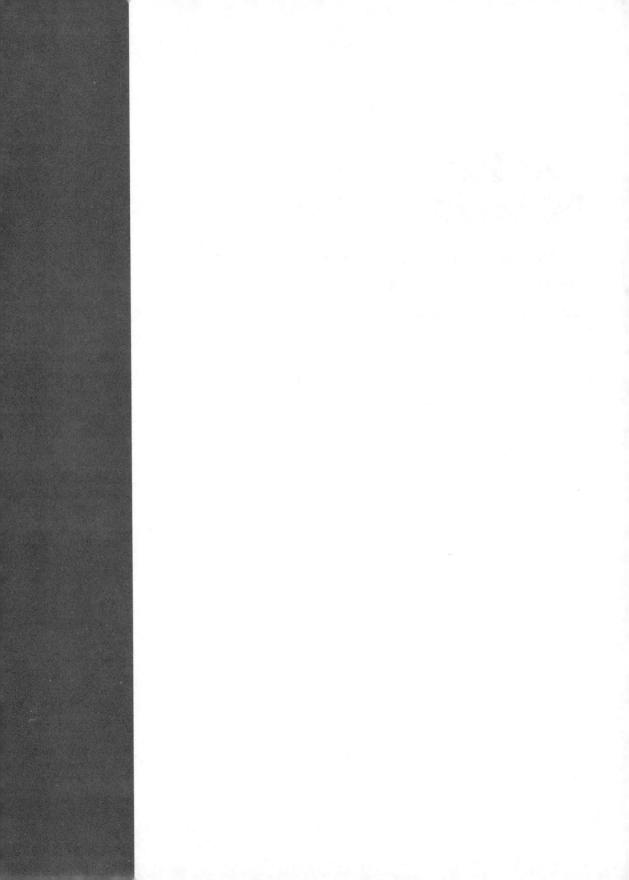

CHAPTER

21

Maintenance, Speed Tweaks & Troubleshooting

Your computer requires periodic checkups and preventive maintenance—pretty much like you, its human sidekick. Fortunately, Microsoft has put quite a bit of effort into equipping Windows 8 with special tools, all dedicated to keeping your system stable and fast. Here's a crash course in keeping your PC—and its hard drive—humming.

The Action Center

If you're looking for the best place to go for at-a-glance information about the current state of your PC's maintenance and Internet security, open the Action Center (it was called the Security Center in Windows Vista). To open it, click the tiny ⚑ or ⚐ on your system tray.

Here, all in one place, are all the security and maintenance messages that Windows wants you to see. Be grateful; they *used* to pop up as individual nag balloons on the system tray all day. Now they accumulate here.

Color coding lets you know what steps Windows thinks you should take. Messages marked with a *red* vertical bar are things you should fix right now, like not having a virus program installed. Items with a yellow bar are less urgent; they're maintenance recommendations, for example.

You can read the full scoop on the Action Center on page 453. For now, it's enough to remember that here's the place to check to see how your Windows Updates and PC backups are doing.

Disk Cleanup

As you use your computer, Windows litters your hard drive with temporary files. Programs, utilities, and Web sites scatter disposable files everywhere. If you could see your hard drive's surface, it would eventually look like the floor of a minivan whose owners eat a lot of fast food.

To run Windows 8's built-in housekeeper program, the quickest route is this: Open the Start screen. Type *disk cleanup* and select Settings under the search box. In the search results, click "Free up disk space by deleting unnecessary files." (Disk Cleanup is also available in the Control Panel.)

The Disk Cleanup program dives right in. If you have more than one drive, it lets you choose the one you want to work on; then it goes to work, inspecting your drive and reporting on files you can safely remove.

Left to its own devices, it will clean up only *your* files. But if you'd like to clean up all the files on the computer, including Microsoft's own detritus, click "Clean up system files." Authenticate if necessary.

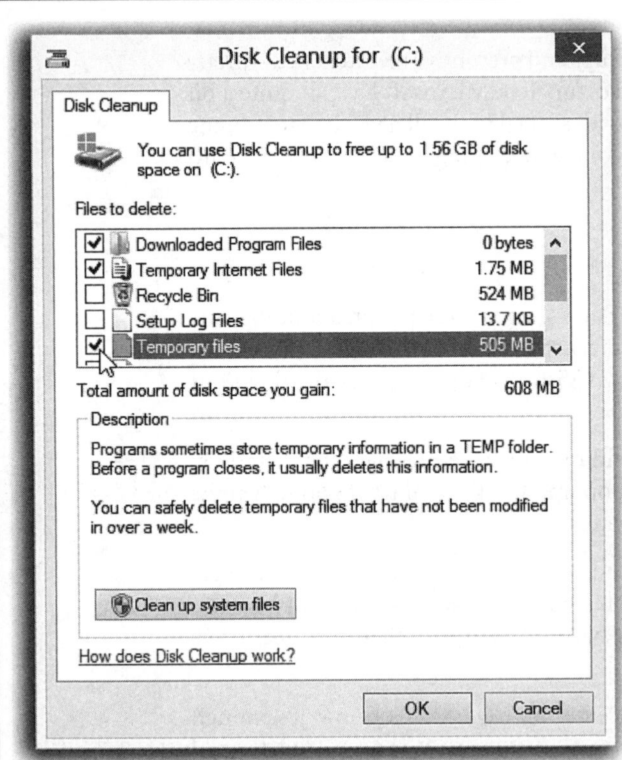

Figure 21-1:
Disk Cleanup announces how much free space you stand to gain. After you've been using your PC for a while, it's amazing how much crud you'll find there–and how much space you can recover.

The Disk Cleanup dialog box shown in Figure 21-1 appears when the inspection is over. Turn on the checkboxes of the file categories you'd like to have cleaned out, and then click OK to send them to the digital landfill. It's like getting a bigger hard drive for free.

Disk Defragmenter

When you save a new file, Windows records its information onto the hard drive in small pieces called *blocks*. On a new PC, Windows lays the blocks end-to-end on the hard drive's surface. Later, when you type more data into a document (thus enlarging it), the file no longer fits in the same space. Windows puts as much of the file in the original location as can fit, but it may have to store a few of its blocks in the next empty spot on the hard drive.

Ordinarily, you'll never even notice that your files are getting chopped up in this way, since they open promptly and seamlessly. Windows keeps track of where it has stored the various pieces and reconstitutes them when necessary.

As your drive fills up, though, the free space that's left is made up of smaller and smaller groups of blocks. Eventually, a new file may not fit in a single "parking place" on the hard drive's surface, since there are no free spaces left large enough to hold it. Windows may have to store a file in several different areas of the disk, or even hundreds.

When you try to open such a *fragmented* file, the drive heads (which read the disk) must scamper all over the disk surface, rounding up each block in turn, which is slower than reading contiguous blocks one after the other. Over time, this *file fragmentation* gets worse and worse. Eventually, you wind up griping to your buddies or spouse that you need a new computer, because this one seems to have gotten *so slow*.

The solution: Disk Defragmenter, a program that puts together pieces of files that have become fragmented on your drive. The "defragger" also rearranges the files on your drives to make the operating system and programs load more quickly. A freshly defragged PC feels faster and more responsive than a heavily fragmented one.

Windows' disk-defragging software runs *automatically* at regular intervals, in the tiny moments when you're not actually typing or clicking. It's like having someone

POWER USERS' CLINIC

Beyond Disk Defragmenter

Disk Defragmenter isn't the only tool for the defrag job; the world is full of disk-defragmenting programs that offer additional features.

For example, some of them track how often you use the various files on your drive, so they can store the most frequently used files at the beginning of the disk for quicker access. In some programs, you can even *choose* which files go at the beginning of the disk.

Do these additional features actually produce a measurable improvement over Windows 8's built-in defragger? That's hard to say, especially when you remember the biggest advantage of Disk Defragmenter–it's free.

take out your garbage for you whenever the can is full. Slow-PC syndrome should, therefore, be a much less frequent occurrence.

Tip: Fragmentation doesn't become noticeable except on hard drives that have been very full for quite a while. Don't bother defragmenting your drive unless you've actually noticed it slowing down. The time you'll spend waiting for Disk Defragmenter to do its job is much longer than the fractions of seconds caused by a little bit of file fragmentation.

And if you're the lucky owner of a solid-state drive (SSD)—fast, quiet, super-expensive—you'll find that fragmentation has only a minimal hit on your computer's speed. In fact, if Windows 8 detects that you're using an SSD, it disables automatic defragmentation.

Defragging Settings

Even though Windows defrags your hard drive automatically in the background, you can still exert some control. For example, you can change the schedule, and you can trigger a defragmentation manually when you're feeling like a control freak.

Start by opening the Disk Defragmenter main screen. You can get there via the Control Panel, or from the Start screen. Type *disk defrag* and select Settings under the search box. In the search results, click "Defragment and optimize your drives."

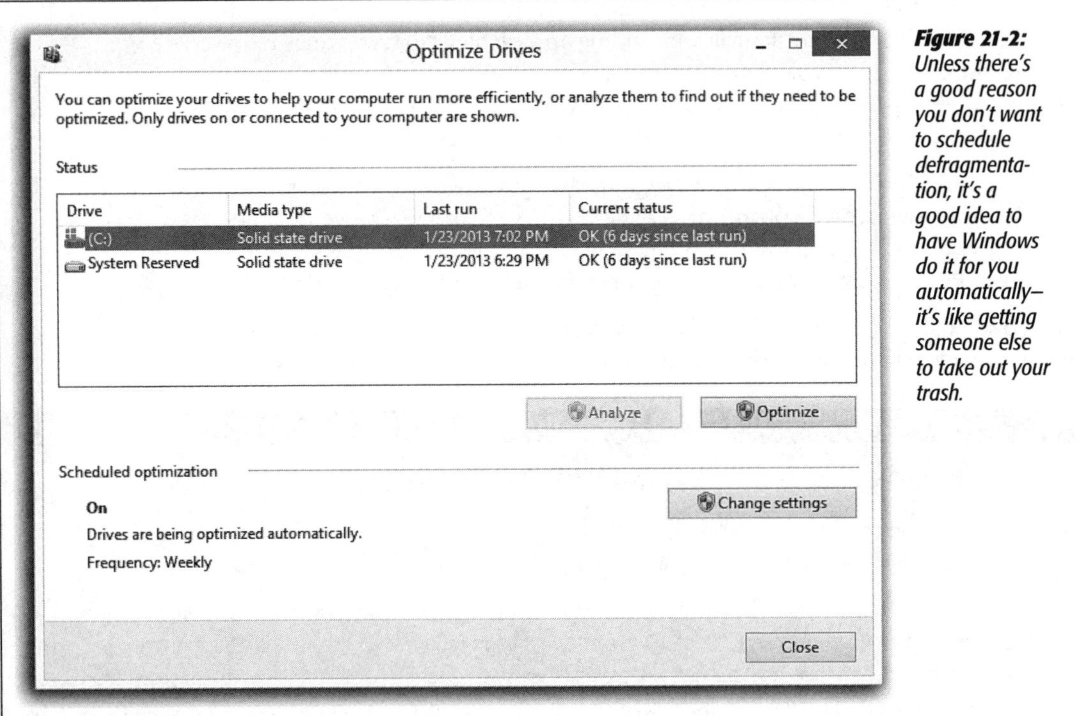

Figure 21-2: *Unless there's a good reason you don't want to schedule defragmentation, it's a good idea to have Windows do it for you automatically—it's like getting someone else to take out your trash.*

Tip: Throughout Windows, and throughout its book and magazine literature, disks are referred to as *volumes*. Usually, "volume" means disk. But technically, it refers to *anything with its own disk icon* in the Computer window–including disk partitions, flash drives, and so on.

The Disk Defragmenter window opens (Figure 21-2). From here, you can either adjust the schedule or trigger defragmentation manually:

- Adjust the schedule. Click "Configure schedule." Authenticate if necessary. A screen appears, showing that Windows 8 ordinarily defrags your disk late every Wednesday night (at 1:00 a.m., in fact). You can use the pop-up menus here to specify a Weekly, Daily, or Monthly schedule, complete with day-of-week and time-of-day options. Click OK, and then OK again.
- Manually. Click "Defragment disk"; the defragmenter does its work. Depending on the size of your hard disk, your processor speed, and the amount of fragmentation, it will take anywhere from several minutes to several hours.

Tip: During the defragmentation process, Windows picks up pieces of your files and temporarily sets them down in a different spot, like somebody trying to solve a jigsaw puzzle. If your hard drive is very full, defragmenting will take a lot longer than if you have some empty space available–and if there's not enough free disk space, Windows can't do the job completely. Before you run Disk Defragmenter, use Disk Cleanup and make as much free disk space as possible.

Hard Drive Checkups

It's true: Things can occasionally go wrong on the surface of your hard drive. Maybe there's a messed-up spot on its physical surface. Maybe, thanks to a system crash, power outage, or toddler playing with your surge suppressor, your computer gets turned off without warning, and some files are left open and stranded.

In the olden days, way back even before Windows XP, fixing your disk required running a program called ScanDisk, a utility designed to detect and, when possible, repair drive damage.

ScanDisk doesn't exist in Windows 8. But its functions, and many more, have been overhauled. Many disk problems are automatically detected and automatically fixed—and most of them don't require you to wait while the PC repairs itself. There's a lot less downtime.

The Three Action-Center Messages

To see how your computer is doing, open the Action Center described earlier. Near the top, you'll see one of these messages (Figure 21-3):

- No issues have been detected by Action Center. All is well.
- Scan drive for errors. This message appears under the Maintenance heading. It means Windows has found something it doesn't like. It's going to check out the damage and mark it for fixing at the next restart. Anyway, click "Run scan."

- Restart to repair drive errors (important). This message, also under Maintenance, comes after the previous one, and it means Windows found stuff that needs fixing—stuff that can be fixed only by restarting your machine. Click Restart.

Manual Checks

You can also check your disk on command, without requiring the Action Center's prompting. (This is the old disk-checking procedure.)

Right-click the icon of the hard drive you want to check (in the Computer window). From the shortcut menu, choose Properties; click the Tools tab, and click Check. Authenticate yourself if needed.

Note: Geeks fondly refer to the feature described here as *chkdsk* (apparently named by someone with no vowels on his keyboard). You get to the geek-friendly, text-only version of it by typing *chkdsk* in a Command Prompt window. But the method described here is much better looking.

FREQUENTLY ASKED QUESTION

When Good Drives Go Bad

I was surprised when the Action Center found some problems with my hard drive. I don't understand what could have gone wrong. I treat my PC with respect, talk to it often, and never take it swimming. Why did my hard drive get flaky?

All kinds of things can cause problems with your hard drive, but the most common are low voltage, power outages, voltage spikes, and mechanical problems with the drive controller or the drive itself.

An inexpensive gadget called a *line conditioner* (sold at computer stores) can solve the low-voltage problem. A more expensive gizmo known as an *uninterruptible power supply* (UPS) maintains enough backup battery power to keep your computer going when the power goes out completely–for a few minutes, anyway, so you can shut it down properly. The more expensive models have line conditioning built in. A UPS is also the answer to power outages, if they're common in your area.

Voltage spikes are the most dangerous to your PC. They frequently occur during the first seconds when the power comes back on after a power failure. A surge suppressor is the logical defense here. But remember that the very cheap devices often sold as surge suppressors are actually little more than extension cords. Furthermore, some of the models that do provide adequate protection are designed to sacrifice themselves in battle. After a spike, you may have to replace them.

If you care about your computer (or the money you spent on it), buy a good surge suppressor, at the very least. The best ones come with a guarantee that the company will replace your equipment (up to a certain dollar value) if the unit fails to provide adequate protection.

On the other hand, insufficient power is just as dangerous as a voltage spike. If you own a desktop PC, chances are good that the built-in power supply is strong enough for whatever components your PC was born with. But if you've upgraded–adding a faster hard drive or a beefier video card, for example–you may be pushing your PC's power supply to its limits.

If you're doing a bunch of upgrades to convert an entry-level office PC into a gaming powerhouse, then make sure you're including a newer, stronger, power supply among those upgrades.

Disk Management

"Disk management" isn't just a cool, professional-sounding skill—it's the name of a built-in Windows maintenance program that lets you perform all kinds of operations on your hard disk.

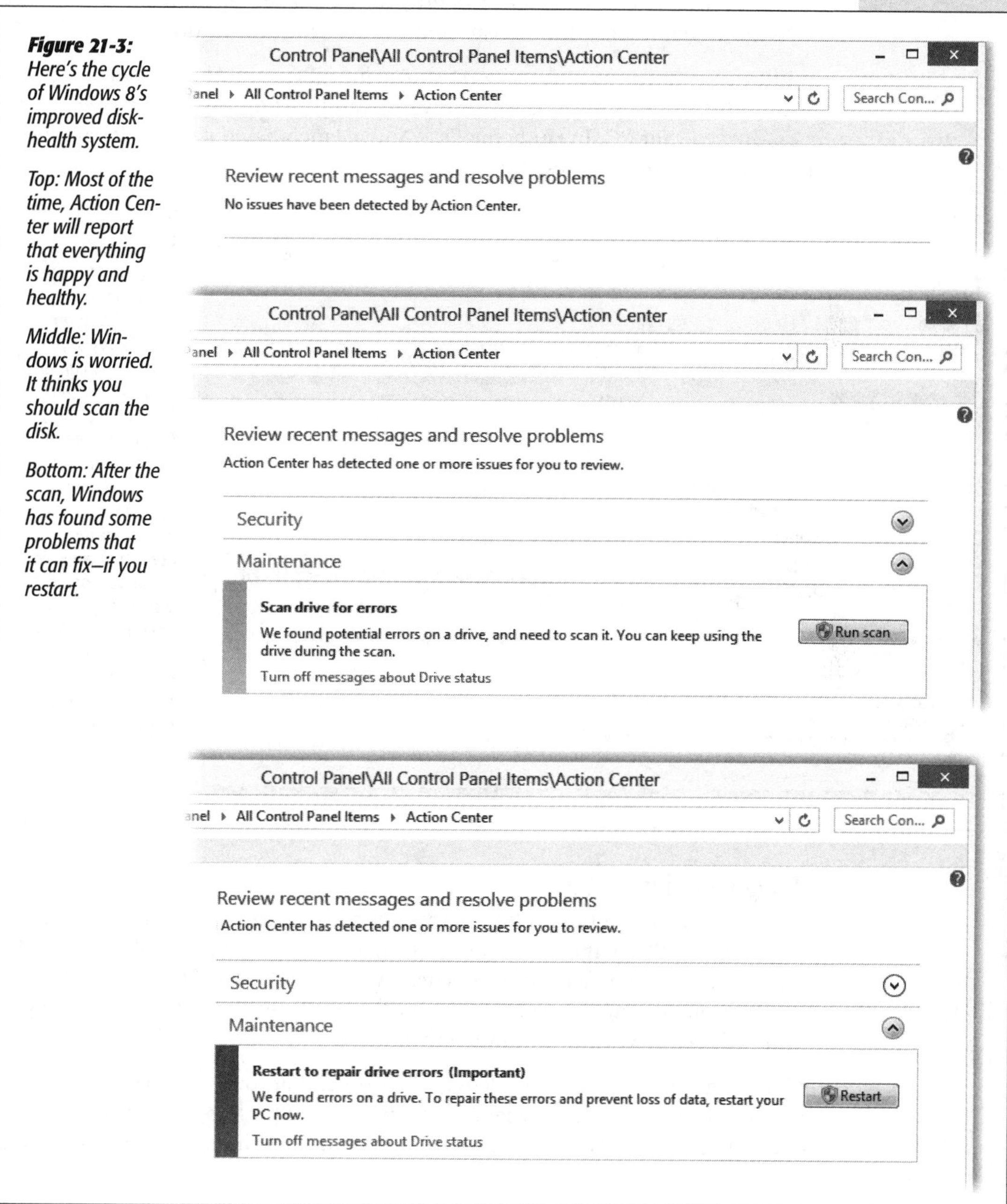

Figure 21-3: *Here's the cycle of Windows 8's improved disk-health system.*

Top: Most of the time, Action Center will report that everything is happy and healthy.

Middle: Windows is worried. It thinks you should scan the disk.

Bottom: After the scan, Windows has found some problems that it can fix–if you restart.

To open this technical database of information about your disks and drives, you can use either of these two methods:

- In the Control Panel, click System and Security. Click"Create and format hard disk partitions." (It's at the very bottom of the window.)
- Open the Start screen. Type *disk manage* and select Settings under the search box. In the search results, click "Create and format hard disk partitions."

In either case, you arrive at the window shown in Figure 21-4. At first glance, it appears to be nothing more than a table of every disk (and *partition* of every disk) currently connected to your PC. In truth, the Disk Management window is a software toolkit that lets you *operate* on these drives.

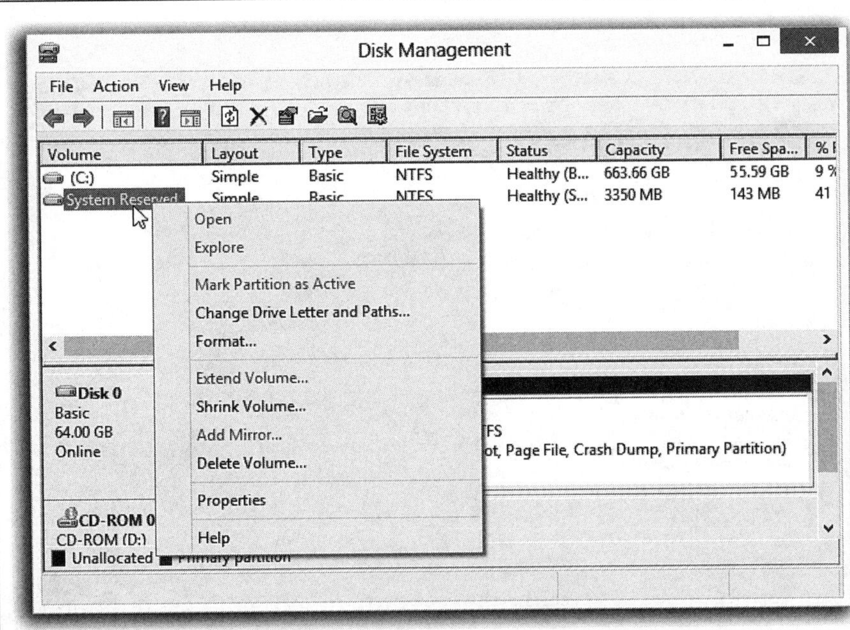

Figure 21-4: *The Disk Management window does more than just display your drives; you can also operate on them by right-clicking. Don't miss the View menu, by the way, which lets you change either the top or the bottom display. For example, you can make your PC display all your disks instead of your volumes. (There's a difference; see page 706.)*

Change a Drive Letter

As you've probably noticed, Windows assigns a drive letter to each disk drive associated with your PC. In the age of floppy disks, the floppy drives were always A: and B:. The primary internal hard drive is generally C:; your CD/DVD drive may be D: or E:; and so on. Among other places, you see these letters in parentheses following the names of your drives in the Computer window.

Windows generally assigns these letters in the order that you install new drives to your system. You're not allowed to change the drive letter of the floppy drive or any startup hard drive (the C: drive and, if you're set up for dual booting, any other boot drives).

You can, however, override the *other* drives' unimaginative Windows letter assignments easily enough, as shown in Figure 21-5.

Note: If Windows is currently using files on the disk whose drive letter you're trying to change, Disk Management might create the new drive letter assignment but leave the old one intact until the next time you restart the computer. This is an effort to not pull the rug out from under any open files.

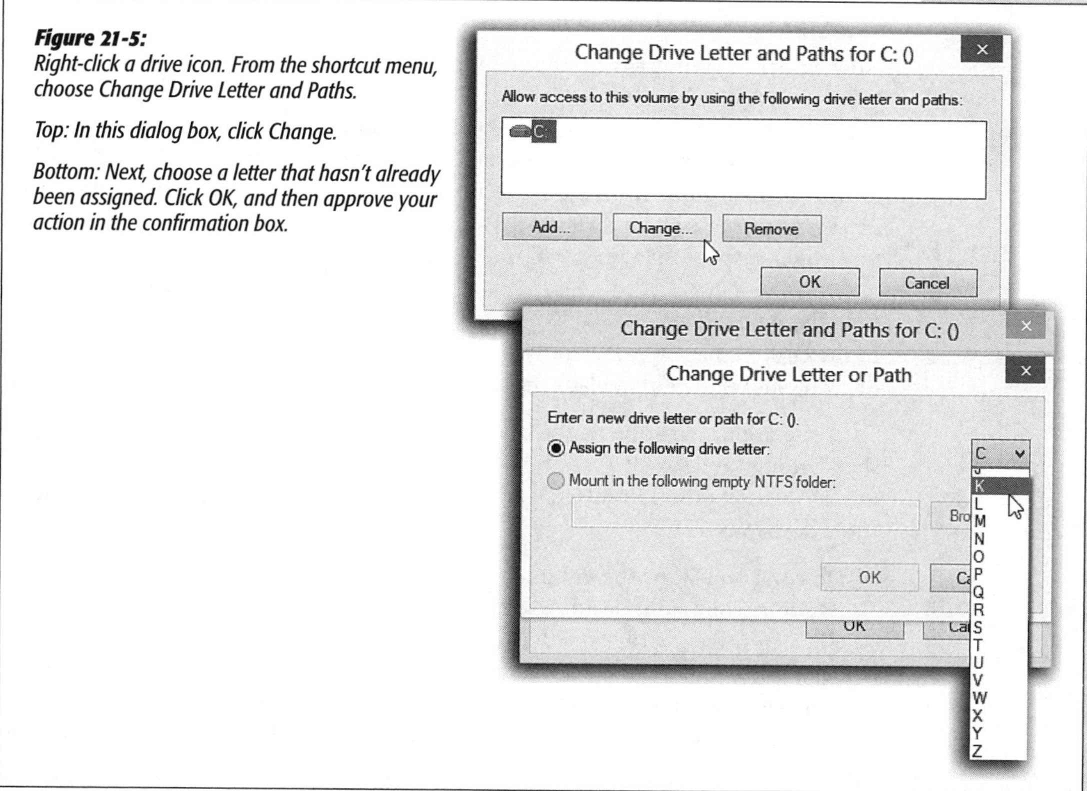

Figure 21-5: *Right-click a drive icon. From the shortcut menu, choose Change Drive Letter and Paths.*

Top: In this dialog box, click Change.

Bottom: Next, choose a letter that hasn't already been assigned. Click OK, and then approve your action in the confirmation box.

Partition a New Drive

The vast majority of Windows PCs have only one hard drive, represented in the Computer window as a single icon.

Plenty of power users, however, delight in *partitioning* the hard drive—dividing its surface so that it appears on the screen as two different icons with two different names. At that point, you can live like a king, enjoying the following advantages (just like people who have two separate hard drives):

- You can keep Windows 8 on one of them and Windows 7 (for example) on the other, so you can switch between the two at startup. (This feature, called *dual booting, is* described on page 841.)

- Two partitions make life much easier if you frequently install and reinstall the operating system, or different versions of it. Having the partitions allows you to keep all your files safely on one partition, confining all the installing/uninstalling activity to the other.
- You can use multiple partitions to keep your operating system(s) separate from folders and files. In this way, you can perform a *clean install* of Windows (page 841) onto one partition without having to worry about losing any of your important files or installation programs.

Now, in earlier Windows days, partitioning a hard drive using the tools built into Windows required first erasing the hard drive completely. Fortunately, Windows 8's Disk Management console can save you from that hassle, although making a backup before you begin is still a smart idea. (The short version: Right-click the disk's icon in Disk Management; from the shortcut menu, choose Shrink Volume. In the Shrink dialog box, specify how much space you want to free up, and then click Shrink. Then turn the free space into a new volume, as described next.)

Creating a partition

In the Disk Management window, free space (suitable for turning into a partition of its own) shows up with a black bar and the label Unallocated.

To create a new partition, right-click one of these unallocated segments. From the shortcut menu, choose New Simple Volume (if this option isn't available, right-click the disk and choose Initialize Disk). A wizard appears; its screens ask you to make some decisions:

- How big you want the volume to be. If you're dividing up a 500 GB drive, for example, you might decide to make the first volume 300 GB and the second 200 GB. Begin by creating the 300 GB volume (right-clicking the big Unallocated bar). When that's done, you see a smaller Unallocated chunk still left in the Disk Management window. Right-click it and choose New Simple Volume *again,* this time accepting the size the wizard proposes (which is *all* the remaining free space).
- What drive letter you want to assign to it. Most of the alphabet is at your disposal.
- What disk-formatting scheme you want to apply to it. Windows 8 requires NTFS for the system drive. But if you're just using the drive to store data (and not to contain a copy of Windows 8), the old FAT32 format is fine. In fact, if you plan to dual-boot Windows 8 with Linux, Mac OS X, or an old version of Windows, then FAT32 might be the only file system all those operating systems can recognize simultaneously.

When the wizard is through with you, it's safe to close the window. A quick look at your Computer window confirms that you now have new "disks" (actually partitions of the same disk), which you can use for different purposes.

Turn a Drive into a Folder

Talk about techie! Most people could go their entire lives without needing this feature, or even imagining that it exists. But it's there if you're a power user and you want it.

Using the Paths feature of Disk Management, you can actually turn a hard drive (or partition) into a *folder* on another hard drive (or partition). These disks-disguised-as-folders are technically known as *mounted drives, junction points,* or *drive paths.*

This arrangement affords the following possibilities:

- In effect, you can greatly expand the capacity of your main hard drive—by installing a second hard drive that masquerades as a folder on the first one.
- You can turn a burned CD or DVD into a folder on your main hard drive, too—a handy way to fool your programs into thinking the files they're looking for are still in the same old place on your hard drive. (You could pull this stunt in a crisis—when the "real" folder has become corrupted or has been thrown away.)
- If you're a *power* power user with lots of partitions, disks, and drives, you may feel hemmed in by the limitation of only 26 assignable letters (A through Z). Turning one of your disks into a mounted volume bypasses that limitation, because a mounted volume doesn't need a drive letter at all.
- A certain disk can be made to appear in more than one place at once. You could put all your MP3 files on a certain disk or a partition—and then make it show up as a folder in the Music folder of everyone who uses the computer.

Note: You can create a mounted volume only on an *NTFS-formatted* hard drive.

To bring about this arrangement, visit the Disk Management window, and then right-click the icon of the disk or partition you want to turn into a mounted volume. From the shortcut menu, choose Change Drive Letter and Paths.

In the Change Drive Letter and Paths dialog box (Figure 21-6, top), click Add; in the next dialog box, click Browse. Navigate to and select an empty folder—the one that will represent the disk. (Click New Folder, shown at bottom in Figure 21-6, if you didn't create one in advance.) Finally, click OK.

Once the deed is done, take time to note a few special characteristics of a mounted volume:

- The mounted volume may behave just like a folder, but its icon is a dead giveaway, since it still looks like a hard drive (or a CD drive, or a DVD drive, or whatever).

  Still, if you're in doubt about what it is, you can right-click it and choose Properties from the shortcut menu. You see that the Type information says "Mounted Volume," and the Target line identifies the disk from which it was made.
- Avoid circular references, in which you turn two drives into folders on *each other.* Otherwise, you risk throwing programs into a spasm of infinite-loop thrashing.

- To undo your mounted-drive effect, return to the Disk Management program and choose View→Drive Paths. You're shown a list of all the drives you've turned into folders; click one and then click Remove.

  You've just turned that special, "I'm really a drive" folder into an ordinary folder.

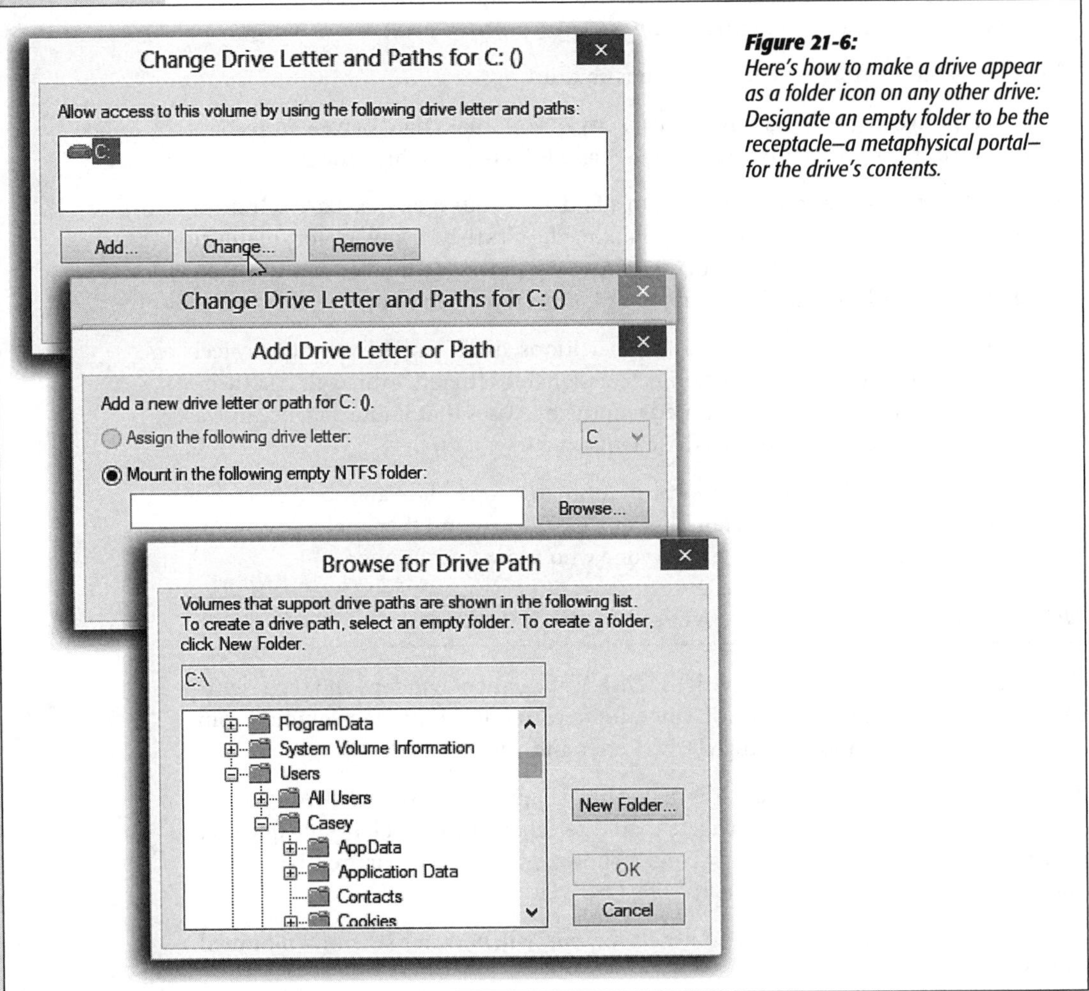

Figure 21-6: *Here's how to make a drive appear as a folder icon on any other drive: Designate an empty folder to be the receptacle–a metaphysical portal–for the drive's contents.*

Task Scheduler

The Task Scheduler, another power-user trick for techies, lets you set up programs and tasks (like disk defragmentation) so they run automatically according to a schedule you specify. Both mere mortals and power geeks may find it useful. For example:

- Create an email message that gets sent to your boss each morning, with yesterday's sales figures attached automatically.

- Have the Recycle Bin emptied automatically once a month.
- Create a phony dialog box that appears every time the office know-it-all's PC starts up. Make it say: "The radiation shield on your PC has failed. Please keep back seven feet." You get the idea.

Adding a Task

Here's how you add a new task:

1. Open the Task Scheduler.

   To do that, open the Start screen. Type *schedule* and select Settings under the search box. In the search results, click "Schedule a task." The Task Scheduler window appears (Figure 21-7).

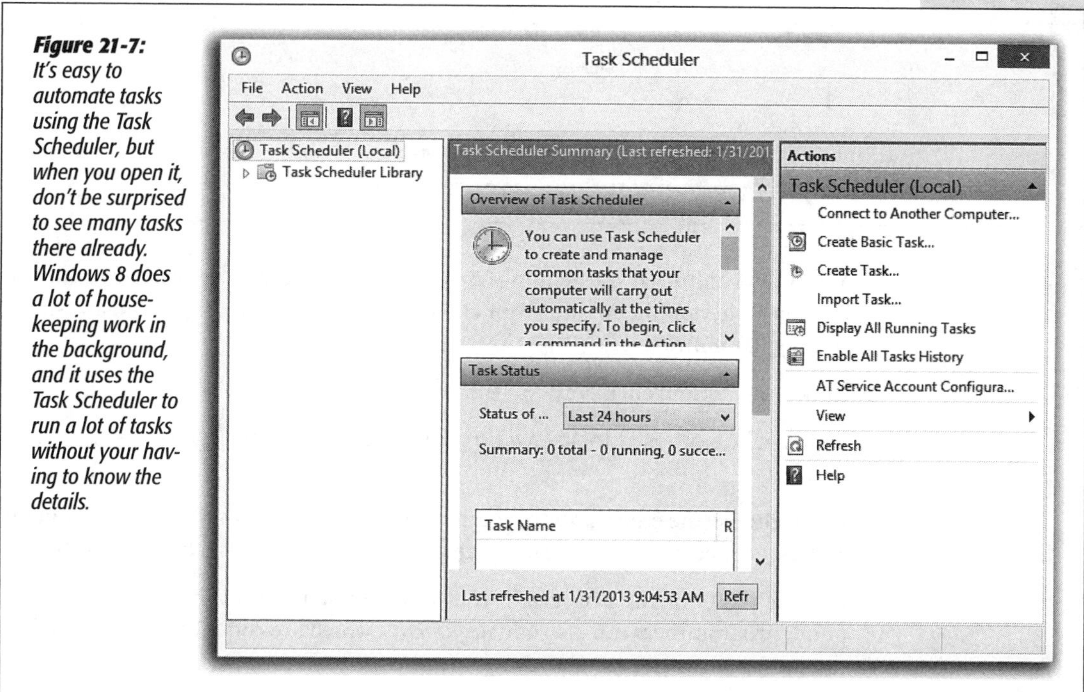

Figure 21-7: *It's easy to automate tasks using the Task Scheduler, but when you open it, don't be surprised to see many tasks there already. Windows 8 does a lot of housekeeping work in the background, and it uses the Task Scheduler to run a lot of tasks without your having to know the details.*

2. Click Create Basic Task.

   This link appears on the right-hand pane of the Task Scheduler. A wizard appears.

3. Type a name for the task and a description, and then click Next.

   Now you're supposed to choose what Windows calls a "trigger"—in plain English, when to run the task (Figure 21-8). You can specify that it run daily, weekly, monthly, or just once; every time the computer starts or every time you log in; or when a specific event occurs—like when a program starts.

4. Choose a trigger, and then click Next.

   The next screen varies according to the trigger you chose. If you chose to run the task on a daily, weekly, or monthly basis, you're now asked to specify *when* during that day, week, or month. Once that's done, click Next.

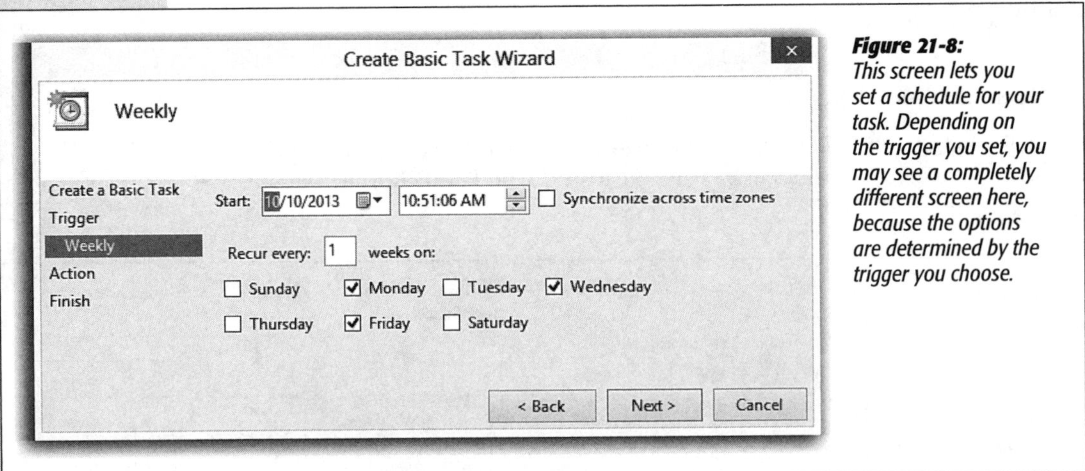

***Figure 21-8:** This screen lets you set a schedule for your task. Depending on the trigger you set, you may see a completely different screen here, because the options are determined by the trigger you choose.*

   You now wind up at the Action screen. This is where you say *what* you want to happen at the appointed time. Your choices are "Start a program," "Send an e-mail," or "Display a message."

5. Choose an action; click Next.

   Now you're supposed to say *what* program, email, or message you want the PC to fire up.

   If you choose the email option, you now fill out a form with the recipient's name, address, subject line, message body, and so on; you can even specify an attachment.

   If you choose to run a program, you now browse to select the program. At this point, programmers can also add *arguments*, which are codes that customize how the program starts.

   And if you opt to display a message, you get to type a name and text for the message. At the appointed time, an actual Windows dialog box will appear on the screen—except that it will contain text that *you* wrote.

6. Complete the details about the email, program, or phony dialog box, and then click Next.

   Finally, a screen appears, summarizing the task, when it will run, and so on. To edit it, click the Back button.

7. To confirm the automated task, click Finish.

   You return to the Task Scheduler window. Although you may have to scroll down to see it, your new task appears in the Active Tasks list at the bottom of the window. If all goes well, Windows will fire it up at the moment you specified.

Editing Scheduled Tasks

To change a scheduled task, you first need to find it in the Task Scheduler Library, which is on the left side of the window. Click Task Scheduler Library, and then look at the topmost pane in the middle part of your screen (Figure 21-9). You see a list of scheduled tasks. Highlight the one you want to change.

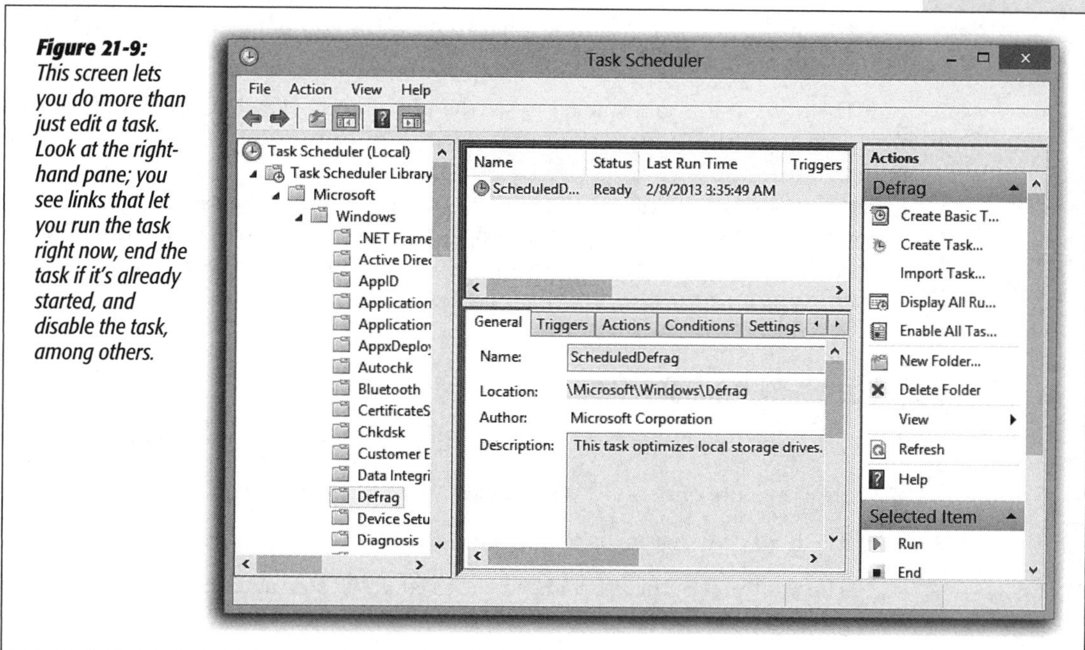

Figure 21-9: *This screen lets you do more than just edit a task. Look at the right-hand pane; you see links that let you run the task right now, end the task if it's already started, and disable the task, among others.*

Delete the task by simply hitting the Delete key. To edit a task, click it and then click the Properties link at the right side of the screen. The tabs in the resulting dialog box (General, Triggers, and so on) may sound familiar, but they actually give you far more control over how each task runs than the basic controls you saw when you first set the task up.

Here are some examples of what you can do on each tab:

- General. Select which user account should run the task, and tell Windows whether or not to run when the user is logged in.

- Triggers. You can delay the task's execution by a few minutes or until a certain date; have it repeat automatically at regular intervals; stop it after a certain time period; and so on. The "Begin the task" pop-up menu offers a wealth of new triggers, like "On idle" and "On workstation unlock."
- Actions. Change the action.
- Conditions. Specify that the task will run only under certain conditions—for example, after the computer has been idle for a certain amount of time, when the computer is on AC power, or when it switches to battery power, and so on. You can even say you want to run the task if the PC is sleeping (by waking it first).
- Settings. Here's a miscellaneous batch of additional preferences: what actions to take if the task doesn't work, what to do if the computer was turned off at the appointed time, and so on.
- History. On this tab, you get to see the task's life story: when it ran and whether each attempt was successful.

Note: Lots of tasks are already present on your PC. Microsoft set them up to ensure the proper running of your computer. To see them all, expand the flippy triangle next to the words "Task Scheduler Library" and then expand Microsoft, and then Windows. You see dozens of tasks in many different categories. In other words, your PC is very busy even when you're not there.

Three Speed Tricks

It's a fact of computing: Every PC seems to get slower the longer you own it.

There are plenty of reasons. When the PC is new, consider that:

- The hard drive has loads of free space and zero fragmentation.
- The boot process hasn't yet been cluttered up by startup code deposited by your programs.
- Few background programs are constantly running, eating up your memory.
- You haven't yet drained away horsepower with antivirus and automatic backup programs.

Also, remember that every year, the programs you buy or download are more demanding than the previous year's software.

Some of the usual advice about speeding up your PC applies here, of course: Install more memory or a faster hard drive.

But in Windows 8, here and there, nestled among the 50 million lines of code, you'll find some *free* tricks and tips for giving your PC a speed boost. Read on.

SuperFetch

Your PC can grab data from RAM (memory) hundreds of times faster than from the hard drive. That's why it uses a *cache,* a portion of memory that holds bits of software code you've used recently. After all, if you've used some feature or command once, you may want to use it again soon—and this way, Windows is ready for you. It can deliver that bit of code nearly instantaneously the next time.

When you leave your PC for a while, however, background programs (virus checkers, backup programs, disk utilities) take advantage of the idle time. They run themselves when you're not around—and push out whatever was in the cache.

That's why, when you come back from lunch (or sit down first thing in the morning), your PC is especially sluggish. All the good stuff—*your* stuff—has been flushed from the cache and returned to the much slower hard drive, to make room for those background utilities.

SuperFetch attempts to reverse that cycle. It attempts to keep your most frequently used programs in the cache all the time. In fact, it actually *tracks you* and your cycle of work. If you generally fire up the computer at 9 a.m., for example, or return to it at 1:30 p.m., SuperFetch will anticipate you by restoring frequently used programs and documents to the cache.

There's no on/off switch for SuperFetch, and nothing for you to configure. It's on all the time, automatic, and very sweet.

ReadyBoost

Your PC can get to data in RAM (memory) hundreds of times faster than it can fetch something from the hard drive. That's why it uses a *cache,* a portion of memory that holds bits of software code you've used recently. (Does this paragraph sound familiar?)

The more memory your machine has, the more that's available for the cache, and the faster things should feel to you. Truth is, though, you may have a bunch of memory sitting around your desk at this moment that's *completely wasted*—namely, USB flash drives. That's perfectly good RAM that your PC can't even touch if it's sitting in a drawer.

Note: ReadyBoost can also work with memory cards, like SD and Compact Flash cards from digital cameras—but only *if* your PC has a built-in card slot. (All the descriptions below apply equally to these memory cards.) External card readers don't work. PlaysForSure music players don't work, either—although Apple's iPod Shuffle does!

That's the whole point of ReadyBoost: to use a flash drive as described above as additional cache storage. You can achieve the same effect by installing more RAM, of course, but that job can be technical (especially on laptops), forbidden (by your corporate masters), or impossible (because you've used up all your PC's RAM slots already).

To take advantage of this speed-boosting feature, just plug a USB flash drive into your computer's USB jack.

Note: Both the flash drive *and* your PC must have USB 2.0 or later. USB 1.1 is too slow for this trick to work.

In any case, the AutoPlay dialog box now opens, as shown in Figure 21-10 (left).

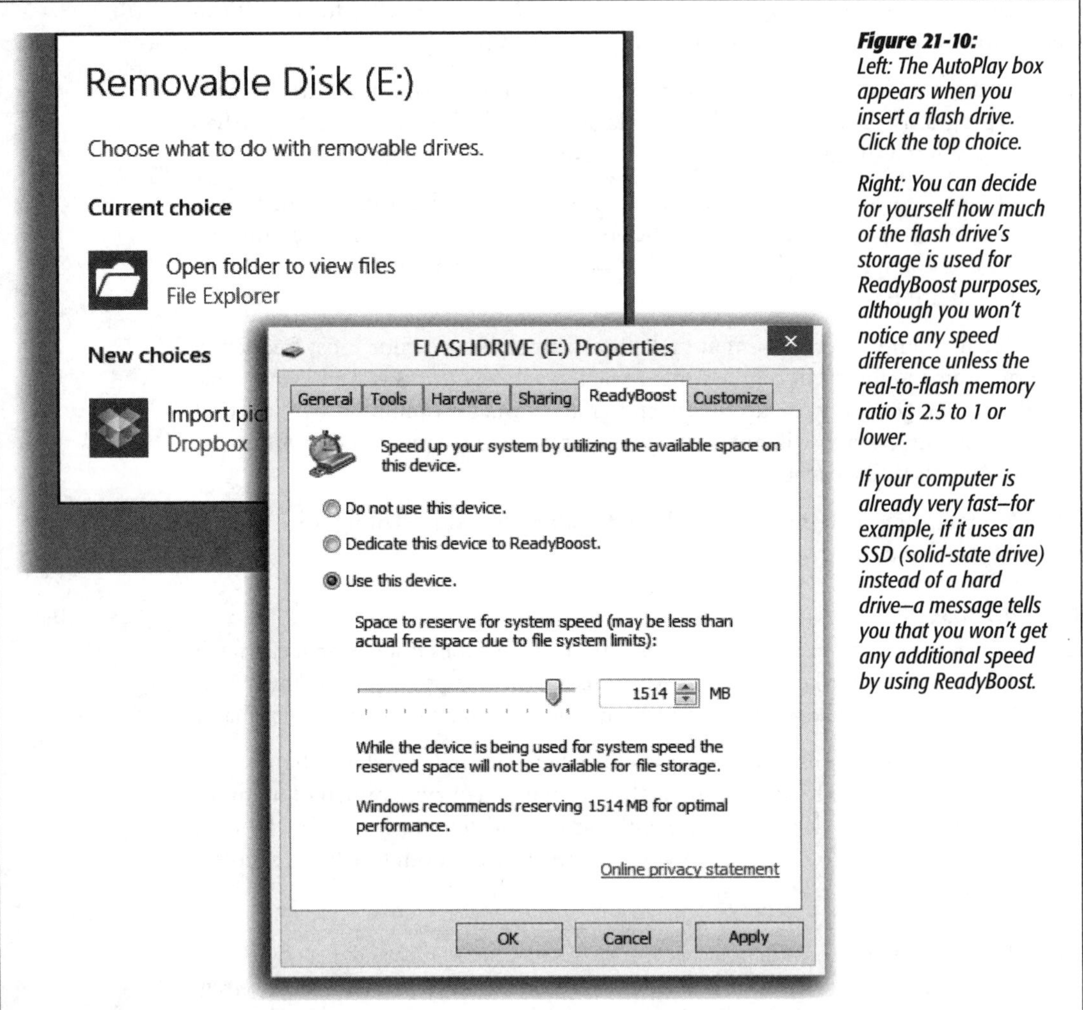

Figure 21-10:
Left: The AutoPlay box appears when you insert a flash drive. Click the top choice.

Right: You can decide for yourself how much of the flash drive's storage is used for ReadyBoost purposes, although you won't notice any speed difference unless the real-to-flash memory ratio is 2.5 to 1 or lower.

If your computer is already very fast—for example, if it uses an SSD (solid-state drive) instead of a hard drive—a message tells you that you won't get any additional speed by using ReadyBoost.

Click "Open folder to view files"; in the flash device's window (which opens automatically), click Properties on the Ribbon, and then click ReadyBoost. That box is shown in Figure 21-10 (right). Turn on "Use this device."

That's all there is to it. Your PC will now use the flash drive as an annex to its own built-in RAM, and you will, in theory, enjoy a tiny speed lift as a result.

Note: You won't run into problems if you yank out the flash drive; ReadyBoost stores a *copy* of the hard drive's data on the card/flash drive.

You also don't have to worry that somebody can steal your flash drive and, by snooping around the cache files, read about your top-secret plans for world domination. Windows 8 encrypts the data using CIA-quality algorithms.

And now, the fine print:

- Not all flash drives are equally fast, and therefore not all work with ReadyBoost. Look closely at the drive's packaging to see if there's a Windows ReadyBoost logo. (Technically speaking—very technically—its throughput must be capable of 2.5 MB per second for 4 KB random reads, and 1.75 MB per second for 512 KB random writes.)
- ReadyBoost works only with memory gadgets with capacities from 256 megabytes to 4 gigabytes.
- If Windows decides that your drive is fast enough *without* ReadyBoost, it disables ReadyBoost entirely. If you're the lucky owner of a computer with a solid state disk (SSD), for example, don't bother with ReadyBoost.
- If you choose "Dedicate this device to ReadyBoost," then you can't use it for storing everyday files. If you choose "Use this device" and then adjust the slider, you can leave some space for files as well (although it won't be quite as much as you expect).
- You can use one flash drive per PC, and one PC per flash drive.
- Ordinarily, saving files and then erasing them over and over again shortens a flash drive's life. Microsoft insists, however, that you can get 10 years out of one flash drive using ReadyBoost.
- ReadyBoost doesn't give much of a boost if your computer has a lot of RAM to begin with—more than 1 gigabyte, say. The biggest speed gains appear when you have a 1-to-1 ratio between real PC memory and your flash drive. For example, if your PC has 1 gigabyte of RAM, adding a 1-gig flash drive should give you a noticeable speed boost.

  The speed gains evaporate as you approach a 2.5-to-1 ratio. For example, suppose your PC has 1 gigabyte of RAM and you add a 256-megabyte flash drive. That's a 4-to-1 ratio, and you won't feel any acceleration at all.

Shutting Off Bells and Whistles

Windows, as you know, is all dressed up for "Where do you want to go today?" It's loaded with glitz, glamour, special effects, and animations. And every one of them saps away a little bit of speed.

With any luck, your PC is a mighty fortress of seething gigahertz that brushes off that kind of resource-sapping as though it were a mere cloud of gnats. But when things start to bog down, remember that you can turn off some of the bells and whistles—and recover the speed they were using.

Here's how.

Right-click the lower-left corner of the screen. From the shortcut menu, choose System. In the System control panel that appears, click "Advanced system settings" at left. Authenticate yourself if needed.

Now, on the Advanced tab, click the uppermost Settings button. You've just found, in the belly of the beast, the complete list of little animations that make up Windows' window dressing (Figure 21-11). For example, "Animate windows when minimizing

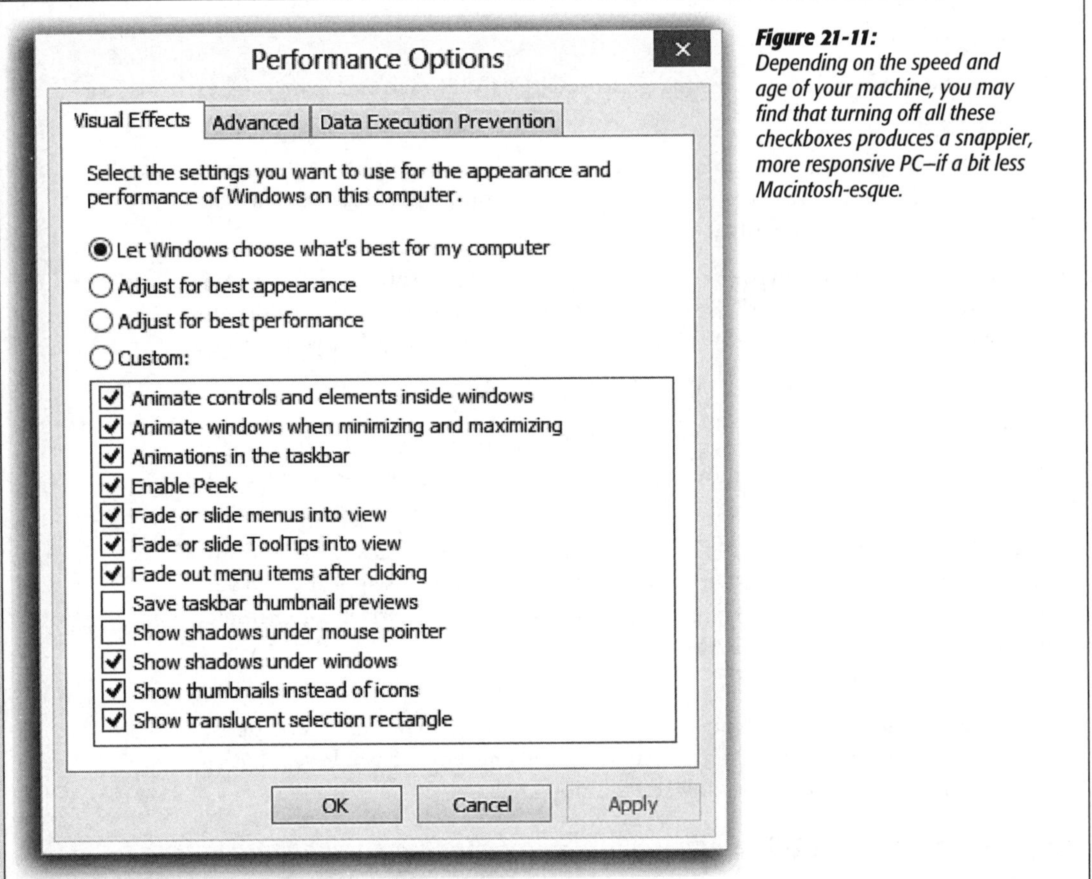

Figure 21-11:
Depending on the speed and age of your machine, you may find that turning off all these checkboxes produces a snappier, more responsive PC–if a bit less Macintosh-esque.

and maximizing" makes Windows present a half-second animation showing your window actually shrinking down onto the taskbar when you minimize it. "Show shadows under mouse pointer" produces a tiny shadow beneath your cursor, as though it were floating a quarter-inch above the surface of your screen.

With one click—on "Adjust for best performance"—you can turn off all these effects. Or, if there are some you can't live without—and let's face it, tooltips just aren't the same if they don't *fade* into view—click Custom, and then turn off the individual checkboxes for the features you don't need.

Windows Update

Windows 8 is more secure than previous versions of Windows, but you may have noticed that Microsoft isn't going so far as to say, "You don't need an antivirus program anymore." The hackers will have a *much* harder time of it, but with so many million lines of code to explore, they're sure to break in somehow.

Microsoft and other security researchers constantly find new security holes—and as soon as they're found, Microsoft rushes a patch out the door to fix it. But creating a patch is one thing; actually getting that patch installed on multiple millions of copies of Windows 8 around the world is another thing entirely.

Note: In fact, it's Microsoft's *patches* that usually alert hackers to the presence of security holes in the first place! They exploit the fact that not everyone has the patch in place instantly. (Which brings up the question: Should Microsoft even be creating the patches? But that's another conversation.)

That's where Windows Update comes in. When Microsoft releases a security fix, it gets delivered straight to your PC and automatically installed. (If you want, you can first review the fix before installing it, although few people have enough knowledge to judge its value.)

Windows Update doesn't deliver patches just to Windows itself; it can also send you better drivers for your hardware and patches to other Microsoft products, notably Office.

Installing Updates

As shown in Figure 21-12, Windows Update has two front ends: one at the desktop, and one in TileWorld.

Windows Update, Desktop Edition

When important updates become available, your Action Center icon on the taskbar (⚐) will let you know. Click it to open the Windows Update panel of the Control Panel (Figure 21-12, top). Of course, you can also open that Control Panel screen whenever you like.

As shown in the figure, you're likely to see two categories of updates: "important" ones (those having to do with bugs or security) and "optional" ones (usually those that offer new features). If you trust that Microsoft knows best, just click "Install updates" to install them. If you'd rather do some research first on what Microsoft is proposing, click the link (for example, "2 important updates are available") to read about the updates. (You can then go Google them to make sure other people have had a good experience with them, for example.)

Windows Update, TileWorld Edition

To see the TileWorld incarnation of Windows Update (Figure 21-12, bottom), open the Charms bar, select Settings, select "Change PC settings," and select Windows Update.

This panel lists only *important* updates. You can click "Check for updates now" to make sure all the latest updates are listed. Or, if Windows indicates that new updates are available ("We'll install 1 important update automatically," for example), click Install to commit to it.

If you'd rather know the details of what you're installing, or if you'd like to see which *optional* updates are waiting, click "Choose important updates to install, or install

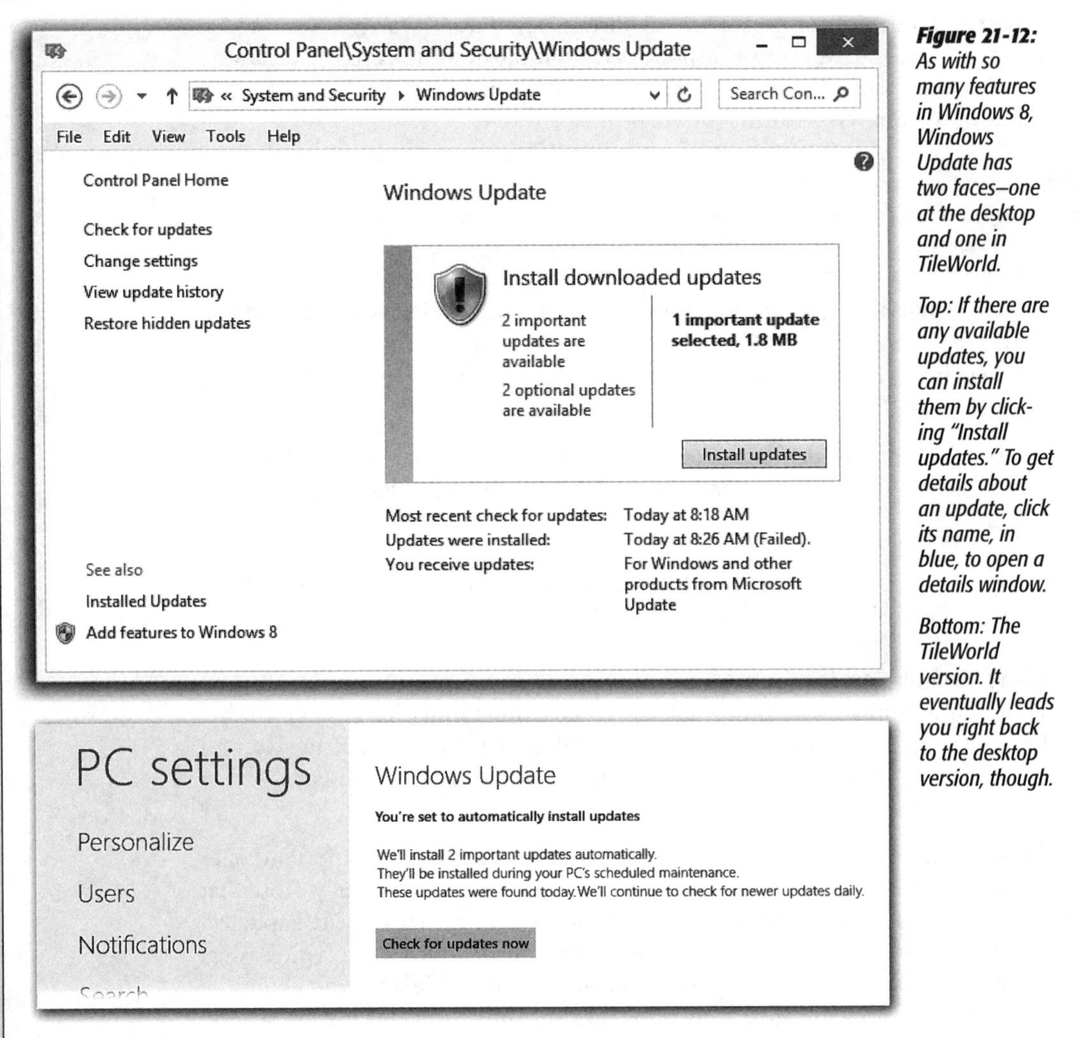

Figure 21-12: *As with so many features in Windows 8, Windows Update has two faces—one at the desktop and one in TileWorld.*

Top: If there are any available updates, you can install them by clicking "Install updates." To get details about an update, click its name, in blue, to open a details window.

Bottom: The TileWorld version. It eventually leads you right back to the desktop version, though.

optional updates." You're sent directly back to the desktop Control Panel screen shown in Figure 21-12 at top.

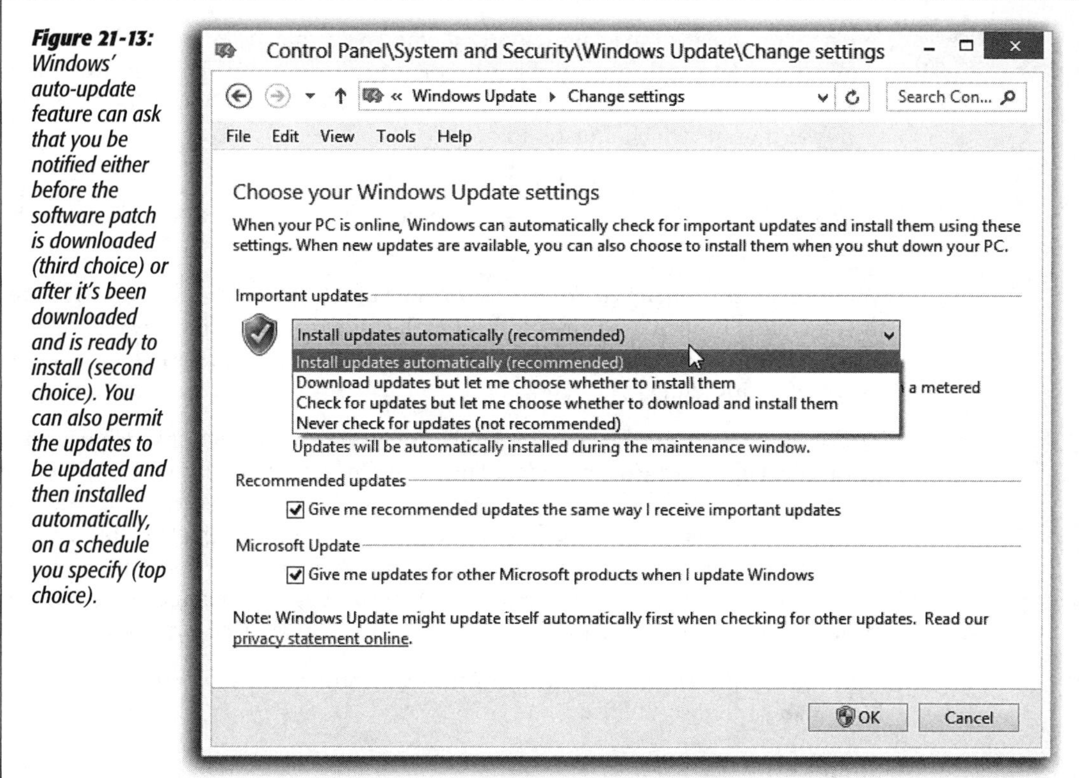
Control Panel\System and Security\Windows Update\Change settings
« Windows Update ▸ Change settings
Search Con...
File Edit View Tools Help
Choose your Windows Update settings
When your PC is online, Windows can automatically check for important updates and install them using these settings. When new updates are available, you can also choose to install them when you shut down your PC.
Important updates
Install updates automatically (recommended)
Install updates automatically (recommended)
Download updates but let me choose whether to install them
Check for updates but let me choose whether to download and install them
Never check for updates (not recommended)
a metered
Updates will be automatically installed during the maintenance window.
Recommended updates
Give me recommended updates the same way I receive important updates
Microsoft Update
Give me updates for other Microsoft products when I update Windows
Note: Windows Update might update itself automatically first when checking for other updates. Read our privacy statement online.
OK
Cancel

Figure 21-13: *Windows' auto-update feature can ask that you be notified either before the software patch is downloaded (third choice) or after it's been downloaded and is ready to install (second choice). You can also permit the updates to be updated and then installed automatically, on a schedule you specify (top choice).*

Windows Update Settings

Microsoft figures most people would like these updates to arrive as quietly and automatically as possible. But you can override that assumption.

To adjust how updates work, open the Windows Update screen of the Control Panel (Figure 21-12), and then click "Change settings." You wind up at the box shown in Figure 21-13.

The four options here correspond to four levels of trust people have in Microsoft, the mother ship:

- Install updates automatically (recommended). Translation: "Download and install all patches automatically. We trust in thee, Microsoft, that thou knowest what thou do-est." (All of this will take place in the middle of the night—or according to whatever schedule you set on this screen—so as not to inconvenience you.)

- Download updates but let me choose whether to install them. The downloading takes place in the background and doesn't interfere with anything you're downloading for yourself. But instead of installing the newly downloaded patch, Windows asks your permission.
- Check for updates but let me choose whether to download and install them. When Windows detects that a patch has become available, a note pops up from your system tray, telling you that an update is available. Click the icon in the system tray to indicate which updates to download and then install.
- Never check for updates (Not recommended). Microsoft will leave your copy of Windows completely alone—and completely vulnerable to attacks from the Internet.

Microsoft hates it when people choose anything but the first option, because it leaves them potentially open to security holes. On the other hand, patches have sometimes been known to be a bit buggy, so some people like to do a Google search on any new patch before installing it.

Notice, at the bottom of Figure 21-13, that there are several sections, two of which affect which updates are downloaded: There's one for recommended updates, and one for Microsoft Update. A *recommended update,* in Microsoft lingo, is an update that isn't required to keep your PC safe or to keep your operating system from blowing up but that can solve "non-critical problems and help enhance your computing experience." That's usually an updated driver or a Windows bug fix or feature enhancement. Turn on recommended updates if you want them to be included in Windows Update.

The *Microsoft Update* section delivers updates for other Microsoft software on your PC, notably Microsoft Office.

Beyond the Basics

There's a lot more to Windows Update than these basics, though. You can take a look at all the updates installed on your PC, for example, and you can even uninstall an update. And you can also restore the mysterious-sounding "hidden updates."

To begin, get back to the screen shown in Figure 21-12 at top. The left side of the screen includes these links:

- Check for updates checks for updates right now—and installs them, if you want.
- Change settings works as described earlier.
- View update history shows you a list of all the updates that have been downloaded and installed. You see the date of each update, whether it was successful, the type of update, and its purpose. Double-click one to get more details.
- Restore hidden updates. As noted below, you can *hide* an update to get it out of your hair. When you click "Restore hidden updates," they reappear so you can reinstall them.

Removing Updates

If an update winds up making life with your PC worse instead of better, you can remove it. Head to Control Panel→Programs→View Installed Updates, click an update, and then select Uninstall.

Note: You can't remove all updates, however. Security-related updates are usually nonremovable.

There's one problem with this action: The next time Windows Updates does its job, it will *re*install the update you just removed.

The workaround is to *hide* the update so that it doesn't get downloaded and installed again. Open Windows Update, and then click "Check for updates."

After Windows finds updates, click "View available updates." Right-click the update you don't want; select "Hide update." From now on, Windows Update ignores that update.

If, later, you change your mind, click "Restore hidden updates," select the update you want installed, and then click Restore.

Reset and Refresh

For years, the most miserable moments of a PC owner's existence have been spent troubleshooting mysterious glitches. You have no idea exactly what went wrong, but something isn't behaving right. And off you go to a weekend of Googling, troubleshooting, and head-scratching. By the end of it, you may just be inclined to do a "nuke and pave"—erasing your hard drive completely and installing everything from scratch.

In Windows 8, none of that is necessary. Microsoft has given you two incredibly powerful, incredibly easy-to-use troubleshooting techniques that perform much the same purpose as a nuke and pave—that is, resetting everything to its original, virginal condition—but requires far less work and effort. They're called Reset PC and Refresh PC:

- Refreshing a PC gives it a fresh, clean copy of Windows 8 and all the programs that came with it. It leaves your files and your TileWorld apps in place, which is a huge improvement over the nuke-and-pave tradition.

  But it erases all your *desktop programs, drivers, and Windows settings.* You have to reinstall your desktop programs and drivers when it's over. (For your reconstructing convenience, Windows leaves a thoughtful list of all the deleted programs on the desktop, with Web links to download them.)

- Resetting a PC *erases it completely*—your programs, apps, files, and settings are all deleted—and leaves it with a factory-fresh copy of Windows 8. It's great for erasing your hard drive before you donate or sell your computer to somebody new.

Both of these functions are available only from TileWorld.

Tip: Well, "only" is a very strong word. Actually, the Refresh and Reset commands are also available from the Advanced Startup menu sequence illustrated in Figure 21-15.

Refreshing Your PC

Here's how to go about the new Refresh process:

1. **In TileWorld, open the Charms bar.**

   For example, swipe in from the right side of the screen, or press ⊞+C.

2. **Select Settings, and then "Change PC settings."**

   The TileWorld control panel opens.

3. **In the settings list, select General.**

   Scroll down to "Refresh your PC without affecting your files."

4. **Under "Refresh your PC," click "Get started."**

   You see the warning shown in Figure 21-14. Make sure you understand that you'll have to reinstall all your desktop apps and reestablish all your settings.

5. **Click Next.**

   You're asked to insert your Windows 8 DVD or flash drive so that Windows can reinstall itself.

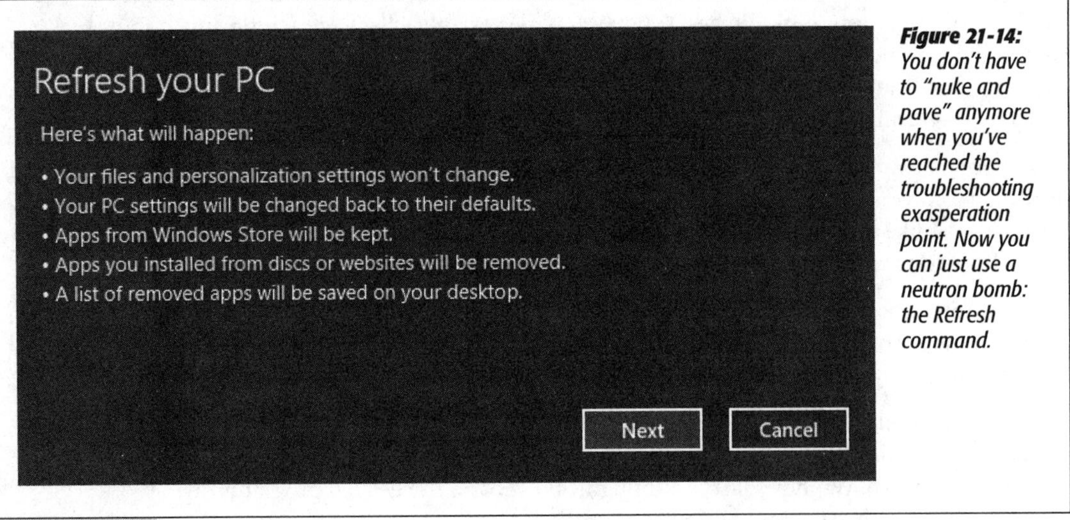

Figure 21-14: *You don't have to "nuke and pave" anymore when you've reached the troubleshooting exasperation point. Now you can just use a neutron bomb: the Refresh command.*

6. **Insert the Windows 8 disc or drive, and then click Refresh.**

   Windows goes to work, restarting the computer as necessary; the process takes 15 to 30 minutes.

Tip: When the computer starts up again, if the Windows DVD is still in the drive, it may try to start up from the DVD's copy of Windows instead of your computer's. When you see "Press any key to boot from disc," don't.

When it's all over, things should work a lot more smoothly—your headaches are over—but of course you have some reinstalling ahead of you. Open the link on the desktop called Removed Apps; it's a Web page that lists all the programs your PC used to have that got deleted during the refresh. You have to fetch their original installers to put them back on your machine. You'll also have to rejoin your network and Homegroup, if you were on those.

Resetting Your PC

In more dramatic situations—for example, you're about to get rid of your computer and want to make sure none of your stuff is going along for the ride to the new owner—you can also *reset* your PC. In other words, you're sending it back to its factory-fresh

POWER USERS' CLINIC

Refreshing to a More Complete Point

Ordinarily, the Refresh command gets rid of all your desktop apps and settings, in the name of giving you a more stable system. Unfortunately, you're then left with the task of re-installing all your desktop apps and reestablishing all your settings and preferences.

But if you're clever, you can get Refresh to rewind instead to a time when everything was working fine, instead of all the way back to the dawn of time. That is, Refresh can preserve your desktop programs and settings, too!

You can do this only, however, if you take a snapshot when your machine is working *well*. Later, you can Refresh back to this point. (In this scenario, only a few settings don't make the transition: any custom file associations, and changes you've made in the Display or Windows Firewall panels of the Control Panel, for example.)

The other requirement: not to be terrified of typing out instructions at the command line.

To create the snapshot, right-click the lower-left corner of the screen; from the shortcut menu, choose Command Prompt (Admin). Authenticate. Now, your old, old friend, the DOS prompt appears (c:\windows\system32:). Type this:

mkdir c:\refreshpt

and then press Enter. You've just made a new folder that will contain your snapshot file. (If you know your way around the command line, you can create this file on another hard drive, if you like.)

To make the snapshot file itself (the refresh point), type this, being careful to type the correct slashes:

recimg /createimage c:\refreshpt

Now Windows makes a big file (about 4 gigabytes) called install.wim. (The suffix stands for Windows Installer Image.) This process can take several *hours*.

When it's all over, though, you'll be able to rewind a malfunctioning PC back to this happier day. Follow the steps on page 690. Instead of rewinding all the way to your PC's virginal state, Windows will rewind only as far as the installer-image snapshot you made.

condition, with nothing on it except Windows and the software programs that came with it. All your files, settings, and software are completely wiped out.

Follow steps 1–3 of the previous instructions. Then:

4. **Under "Remove everything and install Windows," click "Get started."**

   Again, a warning. "All your personal files and apps will be removed. Your PC settings will be changed back to their defaults."

5. **Click Next.**

   You may be asked to insert your Windows 8 DVD or flash drive, so that Windows can reinstall itself. If you have multiple drives, you're also asked if you want to erase only the Windows drive or all the drives. Click your choice.

6. **Insert the Windows 8 disc or drive, and then click Reset.**

   Windows goes to work, restarting the computer as necessary; the process takes 15 to 30 minutes. When it's all over, you know what you'll have: a computer containing nothing but Windows and its accompanying included software. Nothing of yours.

Windows Recovery Environment (WinRE)

You might play by all the rules. You might make regular backups, keep your antivirus software up to date, and floss twice a day. And then, one day, you get your reward: The PC won't even start up. You can't use any of Windows' software troubleshooting tools, because you can't even get to Windows.

In that most dire situation, Microsoft is pleased to offer what's known to techies as WinRE (Windows Recovery Environment). It's a special recovery mode, loaded with emergency tools: System Reset, System Refresh, System Restore, System Image Recovery, Safe Mode, and on and on.

Windows Recovery Environment is a pure, protected mode that's separate from the normal workings of Windows—a place to do troubleshooting without worrying about changes that have been made by any software, good or bad.

If the problems you're having are caused by drivers that load just as the computer is starting up, for example, then turning them all off can be helpful. At the very least, WinRE allows you to get into your machine to begin your troubleshooting pursuit. It's a menu most people never even know exists until they're initiated into its secret world by a technically savvy guru.

It used to be easy to open this screen; you just pressed the F8 key at the right moment during startup. But that trick doesn't work in Windows 8. Some Windows 8 machines start up so fast that you'd have only milliseconds to hit the F8 key at just the right time.

In Windows 8, the Recovery Environment (Figure 21-15) appears *automatically* if the computer hasn't successfully started up after two attempts. If it doesn't, or if you're impatient, you can get to it using any of these methods:

***Figure 21-15:** Welcome to the Windows Recovery Environment. Somewhere in this series of screens, you'll encounter every conceivable troubleshooting tool.*

The first one is the "Choose an option" screen. If you select the Troubleshoot option here, you get the Troubleshoot screen (second from top). Here, for your troubleshooting pleasure, are duplicates of the Refresh and Reset commands.

But if you click "Advanced options," you arrive at the "Advanced options" screen (third from top). This is a good place to recover data from a System Restore backup.

But if you choose Startup Settings, you open the actual, true-blue Startup Settings menu.

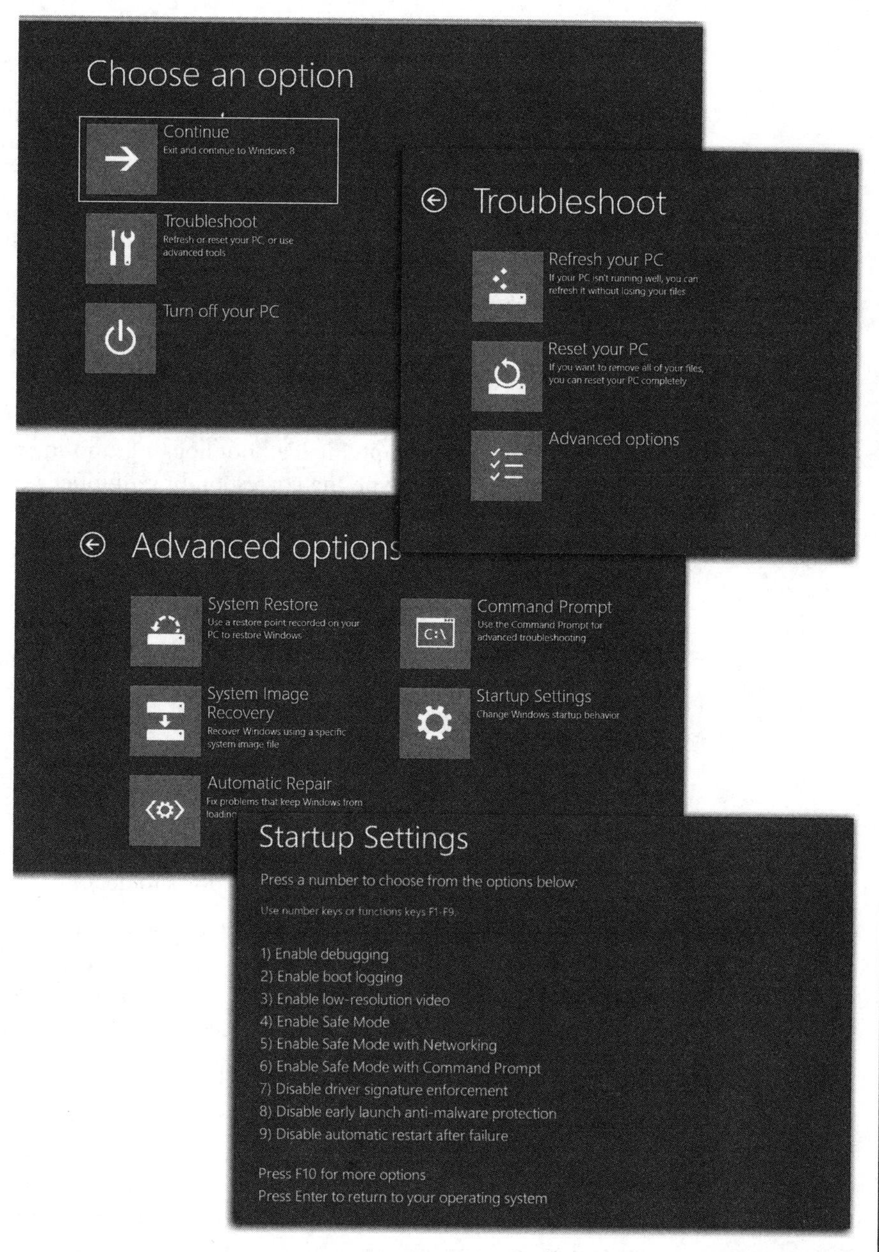

The steps differ depending on how much trouble you're having getting the computer going. Choose *one* of these three techniques:

- Hold down the Shift key as you click Restart. (To find the Restart button, open the Charms bar, select Settings, and select Power.)
- In the Settings panel of the Charms bar, select "Change PC settings." Select General, and then scroll down to "Advanced setup" and click "Restart now."
- Start up from a Windows DVD or a flash drive. At the Windows Setup screen, hit Next; then choose "Repair your computer." (This technique works even if the computer is too sick to start up normally.)

Tip: If you're a command-line kind of person, here's how you open the Recovery Environment from the command console. Type *shutdown.exe /r /o* and press Enter.

In each case, you arrive at the "Choose an option" screen. Follow the sequence shown in Figure 21-15 to find the Startup Settings screen.

The Startup Settings options include Safe Mode, Safe Mode with Networking, Safe Mode with Command Prompt, Enable Boot Logging, and so on. Use the arrow keys to walk through them, or type the corresponding number key or function key to choose one.

Here's what the Startup menu commands do:

1. **Enable debugging.**

   Here's an extremely obscure option, intended for very technical people who've connected one PC to another via a serial cable. They can then use the second computer to analyze the first, using specialized debugger software.

2. **Enable Boot Logging.**

   This startup method is the same as Normal, except that Windows records every technical event that takes place during the startup in a log file named *ntbtlog.txt* (located on the startup drive, in the Windows folder).

   Most of the time, you'll use the Boot Logging option only at the request of a support technician you've phoned for help. After confirming the operating system startup, the technician may ask you to open ntbtlog.txt in your Notepad program and search for particular words or phrases—usually the word "fail."

3. **Enable low-resolution video.**

   In this mode, your PC uses a standard VGA video driver that works with all graphics cards, instead of the hideously ugly generic one usually seen in Safe Mode. Use this option when you're troubleshooting video-display problems—problems that you're confident have less to do with drivers than with your settings in the Display control panel (which you're now ready to fiddle with).

Of course, VGA means 640 × 480 pixels, which looks huge and crude on today's big monitors. Do not adjust your set.

4. **Enable** Safe Mode.

   Safe Mode starts up Windows in a special, stripped-down, generic, somewhat frightening-looking startup mode—with the software for dozens of hardware and software features *turned off.* Only the very basic components work: your mouse, keyboard, screen, and disk drives. Everything else is shut down and cut off. In short, Safe Mode is the tack to take if your PC *won't* start up normally, thanks to some recalcitrant driver.

   Once you select the Safe Mode option on the Startup menu, you see a list, filling your screen, of every driver Windows is loading. Eventually, you're asked to log in.

   Your screen now looks like it was designed by drunken cavemen, with jagged, awful graphics and text. That's because in Safe Mode, Windows doesn't load the driver for your video card (on the assumption that it may be causing the very problem you're trying to troubleshoot). Instead, Windows loads a crude, generic driver that works with *any* video card.

   The purpose of Safe Mode is to help you troubleshoot. (Windows Help opens automatically when you arrive at the desktop, offering a description of Safe Mode.) If you discover that the problem you've been having is now gone, you've at least established that the culprit was one of the now disabled startup items or drivers. If this procedure doesn't solve the problem, then contact a support technician.

5. **Safe Mode with Networking.**

   This option is exactly the same as Safe Mode, except that it also lets you load the driver software needed to tap into a network, if you're on one, or onto the Internet—an arrangement that offers a few additional troubleshooting possibilities, like being able to access files and drivers on another PC or from the Internet. (If you have a laptop that uses a PC Card networking card, however, this option may still not help you, since the PC Card driver itself is still turned off.)

6. **Safe Mode with Command Prompt.**

   Here's another variation of Safe Mode, this one intended for ultra–power users who are more comfortable typing out text commands at the command prompt than using icons, menus, and the mouse.

7. **Disable driver signature enforcement.**

   As a way to protect your PC, Windows uses a technique called driver signature enforcement, which is designed to load only drivers that are verified to be valid. Of course, there are plenty of times when drivers aren't verified but are in fact usable. If you suspect that to be the case, choose this option; Windows will load all your drivers.

8. **Disable early launch anti-malware protection.**

   It's an increasingly common trick by the bad guys: They release a *rootkit* (a virus-like bit of software) that installs a driver that loads into memory right when your computer starts up. Since it's there before your antivirus software has loaded, it's very difficult to detect and remove.

   In Windows 8, Microsoft created Early Launch Anti-Malware Protection (ELAMP), a window of opportunity for certain antivirus programs to load before all other drivers. That way, the antivirus software scan any other drivers that load and, if they're malware, block them from loading.

   Ah—but what if one of these antivirus programs identifies a driver as evil but it's actually not? Then you won't be able to start up at all. In that situation, you'd want to turn ELAMP off using this option.

   Once you've started up, update your virus software or remove the questionable driver. The next time you start up, ELAMP will be turned on again.

7. **Disable automatic restart on system failure.**

   Under normal conditions, Windows automatically reboots after a system crash. Choose this option if you don't want it to reboot.

If you press F10, you go into the Windows Recovery Environment, described in Figure 21-15.

If you press Enter, you start the operating system in its usual fashion, exactly as though you'd never summoned the Startup menu to begin with. It lets you tell the PC, "Sorry to have interrupted you...go ahead."

Thanks to these powerful startup tools, there's less reason than ever to pay $35 for the privilege of talking to some technician named "Mike" who's actually in India, following a tech-support script that instructs you to first erase your hard drive and reinstall Windows from scratch.

Troubleshooting Tools

These days, a first-time Windows user probably doesn't even know what you mean by the phrase "blue screen of death." PCs don't crash nearly as often as they used to.

But there are still a million things that can go wrong—and about a million troubleshooting tools to help you, or somebody you've begged to help you, solve them. Here's the, ahem, crash course.

Automatic Error Reporting

In the Windows XP days, every time a program crashed, a dialog box asked if you wanted to send details of the crash, anonymously, to Microsoft. Maybe, just maybe, the cumulative stream of these reports might lead some programmer somewhere to detect a pattern—and fix his darned bug.

In Windows 8, you can tell your PC to send those reports to Microsoft automatically—without interrupting or bothering you—or not to send them at all. You can also look over a running diary of all the crashes you've had.

To fiddle with these settings, open the Action Center. (Click the ⚐ on your taskbar system tray, and click Open Action Center.) Expand the Maintenance section, if necessary, and then click Settings. Proceed as shown in Figure 21-16.

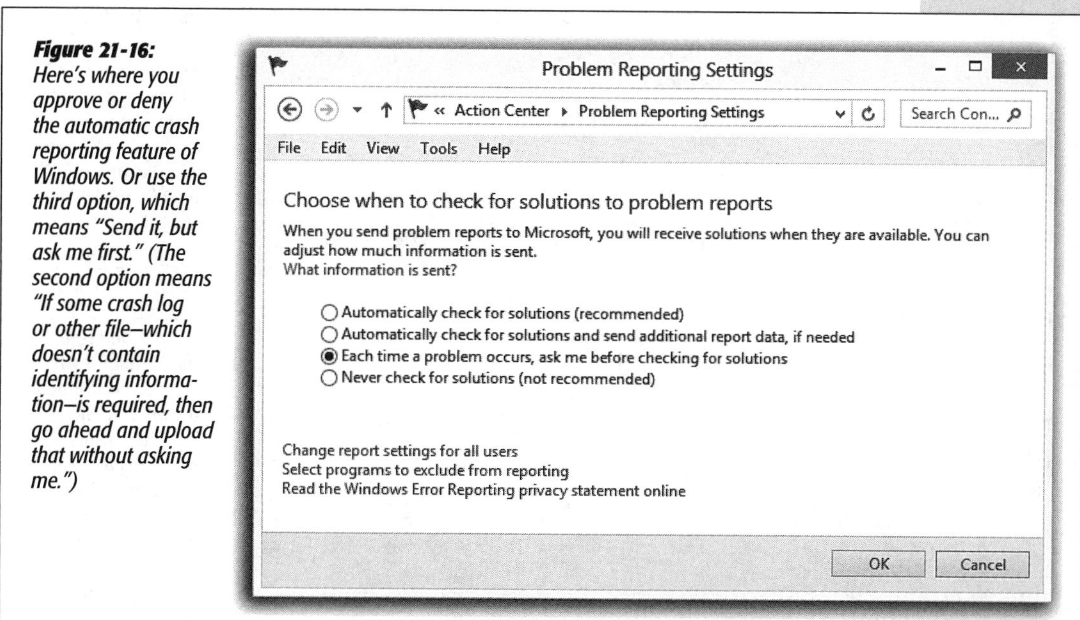

Figure 21-16: *Here's where you approve or deny the automatic crash reporting feature of Windows. Or use the third option, which means "Send it, but ask me first." (The second option means "If some crash log or other file–which doesn't contain identifying information–is required, then go ahead and upload that without asking me.")*

Automatic Solution Reporting

It doesn't happen often, but it's conceivable that all those millions of crash reports that Microsoft collects might one day result in a patch that fixes the problem—maybe even a problem *you* reported. If Windows finds out that some bug-fix update is available for a crash you've had, a message in the Action Center will let you know and offer you the chance to download it.

The Diary of Windows Crashes

Windows maintains a tidy list of all the problems you've been having with your machine. Needless to say, this little item isn't featured very prominently in Windows, but it's there.

To see it, type *reports* at the Start screen; select Settings under the search box. In the search results, click "View all problem reports." You get the astonishing box shown in Figure 21-17 (top).

Tip: For techies, Windows includes an even more technical list of the goings-on on your PC: the Event Viewer. Open it by typing *event viewer* at the Start screen; then click Settings and click "View event logs." Enjoy looking over eye-glazing lists of every log Windows keeps—lists of happenings concerning programs, setup, security, services, and more. You can sort, filter, and group these events—but if you can understand the significance of these obscure messages, you shouldn't be reading a Windows book—you should be writing one.

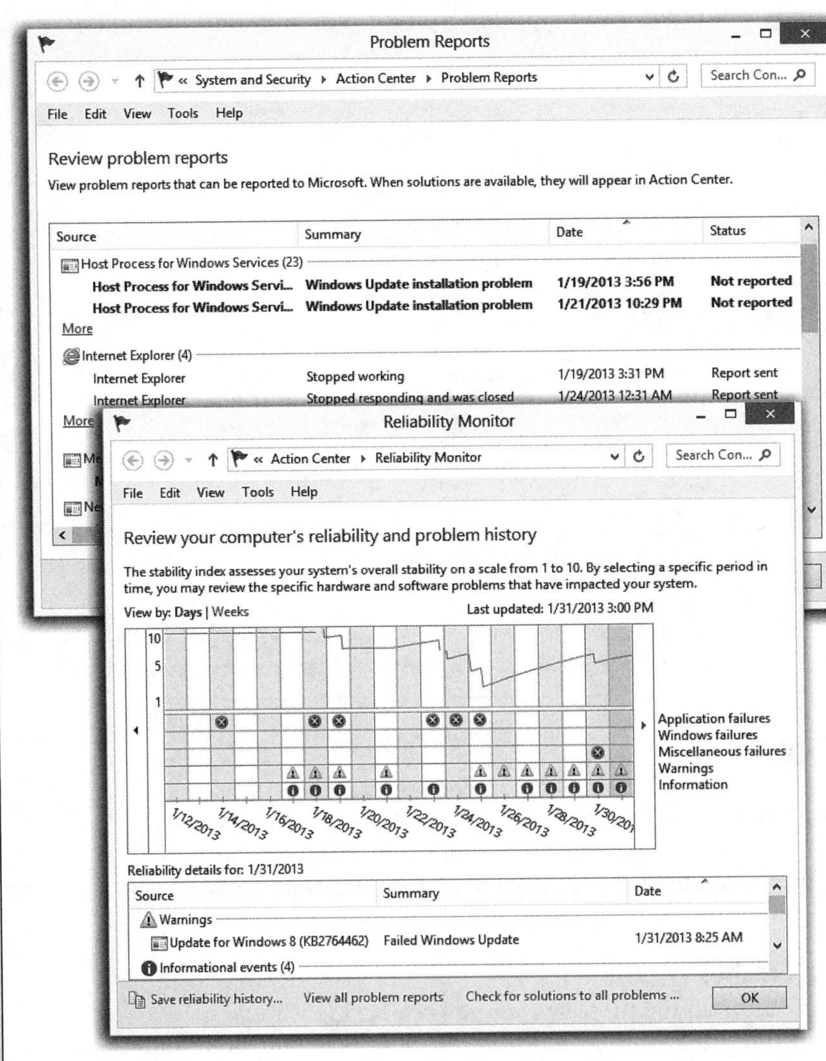

Figure 21-17: *Top: Diary of a typical Windows 8 machine. It's a list of all the things that have gone wrong recently. Double-click one to open a screen of techie details that could be useful to a tech-support rep.*

Bottom: Here's a mighty graph of your crashes stretching back one year, which explains why your PC has seemed so cranky lately. Each icon shows something that went wrong—a crash, a freeze, an error message. Click a column to see everything that happened that day.

If you see a lot of crashes following, for example, an installation or system change, you might have spotted yourself a cause-and-effect situation. You now have a clue to your PC's recent instability.

Reliability Monitor

If you prefer to get the bad news in visual form, try the Reliability Monitor (Figure 21-17, bottom). To see it, type *history* at the Start screen. Click "View reliability history."

Just say the words "startup items" to a Windows veteran, and you're sure to witness an involuntary shudder.

Startup Items Revealed

Startup items are programs that load automatically when you turn the computer on, without your invitation. Some of them are icons in the system tray. Some are designed to assist antivirus or iPod syncing apps. Some of them run in the background, invisibly.

But all of them use memory, and sometimes they can slow down your machine. And until Windows 8 came along, they were annoying and complex to manage.

Now, sometimes, there are on/off switches for the startup items in the programs themselves, in menu called Settings, Preferences, Options, or Tools. That's a clean, direct way to shut something up, but it won't help you with invisible startup items—those you didn't even know are running.

In the pre–Windows 8 days, you could have a look at all your startup items, and even turn off the ones you didn't think were necessary, using a command-line program with the cheerful name MSConfig. Fortunately, that's no longer necessary; a much more visual, easy-to-understand method awaits in Windows 8: a little program called the Task Manager.

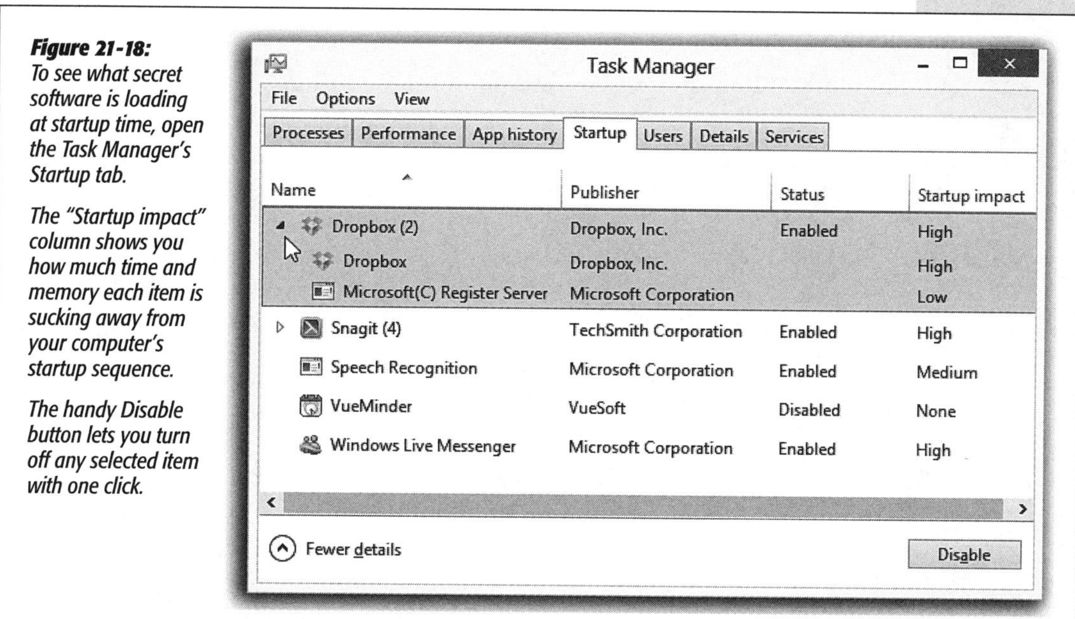

***Figure 21-18:** To see what secret software is loading at startup time, open the Task Manager's Startup tab.*

The "Startup impact" column shows you how much time and memory each item is sucking away from your computer's startup sequence.

The handy Disable button lets you turn off any selected item with one click.

Yes, it's the same program described on page 335. But in Windows 8, the Task Manager has a new tab called Startup Items. It's a startup/shutdowner's dream come true.

To open the Task Manager, type its name at the Start screen. Or right-click the lower-left corner of the screen and, from the shortcut menu, choose Task Manager. Now click its Startup tab, and proceed as shown in Figure 21-18.

CHAPTER 22

Backups & File History

There are two kinds of people in the world: those who have a regular backup system—and those who *will.*

You'll get that grisly joke immediately if you've ever known the pain that comes with deleting the wrong folder by accident, or making changes that you regret, or worst of all, having your hard drive die. All those photos, all that music you've bought online, all your email—gone.

Yet the odds are overwhelming that at this moment, you do not have a complete, current, automated backup of your computer. Despite about a thousand warnings, articles, and cautionary tales a year, guess how many do? About *four percent.* Everybody else is flying without a net.

If you don't have much to back up—you don't have much in the way of photos, music, or movies—you can get by with burning copies of stuff onto blank CDs or DVDs or using a free online backup system like Dropbox or your SkyDrive. But those methods leave most of your stuff unprotected: all your programs and settings.

What you really want, of course, is a backup that's rock-solid, complete, and *automatic.* You don't want to have to remember to do a backup, to insert a disc, and so on. You just want to know you're safe.

If you use Windows in a corporation, you probably don't even have to think about backing up your stuff. A network administrator generally does the backing up for you.

But if you use Windows at home, or in a smaller company that doesn't have network nerds running around to ensure your files' safety, you'll be happy to know about the various tools that come with Windows 8, all dedicated to the proposition of making safety copies. You have System Images and System Restore, for your entire system, and you have the new File History, for rewinding individual documents to earlier drafts—or recovering them if they've gotten deleted or damaged them.

Windows Backup and Restore

The dedicated backup program that used to come with Windows, Backup and Restore, has been "deprecated" by Microsoft. That's geek slang for "taken out behind the barn and shot."

Microsoft still includes it in Windows 8, for the benefit of people who created backups in Windows 7 that they might like to restore someday on their Windows 8 machines. But you'd never know it; there's no icon for it, you can't search for it, and even its actual hidden location has been trickily renamed.

If you want to use this backup program, open the Control Panel. Under the System and Security heading (in Category view), click "Save backup copies of your files with File History." When the corresponding screen appears, click "Windows 7 File Recovery." Yes, that's the new name for Windows Backup and Restore (and, no, it's not just for Windows 7; it works fine in Windows 8).

This program creates a system image (described below), or just backs up any folders and files you choose, onto any other disks—other hard drives, CDs or DVDs, or other computers on the network. To get started, click "Set up backup."

If you can't figure out how to proceed from there, download the free bonus Appendix to this chapter, "Windows 7 File Recovery (Backup and Restore)" from this book's "Missing CD" at *www.missingmanuals.com.*

So if Microsoft doesn't want you to use Backup and Restore anymore, what does it expect you to use instead? Two tools: System Images (snapshots of your entire computer) and File History (snapshots of individual documents). Both are described in the following pages.

System Images

When your hard disk crashes, you lose more than just your personal files. You also lose your operating system—*and* all the programs you've installed, *and* all their updates and patches, *and* all your settings and options and tweaks. It can take you a very long time to restore your PC to that state.

A *system image* solves the problem easily. This feature (called Complete PC Backup in the Windows Vista days), creates a perfect snapshot of your *entire* hard drive at this moment: documents, email, pictures, and so on, *plus* Windows, *and* all your programs and settings. Someone could steal your *entire hard drive,* or your drive could die, and you'd be able to install a new, empty one and be back in business inside of an hour.

It's a good idea to make a fresh system image every few months, because you'll probably have installed new programs and changed your settings in the interim.

Note: For the techies scoring at home, a system image is a .vhd file, the same kind that's created by Microsoft's Virtual PC software—and, therefore, you can mount it using Virtual PC, if you like.

Make the Image

To make a system image, open the Control Panel. Under the System and Security heading (in Category view), click "Save backup copies of your files with File History." When the corresponding screen appears, click Windows 7 File Recovery. You arrive at the Windows 7 File Recovery box. Continue as shown in Figure 22-1.

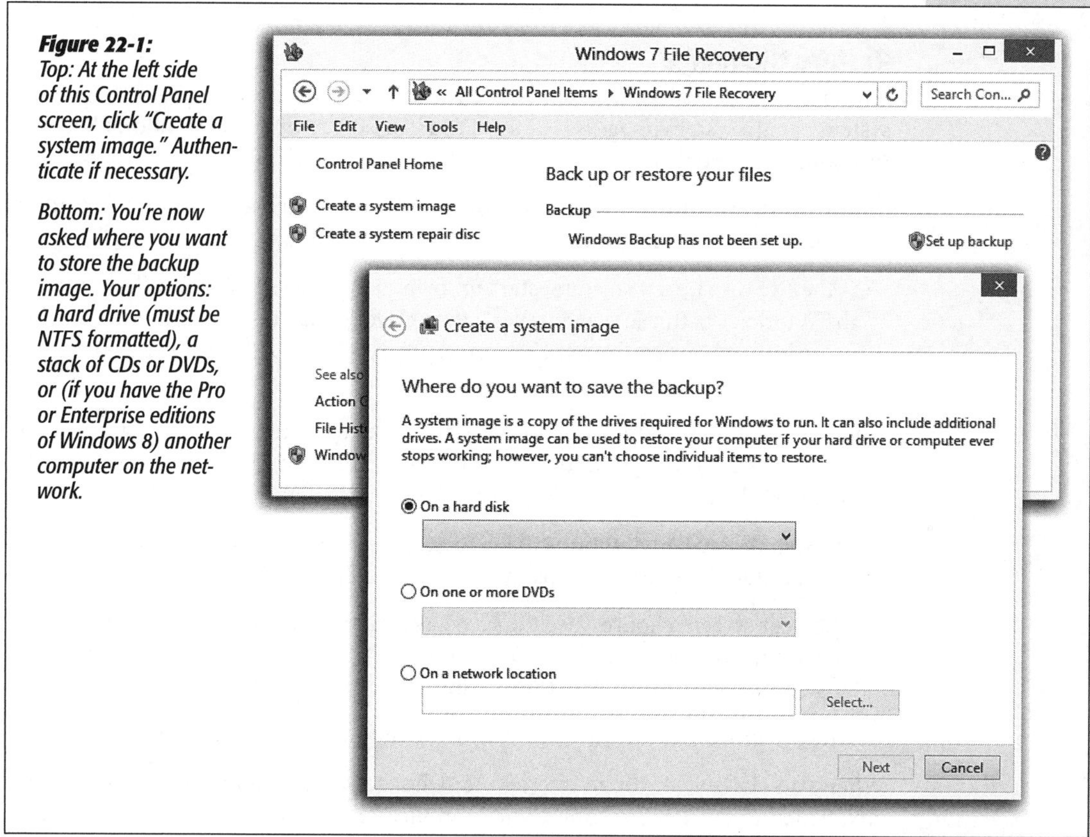

Figure 22-1:
Top: At the left side of this Control Panel screen, click "Create a system image." Authenticate if necessary.

Bottom: You're now asked where you want to store the backup image. Your options: a hard drive (must be NTFS formatted), a stack of CDs or DVDs, or (if you have the Pro or Enterprise editions of Windows 8) another computer on the network.

No matter where you store the image, you'll need a *lot* of empty disk space. Not as much as your entire PC drive, because you won't be backing up empty space or temporary files. But a lot.

Note: You can keep multiple system images around—representing your PC's world at different times—if you back up to discs or hard drives. If you save to a network location, though, you can keep only the most recent system image.

When you click Next, you're offered a list of all your computer's drives. You may, if you wish, include other drives as part of the system image, so that they'll be restored, too, if the worst should come to pass. (Your Windows drive is automatically selected; you're not allowed to include the drive you're saving the image *onto*.)

Click "Start backup"; the backup begins. You'll be prompted when you need to insert new discs.

Tip: At the end of the backing up, Windows asks if you'd like it to burn a system repair disc—a CD or DVD that can start up your PC when it won't start up from the hard drive. It's an excellent idea.

Restore the Image

Suppose disaster strikes: Your hard drive is trashed. Fortunately, restoring your entire system using a system image is very easy. You just have to open the Windows Recovery Environment, like this:

- If your PC is running, hold down the Shift key as you click Restart. (To find the Restart button, open the Charms bar, select Settings, and select Power.)
- If the PC won't even start up, start up from a Windows DVD or a flash drive. At the Windows Setup screen, hit Next; then choose "Repair your computer." (Alternatively, just boot up from the system repair disc you made when you created the system image.)

Once you see the "Choose an option screen," click Troubleshoot, then "Advanced options," then System Image Recovery. (You can see this sequence of screens illustrated in Figure 21-15.)

In the System Recovery Options dialog box that appears, choose an administrator's account. Enter the appropriate password, and then click Continue.

On the next screen, choose "Use the latest available system image (recommended)," and click OK. (Of course, if you have some weird agenda, you can also choose an older system image, using the other option here.)

When prompted, find the drive or disc that contains your system image.

When you click Next, you're offered the "Choose additional restore options" dialog box, which offers some complex and complicated options. The key element worth inspecting is the "Format and repartition disks" option.

- If it's turned on, then every disk and partition will be formatted and partitioned to match the system image. (If this box is turned on and dimmed, then you have no choice; the disk will be formatted and partitioned to match the system image.)
- If you can't turn on this checkbox—it's dimmed and unchecked—then you're probably restoring a system image from one partition to another on the same disk. Clearly, Windows can't erase the disk it's operating from.

The "Only restore system drives" option does what it says: leaves your other drives alone.

When you click Finish and then Yes in the confirmation box, the long, slow restoration process begins. And the rest, as they say, is history recreated.

Just remember that this process *reformats your hard drive,* and in the process *wipes out all your data and files.* They'll be replaced with the most recent snapshot (system image) you've made. Of course, you may well have a *regular* backup that's more recent; you can restore that as the final step.

Note: If you were thinking of using a system image to turn a new PC into a replica of your old, crashed one, be warned: You can't restore a system image to a new PC's hard drive if it's smaller than the old one. (Yes, even if the data on the backup drive would easily fit on the target drive.)

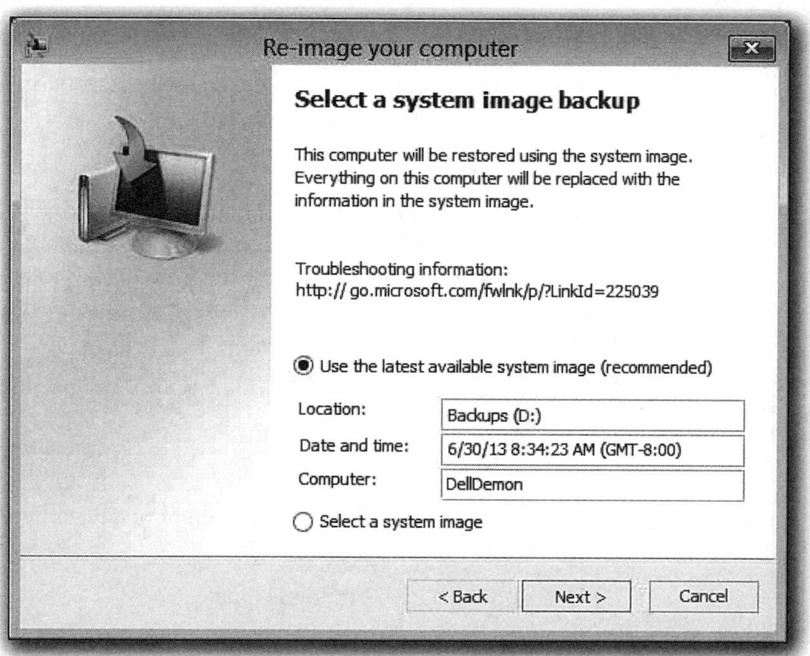

Figure 22-2: *Here's the payoff for your diligent system imaging. Windows is about to turn your current, messed-up computer back into the model of PC health that it was the day you made the image.*

System Restore

As you get more proficient on a PC, pressing Ctrl+Z—the keyboard shortcut for Undo—eventually becomes an unconscious reflex. In fact, you can sometimes spot veteran Windows fans twitching their Ctrl+Z fingers even when they're not near the computer—after knocking over a cup of coffee, locking the keys inside the car, or blurting out something inappropriate in a meeting.

Windows offers the mother of all Undo commands: System Restore. This feature alone can be worth hours of your time and hundreds of dollars in consultant fees.

The pattern of things going wrong in Windows usually works like this: The PC works fine for a while, and then suddenly—maybe for no apparent reason, but most often following an installation or configuration change—it goes on the fritz. At that point, wouldn't it be pleasant to be able to tell the computer, "Go back to the way you were yesterday, please"?

System Restore does exactly that. It "rewinds" your copy of Windows back to the condition it was in before you, or something you tried to install, messed it up. Best of all, System Restore *doesn't change your files.* Your email, pictures, music, documents, and other files are left up to date.

Tip: If your PC manages to catch a virus, System Restore can even rewind it to a time before the infection–*if* the virus hasn't gotten into your documents in such a way that you reinfect yourself after the system restore. An up-to-date antivirus program is a much more effective security blanket.

In fact, if you don't like your PC after restoring it, you can always restore it to the way it was *before* you restored it. Back to the future!

About Restore Points

System Restore works by taking snapshots of your operating system. Your copy of Windows has been creating these memorized snapshots, called *restore points,* ever since you've been running it. When the worst comes to pass, and your PC starts acting up, you can use System Restore to rewind your machine to its configuration the last time you remember it working well.

Windows automatically creates landing points for your little PC time machine at the following times:

- Once a day.
- Every time you install a new program or install a new device driver for a piece of hardware.
- When you install a Windows Update.
- Whenever you feel like it—for instance, just before you install some new component.

The System Protection Dialog Box

The central command center for the System Restore feature is the System Protection dialog box. Here are two good ways to open it:

- **Open the Start screen.** Type *restore* and select Settings under the search box. In the search results, click "Create a restore point" (yes, even though you're not creating one—you're using one).
- **Right-click the lower-left corner of the screen;** from the shortcut menu, choose System. In the resulting dialog box, click "System protection."

Either way, you now see the dialog box shown in Figure 22-3.

Creating a Manual Restore Point

To create one of these checkpoints *manually*, open the System Protection tab on the System Properties dialog box (follow the steps above). At the bottom of that box, the Create button lets you create and name a new manual restore point. (Windows adds a date and time stamp automatically.)

Note: As you can imagine, storing all these copies of your Windows configuration consumes quite a bit of disk space. That's why System Restore lets you limit how much of your drive is allowed to fill up with restore points. Click Configure in the System Protection tab of the System Properties dialog box (Figure 22-3); you get a slider that lets you cap the percentage of the drive that can be swallowed up with restore-point data. When your drive gets full, System Restore starts *deleting* the oldest restore points as necessary.

Figure 22-3:
Here's your command center for all System Restore functions. Its layout is, more or less, upside-down.

For example, starting from the bottom of the box: Click the Create button to make a restore point right now, manually; click Configure to delete all restore points and limit disk space; click System Restore to perform the actual rewinding of your system.

It probably goes without saying, but System Restore works only if the master System Protection switch is turned on. It's hiding behind the Configure box shown here.

Performing a System Restore

If something goes wrong with your PC, here's how to roll it back to the happy, bygone days of late last week—or this morning:

1. **Open the System Protection tab on the System Properties dialog box (Figure 22-3).**

   The steps are described on the previous pages.

2. **Click System Restore. At the "Restore system files and settings" welcome screen, click Next.**

   The list of memorized restore points appears (Figure 22-4, top).

3. **Look over the restore points; click the one you want to rewind to.**

   As you survey the restore points, try to remember when, exactly, your system went wonky. Double-click a restore point (or click "Scan for affected programs") to help

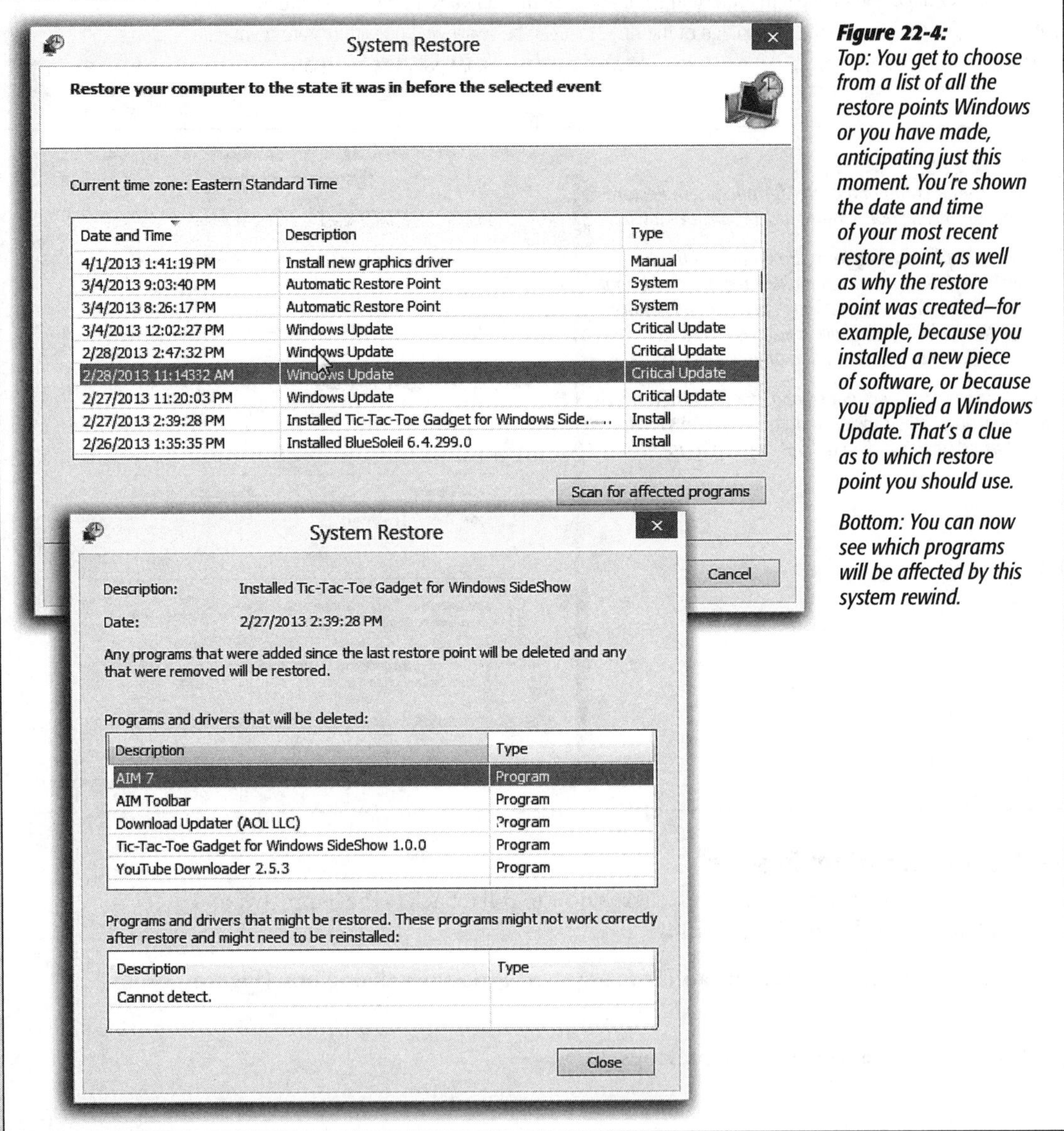

Figure 22-4:
Top: You get to choose from a list of all the restore points Windows or you have made, anticipating just this moment. You're shown the date and time of your most recent restore point, as well as why the restore point was created—for example, because you installed a new piece of software, or because you applied a Windows Update. That's a clue as to which restore point you should use.

Bottom: You can now see which programs will be affected by this system rewind.

you figure out which apps and drivers will be affected if you go through with the restore (Figure 22-4, bottom).

3. **Click Next.**

   You have one more chance to back out: Windows displays the date and time of the restore point, shows you which drives will be affected, gives you another chance to create a password-reset disk, and asks if you *really* want to go back in time.

4. **Click Finish. In the confirmation box, click Yes.**

   Windows goes to town, reinstating your operating system to reflect its condition on the date you specified. Leave your PC alone while this occurs.

   When the process is complete, the computer restarts automatically. When you log back in, you're back to the past—and with any luck, your PC runs smoothly again. (None of your email or files are disturbed.)

POWER USERS' CLINIC

System Restore vs. Your Hard Drive

Ever wonder where Windows stashes all these backup copies of your operating system? They're in a folder called System Volume Information, which is in your Local Disk (C:) window. Inside *that* are individual files for each restore point. (System Volume Information is generally an invisible folder, but you can make it visible by following the instructions on page 224. You still won't be allowed to move, rename, or delete it, however—thank goodness. In fact, you won't even be able to look inside it.)

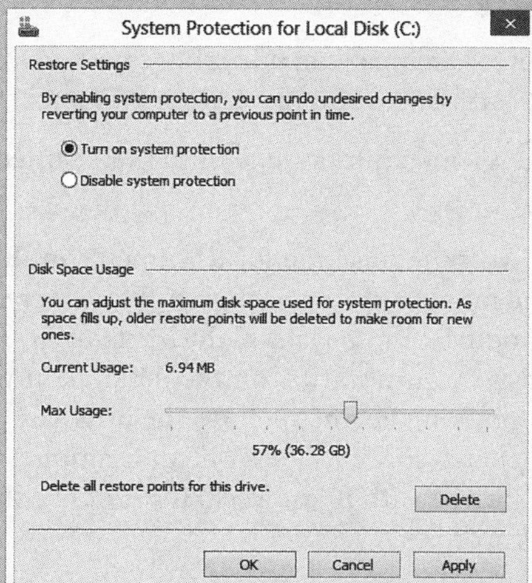

You can turn off System Restore entirely, or you can limit it to eating up a certain percentage of your hard drive space.

Open an Explorer window. Right-click Computer; from the shortcut menu, choose Properties.

In the resulting dialog box, click "System protection" in the left-side panel. Authenticate yourself if necessary. On the System Protection tab, click Configure. You get the dialog box shown here.

Use the Max Usage slider to put a cap on how much drive space all these restore points are allowed to eat up.

In times of strife, there's also a nuclear option here: the Delete button.

Note, however, that this button deletes not just all your restore points, but also the backups of all your *documents* (those created by the File Histories feature described on the following pages).

You've been warned. Be careful out there.

If it didn't work—if you only made things worse—repeat step 1. At the top of the System Restore welcome screen, you'll see an option called Undo System Restore. It lets you *undo* your undoing.

Or, of course, you can click "Choose a different restore point" if you think that maybe you didn't rewind your PC far back *enough* and want to try again with a different restore point.

Turning System Restore Off

You really shouldn't turn off System Restore. You really, really shouldn't. It's just so incredibly useful, when you're pressed for time and things start going wacky, to be able to hit rewind and grant yourself a perfectly smooth PC, even if you never do find out what the trouble was.

But if you're an advanced power user with no hard drive space to spare—is there such a person?—open the System Protection tab of the System Properties box (shown in Figure 22-3). Click Configure, click "Disable system protection," and click OK. (See the box on page 695 for details.)

In the "Are you sure?" box, click Yes. That's it. You're flying without a net now, baby.

File History

System Restore is an amazing, powerful, career-saving feature—but it's awfully self-interested. It cares only about protecting *Windows.*

How can you rewind your *documents* to their earlier, healthier, or pre-edited conditions?

File History is a time machine for documents in the same way System Restore is a time machine for your system software. It's an incredible safety net against damage, accidental modification, or late-night bouts of ill-advised editing. It automatically backs up files in your libraries, on the desktop, in your address book, and on your SkyDrive. If anything bad happens to the originals, you're covered. You can also rewind documents to specific dates—if, for example, you decide your novel was better before you tinkered with it last week. It's a lot like the Time Machine feature on the Mac, in other words.

Note: There was a similar but less sophisticated feature in Windows 7 called either Previous Versions or Shadow Copy. They're gone now.

The beauty of File History is that it's automatic and invisible. It's *part* of System Restore, actually, meaning that unless you've turned System Restore *off,* File History is protecting your documents, too. To save time and disk space, File History bothers copying only the files that have changed since the last restore point was created.

Set Up File History

The File History feature has its own dashboard in the Control Panel. You can get to it either from TileWorld or the desktop:

- **From TileWorld.** Open the Start screen. Type *file history* and select Settings under the search box. In the search results, click "File history."
- **From the desktop.** Open the Control Panel (for example, right-click the lower-left corner of the screen; choose Control Panel from the shortcut menu.) In Category view, choose "Save backup copies of your files with File History."

Either way, welcome to Figure 22-5.

***Figure 22-5:** Here's the master panel for File History. It's where you turn the thing on or off; rewind documents; and leave out folders of stuff you'll never need to rewind, to save disk space.*

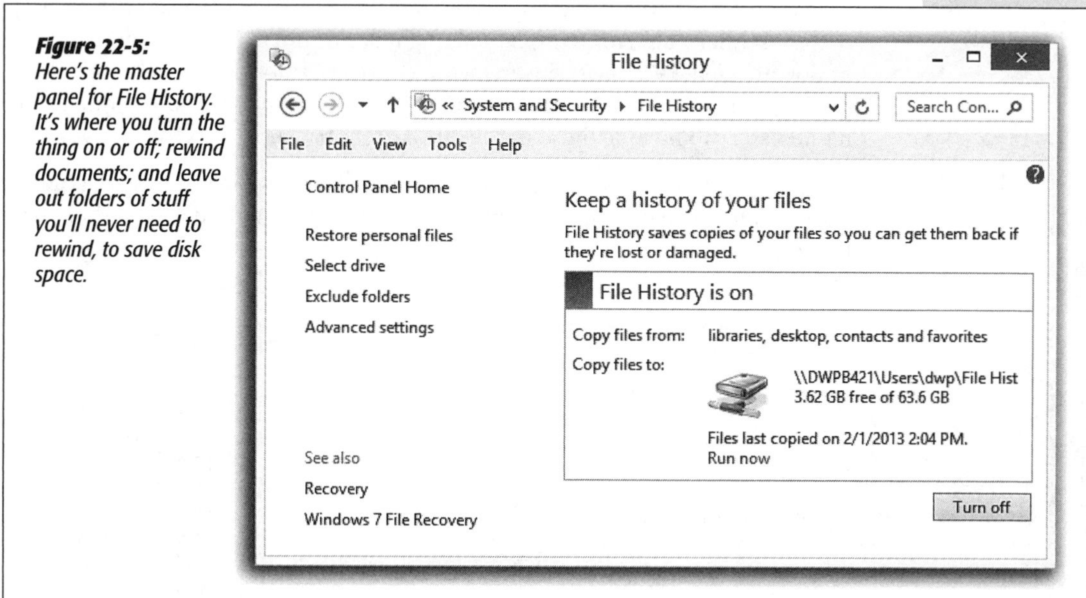

File History works best if you direct it to create its backups on some other drive—not the one the files are on now. The whole point, after all, is to provide protection against something going wrong—and disk failure is a big something. So you're supposed to use an external drive or another computer on the network.

Here goes:

- **Use an external drive.** When you connect an external drive, an AutoPlay message appears. When you tap or click it, you're offered the unusual option "Back up your files on this drive." That's what you want.
- **Use another machine on the network.** Open the File History Control Panel (Figure 22-5). Click "Select drive." The resulting dialog box shows the available network disks for File History backups that Windows knows about; click "Add network location" to choose a computer, drive, and folder for storing your backups.

Note: If this window is empty, you may see a message at the top of the dialog box that tells you about network computers and devices not being visible. That's because network discovery isn't turned on. Select the message, and then select "Turn on network discovery and file sharing."

While you're visiting the File History controls, you may also want to set up these items:

- **Exclude files.** The whole point of File History is to have a backup of all your files. It's conceivable, though, that you might want to exclude some files or folders from the File History treatment. First, you might not want certain, ahem, private materials to be part of your incriminating data trail.

  Second, you might want to save space on the backup drive, either because it's not as big as your main drive or because you'd rather dedicate its space to more backups of the essential stuff. For example, you might decide not to back up your collection of downloaded TV shows, since video files are enormous. Or maybe you use an online photo-sharing Web site as a backup for all your photos, so you don't think it's necessary to include those in the File History backup.

  To omit certain files and folders, click "Exclude files." In the resulting dialog box, click Add to navigate your computer and choose files and folders you don't need backed up.

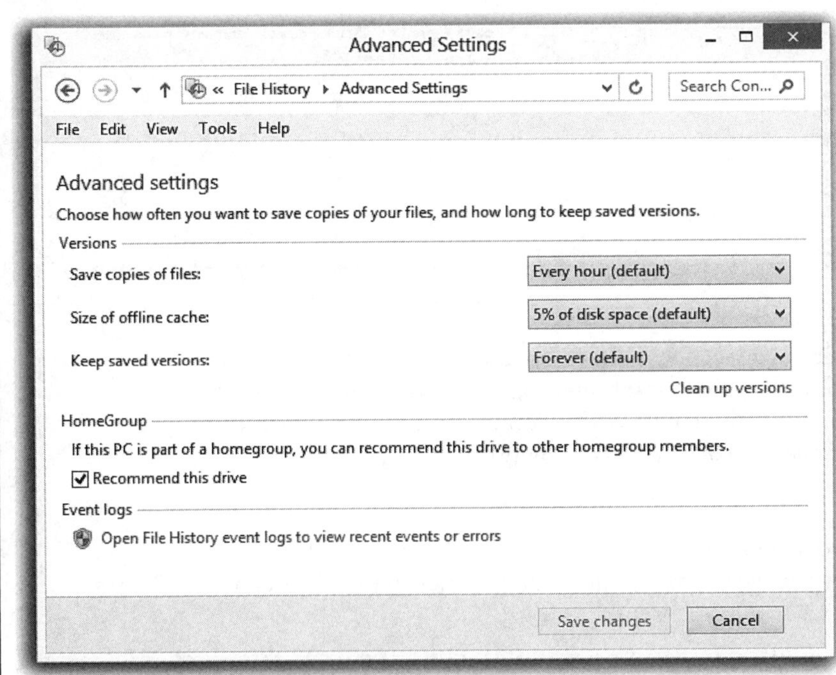

***Figure 22-6:** This important Settings box lets you specify how often Windows backs up your files (from once a day to once every 10 minutes); how much of the backup disk's space is allowed to be dedicated to the backups (from 2 to 20 percent); and how long Windows should keep the old versions of your documents (from "Until space is needed" to "Forever").*

- **Adjust the frequency.** Ordinarily, File History quietly and automatically checks your computer once an hour. If any file has changed, it gets backed up at the end of the hour. These follow-up backups are quick; Windows backs up only what's changed.

  So, should disaster strike, the only files you can lose are those you've changed within the past 59 minutes.

  And even then, you can force more frequent backups if you want to, as described in Figure 22-6.

Tip: The box in Figure 22-6 also shows that you can specify how long you want Windows to hang on to the old versions of your documents. Maybe after a year, for example, it's OK for those old backups to start self-deleting.

Recovering Files

All right, you've got File History on the job. You sleep easy at night, confident that your life is in order—and your stuff is backed up.

Then, one day, it happens: Your hard drive crashes. Or you can't find a file or folder you know you had. Or you save a document and then wish you could go back to an earlier draft. Some kind of disaster—sunspots, clueless spouse, overtired self—has befallen your files. This is File History's big moment.

Open the Control Panel pane shown in Figure 22-5. Click "Restore personal files."

Now you see the fascinating new window shown in Figure 22-7 (top). Your job is to find the file in questions, either because it's been deleted or because you want to rescue an older version of it. There are three ways to go about it: browsing, Ribboning, or searching.

Browsing for the file

Double-click folders as usual, looking for the file in its usual place.

If it's been deleted, of course, you won't find it—at least, not in *today's* listing. But if you click the ⊖ button, the entire window slides to the right; you're viewing endlessly scrolling *versions* of the current window, going back in time.

If you scroll back far enough this way, you'll eventually see the missing file reappear. You've rewound time to a point before it went missing.

Scrolling back in time is also useful when you want to find an earlier *version*, or draft, of a document. And how will you know which version you're looking at? Because you can *double-click* an icon to open it, right within this window (Figure 22-7, bottom). You can keep clicking the ⊖ button even when the document is open, so you can watch its contents change in real (backward) time.

Once you've found the file in question, click the big green Restore button at the bottom of the window. Magically enough, the lost file or folder (or outdated document) is brought back from the dead.

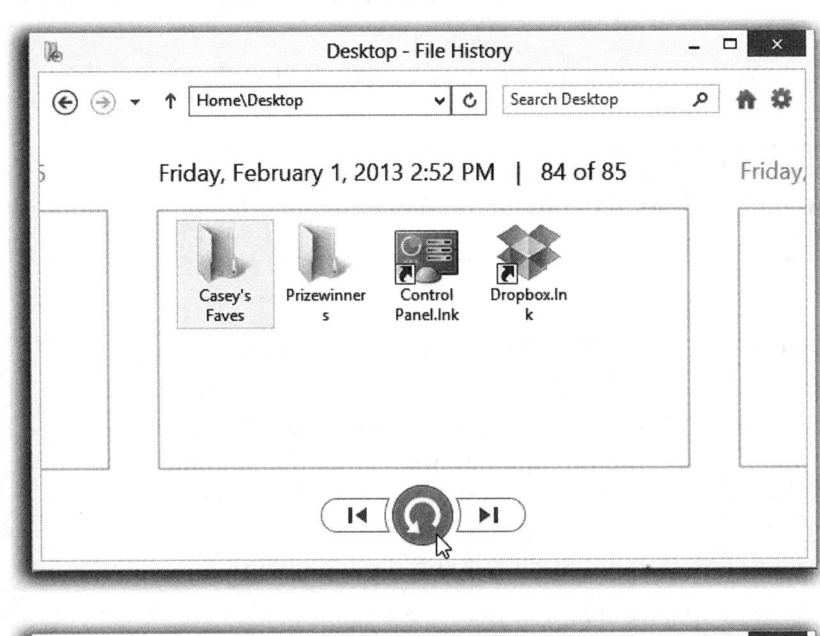

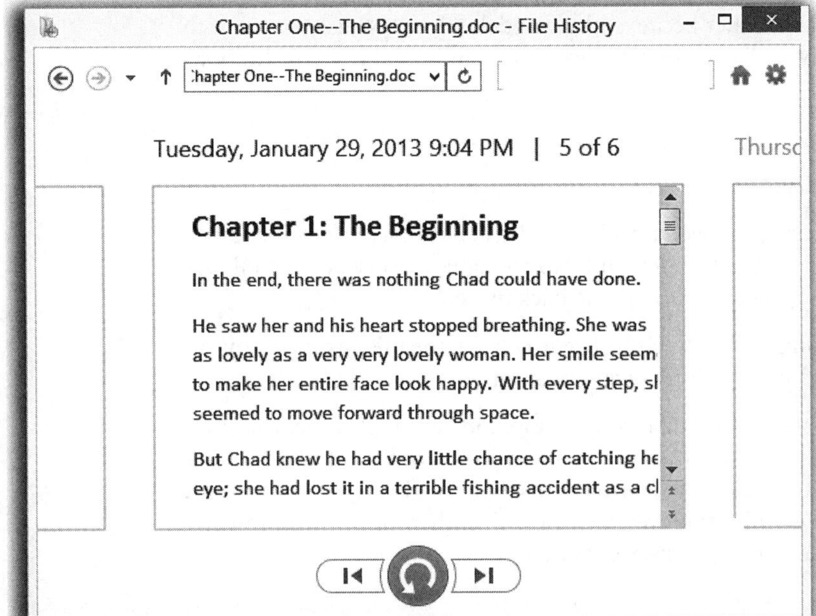

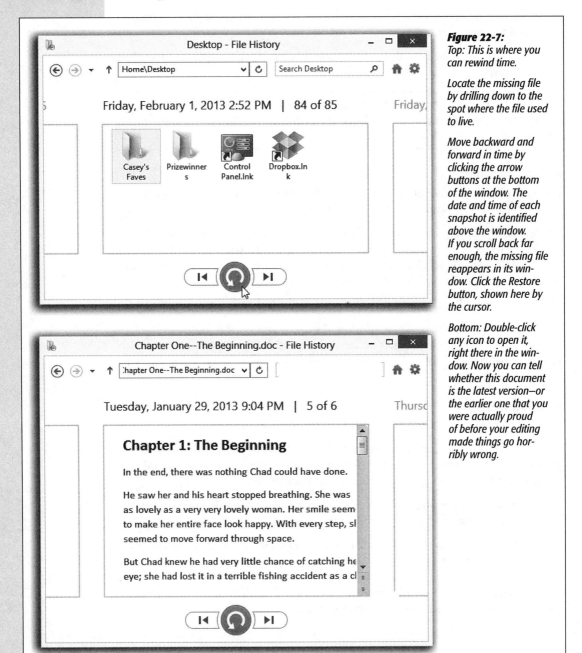

Figure 22-7:
Top: This is where you can rewind time.

Locate the missing file by drilling down to the spot where the file used to live.

Move backward and forward in time by clicking the arrow buttons at the bottom of the window. The date and time of each snapshot is identified above the window. If you scroll back far enough, the missing file reappears in its window. Click the Restore button, shown here by the cursor.

Bottom: Double-click any icon to open it, right there in the window. Now you can tell whether this document is the latest version—or the earlier one that you were actually proud of before your editing made things go horribly wrong.

File History prides itself not just on recovering files and folders, but also on putting them back where they came from.

Tip: You can also tell File History to put the file or folder into a *new* location. To do that, right-click its icon; from the shortcut menu, choose "Restore to," and choose the recovered folder location.

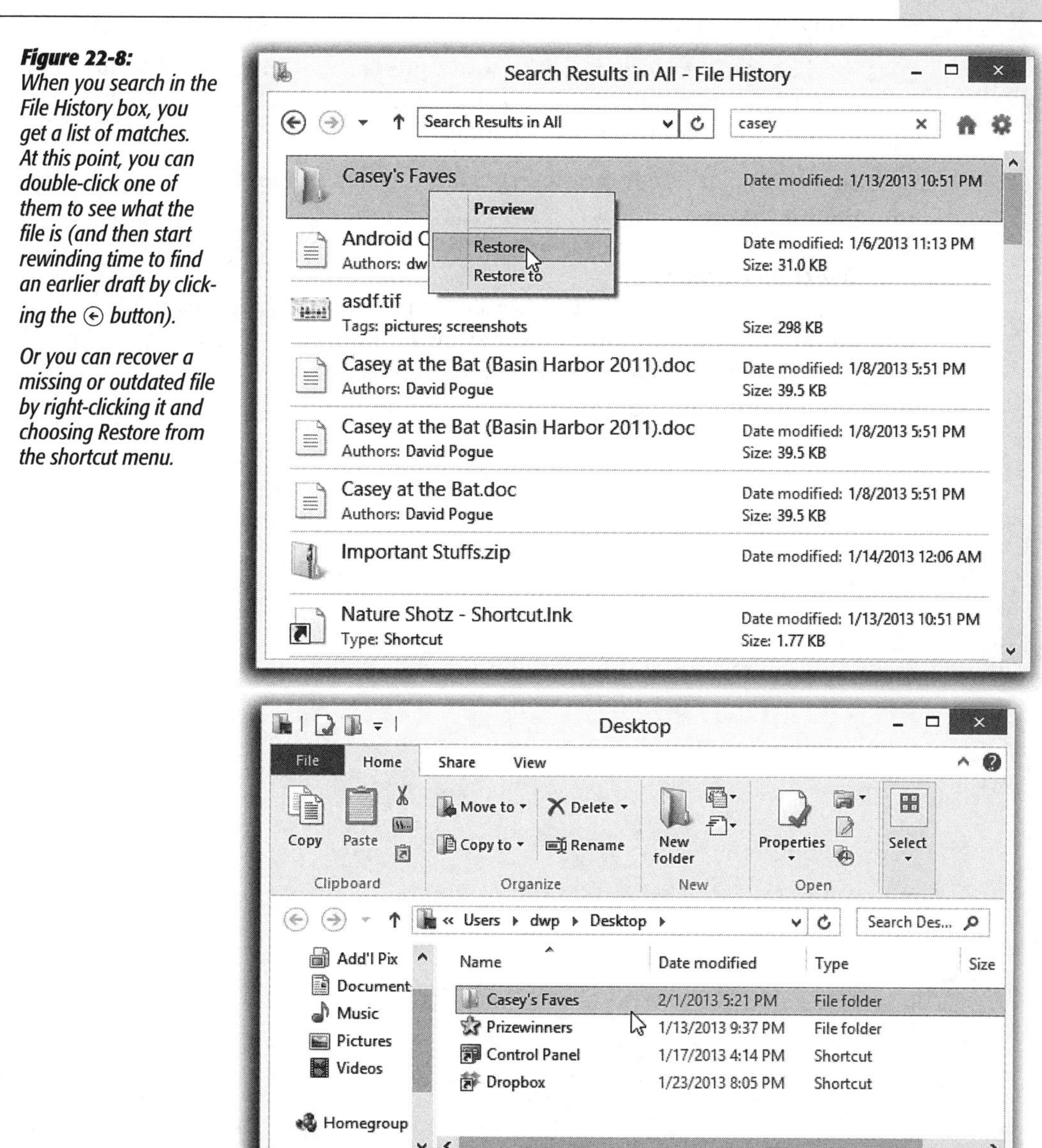

Figure 22-8: *When you search in the File History box, you get a list of matches. At this point, you can double-click one of them to see what the file is (and then start rewinding time to find an earlier draft by clicking the* ← *button).*

Or you can recover a missing or outdated file by right-clicking it and choosing Restore from the shortcut menu.

If you recover a different version of something that's still there, Windows asks if you want to replace it with the recovered version—or if you'd rather keep both versions.

Ribbon rewinding

You don't actually have to bother with the Control Panel when you want to restore a file. Turns out there's a History button on the Ribbon's Home tab right in every File Explorer window.

In other words, you can start the recovery process by opening the folder that contains (or used to contain) the file you want. Or find the icon of the file you want to rewind. In either case, click that History button.

You wind up in exactly the same spot illustrated in Figure 22-7; the recovery process is the same.

Searching for the file

Once you've opened the – window shown in Figure 22-7, here's another way to find the missing or changed file: Type into the search box at the top of the window. That's handy if you can't remember what folder it was in. See Figure 22-8.

CHAPTER
23

The Disk Chapter

Files and folders, as you've probably noticed, have a tendency to multiply. Creating new documents, installing new software, and downloading new files can fill up even the largest disk drives in no time—especially if, as Microsoft fervently hopes, you get heavily into music, pictures, and video.

Fortunately, Windows offers a number of ways to manage and expand the amount of space on your hard drives. You can subdivide your drives' storage into individual partitions (sections), save space using disk compression, encrypt the contents of your drives for security, and so on.

You can skip this entire chapter, if you wish, and get along quite well without using any of these features. They're strictly optional. But if you aspire to wear the "Power User" T-shirt, then read on.

Note: Three of the features described in this chapter–dynamic disks, disk compression, and EFS (encrypting file system)–all require the *NTFS file system* on your computer's disk drives. That's probably what you're using on your main hard drive, because Windows 8 requires it.

But many other kinds of disks–memory cards, iPods, external USB disks, and so on–use the older Fat 32 file system instead. You won't be able to use NTFS tricks on them.

Storage Spaces

If you have a few strands of nerd DNA in your body, this one's for you. It's a new Windows 8 feature that lets you slice and dice various physical disks (hard drives and flash drives) into any number of virtual ones, for reasons of convenience or data safety.

For years now, the data centers of big corporations have used RAID systems (Redundant Array of Independent Disks). A RAID array is a bunch of drives installed inside a single metal box; clever software makes them look to a computer like one big drive. Or three smaller ones, or fifty little ones—however the highly trained system administrator decides to chop them up.

And why bother? Because the files on a RAID system can be recovered even if one of the hard drives dies, thanks to a fancy encoding scheme. (Thus, the "redundant" in the name.)

But RAID systems are complicated to set up, and incredibly inflexible; you generally have to install all drives of the same type and capacity simultaneously. And if you decide to expand your array, you have to erase all of the existing drives and reformat them.

Storage Spaces offers the same benefits as RAID systems—for example, data safety even if one of the drives croaks—without anywhere near the same complexity or inflexibility. Your setup doesn't require matching drives, and you can fiddle with the capacity at any time without having to reformat anything.

Note: A Storage Space can't be a startup drive.

Here's how to set up Storage Spaces.

1. **Round up your drives.**

   They can be internal or external; they can connect to the computer with any connector type; they can be spinning hard drives or solid-state drives.

   This motley bunch of drives is what Microsoft calls a *pool.*

2. **In the Control Panel, open Storage Spaces.**

   Click the System and Security heading to find it. The dialog box shown at top in Figure 23-1 appears.

3. **Click "Create a new pool and storage space." Authenticate if you're asked. Confirm that yes, you want to do this.**

   Now you're shown a list of all drives attached to your computer that will work with Storage Spaces (Figure 23-1, middle). (For example, they have to be NTFS-formatted.) As Windows warns you, *they'll all be erased.* Might be a good idea to click "View files" next to each drive, to make sure you won't miss whatever files are on it now.

   Windows is about to *combine* these drives' space into one gigantic pool, which you'll be able to chop up as you please in just a moment. (You won't be able to use these drives on their own anymore.)

Note: Nobody's found the upper limit to the number of actual drives that you can incorporate into a pool. Microsoft says that it's successfully tested this feature with "hundreds of drives." Can you imagine the size of their power strip?

---

4. Turn on the checkboxes of the drives you want pooled, and then click "Create pool."

   The dialog box shown in Figure 23-1, bottom, appears now.

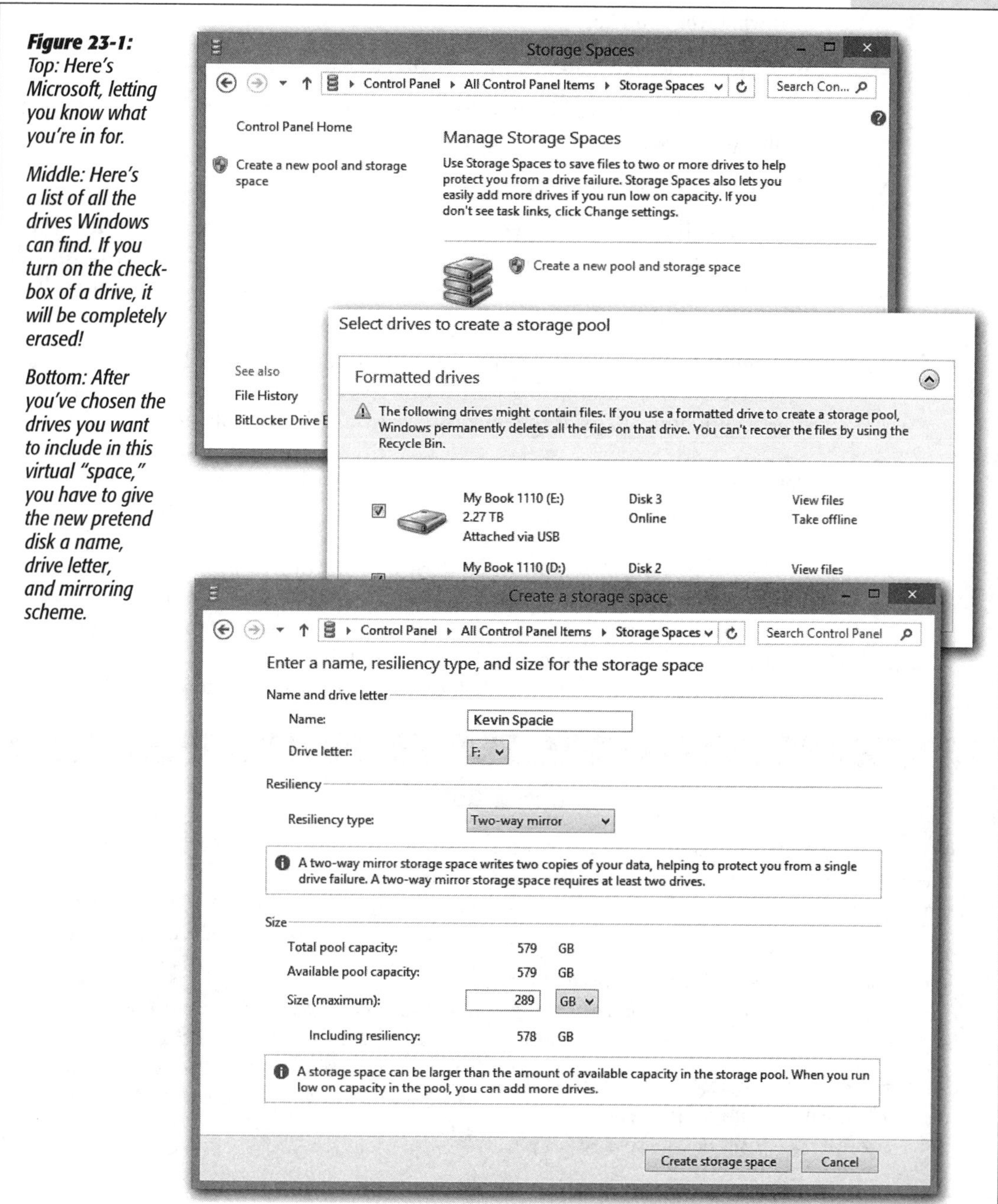

Figure 23-1: *Top: Here's Microsoft, letting you know what you're in for.*

Middle: Here's a list of all the drives Windows can find. If you turn on the checkbox of a drive, it will be completely erased!

Bottom: After you've chosen the drives you want to include in this virtual "space," you have to give the new pretend disk a name, drive letter, and mirroring scheme.

5. **Type a name for your storage space.**

   A *space*, in Microsoft lingo, is "one of the virtual drives you'll carve out of the pool." It can be one big "drive," made up of all the component drives behind the scenes, or it can be five, or ten, or whatever. Each is called a storage space. Name it whatever you like.

6. **Assign a drive letter to your new virtual disk.**

   The letter is up to you. You have a whole alphabet to choose from (except for letters already in use). You can change it later.

7. **Choose the *resiliency* type you prefer.**

   Ah, now this is where it gets good (and complicated). This option lets you set up that magical redundancy feature, in which Windows will duplicate your files across multiple physical drives. That way, if one drive dies, your files are still safe. Here are your choices.

   "*Simple (no resiliency)*" doesn't create any duplicate copies. It just turns all your selected drives into one big virtual disk in your Explorer windows, or several, if you chop it up. (This is the only choice if you selected only one disk in step 4.)

Note: If you use this option, then when of these drives dies, you lose the contents of *all* of these drives. In other words, don't use a "Simple (no resiliency)" storage space for anything important.

   "*Two-way mirror*" requires two drives. (They don't have to match.) Your files are stored in duplicate, one copy on each drive, for safety purposes. In Explorer, you'll still see only one "disk," with only half the capacity of the actual disks you've attached. That's because Windows is maintaining a second copy of everything. (Actually, you'll have less than half the space, because Storage Spaces requires some

UP TO SPEED

Volumes Defined

You won't get far in this chapter, or at PC user group meetings, without understanding a key piece of Windows terminology: *volume.*

For most people, most of the time, volume means "disk." But technically, there's more to it than that—a distinction that becomes crucial if you explore the techniques described in this chapter.

If you open your Computer window, you see that each disk has its own icon and drive letter (C:, for example). But each icon isn't necessarily a separate disk. It's possible that you, or somebody in charge of your PC, has split a single drive into multiple *partitions* (Appendix A), each with a separate icon and drive letter. Clearly, the world needs a term for "an icon/drive letter in the Computer window, whether it's a whole disk or not." That term is *volume.*

The Storage Spaces feature of Windows 8, in other words, can display many actual hard drives as one volume on the screen, with one drive letter. (It can also do the reverse, although you're likely to get a migraine if you think about it too much.)

file storage of its own. And if the two real drives don't match in size, you get only the available space of the smaller one.)

"*Three-way mirror*" means that every file is stored in *triplicate*, on three different actual drives, for incredible safety. Even if *two* of your drives die simultaneously —*wow*, are you having a rotten day—your data marches on, unaffected. (This option requires at least five actual drives.)

Suppose you have six drives, of capacities in 1, 1, 2, 2, 2, and 4 terabytes. That adds up to 12 terabytes of storage. With three-way mirroring, in Explorer, you'll see only *one* drive on the screen, with only a 4-terabyte capacity. That's because the rest of the storage is being used for your safety copies.

Finally, there's "Parity." This clever scheme, available if you have three or more real disks in the pool, duplicates your files for safety, just like mirroring. But somehow, using fancy coding, this arrangement uses *less* than twice the physical storage to do it. If you have 2 terabytes of files, for example the Parity setting will use only 3 terabytes for this duplication, not 4. The downside: saving files takes longer.

8. **Choose the maximum size for this pool.**

   You can actually choose a size that's greater than the total storage of your physical disks. If you ever run low on storage in your pool, you'll be able to buy another drive and add it to the others without having to erase or reformat anything. (That's a feature the geeks called *thin provisioning*. See if you can work that term into a conversation at your next party.)

9. **Click "Create storage space."**

   Windows creates your new storage space, summarizes it in a window , and proudly opens an Explorer window for the new virtual disk. You can use this disk just as you would any drive. You can share it on the network, encrypt it with BitLocker, and so on.

And if one of the component drives should stop working, guess what? You won't care. (At least not if you chose one of the "resiliency" options.)

Your taskbar sprouts a message that says, "Check Storage Spaces for problems," but you'll keep right on working. Not a single file is lost or damaged.

Of course, you're flying without a net now, so you should replace the broken drive as soon as you can, with one that's as big or bigger than the dead one. Open the Storage Spaces Control Panel again, where you'll see a yellow exclamation-point icon to indicate the dead drive. Connect a new drive to your PC, click "Add drives," introduce the new blank drive to the mix, and you're back in business. (Now you can click Remove next to the dead drive's icon and uninstall the thing.)

Important: Remove the dead drive only *after* connecting up the new drive. Otherwise, you'll lose all your files on all the drives.

Dynamic Disks

Before Storage Spaces came along, there were other ways to tell Windows to treat multiple drives as one. There was Drive Extender, a more technical version of what we know today as Storage Spaces.

That feature is gone now, but *dynamic disks, basic disks,* and *spanned volumes* are still around—another way of slicing and dicing your actual disks in clever ways.

If this older, more complex, decidedly more advanced topic interests you, a free bonus appendix to this chapter awaits, called "Dynamic Disks.pdf." You can download it from this book's "Missing CD" page at *www.missingmanuals.com.*

Compressing Files and Folders

The hard drives made these days have greater capacities than ever, but programs and files are much bigger, too. Running out of disk space is still a common problem. Fortunately, Windows 8 is especially effective at compressing files and folders to take up less disk space.

Compressing files and folders can also be useful when you want to email files to someone without dooming them to an all-night modem-watching session. That's why Microsoft has endowed Windows 8 with two different schemes for compressing files and folders: *NTFS compression* for storing files on your hard drive, and *zipped folders* for files that might have to be transferred.

NTFS Compression

If you have Windows 8, then your hard drive is formatted using a file system called *NTFS* (short for *NT file system).*

Most people can live a long and happy life without knowing anything about NTFS. If you work in a corporation, you might be grateful for the additional security it offers to Windows fans (Chapter 24), and leave it at that. Now and then, however, you'll read about features that are available *only* if your hard drive was prepared using NTFS—and this is one of those cases.

Tip: The hard drive that's running Windows 8 has the NTFS format; Windows 8 requires it. To find out what formatting some other drive uses (a flash drive or external hard drive, for example), open your Computer window. Right-click the drive icon in question; from the shortcut menu, choose Properties. In the resulting dialog box, you see either "File system: NTFS" or "File system: FAT 32." Unfortunately, special NTFS features like automatic compression aren't available to you unless you upgrade the drive formatting to NTFS.

For instructions, download the free appendix to this chapter from this book's "Missing CD" page at *www.missingmanuals.com.* The file is called NTFS Upgrade (pdf). (Note, however, that if you convert a flash drive to NTFS, you may no longer be able to use it with non-Windows computers and devices like digital cameras.)

The NTFS compression scheme is especially likable because it's completely invisible to you. Windows automatically compresses and decompresses your files, almost instantaneously. At some point, you may even forget you've turned it on. Consider:

- **Whenever you open a compressed file,** Windows quickly and invisibly expands it to its original form so you can read or edit it. When you close the file again, Windows instantly recompresses it.
- **If you send compressed files via email** or copy them to a PC whose hard drive doesn't use NTFS compression, Windows 8 once again decompresses them, quickly and invisibly.
- **Any file you copy into a compressed folder or disk** is compressed automatically. (If you only *move* it into such a folder from elsewhere on the disk, however, it stays compressed or uncompressed—whichever it was originally.)

Compressing files, folders, or disks

To turn on NTFS compression, right-click the icon for the file, folder, or disk whose contents you want to shrink. Choose Properties from the shortcut menu. Click the Advanced button (if it's a file or folder), and in the resulting dialog box, turn on "Compress contents to save disk space" (Figure 23-2), click OK, and then click Apply or OK when you return to the Properties dialog box. If you have selected a folder for compression, you're prompted as to whether you also want to compress the files and subfolders within it.

Many Windows veterans wind up turning on compression for the entire hard drive. It can take Windows 8 several hours to perform the initial compression of every file on the drive.

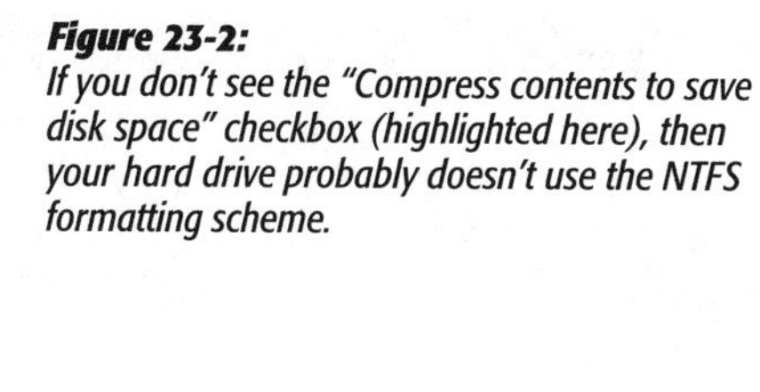

Figure 23-2:
If you don't see the "Compress contents to save disk space" checkbox (highlighted here), then your hard drive probably doesn't use the NTFS formatting scheme.

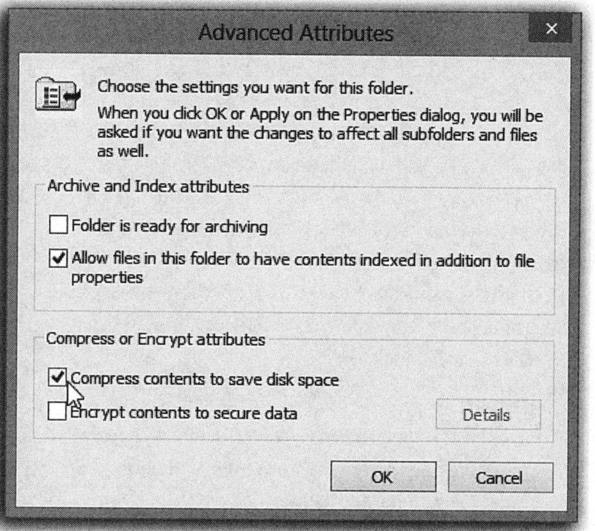

If you do this, or even if you try to compress a large folder such as *C:\Program Files*, you will invariably run into a few files that can't be compressed because they're currently in use. Short of opening up the Task Manager and shutting down nearly every process on your system (not recommended), you won't be able to avoid a few of these. Your best bet is to select Ignore All the first time Windows 8 notifies you about this problem. Then you can safely walk away from your computer and let the compression continue.

When Windows is finished compressing, the compressed file and folder icons appear in a different color, a reminder that Windows is doing its part to maximize your disk space. (If they don't change color, then somebody—maybe you—must have turned off the "Show encrypted or compressed NTFS files in color" option described on page 226.)

When you look at the Properties dialog box for a compressed file (right-click the file and choose Properties from the shortcut menu), you see two file sizes. The Size value indicates the actual (uncompressed) size of the file, while the Size On Disk value is the compressed size of the file—that is, the amount of disk space it's occupying.

Note: It's probably worth noting that you can't save a system image backup onto an NTFS compressed disk.

Zipped Folders

As noted above, NTFS compression is great for freeing up disk space while you're working at your PC. But when you email your files to somebody else or burn them to a CD, Windows 8 always decompresses them back to their original sizes first.

Fortunately, there's another way to compress files: Zip them. If you've ever used Windows before, you've probably encountered Zip files. Each one is a tiny little suitcase,

UP TO SPEED

Data Compression

Data compression is the process of replacing repetitive material in a file with shorthand symbols. For example, if a speech you've written contains the phrase *going forward* 21 times, a compression scheme like the one in NTFS may replace each occurrence with a single symbol, making the file that much smaller. When you reopen the file later, the operating system almost instantaneously restores the original, expanded material.

The degree to which a file can be compressed depends on what kind of data the file contains and whether it's already been compressed by another program. For example, programs (executable files) often shrink by half when compressed. Bitmapped graphics like TIFF files squish down to as little as one-seventh their original size, saving a great deal more space.

The PNG and JPEG graphics files so popular on the Web, however, are already compressed (which is why they're so popular–they take relatively little time to download). As a result, they don't get much smaller if you try to compress them manually. That's one of the main rules of data compression: Data can be compressed only once.

In short, there's no way to predict just how much disk space you'll save by using NTFS compression on your drives. It all depends on what you have stored there.

an *archive,* whose contents have been tightly compressed to keep files together, to save space, and to transfer them online faster (see Figure 23-3). Use Zip files when you want to email something to someone, or when you want to pack up a completed project and remove it from your hard drive to free up space.

Creating zipped folders

In Windows 8, you don't even need a shareware program like PKZIP or WinZip to create or open Zip files. You can create a Zip archive in either of two ways:

- Right-click any blank spot on the desktop or an open window. From the shortcut menu, choose New→Compressed (zipped) Folder. Type a name for your newly created, empty archive, and then press Enter.

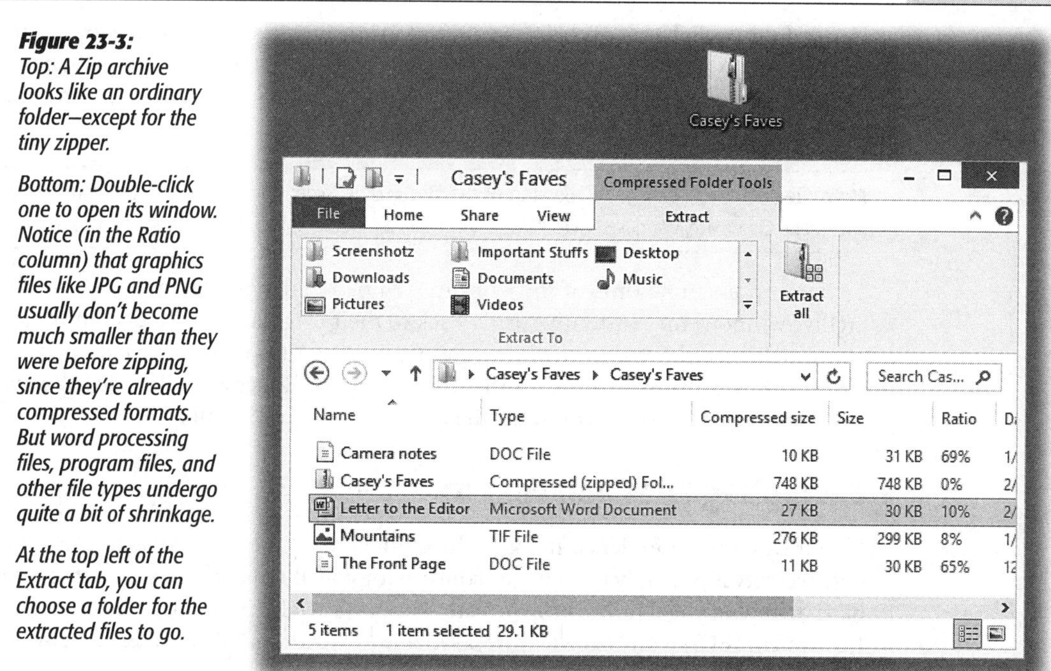

Figure 23-3: *Top: A Zip archive looks like an ordinary folder–except for the tiny zipper.*

Bottom: Double-click one to open its window. Notice (in the Ratio column) that graphics files like JPG and PNG usually don't become much smaller than they were before zipping, since they're already compressed formats. But word processing files, program files, and other file types undergo quite a bit of shrinkage.

At the top left of the Extract tab, you can choose a folder for the extracted files to go.

Now, each time you drag a file or folder onto the archive's icon (or into its open window), Windows automatically stuffs a *copy* of it inside.

Of course, you haven't actually saved any disk space, since now you have two copies of the original material (one zipped, one untouched). If you'd rather *move* a file or folder into the archive—in the process deleting the full-size version and saving disk space—then right-drag the file or folder icon onto the *archive* icon. Now from the shortcut menu, choose Move Here.

- To turn an existing file or folder *into* a zipped archive, right-click its icon. (To zip up a handful of icons, select them first, then right-click any *one* of them.) Now, from the shortcut menu, choose Send To→Compressed (zipped) Folder. You've just created a new archive folder *and* copied the files or folders into it.

Tip: At this point, you can right-click the zipped folder's icon and choose Send To→Mail Recipient. Windows automatically whips open your email program, creates an outgoing message ready for you to address, and attaches the zipped file to it–which is now set for transport.

Working with zipped folders

In many respects, a zipped folder behaves just like any ordinary folder, in that you double-click it to see what's inside.

If you double-click one of the *files* you find inside, however, Windows 8 opens up a *read-only* copy of it—that is, a copy you can view, but not edit. To make changes to a read-only copy, you must use the File→Save As command and save it somewhere else on your hard drive first.

Note: Be sure to navigate to the desktop or the Documents folder, for example, before you save your document. Otherwise, Windows saves it into an invisible temporary folder, and you may never see it again.

To decompress only some of the icons in a zipped folder, just drag them out of the archive window; they instantly spring back to their original sizes. To decompress the entire archive, right-click its icon and choose Extract All from the shortcut menu (or, if its window is already open, click the "Extract all files" link on the Ribbon). A wizard asks you to specify where you want the resulting files to wind up.

Encrypting Files and Folders

If your Documents folder contains nothing but laundry lists and letters to your mom, data security is probably not a major concern for you. But if there's some stuff on your hard drive that you'd rather keep private, Windows can help you out. The Encrypting File System (EFS) is an NTFS feature, available in Windows 8 Pro and Enterprise, that stores your data in a coded format that only you can read.

The beauty of EFS is that it's effortless and invisible to you, the authorized owner. Windows 8 automatically encrypts your files before storing them on the drive, and decrypts them again when you want to read or modify them. Anyone else who logs onto your computer, however, will find these files locked and off-limits.

If you've read ahead to Chapter 24, of course, you might be frowning in confusion at this point. Isn't keeping private files private the whole point of Windows's *accounts* feature? Don't Windows's *NTFS permissions* (page 755) keep busybodies out already?

Yes, but encryption provides additional security. If, for example, you're a top-level agent assigned to protect your government's most closely guarded egg salad recipe, you can use NTFS permissions to deny all other users access to the file containing the information. Nobody but you can open the file in Windows 8.

However, a determined intruder from a foreign nation could conceivably boot the computer using *another* operating system—one that doesn't recognize the NTFS permissions—and access the hard drive using a special program that reads the raw data stored there. If, however, you had encrypted the file using EFS, that raw data would appear as gibberish, foiling your crafty nemesis.

Using EFS

You use EFS to encrypt your folders and files in much the same way that you use NTFS compression. To encrypt a file or a folder, open its Properties dialog box, click the Advanced button, turn on the "Encrypt contents to secure data" checkbox, and then click OK (see Figure 23-4). (To build a quicker way, see page 855.)

Figure 23-4:
To encrypt a file or folder using EFS, turn on the "Encrypt contents to secure data" checkbox (at the bottom of its Properties dialog box). If you've selected a folder, a Confirm Attribute Changes dialog box appears, asking if you want to encrypt just that folder or everything inside it, too.

Depending on how much data you've selected, it may take some time for the encryption process to complete. Once the folders and files are encrypted, they appear in a different color from your compressed files (unless you've turned off the "Show encrypted or compressed NTFS files in color" option; see page 226).

Note: You can't encrypt certain files and folders, such as system files, or any files in the system *root folder* (usually the Windows folder). You can't encrypt files and folders on Fat 32 drives, either.

Finally, note that you can't both encrypt *and* compress the same file or folder. If you attempt to encrypt a compressed file or folder, Windows needs to decompress it first. You can, however, encrypt files that have been compressed using another technology, such as Zip files or compressed image files.

After your files have been encrypted, you may be surprised to see that, other than their color change, nothing seems to have changed. You can open them the same way you always did, change them, and save them as usual. Windows 8 is just doing its job: protecting these files with the minimum inconvenience to you.

Still, if you're having difficulty believing that your files are now protected by an invisible force field, try logging off and back on again with a different user name and password. When you try to open an encrypted file now, a message cheerfully informs you that you don't have the proper permissions to access the file.

EFS Rules

Any files or folders you move *into* an EFS-encrypted folder get encrypted, too. But dragging a file *out* of one doesn't unprotect it; it remains encrypted as long as it's on an NTFS drive. A protected file loses its encryption only in these circumstances:

- You manually decrypt the file (by turning off the corresponding checkbox in its Properties dialog box).
- You move it to a Fat 32 or exFAT drive.
- You transmit it via a network or email. When you attach the file to an email or send it across the network, Windows decrypts the file before sending it on its way.

By the way, EFS doesn't protect files from being deleted. Even if passing evildoers can't *open* your private file, they can still *delete* it—unless you've protected it using Windows's permissions feature (Chapter 24). Here, again, truly protecting important material involves using several security mechanisms in combination.

BitLocker Drive Encryption

EFS is a great way to keep prying eyes out of individual files. But Microsoft wouldn't be Microsoft if it didn't give you six variations on a theme. And BitLocker, available on Windows 8 Pro, goes much farther than protecting individual files or folders; it can encrypt an entire drive.

HISTORY CLASS

PKZIP

The Zip archive format was developed in the late 1980s by Phil Katz, a pioneer of PC compression technology. Katz's original product, PKZIP, was a DOS-based archiving program that soon became an industry standard.

There have been many other archive compression standards over the years, but none of them became as ubiquitous as the Zip format. Every program today that creates or manipulates Zip files, including Windows 8, owes a debt of thanks—if not a free T-shirt or two—to Phil Katz.

After all, when million-dollar corporate secrets are at stake, a determined, knowledgeable thief could swipe your laptop, nab your flash drive, or even steal the hard drive out of your desktop PC.

If security is that important for you, then you'll be happy to know about BitLocker Drive Encryption, a feature of the Pro and Enterprise versions of Windows 8. When you turn on this feature, your PC automatically encrypts (scrambles) everything on an *entire drive,* including all of Windows itself.

If the bad guy tries any industrial-strength tricks to get into the drive—trying to reprogram the startup routines, for example, or starting up from a different hard drive—BitLocker presents a steel-reinforced password screen. No password, no decryption.

In Windows 8, you also get BitLocker to Go—a disk-encryption feature especially for removable drives like USB flash drives. Even if you lose it or leave it behind, it's worthless to anyone without the password.

You don't notice much difference when BitLocker is turned on. You log in as usual, clicking your name and typing your password. But if a malefactor ever gets his hands on the actual disk, he'll be in for a disappointing surprise.

BitLocker for a Hard Drive

Here's how to encrypt a hard drive (as opposed to a removable drive):

1. **Open the Control Panel, and select System & Security→BitLocker Drive Encryption.**

   You see the display shown in Figure 23-5 at top, listing each of your disks. (Under a separate heading, you see the icons of removable disks like flash drives. For them, see "BitLocker to Go," below.)

2. **Click Turn On BitLocker.**

   Chances are pretty good that you'll get an error message saying, "This device can't use a Trusted Platform Module," bummer; your computer doesn't have a TPM, a special circuit that's built onto the system boards of BitLocker-compatible PCs.

   However, there's a sneaky, rather silly workaround if your PC doesn't have this item; see the box on the next page.

   When it's all over, you wind up with the message shown in Figure 23-5, middle. It's asking what you want to use as your master key. Yes, you can make up a password. But you can also turn a USB flash drive into a physical key that can unlock your hard drive.

   Either way, don't mess around here. You're about to take the extraordinary step of encrypting your entire hard drive. If you lose that password or that flash drive, *all your files are gone forever.* Nothing can get them back.

3. **Click either "Insert a USB flash drive" or "Enter a password."**

   If you chose the flash-drive option, a window opens and shows you all the flash drives Windows can find. Click the one you want to use, and then click OK. Do not lose the flash drive.

   If you chose the password option, a window opens and asks you to enter a complex password. Twice. Do not forget it.

4. **Click Next.**

   Now you see the box shown in Figure 23-5 at bottom. Microsoft is giving you an out—a backup emergency recovery method—in case you lose your flash-drive "key" or forget the BitLocker password. It's allowing you to create a recovery key: a back door.

   The recovery key is a 48-digit serial number. You have four ways to save it: to your Microsoft account (that is, you're saving the key online); to *another* flash drive; to a file on the computer; or as a printout.

Note: You can choose more than one of these options. You can save it *and* print it, for example. The dialog box doesn't go away until you click Next.

5. **Choose where to save the recovery-key number, and then click Next.**

   Now you see the box shown in Figure 23-5, bottom. Windows is offering to encrypt only the part of the disk that actually has files on it (a new option in Windows 8), which is much faster than encrypting the entire disk including empty space. Better

POWER USERS' CLINIC

The Trusted Platform Module Workaround

If you can't turn on BitLocker–if a note explains that you don't have a Trusted Platform Module (TPM) chip–here's the workaround.

Press ⊞+R to open the Run dialog box. Type *gpedit.msc*. Press Enter. You've just opened the Group Policy Object Editor, a program you can use to configure advanced settings on Windows.

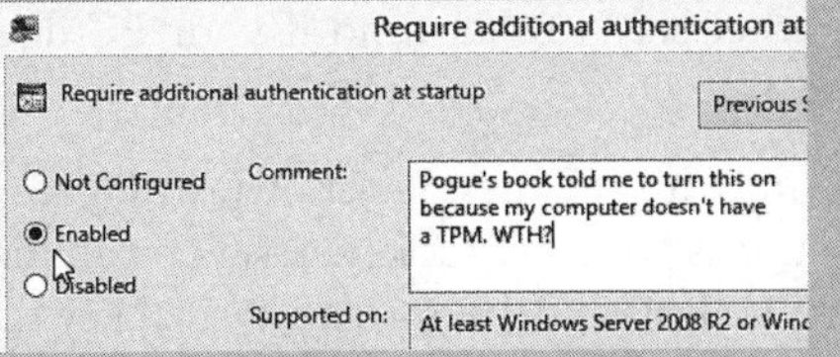

Drill down to Local Computer Policy→Computer Configuration→Administrative Templates→Windows Components→BitLocker Drive Encryption→Operating System Drives.

On the right side of the window, find "Require additional authentication at startup," and double-click it.

The Properties dialog box appears. Select Enabled. Make sure "Allow BitLocker without a compatible TPM (requires a startup key on a USB flash drive)" is turned on. Click OK.

Now you can proceed with the BitLocker features as described on these pages.

(Of course, in a corporation, a system administrator might have done all of this for you–or prevented you from doing it.)

yet, even if you choose "used disk space only," any new files you add later will be encrypted automatically.

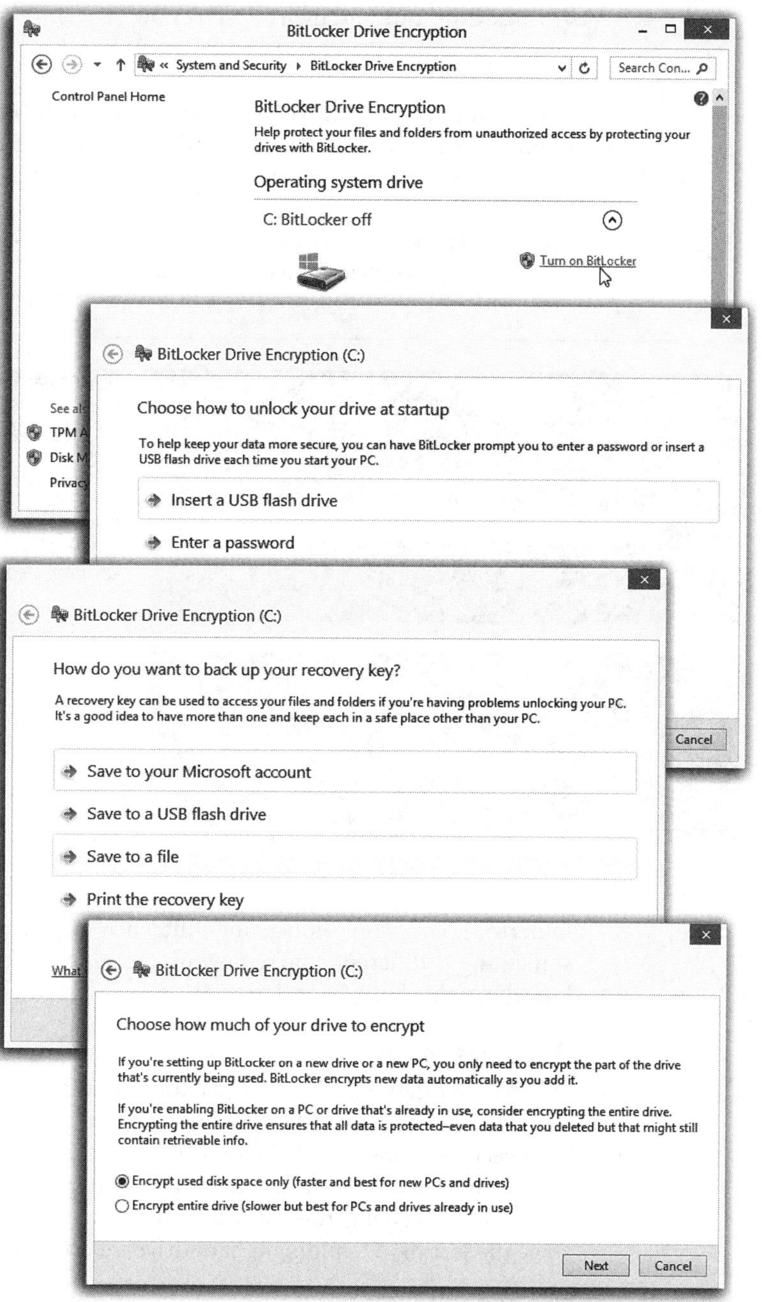

Figure 23-5:
Top: You get a separate "Turn On BitLocker" link for each drive listed in the Control Panel.

Second from top: Make up your primary password. It has to have capitals and lowercase letters, and numbers too. Or turn a flash drive into a physical key.

Third from top: Where do you want to store your last-ditch recovery key? Whatever you decide, don't lose the darned thing. You'll feel like an idiot if you attempt to stop a bad guy from getting to your files–and wind up stopping yourself from getting to them because you lost the passwords.

If you choose "to your Microsoft account," go here if you ever have to recover that key:

https://skydrive.live.com/RecoveryKey

Bottom: There's not much point to encrypting the empty space.

6. **Click Next.**

   Windows asks if you're ready to begin, and warns you that the PC might feel sluggish while the encryption is going on. (This can take some time.)

7. **Click Continue and then "Restart now."**

   The computer restarts.

From now on, every time you turn on the computer (or, more specifically, every time Windows tries to access the encrypted drive, you see the box in Figure 23-6. Now you have *two* passwords to type each morning instead of one.

Tip: For drives *other* than your Windows drive, you can turn on "Automatically unlock," which saves you that additional password-entering business; see page 722.)

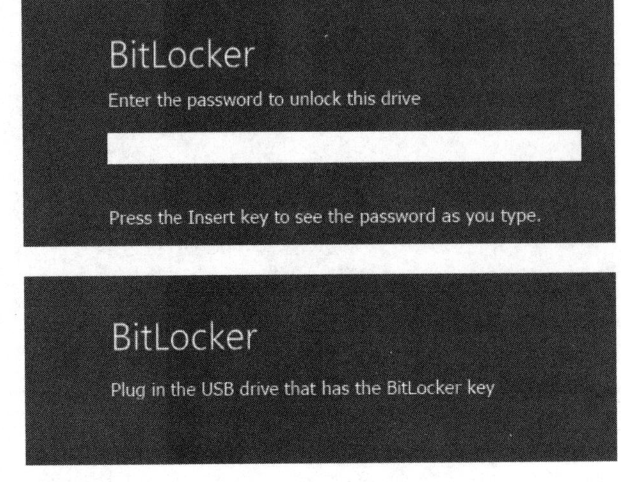

Figure 23-6:
From now on, you have to supply your BitLocker password (or insert the flash drive "key") every time you want to access your encrypted drive.

If you don't have the password or flash drive (gulp), press the Esc key to use the recovery key from step 5. That's your last chance.

Otherwise, you won't notice any difference in your usual routine. But, of course, something is different: you're now protected, even from the most determined and knowledgeable hard drive thieves.

BitLocker to Go

Windows 8 offers a new feature just for removable drives (mainly USB flash drives): BitLocker to Go. It works the same way—you create a password and a backup password (recovery key), and then Windows encrypts the drive—but it's arguably even more useful, because removable drives are portable. It's understood that you'll be taking it out into the big dangerous world. You're much more likely to lose a flash drive than to be the victim of a midnight hard drive–removal raid.

The steps go like this:

1. **Open the Control Panel, and select System & Security→BitLocker Drive Encryption.**

   You see the display shown in Figure 23-5 at top, listing each of your disks.

2. **Under "Removable data drives —BitLocker to Go," find the icon of the drive you want to encrypt. Click "Turn On BitLocker" next to it.**

   After a moment, you wind get the message shown in Figure 23-7. It's asking whether you want to use a password as the unlocking key, or a smart card that's been issued to you by your corporate network geek.

Figure 23-7: *You don't need that mysterious Trusted Computing Module chip when you're trying to BitLocker a flash drive, thank goodness.*

The decision you have to make here is easy: use the "smart card" option only if you work in a corporation where somebody gave you a smart card to use.

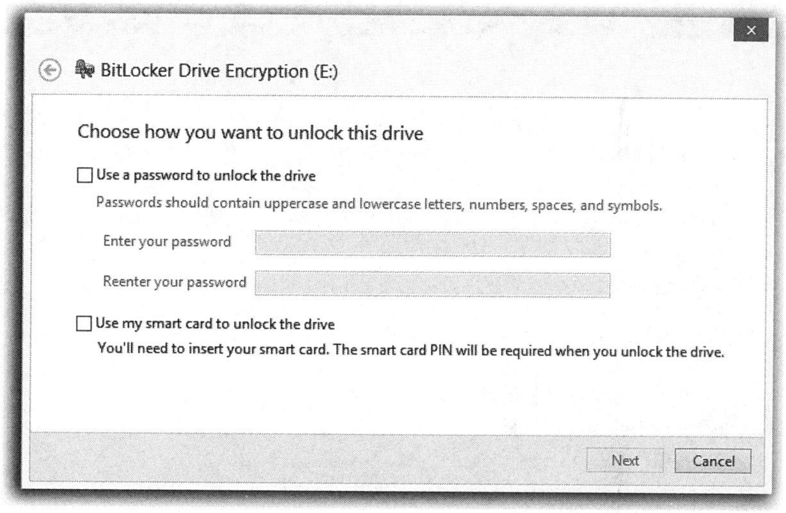

3. **Make your selection.**

   If you choose the password option, you're now asked to make up a hard-to-crack one. Enter it twice.

   If you chose the smart card option, insert the card into your computer's reader.

4. **Click Next.**

   Now you see a box like the one in Figure 23-5, third from top. Here again, Microsoft is helping you create a backup key, in case you forget the BitLocker password. It's a 48-digit serial number. You have three ways to save it: to your Microsoft account (that is, you're saving the key online); to a file on the computer; or as a printout.

Note: A reminder: You can choose more than one of these options.

5. **Choose where to save the recovery-key number, and then click Next.**

   Now Windows wants to know if it should encrypt only the part of the disk that actually has files on it (theoretically faster), or the entire drive. For a flash drive, there's not much difference in speed.

6. **Make your selection and click Next.**

   Windows warns you that the PC might feel slow while the encryption is going on.

7. **Click "Start encryption."**

   That's it. Once your flash drive is encrypted, Figure 23-8 shows what you'll see when you insert it into any Windows computer (Vista, Windows 7, Windows 8).

POWER USERS' CLINIC

Disk Quotas

Does one of your account holders have a tendency to become overzealous about downloading stuff, threatening to overrun your drive with shareware junk and MP3 files? Fortunately, it's easy enough for you, the wise administrator, to curb such behavior among holders of Standard accounts.

Open the Computer window (click Computer at the left side of any Explorer window). Right-click the hard drive icon; from the shortcut menu, choose Properties. In the Properties dialog box, click the Quota tab. Click Show Quota Settings to bring up the Quota Settings dialog box, shown here, and then turn on "Enable quota management."

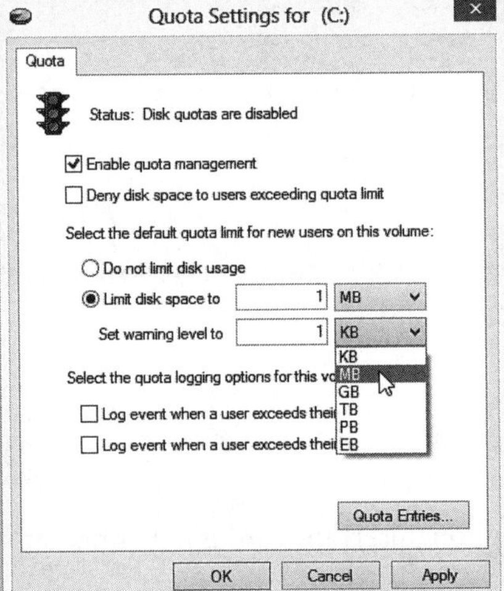

You might start by turning on "Deny disk space to users exceeding quota limit." This, of course, is exactly the kind of muzzle you were hoping to place on out-of-control downloaders. The instant they try to save or download a file that pushes their stuff over the limit, an "Insufficient disk space" message appears.

Use the "Limit disk space to __" controls to specify the cap you want to put on each account holder. Using these controls, you can specify a certain number of kilobytes (KB), megabytes (MB), gigabytes (GB)—or even terabytes (TB), petabytes (PB), or exabytes (EB). (Then write a letter to *PCWorld* and tell the editors where you bought a multi-exabyte hard drive.)

You can also set up a disk-space limit ("Set warning level to ____") that will make a *warning* appear—not to the mad downloader, but to you, the administrator. By clicking the Quota Entries button, you get a report that shows how much disk space each account holder has used up. (This is where you see the warning as a written notation.)

If you just want to track your underlings' disk usage without actually limiting them, then set the warning level to the desired value, but set the Limit Disk Space value to something impossibly high, like several exabytes.

When you click OK, Windows warns you that it's about to take some time to calculate just how much disk space each account holder has used so far.

Tip: Don't miss the fact that you don't have to enter a password for this flash drive every darned time you insert it. As shown at bottom in Figure 23-8, you can opt to have it unlocked automatically every time you connect it to *your* PC. (A bad guy who steals the drive won't have any luck on *his*.)

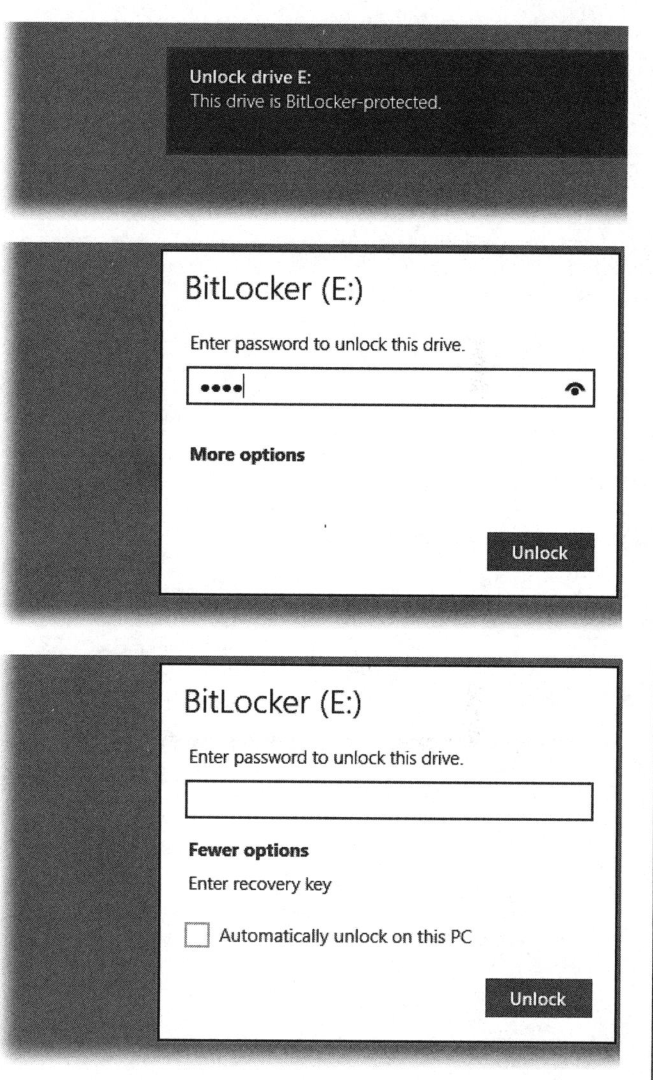

Figure 23-8:
When you insert a BitLockered flash drive into a Windows 8 computer, this is what you see (top). (On Windows Vista or Windows 7, the box looks a little different.)

Click that message. Now you see the "Enter password" box (middle).

Only if you type the password correctly will Windows let you access the drive.

(On Windows XP and Windows Vista, you can open what's on the drive, but you can't make changes, save new files, or delete anything. It's read-only.)

Bottom: The "More options" link offers you the chance to enter your recovery key. It also offers a way to unlock this disk on this PC automatically–a huge effort-saver.

BitLocker Options

Once you've turned on BitLocker for a drive—any drive—the same Control Panel panel that began your adventure now shows a list of useful commands next to the drive's icon. You can change the password, remove the password, turn off BitLocker, and so on. After all, you probably won't work for the CIA forever.

One of the most useful is "Turn on auto-unlock." It means that, yes, you won't have to enter your BitLocker password for the corresponding drive every darned time you turn on the PC. As you can see in Figure 23-9, it's available for any drive *except* the one you're running Windows from.

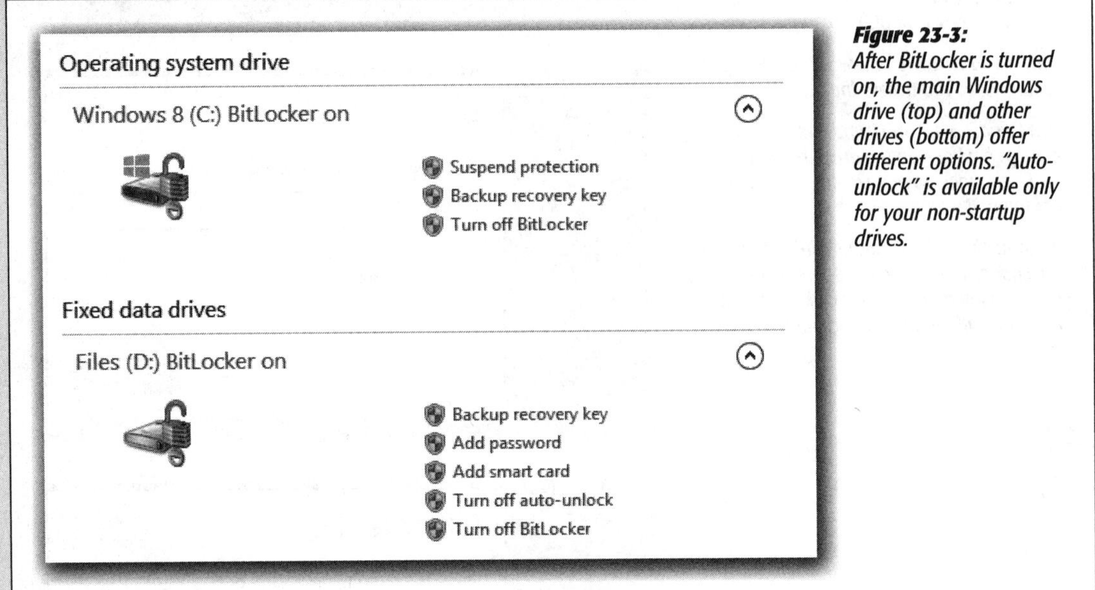

Figure 23-3:
After BitLocker is turned on, the main Windows drive (top) and other drives (bottom) offer different options. "Auto-unlock" is available only for your non-startup drives.

7

Part Seven: The Windows Network

CHAPTER

24

Accounts (and Logging On)

For years, teachers, parents, tech directors, and computer lab instructors struggled to answer two difficult questions: How do you rig one PC so several different people can use it throughout the day, without interfering with one another's files and settings? And how do you protect a PC from getting fouled up by mischievous (or bumbling) students and employees?

Easy: Use a multiple-user operating system like Windows 8. Anyone who uses the computer must *log on*—supply a correct name and password—when the computer turns on.

Since the day you installed Windows 8 or fired up a new Windows 8 machine, you've probably made a number of changes to your setup—fiddled with your Start screen, changed the desktop wallpaper, added some favorites to your Web browser, downloaded files onto your desktop, and so on—without realizing that you were actually making these changes only to *your account.*

Ditto with your Web history and cookies, Control Panel settings, email stash, and so on. It's all part of your account.

If you create an account for a second person, who's never used Windows 8, then when she turns on the computer and signs in, she'll find the desktop looking the way it was factory-installed by Microsoft: basic Start screen, standard desktop picture, default Web browser home page, and so on. She can make the same kinds of changes to the PC that you've made, but nothing she does will affect your environment the next time *you* log on.

In other words, the multiple-accounts feature has two benefits: first, the convenience of hiding everyone else's junk, and second, security that protects both the PC's system software and everyone's work.

Behind the scenes, Windows stores *all* these files and settings in a single folder—your Personal folder, the one that bears your name. You can open it easily enough; at the desktop, it's listed in the Favorites list at the left side of every Explorer window. (Technically, your Personal folder is in the Computer→Local Disk (C:)→Users folder.)

Tip: Even if you don't share your PC with anyone and don't create any other accounts, you might still appreciate this feature because it effectively password-protects the entire computer. Your PC is protected from unauthorized casual fiddling when you're away from your desk (or if your laptop is stolen)—especially if you tell Windows to require your logon password after any time the screen saver has kicked in (page 307).

If you're content simply to *use* Windows, that's really all you need to know about accounts. If, on the other hand, you have shouldered some of the responsibility for *administering* Windows machines—if it's your job to add and remove accounts, for example—read on.

Local Accounts vs. Microsoft Accounts

Until Windows 8, any account you created on your PC was a *local* account, meaning *stored on the computer itself.* All your stuff—your files, email, settings, passwords—sat on the PC itself.

Seems obvious, right? Where else would you store all those details?

Today, there's an answer to that: online.

In Windows 8, you have the option to have your account details stored by Microsoft, online ("in the cloud," as the marketing people might say). You don't log in with a name like Fizzywinks; instead, you log in with an *email address* that you've registered with Microsoft. If your name and password are correct, you've just succeeded in logging in with your *Microsoft account* instead of with a local one.

And why is that a good thing? Because it means you can sign into *any Windows 8 computer anywhere*—your other laptop, a friend's PC, another company's—and find yourself instantly at home. You won't have your files, music collection, and movies, of course (unless you've stored them on your SkyDrive). But you will find every possible account-related element ready and waiting, even on a computer you've never used before. Here's what you'll find:

- **Your Twitter, Facebook, LinkedIn, Hotmail, and other accounts.** You're supposed to link *these* to your Microsoft account. After that, no matter what computer you use, your People app, Skype program, and other address books will always be up to date and fully loaded.

- **Your online photos.** Once again, your Microsoft account can store your links to services like Flickr and Facebook, so their contents are automatically available when you sign into any Windows 8 machine.
- **Your SkyDrive.** Any files you've stashed on the SkyDrive (page 161) are available to you.
- **Your settings.** Your wallpaper, color scheme, and many other settings. Many programs store their settings as part of your Microsoft account, too.
- **Your Web world.** Your Internet Explorer bookmarks (Favorites), browsing history, and even Web-site stored passwords will be there waiting for you.

Note: Your passwords don't get synced until you make each Windows 8 computer a "trusted PC." See the box below.

- **Your TileWorld apps.** You can install a TileWorld app on up to five Windows 8 machines. They don't show up automatically when you log into a brand-new computer, but you can open the Store app and click "Your apps" to re-download them.

UP TO SPEED

That "Trusted PC" Business

When you first sign into a new Windows 8 machine, a peculiar message sprouts from your taskbar. It's an "important message" that says "Trust this PC." (A similar link appears on the PC Settings screen when you click Users or "Sync your settings" for the first time.)

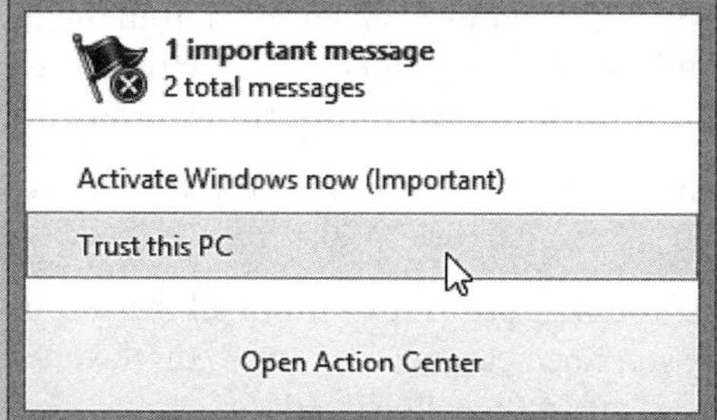

When you click it, the Action Center opens, bearing a button called, once again, "Trust this PC." When you click it, you go online to your Microsoft Account Settings page (*account.live.com*); here you're asked to name your new computer. Shortly thereafter, you get an email or a text message at the address or phone number you specified when you created the Microsoft account. If it's a code sent to your phone, then your Microsoft account Web page (page 736) offers a place to type it in.

If it's an email, it says something like "It looks like you added some security info to your Microsoft account." It displays the name of the new PC and offers a big, fat "Confirm [computer name]" button. Once you click it, the new computer is verified as yours.

By adding a trusted PC to Microsoft's database, you gain two features.

First, from now on, your saved passwords (for Web sites, networked computers, and so on) can sync automatically among trusted PCs, as described in this chapter.

Second, the Microsoft Account Settings page offers an option that lets you change your account password—but you're allowed to do that only from a trusted PC. That's a measure intended to stymie evil teenage hackers who might otherwise try to hack your account online.

You'll also be allowed to sync your password settings between this computer and any others you've established as "trusted."

A Microsoft account is also, of course, your Microsoft wallet; you can use your Microsoft ID to buy apps, music, videos, and games from Microsoft. It's also what you use to sign in if you have an Xbox (possible) or a Windows Phone (unlikely).

There are even synergies there. If you've signed into both your Xbox and your Windows 8 machine with the same Microsoft account, you can do things like using the Share button.

A Microsoft account still lets you into your PC when you don't have an Internet connection. You can turn off as many of the syncing features as you like, for privacy's sake. The company swears it won't send anything to the email address you use. And it's free. In general, it's the best way to log into Windows 8.

And what about the alternative—a local account? If you have only one computer (and therefore don't need the syncing business) and don't plan to buy anything online, it's fine, too.

You can always convert any account—from Microsoft to local or vice versa.

Accounts Central

In keeping with Windows 8's schizophrenic nature, there are two places to work with accounts: TileWorld and the desktop Control Panel.

- **TileWorld.** Open the Charms bar. Select Settings; select "Change PC settings"; select Users. You see the panel shown at left in Figure 24-1.
- **Desktop.** Open the Control Panel (for example, right-click the lower-left corner of the screen and choose Control Panel from the shortcut menu). Click "User Accounts and Family Safety," then "User Accounts," then "Manage another account." You arrive at the Control Panel pane shown at right in Figure 24-1.

  Or, another approach: At the Start screen, type *accounts*. Click Settings under the search bar; in results, click "Make changes to accounts."

In each case, you now get to see a list of all the accounts you've created so far. Here, too, is where you can create new accounts, edit the ones you've already made, or delete them, as described in the following pages.

First, though, it's important to understand the difference between the two account types you may see in the Control Panel: *Administrator* or *Standard*. Read on.

Administrator vs. Standard Accounts

It's important to understand the phrase that appears just under your name in the panel shown in Figure 24-1 at bottom. On your own personal PC, the word "Administrator" probably appears here.

Because you're the person who installed Windows 8, the PC assumes that you're one of its *administrators*—the technical wizards who will be in charge of it. You're the teacher, the parent, the resident guru. You're the one who will maintain this PC and who will be permitted to make system-wide changes to it.

You'll find settings all over Windows (and all over this book) that *only* people with Administrator accounts can change. For example, only an administrator is allowed to do the following:

- Create or delete accounts and passwords.
- Make changes to certain Control Panel programs.
- See and manipulate *any* file on the machine. Install new desktop programs (and certain hardware components).

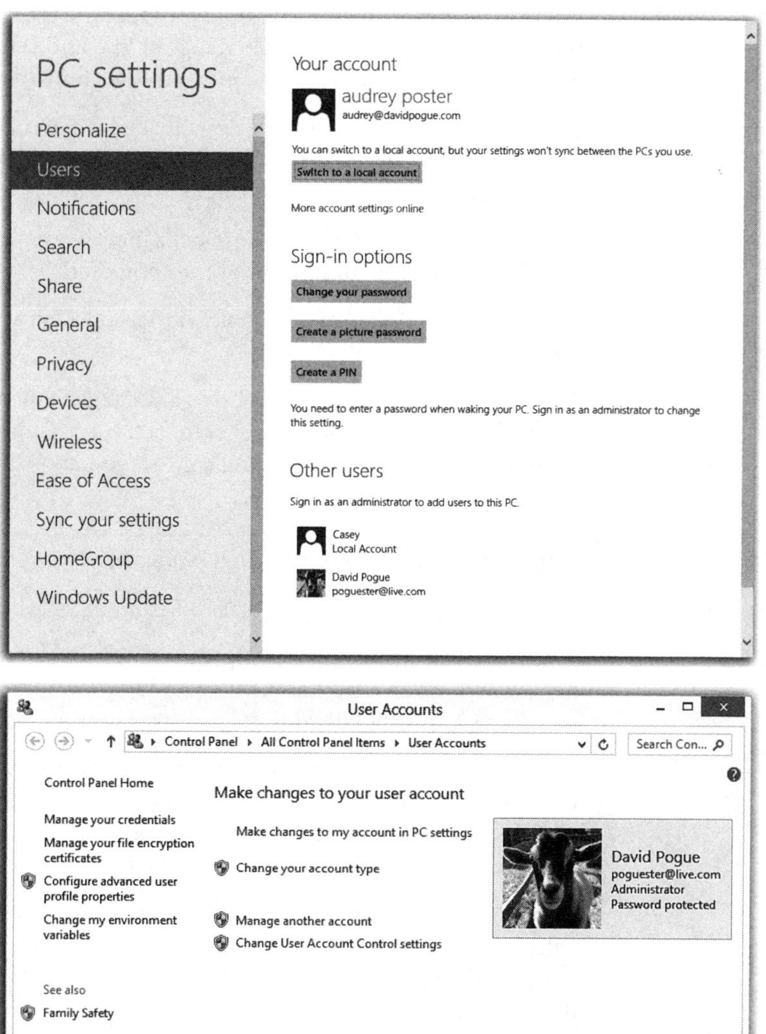

Figure 24-1: *Windows 8 offers two places to do much the same thing: in TileWorld (top) and at the desktop Control Panel (bottom). For various functions, at different times, you'll need both.*

- Install new desktop programs (and certain hardware components).

Note: You don't need an administrator to install a TileWorld app.

There's another kind of account, too, for people who *don't* have to make those kinds of changes: the Standard account.

Now, for years, people doled out Administrator accounts pretty freely. You know: The parents got Administrator accounts, the kids got Standard ones.

The trouble is, an Administrator account *itself* is a kind of security hole. Anytime you're logged in with this kind of account, any nasty software you may have caught from the Internet is *also,* in effect, logged in—and can make changes to important underlying settings on your PC, just the way a human administrator can.

Put another way: A virus you've downloaded while running a Standard account will have a much harder time infecting the rest of the machine than one you downloaded while using an Administrator account.

Today, therefore, Microsoft recommends that *everyone* use Standard accounts—even you, the wise master and owner of the computer!

So how are you supposed to make important Control Panel changes, install new programs, and so on?

That's gotten a lot easier in Windows 8. Using a Standard account no longer means you can't make important changes. In fact, you can do just about everything on the PC that an Administrator account can—if you know the *password* of a true Administrator account.

Note: Every Windows 8 PC can (and must) keep at least one Administrator account on hand, even if you rarely log in with that account.

Whenever you try to make a big change, you're asked to *authenticate yourself.* As described on page 743, that means supplying an Administrator account's password, even though you, the currently logged-in person, are a lowly Standard account holder.

If you have a Standard account because you're a student, a child, or an employee, you're supposed to call an administrator over to your PC to approve the change you're making. (If you're the PC's owner, but you're using a Standard account for security purposes, you know an administrator password, so it's no big deal.)

Now, making broad changes to a PC when you're an administrator *still* presents you with those "prove yourself worthy" authentication dialog boxes. The only difference is that you, the administrator, can click Continue (or tap Enter) to bypass them, rather than having to type in a password.

You'll have to weigh this security/convenience tradeoff. But you've been warned: The least vulnerable PC is one on which everyone uses a Standard account.

Adding an Account

To create a new account, open the Charms bar; hit Settings; hit "Change PC settings"; and select the Accounts, as described above (Figure 24-1, top). If you're new at this, there's probably just one account listed here: yours. This is the account Windows created when you installed it.

Note: The desktop Control Panel also offers a link called "Add a new user in PC settings"—but it just takes you right back here, into the TileWorld panel.

Scroll down, or look down, to the "Other users" heading. If you see more than one account here—not just yours—then one of these situations probably applies:

- **You created them** when you installed Windows 8, as described in Appendix A.
- **You bought a new computer** with Windows 8 preinstalled and created several accounts when asked to do so the first time you turned on the machine.
- **You upgraded from an earlier version** of Windows, and Windows 8 gracefully imported all your existing accounts.

To add another one, proceed thusly.

Note: If this is the first account—if you're using a new PC for the very first time—the setup process is longer than what you'll read here. You'll also be asked to choose a color scheme, opt to send automatic crash data back to Microsoft, and so on. Appendix A walks you through this one-time process.

---

1. **Select "Add a user."**

   This button doesn't even appear unless you have an Administrator account.

   Now you see the screen shown in Figure 24-2. Here's where Microsoft is trying to sell you on the virtues of having a Microsoft account.

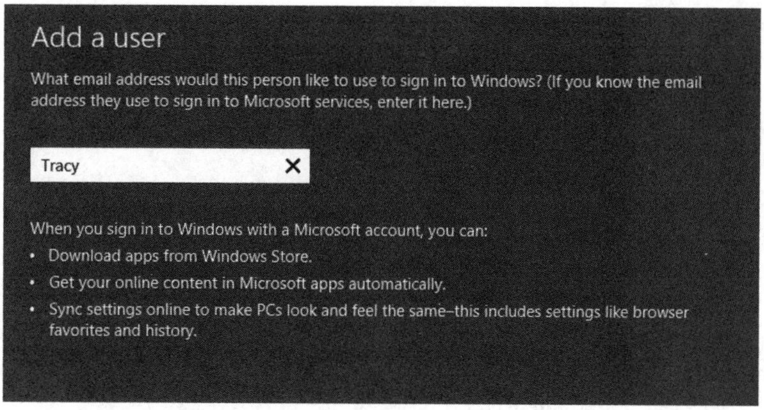

Figure 24-2: *Enter the email address of the new account holder. It doesn't matter if this person already has a Microsoft account or not. (If not, you'll be asked for a password in a subsequent step; if so, great! You've just added that Microsoft account to this PC.)*

Add a user
What email address would this person like to use to sign in to Windows? (If you know the email address they use to sign in to Microsoft services, enter it here.)
Tracy
When you sign in to Windows with a Microsoft account, you can:
• Download apps from Windows Store.
• Get your online content in Microsoft apps automatically.
• Sync settings online to make PCs look and feel the same—this includes settings like browser favorites and history.

2. **To create a new Microsoft account, type the lucky person's email address into the box.**

   You don't *have* to. If you'd prefer a local account, choose "Sign in without a Microsoft account" at the bottom of the screen. Microsoft tries one more time to win you over with a screen that touts the advantages of a Microsoft account; if you're still unconvinced, click "Local account" to continue. Make up a password on the next screen (or leave it blank, if you're not worried about other people snooping), and boom—you're finished.

Tip: If you sign up for a local account, there's no particular need to dream up a convoluted password. In fact, you may want to consider setting up *no* password–leaving both password blanks empty. Later, whenever you're asked for your password, just leave the Password box blank. You'll be able to log on and authenticate yourself that much faster each day.

   If you provide a password, you can also provide a *hint* (for yourself or whichever coworker's account you're operating on). This is a hint that anybody can see (including bad guys trying to log on as you), so choose something meaningful only to you. If your password is the first person who ever kissed you plus your junior-year phone number, for example, your hint might be "first person who ever kissed me plus my junior-year phone number."

   Later, when you log in and can't remember your password, leave the Password box empty and hit Enter. You wind up back at the Login screen to try again—but this time, your hint will appear just below the Password box to jog your memory.

   If you don't have an email address, you can get one of those here, too (select "Sign up for a new email address").

3. **Hit Next.**

   Welcome to the "Set up a Microsoft Account" screen. Microsoft wants you to make up a password and supply your contact information. (It promises never to send you junk mail.)

4. **Make up a password.**

   A Microsoft account requires a beefy password. It must be at least eight characters long and include at least two of these: capital letters, lowercase letters, symbols, and numbers.

   That's going to be a drag to remember, and even worse to enter every time you use the computer. Fortunately, if you share the PC only with a spouse or a few trusted colleagues in a small office and have nothing to hide, you can eliminate the requirement to enter the password with each login; see page 55.

5. **Fill in your name, country, and Zip code. Choose Next, and then fill in your birthday, phone number, an alternate email address, and a secret question and answer.**

You're required to fill in at least two of these alternate avenues. They give Microsoft a way to reach you, or to prove you're the legitimate owner of this account, if you ever forget your password.

6. **Choose Next. On the "Finish up" screen, tell Microsoft how enthusiastic you are about getting its spam.**

   The two checkboxes grant Microsoft permission to send you ads.

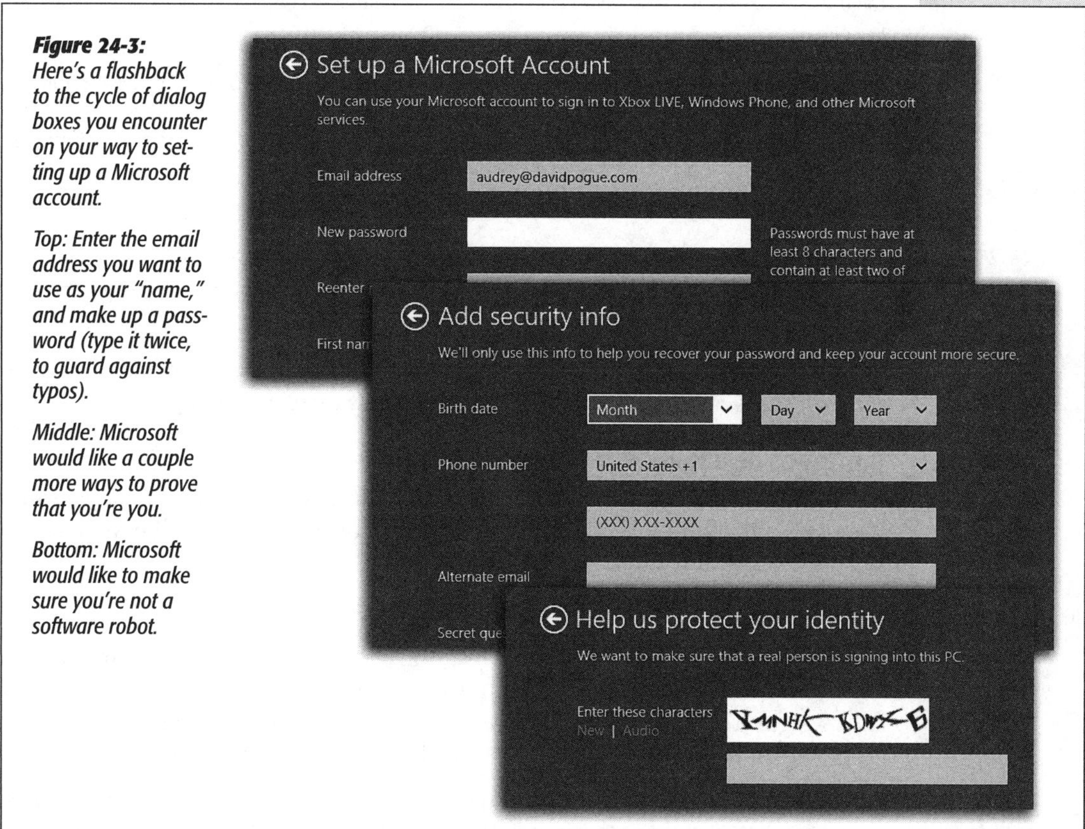

***Figure 24-3:** Here's a flashback to the cycle of dialog boxes you encounter on your way to setting up a Microsoft account.*

Top: Enter the email address you want to use as your "name," and make up a password (type it twice, to guard against typos).

Middle: Microsoft would like a couple more ways to prove that you're you.

Bottom: Microsoft would like to make sure you're not a software robot.

7. **Choose Next. Type in the scrambled letters.**

   This screen is intended to thwart automatic software robots that sign up for Microsoft accounts by the thousands for spamming purposes. Generally, software can't read these gibberish characters—only a person can.

8. **Choose Next.**

   This is your chance to turn on the parental-controls feature described on page 475. If that's appropriate for the person whose account you're creating, then turn on the checkbox.

9. Choose Finish.

After a moment, you return to the Accounts screen, where the new account holder's name joins whatever names were already there. You can continue adding new accounts forever or until your hard drive is full, whichever comes first.

Tip: If you never had the opportunity to set up a user account when installing Windows–if you bought a PC with Windows already on it, for example–you may see an account named Owner already in place. Nobody can use Windows at all unless there's at least *one* Administrator account on it, so Microsoft is doing you a favor here.

Just double-click it and click "Change the account name" to change the name "Owner" to one that suits you better. Make that account your own using the steps in the following paragraphs.

Editing an Account

Although the process of creating a new account is swift and simple, it doesn't offer you much in the way of flexibility. You don't even have a chance to specify the new person's account picture (rubber ducky, flower, or whatever).

That's why the next step in creating an account is usually *editing* the one you just set up. As it turns out, the options are scattered across three different places.

Settings You Change in PC Settings

On the main Users screen (Figure 24-1), you can make changes *only to your own account.* So if you've just created a new account for somebody, she'll have to log in, open this panel, and make the changes herself.

Here are the kinds of changes someone can make after logging in:

- **Add an account picture.** The usual sign-in screen displays each account holder's name, accompanied by a little picture. When you first create the account, however, it assigns a generic silhouette to you, meaning that everybody is identical—not exactly the sort of "I'm a PC" message Microsoft probably hopes to spread.

  To choose something more personal, select Personalize, and then click "Account picture." You can select either Browse (to choose an existing picture from your hard drive) or "Create an account picture" (meaning "Let's take a picture of your head right now, using the computer's camera").

- **Switch to a different account type.** If you have a local account, you can switch to a Microsoft account, or vice versa. The "Switch to a local account"/"Switch to a Microsoft account" button is staring you in the face at the top of the Users panel in PC Settings.

- **Change your password, PIN, or picture password.** As you know from Chapter 1, Windows 8 lets you log in with either a regular typed password, a four-digit number, or a picture password (you draw lines on a photo you've selected). Here's where you can create or change whatever you've set up.

- **Eliminate the need for a password.** See the Change button ("Any user who has a password must enter it when waking this PC")? If you click it, and dismiss the warning message, then nobody will have to enter a password when waking this computer. It will jump right into whatever account was open.

  That, of course, is not an ideal situation in a business (or in a family with teenagers); sometimes, protection is needed. But if nobody uses this PC but you, or maybe you and a partner without a lot of secrets, then the password is just red tape you might prefer to do without. This option is for you.

- **Change the wallpaper, color scheme, notifications, and other settings.** All the settings you make on the Personalize tab of PC Settings apply *only to your account*. In fact, *all* the settings you make in PC Settings apply only to your account.

POWER USERS' CLINIC

Sync Settings

It's one of the best parts of the Microsoft account system: Whenever you log into a Windows 8 computer, all your settings are in place. Your desktop picture, your color scheme, your Web bookmarks—the works. If you have a desktop PC at home and a laptop on the road, well, you're all set; everything is consistent as you move from computer to computer.

There are two reasons you may not love this idea, however. Maybe there's some reason that you don't want a certain setting synced. Maybe you use your laptop exclusively when you're in France and don't want your English-language preference synced. Maybe you want independent bookmarks on each machine.

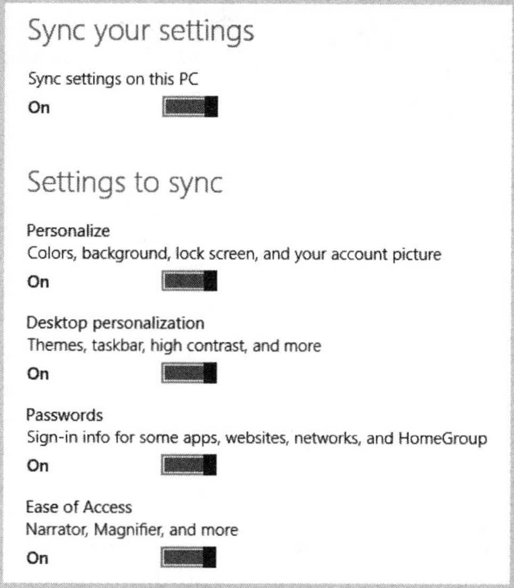

Or maybe the privacy implications just freak you out. Maybe you don't want your laptop browsing History showing up on the family PC in the living room. Or maybe you just don't want Microsoft knowing about your activity.

In any case, there are on/off switches for most of the synced settings. To find them, open the Charms bar. Select Settings, then "Change PC settings," then "Sync your settings."

Sync your settings

Sync settings on this PC
On

Settings to sync

Personalize
Colors, background, lock screen, and your account picture
On

Desktop personalization
Themes, taskbar, high contrast, and more
On

Passwords
Sign-in info for some apps, websites, networks, and HomeGroup
On

Ease of Access
Narrator, Magnifier, and more
On

At the top, you have a master on/off switch for the whole concept of syncing your settings. That's the one to flip if the whole idea just creeps you out.

Below that, you get individual switches for various categories of settings. In most cases, the descriptions tell you just what gets synced for that on/off switch. But here are some additional settings that you might not guess:

The Personalization settings include not just the look of TileWorld, but also file-type associations you've set up (page 355). "Desktop personalization" governs your choice of theme, yes, but also your screen-saver setting and taskbar configuration. And "Language settings" also stores your preferences for the TileWorld spell checker.

And if you've created a Microsoft account, guess what? Most of these settings are stored online—and if you sign into another Windows 8 computer somewhere, you'll find all your settings instantly recreated on that machine.

Settings You Change Online

Remember—a Microsoft account is stored on the Internet. It should come as no surprise, then, that Microsoft offers a Web site where you can make a lot of additional changes to your account.

On the Users screen of PC Settings (Figure 24-1), click "More account settings online." Off you go into Internet Explorer, where you're asked to sign in with your email address and password. Then you arrive at the peculiar page shown in Figure 24-4, where the tabs at left let you change things like these:

- **Overview.** Edit your name, birthday, password, security questions, and so on. If you click "Edit personal info," you can add new information to Microsoft's dossier on you: your gender, profession, mailing address, and so on.

  Here, too, is your opportunity to delete your Microsoft account—for example, when you buy that Mac you've always wanted. (Joke! That's a joke.)

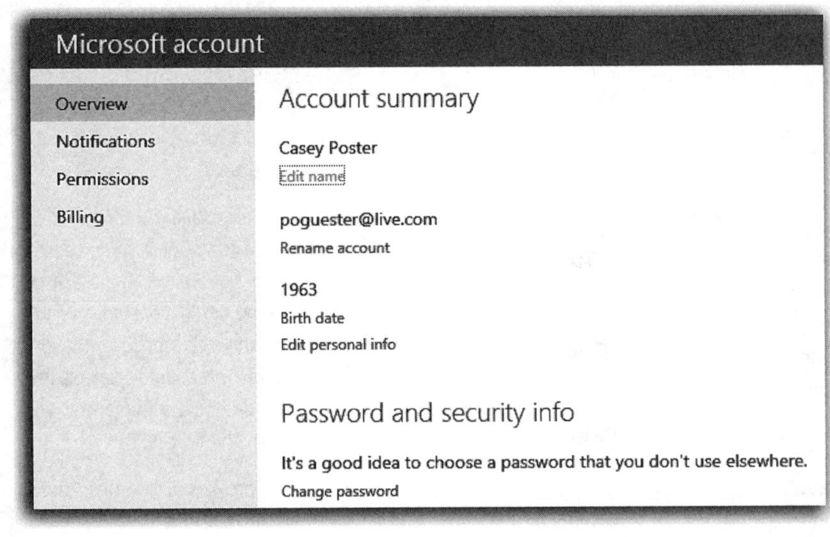

Figure 24-4: *Here's the central storage locker for all the information in your Microsoft account. If your computer gets broken or stolen, who cares? Your settings will be restored instantly the next time you log in with a Microsoft account.*

- **Notifications.** Where do you want Microsoft to send important updates and alerts? And can Microsoft *please* send you junk mail?

- **Permissions.** The options here are actually extremely important—and very powerful.

Manage Linked Accounts. Over time, you might have collected quite a few email addresses from Microsoft's various services. Maybe you're casey@hotmail.com, casey23@outlook.com, and BigCase@live.com. Using this link, you can associate all those addresses with one another.

Thereafter, you can switch from one account to another on any Microsoft Web site—Outlook.com, say—just by choosing a different one from the name/photo pop-up menu at the upper-right corner of the screen. You won't have to log out/log in over and over again. (This really has nothing to do with Windows 8, but it's handy.)

Manage parental permissions. This item actually has nothing to do with the Family Safety feature described in Chapter 25. Instead, it refers to accounts you've set up for under-14-year-olds for Microsoft's online services, like Outlook.com.

Add accounts, Manage accounts. Remember how you can link online accounts (like Facebook and Twitter) to your Microsoft account? How Windows 8 cleverly incorporates all your friends' updates into the People app?

Here's where you can hook up additional accounts to your Microsoft account, and see which accounts you've already liked with it. You can edit their name/password combinations, limit what information they exchange with Windows, and delete the accounts when necessary.

- **Billing.** Here's the master dashboard for buying stuff online from Microsoft: music, movies, apps, and so on. You can see your past purchase history, change your credit-card info, cancel subscriptions, and so on.

Settings You Change in Control Panel

The most useful options for changing account info are at the desktop, in the Control Panel. (Click User Accounts and Family Safety, then User Accounts.)

On this pane (Figure 24-1, bottom), you see only the details of your account. You can't even see who else has accounts on your PC. At this point, here's all you can do:

- **Make changes to my account in PC settings.** That's right: This link takes you *back* into TileWorld to make the kinds of changes described in the previous paragraphs.
- **Change your account type.** Here's where you can convert your own account between Standard and Administrator. (There must always be at least one Administrator account on a PC. Otherwise, everyone would be a Standard nobody, and nobody could make any important changes.)
- **Manage another account.** Ah, now we're talking. You, as administrator, can make changes here to *other* people's accounts (Figure 24-5). That, after all, is why you were elected administrator.

  Click the icon of the person whose account you want to tweak. As you can see in Figure 24-5, the links here offer you the opportunity to change, for example, this person's name—just the ticket when one of your coworkers gets married or joins the Witness Protection Program.

- **Change User Account Control settings.** Long story. See page 743.

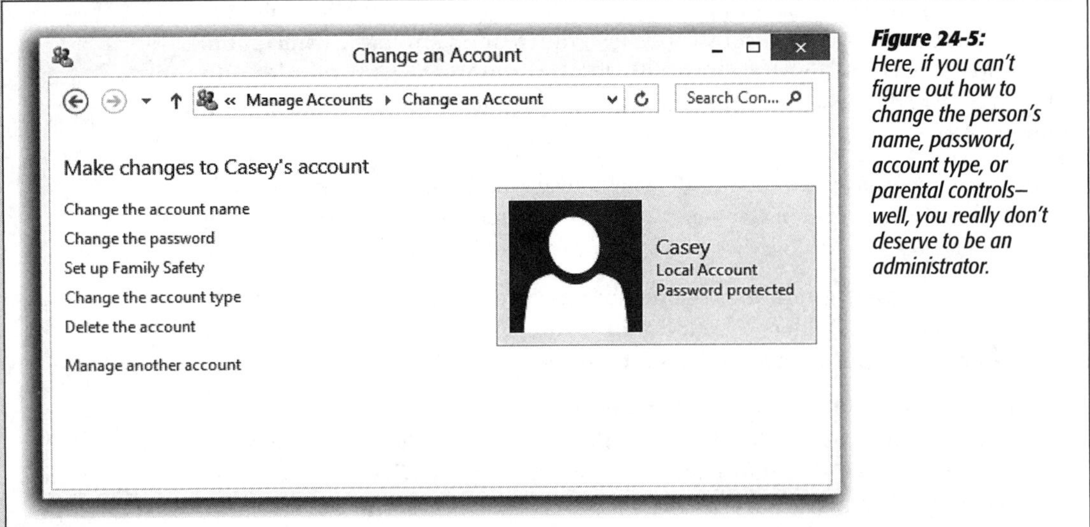

Figure 24-5: *Here, if you can't figure out how to change the person's name, password, account type, or parental controls—well, you really don't deserve to be an administrator.*

You're free to make any of these changes to any account at any time; you don't have to do it immediately after creating the account.

The Forgotten Password Disk

As described above, Windows contains a handy *hint* mechanism for helping you recall your password if you've forgotten it.

But what if, having walked into a low-hanging branch, you've forgotten both your password *and* the correct interpretation of your hint? In that disastrous situation, you don't have to fling your worthless PC into the freezing river quite yet. You have a few more options:

- On a corporate domain network, the system administrator can reset your password.
- Someone with an Administrator account can sign in and change your password for you. Even *you* can do that, if you remember the password for another Administrator account.
- Use the Password Reset Disk.

This disk is a clever solution-in-advance. It's a USB flash drive that you can use like a physical key to unlock your account in the event of a forgotten password. The catch: You have to make this disk *now,* while you still remember your password.

Tip: This drive can get you into a *local* user account, one stored on the computer—not a Microsoft account. If you've forgotten your Microsoft account password, you can reset it at *https://account.live.com/password/reset.*

To create this disk, insert a USB flash drive. Then, at the Start screen, type *forgot.* Select Settings under the search box, and, in the results, select "Create a password reset disk."

The Forgotten Password Wizard appears (Figure 24-6). Click through it, supplying your current password when asked. When you click Finish, remove the disk or flash drive. Label it, and don't lose it!

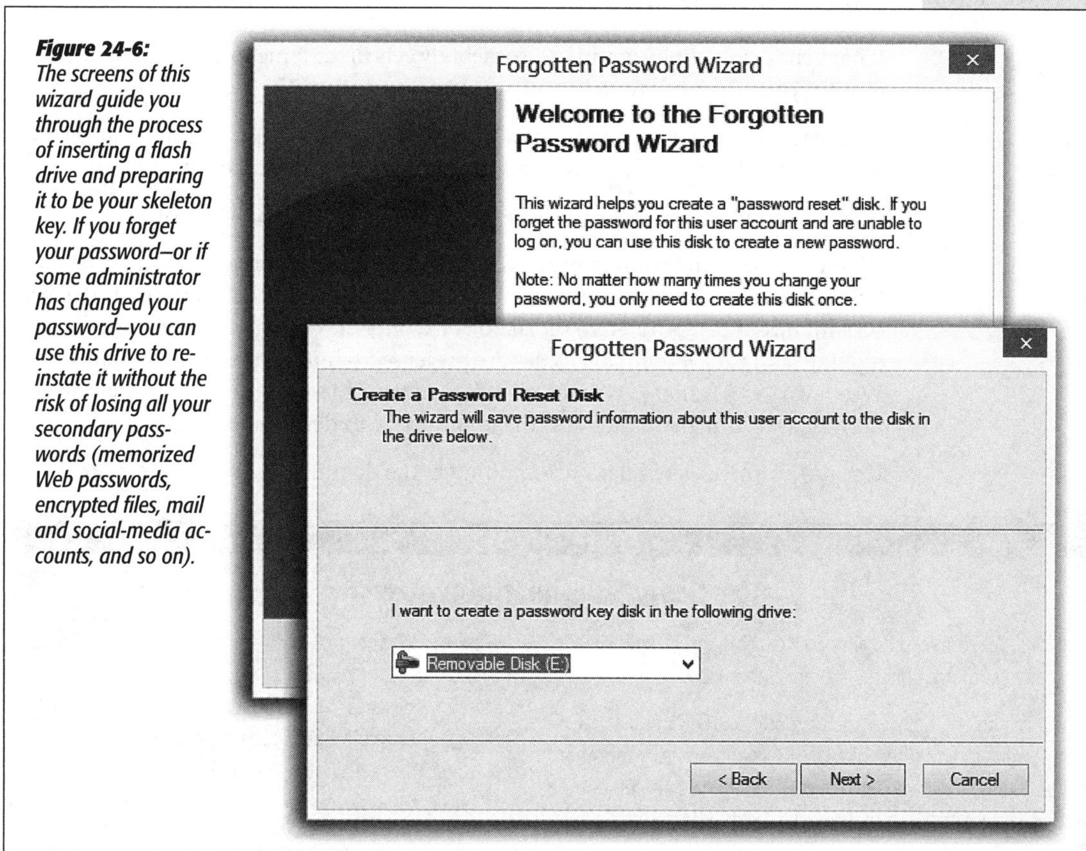

Figure 24-6: *The screens of this wizard guide you through the process of inserting a flash drive and preparing it to be your skeleton key. If you forget your password—or if some administrator has changed your password—you can use this drive to reinstate it without the risk of losing all your secondary passwords (memorized Web passwords, encrypted files, mail and social-media accounts, and so on).*

Don't leave it in plain sight, either, though; anyone with that drive can now get into your stuff.

Tip: Behind the scenes, Windows saves a file onto the flash drive called *userkey.psw.* You can guess what that is.

When the day comes when you can't remember your password, leave the Password box empty and hit Enter. You wind up back at the Login screen; this time, in addition to your password hint, you see a link called "Reset password." Insert your Password Reset flash drive and then click that link.

A Password Reset Wizard now helps you create a new password (and a new hint to remind you of it). You're in.

Even though you now have a new password, your existing Password Reset Disk is still good. Keep it in a drawer somewhere for use the next time you experience a temporarily blank brain.

Deleting User Accounts

It happens—somebody graduates, somebody gets fired, somebody dumps you. Sooner or later, you may need to delete an account from your PC.

To delete a user account, open the Control Panel. Click "User Accounts and Family Safety"; then (under "User Accounts") click "Remove user accounts."

Click the appropriate account name, and then click "Delete the account."

Windows asks if you want to preserve the contents of this person's Documents folder. If you click the Keep Files button, you find a new folder, named for the dearly departed, on your desktop. (As noted in the dialog box, only the documents, the contents of the desktop, and the Documents folder are preserved—but *not* programs, email, or even Web favorites.) If that person ever returns to your life, you can create a new account for him and copy these files into the appropriate folder locations.

If you click the Delete Files button, though, the documents are gone forever.

POWER USERS' CLINIC

The Other Administrator Account

This will sound confusing. But there's another kind of Administrator account: *the* Administrator account.

This is an emergency backup account with full administrator powers and *no password.* Even if you delete all your other accounts, this one still remains, if only to give you some way to get into your machine. It's called Administrator, and it's ordinarily hidden.

Most people see it only in times of troubleshooting, when they start up their PCs in Safe Mode. It's the ideal account to use in those situations. Not only does it come with no password assigned, but it's also unlimited. It gives you free powers over every file, which is just what you may need to troubleshoot your computer.

In Windows XP, the problem was, of course, that anyone who knew about it could get into Windows with full administrator privileges–and no need to know a password. Your kid, for example, could blow right past your carefully established Parental Controls–and let's not even consider what a virus could do.

So in the more security-minded Windows 8, the secret Administrator account is still there. But it's ordinarily disabled. It comes to life *only* if you're starting your PC in Safe Mode.

(That's on a standard home or small-office PC. On a corporate domain network, only a networking geek who's got a Domain Admins account can start up in Safe Mode. You know who you are.)

A few more important points about deleting accounts:

- You can't delete the account you're logged into.
- You can't delete the last Administrator account. One must remain.
- You can create a new account with the same name and password as one you deleted earlier, but in Windows' head, it's still not the same account. As described in the box on the next page, it won't have any of the original *secondary* passwords (for Web sites, encrypted files, and so on).
- Don't manipulate accounts manually (by fooling around in the Users folder). Create, delete, and rename them only using User Accounts in the Control Panel. Otherwise, you'll wind up with duplicate or triplicate folders in the Users folder,

GEM IN THE ROUGH

The Secret, Fully Automatic Logon Trick

You're supposed to do most of your account-editing work in the User Accounts pane of the Control Panel, which is basically a wizard that offers one option per screen. That requirement may not thrill veteran Windows 2000 fans, however, who are used to the much more direct—and more powerful—User Accounts screen.

Actually, it's still in Windows 8. To make it appear, press ⊞+R to open the Run dialog box, type *netplwiz*, authenticate yourself if necessary, and then press Enter. You see the program shown here.

Most of the functions are the same as what you'd find in the User Accounts control panel—it's just that you don't have to slog through several wizard screens to get things done. Here you can add, remove, or edit accounts, all in a single screen.

This older Control Panel program also offers a few features that you don't get at all in the new one. For example, you can turn off the checkbox called, "Users must enter a user name and password to use this computer." When you do so and click OK, you get a dialog box called Automatically Log On, where you can specify a user name and password of one special person. This lucky individual won't have to specify any name and password at logon time and can instead turn on the PC and cruise directly to the desktop. (This feature works only at *startup time*. If you choose "Sign out" at the Start screen, the standard Logon dialog box appears so that other people have the opportunity to sign in.)

This automatic-logon business is ordinarily a luxury enjoyed by solo operators whose PCs have only one account and no password. By using the secret User Accounts method, however, you can set up automatic logon even on a PC with several accounts, provided you recognize the security hole it leaves open.

with the PC name tacked onto the end of the original account name (Bob, Bob.DELL, and so on)—a sure recipe for confusion.

Tip: If you're an administrator, don't miss the Users tab of the Task Manager dialog box. (Press Ctrl+Shift+Esc to get to the Task Manager.) It offers a handy, centralized list of everybody who's logged into your machine and contains buttons that let you log them off or disconnect them. All this can be handy whenever you need some information, a troubleshooting session, or a power trip.

Disabling Accounts

If you *do* expect that your colleague may one day return to your life, you might consider *disabling* the account instead of deleting it. A disabled account doesn't show up on the Login screen or in the User Accounts program, but it's still there on the hard drive, and you can bring it back when necessary.

There's no pretty Control Panel link for disabling an account; you'll have to get your hands greasy in the power-user underpinnings of Windows. See "Account is disabled" on page 747 for details.

UP TO SPEED

Passwords Within Passwords

The primary password that you or your administrator sets up in the User Accounts program has two functions. You already know that it lets you log on each day so you can enter your Windows world of desktop clutter, Start-screen tailoring, Web bookmarks, and so on.

But what you may not realize is that it's also the master key that unlocks all the other passwords associated with your account: the passwords that Internet Explorer memorizes for certain Web sites, the passwords that get you into shared disks and folders on the network, the password that protects your encrypted files, and so on. The simple act of logging onto your account also unlocks all these other secure areas of your PC life.

But remember that anyone with an Administrator account can change your password at any time. Does that mean that whoever has an Administrator account–your teacher, boss, or teenager, for example–has full access to your private stuff? After you leave the school, company, or household, what's to stop an administrator from changing your password, thereby gaining access to your electronic-brokerage account (courtesy of its memorized Internet Explorer password), and so on?

Fortunately, Microsoft is way ahead of you on this one. The instant an administrator changes somebody else's password, Windows wipes out all secondary passwords associated with the account. That administrator can log onto your account and see your everyday files, but he can't see Web sites with memorized passwords and so on. (The bad news is that he'll also wipe out your stored passwords for EFS-encrypted files, if any.)

Note that if you change your *own* password–or if you use a Password Reset Disk, described in these pages–none of this applies. Your secondary passwords survive intact. It's only when *somebody else* changes your password that this little-known Windows security feature kicks in, sanitizing the account for your protection.

The Guest Account

Believe it or not, Administrator and Standard aren't the only kinds of accounts you can set up on your PC.

A third kind, called the Guest account, is ideal for situations where somebody is just visiting you for the day. Rather than create an entire account for this person, complete with password, hint, little picture, and so on, you can just switch on the Guest account.

To find the on/off switch, open the Start menu and type *guest*; click "Turn guest account on or off" in the results list. Authenticate yourself if necessary.

In the Manage Accounts window, click Guest, and then click Turn On.

Now, when the visitor tries to log in, she can choose Guest as the account. She can use the computer but can't see anyone else's files or make any changes to your settings.

When the visitor is finally out of your hair, healthy paranoia suggests that you turn off the Guest account once again. (To do so, follow precisely the same steps, except click "Turn off the guest account" in the final step.)

Authenticate Yourself: User Account Control

You can't work in Windows 8 very long before encountering the dialog box shown in Figure 24-7. It appears anytime you install a new program or try to change an important setting on your PC. (Throughout Windows, a colorful 🛡 icon next to a button or link indicates a change that will produce this message box.)

Clearly, Microsoft chose the name User Account Control (UAC) to put a positive spin on a fairly intrusive security feature; calling it the IYW (Interrupt Your Work) box probably wouldn't have sounded like so much fun.

Why do these boxes pop up? In the olden days, nasties like spyware and viruses could install themselves invisibly, behind your back. That's because Windows ran in *Administrative mode* all the time, meaning it left the door open for anyone and anything to make important changes to your PC. Unfortunately, that included viruses.

Windows 8, on the other hand, runs in *Standard* mode all the time. Whenever somebody or some program wants to make a big change to your system—something that ought to have the permission of an *administrator* (page 728)—the UAC box alerts you. If you click Continue, Windows elevates (opens) the program's permissions settings just long enough to make the change.

Most of the time, *you* are the one making the changes, which can make the UAC box a bit annoying. But if that UAC dialog box ever appears by *itself*, you'll know something evil is afoot on your PC, and you'll have the chance to shut it down.

How you get past the UAC box—how you *authenticate yourself*—depends on the kind of account you have:

- **If you're an administrator,** the UAC box generally doesn't appear at all. Even when you click a link marked with a 🛡 icon, you generally blow right past it. (That's a welcome change from Vista, when you'd see the UAC box for no good reason—you'd hit Enter to dismiss it.)

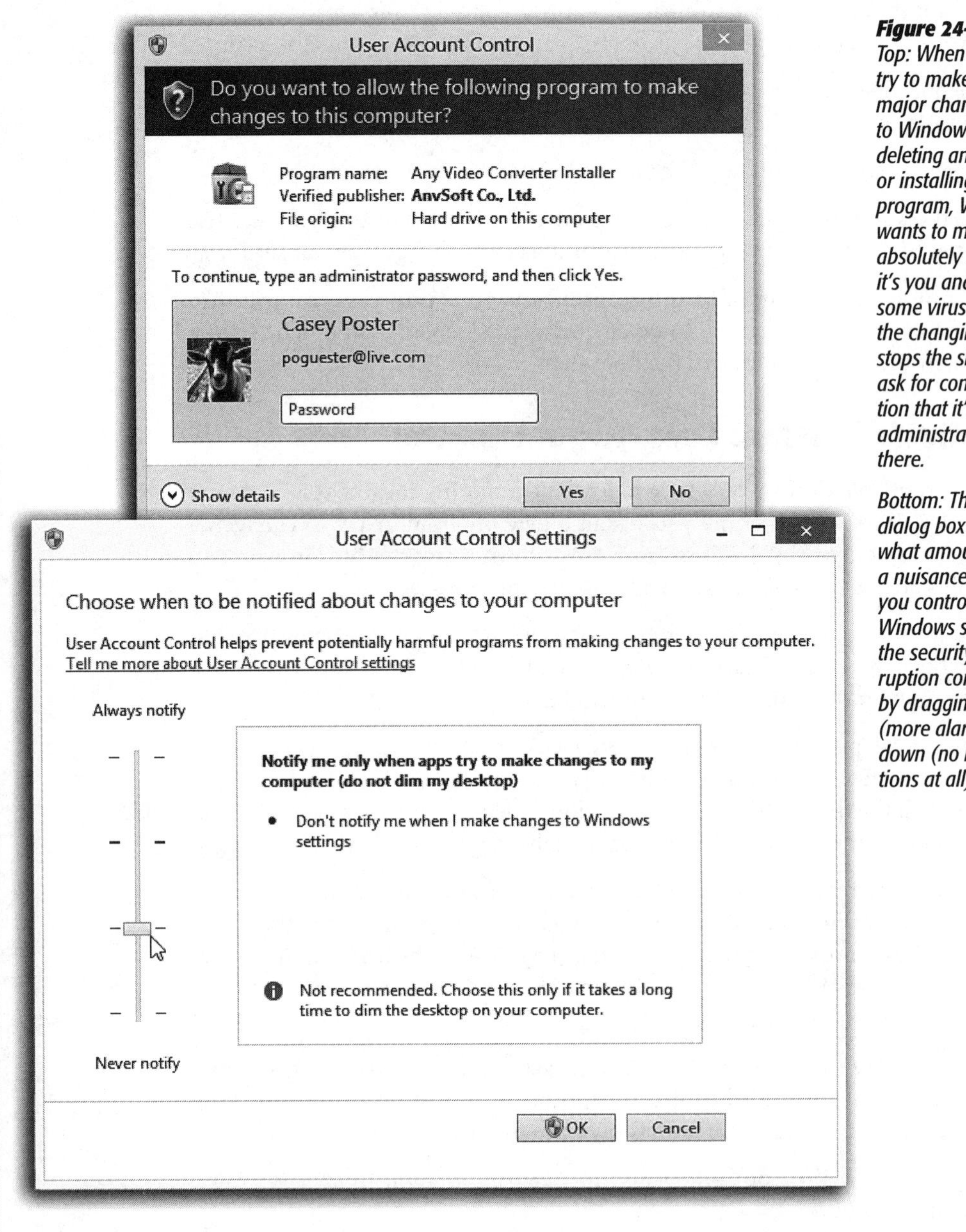

Figure 24-7: *Top: When you try to make a major change to Windows, like deleting an account or installing a new program, Windows wants to make absolutely sure that it's you and not some virus doing the changing. So it stops the show to ask for confirmation that it's you, an administrator, out there.*

Bottom: This dialog box offers what amounts to a nuisance slider; you control where Windows stands on the security/interruption continuum by dragging it up (more alarmist) or down (no interruptions at all).

- **If you're a Standard account holder,** the UAC dialog box requires the password of an administrator. You're supposed to call an administrator over to your desk to indicate his permission to proceed by entering his own name and password.

Questions? Yes, you in the back?

- **Why does the screen go dark around the dialog box?**

  That's another security measure. It's designed to prevent evil software from tricking you by displaying a *fake* Windows dialog box. Windows darkens and freezes everything on the screen except the one, true Windows dialog box: the UAC box.

- **Can I turn off the UAC interruptions?**

  Well, yes. But listen: You should be grateful that they don't appear *nearly* as often as they used to, when they became a profound nuisance.

  All right then. If even the few remaining interruptions are too much for you, you can turn them off altogether. Open the Start screen. Type *uac;* select Settings, and then "Change User Account Control settings."

  You get the dialog box shown at bottom in Figure 24-7. If you drag the slider all the way to the bottom, you won't be interrupted by UAC boxes at all.

  This truly isn't a good idea, though. You're sending your PC right back to the days of Windows XP, when any sneaky old malware could install itself or change your system settings without your knowledge. Do this only on a PC that's not connected to a network or the Internet, for example, or maybe when you, the all-knowing system administrator, are trying to troubleshoot and the UAC interruptions are slowing you down.

Local Users and Groups

The control panels you've read about so far in this chapter are designed for simplicity and convenience, but not for power. Windows offers a second way to create, edit, and delete accounts: an alternative window that, depending on your taste for technical sophistication, is either intimidating and technical or liberating and flexible.

It's called the Local Users and Groups console.

Opening the Console

The quickest way to open up the Local Users and Groups window is to press ⊞+R to open the Run dialog box, type out *Lusrmgr.msc,* and authenticate yourself if necessary. (Microsoft swears that "Lusrmgr.msc" is *not* short for "loser manager," even though network administrators might hear that in their heads.)

The Local Users and Groups console appears, as shown in Figure 24-8.

In this console, you have complete control over the local accounts (and groups, as described in a moment) on your computer. This is the real, raw, unshielded command center, intended for power users who aren't easily frightened.

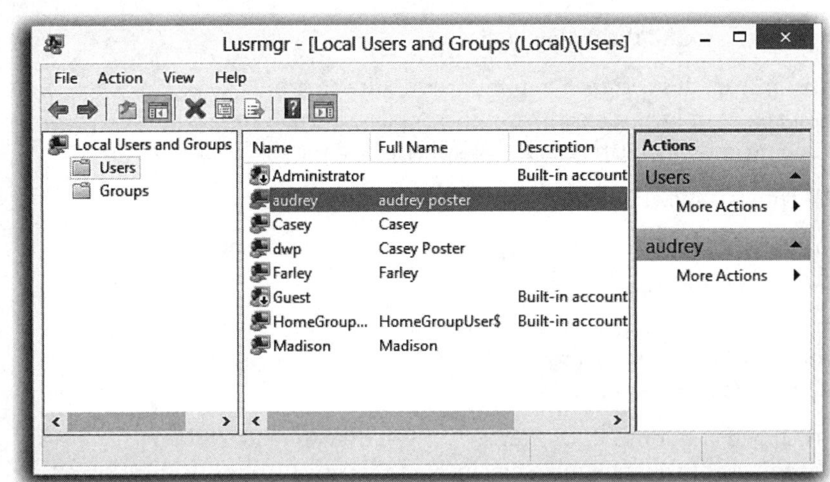

***Figure 24-8:** Local Users and Groups is a Microsoft Management Console (MMC) snap-in. MMC is a shell program that lets you run most of Windows' system administration applications. An MMC snap-in typically has two panes. You select an item in the left (scope) pane to see information about it displayed in the right (detail) pane.*

If you're on a small network, remember that you'll have to create a new account for each person who might want to use this computer—or even to access its files from across the network. If you use the Local Users and Groups console to create and edit these accounts, you have much more control over the new account holder's freedom than you do with the User Accounts control panel.

Creating a New Account

To create a new account in the Local Users and Groups console, start by double-clicking the Users folder in the middle of the window. It opens to show you a list of the accounts already on the machine. It includes not only the accounts you created during the Windows 8 installation (and thereafter), but also the Guest and secret Administrator accounts described earlier in this chapter.

To create a new account, choose Action→New User. In the New User dialog box (Figure 24-9), type a name for the account, the person's full name, and, if you like, a description. (The description can be anything you like, although Microsoft no doubt has in mind "Shipping manager" rather than "Short and balding.")

In the Password and Confirm Password text boxes, specify the password your new colleague will need to access the account. Its complexity and length are up to your innate sense of paranoia.

Tip: If you can't create a new account, it's probably because you don't have the proper privileges yourself. You must have an Administrator account or belong to the Administrators *group* (page 728).

If you turn off the "User must change password at next logon" checkbox, then you can turn on options like these:

- **User cannot change password.** This person won't be allowed to change the password you've just made up. (Some system administrators like to maintain sole control over the account passwords on their computers.)

Figure 24-9: *When you first create a new user, the "User must change password at next logon" checkbox is turned on. It's telling you that no matter what password you make up when creating the account, your colleague will be asked to make up a new one the first time he logs in. This way, you can assign a simple password (or no password at all) to all new accounts, but your underlings will still be free to devise passwords of their own choosing, and the accounts won't go unprotected.*

- **Password never expires.** Using software rules called *local security policies*, an administrator can make account passwords expire after a specific time, periodically forcing employees to make up new ones. It's a security measure designed to foil intruders who somehow get hold of the existing passwords. But if you turn on this option, then the person whose account you're creating will be able to use the same password indefinitely, no matter what the local security policy says.

- **Account is disabled.** When you turn on this box, the account holder won't be able to log on. You might use this option when, for example, somebody goes on sabbatical—it's not as drastic a step as deleting the account, because you can always reactivate the account by turning the checkbox off. You can also use this option to set up certain accounts in advance, which you then activate when the time comes by turning this checkbox off again.

Note: When an account is disabled, a circled ↓ badge appears on its icon in the Local Users and Groups console. (You may have noticed that the Guest account appears this way when you first install Windows.)

When you click the Create button, you add the new account to the console, and you make the dialog box blank again, ready for you to create another new account, if necessary. When you're finished creating accounts, click Close to return to the main console window.

Groups

As you may have guessed from its name, you can also use the Local Users and Groups window to create *groups*—named collections of account holders.

Suppose you work for a small company that uses a workgroup network. You want to be able to share various files on your computer with certain other people on the network. You'd like to be able to permit them to access some folders but not others. Smooth network operator that you are, you solve this problem by assigning *permissions* to the appropriate files and folders.

In fact, you can specify different access permissions to *each file for each person.* But if you had to set up these access privileges manually for every file on your hard drive, for every account holder on the network, you'd go out of your mind.

That's where groups come in. You can create one group—called Trusted Comrades, for example—and fill it with the names of every account holder who should be allowed to access your files. Thereafter, it's a piece of cake to give everybody in that group access to a certain folder, in one swift step. You end up having to create only one permission assignment for each file, instead of one for each *person* for each file.

Furthermore, if a new employee joins the company, you can simply add her to the group. Instantly, she has exactly the right access to the right files and folders, without your having to do any additional work.

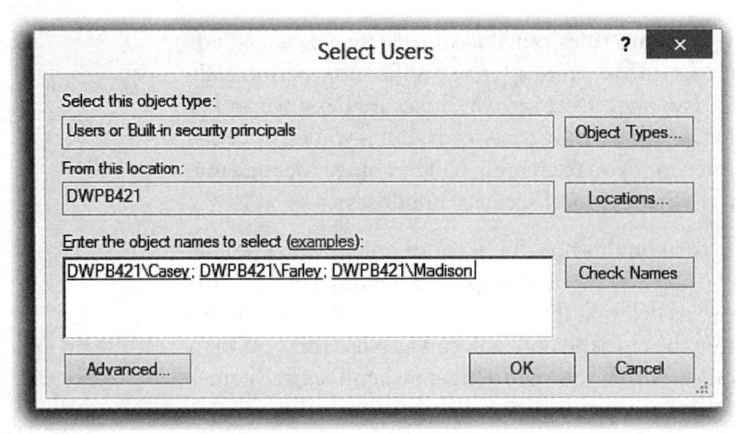

Figure 24-10: *The New Group dialog box lets you specify the members of the group you're creating. A group can have any number of members, and a person can be a member of any number of groups.*

Creating a group

To create a new group, click the Groups folder in the left side of the Local Users and Groups console (Figure 24-8). Choose Action→New Group. Into the appropriate boxes (Figure 24-10), type a name for the group, and a description, if you like. Then click OK.

A Select Users dialog box appears. Here you can specify the members of your new group. Type the account holders' names into the text box, separated by semicolons, and then click Check Names to make sure you spelled them right. (You can always add more members to the group, or remove them, later.)

Finally, click OK to close the dialog box, and then click Create to add the group to the list in the console. The box appears empty again, ready for you to create another group.

Built-in groups

You may have noticed that even the first time you opened the Users and Groups window, a few group names appeared there already. That's because Windows comes with a canned list of ready-made groups that Microsoft hopes will save you some time.

For example, when you use the User Accounts control panel program to set up a new account, Windows automatically places that person into the Standard or Administrators group, depending on whether or not you made him an administrator. In fact, that's how Windows knows what powers and freedoms this person is supposed to have.

Here are some of the built-in groups on a Windows 8 computer:

- **Administrators.** Members of the Administrators group have complete control over every aspect of the computer. They can modify any setting, create or delete accounts and groups, install or remove any software, and modify or delete any file.

  But as Spider-Man's uncle might say, with great power comes great responsibility. Administrator powers make it possible to screw up your operating system in thousands of major and minor ways, either on purpose or by accident. That's why it's a good idea to keep the number of Administrator accounts to a minimum—and even to avoid using one for everyday purposes yourself.

Note: The Power Users group was a big deal in Windows XP. Power Users had fewer powers than Administrators but still more than mere mortals in the Users group. But Microsoft felt that they added complexity and represented yet another potential security hole. In Windows 8, this group is abandoned.

- **Users.** Standard account holders are members of this group. They can access their own Start screen and desktop settings, their own Documents folder, the Shared Documents folder, and whatever folders they create themselves—but they can't change any computer-wide settings, Windows system files, or program files.

  If you're a member of this group, you can install new programs—but you'll be the only one who can use them. That's by design; any problems introduced by that program (viruses, for example) are limited to your files and not spread to the whole system.

If you're the administrator, it's a good idea to put most new account holders into this group.

- **Guests.** If you're in this group, you have pretty much the same privileges as members of the Users group. You lose only a few nonessential perks, like the ability to read the computer's *system event log* (a record of behind-the-scenes technical happenings).
- **In addition to these basic groups,** there are some special-purpose groups like Backup Operators, Replicator, Cryptographic Operators, Event Log Readers, and so on. These are all groups with specialized privileges, designed for high-end network administration. You can double-click one (or widen its Description column) to read all about it.

Note: You can add an individual account to as many groups as you like. That person will have the accumulated rights and privileges of all those groups.

Figure 24-11:
In the Properties dialog box for a User account, you can change the full name or description, modify the password options, and add this person to or remove this person from a group. The Properties dialog box for a group is simpler still, containing only a list of the group's members.

Modifying Users and Groups

To edit an account or group, just double-click its name in the Local Users and Groups window. A Properties dialog box appears, as shown in Figure 24-11.

You can also change an account password by right-clicking the name and choosing Set Password from the shortcut menu. (But see page 742 for some cautions about this process.)

Fast User Switching

Suppose you're signed in and you've got things just the way you like them. You have 11 programs open in carefully arranged windows, your Web browser is downloading some gigantic file, and you're composing an important speech in Microsoft Word. Now Robin, a coworker/family member/fellow student, wants to duck in to do a quick email check.

In the old days, you might have rewarded Robin with eye-rolling and heavy sighs, or worse. If you chose to accommodate the request, you would have had to shut down your whole ecosystem—interrupting the download, closing your windows, saving your work, and exiting your programs. You would have had to log off completely.

Thanks to Fast User Switching, however, none of that is necessary. See Figure 24-12.

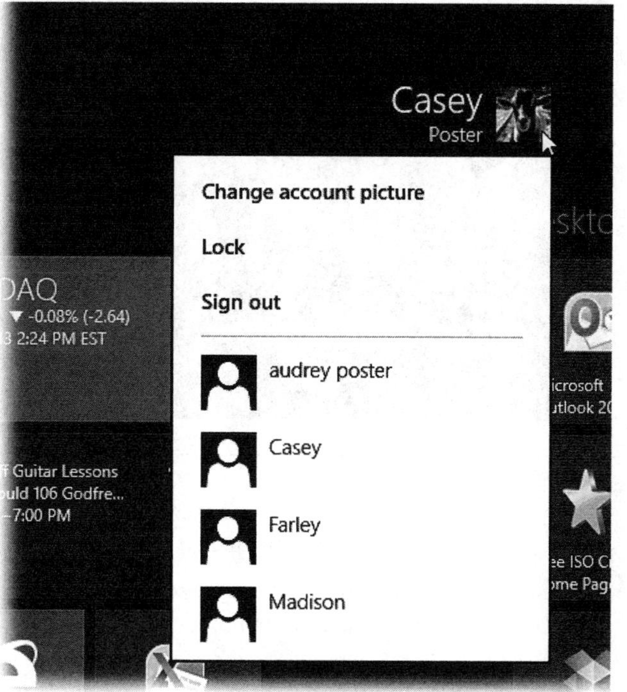

***Figure 24-12:** To log in while someone else is logged in, just press the magic keystroke ⊞ (to return to the Start screen), and then click the current user's account photo.*

The words "Signed in" beneath your name indicate that you haven't actually logged off. Instead, Windows has *memorized* the state of affairs in your account—complete with all open windows, documents, and programs—and shoved it into the background.

Robin can now click the Robin button to sign in normally, do a little work, or look something up. When Robin logs out, the Accounts screen comes back once again, at which point *you* can log back on. Without having to wait more than a couple of seconds, you find yourself exactly where you began, with all your programs and documents still open and running—an enormous timesaver.

Logging On

When it comes to the screens you encounter when you log onto a Windows computer, your mileage may vary. What you see depends on how your PC has been set up. For example:

You Get the Accounts Screen

This is what people on standalone or workgroup computers see most of the time (Figure 24-13).

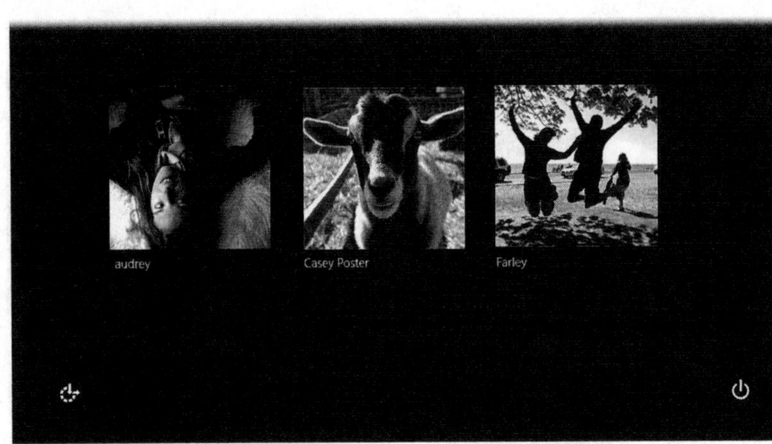

Figure 24-13: *If you click the ⏻ button (lower-right corner of the screen), you can make the computer turn off, restart, sleep, and so on—maybe because you're in a sudden panic over the amount of work you have to do. Or you can just log in. If you click the lower-left button, you access Narrator, Magnifier, and other accessibility tools.*

To sign in, click your account icon. If no password is required for your account, then you proceed to your Start screen with no further interruption.

If there *is* a password associated with your account, you see a place for it. Type your password and then press Enter.

There's no limit to the number of times you can try to type in a password. With each incorrect guess, you're told, "The user name or password is incorrect," and an OK button appears to let you try again. The second time you try, your password hint appears, too.

Tip: If your Caps Lock key is pressed, another balloon lets you know. Otherwise, because you can't see anything on the screen as you type except dots, you might be trying to type a lowercase password with all capital letters.

You Zoom Straight to the Desktop

If you're the *only* account holder, and you've set up no password for yourself, you can cruise all the way to the desktop without any stops. The setup steps appear in the box on page 741.

This password-free scenario, of course, is not very secure; any evildoer who walks by your machine when you're in the bathroom has complete access to all your files (and protected Web sites). But if you work in a home office, for example, where the threat of privacy invasion isn't very great, it's by far the most convenient arrangement.

You Get the "Press Ctrl-Alt-Delete to Begin" Message

You or your friendly network geek has added your PC to a domain while installing Windows 8 and activated the Require Users to Press Ctrl-Alt-Delete option. This is the most secure configuration, and also the least convenient.

Profiles

As you read earlier in this chapter, every document, icon, and preference setting related to your account resides in a single folder: By default, it's the one bearing your name in the Local Disk (C:)→Users folder. This folder's friendly name is your Personal folder, but to network geeks, it's known as your *user profile.*

The Public Profile

Each account holder has a user profile. But your PC also has a couple of profiles that aren't linked to human beings' accounts.

Have you ever noticed, for example, that not everything you actually see on your Start screen and on your desktop is, in fact, in *your* user profile folder?

Part of the solution to this mystery is the Public profile, which also lurks in the Users folder (Figure 24-14). As you can probably tell by its name, this folder stores many of the same kinds of settings your profile folder does—except that anything in (C:)→Users→Public→Desktop appears on *everybody's* desktop.

All this is a long-winded way of suggesting another way to make some icon available to everybody with an account on your machine. Drag it into the Desktop folder inside the Public folder. (This folder is ordinarily hidden; it appears only when you un-hide Windows' protected files and folders; see page 224.)

But if you're wondering where the common Start-screen items are, you'll have to look somewhere else. If you're prowling around your hard drive, you'll find them in (C:)→ProgramData→Microsoft→Windows→Start Menu. (The ProgramData folder is also ordinarily hidden.)

Whose software is it, anyway?

These locations also offer a handy solution to the "Whose software is it, anyway?" conundrum, the burning question of whose Start screen and desktop reflect new software that you've installed using your own account.

Some software installers ask if you'd like the new program to show up only on your Start screen, or on *everybody's* Start screen. But not every installer is this thoughtful. Some installers automatically deposit their new software into the ProgramData and Public folders, thereby making its Start screen and desktop icons available to everybody when they log on.

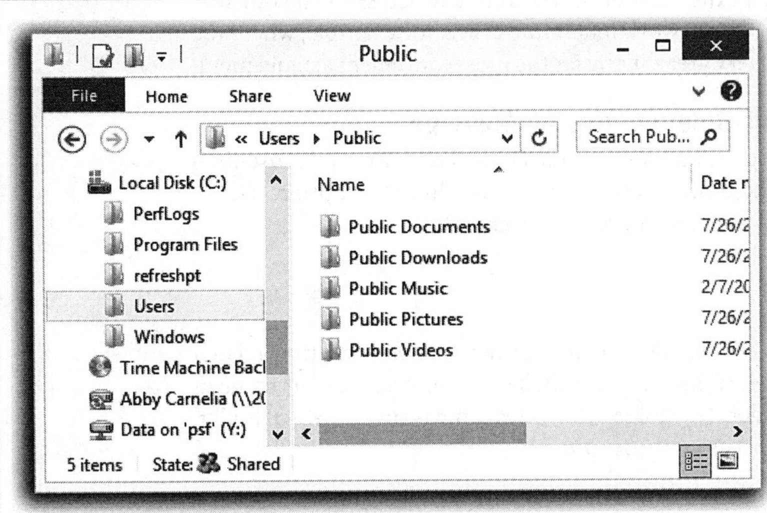

***Figure 24-14:** Behind the scenes, Windows maintains another profile folder, whose subfolders closely parallel those in your own. What you see—the contents of the Desktop folder, Documents folder, Favorites list, and so on—is a combination of what's in your own user profile folder and what's in the Public folder.*

On the other hand, some installers may deposit a new software program only into *your* account (or that of whoever is logged in at the moment). In that case, other account holders won't be able to use the program at all, even if they know it's been installed, because their own Start screens and Desktop folders won't reflect the installation. Worse, some people, not seeing the program's name on their Start screens, might not realize that you've already installed it—and may well install it *again*.

One possible solution is to open *your* Programs folder (into the address bar at the top of an Explorer window, type *C:\Users\username\AppData\Roaming\Microsoft\Windows\Start Menu\Programs)*. Copy the newly installed icon, and then paste it into the "everybody" profile folder (C:\ProgramData\Microsoft\Windows\Start Menu\Programs).

Repeat with the Desktop folder, if you'd like everyone to see a desktop icon for the new program. To open the shared desktop folder, open (C:)→Users→Public→Desktop. (You'll have to make the Desktop folder visible first—see "Show hidden files, folders, and drives" on page 224—and then make it invisible again afterward.) You've just made that software available and visible to everybody who logs onto the computer.

The Default User Profile

When you create a new account, who decides what the desktop picture will be—and the Start screen configuration, the assortment of desktop icons, and so on?

Well, Microsoft does, of course—but you can change all that. What a newly created account holder sees is only a reflection of the Default user profile. It's yet another folder—this one usually hidden—in your (C:)→Users folder, and it's the common starting point for all profiles.

If you'd like to make some changes to that starting point, turn on "Show hidden files, folders, and drives" (page 224). Then open the (C:)→Users→Default folder, and make whatever changes you like.

NTFS Permissions: Protecting Your Stuff

There's one final aspect of user accounts that's worth mentioning: *NTFS permissions,* a technology that's a core part of Windows 8's security system. Using this feature, you can specify exactly which coworkers are allowed to open which files and folders on your machine. In fact, you can also specify *how much* access each person has. You can dictate, for example, that Gomez and Morticia aren't allowed to open your Fourth-Quarter Projections spreadsheet at all, that Fred and Ginger can open it but not make changes, and George and Gracie can both open it and make changes.

Your colleagues will encounter the permissions you've set up like this in two different situations: when tapping into your machine from across the network or when sitting down at it and logging in using their own names and passwords. In either case, the NTFS permissions you set up protect your files and folders equally well.

Tip: In Chapter 27, you can read about a very similar form of access privileges called *share permissions.* There's a big difference between share permissions and the NTFS permissions described here, though: Share permissions keep people out of your stuff only when they try to access your PC from *over the network.*

Actually, there are other differences, too. NTFS permissions offer more gradations of access. And using NTFS permissions, you can declare individual *files*—not just folders—accessible or inaccessible to specific coworkers. Read on for details.

Using NTFS permissions is most decidedly a power-user technique because of the added complexity it introduces. Entire books have been written on the topic of NTFS permissions alone.

You've been warned.

Setting Up NTFS Permissions

To change the permissions for an NTFS file or folder, you open its Properties dialog box by right-clicking its icon and then choosing Properties from the shortcut menu. Click the Security tab (Figure 24-15).

Step 1: Specify the person

The top of the Security tab lists the people and groups that have been granted or denied permissions to the selected file or folder. When you click a name in the list, the Permissions box at the bottom of the dialog box shows you how much access that person or group has.

The first step in assigning permissions, then, is to click Edit. You see an editable version of the dialog box shown in Figure 24-15.

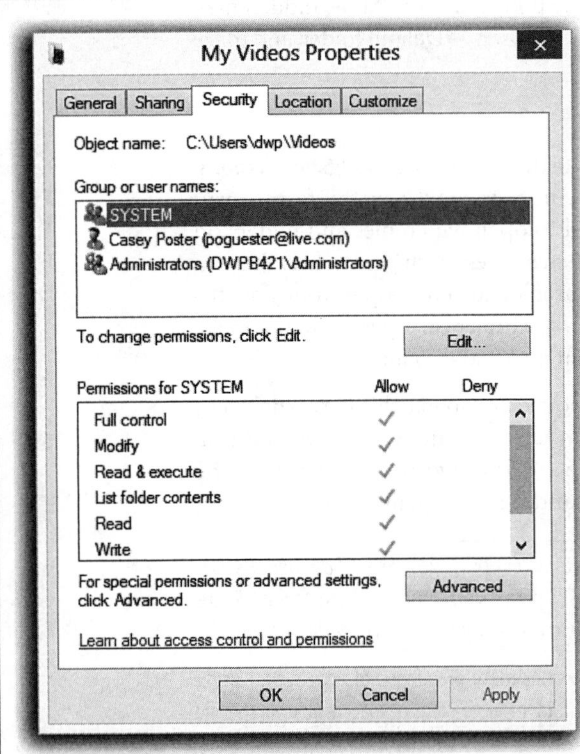

Figure 24-15:
The Security tab of an NTFS folder's Properties dialog box. If you have any aspirations to be a Windows power user, get used to this dialog box. You're going to see it a lot, because almost every icon on a Windows system–files, folders, disks, printers–has a Security tab like this one.

If the person or group isn't listed, then click Edit, then Add to display the Select Users or Groups dialog box, where you can type them in (Figure 24-16).

Tip: Instead of typing in names one at a time, as shown in Figure 24-16, you can also choose them from a list, which lets you avoid spelling mistakes and having to guess at the variations. To do so, click the Advanced button to display an expanded version of the dialog box, and then click Find Now to search for all the accounts and groups on the computer. Finally, in the resulting list, click the names of the people and groups you want to add (Ctrl-click to select more than one at a time). Click OK to add them to the previous dialog box, and then click OK again to add the selected users and groups to the Security tab.

If you've used Windows 2000, you might wonder why this process is so much more convoluted in Windows 8. The answer is: Good question!

Step 2: Specify the permissions

Once you've added the users and groups you need to the list on the Security tab, you can highlight each one and set permissions for it. You do that by turning on the Allow or Deny checkboxes at the bottom half of the dialog box.

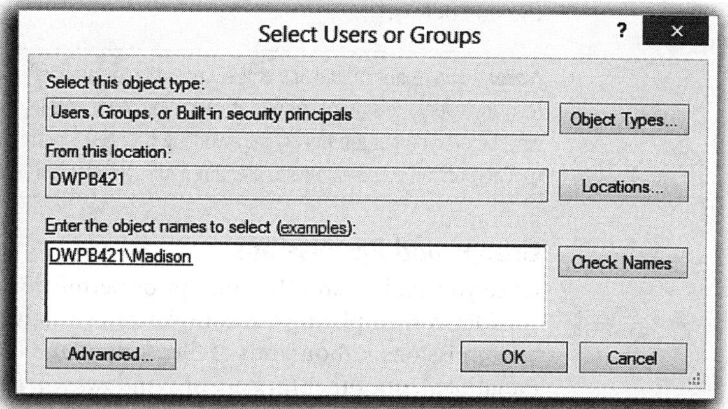

Figure 24-16: *Type the names of the people or groups in the "Enter the object names to select" box at the bottom, trying not to feel depersonalized by Microsoft's reference to you as an "object." If you're adding more than one name, separate them with semicolons. Because remembering exact spellings can be iffy, click Check Names to confirm that these are indeed legitimate account holders. Finally, click OK to insert them into the list on the Security tab.*

The different degrees of freedom break down as follows (they're listed here from least to most control, even though that's not how they're listed in the dialog box):

- **List folder contents,** available only for folders, means the selected individuals can see (but not necessarily open) the files and folders inside. That may sound obvious—but believe it or not, if you *don't* turn on this option, the affected people won't even be able to see what's in this folder. The folder will just appear empty.
- **Read** lets people examine the contents of the file or folder but not make changes. (They can also examine the permissions settings of these files and folders—the ones you're setting up right now.)
- **Read & Execute** is a lot like Read, except that it also lets people run any programs they find inside the affected folder. When applied to a folder, furthermore, this permission adds the ability to *traverse* folders. (Traversing means directly opening inner folders even when you're not allowed to open the outer folder. You might get to an inner folder by double-clicking a shortcut icon, for example, or by typing the folder's path into the address bar of a window.)
- **Write** is like Read, but it adds the freedom to make and save changes to the file. When applied to a folder, this permission means that people can create new files and folders inside it.
- **Modify** includes all the abilities of the Write and Read & Execute levels, plus the ability to *delete* files or folders.

- **Full control** confers complete power over the file or folder. The selected person or group can do anything they like with it, including trashing it or its contents, changing its permissions, taking ownership of it (away from you, if they like), and so on.

Of course, turning on Allow grants that level of freedom to the specified user or group, and turning it off takes away that freedom. (For details on the Deny checkbox, see the box below.)

Note: If you're not careful, it's entirely possible to "orphan" a file or folder (or even your entire drive) by revoking everyone's permission to it, even your own, making it *completely* inaccessible by anyone. That's why, before you get too deeply into working with NTFS permissions, you might consider creating an extra user account on your system and granting it full control for all your drives, just in case something goes wrong.

Groups and Permissions

Once you understand the concept of permissions, and you've enjoyed a thorough shudder contemplating the complexity of a network administrator's job (six levels of permissions × thousands of files × thousands of employees = way too many permutations), one other mystery of Windows will fully snap into focus: the purpose of *groups*, introduced on page 748.

On those pages, you can read about groups as canned categories, complete with predefined powers over the PC, into which you can put different individuals to save yourself the time of adjusting their permissions and privileges individually. As it turns out, each of the ready-made groups also comes with predefined *permissions* over the files and folders on your hard drive.

Here, for example, is how the system grants permissions to the items in your Windows folder for the Users and Administrators groups:

FREQUENTLY ASKED QUESTION

Allow vs. Deny

Why do I see both Allow and Deny checkboxes in the Permissions dialog box? Isn't not allowing permission the same as denying it?

In this case, no. "Deny" permissions always take precedence over "Allow" permissions.

For example, if somebody has been granted access to a file or folder because he's a member of a group, you can explicitly revoke his permission by using the Deny checkboxes for his account. You've just overridden the group permission, just for him, leaving the rest of the group's permissions intact.

You can also use the Deny checkboxes to override permissions granted by inheritance from a parent folder. For example, you can grant somebody access to the C: drive by sharing it and assigning her Allow permissions to it, but then prevent her from accessing the C:\Program Files folder by sharing that and denying her permission.

	Users	Administrators
Full Control		X
Modify		X
Read & Execute	X	X
List Folder Contents	X	X
Read	X	X
Write		X

If you belong to the Users group, you have the List Folder Contents permission, which means you can see what's in the Windows folder; the Read permission, which means you can open up anything you find inside; and the Read & Execute permission, which means you can run programs in that folder (which is essential for Windows itself to run). But people in the Users group aren't allowed to change or delete anything in the Windows folder, or to put anything else inside. Windows is protecting itself against the mischievous and the clueless.

Members of the Administrators group have all those abilities and more—they also have Modify and Write permissions, which let them add new files and folders to the Windows folder (so that, for example, they can install a new software program on the machine).

When Permissions Collide

If you've successfully absorbed all this information about permissions, one thing should be clear: People in the Administrators group ought to be able to change or delete any file in your Windows folder. After all, they have the Modify permission, which ought to give them that power.

In fact, they can move or delete anything in any folder *in* the Windows folder, because the first cardinal rule of NTFS permissions is this:

NTFS permissions travel downstream, from outer folders to inner ones.

In other words, if you have the Modify and Write permissions to a folder, then you ought to have the same permissions for every file and folder inside it.

But in Windows XP, there was something called the Power Users group. It's been turned off in Windows 8, but for the sake of illustration, let's say you're part of it. You'd find that you can't, in fact, delete any files or folders in the Windows folder. That's because each of them comes with Modify and Write permissions turned *off* for Power Users, even though the folder that encloses them has those permissions turned on.

Why would Microsoft go to this trouble? Because it wanted to prevent people in this group from inadvertently changing or deleting important Windows files—and yet it wanted these people to be able to put *new* files into the Windows folder, so they could install new programs.

This is a perfect example of the second cardinal rule of NTFS permissions:

NTFS permissions that have been explicitly applied to a file or folder always override inherited permissions.

Here's another example: Suppose your sister, the technical whiz of the household, has given you Read, Write, Modify, Read & Execute, and List Folder Contents permissions to her own Documents folder. Now you can read, change, or delete any file there. But she can still protect an individual document or folder *inside* her Documents folder—the BirthdayPartyPlans.doc file, for example—by denying you all permissions to it. You'll be able to open anything else in there, but not that file.

Believe it or not, NTFS permissions get even more complicated, thanks to the third cardinal rule:

Permissions accumulate as you burrow downward through subfolders.

Now suppose your sister has given you the Read and List Folder Contents permissions to her Documents folder—a "look but don't touch" policy. Thanks to the first cardinal rule, you automatically get the same permissions to every file and folder *inside* Documents.

Suppose one of these inner folders is called Grocery Lists. If she grants you the Modify and Write permissions to the Grocery Lists folder so you can add items to the shopping list, you end up having Read, Modify, *and* Write permissions for every file in that folder. Those files have *accumulated* permissions—they got the Read permission from Documents, and the Modify and Write permissions from the Grocery Lists folder.

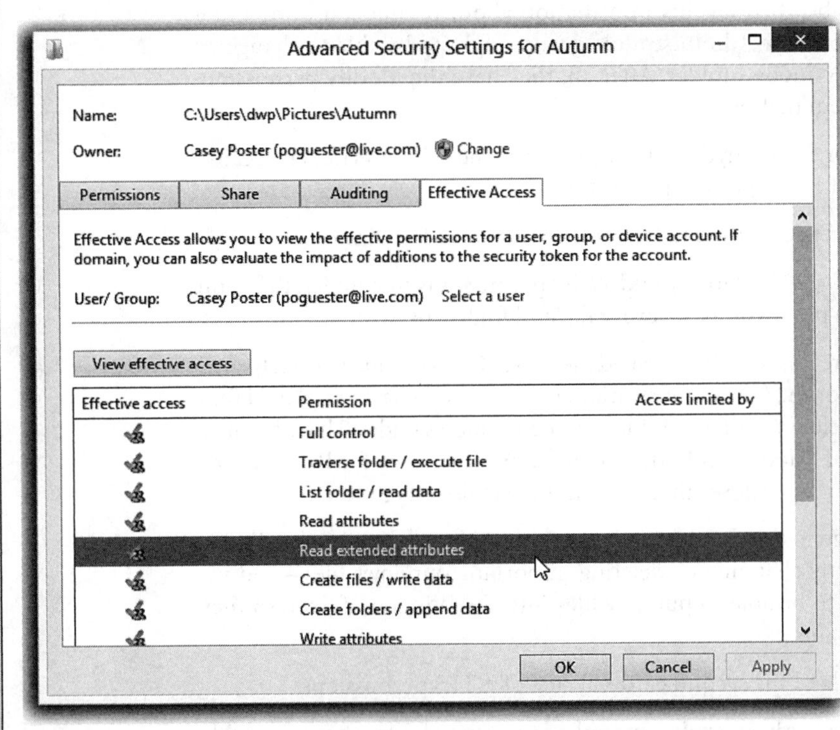

Figure 24-17: *The Effective Permissions tab for an NTFS folder. Note that you can't turn these checkboxes on or off; this is a read-only screen that tells you what permissions the selected user or group has for the file or folder. You can't modify the permissions here. You can't tell from this display how these effective permissions have been calculated, either (that is, where the permissions have been inherited from).*

Because these layers of inherited permissions can get dizzyingly complex, Microsoft has prepared a little cheat sheet, a dialog box that tells you the bottom line, the net result—the *effective* permissions. To see it, follow these steps:

1. **Click the Advanced button on the Security tab.**

   The Advanced Security Settings dialog box appears.

2. **Click the Effective Access tab; click "Select a user."**

   Now you see the same Select User or Group dialog box you saw earlier when you were creating permissions.

3. **Click the user or group whose effective permissions you want to see, and then click OK.**

   You return to the Effective Access tab.

4. **Click "View effective access."**

   You now see checkmarks next to the permissions that are in effect, taking into account folder-permission inheritance and all other factors for the user or group of that particular file or folder (Figure 24-17).

CHAPTER

25

Setting Up a Small Network

It's a rare Windows machine indeed that isn't connected, sooner or later, to some kind of home or office (known to nerds as a *local area network,* or *LAN*). And no wonder: The payoff is considerable. Once you've created a network, you can copy files from one machine to another just as you'd drag files between folders on your own PC. You can store your music or photo files on one computer and play them on any other. Everyone on the network can consult the same database, phone book, or calendar. When the workday's done, you can play games over the network.

Most importantly, you can share a single printer, cable modem or DSL Internet connection, fax modem, or phone line among all the PCs in the house.

If you work at a biggish company, you probably work on a *domain network*—the big, centrally managed type found in corporations. You, lucky thing, won't have to fool around with building or designing a network, because your job, and your PC, presumably came with a fully functioning network (and a fully functioning geek responsible for running it).

If you work at home, or if you're responsible for setting up a network in a smaller office, this chapter is for you. It guides you through the construction of a less formal *workgroup network,* which ordinary mortals can put together.

Setting up a network has never approached the simplicity of, say, setting up a desk lamp. But in Windows 8, there's some terrific news on this front. A feature called *Homegroups* makes the setup incredibly fast and easy—*if* all your PCs are running Windows 7 or 8, and *if* you have no particular need to keep your music, photo, and video collections private from the rest of your family members.

If you don't meet those requirements, you can still use the older, more complex Windows networking methods. They'll take you an afternoon to set up and understand—but this chapter will hold your hand.

Kinds of Networks

You can connect your PCs using any of several different kinds of gear. Many of the world's offices are wired with *Ethernet cable,* but, as you probably know, wireless networks are very popular for small offices and homes. Here and there, a few renegades are even installing networking systems that rely on the phone or power lines already in the walls. Here's an overview of the most popular networking systems.

Note: Be sure that whatever networking gear you buy is compatible with Windows 8, either by checking logos on the package or by checking the maker's Web site. Networking is complicated enough without having to troubleshoot some gadget that's not designed for Win8.

Ethernet

Ethernet is the world's most popular networking protocol. It gives you fast, reliable, cheap, trouble-free communication. All you need are three components:

- **Network adapters.** An Ethernet jack is built into virtually every Win8-compatible PC. That's your *network adapter*—the circuitry that provides the Ethernet jack (Figure 25-1). You may also hear a network adapter called a *network interface card* or NIC ("nick").

  If your machine doesn't have an Ethernet jack—plenty of laptops and tablets don't—you can add one. Adapters are available as internal cards, external USB attachments, or laptop cards.

- **A router.** If you have a cable modem or DSL connection to the Internet, a *router* (about $60) distributes that Internet signal to all the computers on your network. (The dialog boxes in Windows call these devices *gateways,* although almost no one else does.)

  Routers with four or eight ports (that is, Ethernet jacks where you can plug in computers) are popular in homes and small offices.

  It's worth noting that you can inexpensively expand your network by plugging a *hub* or *switch* into one of the router's jacks. Hubs and switches are similar-looking little boxes that offer *another* five or eight Ethernet jacks, connecting all your computers together. (A *switch* is more intelligent than a hub. It's more selective when sending data to the right PCs on your network; as a result, the bits and bytes move a little faster.)

Tip: There's also such a thing as a router with both physical Ethernet jacks *and* wireless antennas that broadcast the signal throughout your place.

To set up a router, plug it into your cable or DSL modem using an Ethernet cable. Restart the cable modem. Now use whatever software came with the router to set up its security features. Often, the software is actually built into the router; you're supposed to view it by opening up a special page in your Web browser, of all things.

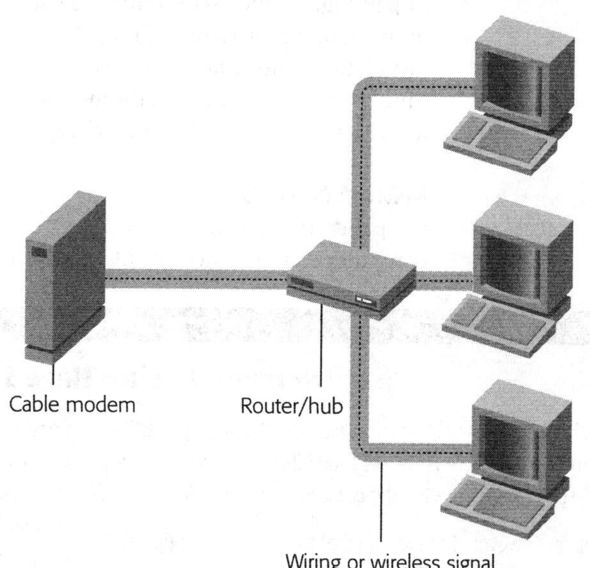

Figure 25-1:
Top: The Ethernet cable is connected to a computer at one end, and the router (shown here) at the other end. The computers communicate through the router; there's no direct connection between any two computers. The front of the router has little lights for each connector port, which light up only on the ports in use. You can watch the lights flash as the computers communicate with one another.

Bottom: Here's what a typical "I've got three PCs in the house, and I'd like them to share my cable modem" setup might look like.

The router then logs onto your Internet service and stands ready to transmit Internet data to and from all the computers on your network.

As a bonus, the router provides excellent security, serving as a firewall that isolates your network computers from the Internet and keeps out hackers. (See Chapter 14 for much more on firewalls.)

- **Ethernet cables.** The cables used for most Ethernet networks look something like telephone cables, but they're not the same thing—and they're definitely not interchangeable. Both the cable itself (called *10BaseT, 100BaseT,* or *Cat 5*) and the little clips at each end (*RJ-45 connectors*) are slightly fatter than those on a phone cable. You can buy Ethernet cables in a variety of lengths and colors. Each computer must be connected to the hub, switch, or router with a cable that's no longer than about 100 yards.

Tip: If you've got a computer that sits in one place, like a desktop PC, you should use an Ethernet cable even if you have a wireless network.

One reason is security (wired networks are harder for the baddies to "sniff"). Another is speed. Yes, wireless technologies like 802.11n promise speeds of 300 megabits per second, which is very, very fast. But, first of all, the real-world speed is about a third of that; second, that speed is shared among all computers on the network. As a result, if you're copying a big file across the network, it will probably go twice as fast if it's going between one wireless and one wired PC than between two wireless PCs.

Ethernet gear can be shockingly inexpensive; a search at *www.buy.com,* for example, reveals five-port Ethernet hubs for $30 from no-name companies. If you're willing to pay slightly more—$20 for the card, $50 for the hub, for example—you can get brand-name gear (like D-Link, NETGEAR, 3Com, or Linksys) whose support with installation, phone help, and driver updates through the years may reward you many times over. Setting up an Ethernet network generally goes very smoothly, but in the few cases where trouble arises, cheapo equipment is often the problem.

Network hookups

On paper, the hardware part of setting up the network is simple: Just connect each computer to the router or hub using an Ethernet cable.

UP TO SPEED

Network Devices Have Speed Limits

Ethernet cards and hubs are available in different speeds. The most common are *100BaseT* (100 Mbps, sometimes cleverly called *Fast Ethernet*) and *gigabit Ethernet* (1,000 Mbps).

Note, however, that the speed of the network has no effect on your computers' *Internet* speed–Web surfing, email downloading, and so on. The reason: Even the slowest network operates far faster than your Internet connection. Remember, the top speed of a typical broadband Internet connection is around 5 or 10 megabits per second–still many times slower than the *slowest* home network.

So why does a faster network matter? Primarily to save time when you're transferring big files between the PCs on the network. For example, you can play MP3 music files stored on another computer over a 10BaseT connection with no problems at all. However, if you plan to install video cameras all around your palatial estate and want to watch all the video feeds simultaneously, opt for Fast Ethernet–or even Gigabit Ethernet, the current Ethernet speed champ at 1,000 Mbps.

The bottom line? As you shop for gear, you may as well go for the higher speeds so you'll be ready for any high-bandwidth application that comes down the pike.

It's that "using an Ethernet cable" part that sometimes gets sticky. Depending on where your PCs are and how concerned you are about the network's appearance, this wiring process may involve drilling holes in floors or walls, stapling cables to baseboard trim, or calling in an electrician to do the job.

When all your computers are in the same room, you can run the cables along the walls and behind the furniture. If you have to run cables between rooms, you can secure the cables to the floor or baseboards using staples—use the round kind that won't crush the cables—or plastic "raceways" with adhesive backing.

Of course, you might not be thrilled about having *any* exposed cables in your home or office. In that case, the installation process can be much more complicated. You should probably hire a professional cable installer to do the job—or don't use cables at all. Read on.

Wireless Networks (WiFi or 802.11)

So far, this discussion has focused on using wired Ethernet to hook up your computers. Millions of people, however, have embraced the flexibility of *WiFi* (802.11), a *wireless* networking system.

Every laptop sold today has a WiFi antenna built in. You can also add it to a desktop in the form of a wireless card or USB adapter. Once all your equipment is wireless, that's it: Your PCs can now communicate with one another.

To get onto an *existing* wireless network, follow the steps on page 438.

But if you want your *own* wireless network, right there in your own home or office, you also need a *wireless router* (about $50)—a box that connects to your router or hub and broadcasts the Internet signal to the whole building. The usual suspects—Linksys, NETGEAR, D-Link, and others—sell these routers. They're also called base stations or access points.

Now, 802.11 equipment has a range of about 150 feet, sometimes even through walls. In concept, this setup works much like a cordless phone, where the base station is plugged into the wall phone jack and a wireless handset can talk to it from anywhere in the house.

Wireless networking is not without its downsides, however. You may get intermittent service interruptions from 2.4-gigahertz cordless phones and other machinery, or even the weather. Furthermore, big metal things, or walls *containing* big metal things (like pipes) can interfere with communication among the PCs, much to the disappointment of people who work in subways and meat lockers.

A wireless network isn't as secure as a cabled network, either. It's theoretically possible for some hacker, sitting nearby, armed with "sniffing" software, to intercept the email you're sending or the Web page you're downloading. (Except secure Web sites, those marked by a little padlock in your Web browser.)

Still, nothing beats the freedom of wireless networking, particularly if you're a laptop lover; you can set up shop almost anywhere in the house or in the yard, slumped into any kind of rubbery posture. No matter where you go within your home, you're online at full speed, without hooking up a single wire.

Other Kinds of Networks

There are a couple of other network types that are worth looking into. Both are wired networks, but they use the wires you already have.

Phone line networks

Instead of going to the trouble of wiring your home with Ethernet cables, you might consider using the wiring that's already *in* your house—telephone wiring. That's the idea behind a kind of networking gear called HomePNA. With this system, you can use the network even when using the modem or talking on the phone, although you can't make a modem and a voice call simultaneously.

Unfortunately, the average American household has only two or three phone jacks in the *entire house*, meaning you don't have much flexibility in positioning your PCs.

UP TO SPEED

802.11 Networks: Regular or Supersized?

Wireless gear comes in several flavors, each offering different degrees of speed, distance, and compatibility. They have such appetizing-sounding names as 802.11b, 802.11a, 802.11g, and 802.11n.

So what's the difference? Equipment bearing the "b" label transfers data through the air at up to 11 megabits per second; the "g" system is almost five times as fast. (Traditionally, geeks measure network speeds in megabits, not megabytes. Here's a translation: The older "b" gear has a top speed of 1.4 megabytes per second, versus more than 6 megabytes per second for the "a" and "g" stuff. Remember, though, you'll usually get around half that speed. Your wireless network uses a lot of the bandwidth for such network housekeeping chores as correcting transmission errors.)

The beauty of 802.11g gear, though, is that it's backward-compatible with the older "b" gear. If your laptop has an 802.11b card, you can hop onto an 802.11g base station simultaneously with people using "g" cards. And if you have an 802.11g card, you can hop onto older base stations. You won't get better speed, of course, but at least you won't need a separate base station.

The current standard is 802.11n, which offers better speed *and* better range than its predecessors (thanks to multiple antennas). Remember, though, you won't get the better speed unless *both* your base station *and* your networking cards speak "n."

Faster equipment doesn't speed up your email and Web activity, though. A cable modem or a DSL box delivers Internet information at a fraction of the speed of your home or office network. The bottleneck is the Internet connection, not your network.

Instead, the speed boost you get with "g" gear is useful only for transferring files among computers on your network, streaming video or audio between computers (or PCs and your TV), and playing networked games.

Finally, the great thing about wireless networking is that it all works together, no matter what kind of computer you have. There's no such thing as an "Apple" wireless network or a "Windows" wireless network. All computers work with any kind of access point.

If you're trying to avoid the plaster-dust experience of installing additional wiring, consider WiFi or Powerline networking.

Power outlet networks

Here's another way to connect your computers without rewiring the building: Use the electrical wiring that's already in your walls. Unlike phone jacks, electrical outlets are usually available in every room in the house.

If you buy *Powerline adapters* (also called HomePlug adapters), you get very fast speeds (from 14 up to 100 Mbps), very good range (1,000 feet), and the ultimate in installation simplicity. You just plug the Powerline adapter from your PC's Ethernet or USB jack into any wall power outlet. Presto—all the PCs are connected.

Powerline adapters are inexpensive (about $40 apiece) and extremely convenient.

Sharing an Internet Connection

If you have high-speed Internet service, like a cable modem or DSL, you're a very lucky individual. Not only do you get spectacular speed when surfing the Web or doing email, but you also have a full-time connection. You never have to manually connect or disconnect.

But you'd be nuts to confine that glorious connection to *one* PC. Share it! Make it available to the whole house!

Your broadband company probably supplied you with a router (probably both wireless and wired) that shares the Internet connection with more than one computer. If not, there are two ways to do it yourself.

Get a Broadband Router

As noted earlier, a router (a *gateway* in Microsoft lingo) is a little box, about $60, that connects directly to the cable modem or DSL box. It generally doubles as a hub,

UP TO SPEED

Ad Hoc: PC-to-PC Micronetworks

If your network has modest ambitions—that is, if you have only two computers you want to connect—you can ignore all this business about hubs, routers, and wiring. Instead, you can create a tiny, two-computer wireless network between them.

These so-called ad hoc networks are great when you want to grab a folder full of files from a friend on a plane, for example. (You can also create a wired ad-hoc network, using an Ethernet crossover cable, instead of going wireless.)

Unfortunately, in Windows 8, Microsoft removed the "Create ad hoc network" option from the Network and Sharing Center. Now creating one requires one of two tools.

First, you can follow along with a guided tour through the necessary command-line typed commands, like this tutorial here: *http://j.mp/YEIsrd*

Second, you can use a piece of free software to do the job for you, like Wi-MAN. You can download it from this book's "Missing CD" page at *www.missingmanuals.com*.

providing multiple Ethernet jacks to accommodate your wired PCs, plus WiFi antennas that broadcast to your wireless PCs. The Internet signal is automatically shared among all the PCs on your home network.

Use Internet Connection Sharing

Internet Connection Sharing (ICS) is a built-in Windows feature that distributes a single Internet connection to every computer on the network. It's like the way a smartphone's tethering feature can distribute wireless Internet to nearby WiFi gadgets—but without the monthly fee. You just fire ICS up on the *one* PC that's connected directly to your cable modem or DSL box—or, as networking geeks would say, the *gateway* or *host* PC.

But there's a downside: If the gateway PC is turned off or goes into Sleep mode, nobody else in the house can go online.

Also, the gateway PC requires *two* network connections: one that goes to the cable modem or DSL box, and another that connects it to your network. Usually, that's one Ethernet connection and one WiFi card. One connects to the Internet (for example, via a cable modem), and the other distributes the Internet signal to the other computers.

Set up the sharing PC

If you decide to use Internet Connection Sharing, start by making sure the gateway PC can already get onto the Internet on its own. Then:

1. **Right-click the Network icon on your system tray; from the shortcut menu, choose Open Network and Sharing Center. Click the "Change adapter settings" link at the left side.**

   Now you see a window containing icons for every network connection. It's probably one or two at most.

2. **Right-click the icon of the connection you want to share; from the shortcut menu, choose Properties.**

   Authenticate if necessary. You wind up at the Properties dialog box shown in Figure 25-2.

3. **Click the Sharing tab. Turn on "Allow other network users to connect through this computer's Internet connection."**

   If there's no Sharing tab, it's because you have only one kind of network connector (only WiFi, for example).

   When all that looks good, you can close the windows.

Now, the other computers on the network can share the gateway PC's Internet connection, even if they're running earlier versions of Windows, or even Mac OS X or Linux. In fact, they don't need to be computers at all: You can use ICS to share your Internet connection with a video game console, a tablet, or a smartphone.

Tip: If you've created a VPN (virtual private network) on the gateway machine, *all* the PCs sharing the Internet connection can get onto the corporate network!

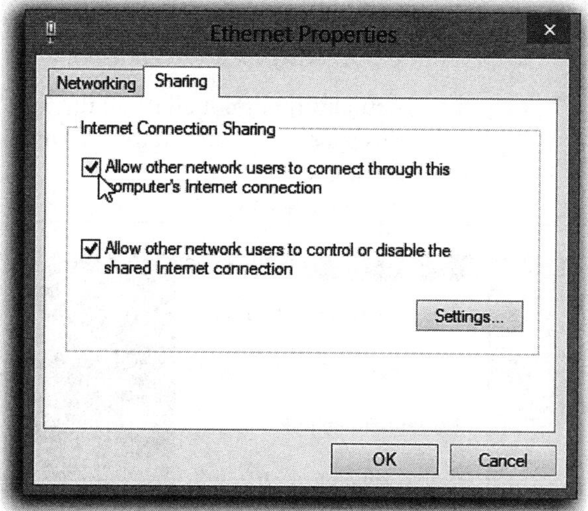

Figure 25-2: *Internet Connection Sharing lets you broadcast your cable modem/DSL's signal to all the grateful, connectionless computers in the house. Your savings: the price of a hardware router.*

Set up the other PCs

If the other computers can't just hop onto the shared network as though it's any other WiFi hotspot, you may have to adjust some of their settings, too. Follow these steps on the machines that will be using the shared connection (not the one you set up before):

1. **Open the Start screen. Type *options* and select Settings under the search box. In the search results, select Internet Options.**

   The Internet Options dialog box opens.

2. **Select the Connections tab. Select "Never dial a connection." Click "LAN settings."**

   Now the Local Area Settings dialog box appears.

3. **Turn off all checkboxes and then hit OK. Restart all the computers.**

And now the fine print:

- Internet Connection Sharing doesn't work with domain networks, DNS servers, gateways, or DHCP servers (you know who you are, network geeks).
- The "receiving" PCs (the ones that will share the connection) can't have static (fixed) IP addresses. (You'll know if you have one, because you're the one who set it up.)

Managing Your Network

Network management is another one of those two-headed beasts in Windows 8. You can take care of many tasks in the Charms panel that belongs to TileWorld; but more detailed work still requires the Network and Sharing Center back at the desktop. Here's a look at both mechanisms.

The Charms Bar

As you'll soon discover, the Networks pane of the Charms bar offers all the basics. It lists available networks, lets you hop onto one, stores the password, and lets you specify whether a WiFi hotspot is a public or private one.

Actually, that's not all it can do, though. There's a secret shortcut menu awaiting on this panel, filled with additional network management options. Figure 25-3 describes getting to it.

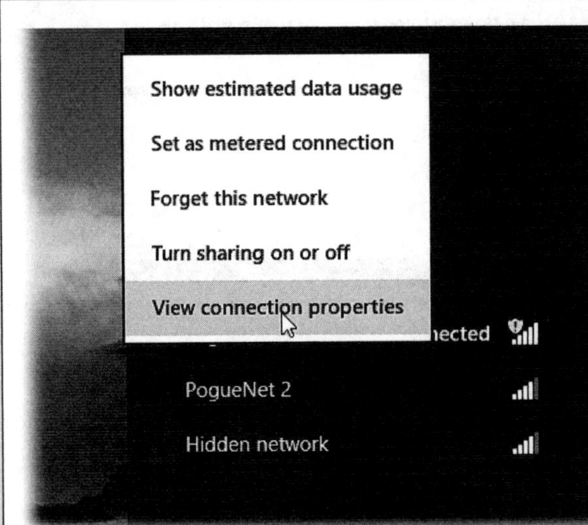

Figure 25-3:
Few people suspect that this shortcut menu even exists. But it does, and they should.

To get here, open the Charms panel. Select Settings. Select the network icon at the bottom.

Then, to make this menu appear, right-click a network's name (if you have a mouse) or hold your finger down on it for a second (if you don't).

Once you've opened this secret shortcut menu, here are your options:

- **Show estimated data usage.** How many megabytes have flowed over this connection since you joined it? In this age of monthly data limits, that can be useful information. (The Reset button lets you wipe the slate clean and start counting anew.)
- **Set as metered connection.** Declares this connection to be a *metered* one—that is, one where you're billed by the minute or by the kilobyte. (Almost always, that means a cellular connection.)

  And why should you identify it that way? Because once Windows knows that you're on a data diet, it offers various ways to avoid running up your bill. Here and there, in Windows 8's settings, you'll find on/off switches for things like "Download over metered connections." In other words, whenever you're connected to a connection where it's important to conserve, Windows will do its best to help you.

  (Once you use this command, it changes to say "Set as non-metered connection.")

- **Forget this network.** Page 441 shows you how to make Windows memorize a connection so that you can hop onto it easily next time. This command tells Windows to forget that connection so that its name no longer clutters up your lists of hotspots. (That's handy when a WiFi hot spot's settings get messed up, as sometimes happens.)
- **Turn sharing on or off.** This option is available only for the connection you're actually using right now. It presents the same question posed on page 439, lower right: Are you in a public place or a private place? If the answer is "private," like your home, then it's safe to turn on file sharing among computers. If it's "public," best to leave file sharing turned off so that evildoers lurking with latté grandés in the corner can't hack into your files.
- **View connection properties.** Opens the Properties dialog box shown in Figure 25-2, so that you can (for example) turn on Internet Connection Sharing or make other adjustments.

The Network and Sharing Center

Several times in this book, you'll read about the Network and Sharing Center. Until TileWorld came along, this was the master control center for creating, managing, and connecting to networks of all kinds (Figure 25-4). Now that you can do most network tasks right in the Charms bar, the N.a.S.C. isn't quite as essential.

But it's still where you set up the sharing of files, folders, printers, and multimedia files over the network, as you'll discover in Chapter 27.

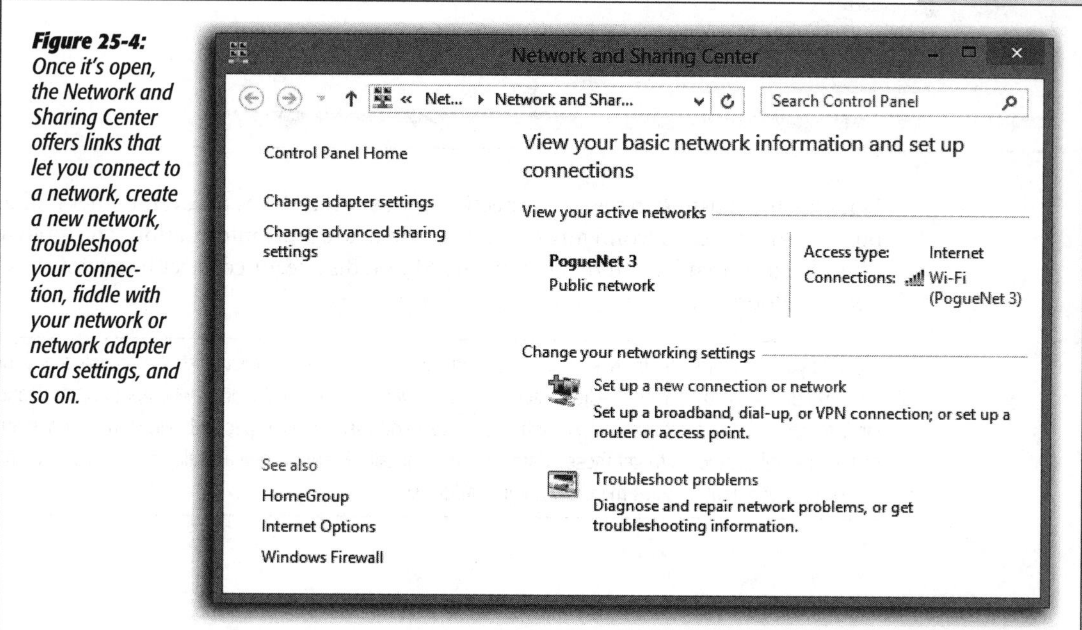

***Figure 25-4:** Once it's open, the Network and Sharing Center offers links that let you connect to a network, create a new network, troubleshoot your connection, fiddle with your network or network adapter card settings, and so on.*

There are all kinds of ways to get there, but the quickest is to right-click the or icon on your taskbar system tray. From the shortcut menu, choose Open Network and Sharing Center.

You can also get there from the Start screen by typing *network and*; select Settings; and then select Open Network and Sharing Center.

To *do* anything with your network, you need to click one of the links in blue. They include these:

Change adapter settings

Click this link to view a list of all your network adapters—Ethernet cards and WiFi adapters, mainly—as well as any VPNs or dial-up connections you've set up on your computer (Figure 25-5).

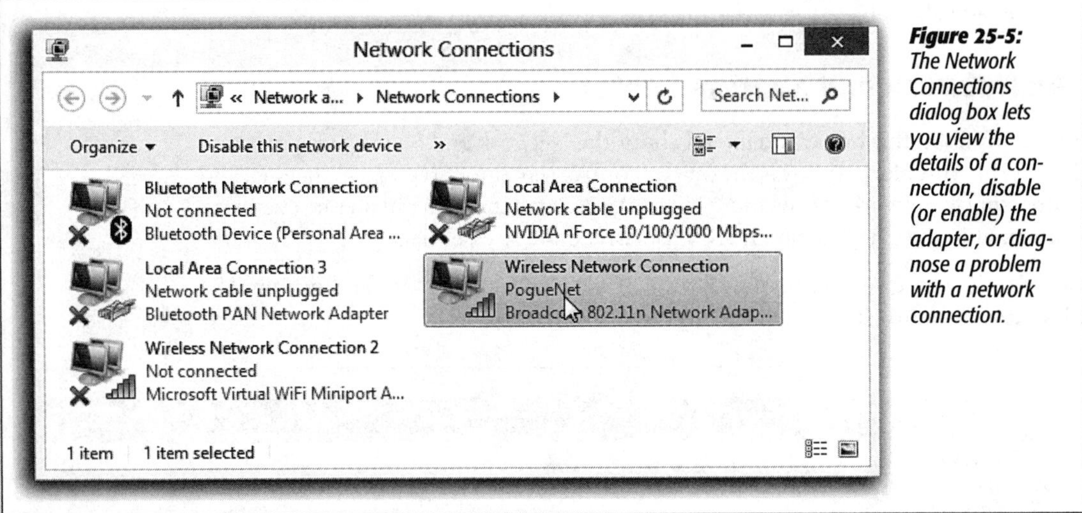

Figure 25-5: *The Network Connections dialog box lets you view the details of a connection, disable (or enable) the adapter, or diagnose a problem with a network connection.*

Double-click a listing to see its connection status, which leads to several other dialog boxes where you can reconfigure the connection or see more information. The toolbar offers buttons that let you rename, troubleshoot, disable, or connect to one of these network doodads.

Note: If you right-click one of these icons and then choose Properties, you get a list of protocols that your network connection uses. Double-click "Internet Protocol Version 4" to tell Windows whether to get its IP and DNS server addresses automatically, or whether to use addresses you've specified. Ninety-nine times out of 100, the right choice is to get those addresses automatically. Every once in a while, though, you'll come across a network that requires manually entered addresses.

Change advanced sharing settings

This section is the master control panel of on/off switches for Windows' *network sharing* features. (Most of these have on/off switches in other, more scattered places, too.) Here's a rundown.

Note: The options here are actually listed twice: once for networks you've designated as Home or Work networks, and one for Public networks. (Page 439 has details on these differences.)

- **Network discovery** makes your computer visible to others and allows your computer to see other computers on the network.
- **File and printer sharing** lets you share files and printers over the network. (See Chapter 27.)
- **Public folder sharing** lets you share whatever files you've put in the Users→Public folder. (See Chapter 27.)
- **Media streaming** is where you listen to one PC's music playing back over the network while seated at another. (See Chapter 18.) It appears here only if you've turned this feature on.
- **File sharing connections** lets you turn off the super-strong security features of Windows file sharing, to accommodate older gadgets that don't recognize it.
- **Homegroup connections.** Here's the master on/off switch for the delightful Homegroup feature described in Chapter 27.

Links in the Main Window

In the main part of the Network and Sharing Center window, the "Change your networking settings" heading offers a few more handy tools:

Set up a new connection or network

Most of the time, Windows does the right thing when it encounters a new network. For example, if you plug in an Ethernet cable, it assumes you want to use the wired network and automatically hops on. If you come within range of a wireless network, Windows offers to connect to it.

Some kinds of networks, however, require special setup:

- **Connect to the Internet.** Use this option when Windows fails to figure out how to connect to the Internet on its own. You can set up a WiFi, PPPoE broadband connection (required by certain DSL services that require you to sign in with a user name and password), or a dial-up networking connection.
- **Set up a new network.** You can use this option to configure a new wireless router that's not set up yet, although only some routers can "speak" to Windows in this way. You're better off using the configuration software that came in the box with the router.

- **Manually connect to a wireless network.** Some wireless networks don't announce (broadcast) their presence. That is, you won't see a message popping up on the screen, inviting you to join the network, just by wandering into it. Instead, the very name and existence of such networks are kept secret to keep the riffraff out. If you're told the name of such a network, use this option to type it in and connect.
- **Connect to a workplace.** That is, set up a secure VPN connection to the corporation that employs you, as described on page 823.
- **Set up a dial-up connection.** If you connect using a dial-up modem, you're in luck. Actually, not really.

Troubleshoot problems

Very few problems are as annoying or difficult to troubleshoot as flaky network connections. With this option, Microsoft is giving you a tiny head start.

When you click "Troubleshoot problems," Windows asks what, exactly, you're having trouble with. Click the topic in question: Internet Connections, Shared Folders, Homegroup, and so on. Invisibly and automatically, Windows performs several geek tweaks that were once the realm of highly paid networking professionals: It renews the DHCP address, reinitializes the connection, and, if nothing else works, turns the networking card off and on again.

If the troubleshooter doesn't pinpoint the problem, check that all the following is in place:

- Your cables are properly seated in the network adapter card and hub jacks.
- Your router, Ethernet hub, or wireless access point is plugged into a working power outlet.
- Your networking card is working. To check, open the Device Manager (type its name at the Start screen). Look for an error icon next to your networking card's name. See Chapter 20 for more on the Device Manager.

If that doesn't fix things, you'll have to call Microsoft, your PC maker, or your local teenage PC guru for help.

CHAPTER 26

Corporate Networks

Windows 8 was designed to thrive in two very different kinds of network worlds: the *workgroup* (an informal, home or small-office network) and the *domain* (a hard-core, security-conscious corporate network of dozens or thousands of PCs). Depending on which kind of network your PC belongs to, the procedures and even dialog boxes you experience are quite a bit different.

Chapter 25 guides you through the process of setting up a workgroup network, but no single chapter could describe setting up a corporate domain. That's a job for Super Geek, otherwise known as the network administrator—somebody who has studied the complexities of corporate networking for years.

This chapter is designed to help you learn how to *use* a corporate domain. If your PC is connected to a workgroup network or no network at all, on the other hand, feel free to use these pages as scratch paper.

Note: In the context of this chapter, the term *domain* refers to a group of Windows computers on the same network. It's not the same as an *Internet* domain, which you may occasionally see mentioned. An Internet domain is still a group of computers, but they don't have to be connected to the same network, and they don't have to be running Windows. In addition, the domain name (like *amazon.com*) must be registered to ensure that there's no duplication on the Internet. Because Windows domains are private, they can be named any way the administrator chooses.

The Domain

On a regular small-office network, nobody else on a workgroup network can access the files on your PC unless you've created an account for them on your machine. Whenever somebody new joins the department, you have to create another new account; when people leave, you have to delete or disable their accounts. If something goes wrong with your hard drive, you have to recreate all of the accounts.

You must have an account on each shared PC, too. If you're lucky, you have the same name and password on each machine—but that isn't always the case. You might have to remember that you're *pjenkins* on the front-desk computer, but *JenkinsP* on the administrative machine.

Similarly, suppose there's a network printer on one of the computers in your workgroup. If you want to use it, you have to find out whose computer the printer is connected to, call him to ask if he'll create an account for you, and hope that he knows how to do it. You either have to tell him your user name and password, or find out what user name and password he's assigned to you. In that case, every time you want to use that printer, you might have to log on by typing that user name and password.

If you multiply all of this hassle by the number of PCs on a growing network, it's easy to see how you might suddenly find yourself spending more time managing accounts and permissions than getting any work done.

The Domain Concept

The solution to all of these problems is the network domain. In a domain, you only have a single name and password, which gets you into every shared PC and printer on the network that you're authorized to use. Everyone's account information resides on a central computer called a *domain controller*—a computer so important, it's usually locked away in a closet or a data-center room.

A domain controller keeps track of who is allowed to log on, who *is* logged on, and what each person is allowed to do on the network. When you log onto the domain with your PC, the domain controller verifies your credentials and permits (or denies) you access.

Most domain networks have at least two domain controllers with identical information, so if one computer dies, the other one can take over. (Some networks have many more than two.) This redundancy is a critical safety net, because without a happy, healthy domain controller, the entire network is dead.

Without budging from their chairs, network administrators can use a domain controller to create new accounts, manage existing ones, and assign permissions. The domain takes the equipment-management and security concerns of the network out of the hands of individuals and puts them into the hands of trained professionals. You may sometimes hear this kind of networking called *client/server networking*. Each *workstation*—that is, each mere mortal PC like yours—relies on a central server machine for its network access.

If you use Windows in a medium- to large-sized company, you probably use a domain every day. You may not even have been aware of it, but that's no big deal; knowing what's been going on right under your nose isn't especially important to your ability to get work done. After all, it's not your job—it's the network administrator's. But understanding the domain system can help you take better advantage of a domain's features.

Active Directory

As you know, Microsoft sells two primary versions of Windows 8: the Pro and the regular. One key difference is that computers running the plain Windows 8 edition can't join a domain.

There are other versions of Windows, however: the specialized ones that run on those domain-controller computers. To create a domain, at least one computer must be running Windows Server (version 2000 or later). These are far more expensive operating systems (the price depends on the number of machines that they serve) and they run only on high-octane PCs. They also require high-octane expertise to install and maintain.

One key offering of these specialized Windows versions is an elaborate application called *Active Directory*. It's a single, centralized database that stores every scrap of information about the hardware, software, and people on the network. (The older operating system called Windows NT Server can create domains, but it doesn't include Active Directory.)

After creating a domain by installing Active Directory on a server computer, network administrators can set about filling the directory (database) with information about the network's resources. Every computer, printer, and person is represented by an *object* in the database and *attributes* (properties) that describe it. For example, a *user object's* attributes specify that person's name, location, telephone number, email address, and other, more technical, elements.

Active Directory lets network administrators maintain an enormous hierarchy of computers. A multinational corporation with tens of thousands of employees in offices worldwide can all be part of one Active Directory domain, with servers distributed in hundreds of locations, all connected by wide-area networking links. (A group of domains is known as a *tree*. Huge networks might even have more than one tree; if so, they're called—yes, you guessed it—a *forest*.)

The objects in an Active Directory domain are arranged in a hierarchy, something like the hierarchy of folders within folders on your hard drive. Some companies base their directory-tree designs on the organization of the company, using departments and divisions as the building blocks. Others use geographic locations as the basis for the design, or use a combination of both.

Unless you've decided to take up the rewarding career of network administration, you'll never have to install an Active Directory domain controller, design a directory tree, or create domain objects. However, you very well may encounter the Active Directory at your company. You can use it to search for the mailing address of somebody else on the network, for example, or locate a printer that can print on both sides of the page at once. Having some idea of the directory's structure can help in these cases.

Domain Security

Security is one of the primary reasons for Active Directory's existence. First off, all of the account names and passwords reside on a single machine (the domain controller), which can easily be locked away, protected, and backed up.

Active Directory is also a vital part of the network's other security mechanisms. When your computer is a member of a domain, the first thing you do is log on, just as in a workgroup. But when you log into a domain, Windows 8 transmits your name and password (in encrypted form) to the domain controller, which checks your credentials and grants or denies you access.

Four Ways Life Is Different on a Domain

The domain and workgroup personalities of Windows are quite different. Here are some of the most important differences.

NOSTALGIA CORNER

The Double-Thick Security Trick

If you use Windows in a corporation, the Lock screen probably bears a message at the top left corner when you first turn on the machine. You don't proceed to the regular Login screen until you first press Ctrl+Alt+Delete.

This somewhat inconvenient setup is intended as a security feature. By forcing you to press Ctrl+Alt+Delete to bypass the initial Welcome box, Windows rules out the possibility that some sneaky program (such as a Trojan-horse program), designed to *look* like the regular Login screen, is posing as the regular Login screen—in order to "capture" the name and password you type there.

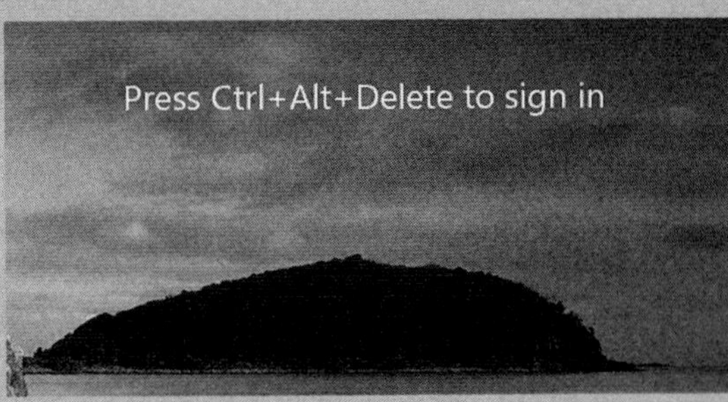
Press Ctrl+Alt+Delete to sign in

This two-layer login system is what you get when you add your PC to a network domain during the Windows installation. If you want to use it on a workgroup machine, you can, but you have to do a little digging to find it. Press ⊞+R to open the Run dialog box; type *control Userpasswords2*, and then press Enter. Authenticate yourself. You see the program shown on page 740—the old-style User Accounts box. Click the Advanced tab.

At the bottom of the Advanced tab, turn on "Require users to press Ctrl+Alt+Delete," and then click OK. From now on, turning on the PC greets you not with a Login screen, but with the unfakeable Lock screen shown here.

Logging On

What you see when you log onto your PC is somewhat different when you're part of a domain. Instead of the standard Welcome screen, you generally encounter a two-step sign-in process:

- First, the Lock screen instructs you to press Ctrl+Alt+Delete to log on. (This step is a security precaution, described in the box on the facing page.)
- When you click ⊛ at the Login screen, you can click "Other User" and then log into the domain you joined (see Figure 26-1).

Tip: You can turn off the requirement to press Ctrl+Alt+Delete, if you like. Open the Control Panel; then click User Accounts and Family Safety→User Accounts. Next, click Manage User Accounts. Authenticate if asked. Now select the Advanced tab and turn off the "Require users to press Ctrl+Alt+Delete" checkbox.

Figure 26-1: *Even if your computer is part of a domain, you can still log in to a local account. But to connect to the domain, you have to click the ⊛ button and choose Other User.*

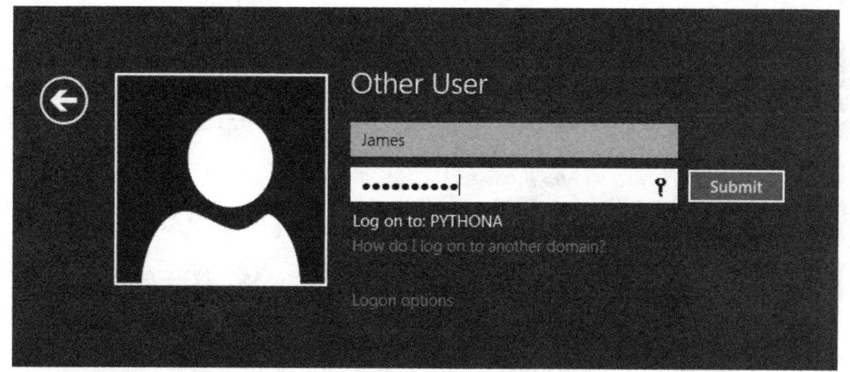

UP TO SPEED

Knowing What You're Logging Onto

There are two kinds of accounts on a corporate PC: *domain* accounts, maintained by a highly paid professional in your company, and *local* accounts–accounts that exist only on the PC itself. It's actually possible to find domain accounts and local accounts that have the same name–a perennial source of confusion for beginners (and occasionally experts).

For example, you know that every Windows computer has an Administrator account, which the Windows 8 installer creates automatically. The trouble is, so does the domain controller.

In other words, typing *Administrator* into the User Name text box might log you onto either the local machine or the domain, depending on what password you supply. (With luck, the two accounts won't have the same password, but you never know.)

To avoid this kind of confusion, Windows 8 lets you specify which domain to log onto. Just prefix the account name with the domain name, like this: *2K3DOMAIN\Administrator.*

And if you forget this secret code, you can always click the link marked "How do I log onto another domain?" at the Login screen.

As you see in Figure 26-1, you can now type your user name and password. To save you time, Windows fills in the User Name box with whatever name was used the last time somebody logged in.

Browsing the Domain

When your PC is part of the domain, all of its resources—printers, shared files, and so on—magically appear in your desktop windows, the Network window, and so on (Figure 26-2).

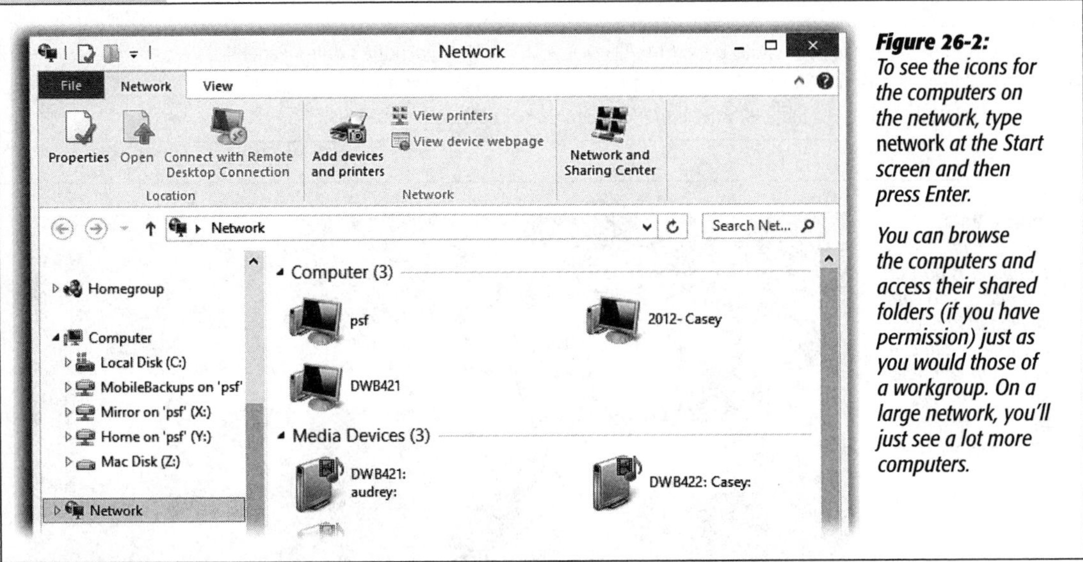

Figure 26-2: *To see the icons for the computers on the network, type* network *at the Start screen and then press Enter.*

You can browse the computers and access their shared folders (if you have permission) just as you would those of a workgroup. On a large network, you'll just see a lot more computers.

Searching the Domain

You can read all about the Search command in Chapter 7. But when you're on a domain, this tool becomes far more powerful—and more interesting.

When you open the Network window as described above, the Ribbon changes to include an option to Search Active Directory. Click it to open the dialog box shown at top left in Figure 26-3.

The name of this dialog box depends on what you're looking for. Your choices are:

- **Users, Contacts, and Groups.** Use this option to search the network for a particular person or network group (Figure 26-3). If your search is successful, you can, for example, find out someone's telephone number, email address, or mailing address, or see what users belong to a particular group.

- **Computers.** This option helps you find a certain PC in the domain. It's of interest primarily to network administrators, because it lets them open a Computer Management window for the computer they find. It also lets them manage many of the PC's functions by remote control.

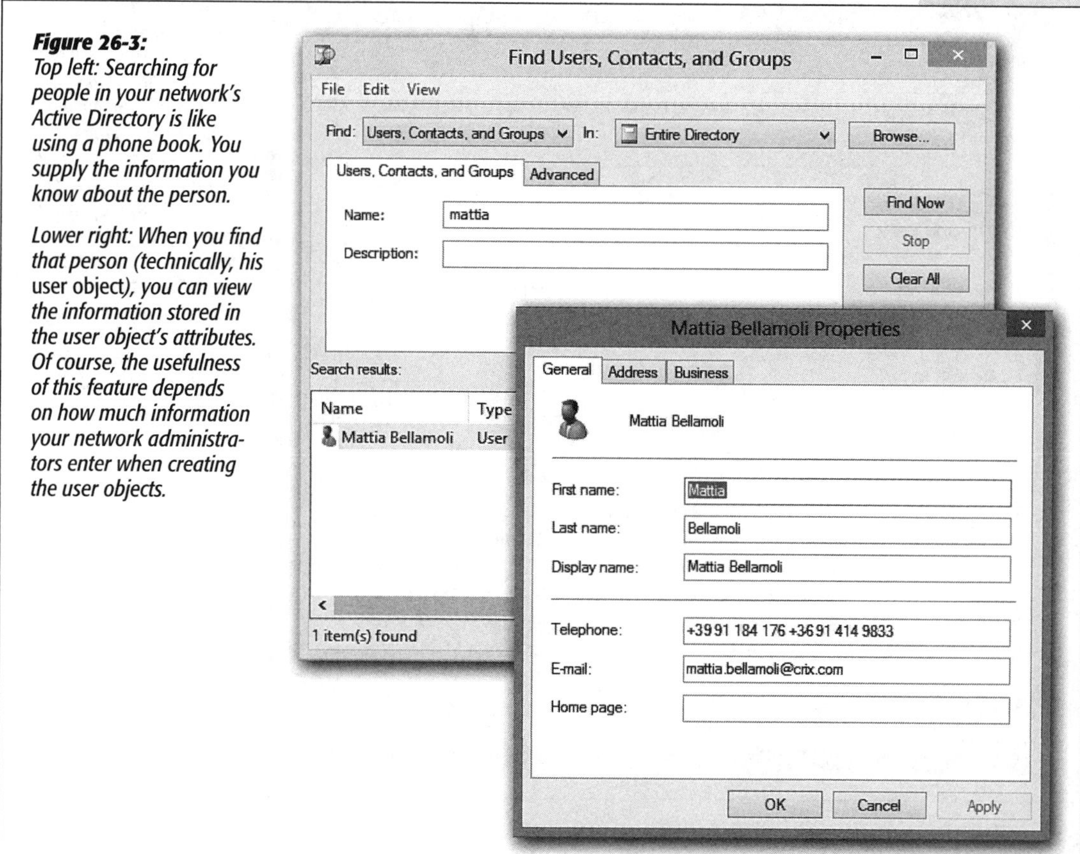

Figure 26-3: *Top left: Searching for people in your network's Active Directory is like using a phone book. You supply the information you know about the person.*

Lower right: When you find that person (technically, his user object), you can view the information stored in the user object's attributes. Of course, the usefulness of this feature depends on how much information your network administrators enter when creating the user objects.

- **Printers.** In a large office, it's entirely possible that you might not know where you can find a printer with certain features—tabloid-size paper, for example, or double-sided printing. That's where this option comes in handy (see Figure 26-4).

- **Shared Folders.** In theory, this option lets you search for shared folders on the domain's computers—but you'll quickly discover that searches for a certain shared folder generally come up empty-handed.

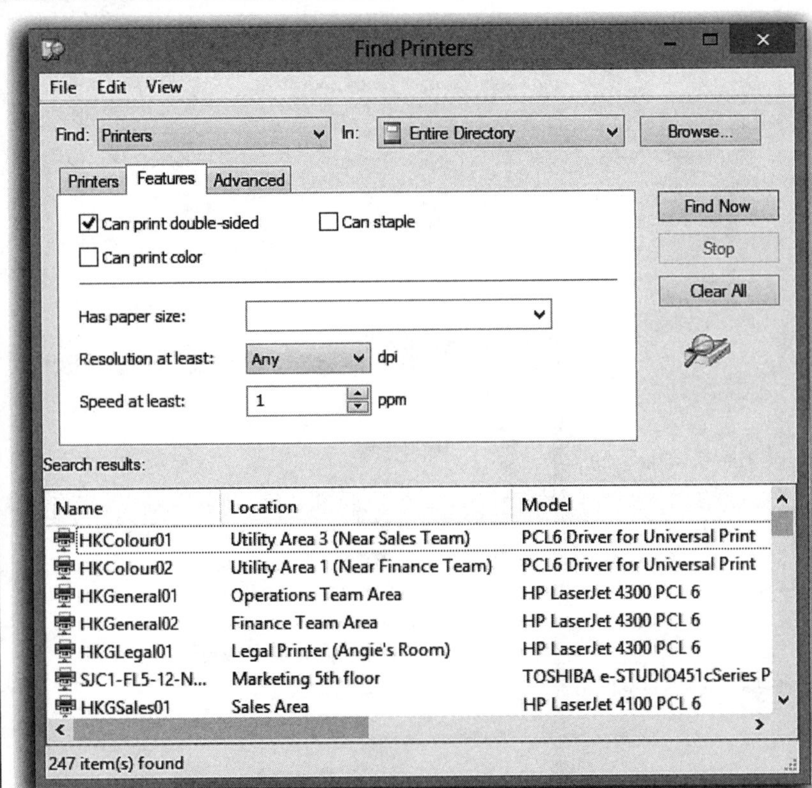

Figure 26-4: *Searching for a printer in Active Directory lets you find the printing features you need. Network administrators may also record the physical locations of the network printers. This way, when your search uncovers a printer that can handle executive paper and also print double-sided, you can simply look at its attributes to find out that it's located on the fourth floor of the building.*

That's because just sharing a folder on your computer doesn't "publish" it to Active Directory, which would make it available to this kind of search. Only network administrators can publish a shared folder in Active Directory.

- **Organizational Units.** You may not have heard of organizational units, but your network administrator lives and breathes them. (They're the building blocks of an Active Directory hierarchy.) You, the mere mortal, can safely ignore this search option.

Custom Searches

In addition to these predefined searches, you can also create a custom search of your own by looking for information in specific fields (that is, attributes) of Active Directory, as shown in Figure 26-5.

When used creatively, these custom searches can be powerful indeed, in ways you might not expect. For example, suppose your car won't start, and you need a ride home from the office. You can open this dialog box, click the Field button, and choose User→Home Phone. Change the Condition drop-down menu to Starts With, and then type your own area code and telephone exchange into the Value text box. When you click the Find Now button, you'll get a list of coworkers who live in your neighborhood (as indicated by the first three digits of their phone numbers).

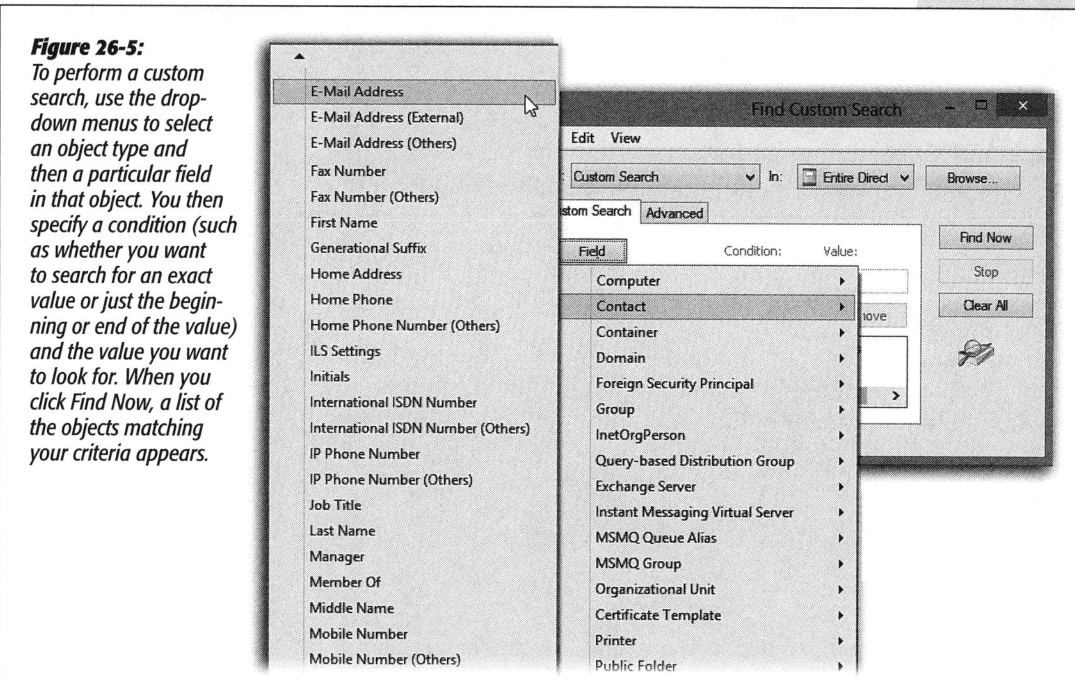

Figure 26-5: *To perform a custom search, use the drop-down menus to select an object type and then a particular field in that object. You then specify a condition (such as whether you want to search for an exact value or just the beginning or end of the value) and the value you want to look for. When you click Find Now, a list of the objects matching your criteria appears.*

Assigning Permissions to Domain Members

Chapter 27 describes the process of assigning permissions to certain files and folders, so that only designated people and groups can open them from across the network. When you're a member of a domain, the process is the same, except that you can select people and groups from the domain as well.

When you open the Properties dialog box for a file or folder, click the Security tab, then click Edit and then Add, you don't get the same dialog box that you'd see on a workgroup network. On a domain, it's called the Select Users, Computers, or Groups dialog box (Figure 26-6). You'll also see this dialog box if you right-click on a folder, click Share, and then select Find from the drop-down menu to the left of the Add button.

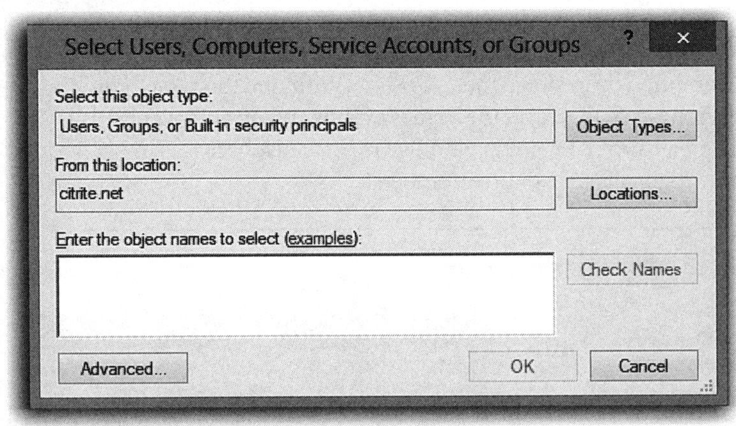

Figure 26-6:
Note that the standard location for the objects is your current domain. You can still click the Locations button and select your computer's name (to specify local user and group accounts), or even choose another domain on the network, if others are available.

CHAPTER 27

Sharing Files on the Network

Whether you built the network yourself or work in an office where somebody has done that work for you, all kinds of fun can come from having a network. You're now ready to share all kinds of stuff among the various PCs on the network:

- **Files, folders, and disks.** No matter what PC you're using on the network, you can open the files and folders on any *other* networked PC, as long as the other PCs' owners have made these files available for public inspection. That's where *file sharing* comes in, and that's what this chapter is all about.

  The uses for file sharing are almost endless. It means you can finish writing a letter in the bedroom, even if you started it downstairs at the kitchen table—without having to carry a flash drive around. It means you can watch a slideshow drawn from photos on your spouse's PC somewhere else in the house. It means your underlings can turn in articles for your small-company newsletter by depositing them directly into a folder on your laptop.

Tip: File sharing also lets you access your files and folders from the road, using a laptop. See Chapter 28 for more information on this road-warrior trick.

- **Music and video playback.** Windows Media Player can *stream* music and videos from one PC to another one on the network—that is, play in real time across the network, without your having to copy any files. In a family situation, it's super-convenient to have Dad's Mondo Upstairs PC serve as the master holding tank for the family's entire music collection—and be able to play it using any PC in the house.

- **Printers.** You don't need a printer for every PC; all the PCs can share a much smaller number of printers. If several printers are on your network—say, a high-speed laser printer for one computer and a color printer on another—everyone on the network can use whichever printer is appropriate to a particular document. You'll find step-by-step instructions starting on page 623.
- **Your Internet connection.** Having a network means that all the PCs in your home or office can share a single connection (Chapter 25).
- **A DVD drive.** Tablets and many laptops don't have DVD drives. So how are you supposed to play movies or install software from a disc? By sharing the DVD drive on another PC in the house.

Note: Your network might include a Windows 8 PC, a couple of Windows 7, XP, or Vista machines, older PCs, and even Macs. That's perfectly OK; all of these computers can participate as equals in this party. This chapter points out whatever differences you may find in the procedures.

Three Ways to Share Files

It's not easy to write *one* operating system that's supposed to please *everyone,* from a husband and wife at home, to a small business owner, to a network administrator for the federal government. Clearly, these people might have slightly different attitudes on the tradeoff between convenience and security.

That's why Windows 8 offers *three ways* to share files. Each is light-years more convenient, secure, and comprehensible than file sharing in the Windows XP days. And each falls at a different spot on the security/convenience spectrum:

- **Homegroups.** The Homegroup feature was invented for families or small-business owners—places where people don't have a lot to hide from one another. This kind of network is *really* easy to set up and use; nobody has to enter names and passwords to use files on other PCs in the house.

  Setup is a one-time deal: You type the same code into each computer, and presto—everyone can see everyone else's Music, Photos, Videos, and Documents folders. Everyone can send printouts to everyone else's printers. Everyone can listen to everyone else's Windows Media Player music collections, too. (You can turn these shared items off individually, if you like.)

  Downsides: A PC can join a Homegroup only if it's running Windows 7 or 8. And Homegroups don't offer the level of security, passwords, and networky red tape that bigger companies require. The idea is to give everyone in the house free access to everyone else's stuff with one click.
- **The Public folder.** There's a Public folder on every PC. It's free for anyone on the network to access, like a grocery store bulletin board. Super-convenient, super-easy.

Downsides: First, you have to move or copy files *into* the Public folder before anyone else can see them. Depending on how many files you wish to share, this can get tedious.

Second, this method isn't especially secure. If you worry about people rummaging through the files and deleting or vandalizing them, or if bad things could happen if the wrong person in your building gets a look at them, well, then, don't use this method (although you can still give the Public folder a password).

- **Any folder.** At the far end of the security/convenience spectrum, you have the "any folder" method. In this scheme, you can make any ordinary folder available for inspection by other people on the network.

  This method means you don't have to move files into the Public folder. It also gives you elaborate control over who's allowed to do what to your files. You might want to permit your company's executives to see and edit your documents but allow the peons in accounting only to see them. And Andy, that unreliable goofball in sales? You don't want him even *seeing* what's in your shared folder.

  Downsides: More complex and inconvenient than the other methods.

The following pages walk you through all three kinds of file sharing.

Tip: These networking types can coexist. So you can have a Homegroup for the benefit of the other Windows 7/8 computers in your house, but still share with Windows Vista or XP machines using the other methods. Nobody said this was going to be simple.

Homegroups

Let's suppose there are two PCs in your house. Setting up a Homegroup is incredibly easy. In fact, it's as easy as 1, 2, 3, 4, 5, 6.

You can do the whole thing either in TileWorld or at the Control Panel; the following pages walk you through both setup procedures.

Creating a Homegroup in TileWorld

Fingers ready? It doesn't matter which PC you start with, although if you're in TileWorld, that pretty much means it's one of your Windows 8 machines.

1. **On the first PC, open the Homegroup panel of PC Settings (Figure 27-1, top).**

   To get to the right screen, open the Charms bar; select Settings; select "Change PC settings"; select Homegroup.

   If you agreed to create a Homegroup on the day you set up this PC, by the way, what you see looks more like Figure 27-2. In other words, your Homegroup already exists. Congratulations!! Skip a couple of pages to "How to Use Your Homegroup."

2. **Click "Create a homegroup."**

   Now the panel shown in Figure 27-1 at bottom appears.

Note: If you get a message that says, "Homegroup is only available on a home network," click "Change sharing settings." In the Networks panel illustrated on page 439, choose "Yes, turn on sharing." You return to the previous screen, where now you can continue as described here.

The point: Homegroups work only when you're on a private network, like at home. In public networks—coffee shops and so on—a bad guy could theoretically "sniff" the open WiFi airwaves and snoop on your stuff.

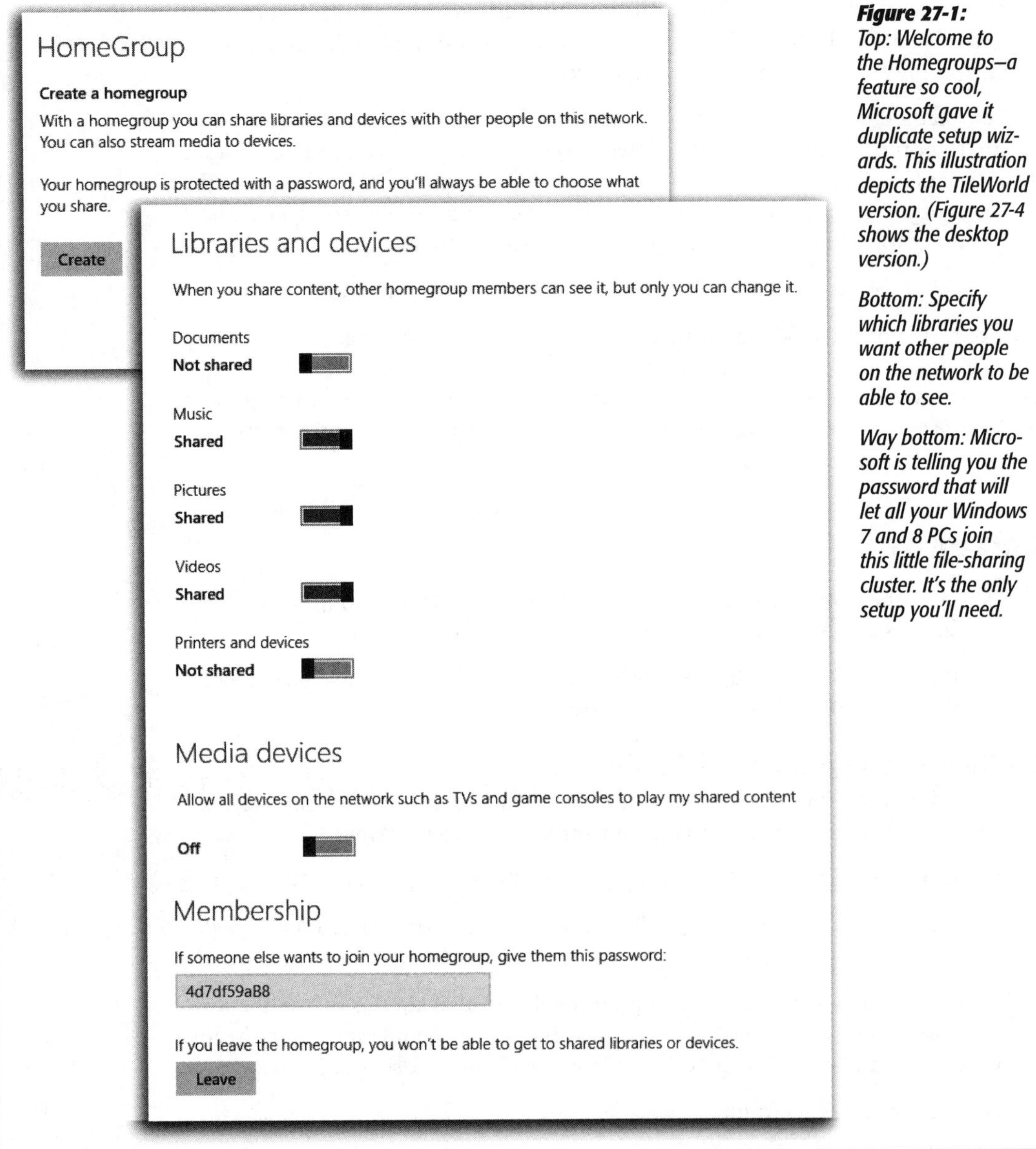

Figure 27-1: *Top: Welcome to the Homegroups—a feature so cool, Microsoft gave it duplicate setup wizards. This illustration depicts the TileWorld version. (Figure 27-4 shows the desktop version.)*

Bottom: Specify which libraries you want other people on the network to be able to see.

Way bottom: Microsoft is telling you the password that will let all your Windows 7 and 8 PCs join this little file-sharing cluster. It's the only setup you'll need.

3. **Turn on the checkboxes for the stuff you want to share.**

   Windows proposes making your Photos, Music, and Videos libraries available for the other PCs in your house to use. If you like, you can also turn on the Documents library. (It starts turned off in case you keep private stuff in there.) And you can share whatever printer is connected to your PC—an inkjet, for example.

   The "Media devices" heading means: "Let me play my music, pictures, and videos on the Xbox."

Tip: You can always change these settings later, as described below.

   At the bottom of this panel, Windows displays a ridiculously unmemorable password, like E6fQ9UX3uR. Fortunately, you'll never have to memorize it. You can also change it to something less dorky, as described on page 793.

4. **Walk to the second PC. Open the Homegroup panel just as you did in step 1.**

   This time, the wording is different. It sees the *first* PC already on the network, already with a Homegroup initiative under way (Figure 27-2).

Figure 27-2: *On the second PC, a dialog box may pop up automatically, announcing that a Homegroup has just been discovered. If not, you can open Homegroup in PC Settings; this is what you'll see there.*

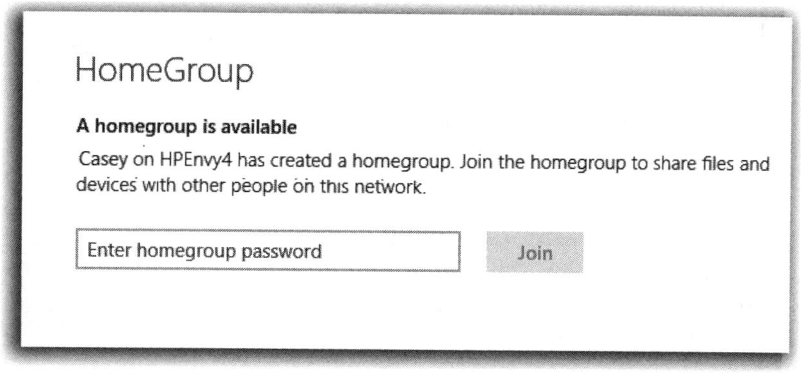

HomeGroup

A homegroup is available

Casey on HPEnvy4 has created a homegroup. Join the homegroup to share files and devices with other people on this network.

Enter homegroup password | Join

UP TO SPEED

The Fine Print of Homegroups

Homegroups work quickly and well. But as with anything that seems too good to be true, there are a few footnotes:

1. If your PC is on a corporate domain network, you can join a Homegroup but you can't create one. You'll be able to access libraries and printers on other computers in the Homegroup, but you can't share your own.

2. If you have Windows 7 Starter, Windows 7 Home Basic, or RT, you can join a Homegroup, but you can't create one.

3. Homegroups don't work unless you turn on network sharing for this network (see page 439).

4. When you share a folder in the Homegroup, all folders inside are also shared.

You've been warned. Sign here, please.

5. **Enter the membership password and hit Join.**

(The membership password is the one shown at bottom in Figure 27-1.)

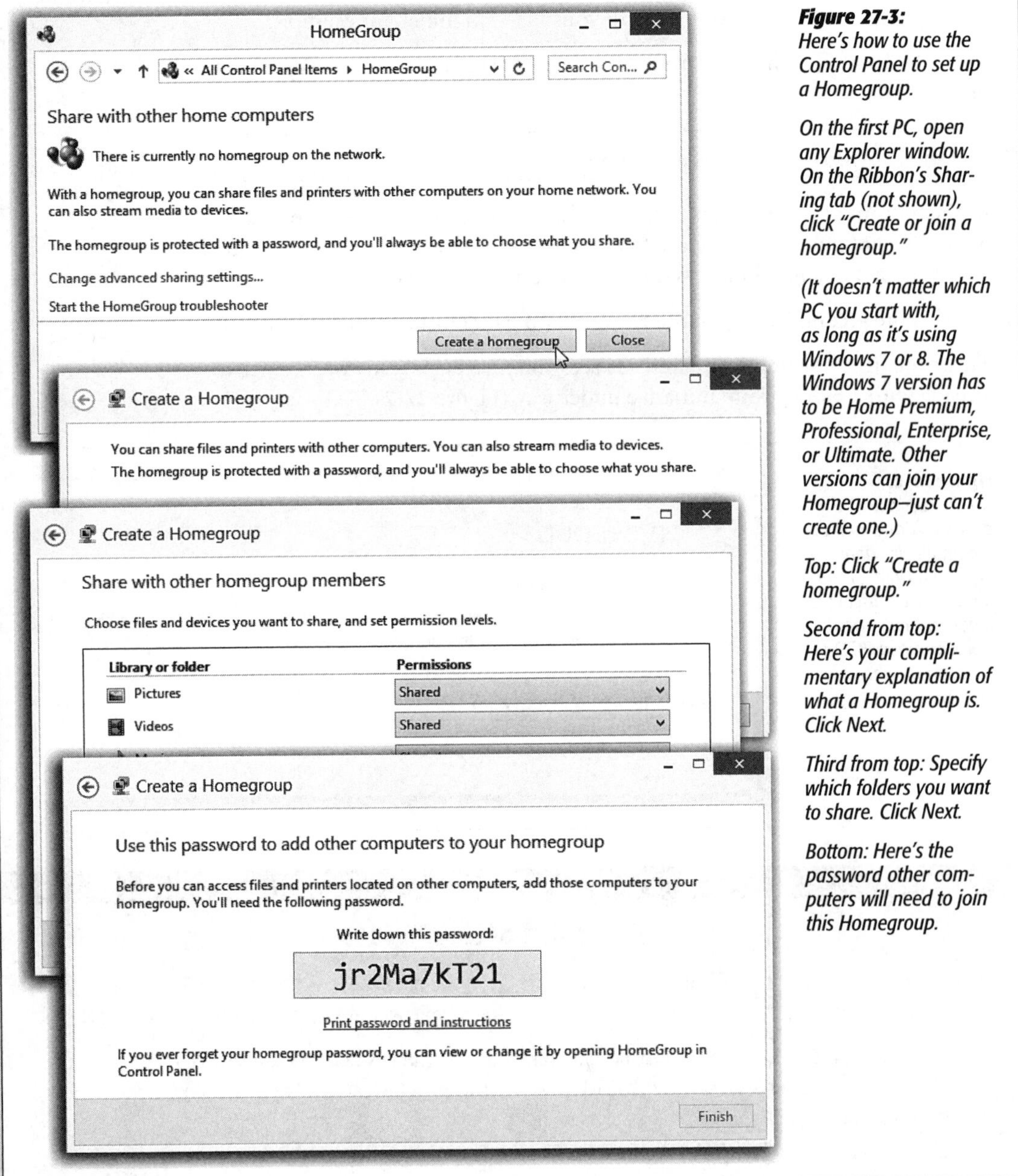

Figure 27-3: *Here's how to use the Control Panel to set up a Homegroup.*

On the first PC, open any Explorer window. On the Ribbon's Sharing tab (not shown), click "Create or join a homegroup."

(It doesn't matter which PC you start with, as long as it's using Windows 7 or 8. The Windows 7 version has to be Home Premium, Professional, Enterprise, or Ultimate. Other versions can join your Homegroup—just can't create one.)

Top: Click "Create a homegroup."

Second from top: Here's your complimentary explanation of what a Homegroup is. Click Next.

Third from top: Specify which folders you want to share. Click Next.

Bottom: Here's the password other computers will need to join this Homegroup.

Now you see a "Libraries and devices" screen that looks just like the one in Figure 27-1 at bottom. This is your opportunity to specify which stuff in *your* account, on *this* computer, you want to share with everybody else.

6. **Slide the bars to indicate which folders you'd like to share.**

   If you have a third PC, or a fourth or a fifth, repeat steps 4–6. If you buy another PC a year from now, repeat steps 4–6.

And that's all there is to it. Your computers are now joined in blissful network harmony.

Creating a Homegroup at the Desktop

You can also create a Homegroup the Windows 7 way—using the Control Panel. You'll find exactly the same options, just presented in a different graphic style and spread out over more dialog boxes. See Figure 27-3.

Tip: One advantage of the Control Panel method: You have far more options.

Open the main Homegroup screen (see Figure 27-3, top). Here, the links let you remind yourself of the password, leave the Homegroup, or view the master sharing control panel for your computer ("Advanced sharing settings.") Best of all, here's where you can *change* the password. Click "Change the password," authenticate if necessary, and make up any new password you like (eight characters or longer). ("Bluefish" is much easier to remember than E6fQ9UX3uR.)

How to Use Your Homegroup

Once a Homegroup is set up, using it is a piece of cake.

- **Root through other people's libraries.** On PC #2, click Homegroup at the left side of any Explorer window. Voila! There are the icons for every PC—in fact, every *account* on every PC (Figure 27-4).

  And if you open one of them, you can see the pictures, music, videos, documents, and whatever else they've made available for sharing.

- **Share each other's printers.** When you go to print, you'll see that *all* the printers in the house are now available to *all* the PCs in the house. For example, if there's a color inkjet plugged into the USB jack of Computer #1, you can send printouts to it from the Print dialog box of Computer #2. (The other computers' shared printers even have their own icons in the Devices and Printers folder, as described in Chapter 20.)

Note: If the printer is a relatively recent, brand-name model, it should "just work"; Windows installs the printer automatically. If not, the Homegroup feature notifies you that a printer is available, but you have to click Install to OK the driver installation.

- **Play each other's music and video.** When you're in Windows Media Player or Media Center, same thing: You'll see the names of all the other computers listed for your browsing pleasure, and inside, all their music, photos, and videos, ready to play. (The other machines are listed in the navigation pane at left, in a category called "Other libraries.")

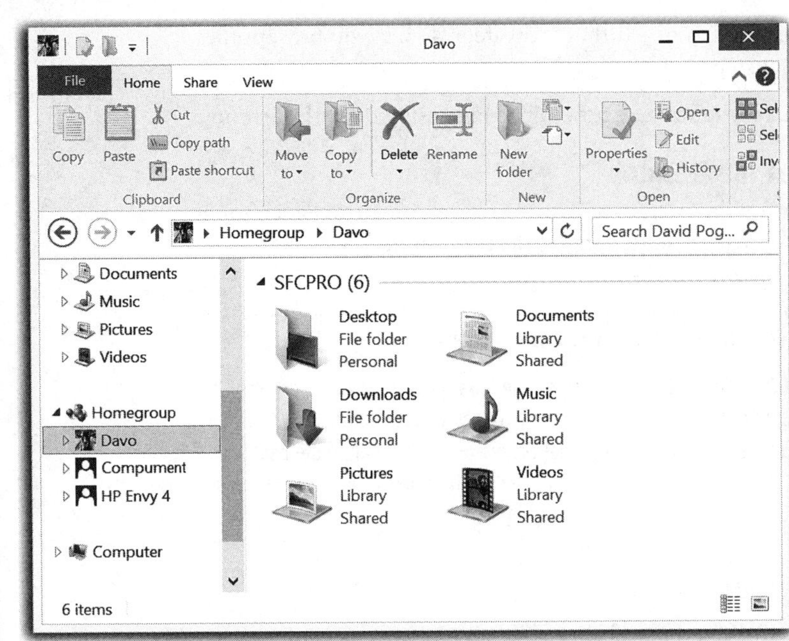

Figure 27-4:
Sitting at PC #1, any Explorer window lets you work with the contents of all the other PCs' libraries. Just expand the Homegroup triangle at the left side of any Explorer window. There they are: individual listings for each account on each PC.

You can click the Homegroup heading and see icons for each account holder/PC, or you can open the flippy triangles in the navigation pane.

In general, you can't change or delete their stuff; this is a "look, don't touch" situation.

How to Share More Files and Folders

Microsoft starts you off by sharing your main libraries—Photos, Videos, Music, Documents. Anything you put in them becomes available immediately.

But that doesn't mean you're limited to sharing those folders. You can share any folder you like, making it available for ransacking by everyone else in the Homegroup.

To do that, open whatever Explorer window it's in. On the Ribbon's Share tab, the tiny scrolling list offers every conceivable way to share the contents of this window (Figure 27-5):

- **Homegroup (view).** Everybody else in the group can see and open these files and folders, but can't delete, change, or add anything.
- **Homegroup (view and edit).** Everybody else in the group can do whatever they like to these files and folders—add, change, delete, whatever. This is a good choice if "everybody" means *you*, moving between computers, or maybe "you and your perfectly trustworthy partner."
- **Robin, Casey, Lee, Dana...** You can also share this window's contents with just *one* person. Select his name here.

- **Specific people.** This option opens a dialog box that lets you add several people to the lucky-invitees list quickly. It's a lot less clunky than adding them one at a time as described in the previous paragraph. See Figure 27-8, later in this chapter.
- **Advanced sharing.** When you've opened the window for a drive or a system folder, the Ribbon doesn't show all of those options. Instead, it shows only one option: Advanced sharing. It opens the Properties dialog box for that drive or folder, open to the Sharing tab, where you can fiddle with the more complex passwords and permissions described later in this chapter.

Figure 27-5: *This tiny scrolling list answers the question: "With whom would you like to share the contents of this folder, master?"*

There's also a "Stop sharing" button on this tab. You probably don't need to be told what it does.

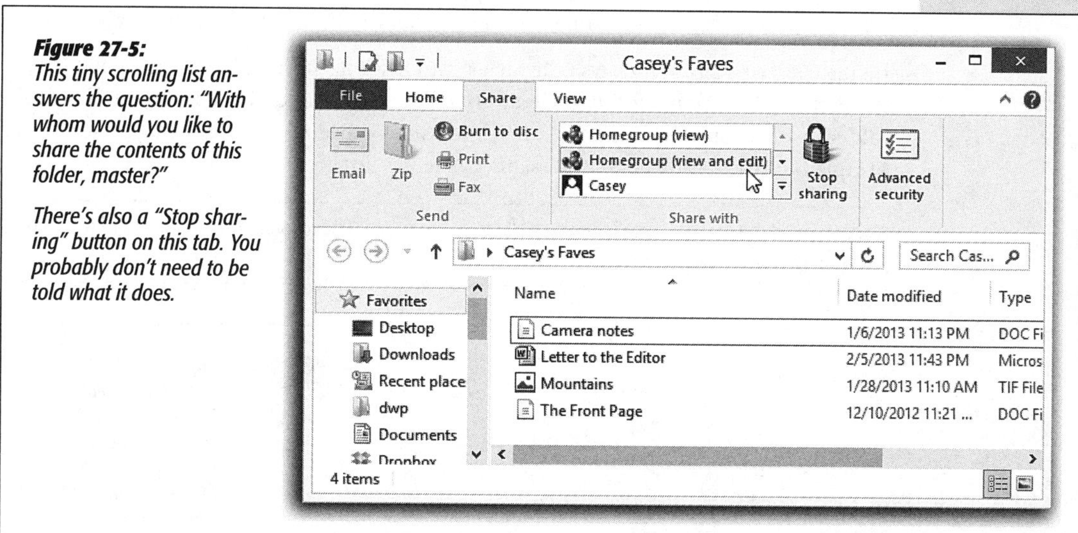

Leaving a Homegroup

If you're feeling a little private, you can remove your PC from the big happy network family, either temporarily or permanently. Just click the Leave button shown in Figure 27-1.

You can rejoin at any time—you'll see a Join button on the Homegroup panel—but you'll need the password. (You can find out the password by opening the Homegroup panel on any *other* PC.)

Tip: If you're not using the Homegroup feature at all, you can also disable it completely. The advantage is that the Homegroup heading won't take up space in your navigation bar anymore.

To do that, switch your network to the Public type ("No, don't turn on sharing"), as shown at lower right on page 439. The next time you start the PC, Homegroup will have vanished from your Explorer windows.

Editing the Shared Homegroup Libraries

Microsoft suggests starting you off by sharing your Music, Pictures, and Videos libraries, as shown in Figure 27-1, plus any USB printer you're connected to; one more click shares your Documents library as well.

If you ever decide to adjust that setup—to turn off your Music, turn on your Documents, or whatever—no biggie. Open the Homegroup panel shown in Figure 27-1 again, and just change the switches.

Sharing the Public Folders

Homegroups are incredibly easy to set up and easy to use. But they're limited to Windows 7/8 computers.

If you have older versions of Windows on hand, Microsoft's *previous* attempt at quick-setup, low-security file sharing is also available: the Public-folders method.

Inside each of your Windows 8 libraries, you'll see a Public folder. You know: Inside the Pictures library is a folder called Public Pictures; inside Music is the Public Music folder; and so on. (See Figure 27-6.) They start out empty, except maybe for some sample files in the Music, Pictures, and Videos folders.

Note: Behind the scenes, these folders are all inside the master Public folder (there's one per PC). It sits in the Local Disk (C:)→Users folder.

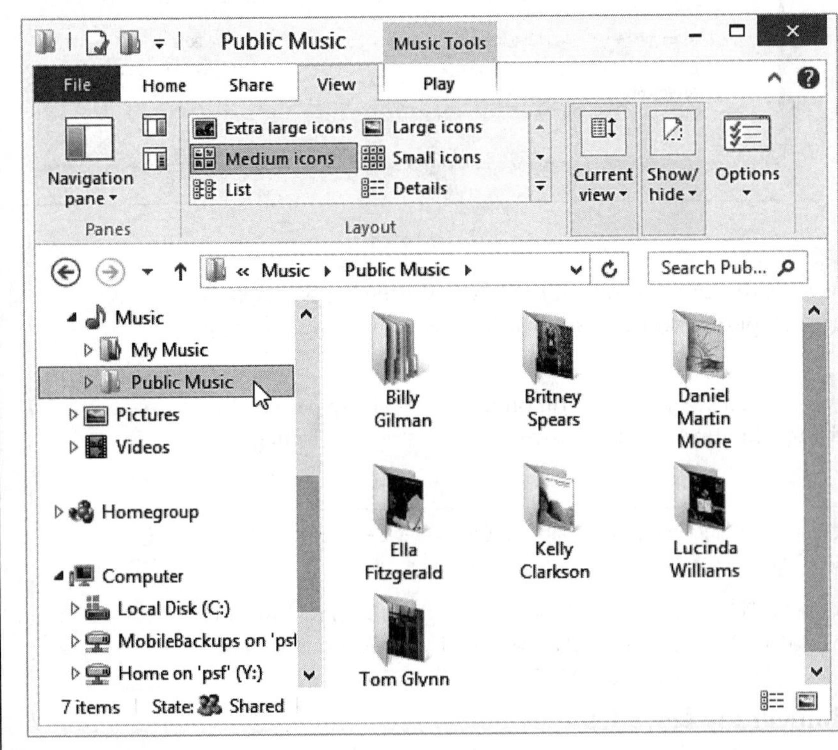

Figure 27-6: *Each Public folder is like a central public square, a shared meeting point for all PCs on the network. Anything in one of these folders is available to anyone on the network–free and clear. You can find the Public folders listed inside each of your standard libraries.*

When you want to share some of your *own* stuff with fellow network denizens, Job One is to drag your files and folders into one of these Public folders.

Before you go live with your Public folder, though, you have a few more options to look over:

- **Set up accounts.** Ordinarily, each person who wants to get into your PC from the network requires an account (Chapter 24). They already have accounts on their own machines, of course, but you need to create corresponding ones on your machine.

Figure 27-7: *Here's how to turn off the requirement for an account password. (Note that in this gigantic, scrolling dialog box, you can set up two sets of options: one for networks you've designated as Home and Work and another for networks you've declared as Public.)*

This illustration is depicted as two different windows, but it's really one gigantic scrolling one; the lower image shows what you see when you reach the bottom.

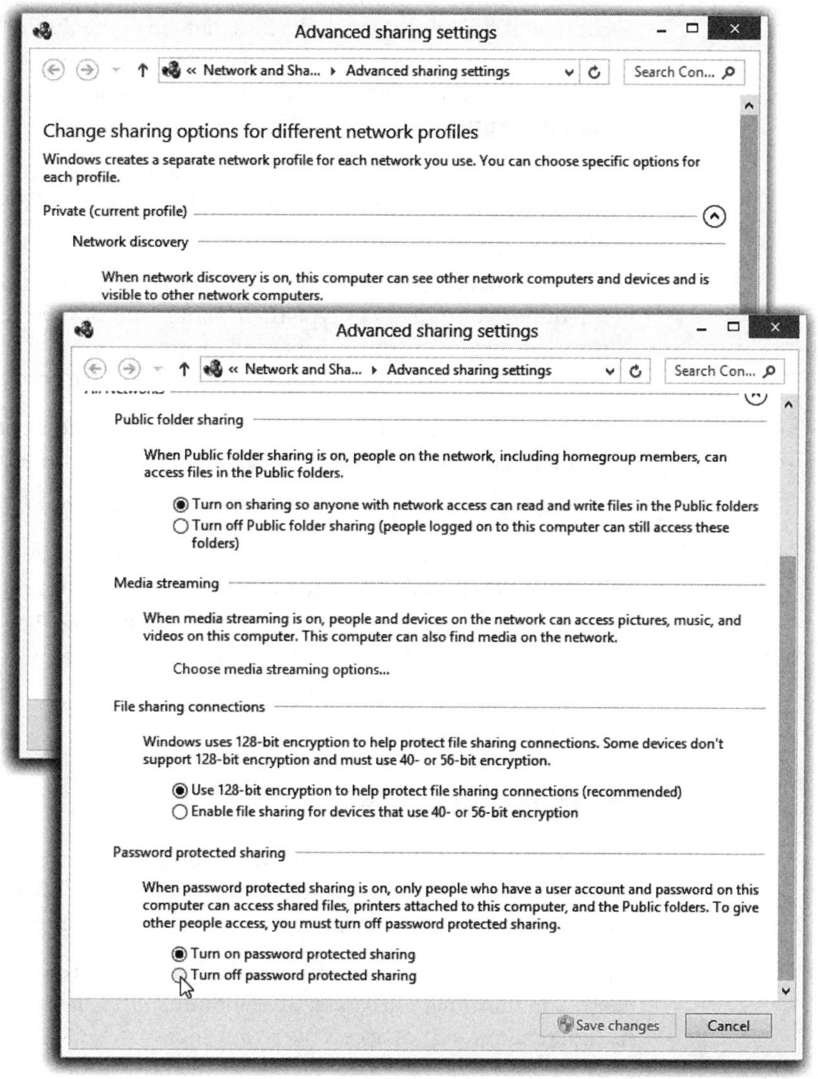

So if, on your own Dell, your name is Casey and your password is *fishsandwich*, then you should see to it that the Toshiba downstairs also has a user account called Casey with the same password.

Tip: When you try to access a shared folder, you can enter any account name and password on that computer. But the beauty of having an account of your own on that machine (with exactly the same name and password) is that you'll breeze right in. You'll connect instantly, without having to encounter the "Connect to" login box every time you connect.

- **Turn off the password requirement (optional).** Anyone who *doesn't* have an account will still be able to see the files that are in the Public folders, open them, and make their own copies of them—but not make changes to them. Such people can't add files, delete anything, or edit anything. (Technically, they'll be using the Guest account feature of every Windows PC.)

  To set up password-free access, open the Start screen and type *sharing;* select Settings under the Search box. In the search results, click "Manage advanced sharing settings."

  As shown in Figure 27-7, "Public folder sharing" comes turned on. Out of the box, it requires your guests to type their names and passwords when connecting. But if you also click "Turn off password protected sharing," then anyone will be able to see what's in your Public folder, even without an account on your machine.

  (Of course, even if you leave passwords on, Windows offers to memorize your name and password when you first connect to a certain computer on the network.)

  To make your changes stick, click "Save changes," and then authenticate yourself if necessary.

- **Turn off Public folder sharing altogether (definitely optional).** Proceed as described above, but click "Turn off Public folder sharing" (shown in Figure 27-7). Now your Public folder is completely invisible on the network.

So now that you've set up Public folder sharing, how are other people supposed to access your Public folder? See page 804.

Sharing Any Folder

If the Public folder method seems too simple, restrictive, and insecure to you, then you can graduate to what Microsoft cleverly calls the "share any folder" method. In this scheme, you can make *any* folder available to other people on the network.

This time, you don't have to move your files anywhere; they sit right where you left them. And this time, you can set up elaborate *sharing permissions* that grant individuals different amount of access over your files.

Better yet, files you share this way are available to other people on the network *and* other account holders on the *same computer.*

Here's how to share a file or folder disk on your PC:

1. **In an Explorer window, open the window that contains the files or folders you want to share. On the Ribbon's Share tab, choose the names of the people you want to share with.**

   The names of this PC's other account holders all appear here, in this cramped scrolling list (Figure 27-8, top). You can click to share with one person.

   Or, to share with more than one person, click "Specific people" to open the "Choose people to share with" dialog box (Figure 27-8, bottom). You wanted individual control over each account holder's access? You got it.

Note: The steps for sharing a *disk* are different. See the box on the next page.

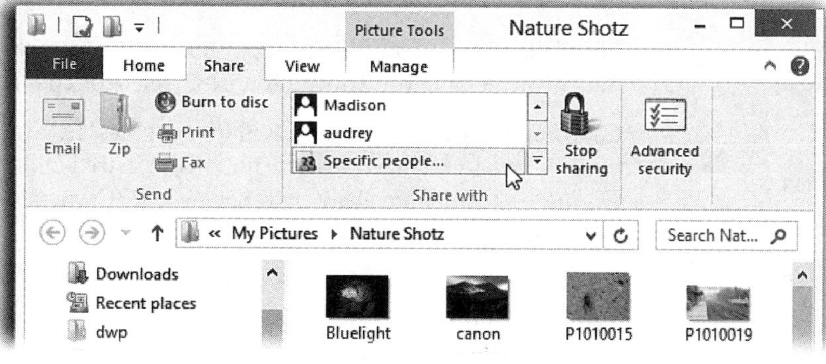

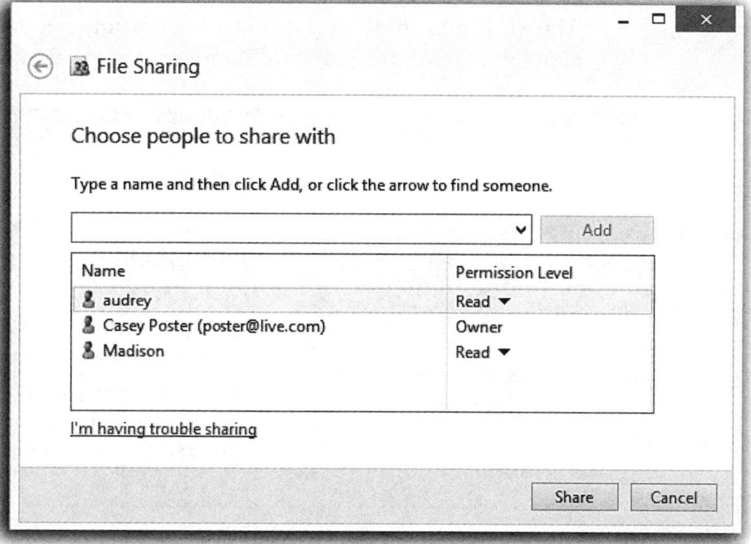

Figure 27-8: *Top: The Ribbon offers insta-sharing with any individual. Or, if you want more than one person to get in on the fun, choose "Specific people" to open...*

Bottom: ...this box.

Use the pop-up menu at the top to choose an account holder's name. Or type it out, if you prefer.

After each name, click Add. Then use the Permission Level pop-up menu to specify either Read ("look but don't touch") or Read/Write ("you can edit and even delete stuff") permissions. Click Share when you're finished.

2. **Choose a person's name from the upper pop-up menu, and then click Add.**

   This is the list of account holders (Chapter 24)—or account-holder *groups*, if someone has created them.

   If the person who'll be connecting across the network doesn't yet have an account on your machine, choose "Create a new user" from this pop-up menu. (This option is available if the PC is *not* part of a Homegroup. Also, "Create a new user" isn't some kind of sci-fi breakthrough. You are not, in fact, going to create a human being—only an account for an *existing* person.)

   The name appears in the list.

   Now your job is to work through this list of people, specify *how much* control each person has over the file or folder you're sharing.

3. **Click a name in the list. Click the ▾ in the Permission Level column and choose Read or Read/Write.**

   Read is that "look, but don't touch" business. This person can see what's in the folder (or file) and can copy it, but can't delete or change the original.

   Contributors (available for folders only—not files) have much broader access. These people can add, change, or delete files in the shared folder—but only files *that they put there.* Stuff placed there by other people (Owners or Co-owners) appears as "look, but don't touch" to a Contributor.

   Read/Write means that this person, like you, can add, change, or delete any file in the shared folder.

Note: Your name shows up here as Owner. You have the most power of all–after all, it's your stuff.

This stuff may sound technical and confusing, but you have no idea how much simpler it is than it was before Windows 8 came along.

GEM IN THE ROUGH

Sharing Disks

You can share files and folders, of course, but also *disks.*

Sharing an entire disk means that every folder on it, and therefore every file, is available to everyone on the network. If security isn't a big deal at your place (because it's just you and a couple of family members, for example), this feature can be a timesaving convenience that spares you the trouble of sharing every new folder you create.

On the other hand, people with privacy concerns generally prefer to share individual *folders.* By sharing only a folder or two, you can keep *most* of the stuff on your hard drive private, out of view of curious network comrades. For that matter, sharing only a folder or two does *them* a favor, too, by making it easier for them to find the files you've made available. This way, they don't have to root through your entire drive looking for the folder they actually need.

4. **Click Share.**

   The "Your folder [or file] is shared" dialog box appears. This is more than a simple message, however; it contains the *network address* of the files or folders you shared. Without this address, your colleagues won't know that you've shared stuff and will have a tough time finding it.

Note: If you've shared some files, you may see an interim message that appears before the "Your files are shared" box, warning you that Windows is about to adjust the access permissions to the folder that encloses them. That's normal.

---

5. **Click "e-mail" or "copy" (Figure 27-9).**

   The "e-mail" link opens a new, outgoing message in your email program, letting the gang know that you've shared something and offering them a link to it. The "copy" link copies the address to the Clipboard so you can paste it into another program—which is your best bet if Mail isn't your email program of choice.

Tip: To stop sharing a folder or file, click it. Then, from the Share tab of the Ribbon of whatever window contains it, choose "Stop sharing."

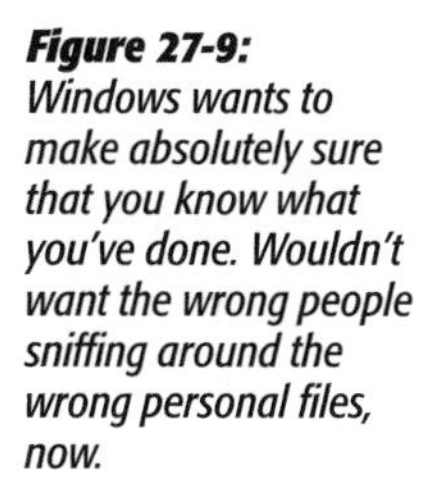

Figure 27-9: *Windows wants to make absolutely sure that you know what you've done. Wouldn't want the wrong people sniffing around the wrong personal files, now.*

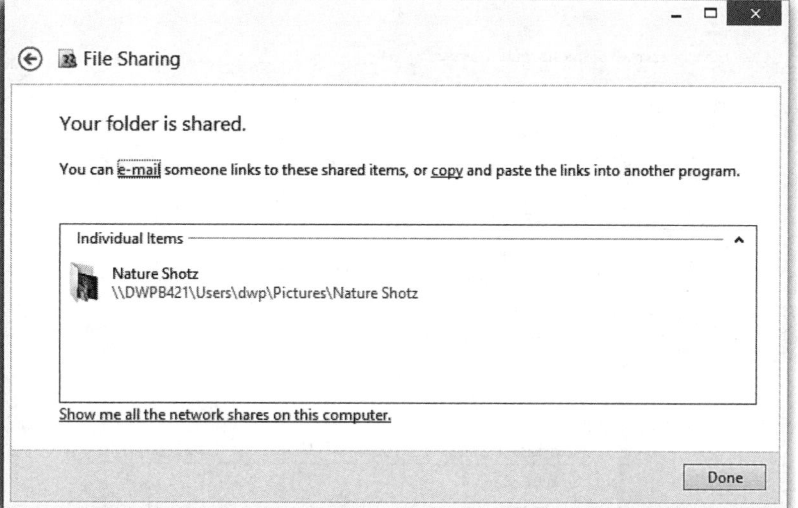

Advanced Folder Sharing–and Disk Sharing

Microsoft made a noble step forward in simplicity with the "share any folder" wizard described in the previous pages. But the older, more complicated—yet more flexible—method is still available. Here's a quick review of this alternate route (which is, by the way, the *only* route for sharing entire *disks):*

1. **Right-click the folder or disk you want to share. If it's a folder, choose Properties from the shortcut menu, and then click the Sharing tab. If it's a disk, choose "Share with"→"Advanced sharing."**

   At this point, you *could* click the Share button (if you're operating on a folder, anyway). You'd arrive at the dialog box shown in Figure 27-8 (bottom) where you could specify the account holders and permission levels, just as described earlier. But don't.

2. **Click Advanced Sharing. Authenticate, if necessary.**

   The Advanced Sharing dialog box appears.

3. **Turn on "Share this folder." (See Figure 27-10, top.) Next, set up the power-user sharing options.**

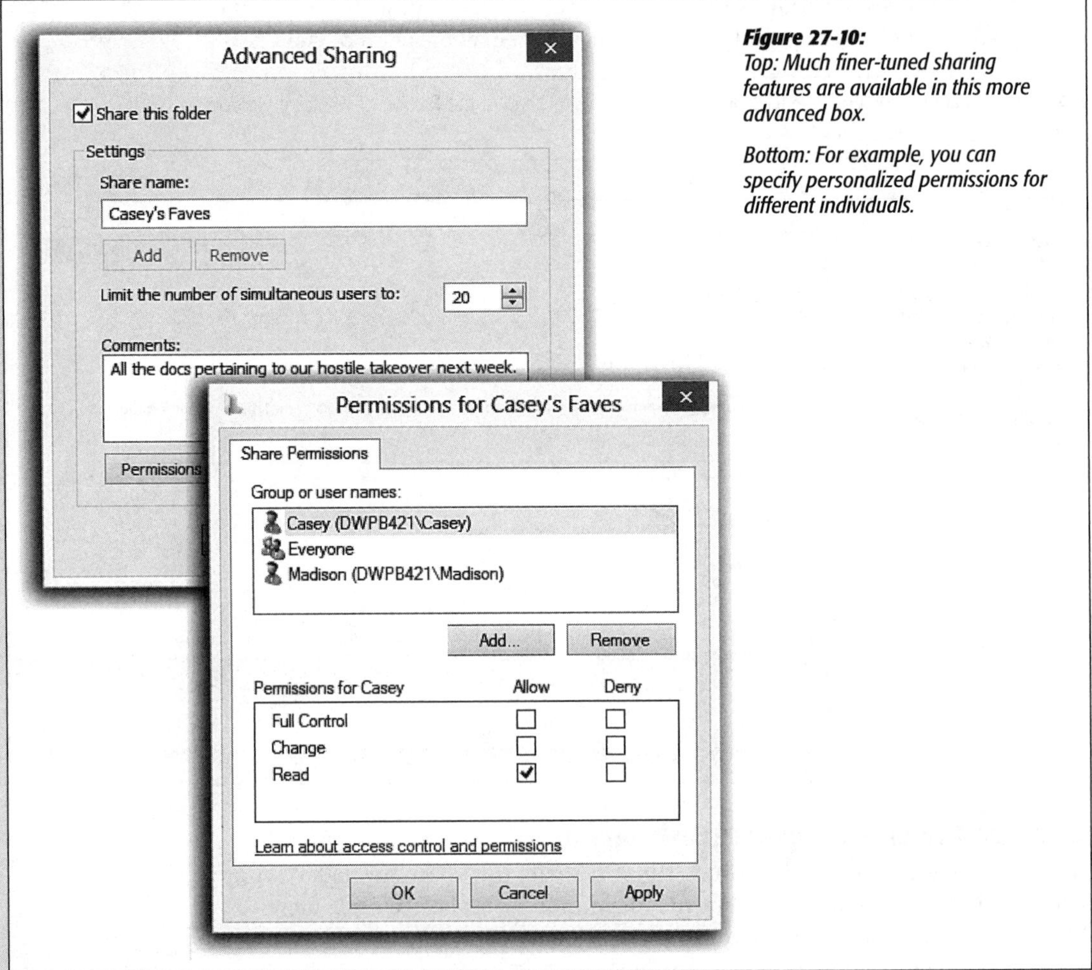

Figure 27-10:
Top: Much finer-tuned sharing features are available in this more advanced box.

Bottom: For example, you can specify personalized permissions for different individuals.

For example, you can limit the number of people who are browsing this folder at once. You can click Permissions to fine-tune who can do what (Figure 27-10, bottom). And you can edit the "Share name"—in fact, you can create *more than one* name for the same shared folder—to make it more recognizable on the network when people are browsing your PC.

Tip: For more on Allow, Deny, and other sharing privileges, see page 755.

Notes on File Sharing

And now, the fine print on sharing files:

- Sharing a folder also shares all the folders inside it, including new ones you create later.

  On the other hand, it's OK to *change* the sharing settings of a subfolder. For example, if you've shared a folder called America, you can make the Minnesota folder inside it off-limits by making it private. To do this, right-click the inner folder, choose Properties, click Sharing, click Advanced Sharing, and use the dialog box shown in Figure 27-10.

- Be careful with nested folders. Suppose, for example, that you share your Documents folder, and you permit other people to change the files inside it. Now suppose that you share a folder that's *inside* Documents—called Spreadsheets, for example—but you turn *off* the ability for other people to change its files.

  You wind up with a strange situation. Both folders—Documents and Spreadsheets—show up in other people's Network windows, as described below. If they double-click the Spreadsheets folder directly, they won't be able to change anything inside it. But if they double-click the Documents folder and then open the Spreadsheets folder inside *it*, they *can* modify the files.

Hiding Folders

If a certain folder on your hard drive is really private, you can hide the folder so that other people on the network can't even *see* it. The secret is to type a $ symbol at the end of the *share name* (shown at top in Figure 27-10).

POWER USERS' CLINIC

Unhiding Hidden Folders

As sneaky and delightful as the hidden-folder trick is, it has a distinct drawback–*you* can't see your hidden folder from across the network, either. Suppose you want to the upstairs PC on the network to open something in your hidden My Novel folder (which is downstairs in the kitchen). Fortunately, you can do so–if you know the secret.

On the upstairs computer, press ⊞+R. In the Run dialog box, type the path of the hidden folder, using the format *\\Computer Name\Folder Name.*

For example, enter *\\kitchen\my novel$* to get to the hidden folder called "My Novel$" on the PC called "Kitchen." (Capitalization doesn't matter.) Then click OK to open a window showing the contents of your hidden folder.

For example, if you name a certain folder My Novel, anyone else on the network can see it (even if they can't read the contents). But if you name the folder *My Novel$*, it won't show up in anybody's Network window. They won't even know it exists.

Accessing Shared Folders

Now suppose you're not you. You're your coworker, spouse, or employee. You're using your laptop downstairs, and you want access to the stuff that's in a shared folder on the Beefy Main Dell computer upstairs. Here's what to do (the steps are the same whether the Public folder or *any* folder was shared):

1. **Open any Explorer window.**

   The navigation pane at left shows a Network heading. Click its flippy triangle, if necessary, to see icons for all the computers on the network (Figure 27-11, top). The same navigation pane is available in the Save and Open dialog boxes of your programs, too, making the entire network available to you for opening and saving files.

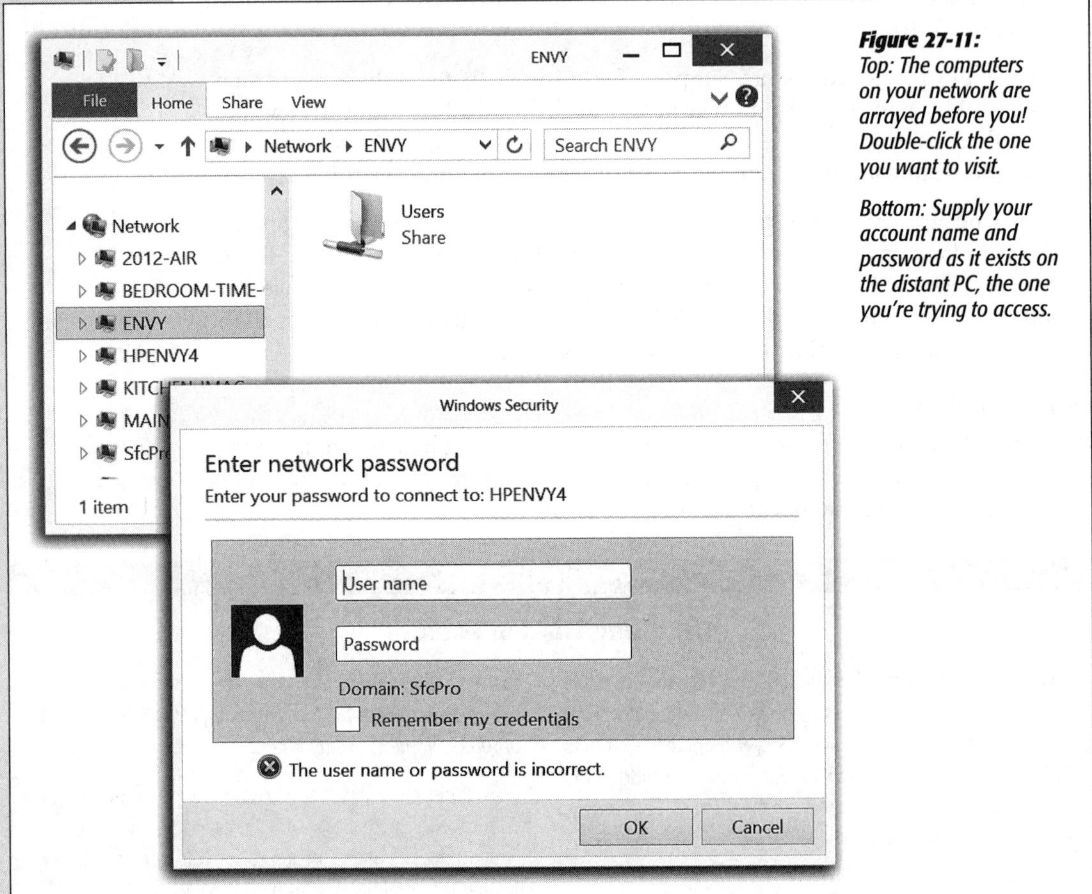

Figure 27-11: *Top: The computers on your network are arrayed before you! Double-click the one you want to visit.*

Bottom: Supply your account name and password as it exists on the distant PC, the one you're trying to access.

Tip: Alternatively, type *network* at the Start screen; press Enter to open the Network result in the results list.

If you *don't* see a certain computer's icon here, it might be turned off, or off the network. It also might have *network discovery* turned off; that's the feature that lets a PC announce its presence to the network. (Its on/off switch is one of the buttons shown in Figure 27-7.)

And if you don't see any computers at *all* in the Network window, then network discovery might be turned off on *your* computer.

2. **Double-click the computer whose files you want to open.**

FREQUENTLY ASKED QUESTION

Accessing Windows 8 from XP, Vista, Mac...

How do I access my Windows 8 PC from my non-Windows 8 machines?

Piece of cake. Turns out all versions of Windows use the same networking scheme, so you can share files freely among PCs using different Windows versions.

Once some files are shared (on any PC), here's how to find them:

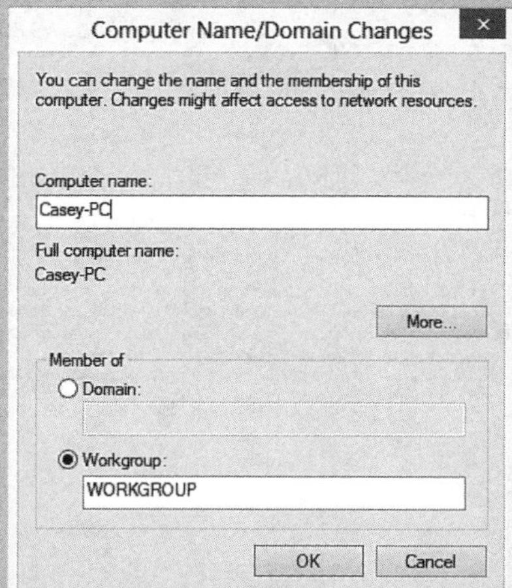

In Windows 7 or Windows Vista: Choose Start→Network.

In Windows XP or Windows Me: Choose Start→My Network Places.

In earlier versions: Double-click the desktop icon called Network Neighborhood or My Network Places.

On the Mac: Just look in the Sidebar of any Finder window in the Shared category. Open the Workgroup icon, if you see it, and then double-click the name of the computer you want. Enter your PC account's name and password. (You'll probably have trouble if your PC account doesn't have a password.) The whole thing looks exactly like Figure 27-11.

Now you see icons that correspond to the computers on your network (including your own machine), much as shown in Figure 27-11. That should be all there is to it.

If you don't see the Windows computers, it may because all the machines don't have the same *workgroup* name. (A workgroup is a cluster of networked machines.) To change your Windows XP computer's workgroup name to match, choose Start→Control Panel, click "Performance and Maintenance," and then open System. Click the Computer Name tab, and then select Change.

To change a Vista PC's workgroup name, choose Start→Control Panel; click System and Maintenance; open System. Under the "Computer Name, Domain, and Workgroup Settings" heading, click Change Settings.

To change a Mac's workgroup name, open →System Preferences→Network. Click Advanced→WINS, and type right into the Workgroup box.

And to change your Windows 7/8 machine's name, type *rename* into the Start screen or menu; click "Change workgroup name" under Settings. Click Change, and enjoy the box shown here.

If you're on a corporate domain, you may first have to double-click your way through some other icons, representing the networks in other buildings or floors, before you get to the actual PC icons.

If you *don't* have an account on the PC you're invading—an account with the same name and password as you have on your own PC—then the Connect To box now appears (Figure 27-11, top).

Here, you have to fill the name and password of an account on the *other* computer. This, of course, is a real drag, especially if you access other people's files frequently. Fortunately, you have two timesaving tricks available to you here.

First, if you turn on "Remember my credentials," then you'll never see this box again. The next time you want to visit the other PC, you'll be able to double-click its icon for instant access.

Finally, if you're trying to get to someone's Public folder, and you don't need to modify the files, but just read or copy them, you don't need a password, ever. Just

GEM IN THE ROUGH

Accessing Macs Across the Network

When it comes to networking, Macs are people, too.

Windows is perfectly capable of letting you rifle through a Mac's contents from across the network. Here's how to set that up (these instructions cover OS X 10.8, Mountain Lion.)

On the Mac, choose → System Preferences. Click Sharing, and then turn on File Sharing. Click Options.

Now you see the dialog box shown here. Turn on "Share files and folders using SMB (Windows)." Then specify *which* Mac user accounts you want to be able to access; enter their passwords as necessary, and then click Done.

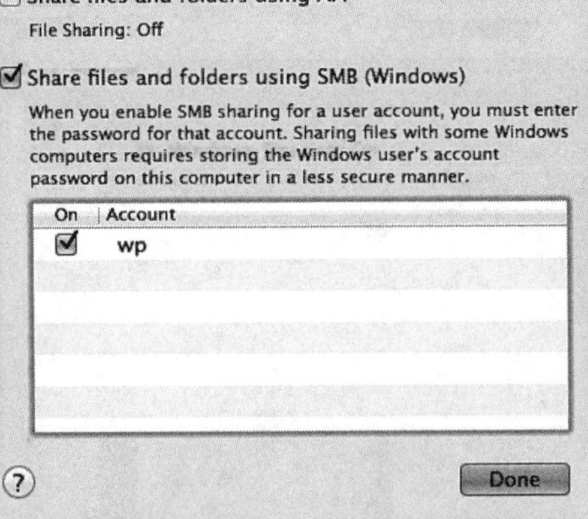

(Before you close System Preferences, you might notice that the line in the middle of the dialog box says: "Windows users can access your computer at smb://192.168.1.203." Those numbers are the Mac's IP address. You'd need it only if you decided to access the Mac by typing its UNC code [page 808] into your Windows address bar, like this: *102.168.1.203.*)

On the PC, proceed exactly as though you were trying to connect to another Windows PC. The Mac's name shows up in the Network section of the navigation pane (left side of any Explorer window).

When you click the Mac's name, you see the dialog box shown in Figure 27-11, bottom. Enter your Mac account name and password, and turn on "Remember my credentials" (so you won't be bothered for a name or password the next time you perform this amazing act of détente). Click OK.

Now your Mac home folder opens on the screen before you. Feel free to work with those files exactly as though they were in a folder on your PC. Détente has never been so easy.

type *guest* into the "User name" box and click OK. You'll have full read-only access. And here again, next time, you won't be bothered for a name or password.

Tip: In the unlikely event that you want Windows to *stop* memorizing your password, open the Start screen. Type *credential* and select Settings under the Search box. In the search results, click Credential Manager. You see a list of every name/password Windows has memorized for you. You can use the options here to add a new memorized name/password, or expand one of the existing items in the list to remove it ("Remove from vault") or edit it.

3. Click OK.

   If all went well, the other computer's window opens, presenting you with the icons of its shared folders and disks.

Tip: Working with the same shared folders often? Save yourself a lot of time and burrowing–make a desktop shortcut of it right now!

Once you've opened the window that contains the shared folder, grab your mouse. Right-click the shared item and drag it to the desktop. When you release the mouse, choose "Create shortcuts here" from the shortcut menu. From now on, you can double-click that shortcut to open the shared item directly.

Once you've brought a networked folder onto your screen, you can double-click icons to open them, drag them to the Recycle Bin, make copies of them, and otherwise manipulate them exactly as though they were icons on your own hard drive. (Of course, if you weren't given permission to change the contents of the shared folder, you have less freedom.)

Tip: There's one significant difference between working with "local" icons and working with those that sit elsewhere on the network. When you delete a file from another computer on the network (if you're allowed to do so), either by pressing the Delete key or by dragging it to the Recycle Bin, it disappears instantly and permanently, without ever appearing in the Recycle Bin.

You can even use Windows' Search feature to find files elsewhere on the network. This kind of searching can be very slow, however.

Extra Credit: Universal Naming Convention (UNC)

For hard-core nerds, that business of double-clicking icons in the Network folder is for sissies. When they want to call up a shared folder from the network, or even a particular document *in* a shared folder, they just type a special address into the address bar of any folder window, or even Internet Explorer—and then press the Enter key. You can also type such addresses into the Run dialog box (press ⊞+R).

It might look like this: *laptop\shared documents\salaries 2014.doc.*

Tip: Actually, you don't have to type nearly that much. The AutoComplete feature may propose the full expression as soon as you type just a few letters of it.

This path format (including the double-backslash before the PC name and a single backslash before a folder name) is called the *Universal Naming Convention (UNC)*. It was devised to create a method of denoting the exact location of a particular file or folder on a network. It also lets network geeks open various folders and files on networked machines without having to use the Network window.

You can use this system in all kinds of interesting ways:

- Open a particular folder like this: *computer name\folder name.*
- You can also substitute the IP address for the computer instead of using its name, like this: *192.168.1.44\my documents.*
- You can even substitute the name of a shared *printer* for the folder name.
- As described later in this chapter, Windows can even access shared folders that sit elsewhere on the Internet (offline backup services, for example). You can call these items onto your screen (once you're online) just by adding *http:* before the UNC code and using regular forward slashes instead of backward slashes, like this: *http://Computer Name/Folder Name.*

Tip: A great place to type UNC addresses is in the address bar at the top of any File Explorer window.

Mapping Shares to Drive Letters

If you access network shares on a regular basis, you may want to consider another access technique, called *mapping shares*. Using this trick, you can assign a *letter* to a particular shared disk or folder on the network. Just as your hard drive is called C: and your floppy drive is A:, you can give your Family Stuff folder the letter F: and the backup drive in the kitchen the letter J:.

Doing so confers several benefits. First, these disks and folders now appear directly in the Computer window. Getting to them this way can be faster than navigating to the Network window.

Second, when you choose File→Open from within one of your applications, you'll be able to jump directly to a particular shared folder instead of having to double-click, ever deeper, through the icons in the Open File dialog box. You can also use the mapped drive letter in pathnames anywhere you would use a path on a local drive, such as the Run dialog box, a File→Save As dialog box, or the Command Line.

To map a drive letter to a disk or folder, open the Computer window. (In any Explorer window, click Computer in the navigation pane at left.) Then, on the Ribbon's Computer tab, click "Map network drive."

The Map Network Drive dialog box appears, as shown in Figure 27-12.

2. **Using the drop-down list, choose a drive letter.**

   You can select any unused letter you like (except B, which is still reserved for the second floppy disk drive that PCs don't have anymore).

3. **Indicate which folder or disk you want this letter to represent.**

   You can type its UNC code into the Folder box, choose from the drop-down list of recently accessed folders, or click Browse.

Figure 27-12: *Top: Choose a letter, any letter. Then choos a folder, any folder.*

Bottom: You've just turned a folder into a drive, complete with it own drive letter—and instant access to the navigation pane.

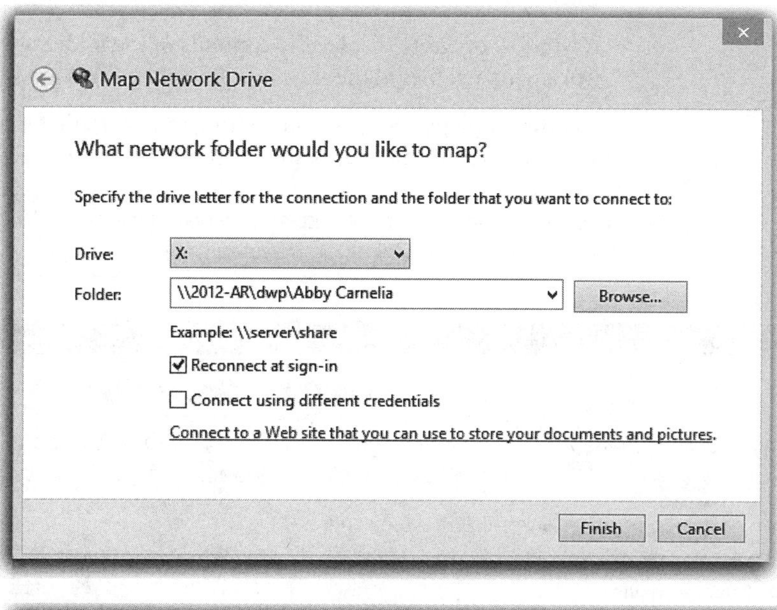

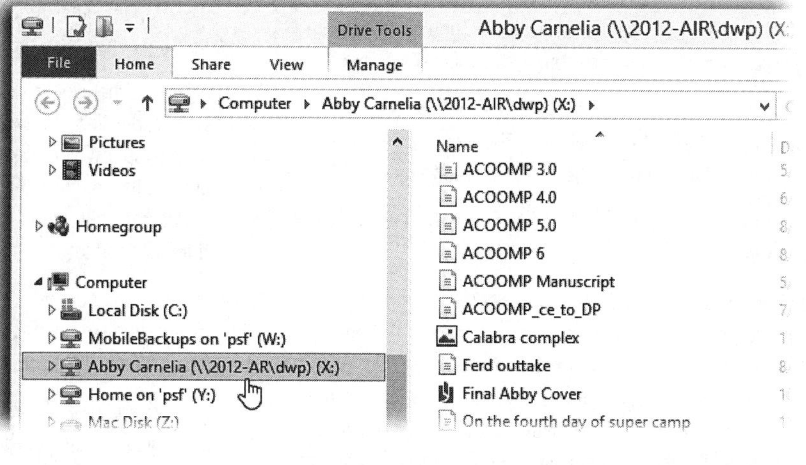

Tip: Most people use the mapping function for disks and drives elsewhere on the network, but there's nothing to stop you from mapping a folder that's sitting right there on your own PC.

4. **To make this letter assignment stick, turn on "Reconnect at sign-in."**

   If you don't use this option, Windows forgets this assignment the next time you turn on the computer. (Use the "Connect using different credentials" option if your account name on the shared folder's machine isn't the same as it is on this one.)

5. **Click Finish.**

   A window opens to display the contents of the folder or disk. If you don't want to work with any files at the moment, just close the window.

From now on (depending on your setting in step 4), that shared disk or folder shows up in your navigation pane, as shown at bottom in Figure 27-11.

Tip: If you see a red X on one of these mapped icons, it means that the PC on which one of the shared folders or disks resides is either off the network or is turned off completely.

FREQUENTLY ASKED QUESTION

FTP Sites and Other Online Disks

How do I bring an FTP server, or one of those Web-based backup drives, onto my PC?

The trick to bringing these servers online is to open the Computer window. On the Ribbon's Computer tab, click "Add a network location."

When the wizard appears, click Next. Then, on the second screen, click "Choose a custom network location." Click Next.

Finally you arrive at the critical screen, where you can type in the address of the Web site, FTP site, or other network location that you want your new shortcut to open.

Into the first text box, you can type any of these network addresses:

The UNC code. As described earlier in this chapter, a UNC code pinpoints a particular shared folder on the network. For example, if you want to open the shared folder named FamilyBiz on the computer named Dad, enter *\\dad\family-biz.* Capitalization doesn't matter. Or, to open a specific file, you could enter something like *\\dad\finances\budget.xls.*

http://website/folder. To see what's in a folder called Customers on a company Web site called BigBiz.com, enter *http://bigbiz.com/customers.* (You can't just type in any old Web address. It has to be a Web site that's been specifically designed to serve as a "folder" containing files.)

ftp://ftp.website/folder. This is the address format for FTP sites. For example, if you want to use a file in a folder named Bids on a company site named WeBuyStuff.com, enter *ftp://ftp.webuystuff.com/bids.*

What happens when you click Next depends on the kind of address you specified. If it was an FTP site, you're offered the chance to specify your user name. (Access to every FTP site requires a user name and password. You won't be asked for the password until you actually try to open the newly created folder shortcut.)

Click Finish. Your network shortcut now appears in the Network Location area in the Computer window. The wizard also offers to connect to and open the corresponding folder.

You can work with these remote folders exactly as though they were sitting on your own hard drive. The only difference is that because you're actually communicating with a hard drive via the Internet, the slower speed may make it feel as if your PC has been drugged.

Sharing a DVD Drive

Clearly, the computer industry thinks the DVD is going away. More and more people rent movies by streaming them from the Internet instead of renting a disc. More and more software comes as a download instead of on a CD or a DVD. And more and more, new laptop models (not to mention tablets) don't even come with DVD drives.

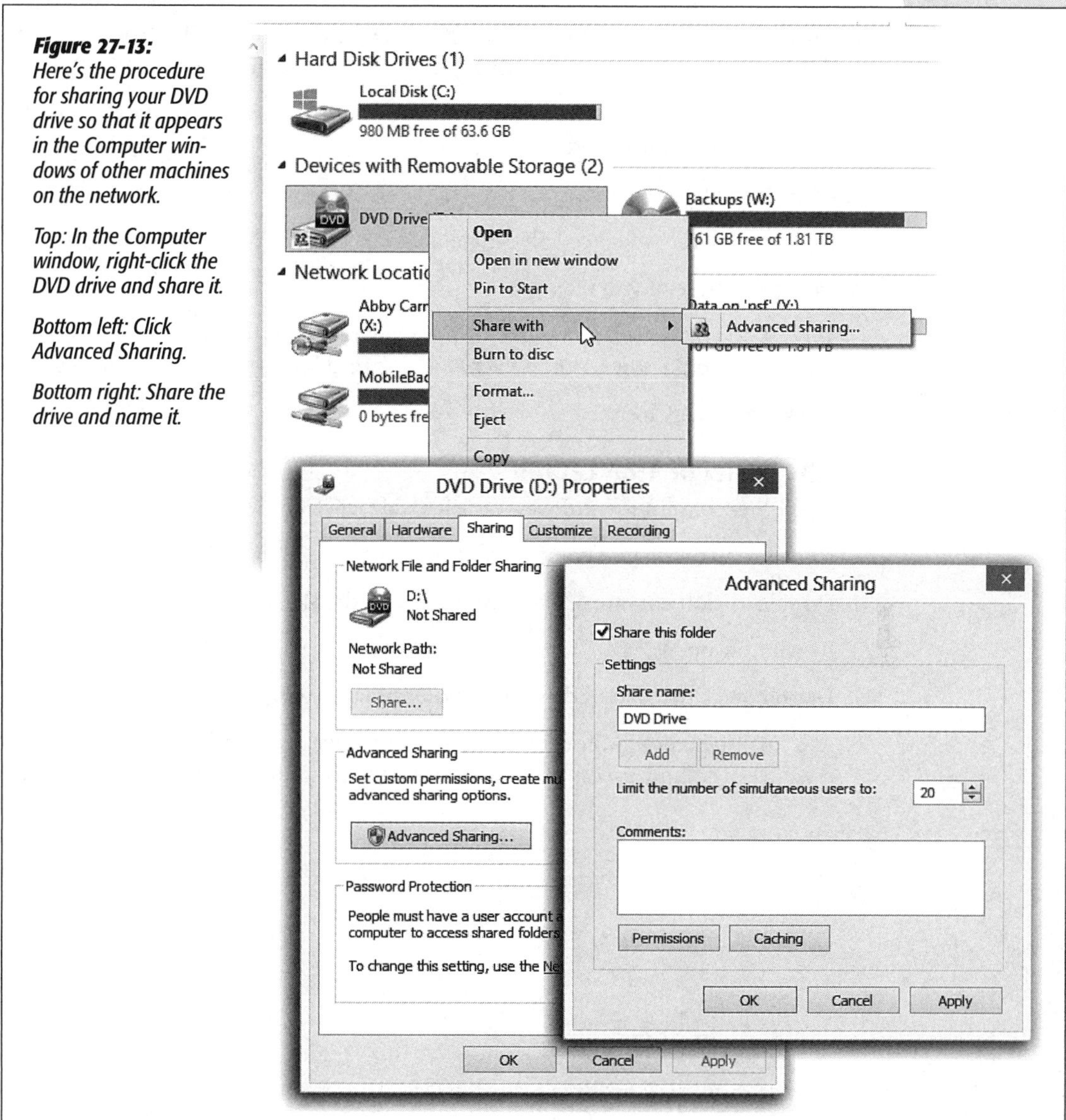

Figure 27-13: *Here's the procedure for sharing your DVD drive so that it appears in the Computer windows of other machines on the network.*

Top: In the Computer window, right-click the DVD drive and share it.

Bottom left: Click Advanced Sharing.

Bottom right: Share the drive and name it.

But discs aren't completely dead. Sooner or later, you might wind up wishing you had a DVD drive in your tablet or superthin laptop.

Fortunately, there's a workaround. If another Windows PC on your network has a DVD drive, you can share it over the network so that it appears on the screen of your laptop or tablet. Here's how to do it (follow along in Figure 27-13):

On the PC with the Drive

1. **In the Computer window (press ⊞+E), right-click the DVD drive; from the shortcut menu, choose "Share with"→"Advanced sharing" (Figure 27-13, top).**

   You've just opened the DVD drive's Properties box, already on the Sharing tab (Figure 27-13, bottom left).

2. **Click Advanced Sharing.**

   Now you see the Advanced Sharing dialog box (Figure 27-13, bottom right).

3. **Name the drive, if you like.**

   Type "DVD drive" or something into the "Share name" box. (If you click Permissions, you should now see that "Everyone" has read access to the drive. That's good.)

4. **Click OK, then Close.**

On the Tablet or Thin Laptop

1. **Open the Computer window. At the left side, click Network.**

   Icons for all the shared computers appear.

2. **Double-click the name of the computer with the shared drive.**

   Its window opens.

3. **Double-click the shared drive; now you can work with whatever disc is inside it.**

   As a final step, though, consider *mapping* this drive, as described earlier. That way, it will always show up on your tablet or laptop as though it were built right in.

CHAPTER
28

The Road Warrior's Handbook

If Windows 8's two-headed design means anything at all, it's that Microsoft is betting on the future of mobile. Fewer and fewer computers will be tethered to desks. More and more will be carried around—and most of them will have touchscreens. Microsoft believes that so strongly, it created TileWorld to be ready.

But the touchscreen simplicity of TileWorld isn't the only nod Windows 8 makes to easing the lives of road warriors. This chapter covers a motley collection of additional tools for anyone who travels.

Windows Mobility Center

The Windows Mobility Center is a handy, centralized hub for managing everything that makes a laptop a laptop (Figure 28-1): battery, wireless networking, external projector connection, and so on. The quickest way to get there is to choose its name from the secret Utilities menu (press ⊞+X, or right-click the lower-left corner of the screen.)

You can also open the Start screen, type *mobility*, and select Settings under the search box. In the search results, click Windows Mobility Center.

Here's the list of tiles that may appear in your Mobility Center. You may not have all of them, depending on what kind of computer you're using and what components it has. And you may have more of them, if your computer company installed its own options.

Note: Of course, many of the functions of this older control panel are now right there on the Charms bar when you tap Settings, which might be quicker to get to.

- **Display brightness.** The slider dims your screen for this work session only, which can save enormous amounts of battery power. If you want to make brightness changes that are always in effect, you can click the small monitor icon to open the Power Options control panel.
- **Volume.** Change your speakers' volume, or mute them entirely. Click the icon to open the Sound control panel.

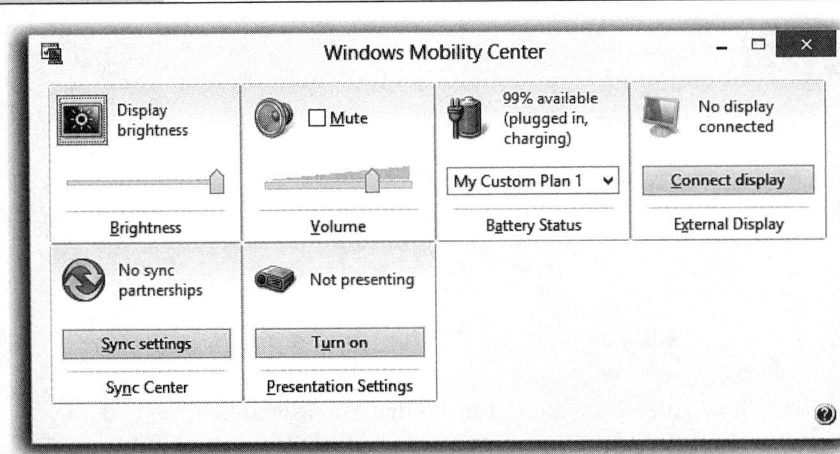

Figure 28-1: *Each setting in Mobility Center is illustrated with a cute little icon—but don't be fooled. This is so much more than an icon! It's also a* button *that, when double-clicked, opens up a Control Panel applet or a configuration page.*

- **Battery Status.** This is your battery's fuel gauge. The drop-down menu lets you choose a power plan setting, like "High performance" (your PC doesn't go to sleep, but uses up battery power faster) or "Power saver" (the laptop goes to sleep sooner to conserve juice). Click the icon to open the Power Options control panel, where you can change the power-plan settings for good.
- **Screen Orientation.** This one appears most often on tablets. It lets you turn the screen image 90 degrees. Click the icon to open the Display Settings control panel for additional screen settings.

Tip: On some laptops and tablets, Ctrl+Alt+arrow key rotates the screen, which saves you a few steps.

- **External Display.** Have you hooked up a second monitor? If so, click "Connect display" to make Windows aware of its new responsibilities. This tile also reveals whether or not Windows "sees" the second screen. Click the icon to open the Display control panel, where you can configure the resolution and other settings of the second monitor.
- **Sync Center.** The Sync Center is the communications hub for *offline files*, the "sync my copies with the network copies" feature described on page 815. This tile shows you the status of a sync that's already under way. Click the icon (or "Sync settings") to open the Sync Center program, where you can set up new "sync partnerships" between your PC and other network PCs.

- **Presentation Settings.** This feature is the answer to a million PowerPoint pitchers' prayers. It makes sure that your laptop won't do anything embarrassing while you're in the middle of your boardroom presentation.

  On the Presentation Settings tile of Mobility Center, click "Turn on." When the tile says "Presenting," your laptop won't go to sleep. No alarms or reminder dialog boxes appear. The screen saver doesn't kick in. You're free to give your pitch in peace. Click the icon to open the Presentation Settings dialog box shown in Figure 28-2.

Tip: Once the Mo' Center is open, you can also open its icons entirely from the keyboard. Try this: See the underlined letter beneath each panel, such as Battery Status or Connect Display? (If not, tap the Alt key.) Press that letter key to highlight the icon, and then press Enter.

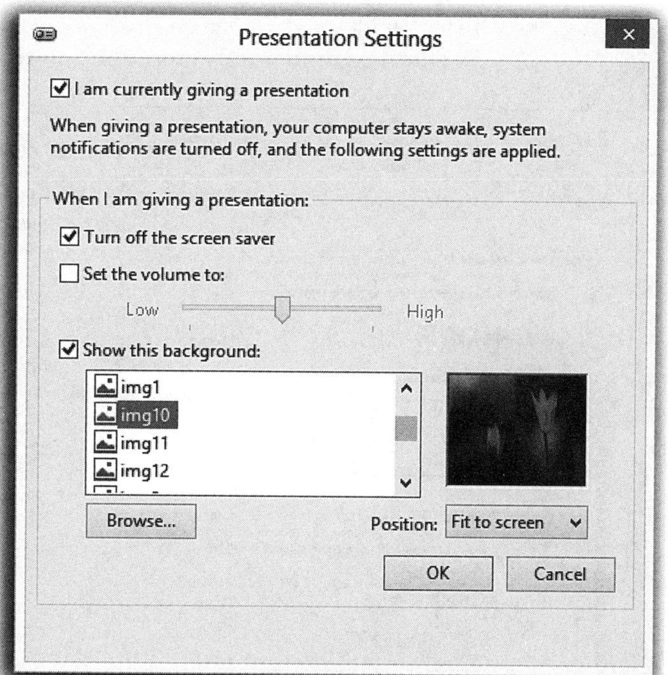

Figure 28-2: *When you're in Presentation mode, your screen saver and system notifications don't appear, and your laptop won't go to sleep. You might also want to specify a piece of uncontroversial artwork for your desktop wallpaper, so your bosses and potential employers won't accidentally spot the HotBikiniBabes.com JPEG you usually use.*

Offline Files and Sync Center

The *offline files feature* is designed for laptop lovers. It lets you carry off files that generally live on your office network, so you can get some work done while you're away.

Then, when you return and connect your laptop to the office network, Windows automatically copies your edited, updated documents back to their original locations on the network, intelligently keeping straight which copies are the most recent. (And vice versa—if people changed the network copies while you were away, Windows copies them onto your laptop.)

Offline Files is a great feature for corporate workers. When you reconnect to the home network, Windows triggers an automatic, seamless, invisible synchronization of the files you worked on while you were away—there's no alert balloon, no need to shut down all programs and manually trigger the sync.

You can also command Windows to sync at more specific times: every time you connect to the network, for example, or at 3:00 a.m.

Turn on the Feature

Before you can use Offline Files, you have to flip its master switch on. See Figure 28-3.

Preparing to Leave the Network

To tell Windows which files and folders you want to take away with you on the laptop, find them on the network. Proceed as shown in Figure 28-4.

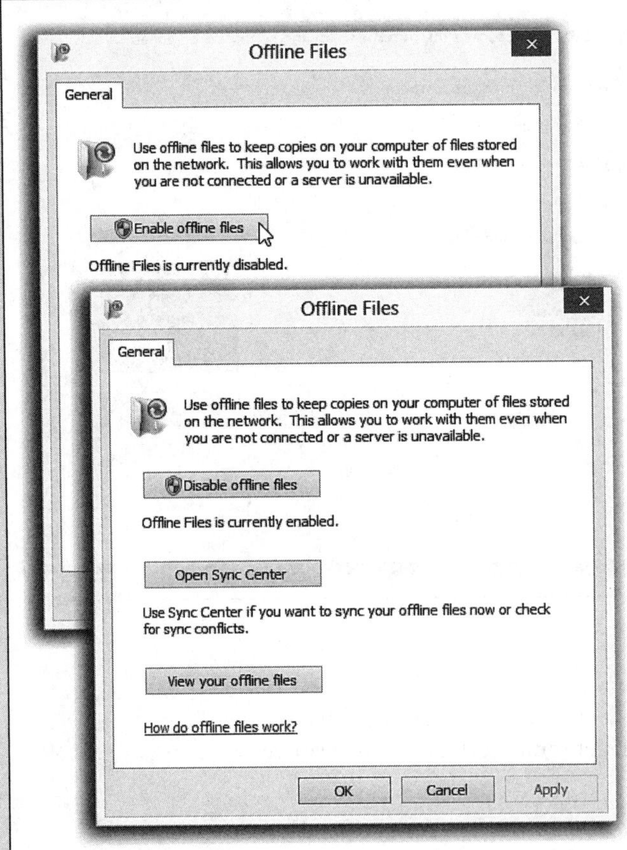

Figure 28-3:
To find this master Offline Files box, open the Start screen. Type offline *and select Settings under the search box. In the search results, click "Manage offline files."*

Top: This box appears. Select "Enable offline files." (Windows may tell you that you have to restart the computer to make the feature come alive.)

Bottom: Now the dialog box looks like this. You'll need the lower two buttons later in your new life with Offline Files.

Windows now takes a moment—well, quite a few moments, actually—to copy the selected files and folders to your laptop. Fortunately, it works in the background, between your mouse clicks and keystrokes.

Note: If somebody on the network is actually using those files right now–has them open–you'll get an error message at this point. Wait until those documents are closed, and then try again.

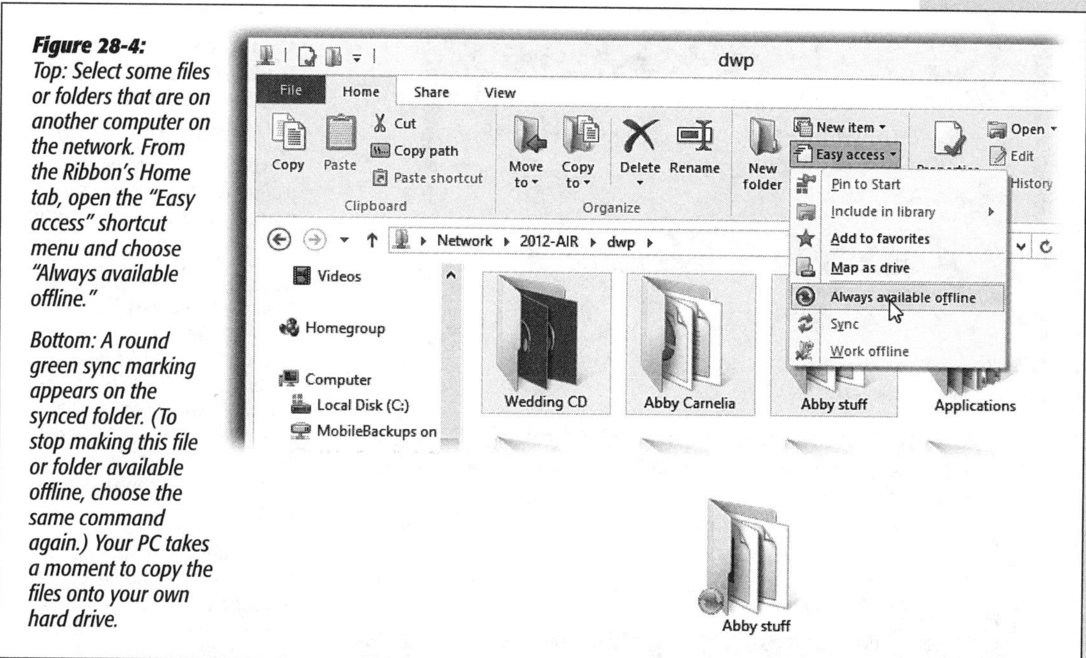

***Figure 28-4:** Top: Select some files or folders that are on another computer on the network. From the Ribbon's Home tab, open the "Easy access" shortcut menu and choose "Always available offline."*

Bottom: A round green sync marking appears on the synced folder. (To stop making this file or folder available offline, choose the same command again.) Your PC takes a moment to copy the files onto your own hard drive.

It's an excellent idea to synchronize your folders manually every time you're about to leave the network, so the files on your laptop are up to date. (In fact, if you're away and you try to edit an out-of-date file, Windows won't even let you open it!)

To trigger the syncing, open that "Easy access" pop-up menu again (Figure 28-4) and choose Sync.

Working Offline

Now suppose you're untethered from the network, and you have a moment to get some work done.

To find the synced folders, open the master Offline Files dialog box (Figure 28-3); click "View your offline files."

A new window opens (Figure 28-5). There before you is a list of all the files and folders to which you "subscribed" before you left the network (Figure 28-5).

Note: In previous versions of Windows, you'd also see the icons of folders you didn't ask for, displayed for context with red X's on their icons. That doesn't happen in Windows 8; Microsoft found that people were just too confused about what those other icons were.

You're free to work with offline files and folders exactly as you would if you were still connected to the network. You can revise, edit, and duplicate files, and even create

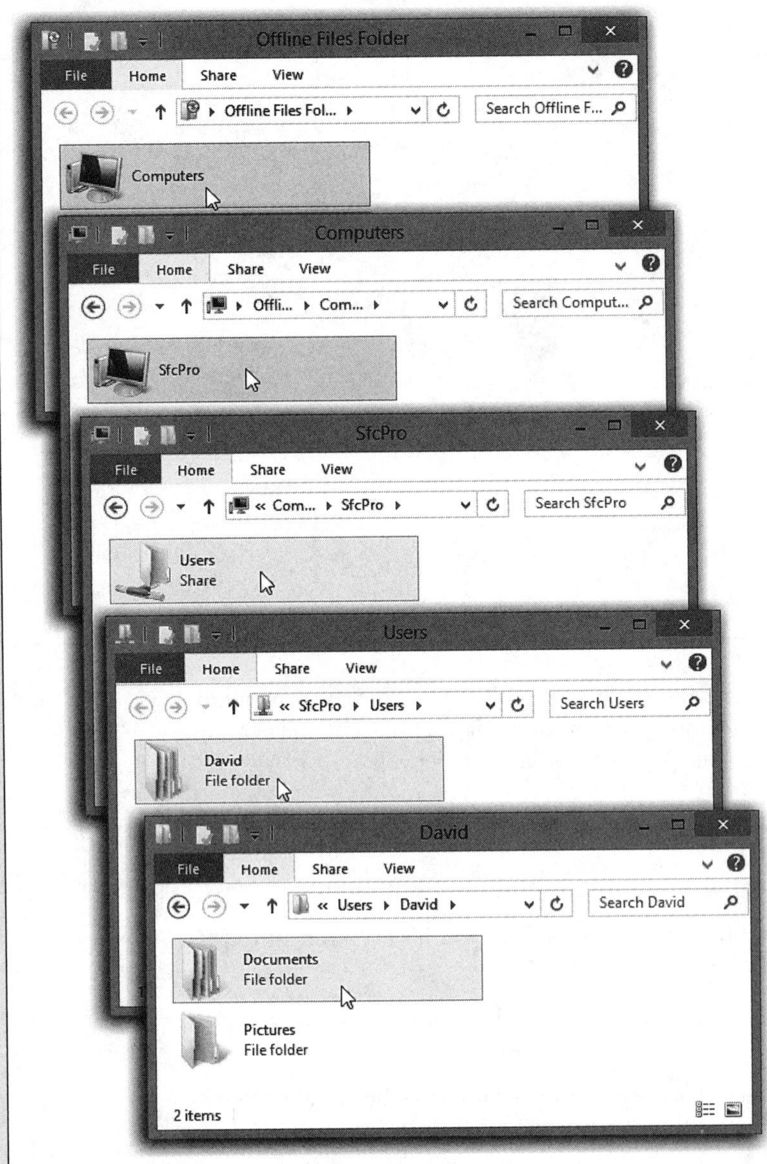

Figure 28-5: *The folders you've subscribed to appear in this window when you click "View offline files."*

However, you're seeing the global view here–you're seeing icons for the entire disconnected network.

It takes some burrowing to get from the Computers icon (top) to the PC these files came from (second from top) to the Users folder on that PC (third), to the Personal folder of the specific account holder (fourth), and finally to the actual folders that contain the copied items (bottom).

No wonder Microsoft suggests that you pin the shared folders to your Start screen. (On the Ribbon's Home tab, the "Easy access" shortcut menu offers a command that does just that.)

new documents inside offline folders. The permissions remain the same as when you connect to the network.

Tip: Sometimes you want to work with your laptop copies (not the network copies) even if you're still *on* the network—if, say, the network connection is not so much *absent* as *slow.* To do that, open the folder on the network that contains the offline files. On the Ribbon's Home tab, open the "Easy access" pop-up menu and choose "Work offline."

Reconnecting to the Network

Now suppose you return from your jaunt away from the office. You plop your laptop down on your desk and reconnect to the network.

Once Windows discovers that it's home again, it whirls into action, automatically comparing your set of offline files and folders with the master set on the network. (Windows copies only the changed pieces of each file—not the entire file.)

Along the way, Windows attempts to handle discrepancies between the two sets of files as best it can. For example:

- If your copy and a network copy of a file don't match, Windows wipes out the older version with the newer version, so both locations have the latest edition.
- If you deleted your copy of a file, or if somebody on the network deleted the original, Windows deletes the corresponding file so that it no longer exists on either machine. (That's assuming that nobody edited the file in the meantime.)
- If somebody added a file to the network copy of a folder, you get a copy of it in your laptop's copy of the folder.
- If you've edited an offline file that somebody on the network has deleted in the meantime, Windows offers you the choice to save your version on the network or to delete it from your laptop.
- If you delete a file from your hard drive that somebody else on the network has edited in the meantime, Windows deletes the offline file from your hard drive but doesn't delete the network copy from the network.
- If both your copy and the network copy of a file were edited while you were away, a balloon in the notification area notifies you of the conflict. Click it to open the Sync Center, where you can decide which version "wins." (Until you do that, the file in question remains offline, on your laptop.)

The Sync Center

As you've discovered, the Offline Files feature requires trips to three different headquarters. You turn on the feature in one place (Figure 28-3); you identify the files you want to sync in another (Figure 28-4); and you view the files in a third place (Figure 28-5). Wouldn't it be nice if Offline Files could get its act together?

It would, and it has. The Sync Center is just what you need. To open it, try one of these methods:

- **Open the Start screen.** Type *sync center* and select Settings under the search box. In the search results, click Sync Center.
- **Click Open Sync Center** in the dialog box shown in Figure 28-3.
- **In the Control Panel, search for *sync*.** Open the Sync Center result.

However you decide to get there, the resulting window looks something like Figure 28-6.

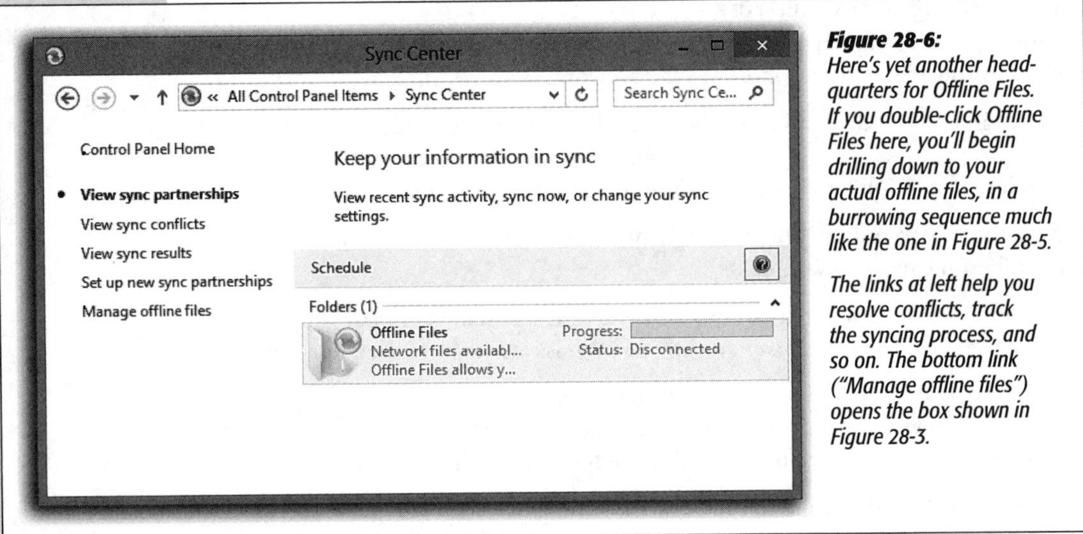

Figure 28-6: *Here's yet another headquarters for Offline Files. If you double-click Offline Files here, you'll begin drilling down to your actual offline files, in a burrowing sequence much like the one in Figure 28-5.*

The links at left help you resolve conflicts, track the syncing process, and so on. The bottom link ("Manage offline files") opens the box shown in Figure 28-3.

Windows to Go

If you work in a corporation—especially if you're in charge of the computers there—you've heard of BYOD. It stands for "bring your own device," and it means "employees bringing their own tablets, laptops, and phones to work."

It sounds like a great idea; why shouldn't the worker bees enjoy the comfort of their own machines? But system administrators hate BYOD. It means that the unsophisticated peons are bringing in all kinds of unsecure, uninspected, unapproved hardware and software into the carefully controlled corporate environment. They'd much rather issue you a nine-pound, kerosene-powered Dell laptop from 2007 that they've personally set up and locked down for your use.

Windows to Go, a new feature in the Enterprise edition of Windows 8, offers a clever solution. It lets your IT overlords create a complete Windows 8 world *on a flash drive* that can be used to start up any laptop—even your own. It contains a copy of Windows, whatever programs the bosses want you to have, documents, the works. (That's why it requires a flash drive that holds 32 gigabytes or more!)

Note: If *you* are the IT overlord, here are the steps for creating a Windows to Go installation for use by your underlings: *http://j.mp/YetpTa*.

Actually, it doesn't have to be a laptop. You could start up *any* recent Windows machine—at home, at work, on the road—from this flash drive and find yourself in the same exact Windows world that your company set up for you.

To use the Windows to Go flash drive, insert it into the not-at-the-office PC's USB jack while it's shut down. When you boot it up again, it should start up from the USB drive automatically. If it doesn't, you may have to adjust your BIOS settings so that it does; ask your network geek or check the PC manufacturer's Web site. (Chances are pretty good that your system admin people turned on the BitLocker encryption feature described on page 714. You'll have to enter that password.)

At this point, you don't see any of your personal stuff. Your laptop's own hard drive doesn't even show up. Don't freak out; this is all in the name of keeping your work stuff and your personal stuff completely separate. When you're using Windows to Go, your laptop belongs to the corporation; everything else is hidden and offline. There's no possibility of cross-contamination.

When you shut down and yank out the flash drive, that same computer once again starts up from your own cluttered copy of Windows. The system administrators couldn't care less. (And if your flash-drive copy of Windows goes wrong somehow—maybe it gets a virus or something—who cares? The system admins can hit a couple of keys and spit out a fresh, virginal copy.)

The fine print goes like this:

- Only some flash-drive brands and models are officially compatible. (The list is here: *http://j.mp/YetAhl.*)
- Some features don't work when you've started up from the flash drive: hibernation, the Windows Recovery Environment, the Refresh and Reset PC commands, and the Windows App Store.
- If you knock the flash drive out of the USB jack—or if someone grabs it unthinkingly—Windows to Go simply freezes everything you were doing. Every document remains suspended; video or music playback pauses. If you reinsert the flash drive within 60 seconds, everything picks up exactly where you left off. If not, the system assumes you've gone home, and the PC shuts down. No trace of your activity remains on it.

Dialing In from the Road

Windows provides several avenues for accessing one PC from another across the Internet. If you're a road warrior armed with a laptop, you may be delighted by these features. If you're a corporate employee who used to think you could escape the office by going home, you may not.

In any case, each of these *remote access* features requires a good deal of setup and some scavenging through the technical underbrush, and each offers slightly different benefits and drawbacks. But when you're in Tulsa and a spreadsheet you need is on your PC in Tallahassee, you may be grateful to have at least one of these systems in place.

And besides—if you're connecting to PCs at your corporate office, your corporate IT people have probably already done all the hard work of getting the computers at work set up for you to connect to them from home or the road.

The two most common scenarios for using these remote access features are (a) controlling your home PC remotely using a laptop and (b) connecting to your office network from your PC at home. To help you keep the roles of these various computers straight, the computer industry has done you the favor of introducing specialized terminology:

- The *host computer* is the home-base computer—the unattended one that's waiting for you to connect.
- The *remote computer* is the one you'll be using: your laptop on the road, for example, or your home machine (or laptop) when you tap into the office network.

This chapter covers two systems of connecting:

- **Virtual private networking (VPN).** Using this system, you use the Internet as a secure link between the host and the remote machine. The remote computer behaves exactly as though it has joined the network of the host system—usually your company's network.
- **Remote Desktop.** This feature doesn't just make the remote PC join the network of the host; it actually turns your computer *into* the faraway host PC, filling your screen with its screen image. When you touch the trackpad on your laptop, you're actually moving the cursor on the home-base PC's screen, and so forth.

Tip: For added protection against snoopers, you should use Remote Desktop *with* a VPN connection.

To make Remote Desktop work, you have to connect *to* a computer running Windows 8, Windows 7 (Professional and above), Vista (Business and above), XP Pro, or Windows Server. But the machine you're connecting *from* can be any relatively recent Windows PC, a Macintosh (to get a free copy of Remote Desktop Connection for Mac, visit *www.microsoft.com/mac/*), or even a computer running Linux (you'll need the free *rdesktop client*, available from *www.rdesktop.org*).

Tip: The world is filled with more powerful, more flexible products that let you accomplish the same things as these Windows features, from software programs like LapLink, Carbon Copy, and pcAnywhere to Web sites like *www.gotomypc.com*.

On the other hand, Remote Desktop is free.

Finally, note that these are all methods of connecting to an *unattended* machine. If somebody is sitting at the PC back home, you might find it far more convenient to connect using Remote Assistance, described in Chapter 9. It's easier to set up and offers the same kind of "screen sharing" as Remote Desktop.

Virtual Private Networking

All over the world, frequent travelers connect to distant homes or offices using *virtual private networking*. VPN is a fancy way of saying, "Your remote computer can become part of your host network over the Internet."

Note: To make VPN work, both computers require Internet connections; that much is obvious.

The one at home (or at the office) is probably all set. You should, however, put some thought into getting the *laptop* online. You'll have to find wireless hotspots, for example, or, if you do this a lot, you can sign up for a cellular modem plan or even a dial-up account.

What corporations like most about VPN is that it's extremely secure. The information traveling between the two connected computers is encoded (encrypted) using a technology called *tunneling*. Your connection is like a reinforced steel pipe wending its way through the Internet to connect the two computers.

To create a VPN connection, the host computer has two important requirements. If you're VPNing into a corporation or a school, it's probably all set already. Otherwise:

- **It must be on the Internet** at the moment you try to connect. Usually, that means it needs a full-time Internet connection, like cable modem or DSL.
- **It needs a fixed IP address.** (See the Note below.)

On the other hand, the remote computer—your laptop—doesn't have any such requirements. It just needs an Internet connection.

Note: Several of the remote-connection methods described in this chapter require that your home-base PC have a *fixed, public* IP address. (An IP address is a unique number that identifies a particular computer on the Internet. It's made up of four numbers separated by periods.)

If you're not immediately nodding in understanding, murmuring, "Ahhhhh, right," then download the bonus document available on this book's "Missing CD" at *www.missingmanuals.com.* The free PDF supplement you'll find there is called "Getting a Fixed, Public IP Address."

Setting Up Your Laptop

In general, the big network bosses who expect you to connect from the road have already set up the VPN software at *their* end. They may even have set up your laptop for you, so that dialing in from the road requires only one quick click.

But if not—if you want to set up your remote PC yourself—here are the steps. Fortunately, in Windows 8, the VPN setup process has been TileWorldified and simplified.

1. **At the Start screen, type *VPN* and select Settings under the search box. In the search results, click "Set up a virtual private network (VPN) connection."**

   The dialog box shown in Figure 28-7 appears.

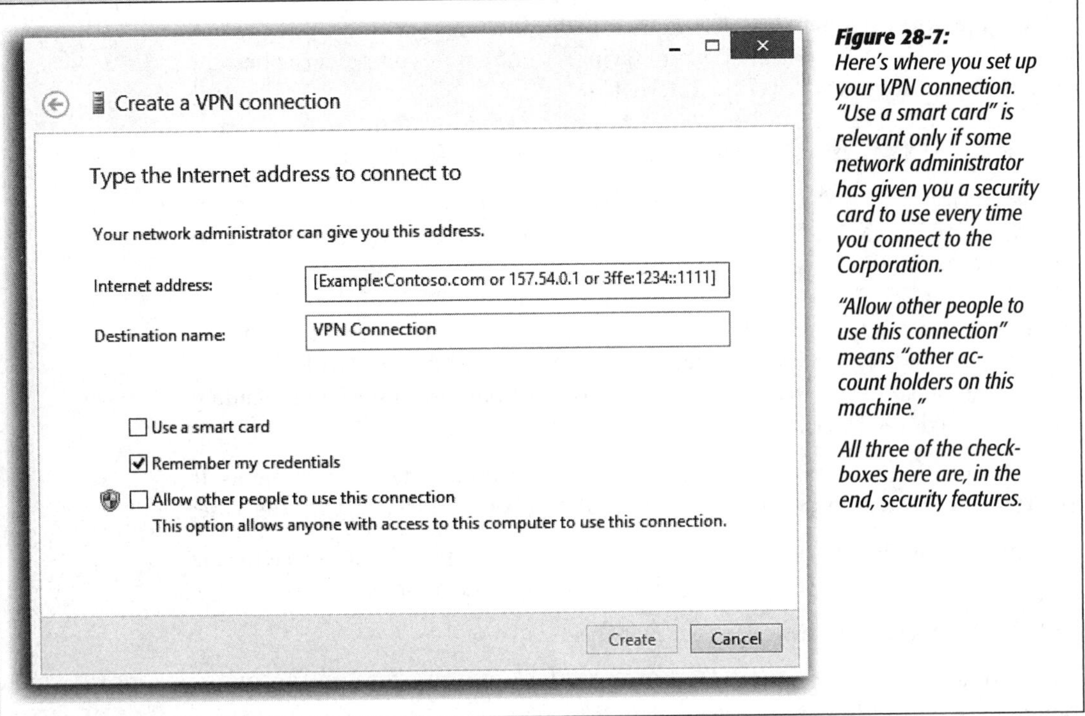

Figure 28-7: *Here's where you set up your VPN connection. "Use a smart card" is relevant only if some network administrator has given you a security card to use every time you connect to the Corporation.*

"Allow other people to use this connection" means "other account holders on this machine."

All three of the checkboxes here are, in the end, security features.

2. **Into the boxes, type the host name or registered IP address of the VPN host—that is, the computer you'll be tunneling into.**

   If you're connecting to a server at work or school, your system administrator can tell you what to type here. If you're connecting to a computer you set up yourself, specify its public IP address. (See the Note on the previous page.)

   This is *not* the private IP address on your home network, and definitely not its computer name (despite the fact that the New Incoming Connection Wizard told you that you would need to use that name); neither of these work when you're logged into another network.

3. **Type a name for your VPN connection.**

   It doesn't matter what you type in "Destination name"; this is just for your reference.

   While you're here, you might also want to turn on "Use a smart card" (if your company issued you one for security) or "Remember my credentials" (if you'd rather not have to enter your name and password every time you connect).

4. **Click Create.**

   You might have noticed, if you're among the technically inclined, that you did not have to specify things like authentication protocols and tunneling setups. Windows 8 can figure that stuff out all by itself, saving you the technical bushwhacking.

Connecting to the VPN

Now, none of what you've achieved so far has actually gotten you online. All you've done is create a *VPN connection*—a stored, clickable icon for connecting to the mother ship. When the time comes that you want to make the actual connection, read on.

1. **Open the Charms bar. Select Settings. Select the network icon (for example, the WiFi icon) at the bottom left.**

   You now see something like Figure 28-8.

Figure 28-8:
The VPN is not a connection to the Internet. You do, however, need a connection to the Internet if you want to use the VPN.

In any case, click the name of the VPN you set up and then click Connect.

2. **Click your VPN's name and then click Connect.**

   If you've done this before, and you turned on "Remember my credentials" when you created the VPN connection, you hop directly onto the distant network. You're in!

   If not, you're asked to enter your name and password—take this final step:

3. **Type your user name, password, and, if required by the network administrator, the domain name. Then click OK.**

When you make the VPN connection, you've once again joined your home or office network. You should feel free to transfer files, make printouts, and even run programs on the distant PC.

When you want to disconnect, right-click the 📶 or 🖥 icon in your notification area, click the VPN Connection from the list that pops up, and then choose Disconnect.

(You can also disconnect using the Network and Sharing Center.)

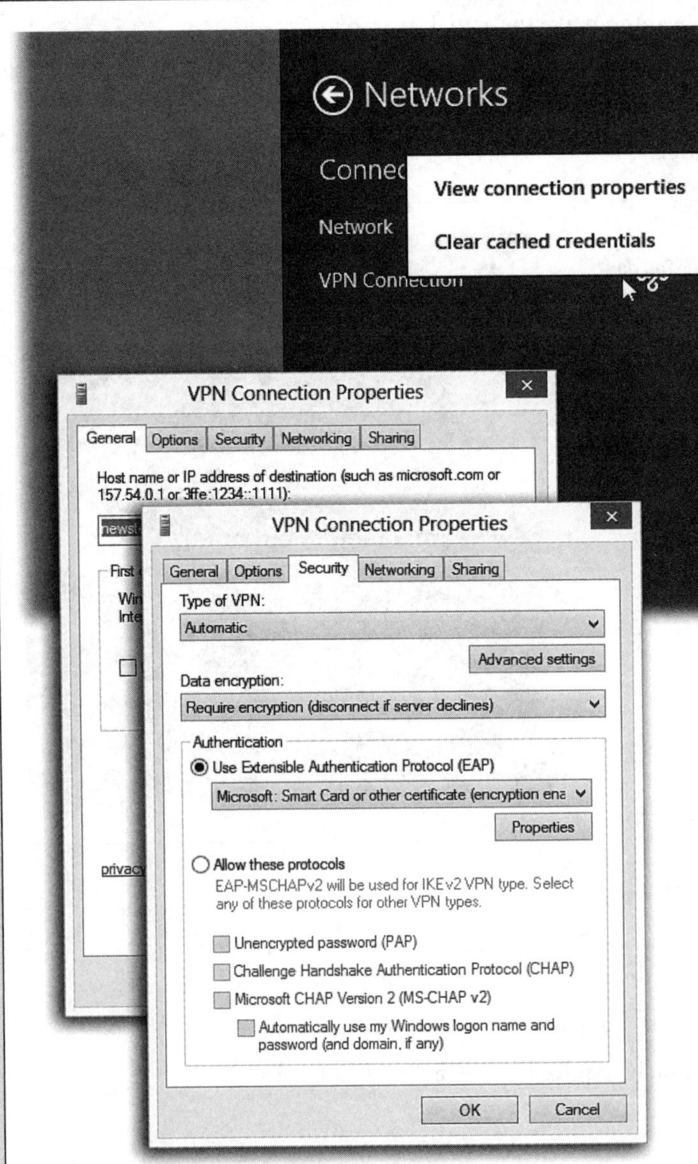

Figure 28-9:
There's a secret shortcut menu awaiting on the Networks panel.

Top: Right-click your VPN connection's name (or, on a touchscreen, hold your finger down on it). From the shortcut menu, choose "View connection properties."

Bottom: The VPN Connection Properties dialog box opens. Its various tabs let you tweak every VPN variable until you finally get the thing to work.

By the way: These instructions describe Windows 8's built-in VPN software. But more often than not, you'll be given software from Cisco or your employer/school to use instead. In that case, pretend you never read these pages.

Changing Your VPN Settings

If the VPN connection doesn't work the first time—it hardly ever does— you can make some adjustments as shown in Figure 28-9. Keep your company's highly trained network nerd nearby to help you.

Remote Desktop

Here's another remote-access option: Remote Desktop. When you use Remote Desktop, you're not just tapping into your home computer's network—you're actually bringing its screen onto your screen. You can run its programs, print on its printers, "type" on its keyboard, move its cursor, manage its files, and so on, all by remote control.

Remote Desktop isn't useful only when you're trying to connect to the office or reach your home computer from the road; it works even over an office network. You can actually take control of another computer in the office—to troubleshoot a novice's PC without having to run up or down a flight of stairs, perhaps, or just to run a program that isn't on your own machine.

If you do decide to use Remote Desktop over the Internet, consider setting up a VPN connection first; using Remote Desktop *over* a VPN connection adds a nice layer of security to the connection. It also means that you become part of your home or office network—and you can therefore connect to the distant computer using its private network address or even its computer name.

Tip: The computers on the *receiving* end of the connections require the fanciest versions of Windows Vista, 7, or 8 (Pro, Enterprise, or Ultimate editions). But the laptop *you're* using can be running any edition. In fact, it can be running any version of Windows all the way back to 95, and even Mac OS X or Linux.

To install the Remote Desktop Connection client on OS X or an older version of Windows, visit the Microsoft Download Center (*www.microsoft.com/downloads/*) and search for "Remote Desktop Connection." For Linux, get the free rdesktop program at *www.rdesktop.org*.

Setting Up the Host Machine

To get a PC ready for invasion—that is, to turn it into a host—proceed like this:

1. **Right-click the lower-left corner of the screen (or press ⊞+X). From the shortcut menu, choose System.**

   The System pane of the Control Panel appears.

2. **At the left side, click "Remote settings."**

   The System Properties dialog box opens to the Remote tab. Set things up as directed in Figure 28-10.

3. **Click OK twice to close the dialog boxes you opened.**

   The host computer is now ready for invasion. It's listening to the network for incoming connections from Remote Desktop clients.

Making the Connection

When you're ready to try Remote Desktop, fire up your laptop, or whatever computer will be doing the remote connecting.

Note: As a first step, you may be required (by your bosses) to connect to the VPN of the distant host computer, as described earlier in this chapter. If the host computer is elsewhere on your local network–in the same building, that is–you can skip this step.

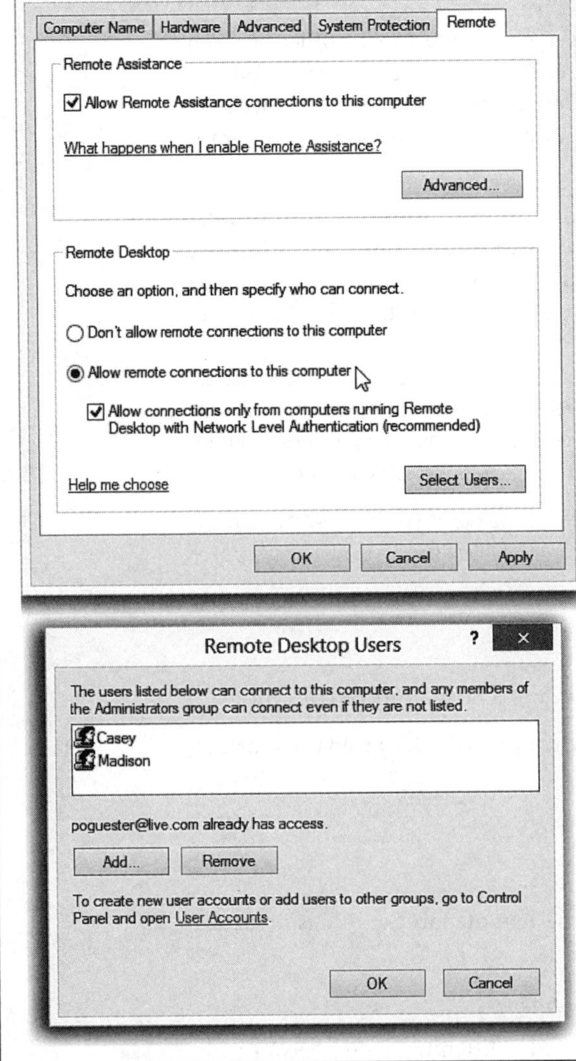

Figure 28-10:
Top: Here's the master switch for Remote Desktop (you're looking at the lower part of the box, not the Remote Assistance section).

Turn on "Allow remote connections to this computer."

A message may warn you that when this computer goes to sleep, people won't be able to connect to it. Click OK–or first click the Power Options link to turn off automatic sleep and hibernation.

For added protection against ruthless hackers, you can also turn on "Allow connections only from computers running Remote Desktop with Network Level Authentication (recommended)." What it means is, "Accept connections only from Windows 7 and Windows 8 machines." Turn this option off if any other kind of machine might want to hook up.

Now click Select Users.

Bottom: You certainly don't want teenage hackers to visit your precious PC from across the Internet, playing your games and reading your personal info. Fortunately, you can specify precisely who is allowed to connect.

Click Add. In the resulting dialog box, type the names of the people who are allowed to access your PC using Remote Desktop.

By default, local users with administrative privileges are automatically given access.

Choose your comrades carefully; remember that they'll be able to do anything to your system, by remote control, that you could do while sitting in front of it. (To ensure security, Windows insists that the accounts you're selecting here have passwords. Although you can add them to this list, password-free accounts can't connect.) Click OK.

1. **Open the Remote Desktop Connection program.**

   Here's one way. At the Start screen, type *remote* and then, when Remote Desktop Connections appears in the results list, click it or press Enter. The Remote Desktop Connection dialog box appears.

2. **Click Show Options to expand the dialog box (if necessary). Fill it out as shown in Figure 28-11.**

   The idea is to specify the IP address or DNS name of the computer you're trying to reach. If it's on the same network, or if you're connected via a VPN, you can use its computer name instead.

Figure 28-11: *Click Show Options (not shown) if you don't see these tabs.*

Once you've made them appear, a few useful settings become available (and a lot of rarely useful ones).

On the General tab (top), you can enter (and tell Windows to remember) your name and password for the connection. If you're connecting to a network outside your building, you'll probably have to type in its IP address—something only the company's network nerds can tell you.

On the Display tab (bottom), for example, you can effectively reduce the size of the other computer's screen so that it fits within your laptop's. On the Experience tab, you can turn off special-effect animations to speed up the connection.

3. **Click Connect.**

   If you get a strange warning that "the identity of the remote computer could not be identified," see the box on the next page.

Now a freaky thing happens: After a moment of pitch-blackness, the host computer's screen fills your own (Figure 28-12). Don't be confused by the fact that all the open windows on the computer you're using have now *disappeared*. (Actually,

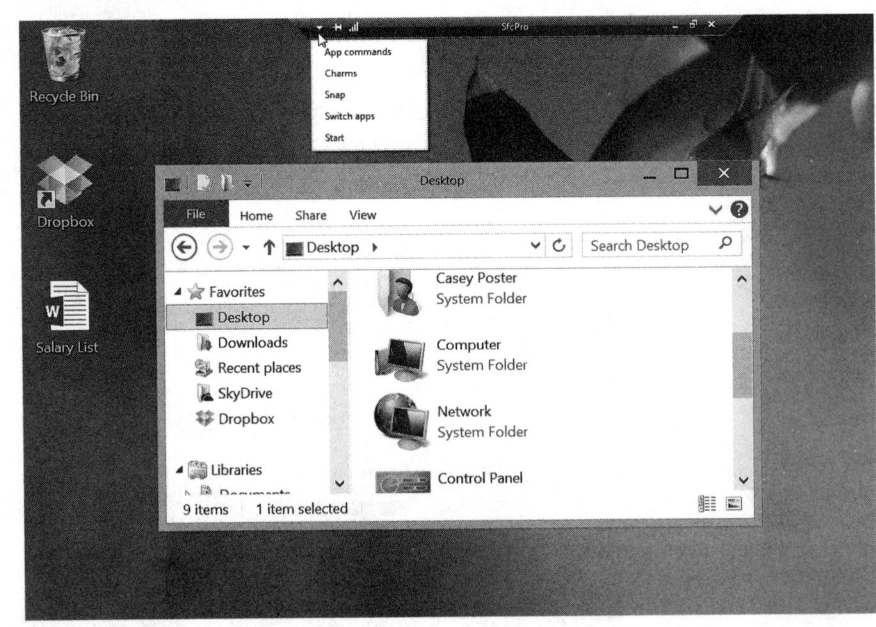

Figure 28-12: *The strange little bar at the top of your screen lets you minimize the distant computer's screen or turn it into a floating window. To hide this title bar, click the push-pin icon so that it (the pin) turns horizontal. The bar slides into the top of the screen, out of your way, until you move the cursor to the top edge of the screen.*

UP TO SPEED

For the Paranoid

If you see an error message indicating that "the identity of the remote computer cannot be verified," it means that you (or your network administrator) haven't obtained a security certificate from a trusted authority. This means you can't be absolutely, positively, 100 percent certain you're connecting to the computer you think you're connecting to.

If you're super paranoid, you can click View Certificate, click the Details tab, and scroll down to look at the thumbprint.

Then, go over to the host machine, open the Start screen, type *mmc*, and click the icon that appears in the results. This brings up the Microsoft Management Console. Click File→Add/Remove Snap-In and add the Certificates snap-in (choose Computer Account when prompted); click Finish, and then click OK.

Now, double-click the Remote Desktop folder on the left pane of the Console window, and then click Certificates. You should see one certificate appear in the middle pane. Double-click it, and examine the details to make sure they're identical to what you're seeing on the remote machine you're connecting from. When you close the Console, click No when it asks you if you want to save changes.

Now you're 100 percent certain and can confidently click the box labeled "Don't ask me again for connections to this computer" when you make a Remote Desktop Connection to the host.

they won't if you click the Display tab and choose a smaller-than-full-screen remote desktop size before you connect.)

You can now operate the distant PC as though you were there in the flesh, using your own keyboard (or trackpad) and mouse. You can answer your email, make long-distance printouts, and so on. All the action—running programs, changing settings, and so on—is actually taking place on the faraway host computer.

Tip: You can even shut down or restart the faraway machine by remote control. Open a Command Prompt and run the command *shutdown /s*. The computer will shut down in less than a minute.

Keep in mind a few other points:

- You don't need to feel completely blocked out of your own machine. The little title bar at the top of the screen offers you the chance to put the remote computer's screen into a floating window of its own, permitting you to see both your own screen and the home-base computer's screen simultaneously (Figure 28-13). You can return to full-screen mode by pressing Ctrl+Alt+Break.

Figure 28-13: *By putting the other computer's screen into a window of its own, you save yourself a little bit of confusion. You can even minimize the remote computer's screen entirely, reducing it to a tab on your taskbar until you need it again.*

- If the host computer is running Windows 8, but you're not, you might wonder: How can I open the App bar, Charms bar, Start screen, and so on? That's the purpose of the ▾ menu at the left end of the control bar, shown open in Figure 28-12. It lists "App commands" (meaning the App bar), Charms, Snap (meaning, "split the screen between two apps"), "Switch apps" (opens the TileWorld app switcher at the left side), and Start (opens the Start screen).
- You can copy and paste highlighted text or graphics between the two machines (using regular Copy and Paste), and even transfer entire documents back and forth

(using Copy and Paste on the desktop icons). Of course, if you've made both desktops visible simultaneously, you can move more quickly between local and remote.

- Even Windows can't keep its mind focused on two people at once. If somebody is trying to use the host machine in person, you'll see a message to the effect that you're about to bump that person off the PC.

  Similarly, if somebody logs on at the host computer, *you* get unceremoniously dumped off. (You just get a message that tells you, "Another user connected to the remote computer.") Fortunately, you don't lose work this way—your account remains logged on behind the scenes, just as in fast user switching. When you connect again later (after the interloper has signed off), you'll find all your programs and documents open exactly as you (or your interloper) left them.

- Back at the host computer, nobody can see what you're doing. The standard Welcome screen appears on the remote PC, masking your activities.

Keyboard Shortcuts for the Hopelessly Confused

When the Remote Desktop Connection window is maximized (fills your entire screen), all the standard Windows keyboard shortcuts operate on the *host* computer, not the one you're actually using. When you press the ⊞ key, for example, you see the host computer's Start menu.

UP TO SPEED

Remote Networking vs. Remote Control

When you connect to a PC using direct dial or virtual private networking (VPN), you're simply joining the host's network from far away. When you try to open a Word document that's actually sitting on the distant PC, your *laptop's* copy of Word opens and loads the file. Your laptop is doing the actual word processing; the host just sends and receives files as needed.

Windows' Remote Desktop feature is a different animal. In this case, you're using your laptop to *control* the host computer. If you double-click that Word file on the host computer, you open the copy of Word *on the host computer.* All the word processing takes place on the distant machine; all that passes over the connection between the two computers is a series of keystrokes, mouse movements, and screen displays. The host is doing all the work. Your laptop is just peeking at the results.

Once you understand the differences between these technologies, you can make a more informed decision about which to use when. For example, suppose your PC at the office has a folder containing 100 megabytes of images you need to incorporate into a PowerPoint document. Using a remote networking connection means you'll have to wait for the files to be transmitted to your laptop before you can begin working–and if you've connected to the office machine using a dial-up modem, you'll be waiting, literally, for several *days.*

If you use a Remote Desktop connection, on the other hand, the files remain right where they are: on the host computer, which does all the processing. You see on your screen exactly what you would see if you were sitting at the office. When you drag and drop one of those images into your PowerPoint document, all the action is taking place on the PC at the other end.

Of course, if the computer doing the dialing is a brand-new Intel i35 zillion-megahertz screamer, and the host system is a 5-year-old rustbucket on its last legs, you might actually *prefer* a remote network connection, so the faster machine can do most of the heavy work.

Note: There's one exception. When you press Ctrl+Alt+Delete, *your* computer processes the keystroke.

But in window-in-a-window mode (Figure 28-13), it's a different story. Now your current computer "hears" your keystrokes. Now, pressing ⊞ opens *your* Start screen. So how, with the remote PC's screen in a window, are you supposed to operate it by remote control?

One solution: On the Local Resources tab of the dialog box shown in Figure 28-11, you can specify which computer "hears" your keyboard shortcuts.

Another: Use Microsoft's alternatives for the key combinations. For example, when the Remote Desktop window isn't full screen, pressing Alt+Tab switches to the next open program on *your* computer—but pressing Alt+Page Up switches to the next program on the *host* computer.

Here's a summary of the special keys that operate the distant host computer—a table that can be useful if you're either an extreme power user or somebody who likes to win bar bets:

Standard Windows Key Combination	Remote Desktop Key Combination	Function
Alt+Tab	Alt+Page Up	Switches to the next open program
Alt+Shift+Tab	Alt+Page Down	Switches to the previous open program
Alt+Esc	Alt+Insert	Cycles through programs in the order in which you open them
Ctrl+Esc (or ⊞)	Alt+Home	Opens the Start menu
Ctrl+Alt+Delete	Ctrl+Alt+End	Displays the Windows Security dialog box

(Actually, you should use the alternative key combination for the Security dialog box whether the Remote Desktop window is maximized or not, because Ctrl+Alt+Delete is always interpreted by the computer you're currently using.)

Disconnecting

To get out of Remote Desktop full-screen mode, click the Close box in the strange little bar at the top of your screen; if you're using the floating window, you can click the usual ✕ in the upper right.

Note, however, that this method leaves all your programs running and your documents open on the distant machine, exactly as though you had used fast user switching. If you log on again, either from the road or in person, you'll find all those programs and documents still on the screen, just as you left them.

If you'd rather log off in a more permanent way, open the Start screen on the other computer, click your account picture, and choose "Sign out."

Fine-Tuning Remote Desktop Connections

Windows offers all kinds of settings for tailoring the way this bizarre, schizophrenic connection method works. The trick is, however, that you have to change them *before* you connect, using the tabs on the dialog box shown in Figure 28-11.

Here's what you find:

- **General tab.** Here's where you can tell Windows to edit or delete credentials (user name and password) from your last login, or to save all the current settings as a shortcut icon, which makes it faster to reconnect later. (If you connect to a number of different distant computers, saving a setup for each one can be a huge timesaver.)
- **Display tab.** Use these options to specify the *size* (resolution) of the host computer's display.
- **Local Resources tab.** Using these controls, you can set up local peripherals and add-ons so they behave as though they were connected to the computer you're using. This is also where you tell Windows which PC should "hear" keystrokes like Alt+Tab, and whether or not you want to hear sound effects played by the distant machine.
- **Programs tab.** You can set up a certain program to run automatically as soon as you connect to the host machine.
- **Experience tab.** Tell Windows the speed of your connection, so it can limit fancy visual effects like menu animation, the desktop wallpaper, and so on, to avoid slowing down the connection.
- **Advanced.** You can control whether Remote Desktop Connection warns you if it can't verify the identity of a computer, and also whether to connect through a special gateway server (if you need to use one of these, your system administrator will tell you).

8

Part Eight: Appendixes

APPENDIX

A

Installing Windows 8

If your computer came with Windows 8 already installed on it, you can skip this appendix—for now. But if you're running an earlier version of Windows and want to savor the Win8 experience, this appendix describes how to install the new operating system on your computer.

Before You Begin

Believe it or not, most of the work involved in installing Windows 8 takes place well before the installation software even approaches your computer. You have a lot of research and planning to do, especially if you want to avoid spending a five-day weekend in Upgrade Hell.

For example, you must ensure that your PC is beefy enough to handle Windows 8. You also have to decide which of two types of installation you want to perform: an *upgrade* or a *clean install.* (More on this in a moment.)

If you opt for the clean install (a process that begins with *erasing your hard drive completely*), you must back up your data. Finally, you have to gather all the software bits and pieces you need in order to perform the installation.

Hardware Requirements

Before you even buy a copy of Windows, your first order of business should be to check your computer against the list of hardware requirements for Windows, as published by Microsoft. Windows 8, as it turns out, requires some fairly decent memory, speed, disk space, and, above all, graphics-card horsepower. Most 2004-era computers (and earlier ones) aren't up to the challenge.

A lower-powered computer can *run* Windows 8. It may feel slow, but you'll get all the other security and feature enhancements.

The hardware requirements include a 1-gigahertz processor (or faster), 2 gigabytes of memory (or more), 20 gigabytes of free hard drive space (or more), and a graphics card that has "DirectX 9 support with WDDM 1.0 driver" (check the packaging or, for laptops, the manufacturer's Web site).

Obviously, the touchscreen features require a touchscreen.

If your computer doesn't meet these requirements, you could consider a hardware upgrade—both memory and disk-space upgrades are reasonably easy and inexpensive upgrades.

The one place where you may be stuck, though, is on the processor issue. The state of the art in processor speeds seems to advance almost weekly, but it's safe to say that a PC running at 1 GHz or less is certifiably geriatric. It may be time to think about passing the old girl on to the kids or donating it to a worthy cause and getting yourself a newer, faster computer. As a bonus, it will come with Windows 8 preinstalled.

The Upgrade Advisor

Once you've had a conversation with yourself about your equipment, it's time to investigate the suitability of your existing software and add-on gear for use with Windows.

If you haven't yet bought Windows 8, your first step would be a visit to *http://windows.microsoft.com/upgradeadvisor*. Click "Can my PC run Windows 8?"

That link downloads the Windows 8 Upgrade Advisor. It scans your system to produce a report on the Windows 8 compatibility of your hardware and software, so that you know exactly how much hardware/software whiplash lies in store.

Almost everybody finds some incompatibilities reported here, because Microsoft is conservative about which programs will work with Windows 8.

But if the report lists a serious incompatibility, it's not worth proceeding with the installation until you've updated or uninstalled the offending program.

The Advisor adventure concludes with an offer to buy and download Windows 8 on the spot. If you take advantage of this option, one of the first things you'll see is the product key—a long serial number. You'll need this later. Write it down, print it, or copy and paste it into an email message or Notepad page.

What You Have to Lose

Upgrading to Windows 8 from an earlier version of Windows doesn't necessarily mean that all your stuff will survive the journey. As the Upgrade Advisor will tell you, starting from an older version of Windows might leave behind some things you care about.

Here's the rundown:

- **Windows 7.** Everything comes through. You lose nothing.

- **Windows Vista.** You get your documents and settings, but your programs don't survive the transition.
- **Windows XP.** You lose your programs and settings; only your documents survive.
- **Windows 8 Release Preview.** You lose your programs and settings; only your documents survive.
- **Windows 8 Consumer Preview, Windows Developer Preview.** Nothing comes into your new installation. However, you'll find a folder on your hard drive called Windows.old, which contains everything from your preview installation.

Decision 1: DVD or Download

You can get Windows 8 either on a DVD or as an Internet download. Since fewer and fewer computers even have DVD drives anymore, the Internet option makes a lot of sense.

This site offers links to both the download and the DVD ordering page: *http://windows.microsoft.com/en-US/windows/buy.*

Note: If you choose the download version, the Upgrade Advisor described above runs automatically.

Decision 2: Upgrade or System Builder

The copy of Windows 8 most people buy is, technically, the *upgrade* edition. It must be installed onto a PC that *already has a copy of Windows.* Usually, that's what you want.

But if you're a hobbyist who's built your own PC from scratch, or you have a PC with an empty hard drive for any other reason, you need to buy the more expensive *system builder* version of the Windows 8 installer. It lets you install Windows onto a new, blank hard drive.

Decision 3: Directly or from External Disk

If you download the Windows 8 installer, you'll be offered three options once the download wraps up:

- **Install now.** That's what most people want, most of the time. As a bonus, the Upgrade Advisor will run automatically and let you know how much of your software and hardware will work after the upgrade.
- **Install by creating media.** This option lets you convert the installer into an ISO disk image (page 294); you're then offered the chance to copy it onto a blank DVD or USB flash drive. That's especially handy if you want to install Windows in a dual-boot setup, a different PC (not the one you're downloading onto), or into a virtual machine.
- **Install later from your desktop.** Windows deposits a shortcut on your desktop. When the time is right to perform the actual Windows 8 installation, double-click it. (Or click the link in the confirmation email you got when you bought Windows 8.)

Each of these options requires that you use the clean-install instructions in the following pages.

Decision 4: Upgrade vs. Clean Install

The next big question is whether you should *upgrade* your existing copy of Windows to Windows 8, or *erase* it and perform a clean install of Windows 8.

Upgrading the operating system retains all your existing settings and data files. Your Favorites list and the files in your Documents folder will all be there after the upgrade. Sounds great, right? Who wouldn't want to avoid having to redo all those settings?

Unfortunately, in past versions of Windows, upgrading from an older copy of Windows often brought along unwelcome baggage: outdated drivers, fragmented disk drives, and a clutter of unneeded registry settings. If all this artery-clogging gunk had already begun to slow down your computer, upgrading to a newer version of Windows only made things worse.

Microsoft says it's drastically improved the upgrade process. Rather than merging the old operating system in with the new, Windows 8's Setup program pushes all the old stuff (programs, settings, and documents) aside, and then wipes the old OS clean. After that, Setup installs the new OS and then brings over your settings, documents, and programs. All of this leads to a cleaner upgrade that should be more stable than previous Windows upgrades.

Even so, some caution is still justified. The upgrade of the operating system itself may go smoothly, but there's no telling what glitches this procedure may introduce in your non-Microsoft programs. In general, such programs prefer to be installed fresh on the new operating system.

The alternative to an upgrade is the *clean install* of Windows 8. During a clean install, you reformat your hard disk, *wiping out everything on it.* You wind up with a fresh system, 100 percent free of all those creepy little glitches and inconsistencies that have been building up over the years. Ask any Windows veteran: The best way to boost the speed of a system that has grown sluggish is to perform a clean install of the operating system and start afresh.

The drawback of a clean install, however, is the work it will take you to back up all your files and settings before you begin.

Tip: One of the most convenient solutions is to install a new hard drive before you upgrade and put your current hard drive in an external enclosure that you've bought online. You can put it on a shelf for safekeeping, and plug it in every time you need to grab a file from your old installation.

You can even do this with some laptops whose hard drives are user-replaceable: inexpensive USB or FireWire enclosures are available in both 2.5-inch (laptop hard drive) and 3.5-inch (desktop hard drive) size, and installation takes only a few minutes. Just be sure you know what kind of hard drive you have (Serial ATA or Parallel ATA, and in some cases, SCSI) before you choose either your new internal hard drive or your enclosure, because both of these must be compatible with whatever you're currently using.

If you have a second computer, you can also consider backing up your stuff onto it, via a network (Chapter 27). In any of these cases, you'll probably want to use Windows Easy Transfer to perform the backup (page 847).

Even having a full backup, however, doesn't mean a clean install will be a walk in the park. After the installation, you still have to reinstall all your programs, reconfigure your personalized settings, recreate your network connections, and so on.

Tip: It's a good idea to spend a few days writing down the information you need as you're working on your computer. For example, keep track of the user names and passwords you need for various Web sites you frequent.

Overall, a clean install is preferable to an upgrade. But if you don't have the time or the heart to back up your hard drive, wipe it clean, and reestablish all your settings, then the upgrade option is always there for you.

Decision 5: Dual Booting

Here's yet another decision you have to make before you install Windows 8: whether or not you'll want to be able to *dual boot*.

In this advanced scenario, you install Windows 8 onto the same PC that contains an older version of Windows, maintaining both of them side by side. Then, each time you turn on the PC, it *asks you* which operating system you want to run for this computing session (see Figure A-1).

Figure A-1: *When you dual boot, this menu appears each time you turn on your PC, offering you a choice of OS. (If you don't choose in 30 seconds, the PC chooses for you.)*

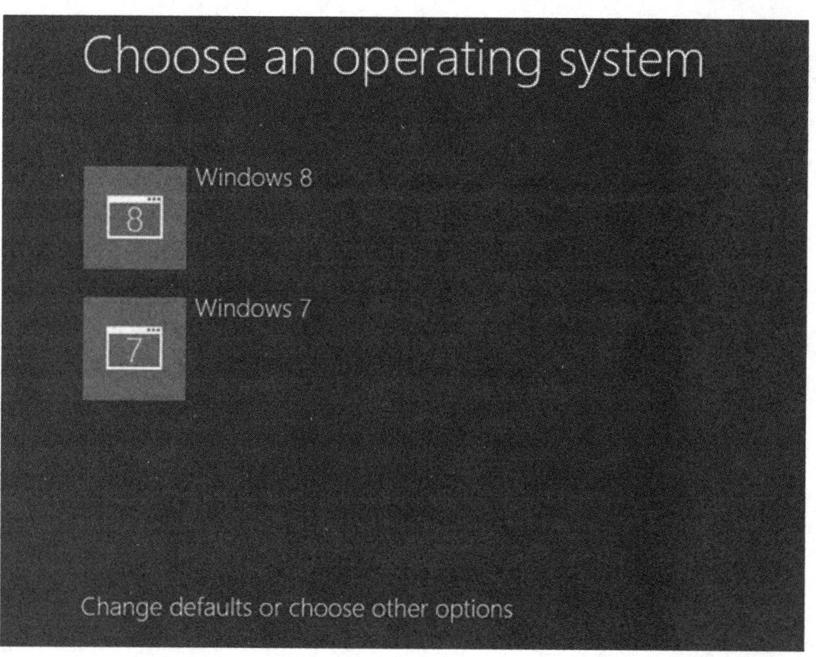

Dual booting comes in handy when you have some program or hardware gadget that works with one operating system but not the other. For example, if you have a scanner with software that runs on Windows Vista but not Windows 8, you can start up in Vista only when you want to use the scanner.

If you intend to dual boot, keep this in mind: *You can't install both operating systems onto the same hard drive partition.* If you did, your programs would become horribly confused.

Instead, keep your two Windows versions separate using one of these avenues:

- **Buy a second hard drive.** Use it for one of the two operating systems.
- **Back up your hard drive,** erase it completely, and then *partition* it, which means dividing it so that each chunk shows up with its own icon, name, and drive letter. Then install each operating system on a separate disk partition.
- **If you're less technically inclined,** you might prefer to buy a program like Acronis Disk Director. Not only does it let you create a new partition on your hard drive without erasing it first, but it's also flexible and easy.

There's just one wrinkle with dual booting: If you install Windows 8 onto a separate partition (or a different drive), as you must, you won't find any of your existing programs listed on the Start screen, and your desktop won't be configured the way it is in your original operating system. You'll generally wind up having to reinstall every program into your new Windows 8 world, and to reestablish all your settings, exactly as though the Windows 8 "side" were a brand-new PC.

Installing Windows 8

Once you've decided to take the plunge and install Windows, you can begin the countdown.

Preparing for the Installation

If you've made all the plans and done all the thinking described so far in this chapter, you have only a short checklist left to follow:

- **Update your virus program and scan for viruses.** Then, if you're updating an existing copy of Windows, *turn off* your virus checker, along with other auto-loading programs like non-Microsoft firewall software and Web ad blockers.
- **Confirm that your computer's BIOS**—its basic startup circuitry—is compatible with Windows 8. To find out, contact the manufacturer of the computer or the BIOS.

  Don't skip this step. You may well need to upgrade your BIOS if the computer was made before mid-2006.
- **Gather updated, Windows 8–compatible drivers** for all your computer's components. Graphics and audio cards are particularly likely to need updates, so be sure to check the manufacturers' Web sites—and driver-information sites like

www.windrivers.com and *www.driverguide.com*—and download any new drivers you find there.

- **Disconnect any gear that's not absolutely necessary** for using your computer. You'll have better luck if you reconnect devices *after* Windows 8 is in place. This includes scanners, game controllers, printers, and even that USB-powered lava lamp you like so much.

If you've gone to all this trouble and preparation, the Windows installation process can be surprisingly smooth. The Windows 8 installer is much less painful than the ones for previous versions of Windows. You won't see the old DOS-style startup screens, the installation requires fewer restarts, and if you're doing a clean install, it's amazingly fast (often 15 minutes or less).

The Upgrade Installation

Here's how you upgrade your existing version of Windows to full Windows 8 status. (If you prefer to perform a clean install, skip these instructions.) It's a series of instruction screens, with a Next button to click at the bottom of each one.

Phase 1: Run the installer

Double-click the installer, whether it's on your hard drive, a flash drive, or a DVD.

Note: If the installer is on a DVD or a flash drive, insert it while running your *old* copy of Windows and then shut down your PC. When you restart it, it should start up from the disc or flash drive. (If it doesn't, go online to read up about how to make your PC start up from a DVD or a flash drive.)

WORKAROUND WORKSHOP

When No Windows Disc Comes With Your PC

It's becoming increasingly common for computer manufacturers to sell you a new PC without including an operating system DVD. (Every 11 cents counts, right?) The machine has Windows installed on it—but if there's no installation CD or DVD or flash drive, what are you supposed to do in case of emergency?

Instead of a physical Windows disc, the manufacturer may provide something called a *restore image*—a CD-ROM or DVD (or more than one) containing a complete copy of the operating system *and* other software that was installed on the computer at the factory. If the contents of the computer's hard disk are ever lost or damaged, you can, in theory, restore the computer to its factory configuration by running a program on the restore image.

Of course, this image is a bit-by-bit facsimile of the computer's hard disk drive, and therefore, restoring it to your computer *completely erases* whatever files are already on the drive. You can't restore your computer from an image disk without losing all the data you saved since you got the computer from the manufacturer. (Talk about a good argument for keeping regular backups!)

Furthermore, some manufacturers put a copy of these installation files right on the hard drive, so you won't even have to hunt for your CDs.

These are the screens you'll encounter:

- **Language.** You're asked to specify your preferred language, currency, time, and keyboard formats right up front—this language, after all, is the one the installer will use to communicate with you.
- **Install now.** Click it (Figure A-2, top).

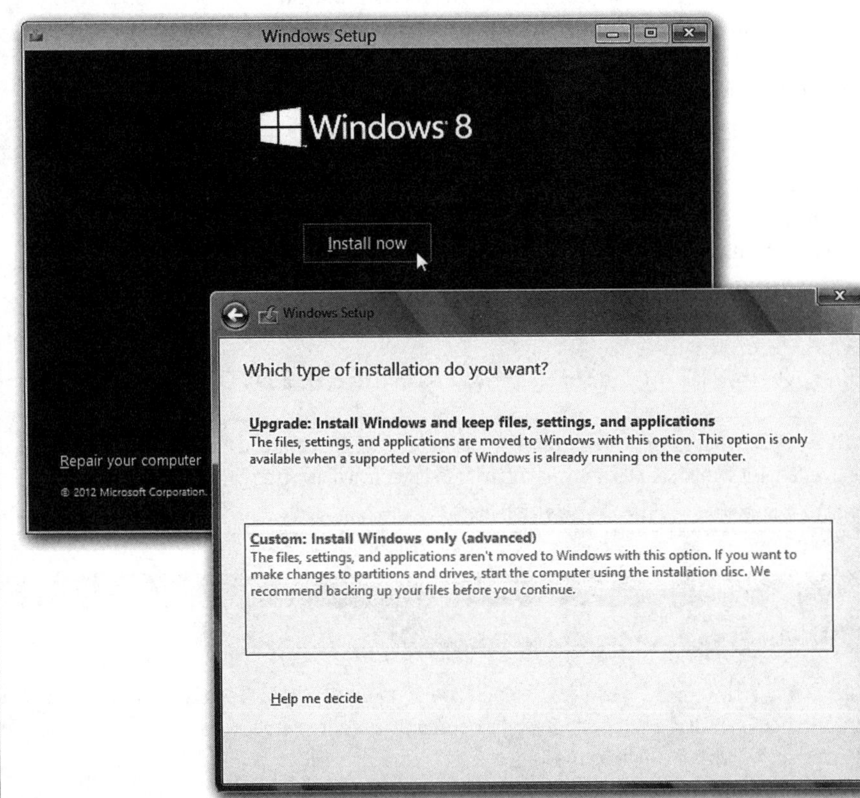

Figure A-2: *Top: The Setup program is ready for action. Close the doors, take the phone off the hook, and cancel your appointments.*

Bottom: Use the buttons on this screen to indicate whether you want a clean installation or an upgrade installation.

- **Product key.** Now you're asked to enter the 25-digit product key (serial number). If you downloaded Windows 8, the Upgrade Advisor displayed your product key, as described above. If you have it on a DVD, the product key is on a sticker on the case.

Note: In some countries, a huge percentage of all copies of Windows are illegal duplicates. To fight that problem, Microsoft invented *activation*—a serial-number system that prevents you from installing one copy of Windows on even *two* computers. That's right: If you have a desktop PC as well as a laptop, you have to have a second product key.

- **License terms.** Review the work of Microsoft's lawyers, and then accept it.
- **Which type?** Here's where you choose between Upgrade and Custom installations (Figure A-2, bottom).

  Upgrade means converting your existing, older Windows installation into a Windows 8 installation, preserving as much of your stuff (files, settings, and programs) as possible.

  Custom gives you the chance to partition your hard drive and create a dual-booting installation, as described above. (Custom is also the only option if your hard drive has no copy of Windows, or a really old one like Windows XP.)

Now the installer itself runs, chugging away quietly.

Phase 2: Establish settings

When the installation is nearly complete, a few more screens ask you to choose the following:

- **A color scheme for the Start screen.**
- **A name for this computer (no spaces or punctuation allowed).**
- **Which WiFi network you want to join.**
- **If you want to accept "Express settings."** These are settings that concern privacy, automatic downloads of Windows patches, security, and local network connections. They're actually fine for most people, but if you'd like to review these factory settings and adjust them, click Customize.

Phase 3: Create your account

Next you're asked to create your account. This is a name and password you'll use to sign in. See page 725 for a walk-through of the account-creation process.

Finally, Windows fills the screen with a weird, repetitive animation that shows you how to open the Charms bar. Against a color-changing solid background, it keeps you posted on its progress, saying things like, "Creating your account," "Finalizing your settings," "Installing apps," "Your PC will be ready in just a moment"—and then boom! There you are at the Start screen, and you're ready to begin.

Performing a Clean Install (or Dual-Boot Install)

To perform a clean installation of Windows 8, or to install it onto an empty partition for the purpose of dual booting, the steps are slightly different.

Begin as described in "Phase 1: Run the installer" on the previous pages. But on the final step described there, where you have to choose Upgrade or Custom, choose Custom.

Now Windows shows you a list of the *partitions* on your hard drive (Figure A-3). Unless you've set up your hard drive for *dual booting* as described earlier, you probably have only one.

Now click to highlight the name of the partition (or choose some unallocated space) on which you want to install Windows 8, and then click Next. Use the Drive Options at the bottom of this window to delete, create, or format partitions. To create a dual-book situation, you have to *erase a partition completely* to make it ready for Windows 8.

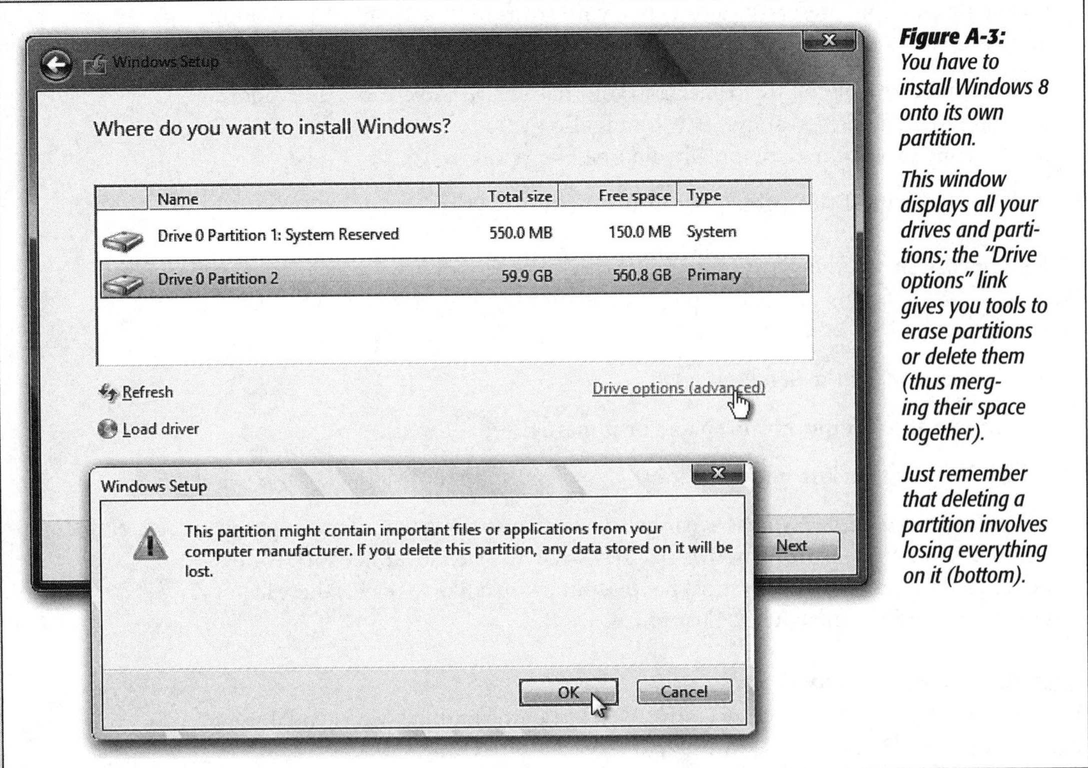

Figure A-3: *You have to install Windows 8 onto its own partition.*

This window displays all your drives and partitions; the "Drive options" link gives you tools to erase partitions or delete them (thus merging their space together).

Just remember that deleting a partition involves losing everything on it (bottom).

After the formatting process is complete, the Setup program begins copying files to the partition you selected and eventually restarts the computer a time or two.

Once that's done, you return to the regular installation process—see "Phase 2: Establish settings" on the previous page.

Jobs Number 1, 2, 3...

Once you've installed Windows 8, you can start using the computer however you like. But if you're smart, you'll make these tasks your first order of business:

- **Transfer files from your old computer** (see "Windows Easy Transfer" on the facing page).
- **Download Windows Essentials,** the free Microsoft software suite that includes excellent programs for managing mail, photos, blog pages, and more (page 375).

- **Put the Desktop tile in the upper-left corner of the Start screen.** From now on, you can jump to the desktop from anywhere by pressing the ⊞ key and then Enter in rapid succession.
- **Restore the Start menu (page 192).**
- **Add users.** That means adding *accounts* to a PC that will be used by more than one person, as described in Chapter 24.
- **Add a Shut Down tile to the Start screen (page 32).**
- **Turn on Windows Defender.** If you have a new PC, and it came with a trial version of antivirus software like Norton or McAfee, you'd be wise to mutter, "But Windows 8 comes with its own antivirus software!" And you might uninstall the trialware.

  Well done! But now go into Windows Defender (page 449) to turn it on.

Windows Easy Transfer

Windows Easy Transfer is a program that's designed to round up the files and preference settings from one computer and copy them into the proper places on a new one. For millions of upgrading Windows fans, this little piece of software is worth its weight in gold.

You can use Windows Easy Transfer in several ways:

- **If you have two computers,** you can run Windows Easy Transfer on the old computer, package its files and settings, and then transfer them to the new computer.

  You can make the transfer over a network connection, a direct cable connection, or via a flash drive or hard drive
- **If you have only one computer,** you can run Windows Easy Transfer before you install, saving the files and settings to a flash drive or a second hard drive. Then, after performing a clean install of Windows 8, you can run the wizard again, neatly importing and reinstating your saved files and settings.

Note: Easy Transfer doesn't bring over your programs—just your files and settings.

Phase 1: Backing Up the Files

To save the files and settings on your old computer (or your old operating system), you'll need a copy of Windows Easy Transfer. If it's not already on your computer (it's included with Windows 8, for example), you can download it from Microsoft's Web site at *http://bit.ly/9rt8eg,* and then proceed like this:

1. **Double-click the file you downloaded.**

   It has a name like "wet7xp_x86.exe." The Setup program opens. Install Windows Easy Transfer.

2. Open Windows Easy Transfer.

   For example, if the old PC has Windows Vista or Windows 7, then open the Start Menu, click All Programs, and choose Windows Easy Transfer (Figure A-4, top).

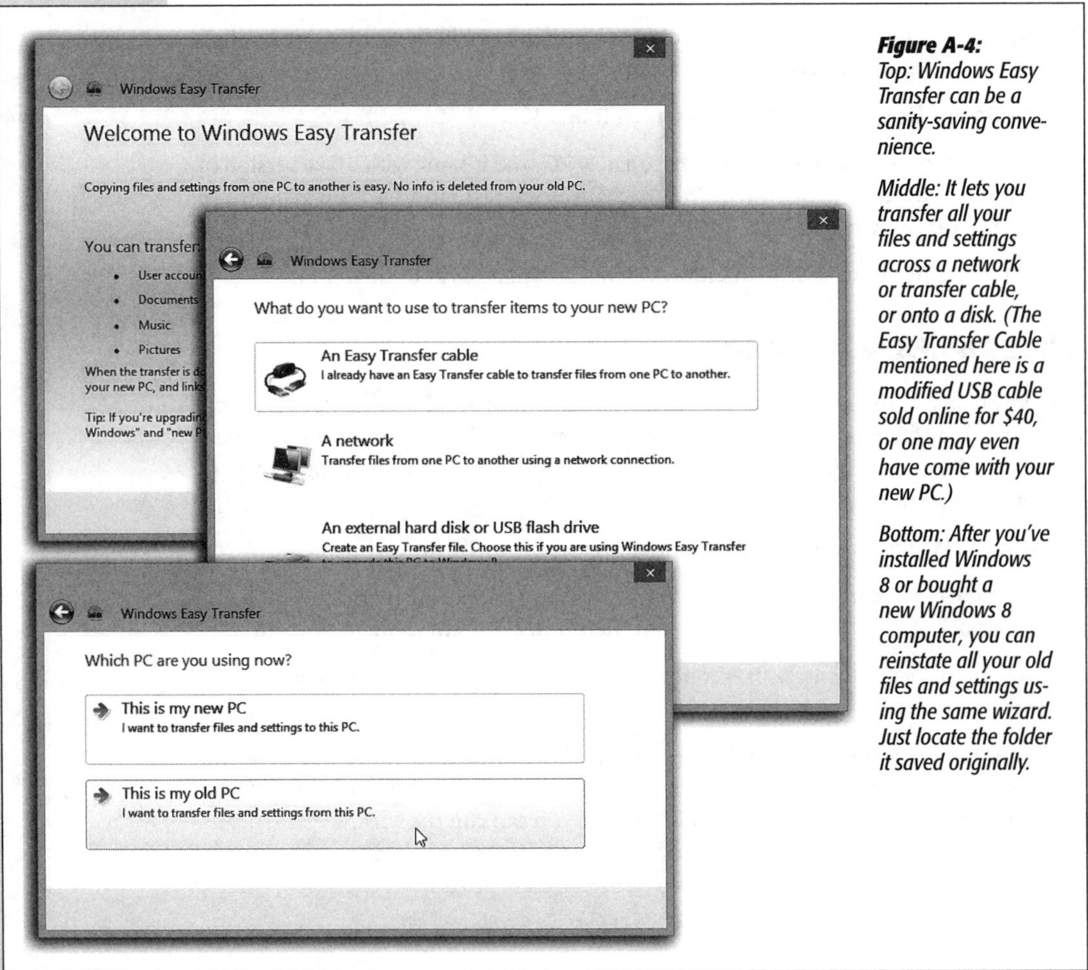

Figure A-4: *Top: Windows Easy Transfer can be a sanity-saving convenience.*

Middle: It lets you transfer all your files and settings across a network or transfer cable, or onto a disk. (The Easy Transfer Cable mentioned here is a modified USB cable sold online for $40, or one may even have come with your new PC.)

Bottom: After you've installed Windows 8 or bought a new Windows 8 computer, you can reinstate all your old files and settings using the same wizard. Just locate the folder it saved originally.

3. Click Next. On the "What do you want to use" screen, specify how you want to transfer the files and settings (Figure A-4, middle).

   You can choose from a link to another computer using a direct cable or network connection, or to a flash drive or external hard disk. The last option also lets you use a network location, which could be a file server or another computer on your network.

4. **Click the option you want to use, and then click Next.**

   The "Which PC are you using now?" screen appears (Figure A-4, bottom).

5. **Click "This is my old PC."**

   The "What do you want to transfer?" screen appears. If you're transferring across the network or a transfer cable, go over to your new computer and run Windows Easy Transfer there. If you're using the network method, you also have to provide the key that appears on this screen.

6. **Specify which information you want to transfer to the other computer.**

   You can elect to transfer all the user accounts on the computer, complete with their files and settings, or just *your* account, files, and settings. (See Chapter 24 for details on accounts.) You can also transfer Shared Items.

   You can use the Customize button (under each user name and under Shared Items) to build a customized list of the *specific* files and settings you want to transfer.

7. **Click Next.**

   If you're saving to a disk, the "Save your files and settings for transfer" screen appears. If you want to password-protect your saved files and settings, then type a password twice. Click Save, and then choose a location to save your files and settings (a hard disk, a flash drive, or even a network location).

8. **Click Next.**

   The progress screen appears. The wizard proceeds to search your drives for the necessary information and send it to the location you specified. If you saved your files and settings to an external disk, flash drive, or network location, Windows Easy Transfer tells you where it saved it; click Next.

9. **Click Close.**

Phase 2: Restoring the Files

To transfer the settings and files, use the following procedure.

If you're doing a clean install, make sure you've put the Windows Easy Transfer file somewhere safe. For maximum peace of mind, you should also have a separate backup of all your files somewhere, because the clean install deletes everything on the selected drive or partition before installing Windows.

If you're moving files to a second computer and are using the transfer cable or network method, you'll have been instructed to start this procedure on your new computer in step 5 of Phase 1.

Let's suppose you're on your Windows 8 machine now.

1. **Open Windows Easy Transfer.**

   At the Start screen, type *transfer*. In the search results, click Windows Easy Transfer to open it.

2. **Click Next. On the "What do you want to use" screen, specify how you want to transfer the files and settings.**

   You can choose from a link to another computer using a direct cable or network connection, or to a flash drive or external hard disk (or network location).

3. **Click the option you want to use, and click Next.**

   The "Which PC are you using now?" screen appears.

4. **Click "This is my new PC."**

   If you're using the network method or transfer cable, the "Do you need to install Windows Easy Transfer" screen appears. Click "I already installed it on my old computer." Click Next and (if you're using the network) enter the key from step 5 of Phase 1.

   If you're using a flash drive, external disk, or network location, you're asked whether Windows Easy Transfer has already saved your old files. Click Yes and choose the location where you saved the files. The location you specify could be a path to a hard drive or a flash drive folder, or a network location. Click Open.

5. **Click Next.**

   Now verify the names of the accounts you're transferring to the new computer. You can either transfer the files and settings into existing accounts or create new accounts (click Advanced Options to change the defaults). If you let it transfer the settings into existing accounts, you'll *replace* their current files and settings. Of course, if this is a fresh install of Windows, those people probably don't have many settings or files yet.

6. **Click Transfer.**

   The wizard copies the files and applies the saved settings to the new computer.

7. **Click Finish to close the wizard.**

   Windows Easy Transfer now reports how the transfer went. If Windows 8 couldn't restore some of your settings, you'll have to recreate them manually. You can also see a list of what was transferred and a list of suggested programs you might want to install. Depending on the settings you saved, you may have to log off and log on again before the transferred settings take effect.

APPENDIX

B

Fun with the Registry

Occasionally, in books, articles, and conversations, you'll hear hushed references to something called the Windows Registry—usually accompanied by either knowing or bewildered glances.

The Registry is your PC's master database of preference settings. For example, most of the programs in the Control Panel are nothing more than graphic front ends that, behind the scenes, modify settings in the Registry.

The Registry also keeps track of almost every program you install, every peripheral device you add, every account you create, your networking configuration, and much more. If you've noticed that shortcut menus and Properties dialog boxes look different depending on what you're clicking, you have the Registry to thank. It knows what you're clicking and what options should appear as a result. In all, there are thousands and thousands of individual settings in your Registry.

As you can well imagine, therefore, the Registry is an extremely important cog in the Windows machine. That's why Windows marks most of your Registry files as hidden and non-deletable, and why it makes a Registry backup every single time you shut down the PC. If the Registry gets randomly edited, a grisly plague of problems may descend upon your machine. Granted, System Restore can extract you from such a mess, but now you know why the Registry is rarely even mentioned to novices.

In fact, Microsoft would just as soon you not even know about the Registry. There's not a word about it in the basic user guides, and about the only information you'll find on it in the Help and Support center is a page that says, "Ordinarily, you do not need to make changes to the registry. The registry contains complex system information that is vital to your computer, and an incorrect change to your registry could render your computer inoperable."

Still, the Registry is worth learning about. You shouldn't edit it arbitrarily, but if you follow a step-by-step "recipe" from a book, magazine, Web site, or technical-help agent, you shouldn't fear opening the Registry to make a few changes.

Why would you want to? Because there are lots of Windows settings that you can't change in any other way, as you'll see in the following pages.

Meet Regedit

Windows comes with a built-in program for editing Registry entries, a little something called (what else?) the Registry Editor. (There are dozens of other Registry-editing, Registry-fixing, and Registry-maintenance programs, too—both commercial and shareware—but this one is already on your PC.)

As an advanced tool that Microsoft doesn't want falling into the wrong hands, the Registry Editor has no icon. You must fire it up by typing its name into the Start screen's search box. Type *regedit* to find the program; select it in the results list.

Authenticate yourself if necessary. After a moment, you see a window like Figure B-1.

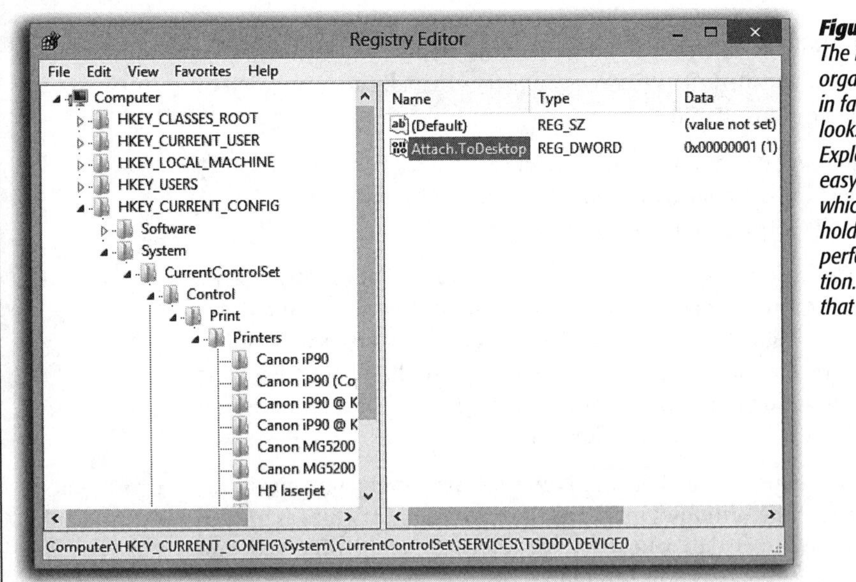

Figure B-1: *The Registry's settings are organized hierarchically; in fact, the Registry Editor looks a lot like Windows Explorer. But there's no easy way to figure out which part of the Registry holds a particular setting or performs a particular function. It's like flying a plane that has no windows.*

The Big Five Categories

It turns out that Microsoft has arranged all those software settings into five broad categories. Microsoft calls them *root keys*, but they look and act like folders in a Windows Explorer window. You expand one of these folders (root keys) just as you would in Explorer, too, by clicking the little flippy triangle button beside its name.

The names of these five categories are not especially user-friendly:

- **HKEY_CLASSES_ROOT.** This root key stores all kinds of information about files: filename extensions, file types, shortcut menus, and so on.

Note: A number of Registry entries appear in more than one place, as live mirrors of each other, for convenience and clarity. Edit one and you make a change in both places.

This root key, for example, is a pointer to the key at HKEY_LOCAL_MACHINE\SOFTWARE\Classes. (More on this slash notation below.)

- **HKEY_CURRENT_USER.** As you'd guess, here's where you'll find the settings pertaining to your account: your desktop arrangement, your wallpaper setting, and so on, plus information about connections to printers, cameras, and so on. (This key, too, is a live mirror—of the identical one in HKEY_USERS, described below.)
- **HKEY_LOCAL_MACHINE.** This one knows all about your PC and its copy of Windows: drivers, security settings, hardware info, the works.
- **HKEY_USERS.** Here's where Windows stores the information about all the account holders (user profiles) on your PC, including the "Current_User"'s. You'll rarely be asked to edit this root key, since the good stuff—what applies to your own account—is in the CURRENT_USER key.
- **HKEY_CURRENT_CONFIG.** Most of this root key is made up of pointers to other places in the Registry. You'll rarely be asked to edit this one.

Keys and Values

If you expand one of these categories by clicking its flippy triangle, you see a long list of inner "folders," called *keys*. These are the actual settings that the Registry tracks, and that you can edit.

Some keys contain other keys, in fact. Keep clicking the flippy triangles until you find the subkey you're looking for.

In books, magazines, and tutorials on the Web, you'll often encounter references to particular Registry subkeys written out as a Registry path, like this:

HKEY_CURRENT_USER→Control Panel→Mouse

(You may see backslashes used instead of the arrows.) That instruction tells you to expand the HKEY_CURRENT_USER root key, expand Control Panel within it, and finally click the Mouse "folder." It works just like a folder path, like C:→Users→Chris→Desktop.

If you actually try this maneuver, you'll find, in the right half of the window, a bunch of keys named DoubleClickSpeed, MouseSpeed, MouseTrails, and so on. These should sound familiar, as they correspond to the options in the Mouse program of your Control Panel. (Figure B-2 clarifies this relationship.)

Each value usually contains either a number or a block of text. DoubleClickSpeed, for example, comes set at 500. In this case, that means 500 milliseconds between clicks, but each Registry value may refer to a different kind of unit.

Tip: Many of the Windows Explorer keyboard shortcuts also work in regedit. For example, once you've clicked a key, you can press the right and left arrows to reveal and hide its subkeys. You can also type the first letter of a subkey's name to highlight it in the left pane–same with a value's name in the right pane. And you can press the Backspace key to jump to the "parent" key, the one that contains the subkey.

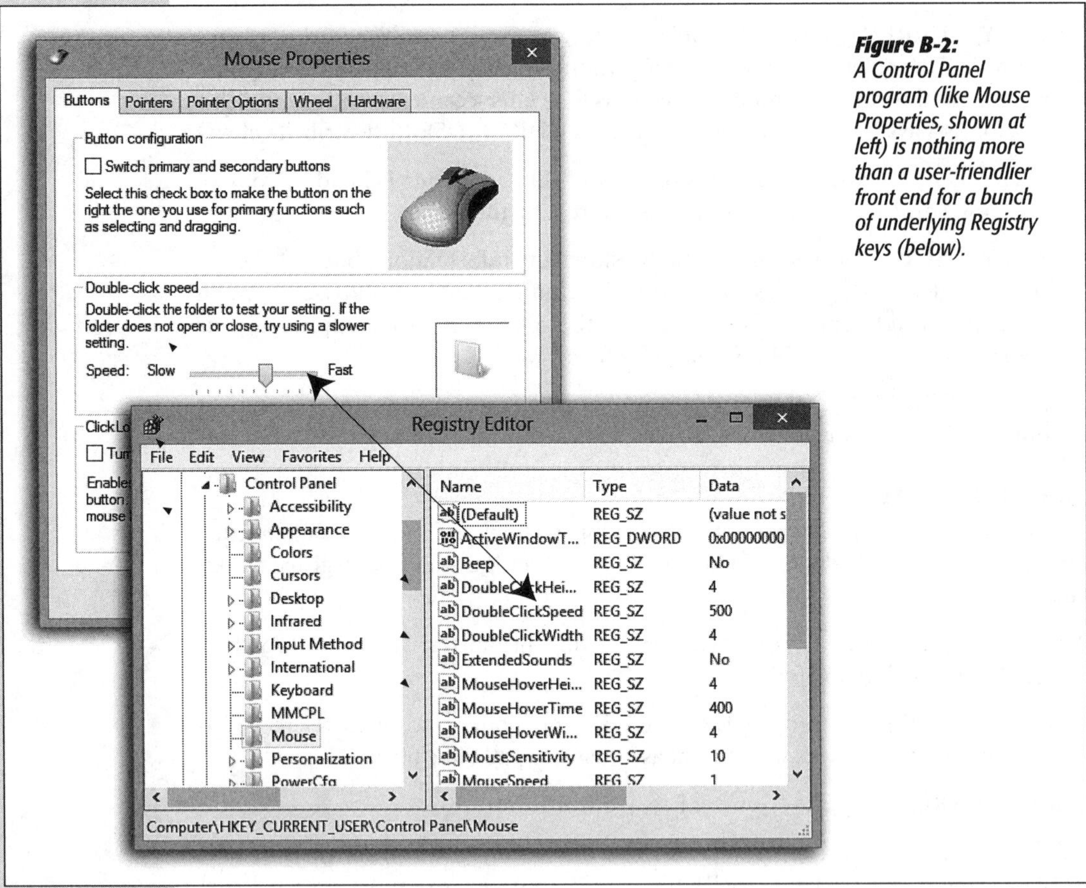

Figure B-2: *A Control Panel program (like Mouse Properties, shown at left) is nothing more than a user-friendlier front end for a bunch of underlying Registry keys (below).*

Backing Up Key Values

In general, you won't go into the Registry unless you truly want to make a change. That's why the program is called "regedit," not "regviewer."

As you know, though, making the wrong change can botch up your copy of Windows—and regedit has no Undo command and no "Save change before closing?" message.

That's why it's essential to *back up* a Registry key—or even its entire root key—before you change anything. Later, if the change you made doesn't work the way you'd hoped, you can restore the original.

To back up a key (including all its values and subkeys), just select it and then choose File→Export. Save the resulting key somewhere safe, like your desktop. Later, you can reinstate the key by double-clicking the .reg file you exported. (Or, if you're paid by the hour, open regedit, choose File→Import, and manually open the .reg file.)

Note: Importing a .reg file merges it with the data already in the Registry. Any values you edited will go back to their original versions, provided you haven't renamed them.

This means, for instance, that if you export a key, rename one of the values in that key, and then reimport the .reg file, the value you renamed will still be there, along with the value by its original name. In other words, a .reg file is a very good idea, but it's not a "get out of jail free card" that undoes all types of changes.

The only way to get a true Registry backup is to back up the Registry files themselves. Only the Backup and Restore program described on page 859 can do this for you. System Restore, described on page 691, can also restore your Registry to a previous time.

Regedit Examples

Here are three typical regedit tweaks, spelled out for you step by step.

Encrypt/Decrypt from the Shortcut Menu

As you know from page 258, one of the perks of using Windows 8 is that you can encrypt files and folders, protecting them from people who try to open them from across the network or using a different account.

If you use this feature quite a bit, however, you'll quickly grow tired of opening the Properties box every time you want to encrypt something. Wouldn't it be much more convenient if the Encrypt and Decrypt commands were right there in the shortcut menu that appears when you right-click an icon?

Of course it would. To make it so, do this:

- **Navigate to:** HKEY_CURRENT_USER→Software→Microsoft→Windows→CurrentVersion→Explorer→Advanced.

  Now, for this trick, you're going to need a key that doesn't actually exist yet. Fortunately, it's easy to create a new key. In this case, just right-click the Advanced "folder," and then, from the shortcut menu, choose New→"DWORD (32-bit) Value." You see "New Value #1" appear in the right side of the window, ready to be renamed; type *EncryptionContextMenu,* and then press Enter.

Tip: The birth of a new Registry entry is a good opportunity to name it, but you can rename any value or key at any time, just the way you'd rename a file icon. That is, you can open the renaming rectangle by right-clicking or by pressing F2.

- **Double-click this value on the right side:** EncryptionContextMenu.
- **Make this change:** In the "Value data" box, type *1*.
- **Wrap up:** Click OK and quit regedit. When you right-click any file or folder icon, you'll see the new Encrypt command in the shortcut menu. (Or, if it's already encrypted, you'll see a Decrypt command.)

A Really, Really Clean Desktop

Windows XP used to nag you every now and then to get unused icons off your desktop. But why stop there? If you've got the world's most beautiful desktop wallpaper set up, you might not want *any* icons marring its majesty.

If you think about it, you can get by just fine without a single icon on the desktop. You can open anything from within an Explorer window or the Start screen. You can put things into the Recycle Bin without dragging them to its icon. (Just highlight icons and then press the Delete key, for instance.)

The following regedit hack doesn't actually remove anything from your desktop. It just hides them. You can still work with the icons on your desktop by using Windows Explorer to view the contents of your Desktop folder, for example.

- **Navigate to:** HKEY_CURRENT_USER→Software→Microsoft→Windows→CurrentVersion→Policies.
- **Right-click the Policies folder:** From the shortcut menu, choose New→Key, and rename it to Explorer.
- **Right-click the Explorer folder:** Choose New→Binary Value, and name the new value NoDesktop. Double-click this value.
- **Make this change:** In the "Value data" box, type *01 00 00 00.* (Regedit puts the spaces in automatically.) Click OK.
- **Wrap up:** Click OK, quit regedit, and then log out and log in. (To reverse the procedure, just delete the NoDesktop value you created, and then log out and log in.)

Slow Down the Animations

Windows' window animations and other eye candy are very cool. But they happen fast; Microsoft didn't want them to get in your way. That's a shame if you want to study the visual-FX majesty of these animations in more detail.

If you make this regedit tweak, you can make the window animation slow down on command—specifically, whenever you're pressing the Shift key.

- **Navigate to:** HKEY_CURRENT_USER→Software→Microsoft→Windows→DWM.
- **Right-click** the DWM folder. From the shortcut menu, choose New→"DWORD (32-bit) Value." Name the new value *AnimationsShiftKey*.

- **Double-click this value on the right side:** In the "Value data" box for the AnimationsShiftKey entry you just made, type *1*. Click OK.
- **Wrap up:** Quit regedit and then log out and log in. (To reverse the procedure, just delete the AnimationsShiftKey value you created, and then log out and log in.)

To see effects in slow motion, press the Shift key just before they start to occur. For example, Shift-click a window's Close box—and watch in amazement as it *slowwwwly* fades into total transparency, like a ghost returning to the world beyond.

Tip: If you find your pulse racing with the illicit thrill of making tweaks to your system, why stop here? You can find hundreds more regedit "recipes" in books, computer magazines, and Web sites. A quick search of "*regedit hacks*" in Google will unearth plenty of them.

APPENDIX
C

Where'd It Go?

As the saying goes, you can't make an omelette without breaking a few eggs. And on the road to Windows 8, Microsoft broke enough eggs to make a Texan soufflé. Features got moved, renamed, and ripped out completely.

If you're fresh from Windows 7, Windows Vista, Windows XP, or even earlier versions of Windows, you might spend your first few days with Windows 8 wondering where things went. Here's a handy cheat sheet of features that aren't in Windows 8 (or aren't where you think they should be).

- **Ad hoc networking.** For some mysterious reason, Microsoft removed the link that lets you set up this PC-to-PC wireless network. The feature is still available—it's just much harder to get to. Page 769 has details.
- **Add or Remove Programs control panel.** The Control Panel applet called Programs and Features performs the software-removal function. No Control Panel applet remains to *add* software, because every program these days comes with its *own* installer.
- **Aero.** Amazing. Microsoft must have spent tens of millions of dollars advertising the animated eye candy known as Aero in Windows 7: see-through window edges, flippy window switching, and so on. It's all gone in Windows 8.
- **Backup & Restore.** Microsoft would much prefer that you use the new File Histories feature and other backup tools; there's no remaining icon for Backup & Restore, and you won't find it by searching. But it's there; see page 859.
- **Briefcase.** This handy tool for syncing files between two computers has, after several decades, finally been taken out behind the barn and shot. It's gone from Windows 8.

- **Calendar.** Windows Calendar, part of Vista, is gone now. The only calendars now are the one built into Windows Live Mail (Chapter 16) and the online Windows Live Calendar site.
- **CardSpace.** This app was supposed to store your online identities, but Microsoft has abandoned it now.
- **Chess Titans.** No games come with Windows 8.
- **Classic theme.** If you really want to make your Windows 8 machine look like it's from 1998, you'll have to rely on shareware to do it; the Classic theme is no longer built in.
- **Clipbook Viewer.** This handy multi-Clipboard feature is no longer in Windows 8.
- **Complete PC Backups** (from Vista) have been renamed "system images," and they're alive and well in Windows 8.
- **Contacts.** This Vista address-book entity is gone. Now the only address book is the one in Windows Live Mail (Chapter 16).
- **Desktop cleanup wizard** has gone away. You can't actually pretend that you'll miss it, can you?
- **Desktop gadgets.** Microsoft removed gadgets from Windows…or did it? (See "Gadgets" on the facing page.)
- **Discuss pane.** This Windows XP panel did nothing unless some technically proficient administrator set up something called a SharePoint Portal Server—a corporate software kit that permits chat sessions among employees. Anyway, it's no longer in Windows.
- **Documents & Settings folder.** Now called Users.
- **DVD Maker.** Its full name is Windows Live DVD Maker, and it's now part of the downloadable Windows Essentials (Chapter 11).
- **DVD playback.** Amazingly, Windows 8 doesn't come with any software that can play DVD movies. You can buy Windows Media Center for $10, or you can download a free DVD movie-playback program like VLC. You can download it from this book's "Missing CD" page at *www.missingmanuals.com*.
- **Explorer bar.** Gone.
- **Favorites folder.** Favorites are still around, in the sense of bookmarks from Internet Explorer. But the Favorites *toolbar* at the desktop is gone. No grieving is necessary, though; you can create exactly the same effect with the Links toolbar or one you create yourself (page 245).
- **Flip 3D.** This animated effect in Windows 7 displayed all open windows as 3-D stacked "cards" floating in space. It really wasn't that useful. It's gone now.
- **File types.** In Windows XP, you could define new file types and associate them with programs yourself, using the File Types tab in the Folder Options dialog box.

In Windows 8, the File Types tab is gone. There's a similar dialog box now (page 355), but it doesn't let you make up your own file types and associations. It doesn't let you define custom secondary actions, either, or ask Explorer to reveal filename extensions for only specific file types.

- **Files & Settings Transfer Wizard.** Renamed Windows Easy Transfer (see Appendix A).
- **Filmstrip view (Explorer windows).** Replaced by the any-size-you-like icon view feature.
- **FreeCell.** All games are gone from Windows 8.
- **Gadgets.** Gadgets, of course, were what Mac or Android fans know as widgets: small floating windows that convey useful Internet information, like current stock, news, or weather reports. They were there in Windows 7, but now they've been retired.

  You can bring them back, though, with the free 8GadgetPack add-on. You can download it from this book's "Missing CD" page at *www.missingmanuals.com.*
- **Games.** Astonishingly, Windows 8 comes without a Games folder—and without any games at all. Not even Solitaire.
- **Gopher.** Removed.
- **Hardware profiles.** Removed.
- **High performance power plan,** for laptops, is no longer listed in the Power icon on the taskbar. It's available, though, if you open the Power control panel.
- **Image toolbar (Internet Explorer).** Removed. Most of the commands that were on this auto-appearing IE6 toolbar, though—Save Picture, E-mail Picture, Set as Background, and so on—are now in the shortcut menu that appears when you right-click any picture on the Web.
- **Inkball.** Inkball is gone, along with all the other Windows games.
- **IP over FireWire.** Removed.
- **iSCSI Initiator.** Gone from Windows 8. Does anybody really use SCSI anymore?
- **Macintosh services.** The software that offered file and print sharing via the AppleTalk protocol (which even Apple has abandoned) is gone.
- **Mahjong Titans.** No games come with Windows 8.
- **Meeting Space.** This was Vista's replacement for NetMeeting, but now Meeting Space is gone, too. If you want to share someone's screen, use Remote Assistance or Remote Desktop. If you want to have audio or video calls, use Skype.
- **Minesweeper.** All games are gone from Windows 8.
- **Movie Maker.** Its full name is Windows Movie Maker, and it's now part of the downloadable Windows Essentials (page 375).

- **My Network Places.** You no longer have to open a special window to see the other computers on your network. They're listed right there in the navigation pane at the left side of every Explorer window.
- **NetMeeting.** Removed. Well, there's always Skype.
- **Network map.** The Network & Sharing Center used to offer a charming visual map, showing the various connections between your computer, your router, and the Internet itself. In Windows 8, the Network & Sharing Center is still there, but the map is gone.
- **Offline browsing/Offline favorites (Internet Explorer).** In Windows XP, you could right-click a Web page's name in your Favorites menu and store it for later perusal when you were no longer online—complete with whatever pages were linked to it. Internet Explorer would even update such pages automatically each time you got back online. This feature is gone from Internet Explorer 10.
- **Outlook Express.** Now called Windows Live Mail and described in Chapter 16.
- **"Parent folder" button.** In Windows XP, you could click this button to go up one folder (that is, to see the folder that enclosed the current one). In Windows 8, it's back—it's the ↑ button next to the address bar in any Explorer window.
- **Parental controls.** They're now called Family Safety, and they've been expanded quite a bit.
- **Password protecting a .zip archive.** Removed. In the window of any open .zip file, there's still a column that indicates whether or not each file is password-protected—but there's no way to add such a password yourself.
- **Phishing filter,** the Internet Explorer feature that shields you from phony banking sites, has been renamed SmartScreen filter.
- **Photo Gallery.** Its full name is Windows Photo Gallery. It doesn't come built into Windows, but it's an easy download as part of Windows Essentials (Chapter 11).
- **Pinball.** Gone, along with the rest of the Windows games.
- **Pointer themes.** You can make your cursor bigger or smaller in Windows 8, but the fun cursor designs like 3D-Bronze, 3D-White, Conductor, Dinosaur, Hands 1, Hands 2, Variations, and Windows Animated have been killed off by the No-Fun Committee.
- **PowerToys.** Microsoft seems to have lost its enthusiasm for these freebie software goodie-bag items; they disappeared back in Windows Vista.
- **Previous Versions.** It's now called File Histories, and it's even better.
- **Purble Place.** No games come with Windows 8.
- **Recent documents.** Gone in Windows 8.

- **Quick Launch toolbar.** Since the entire *taskbar* is pretty much a giant Quick Launch toolbar now, Microsoft took out all visible evidence of the Quick Launch toolbar. But you can resurrect it with a quick hack. See page 244.
- **Reversi.** All Windows games are gone.
- **Run command.** It may seem to be missing from the Start screen, but you can put it right back. Or you can just press ⊞+R to call it up.
- **Search assistant (Internet Explorer).** Replaced by the new search bar at the upper-right corner of the Internet Explorer window.
- **Search pane.** Gone. But the new Start screen's search box (Chapter 3) is infinitely superior.
- **SerialKeys.** This feature for specialized gadgets for the disabled is no longer supported.
- **Sidebar.** In Vista, the small, floating, single-purpose apps known as *gadgets* hung out in a panel called the Sidebar. Both it and its gadgets are gone now.
- **Solitaire.** No games come with Windows. Not even this classic one, which, for many people, *was* Windows.
- **Sortable column headings** in Explorer windows have gone away, except in Details view. That is, there's no longer a row of column headings (Name, Date, Size, Kind…) across the top of every window that you can click to sort the window—except, as noted, in Details view.
- **Spades.** Games are gone.
- **Stacking,** as an activity for organizing similar files in any Explorer window, arrived in Vista and then departed in Windows 7. (You can clump the contents of library windows only, and only by a few criteria.)
- **Start menu.** Gone. Microsoft would like you to use the new Start screen instead—but you can restore the Start menu if you miss it. See Chapter 1.
- **Startup Hardware Profiles.** Removed.
- **Taskbar dragging.** You can no longer drag the taskbar's top edge off the screen to hide it manually. You can't drag the taskbar to the middle of the screen anymore, either. And you can't drag a folder to the edge of the screen to turn it into a toolbar. (One guess: Too many people were doing this stuff *accidentally* and then getting frustrated.)
- **Telnet.** Removed—or so it seems. Fortunately, you can restore it using the "Turn Windows features on or off" feature described on page 426; select Telnet Client.
- **Tip of the Day.** No longer part of Windows. Microsoft must expect you to get your tips from computer books now.

- **TweakUI.** Not available for Windows 8. But there are several billion freeware and shareware programs available to take on the task of making tweaky little changes to the look of Windows.
- **Wallpaper.** Now called Desktop Background. (Right-click the desktop; from the shortcut menu, choose Personalize.)
- **Web Publishing Wizard.** Gone.
- **What's This? button in dialog boxes.** This little link is gone from Windows dialog boxes, probably because it didn't work in most of them. Now, if help is available in a dialog box, it lurks behind the ⑦ button.
- **Windows Address Book.** Gone. The only address book left in Windows now is the one built into Windows Live Mail—and even that doesn't come with Windows. It's a free download, though (Chapter 16).
- **Windows Calendar.** This Vista program is gone. The only calendars now are the one built into Windows Mail (Chapter 16) and the TileWorld app Calendar.
- **Windows Components Wizard.** Now called the Windows Features dialog box.
- **Windows DVD Maker.** Gone. Microsoft must agree with Apple that nobody uses DVDs anymore.
- **Windows Live Mesh.** Replaced by the SkyDrive.
- **Windows Media Center.** This TV-recording program is still around—as a $10 add-on; see page 611.
- **Windows Media Player toolbar** is gone. Now Media Player's taskbar icon sprouts basic commands (although it lacks the old volume slider).
- **Windows Messenger.** Microsoft's chat program no longer comes preinstalled in Windows, thanks to antitrust legal trouble the company encountered. It's an easy download, though, as part of the Windows Essentials suite described at the beginning of Chapter 11.
- **Windows Movie Maker.** It's now part of the downloadable Windows Essentials (page 375).
- **Windows Picture and Fax Viewer.** This old program's functions have been split. Now you view pictures in the free Windows Photo Gallery and faxes in Windows Fax and Scan.
- **Windows Ultimate Extras.** There's no Ultimate version of Windows anymore.
- **Windows XP Mode.** Gone.

APPENDIX

D

Master List of Gestures & Keyboard Shortcuts

Here it is, by popular, frustrated demand: The master list of every secret (or not-so-secret) keystroke in Windows 8. Clip and post to your monitor (unless, of course, you got this book from the library).

TileWorld gestures

To do this	Use this gesture
Open Charms bar	Swipe in from right edge
Open App bar ("right-click")	Swipe in from top/bottom edge
Switch to last app	Swipe in from left edge
App switcher	Swipe in from left edge, then out again (not to edge)
Close app	Drag from top of app to bottom
Split window	Drag from top edge to the right or left
Zoom in/zoom out (Maps, Photos, and so on)	Spread or pinch two fingers

TileWorld keystrokes

To do this	Press this key
Open Start screen	⊞ or Ctrl+Esc
Open Charms bar	⊞+C
Open App bar ("right-click")	⊞+Z
Search for apps (at Start screen)	Just start typing
Search for apps (anywhere)	⊞+Q

Search for files	⊞+F
Search for settings	⊞+W
Open Share panel	⊞+H
Open Devices panel	⊞+K
Open Settings panel	⊞+I
Switch between two split-screen apps	⊞+J

TileWorld mouse shortcuts

To do this	Do this
Open Start screen	Point to lower-left corner of the screen; click the thumbnail
Open previous app	Point to upper-left corner of the screen; click the thumbnail
Open Charms bar	Point to top- or bottom-right corner
Open App bar	Right-click
Open TileWorld app switcher	Point to bottom-left corner, move up—or top-left corner, move down
Close app	Point to top edge, drag all the way to bottom of screen
Split the screen	Drag down from top edge and to the right or left (or inward from left edge, then carefully to the left or right)

File Explorer keyboard shortcuts

To do this	Press this key
Open a new window	Ctrl+N or ⊞+E
Close the current window	Ctrl+W
Create a new folder	Ctrl+Shift+N
Display the bottom/top of the active window	End/Home
Maximize or minimize the active window	F11
Rotate a picture clockwise	Ctrl+period (.)
Rotate a picture counterclockwise	Ctrl+comma (,)
Display all subfolders under the selected folder	Num Lock+* on numeric keypad
Display the contents of the selected folder	Num Lock+plus (+) on numeric keypad
Collapse the selected folder	Num Lock+minus (-) on numeric keypad

Collapse the current selection (if expanded), or select parent folder	←
Open the Properties dialog box for selected item	Alt+Enter
Back to the previous folder	Alt+← or Backspace
Display the current selection (if it's collapsed), or select the first subfolder	→
Next folder	Alt+→
Open the parent folder	Alt+↑
Display all folders above the selected folder	Ctrl+Shift+E
Enlarge/shrink file and folder icons	Ctrl+mouse scroll wheel
Select the address bar	Alt+D
Select the contents of the search box	Ctrl+E, Ctrl+F

General keyboard shortcuts

Open the Start screen	⊞ or Ctrl+Esc
Help	⊞+F1
Copy the selected item	Ctrl+C (or Ctrl+Insert)
Cut the selected item	Ctrl+X
Paste the selected item	Ctrl+V (or Shift+Insert)
Undo an action	Ctrl+Z
Redo an action	Ctrl+Y
Delete the selected item and move it to the Recycle Bin	Delete (or Ctrl+D)
Delete the selected item without moving it to the Recycle Bin first	Shift+Delete
Rename the selected item	F2
Move the cursor to the beginning of the next word	Ctrl+→
Move the cursor to the beginning of the previous word	Ctrl+←
Move the cursor to the beginning of the next paragraph	Ctrl+↓
Move the cursor to the beginning of the previous paragraph	Ctrl+↑
Select a block of text	Ctrl+Shift with an arrow key
Select more than one item in a window, or select text within a document	Shift+any arrow key
Select multiple individual items in a window or on the desktop	Ctrl + any arrow key + space bar

Select all items in a document or window	Ctrl+A
Search for a file or folder	F3
Display properties for the selected item	Alt+Enter
Open a menu	Alt+underlined letter
"Click" a menu command (or other underlined command)	Alt+underlined letter
Make the menu bar appear	Alt or F10
Open the next menu to the right, or open a submenu	→
Open the next menu to the left, or close a submenu	←
Cancel the current task	Esc
Open Task Manager	Ctrl+Shift+Esc
Prevent the CD from automatically playing	Shift when you insert a CD
Switch the input language when multiple input languages are enabled	Left Alt+Shift
Switch the keyboard layout when multiple keyboard layouts are enabled	Ctrl+Shift
Change the reading direction of text in right-to-left reading languages	Ctrl+right Shift or Ctrl+left Shift

Window and program-switching keyboard shortcuts

Close the window	Alt+F4
Open the shortcut menu for the active window	Alt+space bar
Close the document (in apps that let you have multiple documents open)	Ctrl+F4
Switch among open programs	Alt+Tab
Use the arrow keys to switch among open programs	Ctrl+Alt+Tab
Cycle through TileWorld programs	⊞+Tab
Cycle through desktop programs in the order in which they were opened	Alt+Esc
Cycle through screen elements in a window or on the desktop	F6
Display the address bar list in File Explorer	F4
Display the shortcut menu for the selected item	Shift+F10
Refresh the active window	F5 (or Ctrl+R)

⊞-Key shortcuts

Start screen (and back to previous program)	⊞
Open Charms bar	⊞+C
Open App bar ("right-click")	⊞+Z
Search for apps (anywhere)	⊞+Q
Search for files	⊞+F
Search for settings	⊞+W
Open Share panel	⊞+H
Open Devices panel	⊞+K
Open Settings panel	⊞+I
Switch between two split-screen apps	⊞+J
Open App bar ("right-click")	⊞+Z
Open System Properties dialog box	⊞+Pause
Display the desktop	⊞+D
Minimize all windows	⊞+M
Restore minimized windows to the desktop	⊞+Shift+M
Open Computer in an Explorer window	⊞+E
Search for a file or folder	⊞+F
Search for computers (if you're on a network)	Ctrl+⊞+F
Lock your computer or switch users	⊞+L
Open the Run dialog box	⊞+R
Cycle through programs on the taskbar	⊞+T
Open the first, second (etc.) program pinned to the taskbar	⊞+1, ⊞+2, etc.
Open another window in the first, second (etc.) pinned taskbar program	Shift+⊞+1, Shift+⊞+2, etc.
Switch to the last window in first, second (etc.) program pinned to the taskbar	Ctrl+⊞+1, Ctrl+⊞+2, etc.
Open a jump list for the first, second (etc.) program pinned to the taskbar	Alt+⊞+1, Alt+⊞+2, etc.
Cycle through open TileWorld apps	⊞+Tab
Use arrow keys to cycle through open TileWorld apps	Ctrl+⊞+Tab
Switch to the program that displayed a message in the notification area	Ctrl+⊞+B
Maximize the window	⊞+↑
Maximize the window, maintain width	⊞+Shift+↑
Snap window to the left side of the screen	⊞+←

Snap the window to the right side of the screen	⊞+→
Move window to the previous/next monitor	⊞+Shift+←, ⊞+Shift+→
Restore/Minimize the window	⊞+↓
Maximize the window, maintain width	⊞+Shift+↓
Minimize all but the active window	⊞+Home
Stretch the window to the top and bottom of the screen	⊞+Shift+↑
Move a window from one monitor to another	⊞+Shift+← or →
Choose an external-monitor/projector mode (like mirroring)	⊞+P
Lock screen orientation (not all computers)	⊞+O
Open Ease of Access Center	⊞+U
Open Narrator	⊞+Enter
Cycle through recent "toast" alerts	⊞+V (add Shift to reverse)
Open secret Utilities menu	⊞+X
Switch languages, if you've set some up	⊞+space bar
Move Start screen to left/right monitor	⊞+PgUp, ⊞+PgDown

Taskbar keyboard shortcuts

Open a program or another window in a program	Shift-click a taskbar button
Open a program as an administrator	Ctrl+Shift-click a taskbar button
Show the window menu for the program	Shift+right-click a taskbar button
Show the window menu for the group	Shift+right-click a grouped taskbar button
Cycle through the windows of the group	Ctrl-click a grouped taskbar button

Ease of Access keyboard shortcuts

Turn Filter Keys on and off	Right Shift for 8 seconds
Turn High Contrast on or off	Left Alt+Left Shift+PrtScn (or PrtScn)
Turn Mouse Keys on or off	Left Alt+Left Shift+Num Lock
Turn Sticky Keys on or off	Shift five times
Turn Toggle Keys on or off	Num Lock for 5 seconds
Open the Ease of Access Center	⊞+U

Dialog box keyboard shortcuts

Move forward through tabs	Ctrl+Tab
Move back through tabs	Ctrl+Shift+Tab
Move forward through options	Tab

Move back through options	Shift+Tab
Perform the command (or select the option) that goes with that letter	Alt+underlined letter
Replaces clicking the mouse for many selected commands	Enter

Magnifier keyboard shortcuts

Zoom in or out	⊞+plus (+) or minus (-)
Preview the desktop in full-screen mode	Ctrl+Alt+space bar
Switch to full-screen mode	Ctrl+Alt+F
Switch to lens mode	Ctrl+Alt+L
Switch to docked mode	Ctrl+Alt+D
Invert colors	Ctrl+Alt+I
Pan in the direction of the arrow keys	Ctrl+Alt+arrow keys
Resize the lens	Ctrl+Alt+R
Exit Magnifier	⊞+Esc

Remote Desktop Connection keyboard shortcuts

Move between programs, left to right	Alt+Page Up
Move between programs, right to left	Alt+Page Down
Cycle through programs in the order they were started in	Alt+Insert
Open Start menu	Alt+Home
Switch between a window and full screen	Ctrl+Alt+Break
Display the Windows Security dialog box	Ctrl+Alt+End
Display the system menu	Alt+Delete
Place a copy of the active window, within the client, on the Terminal server clipboard (same as pressing Alt+PrtScn on a local computer)	Ctrl+Alt+minus (-) on the numeric keypad
Place a copy of the entire client window area on the Terminal server clipboard (same as pressing PrtScn on a local computer)	Ctrl+Alt+plus (+) on the numeric keypad
"Tab" out of the Remote Desktop controls to a control in the host program (for example, a button or a text box)	Ctrl+Alt+→ or ←

Index

Index

D

E

F

G

H

I

M

N

O

P

S

U

X

Z

Colophon

The book was written and edited in Microsoft Word, whose revision-tracking feature made life far easier as drafts were circulated from author to technical and copy editors. The steps in this book were tested on machines from HP, Toshiba, and Apple . (That's right: Apple. You can't believe how fast Windows 8 runs under the Parallels emulator [virtual machine], on a MacBook Air.)

SnagIt *(www.techsmith.com)* captured the illustrations; Adobe Photoshop CS6 and Illustrator CS6 were called in as required for touching them up.

The book was designed and laid out in Adobe InDesign CS5.5 on a MacBook Pro, and Mac Pro. The fonts used include Formata (as the sans-serif family) and Minion (as the serif body face). To provide symbols like and , custom fonts were created using FontLab Fontographer.

The book was generated as an Adobe Acrobat PDF file for proofreading and indexing, and final transmission to the printing plant.

Windows 8

THE MISSING CD

There's no CD with this book; you just saved $5.00.

Instead, every single Web address, practice file, and piece of downloadable software mentioned in this book is available at *missingmanuals.com* (click the Missing CD icon). There you'll find a tidy list of links, organized by chapter.